MONSIGNOR WILLIAM BARRY MEMORIAL LIBRARY
BARRY UNIVERSITY
D210 .R6313
Romein, Jan, 1893-1962. c   010101 000
The watershed of two eras : Eu

0 2210 0067482 2

D1252423

D
210   192124
.R6313

Msgr. Wm. Barry Memorial Library
Barry University
Miami, FL   33161

ROMEIN

WATERSHED OF TWO...

THE WATERSHED OF TWO ERAS
EUROPE IN 1900

JAN ROMEIN

THE WATERSHED
OF TWO ERAS

EUROPE IN 1900

Translated by Arnold J. Pomerans

WESLEYAN UNIVERSITY PRESS

Middletown, Connecticut

Barry University Library
Miami, FL 33161

Copyright © 1978 by Wesleyan University

The publishers gratefully acknowledge support toward the publication
of this book by the Andrew W. Mellon Foundation and the Friends
of the Wesleyan University Press Publication Fund.

Library of Congress Cataloging in Publication Data

Romein, Jan Marius, 1893-1962.
    The watershed of two eras.

    Translation of Op het breukvlak van twee eeuwen.
    Bibliography: p.
    Includes index.
    1. History, Modern — Addresses, essays, lectures.
I. Title.
D210.R6313   909.82   77-14841
ISBN 0-8195-5026-4

Manufactured in the United States of America
First edition

D
210
.R6313

192124

CONTENTS

A MEMOIR OF JAN ROMEIN

Historians can be classified in various ways. Thus we may distinguish "lumpers" from "splitters", synthesists from analysts, specialists from general historians, and those who stress the continuity of the historical process from those who dwell on its fragmentary nature. To Jan Romein, *change* was the crucial factor. In an address he wrote shortly before his death in 1962, but was unable to deliver to a conference of British and Dutch historians, he explained how he was first introduced to the dialectical change of quantity into quality. As a child, he had been fascinated by the irrigation system in the hothouse of the Zoological Gardens. "A thin stream of water flowed into one of the buckets from a tap. As soon as the bucket was filled it tipped over under its own weight, and the other bucket moved automatically beneath the tap to be filled in its turn. Here I unconsciously acquired the knowledge that a motion in one direction by its very nature prepares for a motion in the opposite direction, a motion that will come about at a certain yet always unexpected moment." *Historia saltat*: history does not run an even course; periods of quick change make way for periods of gradual transformation. That the former often gave rise to great human suffering was something Romein realized only too well, but then, did not the gradual changes take their toll as well?

Romein's language reflected much of his credo. He rarely used "either . . . or" constructions, preferring such phrases as "despite the fact . . . or perhaps because of it"; "those who have eyes to see will detect the first signs of later decay at the height of this very development". Romein expressed this view repeatedly when dealing with European supremacy and colonial power, which seemed to have reached their peak in about 1900 and which, in virtue of this very fact, had begun to decline, albeit very few people realized it at the time. Much the same was true of bourgeois dominance. Romein's style invariably reflects these striking contrasts, and many of the biographical analyses contained in his *Erflaters* (The Testators) owe their impact to this very fact. Moreover, his dialectical approach helped Romein, time and again, to cast doubt on much that was taken for granted and hence to strip it of its so-called timeless character. He also bridged many apparently glaring contradictions, quite particularly with his attempt in the *Erflaters* to reconcile the dynastic and personal ambitions of William of Orange with his unselfish devotion to the Dutch cause. The resulting portrait is remarkable for the tensions it reveals.

My remarks may have suggested that, to Romein, dialectics was, above all, an aesthetic and dramatic principle, from which, as in a sonnet, he extracted a kind of *volta*. There was more to it than that: far more telling was his view that history, and reality in general, are profoundly structured. There is no forward movement without a return, no change without resistance, no oppression without the pursuit of freedom, and no progress without the risk of being overtaken by those who have lagged behind. The concept of the historical handicap, of the privilege of back-wardness, a subject on which Veblen and Trotsky, to mention only two, also dwelled at some length, was central to many of Romein's writings. It is bound up with his idea that history is the record of man's continuous quest for emancipation. This quest takes many a twist and turn, often seeming to follow a retrograde course, but such deviations must not be allowed to obscure the basic direction. Romein tended to pay less attention to what happened at a given historical moment than to the later — often much later — consequences. In short, his historical writings have a strongly anticipatory character, not least the present work, in which he shows that the year 1914, far from being the watershed it is generally assumed to have been, was foreshadowed by much earlier changes. His anticipatory approach explains, in particular, the importance he attaches to early signs of the decline of European colonialism, to which few people paid due attention at the time. Hence the frequently voiced reproach of his opponents that Romein set out to theologize history, to rewrite it in retrospect. This is a point to which I have referred at greater length in my review of the Dutch edition of *The Watershed* in *History and Theory*, 9 (1970), p. 116 f.

Another aspect of Romein's dialectical approach should also be mentioned: Romein was forever engaged in breaking down boundaries and frontiers. He refused to conform to the customary practice of dividing the field of activity between political, social and cultural historians. To him, this compartmentalization of history was responsible for many distortions of the historical picture, for reductions that have done violence to the historical process. His Marxism, heterodox though it may have been, persuaded him early in his career to set his face against this kind of segmentation. He refused to be held back by boundaries resulting from the division of labor amongst historians, invariably turning his attention to the overall view, while at all times attaching great importance to the socio-economic factor, not least because it was neglected by the "bourgeois" historians of his day. It is difficult to say, however, to what extent Romein held that the material factors are of paramount importance, determining all the rest. Here, too, he reserved the right to be less hidebound than orthodox Marxists were prepared to allow. His heterodox approach was the cause of attacks from at least two sides: the orthodox camp treating him as a renegade who had failed to attach due importance to the objective laws of history, one who vaunted his subjectivism; and the "bourgeois" camp despising him as too much of a determinist and theorist, one who reduced the great complexity of historical events to oversimplified theories. Romein was often accused of using his historical writings as a vehicle for purveying Marxist propaganda, though there is little doubt that professional jealousy played its part here. For Romein, though a lone wolf, earned great renown by his writings on Dutch history in the thirties and later, much more than a historian from so small a country might have expected to enjoy.

This explains why Romein, his acknowledged erudition and keen intellect notwithstanding, remained an outsider, locked in battle not only with his erstwhile communist friends, who now considered him a Trotskyite, but also with his fellow historians, who thought he was lacking in historical objectivity. Time and again the man who had stressed the inevitable intervention of the subjective factor in so many of his essays was accused of using this fact as a pretext for his political, that is, Marxist, interpretation, from which he then derived a new "objectivation", namely, the idea that the only history capable of surmounting the historian's inescapable subjectivity was one rooted in the spirit of the age and hence alone capable of interpreting the tasks to be performed. Critics referred to this approach as Romein's dialectical somersault, and were particularly incensed by his use of the Hegelian concept of *Zeitgeist*, or spirit of the age, which, they claimed, was open to so many abuses.

It should not, however, be forgotten that it was the example of Romein's great teacher, Huizinga, which taught him that a scholar who cannot meet the challenges of his day is likely to end up as a cultural pessimist. "Is not every civilization bound to decay as soon as it begins to penetrate the masses?" Huizinga had echoed Rostovtsev, whom, incidentally, he had failed to quote correctly.

Despite the high regard in which Romein held Huizinga, he felt that his teacher had fallen into the trap set for all nineteenth-century cultural historians, to emerge as a *humaniste manqué*, just like Burckhardt, who was overwhelmed by the changes that occurred all around him. Romein spoke of Huizinga's Erasmian longing for safe neutrality (something of which Huizinga himself had accused Erasmus in his biography of the latter). According to Romein, Huizinga went out of his way to deal with non-contentious subjects. "They are deliberately insulated from the aspirations of our age and are redolent of the cloistered atmosphere of the scholar's study, to which no plebeian noises can percolate from the street, and in which the anti-Stoic struggle for a crust of bread cannot be heard" (*Het onvoltooid verleden*, p. 103). Here we can hear the voice of the disappointed student, lamenting the shortcomings of his admired mentor, shortcomings from which Romein believed that he himself was quite free. For though Romein, like Huizinga, came from a well-to-do bourgeois home, he realized what great changes the Russian Revolution had wrought in world history: after 1917, nothing was left untouched by the international civil war that has been raging ever since. This change had passed Huizinga by, at least according to Romein. As a result, he had failed to seize a great opportunity and hence to grasp his own age; worse still, he was driven onto the defensive and filled with the sense of impotence so characteristic of the liberal thinker — again according to the self-confident Romein. For the liberal thinker is caught in the web of his own conflicts. Huizinga's thought, too, was dominated by fear of the masses, or so Romein would have had us believe.

However that may be, Romein himself never sought refuge in safe neutrality. I have already mentioned a number of frontiers he crossed, to his colleagues' undisguised dismay. There were several more. Specialization and the increasing fragmentation of many disciplines filled Romein with as much horror as they did Karl Marx. Radical specialization has the result that historians are driven to write "historians' history" only, and to address themselves exclusively to their professional colleagues, thus stunting the social function of the historian.

A handful of them, however, still knew how to address a wider audience. Romein prided himself on being one of that small band, and throughout his life he searched for ways of halting this continuous shattering of the historical picture. This book is a prime example of his attempt to write integral history. It is difficult to describe the burdens that the attempt brought upon him. Only his unshakable sense of duty kept him at his desk, ignoring his pain, until the very end of his life. I still carry a vivid picture in my mind of this small, emaciated man working on his great project almost to his last breath, until it became physically impossible for him to carry on. From time to time he was plagued by doubts. When I drew his attention to H. Stuart Hughes's *Consciousness and Society* in 1961, he felt that much of his *Watershed* had become redundant. For Hughes, too, had dealt with the growing uncertainty in science and art, and the revolt against positivism as a philosophy dealing in certainties.

Romein always had a predilection for large-scale projects. Even as a schoolboy, he had written a history of the Church, and in his later years much of his time was spent, apart from the *Watershed*, on Part VI of the UNESCO *History of Mankind*. His object was to write the history of our time in such a way as to surmount the historiographic antitheses between East and West, and between North and South. This was the kind of challenge Romein was always glad to accept. He worked in close collaboration with Caroline Ware from the United States and with Panikkar from India. Theirs was a difficult task, and they were often impeded. The Russians, for example, had strong reservations about the work, despite the scholarly research that was carried out, and insisted on adding a piece of their own.

The *History of Mankind* was but one of many projects from which other historians might have shrunk, but into which Romein threw himself with gusto, some might say reckless abandon.

Apart from large-scale projects (another instance is the twelve-part *General History of the Netherlands*), Romein was also attracted by concepts with the broadest possible field of application. His "common human pattern" was just one example; with it, Romein tried once again to express the idea that, seen in historical perspective, the development of Western Europe reflects a relatively recent deviation from the much more common human pattern of thought and life found in most non-European cultures and in economically backward regions of Europe. He first presented this concept during a lecture tour of Indonesia in 1951. Critics have stressed that Romein introduced it as a counter to Eurocentrism but that, in so doing, he ignored the great differences in development of various non-capitalist societies. In other words, they claimed that a concept meant to eliminate the Eurocentric perspective was itself a Eurocentric device *par excellence*. Similar objections were also voiced against Romein's idea of the privilege of backwardness, which many of his colleagues thought much too vague. Wertheim, in particular, tried to show in his *Evolutie en Revolutie* what particular type of backwardness would, in which circumstances, encourage accelerated development, and argued that backwardness was not always a privilege. However, all Romein was trying to do with this idea was to challenge the prevailing belief in European superiority, at a time when other historians still held that Europe alone had a history. It is true that he did not develop his idea and that, in particular, he failed to differentiate it so that it could be applied to specific situations. But then, good Marxist that he was, he never aimed at the formalization of theories or models, something he believed was of little value in the study of historical processes. This explains why he rarely engaged in formal epistemological discussions à la Popper. Max Weber's work, so steeped in historical knowledge, was, next to Marx's, his most important guide. Like Marx, Romein believed that true theories must be elaborated "for concrete conditions and by means of concrete relations" (Letter from Marx, August 25, 1842).

His own term, "theoretical history", provides a key to the objectives of his theoretical studies. By it, he did not refer, like the historians of the Scottish Enlightenment, to "conjectural or hypothetical history", but to something akin to Marx's "theoretical praxis" and to what social scientists refer to as theoretical science. His friendship with the Leyden physicist, Kramers, persuaded him on more than one occasion to try to apply to history many of the ideas he had heard Kramers expound during long conversations. Romein has explained at some length why he chose that particular term in preference to the more customary "theory of history" or "philosophy of history". The concrete nature of the kind of study he had in mind was rooted in substantive history, which was all that mattered ultimately. Theory was a point of view — whence the adjectival use of that word. As against all those of his colleagues who maintained that history deals with practical matters about which we cannot theorize to any large extent, Romein argued that history is concerned with the relationship between the general and the particular, and that it is impossible to know one without understanding the other. It is the historian's task to discover recurrent patterns, regularities, compatible factors, all of which render the idea of unicity, so dear to many historians, far less self-evident that they take it to be.

In 1948, Romein presented his ideas to Anglo-Saxon readers in the *Journal of the History of Ideas.* His article was partly responsible for the decision of several American universities and members of the Rocke-feller Foundation to hold a special conference in Princeton. It was one of Romein's greatest disappointments when it turned out that his political opinions precluded him from entering the United States. He was never to visit that country and all his later contacts with American scholars were made in Europe. Luckily, his trip to Indonesia proved an effective plaster for his wounds.

Little came of his plan to make a closer theoretical study of U.S. historical problems during the late forties. The political climate was not propitious; moreover, the antitheoretical, pragmatic attitude of most American historians was still so marked that it took more than another decade before *History and Theory* could make its first appearance. It goes without saying that American philosophers and sociologists had taken an interest in the problems of theoretical history all along, but their work was frowned upon by most historians. Having had the experience of the sixties, when America awakened to the contributions of the European theorists, and of the Frankfurt school in particular, no less than to those of the previously ignored American Marxists, and when their books were snapped up in large numbers — we find it exceedingly difficult to imagine how deeply antitheoretical the climate was in the forties. Then it was the general consensus that theory is not only irrelevant but dangerous to boot.

When *History and Theory* was founded in the sixties, the Dutch historian invited to join the editorial board was not Romein but his colleague and opponent, Pieter Geyl, whose name was much better known in U.S. historical circles. Though Geyl had shown little interest in theoretical problems, his historiographic studies had not gone unread in the States; indeed, his essay on the causes of the American Civil War (*The American Civil War and the Problem of Inevitability*) was included in many a textbook. Nor had his polemic with Toynbee been forgotten. Romein, by contrast, was a relatively unknown figure.

In a sense it is a tragedy that so small a country as the Netherlands should have produced two historians of rank after World War II, and that they should have been engaged in what, to Geyl at least, was an endless polemic. Time and again, Geyl railed against what he considered the corrosive character of Romein's approach. Romein rarely bothered to answer these charges, even though his own students were accused of repeating their teacher's sins. It was all based on a misunderstanding: Geyl's suspicion that Romein was trying to set up a school of his own. Yet nothing could have been further from Romein's mind. He always went out of his way — and I speak from personal experience — to select assistants whose approach to history no less than to politics, differed widely from his own.

To Geyl, who still devoted his valedictory lecture to the vitality of Western civilization, Romein must have seemed a corrupter of youth, a man all the more dangerous for his intelligence and erudition, which Geyl acknowledged in all his attacks. Geyl's chief objections were Romein's views of the task of the theoretical historian and his political commitment. Geyl often quoted Romein's dictum that no amount of abstract argument is worth a single application, and countered with: "Why not a three-part work on cultural history in the nineteenth century!" Romein rose to that challenge with his *Watershed*, in which he tried to adduce proof of the general validity of his theories.

When Romein drew the attention of his compatriots to Toynbee's work — despite the fact that he differed from Toynbee in many respects, not least in his attitude to religion — Geyl once more uttered a warning against the dangers of this type of theoretical approach. How immoderate his attacks often were became particularly clear in 1961, when Geyl saw fit to turn his wrath against Huizinga. But at the time his championship of the West enjoyed wide support, while Romein was plainly sailing against the wind. Today, however, when we look back at Geyl's most important contributions (the unity of the Dutch people, the adverse role of many Orange *stadtholders*), we are bound to say that few have stood the test of time. Many of his ideas were distorted by his bias, were the offshoots of so many political *idées fixes.* In the fifties, however, Geyl undoubtedly dominated not only the Dutch historical scene but also the face it presented to the outside world. Romein's reaction, over and above his natural disappointment, was "My time will surely come".

I do not maintain, of course, that Romein was always right. Though he changed his ideas about the Soviet Union over the years, and especially in the thirties, fear of, and revulsion from, anticommunism inhibited him from pursuing his critique of Stalinism as far as he might have done. At the very least, he glossed over many important problems. And during the Cold War, he refused to bow down to the proffered alternatives — either this side of the other — and came up with his own solution of *tertium datur.* He refused resolutely to swallow the dichotomous, Manichean world view, and instead paid increasing attention to dissenters, heretics, past thinkers who had rejected the dogmas of their day. One of the last seminars organized by Romein was devoted to Pierre Bayle, whose *Dictionnaire* (1695) had unmasked many prejudices, not least those underlying the mutual recriminations of Protestants and Catholics.

The system of power blocs that emerged after World War II left little room for a third force. Small wonder, then, that Romein, ever the great heretic, was assailed from both sides. There was no hint of the freeze to come; the threat of a third world war divided mankind into two camps and imposed a choice from which only a very few knew how to escape. Romein, for one, did not feel free to voice his reservations about the Soviet Union. He held that in doing so, he would only be serving the other side. Moreover, the Soviet Union, despite everything that had gone wrong, continued to have a strong emotional hold on him. This was a subject on which he wrote numerous polemics.

And, indeed, many of Romein's writings were polemical in character. I remember that, during our first encounter, I could not for the life of me understand how this amiable and gentle man could have been the fierce polemicist I knew from his writings, one whose bluntly heterodox views had lost him so many supporters. Jan Romein's biography is a saga of broken relationships. For all that, he not only kept many old friends but also earned the loyalty of that large circle of men and women who stuck by him to the very last. First and foremost among these was his wife, with whom he collaborated in a host of studies, and who also completed the *Watershed* after his death. Jan and Annie Romein were a well known bi-unity in the post-war Netherlands.

Apart from his wife, there was also his friend Dirk Struik, who had gone to the United States in the twenties. A professor at M.I.T., Struik felt the blast of the Cold War even more sharply and directly than did Romein in the Netherlands. It was Struik who helped Romein with those parts of the *Watershed* that are devoted to the development of the natural sciences.

Romein received no official Dutch recognition for his work. The due of much lesser men was withheld from him. He never complained, however, for he was well aware of the climate in which he worked.

Yet, at a crucial moment in its history, he nevertheless made a great contribution to the country that spurned him. He did so in a lecture he delivered at the University of Amsterdam in November, 1940. Its title was "The Origins, Development and Future of Dutch History". Before a large audience — and under the vigilant eye of the German occupier — he made his position perfectly clear. It was an impressive and solemn occasion, and one that would long be remembered. "Those of us," he said on that occasion, "who are filled with the spirit of the Netherlands . . . know that we are swimming against the stream, but then we are used to that." And he concluded with: "Remember that you are scions of our beloved country; be true to its ideals and do not flinch." No one can doubt that Romein, the convinced Marxist, was also a good and loyal Dutchman.

Intellectual courage informed these carefully considered remarks, voiced during a critical moment in his country's history. His great disappointment came after the war, when the renaissance he so ardently desired failed to materialize, and restoration and reconstruction of the past predominated. It was not until the sixties that there was a drastic change for the better — too late for Romein, who died in the summer of 1962.

— MAARTEN C. BRANDS

PREFACE

When Jan Romein died on July 16, 1962, some of the forty-two chapters in Parts I and II of this book and the whole of Part III — which had been intended as the theoretical demonstration — had not yet been written. I had no wish to see the work to which my husband had, during the last ten years of his life, devoted all his spare time, abandoned in manuscript form, and was glad to agree when the publishers asked me to complete it.

However, none of the theoretical section had been committed to paper and there was nothing from which I could even begin a reconstruction. The basic ideas of Parts I and II had been a familiar strand in my husband's thoughts: "Part III won't take me long," he had said, "I have it all in my head."

Fortunately the publishers shared my belief that even this incomplete sample of what my husband used to call the integral presentation of history would find a response from the general reader, the more so as the theoretical part would, by its very nature, have been addressed to a more specialized circle.

What my husband meant by the integral historical approach is briefly set out in one of the essays constituting his posthumous *Eender en anders* (Like and Unlike). In it, he tried to show that, while historical *studies* have benefited from the modern trend to specialize and to distinguish among, say, political, economic, social, cultural, and art history, the *writing* of history has suffered a great deal from this specialization. He accordingly tried to oppose this trend with a new specialty: a form of historical analysis in which the various "flat" projections are reconstructed into a three-dimensional whole. He was fascinated by the idea that the relatively comprehensive treatment of a large enough number of their facets might lead to an integral understanding of short historical periods.

This book is an attempt at writing this kind of history. The choice of period was not accidental: the most cursory survey of the European scene at about 1900 shows plainly that it marked a turning point in almost every sphere of human endeavor. Moreover, in the preparation and actual writing of each successive chapter, it became increasingly clear that a common thread ran through them all. However cautious the historian must be with material that fits — or seems to fit — his working hypothesis, in the present case the writer felt entitled to think that it did just that, and that the turn of the last century had indeed produced an overall change in the historical pattern.

As I have said, the writing of integral history, too, calls for a degree of specialization. It involves a regulating principle, wide historical knowledge, and a deep interest in historical processes, lest the regulating principle degenerate into a mere schematization. Although Jan Romein was possessed of the last two qualities to a very high degree, he did not feel up to writing two chapters that demanded more specialist knowledge than he — let alone I — commanded. To my great delight, Professor D. J. Struik of Cambridge, Massachusetts, at once agreed to complete the work of his near lifelong friend with a chapter on science, which few are more qualified to write than he. I owe him a great debt of gratitude. I am also indebted to F. Knuttel of Dordrecht for her survey of the history of music during the period under review and for giving me permission to adapt the material to the general structure of this book. I should also like to express my sincerest thanks to Dr. M. Brands and Dr. J. Haak and their colleagues in the Historical Institute, University of Amsterdam, particularly P. B. M. Maas, J. Giele, and my oldest son, J. E. Romein, for their time-consuming bibliographic research, for checking and correcting the manuscript, and for compiling the index. Finally, I should like to put it on record that P. A. L. Oppenheimer proved to be as devoted a secretary in working on my husband's literary estate, as he had been for more than thirty years in Jan Romein's lifetime.

— ANNIE ROMEIN-VERSCHOOR

INTRODUCTION

Ask a serious student of European history if there have been any outstanding Dutch historians in the twentieth century. Predictably, the
student will name Johan Huizinga, possibly adding the name of Pieter
Geyl, the only other Dutch historian apt to be widely known in the
English-speaking world. Publication of the present work in English dress
may lead — no, should lead — to the inclusion of the name of Jan Marius
Romein. The relationship between Romein and Huizinga, and to a lesser
degree between Romein and Geyl, will require some attention.

It would be easy to attribute the relative lack of familiarity with
Romein's work in the English-reading world to his regrettable but understandable habit of writing in his mother tongue, and Dutch is a language
not widely taught in secondary schools outside of Holland, except in
Flemish-speaking areas of Belgium. We have here a simple, clear, and
persuasive explanation, but it won't wash. It is of course true, but language is not the whole story. It would not be impossible for an English
monoglot to acquire some idea of Romein's thought from publications
in English, even some idea of the present book: a forty-four page abstract
appeared, in English, in 1971 in *Acta Historiae Neerlandica*. This annual,
admittedly, is not found next to the almanacs on every newsstand.
Romein's English articles are scattered in several journals, and the one
book by him heretofore available in English, *The Asian Century*, may
have seemed pitched exclusively to specialists in Asian history. Another
book in English bearing his name on the title page must be disregarded.
Volume six of the UNESCO *History of Mankind* (London: George Allen
and Unwin, 1968) lists as authors-editors Caroline F. Ware, K. M. Panikkar, and Jan Romein, but they advise the reader that it is "a joint, not a
composite piece of work," and one could not hope to isolate Romein's
part.

More important than the language limitation was Jan Romein's diver-
gence, to adapt one of his concepts, from "the common historian's pattern." Within the profession Romein was a maverick (and Pieter Geyl a
far more conventional historian and more widely known in the Anglo-

American world). Romein was unconventional as a historian. During the middle third of the twentieth century his leftist politics and his interest in theoretical problems of history set him off from the majority of his profession. A self-declared Marxist, Romein was so consistently unconventional, or more precisely, so uncompromisingly independent, that after a decade of membership the Netherlands Communist Party expelled him. That was in 1927. Excommunication from the Third International as a heretic did not render him more acceptable to conservatives.

Romein published much, and some of these other writings will be drawn upon to show the stages of his thinking that led to his culminating achievement, the book that follows. Since the genesis and development of his ideas inevitably reflected the events of his life, and since he once wrote that "the foundation of all biographical work is a list of the dates of the life to be described," I had better provide a brief chronology of the outward events of his life, after which we can examine his ideas.

Jan Marius Romein was born in Rotterdam on October 30, 1893. Delayed by illness, he entered the University of Leyden older than most beginning students during the First World War. He studied literature and then history, and he met Annie Verschoor, who was born near Nijmegen on February 2, 1895. They were married on August 14, 1920, and by 1921 both of them had passed their examinations. Jan qualified for the doctorate in 1924, Annie eleven years and three children later. In 1939 Jan Romein was appointed associate professor in the municipal University of Amsterdam. The Nazi occupiers of the Netherlands removed him from his post and held him for three months in the Amersfoort prison camp, releasing him and some other prisoners in celebration of the Führer's birthday. Following the liberation of the Netherlands, Romein became a full professor in 1945. He succumbed to a heart attack on July 16, 1962, leaving the manuscript, or most of it, underlying the present book. Annie Romein-Verschoor, with help from friends and some of her late husband's former students, prepared the manuscript for publication. It appeared in two volumes in 1967: *Op het breukvlak van twee eeuwen* (Leyden & Amsterdam: Brill, Querido, 1967). Three years after in effect perfecting her husband's estate Annie Romein-Verschoor looked back in wonderment and wrote her memoirs. (Annie Romein-Verschoor, *Omzien in Verwondering*, 2 v. [Amsterdam: de Arbeiderpers, 1970–71]). She was an independent spirit and a scholar in her own right in the sociology of literature and the arts as well as co-worker and collaborator in several works with her husband. It would be misleading as well as unjust to this consistent feminist to derive her identity from another, to label her merely Jan Romein's wife and widow. Her autobiography, which is also in part a memoir of her husband's life, is candid and revealing and often moving.

Both the Romeins, as is common among Western, and probably not only Western Marxist intellectuals, came from middle-class families. Annie's father was a ship's captain, Jan was well off for a student, thanks to an inheritance from his grandmother. At the university Jan associated with a handful of exceptionally mature student intellectuals who introduced him to Marxism and who later achieved eminence, especially in physics and mathematics. Among them was Dirk Jan Struik, later professor of mathematics at M.I.T., from whose pen came chapter 22 of the present work. The Bolshevik Revolution in November, 1917, excited the enthusiasm of these students, including Jan Romein and Annie Verschoor, and Jan undertook a Dutch translation of Franz Mehring's life of Karl Marx, published in 1921. His scholarly interests initially had centered on literature, and when he shifted to history, the second impetus, I conjecture, derived from the intrinsically historical outlook of Marxism. (The primary impetus had another root which requires longer exposition). Annie Romein later described their continued admiration for Marx's ideas, but always seen "inevitably in historical perspective." She writes that "historical materialism for us was primarily a method of working, never a faith." Nonetheless, in the eyes of the orthodox Communists they had lost the faith; in their own eyes they saw no reason to abjure their working method.

The primary stimulus turning Jan Romein to seek to become a professional historian was the influence of Johan Huizinga, professor of history at Leyden when Jan Romein and Annie Verschoor were students there. Yet the differences between the professor and Jan Romein appeared diametrical. Jan Romein was political to his finger tips, "committed," as we are apt to say nowadays, and specifically a Marxist and a democrat. Huizinga was none of these. He was aloof, non-political. Romein himself characterized Huizinga's ideal of historical writing as "aristocratic-stoic," and instead of commitment Romein found in Huizinga's writings "an Erasmian need for pure neutrality." Politics held no interest for Huizinga.

Huizinga's indifference to politics lasted until May 1940. On the tenth of that month, Nazi armies swept over the Netherlands and on the fourteenth the government capitulated, "He was sixty-eight years old," wrote Professor Rosalie L. Colie of Huizinga, "when he learned that even if a man can ignore politics, politics does not ignore him." (R. L. Colie, "Johan Huizinga and the Task of Cultural History," *American Historical Review*, 69 (April 1964), 629). In his revulsion at the Nazi violation of his country, Huizinga refused obedience to the conquerors, and was confined as a hostage. Yet this came decades after Romein had chosen the profession of historian. What could have drawn the quintessentially political Romein to the profoundly non-political cultural historian?

Romein all his life looked up to Huizinga — but critically. The reader of an essay Romein published in 1931 on Huizinga's views on cultural history could infer from such biting criticism that the two men espoused irreconcilable positions. The professor defended his views against his (apostate?) former pupil. To a reprint of his critical article Romein added an unrepentant postscript, withdrawing none of his critical analysis. "This judgment upon an aging scholar," Romein concluded, "may seem too harsh on the part of one who had the happiness to be his pupil, and who remains grateful to him. He should consider that precisely as his pupil I hold to what Lessing said: 'A miserable poetaster one does not criticize at all; a mediocre poet one treats with forbearance; but to a great poet one is ruthless.' "

When Romein in the early 1920's sought to complete his doctorate — "promoveren" — under Huizinga's supervision he visited his Leyden professor. They exchanged ideas about topics for a dissertation, but to no avail. Jan came back to tell Annie that every topic that Huizinga proposed he found too dull, and every topic he proposed Huizinga found too dangerous. So Romein had to find another professor, Van Wijk, to supervise his dissertation. It treated the Western reception of the works of Dostoyevsky, a topic evidently neither too dull for Romein nor too dangerous for Van Wijk. Yet it was not his dissertation supervisor, Van Wijk, but Huizinga whom he considered his mentor. "All my life," he said, "at the completion of any piece of work, I can never free myself from the thought: what would Huizinga think of it?

One more item on this relationship: when Romein's name at long last was advanced for consideration to fill a vacancy in the faculty of history in the municipal university of Amsterdam, Romein might have hoped for backing from his mentor. Instead, Huizinga wondered whether Romein had any ability as a teacher: he had never faced a class. And when in the spring of 1939 Romein was finally appointed an associate professor at Amsterdam, and a covey of conservative historians addressed a protest to the minister at the appointment of such an enemy of his country, who was it who publicly defended Romein? Not Huizinga, who preferred another man on the ground that he had done archival work, not precisely the source of Huizinga's own fame. It was, among others, Pieter Geyl against whom Romein had polemicized and who had responded in kind against Romein. Geyl published a statement in the press denouncing the use of politics to bar Romein from his chair. Pieter Geyl was unwilling to stoop, even by silence, to endorse the intrusion of what he considered irrelevant slander to block the appointment of a man with whom he disagreed on professional issues. Huizinga's admirers felt shame at his timid behavior; Geyl's critics admired their opponent's honorable conduct.

In view of all these frustrations, how can we account for Jan Romein's continued view of Huizinga as his imperfect but revered mentor? At once, the currently fashionable thought leaps to mind: is this not a nearly classical oedipal relationship? The intellectual son slays his revered intellectual father — his *Doktorvater* — while the father struggles for his life against his threatening son. This explanation will surely satisfy anyone who forgets to ask why Jan Romein envisaged Johan Huizinga as his intellectual father. If we could answer this question, we could justify the Freudian flourishes.

Yet this oedipal hypothesis need not be dismissed if only we can find some evidence for it. It is true that Mrs. Romein says: "My husband had a real '*Schüler-complex*' with respect to Huizinga." But a pupil-master relationship is not necessarily clarified by translating it into a son-father connection. Furthermore, if we wish to picture Huizinga as Romein's "Doctor-Father" — the term is German university jargon, and I do not know whether it is also found in Netherlands universities — we have a difficulty. Van Wijk, not Huizinga, was Romein's dissertation supervisor. We would be compelled, therefore, to identify Van Wijk, the actual "Doctor-Father," as the Surrogate Father, or the Doctor Stepfather who took the place of the "real" Doctor-Father, Huizinga. This leaves us again with the problem of explaining why Romein viewed Huizinga as his "real" Doctor-Father, and we are back at square one. If there is insufficient evidence to support the oedipal hypothesis, neither is there enough evidence to invalidate it. Romein's attitude toward Huizinga was one of great respect tempered with acute critical reserve, which can be placed in a non-father context. The simplest explanation of Romein's attitude toward Huizinga, setting aside this amateurish venture into pseudo-psychohistory, is that although Huizinga had limitations, he had in the eyes of many, including Romein, the attributes of a great historian. The particular modes of his greatness evidently met needs deeply felt by the younger historian.

During the summer of 1946 Romein drafted a lecture on "Huizinga as Historian." He delivered it as part of a lecture series in the auditorium of Amsterdam University on November 7, 1946. For a self-declared Marxist to commemorate the twenty-ninth anniversary of the Bolshevik Revolution with a tribute to Huizinga appears odd, yet it has its rationale, too. The lecturer began with an account of his early personal contact with

Huizinga. The very first course he took with him in 1915 deflected the young man from his previous intentions "and made such an impression on the youthful student that from that moment on he knew what he wanted to become; and further, and more to the point, that . . . for years he would remain the intellectual follower of his mentor." Romein took every course — he lists five more — that Huizinga offered during the next five years. As soon as Huizinga's *Waning of the Middle Ages* appeared in the bookshops in 1919, he bought a copy. "It made the deepest impression on me that a book can make on anyone. This is the way, and no other way, that I want to learn to write, I swore to myself after reading the first pages." The student subsequently devoured the book on twelve successive evenings. He contrived an occasion to relate this to his professor, as if it were an achievement, to which Huizinga, "smiling, but also with a tinge of regret, said: 'And I have worked on it for twelve years.'"

Romein's untarnished admiration for his professor seems to have lasted two full years, and now the lecturer, sketching this personal portrait, adds some crosshatching to deepen as well as to complicate the simple outline thus far. And in so doing, he tips his mortarboard, so to speak, to the calendar that reads November 7, 1946. "Into the honey of my admiration the wormwood of criticism began to mix since 1917, the year of the Russian Revolution." The young man's enthusiastic reception of the news of the November revolution was shared in not the least degree by his professor.

This episode parallels the painful stage in a boy's life when he begins to acquire an identity of his own, when he discovers failings in his heretofore unblemished father. In his study of biography published in 1946, Romein identifies the most fruitful attitude of the biographer to his subject as one of ambivalence. In his Huizinga lecture he places the onset of his ambivalence to his subject in 1917. Huizinga with his magician's wand had lifted the curtain to reveal the wonders of the past; now Marxism appeared to the sorcerer's apprentice to offer a recipe to make the past speak. Huizinga disdained it while Romein possessed himself of it, or was possessed by it. Ambivalence set in.

Romein now cites his sharply critical essay on Huizinga of 1931, from which the ending has already been quoted. "It was fundamentally a rejection, but it was equally an act of admiration; and yet I think not inconsistent," To this criticism, he tells his audience, Huizinga showed no resentment. And now the lecturer presents a startling analogy. He compares his intellectual conflict with Huizinga to Jacob wrestling with the Angel, until the latter blessed him. The text in Genesis (R.S.V. 32:28–30) does not identify Jacob's opponent as an "angel." When Jacob says: "Tell me, I pray, your name," he does not answer the question. Since he had previously told Jacob: "You have striven with God and with men, and have prevailed," Jacob draws the inference: "I have seen God face to face, and yet my life is preserved." If Romein sees himself as having wrestled with God, he is displaying an extraordinary reverence toward his professor, yet he sees himself as prevailing. With this the lecturer ends his personal reminiscences.

What seemed so extraordinary to Romein was Huizinga's symbiotic fusion of two distinct and strong powers, the artistic and the scholarly. As a historian should, Romein places his mentor in historical context, asking "Why should I shrink from applying to Huizinga what he did not shun in applying to Rembrandt?" Huizinga's mind developed in his student years, from 1881 to 1891, "the Indian Summer of liberalism," and although he became "one of the midwives assisting at the birth of the new century," this new age he helped usher in was not to his liking. Because of his liberal nineteenth-century rationality he detested the new century's "hideous excrescence of irrationality" to which he himself had contributed. In Huizinga's abhorrence of twentieth-century irrationality Romein thought he detected a tincture of guilt. "In a scholarly sense, he did not belong to his own times."

Romein shows no doubt that he himself belonged to the twentieth century, thanks to his Marxism. He saw two ways of viewing the contemporary crisis of culture. One way was to penetrate to the causes, "whereby the *structure* of society is not blameless." This was the way of "socialist criticism." Or else one may criticize merely the symptoms, leaving the social structure unchallenged. This was the way of "bourgeois criticism." Huizinga, inescapably, had to pursue the second course. "His fame as a critic of his times rests ultimately upon the completely innocuous character of his criticism." "Huizinga was no thinker," says Romein: he was, instead a seer. His work "is many-sided; it is not inclusive." We shall recall this remark when we consider Romein's concept of "integral history."

Romein did not end his lecture on Huizinga on a negative note. Huizinga, he thought, combined two gifts, one of understanding ("rendering an account"), the other of vision. In turn, they derived from a more fundamental element of his personality structure. "Is 'seeing' anything but rendering an account of the visible? And conversely, is rendering an account anything but 'seeing' the invisible? I have no word for the separate twin-gifts, but if you ask me what was special about Huizinga I do not hesitate to answer: the ineffable." One is tempted to exclaim: "Good God!" After all, "God said to Moses: 'I am who I am.'" The Ineffable.

"And in this ineffable," continues Romein, "I see his importance, his importance for his discipline which is also mine, and beyond that, for both of us, for our Fatherland. Fatherland — for see how the Netherlands comprises both aspects of this quality. I do not have to demonstrate the Dutch [talent] for 'seeing.' You know our painters. And as for rendering an account: Karel van Woestijne well said in speaking of [the poet] Verwey: '*Un Hollandais, c'est un homme qui se rend compte.*"

As a historian and a man of the twentieth century, recognizing the mutability of judgments, Romein anticipates the supersession of his views on Huizinga by some future scholar.

> I have learned only too well that everything human, and hence every-
> thing historical, is always more intricate than even someone who is
> convinced of this truth can imagine. So I can believe that the future
> writer may gloss over the theoretical weakness of Huizinga, showing
> that he was nonetheless the first in our country to consider theoret-
> ical questions. I can imagine him explaining away or acquitting
> Huizinga of the inconsistencies with which I have reproached him.

The future writer may conclude that Huizinga's diagnosis of the crisis of our times was correct. And finally, Romein pictures the future author deleting the words, "He was a great historian," as superfluous. To pursue further the question of why Romein was influenced by Huizinga appears likewise to be superfluous.

Three matters remain to be considered before approaching the present book: first, Romein's idea of "integral history;" second, his Marxism; and third, his concept of the "Common Human Pattern."

On October 19, 1957, less than five years before his death, Romein delivered a lecture "On the Writing of Integral History." It summarized two decades of thinking that concerned the problem of content but was not consciously formulated to permit analysis of it. He was concerned to overcome the traditionally limited scope of Clio's territories. He wanted the range of historical scholarship expanded to encompass "psychology, philosophy, sociology, the arts, political science, economics, religion, the ways in which life, society, and human beings are viewed, the knowledge of all the sciences and literatures, and not least, the connections and interrelationships among groups, families, and generations." Easier said than done: how was the historian to cope with this? One could conduct research into all the "peripheral" fields, but that would imply the exis-tence of a central field, "whereas in fact the concept of integrality, if we think it through, permits no residual field, no specific historical field that would be the 'central field.' " The problem, rather, is to ascertain the interconnections linking human activities in a "holistic" approach. "Holism" — the word comes from the South African general, statesman, and philosopher, Jan Christiaan Smuts — Romein finds everywhere in this century. It is "in the air," but to speak in this way is to summon up a metaphysical phantasm, the "Spirit of the Age," the *Zeitgeist*. "Only integral historiography can transform the *Zeitgeist* from a vague, mystical idea into a scientific insight," Only then can one hope to answer correctly two questions: "What are the dominant elements of a given '*Zeitgeist*'? and what are the political economic, social, and intellectual constellations that give rise to it?"

Everything is connected with everything else. True enough, but this is the heart of the problem. (Huizinga's work was "many-sided" but "not inclusive"). "In this way alone, the idea of integral history arose quite simply out of what Huizinga called 'rendering an account.' " But there was another source as well. "The great impetus to the origin of the integral history concept came, in my opinion, from Karl Marx." His historical outlook contained an integral factor: it was ultimately the mode of production, economics, "with which everything, political, social, and cultural, stood in more or less remote functional connection." Yet Romein quotes George Lukács, himself a Marxist, as saying: "It is not the predominance of the economic motif that decisively distinguishes Marxist from bourgeois scholarship but the viewpoint of totality." Marx's integralism appears defective since there is a central field, the economic, yet, asks Romein, do not the terms "base" and "superstructure" imply a functional relationship? One must perceive the whole: no mountain without a valley, no valley without a mountain. They constitute a single system as inseparably linked as change and continuity.

How can the historian master such a system? Everyone knows, albeit vaguely, that one epoch follows another, yet can anyone imagine that he can really know how the transition occurs? Romein does not tackle this problem explicitly in his lecture on integral history, although the big book that he was then toiling over proves to be a study of precisely such a transition. In the lecture he warned that no one could apply the method of integral history to the totality of the past, but it was not impossible to treat a segment of the past integrally.

> During the war . . . I formulated a plan to write an integral history of the year 1900, in which I would not go back beyond 1889 nor go forward past 1914. Concerning the results I cannot now speak since so far I have not gotten past the first half of the first of the three volumes. Like so many others, I must deplore that the occupa-

tion of professor today leaves one so little time for research. But quite apart from the question of whether it shall fall to my lot to complete this magnum opus, on the basis of what is now completed I feel entitled to say that no matter how difficult it may be, integral historiography is possible. *Quod erat demonstrandum.*

As we know, it fell to Romein's lot to complete, or nearly complete, two of the three volumes. The third, the theoretical part, as he told his wife, was all in his head, and hence no draft existed among his papers. If we wish to know how Romein pictured integral history, the text lies before us. To understand it more fully, we must look at the two further components in the author's outlook.

Romein called himself a Marxist. For a decade after the Bolshevik Revolution he was a member of the Communist Party of the Netherlands, but this did not numb his brain and he proved to be a nettlesome comrade. He more or less withdrew from party activity in 1925, and two years later he was formally expelled. He and Annie Romein continued to think of themselves as Marxists but hewed to their principles instead of the party line. His Marxism, as should be evident already, was hardly doctrinaire. With respect to the U.S.S.R. he was no simple-minded defender of Soviet Russia, right or wrong. He and Annie, for example, found Soviet treatment of Hungary in 1956 utterly indefensible, but neither did they find the actions of the Western powers to be glorious.

What did Romein think about "revolution"? We know that as a young man he had responded enthusiastically to the news of the Bolshevik Revolution, but the views he held as a mature historian can be read in his treatment of the problem of *omslag.* He translated the word into English as "turnover," and used it to refer to the dialectical metamorphosis of a culture, or a segment thereof, into a new form. He does not use the metaphor "mutation," nor does he call the turnover a revolution. To this problem he devoted a paper intended to be delivered to a conference of British and Dutch historians to be held at Utrecht in September of 1962. Since Romein died in July, the paper was presented by a former student of his under the title, "Change and Continuity in History. The Problem of the 'Turnover,'" It was subsequently printed in *Delta* in the spring, 1963, issue.

The essence of Romein's thought is contained in one sentence: "The core of the problem of the 'turnover' . . . rests in the dialectical unity of two seemingly absolute and irreconcilable opposites, continuity and change." He explained, however, that they "are not absolute, but relative, opposites. They belong together like light and shadow . . . . If there were only continuity, everything would stay the same . . . . If on the other hand only change existed, there would be constantly something brand new, without the slightest connection with what had gone on before."

> Historical evolution, if my approach is correct, takes place in a practically infinite series of micro-processes. Some of these micro-processes, so to say in conjunction with one another, then prompt and direct the macro-processes which, again in conjunction, give shape and content to the vast historical drama and are usually the historian's material for study.

Romein then comes to the theme of his big book: "To stick to the turn of the last century: with this approach we may be able to understand what happened then as the resultant of a practically endless but nonetheless describable series of micro-processes operating in the brains and hearts of men," to wit, "the transformation of the traditional forms of domination into those of modern imperialism; the development of classical capitalism into a new type of banking and monopoly capitalism; the great landslide in which the masses for the first time joined the nations to play an active role in world developments."

Romein's Marxism found expression in his sensitivity to class structure, but it is hardly employed to force everything into a simple class-conflict model. His sympathies and antipathies, though controlled, are evident. He thinks dialectically not out of piety toward Marx (or Hegel) but because he believed that reality proceeded dialectically. He was a Dutch patriot — not a nationalist — who wanted Holland's colonial empire dismantled. His ability to understand, to render an account of, Holland's neighboring cultures, and the more remote ones as well, exhibited that empathy which Huizinga, in a lecture delivered in Berlin three days before Hitler was appointed Chancellor (and which I heard), attributed to educated Netherlanders as a consequence of their country's intermediary position in Europe. A Marxist, yes, but as a reviewer of one of Romein's works wrote, some authors ride their hobbyhorses to death, Romein leaves his in the stable.

Debarred from an academic position for twelve years after his expulsion from the Communist Party, denounced by the conservatives as a communist and by the Communists as a "Trotskyite," Romein supported his family by extensive journalism and by writing scholarly articles and books. In 1934 Jan and Annie Romein published a history of their country, *De Lage Landen bij de Zee* (*The Low Lands By the Sea*), a one-volume work of Marxist interpretation aimed at a popular readership.

How Marxist was it? Written by authors denounced by conservatives as "unpatriotic," this book, so several survivors of the Nazi concentration camps in Holland later told them, along with the Bible, helped buoy up the prisoners' anguished feelings.

To condense their country's history from ancient times to the present in a single volume the Romeins had felt obliged to scant the role of individuals. They therefore undertook to prepare a gallery of portrait studies of three dozen individuals who had contributed to the shaping of Dutch culture. This appeared in 1938–1940 under the title *Erflaters van onze Beschaving. Nederlandse gestalten uit zes eeuwen* (*Legators of our Civilization. Dutch Figures From Six Centuries*). *The Low Lands By the Sea* went through four printings before the death of Jan Romein, the last edition being lavishly illustrated in four paperback volumes. By 1959 the biographical portraits achieved eight printings. The authors briefly touched on their Marxism in the foreword. They agreed that the Marxist approach was neither the first nor the only one to connect "great men" with their times, but the question was "what is the nature of the connection"? Connections might be external and superficial; what they sought were the internal and intrinsic connections. They also agreed that Marxism, apart from a few scattered efforts, had failed to address itself to the psychological explanation of individual behavior, essential in understanding any individual, great or small. Such neglect stemmed from the Marxist focus on large scale social relationships rather than on individual ones. History for Marxists examined a series of mutual group relationships "whose ultimate basis is found in the ways they procure their subsistence." Psychology they saw as the study of the ways in which individuals relate to themselves and others and as members of groups, the prerequisite for biography. (In his book on biography, Romein couples the names of Freud and Marx). In short, their Marxism is undoctrinaire, only "ultimately" relating mass phenomena to their economic base, and it is modulated through their authors' considerable acquaintance with Freud's writings, again applied in an undoctrinaire way.

The thirty-six subjects in their biographical book include admirals and generals, poets and painters, musicians, scientists, physicians, colonial administrators, statesmen, political leaders, and an architect, at least half of them of international renown, an extraordinary pantheon of luminaries for one small nation. That they should have included Hugo de Groot, Rembrandt and Van Gogh, Erasmus and Spinoza, reveals the expected. The inclusion of Eduard Douwes Dekker, "Multatuli," the revolutionary writer who championed the cause of the Indonesian people in the Dutch

East Indies, or Ferdinand Domela Nieuwenhuis, anarchist, "the apostle of the workers," points to their political values.

The ambivalence of which Romein spoke in his lecture on "Huizinga as Historian" appears in these biographical sketches. If it brings the subjects to life, it is because when it is sensitively informed it introduces shadings that mold the subject, even in a cameo, into the round. If human beings, as we see ourselves in this century, are perceived as bundles of contradictions, then a biographical method that reveals similar inconsistencies in the illustrious dead revivifies them in a way that neither hagiography nor debunking can achieve. This is no cut-and-slash "Marxist" approach: the founder of the East Indian empire is understood in his times and is not anachronistically damned as an imperialist. The approach is — I shall not say Marxist — dialectical, and hence compatible with Marxism. It is also compatible with other approaches. Herbert J. Muller in his *Uses of the Past* (1952) views the past with two constructs, irony and tragedy, drawn from literary criticism but found in life, past and present, as well as in literature. Muller's "irony" is close to Romein's "ambivalence," recognizing, as I would put it, that there is a dark cloud around every silver lining, no ointment lacks its fly, and that good intentions inevitably pave a stretch of the road to perdition. Romein could concur in Muller's recognition that in the final analysis there is no final analysis. From the concept of "ambivalence" we approach the third of Romein's dominant ideas that the reader of the text that follows needs to keep in mind, the idea of the "Common Human Pattern."

In 1951 Jan and Annie Romein sailed for Indonesia. It was backlash compensation for the frustration he had recently suffered. In the spring of 1948 *The Journal of the History of Ideas* had invited him to submit an article on theoretical history, which was subsequently published. Presently the European representative of the Rockefeller Foundation made his acquaintance and subsequently undertook to arrange a grant for a three-month trip to the United States to lecture on theoretical history at several universities. But in 1949 Romein's request for a visa was denied, over the protests of the Rockefeller people, Arnold J. Toynbee, and the Dutch ambassador in Washington. Evidently his Marxism was powerful enough to intimidate the State Department in the era of McCarthy. So the Romeins were open to an invitation to visit Indonesia.

For her it was a return to the scenes of her childhood and early adolescence. She had lived there from her tenth to her fifteenth year. For him — and the university authorities authorized his leave of absence only reluctantly — it was the first direct contact with the non-European world.

The origins of this visit went back two decades. In 1928 a Dutch publisher had commissioned him to translate and adapt for Dutch readers the eight-volume *Harmsworth's Illustrated History of the World*. Annie Romein rewrote the chapter on modern art and literature. Jan himself wrote three new chapters, on the Revolt of the Netherlands, the Russian Revolution, and the Awakening of Asia. The publisher reprinted the chapter on the Awakening of Asia as a pamphlet and shipped it out to the Dutch East Indies. There the governor-general forbade its distribution. What made it subversive in the eyes of the authorities, its thesis that Indonesia should be free from Dutch colonial rule, a viewpoint shared by very few Netherlanders in 1931 when it appeared, was precisely what ensured its surreptitious circulation among Indonesian nationalists. Now, in 1950 the process of severance of ties to the Netherlands was approaching completion and Indonesian nationalists were more or less in control. University circles in Indonesia arranged an invitation to Romein to come as visiting professor to the university in Jokjakarta for the academic year 1951–52.

The visiting professor offered two courses, complementary in nature, one on Asian, the other on European history, each of which generated a book. The second to be published, *De Eeuw van Azië* (Leyden: Brill, 1956), involved the Romein's firstborn son, Jan Erik, as collaborator. It was translated into German and from this into English as *The Asian Century. A History of Nationalism in Asia* (Berkeley: University of California Press, 1962) with a new chapter covering the years from 1955 to 1960, written with the aid of Dr. J. M. Pluvier, and provided with a foreword by K. M. Pannikar, Romein's collaborator on the UNESCO book. Professor Hilary Conroy of the University of Pennsylvania reviewed the English translation in the *American Historical Review* (69 [October 1963], 152–53). While it contained "some serious defects," chiefly in its unevenness, he found it "immensely stimulating and perceptive in certain areas and ways." He did not fault the book for the author's "frankly anti-colonial" standpoint, which "bias is carefully controlled." One wonders whether Romein's Marxism was suffering from "innocuousness" as he had found Huizinga's "liberalism." The State Department would not concur.

Most important to our present purpose was the volume on European history, a collaboration between Jan and Annie Romein-Verschoor, published as *Aera van Europa* (Leyden: Brill, 1954), with a subtitle that translates as "European History as Deviation from the Common Human Pattern." The interlock between the two books is explicit. In the first paragraph of the author's preface to *The Century of Asia* Romein wrote:

In my book, *Aera van Europa* the story is told of the departure in Europe from the "common human pattern" which elsewhere was still dominant; that departure began with the Greeks, was continued in the Renaissance and was completed in the "Enlightenment," the Industrial Revolution and the French Revolution. In this departure the author believes he has found the final cause of the temporary domination of Asia by the Europeans.

In a later essay Romein tells of the long incubation period. He had long concerned himself with

the Middle Ages, stimulated by Huizinga's fascinating lectures, with Byzantium, and with Russia; subsequently with modern world history, especially of the non-European world. Meanwhile my interest grew in theoretical problems. I acquired a vivid impression of the world of Asia from the writings of contemporaries and the reports of my countrymen who had lived and worked there, and above all from the accounts by my wife and co-worker of her youthful years in Indonesia. And now, finally, I stood in a lecture hall in Jokjakarta before Indonesian students whose interests I believed I could best serve if I chose as my theme the question: how was it possible for Europe, even though only for a limited time, to dominate Asia?

It was the answer to this question that finally led to the conception of the Common Human Pattern. For if European domination began at some given time, then a previous situation must have existed in which this Europe was not yet "Europe." So, proceeding from the similarity between this Europe that had not become "Europe" and from what I knew of Asia, I came to the assumption, which seemed after critical examination to be tenable, that prior to European hegemony there had been a Common Human Pattern, and the inception of this hegemony put an end to the universality of this pattern. Europe began to deviate from it, and out of this deviation drew the power to establish its domination.

We may confidently accept Romein's retrospective account of the origins in his mind of this new, provocative concept as arising, after a long period of gestation, out of the culture shock of his personal encounter with an Asian society. There is no trace of the concept in a book published in the year of his departure from Europe. The book was a concise but comprehensive summary of Romein's ideas about history as he had formulated them on the eve of his voyage of discovery. *In de hof der Historie.*

Kleine Encyclopedie der theoretische Geschiedenis (Amsterdam: Querido, 1951) — *In the Court of History. A Short Encyclopedia of Theoretical History* — opens with a nearly seventy-page section called "Polemic" in which Romein undertook to demolish the critics of his article of 1946 on theoretical history. The remainder of the little book, some eighty pages, is a series of brief chapters suitable for inducting students into the discipline of history. In separate chapters he treats the meanings of the word "history," the concept of history, the psychological foundations, the origins and course of historical writing, and the form, the content, the essence, and the meaning of history. Nowhere can the reader find a trace of the Common Human Pattern.

Oddly enough, and this is not a parenthetical observation, in the chapter called "The Content of History" Romein confines the treatment largely to the meaning of "fact" and ignores what the reader would expect to find, namely, the discussion of content. Romein never raised in this book the question, the great central question that the historical profession, to my knowledge, fails to ask let alone answer, to wit: what is or what should be the subject matter which historians should consider their own? It is not as if the question had never been posed. The philosopher, John Herman Randall, Jr., in 1958 challenged the historical profession to declare itself on what the content of history was. There was no question about the content of histories of art, biology, chemistry, dance, engineering, French literature, and so on down the alphabet. Each could legitimately be offered in the appropriate specialized department. But to what definable content did the department of history devote itself? As far as I am aware, no one picked up the gauntlet. Historians responded with deafening silence. Except, in a manner of speaking, Jan Romein, proleptically and ineffectually. Six years before Randall's book appeared, Romein delivered a lecture on "History as the Bond-Stone of the Scholarly Disciplines." ["De Geschiedenis als Bindsteen der Wetenschappen," reprinted in Romein's *Carillon der tijden* (Amsterdam: Querido, 1953), pp. 74–85.] In essence, he repeated the substance of his views on integral history. One will once more search in vain for some principle of selection that would enable the historian to organize his inquiry into the past. But in 1952 when he delivered this lecture, the absence is all the more curious since in other work he was already beginning to treat this issue. Evidently he was not yet conscious of the general historiographical significance of the concepts that were, even then, guiding his practice of historical work.

As we have already noted, in propounding integral history as the investigation of the relationships among the manifold activities of mankind, Romein had deliberately refrained from assigning priorities. Nor did he articulate this issue in either his little survey book of 1951 or his lecture of 1952. To the reflective reader, the issue of what is to be integrated suffers from neglect. *In the Court of History* discusses periodization. But periodization — it is virtually tautological to say this — presupposes a body of knowledge to be organized into historical periods. If Romein urges integral history, we cannot forget that "integral" entails integration, and integration implies a pattern. In 1954 Romein begins to recognize this issue.

Personal encounter with Indonesian culture teased Romein's mind into awareness of the peculiar pattern of European history. His *magnum opus*, as the reader will discover, embodies Romein's insights into the uniqueness of Europe and its history. Had he lived to complete his great project with the third volume drawing the theoretical consequences of his concentrated study, it is possible that he might have drawn inferences from his work leading to direct confrontation with the question of the appropriate content of historical study, more explicitly with the patterns of content essential to integral history. It is possible.

We have no evidence to show that his constantly active mind would have probed in this particular direction. The grounds for thinking it possible are contained in *The Era of Europe* and in his article published in the *Journal of World History* in 1958. In this article on the Common Human Pattern he carries the clarification of his ideas beyond the stage he had reached four years before, insofar as he now refers to six essential categories in formulating the European and the Common Human Pattern: "attitudes toward *nature, life, thought, time, authority*, and *work*." This is a sharper conceptualization as well as a reduction in number of the "attitudes" he mentions in earlier statements. Now, for the first time since the idea of a pattern of European history surfaced in his mind, Romein seems increasingly if still dimly, aware, of the potential instrumental value of the idea.

A review of the sequence of problems and responses to them may make the progress of Romein's thought visible. Initially filled with admiration for Huizinga's wide range of matter included in "cultural history," he presently sensed its limitations. Romein's response was to set up the utopian goal of including "everything," which he recognized as absurd from the moment of its hatching in his mind. He therefore proposed a practical way of achieving something nearly as comprehensive, the study of the relationships among an extensive list of human activities, for which he offered no principle of selection but only an enumeration, the helter-skelter order itself suggesting the absence of a criterion. During these years, the 1940's, his concept of integral history excluded on principle any notion of a central core around which to organize historical investigation; he could recommend no specific procedure for selecting those segments of human activity that required the historian's attention if he were to pursue integral history. It was at this stage in this thinking that Romein mapped out the vast terrain on which he would test the integral approach, the framework of his *magnum opus* that follows this Introduction.

Romein's forty-two chapters reveal the range of content which he sought to control, yet the reader may find this big book "many-sided" rather than "inclusive." One may wonder, for example, at the omission of consideration of diet, or costume; or why he neglected Felix Hoffmann: he has included three other Hoffmanns and one Hofmann. Why overlook the chemist who discovered the merits of acetylsalicylic acid in 1899, barely in time for the twentieth century to be called the aspirin age? Any principle of inclusion should have coupled with it, dialectically, a corresponding principle of exclusion; but where the principle of selection seems partly below the level of consciousness, to ask for still more would be exponentially absurd. But matters did not rest there.

The jolt of encounter with Indonesia shook these inchoate ideas into a structure, and the structure was the dialectical relationship between European and non-European cultures. He perceived classes of thought-attitude-behavior in limited number; they enabled the scholar to differentiate European history from all other histories. Such was the insight that explicitly governed his *Era of Europe*. Three years after he published this book, seven years after setting foot in the non-European world, Romein replaced a more or less empirical list of areas in which differences clearly emerged with six key fields of investigation.

This invention cut through the earlier impasse. If integral history excluded a central or basic field (and thereby repudiated Marx's programmatic statement of historical materialism in his introduction to his *Critique of Political Economy* of 1859), how was the historian to cope with the multitude of equi-valued fields? Romein's practical program was to devise and revise through comparative studies a minimal set of categories that, applied to two cultures, would reveal significant differences. He did not promulgate the six categories in his article of 1958 as the Six Commandments, or as historical cant might term them, as the Imperative Categories, but put them forward on pragmatic grounds, to be evaluated in the light of their utility. He invited other historians to wrestle with them. It is tempting to advance the notion that a new category on the nature of reality would demonstrate a comprehensive power of discrimination and integration. But this is not the place to conduct such a discussion. Furthermore, such a discussion would have to take account of the utility of this device in introducing method into otherwise diffuse, aimless, and untestable maundering about periodization.

Romein's Common Human Pattern implied a periodization, most simply, Before Deviation and After Deviation. He retained the concept of "the Middle Ages," which shows that he had not yet begun to think through the implications of the Common Human Pattern. He saw the beginning of the deviation variously, as commencing with the Greeks, or with the Renaissance, or with the Reformation, and as proceeding with the Enlightenment, the French, and the Industrial Revolutions. In the twentieth century Romein envisaged two converging phenomena, in the non-European world the onset of a departure from the Common Human Pattern, and in the European world the inception of a departure from its own deviation from the Common Human Pattern.

The roots of the weakening of Europe's commitment to the assumptions that led to its world-wide triumph in the nineteenth century Romein locates in the years on either side of 1900. The Dutch reviewer, Dr. H. W. van der Dunk, (*Tijdschrift voor Geschiedenis*, 81 [1968], 465–478), had reservations about choosing the year 1889 as the starting point. This seems to me, also, to be unnecessarily calendar-ridden, and instead of a specific year it would seem preferable to use the term, "the generation before 1914," vaguer but sufficiently precise. None the less, Romein's focus seems to me essentially sound. One could cite a number of authors of less comprehensive studies — H. Stuart Hughes, Gerhard Masur, J. R. von Salis, Felix Gilbert, and Henry Steele Commager — as well as historians of physics, genetics, literature, international relations, painting, and architecture — whose writings, whether they like it or not, support Romein's thesis. A strong case, to me overwhelmingly convincing, can be made for placing the roots of the present crisis of Western culture in the generation that flourished before the outbreak of the First World War. Romein in detail traces these roots to that generation. The reader who will keep in mind Romein's basic categories as well as his purpose will avoid losing sight of the woods in view of the luxuriant foliage of the trees, and will be able to judge whether he succeeded in achieving his purpose.

— HARRY J. MARKS

THE WATERSHED OF TWO ERAS
EUROPE IN 1900

CHAPTER I

1900: A SYNOPTIC VIEW

In 1900 Britain was the most powerful nation on earth. This small island kingdom with its 41.5 million inhabitants[1] ruled the northern part of North America, where between the eightieth and eighty-fifth parallels its influence stretched amid countless islands, the ice, the snow, and the mists. In Central America Britain held Honduras, exercised great influence in Mexico, and could call the West Indies her own. In South America she owned British Guiana and wielded authority in the most important countries of that continent: it was no exaggeration to call the Argentine an economic dependency of Britain. In Africa no power could compare with the British. In the north Britain ruled Egypt and checked French ambition in the Sudan; in the south she was trying actively to extend the boundaries of the Cape Colony northward; and she nurtured scattered possessions and felt safe in the knowledge that, on the east and west coasts, the Portuguese colonies invariably followed their motherland in heeding the voice of London. In Asia, India with Burma and Baluchistan remained the most glittering pearl in the British crown, and British authority was still reaching out in all directions: across the North West Frontier Province (only just created by the Viceroy, Lord Curzon) to Afghanistan, Siam, Tibet, and Southern Persia. The famine of 1900, by all accounts the worst ever, and the smallpox, cholera, and rabies epidemics were considered so many passing shadows. Singapore, in Malacca, while controlling South-East Asia from its almost impregnable maritime fortress, was also a British springboard toward both the Far East and the Far South. In China and even in Japan no white men were more feared and respected than the ubiquitous and omnipotent British. Finally, Australia, the fifth continent, which had recently been proclaimed a Commonwealth, was a British possession. So, too, were the neighboring islands of New Zealand; the Cook Islands, which formally became part of New Zealand in 1901; Tasmania; part of the Samoa group which had recently been divided between the Powers; part of New Guinea; and the newly discovered continent of Antarctica, where the British Empire faded away amid wind, snow, and ice just as at the other pole.

Here the penguins, and there the seals, were the only subjects of Queen Victoria, whose name seemed more fitting to her position than that of any prince to his.

In 1900, the British Empire was thus still expanding, its power apparently unassailable from within no less than from without. Britain had no allies. In that respect, conditions had barely changed since the turn of the previous century: as then, all Europe from Calais to Constantinople was a hostile camp. Had international sentiment alone — in the New World as well as in the Old — been able to save the Boer Republics, South Africa would never have become a British Dominion. Yet despite this bitter war, waged some 7,000 miles from home, and fought no less strenuously than the campaign against Napoleon a hundred years earlier, the British could afford the luxury of "isolation" better than ever before and even described it as "splendid."

No less solid than Britain's power were the foundations on which it was built. In 1900 British supremacy was still founded on mastery of the sea; that mastery on prosperity, and prosperity in turn, it was generally believed, on free trade. Yet free trade itself was based on a monopoly — covert, but all the more effective and persistent — a monopoly that was the direct result of the dominance Britain owed to her industrial revolution. Thanks to it, she had become the world's factory, so to speak, importing raw materials from, and exporting finished products to, every corner of the globe. She had retained the lead, when others tried to close the gap, by sacrificing her rural classes. And when even this drastic step proved of no lasting avail, Britain endeavored to persuade the other great Powers that the prevailing "division of labor" was in their own best interest. If they demurred — and in 1900 there were signs of marked resistance from both Germany and the United States — then they had to be coerced, in which case, of course, the pretense that Britain's interests were identical with those of the rest of the world would have to be dropped. And when this did happen, the ideological source from which Britain drew her self-confidence quickly dried up. The most striking quality of the British during this period was that their air of infallibility, even at its height, included a healthy dose of self-criticism. No one can say that Britain did not see the danger signs in 1900; indeed, she sensed them even before they appeared. As early as 1886, a Royal Commission published a report on the depression in trade and industry. It reflected the kind of lucid objectivity that, normally, only those can afford who deem themselves invulnerable. For what the Commission had been asked to examine was not simply one of the normal crises of capitalism, but what we should call a structural crisis.

To maintain her lead, Britain had also to make sure that her own laboring classes remained satisfied with working relatively long hours for low wages; in other words, that one third of the population continue to put up with conditions of near-starvation, and that neither the Trade Unions nor social legislation be allowed to upset the wonderful harmony and prosperous independence of industry, commerce, and banking. But here, too, the trend was plain to see in 1900. Finally, and perhaps most important of all, Britain could retain control of the "world factory" only while coal remained the main source of industrial power. And was that the case in 1900? By then, thirty-five years had passed since the publication of Jevons's prophetic *The Coal Question*. Its author had argued that although the exhaustion of Britain's coal deposits was merely a distant possibility, the cost of mining was bound to increase sharply within the foreseeable future when shafts would have to be driven ever-deeper, while foreign coal would remain relatively cheap, not only because of the abundant supplies, but also because of its easier accessibility. In other words, Jevons realized that Britain's very lead in this field was bound, in the long run, to become a handicap. His book led to the appointment of a Royal Commission with the task of reporting on the available coal reserves. This was one of the first symptoms of Britain's doubts in her own supremacy, doubts that had previously been beyond thinking, the more so as, even when Jevons published his widely-read book, Britain still produced eighty million tons of coal a year, while the rest of the world accounted for a mere fifty million (of which the United States produced just under fourteen million, and Prussia twelve million tons). But some forty years later Jevons's arguments must have carried far greater credibility: of the world total of 1,245 million tons of coal mined in 1912, only 265 million tons were Britain's; the United States by that time was producing 485 million tons, while Germany, with 259 million, was hard on Britain's heels. Yet not even Jevons could have foreseen the gravest threat of all to the black fundament of British supremacy — the replacement of coal with other sources of energy: petroleum and water power, not to mention nuclear energy. In 1900 these alternatives did not yet pose a serious threat to coal, but they were already looming ominously in the background. As early as 1879 Siemens had constructed the first practical electric locomotive, which was put into service in the United States in 1895; in 1880 Edison had demonstrated his electric car; three years later the first all-electric track was opened at Portrush, Ireland. For all that, electricity did not become a serious competitor of coal until after 1900, when hydroelectric power first came to the fore — though where this source of power was not available, coal and coal derivates

3

continued to lead all other fuels. True, Standard Oil had begun to produce petroleum in 1882, and in the Caucasus, too, crude oil was beginning to flow steadily with the help of British capital. But Doheny, the friend of Porfirio Diaz, was only just beginning to exploit Mexico's rich oil resources. There is no better proof of the fact that, at the turn of the century, Britain had little cause for anxiety than the type of ship still being constructed in 1914; 89% were stoked with coal, 4.9% were under sail, 2.6% burned oil, and a mere 0.5% were propelled by electricity. Unless we argue from hindsight, we must therefore conclude our survey as we began it: at the turn of the century, Britain was still the greatest power on earth.

That power, however, was based on the circumstances of the time, and circumstances tend to change. As statistical material began to pour in from all sides in ever greater abundance, and as people learned to make increasing use of it, British industrialists, merchants, and bankers must have begun to feel anxious about the future. From the latter half of the eighties, they could have nursed their anxieties at leisure, for it was at this time that men of affairs began to arrive in their offices later in the morning and to leave earlier in the afternoon, to absent themselves for long weekends, and to dismiss all types of competition as unfair. Yet since most of them refused to waste their leisure hours on serious reflection, only a handful could have heeded the coming changes. We have seen that the United States and Germany had begun to challenge Britain's lead in coal-mining. The figures for pig-iron, to mention another example, were no more encouraging. In 1899, Britain with her 9,454,000 tons was still well ahead of Germany with her 8,142,000 tons, but the "law of the diminishing lead" was making itself felt even more strongly here than in the coal fields: since 1860 Britain had increased her production by 147% while Germany had increased hers by no less than 1380%. The race with the United States had been lost ingloriously as early as 1899: as against Britain's 9,454,000 tons the Americans had produced 13,839,000 tons, equivalent to more than half the total European output of 26,196,000 tons. Following the death of Stanley Jevons in 1882, his warnings were taken up by Charles Dilke. In 1868, in the first edition of his *Greater Britain*, the fruit of his trip round the world in the previous year, this prototype of Jules Verne's Phileas Fogg could still boast that the "firm belief in the greatness of my race" had been his constant guide and companion. The same — or was he perhaps a changed? — Charles Dilke entitled the revised, 1890 edition of his book *Problems of Greater Britain*. Pure chance? Hardly. In the nineties, a host of political problems that needed no statistical demonstration had begun to make themselves

4

felt: the French drive toward Siam from Laos, and toward the Nile at Fashoda; German demands in Africa and in the Pacific, and the German naval bills of 1898 and 1900; the Russian penetration of the Middle East and of East Asia; and the entry, with the conquest of Cuba and the Philippines, of the United States into the ranks of the colonizing powers. With these problems, the doubters multiplied. Lloyd George, Ramsay MacDonald, Shaw, and the Webbs began to express their dismay at conditions abroad, while Joseph Chamberlain, the wild man, and even the tame Balfour voiced their anxiety about the state of the economy and found that "isolation" was not nearly as "splendid" as it had been. Balfour sent Kitchener, the hero of Fashoda and South Africa, to India to take command of the British forces. Now that the Empire had signed an alliance with Japan (in January 1902), a confrontation with Russia in Central Asia could be faced with somewhat greater equanimity than before. In 1898 Chamberlain was sent to Berlin to woo the Kaiser, but in vain. "Proud Albion" made the mistake she was to repeat some forty years later under much more critical circumstances: negotiations on much too low a level. A Colonial Secretary is not the man to send to deal with a country that feels it is, if not the greatest power on earth, at least the leader of the most powerful continent. Three years later, in July 1902, Chamberlain shattered the other pillar of British power — free trade — when, at the Imperial Conference of the premiers of the Dominions and self-governing colonies, he tried to tie the bands of empire more firmly in with the idea of imperial preference: "At the present moment the Empire is being attacked from all sides and in our isolation we must look to ourselves." Chamberlain was quite right, of course, in stressing the dangers of isolation, and Britain was careful not to leave it at the one vain attempt to woo Germany or the one successful attempt to woo Japan. Edward VII made personal efforts to win the friendship of France and win it he did, the more readily as, in 1904, the fear of being humiliated by Germany weighed much more heavily with Paris than the desire to humiliate England. Britain was given a free hand in Egypt, France in Morocco. Three years later came an understanding with Russia: Persia was divided into two spheres of influence; the north Russian, the south British with a neutral center; the Russians abandoned their claims to Afghanistan, recognized Britain's special interests in Tibet, and pulled out of both. Russia's concessions reflected her urgent need to win over the ally of Japan, a country that had just dealt her a crushing defeat.

All these British attempts to put an end to isolation may, depending on one's viewpoint, be variously considered as so many demonstrations of British weakness or of British strength, and, in either case, of the growing power of Europe. The compact with Japan, after all, was reached at the cost of China and Korea, that with France at the cost of Egypt and Morocco, and that with Russia at the cost of Persia. And yet, all these treaties — despite the diplomatic skill that had gone into them — also bore witness to, perhaps unavoidable, political shortsightedness. In particular, they ignored the immutable historical law that all concentrations of power invariably attract new challengers. Britain found hers in Germany, Europe in Asia. Thus, though Britain at the turn of the century wanted nothing less than she did war, her policy nevertheless paved the way for a military confrontation that, despite the victory in 1918 and the original appearances to the contrary, eventually displaced her from the pinnacle on which she still rested so proudly in 1900.

While Britain gloried in the present, France basked in the radiance of her glittering past. Sober population records express this fact less poetically but all the more convincingly. In 1866 the number of Frenchmen had just exceeded thirty-eight million; by 1901 the three had remained unchanged and the eight had not yet turned into a nine. Of these close on thirty-nine million people, more than one million were aliens: Belgians and Poles, who worked in the northern factories and mines and Italians, who had settled on the deserted farms in the south. There were three births per family in 1881–1885, but only 2.1 in 1900, with the result that after 1890 the mortality rate was greater than the birth rate, with the sole exception of the years 1897–1899. In a stable world this reduction might have been considered an advantage; in the world of 1900 it was judged a severe drawback, even a disaster. For did it not bode ill that France should have lost some 25,000 of her thirty-eight million citizens during the same year that Germany had added some 800,000 to her fifty-six million? Countless laws were passed to stop this fatal process: the imposition of special taxes on single men and women and on childless couples, and state support for poor but large families — measures of which the proposals made by Senator Piot in 1900 were only one instance, and which worked no better than similar measures elsewhere or at any other time.

Less fatal but much more spectacular was the political unrest that had kept the Republic in an almost perpetual state of upheaval ever since its creation. At the beginning of the period we are considering, in 1889, the Boulanger crises had just been settled, but only because of that would-be dictator's own bungling and impotence. Two years later when Boulanger committed suicide on the grave of his mistress in Brussels, the revanchist idea was buried with him, at least in its most virulent form. True, Poincaré, Clemenceau, Foch, and many others like them only lived for the day when they could safely resurrect it; but until then the defeat of 1871 would have to be borne in silence. That, too, would have been a great boon in a world at peace, but in the prevailing climate it only served to whet Germany's appetite. In 1892–1893, the Panama boil burst wide open, and its pus spattered the good names of de Lesseps and Eiffel among many others, and that of Clemenceau as well; Baron Jacques Reinach, a Jewish banker of German origin, was found dead one day after being called before an investigating magistrate. Strikes increased in virulence and there were hundreds every year, many of them crushed by brute force, as on May 1, 1891 in Fourmies. The bomb attacks by Ravachol and other anarchists, one of whom took the life of President Sadi Carnot in 1894, were cause and consequence at once of an explosive atmosphere that finally discharged itself in the Dreyfus affair and its aftermath. There was the trial and conviction of Déroulède in January 1900. In 1899, Déroulède, poet, soldier, playwright, politician, and the man in whose hands Boulanger had been no more than a puppet, had tried his luck once more by persuading General Roget to stage a *coup d'état* during the funeral of President Faure. However, it was not for this attempt that he was eventually sentenced, but for another plot contrived a few months later. A less notorious but no less typical sequel of the Dreyfus affair was played out in September of that year, in the wake of the government's decision to replace church-trained clerics with state-trained teachers at the military academy of St. Cyr. The republican press rejoiced at this show of republican strength; the nationalist press denounced it just as fiercely as a "masonic" attack on army morale. It would not be difficult to extend the list of these conflicts. In 1900, the idea of a *coup d'état* was still very much in the air and Gallifet, the Minister of War, was able to tell the Chamber that he had repeatedly been invited to participate in them. Moreover, there were few political developments that were not seized upon by one half of the press or the other, and denounced with flaming rhetoric in the best Gallic tradition. In a sense, Premier Waldeck-Rousseau may be said to have stated the core of the problem in October 1900 when he blamed the Church for having split French youth into two camps that did not know, and would soon be unable to understand, each other. His opponents, of course, believed the exact opposite, though they, too could not deny the existence of two distinct French nations, one Rightist, royalist, nationalistic, militaristic, conservative and clerical, and the other Leftist, republican, progressive, and secular. Thus while Waldeck-Rousseau and his even more radical successor, Combes, raised the cry of "Ecrasez l'infâme!", Comte Albert de Mun, a prominent Catholic, declared roundly that the Church

7

and the revolution were irreconcilable enemies. "The Church may not perish and will therefore have to destroy the revolution." And in his way, he was undoubtedly right. For though the existence of two French nations, which dated from the end of the reign of Louis XIV, was not the sole cause of France's fall from greatness, it was a major factor, and one that bedevils French politics to this day.

Nor was France much happier in her foreign policy. In 1900 she was nearly as isolated as Britain but much more threatened from without. Colonial rivalry had led to the clash between Colonel Marchand and General Kitchener at Fashoda, a clash that had driven France to the brink of a war with England, her hereditary foe. When Britain attacked the Boers, France showed her malevolence by a long series of pinpricks: her revenge for Fashoda was a host of obscene caricatures of Queen Victoria by Léandre, who was made a member of the Legion of Honor for drawing them; when the British ambassador lodged a protest, he was informed that Léandre had been honored for his skill at portraiture, not at caricature. On her eastern borders France's relations were no better than they were to the west. By her occupation of Tunis in 1881, she had driven Italy into the arms of the Triple Alliance (with Germany and Austria), thus conjuring up a new danger which could only just be averted by a secret pact, signed in December 1900, giving Italy a free hand in Tripoli and France a free hand in Morocco. The increasing strength of the German empire remained a more serious threat, against which the risky alliance with Russia offered little protection. France had put out tentative feelers to Russia as early as 1891, having first smoothed the way with a series of loans. On July 24 of that year a French squadron had visited Kronstadt, probably in reaction to the Kaiser's State visit to London three weeks earlier, which, had everything gone according to plan, might well have served to reconcile two of France's old enemies.

La Patrie en danger. Alexander III, when the Marseillaise was played to him on board the ships of the French navy, must have had thoughts of his own. But he, too, had weighty reasons of state for an alliance with the Republic he despised and feared. Wilhelm II believed he could see more clearly which way the wind was blowing than Bismarck had done, and accordingly refused to renew the Reinsurance Treaty with St. Petersburg. Instead, he hastened to extend the Triple Alliance, indeed before the original treaty had lapsed. This alliance, coupled with a possible Anglo-German *entente*, posed so grave a threat to French and Russian interests in Europe and Asia that it had to be parried even before it arose. The result was a vague Franco-Russian Treaty, which was only meant to continue while the Triple Alliance remained in force, and it was not until 1899, when there were rumors that the Danube monarchy was in imminent danger of collapse, that this limitation was dropped after a long bout of fresh negotiations. The new objective was the preservation of the balance of power and — needless to say — of peace. Had not Czar Nicholas proved his pacific intentions by sponsoring the recent Peace Conference at The Hague? Even so, Paris could not feel safe, or relatively so, until 1904, when Edward VII, having failed in a final attempt to reach agreement with Germany, bound his country to France by a treaty that became known as the Entente Cordiale. Three years later, the margin of safety was, it appeared, increased — though in practice a new threat was conjured up — when France's ally, Russia, signed an alliance with Britain as well.

However, neither her stagnant population nor her inner division and outer isolation were allowed to dim the radiance of France's great past: she may have been beaten at Sedan, but she was determined to seek, and bound to find, compensation for that defeat beyond the confines of Europe.

In the event, France acquired an overseas empire which was second in size only to the British. By far the greatest and most important part lay close to home: the whole of North-West Africa from Algiers to the Belgian Congo, except for Morocco, Liberia, and small coastal enclaves owned by Spain, Portugal, Britain, and Germany. In 1900, French rule over that "Second France" was still largely nominal, but it was about to be consolidated: an oasis to the south of Oran was soon to be cleared, and a successful expedition against Sultan Rabah of Kousseri, who lost his life as a result, was conducted to Fort Fureau on Lake Chad, and would provide some recompense for the fiasco of Fashoda, two years earlier. The Sultan of Morocco was — rightly — afraid of French designs on the oasis of Touat, and his people grew increasingly hostile to France, although for a long time they did nothing at all about their feelings. Then, French control over West and Equatorial Africa was greatly tightened after fresh discussions with Britain. In addition, French rule was being consolidated on the east coast, where France held part of Somaliland, Réunion, and three other island groups in the Indian ocean. Here, French claims to Madagascar dated back to 1642, but it was not until 1890 that Britain, though not the native population of some two million inhabitants, consented to recognize a French protectorate over that island, and not until 1895 that its annexation became a *fait accompli* with the occupation of the capital; in 1897 the Queen was deposed and exiled, and in 1900 General Gallieni was appointed Governor-General. Of the vast French possessions in America which, in the eighteenth century, had stretched from Canada to Louisiana, cutting off its English colonies from the interior, there now remained only the tiny islands of St. Pierre and Miquelon in the north; Guadalupe and Martinique — where the unexpected eruption of Mt. Pelée claimed 30,000 victims in 1902 — in the center; and French Guiana, a large and desolate country used only as a penal colony, in the south. A boundary dispute with Brazil was settled by arbitration in 1900. Off South America, France still held a large number of small island groups in the Pacific. France's Indian empire, most of which Dupleix had been forced to cede to Clive in the eighteenth century, had shrunk to even smaller proportions: there remained just a few crumbs along the coast, Pondichery among them. For all these losses, France had sought and obtained compensation in Indo-China: under Napoleon III she seized Cochin-China in 1861 and Cambodia in 1862; after the collapse of the Second Empire and encouraged even by Bismarck, who was only too happy to see French attention diverted from Alsace-Lorraine, she had added Annam (1884) and Laos and Tonkin (before 1893). Finally, she owned New Caledonia and the New Hebrides to the east of Australia.

Nevertheless, however mighty the French colonial empire may have been, unlike the British it was not the source of France's real glory in 1900. That source remained France herself, with her great past and with Paris, as ever, the capital of the world, and not only in culture. The 1900 World Exposition proved this clearly. Moreover, French political and economic influence reached beyond the empire as far as Russia, the Balkans, and Turkey, indeed as far as the Belgian Congo and distant Yunnan. The latest discoveries, including automobiles and aeroplanes, while not inconceivable without the contribution of French thought, would have been delayed for many years. The export of luxury articles was on the increase and so was the tourist trade. Still, though the un-balanced times weighed heavily upon the French, to whom poise is second nature, they had probably more reason than any other nation to call themselves fortunate — at least until the turn of the century. Then, the very fact that they lived so much in the past began to tell against them, not least because French disdain of the less cultured foreigners and their contributions, which had acted as a spur in France's heyday, now acted as a brake on further progress. Thus while French leadership in the cultural sphere was still taken for granted, it, too, was beginning to wane.

In retrospect it seems astonishing that, in 1900, very few people thought it odd that so small a part of the globe as Western Europe should have controlled so large a part of the rest. For not only Britain and France, but also Denmark, the Netherlands, and Belgium had important colonial possessions. Denmark owned Greenland and some islands in the West Indies which, incidentally, she sold to the United States in 1902. The Netherlands held Indonesia and the Dutch East Indies in the east, and Surinam and the Dutch Antilles in the west. In Indonesia, van Heutsz had just succeeded in subjugating Atjeh, and in carrying the process of "pacification" to the more remote districts. Taxes and profits from the government plantations, which continued to flourish despite the official abolition of the plantation system in 1870, provided him with all the financial resources he needed. In 1900, these profits still amounted to a good 4.5 million guilders, and taxes accounted for close on 40.5% of the total revenue of 150 million guilders.[2] The financial outlook seemed as unclouded as the Indonesian sky. At the time, van Deventer's famous article in the *Gids* entitled "A Debt of Honor" (1899), which called for an "ethical policy," was still no more than a straw in the wind and one, moreover, that the "unethical" politicians could easily shrug off. Few people in Holland bothered their heads about such questions while the plantations continued with such splendid regularity to yield the same satisfactory results they had produced for so many years — and would, in fact, produce for many years to come. A fracas in Surabaja, started by a drunken sailor, might well have made them think twice, but this is arguing from hindsight: white domination was still considered a law of nature, if only because it had proved so successful.

This law also held in the Congo. The International Association founded by King Leopold II in 1883 was followed in 1885 by a treaty binding the Congo Free State to Belgium under the sovereignty of the King of the Belgians. In 1908, after interminable wrangles about frontiers, loans (1890), and constitutional matters (1893); after two annexation attempts (1894 and 1901); the discovery of notorious crimes and scandals (1903); the dispatch of a special commission of inquiry (1904) and further negotiations, this immense part of Central Africa, which in 1900 was inhabited by some 2,000 Europeans and some 10 million Africans, was finally declared a Belgian colony. In 1900, Moray could still set out to explore the south, and vanish completely for six months; at the time, European explorers could be as lonely in central Africa, central Asia, central South-America, or central Australia as at the North or South Pole. Southern, unlike Western, Europeans were far less certain that white domination would be enduring. True, Portugal had been able to retain fragments of her colonial empire both in Africa — the Cape Verde Islands, Guinea, and Angola — and in Asia — Goa in India, North-East Timor in Indonesia, and Macao in China; but she knew that she would expand no further. Spain was even worse off. She had been forced to cede Cuba,

11

the Philippines, Puerto Rico, and Guam to the United States in 1898, and the Marianas and the Caroline Islands to Germany in 1899. In Africa she still held Rio de Oro and Fernando Po, but these depleted rather than replenished the Spanish coffers. The generation of 1898, as it called itself, tried vainly to make the best of a bad situation by rousing the country out of its lethargy with a call for modernization. The past weighed heavily enough on France; on Spain it weighed more heavily still, so much so, in fact, that Spain was generally considered a non-European country. And, indeed, her position was one that the rest of Europe was not to reach for another half a century: Spain was forward in nothing but her backwardness.

Seen in retrospect, Germany's and Italy's determined attempts to join the ranks of the colonial powers seem totally misplaced, but this was not how things looked in 1900, when few Germans or Italians realized that a quarter or half a century later even that paltry claim to glory would have evaporated. On the contrary, just as France reveled in her past and Britain in her present, so Germany and Italy lived in the future. Both were latecomers to the colonial race. Even so, between 1884 and 1900 Germany seized four slices of the African pudding (Togoland, the Cameroons, South-West Africa, and German East-Africa), large in size, although very poor in plums. During the same period, in 1897, she appropriated Kiaochow in China. In 1900, she played a leading part in the suppression of the Boxer rebellion; in the Near East she was a constant thorn in the flesh of Britain and France. Italy did not fare nearly so well, not least because she was short of raw materials. For a time, however, she led Germany in the imperialist race; in 1882 she took possession of Eritrea, where an Italian company had bought the coaling station of Assab in 1870. She next turned her unwelcome attentions to Abyssinia, where she secured major successes in 1889 and 1895 but suffered the first of many reverses in 1896. On March 1 of that year, the Italians were crushingly defeated by King Menelik of Ethiopia at Aduwa: all 25,000 of the would-be conquerors were taken prisoner or killed. It was probably the greatest setback in colonial history, but the lesson was lost on most Europeans, who preferred to blame chance and circumstance rather than admit that white domination was no more than a temporary phenomenon, and hence itself the child of chance and circumstance. Toward the end of this period, in 1911, Italy was to find compensation in Tripoli, a consummation for which she had worked arduously ever since 1900, when Emmanuel III, succeeding the assassinated King Humbert, had signed that treaty with France, mentioned earlier, which gave Italy a free hand in Tripoli and France a free hand

12

in Morocco. But despite the long preparation, this venture, too, produced little reward. Colonization, when all is said and done, is an art that cannot be learned by the mere wish to master it.

Apparently impregnable from within no less than from without, the House of Romanov ruled supreme over the Russian empire in 1900, when anyone suggesting that Nicholas II would be the last of all the czars would have been thought a madman. Nicholas reigned over more than one seventh of all the land on earth. His empire was larger than the Soviet Union of today, for it included much of Poland, as well as the Baltic countries and Finland in the west, and Port Arthur and Talien — leased from China in 1898, and reorganized into the Kwantung territory in 1899 — in the east. And if we consider Siberia a Russian colony — in fact it was more in the nature of a settlement, for only Bukhara, Khiva, and Kwantung enjoyed full colonial status — then Russia, not Britain, had the world's largest empire. Moreover, the Czar's influence extended far beyond his vast frontiers: in Europe as far as the Balkans; in Asia as far as Persia, Afghanistan, Chinese Turkestan, Mongolia, and Manchuria. Was there not a Russo-Persian Bank and a Russian railway called the Chinese Eastern? Last but not least, Russia had a population of 130 million, 106 million or more of whom lived in European Russia. Of these last, 85 million were Great-Russians. She was only surpassed in population by China (an estimated 400 million) and India (nearly 300 million). The United States and Japan, although their populations were rapidly increasing, lagged far behind with 76 million and close to 44 million inhabitants respectively. And though, in purely cultural terms, Russia was a half-way house between Europe and Asia, her power and ambition were wholly European — not until much later did it become fashionable to deny this fact. France, as we have said, sought Russia as an ally, and did not mind spending billions of francs to that end; in 1907, Britain settled her differences with Russia for similar reasons. If Germany had known what lay in store for her in 1914–1917, and above all in 1941–1945, she would surely have exerted more effort even than France and Britain. We have said that in 1900 Russia seemed impregnable. This is true enough, but merely goes to show how deceptive appearances can be: the ground beneath the feet of the mighty colossus was already being cut away. Russian industry may have developed quickly and grown immensely strong at the turn of the century, but Russian capitalism and the Russian bourgeoisie had remained fragile structures. Russia herself was more of a colony than a colonizing power — or perhaps a semi-colony. It was with West-European capital and technological skills that her railways had been built, that her factory wheels were kept turning, and that her oil was pumped up at Baku. Moreover, the peasants, who accounted for 80% of Russia's population, may have been backward — four out of five Russians could neither read nor write, and the fifth who could was rarely a peasant — but they were not so backward or stupid as to accept their chronic lack of land without protest: hardly a year went by in which a host of noble country houses did not go up in flames. The industrial proletariat, thrown together by the concentration of industry in the large cities, proved even less submissive: strikes were numerous and widespread, and the strikers indomitable. Though few of them had read the Communist Manifesto, they all knew full well that they had nothing to lose but their chains. The bourgeoisie finally was rebellious as well: just as the peasants rose up against the landlords and the workers against their bosses, so the middle class resented the nobility at home and the capitalists from abroad, whom they rightly blamed for their own economic weakness and political impotence. And all three classes were opposed, not openly and often even not knowingly, to czarism as the embodiment of oppression and exploitation. The 3,000 people trampled to death among the crowds who had come to watch the Czar's coronation in Moscow in 1894, may have died by accident, but their deaths were not forgotten. Injustice due to indifference and ignorance would be avenged by resolution steeped in knowledge. Small wonder that, a mere ten years after that coronation, the autocracy, despite the continued support of the nobility and the church, was struck a blow that few people could have expected even in 1900: defeat at the hands of small and insignificant Japan. But human affairs can take such strange courses that one further aspect of Russia's position must be considered before we pass on. Despite all of her backwardness, or rather, because of it, Russia had a future lying ahead of her which at that time seemed to belong more to Germany. Was it simply that the Slavs multiplied numerically, while the Latin and Germanic peoples grew relatively slowly? There was more to it than that. Russia was, in due time, to derive leadership from her very backwardness. The peasants would be freed, the workers transformed into bosses, and Russia would leapfrog over the historical phase of bourgeois rule. But what is of more importance for this survey, Russia had more experience with Asia, more contacts with it, and more interest in it than all the other nations of Europe together. She was to make use of this knowledge before the clock of history had advanced another twenty years.

While it is impossible to follow the vagaries of the colonial policies pursued in Southern and Western Europe without going back to the sixteenth and even to the fifteenth centuries, Central European colonialism was a wholly modern phenomenon, and one that falls entirely within our period. The acquisition in about 1700 of part of the Gold Coast by the Great Elector was an isolated episode. True, Germany had acquired all her African and almost all her Asiatic colonies by 1889, but as late as 1890 she was still so lukewarm about her possessions that she readily ceded to Britain her claim to the Sultanate of Zanzibar and to what later became known as Uganda in exchange for little Heligoland. The same cavalier attitude also explains why the German "protectorates," as they were officially called, remained mere trading stations, albeit under state "protection." They had been founded by such pioneers as Nachtigal in the Cameroons, Lüderitz in German South-West Africa, and Karl Peters in German East-Africa.

Peters, in particular, a forceful personality, was typical of his kind. In 1893, while he reigned as Commissioner over his own province, an English missionary accused him of wild excesses against the native population, and the charges were so grave that Berlin saw fit to drop him — which, indidentally, did not stop London from granting him a share in the exploitation of Rhodesia, or Berlin from restoring him to office after the outbreak of war in 1914. This remarkable act was just another indication of how little importance the Fatherland attached to its colonies: although the German colonial empire measured 2.9 million square kilometers, making Germany the third largest colonial power in 1900 (if we ignore Siberia as a special case), none of her colonies imported a significant volume of industrial products from, or exported a significant volume of raw materials to, the Fatherland. Last but not least, the Germans displayed their lack of colonial acumen in their failure to provide a significant number of settlers. No more than 3,535 Germans lived in all their African colonies combined, and only 500 on the Pacific islands: the Bismarck Archipelago (1885), the Solomons (1886), the Marshall Islands (1886), the Carolines, the Marianas, Samoa (1899), and Kaiser Wilhelmsland in New Guinea (1884), which was still being run by the Neuguinea Kompanie in April 1899. The largest number of Germans, 2352 in all, lived in the garrison of Kiaochow, leased or rather snatched from China in 1897. Hence it is no exaggeration to say that her colonies gave the German Reich just two things: worry, and an excuse for building a large navy. It was not until 1900 that South-West Africa was temporarily "pacified" and that the state of war which had raged in Gobabis since 1896 came to an end. In 1903, however, the Hereros rose up against their harsh masters, and it took the Germans until 1907 to subdue them and to destroy their entire nation. The campaign was not only fierce but earned Germany a bad name even among colonialists. Elsewhere, too, the Germans were hard pressed, for instance in Samoa, where British and United States gunboats opened fire on them, before recognizing their claims to that island in 1899. As late as 1900 Germany had to mount a punitive expedition against the Bangwa in the Cameroons. True, the other powers had their difficulties as well: the British not only in the Cape, but also in Ashanti, where Kumasi lay besieged by rebellious natives for months before it was finally relieved. Nor should the famine in India be forgotten, for it afflicted 22 million people in the British territories alone. And while the French had their hands full along the Moroccan and the Sudanese frontiers, the Dutch were beleagured both in Atjeh and in Bali, as were the Americans in the Philippines, where the guerillas inflicted heavy losses upon them — and all this was only what appeared in print in the newspapers of the day. But what, subjectively speaking, increased the German debit columns was the fact that the credit columns had so few entries — then or later. Germany had arrived too late at the dividing up of the world; the best bits had gone when she appeared on the scene. German South-West Africa may serve as an example. It was obviously no more than a leftover; navigators had hurried past the thousand in-hospitable miles that constituted its coastline, through the heavy swells, the storms, and the mist, and they had been quite right to do so for most of the interior was occupied by the Namib Desert. One of the main causes of Germany's failure to strike in time was purely geographical: she lacked direct access to the Atlantic, the great ocean to which Western Europe largely owed its paramount position. She did have the North Sea, but the latter was of greater importance to the Hanseatic cities than it was to Germany as a whole, and it was only with the utmost reluctance and then only two years before the turn of the century that Hamburg and Bremen had finally submitted to the dictates of Prussia. That the German Reich never acquired a real taste for colonial possessions may also be gathered from the fact that even Hitler's demands for greater *Lebensraum* had no other purpose than to wrest concessions in Europe. German imperialism always set its sights on continental objectives; it never felt truly at home beyond the seas.

In 1900, the world population had risen to about 1,600 million, 400 million living in Europe and of the remaining 1,200 million, half were under European control. This ratio was bound to lead to a collision, and the only surprising thing is that it had not yet done so by the end of the century, when European supremacy still looked inviolable. One of the few who could already read the signs of conflict was the Victorian poet, Wilfrid Scawen Blunt, but then he had lived the kind of life most apt to sharpen a man's sensibilities. Rich, and married to Byron's grand-

16

daughter, he had used their combined fortunes to travel extensively in Egypt and the Middle East. During these travels he had had every chance to see the effects of British imperialism at close quarters and also to witness the Islamic revival. In 1887 he was jailed for two months for his open championship of Irish Home Rule, and his political career was finished — despite their proverbial phlegm, the British upper classes are not given to tolerating a deserter from their own ranks. Blunt's wide experiences and his own rebellious nature were reflected in the extract from his diary, written on December 22, 1900, when he was sixty years old: "All the nations of Europe are making the same hell on earth in China, massacring and pillaging and raping in the captured cities as outrageously as in the Middle Ages. The Emperor of Germany gives the word for slaughter and the Pope looks on and approves. In South Africa our troops are burning farms under Kitchener's command, and the Queen and the two Houses of Parliament, and the bench of bishops thank God publicly and vote money for the work. The Americans are spending fifty millions a year on slaughtering Filipinos; the King of the Belgians has invested his whole fortune on the Congo, where he is brutalizing the negroes to fill his pockets. The French and Italians for the moment are playing a less prominent part in the slaughter, but their inactivity grieves them. The whole white race is revelling openly in violence as though it had never pretended to be Christian. God's equal curses be on them all! So ends the famous nineteenth century into which we were so proud to have been born." And on December 31, 1899, while the nineteenth was making way for the twentieth, Blunt added these prophetic words: "I bid good-bye to the old century, may it rest in peace as it has lived in war. Of the new century I prophesy nothing except that it will see the decline of the British Empire. Other worse empires will rise perhaps in its place, but I shall not live to see the day."[3] He did not — for he died in 1922 — but if he had children and grandchildren, they would indeed have witnessed not only the fall of the British Empire but also the rise of considerably worse ones.

European expansion in the nineteenth century, impinging as it did on most spheres of life,[4] was not limited to the annexation of known regions but also extended to the discovery of unknown territories. So fervent was this pursuit that the most sensational discoveries had all been made before 1889, the beginning of our period. They had come about due entirely to the efforts of those full-bearded, intrepid explorers who set out in sailing ships, carried rifles and had their likenesses immortalized in the woodcuts illustrating their travelogs. They included Speke, Livingstone, Burton, Baker, and Stanley, among the most famous

17

explorers of the Dark Continent. Stanley lived on until 1904, but by 1889 he had returned from his last great journey, through the primeval forests of the upper Aruwimi, which he had made to escort Eduard Schnitzer, or Emin Pasha as he was called, a German in the Egyptian Service, from the East Sudan, thereby preparing the way for the British annexation of that territory. By then, Australia and Greenland had already been traversed, the first before 1875 and from five different points, the second from east to west by Nansen and Swerdrup in 1888, the same year in which Doughty published his *Arabia Deserta*. Nearly ten years earlier, in 1879, Nordenskjöld had discovered the Northeast Passage, but it was not until 1906 that Amundsen opened the Northwest Passage.

This does not, however, mean that no unknown or little-known territory was opened up between 1889 and 1914. On the contrary, the Golden Book of the Royal Geographical Society was far from closed, and "white spots" still abounded throughout the world — neither Australia nor New Guinea, neither Central Asia nor Tibet, neither the Arabian interior nor the Congo had been fully explored, let alone mapped; and of the Amazon river basin and the Gran Chaco little more was known at the time than Von Humboldt had known a hundred years earlier. Yet however important all the latest explorations may have been, the only true mysteries and hence the only sensational discoveries left were confined to the two most extreme points on earth: the North and South Poles.

Somewhat less dramatic explorations were proceeding apace, particularly in Central Asia, no doubt encouraged by the friction between Britain and Russia, for a great many were closely bound up with border disputes. Explorer after explorer made for the inhospitable Himalayas, among them Conway, Bruce, the Duke of the Abruzzi, and Longstaff, who discovered the most important glacier of the mighty Karakoram system in 1909. Nine years earlier, Sir Aurel Stein, the great archaeologist and explorer, discovered the sand-covered towns and villages of Khotan, a lost civilization and an ideal hunting ground for antiquarians. It was also in 1900 that Evans began to dig into the past of another lost civilization in the palace of Knossos on Crete. Similar discoveries in Sumeria and the Indus valley had to wait for several decades. Stein himself made his greatest discovery, one that opened up a new chapter in the history of Eastern art, six years later at Tunhuang: the Caves of a Thousand Buddhas with hundreds of rock temples, early Chinese paintings, and historic relics that had lain hidden for 900 years; from the buried library it became clear that block-printing was known in the ninth century, at least one century earlier than was previously believed. In 1913, Stein travelled through the heart of Asia for the last time — from the Tien mountains in the north to Kunlong in the south, and from the Pamir plateau in the west to the Gobi Desert and beyond in the east. His travels took him more than once to the mysterious Lop Nor on the western edge of that desert. Its mystery, however, was not solved by Stein but by Sven Hedin in 1900. Just as laconically as Speke had once wired "The Nile is settled," so Sven Hedin now wired that the Lop Nor problem was solved. He was able to show that the location of the terminal lake had steadily shifted over the centuries, thus correcting the earlier mistake of his predecessor, Prjevalsky. Sven Hedin also succeeded in crossing into Tibet, where he tried to enter the Forbidden City of Lhasa disguised as a shepherd, and failed as Rockhill, Bonvalot, Bower, de Rhins, Little-dale, Wellby, Malcolm, and Deasy had failed before him — no one could accuse Europeans of being faint-hearted. In 1904, Younghusband succeeded at long last, but he arrived in Lhasa at the head of an armed force sent to ensure the implementation of a treaty signed in Darjeeling in 1890. Like Stein, Sven Hedin, too, crossed the Gobi Desert, followed by the Russians Kozlov and Gadygin in 1900; but these were not true voyages of discovery, since, in his day, Marco Polo had described the desert so accurately that Stein had little to add to his account. This, by and large, applies to all the other overland journeys of discovery in our period. And though we could easily mention other explorers in Central Asia or the Near East,[5] we shall refrain from doing so, if only because none of them had the magnetism of Stein or Sven Hedin.

Much as Lhasa was the great attraction in Asia, so Lake Chad was the great attraction in Africa. This was once again not unconnected with political friction, here between "Greater Britain" and "La Nouvelle France." In particular, France was anxious to prevent a possible British linkage of Nigeria with the Egyptian Sudan, which would have frustrated her own designs on Equatorial Africa. Voulet and Chanoine accordingly set out for Lake Chad from the north; their expedition is chiefly remembered for the mutiny that cost the life of Captain Klobb, who had gone to their aid. Gentil then set out for the lake from the French Congo in the south, while Joalland and Meynier started from the Niger in the west. That same year (1900), Foureau and Lamy made a crossing of the Sahara from Algiers to the mouth of the Congo; Lamy died in the course of this important expedition. A few months earlier, Flamand and Pein had reached Tidikelt; their arrival marked the beginning of many long French attempts to subdue the Touareg tribe. France now seemed firmly entrenched in North-West Africa. "Logically," the next step should have been the construction of a Trans-Sahara railway, and, in fact, *Le Matin*

19

offered one million francs to encourage preliminary work on that project. But no more came of it than had come of the projected railway from In Salah to Timbuktu; the advent of aviation was to bury both projects. The Russians, by contrast, had gone so far with their Trans-Siberian railway, on which they had worked for nine long years in the belief that it would help to make Siberia a strong competitor of the United States,[6] that they could no longer withdraw. The great dream of a Berlin-Baghdad Railway, too, was at long last realized, after a host of technical difficulties had been surmounted. However, two other ambitious projects succumbed to technical progress: neither the line between Cape Town and Cairo nor that between New York and the South American capitals of Santiago, Buenos Aires, and Rio de Janeiro was ever completed. Of the second there only remains a seven-part report published in 1898;[7] of the first, nothing at all.

While all these explorations were inspired by commercial ambitions, either directly or by implication — an excellent case in point was Moore's expedition in 1900 to Lake Tanganyika which established that the Lake lay more to the west than was previously believed, with the result that German East-Africa gained some 10,000 square kilometres at the expense of the Congo[8] — polar expeditions seem clearly to have been inspired solely by the lure of adventure and glory, which does not, of course, mean that they produced no material advantages. It was no doubt more than pure chance that it should have been during the period under review, when Europe's star shone at its brightest, that the drive to the poles became an almost obsessive preoccupation, so much so that it appeared as if Europeans were determined to prove, at the eleventh hour as it were, that the white race had an unquenchable thirst for knowledge and hence a perfect moral right to rule over the rest of the world. Not since the Crusades had there been so concerted an effort by the white race. The circumpolar stations in the Arctic, first envisaged in 1875 and set up in 1882, were built by Scandinavians, Russians, Dutchmen, Britons, Germans, Austrians, and Americans; during the actual journeys Italians and Frenchmen participated as well. The Iberians were missing from this last chapter in the history of discoveries, but they had, after all, written the first. The chronological summary of the polar expeditions which follows can in no way hope to do justice to the heroic spirit and tenacity of the men involved, but there is probably no better way of underlining how strong and widespread the mysterious urge to reach these two formidable and inhospitable points on the earth's surface really was. In 1895, Nansen and Hjalmar Johansen, having left their ship, the *Fram*, in charge of Sverdrup, reached a latitude of 86° 14′ N., and established

20

a record. At the same time, Jackson and Harmsworth were busily exploring Franz Josef Land, an archipelago discovered some twenty years earlier. Franz Josef Land was also explored by Baldwin (1898) and Wellmann (1898 and 1900), and a wealthy American, W. Zeigler, sent further expeditions there in 1901–1905. In 1897, Andrée went up in a balloon from Danes Island, Spitsbergen; he made it as far as Kvitöya (White Island) in the Barents Sea, where his headless body was discovered in 1930. That same year, Conway and Nathorst explored the interior of Spitsbergen. In 1898, Sverdrup set out to circumnavigate Greenland, and in 1899 he explored the Arctic archipelago north of Canada. At the same time, the Russian admiral, S. O. Makarov, made a trial run on the icebreaker *Yermak* to test the force of the Arctic ice, and though he failed to reach a high latitude, he concluded that a large and strong enough ship could force a passage to the Pole. And as if to reach that objective at all costs before the century was out, the Duke of the Abruzzi made yet another attempt in 1899, and he was still pursuing the Pole in 1900 when he learnt of King Humbert's assassination. Disabled by frostbite, the Duke handed over to Captain Umberto Cagni, who broke Nansen's record: he reached a latitude of 86° 34′ N, roughly 200 miles from the Pole, having first covered some 700 miles by sled. In 1900, Arndrup completed the map of Greenland's east coast. The new century began with Peary's failure: moving ice floes blocked his path of the Pole. Undaunted, he returned five years later with Bartlett and apparently reached a latitude of 87° 6′; but this claim does not stand up to a closer investigation, no more so, in fact, than his assertion that he reached the Pole on April 6, 1909. In 1907, his competitor, Cook, also set out for the Pole and claimed to have reached it on April 20, 1908; but he, too, was unable to substantiate his claim. By the time the First World War was declared none of the co-operating or competing nations had been able to plant its flag on the North Pole; for the Anglo-American polar expedition led by Mikkelsen, Leftingwell, and Stefansson (1906–1908) had also failed. Our account of Arctic explorations is far from complete: a host of Canadians and Russians, too numerous to mention, also laid claim to the Arctic on behalf of their respective countries. And while Rasmussen and many others crossed Greenland in all directions — in 1912 alone the Eskimos were treated to four teams of visitors — others turned their attention to Spitsbergen, which Count Zeppelin explored in 1911 from his airship, the *Mainz*. Around the South Pole, the crush was equally great, the more so as the Sixth International Geographical Conference, held in London in 1895, had described the exploration of the Antarctic as the most urgent geographical task of the age. Between 1893 and 1914, there were at least eighteen Antarctic expeditions, including Shackleton's in the *Endurance* and Mackintosh's in the *Aurora*, both of which set out in 1914 with plans for a rendezvous. Other Antarctic explorers were Larsen (1893) and Kristensen (1894), two Norwegians; de Gerlache (1897-1899), a Belgian; and Borchgrevink (1898-1900), another Norwegian. On April 1, 1900 Borchgrevink cabled from Bluff in New Zealand that the task of the expedition had been completed, that the exact location of the magnetic south pole had been determined (by calculation), and that the highest latitude reached had been 78° 50', and that the zoologist Hansen had died. "Else all's well on board." For the first time, an expedition had wintered on the Antarctic mainland. Next came Drygalsky (1901-1903), a German; Nordenskjöld (1901-1903), a Swede; Scott (1902-1904) and Bruce (1903-1905), two Britons; Charcot (1903-1905), a Frenchman; and Shackleton (1907-1909), another Briton. British too were Mawson and Mackay (1908-1909), who, on January 16, 1909 hoisted the Union Jack on the magnetic pole some 1,200 miles from the South Pole. The South Pole was first reached on December 16, 1911 by Amundsen, who planted the Norwegian flag. As in the Arctic, the search for the South Pole had become an international race: Scott, who like Amundsen had set out in 1910, reached it early in 1912, only to perish with his companions a few months later. The Japanese explorer Choku Shirase (1910-1912) also set out for the South Pole, but turned back when he learnt that Amundsen had reached it before him.

The current political map of Antarctica reflects this international race most faithfully: Britain claims all the territory between 20° and 80° W, incidentally not without protests from Argentina, and between 150° and 180° E; Norway "owns" everything between 20° W and 45° E; Australia "owns" everything between 45° and 160° E, except for a small French triangle. The remainder, between 80° and 150° W, finally, has been unofficially claimed for the United States by Bird and Ellsworth. This strange division of "empty space" is perhaps more typical than anything else of Europe's explosive energy, in which noble and ignoble motives were so inextricably intertwined.

Other expeditions set out at about the same time, not so much to hoist flags, those symbols of political power, as to extend human knowledge, though to the Western mind these two concepts had become identical once Bacon had declared that "knowledge itself is power." Three of these attempts were directed to oceanography and deserve special mention: the German *Valdividia* expedition (1898-1909) to the Atlantic and the Indian oceans, the U. S. *Albatross* expedition (1899-1900) to the Pacific, and the Dutch *Siboga* expedition (1899-1900) to the

Indonesian archipelago. All three eradicated a mass of prejudices and corrected a host of misconceptions; in particular they confirmed the earlier findings of the *Challenger* expedition (1872–1876) that, popular opinion to the contrary, life could be sustained below a depth of 250 fathoms. The scientific studies of the deep-sea flora and fauna by Weber alone filled 150 volumes. This is not the place to discuss them in detail, except perhaps to mention the result that exemplified a whole series designed to extend the extreme limits of human knowledge: the greatest depth plumbed by the expedition was some 18,500 feet in the Banda Sea. This "record" was not, however, as spectacular as it might have been, since Ross had previously sounded a depth of some 16,000 feet during his 1840 Antarctic expedition, and certainly not when we compare it with the 26,000 feet plumbed by the *Challenger*, or the close on 30,000 feet that Agassiz had plumbed on the *Albatross* shortly before, let alone with the results obtained subsequently in the trenches east of the Philippines where depths of more than 33,000 feet were recorded. These submarine explorations greatly stimulated the search for the deepest and highest point on land accessible to men. The deepest mine in 1900 was almost 5,000 feet below the surface, the highest peak ever climbed close on 18,000 feet above sea level; but this far from quenched the thirst for new records that had begun to haunt Western man. The slogan was higher and higher and faster and faster. For had not Marinetti proclaimed in his futurist manifesto of 1909 that speed had graced the world with a fresh beauty? The highest mountain top merely served to point the way to the empty sky which men made the first attempt to enter in a dirigible as early as 1851. An improved version was launched in 1885, but it was not until 1898 that the first serviceable airship was constructed, thanks largely to the development of suitable internal combustion engines by Santos Dumont in France and Count Zeppelin in Germany. Five years later, Orville Wright was the first to leave the ground in a heavier-than-air machine. Though he stayed up for a mere twelve seconds, men had conquered the air in principle. From 1903, planes began to climb higher and to go faster over ever-longer distances. And still the race went on: Western man was determined not only to leave the earth itself, but also its atmosphere, though for the time being he would only do so in his imagination. Again, when the theory of the expanding universe was eventually constructed, its advent had been foreshadowed, at least subjectively, by the discovery that the universe was much larger than had previously been thought. In about 1800, the size of the universe was expressed in fourteen figures; by 1900 it was expressed in seventeen. And that was only a beginning — fifty years later the figure had risen to one, followed by twenty-seven zeros, expressed in kilometers.

In 1900, the expansion of European thought was as boundless as the expansion of European deeds. If it was ever true to speak of world supremacy, then that term applied with particular force to Europe at the turn of the century, and that is exactly how Europeans themselves saw it at the time. And how could it have been otherwise? The whole world had been parceled out among the European powers. Whatever did not belong to Europe politically was bound to her by economic, and certainly by cultural, ties. Culturally, North America was still British, Central and South America still Spanish; politically most of Africa, with the exception of Abyssinia, had been carved up by the Great Powers, and the remaining strip of "no man's land" was about to be colored British red. In those parts of Asia that had managed to retain their independence, European influence was steadily growing: Germany kept extending her hold over the Turkish Empire; Great Britain and Russia exerted increasing pressure on Persia and Afghanistan; and it seemed only a matter of time before London laid hands on Siam. Yet even while the European tree was bearing such rich fruit, its roots were being sapped and its foliage had begun to wilt. In 1901, when the Anglo-American Treaty and with it the future of the Nicaragua Canal came up for renewal, Britain was at a disadvantage: the United States had in 1899 bought the Panama Canal concession from an insolvent French company. Worse still, there was no new Disraeli to acquire a lion's share in a passage more important than even the Suez Canal. The Spanish Empire had just fallen into American hands. Britain was about to recognize Japan as her equal and ally, and that new ally was about to deliver a crushing blow to Russia. A chill wind was blowing from the west and another from the east. Within Europe herself tension kept increasing: the summer of European supremacy was making way for the autumn.

CHAPTER II

FIN DE SIÈCLE

Fin de siècle: the origins of this phrase are obscure, and all we can be certain of is that the last decade of the nineteenth century applied it to itself. Since it is unusual for a particular period to assume such labels, we must take it that there was a special reason for doing so at the time. That reason was not simply that the end of a century was in sight, although this fact probably played some part; the context in which the phrase is generally used suggests that much more than that was involved. For *fin de siècle* often went hand in hand with the word "decadent," and not merely in the writings of Max Nordau, that latter-day Jeremiah. There was a smell of autumn about those years, or more precisely of an Indian summer, of those September days still bathed in summer sunshine though wreathed in autumnal mists.

Was Europe in 1900 really finished, or did people believe that it was? Undoubtedly there were some who did, who endorsed Max Südfeld's diagnosis that the age was sick and decadent (*Krankheit des Jahrhunderts*, 1889; and *Entartung*, 1892); but if there is any truth at all in our claim that the turn of the century was marked by a sense of expansion, not of tired resignation, then *fin de siècle* could not possibly have expressed a belief in the collapse of a continent that, more than ever before, was determined to impose its will on the rest of the world. In fact, our period was also known as the Gay Nineties or as *La Belle Epoque;* and Holbrook Jackson, one of the great connoisseurs, was quick to point out that "side by side with the prevailing use of the phrase [*fin de siècle*], and running its popularity very close, came the adjective 'new'; it was applied in much the same way to indicate extreme modernity."[1] Blaikie Murdoch, another expert on late nineteenth-century literary and artistic trends, was to speak of the "Renaissance of the nineties." And, indeed, there was an atmosphere of spring and renewal no less than of autumn and decline. *Fin de siècle*. That phrase must have been coined by someone with an uncommonly fine dialectical sense of circumstance and language, for besides the note of decline it undoubtedly strikes one of high achievement as well. It was as if the world were teetering on the brink, uncertain whether it ought to climb higher still, or descend: an epoch in the true sense of the word. *Fin de siècle*, the great turning point.

The key to this uncertainty must be sought in social, not in political history. At the time, the bourgeoisie was by far the most powerful class. To its right, or if you like, on its shoulders, there still stood the nobility, although its influence had greatly declined during the past century. England was perhaps the exception, for in that country a number of aristocrats still held power in government, in the business world, and in the leading clubs. England still boasted a House of Lords and the gentry still seemed unassailable in their vast landed estates; though appearances, as we have seen, are often deceptive. The English had for centuries made a habit of ennobling deserving commoners. Disraeli, to mention just one famous example, was made Earl of Beaconsfield, although despite the change of name he remained the same Benjamin whose grandfather had come to England from Italy, where the Jews had been sorely pressed. Also, the lush acres of the gentry did not betray the heavy burden of debt that had begun to press down upon their owners. The gentry itself, however, was well aware of mounting problems. Lord Randolph Churchill, Winston's father and a descendant of the Duke of Marlborough, married Miss Jenny Jerome, the daughter of one of New York's "Four Hundred Families," Lord Curzon, who at Oxford had called himself "a most superior person," married the daughter of Levi Z. Leiter, a millionaire from Chicago. They did not contract these profitable marriages simply because their love of horses had taught them the dangers of inbreeding.

In France as well the world of diplomacy and of *haute finance* was still replete with barons, counts, and dukes, and it was not by chance that Daniel Halévy called one of his books *La République des ducs*. But though *Le Gaulois* may have described the dress, toilette, and perfumes of their wives and daughters as they rode in the Bois, and *Gil Blas* their duels in the misty mornings, they nevertheless had few guaranteed privileges left. Thus when M. le Comte Boni de Castellane, who was still accustomed to serve 250 guests dinner on rococo plate lit by silver chandeliers almost every Sunday, saw the bottom of his money chest, he had no alternative but to escape to America. Again, in Germany, though the Junkers still wielded real power behind the Elbe both in the army and in the state, they, too, no longer drew the revenue from their great estates they had been taught to expect. What few large incomes remained were fast being dissipated. The Union Club in Berlin, which was meant to do for Germany what the Jockey Clubs of London and Paris did for Britain and France, became so notorious a gaming den that the garrison commander was forced to order his officers to choose between the Club and the Army. At the same time,

26

marriages with the daughters of industrial barons from the west had become so numerous as to constitute a *de facto* form of defeudalization. Much the same thing had happened among the scions of the Danube monarchy, whose decline is described so eloquently in Roth's *Radetzkymarsch*. Even in Russia, where the nobility was still all-powerful, family fortunes had been sorely depleted by the "emancipation" of the serfs in 1861. In his *The Goloveyous*, Saltykov (Shchedrin) describes the sorrows of a Russian noble family with a master's hand, and the work of Chekhov, a quarter of a century later, has rightly been called the swan song of the Russian nobility. Nor were these novelists alone in painting this gloomy picture: the historical record tells much the same tale. Between 1861 and 1892, as many as one third of the landed estates were sold off, and no less a personage than Count Witte, the Prime Minister, passed a judgment on members of his class that no outsider could have framed more astringently: he called them degenerates who indulged their jaded appetites at the taxpayers' expense.[2] It could hardly have been his Dutch descent alone that caused him to sound so bourgeois a note of indignation. Finally, the United States had never boasted a formal aristocracy of its own; although the Daughters of the American Revolution did their best to assume that role, they nevertheless remained the daughters of perfectly bourgeois mothers. Hence, if anything at all was drawing to a close at the turn of the century, it was the nobility and its culture, or what went by that name; so that it is not at all unlikely that the term *fin de siècle* was coined in these very circles, just as the cry of bloody revolution had first gone up in the noble salons of a century earlier. The difference in tone between these two epithets shows, if anything, that, at the turn of the century, the European bourgeoisie had little to fear from absolute monarchs or privileged nobles.

In addition, much as the bourgeoisie was no longer threatened from on high by the "second estate," so it was not yet challenged from below by the third. For although the working class had begun to develop a measure of class consciousness and had started to close its ranks, it was still quite powerless even where it was numerically strong, and even where — as in Germany — it could boast a strong party and a trade union movement. As a result, the bourgeoisie could afford the luxury of entertaining all sorts of bizzare and exotic notions. To them, the idea of a *fin de siècle* was a pose rather than a fact. For had not the bourgeosie despite all their self-confidence been aping the manners and language of the aristocracy for centuries, and had they not vied for noble titles to boot? Hence was it not quite natural that they should have shared the ideas of those who still seemed to be the great of the earth, particularly as many a convinced republican shared the nostalgic love of exiled kings? The European bourgeoisie could afford to indulge in these yearnings the more because its rule, as we have said, seemed unassailable from within no less than from without. True, the United States was a rising power in the West, and Japan a rising power in the East, but Europe still stood so supreme that the advance of these two extra-European nations seemed no more than a temporary irritation, particularly now that the leading European countries were at peace with one another. The Franco-German war of 1870–1871 seemed to have been the last of a long series of internecine struggles, and had in any case been very short and relatively mild. The terror of the Commune had been forgotten; and peace, order, and progress seemed assured for all time. Science and technology were gaining one victory after another, as the 1900 Paris Exposition showed most graphically and dramatically. Small wonder then that optimism was so rife that the pessimists were if anything even more sanguine than the boldest of the optimists: their objections did not so much reflect the feeling that things were going badly as the view that they might be going much better still. In any case, it was generally felt that European achievements were permanent and hence bound to spread to the rest of the world. Politically, these achievements were thought to rest on the triple pillars of nationalism, liberalism, and parliamentarianism. The third of these sacrosanct pillars had recently been imported, or was about to be imported even by Russia, Turkey, Japan, and Persia; and the first two pillars were generally believed to be either its direct cause or else its direct consequence. The fact that all three stood on shaky foundations merely served to kindle the hope that they would soon be suitably buttressed. And while the great political ideals still needed three pillars, the economic ideal rested on but one, rarely mentioned by name — capitalism. For although Marx may have taught that capitalism, too, was a historical phenomenon, and as such bound, sooner or later, to make way for a different mode of production, those who profited from it and therefore had no need to study Marx before opposing his ideas considered capitalism one of the eternal verities, the sole expression of *the* economic truth. Finally, the social ideal of the bourgeoisie was not supported by three pillars or even by one, for the very good reason that it simply did not exist. The general mood of the European bourgeoisie before the turn of the century can therefore be summed up, with no more exaggeration than attaches to any generalization, as one of complete self-assurance, based on the firm conviction that they should, nay must, reign over Europe and the rest of the world.

In 1900, this self-assurance began to be shaken, however slightly, by the first distant rumblings from the industrial working class. That class

28

had grown apace with growing mechanization. Characteristic of Britain as early as 1800, the effects of this combined growth first made themselves felt in France and Belgium about 1850; after 1870 in Germany and the Netherlands as well; and by 1900 had spread to northern Italy, Austria, and Russia. Large groups of industrial workers had embraced socialist ideas, particularly in the chiliastic mold in which Karl Marx had cast them. The original ban on associations of workers, passed on the grounds that they posed a threat to free enterprise and hence to one of the greatest achievements of the French Revolution, had to be rescinded in country after country. Trade unions were officially recognized, first here and there and eventually everywhere, and the fight for the eight-hour day was on. That fight and the struggle for higher wages struck the workers as the only possible means of attaining a decent life, one in which they would have time and energy to organize the subsequent and all-important struggle for a socialist society. But while this was their common social and economic objective, they were not yet agreed on the best method of attaining it. One wing of the organized working class based its political campaign on the struggle for universal adult suffrage, then still so untried in practice as to remain a great panacea for social misery. Members of this wing considered that it was not only possible to obtain a majority in parliament with the help of the ballot box but also believed that once achieved this majority would lead straight to the creation of heaven on earth.

The differences between this and the second group, which considered violent social revolution an essential part of the general transformation of society, were not yet nearly as sharp as they were to become later. Both groups still called themselves Marxists. For while Marx had taught that only a social revolution would ensure the transfer of power from the bourgeoisie to the proletariat — a prerequisite of the "expropriation of the expropriators" — he had also taught that, by virtue of the concentration of capital into ever fewer hands, this transfer was unlikely to be opposed by any sizeable section of the community. In his writing during the nineties, Engels, too, no doubt impressed by the spectacular successes of the German Social Democrats at the polls, had conceded the possibility of a transformation of society that, though radical in essence, might be gradual in form.

While the ideas advanced by these two groups worried the bourgeoisie increasingly, the deeds of a third group — the anarchists — worried them even more. There was no clear dividing line between them and the other two, or else the bourgeoisie might have slept peacefully in the knowledge that their divided class enemy was rendered harmless by its very division. However, the syndicalists, who were most active in France and who may be considered a link between the Marxist and anarchist wings of the working-class movement, proved to the bourgeoisie that despite all their ideological and organizational differences, the entire class-conscious part of the proletariat shared a single ideal. Among the anarchists, the Russians Bakunin and Kropotkin, the Italian Malatesta, and the Dutchman Domela Nieuwenhuis were the best known; their names evoked as much fervor among their supporters and as much hostility among their opponents as the names of Lenin, Stalin, and Mao Tse-tung were to evoke among theirs. What concerns us here, above all, is that some of these anarchists, just like the Russian "nihilists of the deed," did not shrink from individual terror to obtain the common aim. Under their hands died more Russian dignitaries, from Czar Alexander II in 1881 to Prime Minister Stolypin in 1911 than this period counted years; they also slew an empress of Austria, a king of Italy, a president of France, and a president of the United States. All these assassinations filled the ruling class with more terror than the actual situation justified, and terrified people rarely make fine distinctions. Rightly or otherwise, after the Paris Commune of 1871 and the Russian Revolution of 1905, the proletariat had begun to pose what many hoped was a far-distant, but what was in fact an already tangible, threat to the power and possessions of the rich. The specter rose up anew and more forcibly each May Day celebration, the first of which had been organized by the International Working Men's Association in 1890. Would the general strike, that mythically exalted and at the same time mythically vilified test of strength, which was to ring in the social revolution, be declared this time? For were "they" not already intoning: "And all the mighty wheels stand still, but for your muscle and your will"? And even if, as the most level-headed believed, all this was no more than an attempt by the workers to bolster up their courage in the face of repeated police and cavalry charges, it was bad enough in all truth. This then was the main fear of the bourgeoisie.

Their second fear which, like the first, was beginning to gnaw at their self-assurance and, worse still, was making inroads into their purse, was the growing arms race. Germany, with a population of seventy million, had more manpower than France, with her forty million citizens. To offset this deficit, France had to keep a larger standing army if she was not to be hopelessly outnumbered in time of war, while Germany had to expand her navy lest she succumb to Britain at sea. By a law of 1882, extended in 1889 and again in 1892, France introduced three years' compulsory military service — except for students and seminarists, who were expected to serve for one year only. By 1900, the peacetime establishment of the French army, including the Algerian and Tunisian contingents,

30

was made up of 590,000 officers and men, as against the Germans' 490,000, laid down by the law of 1899.[3] Yet despite this advantage, Pelletan, Chairman of the Estimates Committee, saw fit to strike a sour note in the Chamber in February, 1900. France, he said, spent proportionately more on her army and navy than any other country: 1,080 million francs, of which 707 million went to the army alone, compared with Britain's 1,098 million, Russia's 1,084 million, and Germany's 1,000 million. Nevertheless mismanagement was so rife that she did far less with these sums than her potential rivals. It was also in 1900 that Germany presented her Navy Bill, thus opening the way for a further extension of the arms race. The official justification advanced by von Tirpitz, Secretary of the Navy since 1897, was the so-called "Risk Theory": the risk of attacking a strong German fleet would be so great as to deter any would-be aggressor. In the event, that theory did introduce a new risk, not least for Germany herself, as the future was to show only too plainly. Except for the military experts, however, few people anticipated a fresh European conflict at the time, though the few who did found the situation ominous enough, the more so as airships, submarines, and the new weapons had added a fresh dimension to war. It was in 1898 that Santos Dumont in France and Count Zeppelin in Germany had launched the first serviceable dirigibles and in 1900 that the first modern "submersible" had made its debut (although the Swedish engineer Nordenfeldt had supplied the Turkish navy with a useful sample as early as 1878). By 1902, the French navy owned fourteen submarines and had a further twenty under construction.[4] The army and navy estimates of most of the Great Powers took up an ever-increasing share of the ever-increasing annual budgets: in France they swallowed up 29% of the 1901 budget (1,020 million francs out of a total of 3,500 million francs).[5] Seen in retrospect, this may seem an extremely modest proportion, but compared with the past it was vast indeed.

Against this threatening background, the seven to eleven-year trade cycles and *a fortiori* the recurring international political crises constituted two further sources of anxiety. The economic crises, admittedly, were generally shrugged off because people had grown to accept them as "unavoidable" or even "salutary" concomitants of prosperity. Moreover, in the middle of the nineties, the so-called third economic wave was still on the ascendant (it continued until 1914, and what few depressions occurred in the course of it seemed relatively short and slight). Hence the growing specter of war seemed all the more ominous. In 1899, at the very beginning of this period, American and German naval units had nearly opened fire on each other off Samoa. In 1898, France and Britain had almost gone to war following the clash at Fashoda between Colonel Marchand and Lord Kitchener. One year earlier Russia and Austria, and also Britain and Russia had all but opened hostilities, the first in connection with the Greco-Turkish war of 1897, the second as a result of a common thirst for possessions in China.

In 1904–1905 came that great shock to European self-confidence which went by the name of the Russo-Japanese war. Trotsky was not exaggerating when he remarked on January 2, 1905, on the occasion of the fall of Port Arthur, that progressive Asia had delivered an irreparable blow to reactionary Europe — the fall of Port Arthur was the prologue to the collapse of Czarism. The Russian autocracy had severely misjudged the strength of the masses, much as others after them were to underestimate the strength of the Mexican and the Chinese masses. Mass movements were something quite new in 1900–1914, and nobody would have believed that, before long, unknown men would lead the masses to victory: the masses were beyond anyone's understanding; they could not be told apart, let alone from a disciplined body. The shock waves of the war and the 1905 revolution spread quickly beyond the Czar's western frontiers. Count von Schlieffen, Chief of the German General Staff from 1891 to 1906, was one of the first to learn the lesson. Russia, he argued, would be unable to wage war on two fronts, against Japan as well as against Germany, just as Germany would be unable to take on the combined forces of France and Russia. Now that Britain had not yet recovered from the exertions of the Boer war, the time was right for declaring a preventive war against Russia. But his plea fell on deaf ears; the Kaiser would not hear of upsetting his "cousin Nicky," and von Bülow was totally opposed to such a war. All he wanted was to humiliate France, and to weaken the recent entente between France and Great Britain.

He thought his chance had come at the beginning of 1905, during the "First Moroccan Crisis" (1905–1906). As Reichs Chancellor and Prime Minister of Prussia (1900–1909), he persuaded the vacillating Kaiser to pay his inglorious visit to Tangiers — there was no proper landing place and not even a decent horse — and to deliver a speech in support of the Sultan, from whom France was busily trying to extract fresh concessions. To this manoeuvre, von Bülow owed his noble title, but the Algeciras Conference, in which the "crisis" culminated early in 1906, yielded no plums — quite the contrary. Von Bülow had instigated it all with the secret objective of testing the strength of the Anglo-French entente, only to find that his efforts were crowned by a strengthening of that alliance and by closer liaison between the Anglo-French general staffs. And if Germany had merely wanted to exploit the situation in order to gain harbor facilities in Morocco, then she failed on that account as well. Count Tattenbach was no match for Britain's Sir Arthur Nicholson, who found him "really a horrid fellow, blustering, rude and mendacious, the worst type of German I have ever met."[6] This description could have applied to quite a few German diplomats, and their foreign colleagues might well have been grateful to these Germans for making them look so intelligent and polished by comparison. Neither the Russians nor the Americans nor even the Italians sided with Germany. The Russians and Italians, incidentally, were not simply reacting to Tattenbach's boorishness; St. Petersburg was tied to Paris and London with golden ropes, and Rome had the understanding with Paris: Morocco for you, Tripoli for us. Consequently von Bülow was thwarted on every front — he had tried to avoid German isolation at any cost, and had achieved the precise opposite. Holstein, the "gray eminence" acting behind the scenes, was dismissed; and when Bebel took von Bülow to task for his part in the whole affair, the Chancellor made a very poor showing in the Reichstag. It was also at the time of the Algeciras Conference, on February 10, 1906, that Lord Fisher, the British counterpart of von Tirpitz, launched the first Dreadnought, an event that was of more than purely symbolic importance. This battleship of 17,950 tons with its ten great guns, all of the same caliber (twelve inches), and with a speed of eighteen to twenty knots, revolutionized shipbuilding as well as international relations.

The year 1907 was called calm, notwithstanding the fact that Russia and Britain agreed to divide Persia into two spheres of influence separated by a small, neutral, buffer zone, and that France, Britain, and Spain signed the treaty of Cartagena to frustrate any possible German designs on the Balearic or the Canary Islands. Two points for Britain and her allies.

In 1908, by contrast, two points for Germany and hers: the uprising of the Young Turks and the annexation of Bosnia and Herzegovina by Austria-Hungary. At the time, few people could have forecast that the phrase *fin de siècle* was about to express the true state of affairs in that part of the world. Vienna was still the capital of eastern Europe, much as she had been since the retreat of the Turks in the seventeenth century; the annexation of Bosnia and Herzegovina must have seemed the final move in the expulsion of Islam from Europe, and the Turkish revolution the death-throes of the "sick man of Europe." Vienna was still the gay city in which Stefan Zweig had spent his youth and which he had described so evocatively in his *Welt von Gestern.* But it was also the city that Cohen-Portheim was to examine more profoundly some twenty-five years later in his *Die Entdeckung von Europa:* the last aristocrat among European capitals, where time seemed to stand still and where overrefine-

33

Barry University Library
Miami, FL 331 1

ment went hand in hand with forebodings of the approaching doom, much as they had done in Paris before the Great Revolution. Vienna wore a gay and lively face to hide her nostalgia, and this was reflected in her music, from Mozart to Lehar, and from Schubert's *Unfinished Symphony* to Strauss's *Blue Danube.*[7] It was the Vienna of 1900, whose rulers, according to Viktor Adler, still reigned like despots, but despots whose depredations were tempered by old-style misgovernment. Yet the storm signals had already gone up, for was it not in Vienna that Freud's psychoanalysis and Herzl's Zionism had seen the light of day?

A whole book could be written on the year 1908, every sentence deflected by the magnet of 1914. Much as von Schlieffen had pleaded for a sudden attack on France in 1904, while France's ally was tied down in the Russo-Japanese War, so now Sir John Fisher, the First Sea Lord, advocated a preventive strike against the German Navy. The moment was propitious, for Germany's loyalties were divided between Austria, her ally, and Turkey, her friend; and unless Britain struck at once, the German Navy would gain the upper hand, at the latest by August 1914, the proposed date of the completion of the Kiel Canal. From the other side of the fence, Conrad von Hötzendorf, Chief of the Austro-Hungarian General Staff, was calling for the subjugation not only of Bosnia and Herzegovina but also of Serbia, by an unexpected attack.

1908 was also the year in which the *Daily Telegraph* published a "personal interview" with the Kaiser. While the House of Commons was still laughing at Wilhelm's boasts, many Reichstag members were deeply incensed by them. Maximilian Harden lifted the lid of a cesspool in his *Zukunft* when he published what von Holstein had merely been whispering about the homosexual activities of von Eulenburg, recently restored to the Kaiser's circle of intimate friends. But though the Social Democrats, "those unpatriotic louts," had collected 3¼ million votes at the polls, and were flexing their muscles, Wilhelm continued to pose as the great Kaiser and von Bülow as the great statesman and the German people, who mistook all this fools' gold for the real thing, as the "great nation." In brief, 1908 was a turning point, one at which what might still have been an avoidable catastrophe was converted into certain disaster for the bourgeoisie. Diplomatic activities became so precipitate as to appear so many aimless improvisations. The house was divided against itself, and this time for good.

Fresh storm signals went up at the beginning of 1911. French forces occupied Fez, the capital of Morocco, and the German Foreign Secretary, von Kiderlen-Wächter, reacted with his "leap of the Panther" to Agadir, and a demand for compensation in the French Congo. The second Morocco crisis had begun. Caillaux, who was to become Prime Minister of France soon afterward, made feeble attempts to patch up the quarrel, but Lloyd George, speaking at a dinner in the Mansion House, warned Germany not to count on British compliance at any price, and Germany was duly impressed by the voice of one respected by the British masses. French moderation and British determination were thus able to save the situation once more: accepting a small part of the compensation they had originally demanded, the Germans conceded that France had special rights to Morocco. Nevertheless, the course of events could no longer be stemmed by diplomatic niceties: the first fire had barely been put out before another was lit elsewhere. When France prepared to occupy Morocco, Italy thought it was high time to seize Tripoli, as her secret agreement with France entitled her to do. On November 4, when the Franco-German compromise was reached, Italy had been at war with Turkey for over a month, and there was a widespread feeling in all European capitals that this last move on the international chess board might have unpredictable consequences. However, by then Europe was too bogged down in the traditional diplomatic game to realize that what mattered was no longer the right move — that whoever won, mankind as a whole was bound to be the loser.

Haldane's mission to Berlin at the beginning of 1912 was the only even half-serious attempt to avert the coming calamity, but this eleventh-hour manoeuvre to patch up Anglo-German differences foundered on the rocks of the new German Navy Bill. The net which the European bourgeoisie was drawing over its head was of mesh not large enough to escape through. And just as the second Morocco crisis had led indirectly to the Tripolitanian war, so the latter led indirectly to the two Balkan wars. On the very day — October 18, 1912 — that Italy and Turkey made peace, the Balkan nations decided to grasp the crescent moon by its horns. Once again fate played one of her sinister tricks, for one year after these latest flames had been put out by the Treaty of Bucharest, signed on August 10, 1913, a far greater conflagration blew up nearby, kindled by the assassination of the Archduke Franz Ferdinand of Austria in Sarajevo. This time the blaze could no longer be contained; on the contrary, crises, fears, and envy all served to stoke the flames in which Europe's supremacy was to perish and with it the reign of the European bourgeoisie over both the proletariat at home and the colonial subjects abroad. Europe's leadership, still taken for granted in 1900, was about to be consumed in the struggle, as the French historian, Ernest Lavisse, had predicted it would. "Every force becomes spent," he had written. "Historical leadership is not an eternal gift. Europe inherited it three

35

thousand years ago from Asia, but cannot maintain it forever."[8] *Fin de siècle*: within two decades a mere presentiment had been transformed into a harsh reality, and the end of a century into the end of an entire world.

With the breakdown of external security, it was, of course, impossible that the inner security of the European bourgeoisie, still firm at the turn of the century, should have remained unshaken. And, indeed, it was at this very time that a formal change in the bourgeois outlook could first be discerned — a loosening of the mental structures and a fraying of the emotional tissues, both the direct effects of rising doubts about the old religious, intellectual, and moral truths, norms, and values. This change is one by which any serious student of history and sociology is bound to be struck. For it was no accident that the old social approach, which had been so solidly entrenched throughout the nineteenth century and which was considered so self-evident, except by the few Jeremiahs who appear in every period of history, should suddenly have been assailed by so many social critics, ranging from cautious skeptics to wholehearted opponents of the bourgeois system.[9] Their ranks were swelled further by philosophers, scientists, and writers who, like them, were having second thoughts about what not so long ago were considered to be "eternal verities." In this preliminary section we can do no more than mention a few straws in the wind. Thus while Haeckel, in his *Welträthsel* of 1899, had argued that the mystery of the universe was as good as solved, after the turn of the century it seemed very doubtful that science held or ever could hold all the answers to mankind's most perplexing problems. In philosophy, Bergson began to cause a stir with his *élan vital*, or mysterious vital force. Driesch, for his part, insinuated neovitalism into Haeckel's own biological preserve. In the historical field, Berr founded his *Revue de Synthèse Historique* in 1900; Breysig published his *Kulturgeschichte der Neuzeit* in 1901; Croce brought out his *Critica* in 1903, and Lamprecht his *Moderne Geschichtswissenschaft* in 1905 — all signs of a historical revival but also of dissatisfaction with the prevailing academic approach. In psychology, Freud — whose *Interpretation of Dreams* appeared in 1900 — opened up new horizons. He had become disillusioned with the old psychology, which he had found floundering in a sea of sham-experiments, as the historians we have just mentioned had lost their faith in the nineteenth-century pseudo-objectivity of their discipline. In 1907, Brouwer published a thesis that was to lay the foundations of mathematical intuitionism in opposition to the prevailing logistic and formalistic approach. It could not have been by chance that Bergson, too, set intuition above practical reason. At the same time, there also appeared

36

cracks in the Newtonian edifice: Planck's principles of quantum mechanics were first formulated in 1900, and Einstein published his special theory of relativity in 1905. While Kautsky was still advancing a mechanical interpretation of Marxism, his views were being challenged from two quarters: from Bernstein, whose *Voraussetzungen* (1899) had ceased to treat the victory of socialism as part of an inevitable historical process, and from Rosa Luxemburg and Lenin, who, though still convinced that socialism was bound to come, added that its advent called for the conscious exertion of the working class. A voluntaristic conception of Marx's doctrine had thus ousted the deterministic approach and, what is more, in two bitterly opposed camps. Voluntarism, relativism, intuitionism, the unconscious, subjectivism, synthesis, vitalism — all these were but different names for a new mode of thought ushered in at the turn of the century.

Because social historians, rather than scientists, were so quick to attribute these changes and shifts in emphasis to a loss of rationality and objectivity, they can rightly be accused of having mistaken the true nature of the latest scientific advances. Nevertheless, this very lapse on their part corroborates our own view that the bourgeoisie was losing its traditional composure, that its uncertainty was general and something quite distinct from what science itself was later to embrace in special form under the name of the uncertainty principle. The same process also made itself felt in the arts, where naturalism yielded to a host of new and more fluid schools. Impressionism, though still regarded as no more than the latest "style," was already paving the way for new patterns of perception that were to prove as fruitful in the arts as better methods of observation were in science. To the artist, less bound to tradition and convention, indeed in constant revolt against them, uncertainty became a fixed motif. Munch's woodcut, *Angst* (1895), was one of the earliest manifestations of this trend. After impressionism, firm lines disappeared from art and literature, and though some traces of the old realistic forms lingered on, neo-symbolism gained in strength and adherents. These adherents turned their backs on a world they found too painful to bear, and took refuge instead in the magical powers of the spirit. But those who took this road conveniently forgot that the spirit wilts if it is robbed of its foundations: the earth and her children.

At the same time, the old moral code was perceptibly relaxed. The advances of rationalism, which had dogged the steps of the church throughout its long history, became so forceful and dramatic at the end of the nineteenth century, that "modernism" spread rapidly among Catholics and Protestants alike. The secular ideas it introduced were not so much rooted in atheism as in doubt and uncertainty. Nor was this moral crisis confined to the church. All authority based on tradition (as wielded by the state, the family, convention, and so forth) began to crumble; all fixed values became relative, just as truth itself began to be judged by its relevance to the present or its promise for the future and no longer by its perennial appeal. The present was determined to make a complete break with the past, and to recognize no authority beyond itself or the future; but because recent developments had shown that the future was uncertain, the soul of Europe turned into a tortured reflection of its former self.

CHAPTER III

THE DRAGON AWAKES

The year 1900, the "Keng" year of the Chinese sixty-year cycle and also the twenty-sixth year of the reign of Kuang Hsü, the nominal emperor, turned out to be portentous for China. Diviners had long been predicting that the year would bring many disasters, and an event on its very eve proved them right: on December 30, 1899, a British missionary named Brooks was found murdered near Tsinan. The consequence of this act was something against which Lord Salisbury, the British Prime Minister, was to issue a warning a few months later, although in a different connection. At a meeting chaired by the Archbishop of Canterbury, he stated bluntly that missionaries would do well to use greater circumspection, lest their work claim much human life, and their religion appear a tool in the conqueror's hands.[1] Of the seven Chinese culprits in the Brooks affair, three were beheaded, one was strangled, one received life imprisonment, one a sentence of ten years' hard labor, and one was banished for two years; four village elders in whose district the crime had been committed were let off with a flogging. In addition, a fine of 9,000 taels was imposed, and a monument to the murdered missionary ordered to be set up at a cost of a further 500 taels.[2] Whether this monument still stands we cannot tell, but we do know that the murder was not premeditated. It was a symptom of the increasing reaction of the East to the action of the West.

However, the Tsungli Yamen, the office which since 1860 had been administering foreign affairs on behalf of the Emperor, had to deal not only with the symptom but also with its inevitable repercussions. In particular, the Tsungli Yamen realized that the foreigner was too entrenched in the country to turn a blind eye to the Brooks murder. The sentences passed on the assassins by F. A. Campbell, of the British Consulate in Shanghai, and his two missionary secretaries — with the provincial judge of Shantung as assessor — were to be expected. The Chinese authorities knew full well that much smaller provocations had been used to extort much larger concessions, but also that these very concessions were the main causes of the present state of unrest and of the kind of

39

excesses that had claimed the life of Brooks. An Imperial Decree of January 4, 1900, which tried to pour oil on all these troubled waters, was followed by another on January 11 which unintentionally but inescapably poured oil on the smoldering fires; for it stated that murder and pillage had been increasing as a direct result of the activity of armed gangs and called for their ruthless suppression. At the same time, however, it offered increased protection to all those associations of loyal subjects who were busily organizing whole villages into self-defense units.[3] The Europeans could hardly find words to express their dismay at this "two-edged" decree, though as closer studies have since shown it was perfectly justified. Brooks had indeed been killed by the Boxers, but the Boxer movement was, in the main, made up of two factions which Westerners failed to tell apart, firstly because they were badly informed — at the time, Peking was not a place to which respectable countries sent their top diplomats — and secondly because they knew nothing at all about the nature of mass movements in general and of extreme right-wing associations in particular. And the Boxers were just that. One wing of their movement was a legitimate People's Militia, known as the I Ho Tu'an ("Patriotic Harmony Bands") or the I Ho Ch'üan ("Righteous Harmony Fists"). The second wing, which had infiltrated the first in a manner that European history was to reflect so amply, and which made the whole organization seem a mere cover for their activities, consisted chiefly of members of the kind of secret society which China had known in such numbers in the course of her long history: the Taiping, the Black Flag, the White Lily, or the Triads. This time it was the Ta Tao Hui, or "Band of the Great Sword," the Boxers in the strict sense. They were infused with a patriotic mystique, and like the regular army with their German and Japanese drill, engaged in long bouts of physical exercises, whence their name of "Boxers." In addition, they relied on rites and incantations to render them invulnerable. The "uniforms" were streaked with red; their banners were yellow and bore the slogan "Long Live the Dynasty. Destroy the Foreigner." Patriotism was their mainspring; their main weakness was their lack of a program or of any desire to reform their country. How, indeed, could they have had this desire, uneducated peasants and proletarians that they were, with Prince Tuan and Yü Hsien, two arch-reactionaries, urging them on from behind the scenes? Another of their weaknesses was that these poorest of the poor were unwittingly and helplessly tied to the pursestrings of the West they so bitterly loathed, for the West supplied them with the cheap textiles and other manufactured goods they urgently needed.

To appreciate why anti-Western sentiment assumed such violent forms at the turn of the century, we must look back to the years 1894–1895, when the Japanese victory had laid China wide open to concession hunters. The result was a spate of new "leases," as one railway concession followed upon another and as piece after piece was carved out of the Chinese Empire. The Germans started it all by pocketing Kiaochow. They had first planned to do so in the summer of 1897, and the murder to two Catholic missionaries had played straight into their hands. When they struck, in March 1898, they not only gained that coveted trophy but also preferential rights in Shantung (where, according to tradition, Confucius was born) — and all this "in grateful acknowledgment of the friendship Germany had shown to the Imperial Chinese Government." The Russians, who had been gnawing at Korea and Manchuria, followed on that very month by occupying Port Arthur and a portion of the Liaotung peninsula. One month later the French "leased" the Bay of Kwangchow; the British made this an excuse for "leasing" an additional portion of the Kowloon promontory, opposite Hong Kong, and in the summer, after having first protested about the predatory behavior of their rivals, went on to ensconce themselves in Weihaiwei, between the Germans and the Russians. The Italians, too, staked their claims: in March 1899, they demanded the lease of San Men Bay and the setting aside of the greater part of Chekiang province as a sphere of their influence.[4]

The general auction had started, but some of the goods remained unsold. The Italians went away empty-handed despite the fact that their "request" had been underwritten by four cruisers carrying 110 guns, sent out most improperly, it was felt, because "the Italians did not even wait for a missionary to be killed before demanding a naval station."[5] Asia, in fact, had two means of defense against Western penetration: total isolation and preservation of the status quo, or adaptation to the West the better to fight it with its own weapons. Japan was the classic example of the successive and successful application of both methods, and China, too, was familiar with them, although in her case things were not nearly so straightforward. The "Hundred Days of Reform," June 10 to September 20, 1898, had been an attempt to resist the enemy through adaptation. The movement had had many champions, Sun Yat-sen and K'ang Yu-wei chief among them. There was, however, a considerable difference between these two. While the first, who worked in anti-dynastic Canton, felt that the enemy at home must be subdued before the foreigner, or, alternatively, that modernization demanded a revolutionary struggle against both, the second believed in more gradual reforms. K'ang Yu-wei had the ear of the Emperor but not — what was far more important — of Tz'u Hsi, the Empress Dowager, or the "Old

Buddha" as she was called. As soon as she got wind — and she had a fine nose — of the fact that the Reformers were plotting against her and her leading henchman, Commander Jung Lu, she squelched the incipient rebellion, forcing Kuang Hsü to declare in writing that he was not the legal emperor, that he was, moreover, ill, and that he was only too happy to leave the reins of government in her capable hands. Thus, in September 1898, the Old Buddha brought to an end the Chinese reform movement, exploiting anti-Western popular sentiment to save her own skin and hence the dynasty. She went no further than that, and was always very careful not to identify herself too closely with the masses on whom whe might well be forced to turn as well. Indeed, when that eventuality arose, she struck at them without hesitation. The equivocal make up of the popular movement — loyal militiamen on the one hand and fanatical mystics on the other — provided her with an excellent chance to pursue a double policy. Count Ito, the Japanese Prime Minister, was one of those who understood her. Thus when he gave an interview to Sir Valentine Chirol, the correspondent of the *Times*, soon after the suppression of the "revolt," he expressed the view that Britain had been quite wrong to come to the aid of the Manchu dynasty after the Taiping rebellion, for the shrewd old lady had quickly turned the spearhead of the movement against the West. The wind she had sown was bound to grow into a storm that would sweep every foreigner out.[6]

History had thus provided the basic condition of the rise and eventual collapse of the popular resistance movement: the ever-more shameless and hypocritical behavior of the West, beginning with the Opium War sixty years earlier. Anti-Western feeling flared up as fiercely as ever it had done during the Taiping rebellion, fed as it now was by the belief that the flooding of the Yellow River and the ensuing famine had been unleashed by the gods in their fight against the Christian God whose power the missionaries constantly vaunted. His disciples had desecrated the ancestral burial places by running railway tracks through them; the real struggle was waged in the Paoting-Tientsin-Peking railway triangle. The railways themselves terrified the Chinese peasants, much as they had earlier terrified European peasants. Then there were telegraph poles that protruded into the realm of the spirits, steamboats that stole the bread out of the mouths of junk builders and river boatmen, new machinery that threw honest artisans onto the streets; and a host of other encroachments by the growing number of foreign firms with names no honest man could pronounce even if he could have read them. Although few Chinese could have known that there were nearly 1000 of these firms giving employment to almost 20,000 people,[7] they felt that there were too many of them by far. All these horrors were the work of "foreign devils" affecting an insufferable air of superiority and spreading a strange religion which preached one thing on Sunday and did the very opposite throughout the week.[8] As for the feeling of superiority, not even the Americans were immune to it (as witness their exclusion in 1892 of Chinese immigrants, previously welcomed as a source of cheap and tractable labor) and this despite their genuine dismay at the greed of their European allies. The dismay was real enough, but not so their alleged lack of self-interest: in December 1900, John Hay, the U. S. Secretary of State, under pressure from the American Navy, tried to carve yet another slice out of China by asking for a naval coaling station at Samsah Inlet, north of Foochow on the coast of Fukien province. Nothing came of the request, not because of Chinese opposition but because Japan blocked the move by reminding Hay of his own recent efforts to preserve the territorial integrity of China.[9]

It has often been alleged that the Chinese were determined to destroy Christianity, when in fact their fury was never directed at the church or even at the missionaries as such. True, the latter were not always the most tactful, and often, in their zeal, they lovingly if somewhat haughtily lumped all heathens together — one of many lapses for which Henri Borel took them severely to task.[10] But the only reason they became the chief victims was that they were the sole foreigners in China who lived outside the range of white bayonets; had Barnum and Bailey toured the country at the time, they also would have paid with their lives.

Anti-foreign sentiment was, in any case, the main inspiration of the popular movement; another was the belief that, unlike its predecessors, the movement enjoyed the tacit support of the government. This was a source of strength, but also a source of weakness — of strength because after the outbreak of hostilities the better-armed official forces made common cause with the "rebels," and of weakness, because the support of the dynasty confined the movement to the four loyal provinces of Shantung, Chihli, Shansi, and Shengking (Southern Manchuria). Chihli was the main center; the rest of China was not prepared to join a movement compromised by the support of a dynasty from which they believed the "heavenly mandate" had long since been withdrawn. Moreover, dynastic support hampered the movement because it was clear from the outset that the Manchus would desert it the moment it ceased to serve their own purpose. A final, if paradoxical, cause of the mass uprising was the initial indifference of the European chancelleries, due either to lack of insight or to selfish designs. Many must have told themselves that this was not the first time a minor and temporary setback had

43

promised great advantages in the long run. Thus the Russian Minister of War was heard to declare at the beginning of the outbreak: "This will give us an excuse for seizing Manchuria."[11] Indeed, it seems probable that Russia spent quite a few roubles on stoking up this promising little fire. We also know that the Kaiser was furious when he learned, shortly before the dispatch of von Waldersee, that all the ambassadors were still alive and that the Allies, under the Russian commander, General Linievich, had relieved the foreign legations without German help.[12]

In discussing the circumstances which gave rise to the Boxer movement we have, here and there, anticipated the developments. Hence a short summary of the actual course of events may not be out of place. It can be short, because we are not so much concerned with the uprising as such as with the reactions of the European powers which were so deeply involved that, for a time, news from China took precedence in the headlines over news from the South African front. The "two-edged" decree of January 11th was followed on the 27th by a demand jointly presented by the ambassadors of Britain, France, Germany, and America: the *entire* Boxer movement had to be banned. There was no reply. A month later came a fresh ultimatum. This time there was a formal reply together with a copy of an edict by Yü-lu, Governor of Chihli, banning the I Ho Tu'an but deliberately ommitting any mention of the Ta Tao Hui — quite reasonably from the Chinese point of view since the latter were outlawed in any case.[13] This did not satisfy the European ministers, who on March 7 sent a telegram to their several governments asking for what had always worked in the past: a show of naval strength in the North China Sea. The ships duly arrived. Next came a strongly worded demand for additional guards to protect the diplomatic quarter of Peking, in reply to which the Powers were informed that Yühsien, the Governor of Shantung, who as such bore ultimate responsibility for the murder of Brooks, had been transferred to the Governorship of Shansi. On May 14 the situation deteriorated further. Anti-foreign placards went up in the streets of Peking, and Bishop Favier informed the French ambassador, Pichon, and through him all the other legations, that Peking was surrounded, that anti-Christian agitation was merely an excuse, and that the Boxers were really out to kill all foreigners, as their banners made only too plain. A new protest was lodged on May 21. The reply, on May 24, stated that there must be some misunderstanding, since all earlier demands had been met on the 18th. On May 26, came a fresh ultimatum and a fresh reply which only served to convince the most intelligent among the Boxers that their government always capitulated in the end, however reluctantly. From then on it was no longer the mystical but the radical element that set the tone. It spoke the language of Sun Yat-sen, who was still away on his great tour, in the course of which he braved violent death for seventeen years, from 1895 to 1912. The Boxer reply to the latest humiliation was an attack on the railway works at Tengt'ai near Peking, and the Chinese soldiery, not particularly anxious to protect foreign possessions, made common cause with the "rebels." When engineers from the Franco-Belgian Railway Company at Paoting and their families tried to escape to Tientsin, four of them were killed, and on June 1 two missionaries lost their lives as well. Admittedly, theirs was the only European blood that had flowed since Brooks's death — Chinese Christians fared worse — and these incidents were the only attacks on unarmed foreigners, but when the guards were posted in the legations on May 31 with the agreement of the Chinese government, they came only just in time. The only question was whether this contingent of some 300 men and 12 officers would be large enough, now that the Boxers were massing outside the city, red scarves tied round their heads, red ribbons at their wrists and ankles, red sashes round their waists, armed with daggers and lances, and carrying red flags and yellow banners inscribed with battle-slogans and demands. There was good reason to fear them, and on June 10, Admiral Seymour, at the head of a force of some 2,000 men, left Tientsin for the relief of the capital. Halfway there, he discovered that the railway line had been cut, and that he must either proceed on foot or return. Finding that the weight of numbers barred the first course, he retreated.

The first armed clash served to aggravate the situation more than anything that had gone before. The Old Buddha enlisted the help of Li Hung-chang, China's most experienced politician; appointed Prince Tuan, the semi-official protector of the Boxers, as co-president of the Tsungli Yamen; and sent a letter instructing all viceroys and governors to meet force with force. Greatly encouraged, the Boxers now broke into Peking and Tientsin, and, on June 16, the Powers replied by capturing the Taku forts near the mouth of the Peh Ho. The Chinese took this for a declaration of war.

The next act in the drama was played out in Peking. Here Sugiyama, head of the chancellery in the Japanese legation, was murdered on June 11, while looking in vain for the relief force from one of the city gates. On June 19, the Chinese government asked the foreign ministers to leave the city within twenty-four hours for their own safety. When Baron von Ketteler, the fearless German ambassador — he had previously warded off an armed Boxer with his walking stick — set out next morning in his green and red official chair, accompanied by an armed Chinese guard, to

45

protest to the Tsungli Yamen against the explusion order, he was shot
dead on the way by a sergeant in the regular Chinese army. This incident
was clearly connected with the aggressive behavior of the legation guards,
remarked upon even by European eyewitnesses.[14] That day, xenophobia
reached new heights, and changed tragedy into farce: a government decree
proscribed the use in literary examinations of any characters representing
the allied countries.[15] That day also marked the beginning of the siege
of the legations. It was to continue until August 14, eight anxious weeks
for those inside: some 450 civilians, the same number of soldiers, and
a few thousand Chinese converts who had sought refuge among them.
Yet we must ask whether their fears were justified. The letters of Putnam
Weale[16] indicate that they were; Allen's account merely suggests that
they may have been. But when we consider that all these buildings,
though fortified, were anything but strongholds; that throughout all these
weeks not one of them was captured or completely destroyed; and that,
when the legations were finally relieved, no more than fifty of the besieged were found dead, even though the Chinese were equipped with
modern Männlicher rifles and Krupp field-guns, then we cannot but
conclude that the Chinese government did its utmost to avoid bloodshed.
There are other pointers in the same direction. On July 3 the Grand
Council addressed a letter to the Tsungli Yamen which stated that what
crimes had been committed were the work of bandits and that help —
from the foreigners — must be enlisted to bring these bandits to justice.
On July 19, letters were courteously presented to the various heads of
state by their Chinese ambassadors, who had strict instructions to observe
the usual diplomatic civilities. These letters repudiated the Boxer rebels,
and called upon the Great Powers to restore order.[17] On July 27, fifteen
trucks with provisions reached the embassies. By then, official China
had given way, no doubt in the wake of the fall of Tientsin on July 14
and probably no less because the reactionary government feared a revolutionary victory more than it feared the foreigners.

The request to restore order was met by the Great Powers with
immediate action. Having cleared Tientsin and its environs of "rebels,"
they started their march on Peking on August 4, and reached the capital
in the early morning of August 13. The fall of Peking will not be described here. It followed the classical pattern of the conquest of cities
in which there is no special reason for sparing the enemy: the color of
smoke and blood, the smell of burning flesh, and the silence of lust
and mortal anguish. Putnam Weale reported — though he was speaking
of the Germans alone — that even the officers took a hand in the looting,
but in a modified way: "They force their way into the remains of the

curio shops, take the few pieces that are left, place a dollar or so on the counter and then walk out. This makes a legitimate purchase."[18] Compared with the share destined for their Kaiser, the officers' spoils were modest enough: Wilhelm would have received a whole trainful of "tribute," had the train not caught fire by "accident" soon after it was loaded.[19]

Even more revealing was the eyewitness account by Baron d'Anthouard, First Secretary of the French Legation, of the occupation of the Imperial Palace on August 28. The Court had fled to Sian in the heart of distant Shensi; but though she had obviously been in a great hurry, the Old Buddha had still managed to get rid of the emperor's favorite wife by having her thrown into a well.[20] The Court was not to return until the beginning of 1902, and the immense reception halls, apartments, fortifications, barracks, and prisons which, together with the forecourt and inner courts, covered an area of just under sixty acres, lay deserted. The great gilded lion with its yawning mouth, at the foot of the stairs leading to the inner palace, did not impress the enlightened Westerners — its grandeur merely emphasized the desolation all round.[21] The occupation was unnecessarily theatrical. General Linievich and his staff marched in first, followed by the whole diplomatic corps drawn up in order of precedence, and the most motley crew of soldiers and marines that has ever been assembled: Russians, Japanese, Sikhs representing Britain, Annamites representing France, Germans, Italians, and Austrians. The mighty, red-laquered doors with their unwieldy gilded handles turned ponderously on their massive hinges, as eunuchs flitted about discreetly in the imperial staterooms to attend to the visitors. Members of the Tsungli Yamen acted as guides and offered refreshment. The intruders thought it contemptible servility, but the Chinese were merely trying to save face by pretending they were receiving visitors. Significantly enough, the visit was broken off prematurely as soon as it was discovered that some of the "honored guests" had begun to loot the Palace.

On September 25, one month after this historic but inglorious spectacle — the one does not necessarily exclude the other — Count von Waldersee and his army finally arrived in Tientsin. By diplomatic pressure and skulduggery — a German minister *had* been murdered, after all — Wilhelm had finally succeeded in having his Field Marshal appointed Chief Commander, or "World Marshal," of the Allied Armies, even though the French refused to recognize him as such and others did so with bad grace. His original orders had been unexceptionable: to avenge the dead ministers, to save those still alive, and to exert exemplary punishment;

but his late arrival turned his punitive expedition against the now de-feated[22] Boxers into what would later be termed a "police action." "That an old warrior like me" — he was 68 — "should have been forced to play a diplomatic guest role is something I should never have believed a year ago," he recorded in his diary on November 9.[23] With a mere 60,000 men, however, he was able to play that role so well that Wilhelm's alleged reference to him as a "maid of all work"[24] seemed only too fitting. It was without a spot on his uniform — Chinese blood did not count — that he returned to the Fatherland one year later, in August 1901, his mission completed.

Although that mission had been far from glorious, neither had it been simple. To begin with he had to avenge the deaths of 250 mission-aries and civilians. Foreigners had been killed in twenty-seven towns, severely maltreated in another fourteen, robbed and driven out from another three, all spread over five provinces. In addition, the list included another three towns marked down for punishment without apparent cause.[25] The Kaiser's orders were followed to the letter: "No mercy will be shown. All prisoners are to be bayonetted."[26] But while von Waldersee made light of his punitive expeditions against the enemy, conducted with one finger on the map, he had trouble with his squabbling allies. He was full of complaints about them, and understandably so, for the clash of interests, which capable diplomats had been able to sweep under the carpet at home, now came into the open. As a prelude, Russia, Japan, and the United States objected to Germany's insistence that no nego-tiations could start before the Chinese had handed over every one of the "criminals." The Russians even threatened to withdraw altogether, a step by which they hoped to curry favor with Peking, thus playing the same trump they had used in 1860. A grateful Chinese government, they believed, would be only too happy to give them a free hand in Manchuria. The Japanese, too, did not wish to fall foul of the Chinese — they were already anticipating war with Russia. Throughout the Boxer campaign they had done rather more than their share of real fighting, yet had distinguished themselves by their humane treatment of non-combatants.[27] The Americans, who were still unfamiliar with the im-perialist game, merely insisted on fair trading opportunities, realizing full well that this policy would favor their own cheap exports. France steered a middle course, somewhat closer to the German than to the Russian, when, on October 4, she proposed that the Powers present China with the following demands: punishment of the criminals; com-pensation; and guarantees against any repetition. Britain, finally, sided largely with the Germans, lukewarm as she felt toward the French and definitely hostile to the Russians. We shall pass over the minor differences, including those of a personal kind, though they were real enough and often so violent that von Waldersee more than once feared armed clashes between the Allies and had to use all his tact to prevent them. The only people to benefit from all these squabbles were the Chinese; Li Hung-Chang and Prince Ching, the Chinese negotiators, did not hesitate to exploit them and did so from the very moment that negotiations were opened, on October 15. They lasted for nearly a year. On September 7, 1901, the Chinese representatives agreed to the final protocol with the eleven plenipotentiaries. The terms were harsh indeed, and ran to twelve articles: humiliating punishments for the murders of the hated foreigners, especially of von Ketteler and Sugiyama; death sentences to be passed on various Chinese dignitaries; a ban on the importation of firearms; the establishment of permanent legation guards; the dismantling of several Chinese forts; the occupation by the Powers of several points between Peking and the sea; revision, in favor of the Powers, of the detested treaties; and finally an indemnity fixed at the sum of 450 million taels. The greatest humiliation of all was the demand that all these conditions be met and published even before the protocol was signed. As in 1842, 1858, 1860, 1885, and 1895, China had failed to stand up to the West. In 1901 she ceased to be a power, and was reduced to a state of total impotence.

When he signed the protocol on September 7, Li Hung-Chang was already fatally ill. He died two months later. His coffin was taken to the inner court of the Palace of Su I, Viceroy of Chihli, Grand Secretary and Count of the First Rank, where it rested behind a white curtain and a white shrine. On the shrine stood a yellow tray, and the black-on-red imperial decree of mourning, flanked by two gigantic candles in cloisonné enamel candlesticks to light the dead man's way on his last journey. In front of the shrine stood a large censer into which all the mourners, after kneeling on a carpet and bowing reverently to the ground, placed incense sticks before pouring a little wine from a heron-headed ewer, first into a cup and then, with a circling motion of the right hand, into a blue bowl.

With Li Hung-Chang the old China had died. The old China, not China herself. Her nadir became a turning point in her relations with Europe. It was purely by chance that the peace protocol was signed in the Spanish legation, for de Cologan happened to be the oldest diplomat and hence the doyen of the diplomatic corps; but it amounted to a symbolic choice of venue, for Spain had been the first European colonial power to fall victim to inner weakness and external pressure. Infinitely more crucial was the fact that the conservative Boxer movement contained the germ of the Chinese revolution. Among the Europeans there were some who already felt rather than said this. Zabel warned his readers not to underestimate China, or, for that matter, Japan, Russia, and the United States. A Russian victory in the coming conflict would be far worse for Europe than a Japanese one, though those to profit most from a victorious Japan would undoubtedly be the Americans.[28] Netscher had similar presentiments when he wrote that "if the Chinese should win, and if in more or less secret compact with Russia, a country more Asiatic than European, they should gain the upper hand over Europe, then all the fears of the 'Mongolian peril' will doubtless be justified."[29] Borel, who was much better informed, wrote this of China before he learned of the collapse of the Boxer movement: "The revolutionary party is likely to do just what the Japanese have done: rid the country of all foreign influences and turn it into an independent power in the East. If the movement succeeds, the West is as good as finished and the future belongs to China and Japan, to the East."[30] Among the Chinese, too, there were some who took the same view. Thus on November 26, 1900, Angier, Editor-in-Chief of the *London and China Express*,[31] reported a conversation he had had with a "native." When he reminded him of the occupation of Peking forty years earlier, his Chinese interlocutor looked incredulous. Occupation? He had lived in the capital at the time, and no one had occupied Peking. True, there had been a great many troops, but when they were asked what they were doing, they had said that they were short of money and the Chinese government, anxious to avoid any unpleasantness, had paid them off. Angier was amazed at this strange denial of the hard historical facts, but was there not more truth in this myth than in the facts themselves? Was it not true that brutal foreigners had come knocking at the Chinese door, like so many beggars? That episode was now past. How long had it lasted? A mere century. Fifty years after China's deepest humiliation, the roles were reversed. Every trace of European influence had disappeared. Behind the rebellious Boxers with their primitive swords, there loomed as in a Chinese shadow play, the gigantic figure of Sun Yat-sen, behind him that of Marshal Chiang Kai-shek, and behind the Marshal that of Mao Tse-tung.

CHAPTER IV

CAPE TO CAIRO

On January 10, 1900, Field Marshal Roberts disembarked in Cape Town. He was the new British Commander-in-Chief, accompanied by General Kitchener, his chief-of-staff. Their orders were to free the war machine, bogged down in the veld. Both had earned their laurels; both were experts in conducting the tough colonial campaigns on which great empires are built. Lord Roberts of Kandahar and Waterford had waged them in India and Afghanistan, Lord Kitchener of Khartoum in the Sudan and in Egypt. Britain had no sharper blades, and she had to be in grave difficulties to send these two veterans — at the time Roberts was past 68. Similarly, France would one day call on Foch in her hour of need and Germany on Hindenburg, two other graybeards in their sixties.

Were conditions in South Africa as desperate as those prevailing during the First World War, when everything had to be staked? They were serious enough, in all truth. From the outbreak of the Boer War on October 12, 1899, Roberts's predecessor, Sir Redvers Buller, had suffered defeat after defeat, allowing what few successes he had had to slip out of his hands soon afterward. Ladysmith, Mafeking, and Kimberley were besieged. During "Black Week" (9–15 December) General Gatacre had been defeated at Stormberg, while Cronjé had scored a great victory over Methuen at Magersfontein, and the British Commander-in-Chief himself had been repulsed by Joubert and Botha at Colenso. As a result of the first defeat, the Cape Colony lay open to invasion from the north; as a result of the second and third, the relief of Kimberley and the relief of Ladysmith were impeded. The fact that Buller's head had been some-what prematurely stamped out on the issue of emerald-green biscuit tins made the situation all the more embarrassing.[1] As always in such precarious situations, morale at home was boosted with tales of great heroism. On New Year's Eve a skirmish had claimed 80 of a force of 120 men; they had refused to abandon their wounded comrades, had braved the onslaught of 800 Boers, and had eventually been relieved by 115 Cape Mounted Riflemen. On New Year's Day, Londoners rushed the recruiting offices to sign up with the City Imperial Volunteers.[2]

51

While Buller's setbacks had many objective causes, he himself was undoubtedly at fault as well, for he had badly underestimated his opponents. The original British force of 25,000 faced some 60,000 Boers. In addition, the Boers were led by men who had long ago realized that war was inevitable and had made every possible preparation for it, while the British had not — some financial magnates may have anticipated this war for a long time, but the nation as a whole was quite uninvolved. Facing the Boer commandos, who were defending their soil and their homes and who were totally convinced of the justice of their cause, stood soldiers who had come from a distant land and who were expected to right alleged wrongs that meant nothing to them at all. And while the Boers were led by "veldkornets," men whom they had learned to trust over the years, the British officers had been chosen through favor rather than merit: social and political considerations weighed more heavily than professional qualifications. Last but by no means least, the Afrikaners were in a majority in the Cape Province,[3] and it was on the wobbly plank of their loyalty that there drifted what little British prestige had been saved from the shipwreck. Luckily for Britain, the Afrikaners in the Cape Colony, though bound to their brothers in the Transvaal by ties of blood, also had special interests which set them apart. Was it not the Afrikaanderbond which had helped Rhodes to the premiership in Cape Town and had kept him there for six long years? It was the rich landowners and wine-growers in the south who had benefited from the prosperity he had brought to the Cape, not the cattle farmers in the north of the Province. And it was from the north that the greatest danger threatened. In 1900 there was a serious uprising, followed by noisy meetings held by sympathizers of the republic; the Cabinet itself was divided. Milner, High Commissioner since 1897, who would have been the standard-bearer of British imperialism in South Africa had he not, sober businessman that he was, been overshadowed by the far more romantic Rhodes, was only just able to hold on to office, while Schreiner had to resign the premiership and make way for Sir Gordon Sprigg. On December 6, an Afrikaner Congress held in Worcester demanded an end to the war and independence for the republics; but when they called on Milner a few days later, he brushed aside their claim that a continuation of the war would lead to the destruction of the entire white race. The annexations were there to stay; there was no going back now. Two days later Milner was appointed Governor of the two republics; and when de Wet invaded the Cape Colony within the week, he came too late: martial law had been tightened and his supporters, to whom he looked for men and supplies, lay low.

In general, Britain's international position at the end of 1899 was no happier than it was in the veld; the setbacks in the latter were sharply reflected in the former. The view that England would lose the war was widespread; and although the wish may have been father to the thought, there were many objective reasons for pessimism. Thus some claimed that the recent increase in insurance premiums and the consequent rise in freight charges would produce a social crisis of unprecedented dimensions. Others contended that so many men would have to be called up that Britain would run short of merchant seamen, policemen, and postmen. Moreover, would the tramway system not collapse in view of the fact that 200 horses had been requisitioned in Liverpool alone?[4] While people reassured one another that Britain had never lost a war, quite a few had nagging doubts about the outcome of this particular one. England was playing poker, people said. Modern imperialism may have been an indigenous European product, but it nevertheless bore a striking similarity to that game of chance, recently imported from America. Thus Britain had gained the upper hand over Portugal by giving out that she had reached an agreement with Germany on the division of the Portuguese colonies in Africa — a simple bluff. But though all sorts of other wishes, too, were presented as established facts, reality seemed at long last to have been dealt a winning hand, with the result that the legend of British invincibility was fast losing its credibility. It very much looked as if Bismarck had been right to assert that South Africa would become Britain's graveyard.[5] As the nineteenth century was being rung out, few would have wagered that Britain might yet win the game, that the Boers, abandoned by all the other Powers, would finally throw in their hand.

That is how matters stood on January 10, the date with which we began this chapter. Roberts, having learned from his predecessor's mistakes, realized that if only he could convince the doubters and satisfy the dissatisfied, morale could be speedily restored. To that end he needed a spectacular success. His plan was as simple as it was daring: he would capture Bloemfontein, the capital of the Orange Free State, some two-thirds of the way from Cape Town to Pretoria, then follow the railway line first to Kroonstad and then on to Johannesburg and finally to Pretoria, the two most important cities in the distant Transvaal. Once these objectives were reached, the rest would be child's play. Roberts accordingly did what he could to mechanize his forces. Moreover, he discarded the conspicuous scarlet in which his men had been fighting and put them all into khaki. He demanded the most up-to-date field pieces and as many of them as possible; he built block houses along

53

the railway line; introduced armored trains, and brought in more and more horses to replace the losses — on one occasion 6,000 of them were transported over a distance of some 850 miles within five weeks; the South African war was fought chiefly on horseback. It also swallowed up men, for although Roberts with his 70,000 already outnumbered the Boers, he would ultimately command three times that number. British imperialism must win and would win. Parliament, with a weak Liberal Opposition, gladly paid the price: first £10 million then another £13 million, followed by a further £7.5 million and, after the "Khaki Elections" of December 1900, when the war had passed into its third and last, guerilla, phase, by yet another £16 million.[6] Altogether the war was to cost Britain £250 million.

So the tide turned. On February 15, French relieved Kimberley. That very night, Cronjé broke camp at Magersfontein — too late because he was even more obstinate than Kruger himself; three days later he had to surrender at Perdeberg, whence he and a thousand of his companions were sent into exile to St. Helena, much to the disgust of the French, who felt that island was fit only for a Napoleon. On February 18, Buller, after three abortive attempts, succeeded in crossing the Tugela, and at the end of the month he was able to raise the siege of Ladysmith. From then on, try as they might, the Boers were unable to wrest the initiative from Roberts. His was a daring game, for after every fresh success his army was close to exhaustion; what saved him was that the enemy now had no plans other than to frustrate his own. Bloemfontein fell on March 13; Kroonstad on May 12. The Orange Free State was officially annexed on May 24, and soon afterward — on the very day Roberts had promised — Mafeking was relieved. It was now the Transvaal's turn. Johannesburg fell on May 31; and on June 5 the Union Jack was hoisted over the Raadzaal in Pretoria, Kruger's own capital. The flag had been buried in 1881, in a coffin on which they had written the word "Resurgam."[7] Nineteen years later, on September 3, 1900, it was indeed resurrected, and the last free Boer Republic ceased to exist. On the Sunday following Roberts's triumphal entry, the Rev. H. J. Batts, who had been allowed to stay in Pretoria throughout the war, delivered a sermon. His text was Luke XV, 32: "It was meet that we should make merry and be glad: for this my brother was dead and is alive again: and was lost and is found."[8] The brother in question was no doubt of British nationality, though once the peace of Vereeniging was signed, on May 31, 1902, he might equally have been a Boer: the peace terms were mild enough, not least for fear of the black "brother." Eight years later to the day, the Union of South Africa was born, though, in 1900, that great "reconciliation" still seemed very far off, the more so as the Boers kept up the fight, and not without local successes, for twenty long months after the annexation of the Transvaal. Still, all their efforts, in the field no less than on the diplomatic stage, did not avail them in the end. Leyds, Fischer, Wessels, Wolmarans, and finally Kruger himself had gone to Europe to plead their cause, but all in vain. Yet their fight had not been without historical importance. It had driven home that men certain of their cause will sacrifice their lives and possessions, even against overwhelming odds. Moreover, the guerilla tactics of General Botha, Joubert's successor, forced Kitchener, who had taken over from Roberts in November 1900, to wage what can only be called a prelude to the "total" wars of the twentieth century. Nor was it by chance that this should have happened in a war that brought imperialism face to face with fervent nationalism. The British system of blockhouses spanned the entire territory of the two former republics — twelve-and-a-half times the size of the Netherlands. The scattered farms, so many foci of resistance, were razed to the ground; cattle and supplies were "confiscated"; 120,000 women and children were herded into concentration camps behind barbed wire, where one in six of them perished from disease or exposure. Was all this deliberate policy? Not maliciously so, but only inasmuch as it served the final objective: to smash all resistance. The new type of warfare had posed problems that Britain could not solve in the traditional way. She could proffer a very good excuse for the concentration camps: without them, now that their farmsteads had been burned down — so many columns of smoke against the blue sky by day, and so many pillars of fire at night under the twinkling stars — a vastly greater number of women and children would have perished from hunger and thirst. For all that, public opinion refused to swallow this particular piece of sophistry. Indignation in a world that had not yet grown as accustomed to injustice as our own flamed up higher than the fires in the veld, not least in Britain herself. An English clergyman even denounced Campbell-Bannerman as a traitor, a coward, and a murderer. No doubt he went too far, but one must sympathize with him when one recalls that this Liberal leader, who had opposed the war so bitterly, settled for "moderation" once it had started. Other Liberals, by contrast, stuck to their principles, among them William Harcourt, John Morley, James Bryce, Lord Kimberley, and Lloyd George, who had to be smuggled out of a peace meeting, disguised in police uniform, on December 18, 1901, in Birmingham, where he had tried to confront Joseph Chamberlain on his own ground.[9] Labour, too, opposed the war under the leadership of Keir Hardie, but his Party had not been formed until 1900 and still had little influence. MacDonald, its first secretary and Keir Hardie's eventual successor, was a staunch pacifist and suffered the consequences, much as he was to do during the Great War — unlike Lloyd George. The man who gave unflinching support to the Boers from the beginning to the end of the war was W. T. Stead, editor of the *Review of Reviews*. In 1903, in a preface to Frederic Rompel's *Heroes of the Boer War*, he did not mince his words and rounded on the British government for having stained "the annals of the Empire at the dawn of the twentieth century."[10]

A crime was committed, and the cost computed: £250 million. But what had been the real motive? We can tell it in figures. On October 3, 1899, Consolidated Goldfields shares were quoted at £27.10s.; on October 20, after the outbreak of war, they had gone up to £28.10s.[11] We can also say it in words, but it all comes back to the same thing. In 1900, the Powers identified strength with railroads. Behind the Boer war loomed the imperial dream of Cecil Rhodes: a railway from Cape Town to Cairo that would cross and command the entire continent. This majestic plan was part of an even wider dream. We know it as well as any dream can ever be known. In 1877, Rhodes, then twenty-four years old, drew up his first will in South Africa, a country to which he had come seven years earlier in the hope of restoring his poor health — it was feared he might be suffering from consumption. The will spoke of "the extension of British rule throughout the world . . . the colonization by British subjects of all lands wherein the means of livelihood are attainable by energy, labour and enterprise and especially the occupation by British settlers of the entire continent of Africa, the Holy Land, the Valley of the Euphrates, the islands of Cyprus and Candia, the whole of South America, the islands of the Pacific not heretofore possessed by Great Britain, the whole of the Malay Archipelago, the sea-board of China and Japan, the ultimate recovery of the United States of America as an integral part of the British Empire . . . colonial representation in the Imperial Parliament, which may tend to weld together the disjointed members of the Empire, and finally, the foundation of so great a Power as to hereafter render wars impossible and to promote the best interests of humanity."[12] It was all a strange mixture of childish fantasy and prophetic vision. We do not have to look far for its philosophic and ethical sources — they were ill-digested pronouncements by Aristotle, picked up in Oxford, or culled from Darwin and from Reade's *Martyrdom of Man*, a book published in 1872 that had lifted Africa from historical obscurity. In addition, Rhodes shared the belief of so many of his compatriots that God had selected Englishmen to govern the world on His behalf and to His greater glory. What mattered for more was Rhodes's

56

determination to make his dream come true and his personal charisma that helped to press men into its service, for Rhodes was much more — or much less — than a dreamer. The dream may have been his inner mainspring, but it was not for its sake that he was so greatly admired. Men followed him not only because, time and again, he had proved his mastery in their own world, but above all because he excelled in a world they did not share with him: to his Oxford connections he was the diamond king, the Prime Minister, the founder and governor of Rhodesia; to his friends in the diamond world he was the scholar, the statesman, and the hero; to his fellow politicians he was the financier and the richest man in the world. And he was all those. To his enemies, he was a man who misused politics to enrich himself and who misused his riches to sully politics, and he was that as well.

British politicians had done the spadework by blocking every Boer attempt to reach the sea; in 1914 Leyds showed just how this was done. In the east, the ring round the Boers extended to the southern border of Portuguese East Africa; in 1895 the last outlet, Tongaland, had been declared a British Protectorate.[13] In the west, Griqualand West had been annexed as early as 1880, the Bechuanaland Protectorate had followed some five years later, and in May 1895, when all the territories that Rhodes's Chartered Company had acquired since 1889 — Matabeleland, Mashonaland, and Barotseland — were officially renamed Rhodesia in honor of their "founder," another outlet was effectively closed. Since Nyasaland in the northeast had been a British protectorate since 1891, Rhodes's dream had been realized as far as Lake Nyasa in the east and Lake Tanganyika in the north. Beyond that, the Congo Free State and German East Africa barred the way, at least in Rhodes's own lifetime — he died in 1902. He had done what he could. In 1893, when he had learned of the defeat of Lobengula, King of the Matabele, he had sent a telegram to Jameson: "Luke XIV, 31."[14] No doubt that message had a bearing on the raid by Jameson two years later. In any case, the only obstacle to the implementation of the next part of the dream, the creation of the Union of South Africa, was the continued existence of the two independent Boer republics. Its removal was the more important because Rhodesian gold had proved something of a disappointment — the Witwatersrand would, as far as anyone could tell, remain the most important gold field in the foreseeable future, and unfortunately — or fortunately? — it happened to lie in the Transvaal. We have seen how this final hurdle was cleared two months after Rhodes's death.

And what of the railways, those symbols of his unswerving ambition, which only wavered when refractory nature or man refused to bend to his will? Here, too, the spadework had been done by the time Rhodes appeared on the scene. The first section, from Cape Town to Wellington, had been built as early as 1859; it was extended to Kimberley in 1885 following the discovery of the local diamond fields in 1867. The Rhodesia Railways Company, founded in 1893, continued the line as far as Mafeking only one year later, and within a further three years the track had been extended as far as Bulawayo, the capital of Matabeleland. Here amid the Matopo Hills, which the Matabele call "View of the World," Rhodes lies buried in his chosen resting place. Two years after his death, the line was continued as far as Victoria Falls, a western detour designed to entice tourists to the greatest waterfalls in the world. Kalomo was reached in 1905; Broken Hill, some 1,800 miles from Cape Town and a five-and-a-half days' journey by train, in 1906. Here the line stopped dead, as if uncertain whether to continue to the copper mines in Bwana Mkubwa and Kasanshi or to turn eastward toward Lake Tanganyika, but in 1909 commercial interests prevailed and the line was extended to Kambove in the rich Katanga district of the Belgian Congo. For the rest, the advent of airplanes and motor cars saw the abandonment of Rhodes's dream of a Cape-to-Cairo railway.

Rhodes had also wanted to build a telegraph line all along his track, and had even felt that it must come first. Originally he had wanted it to run along the eastern shore of Lake Tanganyika, where he also proposed to set up British posts, but this idea was fiercely resisted by the Germans, who had been in possession of that shore since 1891.[15] Rhodes next approached King Leopold II for wayleaves along the western shore against a lease of the Lado Enclave, a region west of the Upper Nile and northwest of Lake Albert. However when both the Wilhelmstrasse and the Quai D'Orsay reminded the King of the Belgians that, as co-signatories of the Congo Treaty, they would have to be consulted first, this plan, too, had to be dropped. During a visit to Berlin in February 1899, Rhodes was not afraid to broach the subject with the Kaiser in person. They seemed to hit it off extremely well, so much so that Wilhelm even presented his visitor with one of the innumerable plaster busts of himself with which this most modest of monarchs tried to enchant the world. So the telegraph line was built after all, albeit without British guard posts.

Rhodes's great railway plan must have been conceived as early as 1884, for when General Gordon asked him to join the Sudan expedition against the Mahdi, he replied that he had no time just then, though, no doubt, they would meet in Khartoum one day. Meanwhile the northern branch, too, was making progress in response to local demand. As early as 1856, a small stretch of railroad, from Alexandria to Benha, had been

opened up, and in the nineties the work was speeded up: Wadi Halfa
on the Sudanese border was reached in 1897, Berber in 1898, and Khartoum, a good 1,200 miles from the start of the line, in 1899. That the
line stopped there was due to political reasons, though not exclusively so.
True, Britain had agreed in 1884 to evacuate Egypt by January 1, 1888
at the latest, but promises are one thing and actions quite another. In
this particular case, it was the rebellion led by the Mahdi Mohammed
Ahmad in the Sudan that was to change the actions into the very opposite
of the promises. The Egyptian Army was unable to stand up to that
zealot, and so, at first, was the British Army; in 1885, Gordon Pasha was
killed in Khartoum, two days before Lord Wolseley was due to relieve
the beleaguered city. Although the Mahdi, also, died a few months later,
Abdullahi continued the fight with unabated ferocity. This was all the
more awkward for Britain because the Belgians, too, had begun to press
forward in this area, van Kerckhoven's contingent having reached the
Nile at Wadelai in 1892, and because the French, alerted in their turn,
had sent out Monteil in 1893 with orders to occupy the entire territory
between the Bomu and the Nile. Kitchener had to come to the rescue
once again. He only just succeeded, for although the Belgians had returned
to the Nile in 1897, this time at Rejaf, their progress was cut short by
an uprising in the Upper Congo. Kitchener was faced with a much greater
problem in 1898, when Marchand hoisted the French flag over Fashoda,
while the Ethiopians occupied the eastern bank of the Nile. In any case,
it was only after the Mahdi's successor was killed in 1899 that the British
Proconsul could put an end to the Mahdi empire for good. In January
of that year, the British and Egyptian governments regulated the political
status of the Sudan by giving a valid title to the exercise of sovereign
rights in the Sudan by the King of England in conjunction with the
Khedive, based on the right of conquest.[16] In practice, this agreement
meant the extension of British rule from Cairo to Uganda.

The Imperial British East Africa Company, founded by Sir William
MacKinnon in 1877 and chartered in 1888, had tried to entrench itself
both in the Sudan — that essential link of the Trans-Africa railway and
telegraph systems — and also in Kenya to the east. By 1892, however,
the Company was in such difficulties that, without government intervention, the entire area would have been lost to Britain, the more so as
other contenders were already queuing up: the Italians in Somaliland
and the Germans in German East-Africa, where they had seized control
in 1891. Rhodes, as ever on the alert, was afraid of an imminent German
incursion. Happening to be in London at the time, he called on Gladstone
and Harcourt, armed with a large map with the threatened area colored in

red. He offered to run Uganda for £25,000 a year "though he admits there is nothing to be made of it commercially."[17] The Christian Missionary Society helped him as best it could, for it, too, was in need of Government support, not so much against the "heathens" as against its Catholic rivals from France.[18] When Lord Rosebery spoke up for Rhodes's plan, a Government Mission, which included Rhodes's brother Frank, was sent to the spot with instructions to report on the outlook. As a result, Uganda was declared a temporary British protectorate on April 1, 1893, and a formal protectorate one year later. Harcourt, at first a firm opponent of the plan, himself introduced a bill to subsidize the Uganda railway: on December 20, 1901 the first train from the north pulled into Kisumu, on Lake Victoria, where the line joined the Kenya branch from Mombasa and Nairobi.[19] Though it was not yet the "great" railway, it was nevertheless something that must have seemed a pipe dream only ten years earlier. Even so, it would have been no more than a branch line had the Broken Hill-Kisumu gap ever been closed. Had that happened, Britain would have owned a railway line close to 6,000 miles long, spanning an entire and still largely unexplored continent, longer even than the Trans-Siberian Railway from St. Petersburg to Vladivostok, which covered a "mere" 5,500 miles. But, alas, by November 22, 1901, when Count Witte was able to wire the Czar his congratulations on the near-completion of the Siberian (all that was still missing was a short stretch round Lake Baikal which was added during the Russo-Japanese war) less than half of the Trans-African Railway had been completed.[20] Accident? Natural obstacles? Political problems? All three were involved: the accident (?) that the car and the airplane were developed during the very years that the fate of the central section hung in the balance; a host of natural obstacles that seemed almost insurmountable with the available technical means; and above all the intractable political problems we have noted — in the south, the north, and the center of the African continent.

All the same, it would seem that the most important cause lay elsewhere. In fact, British imperialism had begun to waver even while celebrating its latest victories, the accelerated tempo of these British conquests betraying the fear that time was running short. Every one of them had been, in a sense, a rearguard action. Rhodes said just that, when he appeared before the British South Africa Committee of the House of Commons to answer for his part in the Jameson raid. He proudly admitted responsibility for it, but added that he had acted in the certain knowledge that the Transvaal government was intent upon dragging another foreign power into South African affairs.[21] Although the whole truth did not come out — after all the Duke of Fife, son-in-law of the future king,[22] was one of the directors of the Chartered Company, and neither Chamberlain nor Lord Rosebery was completely vindicated during the Inquiry — Rhodes, no doubt, believed in the truth of his own defense, or, if not, he nevertheless realized that his excuse was plausible enough to impress his peers. Despite his flair for business, Rhodes was first and foremost a great romantic; yet he was not the only one to fear the rising star of Germany. Thus, in May 1900, Darcy contended that Germany posed a much graver threat to British interests in Africa than did his native France.[23] And Arvède Barin, in an article in the authoritative *Revue des Deux Mondes*, quoted Edwin Williams's view that the industrial supremacy of Great Britain, so long taken for granted, had turned into a myth, with the ominous "Made in Germany" looming ever more threateningly on the horizon. The threat was real enough: kitchenware and toys, beer mugs and coal scuttles, indeed whole operas complete with singers, orchestras, conductors, and all the rest, kept pouring out of Germany.[24] Still, in the same journal, J. Depelley also pointed out that the censorship of telegrams from South Africa was only possible because all the telegraph lines were in British lands, and he suggested it was high time to put an end to this unsavory state of affairs.[25]

Nor did the threat come from Germany or France alone. In 1899, the *North America Review* published a long article, full of statistics and documents dealing with the decline of British trade, and concluded that Britain might well have to take third place, behind the United States and Germany.[26] This was no empty boast. Thanks largely to Morgan's manipulations, the United States was already producing three times as much steel as the United Kingdom. At the same time, the Cunard Line could compete against Morgan's fleet of ships only with the help of a government subsidy.[27] The *Daily Mail* mentioned a further disturbing example of American trade expansion: U. S. firms not only lay in wait for commissions to reconstruct the bridges which the Boers had destroyed behind them during Buller's advance but, acting on fairly detailed information, were already preparing the necessary parts for immediate shipment.[28] In 1900, the British balance of trade was negative for the first time.

Seeley had sounded the alarm even earlier. His lectures, delivered in 1883, were published that same year under the title of *The Expansion of England;* the twelfth edition, which appeared in 1900, contained the gloomy prophecy that the United States and Russia might soon leave the "great" European powers behind.[29] Seeley did not think it likely, though he thought it possible, that a war might one day force Britain to pull her troops out of India. It was not difficult to guess what would

61

happen to the Raj then, or to the 300,000 Britons submerged in a sea of 300 million Indians.[30] Farther away still, but much too close for British comfort, lay Japan. As early as 1897, warnings about Japanese competition had been pouring into the Colonial Office from the Straits, from Hong Kong, and even from Australia (in Victoria, one-third of all the handkerchiefs sold were of Japanese make).[31]

Since her war with China, five years before the turn of the century, Japan had increased the capacity of her navy from 200,000 tons to 260,000 tons and, worse still, during the same period, she had more than quadrupled that of her merchant fleet (from 150,000 tons to 650,000 tons). Although most of the ships had been built in British yards, no one knew how long this state of affairs would continue — the shipyards of the Mitsubishi Engine and Iron Works already employed a labor force of 30,000.[32] In 1902, Britain nevertheless felt impelled to enter into a defensive alliance with Dai Nippon.

Seeley had been an imperialist, but no Primrose Leaguer, no admirer of Benson's "Land of Hope and Glory," no disciple of Rudyard Kipling, that bard of British imperialism who, in fact, was singing its swan song, however hard he strained his voice with the self-satisfied refrain of "*civis Britannicus sum.*" "Bombastic," Seeley called this entire "school," which he contrasted with the pessimistic, one that pleased him little more but that, on the whole, struck him as the better of the two.

A later student of imperialism was to view this situation in the light of what, in 1900, was still the future. For as long as the urge for action and the hunger for land could be satisfied on African soil, he wrote, Central and Western Europe could bury their arms at home — Britons, Frenchmen, and Germans could content themselves with sharing the spoils of the "Dark Continent." These treaties were so many devices for delaying a war none of them wanted, but that they brought about by the very ruses they dreamed up to prevent it.[33]

And because Rhodes was one of them, his Cape-to-Cairo railway, too, had to remain a dream. Fifty years later nothing more was left of his scheme for British world domination than the paper on which it was written. Asia was free and Africa about to throw off the last traces of foreign rule. History had clearly chosen Seeley's sober predictions, not Rhodes's castles in the air.

CHAPTER V

BERLIN TO BAGHDAD

Three far-reaching events occurred during the last week of the first month of the year 1900, events that may have seemed to be of little historical importance at the time but that nevertheless helped to pave the way for the catastrophe of 1914. The first was von Tirpitz's Navy Bill, which reached the German Reichstag on January 25. It came unexpectedly soon after the Navy Bill of April 1898, was much more sweeping than the latter, and in any case contradicted von Tirpitz's own statement of a year before. Yet when a Center Party deputy reminded the Reichstag of this glaring breach, his protests fell on deaf ears and not surprisingly so, for the extension of the German Navy was a very popular idea. The deputies were only too happy to forget von Tirpitz's glib "never has there been the slightest intention to draw up new naval plans; on the contrary everybody concerned is determined to . . . observe all the limitations set forth therein."[1] The new Bill provided for an extension of the existing fleet in less than twenty years, with one flagship, two squadrons of eight ships of the line each, two large and eight small cruisers for the Home Fleet, five large and as many small cruisers for service in foreign waters, and a reserve force of two ships of the line in addition to one large and two small cruisers. The naval estimates were to be increased by successive increments from 160 million marks in 1900 to 323 million marks in 1916, making a total of 2.5 billion marks.[2] Actually, the estimates were greatly exceeded and without much opposition — what had seemed impossible one year was taken for granted the next.

And with good reason. Germany's unprecedented economic expansion was such that the cost could be borne without undue strain. Thus Count Posadowsky, Minister of the Interior, could inform a delirious Reichstag that German imports had risen by 900 million marks between 1889 and 1899 and that more than half of this amount had been spent on raw materials for Germany's ever-growing industries. He might equally well have pointed to the spectacular population growth: from less than fifty million in 1890 to over fifty-six million in a mere ten years; by 1914 the figure would have leaped to sixty-eight million — an infallible sign of greater prosperity, the more so as most of these new millions earned higher wages and enjoyed better housing conditions than the lesser millions that had gone before[3] . Or Posadowsky might even have mentioned the increase in the number of millionaires — from 5,256 in 1895 to 9,341 in 1910, and the increase in their average fortunes, during the same period, from 6 to 6.5 million marks.[4] Had he sacrificed political caution, he might also have pointed out that these sober figures showed to what extent German bankers, industrialists, and merchants had already encroached upon hitherto closed preserves. The newly-formed limited companies, he might have added, were closely linked to the great industrial banks, older institutions whose coffers were now being filled at an unprecedented rate, not least with coins and banknotes which had previously been hidden in stockings and under mattresses. In particular, he might have mentioned the links between the Deutsche Palestina Bank (1898) and the Osteuropäische Telegraphengesellschaft (1899), or between the Orient Bank and the Deutsche Levant-Linie (1891);[5] and, more generally, the investment of German capital in foreign ventures. In 1914, this investment would stand at some twenty-five billion marks, of which some ten billion had gone into East European securities, so that it would have been true to say that the whole of Europe east of the Rhine had become part and parcel of the German industrial sphere.[6] Finally, he might have ended with the peroration: We Germans intend to conquer the world, and we shall conquer it because we will to do so.

The Germany of Wilhelm II was no longer the Germany of Bismarck. The Kaiser was determined to add great deeds to great words, and while his great deeds fulfilled the dream of Bismarck in part, they also betrayed it. The deeds fulfilled the dream because their mainspring was the will to power, and because they served to keep the middle classes powerless no less effectively than the Iron Chancellor had done; they betrayed it because, while Bismarck had eventually come to the view that Germany must expand in peaceful ways, Wilhelm and von Tirpitz with their Navy Bill were willy-nilly dragging Germany into war. Count Yorck, though still only a captain, had put it all quite bluntly when he said after Bismarck's dismissal that "with him the main obstacle to the proper course, namely war, has been surmounted."[7] While many others were unhappy about the change, they, too, acknowledged that it was an accomplished fact. Herbert, Bismarck's son, may have exaggerated his father's influence, but he did not misjudge the situation when, on the lapse of the Reinsurance Treaty with Russia, he wrote: "This spells the disintegration of the Reich. It will not survive for twenty years."[8] The French *Débats* took a no less gloomy view when it said of Bismarck's dismissal that "the role of chance and surprise in European politics has grown much greater than it was but yesterday."[9] The Russian *Grazhdanin* ("The Citizen") showed even more astonishing insight when it said of European affairs at the turn of the century: "Now, all that was bright has suddenly grown dark. It is no longer possible to predict the outcome of, or advise upon, any one course of action. Europe is in the grip of the inevitable but unexpected — in ideas no less than in events."[10]

One of the main reasons, if not the sole one, for this decline in international confidence was undoubtedly the new attitude adopted by the German Reich, of which Bismarck's departure was a symptom rather than a cause. Another was Germany's sudden economic expansion, and the ineptitude of her diplomats in allaying foreign fears about these developments. At home, by contrast, Germany could feel safe in the knowledge that she had developed an up-to-date and highly efficient productive machine, run by an intellectually mature, although politically immature, bourgeoisie. Theodor Mommsen blamed their immaturity on Bismarck. "The harm done by his rule," he wrote prophetically, "is infinitely greater than the benefit, for the gain in power it has brought can be lost during the first storm, while the subjection of the German personality and of the German spirit is a disaster that can never be repaired."[11] True enough, but by no means the whole truth. For though the German bourgeoisie lived in a country that enjoyed the trappings of parliamentary democracy, its foreign policy was dictated by an obstinate autocrat presiding over a government made up of feudal Junkers from behind the Elbe, men who, though energetic, lacked a will of their own — a fact that Bismarck could not possibly have hoped to change, even had he, a Junker himself, wanted to do so. Their noble blood may already have been diluted by marriages of convenience with the daughters of industrial barons, but such connections served to render them more powerful still. It was precisely the mixture of modern technology with the feudal spirit that proved so explosive in Germany — and later in Japan.

While the first of the three crucial events we mentioned at the beginning of this chapter, the German Navy Bill of 1900, is recorded in most general history books, the reader will look in vain for the other two even in some of the most detailed studies. None of them will tell him that even while the Reichstag was unwittingly deciding the fate of the world for the next few decades, a technical commission arrived in Basra. It had been sent out from Constantinople by the Société du Chemin de Fer Ottoman d'Anatolie (Anatolian Railway Company), a predominantly German enterprise despite its French name, that had been founded some ten years earlier (on March 23, 1889) and was then running a railway over a distance of some 600 miles from the port of Haidar Pasha (opposite Constantinople) to Konya. The commission had been instructed to look into the possibility of extending the line to Baghdad and the Persian Gulf. Its composition was instructive. Its leader was Stemrich, the German Consul-General at Constantinople, and its members included Dr. Mackensen, Director of the Prussian State Railways; von Kapp, Surveyor of the State Railways of Württemberg; Major Morgen, the German Military Attaché in Constantinople; and representatives of the Ottoman Ministry of Public Works.[12] The recommendations of the commission, though favorable, were not very strong, possibly because there had just been another uprising in the vilayet of Bassora (Basra).[13] The extension of the line, the commission reported, would be arduous, and the railway would, in any case, have to be run at a loss, unless Turkey guaranteed a subsidy.[14]

While the first event described in this chapter impinged upon the military and political spheres, and the second, to which we shall be referring at some length, on the economic and political, the third was initially of a purely political nature. But only initially so; later it was to demonstrate that the military, economic, and political spheres are so inextricably intertwined that none of them can be studied in isolation. Thus even the third event, which as we have said seemed at first to be of purely political relevance, was to have such marked economic and military repercussions that it is no exaggeration to say that, inconspicuous though it seemed at the time, it came to overshadow the other two events in general importance.

But it is time to call it by its proper name: it was the publication, by the Young Turks, of their Cairo manifesto, during the same month that the new Navy Bill was presented to the Reichstag and that a German study commission completed its report on the economic and strategic possibilities of the Baghdad railway. The name "Young Turks" was a misnomer, for it was not until eight-and-a-half years later, by which time many of its members were mature men, that their movement helped to revolutionize Turkey. However, all historical events arise out of their past, and the prehistory of this particular event was one with which most newspaper readers were familiar at the turn of the century. Thus in 1899, the *Hollandsche Revue* devoted one of its widely-read biographical sketches to a profile of Ahmed Riza Bey, leader of the Young Turks. He was the son of a Turkish dignitary, and having completed his studies in France, where he attended the Institut Agronomique, he was appointed Director of Public Education and then Government Censor in Asia Minor, in which capacity he contributed articles himself to the very press whose liberality he was supposed to temper. Reprimanded by the Sultan, he made bold to proffer his honest opinion: that it was high time to restore the 1876 constitution. He did not wait for the Sultan's predictable reaction but left for Paris and other European cities, where he continued his campaign. Among other activities, he attended the 1899 Peace Conference in The Hague to protest the presence of the official Turkish legation. He was not a welcome foreigner in the Netherlands nor, for that matter, in Brussels or Paris, for his ruler's arm had a long reach. Van Kol spoke up for him in vain, and even the *Handelsblad* suggested that official Dutch tolerance of the Turkish "butcher" might well be a way of rewarding the Sultan for his efforts to suppress the Pan Islamic movement in the East Indies.[15] This was a possible but unnecessary explanation: at the time, all those in power were still united enough and already sufficiently under threat to render one another what little services they could, provided only that such services did not clash with their own foreign ambitions. Hence Riza Bey and his fellow-exiles had to live the most precarious of lives, first in Paris, until the henchmen of the Turkish ambassador made things too hot for them, and then in Geneva and London, the safest but also the most expensive refuge of all.[16] Here Ahmed Riza edited *Meşverèt* ("Deliberations"), the organ of the Young Turk movement, which his fellow-conspirators smuggled into the Ottoman empire with all the attendant dangers. One of the most avid readers of the paper was Abdullah Cevdet, a Kurdish doctor from Diyarbakir who had studied Büchner, Haeckel, Spencer, and le Bon and who was one of the founders of the group that later became the Committee of Union and Progress and inspired Gökalp to compose his revolutionary songs.[17] So unchallenged was Riza's authority that in 1908 he became the first president of the resurrected Ottoman parliament.[18] In 1899, the able Constantinople correspondent of the *Nieuwe Rotterdamse Courant* drew his readers' attention to the Young Turk movement by associating it with the sensational escape of Mahmud Pasha, the Sultan's brother-in-law. The same journalist also pointed out that the greatest threat to the Sultan no longer came from Paris or any other European capital but from Cairo, where the British had turned a blind eye on *Cür'at* ("Audacity"), the local organ of the Young Turks; having by then gained a firm foothold in Egypt, Britain had lost all interest in Turkey.

It was *Cür'at* which first published the manifesto we have mentioned. Though written in measured tones, it nevertheless presented an ultimatum to the Sultan-Caliph. Of its seven demands, the fifth was the most remarkable: the withdrawal of all privileges from such bodies and institutions that, instead of doing real service to the country, sucked it dry for

67

the benefit of greedy foreign capitalists. This passage was obviously aimed at the Dette Publique Ottomane and the Banque Ottomane, both under Anglo-French control, but no less so at the right of foreigners to try their own subjects, at the foreign-owned post offices and tobacco monopoly, at foreign shipyards and docks, and finally, at the proposed Baghdad railway concession, which by then had been under negotiation for several years.[19] The Young Turks were not, of course, opposed to the railway as such, but to the enriching of the Sultan by the 200,000 Turkish pounds the concessionaries were expected to produce as an interim payment, and by the 300,000 Turkish pounds the Damascus Railway Company had promised for a similar privilege. The Young Turks, whether in Paris or in Cairo, whether plotting their revolt in secret or working openly in Constantinople, were convinced that, things being what they were, all these schemes merely served to bolster up the Sultan's waning authority and were thus an impediment to genuine reform and modernization. Abdul Hamid II, thirty-fourth ruler of the House of Osman and twenty-eighth ruler of Turkey since the capture of Constantinople, was, in fact, the best advertisement for the revolution. Buxton saw him in that light and aptly entitled the first chapter of his book "The Sultan as Revolutionist."[20] After a liberal beginning with a parliamentary constitution in 1876, he had grown steadily more despotic. According to Buxton, 10,000 persons were sentenced to death during his reign for purely political offenses; many more perished "unofficially." The number of victims was exceeded only by the number of spies in the Sultan's employ, which Buxton estimated at 40,000.[21] This arch-schemer[22] was also extremely shrewd. No one knew better than Abdul Hamid how to exploit Islamic sentiments against the Christian powers, or how to play these powers off against one another by favoring the weakest party until it became the strongest. As a result, he was able to preserve a precarious balance and stay in office where lesser men would have been overthrown long since. Furthermore, if a capable ruler is one who can press the most powerful foreigners no less than the poorest of his own subjects into his service, then Abdul Hamid was a capable ruler indeed; Kurdish or Albanian bandits served his purposes as effectively as English and French bankers, or German engineers and generals. For all that, his skillful balancing act, and even the Kaiser's friendship, failed to save him in the end. The upkeep of Yildiz Kiosk, his sumptuous country retreat, of a host of palaces in which his favorites luxuriated, and of the countless dungeons in which his victims languished, swallowed up sums of money that could not be squeezed out of the Turkish peasants indefinitely or out of the Sultan's oppressed Christian subjects; and what few Greek, Armenian, and Jewish merchants might have helped were careful to keep the tax officials at arm's length.

This goes a long way toward explaining the violent language of his opponents: "The Young Turks are convinced that they will achieve nothing by Platonic means. They are therefore firmly resolved to pass from idealism, from propaganda by the pen and the word, to the realism of the deed."[23] To that end they established a Supreme Council, compiled lists of "condemned persons," and drew lots for the executioner's job — in short, they took to individual terrorism.

There was also a quite specific reason for stepping up the campaign at this particular time. That reason was the Boxer rebellion, which made a deep impression on a people with an instinctive sympathy for the oppressed Chinese masses. Needless to say, the ruling clique, too, tried to exploit this sentiment. Thus the Turkish press gave full coverage to the events in the besieged diplomatic quarter, but was careful to omit any critical remarks about the "Old Buddha." On July 12, 1900, the two leading dailies, *Ma'lûmât* and *Servèt*, both poured scorn on the Great Powers, who, even while preparing to appear as champions of peace in The Hague, had started bloody wars in South Africa and in China, and were about to add a third one in Morocco. "At the very moment," the papers concluded, "that the West is opening the Universal Exposition in Paris, meant to celebrate the reign of Labor and Reason, the Far East is creaking under the weight of an attack that is as treacherous as it is untimely."[24]

Russia retaliated at once by reminding the Turks that St. Petersburg was closer to Constantinople than it was to Peking. The French and the Germans reacted more politely but no less effectively: they let it be known that unless both newspapers recanted forthwith, Turkey's credit could suffer. In particular, advances against future state revenues might easily become things of the past. No wonder that the Turkish press not only apologized but bent over backward to placate the West. They now reported with satisfaction that the Sublime Porte was thinking of sending Turkish troops to the aid of the other Powers, thus putting an even speedier end to the Chinese horrors. Although the troops were never sent, the Sultan's blatant *volte-face* drove it home to thinking members of the Turkish nation that they would not be able to throw off the foreign yoke and achieve true freedom while Abdul Hamid, now clearly unmasked as a mere puppet of these foreigners, remained their Sultan.

At the time, it was German militarists, above all, who had bound the Sultan in chains of iron, and German capitalists who had bound him in chains of gold. In 1883, von der Goltz had been appointed military

69

instructor to the Turkish Army, though the post had originally been reserved for a Frenchman. The change in plan was widely blamed on a reactionary French officer in the Turkish service who did what he could to discredit the Third Republic.[25] German businessmen made full use of this unexpected opportunity. Thus while von der Goltz was quite content to leave the Turkish Army equipped with French Martini-Henry rifles, he received orders in 1887 from Berlin to replace them with German Mausers. It may have been pure chance that Wilhelm von Pressel, an engineer in the Turkish service for several years, was a German citizen, but it was no chance at all that in 1887 he tried to interest the Deutsche Bank, through Georg Siemens, the congenial nephew of the great Werner, in the railway plans mentioned at the beginning of this chapter. Siemens demurred: the project was not in his line of business and, moreover, seemed politically undesirable. In other words, Bismarck had told him not to rush into a venture that might cause unnecessary friction with Britain and Russia. When a certain Herr Coch from Vienna approached Siemens a year later, he received much the same answer: a banker could not possibly go further than the public, whose funds he administered, would allow him to go.[26] A fresh approach was made in May, this time by Dr. Alfred Kaulla of the Württembergische Vereinsbank. He wrote to Siemens from Constantinople, where he was negotiating the delivery of guns and munitions from the Mauser factory in Oberndorf, with which his bank was associated, and he too received a negative reply.Their capital had grown so large, he was told by Siemens, that they must invest the bulk of it in interest-bearing securities — an extra 1% from these would earn them more money than even the most promising risky enterprise.[27] This was Siemens in his pre-imperialistic phase. Still, the many appeals to him had not gone unheeded: the more closely he examined the plan that was being pressed upon him so insistently, the more tempted he felt to shoulder this "permanent cultural task," one that promised to redound not only to the advantage and glory of the Deutsche Bank but also to that of Germany at large. On August 9, Siemens informed Kaulla that the scheme was, after all, worth looking into and that he was now giving it his full attention.[28] On August 14, at 7:45 P.M., the first direct train from Budapest drew punctually into Stamboul station carrying passengers from various European capitals. This was the famous Orient Express.[29] That same day, a letter from the Deutsche Bank reached the German Ministry of Foreign Affairs. It stated that the Ottoman Government proposed to engage in large-scale railway construction in Asia Minor, as witness the appended copy of a letter from Dr. Kaulla, suggesting, inter alia, that the Turkish Government would like to place the work in

German hands. Did the German Government have any objections and could the German Embassy in Constantinople perhaps be instructed to support Herr Kaulla's endeavors in every possible way? The reply arrived on September 2. There were no objections whatsoever, and the German Embassy had already received the necessary instructions. But would the petitioner kindly remember that the German Government was not prepared to indemnify anyone who incurred losses abroad in pursuit of his business interests? The letter was signed personally by Bismarck.[30] It may have been imperialism by half measures, but it nevertheless pointed the way to the future.

The ground having been prepared with German thoroughness in the very year Wilhelm II came to the throne, the great new German adventure was begun on October 4, 1888, with the acquisition of the first concession: the purchase of the Haidar Pasha-Ismit line,[31] and permission to extend it as far as Angora (Ankara). On March 23, 1889, the Anatolian Railway Company was founded. That same year, Persia opened the Karun River to international navigation, and the Lynch Brothers, with the support of the British Government, began to run steamers from the Persian Gulf to Basra. In 1889, the Deutsche Levant-Linie was established; the new Kaiser paid his first state visit to the Near East; a Russian syndicate tried to obtain a Persian concession to build a railway from Rasht via Teheran to the Persian Gulf; Baron Julius de Reuter founded the Imperial Bank of Persia; and Cotord presented his plans for the construction of a French railway line from Samsun to Basra.[32] All the pieces needed for the game that would last for twenty-five years and turn out much bloodier than anyone had intended were now in play. Ten years later, in 1898, by which time the Anatolian Railway Company had brought Asia Minor a measure of prosperity — not least by setting up model farms all along the line[33] — and all Germany was debating whether this area was suited to colonization by the Deutsche Kolonialgesellschaft,[34] the first German Navy Law was passed, and the Kaiser paid his second visit to the Near East, this time travelling as far as Palestine. He took the occasion to deliver a speech in Damascus, proclaiming himself the champion of the 300 million Mohammedans and, incidentally, of all German Catholic institutions in the Turkish Empire, previously under French protection.[35]

Imperialism had been forced from a seedling into a full-blown plant. In the hothouse atmosphere the Anatolian Railway Company had gone from strength to strength; and as it expanded, so it also posed an ever-greater threat to world peace. In 1893, plans were ready to extend the line to Konya in the south, and three years later the new terminal wel-

71

comed its first train. By then the Sultan, having come to appreciate the strategic importance of the railway during the suppression of the Armenian uprising in 1897 and also during the war against Greece, was clamoring for its extension to Baghdad, Basra, and the Persian Gulf. While Siemens had begun to realize to his dismay that the Sultan's thirst for blood made the entire enterprise far less profitable and infinitely more risky than it ought to have been, Abdul Hamid, for his part, had become convinced that no one could beat the Germans at the great railway game: Krupp's rails had proved their worth during the transport of troops to the Greco-Turkish theater of war,[36] while those supplied by the French had turned out to be a grave disappointment. Moreover, was any other country more trustworthy than Germany, whose monarch Abdul Hamid could call his close friend, and who had even suggested a blockade of the Greek ports, a proposal that had only been thwarted by the intervention of English meddlers?

So the Sultan was anxious for action. Early in 1898, he discussed the construction of the Baghdad line with the new German ambassador, Freiherr Marschall von Bieberstein. That energetic imperialist was determined to move from the supporting role he had been playing in Constantinople into the lead, and accordingly urged the German Government to put its full weight behind Siemens. In this he was ably assisted by Major Morgen, the military attaché referred to earlier.[37] Siemens allowed himself to be talked around once again but with an apparently small yet characteristic proviso: while he had previously contented himself with the moral support of the German Government he now demanded active assistance. He was quite happy to negotiate a concession for the Baghdad railway, but the "Seehandlung," i.e., the Prussian State Bank, would have to be associated with the issue of the bonds.[38] The objections of the Prussian Minister of Finance, justified though they were — for Siemens was expecting the German state to do no less than shoulder responsibility for an enterprise with unpredictable risks — were brushed aside on political grounds.[39] Imperialism had its own ethos: "allons-y," as an anti-Dreyfusard summed it up at the time, or "immer feste drauf," as his German counterpart put it. It all came down the same — namely, expansion, power, riches, and supremacy.

And so the commission to which we referred at the beginning of this chapter was sent out. However, even before it was ready to publish its conclusions — time plays a crucial part in the imperialist race for world domination — higher powers had already moved in, and had even taken a decisive step. On December 23, 1899, following an irade by the Sultan, Siemens had signed a preliminary contract, on behalf of the

Deutsche Bank, with Zikni Pasha, the Turkish Minister of Trade, to build a railway from Konya to Baghdad and on to Basra — a double-edged Christmas present to the German people, most of whom welcomed it with open arms. Thus when the Navy Bill came up for discussion one month later, even Bebel, however perturbed by the general trend, said not a word about the dangers of the proposed construction of the new line.[40] The final contract was signed on January 21, 1902. It empowered the Anatolian Railway to set up a special company to exploit the concession; and that company was duly founded on March 5, 1903.[41] It was instructed to extend the line (gauge: 1.44 m.) to the Persian Gulf; the Turkish Government, for its part, guaranteed a minimum profit. The notorious Baghdad Railway Company had been born, with the German group holding 40%, the German-controlled Anatolian Railway 10%, the French Banque Ottomane 30%, and four other countries — Austria, Switzerland, Italy, and Turkey — the remaining 20% of the shares. President of the Board of Control was Dr. A. von Gwinner, the leading spirit in the Deutsche Bank after Siemens's death in 1901.[42]

All the gentlemen involved in this great plan were powerful gentlemen, indeed; for the Siemenses of the Deutsche Bank were not only allied to the other great Siemenses, but also to Ballin, Rathenau, Thyssen, and Rouvier, a private banker who later became the French Minister of Finance and Prime Minister.[43] No one took a greater interest in the plan than the Kaiser himself. A glance at the international situation explains why. The German colonies had proved a great disappointment, and yet the clamor of the German Colonial Association, the Navy Union, and, above all, of Lagarde's All-Deutscher Verband continued unabated. Most of this clamor was laughable, but the laughter dies on one's lips when one considers that tens, indeed hundreds of thousands of Germans inhaled this type of laughing gas in an effort to drown their growing fears. At sea, the British Navy was an effective barrier to German expansion and this without having to burn one extra ounce of coal; in the west the Netherlands, Belgium, and France continued to bar the way; in the east stood the Russian bear. All that was left, therefore, was the southeast, where Austria-Hungary, Germany's ally, was firmly entrenched, and where Turkey, moreover, had let it be known that she preferred the Germans, whose objectives were still purely economic, to the British, the French, and the Russians, whose aspirations were more blatantly political, as the Turks had learned to their cost and sorrow. As the southeast was her only outlet, Germany could not afford to ignore it.

In the autumn of 1899, Britian was licking her wounds in South Africa, while Russia, who since 1891 had had her hands full with the

73

Trans-Siberian Railway, was obviously much too involved in the Far East to be diverted to Anatolia, particularly as she had reached agreement with Austria-Hungary in 1897. Although the Dual Monarchy was no longer as formidable as it had been in its heyday, Germany felt that she herself had nothing to lose: Austria-Hungary would either founder on the sharp rocks of minority nationalism, in which case the Hohenzollerns would take over the Hapsburg heritage, or else the Dual Monarchy would hold up and eventually absorb Bosnia, Herzegovina, and Serbia, in which case an essentially German power would border on Turkey. Also, France would be unable to halt the German drive, for much as Britain was afraid to alienate Germany for fear of Russia, so France was afraid of alienating her for fear of Britain. Fashoda was not yet forgotten, and the French themselves were still divided by the Dreyfus affair.

So German imperialism grasped its unique chance, and the only reason it did not exploit it to the full was that it came up against almost insurmountable natural obstacles — in 1909, by which time the entire line should have been completed, the track had not yet progressed beyond Bulguluk, in deepest Anatolia.[44] The great German dream — the exploitation of the rich coalfields of Ereğli and Palu in Kurdistan; the tenfold increase of the cotton harvest in Adana and Ain Tab; endless streams of oil from Arbela and Kirkuk (Mosul); and, above all, the transformation of Mesopotamia from the bleak desert it had become during past centuries into a rich land of milk and honey — had suddenly evaporated. For though the Anatolian Railway and its offshoots would soon carry 40,000 tons of textiles, 100,000 tons of rock salt, and 250,000 tons of grain every month — a cargo worth $300,000[45] — the great German dream first voiced by Friedrich List in the middle of the nineteenth century, and by the orientalist, A. Sprenger, in 1886,[46] had foundered as inexorably as the great British dream of a Cape-to-Cairo railway. It remained a dangerous dream nevertheless. Nazim Bey was quite right to argue that Germany's geographical position made her lend a ready ear to plans of conquest;[47] and the new Turkish Parliament re-echoed his views on many occasions.

Yet no other project was pursued more ardently than the Baghdad Railway. Every inch of the way had to be fought for; and though it was not to the clash of arms, it was open warfare all the same. The weapons were economics, diplomacy, and cultural exchanges; the ammunition was finished goods, raw materials, notes, memoranda, telegrams, and newspaper articles; the contestants were agents, consuls, missionaries, manufacturers, and bankers; the trenches were embassies, consulates, mission-posts, and schools;[48] and the ultimate stakes power and riches.

The other knights errant of imperialism may have been unable to resist Germany in her supreme moment, but they missed no opportunity to undermine the position of their rival in a market that had only just eluded them. Also, much as Siemens had placated the landed gentry at home, to whom a Mesopotamian granary was no inducement at all,[49] with the assurance that he was not out to colonize the Middle East, so he now tried to placate foreign opinion by proposing that the Baghdad Railway be given an international board with a German director. But though he had the ear of Balfour and though he had shrewdly engaged Chamberlain's daughter as a traveling companion for his own, the British Opposition, ably supported by the *Times*, would hear nothing of it, and, in the end, had its way.[50] There must be no new competitor in Asia — Russia was quite enough; no competitor for the Suez Canal; no one to frustrate such plans for the future as Lord Curzon's cherished hope for a railway from Cairo to Calcutta. Moreover, Britain also had interests in Kuwait, which the German technical commission had suggested as a possible railway terminus. The Sheik may have called the Sultan of Turkey his "master," but soon after he was reputed to have done so, Sir Edward Law informed Siemens by letter that the relationship between the Sheik and Britain was extremely close and that anyone ignoring this fact would be sorely disappointed.[51] Even personal discussions between Siemens and Sanderson, the Under-secretary of State, held at the beginning of 1901, proved of no avail.[52] Germany could go so far and no further.

A Russian consortium, too, showed interest in Siemens's plan, but St. Petersburg turned it down. A Baghdad railway could serve only to strengthen Turkey. When the work could no longer be stopped, Russia was able to insist that the track run through Konya and not through Angora and, after Mosul, along the right, not the left bank of the Tigris. But first, Russia had given Turkey a model lesson in imperialist method. Do you not think, a polite note had asked the Turks, that it is high time to repay the fifty-seven million francs you have owed us ever since the Congress of Berlin? You are short of money? Fair enough, but then please give us a railway concession near the Black Sea equal in area to that granted to the Baghdad Railway. And what could Abdul Hamid do other than to agree? Actually, the concession was allowed to lapse, but German and other foreign railway companies were kept away from the Russian borders.[53] When fresh rumors of Russian participation made the rounds in 1901 — the subject must certainly have been broached during the meeting of Wilhelm and "Cousin Nicky" in September of that year — they turned out to be nothing but a wishful dream of the Quai

75

d'Orsay, which had hopes of consolidating the French position with Russian help.[54]

France herself, as her participation in the Baghdad Railway showed very clearly, was by no means hostile to the German scheme; she lacked the financial resources to launch independent programs on so large a scale, and German influence in Turkey still struck her as being greatly preferable to British. A special circumstance served to cast aside what reservations she may still have had: the Banque Ottomane had run into financial difficulties, partly as a result of speculation in South African mining shares, and the Deutsche Bank was ready to come to the aid of its distressed colleague, all the more so if, in exchange, the Banque agreed to participate in the Turkish plans.[55] In all truth, however, French support was never more than half-hearted.[56] Paris was anxious not to alienate Russia and, after 1904, not to offend Britain. Even earlier, in 1903, Delcassé had advised the Cabinet against participation in the railway project and had even been able to persuade the French Government to prohibit dealings in the company's shares on the Bourse. Russian pressure? The Germans, for one, thought that it was.[57]

France and Britain had another lever in the Dette Ottomane Publique, a body founded in 1882 and composed almost entirely of representatives of foreign bondholders. Without agreement from these gentlemen, Turkey could not increase her customs duties, and without increased customs duties, she could not produce the railway subsidies she had promised. In 1907, when Germany finally managed to have the customs duties raised from 8% to 11%, Britain stipulated that all the extra revenue must be used exclusively for reforms in Macedonia.[58] By that time, Britain was also forced to consider the interests of her latest ally, Russia, with whom she had just divided Persia.

Barely had this obstacle been surmounted when new clouds gathered over the pet project of the German imperialists. On June 6, 1908, the Young Turks struck at last, and the Sultan was forced to restore the constitution. His absolute rule was finished for good. Had friendship with Germany in general and the Baghdad Railway in particular been his will and work? Well then, away with them. Long live British and French democracy! Exactly four months later, before these clouds had been blown away, came the annexation of Bosnia and Herzegovina by Austria-Hungary, and with it a fresh wave of anti-German sentiment. This, too, the railway managed to survive, and in 1909, when the Sultan made his attempt to restore his absolute rule, thus helping the military — and despite everything this meant the pro-German — wing of the Young Turks to gain the upper hand, the threat to German imperialism seemed to have receded again, as the Kaiser himself had guessed it would.[59] However, the outbreak of the Italo-Turkish war once again rendered the German position in Turkey precarious. But by then the railway had been built through Ulukişla and on to Karapınar, northwest of Adana,[60] and the Germans were more firmly entrenched than ever before, even though von Bieberstein had to be replaced by von Wangenheim in 1912. Everything seemed to be going well once again, for in February 1914 a Franco-German agreement on the Baghdad Railway was signed, followed in June, after Anglo-Turkish discussions[61] and three years of negotiations,[62] by an Anglo-German agreement, which reflected the earnest desire of all parties to solve the many outstanding colonial problems in peaceful ways. Then, a shot fired by a fanatic in Sarajevo destroyed everything Germany had built up so meticulously over the years. The British could easily have saved themselves all the effort they had made to stir up trouble in Southern Mesopotamia.[63]

Von Bülow was struck by this strange twist of fate. In his memoirs he tells us, in the somewhat slipshod and histrionic manner so characteristic of the man, that Lichnowsky, the German ambassador to the Court of St. James, received the sumptuous gilt-edged ratification instrument of the Anglo-German treaty on the same day as he received the British declaration of war.[64] In reality, matters were somewhat less dramatic,[65] for an interval of two days separated the two events. Still, it cannot be denied that at the very moment that the dream of German imperialism seemed finally to have come true after twenty-five years of sweat and toil, and that the first train was ready to steam into Kuwait after the removal of the last British obstacle, the German dream was ended in the smoke of the great catastrophe now called the First World War. European imperialism, after pushing outward and thus provoking a military clash, was thrown back by the very war it had caused. Inasmuch as the Baghdad Railway was an integral part of that outward thrust, it helped to turn what might have been a blessing for Asia into a curse for Europe. By the time the subject of the Baghdad Railway could again be brought up for discussion, Asia had become sophisticated enough not to accept its completion as a "gift" from Europe.

*The Berlin–Baghdad railway was still a
great project, regardless of who built it and why*

CHAPTER VI

ORIFLAMME AND TRICOLORE

On January 4, 1900, the French Senate in its capacity of Supreme Court of Justice sentenced Paul Déroulède and André Buffet to ten years' banishment and two other royalists, Jules Guérin and de Lur-Saluzes, to ten years' imprisonment, for conspiracy against the State. Déroulède, for one, had certainly been guilty, and not of that crime alone. During the funeral on February 23, 1899, of Félix Faure, the sixth President of the Republic, this ex-poet, his pockets full of proclamations and bank notes, had gone to the Place de la Nation with his lieutenant Marcel Habert, Barrès, and other associates to lie in wait for the black-plumed helmet of General Pellieux, a fellow-conspirator who was due to pass through the square at the head of a military escort returning from the funeral. In the event, the escort was led by General Roget, who was in no way privy to the plot — a fact that did not, however, deter the hot-headed conspirators from seizing the reins of his horse and shouting: "To the Elysée, General! Follow us, General!".[1] Déroulède and Habert were arrested and taken to the Conciergerie, from whence Déroulède sent an accusatory letter to Prime Minister Dupuy two months later: if there had been irregularities in the Dreyfus affair, as Dupuy had claimed there had been, then Dupuy, Premier then as now, must bear the responsibility.[2] *Le Temps* published the letter in full. Déroulède's acquittal by a jury within six weeks — a verdict which would have been astonishing had anything about French justice at the time still astonished anyone — fully restored his spirits, if indeed they had been cast down. For in July, when preparations for Dreyfus's retrial were well under way, Déroulède made preparations to launch a fresh coup d'état, this time in Rennes. It was to start just as soon as General Mercier had finished addressing the court.[3] The Duke of Orleans, Pretender to the French throne, had by then left Brussels for Paris, with a promise to destroy "that gang of Jews, cosmopolitans and Freemasons." Another of Déroulède's supporters, Guérin, leader of the Anti-Semitic League, barricaded himself in "Fort Chabrol," the headquarters of the League, with 2,000 bottles of mineral water, a cellarful of provisions, an ambulance, a printing works — after all, writers must ply their trade — and forty men.[4] Déroulède was arrested, a few hours before the intended coup, together with thirty-five assorted members of the League of Patriots, the Anti-Semitic League, and the League of Young Royalists. Although his second trial was even more farcical than his first, this time he received the sentence mentioned at the beginning of the chapter. It looked as if the Republic had at long last scored a victory over its enemies.

It was also in 1900 that *L'Aiglon* had its premiere in Paris. It was a sensational occasion, even for Paris. Outwardly, the play owed its success to Edmond Rostand's scintillating historical verses, to Sarah Bernhardt in the title role, and to Lucien Guitry, the father of Sacha. But while the play was ostensibly a mere cascade of brilliant phrases, it was, in fact, highly political in content: it dealt with the triumph of Bonapartism, and hence with the humiliation of the Revolution and the Republic. Prince Victor, of the House of Jerome, the acknowledged head of the family and now resident in Brussels, was said to have asked a friend to wire him the number of curtain calls after each act; after the last one the telegraph tapped out twenty. Morand may have been exaggerating, but he was not far from the truth, when he wrote that had Rostand wanted to, he could easily have marched on the Elysée that night.[5]

These two typical examples of French life at the turn of the century, chosen at random from a host of others, may serve to illustrate how deeply France was divided at the time: there was the France of the Right and the France of the Left; the France of the Lily or the Eagle and the France of the *Tricolore;* the France of the *ancien régime* or the Empire and the France of the Great Revolution; the France of the Monarchists and the France of the Republicans. The two were set apart politically as well as spiritually: while one stood for order imposed from above, for divine authority and divine revelation, the other stood for order from within, for human authority and for reason. Moreover — the same difference put into other words — there was also a vague social division between the aristocrats, the military establishment, the clergy, the upper classes, and the embittered middle classes on the one hand, and the intelligentsia, the radical bourgeoisie, the peasants, and the workers on the other. A vague division, we have said, for the situation was so confused as to embrace every conceivable gradation, but not so elastic as to change the basic features of either camp, let alone bridge the gap between them.

In 1900, that rift was nothing new, for the two camps had first appeared in the eighteenth century, although with different names and champions: the Enlightenment versus Absolutism — the second camp, however bourgeois its champions may have become, convinced of the rightness of the established order; and the first, determined to carry the work of the Renaissance to its full term. It was the efforts of the first that had culminated in a revolution of which, when all is said and done, even Napoleon was a servant, though his latter-day disciples may have thought otherwise. Napoleon's fall gave the other, progressive, France, a new chance — one it failed to exploit to the full. The Second Republic wanted to revive the First. Following it, Napoleon III restored the Empire which, seen in retrospect, amounted to no more than an enforced truce; in any case, when this regime, too, eventually collapsed, the Third Republic took over in 1871 but could do no more than bring the struggle to a temporary halt.

When Marshal MacMahon, a duke and a staunch monarchist, was elected President of France upon Thiers's resignation in 1873, and the royalist-clerical majority of the National Assembly gave him a clear mandate to restore the monarchy, he failed only, so it was said, because the Comte de Chambord — formerly the *enfant du miracle* but now the *enfant terrible* of his party — insisted that only the Lily of the Bourbons was fit to flutter over France. While this very demand proved the existence of the one France, its rejection, even by the royalists, demonstrated the strength of the other. In 1880, after MacMahon's resignation, Parliament acknowledged this fact in three ways: by declaring July 14, the day on which the Bastille was stormed in 1789, a national holiday; by extending a pardon to all Communards; and by expelling the Jesuits from France.

All this happened under the presidency of Grévy, who was still in office in 1886 when the Boulanger crisis burst upon the country to keep it teetering on the brink of civil war for three long years. The popular but politically inept General Boulanger had gained a striking victory for his revanchist party at the polls; and on January 27, 1889, one hundred years after the Revolution seemed to have settled the struggle between the monarchy and the republic once and for all, Déroulède made an attempt to seize power on the General's behalf. But while the vain politician-poetaster showed the kind of courage that is not normally associated with his profession, the vain general lacked the heroism expected of his. He explained that Madame de Bonnemain, his mistress, would be sorely disappointed if anything should happen to him. This, at least, is how many contemporary observers tried to explain the failure of the coup d'état. The historian, by contrast, must conclude that the time for the restoration of the monarchy was long past, that other classes than the feudal had long since taken the social stage.

Carnot, President of France from 1887 to 1894, was not only forced to clear up the Boulanger affair but, immediately afterward, had to deal with the Panama scandal, which was to make the headlines for five years and again cause the Republic to tremble to its very foundations. The anti-republicans led by the Comte de Paris and the Marquis de Rochefort, in turn, had been attacking the Left for failing to give wholehearted support to the "great work" of the Panama Company, when the bubble suddenly burst: the year that Boulanger pulled out, de Lesseps also withdrew — the first for lack of courage and the second for lack of money. The financial losses were appalling, but financial scandals were not so unusual during this stormy period of capitalist expansion, and the whole matter could easily have been hushed up had not the monarchists and anti-Semites faced about in an attempt to squeeze political capital out of the fiasco. Early in 1893, the two de Lesseps, father and son, together with Alexandre Gustave Eiffel, whose proud tower had dominated the Paris skyline for the past four years, were found guilty of fraud. The Jewish banker, Baron Reinach, committed suicide; and two other financiers, Herz and Arton, had to flee the country. But they were not the only ones to be blamed: 500 politicians were said to have been bribed by the Panama Company, not least to support the fight against Boulanger. The government, moreover, was accused not only of having granted these bunglers all sorts of favors but also of quashing all attempts to investigate their nefarious activities. The radicals involved felt the whiplash during the August elections: Freycinet, Floquet, Rouvier, and Clemenceau all lost their seats.

The year of the Panama scandal also happened to be the year in which the cards were being dealt for the first hand of an even greater and more devilish game of chance. On January 1, 1893, Alfred Dreyfus, a Jewish Captain in the 21st Artillery Regiment, was assigned to the General Staff; on the last day of that year the Counter-Espionage Bureau attached to the French Ministry of War, under Colonel Sandherr, intercepted a telegram from Berlin to Herr von Schwartzkippen, the German military attaché in Paris — one of a series of documents used to establish Dreyfus's "guilt."[6]

Sadi Carnot himself was no longer there to play this hand. He had been stabbed to death by the Italian anarchist, Santo Caserio, during a presidential tour of an exhibition in Lyons. It had all happened on June 24, 1894, and it was not until the end of September that the Counter-Intelligence branch came into possession of a memorandum in which Colonel Fabre believed he could recognize Dreyfus's handwriting.[7] This was the notorious *bordereau*, the first round to be fired in the Dreyfus affair.

At the time, vigilant nationalism and growing international tension

81

ensured that tales of espionage made the headlines at least as often as the ever-recurring financial scandals. No doubt this case, too, would eventually have been forgotten, much like the defection of Boutonné, a civil servant in the Ministry of War who had been quietly carted off to serve a five-year prison sentence in 1890, or that of another official two years later.[8] But Dreyfus, the reader may object, was an innocent man, so that there was good reason to remember the wrong that had been done to him.

If only that had been the true explanation! His innocence undoubtedly played some part, but had it been the chief reason, how can one explain the many innocent people who have been convicted without anyone lifting a finger? No, there were very special reasons why the Dreyfus affair produced such a stir.

The first of these was the fact that the culprit was not just anybody, but a French officer with access to the Ministry of War. Once that news had leaked out, the entire officer corps was determined to vindicate its honor at all costs and with it the honor of France. The second reason was that the suspect was a Jew, something that had made him the chief suspect in the first place. Anti-Semitism was more virulent and pernicious at the turn of the century than it had ever been, and this for reasons we shall be examining at some length in the next chapter. In the army command, with its feudal *esprit de corps* and its equally feudal clericalism, anti-Semitism was, if anything, even more pronounced than it was in society at large, so that the position of ordinary Jewish officers, let alone of Jewish staff officers, was extremely precarious. Newspaper readers in 1892 who knew that more than one Jewish officer had fought duels with anti-Semitic journalists, and that Captain Mayer had been killed after challenging the Marquis de Morès, who had called him a dirty Jew,[9] did not need great divinatory powers to realize that Dreyfus's latest appointment was no cause for congratulation. All this caused great astonishment and indignation at the time and even we, who have learnt the lessons of the twentieth century, may still feel indignant, though no longer astonished.

The third reason is much more difficult to pinpoint. France, as we saw, was divided into two hostile camps, and the Dreyfus affair must have appeared to both a final chance to settle their country's fate one way or the other. The monarchists sensed that their every victory had turned sour — hence their hysterical tone; the republicans had not yet consolidated their conquests, but felt they were about to do so — hence their more self-assured and less strident voice. The elections held in August 1893 had admittedly unseated a number of radicals, but, in general, the Right had lost ground to the moderate republicans, and what was even more crucial, the socialists had forced the gates of the Palais Bourbon: instead of sixteen deputies they now had fifty, including Jaurès and Guesde. What chances, the royalists must have asked themselves, were there now of applying the revanchist doctrine, that "invisible queen" as Charles Maurras and Daniel Halévy had called it, a doctrine that had reigned supreme from 1871 to 1898?[10] Germany kept growing richer and more populous, Austria and Italy were in the German camp, Britain was an enemy, Russia was France's only ally, and an uncertain one at that. Isolated abroad, the Republic was impotent at home. Had not the workers been taking to the street on every May Day since 1890, acting as if they owned all Paris? Were the anarchists not perpetrating one outrage after another? The Republic could not even protect its own President from Caserio, Ravachol, Emile Henry, Auguste Vaillant, and God alone knew what other assassins. In less than one hundred years, France had suffered three revolutions. Would the fourth be far away if the old order was not quickly restored? And who could do this better than the army? Was not the maintenance of authority worth some small sacrifice such as the deportation of a mere Jew? Was it any wonder, in these circumstances, that the Right brushed aside all opposition with: "Ye know nothing at all, nor consider that is is expedient for us, that one man should die for the people, and that the whole nation perish not"?[11]

What was at stake in the Dreyfus affair was nothing less than authority, for the one France, and also for the other. "Authority in our Republic," Clemenceau declared in 1898, "has broken down as badly as it did under the monarchy."[12] The two camps, for all that, did not mean quite the same thing by "authority." One used it to refer to power tempered if possible by reason, the other to reason supported if necessary by power. What was being posed was the old question of whether or not authority should be vested in the people. That question had also just been posed in Dostoyevsky's *Brothers Karamazov* with its famous parable of the Grand Inquisitor, a first French translation of which had appeared in 1888.[13] Not that General Gonse, for instance, had necessarily read the book, but Père du Lac, the leader of the Parisian Jesuits, undoubtedly had.

The clash between two principles of authority was bound to lead to a general loss of respect for authority. Those who shouted "Long Live the Army!" were proclaiming their contempt for the law, and those who roared "Long Live the Law!" were challenging traditional virtues that seemed so many obstacles on the road to the future. D'Axa, whose anarchist views caused him to welcome this collapse of authority, put it very well when he wrote: "The wind that was sown this winter has swept away so many prejudices that the century-old order has been blown to the moon."[14] He added, no less shrewdly, that if all that was being whispered from the Left no less than from the Right were put on a gramophone record, that record would surely be banned as dangerous anarchist propaganda.[15] Respect and discipline had become things of the past. D'Axa expressed all this in flowery, almost untranslatable, French phrases, which he had pasted all over Paris, richly adorned with cartoons by Steinlen, Willette, Léandre, Hermann-Paul, Couturier, Anquetin, and Luce. If anything was likely to prepare the smug nineteenth-century bourgeois Frenchman for the doubt and despair that were to become his lot in the twentieth century, then it was indeed the Dreyfus affair, which so divided his own camp that socialists of all shades of opinion saw fit to keep out of what they at first considered a purely factional struggle. According to them, the Jesuits were royalists and the Jews republicans; but to the starving masses both were tarred with the same brush. When the storm first broke, Jaurès himself, no less than Clemenceau and most other socialists, was firmly convinced of Dreyfus's guilt; if they were perturbed at all, it was because this rich staff captain had been sentenced to no more than exile, while Charles Hartier, a twenty-year old trooper, had recently been shot by a firing squad for tearing a button from his uniform and throwing it at the President of the Court Martial. "To put an end to all the sordid scandals in which so many officers have distinguished themselves," d'Axa wrote bitterly, "an example had to be made, and what better way of doing that than to kill off a humble soldier?" A moving illustration by Steinlen accompanied this indictment — in the foreground, a lonely boy tied to a stake; in the background a firing squad, an officer with raised sword, and flags fluttering in the light of the setting sun.[16] The etching was a controlled, but all the more forceful, for that protest against the evils of "caporalism"; against murder with a clear conscience; against the unholy alliance between the barracks and the church; against the "tonsure under the kepi," as d'Axa had called it. Later Jaurès, like so many others, changed his mind and not only used, but needed, all his eloquence to convince the Guesdists, and many of his own supporters as well, that the vindication of Dreyfus was the vindication of their own cause. This explains in part why this particular affair became *the* affair. Its outcome would decide whether or not France could step bravely into the twentieth century.

But what exactly was *the* affair? Complicated though its course undoubtedly was, it can all be summed up in a few brief words. A leak

84

of military secrets was discovered through the interception of the telegram to von Schwartzkoppen we mentioned earlier, and envious "comrades" straight away pointed the finger of suspicion at their ambitious rival, Dreyfus, who also happened to be a rich Alsatian Jew. At the time, no one bothered to ask who had started this rumor, particularly as the guilt of a single Jew could not conceivably be called a blot on the "honor of the army." From then on matters ran their own course: a judicial error which, all official disclaimers notwithstanding, was based on xeno- phobia and anti-Semitism;[17] a wave of racial self-delusion that infused even the lowliest French shopkeeper with the conviction that he was of great account; an old feudal tradition asserting its rights over a young bourgeois state; a church determined to abrogate the hated *constitution civile du clergé*; a clash between proto-Fascist and humanitarian ideas, and between the parties and organizations that championed them; a veritable hornet's nest of suspicions, fears, corrupt practices, falsifications and perjuries that carried the country to the brink of war; the firm conviction that the end sanctifies the means; yet, against this tide of filth, a veritable flood of courage, self-sacrifice, and endurance. The result was a *comédie humaine* on a larger stage and far more poignant than even the genius of a Balzac could have created.

As for the details, Herzog needed a good 600 pages merely to list the relevant documents and bare facts;[18] Kayser, who confined himself to the most important data, needed 200 pages to set them out;[19] De- sachy's bibliography, which only takes us as far as 1905, listed more than 700 items.[20] Still, if we ignore the many open questions[21] and steer carefully through the countless twists of this muddy stream, we finish up with the following account:

It was known that von Schwartzkoppen, the German military attaché — and his Italian colleague Panizzardi, too, for that matter — were engaged in espionage; that the Germans ran a special bureau in Brussels and another in Strasbourg; and the French thus had good reason to feel nervous about their activities. During the last week of September 1894 — Schwartzkoppen's telegram had been intercepted late in 1893 — an agent of the French Counter-Espionage Bureau was handed a letter by the caretaker of the German Embassy. This letter — the *bordereau* — which was undated, unsigned, and had been left by an unknown person, referred to five national defense secrets and to a proposed French expedition to Madagascar. Who could have written it? It had to be Dreyfus, the Alsatian Jew, the more so as, according to rumor, there were many other "facts" to inculpate him.[22] The writing of the *bordereau* was at once compared with Dreyfus's; and though the graphologist of the Banque de

85

France declared that the two were similar but by no means identical, other "experts" knew better what was expected of them and "proved" the case against Dreyfus conclusively. A council of ministers advised against a trial which, they felt, might cause international complications. This was particularly the view of the nationalist historian, Hanotaux, who was then Minister of Foreign Affairs. Instead the council ordered an examination of the suspect, a task that was entrusted to Major du Paty de Clam. On October 15, Dreyfus was arrested, having first been asked to write several passages resembling the contents of the *bordereau*, so that the writing could be compared once again: it was better to be safe than sorry. That was the first act.

Unfortunately for the Army, news of the story leaked out, and Drumont's *Libre Parole*, the anti-Semitic, anti-Masonic, and anti-Protestant mouthpiece founded with Jesuit money,[23] got hold of it two weeks later. The paper called for the outlawing of all Jews and predicted a new St. Bartholomew's Massacre. Other papers entered the fray, and with such vigor that a public airing could no longer be avoided; it had all turned into an "affair" even before December 22, when Dreyfus, defended by Maître Demange, was sentenced by a court martial, mainly on the basis of another secret document which General Mercier, then Minister of War, handed to the members after the examination but before sentence was passed. Little did the General suspect that when he lit this anti-Semitic fuse, he was about to cause an explosion that would destroy his entire caste. The sentence was: reduction to the ranks and deportation for life. The appeal by the accused, who continued to protest his innocence, was turned down within ten days. His plea that there was nothing in his life that might have caused him to act in so despicable a way, that he was rich and well satisfied with his position in the army, and that he was the last man to jeopardize his promising career by treason, let alone treason for financial reward, fell on deaf ears. On January 5, 1895, his epaulettes were torn from his shoulders, and his sword was broken over his head. The excited mob pressing against the railings of the Military Academy yelled "*À mort!*" and jeered at his torn uniform. That evening, Léon Daudet, then thirty-one years old, was able to tell his father with wild joy how glorious it had all been. Alphonse merely shrugged his shoulders — he refused to take sides, then or later.[24] But Emile Zola, who was dining with the Daudets, felt a stab of pain. Dreyfus's "I am innocent" had made a deep impression on him.[25] That was the second act. For the *entr'acte*, Gustave le Bon wrote his now famous *Psychologie des foules* in 1895, developing an argument first propounded in 1892 by Scipio Sighele in *La folla delinquente*. They were the first to warn the world against the masses, who had just stepped into the political limelight.[26]

The third act began in the summer of 1896. Dreyfus was still languishing on Devil's Island, counting off the black nights and the white days and as certain as ever that he would be vindicated within three years of his first ordeal. Picquart, who had meanwhile taken over from Sandherr as head of Counter-Intelligence, was another anti-Semite but otherwise a decent man. He now informed his chief that in his considered judgment the author of the *bordereau* was one Major Esterhazy, and pressed for a retrial, adding that the Dreyfus family might otherwise come out with a whole series of unpleasant revelations. His suspicions had been aroused when a wastepaper basket from the German Embassy yielded a telegram torn into thirty-one crumpled pieces — the so-called *petit bleu*. It had been addressed to Esterhazy; and when Picquart had looked more closely into the Major's life, his suspicions had hardened. More Hungarian than French, an illegitimate child who described himself falsely as a count, Esterhazy was a gambler and a womanizer, deep in debt, and had so violent a temperament that he might well have spoken the truth when he called himself a descendant of Attila. The classical question, *cui prodest*, pointed clearly in his direction, as it had never pointed in Dreyfus's. Moreover, espionage against France was a relatively mild expression of his hatred for a country of which Esterhazy had once written: "If I were told that I would die tomorrow as a Captain of Uhlans mowing down Frenchmen, I should be perfectly happy. And what a great feast it would be, were Paris, under a red sun of battle, taken by assault and delivered over to be looted by a hundred thousand drunken soldiers."[27]

Picquart lost what few doubts he may still have had as soon as he obtained a sample of Esterhazy's handwriting and compared it with the *bordereau*. We know how right he was from Esterhazy's full confession,[28] and particularly from the claim, corroborated by von Schwartzkoppen,[29] that some 600 of the 1,000 or so documents produced during the trial were blatant forgeries. But Picquart was not allowed to reveal the truth; his superiors, General Gonse, General Boisdeffre, whose real name was Mouton,[30] and Billot, then Minister of War, saw to that. On September 15, *L'Eclair*, an army paper, published the secret document that had earlier convinced the Court Martial of Dreyfus's guilt. And it published it to excellent effect, for none of its readers knew that this document was a forgery perpetrated by Major du Paty. The opposition countered on November 10 with the publication in *Le Matin*, then in its eleventh year and known for its accuracy,[31] of the *bordereau*,

87

which the public could thus compare for itself with Dreyfus's own hand-writing. But this helped neither Dreyfus nor Picquart, who had mean-while fallen into disgrace. In June 1897, after having wrestled with his conscience for many a bitter month, Picquart had finally decided to confide in Maître Lablois, who in July handed the information to Scheurer-Kestner, Vice-President of the Senate, possibly because Scheurer-Kestner, like Picquart and Dreyfus, was an Alsatian and as such likely to be sympathetic to the exile.

On Kestner's advice, Mathieu Dreyfus, who had never lost hope in the fight for his brother's vindication, now took a step that would have proved crucial had justice still been meted out in France during those years. Mathieu knew, of course, that when the young anarchist journalist Bernard Lazare[32] had written his attack on anti-Semitism in 1894,[33] and a brochure in defense of Dreyfus in 1896, his voice had fallen on deaf ears, but Mathieu felt that his own letter to the Minister of War in November 1897, containing detailed charges against Esterhazy, was something the authorities could not ignore. And, indeed, Esterhazy was duly examined. First things, however, still had to come first, and most important now, as before, were the honor of the army, of the church, of the state, and the law. Consequently, Esterhazy's acquittal was a foregone conclusion. Did not all his superiors speak very highly of him, and was he not garrisoned in distant Rouen and hence far away from all the spying that went on in Paris? — a wonderful discovery by the military geographers, as Clemenceau pointed out scathingly in his *Aurore*.[34] It was at this point that Maître Labori, soon afterward raised to fame by his brilliant defense of Zola, first became involved in the affair.

On the night following Esterhazy's acquittal on January 12, 1898, police agents prepared to arrest Colonel Picquart and to take him to Mont-Valérien. That same night, Emile Zola decided to throw caution to the wind and wrote his now famous letter to President Félix Faure. Next day his letter was blazoned across the front page of *L'Aurore*, beneath the two words that were to make history and ensure their author a permanent place in it — *"J'accuse"*. Zola had become firmly convinced that by striking a blow for a lonely stranger, for the innocent victim of scheming men, he was also striking a blow for humanity.

So the curtain went up on the fourth act. Zola's unquestioned in-tegrity, keen nose, and fine pen all combined to turn his letter into a bombshell. On the morning of January 13, Parisians tore the 300,000 copies of Clemenceau's daily from the vendors' and from one another's hands. Zola's accusations ranged far and wide; the refrain of *"J'accuse"* at the beginning of every paragraph was directed at Lieutenant-Colonel du Paty de Clam, at General Mercier, at General Billot, at Generals Bois-deffre and Gonse, at General Pellieux, at Commander Ravary, at the three graphologists, at the War Office, and at the one court martial that had condemned Dreyfus and at the other that had compounded the crime by acquitting Esterhazy, the real culprit.[35]

Zola had chosen to run a calculated risk. He realized that with those few strokes of the pen he had taken on the army, one of whose spokesmen had once declared that, sooner or later, it would have to overthrow the Republic and shoot the republicans; the church, which, having tripled the size of its estates from 1881 to 1898, foresaw the loss of land worth some ten billion francs if anticlericalism were to triumph; capitalism, which felt no less threatened; and finally the government, which was working hand in glove with these three institutions. He knew that because of his open letter he was bound to be hounded like Dreyfus and Picquart; that those who must needs deny the justice of his charges would drag him through the courts. Indeed, this is precisely what they did do; although to frustrate Zola's declared objective of using his own trial to obtain a review of the Dreyfus case, the jury, under pressure from the generals, the politicians, the priests, the anti-Semitic press, and the public, gave him short shrift: as early as February 23, Zola was found guilty of libel and received the maximum sentence, one year in prison. Perreux, the editor of *L'Aurore*, was given four months — as an ex-Communard he could count himself fortunate in getting off so lightly. In addition, each was fined 3,000 francs. Long live the army, away with Zola, death to the Jews! "Cannibals, all of them," Zola said in disgust. The climax had been reached. Sandwichmen paraded through the streets, while pamphlets and posters covered the walls of Paris. One of these has been preserved. It shows Drumont as Charles Martel in shining armor, driving the latter-day Jewish Saracens from the banks and the Bourse. There were pro-cessions, riots, and book-burnings in Paris, Lyons, Marseilles, Rennes, Nantes, and a real pogrom in Algiers during which, as *La Croix* rejoiced, Christ reigned supreme over the city.[36] The attempt to right a legal wrong had turned into open political and ideological warfare, and it looked very much as if its outcome would decide the future of France.

Zola was no longer alone; the "Ligue pour la defense des droits de l'homme et du citoyen" had been founded on February 20, 1898, during his trial. It held its first public meeting on June 4, and threw a whole phalanx of intellectuals, authors, and artists into the battle. Herzog mentions some sixty of them, including Anatole France, Gaston Paris, Ducleux — the successor and biographer of Pasteur — Charles Péguy, Romain Rolland, Marcel Proust, Marcel Prévost, Daniel Halévy, Joseph

Reinach, Lucien Herr, Octave Mirbeau, Charles Andler, Gabriel Monod, Claude Monet, Elie Reclus, and Briand. Léon Blum and Paul Langéries were among the younger members. Herzog has also named the leading anti-Dreyfusards, some forty of them all told. Of these the most vociferous were Maurice Barrès, Charles Maurras, Gyp, Arthur Meyer, Ernest Judet, Francois Coppée, Paul Valéry — a sad lapse but not on Herzog's part, Jules Lemaître, Ferdinand Brunetière, Forain, Caran D'Ache, and Vincent d'Indy.[37] Dégas, too, belonged to this camp, and so staunch a member was he that on one occasion he dismissed a model who had expressed doubts of Dreyfus's guilt.[38] The great majority of intellectuals, however, preferred to keep their own counsel. Ajalbert specially mentioned Rodin and Lavisse[39] among these, and Daudet *père* was another. Some thirty years later, Cécile Delherbe wrote a thesis on the leading figures in both camps and on the influence of the "affair" on French writers, from Anatole France and Zola, via Beaunier, whose Dreyfus novel was published in 1900, to J. R. Bloch.[40] Indeed, the affair had taken the intellectual world by storm, and in France this meant the center of the stage. Politics, according to Morand, [41] had become the most effective way of succeeding in literature; but the converse was equally true: literature or journalism had become the best way of succeeding in politics.

Yet much as Zola's brave act had failed to help Dreyfus directly, so the "Ligue" was unable to come to Zola's direct rescue. True, Zola's case was reviewed, but on July 18, the Appeal Court merely confirmed the sentence passed on February 3. Zola decided to flee to London that very night, carrying nothing but an overnight bag and a newspaper.

The tide, however, was about to turn. In May 1898, a radical majority was swept into office; when it came to the point, the French peasant and man in the street still voted for what, though it was not yet *his* revolution, looked as if it might become just that. Moreover, however many blackguards may have appeared in the affair, there were always more than enough honorable men to oppose them. This time Brisson, the new Prime Minister, was among them, and so was Cavaignac, who, vain though he may have been, did what had to be done just as soon as he became Minister of War in June. As the son of the man who had beaten down the workers of Paris in June 1848, he might have been expected to crush not only Zola but also the other members of the so-called "Syndicate" — the alleged Jewish plotters whom the Right accused of recruiting Dreyfusards by bribery and corruption. Probably he would have done just that, or at least have tried, had an official investigation led by Captain Cuignet not revealed that the only secret document in which the name of Dreyfus appeared in full, and which Cavaignac himself had recently made known to the Chamber and had ordered all French mayors to post in prominent places, was a crude forgery, as Picquart had said all along that it was. When even Colonel Henry, driven into a corner by the Minister, admitted responsibility for the fraud, Cavaignac, though he knew full well that he was sacrificing his political career and, indeed, damaging his entire cause, unhesitatingly handed the story to the press. His honesty cost him the presidency and made him one of the ten Ministers of War who lost office in the wake of the Dreyfus affair. But before he resigned, he ordered the arrest of Colonel Henry, who, at noon on August 30, was taken to Cherche Midi, where Dreyfus himself had been imprisoned. That night Henry cut his throat with two strokes of the razor they had left him. Or so the official record stated.[42]

Colonel Henry's confession and suicide were the prelude to the fifth act: the revision of the Dreyfus case. General Boisdeffre, the darling of the Jesuits, and General de Pellieux begged leave to resign their commissions. The first had his request granted because he insisted; the second withdrew his application at the government's request. Esterhazy, arrested in July, was discharged from prison but from the army as well. His excuse, which was also his confession, namely that he had acted on the orders of Sandherr and Henry,[43] was not accepted. He disappeared to London, where he was last heard of in 1923, living as Count Jean de Voilemont. Paty de Clam, too, was discharged after an examination. Six hundred members of parliament, whose number included just one Dreyfusard, now that Jaurès had been defeated at the polls, began to feel the first pangs of doubt. The republicans, in particular, suddenly woke up to the fact that the Dreyfusards were not nearly as unworldly and ingenuous as they had believed them to be. When the blow of Fashoda fell upon France that same month, a retrial seemed inevitable.

However, even now the anti-Dreyfusards refused to lie low. Charles Maurras proclaimed Colonel Henry a great patriot, and there was a collection for a monument in his honor. Among the letters accompanying the donations of some 15,000 contributors there were some that anyone anxious to preserve his faith in mankind had best leave unread. Nothing was bad enough for the Jews,[44] and it was only because the necessary equipment was not yet available that gas chambers were not mentioned. The generous donors included the "flower" of the French nobility: nine counts and countesses, one marquis, eight dukes and duchesses, and even three princes and princesses. It was probably the last public demonstration of this doomed estate. The lesser ranks included one Captain Weygand, who, some twenty years later, helped to extricate the Poles from the consequences of their war of aggression against the Soviet Union, and who, some forty years later, was to bear part of the blame for his country's shameful capitulation to Hitler.

Meanwhile, Picquart was still languishing in prison, and Madame Dreyfus's fresh appeal for a revision was turned down. But not for long — at the end of October the Court of Cassation announced that it would accept the case, and on June 3, 1899, it suspended Dreyfus's original sentence. Two days later, Zola returned home, followed that same month by Dreyfus himself, due to be re-tried in Rennes in August. The entire world held its breath. All the best-known journalists reported the proceedings: Max Nordau for the Viennese *Neue Freie Presse;* Daniels for the London *Daily Mail;* Wolff for the *Berliner Tageblatt.* During the open sessions they listened to the evidence of hundreds of witnesses for the prosecution and of more than forty-five witnesses for the defense. There were demonstrations for Dreyfus in London's Hyde Park, attended by 50,000 people, and in Washington, as well. In Budapest the windows of the French Consulate were smashed. In Jerusalem there were daily prayers for the accused, whose portrait graced the walls of many Jewish homes as far away as distant Bukovina. All this support helped to relieve pent-up passions, but did not avail Dreyfus himself. For the fifth act in the drama was an unbelievable verdict: on September 9, by a vote of 5–2, the Court again condemned Dreyfus, this time with "extenuating circumstances" thanks to which his mandatory life sentence was changed to one of ten years. Father Bailly, of the Augustinian Order of the Assumption in Algiers, explained in *La Croix* that the new sentence was the direct result of the miraculous intervention of the Holy Virgin.[45]

The sixth, and final, act, however, was ushered in by a less miraculous form of intervention. A week after the verdict was announced, the new Government of Republican Concentration — with Gallifet, the butcher of the Communards, on the Right; Millerand, the first socialist minister, on the Left; and Waldeck-Rousseau in the center — urged President Loubet to offer Dreyfus a pardon, and succeeded in their plea. The resulting compromise may have been unsatisfactory on human grounds, but it was politically expedient, at any rate at home; the world at large remained outraged, so much so that the Prince of Wales even threatened to boycott the Paris World Exposition. In any case, this compromise earned Waldeck-Rousseau the title of "Richelieu of the Third Republic"[46] Nor is it unlikely that Péguy, having spoken up for Dreyfus with religious fervor, took this half-hearted insult to his need for wholeness very badly — it was the reason why he returned to the bosom of Mother Church, finally to end up with the Action Française, where, incidentally, he also failed to find what he had sought his whole life.[47] "The incident is closed," declared an order of the day. That same September 18, 1899, the Government instructed the Senate to try a group of plotters against the Republic. The Senate's pronouncement, on January 4, 1900, has been recorded at the beginning of this chapter.

The rest is an epilogue. The waves subsided; other matters claimed public attention: the Universal Exposition, the Boer War, the German Navy Law, and the Boxer rebellion. Or perhaps it was not even that. The ordinary Frenchman had grown so sick of the whole affair, of the constant quarrels it had caused him to have with his family, neighbors, and colleagues that he was only too happy to turn his back on politics. All politicians, be they Rightists or Leftists, were tarred with the same dirty brush. So he chose less contentious diversions. If he belonged to the practising half of that quarter of the population that, according to church estimates, was still formally Catholic, he went to church on Sundays and prayed God that the next century might be happier than the last. If he was one of the remaining seven-eighths who, perhaps due to the "affair", had become wholly or partly disillusioned with the church, he sought his Sunday pleasures in a *café-chantant*. There ladies of doubtful virtue entertained him with the latest bawdy ballads; the next day, as a suitable token of remorse, he went to buy a new hat for his wife or toys for his children — perhaps one of those china figurines with turned-up skirts which gave off bursts of scent and were quite the latest thing, according to Morand. By contrast, Russian toy soldiers, the great favorite of yesterday, had become most unfashionable. Russian securities, too, had had the bottom knocked out of them, not only by the great St. Petersburg crash of September 1899,[48] but also because confidence in Russia had collapsed along with the authority of the French General Staff, which had previously moved heaven and earth to draw France into an alliance with the "bloodstained Czar."[49] The stock of the Russian revolutionaries rose in proportion. Everyone on the Left mocked at the unsuccessful Peace Conference in The Hague and swore at Siberia.

While the rest of our story was an epilogue, its very duration underlined the seriousness of the play that had gone before. All the scenes were re-enacted, if on a smaller stage. The amnesty of the innocent and guilty alike, late in 1900, was anything but a triumph of justice. The complete rehabilitation, six years later, of Picquart and Dreyfus was a backstairs manoeuvre and an embarrassing one at that: Dreyfus's decoration with the Légion d'Honneur must have left a bitter taste in his mouth — that honor had been abused so often to reward his detractors that many people would have liked him to refuse it. But history, unlike the cinema, knows no happy endings. True, Waldeck-Rousseau's Government of

93

Republican Concentration and Combes's *bloc des gauches*, an alliance of radicals and socialists, greatly reduced the political influence of the General Staff, confined the jurisdiction of courts martial to cases of insubordination and desertion, closed the Catholic Soldiers' Centers, secularized public education, and completed the separation of church and state. It may therefore be said that the Dreyfusards had won, but only in the sense that they had not been beaten. De Pressensé refused to admit even that. "Ultimately," he told a congress of the *Ligue des Droits de l'Homme* in 1910, "we lost. We were able to see that justice was done to a wronged individual, but what else? Social inequality has merely grown more pronounced."[50] Indeed, all the old problems had not only remained but had been aggravated by the affair. Under other flags and other leaders, the anti-Dreyfusards have kept returning to the fray,[51] as witness the formation of the *Ligue de la Nation Française* toward the end of 1898; the appearance of its mouthpiece, *L'Action Française*, in 1889; and its first public meeting in Lyons on July 5, 1900.

As late as 1924 there appeared a reprint of a book written fifteen years earlier by two anti-Dreyfusards. They took nearly 700 pages to present their case.[52] Another fifteen years later men like them could prove to a world at war that *their* France was far from dead. The members of the "Croix de Feu" and the "Cagoulards" were the direct successors of the "Camelots du Roi," and when the Third Republic was smarting under the German whip, Vichy still flew the oriflamme of St. Denis, though it had grown so thin and frayed that the swastika shone through it. In the final analysis, the Dreyfus affair was just one chapter in the story of the bitter struggle between one France and the other, a struggle that continues to this day.

CHAPTER VII

CHAUVIN'S LEGACY

Early in April 1900, *La Libre Parole*, Drumont's anti-Semitic daily news-paper, then in its eighth year and according to an advertisement[1] the most widely read paper in Paris, opened a subscription list. With the proceeds it proposed to purchase a matched pair of swords to be presented to Raphael Viau on the occasion of his twelfth duel for the good cause. In due course, the swords were handed over to him, beautifully damascened and with an inspiring inscription; but alas, the "master's" devout wish that they "might not remain virgins for long" was not fulfilled: Viau never made use of the gift.[2] There were also less singular but all the more characteristic signs that the wave of French anti-Semitism, which had reached its peak during the Dreyfus affair, was about to recede: the circulation of *La Libre Parole* shrank by more than a third, and a fresh insult to Henri de Rothschild resulted in a fine of more than 20,000 francs—Maître Ménard's great eloquence notwithstanding.[3] Above all, the congress of the anti-Semitic Christian Democrats held on July 14, 1900 was the fifth but also the last.

Things were quite different abroad. In his opening address to the Fourth Zionist Congress, held in London on August 13, 1900, Theodor Herzl said, and this was more than diplomatic politeness, that England was one of the few places free of the scourge of anti-Semitism, and that this very fact highlighted the plight of the Jewish people.[4] He was right. In the preceding spring, a fresh stream of refugees had fled Roumania, leaving a trail of blood all over Europe.[5] On November 14, a Czech jury, after a trial lasting seventeen days, unanimously passed the death sentence on one Leopold Hilsner from Polna in Bohemia for the alleged ritual murder of Agnes Hruza and Marie Klima. The sentence was nothing short of judicial murder, and, as Masaryk observed, a psychological sequel to the Dreyfus case.[6] A similar tragedy was enacted that very year in Konice, Moravia.[7]

The Hilsner affair was neither the beginning nor the end of the de-mented belief that Jews were in the habit of slaughtering Christian chil-dren for ritual purposes: in 1818 the series of modern witch trials had been inaugurated in Tisza-Eszlar in Hungary; in 1892 another such drama had been played out at Xanten in Germany, where Buschoff, a butcher's boy, was accused of the murder of five-year-old Johann Hegmann, and in 1911-1913 Mendel Beilis was tried in Russia on a similar charge.[8] We might add that not all the accused had the same tragic end as the mentally handicapped Hilsner. In Hungary, Eötvös, one of the most gifted parliamentary speakers, was able to save the accused; in Russia, three famous Russian lawyers ensured that justice triumphed in the Bellis case;[9] and in Germany, too, Buschoff was acquitted, despite the fact that the jury had succumbed to an artificially stimulated wave of mass hysteria.

Like most intellectual trends in the nineteenth century, modern anti-Semitism was of French origin. Its earliest manifestation was Alphonse Toussenel's *Les Juifs, rois de l'époque* (1845). The author, a disciple of the Utopian socialist Charles Fourier, gave his "left wing" book the telling subtitle of "History of Financial Feudalism." His anti-Semitism was both curiously "narrow" — it was based on resentment of the lonely success of the Rothschilds and on the presence of Jews among the followers of Saint-Simon — and strangely "broad" in that it greatly exaggerated the importance of Jews in general. Moreover, his charges were leveled at French Protestants as well, who, according to him, showed the same contempt as the Jews for the rights of the working class.[10] In 1869, the Right entered the fray with Gougenot des Mousseaux's *Le Juif, le judaïsme et la judaïsation*, which beat the same drum, but was all the more dangerous because Gougenot, a Catholic bigot, was the first to dig up the medieval blood libel. To him, the Jew was an ally of the Protestant and the Freemason in the hateful struggle for progress.[11]

Meanwhile, Germany had produced her first anti-Semitic "classic"; D. H. Naudh's *Die Juden und der deutsche Staat* ("The Jews and the German State") was published in 1861.[12] It was followed, ten years later, by *Der Talmud-Jude* ("The Talmud-Jew") by August Rohling, then still a modest priest in the Rhineland, and in 1873 by *Der Sieg Des Judenthums über das Germanenthum* ("The Victory of Judaism over Germanism") by the journalist Wilhelm Marr.[13] Marr's subtitle ("Considered from a Non-Religious Point of View") alone showed that he proposed to go much further than his predecessors had done. He had read Gobineau's *Essai sur l'inégalité des races humaines* (1851-1854) and immediately applied its finding to his own country, which was ripe for the new message. Germany in her so-called "founders' years," (1871-1873) was a country in which capitalism had begun to make deep inroads into the old pattern of life, ruining the old middle classes by a series of financial swindles. Bismarck's attempt, early in the eighties, to break the liberal bourgeoisie, was born of the same resentment.

96

Modern anti-Semitism had ceased to be a purely literary affair, so much so that Marr became frightened by his success and turned his back on it with horror and revulsion.[14] Not so the orientalist and "theological father of Germanic anti-Semitic Christendom," Paul de Lagarde, according to whom Paul the Jew had insinuated the Old Testament and hence the "Jewish poison" into Christianity;[15] or the Lutheran court chaplain, Adolf Stöcker,[16] leader of the Christian Social Workers' Association, who with Adolf Wagner founded an anti-Semitic party in 1887, attracting 47,500 votes in 1890 and 285,000 votes in 1898;[17] or Treitschke, the historian, who coined the slogan "The Jews are our misfortune" and inspired large sections of the academic world envious of the Jewish intellect; or Hermann Ahlwardt, who took over from Stöcker in the early nineties. With Ahlwardt, the movement may be said to have fallen into a decline, for he was nothing better than an adventurer. Nevertheless, the Conservatives adopted his program in the 1893 elections, and it was not until 1896 that Ahlwardt dragged their leader, Baron von Hammerstein, down with him — both were drowned in a sea of fraud.[18]

In France, too, anti-Semitic "literature" had paved the way for the rise of a political movement. The change occurred after the publication in 1886 of *La France juive* by Edouard Drumont, a man who despite all his radical noises was, at heart, a pessimistic conservative. Thanks largely to the controversy it unleashed in the press and among the public, his obscure book sold a hundred thousand copies within one year of its publication; and within another two years some seventy other authors had repeated its vicious remarks. Even some socialists were duped, though not for long. The *Du molochisme juif* by Tridon, an atheistic Communard, had even predated Drumont's anti-Jewish gospel by two years; and Paul Lafargue, for instance, claimed in 1886 that "the real republic will not exist until the day that Rothschild is at Mazas [a prison in Paris] or before the firing squad"![19] While some radicals were duped, the National Socialists rejoiced, among them Jacques de Biez, Drumont's first disciple and the vice-president of the French National Anti-Semitic League, who called himself a nationalist — France for the French — and a socialist because he was against the financial feudality;[20] and Morès, whom Byrnes has rightly described as "not only the first National Socialist but also the first storm trooper."[21] "Life is valuable only through action, so much the worse if the action is mortal," was one of his dicta.[22] So the story continued until Guesde finally woke up and proclaimed that, to every true worker, anti-Semitism was synonymous with economic and social reaction.[23] In France, too, it was not the workers but the petit-bourgeois Christian Democrats, led by Fathers Fesch, Gayraud, Naudet, and Garnier, who kept the torch of anti-Semitism ablaze until 1900.[24] It was Father

Gayraud who had called the Jews "an evil and parasitic nation" in his *Les Démocrates-Chrétiens* (1899), and he was by no means the most vituperative among the clergy.[25]

Worse than in France, where, apart from Algiers, Dijon, Langres, and Paris (1898 and 1899), real persecution was kept within "reasonable" bounds, no matter how deeply the anti-Semitic movement had inflamed the people; worse even than in Germany — where physical excesses occurred in several towns during the eighties, and particularly in Xanten following the Buschoff trial in 1892 and in Neustettin where the synagogue was burned down in the same year — was the plight of Jews under the Danube monarchy. Here, too, a liberal party for which most Jews had cast their votes, insofar as they enjoyed the franchise, was opposed by a number of reactionary and clerical groups who despised the modernistic, secular tendencies of the bourgeoisie. The reason why anti-Semitism was particularly virulent in Austria-Hungary was, on the one hand, the prominence of Jews in the industrial, commercial, and cultural life of the capital and, on the other hand, the large influx of Jewish workers from Eastern Europe. Thus while Jews accounted for no more than 1.04% of the total population of Germany in 1900, in Austria-Hungary they made up a good 4.5%. In this touchy atmosphere, the collapse in 1878 of the Parisien Union Générale made a greater impact than it did even in Paris. This "Christian bank" had been founded a few years earlier by the swindler Eugène Bontoux, who had sensed which way the wind was blowing. The Union Générale, he claimed, had been founded for the express purpose of protecting its clients from the "rapacity of the Jewish banks." Bontoux's victims, who naturally blamed the crash on the same Jewish bankers against whom Bontoux had promised to protect them, included the Pretender to the French throne, the Comte de Chambord, and his Austrian wife, the Archduchess Maria Theresa. The latter, who took her loss as a personal insult, dispatched one of her paladins to Germany with express instructions to make a study of anti-Semitism on the spot. The messenger duly contacted Stöcker and returned with a case full of pamphlets from which the Archduchess quickly learned how the Jews had got the better of her. The Cardinal Archbishop of Prague, Count Schönborn, had meanwhile seen to it that August Rohling, now a full canon, was appointed Royal Professor of Hebrew and Antiquities in his see.

From Austria the movement spread to Hungary, where it produced its first bitter fruit in 1882 — the Tisza-Eszlar trial, to which we have referred. The fact that the missing girl — or her body — was never discovered did not prevent von Onody, a member of parliament, from displaying her portrait and alluding to her as a martyr before the first anti-Semitic congress in Dresden. At the same time, one of the foremost Austrian nobles, Count Beleredi, tried to divert the socialist movement into anti-Semitic channels with the help of paid demagogues, who proclaimed to the people at large that all their misery was the direct result of Jewish machinations. The National Party, a mixture of noblemen and shopkeepers, soon afterward joined in the chorus; but in Austria, as in Germany, the main champions of anti-Semitism were the Christian Socialists, a clerical party with radical pretensions, founded by Count Alois von Liechtenstein and Dr. Karl Lueger. From 1889, accusations of ritual murder followed one upon the other; and though all the accused were acquitted, even by anti-Semitic judges, no great imagination is needed to appreciate that Austrian Jews went in fear of their lives, the more so as the votes cast for their detractors increased with every new election and even earned the Christian Democrats a parliamentary majority in 1895.

While anti-Semitism still had relatively well-manicured claws in Austria, in Roumania and Russia it struck with undisguised ferociousness. Here the movement, which enjoyed official backing, was given a great boost by the assassination of Czar Alexander II: in 1882 Jews were forbidden to acquire land and a strict *numerus clausus* was introduced into public education; in 1890 they were forcibly removed to the western provinces and placed under police surveillance; and in the interval they were exposed to regular but increasing violence from below. At the Sixth Zionist Congress, held in Basel on Sunday, August 23, 1903, Herzl, the Kishine pogrom[26] in April of that year still fresh in his mind and no doubt the Gomel pogrom[27] during the same month as well — both far bloodier than even the bloodiest anti-Jewish excesses in the eighties — exclaimed bitterly that "many of us had believed that things could not grow worse, but worse they have grown all the same. A tide of unprecedented misery has been unleashed over our people, and has already swept the lowlier of them away."[28] To compound the disaster, the massive exodus of the victims was helping to stoke the — by then dying — embers of anti-Semitism in the West.

I disagree

Why pick on the Jews? Jewish and non-Jewish experts alike are agreed that anti-Semitism is not based on the racial or national characteristics of the Jews, nor on their political, economic, and social circumstances at any one time or in any one place. True, the new wave of anti-Semitism, like so many that had gone before, was not altogether unconnected with popular resentment, based on a mixture of old prejudices and unhappy personal experiences, but *the* anti-Semitic movement was, as ever, a deliberate political artifact, and as such quite unconnected with what Jews themselves did or failed to do.[29] All the anti-Jewish arguments were shallow, as

99

those who used them realized full well. Their shrewdness was not that they used them all the same, but that they used them for that very reason — the shallower the argument, the more easily it can be fobbed off on the masses. The lower middle class, in particular, who at the turn of the century had fallen between the hammer of capital and the anvil of labor, lent a willing ear to anyone prepared to identify the cause of their misfortune. That cause had to be both tangible and hence identifiable at home, and also intangible and hence international. It had also to be powerful and yet impotent — powerful enough to be a credible bogey, and impotent enough to be overcome. International capitalism might have served the purpose equally well had the anti-Semitic movement been able to dispense with its chief financial backers, and so might the International Working Men's Association had not its members been a reservoir of potential recruits. The Freemasons were not powerful enough, the Jesuits not secretive enough; moreover, the former made poor scapegoats in Protestant, and the latter in Catholic, countries. Therefore, perhaps less deliberately than we have suggested but with an unerring instinct, the wire-pullers hit upon the Jews, who, if necessary, could be associated with the real enemies of the petit-bourgeoisie: international capital and organized labor, which made it possible to rail against Jew-infested international finance, the Jew-infested Left, the Jew-infested army, bench, and science, and even against Jew-infested Christianity and the Jew-infested state. The recent emancipation of the Jews in Eastern and Central Europe offered these men a golden opportunity.

Even those authors, most of them disciples of Freud, who deny that anti-Semitism is an unconscious creation, nevertheless trace it back to the unconscious minds, not of Jews but of non-Jews.[30] However, all those who examine the rise of anti-Semitism at the turn of the century in historical rather than psychological or sociological terms cannot but conclude that its founders were at least partly conscious of what they were doing. This point was first made by a great scholar and sage, a man who has experienced anti-Semitism at close quarters and who devoted his whole life to the courageous fight against it: Rabbi Dr. Joseph Samuel Bloch, from Florisdorf in Vienna. His grasp of the subject was much sharper than that of Novikow, the Russian sociologist and pacifist,[31] of Luschan, the Austrian anthropologist; of Bernard Lazare, the Belgian anarchist;[32] or of Lombroso, the famous Italian criminologist.[33] As early as 1882, when Rabbi Jellinek, the father of the great jurist, thought it best to leave well alone, Bloch took the redoubtable Rohling to court, and conducted his case so successfully that Rohling eventually had to run away in disgrace.[34]

The shabby political motives of the anti-Semites were laid bare even more clearly in Bloch's lawsuit against Pastor Deckert, a Viennese clergy-man. In 1893, when accusations of ritual murder had been proved un-founded in court after court, Deckert had gone to the trouble of searching the historical records for "irrefutable proof." To that end he had trans-lated several documents from a "trial" held in 1475, when the Jews of Trent had been found guilty of the ritual slaughter of Simon Gerber, a boy whose blood they were said to have mixed into their Passover dough. When Deckert was silenced by Bloch's incontrovertible demonstration that this trial, too, had been rigged, so much so that both the Doge of Venice and even Pope Sixtus IV had refused to sanction the verdict, Deckert produced one Paulus Meyer, a converted Russian Jew and an international swindler, who claimed that as a youth he himself had partic-ipated in a ritual murder conducted by the Chassidim. However, so strong was the Austrian sense of justice at the time, and so skillful and persistent was Bloch, that the Deckert trial was turned into the clearest possible demonstration of the fact that the instigators of modern anti-Semitism did not believe in their own accusations or, at any rate, in the means they used to prop them up.[35]

Bloch also exposed anti-Semitism in a masterly pen sketch of Dr. Karl Lueger, the Christian-Socialist who had risen to become mayor of Vienna in 1847 by climbing over the backs of "his" Jews. Bloch's sketch just had to be true, if only because it had the genuine Viennese ring to it: when a Jewish café owner came to complain to the mayor that the tramway lines were being laid right in front of her door and that she was losing customers as a result, Lueger at once had the rails moved; and when the woman, having promised to pray for him if he intervened on her behalf, came back to thank him, he asked, with a twinkle in his eye, if she would now make good her promise.[36]

However pleasant and human this anecdote may appear to be, the underlying reality was anything but that. It was horrifying that one group of human beings — the Christian Social Party — should have constantly slandered another, the Jews, no more innocent or guilty than the rest, by accusing them of every possible crime, from ritual murder to international conspiracy, simply to advance their own political fortunes; and that they should have succeeded, thanks to the prejudice, the credulity, the misery, and the uncertainty of a still larger group — the petit-bourgeoisie.

Small wonder that Bloch's exposures of anti-Semitism should have led many Jews to seek a more radical solution than Bloch's. Bloch gained all the courage he needed for his lifelong and heroic struggle from his opti-mistic faith that, provided only the struggle was waged by all Jews capable of waging it and with the same zeal as his own, emancipation would even-

101

tually make way for the complete assimilation of Jewry — unless, of course, the Jewish "oil" refused to mix with different fuels.[37] Others sought a separatist solution, but in two distinct ways. While some advocated "autonomism," the creation of autonomous, self-governing, political, and social institutions in every country with a Jewish minority, others called for the creation of a Jewish homeland, and proudly displayed the old name of Zion on their banner. Simon Dubnow was the champion of autonomism, and Theodor Herzl of Zionism.

Each of these prophets quite naturally drew on his own background and experience. Bloch was thirty years old in 1881, when the pogroms started in Russia and when masses of fugitives unwillingly carried the virus of crude anti-Semitism to the rest of Europe. For all that, he lived at a time when the tree of emancipation had begun to bear fruit in the growing assimilation of the Jews. Although he was a rabbi, he became, if not an influential, at least a respected member of the Austrian parliament, in which he served from 1891 to 1895, staunchly supported by the representatives of other minorities, all of whom felt the lash of German domination. This fact no less than his successes in the legal and literary battle against anti-Semitism was bound to render him almost totally deaf to the more radical approach of Dubnow, let alone to the most radical view of all, that of Herzl. His relationship with the latter was anything but cordial, and by 1900 it had turned completely sour.[38]

Dubnow, like Bloch, was the child of well-to-do parents and might therefore have been expected to hold similar views. But he was ten years younger than Bloch, had spent his whole life in Russia, and hence reacted differently to the new wave of violence. He was still a student when terrorists threw their well-aimed bomb at the Czar's carriage in St. Petersburg in 1881, and he knew little of the world outside. True, in Russia, too, the Jews had many friends, priests and even generals among them — we know all of them by name[39] — but their voices were drowned in an ocean of hatred. In his autobiography, Dubnow tells us how, as a talmudic scholar, he reacted against his upbringing, first by adopting assimilatory and cosmopolitan ideas and then by embracing autonomism — at about the same time that the working-class Jewish immigrant Zhitlovsky embraced the same solution in Switzerland.[40] On New Year's Day, 1901, Dubnow wrote the following pessimistic note in his diary: "We are entering the twentieth century. What does it have in store for humanity, and for Jewry in particular? To judge by the last few decades, it seems as if humanity might be entering a new Dark Age with horrifying wars and national struggles." He added: "But the mind refuses to believe it."[41] Was it in order to preserve a semblance of hope that, in his vehement polemics with

Ahad Ha-am and the poet Nahum Bialik in Odessa, he finally declared himself an opponent of Zionism, a movement that the venerable Leon Pinsker had joined as early as 1881[42] and of which the young Jabotinsky, born in 1880, was one of the most fiery spokesmen? Or was he too deeply rooted in the Russian Pale — though no longer an orthodox, and hardly even a religious, Jew — to imagine any future for his people outside of what to him was home, even though it was hardly a home at all? From his *Essays on Old and New Judaism* (1897-1907), we can see that not even the Kishinev pogrom during Easter, 1903, however deeply it shocked him, was able to shift him from his entrenched position, except that he now extended his call for autonomous civil and cultural rights with one for mass emigration to America as a temporary expedient. "Twenty-two years ago," he wrote, "those of us who believed in linear historical progress saw with astonishment and dismay how sharply the lines had been twisted back in the most recent past . . . now the circle has been closed." But even then he refused to renounce the irrepressible optimism that was probably still part and parcel of his Jewishness and certainly characteristic of his generation: "But the latest twist finds us better prepared . . . we can now rely on national self-help."[43] The trickle of emigrants to America had meanwhile turned into a tide: more than 1,600,000 Russian Jews escaped to the New World in 1880-1914 and more than 2,500,000 from Europe, including Russia.[44] Of those who remained behind, neither the Jewish socialites — the older ones in the Polish Bund and the younger ones in the Poale Zion movement — who had played an active part during the first Russian revolution, nor the "Seymists," who were striving for a Jewish parliament, were able to stem the anti-Semitic tide, no matter how hard they tried. This may explain why Dubnow is chiefly remembered not for his political ideas but for his cultural contribution to the *Jewish Encyclopaedia*, a co-operative work by Jewish scholars in the United States (1901-1906), and above all for his *Weltgeschichte des jüdischen Volkes* ("History of the Jewish People"; 10 vols.),[45] for which he began to gather material as early as 1887. During the more than fifty years remaining to him, he continued to pursue his historical studies, until 1941 — when a drunken Lithuanian Nazi battered him to death in Vilna.

There was a world of difference not only between Dubnow and Bloch but also between Dubnow and Herzl, who raised the Jewish question from the sphere of synagogal liturgy and legend to the plane of political reality.[46] Herzl was able to do so because, born in 1860 of prosperous and assimilated parents resident in Pest, he was spared the rigors of an orthodox upbringing. So unfamiliar was he with the Jewish tradition that he apparently did not know the writings of Bodenheimer (1891) and Birnbaum

(1893), both of whom had advocated a Zionist solution.[47] Moreover, Herzl succeeded where Dubnow and Bloch had failed because, never having been mocked or humiliated, and being a clever, gifted, and celebrated journalist and playwright, he could hold his head high and speak freely to the great of the earth. Last but not least — because he was one of the first of that new type, the organizer — he turned his people's lamentations into a hymn of hope and their stammered protests into a political goal.

Herzl became a Zionist not through deep thought and study, but in the wake of a professional experience that might have been called accidental had the anti-Semitic wave of those years not rendered such accidents everyday occurrences. As correspondent of the Viennese *Neue Freie Presse*, he was sent to cover the first Dreyfus trial in 1894; and the fact that so grave an injustice could be perpetrated in the France he revered, the country of the Revolution and the Enlightenment, very greatly shocked him. If Paris could be the scene of such anti-Semitic spectacles, there was no salvation for his people anywhere in Europe. He was suddenly struck, as if by lightning, by the tragedy of the Jewish people: there was no way of escape for them because they carried anti-Semitism with them in their baggage. Their only hope was a national home of their own, a view he put forward in his *Der Judenstaat* ("The Jewish State"), a short book written in the summer of 1895 and published one year later.[48]

In a sense, the ground he trod had been well prepared, in words no less than in practice. In 1862, Moses Hess had expressed similar views in his *Rom und Jerusalem*, and Pinsker had done much the same twenty years later in his *Autoemanzipation*. Many others, too, had written in similar vein.[49] On the practical side, wealthy Jews, Baron Maurice de Hirsch and Baron Edmond de Rothschild among them, had made generous grants to facilitate Jewish colonization, be it in Palestine or elsewhere. The Lowenthal-Hirsch plan to purchase some 25,000 square kilometers of ground in Argentina and to settle half a million Russian Jews there had been put forward in 1890. In 1891, Hirsch had also founded the Jewish Colonization Association with an initial capital of £2,000,000, later increased to £10,000,000.[50] However, the theoretical spadework had remained a purely academic exercise and the financial contributions had never even been intended to be more than a palliative.

Herzl's solution, by contrast, was eminently practical and not philanthropic. He refused to be discouraged when a friend to whom he read his manuscript called him a madman, especially as the famous psychiatrist, novelist, and phosopher, Max Nordau, also from Pest but established in

104

Paris, soon afterward not only attested to Herzl's sanity but also offered his personal support. Herzl faced the arduous annual congresses that followed — the first held in Basel in 1897 — with equanimity; he braved the hostile halls packed with opponents and voluble know-alls. He also braved all the obstacles in the way of the Jewish Bank, an institution he was determined to establish with the help of Jacobus Kann, a Jewish banker from The Hague, and of the Jewish National Fund, which had been set up for the express purpose of acquiring land in Palestine. Nor was he discouraged when all those powerful men to whom he turned for help — Baron de Hirsch; Baron de Rothschild; the Maccabeans to whom Israel Zangwill introduced him in London; the German and Austrian emperors; Plehve, the Russian Minister of the Interior; the Czar; the King of Italy; the Pope; and the Sultan — turned him down.[51]

It was probably these reverses and the ever-worsening situation of East European Jewry that persuaded him to lower his sights and to accept Joseph Chamberlain's offer of an alternative Jewish home, first in Cyprus, then in El Arish in the Sinai peninsula, and finally in Uganda. Yet, although he told the delegates to the Sixth Zionist Congress that this last alternative to the Holy Land was only intended as a way station — a "night shelter"[52] for the most sorely oppressed, who might gather their forces there before setting out for the land of their fathers — the opposition, particularly from the Russian delegation, was so fierce that it took a whole year to patch up the quarrel. Herzl himself was not allowed to savor the joys of reconciliation for long; he had given too much of himself[53] and died on July 3, 1904, while still in his early forties. Like Moses, he had led his people out of servitude, and like Moses he, too, did not see the Promised Land. But the Jewish people, appreciating the similarity, and forty-five years after his death once again in possession of Eretz Israel, have continued to revere him as a second Moses.

It was not only this final achievement which proved that Herzl was much less naive than so many of his contemporaries had believed him to be. True, his movement counted only 10,000 members all told, a small enough band when one remembers that there were ten million Jews then living, including the hundred thousand Jewish emigrants who left their homes every year.[54] However, his was a band of Gideonites. Its money came from the West, its fire from the East. Nor had Herzl been ingenuous to seek the support of crowned and uncrowned heads of state; at the time, great men had much more to offer than they have today, and mass movements much less. Palestine, moreover, was the right place to build a Jewish home for both traditional reasons and for very practical ones as well. At the time, it appeared — and not only to Herzl — to be a ripe fruit which

105

would sooner or later drop from the Turkish tree straight into the lap of either France or Britain. This is what Herzl meant when he told the Fourth Zionist Congress held in 1900 that "in the near future a cultural and a trade route will lead through Palestine into Asia, making this part of the world the chief diplomatic nut to be cracked in the coming decade." These words, first spoken in 1898, had acquired a much more convincing ring by 1900.[55] Herzl could not of course, have known that the Young Turk revolution of 1908 was to delay matters for a while.[56] All in all, however, his national solution of the Jewish problem was completely in keeping with the spirit of the time.

While the connection between anti-Semitism and Zionism was obvious, few people appreciated the links between these two currents and the rise of neo-nationalism. Yet these links were very strong as well, and we could do worse than to look more closely at them.

The title of this chapter was chosen with care. Chauvin was a grenadier in Napoleon's Grande Armée, noted for his devotion to the Emperor and for the many wounds he had collected in his service. His name first appeared in propaganda pamphlets after Napoleon's return from Elba, and quickly became a symbol of blind devotion to the cause of national glory. Chauvinism has ever since been synonymous with rabid nationalism. It is a new phenomenon, one that took the place of the tempered nationalism of the liberal bourgeoisie which welcomed rather than abhorred international ties. Nationalism did not become "integral" — as Maurras put it — until the eighties. Maurras not only qualified it thus, but also defined it as the "exclusive pursuit of national policies, the absolute maintenance of national integrity, and the steady increase of national power."[57] To the neo-nationalists, the nation had thus become an end in itself. National needs, or what was taken for such, were upheld as transcending the needs not only of the individual but also of humanity. A direct result was resentment of all other nations and the suppression of minorities, no matter whether they were religious, ethnic, or, indeed, political. One law, one language, one religion, no longer on a world scale but on the national level, was the new ideal. The national flag became an idol. A new loyalty bound men together even against reason. "Totalitarian nationalism" — as Hayes has called it[58] — was one of the chief elements of the rise of modern militarism, protectionism, and imperialism at about the turn of the century. Its heavy hand could be felt in the Ligue des Patriotes in France (1882), in the Primrose League in England (1883), and above all in Germany, where the Kolonialverein, which began its life in 1882 with 200 members, had increased that number to 25,000 by 1900, where the Alldeutscher Verband (Pan-German League), founded in 1894, could

106

boast 100,000 members, and where the Flottenverein (Navy League), founded in 1898 and joined two years later by the Evangelic Workers' Unions[59], had as many as 600,000 members.

In Germany, as in Italy earlier, nationalism was given a tremendous boost by the country's unification. Together with the economic boom following the Franco-German war, unification had opened up unsuspected vistas of power and world domination and helped to submerge the individual concerns of the member states in a swell of Pan-Germanic enthusiasm. Bismarck's *Kulturkampf* made it clear how far the new nationalism had already advanced but also how divided its forces still were. In his attempts to create an absolute state, on the pattern of Prussia and in accordance with the great Hegelian doctrine that the State is a near-divine institution, Bismarck was thwarted time and again by the recently formed *Zentrumspartei*, a political organization that though loyal to the state felt a "higher" obligation to an international, and hence anti-national, institution — namely to Rome, where the Pope had of late been declared infallible. Bismarck's supporters, by contrast, included many liberals who had grown indifferent to the church and whose economic interests could be more readily satisfied in a Greater Germany; Protestant Conservatives, including the anti-Semitic court chaplain, Stöcker, who dreamed of the creation of an "Evangelical German Empire"; and not least the rationalists of the *Fortschrittspartei* (Progressive Party), together with a host of academics, among them Virchow and Mommsen, two sons of the Enlightenment, and as such so staunchly opposed to clerical conservatism and race delusion that it did not take Stöcker long to realize that he had more in common with the Catholics in the *Zentrumspartei* than with these heathens and Social Democrats. In 1914, incidentally, it became very clear that not even the latter were immune to the neo-nationalist virus.

A more telling proof of the virulence of neo-nationalism was the fact that it not only infected the masses but also those individuals who might have been supposed to command the necessary antibodies. In 1877 Kropotkin, for instance, welcomed the Russian campaign against the Turks on the exceedingly shallow ground that the liberation of the Balkan Slavs was bound to weaken czarism. And in 1912, he drew so exaggerated a picture of the oppression of the Slavs by the Danube monarchy that even Max Nettlau, his great admirer, who was also not entirely immune to the nationalist virus, felt impelled to speak up for "his" government.[60] Henri Rochefort, who had been at home on the extreme Left during the days of the Commune, was another to strike an extreme nationalist note in his paper *La Patrie*.[61] His opponent, Jaurès, wove his own thread of lyrical nationalism as expressed, for instance, in his *Armée Nouvelle*

107

(1910), into the legend that neither the French nor the British Empire "inspired as they are by the ideals of freedom and justice",[62] could be accused of oppressing their subject peoples. Even Shaw and Wells, those two great non-conformists, lent their support to the war "their" empire was waging against the Boers, and rationalized that act of brigandage by claiming that it was "in the interest of civilization."[63]

What were the causes of this virulent disease? When we attempt to plumb the depths of this muddy stream we discover that, paradoxically, it had a progressive undercurrent: the emancipation and consequent absorption into the nation of popular strata that had not previously played an active part in political and social life. Responsible for this development were a certain degree of prosperity and the spread of "democracy." Once officially recognized as full members of the nation, these strata, the lower middle classes followed by the workers, began to press their special claims upon the liberal state; and whenever the latter, hampered by economic and social restraints, could not or would not come to their aid, they became receptive to the lures of demagogues or turned almost instinctively to the conservatives. At this point, the progressive undercurrent was dramatically reversed. A new creed, which made a spurious appeal to science — and what could be more authoritative than science? — seemed as if tailor-made to the needs of these rising groups. That new creed was racism, the doctrine of the innate superiority of the white man. Its appeal is easily explained: never before had Europe been so far ahead of the rest of the world as she was during this period. Now that modern psychology has made us familiar with the process of over-compensation, few people still doubt that the sudden burst of self-confidence was, in fact, anything but displaced anxiety. Indeed, from its modest origins modern racialism has been Janus-faced. Thus during the French Revolution, the hard-pressed French aristocrats tried to justify their superiority over the "Celtic" plebeians by stressing their own "Germanic" descent. It was not by chance that de Gobineau's book did not catch on until 1884, or that when it did it should have given rise to a veritable cult in Germany. To Richard Wagner, de Gobineau was a kind of god; a Gobineau Museum was opened in Strasbourg; and a Gobineau Association in Freiburg (1894).[64] Houston Stewart Chamberlain became the new prophet of this movement, and his *Gundlagen des neunzehnten Jahrhunderts* (1899) the bible of Germanic, Teutonic, or Aryan racialism. P. de Lagarde, who died in 1891, had by then tried to wed the new doctrine to anti-Semitism (see page 97). In Britain, Seeley, with his *Expansion of England*, advanced similar, if less extreme, views on the superiority of the

Anglo-Saxon race in 1883; Sergi did the same for the Mediterranean race two years later; the Aksakovs and Katkov, for the Slavs; and Vacher de Lapouge with his *L'Ayrien — son rôle social* (1889), once again for the Aryan race as a whole. J. H. Rosny (pseudonym of the brothers Boëx), originally a follower of Zola, later took to writing "novels" set in the Stone Age and based on the abduction of a brachycephalic brown-haired pre-Aryan, by a dolicocephalic, tall, and blond Aryan.[65] The racial doctrine was so subjective that there was not even a hint of agreement between its various proponents, and this despite, or rather because of, the enthusiastic attempt by some fifty scholars to give it "objective foundations"[66] — the results showed that, their avowed "realism" notwithstanding, they all believed in fairy tales. Unfortunately, the effects of these fairy tales were only too real, as the oppressed minorities learned to their cost. Their call for emancipation had kept step with their mounting oppression. True, they did not (yet) aim at domination in their turn, but their own brand of nationalism was no less virulent than that of their oppressors. Among them, too, lack of self-assurance was both cause and effect of a swaggering stance. Less known and general than the struggle of the Jewish people, that of the other national minorities was no less bitter or dramatic, and it, too, was played out in every part of Europe.

Thus Great Britain, so concerned with the fate of oppressed minorities on the Continent, saw fit to suppress the Irish, and could do so the more readily as many Irishmen were taken in by the myth of the "inferior" Celtic race. One who was not was Arthur Griffith. Returning from South Africa, where he had been a war correspondent, he organized the Sinn Fein passive resistance movement in 1900, and called for a boycott of British goods for the sake of Irish industry.[67] The Norwegian "peasants," rebelling against their "aristocratic" Swedish overlords, scored their first success in 1890, when their language was first introduced in all schools,[68] but did not achieve full independence until 1905. Their nationalism, incidentally, was so aggressive that they demanded control even of Greenland and the Faroe Islands. The Flemish had a harder time of it in Belgium; their struggle coincided more or less with the decline of liberalism and the rise of Catholic power. In 1887 came their first public demonstration: the commemoration of the Battle of the Spurs. In 1889 Brussels reluctantly allowed Flemish litigants to plead in their own language, and in 1898 Belgium was officially declared a bilingual country. The *Algemeen Nederlandsch Verbond*, founded that same year, gave full support to the Flemish movement. August Vermeylen, whose first attack on "Belgian tyranny" was launched in 1895, combined his original campaign with hostility to parliamentarianism and democracy;[69] and though van Cauwelaert, Camille Huysmans, and Franck did not share his other political views, they joined his fight against the predominance of the French language. Regional nationalism in France, though less clear-cut, made itself felt in Provence, where Amouretti and Maurras first called for independence in 1892, and also in Brittany and Corsica. In Spain the Catalans and the Basques fought vainly for their own language and for a separate state. In Germany, the Alsatians, the Lotharingians, the Danes, and above all the Poles in Posen and West Prussia struggled vainly against their oppressors, who in 1894 founded a special association to keep them in their places. It was called the *Ostmarkenverein*, and was led by Hansemann, Kennemann, and Tiedemann.[70] Of all these minorities, the Poles probably suffered most, divided as their country was between Germany, Austria-Hungary, and Russia. Their fate was much less arduous under the Danube monarchy, which played one national minority off against the next, protecting each in turn. Franz Josef's supra-national empire was a Europe in miniature. The Czechs, in particular, gave it no peace; and since Kramář's Young Czech Movement first appeared on the scene, they had been able to wrest one concession after another from their overlords: a Czech university in 1882; a Czech majority in the Bohemian Diet in 1883; the recognition of Czech as a semi-official language in 1886. Yet here, too, there was a strong backlash. In 1893 a state of siege was declared in Prague following a court ruling against the Czech Youth Movement; the jury system was abolished and so was the freedom of the press. When the Czechs resorted to parliamentary obstruction, they were obstructed in turn. Otto Lecher, a Sudeten German, spoke for twelve hours at a stretch to prevent the name of Brünn being changed to Brno. Even the moderate Mommsen sided with him.[71] In 1899 a Czech Academy of Science was founded, and soon afterward the Czechs, too, displayed the kind of nationalist aggression that had lately been so characteristic of oppressed nationalities: some of them laid claim to Lower Austria "for historical reasons."

It was in this seething atmosphere that Thomas Masaryk learned his politics; he was born in 1850, and, despite his age, was proclaimed the first president of the new republic when it was founded after the First World War.[72] Hungary, for her part, having been granted partial freedom in 1867, made certain that the Slovaks, Croats, Serbs, and Roumanians had no freedom at all. By a decree of 1891, Hungarian instruction was made compulsory even in nursery schools, and anti-Semitism among the subject people was partly due to the continued support the Hungarian Jewish bourgeoisie lent to this policy of "magyarization,"[73] a support that earned them little gratitude from their Hungarian "allies." In the Balkans, the newly awakened nationalities fought no less fiercely against one another than they fought against the vestiges of Turkish supremacy. Here the struggle for language and race went hand in hand with religious fervor, which far from assuaging the bitterness added to the dissensions. In Russia the Czar's hand continued to press down on all national minorities, whose list was as long as the Czar's arm was far-reaching. By 1899, members of the Finnish independence movement had been reduced to writing protests in exile, and their country had become a Russian satellite. The Ukrainians scattered through Russia, Poland, and Austria-Hungary were no better off; their oppression grew fiercer all the time until the revolution of 1905 brought them — and the Finns as well — temporary surcease. Things were no better for the White Russians, the Lithuanians, the Estonians, the Latvians, the Georgians, and the Armenians, not to mention the Czar's countless oriental subjects.[74]

Every sentence devoted to the epic struggle of the European minorities at the turn of the century would have to be extended into a page, and every page into a book, to give the reader even a vague idea of its poignancy and complexity. That struggle was both a groping search for new forms and also a reversion to the old; it aroused hundreds of thousands from their sleep of ages, even while dooming tens of thousands to eternal sleep. It was a struggle that, with all its triumphs and tragedies, was nevertheless no more than one chapter in the history of neo-nationalism, a movement that tried to base itself on science and ended up as rank superstition. Two of its great aspirations — pan-Germanism and pan-Slavism — were honored with names, but others reflecting the hopes of pan-Anglo-Saxons and pan-Latinists remained anonymous, though no less pernicious. All of them were based on vague racial stirrings, and provided grist for the mills of the wider chauvinism of the Great Powers, who, though they thought these stirrings of little account, would nevertheless parade them, whenever necessary, to spread fear among their own enemies.[75] Europe was living in a fog of national arrogance covering a vast sea of individual and social despair. While Europe presented a calm front, underneath it was quivering with fear of the future.

In October 1900, Thomas Masaryk, the great humanitarian scholar, wrote an article for his paper, *Čas.* "Superstition," he declared, "turns the heart of the nation into stone, and affects its brain and vision. This process will serve future historians as a yardstick of the civilization and morality not only of the Bohemian nation but of present-day society as a whole; it is the cultural hallmark of the dying nineteenth century."[76] He wrote these sentences on the occasion of the Polna ritual murder trial, which he rightly considered a blot on civilization. So great was his faith in progress, however, that he blamed the trial on the "dying nineteenth century." The fact that it never occurred to him to blame it on the century about to be born was perhaps more characteristic than anything else of the mental climate that prevailed in the year 1900. This rider may seem trivial, but, in fact, covers a whole world of illusion.

Nationalism is the curse of the twentieth century.

CHAPTER VIII

THE GREAT ILLUSION

The July 1900, issue of the *Journal des Economistes*[1] contained an article by Frederich Passy on the "heritage of the nineteenth century." Its author demanded an "August 4" for humanity. Much as the French nobility had, in the name of duty, renounced all its privileges on that day in 1789, so Europe must, at the dawn of the new century, forswear the national privilege of going to war. If she did not, the scepter of civilization would certainly pass to others across the sea, men who devoted themselves to life and not to death. Passy finished with Michelet's claim that France would declare peace on the world in the twentieth century.

Passy did not live to see the First World War. He was nearly eighty when he wrote the article, a staunch pacifist who shared the first Nobel Peace Prize with Henri Dunant in 1901. In 1867, he had founded the Peace League, which changed its name but not its aims in 1889, and also the Interparliamentary Union for Peace and Arbitration, in which he was ably assisted by William Cremer, who was awarded the Nobel Peace Prize in 1903. The Union held its tenth congress on July 31– August 2, 1900, in the Luxembourg Palace, to coincide with the Great Exposition. The deliberations were opened on behalf of the French Government by the Keeper of the Great Seal and were chaired by Fallières, President of the Senate.[2] Passy had good reason to be satisfied; the day when the friends of peace, in their impotence, evoked nothing but contempt or pity, or when Abel Hermant's famous anarchist antiwar novel, *Le Cavalier Miserey*, was greeted with nothing but mockery, seemed long past.

The cause of peace, by contrast, seemed clearly on the ascendant, the more so as the World Peace Congress, held on September 30– October 5, 1900 in the Great Congress Hall of the Exposition (right next to the Army and Navy Pavilion), was attended by some 400 delegates from Peace Leagues all over the world. Passy himself was its honorary president. Millerand delivered the opening address, and the famous physiologist, Charles Richet, was in the chair. Moreover, the first Inter-

113

national Peace Conference in The Hague, held the year before, had finally agreed to set up an international court of arbitration. True, this World Peace Congress was forced to reprove the signatories of The Hague treaty for their apparent lack of haste in fulfilling their contractual obligations, and to acknowledge that the wars in South Africa and China and the massacre in Armenia were painful and disturbing events, but Rome had not been built in a day, still less the glorious new city of peace!

In any case, no one had condemned the South African war more harshly than the British delegate to the Congress, at which Bloch had, moreover, proved once and for all that modern wars were no longer worth fighting.[3]

Ivan, Johann, or Jean de Bloch, who had started life as a poor Polish Jew but had made his fortune as a banker, had decided to devote the last years of his life — he died in 1902 — to the cause of peace. Unlike Nobel and Carnegie, he contributed not only money but also his intellect and energy. In 1898, the six volumes of his great *The Technical, Economic and Political Aspects of Future War* were published in St. Petersburg; a German translation followed in 1899, a French translation in 1900. W. T. Stead, the indefatigable English pacifist who had founded the *Review of Reviews* in 1890 for the express purpose of popularizing the cause of internationalism, wrote a preface to the English translation of the sixth, synoptic volume, and so well was it received that a second impression was brought out in 1900. An anonymous Dutch translator produced useful abstracts of the work in 1899. Bloch's was thus a famous book, and it was even said that it caused the Czar to publish the peace manifesto that eventually led to The Hague conference. Admittedly, others claimed that the real cause of the Czar's manifesto was the Congress held in Budapest, of which the Russian consul had sent extremely favorable reports to Muravyov, the Russian Minister of Foreign Affairs; or that the credit must go to Count Witte, the Russian Minister of Finance, who saw his country slipping behind in the arms race, and therefore championed peace. Still, these different causes did not necessarily exclude one another and, in any case, Bloch's monumental work provided the peace movement not only with emotional and religious arguments, but also with rational foundations that its opponents could not easily shrug off. With a wealth of data, most of them taken from German military historians, Bloch showed that such recent inventions as the quick-firing gun, smokeless gunpowder, lyddite, melinite, and nitroglycerine had so strengthened the powers of defense that any war between determined opponents was bound to end in a stalemate. In addition,

114

any future war would drag on for so long that the number of victims and also the costs would reach intolerable levels, unless — and this alternative probably made the greatest impression on Bloch's readers — war made way for social revolution. While his claims, re-echoed in Mendeleev's dictum, that the desire to wage war is in direct proportion to the range of the weapons with which it is being waged,[4] may be challenged by the modern reader, the massive sacrifices in money and life claimed by the Boer War two years after the appearance of his book certainly seemed to prove Bloch right in the short run, as he himself noted in the *Review of Reviews*.[5] Moreover, the Russo-Japanese War, and to some extent the First World War and the Russian Revolution of 1917, and even the Second World War, also confirmed rather than refuted his thesis.

As well as being the author of this message, Bloch was its chief apostle. During the World Peace Congress he depicted the misery and the cost of future wars on thirty-two large plates, graphic demonstrations of horrors with which we are only too familiar now but which at the time were merely portents of the future: trench warfare, barbed wire entanglements, huge warships, together with tables and graphs of the costs, casualties, epidemics, and so on. According to the Italian General Türr, one of Garibaldi's brothers-in-arms who later became a pacifist, this impressive display of plates and tables was aptly called "The Armed Peace." The *Journal des Economistes*, to which Passy had contributed the article we mentioned at the beginning of this chapter, was so impressed that it published a comprehensive account of Bloch's exhibits in its September edition.

Bloch was ably seconded by Baroness Bertha von Suttner, née Countess Kinsky, who was to receive the Nobel Peace Prize in 1905, and whose *Die Waffen nieder* ("Lay Down Your Arms") made her famous almost overnight. On February 5, 1900, she gave a Munich audience a soberly modest account of the ethical and rational basis of her work for peace.[6] She was also the semi-official center of attraction at The Hague Peace Conference, which she described at some length both in her memoirs and in another book. In 1892 she had founded her own paper, which bore the title of her novel. In it, as well as in Alfred Fried's *Friedenswarte*, founded in 1899, and in many other newspapers established in the eighties, she continued, until her death on the eve of the catastrophe against which she had fought so bravely, to comment on the daily fortunes of war and peace. Two large tomes bear witness to her indefatigable zeal.[7] It was Bertha von Suttner who in 1900 was the first to tell the story of Crook, the editor of the *English Echo*, who had resigned his post

115

rather than support the Boer War in the paper's columns. A banquet in his honor was attended by 200 leading British intellectuals. Lord Coleridge delivered the after-dinner speech, and Herbert Spencer sent his tribute by telegram.[8] Those present, as the Baroness was quick to point out, were not drawn merely from the middle classes: the Labour Union, precursor of the Labour Party, was also represented, and Keir Hardie, MacDonald, Glasier, and Snowden were to play a very active part in the "Stop the War" movement,[9] even going to prison for the cause.

How intensively Bertha von Suttner followed everything with the slightest bearing on the movement may be gathered from the list of subjects on which she commented during that May of 1900. She reported that Irishmen sympathetic to the Boers had set fire to two Canadian towns, but explained that the real blame lay with Chamberlain, who had kindled the fires of war, and with those who had failed to put them out: "with you and me." She noted that Boer deputations had been turned away by all the European powers they had approached. The militarists were saying that England could not possibly draw back now, and a sheepish press repeated that slogan. On May 6, she published a long account of the celebrations to mark the eighteenth birthday of the German Crown Prince. By parades, tattoos, sharpshooting trials, the demonstration of a new howitzer that could hit a covered target, the playing of the "Radetzky March" (thirty-two years later, Joseph Roth was to reconstruct the decline of the Dual Monarch in a brilliant book with that title) — that was how his future duties were presented to a youth who had only just reached manhood. Yet an inspired leader-writer of a Viennese newspaper had seen fit to call these festivities "a true peace congress"! During the first anniversary of The Hague conference — on May 18 — the Baroness pointed out that the conference was no longer mentioned in political speeches or in newspapers, and that those in high office were obviously trying to shelve the ratification of the treaty. She called on men of goodwill in and out of parliament to break this conspiracy of silence. Exaggerated optimism was not a fault of hers: one day later, Russia ratified all the clauses of the treaty, and half a year later the rest of the world, apart from Turkey and China, had followed suit. The fact that the treaty placed no obligations on any of the signatories was, incidentally, one reason for this belated show of good will. The baroness also wrote a commentary on Chamberlain's proclamation of the annexation of the two Boer republics. With bitter irony she added that people continued to question the need for a peace movement now that wars of conquest were things of the past. She took Lord Salisbury, the British Prime Minister, severely to task for declaring, during a Primrose

League Banquet, that not only the Boers but the Irish, too, could never be granted their independence. "We are only as safe as we are strong," he had added on that occasion, implying that there was no safety at all for the weak. But since the protection of the weak and oppressed was the true measure of civilization, Lord Salisbury's remark could only mean that he had turned his back on humanity. Small wonder that the rest of the world had condemned England, in a wave of indignation the noble Lord alone found inexplicable. Fifty, thirty, or even ten years earlier, the Boer War would not have caused anything like the revulsion it produced now that so much had been printed and spoken about it, not least by the English themselves, including Lord Salisbury. A few days later a howitzer was being paraded before the Emperor Franz Josef in Güterbog. The *Berliner Nachrichten* extolled its merits, and congratulated the Austrian artillery on its choice of this fine new weapon. Bertha von Suttner replied by telling her readers that a Hungarian deputy, a member of the Interparliamentary Union, had urged the Chamber to eschew short-term cures for the immediate political situation, which might change as the weather, and to work instead for the adoption of an agreed international code of conduct. The world could only enjoy the blessings of true peace if it put an end to the "armed peace" in which it lived and which lay like a curse over Europe. That this Hungarian deputy was a figment of the Baroness's imagination was something she thought her readers would grasp without further explanation. She predicted that by the end of the month the hostilities in the Transvaal would draw to a bitter close. When, much later, incidentally, than she had foretold, they did end, she noted that the Lord of Hosts had failed to carry the cause of freedom to its just conclusion as the Boers had been certain He would. However, perhaps people throughout the world had now learned the lesson that all wars were bloody and brutish and that no divine blessing rested on murder. Yes, Bertha von Suttner, too, believed in divine providence but, to her mind, God had intended His creatures for higher things than battle — for the clash of minds, not of guns.[10]

Ivan Bloch and Bertha von Suttner, though two of the leading champions of peace in their day, were by no means lone voices. Fried appended a "Who's Who in the Peace Movement" to the second volume of his *Handbook*.[11] In it he listed about three hundred well-known names, followed by a systematic guide to the relevant literature, which covered twenty-six pages and made it clear that this period was the heyday of bourgeois pacifism.[12] For the years 1893–1912, the guide included no fewer than twenty-five books devoted to the history of the arms race.

During these very years, history itself entered a new phase, masterfully described in Beales's *History of Peace*.[13] International co-operation spread to all spheres of human endeavor, with the sole exception of politics. Interdependence had become a recognized moral desideratum and proved a powerful lever against the irrational belief in the benefits of isolation. Peace, people began to realize, was not merely the absence of war, but also the creation of a durable and just international forum in which individual states could settle their differences amicably. The resulting arbitration movement was fed by the persistence of wars no less than by the growth of democracy in Europe and America, which to all intents and purposes constituted the entire "civilized" world — even as late as 1931 when Beales wrote his book. Above all, however, the spread of internationalism no less than the use of increasingly murderous weapons was the direct result of the development of speedier means of transportation and communication. In any case, Beales was right to claim that internationalism had made great headway by 1900, in the private no less than in the public sector. Workers, Freethinkers, Esperantists, and women all boasted peace organizations of their own and held regular international congresses — the Freethinkers beginning in 1880, and the Esperantists in 1905. The number of such congresses increased: from 469 in the nineties to 1,082 in the first decade of the new century.[14] International co-operation, which had always existed in the religious field, was extended to culture and sport, with a host of international exhibitions and the revival of the Olympic Games. While international trade contacts may not have been new in themselves, they had never before been as intense, with the armaments industry setting the pace.

International co-operation between governments, too, was growing. There was an international postal union; various states co-operated in railway projects, in the distribution of electricity, in protecting copyrights, in agriculture, in laying submarine cables, and in maintaining lighthouses and buoys.[15] The most striking development of all, however, was the increase in the number of arbitration agreements. Between 1794, when Great Britain and the United States signed the Jay Treaty, and the year 1900, 177 similar treaties had been signed, 90 of them during the last twenty years. While it is quite true that most of the disputes settled by international arbitration were so small that one almost has to search for them in history books with a magnifying glass,[16] the fact that none of them led to war, as otherwise many might have done, was justification enough for the new procedure.

The most important development, despite all the objections to it that were raised at the time and that can be still raised today, was the official Peace Conference which opened on May 18, 1899 — the Czar's

118

birthday — in the Huis ten Bosch in The Hague and continued until July 29. The twenty-six governments represented — to placate Britain, the Boer republics had not been invited, and the Curia had been excluded so as not to upset Italy — did not, as everyone agreed, achieve a great deal.[17] Indeed, their deliberations were more concerned with war than with peace. The proposed arms limitation treaties were conveniently allowed to lapse, and the permanent arbitration court which was eventually established had no bite to it. Even so, the whole idea was bitterly opposed, particularly by the German delegate, Professor Stengel, who did no more than say in plain German what many other delegates were thinking in their own languages. Good nationalists that they all were, they considered any advance commitment to international arbitration an infringement of their sovereign rights, and national sovereignty was their dogma of dogmata. Worse still, arbitration could be used by opponents to gain time while preparing for war. Its failures notwithstanding, the Conference was of great historical importance, if only because it had taken place at all.[18] It was and remains the first step on the road to the creation of the kind of supra-national organization that would seem so desirable twenty years later, and so indispensable after a further twenty-five years.

The ablest exponent of the federative idea was the Russian sociologist, Jakov Alexandrovich Novikov. His intellectual development was the more remarkable because, although he ended as one of its severist critics, he started his academic career as a Social Darwinist — much like Benjamin Kidd, whose *Social Evolution* (1894) sold some 250,000 copies, and Karl Pearson, who was to achieve fame in 1900 with his *National Life from the Standpoint of Science*. Thus, as early as 1894, Novikov declared in his *La Guerre et ses prétendus bienfaits* that "the popular masses have not been improved by wars of conquest, and this despite the fact that the masses themselves believe the contrary." The Spanish-American War next persuaded him to write his *La Fédération de l'Europe*, in which he set out all the pro-war arguments with controlled passion and deep seriousness, weighed them and found them wanting. The only alternative was a federation of all mankind. In 1900 he published *Der ewige Krieg* ("Eternal War"), a pamphlet written for the express purpose of refuting Stengel's *Der ewige Friede* ("Eternal Peace"). Together with Bloch, he may be said to have paved the way for a book to which Norman Lane, then still a gold prospector and a journalist, would one day owe his world renown and Nobel Prize (1933). That book was *The Great Illusion*,[19] and it sold more than a million copies. Norman Lane had by then become Norman Angell, and the great illusion he exposed was that war was profitable to the victors. For his pacifist ideals, Angell was prepared not only to fight but also to suffer: he spent several years in prison during the First World War.

Alfred Bernhard Nobel was another convert to the cause of peace, possibly under the influence of Bertha von Suttner, who had worked with him for a time, or perhaps because his business acumen had taught him the advantages of international co-operation. The Nobel Dynamite Trust Company Limited, into which he combined all his British and German dynamite factories in 1886 — the first trust and the forerunner of the mighty Imperial Chemical Industries and of the even more famous (or infamous) I. G. Farbenindustrie — was far from absorbing all his time and energy. Through his brother, he also participated in the development of the Russian petroleum industry in Baku, and he would even have joined his other interests to the large-scale manufacture of guns — he took over Bofors in 1894 — had he not died first. Oddly enough, the deadly nature of his business did not prevent him, both during his life and after his death, from rendering financial as well as moral support to the peace movement.[20]

Andrew Carnegie, an American industrialist of Scottish descent, followed much the same path. Once he had acquired a fortune of more than a quarter of a billion dollars in railways and steel, he retired from business and looked around for the best way of investing the forty million dollars he had decided to set aside for the good of mankind. To that end, he spent a great deal of trouble and energy, for he firmly believed that riches should be spent with greater wisdom, and to better effect, than had gone into their accumulation. Stead has described this quest in *Mr. Carnegie's Conundrum* (1899). Carnegie put his problem to many experts, including Fiodor Fiodorovich Martens, a professor in constitutional law and a well-known diplomat who had represented Russia at two Peace Conferences in The Hague. The professor advised the building of a Peace Palace and mentioned the matter to Andrew D. White, American ambassador in Berlin and leader of the U. S. delegation to the 1899 Peace Conference. In June 1900, White urged Carnegie to take Professor Martens's advice and though Carnegie felt little enthusiasm for the project at first, he nevertheless agreed in the end.[21] The Palace, designed by the French architect Cordonnier, and modified by the Dutch architect van der Steur, was completed in 1913. During the opening ceremony, C. von Vollenhoven called for an international police force, army and navy, and Ludwig Quidde for an arms limitation treaty.[22] Valuable gifts were donated to the Palace by many countries, including a fine library, directed for many years by Jacob Ter Meulen, who also served the peace movement with his *Der Gedanke der internationalen Organisa-tion in seiner Entwicklung* ("The Development of the Idea of Inter-national Organization").[23]

How was it possible that despite all these keen demonstrations of pacific intent, the Peace Palace should have given the impression of being nothing so much as a fairy-tale castle still awaiting the arrival of the Prince to awaken the beautiful Princess? In retrospect, the whole peace movement looks unreal, for no sooner was it at its height than the First World War broke out. Was peace, not war, the "great illusion," after all? Or was there something real about all this unreality; was it merely the shadow that clings to all great ideals? Or was it perhaps a sign that Europe had advanced sufficiently to toy with the ideal of peace but not yet far enough to implement it? Or, finally, was the Labor Movement correct when, from the Anarchists to the Revisionists, it looked upon war as the inevitable consequence of capitalism and imperialism, and hence thought it pointless to fight against what it considered a symptom of a much more serious disease?

Yet, despite this argument, part, at least, of the Labor Movement was deeply involved in the fight for peace. That part was imbued with religious ideals, albeit in secular form. Not only Domela Nieuwenhuis's pamphlets against militarism, written in 1901, but also the Rev. G. F. Haspes's *De Weerloosheid* (Passive Resistance), published that same year in response to a competition organized by the Stolpiaan Bequest on the urgings of such Tolstoyans as Bähler and van der Veer, and the Rev. Adin Ballou's *Christian Non-resistance*, first published half a century earlier, and reprinted at the turn of the century, were widely read in left-wing labor circles. They also took a keen interest in the case of the German conscientious objector, Dr. H. Welzel, who, in 1905, justified his pacifism with a whole series of anarchist arguments culled from the great of all ages — from the Taoists to Tolstoy.[24] Tolstoy himself had a large number of adherents in pacifist circles: Biryukov, Tregubov, and the two Chertkovs in Russia, and in Austria Eugen H. Schmitt — a man whose examination of the cultural basis of the Christian dogmas was banned in 1901. There were prominent Tolstoyans among the Bulgarian pacifists[25] no less than among the Dutch contingent, which included, apart from Bähler and van der Veer, such well-known figures as Lode-wijk van Mierop, Felix Ortt, and Professor J. van Rees. Anarchists and trade unionists were equally loud in their anti-militarist protestations, and in 1901 the trade unions held an antiwar congress in London.

Only the Social Democrats, who had a more solid theoretical ground-ing, took the line we mentioned earlier: they considered it futile to fight against war as such, rather than against capitalism. Keir Hardie of the Independent Labour Party, who advocated the general strike as an anti-war weapon during the congress of the Second International in Copenhagen (1910),[26] and Gustav Hervé, a vociferous anti-militarist — at least until 1914 — were marked exceptions. However, even they believed that war was an inevitable concomitant of capitalism. The subject was discussed at length in Paris in 1900, and again in Amsterdam in 1904. In 1907 — while the second Peace Conference was meeting in The Hague — the problem of war and peace and the colonial question were the two most important subjects raised at the Stuttgart International Labor Congress, the first and also the last to be held in Germany. That congress was deeply influenced by the continuing reverberations of the Russian Revolution of 1905. Its radical resolution on militarism and international conflicts was a carefully framed compromise between three French resolutions proposed respectively by Hervé, Guesde, and Jaurès-Vaillant, and a German resolution proposed by Bebel, to which Rosa Luxemburg, Lenin, and Martov had added five amendments. The compromise stood in the name of Vandervelde; and when it was adopted by acclamation during the last day of the congress, the delegates waved their handkerchiefs in a burst of enthusiasm. It was the longest resolution ever adopted by an international congress,[27] and while it referred to the "serious practice of international arbitration," and the "benefits of general disarmament," its real importance lay in the affirmation that "all means deemed appropriate by the parties" must be used in the struggle against war. These means — the general strike and the refusal to do army service among them — were not, however, mentioned by name. More important still, at least in retrospect, was Lenin's amendment calling on international socialists to make war a stepping-stone toward the social revolution; we may take it that the future founder of the Soviet state had read his Bloch as well as his Marx. Just as the Russian leader was in earnest with his final amendment, so Jaurès was in earnest with his central resolution. Seven years later he was to seal the spirit of Stuttgart with his death.

The enthusiasm of the delegates did not impress historians. Van Ravensteyn called it an illusion, if not worse,[28] and Charles Andler considered Stuttgart the preparation for the shipwreck of one of the greatest hopes the world has ever entertained.[29] Drachkovitch spoke more soberly of the "ambiguous radicalism" of Stuttgart.[30] But though the Social Democrats kept their Stuttgart promises no better than the promises they made in Basel five years later, that does not mean that these promises were illusory or made in bad faith. Lenin, for one, stuck to his guns, and fifty years later not even his bitterest enemy, indeed he least of all, would have called the Soviet Union an illusion.

After one great illusion came another — after the illusion of peace, the illusion of war. There is one type of history that, by and large, is printed in the newspapers, though not in the most important ones, and another that, by and large, is not. The activities of the friends of peace was of the first type; those of the armament manufacturers of the second. Nevertheless, both were part of history, and this chapter would be sadly incomplete if it made no mention of the arms industry, if only to provide a picture of the obstacles in the path of the peace movement. Not that the war industry is unworthy of consideration by itself. In particular, it helped to develop those new techniques and methods that made the twentieth century so different from all its predecessors; it also helped to usher in those new economic structures that will be the subject of a later chapter. We cannot tell even today which of the two — the men of peace or the weapons of war — will prevail in the end.

In 1899, the arms race was begun in earnest. In his carefully researched *Militarismus und Antimilitarismus*, published during the year of the Stuttgart Congress, Karl Liebknecht, basing his work on figures taken from the *Nouveau manuel du soldat*, showed that war preparations were costing Europe some $1,240 million in 1899.[31] According to the *Nouveau manuel*, a conservative source, the six great European powers *alone* were spending roughly that amount on war preparations in 1899, and by 1913 they had increased that figure to nearly two billion dollars.[32] Needless to say, with the approach of war this expenditure was stepped up even more dramatically. Thus, while the *Nouveau manuel* put the military expenditure of Britain, France, and Italy at 930 million dollars in 1913, a third source put it at $1,191 million in 1913–1914.[33] By themselves these figures only tell half the story or even less, for they do not include the loss of production caused by the absence from work of the many conscripts.

Those who gained most from these billions were Krupp in Germany, Vickers-Armstrong in Britain, Schneider-Creusot in France, Cockerill in Belgium, the Skoda Company in Bohemia, and the Putilov Company in Russia. In their defense, we might point out that they were more interested in the arms race than in war as such. Yet quite apart from the fact that none of them went out of its way to promote peace and goodwill among men, their claim that by manufacturing "deterrents" they were in fact serving the cause of peace was altogether spurious: if military history proves anything, it is precisely that the accumulation of arms leads to war. Every move by Sir John Fisher (later Lord Fisher of Kilver-stone) evoked a countermove by Admiral von Tirpitz, and so on; and the resulting escalation was often helped along by the skillful machinations of the arms suppliers. The closer they were to the seats of power, the greater was their nefarious influence. The German naval program of 1900 provoked an appropriate response in Britain and Russia; the British response provoked the Germans, the French, and the Russians; the Russian response provoked the Japanese, the French, and the Italians, and so it went. During the first Morocco crisis, Britain launched her first dreadnought; and when the Russian fleet was nearly wiped out during the Japanese war, German, French, and British arms manufacturers vied with one another to rebuild it. Moreover, Ballin of the Hamburg-America Line sent a special agent to Russia as early as 1903, just as soon as he realized a war was approaching. As a result, he was able to fob off his antiquated ships, and also came away with a contract to supply the coal for them. The profit from the last transaction was 22 million marks in 1904, and 38 million marks in 1905.[34] The same gentlemen were also past masters in the art of creating panic. Thus the Deutsche Waffen- und Munitionsfabriken in Karlsruhe, which specialized in the manufacture of machine guns, "persuaded" the Paris *Figaro* to publish an article informing its readers that the French High Command had decided to double the number of machine guns. The idea was to make the German Government more "machine-gun minded," and, in fact, between 1908 and 1910 the German nation spent 40 million marks on these weapons, causing the dividends of the firm to leap from 20% to 32%.[35] In 1908, Mulliner of the Coventry Ordnance Works, part of the John Brown consortium, was able to fool the British Government into thinking that the German naval construction program was twice as great as it really was, where-upon the British program was doubled;[36] and the arms manufacturers made a good thing out of it — the profit on a single dreadnought was £250,000.[37] In the Balkans, Sir Basil Zaharoff sold the first serviceable submarine to his Greek compatriots; and soon afterward he sold two more to their arch-enemies, the Turks.[38]

All these machinations, however, were isolated incidents; the real and insuperable strength of the armament kings lay, and lies, not in trickery, however indispensable it may have been and still is, but in the sheer size of their industry and its international ramifications. Shortly after the end of the First World War, Wehberg estimated the capital of Armstrong and Vickers at 400 million marks; that of the ten next largest companies at 480 million; that of the three largest French arms concerns — Creusot, Aciéries de la Marine Homécourt, and Châtillon-Commentry

— at 320 million; and that of Krupp at 180 million (the last figure was, if anything, much too low since, even in 1902, the private fortune of Fritz Krupp, as submitted to the tax office, was put at 187 million marks,[39] and capitalists are not in the habit of exaggerating their fortunes to the revenue office). These figures add up to a grand total of 1,380 million marks, and this type of investment rarely yielded less than 10%.[40] Liebknecht said that the size of these dividends was in direct proportion to the spread of hatred among the nations. We might add that it was also directly proportional to the degree of co-operation among the arms manufacturers, both nationally and internationally. In the field of national co-operation, the Dortmund Marine Verständigungskonzern (Marine Alliance) made certain that none of its affiliated companies signed independent contracts. Moreover, before passing an order to any of these companies, the Alliance added a 10% surcharge, which was shared out among the rest.[41] In the international field, things could not be worked as smoothly as that; but though competition rendered co-operation more difficult, it in no way prevented it. Here the main rivals were the makers of guns and the makers of armor plate — an instructive example of human logic and also of human stupidity and crime. This rivalry was greatly attenuated in 1901–1903, when the United Harvey Steel Company provided the greatest armor and gun manufacturers with an institution in which they could happily merge their conflicting interest; the list, to mention only the most famous, included Armstrong and Vickers, Schneider-Creusot, Krupp, the Dillinger-Hütte, the Società degli Alti Forni Fondiere Acciaine di Terri, and Bethlehem Steel Limited, each with its own affiliates, including the Skoda and Putilov Works, the Spanish Naval Construction Establishments, and even a Portuguese naval construction syndicate.[42] Co-operation was not confined to the distribution of iron and steel, but also covered nickel, copper, aluminum, rubber, coal, nitrogen, and later even petroleum — nothing with the slightest connection to war was allowed to slip through the net. No wonder that, in the Russo-Japanese War, both sides were fired upon with identical cannons supplied by Krupp, or that ten years later the Turks could kill British soldiers with British guns, while the Austrian field pieces supplied to Russia mowed down Austrian soldiers in Galicia. But, then, the tears of the victims' mothers had the same composition as well, and few of them were wise enough to accept the arms manufacturers' irrefutable argument that only by supplying arms to potential enemies could the arms industry stay in business and supply the home market.

Europe was drifting toward war. There were a few who saw it, and most of these were critics of the established order. Max Nordau was one of them. On January 1, 1914, the *Neue Freie Presse* published his general survey.[43] He concluded it with the following observation: "Europe looks like a nightmare. The whole continent is covered with training camps, barracks, millions of men armed to the teeth, men on foot, on horse, on bicycles, in motor cars and in the air; the sea is teeming with dreadnoughts, super-dreadnoughts, and submarines. Everywhere, national pride wells up in torrents and bursts the banks. Everywhere, taxes loom up like specters, like Faust's poodle, who appeared from behind the stove to grow ever larger and wider until it looked like a hippopotamus. Everywhere, war loans swallow up the fruits of productive labor; everywhere immeasurable cost increases render the life of the masses more onerous and careworn, and richer only in deprivation. Everywhere, enraged minorities defy a majority too timid to contradict them, with furious proclamations of their cannibal ideal of domination, of conquest, of the division of continents and, above all, of war, of glorious and holy war. In international dealings, morals have never played a part, but now even reason has been banished from them, so much so that those few who have kept their heads, gaze with horror at this mass delirium, and would dearly love to shut their eyes before the spectacle of civilized men rushing heedlessly toward an abyss of destruction . . ."

It is possible and even probable that most of the people who read this message in their favorite paper did not allow it to disturb their equanimity and, in any case, considered it grossly exaggerated. They might well have recalled it six months later, when one great illusion, that of peace, had made way for another — that of war. Clearly, men cannot live without illusions.

CHAPTER IX

LET CANDLES BE BROUGHT IN

On Monday, June 21, 1900 at 10 A.M., G. Cauchy graduated from the
University of Paris with a thesis entitled *L'Organisation de suffrage
politique*,[1] a subject that had begun to engage the attention of many
of his contemporaries. Charles Benoist, too, devoted much time and
effort to the extension of the suffrage. On February 2, 1900, he delivered
a lecture on the subject in Paris, followed by another in Lyons fourteen
days later, and a third in Reims one month after that.[2] He had first
broached the subject in 1891, in his *Croquis parlementaires* written under
the nom-de-plume of Sybil, and again in 1892, in his *Sophismes politiques
de ce temps*. He even flattered himself into thinking that the widespread
use of the word "sophism" by his contemporaries was due to the impact
of his own writings.[3] And, indeed, as editor of *Le Temps* and the *Revue
des Deux Mondes*, he had acquired an influential voice. His views on
parliamentarianism in general and the burning question of the franchise
in particular were summed up in his *Crise de l'état moderne*, the first
part of which appeared in 1897, and on the rest of which he continued
to work until his death in 1936.[4]

It is not an exaggeration to say that at the turn of the century the
parliamentary idea was being challenged from all quarters. We have met
some of its sharpest French critics; their list also included Ferneuil and
Lebon (1894), Bonghi and d'Eichtal (1895), Graux and Picot (1898),
and Thuillier, who wrote a thesis on the subject in 1899.[5] In 1901, an
idea expressed in the French constitution of 1791 was resurrected: that
no parliamentary candidate could serve for more than one term of office.
On March 8, Gelle, a deputy from the Somme Department, moved a
resolution to that effect, and though it aroused little enthusiasm at the
time, Morin and Villey revived the idea in 1910. A year later Mlle. J.
Sabatier wrote a thesis on the subject. She was close to the Ligue Républicaine de Moralité Publique, founded that same year by C. Sabatier,
her father, and Abelons. Charles Gide was among its champion.[6] And
we have not mentioned the names of those who were antiparliamentarian
in principle, such monarchists or anarchists as de Vogüé (*Les Morts qui*

parlent, of 1899); Zola's friend and admirer Paul Alexis (Vallobra); Abel Hermant; Léon Daudet, Barrès, Mirbeau; or Sébastien Faure and Jean Grave, whose *La Société mourante et l'anarchie* (1893) re-echoed Rousseau's view that the sovereign people had no need of any form of "representation." Finally, there were the democratic antiparliamentarians, including Micelli, who published a sensational article on the "tyranny of the chamber,"[7] and Scipio Sighele in Italy.[8]

What we have here was not just a clash of opinions but also a clash of men with all the bitterness that entailed. The riots in Fourmies on May 1, 1891, claimed ten dead, two of them children aged 11 and 13. Paul Lafargue was sentenced for his part in the affair; but in November when his supporters elected him deputy for Lille in protest against the authorities, he was set at liberty. "The victims of Fourmies revenged," was Rochefort's ironic comment in *La Révolte*. "Will the voters have to be gunned down in future before they go to the polling booth?"[9]

Nor was this criticism confined to France. In Belgium, a country that had pioneered parliamentary democracy on the Continent, Jules Destrée delivered on October 14, 1901, a lengthy and thoughtful lecture on the "end of parliamentarianism,"[10] He told his audience that complaints about parliament were rife, not only in every parliamentary country, but also in every party, so much so that it was true to say that this particular form of government had begun to crumble at its very foundations.[11] That same year Zenker published a pamphlet in Vienna in which he spoke of the bankruptcy of parliament,[12] a phrase he repeated in 1914.[13] In 1904, F. Norikus claimed that parliamentarianism was in a decline, indeed on the point of collapse,[14] and, like Destrée, he was neither the last nor the first to say so. As early as 1898, E. L. Godkin, an American, had explained in his *Unforeseen Tendencies of Democracy* that complaints about legislators were widespread in every country with a parliamentary form of government.[15]

What precisely were these complaints? They were of different types and often contradictory, as invariably happens with institutions in a state of crisis and, moreover, under attack from every side. De Laveleye listed a number of them in 1882 and again in 1887. He spoke of instability all round: ministries were too short-lived to take stock of what had to be done — in France alone there had been eighteen Ministers of War and fourteen Ministers of Foreign Affairs within fifteen years; constant shifts in the alliances of the various parliamentary groups meant that no single ministry was ever assured of a majority; there was constant sacrifice of the national to party interest; a parliamentary system could only function smoothly if two clearly distinct and highly organized parties took turns in office, which was no longer the case in Belgium or elsewhere. Moreover, even if it had been, the party spirit would have triumphed, riding roughshod over every principle and thwarting all new ideas, all independent institutions, and all serious reforms. Without strong parties, however, there was bound to be national impotence and chaos. And wherever these two problems had been solved, as for instance in the United States, which had adopted despotic committee rule, or in Switzerland, which had adopted the referendum, the parliamentary system existed in name only.[16]

One complaint not mentioned by de Laveleye, but nevertheless voiced repeatedly at the time, was that parliament, though originally designed as an economic watchdog, had, by currying favor with the voters, become a spendthrift: the state squandered vast sums of money on higher wages in the protected industries and in the public sector. This charge was made by Paul Leroy-Beaulier in 1886, by Vaudal in 1897, and by Michon in 1898.[17] The extension of the franchise — in Italy in 1882, in Britain in 1884 and 1885, in the Netherlands in 1887 and 1896 — and a fortiori the introduction of the general franchise — in France and in Spain in 1890, in Belgium in 1893, in Norway in 1898, in Germany and soon afterwards in Hungary in 1905, and in Austria in 1907 — only seemed to make matters worse. Max Weber called universal suffrage the "Danaidean gift of Bismarckian Caesarism."[18] The increase of the national debt through social contributions had by then become the conservatives' greatest nightmare.

Another objection not mentioned by de Laveleye, but more widespread than even the charge of profligacy, was to the growing incompetence of parliamentarians in tackling a whole series of tasks which they felt themselves qualified to handle. The results were derided by Kropotkin in his *Paroles d'un révolté* (1885), a book to which Elisée Reclus wrote the preface.[19] Kropotkin, the greatest anarchist of his age, claimed that the deputies had to voice opinions and cast votes on an infinitely varied range of topics. "They must decide on dog taxes without ever having kept a dog; on academic reform without ever having seen the inside of a university; on the qualities of a new gun or on the location of a state stud farm. They must vote on vine disease, artificial fertilizers, and tobacco; on Indo-China and Guiana; on chimneys and observatories. Without ever having seen a soldier, except on parade, they must create army corps; without ever having smelled an Arab, they must pronounce on land distribution in Algeria. They must decide the cut of uniforms and caps, and do so by relying on their wives' tastes. They must protect sugar and let wheat go by the board. They destroy the grape in the firm belief

129

that they are saving it. One day, they are in favor of re-afforestation and against meadowland; next day, they take the opposite stand; today they are for canals, tomorrow for railways, without the least idea where the canal must be dug or the railway line will run. They must be experts on banking, and add new clauses to the penal code without knowing anything about the rest. In short, each deputy must be a veritable Proteus, omniscient and omnipotent, today a soldier and tomorrow a pigman, successively a banker, an academician, a street sweeper, a doctor, astronomer, drug-manufacturer, tanner, or contractor according to the order of the day in parliament. . . . Accustomed in his capacity as lawyer, journalist, or public orator to speak of things he knows nothing of, he votes for all these and other questions as well."

how true!

Another list of grievances which, however, repeated all the old objections — those voiced by Rittinghausen halfway through the previous century, and by Girardin, Spencer, Lombroso, Sébastien Faure, and Octave Mirbeau, but also by Multatuli, Abraham Kuyper, and Troelstra — together with fresh criticisms based on the author's own parliamentary experiences in 1888–1891, was published by Domela Nieuwenhuis in 1906.[20] Fundamental also was the objection by Julius Ofner that parliamentarianism posed a grave threat to justice.[21]

Other criticisms were less basic, but real enough all the same, though many of them cancelled one another out. Thus some argued that deputies, once elected, ceased to care about their electors; while others maintained that the deputies were much more concerned with wooing their voters than with the general weal; and yet others contended that they cared neither for the voters nor for society at large, but only for their own pockets. While some blamed the deputies for their absenteeism, others complained that they were wasting their time in the Chamber when there were better things to do. Some said that parliament was too small for its manifold tasks; others, that it was too large to pass adequate laws. Some claimed that parliament was too strong; others that it was too impotent, kowtowing to capital, to the press, to secret diplomacy, or to the army, which, when it came to the crunch, always did as it pleased, parliament or no parliament. Some believed that parliament dispensed so much freedom that chaos was bound to ensue, while others claimed that parliament destroyed the very freedom it was meant to protect. They mentioned the continuous lies, the vicious rivalry, the deplorable venality, the miserable narrow-mindedness of the deputies, and the resulting scandals that occurred at regular intervals. Some of these critics blamed all on their political opponents or on certain individuals; others

130

— and they were the more reasonable - blamed the circumstances that made individuals what they were.

From all these objections we gain the impression that parliament was under particularly fierce attack at the turn of the century, when, in fact, similar criticisms had been voiced long before and would be voiced for a long time to come. The feeling of the time might be summed up as: parliament thinks it all-important, yet does nothing. Many of the critics mockingly recalled the old English saying that parliament could do everything except change a man into a woman, or the Arab saying: "I can hear grinding but I see no flour."

The historian, however, cannot leave it at that. He knows that every form of government has its critics and that parliamentary democracy could not expect to fare better. So after having examined the various objections, he must go on to look at the proposed cures; for the latter are a much clearer indication of the spirit of the times than most of the evils they were meant to eradicate.

For if parliament was sick, there was no lack of doctors to come to its aid. Some, as we saw, prescribed the non-renewability of a parliamentary mandate; others, the gradual extension of the suffrage to all sections of the population, though not yet generally to women. Still others advocated proportional representation as the best means of off-setting the loss of votes cast by minorities or even by majorities who, the distribution of seats being what it was, could fare second best in the polls, as happened during the Dutch elections in 1905.[22] Proportional representation was not merely being advocated by Professor Molengraaf in the *Hollandsche Revue*[23] but had already been introduced in five Swiss cantons (1892–1895) and also in Belgium (1899).

Some even advocated a multiple franchise on the Belgian model, or the compulsory vote, thus rejecting the old idea that voting was the free exercise of a natural right. Ritchie became the leading spokesman of this view.[24]

More egregious was the suggestion that various interests or professions should be represented corporatively. Oddly enough, it was the socialists who attached the greatest importance to this particular reform of the representative system. In Belgium, for instance, it was championed by Prins (1884), Hector Denis (1891), de Greef (1892), and above all by Emile Vandervelde (1892). Fournière (1887 and 1898), Jaurès and de Paape (1895), Destrée, and in the Netherlands van Kol, must also be included in this group, not least because they demanded the separation of the economic from the political executive. The corporative idea was also upheld by Kropotkin (1892), Merlino (1898), and Jean Grave (1899). George Sorel was another of its champions. In opposing the spread of state influence and in trying to liberate men from outworn political constraints, the Belgian reformers, he claimed, were true disciples of Marx.[25] Nor was the Right averse to the corporative idea, in which it saw a resurrection of the guild system of blessed feudal memory. This was particularly true of the Christian Social Party in Austria, and of its namesake in France where the message was clearly expressed by La Tour du Pin and then carried into parliament by the Count de Mun and into the streets by the eccentric Mazaroz.[26] In Germany, F. Norikus published his *Gegen den Strom* ("Against the Current") in 1904, a powerful plea for "vocational representation." He, too, was only one voice among many; Schäffle was another and his treatise the most important scientific document published by that entire school of thought.[27] By contrast, such orthodox Marxists as Kautsky held fast to the view that large countries needed centralized parliamentary institutions.[28] Destrée's objections failed to move him, though they did make him more aware of the authoritarian current in the German Social Democratic movement,[29] and caused him to reject the idea of direct popular legislation — another cure for parliamentary ills prescribed in certain socialist circles. It was not a new idea. Rittinghausen seems to have been the first to propose it, soon after he escaped to Paris following the collapse of the German revolution of 1848.[30] The subject was keenly debated by leading French socialists in the 1850s. Kautsky consigned it to the "inventory of the state of the future," which meant that he did not take it very seriously, though seriously enough to oppose it.[31] Esmein did likewise in 1896,[32] while Domela Niewenhuis considered the idea so worthwhile that he set it out at length ten years later.[33] Their interest is, moreover, not surprising. The idea of direct popular legislation was, after all, closely linked to another favorite idea of the times: that of the popular referendum.

It may seem odd that with so many objections and so many proposals for basic reforms, no parliament anywhere was abolished or even radically overhauled. The fact is, however, that that though criticism and plans for reform may undermine institutions, they cannot really transform, let alone destroy them in the absence of profound social changes that make such institutions redundant. And no such changes had occurred. Nineteenth-century parliamentarianism had grown up side by side with the bourgeoisie; and while that class continued in power, parliament remained the true symbol of its dominance. Hence all attempts at reform were strangled at birth with the perennial rejoinder: you may be right but what is the alternative?[34] True, the entry of the working class into parliament and the radically new demands its representatives put forward rendered the work of parliament more difficult; but it also added to its general authority, and helped to bind the working class more closely to the rest of the nation — as they grew stronger, the workers, far from growing more intractable, proved more and more adaptable. It was this very fact that ultimately saved parliament, just as it saved the life of its twin brother, liberalism. In the same way that a beam of light is diffracted by moving water, so the beam of liberalism was scattered by the flow of time, casting its refracted brightness over every field of human endeavor.

Nevertheless, the crisis of parliamentarianism to which this chapter is devoted was ultimately caused by the introduction of illiberal principles. The reason parliament had functioned so well until the beginning of our period was that what difference of opinion there had been until then had always involved two or more factions of the bourgeoisie — they might have disagreed about side issues, but they were always united on matters of real importance. An opposition, by contrast, that held fundamentally different views and was determined to bring these differences into the open threatened to bring the parliamentary machine to a standstill.[35]

This can be taken quite literally. Enrico Ferri, who delivered a lecture in the Brussels Volkshuis two weeks after Destrée had delivered his, pointed out that parliamentary minorities now wielded a new weapon in defense of freedom and justice: obstruction.[36] This weapon was, in fact, being used quite freely, both by way of raising points of order and also by ignoring procedure. Here, the old idea that the rights of minorities must be protected was extended into the absolute refusal to allow the expression of unwelcome opinions. It was used both by fervent socialists and even more so by fervent nationalists. Open discussion was the chief pillar of parliamentarianism,[37] but as soon as the chamber admitted bitter enemies of the regime as well as polite dissenters, parliamentary debates degenerated into farce. It had all started in the Mother of Parliaments with Parnell and his Irishmen in the 1880s; but in the Hungarian and Austrian parliaments, too, there were many who felt too strongly about their cause to play the parliamentary game. Thus Domela Nieuwenhuis reported, and not without some satisfaction, that one of the members of the Hungarian Parliament, after spitting at several of the ministers, had gone on to express his regret that he had not had enough spittle to cover them all.[38] In the Austrian Parliament, as well, nationalism was the mainspring of revolt. In 1897, when the Badeni government supported the Czechs in the hope of solving the Hungarian problem, the Germans obstructed the work of the House, and when the Czechs retaliated, the resulting tumult was so great as to make the activities of our spitting specialist seem mild by comparison. Much the same happened in France, in Italy, and even in the German Reichstag, though in less virulent form. In a letter dated December 4, 1899 and addressed to the Reichs Chancellor, the German ambassador to France referred to it all as "a new invention by various parliaments." Indeed, nowhere did the power of the majority exceed the willingness of the minority to submit to them. Still, only those who think that the sole legitimate role of a minority is to wait until it becomes a majority, will condemn this desperate form of resistance as rank lawlessness — things being what they were, few minorities could hope to gain their ends by tried parliamentary methods.[39]

Some even went so far as to deny the rights of the majorities. According to them, the minority, however small, was always in the right. By the turn of the century, this romantic and élitist idea had begun to have an irresistible attraction for quite a number of people, all of them incensed by what Emil Faguet was to call the "cult of incompetence."[40] The clear stream he saw emerging from the mental purification plants of his supporters' intellects was in fact drawn from three murky sources: from aristocrats who had married money and saw their privileges crumble away; from hypersensitive objectors to the coarse clamor of the masses out to destroy all the old values; and finally from the imperialists whose praetors and proconsuls objected to parliamentary interference in their activities[41] — Milner called the Mother of Parliaments "that mob at Westminster."[42]

That this élitist approach should have arisen at that particular time was not in the least surprising. The work of Nietzsche was full of it,[43] and it also lurked in the studies of mass psychology by Sighele and le Bon (1892 and 1895). Delafosse adopted it explicitly in 1907 when he described members of parliament as "products of negative selection."[44] The same trend was also to be seen in the work of Pareto, Mosca, and Michels. Pareto, as David Spitz has shown, looked upon the ruling élite as an essential element of effective social organization; to Mosca it was a necessary consequence of political order; according to Roberto Michels, whose famous book on the oligarchic tendencies of democracies appeared in 1911,[45] it was inexorably thrown up by every larger group.[46]

The names of these authors make it clear that the élitist approach was not a mere vestige of monarchist or absolutist ideas — which incidentally were still rampant, particularly in Central and Eastern Europe — but the opening up of new social and political structures with the aid of social psychology. In the process, eighteenth-century pessimism came to prevail over nineteenth-century optimism. Though belief in the élite was not particularly confined to traditionalists, it nevertheless had its staunchest defenders among the latter. In Britain its chief spokesman was Carlyle, followed by Sir James Stephen and Sir Henry Maine, Sir Charles Dilke, Cecil Rhodes and, last but not least, by Rudyard Kipling.[47] Its chief Dutch proponent was Bolland, to whom the sovereignty of the people was nothing but "society stood on its head, with the lowest at the top." Machayski, the Russian socialist, who used the nom-de-plume A. Volski and who may be called the precursor of managerialism, took a similar view;[48] and so did Georges Sorel. On the extreme Right, élitism was often wedded to "biological racism," and democratic equality rejected as contrary to the natural order. This, for instance, was the view expressed by W. H. Mallock in his *Aristocracy and evolution* (1898) and other books. (Mallock, incidentally, is remembered not so much for his own writings as for the fierce rebuttal with which Shaw saw fit to honor him.[49]) The champions of the old or — preferably — of a new aristocracy also included not only Ludovici, not by chance a translator of Nietzsche, but also such famous men as W. E. Lecky, the British historian, whose *Democracy and Liberty* was published in 1896. Unlike earlier Victorian critics of democracy such as Stephen and Maine, Lecky had resigned himself to its existence but protested all the more strongly against what he considered its most unsavory aspect: the curtailment of liberty. For the admission of the lower classes to the suffrage was bound to lead to class legislation, and hence to the collapse of the parliamentary system.[50] With Lecky we must also bracket Irving Babbitt and Karl Pearson, despite the fact that Babbitt styled himself a neo-humanist and believed that Madame Blavatsky had overcome the laws of gravity,[51] and that Pearson in his *National Life from the Standpoint of Science* (1901) went far beyond even the biological élitism of Galton, the founder of eugenics. Thus in his *Nature and Nurture* (1910) Pearson declared in favor of nature[52] — no amount of education could make up for the lack of the right type of genetic material. And the right genetic material, oddly enough, was generally found to go hand in hand with massive wealth. Two other famous names must also be mentioned here, both of them Spaniards who had enjoyed a Catholic education: Santayana [53] and Ortega y Gasset.[54] Although the latter was still a student in 1900, he was no less a champion than the former of those "natural aristocrats" whose ranks seemed to grow larger as those of the "real" aristocrats declined, and whose "nature" caused them to despise "democracy" in general and parliamentary institutions in particular as instruments of mediocre, if not totally inferior, men.

Fierce condemnations of parliament as a form of bourgeois dictatorship; passionate pleas to reform it root and branch; rejection of parliamentary institutions as tools of an inferior majority — Western Europe could survive all these attacks on its institutions and political philosophy precisely because it still felt so strongly about the liberal ideas both reflected.

East of a line running from Stockholm via Milan to Barcelona, however, this blessed state of affairs made way for something far less inspiring. For although Germany and Austria-Hungary also had their parliaments, they lacked a true parliamentary system; the middle classes were still fettered by feudalism and absolutism and hence hankered all the more fervently after the great parliamentary ideal: free speech.

Russia and Turkey differed even more strikingly from Western Europe. Czar and Sultan with their cliques of courtiers still ruled as arbitrarily as ever they had done in the past; here parliamentary rule was still in its infancy or unborn. Here, an idea that had long since lost its glamor in the West, still exercised its magic spell to the full — that the clash of opinion in parliament ensures harmonious government, and the clash of economic and social interests a more equitable society. Here the newly born bourgeoisie and, above all, the intelligentsia were still yearning for a revolution that would crush the hated autocracy, on whose ruins would be built the new parliament, inspired with the same pure and untarnished ideals as had once guided the West in its struggle against the crown. Here, the bourgeoisie still looked upon the French Revolution as a source of inspiration.

Such was the situation, not only in Russia and Turkey, but also in Persia and even in distant China and Japan. Japan had had a parliament ever since 1890. Originally, only one in a thousand inhabitants had been enfranchised there, and though that number was nearly trebled during the reforms of 1900,[55] the Japanese parliament remained deep in bribery and corruption — the direct result of the fusion of super-antiquated feudalism with super-modern capitalism. China, too, though beset by imperialist fortune hunters, was seeking a constitutional cure for its impotence — it was not by chance that K'ang Yu-Wei the reformer, wrote *A History of the Constitutional Changes in England.*[56] And in 1905, even the Empress, having learned from the Japanese victory over Russia that powerful states have great constitutions while those which are sickly have not, decided that China, too, must follow the parliamentary path,[57] the more so as Japan offered the pleasing prospect of "a strict despotism combined with absolute equality."[58]

In the same year the Czar of All the Russias was forced to much the same conclusion. If we dwell on its antecedents rather than its consequences, then the Russian Revolution of 1905 must indeed be called a chapter in the victorious history of parliamentarianism. The fact that the workers, instead of being shock troops of the bourgeoisie as they had been in all previous revolutions, played an independent, and leading, part in that revolution, was something few people remarked upon at the time. Fewer still could have realized that this great fight for bourgeois democracy was likely to unleash forces that would twelve years later sweep away not only the autocracy but the bourgeoisie as well. In any case, from early November 1904, when the movement began at a *zemtsvo* congress, to the end of October 1905, when the Czar issued his manifesto, its chief demands were the promulgation of a liberal constitution and hence the creation of a parliament. Even Trotsky, writing his first impressions of November 1905, had to admit that Russia had just passed through a bourgeois revolution, one that had set out to rid society of the fetters of absolutism and feudal property relations. It was only fair, however, to add, as indeed he did, that since the proletariat had been the main driving force, the revolution had been proletarian in its method.[59]

Rudimentary parliamentary ideas, incidentally, had existed in Russia for quite some time. The outcome of the Crimean War had forced the Czar not only to emancipate the serfs, but also, three years later, to allow the setting up of *zemtsvos*, provincial and district assemblies, on which all classes were to be represented, each class electing its deputies separately. The district assemblies were elected in three electoral colleges, nobility, townsmen, and peasants, and in 1870 municipal councils were added. In the 1880s, industries had been concentrated increasingly in the larger cities but, despite a few rudimentary measures, the Russian workers had few if any rights, and were paid less and worked longer hours than anyone else in Europe. The results were strikes and industrial sabotage, long before the revolution. In 1902, strikers in Rothschild's oil refinery in Batum were forced back to work at gunpoint; and in 1903, the South was swept by a general wave of strikes involving 240,000 workers, some seventy-five of whom lost their lives. But it still needed a great deal of optimism, and the youthful vigor of a Lenin — he was twenty-four years old at the time — to write, as early as 1894, that the Russian worker, placing himself at the head of all democratic forces, would overthrow absolutism and lead the Russian proletariat to a victorious communist revolution.[60] Lenin was convinced that that revolution was just round the corner and made all the necessary preparations: even before his party was born, he infused his followers with the élitist ideas so characteristic of the Bolshevik movement. At the same time, following

137

in the footsteps of Marx and Plekhanov, he provided them with the theoretical, tactical, organizational, and historical foundations they needed by a spate of books and pamphlets written during 1894–1899. The Social Democratic Party was founded in 1898, the Social Revolutionary Party in 1901, and the bourgeois League of Liberation in 1903; at the time it was the most important of the three, with its economic roots in industry and its political roots in the *zemstvos* and the municipal councils.

When the war against Japan started in February 1904, the revolutionary movement was given an unsuspected new impetus. The *zemstvos* immediately volunteered to tend the wounded, but Plehve, the Minister of the Interior, declined their generous offer; in July, he fell victim to a bomb thrown under his carriage by Sazonov, a Social Revolutionary. A few weeks earlier General Bobrikov, the Governor of Finland, had provided an example of what the great of the land had to expect in those days. Plehve's successor, Count Svyatopolk-Mirski, had slightly more liberal tendencies, and he let it be known that his policies would be guided by "confidence in the public." As far as possible, of course. Thus he, too, objected to the holding of the *zemstvo* congress which had been called for November in St. Petersburg. The congress nevertheless took place and continued for three days. By a vote of seventy to thirty it adopted eleven "theses," which included a demand for local self-government by the national minorities, freedom of conscience, and a legislative assembly. While *zemstvo* delegates and the members of the League of Liberation vied with each other in presenting these demands, with liberal speeches in the French style of 1830, generally at banquets, students demonstrated against the war (which was going badly), called for an amnesty and demanded a constitution. The first crack in the stronghold of the past, which had looked so impregnable shortly before, appeared with a Czarist *ukase* in December, promising agrarian reforms. For the peasants, too, had not been idle. They had all along resented the high compensation they had been forced to pay in 1861 for the privilege of their emancipation from serfdom. Moreover, in 1900, the land they had been sold (an average of 2.5 desyatin or some 6 acres) produced less than half the yield of the noblemen's acres. Even then, only too few could call their miserable parcels of land their own; seven million peasants were landless, and it was not only during the famines of 1891–1892, 1895–1896, 1897–1898, and 1901 that they had to mix their flour with bark or acorns.

On the subject of a constitution, the December *ukase* said nothing at all. And the less it satisfied the popular demands, the more it infuriated the people, as all half measures are wont to do in revolutionary times. That month, a one-day strike was declared in Baku. On January2, General Stössel capitulated to Nogi at Port Arthur. A breath of freedom wafted through the Russian capital. High-school boys went on strike, demanding the removal of Greek from their curriculum.[61] On January 9, four workers were dismissed from the Putilov Works; seven days later twelve thousand men had come out in sympathy, demanding the dismissal of the manager. Most of them were members of an organization founded by Father Gapon in 1903, apparently with the blessing of the secret police, for the express purpose of keeping the workers out of the clutches of the socialists. But the movement developed a momentum of its own; on January 20 St. Petersburg was in the throes of a general strike involving 140,000 workers. Their demands: the right to strike and an eight-hour day. January 22 had entered into history as "Bloody Sunday." That day, Father Gapon led a march to the Winter Palace from which the Czar had already fled — some of the palace windows had been smashed during "target practice" in the Peter and Paul Fortress across the Neva. Beneath banners and icons and a large portrait of the Czar — for Gapon had adopted the old fiction of the misled prince — the marchers advanced until, suddenly, the Cossacks were upon them. The infantry fired into the crowd, and the demonstrators fell like grain under a scythe. Three other processions fared no better: nine hundred dead and five thousand wounded.[62] "Russia is not yet a revolutionary country," Peter Struve had written on January 20.[63] He was one of the founders of the Social Democratic Party, which in 1900 still rejected the philosophy and politics of Karl Marx. But he was living abroad at the time, and did not realize the true situation in Russia. The general strike flared up again in St. Petersburg, and sympathy strikes were held in most other large cities of the far-flung Czarist empire. The assassination of the Grand Duke Sergei, Governor-General of Moscow and uncle of the Czar, on March 3 gave the constitutional movement a new lease of life. When Bulygin, the new Minister of the Interior, announced the emperor's decision to set up a consultative assembly, his announcement came too late and was, in any case, found wanting. The popular movement made common cause with the bourgeoisie, and Lenin called for armed resistance from far-away Switzerland. In May, the "Union of Unions" was established. Its declared aim was to coordinate the aspirations of the various political pressure groups, an event that was doubtless connected with the destruction of the Russian fleet in the Bay of Tsushima. In June came the creation of the all-Russian Peasant Union with rent-reduction written large on its banner; fires in the granaries and the homes of the landowners were to underline their demands. Even

139

the army and the navy did not remain immune: there were riots among the soldiery returning from the badly dented front, followed by the sailors' mutiny on the battleship Potemkin, off Sebastopol.

Throughout this period, the Constitutional Democrats, or Cadets, had been rallying their forces as well. At the end of April, yet another *zemstvo* congress reiterated the old demand for a constitutional assembly, and on June 19, the Czar gave an audience to its delegates, led by Prince Sergei Trubetskoy, at Peterhof. Nicholas was not at all unfriendly, but he listened more readily to Count Bobrinski, who had countered Trubetskoy's call with his own "to preserve the sacred traditions of the past." That same month Moscow was host to a congress of eighty-six councils, which supported the *zemstvo* demand for civil liberties and a legislative assembly elected by universal suffrage. One month later, both groups held a joint congress in defiance of the Governor-General and the head of the police, and adopted the draft constitution prepared by Kokoshkin, a leading member of the League of Liberation. Mustard was added to this peppery dish on August 19, when Bulygin's proposals were incorporated in an imperial decree. As before, the electorate was to be divided into the three established classes: nobility, townsmen, and peasants. Elections would be indirect, in two stages for the first two classes and in three stages for the peasants. The assembly's powers were to be confined to submitting measures to the Council of State for consideration as laws.[64] All this merely served to fan the flames of unrest, with the universities at their center. The heady wine of freedom was dispensed in overflowing halls, while the thunder of the peasant uprisings rumbled on in the background.

On September 5, a peace treaty was signed in Portsmouth, New Hampshire, but although Russia was granted terms that exceeded her wildest expectations — thanks largely to European and American fears of Japan — it brought her little peace at home. The reform movement had developed its own momentum. At the end of September, a congress of railwaymen was held in Moscow, and a railway strike was declared in October; by the end of that month the Russian railway system was almost totally paralysed. Altogether, the strike movement had the active support of some 750,000 workers, a great wave that produced the first St. Petersburg Soviet of Workers' Deputies. Even revolutions are produced by stages. The movement had started very modestly with a central strike committee of 40 men; a month later that number had grown to 562 elected deputies — of whom 362 were from the metallurgical industry (including six women) — representing 147 factories, 34 workshops, and 16 trade unions, each having elected one deputy for every 500 workers.

The executive committees of 31 included 22 workers. It called for a constituent assembly, to be elected by direct, universal, and secret franchise, and assumed the functions of a semi-official council of state, thus laying the foundations of a political structure that was to incite so much discussion in the West: an "organic" assembly whose members were chosen, not as atomized, abstract citizens, but in terms of their social function. On October 17, armed workers, having seized a large printing plant, published the first issue of *Izvestia*, the official organ of the St. Petersburg Soviet.

No one could have called any of these developments "liberal," but then the world had drifted into the twentieth century. The liberals had to content themselves with basking in the reflected glory of the latest developments, taking full credit for the Czar's latest manifesto, issued on October 30. It was thanks to this manifesto that Count Witte, restored to favor after his fall in 1903, was able to present the Russian nation with a rudimentary constitution. The new legislature was to consist of two Chambers — a State Council and a State Duma[65] — and to that extent the parliamentary movement may indeed be said to have scored a temporary victory. However, its candles flickered ominously and had, in any case, been paid for with the victims of the "Black Hundred": 15,000 dead, 18,000 wounded, and 70,000 prisoners. Because of these high costs, the victory was all the more precious to those who believed in gradual progress, and all the more galling to those who were not deceived by appearances. The result was a split with a crucial bearing on the future — Kropotkin was able to predict it all twenty years before it came to pass.[66]

It was also in 1905 that the Persian revolution broke out. Originally it had followed the old pattern: resentment by the mullahs whose legal powers and privileges were being threatened by the Grand Vizier, Ayn Al-Dawlah, a man as all-powerful as he was dishonest. But new elements had come to inspire the traditional resistance movement in the 1890s. In particular, the nationalist message of Jamal al-Din al-Afghani had not fallen on deaf ears, nor had the enthusiastic reports brought back by young Persian visitors to Europe who had tasted the delights of modern civilization. But even these men did not at first call for parliamentary democracy, as we know from David Fraser of the *Times*, one of the great journalists of his day.[67] Hence it seems likely that it was largely under the influence of the Russian revolution that what had originally been a reactionary movement became a revolutionary one within the short space of a year. The new movement was supported by Britain; in July 1906, the British Embassy offered asylum to all who fled the wrath of the Grand Vizier. Fearing that worse was still to come, Muzaffar ed-Din, the Shah, dismissed Ayn-al-Dawlah and on August 5 promised to convoke a *majlis*, or national parliament, a promise he fulfilled on October 7. It was admittedly not so much a parliament as a traditional assembly elected indirectly through electoral colleges based on social classes, and moreover one in which the landed nobility took pride of place,[68] but the constitution it introduced was nevertheless of the usual liberal type. On December 30, shortly before his death, the Shah put his signature to it with ill-concealed reluctance.

His successor, Mohammed Ali, who had been hostile to the movement since its inception, did not rest until he had stemmed the tide of reform. After a vain attempt in 1907, he succeeded on June 22, 1908, with the tacit support of the Russians, who had by then staggered out of their liberal period, and now ordered the Cossack brigade in Persian service to bomb the *majlis* out of the way. The dream of a Persian parliament would have been shattered for many years to come had not the Young Turk revolution given the young Persians fresh courage in July.[69] Helped by Russian and Turkish revolutionaries, Tabriz and Resht in the north and Isfahan in the south rose up in January 1909. Although Tabriz was blockaded and eventually entered by the Russians, the Bakhtiari rebels led by Ali Kuli chan started a march on Teheran in June, and took it on July 12. The Shah was deposed, and his eleven-year old son lacked the force to stand up to the resurrected *majlis*. Persia, too, had come to realize that resistance to Western penetration was no longer possible except by imitation of the West.

Though the Young Turks had come into existence long before they made their forcible entry on the political scene in 1908, Sultan Abdul Hamid had previously given them short shrift. He could proudly boast that no dog could bark in his empire without his hearing it. But that very boast was to become his downfall. His victims took full advantage of the bad reputation he enjoyed in Europe and could also count on the support of the suppressed nationalists at home. The postal services, which were in the hands of foreign powers as one of the results of the Peace of Belgrade of 1739, closed their eyes to all "un-Turkish" activities, and the protests of the Turkish government only served to do what similar protests by a reactionary government had done in China: they stoked up hatred of foreigners and in so doing strengthened the very nationalist forces they meant to confine. At the end of 1907, when the Shah of Persia had launched his first, still vain, attack on the *majlis*, a number of Young Turks had assembled in Paris. They prepared a plan of campaign

142

and made contact with various Masonic lodges in Salonika and other cities. The troubles in Macedonia did the rest. When Edward VII and Nicholas II met in Tallinn on June 10, 1908, and the Russians agreed to the British proposals for Macedonian reforms, they provoked further resentment. The Young Turks, irritated by the presence of European gendarmes under Italian command, now feared that the free Macedonian provinces would be lost to the Turkish empire for good.[70] On July 4, Niazi Bey planted the flag of resistance in Resna; three days later Enver Bey himself stood by his side. Government troops sent against the rebels went over to them. Within another five days, the Committee for Union and Progress took command of the struggle. During the night of July 22, it seized the telegraph office in Salonika and sent telegrams to all local committees, instructing them to proclaim constitutional government next day.[71] A young officer, Kiazim Bey, wrote and produced a play dealing with the latest achievements of the revolutionary movement. It was called "How It Came About," and was received with great acclaim.[72] On July 24, after many days of discussion with his Council of Ministers, the Sultan realized that he had no alternative but to restore the constitution of 1876. He decided to play the part of the good prince who had been misled by evil counselors, and as a result was able to cling to office for another nine months, not least because the constitution in no way challenged his authority or his private fortune, safely tucked away in banks all over Europe and America and estimated at fifteen billion francs.[73]

The amnesty, the abolition of the hated espionage system,[74] the restoration of the constitution and with it of the *majlis*, which reassembled on December 17, were all greeted with what eyewitnesses have called inordinate scenes of joy and enthusiasm. One who tried to describe the indescribable was Sir Valentine Chirol.[75] Freedom, equality, and fraternity were not enough. The flag of the revolution bore "Justice" in its fourth corner and across the central field of red the slogan "Long Live the Constitution."[76] On July 25, every Turkish newspaper sang paeans of praise to freedom.[77] All races, all classes, all creeds bowed down to the new flag as before a goddess of salvation: Turks, Greeks, Bulgars, Albanians, Jews, (only the Armenians were missing), mullahs, priests, students, and scholars marched through the streets singing the Hymn of the Constitution, sometimes halting to admire a gaily beflagged newspaper office, to listen to a revolutionary speech at a street corner, or to embrace a fellow revolutionary. This was a real honeymoon, following the marriage of faith and hope. But then came the inevitable disillusionment. Yusuf Fehmi was one of many writers to voice his disappointment.

It was all the fault of the Freemasons, who had subverted the new rulers. In an appendix, he reprinted the whole constitution, with the comment "violated" added to practically every article.[78]

At first, however, the new foundations seemed solid enough. Then on October 5, Bulgaria, with the connivance of Germany and Austria, declared her independence. Prince Ferdinand proclaimed himself Czar of the Bulgars. The following day Aehrenthal annexed Bosnia and Herzegovina. Not even Abdul Hamid, though he commanded the support of large sections of the army, could stem the tide this time. He was deposed on April 26, 1909, and succeeded by his younger brother, Mohammed V, who had been kept a state prisoner for as long as he could remember, still bore thumbscrew marks on his hands, and had not read a newspaper for ten years.[79] Despite his proud title, the new sultan was a gentle and retiring man, completely out of his element: a symbol of the decline of feudal autocracy. By his side, the *majlis*, a symbol of popular government though still only in name, was already making itself felt as a symbol of the new enlightenment. Ever since 1717, the Mother of Parliaments on the Thames had resounded to the cry of "Let candles be brought in" as soon as the light of day began to fade.[80] And the parliamentary system did indeed become a source of light for many who had been deprived of it at the very moment that those who had been enjoying it started to point to the many shadows it cast.

CHAPTER X

UNDER THE BLACK FLAG

On August 11, 1900, one Albert, better known as Libertad — the man who was to launch the weekly *L'Anarchie* in 1905 — wrote a letter to the Police Prefect in Paris complaining of harassment by plain-clothes men. He added that he had nothing to hide; and that while he fully sympathized with libertarian ideas, his life was as respectable and orderly as could be. That claim was true enough, depending, of course, on one's definition of respectability and order. In fact, it was by no means certain whether Libertad was a genuine anarchist of the individualist type, so fashionable in Bohemian and artistic circles at the time, or whether he was in the service of the police. Rochefort claimed that even Louise Michel, "la vierge rouge," was convinced that Libertad was a stool pigeon, and she ought to have known: pure idealism had more than once led her into police traps. Jean Maitron, a later and also the best historian of French anarchism, on the contrary, took him for an honest comrade.[1] Perhaps this contradiction reflected the strange mixture of hypersensitivity and indifference which characterized so many of these detached and isolated men, no less than their incredible openness to "sympathetic" strangers.

Similar doubts were also voiced about the notorious Ravachol, who, on July 11, 1892, was made to pay on the guillotine for the many robberies, desecrations of tombs, and bomb attacks he had perpetrated. Kropotkin, while leaving the question of possible police complicity open, repudiated Ravachol's deeds as being of no value to the social revolution; Malatesta took the opposite view, contending that the stranglehold of the state could not be broken with holy water.[2] Others, too, continued to look upon Ravachol as a fighter for social justice. They recalled that, as a mere boy, he had been a true father to his brother and sister; that he had taught reading and writing to the child of the man in whose home he had taken refuge; that he had gone short himself to help the widow of a fellow anarchist; and that, during his trial, he had attempted to save one of his fellow-defendants by taking the entire blame upon himself.[3] Many revered him as a martyr, so much so that they referred to the "anarchist Marseillaise," composed by the shoemaker Marie Constant and containing the wild refrain "Dynamitons, dynamitons," as "La Ravachole."[4] Others voiced doubts about his character and, for that matter, about that of Vaillant, who was executed on February 5, 1894, after having thrown a bomb into the French Chamber of Deputies. For though most anarchists applauded his action, Alexander Cohen, for instance, maintained that Vaillant was an *agent provocateur* in the pay of the French government.

This conflict of views throws light not only on the individuals concerned, but also on the ambiguous character of all the "social guerillas" who, at the turn of the century, challenged authority in the name of freedom. Their character was ambiguous not so much because it is impossible to tell on which side of the barricades they were actually fighting but because it is hard to say, on balance, who was bound more closely to the state — the anarchists, its sworn enemies, or the majority of citizens, who were forced to bow to its dictates. For the bond of hatred is often stronger than the bond of love, let alone the bond of tradition or conformity.

The true anarchists amongst them, in any case, regardless of which particular hue of the broad libertarian spectrum they represented, were filled with an obsessive love of individual freedom and the determination to achieve social justice. Hence their double hatred of the state which *still* paid lip service, but no more, to the first of these aims and had *not yet* translated the second into action. The particular virulence of their hatred thus reflected a realization that the growing strength of the state and the increasing interpenetration of state and society, far from rendering the struggle for individual freedom and social justice superfluous, made it all the more necessary. What caused the rise of anarchism, and at the same time doomed it to failure, was the vain attempt to wed nineteenth-century liberalism, then in its death throes, to the tenets of the nascent socialist mass movement — a synthesis that would have been difficult to achieve at the best of times. Moreover, though the ideals of anarchism may have been attractive, its methods served to repel most people. For not only were these methods singularly inappropriate, but they were also so chilling that what comfort the authorities could have derived from their political irrelevance was overshadowed by the alarm they spread. The lack of self-confidence the bourgeoisie evinced during these years was due in no small part to the spasmodic anarchist outrages perpetrated in the two decades round the turn of the century.

A list compiled by Maitron[5] shows that France alone suffered thirteen anarchist attacks in 1892–1894, not including those committed by foreigners with no direct links to the French movement. The list was opened by George Etiévant, Ravachol's accomplice in the theft of dynamite from Soisy-sous-Etiolles. After his sentence, he told the court that he could not

146

see why, if the laws were good, there was the least need for deputies and senators to change them, and why, if they were bad, there had to be judges and policemen to implement them. The most famous anarchist outrages were, apart from Ravachol's, those by August Vaillant, who threw a bomb from the gallery of the Chamber of Deputies on December 9, 1893, and was executed on February 5, 1894;[6] and by Emile Henry, who on February 12, 1894, threw a bomb into the Café Terminus in Paris, having first deposited another bomb in the Paris offices of the Société des Mines de Carmaux. The second bomb was discovered and taken to the nearest police station where it exploded. For these attacks, Henry was executed on May 21.[7] Subsequently, Santo-Jeronimo Caserio took his revenge upon President Sadi Carnot, who had refused to grant Vaillant a pardon, by stabbing him to death on June 24, 1894, following the state opening of an exhibition in Lyons. The culprit was guillotined on August 15.[8] Nor did the hapless French government leave it at these four death sentences; it also passed four extremely oppressive laws during the same three years.[9] In addition, during 1890–1896, it handed out prison sentences totalling 322 years and 3 months.[10]

Thanks to the interest the police and the press took in them and also because of the intellectual exhibitionism to which so many champions of "propaganda of the deed" were prone, we know hundreds of them who were sentenced to death, to incarceration, or to forced labor by name, and of tens of them we know their first names together with other details. Of all these, Vaillant and Henry were more fascinating than most fictional characters, the first because of his experiences before he threw his bomb, the second because of what followed; the first because his action was so comprehensible, the second because it was so inexplicable.

Vaillant was an outcast, an illegitimate child rejected by both his parents, and also by the poor peasants who fostered him. When he was thirteen, an aged aunt advised him to have himself picked up for vagrancy, so that he would be sent back to his own father, but his father refused to have anything to do with him. The child then tried to fend for himself, and by the time he was seventeen he had come up against the police more than once. On one occasion he filled his empty belly with ninety centimes' worth of food, but could not pay for the meal: he was given six days in prison. Six months later, having vainly tried to find work in Marseilles, he was given three days in prison for begging. Soon afterward, he received a month in prison for stealing a pair of shoes in Algiers. He lost his job in the local rope-yard, and fell in love; but when his girl abandoned him, a stay in a mental home put an end to that romantic interlude. After his release, he fared reasonably well for a short time. He became a socialist;

147

but finding socialism too full of gray theories, he turned to anarchism, and soon afterward decided to start a new life in Argentina. However, all that awaited him there was more hunger and misery, and so he returned in 1893, a disappointed old man of thirty-two. After several vain attempts to find work, his future looked black; blood up, he decided to follow Ravachol's example and to strike back at oppressive society. Just for once he would cease to be a number, just for once he would be a man who, if he could not gain their respect, would at least attract the attention of his callous compatriots. We know all this from the diary he kept shortly before he struck, the so-called "diary of my explosion." He had himself photographed and sent his likeness to everyone he knew. He was obsessed, to the exclusion of all else, by his bomb, by its smell and its smoke.[11] His protest, he recorded the night before he struck, would not merely be the cry of rebellious Vaillant but the cry of "that whole class which demands its rights."

Though his deed sprang from his life as naturally, one might say, as a flower springs from a bud, many of his contemporaries were deeply puzzled by it. Gouzer blamed it on Vaillant's egoism and vanity; Lombroso, true to his theory, considered it a symptom of a hereditary taint; Bertrand dismissed Vaillant as a common criminal — but then he was an officer of the law. Jaurès was more sympathetic and so was Tarde, who, after Vaillant's trial, introduced the distinction between subjective and objective criminality. Bourdau described Vaillant as a philanthropic murderer who "raged against mankind out of love." Maître Labori probably came closest to the truth when, in his defense of Vaillant, he claimed that far from telling against him, as the prosecution had alleged, Vaillant's previous convictions mitigated his crime, for they were so many signs of his misery and despair.[12] With these words, one of the greatest French experts in criminal law had put the blame squarely where it belonged, at the same time laying bare the connection between social injustice and crime.

In Henry's case no such connection could be shown. It may be true that his father was a Communard who had escaped the wrath of the reaction by fleeing to Spain, where his son was born in 1872; but when a general amnesty was declared ten years later, he had returned home and become a good bourgeois who gave young Emile the best education France had to offer. No doubt Emile, like every other child, suffered disappointments, but none so bad as to warrant his violent reaction. No, if Emile suffered from anything, it was lack of contact with life. The fact that he was late in reaching puberty may be part of the explanation; Henry became an anarchist at eighteen and was beheaded at twenty-one. Moreover, his intelligence — he was awarded four prizes at school, including two firsts[13] — was such that blind obsession with a theory seems puzzling. Not that his choice of anarchism as such was in the least surprising — at the time anarchism stood for total renewal in the street, in the salon, in the workshop, and in the university, and its very radicalism must have struck the young as a token of its deep sincerity. In his introduction to the works of the art critic Félix Fénéon, Jean Paulhan had this to say: "Of the great struggle for free verse waged in the nineties, the public and the Chamber of the Third Republic knew nothing but the result: the anarchist attacks."[14] No doubt this man of letters took too exaggerated a view of the role of literature, but his opinion was not at all unusual in a period when their irrepressible love of freedom united anarchists and artists in a single Bohemia. Fénéon, who appeared by Henry's side in the "Trial of the Thirty" as did Sébastien Faure, was a minor official in the Department of War, a man in whose desk the police had discovered a store of explosives. From 1895 to 1903, he was also the editor of the *Revue Blanche*, which published and discussed the work of every modernist of note. This does not, of course, explain his violence; it merely shows that their very fear of action will sometimes propel even the most sedentary theorists into a "forward flight" toward hostile reaction. This is borne out by the declaration Henry made in a clear and calm voice, in April 1894, to a jury determined to sentence him to death. That declaration was a mixture of cold logic and flowing eloquence, in which every lash of the whip struck home and every argument seemed irrefutable. It bore witness to an unbearable struggle between heart and brain and, incidentally, provides us with a clue to the most likely motive of his deed: a death wish of which Henry himself was probably quite unaware.

His declaration was not meant to be a defense. "I rely on one judge only — myself," he exclaimed. All he was offering was an explanation. In his youth he had come to learn that "all the great words I was taught to revere: honor, devotion, and duty, were so many smoke screens for the most infamous scandals." The manufacturer who makes a fortune by exploiting his workers is a respectable man; the officer who tries out a new gun on seven-year olds — a reference to the massacre in Fourmies on May 1, 1891 — is praised for his devotion to duty; the venal minister is considered a devoted servant of the general public. Henry went on to explain that he had been attracted by socialism for a short time but that it had not taken him long to realize that socialism was too authoritarian to produce a free society. As a materialist and an atheist, he had been taught by science that religious and authoritarian morality was built on false foundations and had to be destroyed. It was then that the anarchists —

149

the men round Sébastien Faure — had begun to impress him with their "great seriousness, complete frankness, and their hatred of all prejudices." He was quite indifferent to his own prospects. "All thoughts of self-preservation," he was inclined to say with Souvarine in *Germinal*, "are criminal because they stand in the way of pure destruction." He himself had become revolted "by the horrible spectacle of a society in which everything is vile, insipid, and ugly." He had placed his bomb in the offices of the Mines de Carmaux to persuade the workers that instead of striking peacefully and pitting their few miserable francs against the millions owned by the company, they ought to "burn the coal supplies, smash the machines, and stop the pumps." In the event, the company, mightier than ever, had continued its work of exploitation. "It was then that I decided to break into the consort of harmonious sounds with a voice that the bourgeoisie had heard before but believed had been silenced for good upon the death of Ravachol: the voice of dynamite." During the attack on the Café Terminus he had held back for a moment, for fear of killing innocent people. But "just as the bourgeoisie does not distinguish between guilty and innocent anarchists, so also the anarchist cannot distinguish between guilty and innocent bourgeois." Moreover, all the clients of the café were good little officials earning 300 to 500 francs a month, men "more reactionary than their masters, who hate the poor and range themselves on the side of the strong." "You have hanged in Chicago, beheaded in Germany, garotted in Jerez, shot in Barcelona, guillotined in Montbrison and Paris. At least have the courage of your crimes, *Messieurs les bourgeois*, and admit that our revenge is just. In the pitiless war which we have declared on the bourgeoisie we ask for no single pardon." He concluded with a proud statement from which one must deduce that he did not wish to be saved: "What my defending counsel may say to you in no way detracts from anything I myself have said. My own declaration is the faithful expression of my thoughts. I do not take back one single word."[15]

In the same month that this proud credo resounded in Paris, ten anarchists were sentenced in Barcelona. They had been guilty of two attacks: the first on the Military Governor of the city during a parade in September, 1893; the second on Barcelona socialites who had gathered on November 7 in the new Liceo Theatre for the opening of Rossini's *Wilhelm Tell*, accidentally — or perhaps not — the same opera Orsini had once chosen for his attempt of the life of Napoleon III.[16] The results were more devastating than those of any other example of the "propaganda of the deed": sixty-three dead and wounded, not including the victims of the panic that started after the explosion. The first attack had been led by a man called Pallas, the second by Salvador Franck. Pallas's motive was revenge for the vicious suppression of the anarchist peasant uprising of 1899 in Jerez; Franck's motive, revenge for the death of Pallas. In these cases, too, there had been a vicious circle of repression, revolt, reaction, revenge, execution, and more revenge.

Italy was the scene of similar spectacles. From their headquarters in the ruins of Castel del Monto, Cafiero and Malatesta,[17] followers of Bakunin, had tried as early as 1874 to start an uprising. Three years later, they made a fresh attempt on a much larger scale in Benevento.[18] Count Cafiero, who sacrificed his entire fortune for the good cause, died of a mental illness in 1883. Malatesta outlived him by half a century, revered as the knight errant of anarchism; the worst even Mussolini dared to do to him was to place him under house arrest. The fierce suppression of their movement was partly responsible for Passanante's attack on King Humbert in 1897, the year of his coronation. Thereafter, the House of Savoy could no longer boast that, from its origins in the eleventh century, none of its reigning members had ever been assailed. Indeed, when he was attacked once again in April 1897, this time on his wedding anniversary, the king jumped aside and remarked with a shrug to his escort, *"sono gli incerti del mestiere"* ("These are the risks of the job"). After Sunday evening, July 29, 1900, he was to say nothing at all. Returning from Naples, where he had seen his troops off to China, and on the way to Monza, the royal summer residence near Milan, he was shot four times by Gaetano Bresci. The assassin had come from America with the intent, as he said during his trial, "not to kill Humbert but to kill a principle."[19] There were wide repercussions. Even Leyds, the South African ambassador, was indirectly accused of having had a hand in the affair.[20]

The King of Italy was not the only crowned head to run "vocational risks" in those days. In August 1900 it was the turn of the Shah of Persia, on a visit to Paris, and in November, of the Prince of Wales on a visit to Brussels. The man responsible for the last attack, Sipido, was given a life sentence but managed to escape to Paris. Leopold II went there himself to demand his extradition, but was unsuccessful.[21] Elnikov's assassination of Czar Alexander II in 1881 set off a spate of similar attacks in Germany, Austria, Spain, France, the Balkans, and the United States. Some of these were successful. We have just mentioned Bresci's assassination of King Humbert. In 1894, Caseno stabbed President Sadi Carnot of France to death; in 1898, Luigi Luccheni killed the Empress Elisabeth of Austria in Geneva; and on September 6, 1901, Leon Czolgosz took the life of President McKinley while the organ was playing Bach's Sonata in F.[22] Of all these assassins, Luigi Luccheni was without doubt the most interesting both from a sociological and psychological point of view. He, too, was an illegitimate child, and had been left by his mother in a poorhouse in Parma and given the number 29,239. When he went to prison in Geneva after his crime, he became No. 1,144. His life lay between these two numbers, and might be considered a protest against that fact. When the judge suggested to him that he had never suffered real deprivation, he replied: "When my mother abandoned me in infancy, wasn't that a deprivation real enough to avenge all my life long?"

The last attack in this series came on May 31, 1906, when Matteo Morral threw a bomb at the royal coach as it passed through the Calle Mayor in Madrid. King Alfonso and his young bride, Ena von Battenberg, were returning to the palace from the church in which their marriage had just been solemnized. This grande finale — for in Spain, too, it had been preceded by a great many others[23] — of the anarchist fireworks display deserves special mention for three reasons. First, its failure highlighted the failure of this type of "social agitation"; second, the culprit was the son of a rich cotton manufacturer from Catalonia, and the Catalan bourgeoisie had at least as many nationalist reasons to hate the centralized Spanish state and its symbol as had the red workers; and third, this outrage became linked with the name of Francisco Ferrer, and this very link threw a great deal of light on the transition that was taking place at the turn of the century.

It so happened that Morral was for a time in charge of the bookshop and publishing company associated with Ferrer's *Escuela Moderna* in Barcelona. Though the two men had become estranged, because they loved the same woman, or else because Ferrer had gone back on his anarchist views, the Catalan clergy nevertheless used Morral's attack as a pretext for drawing the attention of the temporal authorities to Ferrer's anti-clerical activities. Ferrer was put in prison, but released soon afterward — an unacceptable outcome for which the Dominicans never forgave him. In July 1909, when an uprising in Barcelona followed one of the many Spanish defeats in Morocco, Ferrer was dragged before the courts again.[24] As had happened with Dreyfus ten years earlier, Ferrer's case also attracted world-wide attention and raised a storm of protest. Although the innocence of the Spanish schoolmaster was even more obvious than that of the French captain, this time the protests were of no avail: Ferrer was sentenced to death and was executed by a firing squad at Fort Montjuich in Barcelona. And there was no one to avenge his death; the vicious circle of semi-official and official violence had run its course. The torch of human rights, still bright enough to allow "the conscience of the world" to triumph in 1899, had grown exceedingly dim by 1909. During the interval, liberalism had lost much of its appeal to the bourgeoisie; and socialism, though it had gained considerably in influence, had done so at the expense of its revolutionary élan. It was no accident that, the year after Ferrer's death, the Parisian trade union movement dropped its plan for an unprecedentedly massive May Day demonstration just as soon as the Prime Minister, Aristide Briand, himself a former socialist, announced drastic countermeasures. There is no clearer way of demonstrating the threat ministerialism had begun to pose to revolutionism, despite the fact that in the prevailing social climate, ministerialism was the natural fruit of revolutionism. An apple rolls furthest from the tree that stands on a mountain top. Similarly, it is the highest political ideals that so often lead to the worst practices — a fact that can be referred to as the "heterogeneity of means and ends."[25]

This digression was not a detour, but an integral part of our argument. For the moderation that had crept into socialism during these years gave anarchism its last chance, and also transformed it. The social uprisings typical of the 1870s and 1880s had become things of the past, no less so than the individual terror typical of the 1890s.

Anarchism was to live on in French syndicalism until 1914, and in Spanish syndicalism until much later, though more in a psychological than in a social or political form. The Anarchist International founded in Amsterdam in 1907 never went beyond the planning stage; the social revolution it intended to organize was stillborn. Yet syndicalism remained conscious of its anarchist origins not only in its revolutionary method but also in its view of the society of the future, its treatment of trade unions as non-party training centers for the revolution, its antiparliamentarianism, its antimilitarism, and finally and above all, its mystical belief in the revolutionary powers of "direct action" and the general strike. The thoughts of Fernand Pelloutier, the founder of French syndicalism; of the leaders of the French Confédération Générale du Travail (founded in 1895 and publishers of the weekly La Voix du Peuple since 1900); of such men as Pouget, Griffuelhes, Delesalle, Guérard, Fortellier, Merrheim, Monatte, Niel, and Yvetot; of the Spanish Confederatión Nacional de Trabajo; of the Unione Sindicale Italiana; and of the Dutch National Arbeids Secretariaat, were all of them rooted in anarchist principles. Thus whatever differences the theorists of the movement — Lagardelle, Sorel, or Berth, for instance — may have had,[26] their views never belied their descent from the noble line of Godwin, Proudhon, Stirner, Bakunin, and Kropotkin.

Of the founding fathers of anarchism, only Kropotkin was still alive in 1900. In spite of that, French workers had not forgotten their Proudhon (d. 1865), the less so as each one of them could cull his own gospel from

153

that great man's oracular writings. Nor had the memory of Bakunin's wild and brave life, ended in 1876, faded from their memories and hearts. Moreover, it was only now that Stirner's extremely individualistic credo, *Der Einzige und sein Eigentum* ("The Ego and His Own"), written in 1845, became more widely available. A cheap pocket edition of his greatly misunderstood work was published in 1892, together with a host of extracts. In the same year, many papers were devoted to his work, and his relationship with Nietzsche was analyzed.[27] In 1898, his disciple, the individualist-anarchist John Henry Mackay, published Stirner's minor writings followed by a biography which encouraged a spate of further writings. In 1900 two French, in 1902 an Italian, and in 1907 an English translation saw the light of day.[28] Eltzbacher, in his classic study of anarchist thought (1900), devoted a whole chapter to Stirner;[29] while Victor Basch wrote a long article on Stirner in 1901 and devoted a whole book to him in 1904.[30] Stirner's case was a striking example of "delayed glory"; for Johann Kaspar Schmidt — his real name — has not only retained a place in the history of philosophy, but his position has been greatly consolidated.[31]

At the turn of the century, however, it was neither Stirner nor such leading anarchist theorists as Sébastien Faure, Jean Grave, Malatesta, Mackay, Malato, Merlino, Johan Most or even Elisée Reclus, Cherkessov, and Tucker, let alone the memory of Proudhon and Bakunin, but the heart and brain of Kropotkin which had captured the imagination of the anarchist movement. No wonder, for he surpassed his contemporaries in resolution and knowledge, even while combining in his person the greatest qualities of his predecessors: the inspirational ideas of Proudhon, the staunch radicalism of Stirner, and the unequaled boldness of Bakunin. Kropotkin's noble descent was partly responsible for earning him authority he had never sought; much more so, however, it was the sovereign ease with which he turned his back on his aristocratic heritage. Neither his military nor his scientific career meant very much to him; uppermost in his mind was always the determination to improve the lot of the disinherited. Not that he was an undistinguished scholar — far from it. Two scientific discoveries of great importance stand in his name: that the structural lines of Asia run from the southwest to the northeast and that the ice cap had once reached down to Central Europe. He discussed the last of these discoveries in 1874, just before his arrest by the "Third Section."[32] Rarely had there been a more poignant renunciation of a scientific career to a political idea, and it is small wonder that Hamon should have chosen Kropotkin as the subject of his brilliant psychological portrait of the ideal socialist anarchist[33] in 1895. Franz Oppenheimer, who shared none of

154

Kropotkin's ideas, nevertheless said that "in our age of dull resignation, of listless despondency, of vulgar materialism and brutal self-seeking, it is nothing short of rejuvenation to read Kropotkin's *Memoirs of a Revolutionary.*" That book, which had appeared in England in 1899, was "full of pugnacity but free of hatred and vengefulness, and reflected the author's unflinching faith in the world-liberating role of science and the goodness of human nature."[34]

Science is an instrument of liberation only if it is practiced without prejudice; man is good in essence only if he is given the opportunity to follow his nature: this was the message Kropotkin tried to convey in his *La Science moderne et l'anarchie*, which appeared in 1913 as a revised translation of the 1901 Russian original.[35] Although that message may have had an eighteenth-century ring to it, Kropotkin contended that it was vindicated not only by the old but also by the most recent scientific discoveries, in which he, like Marx before him, took a keen interest because he, too, made science the cornerstone of his philosophy. To him, anarchism was a "conception of the universe based on a mechanical interpretation of those phenomena which make up the whole nature, social life included."[36] In other words, it called for an examination of the universe by the methods of natural science. No wonder that he rejected the debasement of science by "mystical intuition" and the "misuse of the dialectic" on the part of Bergson.[37] Although he did not die until 1921, at the age of seventy-nine, Kropotkin was not a twentieth-century thinker. But he always kept an open mind, as witness not only his refutation of Bergson, that new star in the philosophic sky of France, but also the second part of his *La Science moderne*, in which he examined the role of the state in the creation of monopolies for the benefit of a privileged minority, with all the imperialist consequences that creation entailed. Kropotkin was also historian enough to draw the lessons of the past in his *La Grande Révolution* of 1909. He was one of the first to warn against gathering clouds of war, predicting as early as 1911, when the world had only just escaped from one holocaust, that another, far more ominous one, lay around the corner.[38]

La Grande Révolution would not have been the thoughtful and stimulating book it turned out to be had the way for it not been cleared by two greater and even more important works: *Fields, Factories and Workshops* (1898) and *Mutual Aid* (1902). Much as Malthus's somber prophecies had, in their day, been written to refute Godwin's message of hope, so the first of these two books was written to refute Malthus's pessimistic prophecies. Kropotkin, mustering an impressive set of facts and figures, showed that economic conflict was not a necessity of life. General pros-

155

perity, he claimed, was a real possibility, and could be achieved if every-one between the ages of twenty and fifty worked a five-hour day. Utopian though this may have sounded when it was written sixty years ago, we who are faced with the problem of what workers and retired people are to do with their leisure, know that it was anything but that. In this thought-ful book, Kropotkin not only attacked the prevailing and extreme division of labor but also the division of the world into an over-industrialized Western Europe and North America and a predominantly agricultural remainder. He believed that small enterprises were more efficient than large, and that federative associations were more salutary than the al-mighty state. In addition, just as he wanted to decentralize industry and politics, so he also pleaded for the dispersal of the population packed into the great cities — a plea that did not go unheard and was taken up par-ticularly by Ebenezer Howard, who, after returning to England from America, founded the Garden City movement, and took an active part in the building of the two garden cities of Letchworth and Welwyn at the turn of the century.[39] Kropotkin also advocated an integral form of education designed to develop both intellectual and physical aptitudes the better to prepare the young for life in a better society. However, not even this society could guarantee happiness; it could merely ensure that the happiness of the few was no longer built on the misery of the many.

Kropotkin not only rounded on Malthus, but also challenged Darwin, or rather Darwin's successor, Thomas Henry Huxley, who until his death in 1895 was the chief exponent of the struggle for existence. Not the struggle for existence but "mutual aid" was the real law of nature, at least between conspecifics. While an officer in Siberia, Kropotkin, ably assisted by his brother Alexander, had made a critical study of Darwin's theory and had found it wanting in the light of his own experiences there. Many others shared his view, among them Professor Kessler, the Russian zoologist and animal psychologist.[40] Kropotkin, for his part, showed that mutual aid was a major factor in the evolution of animals, of primitive men, of barbarians, in the life of medieval cities, and in his own environment as well. Mutual aid was the basis of his faith in collective endeavor, the cornerstone of his vision of the society of the future, and also of his conviction that, despite all the prevailing oppression and lack of wisdom, anarchism would eventually carry the day.

It was in the domain of ethics that he put forward some of his most valuable ideas, first of all in his *La Morale anarchiste* (an English transla-tion of which was published in 1890, and for which Laurentius provided a German gloss in 1896).[41] This was a short work which he was unable

156

to develop as fully as he might have done — we all tend to shelve our best work until we have time to perfect it. Even so, the small book showed clearly enough what the *magnum opus* would have been. Wherever official morality holds sway, the human spirit is asleep. Luckily, however, as happened in the twelfth, sixteenth, and eighteenth centuries, and again in Kropotkin's own day, the spirit begins to stir here and there, with youth clamoring for emancipation and an end to the old prejudices. Whenever that happens, a new and better morality emerges. In this connection, Kropotkin mentioned the French moralist Guyau,[42] who had argued in his *Esquisse d'une morale sans obligation ni sanction* (1885) that as soon as man feel capable of doing something, he also feels a vague compulsion to do it, precisely because his sense of duty is essentially an exuberant sense of power; true morality is thus simply a manifestation of life in higher form. Kropotkin's own conception of inner compulsion would nowadays be called a "sublimated search for pleasure." Similar ideas were voiced in 1892 by Felix Adler before the Berlin Gesellschaft für Ethische Kultur.[43]

The new morality was in no way prescriptive; it was thought to rest on purely scientific foundations. In particular, it rejected the idea of teaching individuals to follow abstract ideas, just as it rejected the repression of the human personality by religion, law, or government. It culminated in glorification of life, and hence was just one manifestation of the neo-vitalist spirit which characterized the early years of the twentieth century in so many spheres.[44]

It was because of these vitalist ideas that Laurentius has likened Kropotkin to Nietzsche, and the similarity is striking enough. The work of both men was the typical product of the transition from the nineteeth to the twentieth century. Both had advanced from rationalism to vitalism, but while Nietzsche had done so deliberately, making that advance a central part of his work, Kropotkin had done so unwittingly, in the margin of his conscious ideas, so to speak. Yet there was a much more striking difference between them: while Nietzsche's vital force was at best morally ambivalent, Kropotkin's was a clear force for good. There is no such thing as strong men without ideals, he said,[45] a claim that twentieth-century experiences would unfortunately fail to confirm. The shadow of the new century had already fallen across Nietzsche's vision. Kropotkin, by contrast, caught the last rays of the eighteenth and nineteenth centuries, and made them shine all the more brightly because he brought them into focus.

The life of this unusual Russian mirrored the entire Europe of his day: the narrow life of a page at the court of Czar Alexander II at the

157

time that the Czar was passing from his liberal to his reactionary phase; the glittering existence of an officer in a bureaucratic society; voyages of discovery across the vast Siberian wastes and the Finnish lakes; the scientific triumphs; the Tchaikovsky circle, and soon afterward confinement in the Peter and Paul Fortress, followed by a romantic though carefully planned escape from its hospital. He fled to Switzerland, then the center of the revolutionary movement, with Utin proclaiming his narrow Marxism in Geneva, and Guillaume his equally narrow Bakuninism in the Jura Federation. There were the countless open and secret meetings, described convincingly in Pio Baroja's *El mundo es ansi*,[46] followed by Kropotkin's expulsion in 1881. He went on to France, then still the hub of the world. Here Paul Brousse, Jean Grave, Sébastien Faure, and Elisée Reclus, a fellow geographer,[47] remained his closest associates until he was expelled from France as well. In 1886, he took refuge in liberal England, and found a quiet retreat in the Reading Room of the British Museum — as had Marx before him and as Lenin was to do later. He became a well-known figure in both legal and illegal revolutionary newspaper offices, threw himself wholeheartedly into the work of propaganda and agitation, and founded the anarchist monthly (now weekly) *Freedom*. In retrospect, these poignant years may seem to have been glorious and easy ones, but at the time they seemed mean and hard. Kropotkin even felt impelled to defend individual violence, for although he himself was not a vengeful man, he understood the misery, the confusion, and the frustration from which such acts of terrorism sprang: those who condemned the anarchists because they shed blood, conveniently overlooked the sea of blood shed by nationalists, militarists, colonialists, and imperialists, not over just a few years but over centuries.

Amid all his propaganda and newspaper work, Kropotkin still found the time for theoretical studies. He showed that the great leap forward, begun during the Renaissance and continued in the eighteenth century, was the direct result of scientific progress, and concluded that the new society and the new ethics, too, must be firmly rooted in science. This approach made him a worthy successor of Diderot and Voltaire, of Condorcet and Comte, of Bentham and John Stuart Mill, of Fourier, Owen and Marx, of Godwin, Bakunin, and Spencer, men whose ideas he combined in the shining vision of a new humanity which fosters a harmony of interests whose inner laws become apparent just as soon as the artificial restrictions of power and wealth are removed and man is set free at last.

How dramatically this dream differed from the reality depicted in the novels of John Henry Mackay[48] and other disciples of Proudhon, Stirner, Tucker, and Most![49] The year 1887 was the year of Queen Victoria's

Golden Jubilee, October the month when fog wrapped London in a
clammy yellow cloak. As they had been wont to do for the past thirty-
five years, the unemployed, unfortunate creatures "who had now lost
even their last right, the right of slaving for others," assembled in Tra-
falgar Square. In vain, they had been fighting their daily battle for casual
jobs in the docks. Their ranks included beggars, pickpockets, and idlers,
so much flotsam thrown up by a sea of misery in this great city, as in
all other capitals. Those who lived by the motto of divide and rule were
blaming it all on "those damned Germans," driven out of their fatherland
by Bismarck's anti-socialist law, but the Social Democratic Federation,
for one, knew better and said so quite plainly in its Jubilee Manifesto.
Four million people in Great Britain alone were living on charity; eighty
per cent of the children in the poor schools were half-starved; during
the previous year, fifty-four people were known to have died of starvation
in London alone, where 80,000 women, that is one in every ten, lived by
prostitution.[50]

Suddenly, a man with a red flag climbed on to the plinth of Nelson's
column and began to speak — black police helmets, a sudden charge.
The great wave of humanity flooded back, shouting "Bread or Labor!"
Another speaker recounted the atrocities committed by the British in
India, a third, addressing the crowd from the edge of the immense square,
protested against capitalist oppression at home. Again a great commotion
surged through the masses. Over the dark sea of heads, the red flag could
be seen turning in the direction of Westminster. Without a word being
said, thousands followed it, a somber mass with a will of steel. Along
Whitehall they marched, past the Horse Guards. The Palace of Westminster appeared through the thinning fog. On they went to Westminster
Abbey, and fell upon its doors. Back in the streets once again, they burst
into the immortal song, "The starving poor of England."[51]

Was it not because the reality of these dreamers was so gray, that
their dreams were so rosy and bright? So wide a gulf could only be bridged
in thought, and thought prescribed nothing short of the most radical revolution, one that left no stone of the existing system unturned. It was
this very gulf that had split the anarchists themselves into two distinct
camps: pure idealists and ruthless terrorists. It was often difficult to tell
them apart, so much so that the story Plekhanov told of Herzen's experience might equally well have applied to them: Herzen had, reputedly,
met several priests and bandits in some small Italian town and, to his
astonishment, was quite unable to distinguish between them.[52] Moreover,
both wings agreed that mankind had little to hope for from the State,
not even in the West, where a relatively efficient form of capitalism

159

rendered the State itself more efficient. In Spain, Italy, and even in France, by contrast, the State appeared no more than an organized gang of robbers, to whose licensed violence the hapless inhabitants were exposed. The phase differences in the development of South and West European capitalism were largely responsible for the differences between anarchism and social democracy, between the ideologies of freedom and of authority. What made this fratricidal struggle so bitter — it was fought out daily with sticks, chairlegs, and sometimes even with revolvers[53] — was the fact that while the anarchists felt weak because they could in no way relate to the existing order, the socialists felt strong because they thought that they could.

Still, not even the socialists had come to feel so at home in the existing order as to envisage an alternative to social revolution. This bound the two factions of the workers' movement together despite all their differences. In no single person were the two trends more closely fused than in Ferdinand Domela Nieuwenhuis, whose complex nature and simple spirit helped him to synthesize so many conflicting views. No one showed better than he that free socialism was the spiritual heir of radical liberalism. He was prophet and politician rolled into one. This combination largely explains why Frisian workers called him "our savior," and why the "moderates" were so annoyed when, at one international workers' congress after the other, he consistently rejected their tactical semi-Marxist nostrums and prescribed instead the magical, but to them hateful, cure of the general strike. Nieuwenhuis was, in fact, a true romantic at heart,[54] and though romanticism was in full flower at the turn of the century, it is doubtful whether many others could have embraced it as sincerely as he did. A letter he wrote hurriedly to his wife has come down to us. It must have been written on November 11, the anniversary of the judicial murder of the Chicago martyrs in 1887, the year in which Domela Nieuwenhuis himself was sent to prison. He wrote that "in the hour of their strangulation" he felt oppressed by the walls of his home, and preferred to commune with nature.[55] In his memoirs, *Van Christen tot Anarchist* ("From Christian to Anarchist") which appeared in 1910, one year after the execution of Ferrer, we can read that this incident, too, drove him close to despair.

Although men like Domela Nieuwenhuis were lone figures and though the gulf between anarchism and social democracy grew ever wider and almost unbridgeable, the bourgeoisie remained terrified by what they still considered a united front. Fear of the anarchists was responsible for the repressive measures passed in Germany as early as 1884, in Austria and the United States in 1885, in Belgium in 1886, in France in 1892,

160

in Spain and Italy in 1894, and in Spain once again in 1908. In the 1880s uncontrolled fear pervaded in the otherwise sedate Netherlands, and caused the brutal suppression not only of the Amsterdam "eel riots" (on July 25 and 26, 1886, following the police ban on the removal of live eels from ropes slung across the canals) but also of all major strikes, and the imprisonment of Domela Nieuwenhuis. A proposal by the Italian government for the extradition of all anarchists was frustrated by British public opinion, but various national police forces were already co-operating . Fear was responsible for this wave of repression, but also for the wide influence anarchist ideas had come to enjoy even outside the workers' movement: Spencer, Tolstoy, and Ibsen were not by chance bracketed with the anarchists and described as great prophets in 1900. Indeed, among the contributors to the anarchist journals just before 1900 we discover such unlikely names as Paul Valéry, Henri de Régnier, Rémy de Gourmont, Stéphane Mallarmé, Emile Verhaeren, Octave Mirbeau, Tristan Bernard, Paul Adam, Léon Blum. Fear, finally, was also responsible for the profuse literature devoted to anarchists and anarchist ideas, so profuse in fact, that, as early as 1897, Max Nettlau was able to compile a bibliography running to more than 300 pages.[56] Even Elisée Reclus, who wrote the preface and who was as well informed as anyone could be, expressed his astonishment at this profusion.[57] Three years later came Stammhammer's bibliography, which ran to two volumes.[58]

The bourgeoisie need not have feared, however. The economic boom of 1895–1914 not only gave the reformists among the Social Democrats renewed hope but also stripped revolutionary anarchism of its mass appeal. With Kropotkin it had reached its zenith. The revolution failed to materialize, and the fire of anarchy which had once blazed so fiercely was transformed into a shower of harmless sparks. Active revolutionary anarchism made way for passive dreams of freedom, justice, and greater humanity, so diverse that they could no longer be contained in a single mold. Ever since, the black flag has been flying at half mast.

CHAPTER XI

THE RED TIDE ADVANCES

"Socialism clings to friend and foe alike, waking the inert legions from their sleep. It is being lapped up by Catholic workers and drips down on the narrow circle of the Calvinists. Its denunciations and aspirations have provided libertarians with a new morality. State and society reflect its influence directly or indirectly in a host of new regulations." Thus wrote P. L. Tak in his *Kroniek* of December 29, 1900. Shortly before, Pareto had said much the same, when he recalled in the *Journal des Economistes* what Tertullian had written sixteen hundred years earlier about the rise of Christianity: "We are but of yesterday, but already we fill your entire land."[1]

Tak ended his article, published as the old century was about to be rung out, by expressing the firm belief that the new century would be one of electricity and of socialism. His *Kroniek* was the leading Dutch progressive weekly, but no more socialist than the *Journal des Economistes.* Tak himself was not to embrace socialism openly until three years later, and his article did no more than state a view commonly held by that section of the middle classes which did not shut its eyes to political developments. And not in the Netherlands alone but throughout Western Europe.

Tak may have done so with a measure of satisfaction; others recognized the writing on the wall more reluctantly, but all alike looked upon socialism as the political system of the future. When it had first emerged during the middle of the century, modern socialism, particularly of the French type, had been so novel a concept that it had probably made an even greater impact than it did in Tak's day, despite the fact that at its inception it lacked the closed doctrine, the strict discipline, and the tight organization that were to characterize it at the turn of the century. Friends as well as foes considered the gradual rise of the Marxist tide a much greater threat to the established order than the spasmodic anarchistic wave, which was in any case ebbing even in its more moderate, syndicalist form. The Dutch National Labor Secretariat, for instance, a syndicalist organization founded in 1893, still counted 17,500 members in 1896, but had shrunk to 13,000 by 1898.[2]

To the more thoughtful anti-socialists, the most irritating feature of the red tide was its advance into quarters that had scoffed at it in the past. Thus, even in the Netherlands, traditionally backward in this field, municipal councils had started to concern themselves with such problems as maximum working hours and minimum wages.[3] Elsewhere, too, the red tide had begun to seep into the schools and the universities. Italy had two outstanding "red" professors — Enrico Ferri and Antonio Labriola; in the Netherlands, Frank van der Goes was allowed to deliver a public lecture to the University of Amsterdam on March 3, 1900.[4] In more "advanced" circles, socialism had, in fact, become quite the fashion, as Huret observed, tongue in cheek. In his *Enquête sur la question sociale en Europe,* for instance, he had this to say: "The Pope is a socialist, Wilhelm II is a socialist, Bleichröder, the banker, is a socialist, Nini *pattes en l'air* is a socialist. The greater one's private income, the more idle one's life, the more one plays poker, takes five o'clock tea — the latest Parisian fashion — the more clothes one buys from Redfern or the more haircuts one has at Lenthéric's, the more socialist one becomes."[5] This cynical exaggeration undoubtedly hid a grain of truth, for the two great medieval powers — Pope and Emperor — had both begun to take notice of that modern movement born from the depths of misery. Less exaggerated, and hence more just, was Morand's dictum that, in 1900, French literature, which still led the world, either stood transfixed before social problems, from Curel to Brieux, from Bourget to Prévost, from Coppée to Paul Adam, or else glorified the proletariat, as Zola had done when, rejuvenated by the Dreyfus affair, he wrote his *Four Gospels.*[6] Morand might also have added the names of Péguy and Rolland. There was also a grain of truth in Max Nordau's observation, echoed by Baumont, that the "good workman" had taken the place of the "noble savage." But Nordau and the five hundred strikes that shook France in 1900 notwithstanding, the "good workman" was still very badly off, particularly in France: he had only to raise his voice and the soldiers of the Republic were rushed to the spot to silence him. Still, Nordau was right, inasmuch as no power on earth could halt the remorseless tide.

The most impressive manifestation of this tide was the Socialist Congress of 1900. It met on Sunday, September 23, in the Salle Wagram in Paris. Naturally, not all the delegations were as impressive as the French, with their more than one thousand members (600 from the left and 473 from the right); but the British with 95 delegates; the Germans, with

57; the Belgians, with 37; and the Russians with 24, made their presence clearly felt.[7] There were also a hundred or so smaller deputations from some fourteen European countries, and six from North and South America. All the delegates were still white, however. The first Japanese socialist, Sen Katayama, lacked the money for so long a journey, but he did send a letter of support. At the next Congress, held in Amsterdam in 1904, he was present in person to shake the hand of the leader of the Russian delegation — a most important symbolic gesture, for the Russo-Japanese war had just started.

The Congress as such brought few surprises. Officially it was the fifth, counting from the founding Congress of the Second International in 1889, which had also been held in Paris; but if we include the Congresses of the First International, it was, in fact, the sixteenth or seventeenth. Its historical importance lay not in any innovations but rather in the direction to which it seemed to be pointing. It was the first congress to reveal a trend that was to dominate practically the whole International within less than fourteen years: gradual reform rather than revolutionary overthrow of the existing order. In cannot, however, be said that the Congress took this path with enthusiasm; the fact of the matter was that not even the leaders were conscious of a change of direction. Even Rosa Luxemburg, perhaps the most levelheaded of all the delegates, a staunch revolutionary and hence highly sensitive to what was happening, did not realize the truth at the time.

Historical analysis has a great advantage over political pronouncements, not only because it is retrospective but also because it knows that it is possible to say A while meaning B, or even to say A and to mean A and yet to arrive at B in the end. And that was precisely what was happening at the 1900 Congress, unbeknownst to all but the anarchists, whose acuity would have redounded to their intellectual credit had they not been in the habit of continually denouncing evils even where none existed. Ever since the International Congress held in London in 1896 had voted to exclude them, the anarchists had found nothing good to say of Marxism, be it red or pink. The historian of the Second International, J. Lenz, from his Communist viewpoint, was to rediscover in 1930 the deviation challenged by the anarchists.[8] For non-Communists, the cogency of this criticism is limited. It will probably be more persuasive that van Ravesteyn, the other historian of the Second International, came in 1931 to the same conclusion.[9]

The agenda comprised twelve points, including the search for the best means of fostering international contacts and solidarity; the demand for a maximum working week, a minimum wage, and other improvements;

164

and the call for expropriation and socialization as prerequisites of labor emancipation. The Congress also dealt with the question of war and peace, colonialism, the general suffrage and direct legislation by the people, municipal socialism, the problem of sharing power with bourgeois parties, the problem of trusts, and finally, the general strike. Various subcommittees were given the task of drafting resolutions. It was decided to found an International Labor Bureau with a permanent seat in Brussels. It would house the archives, serve as an information center, deal with disputes and if possible settle them, and, beyond that, keep the doctrine intact. In short, for those who do not consider a comparison between the International and the Church altogether impossible, the Bureau was to be a sort of Curia without an official Pope. The Belgian socialist Camille Huysmans was elected its paid secretary. This was an essential measure if the Bureau was to do its international work properly; but it also contained the germs of bureaucratization, a tendency Michels, then a socialist professor in Turin, was to examine ten years later in a wider context.[10]

There is no need to list all the resolutions since, even at the time, the main attention of the Congress was directed at the ninth item: the burning question of ministerialism. Even the closely connected question of temporary allegiances with bourgeois parties caused far less of a stir, for such allegiances had already been entered into by Belgian Socialists with the Liberals, by Bavarian Socialists with the Clericals and by Italian Socialists with the Republicans. A resolution by Guesde, proscribing all such pacts except in extreme cases and even then with reservations, was quickly passed. In the circumstances, one might have expected the Congress to come down even more resolutely against ministerialism, i.e., against the practice of allowing socialists to serve as ministers in non-socialist Cabinets and hence assuming direct responsibility for government policies. Ministerialism, or "Millerandism" as it was also called (Millerand had, one year earlier, accepted a portfolio in Waldeck-Rousseau's Ministry of Republican Concentration without consulting his party), was an entirely novel phenomenon, and Millerand, though he had served in the same cabinet as Gallifet, the "butcher of the Commune," had joined a government formed for the express purpose of closing the Dreyfus case and hence of consolidating the victory of the Left. Even Jaurès, though undoubtedly opposed to his comrade's appointment, had obviously felt that, in the circumstances, he had best condone it, and he did just that in a lecture on February 10, 1900. This time there had been a noticeable crack in his melodic voice.

The committee appointed by the Congress was divided. After a lengthy discussion, it voted twenty-four to four in favor of a compromise resolution proposed by Kautsky. It condemned ministerialism in principle on the grounds that the presence of a single socialist in a bourgeois government might prevent the party from achieving a majority of its own. Only as an expedient was ministerialism permissible; and, since the Congress was more concerned with principles than with tactics, it was happy to adopt the exclusion clause. Still, it hedged its bets by adding that even temporary ministerial appointments must be endorsed by a large majority of all the parties involved and could only be condoned if the minister concerned agreed to implement party decisions. This shaky resolution ended with an amendment introduced by Plekhanov after consultation with Jaurès: "This Congress declares that a socialist must resign from a bourgeois Government if the organized party is of the opinion that the Government in question has shown partisanship in an industrial dispute between capital and labor." The Congress carried the resolution, twenty-nine votes after Vandervelde had spoken in favor of it on behalf of the Committee and in the face of stiff opposition from Ferri and Guesde, who declared roundly that socialists must never relent in their opposition to bourgeois governments. If France, Italy, and Germany all had their Millerands, the International was bound to collapse. The Ferri-Guesde counterproposal was supported by the Bulgarian and Irish delegations and by half of the French, Italian, Polish, Russian, and North American delegations — nine votes altogether, for each delegation had two votes.

The final resolution, while apparently shutting the door on ministerialism, actually left it wide open. Did the delegates realize it at the time? We shall never know; all we do know is that the door eventually admitted many socialists, including Guesde himself, into government office. Was the door left open deliberately? It seem unlikely; but then the whole discussion was so fraught with emotion that the delegates failed to examine it as carefully as they might otherwise have done. Moreover, the great majority clearly believed Millerand's case to be exceptional. This may explain why the International took a direction in 1900 that would lead, not to the collpase of the movement as an essential feature of modern society — on the contrary — but to its collapse as an international and revolutionary force. Rosa Luxemburg put it all most forcefully in the series of articles she began to write for *Die Neue Zeit* on January 16, 1901.[11]

Another indication of this new direction was the delegates' lukewarm attitude to the weapon of the general strike, which they had previously considered an essential prelude to the social revolution. In London, at least, it had still been part of the official program; in Paris, it appeared

166

at the end of a series of amendments proposed by the Allemanists, the extreme left-wing of the French group. For the rest, the Congress contented itself with a reference to the London resolution,[12] and only Briand, who considered himself the father of the whole idea, made a speech in favor of the tactic.[13] The result was another blow to internationalism. Perhaps the clearest proof of this slide toward the Right, which appeared to those involved as a sensible advance from delusive dreams of paradise to feasible earthly gains (which indeed it was), was provided by the delegates' attitude to militarism and colonialism. Rosa Luxemburg, whose *Miliz und Militarismus*, published the year before, had made her more familiar with the subject than anyone else at the Congress, delivered a magisterial speech although, at thirty, she was hardly of magisterial age. She was the first to identify and offer a theoretical account of the "imperialist" phase of capitalism.[14] The resolutions to which she was speaking were, nevertheless, much weaker than the old party demands for the "abolition of standing armies" and the establishment of a "National Citizen Force." The only new contribution of the Congress, and typical of it, was the decision to form a special youth organization, probably on the model of the Belgian "Young Guards."[15] Here too the "general" had made way for the "particular."

We said earlier that the Red International has often been likened to the Church, but there is a clear distinction between them. For while the Church as a non-political institution could afford to adapt itself to national conditions, socialism as a political movement could not, and it was precisely by its attempts to do so that its internationalism was wrecked in 1914.

The Congress as a whole, let us repeat, was not aware that it was changing tack. Van Kol, who presided over the final session on September 27, spoke of "small differences that were quickly forgotten," and Citoyen Beausoleil — what name could have been more symbolic? — intoned the *Internationale* with the whole Congress joining hastily in the refrain,[16] thus signalling their unity of purpose and confidence in the future.

Next morning, the delegates went on a pilgrimage to the "Mur des Fédérés" in the Père Lachaise cemetery to pay homage to the heroes of the Commune. Vaillant was not allowed to speak for fear of the police; he was a foreigner, after all. But Singer did so, ending with "Vive la Commune! Vive l'Internationale!" There was no incident.

The incidents, many of them, were still to come. For outside the congress hall, the movement was clearly disenchanted with its delegates' work. The cracks that Millerandism had opened in Paris and that had been papered over so skillfully with Kautsky's "caoutchouc resolution" reappeared, and showed that the whole fabric had begun to crumble. Even earlier, in 1899, the same year in which Millerand became a minister, there appeared three books, each of which bore witness to the growing crisis. The first was by Eduard Bernstein, one of the few direct intellectual disciples of Marx and Engels. His *Voraussetzungen des Sozialismus und die Aufgaben der Sozialdemokratie* ("Problems of Socialism and the Tasks of Social Democracy")[17] was a synopsis and elaboration of the articles he had contributed to *Die Neue Zeit* in 1895 and 1896. This theorist, who was then in his late forties and had escaped from Bismark's repressive laws by seeking refuge in London, subjected a number of contemporary Marxist theses to a sharp critique, drawing in part on the experiences of the English labor movement he had gathered during his exile. Without relinquishing Marxism, let alone socialism, he nevertheless challenged Marx's theories of value, surplus value, capitalist concentration, increasing misery, and business crises. Statistics had shown that medium and small-scale industrial concerns had not been swallowed up, nor was the land passing into fewer hands. Moreover, the trade unions had been able to make sure that the workers had not been plunged into a condition of "increasing misery." Capitalist crisis and collapse, finally, was no more than a theoretical possibility. Social reality was much more subtle, he believed, than Marx and Engels had imagined. The new cartels, in particular, provided a means of maintaining social and economic equilibrium. He invoked Kant against Marx. Socialism would emerge victorious, he claimed, not because it was an economic necessity, but because the working class would in due course achieve moral maturity and come to appreciate its desirability. In short, Bernstein was happy to defer the advent of socialism to the Greek calends, a fact he himself expressed in the now famous phrase: "The final aim of Socialism, whatever that may be, means nothing, the movement means everything." In so doing he renounced the use of revolutionary tactics; the movement's real task was to hasten social reforms by participating in the day-to-day work of parliament.[18]

The core of Bernstein's contribution was an attempt to rid Marxism of its eschatological features, which he traced back to Hegelian theory and Blanquist "practice." In any case, Bernstein had the courage of his convictions, for even in 1914–1918, when he was close on seventy, he refused to vote further war credits in the Reichstag, unlike so many of the Majority Socialists who had attacked his revisionist ideas. He had the courage to challenge the authority of Marx and Engels, the better to reconcile socialist thought with what he rightly felt were the practical needs, if not of today then surely of tomorrow. Sorel, who at the time took a keen interest in the revisionist movement — he made several contributions to the revisionist *Sozialistische Monatshefte*, published by Joseph Bloch since 1897 — called Bernstein's revisionism a "return to the spirit of Marxism." Bernstein, he added, had succeeded in re-establishing the unity of theory with practice, whereas Kautsky, his critic, had done no more than produce a hotchpotch of disparate notions wrapped up in revolutionary phrases.[19] In assessing Sorel's own approach, however, we must remember that, as a syndicalist, he preferred to see social democrats as champions of pure reformism. In fact, however, even those who make a careful study of Bernstein's *Voraussetzungen, Wie ist Wissenschaftlicher Sozialismus möglich?* ("How Is Scientific Socialism Possible?"), or *Theorie und Geschichte des Sozialismus* ("Theory and History of Socialism"), all three written at the turn of the century, will fail to gain a coherent picture of his political philosophy. And this is no accident. The quarrel between the revisionists and the reformists may have centered on what was an acceptable degree of flexibility — a problem every intellectual movement has to solve — but it was aggravated by the fact that both factions had willy-nilly been forced to relinquish their overall vision, because both had failed to produce a dialectical response to the dialectical development of capitalism and socialism. This failure was the direct result of their dismissal of Hegelian ideas, with which neither Bernstein nor Kautsky and Victor Adler had ever felt at home. Plekhanov, though two years younger than Adler, three years younger than Kautsky, and seven years younger than Bernstein, had still savored these ideas in Russia, where Hegelianism had proved more resilient than in the West.[20] He was to hand them on to Rosa Luxemburg and Lenin, who rediscovered dialectics. This too was no accident, for both were still young in 1900 — they were both born in 1870 — and hence more open to a method capable of discerning the unity that lies hidden behind opposites. This synthetic approach was, in fact, making a comeback in many other fields as well; for Marxism, though defeated more than once, always rose again; it was like Antaeus, the Libyan giant, who received new strength from his mother, Terra, as often as he was felled to the ground.

In the years under review, Marx-Antaeus had been cut down by more than one enemy. Bernstein may have been singularly courageous, but he was not alone — not even the word "revisionism" was his own — Alfred Nossig had probably been the first to use it in a long since forgotten book, *Die Revision des Sozialismus.*[21]

The second of the three influential books was Paul Weisengrün's *Das Ende des Marxismus* ("The End of Marxism").[22] It called Bernstein the first great neo-Marxist, but criticized him for his lack of consistency,[23] on the grounds that Marxism, however important it may have been for cultural, historical, or psychological reasons, was neither good science nor good politics. It was too mechanical and, in any case, no more than a "metaphysical hypothesis." Socialism would have to find a new theory, or, short of that, a better "metaphysical hypothesis." For just as the atom was no more than a metaphysical hypothesis, it was something physicists could not do without.[24] The unhappy choice of this analogy was never brought home to its happy author, for when the first bomb developed from this "metaphysical hypothesis" was dropped, he was no longer alive. He lived long enough, nevertheless, to see the publication in 1900 of his second and larger book, in which he greatly elaborated his earlier critique of Marxism.[25]

The third book was written by Thomas Masaryk, who later became the first President of Czechoslovakia, but who at the time was still a professor of philosophy in the Czech University of Prague. That book was a revised version of a work he had published the year before under the title of *Krise innerhalb des Marxismus* ("Crisis within Marxism"), a crisis that Masaryk, who like Sorel had never been a socialist, let alone a Marxist, had followed in the columns of the Viennese *Die Zeit*.[26] In his later studies of Russian intellectual life during the nineteenth and early twentieth centuries, Masaryk repeated his devastating charges once again; materialism was unscientific, positivism epistemologically untenable and practically unfeasible; the whole idea of infra- and super-structures vague and pointless, the individual sacrificed to the masses. Bernstein, he added, spoke no more than the truth when he tried to base socialism not on objective but on subjective considerations, not on history but on ethics.[27] In this, too, he was at one with, though not as temperate[28] as, Sorel, who summed up his own views in *La Décomposition du marxisme* (1908).[29] We might add here that the most famous, and most capable, Dutch critic of Marx was M. W. F. Treub, a radical who appeared on the scene a few years later.[30]

With these men, the list of opponents of orthodox Marxism, within or without the Marxist fold, is far from exhausted. In England, the labor movement had always been reformist — neither the Independent Labour Party nor the Fabians, let alone the Labour Party, would have wanted it otherwise. Hyndman and his Social Democratic Federation, who rejected reformism, were too uncompromising to make any headway. Elsewhere, too, revisionism was not a new doctrine. Georg Vollmar, for instance, had anticipated many of Bernstein's later arguments in his *Eldorado-Rede* (1891) and also in his *Staatssocialismus* (1892). This shrewd Bavar-

170

ian had realized that it was impossible to win over peasants to a party that offered them nothing but the liquidation of their own class. In this he was at one with the French *Parti Ouvrier*, which had also promised to protect peasant property against "proletarianization." But the Bavarian, unlike the French peasants, had large holdings, and, in the circumstances, it was not at all surprising that von Bülow should have considered offering Vollmar a post in his Cabinet in 1903.[31] Gabriel Deville, the French translator of *Das Kapital* and a contributor to Jaurès's *Histoire socialiste*, confessed as early as 1895 that the advocates of the old revolutionary methods had been losing ground.[32] S. Merlino, in his *Pro e contro* (1897), called for a broader definition of orthodox socialism.[33] A little later, and more incisively, Tugan Baranovski and Conrad Schmidt joined in the fray. The Russian, whose *Ruskaya fabrika* of 1898 had still been a classical Marxist text,[34] did so in 1901 with his *Studien zur Theorie und Geschichte der Handelskrisen in England* ("On the Theory and History of Trade Crises in England")[35] and with his *Theoretische Grundlagen des Marxismus* ("Theoretical Foundations of Marxism"), published four years later. In particular, he contended that utopian socialism based on ethical foundations was greatly preferable to what he called "quasi-scientific Marxism." Schmidt argued much the same in the series of articles he contributed about 1900 to Bernstein's paper, and also in further writings right up to, and even during, the war. Like Baranovski and Bernstein, he had been an orthodox Marxist, and a book he had written in 1889 still bore a laudatory preface by Engels. Critics, old and new, from the bourgeois camp — such as Diehl, Gävernitz, Herkner, Masaryk, Schmoller, Schulze, Sombart, Wolf, and above all Böhm-Bawerk, whose theory of marginal utility struck heterodox Marxist economists as preferable to Marx's own theory of surplus value — greatly helped to ease the passage of many Marxists into the revisionist, and often into the bourgeois, camp.

A separate development, though closely bound up with the foregoing, was the "return to Kant" movement. For in addition to attacks on its economic and political foundations, Marxism now also suffered an assault on its philosophical groundwork. It all started in 1896 with Hermann Cohen, the neo-Kantian founder of the Marburg school, who in his introduction to Lange's *Geschichte des Materialismus* ("History of Materialism") called socialism an ethical doctrine, and concluded that Kant, not Marx, must be considered the true founder of German socialism. That year also saw the publication of Rudolf Stammler's famous *Wirtschaft und Recht nach der materialistischen Geschichtsauffassung* ("Economics and Justice in the Materialist Conception of History"), which, while granting that historical materialism was the best-known approach to the

171

study of economic developments, insisted that it be fused with an ethical and ideological approach based on Kant. Three years later there appeared *Sozialpädagogik* ("Social Pedagogy") by the even better-known neo-Kantian, Paul Natorp, and also *Ethik und Politik* ("Ethics and Politics") by Franz Staudinger, who, while adhering more strictly to Marxism than the rest, nevertheless supported Stammler's demand for an ethical approach. The classical work on the subject was written in 1900 by Karl Vorländer, the subtitle of whose *Kant und der Sozialismus* ("Kant and Socialism") — "Considered in the Light of the Most Recent Theoretical Movement within Marxism" — emphasized how burning an issue the whole question had become.[36] Mehring hastened to review the book in *Die Neue Zeit*, and did so at length.[37]

Nor did it remain at that. Not only did Vorländer with his *Marx und Kant*, a reprint of a lecture delivered in 1904,[38] and again with his *Kant und Marx* (1911), swear allegiance to Kant, but so too did Max Adler, a member of the radical Austro-Marxistic school, both in his *Kausalität und Teleologie im Streite um die Wissenschaft* ("Causality and Teleology in the Struggle for Science") and in his *Kant und der Sozialismus* ("Kant and Socialism"), two books published in 1904, the centenary of Kant's death and hence a memorable year for one who considered himself a faithful disciple of both Marx and the great philosopher from Königsberg.[39] Similar views were expressed by Otto Bauer, another Austro-Marxist, in his "Marxismus und Ethik," a series of polemical attacks on Kautsky published in *Die Neue Zeit*. Ludwig Woltmann, too, upheld Kant in his *Der historische Materialismus* as the great authority.

If it was not Kant with whom the critics wanted to complete or replace Marx, then it was Dietzgen. Thus Ernst Untermann wrote close on 700 pages to demonstrate that Marxism and logic were as different as chalk and cheese, and argued that old Joseph Dietzgen, a self-educated tanner, had been able to do very much better.[41] Dietzgen was, indeed, making his influence felt. His main work, published in 1869, *Das Wesen der menschlichen Kopfarbeit* ("The Essence of Human Mental Activity") was translated into Dutch in 1903; and in 1910, the year in which Untermann's work was published, Henrietta Roland Holst published a short booklet on Dietzgen's contribution.[42] Benedetto Croce, too, had become disenchanted with orthodox Marxism. In 1896, when his friend Antonio Labriola wrote *Del materialismo storico* ("On Historical Materialism") and Achille Loria came out with his plagiarized version of Marx, Croce began to formulate a host of criticisms, which he collected in 1899 and published under the title of *Materialismo storico*.[43] In it he argued that although theoretical Marxism had enjoyed a brief vogue in Italy after

1895, it was now dead.[44] As early as 1894, Enrico Ferri, at the time
still a Leftist (an American translation of his book was published in 1900),
raised Darwin, Spencer, and Marx to a scientific trinity, thus showing
that he, too, felt that Marx alone was no longer enough.[45] Soon afterward, Mach and Avenarius launched an "attack" on Marxism with their
empirio-critical system. That at least was the view Malinovski (Bogdanov)
expressed in 1907–1908, when reaction was at its height in Russia. Lenin,
whose "terrible logic" made him sniff out the least heresies, much as
Calvin had done before him, rushed into the counterattack with his
Materialism and Empirio-Criticism.[46] Between 1908 and 1912 Vladimir
Simkhovitch tried to keep the readers of the *Political Science Quarterly*
abreast of all the latest developments on the Marxist battle front.[47]

Quite separate and hence somewhat unnoticed was the crucial deviation from Marxism initiated by the Pole, A. Machajski, a deviation that,
seen in retrospect, was at least as important as Bernstein's. In a three-
part work, *Umstvenny rabotchi* ("The Intellectual Worker"), the first
two volumes of which appeared in 1899 and the third in 1904, he distinguished "intellectual workers" (i.e., managers and technicians) from
both capitalists and proletarians, and went on to assert that this rising
"third class" was destined to take control of society — Burnham's "managerial class" of a half-century later. Machajski played some part in the
first Russian revolution.[48] His disciple Lozinski, among others, examined
the religious aspects of socialism at the turn of the century. "Everything
suggests," he wrote in 1902, "that socialism has entered a period of great
ideological change and of ethical and religious creativity."[49] He believed
that this change was inspired by Spinozan ideas; Göhre, for his part, called
for a return to the "original doctrine of Jesus."[50] That year, the Rever-
ends Bruins and Bakker started their "Happier World" campaign in the
Netherlands. All these contributions bore witness to a resurrection of
chiliasm within the labor movement.

Thus revisionism in the wider sense went much further about 1900
than did the movement with which Bernstein's name was directly associated. In Britain, for instance, its roots went back to guild socialism, and
its modern branches included the Fabian Society under the leadership
of Shaw and Sidney and Beatrice Webb.[51] It was not by chance that the
Webbs' history of the British Trade Union movement should have ended
with a postscript by Bernstein (1895) or that the German translation of
James Ramsay MacDonald's *Socialism and Society* (1902) should have
contained a preface by him. In France, the revisionist camp included
Paul Brousse, the champion of "possibilism" in the 1880s, and above
all Jean Jaurès, who tried to replace the materialistic with a materialistic-

cum-idealistic theory of history[52] and, having debated the whole issue with Guesde in Lille in 1902,[53] came out squarely in favor of ministerialism, despite his original reservations. Millerand himself wrote a book on French reformism in 1903,[54] and in Italy the revisionists included not only Croce[55] but also his friend and subsequent enemy, Gentile, who wrote a critique of historical materialism as early as 1897, followed in 1899 by another critique of Marxist philosophy and finally by his conversion to "actualism" and fascism. Then there were Michels and Arturo Labriola, the son of Antonio and, like his father, a university lecturer. In his *Studio sul Marx* (1908) he attacked Marx's doctrine of capitalist stagnation and decay from a syndicalist point of view. (His revisionism, incidentally, did not prevent him from succumbing to Lenin's "terrible logic" in 1917.)[56] Much like Jaurès in France and Turati in Italy, so Emil Vandervelde and Anseele worked for the revisionist cause in Belgium, Troelstra and Vliegen in the Netherlands, and Tugan Baranovski and Peter Struve in Russia. Struve was a member of a Russian group that also included N. Berdyaev and S. Frank, all of whom had started out as Marxists but had ultimately recanted, both individually and also collectively in *Vechi*, a book of essays on the Russian intelligentsia which produced as great a stir in its day[57] as *The God that Failed* by Stephen Spender, Arthur Koestler, and others was to cause forty years later. Then there was Lev Shestov, who followed the same path, though in his own manner, and many, many others as well.

This influx of intellectuals was cause and consequence at once of the sudden blossoming of revisionist and reformist ideas. Emil Vandervelde summed it up during a lecture he delivered on October 22, 1900, to the Amsterdam Socialistisch Leesgezelschap ("Socialist Reading Circle") — he called it a case of "growing pains."[58] This term must be interpreted dialectically: growth of the new, side by side with the death of the old, revolutionary Marxism that had still inspired the delegates to Paris and Amsterdam. Paul Kampffmeyer took a similar view of these changes four years later, when he asked "Have we Social Democrats remained what we were?" and replied: "We have discovered that our main task is to be as practical as we can."[59]

On that occasion he also spoke of the "secret" of the changes that had recently occurred in the social-democratic camp, and traced them back to structural changes within capitalism. Imperialism was beginning to bear its first fruits: the increasing rejection of free competition in favor of monopolies and colonial expansion and the resulting increase in profits, which enabled the system to bribe a thin upper crust of the working class and the petit-bourgeois followers of the socialist parties with higher wages and better living conditions, and hence to divert them from the path of revolution. Carr said much the same thing when he spoke of the nationalization of socialism and of the incipient socialization of the national state.

However, most of the water used to extinguish the fire of revolution poured from the channel of trade unionism. The successful day-to-day work of thousands of trade union officials tended quite naturally to convince them, no less than the millions who had elected them, that the tangible improvements they had wrested from the state in the form of social legislation, or obtained more directly by mutual aid in the form of co-operatives, were lasting achievements, achievements that a revolution could only undo. The sudden influx of intellectuals was another cause and consequence of the general decline in revolutionary ardor. It was not by chance that the *Sozialistische Monatshefte* had been called *Der sozialistische Akademiker* ("The Socialist Academician") during the first two years of its existence, 1896 and 1897. All these factors combined to ensure the victory of revisionism, so much so that in 1902, when the ten-thousandth copy of Bernstein's book came off the presses, Kampffmeyer told Kautsky that the spread of revisionism no longer astonished him.[60]

The "radical" or "orthodox" Marxists put up a stiff resistance, led by Kautsky, Mahring, Cunow, Parvus (Helphand), Hilferding, Rosa Luxemburg, and Lenin. But while Lenin, with his "terrible logic," was quick to draw the lesson of the coming conflict as early as 1903 — at the London congress of the Russian party — and prepared his followers for the advent of Bolshevism,[61] all the rest, insofar as they lived to see the day, succumbed to the "growing pains" sooner or later, and went on to work for social improvements within the capitalist system.

When it rejected this approach, the Sixth International Socialist Congress in Amsterdam was apparently much more "Leftist" than the Paris Congress had been. Delegates' behavior at the outbreak of war ten years later would prove the contrary; still, their radicalism was more than fleeting. At the time, the anarchists were still a force to be reckoned with, particularly in the trade unions. While the moderates were anxious to show that they, the "true" social democrats, were the most reasonable and temperate of all the delegates, the Left reacted with an extra show of revolutionary fervor. A second reason for the Leftist tenor of the Congress was the fact that it was held on the eve of the first Russian Revolution. In his biography of Lucien Herr, Jaurès's teacher, Charles Andler,

175

attached so much importance to this resurgence of the old spirit as well as to the appointment of a Socialist minister in Australia that he described the year 1904 as the beginning of a new epoch.[62]

As it had in Paris, the vexed question of ministerialism figured prominently on the Amsterdam agenda. However, the antagonists were no longer the same. In 1903, at its Congress in Dresden, the German party had passed a resolution condemning revisionism — and hence also ministerialism — out of hand, so much so that Franz Mehring felt entitled to conclude his history of the German Party, published that year, with the remark that "revisionism had never been more than a passing phase in Germany."[63] When Guesde now proposed a similar resolution at a committee meeting preceding the open session, the German delegation and its satellites led by Bebel were only too delighted to support him against Jaurès. The debate that followed was of a standard the Second International would never reach again. All the leading figures took part in it. The Dresden motion was supported by Ferri (Italy), Plekhanov (Russia), Rekovski (Bulgaria), Belfort Bax (Britain), Němec (Bohemia), Rosa Luxemburg and Bebel (Germany). It was opposed by MacDonald, Iglesias (Spain), Hillquit (U. S. A.), Furnémont (Belgium), Renaudel, Knudsen (Denmark), Branting (Sweden), Kringen (Norway), and Jaurès (France). Two compromise amendments, one by Adler and Vandervelde and another by Troelstra, both based on Kautsky's resolution of 1900, were rejected; and the Dresden resolution was adopted for recommendation to the Congress at large — twenty-seven committee members having voted against it and twelve having abstained. On Friday, August 19, the matter was brought up for plenary discussion. Vandervelde, who refused to act as spokesman for the majority, gave an objective account of the work of the Committee, and Jaurès followed with a speech that turned out to be a tour de force. Even the official Congress report spoke of the "great sensation" he caused when, defending his life's work, he took the offensive and declared prophetically: "The greatest threat to Europe and the world, to liberty and the progress of socialism . . . does not come from the so-called compromises, or dangerous experiments of the French socialists . . . but from the political impotence of the German Socialist Party." What, he went on to ask them, are you doing with your three million votes? The reply came from Bebel. He was an honest man and knew that Jaurès had been right to claim that the German party was impotent, but he, like the great majority of the delegates, also realized that of all the socialist parties in the leading countries the French alone had the slightest chance of changing the system from within. To Jaurès's question, he had only this answer: wait until our three million have

176

grown to seven or eight — an answer reflecting his sense of helplessness. For all that, the Dresden resolution was adopted by a vote of twenty-five to five with twelve abstentions:[64] *anathema sit haereticis.*

If we add that the Congress also adopted a radical resolution on the general strike, proposed by Henriette Roland Holst, the leader of the Dutch delegation, and supported by Briand, then it does indeed look as if the "Left" had scored a resounding victory in Amsterdam, while the "Right" had been soundly defeated. But these terms, though indispensable, are at best schematic. Thus the radical Dutch resolution on the general strike was only adopted after two even more radical resolutions had been voted down. Henriette Roland Holst's real triumph had to wait another year, when the revolutionary weapon she championed proved its worth in the Russian Revolution. The problem of militarism was an even thornier one. Jaurès was not wrong: the radical theory imported from east of the Rhine masked the German workers' incapacity for present action — the "Leftist" phrases had "Rightist" origins. And Jaurès's own "Rightist" tactics reflected the fact that, in the West, the socialist movement had far greater chances of making its influence felt: here the "Rightist" deviation was born out of a "Leftist" situation. Furnémont, the Belgian delegate, stressed this contrast at some length, much as Engels had done in 1891; but the divisions between Left and Right ran much deeper. Jaurès had good reason to warn the Congress against Kautsky's claim that socialist participation in government could only be condoned in cases of national danger. Which of these two leaders was closer to the truth, or more to the Left — Kautsky, who by his *dictum* anticipated and indirectly endorsed the sacrifice of peace, and hence of socialism, to the Moloch of war, or Jaurès, who foreseeing the same development said that he felt unable to "follow nationalist ministerialism through thick and thin"? In any case, Jaurès was to pay for his anti-militarism with his death, thus proving the honesty of his convictions. Moreover, thirty years later, when the great majority of German Social Democrats bowed out before Hitler, they demonstrated the hollowness of their revolutionary phrases and proved the truth of the bitter taunt Jaurès had flung at them in Amsterdam: "You mask your impotence for action by escaping into irreconcilable theoretical formulae with which Comrade Kautsky will be happy to supply you while he still has breath to do so." Bitter though this reproach may have been, subsequent events in Germany and Kautsky's own role in them were to show that, if anything, it had not been bitter enough.

August Bebel, the builder of the German party, and a man of sixty-four in 1904, alone came away unscathed, thanks to his innate simplicity

177

and honesty, but above all because he died in 1913, shortly before the movement reached the crossroads and split asunder for good. Jean Jaurès, by contrast, forty-seven years old in 1904, was made to pay a heavy price for his stand. Not only was he not offered the ministerial post he had sought as the best means of spreading the message of peace — the French bourgeoisie picked its "socialist" allies very carefully — but also because on July 31, 1914, when he had already lost the great fight for peace, one Raoul Villain sealed his fate in the Café du Croissant with a bullet. One year later, James Keir Hardie (forty-eight years old in 1904) died; and though his was not a violent end, he was heartbroken by the collapse of the International he had helped to build. Shaw was quite correct in claiming that the war had killed Keir Hardie. Georgi Valentinovich Plekhanov, well into his sixties at Amsterdam, was to die in 1918 an exile in Finland; though a staunch opponent of the October Revolution he had refused as staunchly to make common cause with its enemies. Victor Adler, too, had steered a middle course. Five years older than Plekhanov, he died a few months later, on Armistice Day. But when he died, the Austrian republic was already in sight, and he could comfort himself with the knowledge that he had done much to prepare its advent.

January 15, 1919, was the day on which Rosa Luxemburg and Karl Liebknecht were murdered. When Rosa Luxemburg had addressed the Amsterdam delegates in 1904, dressed in a light summer frock, she, the most gifted of all, had just turned thirty-four. Fifteen years later, her corpse was found floating in a canal. She had been brutally assaulted by reactionary officers, and she, too, may be said to have fallen victim to the conflict we have described, if indirectly. Karl Hjalmar Branting, who had been as unflinching in his views as Rosa Luxemburg had been in hers, died in 1925 at the age of sixty-five, after having formed his third ministry. The fact that circumstances had proved as favorable to his work for peace as they had proved unfavorable for Jaurès's does not increase his merit, but does not detract from it either. Pablo Iglesias died that same year at the age of seventy-five, having done for the Spanish party what Branting did for the Swedish. Though he had remained an orthodox Marxist, he had been unable to prevent the deflection of the Left wing of his party, which joined the Third International in 1921. Enrico Ferri died four years later, an old and sickly man — a fervent Leftist at Amsterdam, when he was forty-eight, he had ended up with the Fascists at seventy. Pieter Jelles Troelstra died within a year, also at the age of seventy. Though he had sided with the Right wing of his party, his heart had remained with the Left, as the railway strike which took place at the time of the Amsterdam Congress had shown and as his stand in 1918 was to prove again. The fact that he could not reconcile this contradiction was the source of his strength, and also of his disappointment. Aristide Briand died two years later. He had been forty-two at Amsterdam, where he had still spoken in favor of the general strike, but once he became a minister he had seen fit to use armed force to defeat a far from general strike. He had been Prime Minister of France on no fewer than eleven occasions and worked for peace with Germany even when the storm troopers were already marching through Berlin. Five years later came the death of James Ramsay MacDonald, twice Prime Minister of Great Britain. During his second term in office, in 1921, he denied his own creation and so presided over his own political destruction. He died a forgotten man while on a cruise meant to restore his health. One year later in the summer of 1938, the last two of these great figures — Karl Kautsky and Emil Vandervelde — were laid to rest. Munich had by then written *finis* to the Second International. Vandervelde, who died at the age of seventy-two, had joined the Belgian War Cabinet in 1914, and had served his country and his party — this, too, had become possible — in as many departments as he had served them in cabinets. Kautsky died under far sadder circumstances, at the age of eighty-four. He had become an exile in the same part of Amsterdam where, thirty-four years earlier, he thought he had celebrated the greatest triumph of his life. He, too, was in a sense a victim of the conflict within the social-democratic camp, for had the movement not been cowed by its fear of communism, it might well have been able to prevent Hitler's seizure of power and hence Kautsky's exile. For all that, it was true of him as of all the rest of these "apostles," that he had pledged his life to the cause of socialism, or to put it as Lombard did in his Zurich lectures of 1896, to "the living force of the coming centuries."[65] But besides this truth there stands another that could well have served as his epitaph. It formed the title of a book written by Valentin Gitermann, published in Zurich during that same tragic year of 1938: *Die historische Tragik der sozialistischen Idee* ("The Historic Tragedy of the Socialist Idea").

179

CHAPTER XII

MODERN MAGNATES

On April 7, 1900, a short but incisive study by Edmund Théry appeared as a preface to Francis Laur's three-part *De l'Accaparement*.[1] According to Théry, the concentration of industry that had occurred at the turn of the century and to which Laur's work was devoted was the logical continuation of a process begun the moment it became clear that a 500 horsepower steam engine was more economical to run than ten 50 horsepower steam engines. He showed that the horsepower available to every Frenchman had doubled since 1880, so that each citizen could now command the strength of three iron slaves, over and above his own muscular power and that of his animals.[2] To be profitable, however, these powerful new engines had to be concentrated in large factories, and the "dead concentration" of small enterprise replaced with the "living concentration" of big business. In this field, France was exceedingly backward: by the side of the seven million workers recorded during the census of 1891, there still existed more than 7.5 million small entrepeneurs. Even if all the workers' dependents were taken into account, France had no more than 125 employees to every 100 employers.

Small wonder then that Laur devoted so much attention to the spread of trusts and cartels. In this field, too, France, the great leader in the cultural and technological spheres, was being rapidly overtaken not only by America and Germany but also by Britain and Austria.[3] True, France had several national "comtoirs," but their number was barely greater than those run by the various international oil, dynamite, sulphuric acid, and soda cartels, each independent of the others. What was the recent concentration of French industry, to which Laur devoted the third part of his work, compared with the German to which he had devoted the second part? Germany, which had boasted some one hundred cartels in 1889, had increased that figure to 300 by 1900, and was to increase it to as many as 600 on the eve of the First World War.[4] Nor was Laur the only Frenchman to attach so much importance to this burning problem; Paul de Rousiers was another. In 1901 he followed his earlier work on American industrial monopolies with one on industrial concentration in the world at large; which cut the ground from under Laur's feet.[5] Though he did not mention him by name, he accused Laur of inconsistency — a charge, incidentally, leveled at him by many participants in a discussion that was as confused as its subject was new.

The term *"accaparement,"* de Rousiers felt, applied exclusively to "corners," "rings," "pools," or "deals" — long-standing practices for cornering certain commodities and holding on to them until they could be sold at grossly inflated rates. The most famous example, Joseph Leiter's attempt in 1897 in Chicago to corner the world's grain supplies, was still fresh in de Rousiers's memory.[6] Genuine trusts and cartels, by contrast, were permanent institutions and hence lacked the temporary and speculative character of the *accaparement.* For the rest, trusts were combinations of enterprises and cartels were combinations of entrepreneurs. Both aimed to control the market by eliminating competition, fixing prices, charing out supplies, buying raw materials *en bloc*, and cutting out middlemen with the help of special distribution centers.[7]

According to de Rousiers, there was nothing mysterious about this whole business; trusts and cartels were genuine "producers" and did not use the methods characteristic of the *accapareurs.* Pierpont Morgan financed the steel trust quite openly; everyone knew that Rockefeller with his Standard Oil Company was the oil king, Havemeyer was the sugar king, and a certain Berlin banker was king of the Silesian zinc mines.[8] Laur, however, could console himself with his rival's conclusion that, historically speaking at least, the distinction between "bad" and "good" industrial and commercial combines was not as absolute as he had suggested in his first chapter. "Rings," de Rousiers also had to admit, were rudimentary trusts; and though they could be distinguished from the latter in essence, they bore all the hallmarks of speculative conspiracies.[9] Laur may also have taken comfort from the fact that it made little difference to the ruined competitors whether they had been squeezed out by temporary or more lasting monopolistic combines. Finally, he may have recalled the dictum of Adam Smith, the father of modern economics, who, paraphrasing Turgot, had claimed that whenever merchants, be they industrialists or traders, were allowed to associate, they invariably plotted against the public good.[10] While working on the last part of his book, Laur might at any rate have read this indictment in the equally thick tome of his compatriot André Colliez.[11]

According to Colliez, most German industries were already run by cartels, while American trusts commanded a combined capital of 30–35 billion dollars, or one quarter of the country's industrial wealth. Although the trend had started much later in England, there too the trusts were growing as strong as they were numerous. In Austria, France, and Belgium, some of the most important branches of industry had been combined into cartels, and the same process was even taking place in backward Russia.[12] Colliez's conclusions were thus not essentially different from those of his predecessors. The leaders of the industrial revolution who had started this process of concentration may have done so reluctantly, but from the pronouncements of Turgot and Adam Smith with which Colliez sent his book on its way, the Manchester Liberals ought to have realized that with the emergence of limited companies, the process of concentration had become irreversible. Henceforth legal measures against the new associations proved of little avail; the state had to give them their head and to keep watch over some of their sharper practices.[13]

Although the French devoted much attention to trusts and cartels, they were neither the only ones nor even the first to write profusely on the subject. They had been anticipated in Austria by Friedrich Kleinwächter, whose *Die Kartelle* had appeared in 1883[14] — the year of Marx's death. Marx himself had predicted, but not lived to see, the modern concentration of capital, which he made the cornerstone of his theory of capitalist collapse.

Die Kartelle was not particularly informative; for when Kleinwächter wrote it, Germany had no more than twenty or so cartels, most of which had existed for less than ten years,[15] so that he was obliged to rely largely on hearsay.[16] Nevertheless, this pioneer was, in a sense, one of the most important of them all, not least because he contended that cartels provided an alternative to the socialist method of solving the social question by the abolition of private property. The aim of the new industrialists was to put an end to anarchy in production and distribution, a state of affairs that was as detrimental to the producers as it was to the consumers. True, state socialism would be able to achieve the same end, and had, in fact, gone quite a long way toward it: the state already ran schools, post offices, railways, banks, and mines; and the municipalities already controlled gas and water works, public transport, and even savings banks. But what really mattered was not ownership but control: all the state needed to do was to supervise the running of privately owned cartels where they already existed and to help to create new ones wherever they were needed. Kleinwächter's was thus the first plea for a reformed type of capitalism, for a controlled economy. This professor in remote Czernowitz, where no cartel or trust had ever made its presence felt, then went on to ask himself what form of society was being foreshadowed by these institutions, thus posing a problem that was to fill volumes in the years to come.

Naturally, socialists, too, took a keen interest in the subject; Adolf Braun devoted a long pamphlet to it as early as 1892.[17] Cartels, according to him, reflected bourgeois dissatisfaction with that *laissez-aller* policy that had first inspired them with the wish for a "national economic policy" and later for cartels, when competition at home seemed as ominous as competition from abroad, leading as it did to a hyper-concentration of capital and to overproduction. He noted that this new trend had begun to tell against the workers: not only because the employers were more united than before but also because the employees had been made even more dependent.[18] State intervention, according to him, was not the panacea it had become for so many bourgeois writers for, even if it could be put into practice, it would turn out to be totally ineffective and irrational.[19] He nevertheless took an optimistic view, if only because the concentration and accumulation of capital was, as Marx had predicted, ushering in the ultimate crisis of capitalism, with society divided into a few dozen owners and hundreds of millions of dispossessed. This very division was bound to lead to the "expropriation of the expropriators."[20] F. M. Wibaut, who was to use much the same approach some ten years later, put it all no less bluntly when he prophesied that the growing pressure of the trusts would either lead to the gradual socialization of industry or to the complete enslavement of the masses.[21]

With the spread of trusts there also came wider knowledge of their intrinsic character. Two years after the publication of Braun's pamphlet three books provided an almost complete survey of the field. The first, like the texts by Braun and Wibaud, was written from a socialist viewpoint, but its author, Rudolf Meyer, was also a Catholic. The most unusual mixture of historical, economic, social, and political observations he produced proved, on closer inspection, to have been based on the novel but by no means illegitimate idea expressed in the title of his work: *Der Capitalismus fin de siècle* ("Fin de siècle Capitalism").[22] In Chapter VI, devoted to modern cartels, Meyer drew attention to their less savory aspects. In particular, he recalled that when the largest U. S. distillery refused to join the newly formed "whiskey trust" in the late 1890s, its competitors planted a bomb that destroyed the distillery together with the hired assassin. When the story eventually leaked out, the instigators of the crime were brought before the courts — and acquitted.[23] By forming cartels, industrialists were trying not only to eliminate competition but also to defend themselves against the enemies of capitalism, both old, like the Catholics, and new, like the Social Democrats. Among Catholic opponents, Meyer mentioned the Abbé Morrel, Bishop von Ketteler, Cardinal Manning, and Pope Leo XIII, whose encyclical *Rerum novarum*, of May 17, 1891, he claimed had been inspired by Wilhelm II's call for an international social conference in Berlin.[24] Stranger still was Meyer's view of the broad historical context in which modern cartels and trusts were being formed. The cartel movement, according to him, was the same phase of antiquated capitalism that had characterized the economic organization of the guilds at the time of their emergence. Just as the development of the latter had culminated in the storming of the Bastille, so the enslavement of the workers resulting from the banding together of employers must lead to a new and victorious struggle for freedom. However, this time there was more than just one force to take over from what had become a bankrupt estate. On the left, the militant "internationalists" waved their Marxist bible; in the center, a large crowd followed a man in a black robe, the modern Montanist, Domela Nieuwenhuis; and to the right, singing psalms, another sizable group followed a priest in vestments holding the encyclical of 1891. But then — so this new Dante concluded his *Inferno* — "the two wings outflank and scatter the procession of ailing anchorites in the center and join forces with their several battle cries: Catholicism-Socialism."

The second book to appear in 1894 was less inspirational, but all the more effective. It was a collective work produced by the so-called academic socialists, and compiled by Gustav Schmoller on behalf of the Verein für Sozialpolitik, of which he himself was the founder.[25] This association was opposed to the "abstract" and "amoral" character of classical economics, and the subject of cartels proved so much grist to its mill. In writing of cartels it could give free rein to its passion for facts no less than for ethics. In fifteen essays, various authors examined the internal structure of ten German and five foreign cartels (in France, Austria, Russia, Denmark, and America). So great was the impact of the book that Max Weber asked Robert Liefmann to write his doctoral thesis on it.[26] It appeared in 1897,[27] and Liefmann returned to the subject in 1900, with a book on the monopolistic associations of employers and workers that were then enjoying a brief vogue in Britain.[28] In 1905, he published his famous *Kartelle und Trusts*,[29] which ran to six impressions, sold 25,000 copies, and was translated into Swedish, French, Dutch, and Russian, becoming the most widely read book on the subject.

The third book published in 1894 came from the pen of J. Stephen Jeans,[30] who like Liefmann wanted to be neither apologist nor judge. He dealt with trusts — he still used the term in its broadest sense — in the food industry (flour, sugar, and whiskey) and in the oil, cotton, copper, and chemical industries, and also in shipping. He attacked the

184

"anarchy" prevailing in these industries — the old critique of the Utopian socialists had obviously spread to men of other persuasions — and showed that technical progress was leading to overproduction and hence to recurrent crises. Moreover, the emergence of new trusts after all such crises suggested that they were intended to prevent slumps by restricting output and maintaining high prices. Trusts, in fact, played much the same role as the American tariff laws or the German Zollverein.[31] Though he did not put it in so many words, Jeans had thus come to see the links between trusts and the growing virulence of nationalism, with all the dangers that entailed. In particular, high prices at home encouraged foreign competitors to dump their goods or, whenever tariff barriers prevented this, to produce the same articles more cheaply for their own markets. A case in point was the British bleaching powder trust, which had kept production down and prices up, with the result that France had been forced to build up her own bleaching powder industry and Britain had lost a valuable customer. The history of the trust movement was full of such pitfalls, all based on a central anomaly, namely that private trusts, though they tried to check production and distribution in their own sectors, failed either to gain complete control or, where temporary control was gained, merely increased production by better organization, thus vitiating their own policy.

A telling example which Jeans, who confined his studies to Britain and the U. S. A., did not mention, was the famous Rheinisch-Westfälisches Kohlen-Syndikat (Rhenish-Westphalian Coal Syndicate), at that time the greatest of all European cartels. If its incubation period was indicative of its size, then it was very large indeed, for that period lasted from 1879 to 1893. Again, the intention was the restriction of output, following the crisis in the wake of the so-called "Gründer" boom — the mushroom growth of new enterprises in 1871–1873 financed with French war indemnities. Yet fifteen years after its foundation, when the syndicate was being run most efficiently by Emil Kirdorf, and the various subsidiaries no longer jeopardized its work by making private arrangements, production began to rise regularly, from just over 35.5 million tons in 1894 to well over 53.5 million tons in 1900.[32] The syndicate's annual reports show that not only did production increase absolutely, it also did so relatively in respect to the coal output of the entire German Reich: while the syndicate accounted for less than half the total output in 1900, by 1912 it accounted for 93.5 million tons out of a total of 177 million.[33] At the same time the industry passed into an ever smaller number of hands: in 1893 the syndicate had 96 members, by 1904 that number had dropped to 84, and ten years later no more than 62 were left. Every one of these 62, however, produced an average of 1,429,000 tons of coal as against 337,000 tons in the initial years.[34]

In view of these figures it is not surprising that contemporary writers, no matter how much they favored or deplored the new trend, should all have agreed that it had become irreversible, and that many of them should even have foreseen the cartellization of cartels, a concentration of industrial power against which the state, though its power too had increased by leaps and bounds, would be impotent to act in the long run. Laur, for one, put it quite plainly in 1900: "It cannot be denied that we have reached a turning point in the economic history, not only of our own country, not only of Europe or America, but of the whole human race."[35] Three years later, F. C. Huber was to speak of a mass phenomenon, a world-historical process that would bring all civilized countries under its spell with irresistible force. Between 1887 and 1890 in Germany alone the number of cartels had increased from 70 to 137, and between 1897 and 1902 from 250 to almost 350.[35] Many books were written which examined this process. We shall pass over two which were published in 1898, and consider the year 1900, which saw numerous writings on the subject. Apart from Laur and Liefmann, three other important books appeared that year. Their authors were Ely,[37] Jenks,[38] and Colliez;[39] and according to Sombart's expert view, everything of theoretical value was contained in their writings and in those of Kleinwächter.[40]

Let us, however, now turn to three historical phenomena that have not been paid the attention they deserve by any of these authors. The first was that the new trend did not remain confined to industrial capital but spread to financial capital as well, to the great benefit of the former. As early as 1905, Riesser in his ten lectures to the Berlin Vereinigung für Staatswissenschaftliche Fortbildung (Association for Political Progress) was able to show that German banking had become concentrated in the hands of the famous eight;[41] and he attributed this development (a) to the emergence of cartels in the 1890s, (b) to the crisis of 1900, (c) to the foundation of the United States Steel Corporation on February 23, 1901, and (d) to the foundation of the Düsseldorf Stahlwerkverband on March 1, 1904.[42] The development had been both direct and indirect: direct as a result of greater capitalization and the consequent swallowing up of smaller private and savings banks, the creation of combines by the formation of daughter companies, and the acquisition of majority shareholdings; indirect by the use of sleeping partners and the formation of agencies, branches, and special deposit banks.[43] As a result of all these manipulations, German banking had fallen into the hands of the Bank für Handel und Industrie, the Berliner Handelsgesellschaft, the Commerz- und Diskonto-Bank, the Deutsche Bank, the Diskonto Gesellschaft, the Dresdner Bank, the Nationalbank für Deutschland, and the A. Schaffhausenscher Bankverein.[44] The last-named was to stay in business until 1914, when it had to surrender its independence except in name. The capital of the four greatest among the great German banks and their subsidiaries was estimated by Riesser (with certain reservations) at close on two billion marks.[45] What interests us more, however, is the entanglement of this capital with that of the large mining, engineering, electrotechnical, and chemical cartels. In mining, Riesser mentioned some sixty companies which had members of the big banks on their boards; in the engineering industry there were twenty-four; in the electrotechnical industry, twenty-nine; and in the chemical industry, nine.[46] Although this current was probably strongest in Wilhelminian Germany, it was by no means confined to that country. In Britain, there were five powerful banks. While the leading French banks were far less involved with industry, Lysis, who did much the same study for France as Riesser had done for Germany, has shown that the special "banques d'affaires" provided financing for big business and particularly for foreign concerns, as native industrial empires were still relatively few.[47] Belgium and the Netherlands, too, experienced a fusion of banking and industry, though slightly later than Germany.[48] Not, incidentally, that *all* the smaller banks suddenly disappeared in its wake or that no new ones founded; as Sombart has shown, there was also an opposite current.[49]

Rudolf Hilferding applied the term "Finanzkapital" to this entire process of concentration, so characteristic of economic developments at the turn of the century. Under that title his famous book, one of the few classics of Marxist science, appeared in 1910, though most of it had already been written by the time Riesser's work was published.[50] An orthodox Marxist at the time, Hilferding concluded that finance capital in its ultimate form set the seal upon the dictatorship of the financial magnates. Their dictatorship in one country was easily reconciled with a similar dictatorship in another, but not with the needs of the masses exploited by capital at home and abroad. "In the tremendous clash of opposing needs, the dictatorship of the financial magnates finally makes way for the dictatorship of the proletariat."[51] Hilferding's book was too scholarly to make a great impact on the masses. Lenin, however, would more than repair this fault when, having read Hilferding, Riesser, Liefmann, J. A. Hobson's *Imperialism* (1902), Hermann Levy's *Monopole, Kartelle und Trusts* (1909), and every other relevant text he could discover during his exile in Berne, he published his *Imperialism: The Highest*

Stage of Capitalism in 1906.[52] Its influence was as great as its size was small.

The second historical phenomenon we must mention, however briefly, is the fact that governments were forced to take a closer look at the activities of trusts as soon as the latter began to manipulate price levels in such crucial economic spheres as the coal and iron industries.[53] State intervention became all the more imperative once consumers had proved unable to stem the tide by the creation of special purchasing centers or by a policy of support for the remaining independent industries.[54] But the state, too, was relatively helpless, since as a capitalist institution it was bound to further the interests of capital and, moreover, because its liberal ideology made it reluctant to interfere. For if there had to be freedom of trade, why should there not be freedom to enter into trade alliances? In fact, the state could adopt one of five possible attitudes toward the trusts: 1) complete indifference; 2) casual intervention; 3) a general ban subject to certain exceptions; 4) recognition subject to certain controls; and 5) manipulation, by bestowing or withholding government contracts from existing cartels or by creating state-run cartels in certain branches of industry.[55] All these options were known, but characteristically enough, only the first three were used in this period, and the third only in the United States, where the idea of free competition was most strongly entrenched.

In 1887, for instance, the United States enacted the Interstate Commerce Act, ostensibly to prevent unjust discriminations by the railroads between persons, places, and commodities, but in fact fostering monopolistic practices. This act was followed in 1890 by the Sherman Anti-Trust Act, which served to "protect trade and commerce against unlawful restraint and monopoly." The use of the term "unlawful" clearly suggested that there existed lawful monopolies, a view that was also reflected in the British legal distinction between "reasonable" and "unreasonable" trade restraints, and in the litigation to which the term gave rise. Between the Sherman Act and the Clayton Act of 1914, four other anti-trust laws were passed in the United States. In 1898, a permanent commission was appointed and made wide use of its powers to investigate infringements of the anti-trust legislation without, however, being able to halt the new trend. On the contrary, by one of those paradoxes in which the history of capitalism is so rich, the very anti-trust laws that were meant to protect the "small man" often resulted in his elimination. Thus preventive legislation often led to the formation of mammoth concerns that, though they were not monopolies in law, were nevertheless controlled by a single company.[56]

In Germany, the process was somewhat slower though it certainly caused no less concern. The Reichstag debated the problem at length in 1897, in 1900, in 1902, and again in 1908. In 1900 there was a demand for state surveillance, and in 1908, for a general policy of control, but nothing came of either. In 1904 a congress of jurists dealt with the relationship between the state and cartels; in 1903 Schmoller and Kirdorf argued it all out in the Verein für Sozialpolitik. While the Americans took positive anti-trust measures, the less individualistic Germans did nothing of the kind. On the contrary, Germany was the first country to grant trusts legal recognition — in 1923, after the war had shown how useful they could be to the state.[57]

Conversely, even before the state realized how useful a contribution industrial combines could make to the war effort, the trusts had come to appreciate that the state could help them not only to capture new markets abroad but also to suppress labor unrest at home. They seized this chance all the more readily because, though they were admittedly in a stronger position to deal with their labor force than individual employers, they were nevertheless vulnerable due to the crisis within capitalism that had arisen about the end of the century and to which the trusts themselves owed their origin. It was this vulnerability that forced them to accumulate reserves for the lean years from the extra profits they made in the fat, a practice that they seemed to think entitled them to boast that they served as so many buffers against recurrent crises. It was also this vulnerability that caused large-scale industry, highly mechanized and organized as it was, not only to make unprecedented demands on the professional skills of its workers, but also to foster the growth of a labor aristocracy and hence to split the working class into a right and a left wing, the right in particular sending its representatives into the various parliaments and thus participating in the deliberations of government. All in all, the capitalist state and monopoly capital were becoming so intertwined that it was often impossible to tell where the one began and the other one ended. More particularly, there was no longer a sharp boundary between the trust or cartel on the one hand, and the semi-public sector of modern industry, a hybrid of private enterprise and state control, on the other. Their vulnerability, finally, also explains the reactionary attitude characteristic of modern magnates,[58] an attitude that contrasts so strikingly with their modern planning methods, efficiency, rationalization, and mechanization. It was no accident, to mention but one example, that Kirdorf, the founder of the Rheinisch-Westfälisches Kohlen-Syndikat, should have had a meeting with Hitler as early as 1927, and that he should have become Nazi Party Member no. 71,032.

189

Vacillation between reactionary and progressive attitudes is also reflected in the many disparate economic theories that sprang up at the time. In 1900 there was little agreement about what was probably the central economic problem,[59] namely the accelerating tempo of capital turnover. Thus while Lexis spoke of a general trend to speed up all economic processes, von Böhm-Bawerk argued that the capitalist mode of production had precisely the opposite tendency.[60] Sombart tried to calm these troubled waters by pointing out that each of the two contenders was right in his own way. In any case, the accelerated turnover of capital was yet another of the contradictions so typical of capitalism: it called for a massive investment of capital in expensive machinery, and that capital could not be recovered for a very long time.[61]

The famous controversy between Gruizel and Gothein took place about the same time. According to Gruizel, cartels were the direct result of recent economic slumps; according to Gothein, they were caused by the latest booms. Huber, for his part, argued that cartels were the direct results of depressions caused by the over-capitalization of industry which had been proceding apace for several decades.[62] Here we have yet another contradiction, for many other authors contended that over-capitalization was the direct consequence of trust operation. In 1900, for instance, the share capital of the United States Steel Corporation was worth close to 1.5 billion dollars, though the actual cost of acquisition of the corporation's property was less then eight hundred million.[65]

All these differences in opinion were signs of the much deeper uncertainty that was threatening to undermine the solid foundations of classical economics. On its ruins, Sombart proposed to build his "three economic doctrines":[64] a guiding or metaphysical theory, a structural semi-scientific theory, and, most important of all, an explanatory theory. It behooved the economist to perform an "egg dance" between all three.[65]

The inherent contradiction of capitalism brought into the open by the emergence of trusts and cartels ushered in a fierce political struggle and a keen academic debate about their true nature. As for the latter, the modern observer must agree with Rudolf Meyer's view that *fin de siècle* employers' combines were milestones on the road to "orderly" capitalism. What Meyer failed to explain, however, or what, at best, he left buried beneath his elegant flow of rhetoric, was why "orderly" capitalism should have appeared in two distinct guises, one tame and the other predatory — tame inasmuch as it checked competition and predatory inasmuch as, in so doing, it gained a stranglehold on the state and hence wielded far greater power than free enterprise had ever done. In the first heat of the struggle there seemed little doubt that the right lay with those who considered it pointless to fight monopolies, the latest phase of capitalist development, while leaving capitalism itself untouched.

The latest phase was also the toughest. The sharp silhouette our own century, with its interminable conflicts and violent clashes, was to cast on the screen of modern history was clearly foreshadowed by the machinations of that new race of industrial empire-builders who were all powerful, not only on the stage of their enterprises but also behind the scenes, through the press and through parliament. They were clever men and hard as stone. True, few of them were as brilliant as Walter Rathenau, poet and scholar, who in 1899 joined his father as a member of the board of one of Germany's biggest trusts, the Allgemeine Elektrizitätsgesellschaft. It was his tragic fate that he fell victim to the very forces he had helped to unleash. While he had fostered them as forces of progress, his assassins tried to exploit them for the most reactionary ends. In 1900 both facets of monopoly capitalism combined to shape the personality of those modern magnates, who were rightly called the industrial barons of our age.

CHAPTER XIII

URBI ET ORBI

A census taken on December 1, 1900, showed that Germany could boast
33 cities with more than 100,000 inhabitants each. In the whole of Europe, there were 147 such cities with a total population of some forty
million. In other words, one in every ten Europeans was a city dweller.
By 1913 the number of large cities had risen to 183, accommodating
about sixty million people or some 13.5% of Europe's total population.
How fast urbanization was spreading in this period, is perhaps best appreciated when we remember that, as late as 1890, Europe had no more
than 120 large cities,[1] so that their number had increased by more than
a third in less than a quarter of a century.

Small wonder that the problem of urbanization attracted the attention
of a vast array of writers. Legoyt, the director of the French Statistical
Bureau, was the first to write an authoritative book on the subject, as
early as 1870.[2] He was followed, seven years later, by the Norwegian
V. E. Gamborg, and about twenty years later again by M. Heins, R. Kuczynski, and P. Meuriot.[3] Later still came Bücher, Hobson Pearson, and
Conrad. At international demographic congresses — for instance at the
eighth, held in Budapest in 1894 — the problem of urbanization was
high on the agenda; and by 1898, von Fircks was able to publish a bibliography of contributions on the subject running to a hundred pages.[4]

The drift to the towns had become quite general, though it was not
equally intense in all parts of the continent. In the west it was much
more pronounced than it was in the east; and it was strongest of all in
Britain where, according to Sombart, 262 people in every thousand lived
in large towns or cities in 1880 and 355 in every thousand in 1910. In
the Netherlands the corresponding figures were 161 and 233; in Germany,
80 and 212; in Belgium, 153 and 195; in Denmark, 133 and 164; and in
France, 100 and 145. By contrast to these six most highly urbanized
countries stood the six least urbanized: Norway, with 100 city dwellers
in a thousand by 1910; Sweden, with 93; the Balkans, with 90; Austria-
Hungary, with 85; Spain, with 82; and Russia, with 60.[5]

The main cause of urbanization was reflected in this order: the drift to the cities was the greater, the higher the degree of industrialization, except in the Netherlands, which had been an urbanized country for centuries, due more to its trade than to its industry.

Urbanization in the years under review cannot, however, be explained in terms of industrial growth alone. Two other factors also contributed. The first was that the mortality rate, and the infant mortality rate in particular, had begun to decline sharply. In Europe as a whole, the mortality figures had receded from 27.5 per thousand in the 1880s to 25.9 per thousand in the 1890s; the corresponding figures in Western Europe were 24 and 22.1 respectively. By 1900 the rate had dropped to around 20 in the eight leading countries, and by 1930 it was down to a mere 14.9.[6] The reasons for this decline are well known: improvements in public health through the construction of sewers, the supply of piped water and the more frequent use of soap; better diagnostic methods; the discovery of more effective drugs and serums with the consequent control of epidemics (by 1892, for example, cholera had disappeared from Western Europe). The rest was done by better nutrition: the general diet became more balanced and food more plentiful. At the same time, the birthrate remained fairly high, though it had begun to drop toward the end of the century, from 36 per thousand, which had been the average for a long time, to 34 per thousand between 1891 and 1900.[7] The combination of lower mortality and relatively stable birth rates led to an unprecedented population increase. The net figures, though impressive enough — 370 million Europeans in 1893, 401 million in 1900, 452 million in 1914 — do not tell the whole story; for between 1891 and 1900 3.5 million and between 1901 and 1910 eight million Europeans left the Old World to seek a better future elsewhere.[8] Even France, from which the exodus was relatively slight, lost 31,000 people by emigration in 1889.[9]

Of still greater importance, however, was the second factor: increase in population was not evenly divided between town and country. Although the rural population increased, it did so to a very much smaller extent than the urban population, except in England where it dropped by some hundred thousand in 1881–1891 and again in 1891–1901.[10] The main reason for this was the agrarian crisis from which Western Europe suffered between the early 1880s and the middle of the 1890s, and which was the direct result of the opening up of vast territories in the United States, Argentina, Canada, and Russia. Europe was unable to compete with countries whose produce was so much cheaper either because of cheap labor — as in Argentina or Russia — or because of the use of improved machinery — as in the United States. The result was

193

that many European farmers went bankrupt and the rest had to cut down their labor force. While many agricultural workers preferred to cling to the land, their sons and daughters migrated overseas or moved to the towns in their thousands. In London, for instance, most of the new arrivals were between the ages of twenty and twenty-five.[11]

Tales of their exciting new experiences, as well as those of soldiers stationed in city barracks, soon reached the relatives they had left behind, many of whom decided to try the great adventure for themselves. Nor was this true only in England; between 1895 and 1900 one million Germans deserted the countryside, most of them crossing the Elbe to seek employment in the large cities in the west.[12] Not all of them prospered, far from it; but once the pleasures and promises of the city — however meager — had been weighed against the monotonous routine and lack of distraction of country life, there was no restraining them, especially as most felt certain they could avoid the rocks on which so many of their predecessors had suffered shipwreck. Indeed, even if they, too, should founder, there was every hope that their children would do better. In any case, the city, whatever its shortcomings, offered entertainment, excitement, and above all freedom of movement both physically and spiritually, while the village offered nothing but the constraint of strict family ties and the unrelenting rhythm of work on the land, lightened only by the harvest festival and Christmas celebrations.

In any case, the major factor remains: as the village could no longer feed everyone, what was left but the city, close by or in a distand land, where at least there was a market for labor, where wages, however low, were higher than in the country, and where relatives and children could earn something extra.

Once the drift had started, it continued almost automatically, even after 1900, by which time European farmers, too, had begun to introduce more efficient agricultural methods and machinery to feed the hungry cities. Moreover, the creation of special land banks and farmers' cooperatives now helped them to survive lean periods that would have ruined them in the past, and also to diversify their crops with an eye to the industrial market with such products as sugar beet, potato flour, and strawboard. It was no accident that the Polish-born American David Lubin decided in about 1900 to set up a clearing-house of world agricultural information, or that his persistence was rewarded five years later with the emergence in Rome of the International Institute of Agriculture.[13]

The contrast between town and country remained characteristic of all industrialized or industrializing countries, but it was never again to be as pronounced as it was at the turn of the century. Country life today

194

is considerably more attractive than it was in the last century. The largest landed estates have been split up, intensive horticulture has taken the place of extensive agriculture, and not least, a good education has ceased to be the exclusive prerogative of the city. In addition, the gulf between town and country has increasingly been bridged by improvements in transport and traffic, thanks to which the rural population, on the increase once again, can find industrial employment nearby and away from the noisy and overcrowded cities.

Much as the contrast between town and country was never more striking than at the turn of the century, so also were the contrasts within the towns themselves. These contrasts have excited the interest of a host of writers, especially of psychologists. They noted, in particular, that while few country folk — with the exception of some landowners — rubbed shoulders with the rich, in the cities the powerful bankers and the rich manufacturers often lived in the same streets and districts as the poorest, occasionally even in the same houses. By the poor we are referring not only to ragpickers, tramps, beggars, and other outcasts, but also to the great majority of workers, the few remaining artisans, to all such minor officials as clerks and schoolmasters, and, of course, to the army of domestic servants which still abounded at the time. It was this crass contrast in city life which Rainer Maria Rilke had in mind when he wrote in his *Stundenbuch* of 1905: "Lost and doomed are the cities . . . and their short spell seeps away."[14] His loathing of the city, shared by almost all who did not have to live in one and many who did, can be understood only if we remember that the gulf between rich and poor townsmen was greater than in any previous or subsequent period of European history. In England, for example, where the contrast was probably sharper than anywhere else, 175,000 people owned ten-elevenths of the land, and forty million people the remaining one eleventh. This was in 1897, the year of Queen Victoria's Diamond Jubilee. Again, five million Britons enjoyed two-thirds of the national income, while the other thirty-five million subsisted on the rest. London alone counted 100,000 paupers, 70,000 vagrants, and some 30,000 prostitutes. Fifteen years later, toward the end of our period, a small group representing less than 5% of the population above the age of twenty-five still owned more than 60% of the national wealth, while 88% owned less than £100 and 98% less than £1,000.[15] Small wonder then that this glaring contrast was beginning to be resented by an increasing number of people, including quite a few of the well-to-do. Most of them differed from Rilke in degree only. "Unhealthy" was by far the mildest judgment, and many writers argued that the towns could not survive without a continual influx of

195

recruits from the countryside. Kuzcynski, for one, produced precise figures: left to itself, Paris would disappear within another 550 years. This may have been an exaggeration, but it was an established fact that townsmen had a shorter life expectancy than their country[16] cousins, not least because of their deplorable housing conditions. So bad were these conditions that many authors spoke of a process of "degeneration." Max Nordau, who liked to paint things in somber colors, was not the only author to study the urban population; the much more sober Dr. Longstaff observed that city dwellers had narrow chests, pale faces, weak eyes, and bad teeth, adding that he knew not a single Cockney whose father had been born in London.[17] Georg Hansen was another to describe the terrible misery that stalked all cities at the beginning of this period.[18] According to him, people born in the towns lived in the worst districts, had the worst jobs, and comprised the greatest number of degenerates, criminals, lunatics, and suicides. Moreover, even that typical and relatively well-off urban class, the bourgeoisie, had become incapable of reproducing its kind. Once again we cannot dismiss this claim as a gross exaggeration; we have only to think of those constantly swooning young daughters from good homes whose strange antics were taken for granted by so many contemporary novelists. While as often as not the swooning was sheer affectation, many of the young women undoubtedly suffered from pernicious anaemia. Nor were they the only victims. A report published in 1902 by a commission of inquiry into the physical decline of the British people was quite outspoken about the appallingly bad health of so many Boer War volunteers. The commission added that though the doctrine of the survival of the fittest might have its merits, if it were allowed to continue unchecked, a general decline in physical health would be the inevitable consequence.[19]

Some writers were more optimistic, but they were the exceptions, and their optimism seemed hollow. One of them was Wirminghaus, who claimed that, on balance, urbanization did considerably more good than it did harm.[20] But so abstract a blessing as the "standardization of the popular character" failed to recompense a single city child for the perpetual lack of sunshine that blighted life in the slums. The famous German anthropometrist, O. Ammon, went even further.[21] According to him and his school, cities had a most positive selective effect in ensuring the dominance of dolicocephalics, people who were mostly found in the liberal professions and were therefore of superior character. As a result, the inferior brachycephalics would eventually die out. Such eccentric views, however, were quite exceptional, for most writers drew a picture of the large city as somber as life in it must have been at the time. Every kind of social evil flourished here, much more so than it did in the country. This was reflected not only in the mortality tables but also in the crime statistics, though it should be noted that most urban crimes were attacks on the state and on property. To mention but one example: of the 56,000 crimes brought to the attention of the London police in 1894, only 3,500 did not fit into these two categories. Illegitimacy, too, which at the time was still considered a sign of depravity, was unusually high in the cities, in part because many unmarried mothers sought anonymity there for their confinements. Prostitution, finally, was much more widespread in urban than in rural districts — which, incidentally, does not prove that the countryside had higher moral standards, but merely that many "fallen" girls ran away to the towns.

In any case, the town, and above all the big town, was a festering sore. But the greatest of its evils was not the higher mortality nor the physical debilities that were soon afterward remedied by better medical care and better nutrition, not even the greater crime rate — for, surprisingly enough, the crimes committed in towns were qualitatively no worse than those committed elsewhere, despite the more glaring social contrasts. The greatest evil was the grinding poverty of most townsmen, or rather the kind of life to which their poverty condemned them, no matter how long and hard they drudged. Poverty was the ultimate cause of the higher mortality rate, of poor health, of crime, and of prostitution, particularly in the six European capitals with a million or more inhabitants, but by no means in them alone.

The worst of the dreadful poverty was not the low wages, the malnutrition, the crime and the vice, but the miserable housing conditions. This was the true ulcer of European society at the turn of the century, if the term "society" can, in fact, be applied to a system in which the classes were the further apart the closer together they lived. Sometimes the workers would live at the back of the courtyards behind the fine houses of their masters. This arrangement varied from town to town, but what did not alter was the fact that the homes of the masters were as spacious and airy as those of the former were cramped and bleak. From the German census of 1900, with which we began this chapter, we not only know that there were 33 German cities with more than 100,000 inhabitants each, but also how the available housing was shared: in Berlin, each one-room dwelling was occupied on average by 3.69 persons; each two-room dwelling by 2.23 persons; each three-room dwelling by 1.16 persons and each private house with ten or more rooms by 0.70 persons.[22]

These figures speak volumes. Yet those who told the truth about the miserable housing conditions were subjected to a great deal of obloquy. One to dare the critics was Bertillon, who established that the proportion of people living two or more to one room in 1895 was 14% in Paris, 20% in London, 28% in Vienna and Berlin, 31% in Moscow and as much as 46% in St. Petersburg.[23] The housing count of 1912 showed that in Berlin, which, as we saw, was at the bottom of the scale for western cities in 1895, 600,000 people lived more than five to a room.[24] Walter Schiff examined Viennese housing conditions in the same year. The cubic capacity available to the hundred or so working-class families he studied proved, on average, to be smaller than that provided in prisons or almshouses. The 600 members of these families had fewer than 450 sleeping places, including sofas and perambulators.[25]

Such conditions were to be found not only in the great capitals. Conditions in Chemnitz, with 5,000 cases of six or more people sharing a single room in 1900, were barely better than in Berlin with 7,060 such cases.[26] In the same year, 15,396 Amsterdamers, or 11.5% of the city's population, still had to live in single-room tenements. In Rotterdam the percentage was the same; in The Hague it was 12%. The Hague still had 900 one-room tenements inhabited by five or more people; in Amsterdam and Rotterdam the figures were 1,907 and 2,068 respectively. In The Hague, 12,326 adults and children (18%) lived in two-room tenements; in Amsterdam, 29,329 (21.5%); and in Rotterdam, 30,925 (34.5%). If one calls one- and two-room dwellings poor accommodation, then 30% of the population of The Hague, 33% of the population of Amsterdam, and 45% of the population of Rotterdam were poorly housed.[27] Usually, there were more rats than children in these houses.

The rooms were, of course, very small. One author has mentioned dimensions of 9'9" x 8';[28] another gave 16' x 10', but this room was occupied by a family of three generations totalling eleven persons.[29] The tenements were not only small and rat-infested but had very few amenities. In Berlin, again according to the 1900 census, 8,416 street-facing houses had water closets, but 73,092 still relied on non-flushing toilets. For the backyard tenements, the figures were 5,973 and 112,116 respectively. As a rule these amenities had to be shared by several families, although things had improved considerably since the 1850s when 7,000 had had to share 33 lavatories in Manchester, which meant that one privy was shared by 212 people.[30] And as late as 1900 many people were still forced to use buckets or earth closets. The tenements not only had an offensive smell but were also riddled with damp from top to bottom. It was usual for old umbrellas to be put out to catch the drips in the cellars and old buckets the rain in the attics — and this at a time when attic and cellar "apartments" were common: in 1874, there were 4,985 of them in the Amsterdam Island District, and twenty-five years later there were still 3,000.[31] Nor was Amsterdam a particularly glaring example; at the end of our period, Berlin had ten times as many cellar tenements as the Dutch capital.[32]

Apart from being rotten, these workers' tenements were also expensive. Normally, the rent amounted to from 12–15% of a man's wages, but quite often the figure ran to 25–33% and even higher.[33] Hermans visited a garret in Amsterdam which had been converted into four "flats" and earned the landlord 3.40 guilders a week. In one of these flats — rent 0.85 guilders a week — lived a 77-year old, near-blind tailor with his ailing wife. He was past earning money, and the poor relief he received — from the municipality, the Assistance Board, and other charities — came to three guilders a week, plus one-and-a-quarter loaves of rye bread. When the visitor gave him 50 cents, the old man respectfully bared his head.[34] The usual way of meeting the rent was to keep lodgers. In 1900, 205.2 Berlin families in every thousand used this method of relieving one misery with another; in Frankfurt the figure was 220.2, and in Dresden 231.6. Elsewhere it was more or less the same, and with the same disastrous results. What little family life the low wages, the long hours, the absence at work of both husband and wife had left intact was usually destroyed by the presence of boarders and lodgers. It was these conditions of which Rühle said that if it was true that people could be killed with them as surely as with an axe, then countless unpunished murders were being committed at the time.[35] For some of the worst consequences of these housing conditions have not been named: pestilence and cholera had indeed disappeared from Europe by about 1900, but tuberculosis was still rife and so were alcoholism and venereal diseases, and these "three great plagues of the present age," as Rénon called them shortly after 1900, afflicted the population of the big cities more than anyone else.

Tuberculosis, most of all, was the twin sister of poverty. In France alone, 150,000 people died of this disease every year, while another 750,000 or so were infected. In Paris things were worse still: 12,000 to 13,000 people succumbed to the disease every year, or 50 out of every 10,000 inhabitants; and in the poorer districts, as for example in Plaisance, the proportion was twice as high.[36] Nor was that the worst example. While in France the average national mortality rate from tuberculosis was 22.13 per 10,000 in 1900–1910 (again according to Rühle), in Norway the corresponding figure was 24; in Switzerland, 24.68; in Ireland, 25.26; in Austria, 30.53; and in Hungary, as high as 37.44. Considerably better off were Spain with 17.62, Germany with 17.53, Italy with 16.73, the Netherlands with 16.56, Denmark with 16.27, Britain with 15.68, and Belgium with 12.88[37] In all big cities where there were people there was tuberculosis.

The main cause of the spread of "consumption," as the disease was still generally called, was the airless and dank tenements in which the unfortunate victims pined away and infected the rest of the family, whose resistance was undermined further by a monotonous diet of potatoes. Things were not much better in the poorly ventilated factories and workshops where people often had to work in tropical temperatures or to stand barefoot in ice-cold water, and where industrial fumes befouled the air with millions of bacteria. Lily Braun has described it all in some detail.[38] We know that in the Limoges potteries, which used lead paint, twenty out of thirty women workers died of tuberculosis and two of pneumonia. In 1907, Delannoy published a heart-rending drawing of their fate in the satirical L'Assiette au beurre.[39]

In brief, there were some who realized what was happening, nor can it be denied that, here and there, they did something about it. A congress held in London in 1901 decided to set up an International Bureau for the Prevention of Tuberculosis, which convened its first meeting in Berlin, in October 1902.[40] An increasing number of sanatoriums and consultation centers were set up, following the example of Calmette; and private associations waged intense propaganda campaigns with pamphlets, placards, cartoons, and press notices. People were warned against spitting on the ground, there were insistent calls for the mandatory notification of tuberculosis, and statistical studies of the disease were compiled in an effort to discover its causes and to tackle them more effectively. But when we read the answers to the questionnaire circulated by the French physician E. Helme among 700 colleagues in 1904,[41] we find that, though the average general practitioner had begun to appreciate that tuberculosis had social origins, he continued to maintain that it was his job to meddle in such problems, either because he had no means of doing so or else because he was afraid to undermine the foundations of a society of which he considered himself an integral part. His own insecurity rendered him despondent or skeptical. This may explain why 312 of the interviewed doctors replied that the fight against tuberculosis was futile, and why the remaining 382, though approving of the fight in principle, voiced a host of reservations. Rénon, by contrast, contended that the time was not far off when therapeutic medicine would make way for preventive medicine, and that doctors would increasingly turn to social medicine, the science of the future.[42]

The scourge of tuberculosis was not the only one to strike at the urban proletariat; alcoholism was another, and the two were closely bound up with each other. Of the 700 doctors questioned by Helme, no less than 552 declared that their own experience had shown them that a successful fight on the second front (alcoholism) was a prerequisite of success on the first. That alcoholism was the most dangerous ally of social misery[43] was also the view of one of the greatest German physicians, Professor Baer, who said so quite bluntly at the Berlin International Congress for the Prevention of Tuberculosis, held on May 24–27, 1900.[44]

Alcoholism aroused so much attention at the turn of the century not only because of its proven links with tuberculosis and because of the growth of social awareness, but also because it was obviously on the increase. According to Gruber, the consumption of pure alcohol in liters per head of population during the successive decades 1885–1894 and 1895–1904 was: France 17.3 and 20.6; Belgium 12.07 and 13.16; Italy 12.34 and 12.48; Denmark 11.17 and 11.35; Great Britain and Ireland 10.55 and 11.02; Germany 9.2 and 9.63; Austria-Hungary 8.2 and 8.86; Sweden 4.6 and 6. A slight drop had been registered only in Russia (where there was a state monopoly), from 2.7 to 2.67, and in Norway (where there was an effective temperance movement), from 2.36 to 2.3.[45]

The cause of this trend posed a problem in itself. As the increase began at the end of the 1880s, it must have been associated with a whole series of new factors. To begin with, the pressure workers suffered as a result of more intense industrialization and competition made them seek relief through drink, often during breaks and even at their benches. Second, the wage packets had begun to expand, however slightly, thus enabling the common man to change from cheap spirits to the more expensive beer. Third, though other diversions and entertainments were increasingly provided, they were still too few and occasional to take the place of the dubious pleasures of alcoholic intoxication. Thus Professor Gruber, writing in 1888, called alcohol one of the pillars of the contemporary society, which, without it, would long since have become intolerable to the most hard-suffering section of mankind.[46] A few years later Kautsky said much the same when he conceded that without his tavern the German worker would not only have no social but also no political life.[47] Max Weber, with his dialectical eye, also referred to the links between "progress" and alcoholism. In particular, his studies of agricultural workers on the eastern bank of the Elbe had shown him that, though meat consumption had increased, it had not been able to make up for the drop in cereal and milk consumption, and that the growing use of alcohol was somehow filling the gap.[48] Grotjahn painted a similar picture for Switzerland, where the growth of the dairy industry was having a most

201

detrimental effect: the butter, milk, and cheese that had previously been consumed at home now went to commercial depots, and the shrinking milk ration was being supplemented with alcohol.[49]

A factor of quite a different kind was the concentration of capital which helped to turn breweries and distilleries into a political force of great importance. In Britain, according to the Brewer's Almanac, that capital amounted to £230 million, for the most part divided into one pound shares. The Almanac also mentioned by name all Members of Parliament known to be for or against temperance and also listed the doubtful cases. The Liberal defeat at the polls in 1896 has often been blamed on the large number of temperance supporters in the party — the publicans still exerted a major influence on the vote.[50] Small wonder that Lord Rosebery declared in 1895 that unless the State took control of the liquor traffic, the liquor traffic would take control of the State.[51] The number of bars remained alarmingly high throughout Europe, even after the passing of special liquor laws. Roubaix, for instance, in 1897 boasted 2,050 licensed premises for its 110,000 inhabitants, i.e., one for every 53 of its citizens; and 29 town councillors out of a total of 36 were publicans.[52] As Britain had a brewers' lobby, so France had a vintners', and both made their presences felt. Finally, the State itself had a direct interest in the sale of alcohol — in France, to mention just one example, excise duty accounted for one billion francs in a budget of 4.5 billion. That similar amounts could equally well have been collected from taxes on coffee and tea was something few governments cared to consider at the time.

To give the reader some idea of how much money Europeans spent on alcohol, we might point out that, in 1899, the total expenditure on alcoholic beverages in the United Kingdom amounted to £162,163,474, a sum equal to all the rents of all the houses and farms, and representing an average of £3.19s. 11½d. for each man, woman, or child, or £19.19s. 9½d. for each family of five persons.[53] Much the same was true in Germany. Germans spent 2,826 million marks on alcohol in 1903, and a total of 1,765 million marks on their army, navy, education, and labor insurance.[54]

In this, too, working-class families bore the heaviest burden. What percentage of his wages the worker spent on drink varied naturally from case to case, but the average figures are well known. Gruber, examining three lower-income groups in seventeen rural communities in Baden, established that the respective percentages of their income spent on alcohol were 5, 12.5, and 26.2; and the respective percentages spent on food were 53.1, 34.8, and 30.7. Four classes of workers in Berlin

202

spent 5.2, 6.4, 7.6, and 7.7 percent of their income on drink, and 50.7, 49.9, 47.9, and 44 percent of their income on food.[55] Grotjahn put the average percentage of his wages the German, English, French, and Belgian worker spent on drink at 5.1, 4.4, 4.7, and 5.2 respectively.[56] August Pieper, no great champion of temperance, established that cigar makers in Baden spent 104 marks out of their annual wages of 450 on beer,[57] and other studies show that this was by no means unequalled.

As is apparent, there was no lack of studies in this field. When we fit these sober figures into their overall sociological context, we can envision a sorry procession of workers, dust-covered, half stupefied by fatigue and the noise in their airless workshops, collecting their wages and rushing to their favorite saloons, where the glasses stood ready for them in long rows, each full of promise. We realize then why it was that on Saturdays the worker would drink away a quarter of his weekly wage and why, on Sundays, he would get drunk all over again to brace himself for the humdrum sobriety that was often his lot for the rest of the week. We see his wife, a few hours later, arriving meekly or irately, depending on her nature, to drag him back dead drunk to a tenement which held nothing that might have caused him to change his ways — quite the contrary. Or else she might send their youngest child, terrified by his father's thick speech, curses, and physical threats. There was misery, and yet more misery caused by vain efforts to break out of this vicious circle. When we imagine the despair of these wives and children, we also realize why the magic bottle with its promise of oblivion should have appealed to them as well, and not rarely so. It alone held the passport to a better world. For however squalid these moments of drunkenness may have been, they offered at least a brief release from the life-long squalor.[58] It may be that women were taking a first tentative step toward emancipation by learning to drink at this period; this was, perhaps, more true of the petit-bourgeois than of the working-class wife.

The picture we have just sketched may not have been the rule, but neither was it the exception. Luckily, there were many who worked to stem this frightful tide. Every country had its temperance league,[59] and some of these organizations — for instance the Dutch Alliance for the Abolition of Alcoholic Drinks[60] — ran coffee-houses or even, adopting the Gothenburg licensing system, took part in the liquor trade, thus trying to improve it from within and applying the profits to such social improvements as would render drinking unnecessary in the long run.[61] There was no government that did not try to temper the evil of alcoholism by restricting the number of licensed premises. The blue temperance badge, however, was still as rare as the blue flower of the Romantics.

Admittedly, the building worker who took a bottle of milk instead of beer onto his site had already been born; but he was still too young to flaunt his convictions, and the same was true of the student or the officer who was more than likely to be cold-shouldered by his peers if he refused to drink their health.

Meanwhile, as the demon drink raged openly and noisily, that of venereal disease worked secretly and stealthily. In fact there was a close connection between soft chancre, gonorrhea, and syphilis on the one hand and drink on the other, just as there was between drink and tuberculosis, and between all three and social conditions in general. For though there is no proof that workers were proportionally more afflicted with venereal disease than anyone else, their daughters undoubtedly supplied the greatest number of prostitutes, and as such both the greatest chance of contracting venereal diseases and of infecting others.

Of the many components that make up the problem of prostitution, this chapter on life in large cities can enumerate only a few. The actual number of prostitutes is impossible to establish, if only because the number of the registered streetwalkers was everywhere insignificant compared to the number of the "free." In 1900 Paris had no more than 50 registered brothels with a total of fewer than 400 girls; 64 more or less supervised "meeting places" with fewer than 250 "pensionnaires"; and some 6,000 "filles en carte." Yet unofficial estimates of unregistered prostitutes in Paris at the time ranged from 20,000 to 80,000[62] In London, the figures even fluctuated between 8,000 and 80,000.[63] Just as unreliable were the figures for Berlin and Vienna. Flexner, who began his thorough investigation shortly before the First World War, put the number of prostitutes in the German capital at 20,000 but added that this estimate was probably too low;[64] for Vienna, he gave a figure of 30,000.[65] Whether the numbers were underestimated or not, each digit represented one more hope lost, one more young girl destroyed in supplying what, at the time, was considered a perfectly natural need. But in 1900, bourgeois society considered a large bunch of fig-leaves an essential part of their everyday wear, and failed to notice how preposterous it was to consider the demand natural while treating the supply as shameful. Worse still was the usual excuse, normally communicated in whispers, that the physical and moral destruction of "loose women" was not too high a price to pay for the treasured virginity of respectable young girls. The subject of whores was not referred to openly by any but declared libertines, and when it came to the associated diseases not even libertines were bold enough to mention them except in whispers. Nevertheless here, too, things were beginning to change; as Havelock Ellis pointed out, prostitution "now appears to a large and growing number of persons not only an unsatisfactory method of sexual gratification but a radically bad method.[66] In particular, revulsion against the "red palaces"[67] was becoming widespread, and there were many attempts to rid them of their most noxious features. The result was a violent clash between "regulationists" and abolitionists. While the first called for the regular and compulsory inspection of prostitutes on hygienic grounds, the second called, not for the abolition of prostitution as such, but of state interference on moral grounds. Alfred Blaschko threw his great authority behind the international abolitionist movement founded by Josephine Butler in 1875,[68] and it was no accident that he should have subscribed to the view that prostitution is a symptom of economic misery. He was ably seconded by Fiaux,[69] the great French expert, but opposed by Lombroso and Tarnowsky, who called for state control of what to them was an ineradicable evil, rooted in the very nature of the "donna deliquenta" or the "prostituta" and hence unlikely to disappear in the wake of greater prosperity or more humane living conditions.[70] At the same time, Willy Hellpach conceived of a future society in which prostitution was no longer a crime, and in which it would even be possible to attend public functions accompanied by one's "liaison."[71] A little later Ivan Bloch, converted to abolitionism, summed up the whole problem in his widely read *Das Sexualleben unserer Zeit* ("Sexual Life in Our Time").[72] He in turn was followed by Eduard Fuchs, who treated the question of "love by piece work" from a Marxist point of view, and accompanied his text with reproductions of the work of Steinlen, Toulouse-Lautrec, Legrand, Gervex, and Guillaume and Félicien Rops.[73]

Science, which at best served as a theoretical weapon in the fight against prostitution, proved its practical worth during these years in helping to alleviate the frightful lot of all who suffered from syphilis. The isolation in 1889–1892 by Ducrey and Unna of the micro-organism responsible for soft chancre was followed by the isolation of the causative organism of syphilis in 1903, when Mechnikov was the first to infect monkeys with it. In 1905 came Schaudinn's sensational discovery of *Treponema pallidum* as the cause of hard chancre; and one year later, Wassermann introduced the reaction bearing his name, which made possible the timely diagnosis of the "Spanish pox." The year after that, Ehrlich's chemotherapeutic studies were rewarded by the discovery and preparation of Salvarsan, a drug that, together with bismuth, was able to cure syphilis during the first two stages, and thus refute the widespread superstition that this disease was a form of divine punishment. Science and reason had thus done much more than overthrow the tyranny of an "incurable" disease.

Nevertheless, in the deep shadows cast by the gas lanterns in the streets of the big cities there still stalked demons of other kinds, crime and suicide among them. It was not by chance that suicide in particular should have aroused the interest of Durkheim,[74] Ferri, Legoyt, Masaryk, and Morselli at that time. Morselli observed that suicide was increasing even faster than the population;[75] Masaryk called it a mass phenomenon.[76] While some blamed it on a loss of faith, others blamed it on education, intellectualism, or individualism, or on the fact that man's needs were increasing more rapidly than the means of satisfying them. Still others felt that suicide reflected the growing severity of the struggle for existence, or linked it with alcoholism. All were right to a degree, though none of them realized that they were dealing with symptoms, not with causes. The most thorough statistical study of all was that by the Jesuit, Father Krose,[77] who was able to show that some 32,000 Europeans had taken their lives in 1889, and more than 40,000 in 1900.[78] How much more would we know about that year if we could know more about those 40,000 lives! As it is, all we can do is to set out the sober facts. France with 239 suicides per million inhabitants in 1900 was followed closely by Denmark (234), Switzerland (225), and Germany (206).[79] In the big cities, these proportions were strikingly higher — Stockholm: 420, Breslau: 396, Bremen: 356, Frankfurt: 348, Paris: 315, Hamburg: 309, Zurich: 303. Conditions were worst of all in the Austrian army where in 1900, 105 out of every 100,000 soldiers committed suicide — the reverse side of the amusing adventures of the Good Soldier Schwejk. This figure suggests that personal despair may have been a more important factor in suicide than social distress, which may explain why, shortly before the First World War, the suicide rate had increased in every European country with the exception of France, which had to cede the doubtful honor of holding first place to Switzerland (240).[80]

Thousands of unfortunates continued to die yearly, with predictable regularity, choosing an exit that could have been called voluntary but was, in fact, imposed upon most of them by conditions of life in the big cities where the chill wind of loneliness blew over the vast crowds, over lonely sickbeds, and over people racked by hunger; over drinkers who had no friend but the bottle; over criminals who knew themselves rejected by all who were not outcasts like themselves; over waifs, whose homes were everywhere and nowhere; over lunatics withdrawn into their own unreal world; over lone eccentrics, who in their ultimate despair, saw no escape other than the gas tap or the bullet. For here, in the big cities, was born that new phenomenon, the man in the street, alienated first from his fellow citizens and ultimately from himself.

Nonetheless, just as in the squares, factories, streets, and houses of the cities the melancholy gas lamps were, at the turn of the century, gradually making way for electric lighting,[81] so the figurative darkness of the great city, too, was gradually being dispelled. God, an old adage has it, created the land, and man created the city. Now it was precisely the creation of the city that served to teach man the art of town "planning," and with it the art of regenerating the countryside. Man's reforming zeal had been, at first, purely aesthetic; and like everything seeking beauty for the sake of beauty, it had stimulated thoughts instead of deeds. It had thus failed where a social passion for reform was eventually to succeed. In 1896 Theodor Fritsch published his *Stadt der Zukunft* ("City of the Future").[82] Not long afterward, two successful workers' villages were built in England: Cadbury's Bournville near Birmingham, and Lever's Port Sunlight near Liverpool. In the Netherlands, J. A. van Marken made a similar attempt with his Agnetendorp near Delft. All this helped to prepare the ground for the seed, carefully raised from the thought of Wakefield, Marshall, Spence, and Buckingham,[83] which Ebenezer Howard was to sow in 1898 with his *Tomorrow*.[84] This book, which joined the ideal of the model city to the practical struggle against land speculation, led directly to the foundation of the Garden City Association on June 10, 1899, and the construction of the first garden city in Letchworth, near London, in 1903.

This development had been forecast in 1899, in A. F. Weber's prophetic *Growth of Cities in the Nineteenth Century*,[85] and it was reflected in the title of a book published by the Belgian socialist leader Emile Vandervelde in 1903: *L'Exode rural et le retour aux champs.* In Part II of that book, Vandervelde predicted that capital would flow increasingly into the mechanization of agriculture as the stormy development of the industrial sector continued to subside, with a consequent reversal of the rural exodus. In his summary he argued that the gulf between town and country would be closed from both sides, as the cities became more "countrified" with spacious suburbs, parks, and gardens; and the country became urbanized with the rise of local industries, the creation of commuter belts, and the appropriate extension of the road and railway networks.[86] All that was still an ideal, and reality lagged far behind. In 1904 Bauer imagined the town of the future in much the same way as Howard had before him: an inner city ringed by factory districts and working-class suburbs, each ring divided from the next not only by parkland and gardens but also by fields which the workers could tend at their leisure.[87] This ideal, which pretended to look into the future but actually looked back into the past, was never realized. Yet it was approached; in the decades after 1900, the *urbs* lost some of its worst horrors while the *orbis* lost much of its isolation. The countryside would feed not only itself but also the city; and the city would shed some of its harsher, alienating qualities and develop a greater degree of cultural cohesion, so much so, in fact, that all culture would henceforth bear an unmistakably urban stamp.

CHAPTER XIV

THE HUMILIATED AND REVILED

On January 8, 1900, notices calling for the election of workers' delegates appeared on the walls of Le Creusot, the famous arms factory.[1] They were posted on the orders of M. Schneider, the proprietor and the son of the founder, Joseph-Eugène, whose statue graced the factory's gloomy forecourt. M. Schneider was also a mayor, a great admirer of the encyclical *Rerum novarum*, and a well-known philanthropist. He did not, however, admire socialism, which he described as just an excuse for transferring money from the employers' pockets into those of a certain type of politician. Like many employers, he might have been a character from a novel by René Bazin: a man who was proud of being "master in his own house" and wanted to remain so.[2] Hence this telling sentence in the notice, culled from a pronouncement by Waldeck-Rousseau, the radical Prime Minister: "The delegates are not only representative of all the workers, but also official conciliators whose task it is to set out the advantages and necessity of the measures taken by the management.[3]

The notice, in fact, was not the result of one of M. Schneider's whims, for it came in the wake of a series of sharp class skirmishes begun in September 1899, and described in detail by de Seilhac.[4] These skirmishes must have taken M. Schneider completely by surprise, for as late as 1896, when Huret questioned 16,000 workers employed in Le Creusot, he found them still sadly resigned to their fate. There had not been a strike in the factory since 1871. "Strikes here? Never! The place is full of company spies. Anyone who opens his mouth gets slung out through the back door. And anyway we are much too tired for that sort of thing," one of them explained.[5] Did the workers have their own houses? "Oh, yes. A house and a garden, ten square meters. It's twenty-five minutes' walk to the wall around the proprietor's park. House and garden are 3,500 francs, repaid at 40 francs a month, leaving 100 francs for the family." What about pensions? "Of course, 20 francs a month from the age of 60." And food? "We've got no appetite; it's much too hot, what with standing in front of the furnaces all day long."

Yet within three years, resignation had made way for resistance. On

September 18, 1899, three workers had been caught drinking in the electrical shop, and had been sacked on the spot. Perhaps because their patience had been strained for too long, or else because they still lacked delegates capable of dilating on the "advantages and the necessity" of this latest dismissal, their comrades had unexpectedly refused to acquiesce in the decision. They had insulted, threatened, and even spat upon the foreman who had reported the men. There were fresh dismissals, which only served to strengthen the workers' resolve. On September 20, a strike was declared in the electrical and artillery workshops and quickly spread to all the other sections. By 3:30 in the afternoon everyone had downed tools. Then courage fed on itself; the hidden grievances boiled over, and angry posters appeared all over the factory. They declared that far from paying the promised increase of 25 centimes, the company had cut the workers' wages; that it invariably met workers' complaints with ridicule and had failed to recognize the trade union, despite having promised to do so. Every day there were fresh provocations, fresh assaults on conscience and liberty. "Away with the factory police! Long live proletarian solidarity! Not one of us will betray our just cause!" Nine thousand of the men decided to march to Paris and to demonstrate in the Place de la Concorde, as the workers of Marseilles had done in 1893. In the end, however, they did not have to go; for at the request of the strike committee, the government decided to intervene and ordered the election of workers' delegates.

The strike had lasted for ninety days; and though it attracted a great deal of attention, it was by no means unique. In the year 1900 there had been 902 strikes involving 222,714 workers in France; 648 strikes involving 188,238 workers in the United Kingdom; 1,462 strikes involving 131,888 workers in Germany; and 303 strikes involving 105,128 workers and affecting more than 60% of the 1500 or so industrial concerns established in Austria. In Belgium, too, the year 1900 produced a record number of strikes, with 32,443 workers participating in 146 labor disputes, many of them violent, for instance the bloody clashes in the Fabre timber yard of August 18. Of the strikes that occurred in the Netherlands during that year, the one at the Holland-America Line has remained famous because women workers sat down on the trolleys and thus brought the unloading of cargo to a stop.[6] Although only the northern part of Italy could be considered industrial, that country had more strikes in 1900 than ever before: 383 involving 94,883 workers.[7]

In 1900 these six countries thus saw some 4,000 strikes involving some 800,000 workers. Now, comparative studies show that that year was by no means exceptional; in fact the number of strikes and of workers involved in them had been increasing steadily since 1898, especially in smaller countries, in which, according to Lavollée, labor disputes had become particularly frequent, long, and violent:[8]

We also know that in the decade around 1900 there was growing concern with the "social question," as the labor problem used to be called in bourgeois circles. Interest in that question had never been totally lacking, but now it not only grew apace but also began to change in its character: what had been mere sympathy, and hence of little practical help, was being transformed into deep personal involvement and concern. The British were the pioneers in this field; Charles Booth, Robert Blatchford, B. S. Rowntree, and R. Sherard experienced the misery they described at firsthand and, moreover, with enough wit to realize that there was a fundamental difference between sharing the lot of the poor for a brief spell and being made to suffer it one's whole life. Where these pioneers led the way, many others followed, if only by writing. Never before had there been so many and such thorough social studies as appeared at that time, and not in England alone. Of the many French writers concerned with the social question, we have encountered quite a few in the preceding pages. In Germany, there were the Academic Socialists; and in the Netherlands, the Comité tot Onderzoek van de Sociale Kwestie (Social Study Committee) was led by Kerdijk, Pekelharing, Quack, and especially Kuyper, who organized a Social Congress in 1891, claiming that the workers "cannot wait a single day or night longer." The leaders were ably assisted by a host of students in Amsterdam, many of whom later became socialists. The new feeling was also reflected in Pope Leo XIII's *Rerum novarum* of 1891, the best known of the later encyclicals.

The social question even entered literature and painting, although it was no more than a small band of writers and artists who had the courage to "debase" their time-hallowed and exalted art into an instrument of social compassion by describing an all-too earthly reality. Zola was probably one of the first to describe a real proletarian, and not simply a poor man, as Dickens, for instance, had done before him. But Zola was extremely sensitive to the signs of the times: in 1885 he had still preached revolution in *Germinal;* but by 1901, in his *Travail,* he had begun to hint at a possible reconciliation between capital and labor. In Russia there was Maxim Gorki; in Germany, Gerhardt Hauptmann; in Norway, Knut Hamsun; in Denmark, Anderson Nexö; in the Netherlands, S. G. van der Vijgh, who died while still young, a few weeks before the publication in 1900 of his *Werkers*, which was a weak cry soon drowned by the much more powerful sound of Heijermans's *Op hoop van zegen* (1901). In painting, it was Vincent van Gogh, whose honest brush turned

211

the protest against social misery into line and color — hard colors and strange lines, but how could they have been otherwise? Eugeen Laermans, too, saw the human faces hidden beneath the drunken and desperate expressions of the rural laborers he liked to paint, of that "sallow crew in drab clothes," as van der Vijgh had called them. Steinlen in Paris and Käthe Kollwitz and Heinrich Zille in Berlin were equally filled with the new compassion, and tried to etch the deep furrows of social misery into the conscience of the bourgeoisie. We must leave it at these few examples, and simply add that for no other chapter in this book was there such a wealth of contemporary material to work from.

Were all their efforts in vain? Did all the shocking accounts, all the penetrating observations, all the burning indignation, all these words, paintings, reports, and even Government Blue Books lead to no real improvements whatsoever, so that the workers had no alternative to striking? There was, in fact, a clear if somewhat odd connection between the two phenomena. To begin with, there was the awakening of the working class, which expressed itself in active resistance — how else? — but could only do so with effect once the workers had enough bread to enable them to stand up and fight back. Their resistance, in its turn, attracted the attention of writers and artists, few of whom were revolutionaries and could therefore not be silenced or shot like criminals. In the long run, they had to be listened to; and some of the worst remaining evils had to be alleviated, if only to avert an even more hostile reaction. Yet these piecemeal reforms highlighted the perniciousness of the whole system, with the result that dissatisfaction grew, not despite but as the direct result of undoubted progress. The rise of the trade union movement and the greater protection it afforded its ever-increasing number of members; the gradual extension of the franchise and the associated increase in the number of working-class parliamentary representatives; the development of intellectual and physical capacities in the wake of wage increases and a shorter working week; and above all, the spread of socialism, which was not content with righting past grievances but also demanded a better future, combined to accomplish the rest.

The dialectical nexus between social improvements and the growth of working-class dissatisfaction was reflected in yet another link: that between the reformist and the revolutionary wings of the organized labor movement. In Chapter XI we gave a theoretical account of these two currents, as set forth in a host of political papers and discussions. When we turn our attention to the practical results, we quickly discover that though the two currents seemed diametrically opposed, they nevertheless served to reinforce each other. For while the revolutionary attitude

212

led to reflection, reflection to improvements, and improvements to reforms, the reformist drive, beset as its path was with obstacles and frustrations, gave rise to a new revolutionary wave. Bearing this in mind, we find that the vacillations of Social Democrats during the period under review look much more comprehensible.

Among the general studies to which we have referred, and which revealed what had been hidden for decades, none proved more seminal or more detailed than that of von Nostitz. His book ran to more than 800 closely printed pages, and on March 7, 1900, he wrote in the preface: "The greatest problem, which we may for brevity call the social one, is not confined to certain countries or nations but dominates our age as *the* world problem."[9] Von Nostitz restricted his studies to England, but others emulated or tried to emulate him in other countries — the Pelloutiers in France,[10] Otto Rühle, preceded by Wurm, in Germany,[11] and Henrietta Roland Holst in the Netherlands.[12] Even earlier, R. Lavallée had attempted to cover the whole of Europe.[13]

The army of the poor, they showed, was still massive, for it continued to include the great majority of the working class. Charles Booth, who with Beatrice Webb, Octavia Hill, and others introduced the sociographic method of social research, divided the 909,000 inhabitants of the particular area in East London he had chosen to study (22% of the city's total population) into eight classes: a) the lowest class of loafer and petty criminal (1.2%); b) the "very poor" with casual earnings (11.2%); c) the poor with intermittent earnings (8.3%); d) the poor with small regular earnings (14.5%), making a total of 35.2%. Next came those living above the poverty line while in good health: namely, e) those with regular standard earnings (42.3%). Only 22.5% were better off: namely, f) the higher working class (13.6%); g) the lower middle class (3.9%); and h) the upper middle class (5%).[14] True, things were not as bad in the rest of Britain, but they were indeed bad enough. Rowntree, too, concluded that almost one-third of the population of York was poor by any standards;[15] and the German, G. F. Steffen, found that 71% of all Englishmen had to be counted among the working classes and that one-third of these lived in permanent poverty. Chiozza Money tells us that more than one-third of Britain's national income went to one-thirtieth of the population and nearly one-half to a mere ninth of the population; 1,400,000 rich persons shared an annual income of £634,000,000, 4,100,000 well-to-do persons shared an annual income of £275,000,000, a total of £909,000,000 between them, while the remaining 39,000,000, poor people, were left with a total annual income of £935,000,000. No wonder that Ruskin had said in 1880: "Blessed

213

are the Rich in Flesh, for theirs is the Kingdom of Earth. Blessed are the Proud for they *have* inherited the Earth. Blessed are the Merciless for they shall obtain Money."[16] Campbell Bannermann, the then leader of the Liberal Party, was to vouch for the accuracy of these figures.

The acute poverty in which one quarter if not more of the population of the richest continent still lived took thousands of forms and was yet formless: there were tremendous differences between the poor, but the overall picture was a uniform gray. The "workman" was easily recognized: by his clothes, his speech, and his sickly smell — he had no underwear and no time or soap for a weekly change of clothes. He also had a very narrow outlook; for until the bicycle brought him some mobility, even the fairly prosperous artisan was tied to his home. Still worse than the lack of space was his lack of prospects: he started work as a child, generally by the age of twelve, though sometimes at the age of six and even at four. By the time he was in his thirties, he began to be plagued by fears, for he knew that no amount of experience was a substitute for his waning physical strength. When he had passed the age of forty-five, he was an old man,[17] facing the awesome prospect of having to spend the rest of his life in a workhouse, though he could console himself with the fact that the chances of his living much longer were extremely slender. In England, the richest nation of all, the average life expectancy in 1900 was forty-four years for men and slightly more for women.[18] And the older the people grew, the poorer they became. Nostitz established that England had 101,000 poor between the ages of 60 and 65, or 13.2% of that entire age group, but 62,000 poor above the age of 80, or 41.3% of that age group.[19] The analysis published by Money produced a similar picture with different figures: in 1891, the United Kingdom had 54 complete paupers per thousand of the population, and 292 complete paupers per thousand of all those above the age of 65.[20]

The causes of poverty were generally held to be incompetence, laziness, and drunkenness; in other words, the poor themselves were still widely blamed for their misery. Today we know better. The working day was extremely long, and to the workers in the dank cellars it must have seemed endless. By 1900 the worst was over, but the English factory worker still worked a 10-hour day and a 55-hour week, year in, year out, for holidays with pay were almost unknown.[21] Much longer hours were still being worked in trades not yet covered by the Factory Acts, especially on the railways and canals. According to the evidence presented to a Royal Commission, canalboatmen worked an average of 100 hours a week (Mersey flats) and even of 120 hours a week (Leeds and Liverpool Canals).[22] Similarly, 10% of the 4,000 guards on passenger trains, and 70% of the 9,000 guards on freight trains, 25% of the 16,000 signal-men, and 82% of the 27,000 footplate men regularly worked more than twelve, and sometimes more than fifteen or even eighteen-hour shifts in 1890.[23] Although things were notoriously bad in Britain, they were not very much better elsewhere. Dutch sales clerks used to work 82 hours a week on the average and often up to 96 hours, and they were expected to remain on their feet throughout that time. In 1886, when Aletta Jacobs began to agitate against these conditions on purely medical grounds, she was attacked not only by the employers but also by most of her medical colleagues in Amsterdam; and it took another twenty years before sales clerks were provided with chairs.[24] On the docks conditions were even worse: on April 3, 1905, *De Noodkreet*, organ of the Rotterdam long-shoremen, spoke of 72-hour shifts as a normal occurrence.[25] Compared with these conditions, the objections of Martin, the chief accused in the 1890 Vienne trial, might seem overstated; but he was speaking for women, for the carders who had to slave from 7:00 A. M. to 5:30 P. M. without any break, and who — as he pointed out to the judge — wore themselves out for one franc a day, and had to count themselves lucky if their poverty did not force them to sell their bodies as well. In any case, the average working day in France was not much below 10.5 hours — Kuczynski put it at 10.3 hours in 1900;[26] and he arrived at much the same figure for Germany.[27] Italians and Russians still worked an average day of 12 and 12.5 hours respectively at the turn of the century.

Conditions were worst under what went by the name of the "contract system" but was better and more appropriately known as the "sweating system." It was widespread in Europe; and though its precise definition may have varied from place to place, basically it consisted of working at home for the lowest possible pay, with or without the intervention of one or more middlemen or subcontractors, who were often as poor and exploited as the workers themselves. Those who blamed the middlemen for the worst excesses of the sweating system were either ignorant of the true state of affairs or else anxious to smear the poor with the claim that they exploited one another with particular viciousness. Just as often, those with a bad conscience would also blame the Jews. Hobson probably came closest to the truth when he inculpated the vast reservoir of un-skilled laborers that had flocked to the cities from the countryside or from abroad; the gradual replacement of artisans by machinery; the increasing use of cheap female and child labor; and finally, competition from the increasingly industrialized rural areas.[28]

Though the sweating system was known in most industries, it was most prevalent in the clothing, laundry, shoe, and furniture trades, and to a lesser extent in the food and pickling industries. In Holland, pea-picking and shrimp-peeling — often under very unhygienic conditions — were among the worst paid jobs done by women and children; during school holidays, Leyden slum-children would often walk round for weeks with red eyes from peeling onions. The sweating system was far from new; in the early nineteenth century, a daughter of Sir Robert Peel, the British Prime Minister, had fallen ill because the sick child of a seam-stress had slept under her new frock. Many abuses by the system were discovered only when they began to threaten the life of the bourgeoisie. In this way, the working day on the railways was originally shortened, not to improve labor conditions, but to make train journeys safer for travelers. Similarly, Upton Sinclair's *The Jungle* caused a sensation in 1906 not so much because it revealed unspeakable social abuses in the Chicago abattoirs, but because it showed that these led to the production of sausages that were bad. Kingsley, too, knew all about sweated labor, and exposed it as early as 1850 in his *Alton Locke*. A few years later, Marx told the story of a milliner who had died after working for more than twenty-six hours at a stretch with thirty other women in a room with enough air for ten. From Hobson[29] and other reliable witnesses, we know that ten to twelve women would slave for ten to twelve hours at a stretch in rooms with a floor space of some ten square yards, heated by a coke stove and lit by gas. An eight-hour day, outside the season, was considered a half-time job and paid accordingly. In 1890, even the House of Lords could stomach it no longer: a special committee had just reported that many women had to labor from 7 A. M. to 4 P. M. to earn five shillings a week, and that two women, one aged fifty-five and the other twenty-four, had managed to earn the princely sum of eight shillings and sixpence a week by starting their chores at 6 A. M. and carrying straight on until midnight. They had something to eat and drink, but did not have to interrupt the work too long, for all they consumed was some tea and a slice of fish and, to be perfectly honest, a little meat as well, though only twice a year. Another family had two rooms in which husband, wife, and six children worked, ate, and slept. Their food: a cup of coffee and a herring each. One witness declared that on one occasion she had had to work forty hours at a stretch: on a fur coat or on a ball gown, she forgot which. Some 18,000 to 20,000 people lived in this manner in London alone, and the noble Lords praised the neighborly love of those men and women who never refused to help any in even greater need.

For the rest, the committee concluded that any attempt to solve this thorny problem was bound to lead to a "maze of difficulties." In fact, they could no more have solved it than jump over their own shadows; for at the time they submitted their report, the social system they represented — the exploitation of man by man — was still to them the only conceivable one. Legislation having gone as far as it could, they felt, the further improvement of conditions called for an increased sense of responsibility on the part of the employers no less than — the Lords were nothing if not impartial — for better habits among the employees.[30]

Although the sweating system may have been most widespread in London, it was by no means unknown in other big cities. Thus when the special Inquiry Commission appointed by the Amsterdam Municipality in 1897 published its report in 1900 — with appendices about conditions in London and Berlin by way of an excuse — it, too, mentioned that, in the season, contract laborers were expected to work for 480 hours a month for an average hourly wage of 17 cents. Coat-makers with a wage of 23–25 cents an hour did best of all. Here, too, there were small and unhealthy rooms; here, too, the irons were heated on open charcoal burners; here, too, the workers were ostensibly protected by a Labor law — the Law of 1899 — which was more often ignored than applied. Thirteen- and fourteen-year olds regularly worked for twelve hours until 11 P. M.; it is small wonder that the mortality rate in the Dutch clothing trade was far above the national average: 10.27 per thousand as against 8.2 per thousand for the 18–50 age group. Though those responsible often pleaded that the clothing industry was the last refuge of weak individuals, that plea was not even an excuse. It is not surprising that the good burghers of Amsterdam went further than the noble Lords in London: instead of appealing to the employers' sense of responsibility, they called for direct state intervention. To be sure, there was an interval of ten years between the publication of the two reports.

Another group of workers with inordinately long hours and low wages were the domestic servants who, in a sense, were even worse off than the "contract laborers" because they were forced to live among strangers, often far from home. They were only "free" when they lay in their beds, though even there they were often disturbed by the master or by his sons; of the three maids kept by most comfortably-off families (in London, nearly one tenth kept more than three),[31] there was usually at least one who was worth the trouble of disturbing. But by 1900, even the maids had begun to resist. Those who could took other jobs; between 1881 and 1901 the number of servants in England decreased by 8% while the population rose by 25%. "It is probable," the *Quarterly Review* had warned in July 1895, "that London servant girls of fair intelligence, will not for long consent to spend their days in cellar chambers and their

217

nights in . . . inhuman attics."[32] In Berlin, domestic servants held a series of public protests in the summer of 1900, complaining about a host of abuses. There is no need to record the outraged reaction of their "mistresses."[33] For more information on the working and living conditions and the lack of rights of German maidservants the reader is referred to Lily Braun's *Die Frauenfrage*.[34]

The worst of the long hours and low wages has now been told; we need merely add that the wages of the working class as a whole were not very much higher. In Britain, for instance, 37.5 out of a total population of 44 million were dependent on breadwinners earning less than £3 per week.[35] The British worker, moreover, was relatively better off than his Continental neighbor; ever since 1880 his wages had been rising slowly but steadily, while the cost of his rent, food, and household goods had been dropping. Thus if we put the average British wage in 1905–1909 at 100, then the corresponding figure for Germany was 75; for France, 64; and for Belgium 52. Again, if we put the cost of rent, food, clothes, fuel, and other necessities at 100, the corresponding figures in France and Germany were 104 and 111 respectively, and only Belgium came off better with 93.[36]

There is little sense in adducing further figures with which, incidentally, the sources from which we have quoted abound. If we nevertheless go on to refer to Rowntree, it is because he provided a yardstick for interpreting these figures. He distinguished between primary poverty caused by insufficient wages, and secondary poverty caused by wages that sufficed, though only just, to keep body and soul together. In York, Rowntree drew the primary poverty line for 1899, a good year, at 21s. 8d. per week for a family consisting of husband, wife, and three children; 7,230 people or 10% of the whole population of the city lived below it, while 13,072 or 18% lived in secondary poverty. In London, both groups together made up 31% of the population.[37] "No civilization," he concluded, "can be healthy or stable that is built on such a mass of stunted human lives."[38]

Who knows but that this joyless life might still have been bearable, despite the long hours and the low wages, had the employers not docked wages by a merciless system of fines, and had there not been the ever-present specter of injury, unemployment, and destitute old age. Industrial accidents were the rule rather than the exception, largely because of the spread of mass-production techniques. Statistics show that at the beginning of this period, in the 1880s, the number of accidents both per worker and per working hour had begun to increase steadily; and this process was not reversed until about 1900, when safety regulations and greater care on the part of the workers led to a gradual decrease. Germany had 0.71 fatal accidents per thousand insured workers in 1889, 0.74 in 1900, and 0.63 in 1914.[39] This was yet another chapter in the martyrdom of the working class. In October 1895, factory accidents alone caused 49 deaths, 147 amputations, 65 fractures, 4 losses of sight, 71 head and 653 other injuries in Britain. That same month, the mines claimed a further 45 dead and 731 injured, and the railways 566 injured, making a total of 2,332 casualties during this arbitrarily chosen month. November 1897, to take another example, produced close on 3,500 industrial accidents;[40] and, in general, the annual figures suggest that Britain had by no means turned the corner in 1900. In 1903, British factories still produced 1,047 fatal accidents, and in 1908 the number was 1,042; the same two years also produced 92,600 and 121,112 injuries. The mines, and the quarries as well, continued to cause some 1,000 fatal accidents and some 5,000 injuries every year.[41]

In Holland, it was the docks which produced the largest number of victims. In 1906, the Port of Rotterdam, which employed an average of 10,000 dockers, produced 3,718 dead and injured; in 1907, the figure was 4,172. After that the annual casualty rate began to drop — to a "mere" 2,800 per annum in 1908–1914.[42] To the longshoreman, the loss of a hand or an eye could be as fatal as death itself, as anyone deprived of any of his skills was bound to fall behind in the murderous race to the dock gates, run every morning, in fair weather and foul. Every gray hair was a stumbling block here, and for that matter in Amsterdam, Hamburg, London, Bremen, Liverpool, Boulogne, and Bordeaux as well. It was better to suffer this race for work, however, than to be out of work and have no chance at all. The constant threat of unemployment haunted the working man, and though it was much more acute in winter than it was in summer, and worse in one year than in the next, it cast its ominous shadow in all seasons and every year. According to Beveridge,[43] unemployment in the United Kingdom during the relatively good years 1894–1907 stood at an average of 4.5%. This figure was, if anything, an underestimate because, while Beveridge put unemployment at 2.9% for 1900, Money put it at 4%, or at 21,496 unemployed members of those trade unions (total membership 540,102) which paid unemployment benefits. For the years 1900–1907 Money arrived at an average unemployment rate of more than 5.5%,[44] while Beveridge put the rate no higher than 4.6%. Even more somber were the figures published by a Select Committee: in 1893 and 1894 the unemployment rate stood as high as 11.4% and 11.3% respectively.[45] But all these figures are on the low side because they cover trade union members only, and these, by and large, were the most highly skilled workers and hence generally among the last to be dismissed. Money was probably right to claim elsewhere that in making an estimate of workers' earnings, it should be remembered that, on average, they were paid for no more than 40–47 weeks per annum, the remaining 5–12 weeks being lost due to short time, sickness, accident, stress of weather, and such.[46] Keir Hardie did not exaggerate when he said that unemployment was a constant threat to every worker; nor did Charles Booth, when he called unemployment a horrible scourge and described its consequences in great detail: the erosion of what small savings there were, the pawning and sale of household utensils and body linen, followed by physical and mental collapse.

Home life might have tempered some of the worse blows, but just as the worker had no fatherland so he had no proper home. As we saw in the last chapter, his dingy and often poorly heated tenement provided him with little relief from the noise of the machines he had to endure all day, unless he sent his children to play in the streets until supper, consisting of cheap fish, potatoes, weak tea, and bread, which took 60 to 70 percent of his wages.[47] As if all these evils were not enough, he had a more than average chance of falling ill; occupational diseases and malnutrition were not the inventions of hypersensitive doctors. Few employers bothered to provide their workers with the statutory fifteen cubic yards of "air space," let alone with the thirty cubic yards the law had laid down for dusty occupations; to maintain tolerable temperature levels in, say, mills or glassworks; or to provide proper lighting or pleasant working conditions. In the United Kingdom, out of every 1,000 workers, 200 were healthy, 200 were ill, and the rest were sickly. Deafness was common among foundry workers, myopia among seamstresses, engravers, and printers; 49% of all metal workers were certain of receiving at least one metal splinter in one of their eyes. In addition to metal dust, rag dust, and brick dust, many workers came into daily contact with lead, arsenic, mercury, zinc, phosphorus, coal damp, sulphuric acid, chlorine, and other toxic substances. There were harmful animal products as well — 49% of all bristle makers died of tuberculosis. Of the 1,700 men engaged in the construction of the St. Gotthard tunnel, only fifty or sixty stuck it out from beginning to end; similarly, miners rarely worked for more than fifteen years before dying, generally of "consumption."[48] Possibly worse off still were those employed in lead works: in 1903, 875 British workers contracted lead poisoning, and as many as 966 in 1908. Of these cases, 69 and 84 respectively proved fatal.

All in all, it was not surprising that the working class should have had a much higher than average death rate. In Central Europe, "consumption" claimed 70-100 workers per thousand, but only 34 per thousand of the more prosperous classes. Measles, diphtheria, typhus, or cholera claimed one rich person for every 30-60 workers. In Britain, during the worst time, there were many factories in which no more than 20 out of a thousand workers reached the age of forty, and 8 out of a thousand lived to see their fiftieth birthday. According to the German doctor from whom we have been quoting, workers had a life expectancy of 30-35 years, but the more prosperous could expect to live to the age of 50-70.[49] Elsewhere things were no different. Even among children, death was anything but the great leveller it is said to be; in its wisdom it passed the rich child by and took the poor. According to Ellen Key, the infant mortality rate in Berlin was 57 per thousand in aristocratic families and 345 per thousand among the poor.[50] The close links between this type of infanticide and the inhuman drudgery to which working-class mothers were subjected are too obvious to need stressing.

In all this misery, however, there was one beacon of light, and one that is far too often forgotten: none of the facts we have set out here would ever have been known had there not been so many resolute men and women determined to bring them to light. We alluded to this fact at the beginning of this chapter, but we have not yet mentioned the most important consequence of this steadily increasing flow of literature on the "social question:" the middle classes themselves began to question their right to exploit the workers, and to examine their own consciences. They had ceased to believe, or to believe unreservedly, that unemployment was synonymous with laziness, that poverty was a sign of moral weakness and of drunkenness, that the poor had no one but themselves to blame for their own lot — the sober working-class budgets compiled, for instance, by Max May told quite a different story.[51] The very fact that Lord Rosebery saw fit, on the occasion of the great miners' strike of 1895, to invite both parties to the dispute to sit around one table, or that Waldeck-Rousseau, the French Prime Minister, intervened in the Schneider-Creusot dispute at the workers' request in 1899, shows clearly that the powerful had begun to grasp the need for minimum concessions, if only to avert worse "excesses." This was one straw in the wind. Another was the increasing concern of industrialists with the social problem, again out of class interest, no doubt, but it was also a sign that they were abandoning the outworn clichés and prejudices of earlier decades. Lord Leverhulme, the founder of Port Sunlight, put it all most succinctly when he declared in 1900 that the highest form of enlightened self-interest is "serving the interest and welfare of all those who work with us."[52] Solid industrialists may still have worn top hats, white waistcoats, gold

221

chains, and gray gaiters, but they were beginning to realize that there
were other things in life than the mad chase after money. In particular,
they had come to realize that the salve of charity could not cure all the
running sores with which society was afflicted; that all the benevolent
fêtes, bazaars, balls, and dinners run by the rich were, if not sheer hypocrisy, at best ridiculously ineffective palliatives; that the working hours
could never be reduced, nor wages be increased, unless the government
compelled the more retrograde employers to improve the conditions
of their workers; that mass unemployment would not be eradicated
with such stop gaps as the breaking of stones, the cleaning of streets,
the clearing of snow, or the sweeping of parks and cemeteries for something like a shilling a day — and even then often collected by public
subscription lest the state or municipality be accused of spoiling the
workers. What was needed instead was systematic labor legislation and
a comprehensive national insurance scheme covering accidents, sickness,
old age, and unemployment. Europe was by then rich enough to make at
least a start with such a scheme; its very riches were opening people's
eyes to the fact that nothing is ever created out of nothing, and that
her supremacy, built on these riches, had not fallen out of the sky, but
had been created by millions of pairs of dirty and despised hands, hands
that still awaited their due reward. This new appreciation, born in the
1890s, did not, of course, mean that the great in the land had decided
to put an end to exploitation, or to return the entire surplus value produced by the worker in the form of wages and social benefits, but it
did mean that some of the worst abuses of exploitation were beginning
to be remedied, however slowly and halfheartedly. According to the
annual report published by the British Ministry of Labour — itself a sign
of the times — 155 industries employing 33,100 workers cut the working
week by an hour in 1893; and 200 industries employing 35,100 workers,
by 2 hours and 17 minutes in 1898. If we include overtime, however,
it is only fair to add that the working week was extended in 1,530 industrial concerns in 1893 and in 900 industrial concerns in 1898.[53] In
1893 came the first attempt to introduce a 48-hour week, but by 1898
the average still stood at 58 hours.[54]

In 1900, France introduced the ten-hour day, and six years later, a
fixed weekly day of rest. Money, who in 1908 compared conditions in
Britain with what they had been forty years earlier, observed that the
average annual wage had risen from £30 to £46, and this at a time when
the price index had dropped from 136 to 102.8 (1900 = 100). During
the same period the death rate fell from 20.8 per thousand to 15.2 per
thousand and the number of paupers from 960,000 to 912,000.[55] Im-

provements in conditions were also mentioned by the Webbs, who discovered that though relatively few people enjoyed a decent standard of living, the absolute number of those who did had increased.

This fact alone shows how relative these improvements still were. For all that, the detestable truck system of supplying goods in lieu of wages, and the equally fraudulent tied shop system which forced working women to buy from company stores, were gradually falling into desuetude. Moreover, the incidence of occupational disease had begun to decline,[56] and paid leave for pregnant factory workers was being introduced in several countries (four weeks before and after confinement in Germany; eight weeks in Switzerland). Here and there workers' committees were allowed to play a part that, in retrospect, looks very much like a restricted form of co-partnership.[57] Ad hoc or permanent arbitration courts were no longer unusual, and bonus or profit-sharing schemes no longer completely unknown. In 1898 there were 93 such schemes in Britain involving some 50,000 workers,[58] and a much smaller number existed in Germany.[59] The worker's child was no longer despised as a guttersnipe, but treated with greater sympathy. School meals ceased to be a mere demand — and not only in Berlin, where an inquiry showed that in the summer and winter of 1908, 36,000 and 22,000 children respectively were sent to school without breakfast, and that 179,000, or 4.9%, had no warm food whatsoever even in winter.[60] Compulsory education, public parks and sports grounds, public reading rooms and special lectures for workers, such settlements as Toynbee Hall, Ons Huis (1892), the Boddaert Homes (1903), the public sanatorium in Hallendoorn, and other social institutions now blossomed, albeit most of them were still run on voluntary contributions and even so were attacked by many public figures. Thus when Snowden, in his *Socialist Budget* of 1907, proposed to increase death duties from 8% to 50%, he was still widely described as a lunatic and a dangerous one at that. Moreover, as late as 1900 old age pensions were being hotly opposed, not least by the Charity Organization Committee, which argued that a grant of five shillings a week would cost the country £20 million per annum and that even a child could see that the costs could not possibly be met when the total national income was £2,000 million, and the "earnings" of the five million richest Britons were a mere £900 million. Eight years later it proved to be possible after all: every British subject over the age of 70 whose annual income did not exceed £31.10s. was granted a pension of from one to five shillings per week. The bill came to just over £8.5 million, and that sum, far from being lost to the system, merely led to a shift in purchasing power.[61] In Germany, Düwell was able to fill a booklet with not always unjustified complaints against the social provisions made at Krupp's,[62] and concluded that the workers greatly preferred straight wage increases to charitable handouts. Diesel told a similar story about his father's social experiments.[63] Money, who, as we saw, granted that there had been some progress, nevertheless observed that, in 1908, 1.5 to 2 million people were still on relief in the United Kingdom, or 1 person in 20; that a third of the population still lived just above the poverty line; and that more than forty people died of hunger every year in London alone.[64] To change this gloomy picture, it took much more than the social contributions of the enlightened middle classes; it called for a concerted effort from the awakening working class on the political no less than on the industrial front. What John Burns had said of the unemployed worker in *The Nineteeth Century* (1892), namely that he was no longer the patient beast of burden who bore its pack in perfect silence and was easily lulled with the soporific of philanthropy,[65] was true *a fortiori* of factory hands. The trade union movement grew irresistibly, not only horizontally but also vertically, embracing skilled as well as unskilled workers, and clerks as well as casual laborers.

It was by moral pressure rather than by numerical force that organized labor was able to improve its lot. We have already spoken of the political wing of the movement,[66] so that we can confine our subsequent remarks to the trade unions. In France, 614,000 out of a total of 3,286,000 industrial workers, or 17%, were trade unionists in 1902;[67] in the United Kingdom, the corresponding figures were 1,502,400 out of just over 10 million in 1892. By 1900 the number of British trade unionists had increased to 1,955,704; and by the end of our period Britain had some 4 million trade unionists in a total labor force of 14 million (28.5%).[68] In 1895, Germany had 259,175 trade unionists (3.5%) in a total labor force of just over 8 million; in 1907 trade union membership had increased to 2 million of a total labor force of 11.5 million (17.5%).[69] According to Sombart, the total number of organized European workers had not reached the eleven million mark by 1912,[70] though the total population had increased by 11 million since 1900, when it had stood at 400 million. But weak though it still was, the trade union movement filled the bourgeoisie with the gravest forebodings and with a deep malaise. Until the turn of the century, the middle classes had been able to suppress any uprisings by these hordes of slaves with the help of the police and if necessary of the army, generally without great bloodshed. Now they were brought face to face with a disciplined movement, and they realized that the old methods would no longer suffice. From the vast masses of the humiliated and reviled, a conscious class had at last

224

arisen in the wake of countless sacrifices. The organized strike, collective labor agreements, social legislation, and all the other concessions the trade unions had wrested from the ruling class, far from weakening the class struggle had merely diverted it into more orderly and effective channels. Slowly but steadily the outcasts of the earth shed the belief that poverty and despair were their pre-ordained lot. They may not yet have implemented the great dream of the 1880s — "eight hours to work, eight hours to play, eight hours to sleep and eight bob a day" — but that dream had ceased to be a wild fantasy. The working class had acquired a new faith; it was no longer seduced by traditional promises of a better hereafter, and was determined to achieve salvation on earth by its own struggle and effort. As one member of the working class said: the people have but to will it and mankind will witness the dawn of a new civilization.

CHAPTER XV

THE SLIPPING MASK

On July 18, 1900, the Prussian Landtag imposed a turnover tax on department stores,[1] whose advantages it nevertheless extolled: their large
capital enabled these stores to buy goods in large quantities and hence
more cheaply than most small shopkeepers could; department stores
carried a wider selection of goods, and, because of their quick turnover,
were content with smaller profits on individual sales. In addition, they
made fuller use of their buildings and staff and could offset slow sales
of one line with speedier sales of another, and losses on one article by
profits from the next. Last but not least, department stores offered the
public a welcome chance of doing all its shopping under one roof.[2] In
other words, according to one writer, they had the same advantages over
corner shops as mass production had over handicraft and the train over
the horse and cart.[3]

In spite of appreciating these advantages, the Landtag was far from
enthusiastic about the new bill — quite the contrary; it was only an amendment limiting the turnover tax to 20% of the net profits[4] that had persuaded the august Prussian legislators not to throw it out. The more
radical opponents of department stores had wanted to go much further
than the government, even though the latter had, by its Bill, seen fit
to violate its own taxing system.[5] One opponent called for an outright
ban on department stores;[6] others went further still and demanded the
proscription of all limited companies in the retail trade.[7]

The retail trade had to be in very great difficulties to press for such
draconian measures, and in great difficulties it was indeed. The department stores were just one, if the most striking, example of an economic
trend that threatened to rob the lower middle class, not only in Prussia
or Germany, but throughout Europe, of its cherished independence
and of the prosperity it had enjoyed during the previous phase of laissez-
faire capitalism.

Department stores, direct factory sales, and ordering by mail were
all French ideas. The Grands Magasins du Louvre were opened in the
days of the Second Empire, and Au Printemps and Au Bon Marché not

much later. In France, laws intended to stem this development were passed in 1880, 1889, 1890, and again in 1893, by which time the Grands Magasins du Louvre were paying some one million francs in taxes. In Germany, where Tietz and Wertheim were to become the symbols of a new age, department stores were first opened in 1895, in the face of even stiffer resistance. The opposition proved fiercer yet in Austria, where the old guild spirit was still alive, and where shopkeepers banded together to preserve their independence and to make sure that big business kept within strict limits.[8]

Both sides made noisy propaganda which was not surprising when we consider that the lower middle class, for instance, looked upon its continued existence and gradual expansion as a guarantee of civilized life and as the only alternative to what it described as "social tuberculosis of the spine."[9] The old Aristotelian view that the best society is one in which the middle class is at the helm and, if possible, more influential than the other two classes put together struck this class as altogether reasonable,[10] not only because middle-class supremacy had been taken for granted ever since the rise of cities in the late Middle Ages, but also and most particularly, because without a prosperous middle class the frightening Marxist prophecy of a final struggle between the rich and the poor was bound to come true. Now, this was a prospect that filled the entire bourgeoisie with the gravest forebodings. It followed, then, that governments throughout the West saw fit to take the kind of countermeasures we have mentioned, and also to initiate statistical studies of the problem — as the Belgian government, for instance, did when it sent a special team to make on-the-spot investigations in the Netherlands.[11] Hence also the heated discussions in the press and journals, pamphlets and books. Important, too, was the decision by leaders of the lower middle class to forget the sacred doctrine of "each for himself" and to convene three international congresses: the first in Antwerp in 1899, the second in Namur in 1901, and the third in Amsterdam in 1902. At the last, Professor Noordtzij, who had also attended the Namur Congress, acted as the official representative of the Dutch government and gave voice to the general feeling that the survival of the middle class was a matter of the utmost social importance.[12]

This general feeling also explains the stormy applause that greeted the address by Gustav Schmoller to the Eighth Evangelical Social Congress held in Leipzig on June 11, 1897.[13] Schmoller not only tried to give the "middle classes" a precise definition but also examined whether or not these classes had grown in importance during the nineteenth century. At last, a man of great authority, one who called himself an ethical econ-

227

omist, proclaimed a purely scientific and socially reassuring message: the old middle class is dead, long live the new! For the old, represented by the artisan, was rapidly making way for the new middle class of administrators, foremen, highly skilled workers, and members of professions. "It very much looks," Schmoller concluded, "as if, in most large industries, the sons of the original founders are being paid off in dividends and replaced with an army of officials, managers, and technicians on good but moderate pay."[14]

When the same message had been proclaimed a year earlier by Julius Vorster,[15] it had gone largely unheard. Now it enjoyed the support of Thomas Masaryk, who made it a cornerstone of his anti-Marxist doctrine,[16] as Treub had done before him.[17] In a special book in 1901 devoted to the same subject,[18] Böttger worked out that the new middle class together with the remains of the old comprised close on five million families in Germany;[19] Schmoller had spoken of 6.5 million. A few years later, Sombart put the combined agrarian, industrial, and administrative middle class in Germany at just over 12.5 million, and the number of workers at just over 35 million.[20]

The differences in these estimates need not detain us, for even the lowest of them suggests that the middle class made up at least a quarter of the population of Europe. All that does concern us here is whether the new middle class acted as a stabilizing element in the class struggle between capital and labor, as some claimed it did, or whether it was simply an appendage of one or the other of these two forces. Although history has failed to provide an unequivocal answer to the question, few modern historians would claim that the new class played an independent role at any time; by its very nature, it lacked the characteristic independence and self-reliance of the old. This does not, of course, imply that none of these supervisors, administrators, bookkeepers, storekeepers, foremen, divisional managers, head clerks, engineers, technicians, agents, and traveling salesmen — in short, none of the officials employed in the public as well as in the private sector of industry — has left his mark on European history.

The transition from the old to the new middle class was as painful as it was emphatic, and no modern historian can ignore it without being guilty of gross distortion. In fact, the very use of the term "transition" is misleading, for though the old and the new middle classes shared their social origins and position, they were essentially distinct from, and even opposed to, each other. In reality it was not so much a transition as a complete transformation: the decline of one world and the rise of another.

Members of the old middle class had a capitalist outlook, for they worked with their own, small capital, and continued to do so until they were assured of an independent existence and a safe old age. This explains their fierce resistance to the new middle class, which relied on extraneous finance and had no need to play the old game. However, members of the new class, too, still thought as capitalists, and even more than did the old, because as servants of finance capital, they identified their own interests with those of the financiers, who provided them with the kind of independence that goes with a decent income.

Again, members of the old middle class had tried to be humane, until it became clear to them that, try as they might, they could not shake off their landlords and creditors. Thus the tailor could only keep his head above water by exploiting his apprentices; the shoemaker had to supplement his income by working as a concierge or an undertaker's man; the cabinetmaker was forced to churn out cheap products for the easy-payments stores; the publican became a servant of the large brewies; the small shopkeeper lost out to the department stores or saw client after client disappear into the co-operative shops across the road, even in countries like Germany, where a law passed in 1896 did not allow co-operatives to sell to anyone but registered members, with the sole result, incidentally, that many occasional buyers decided to sign on.[21] Finally, the small farmer was forever in debt, despite the hard work he and his family put in year in and year out; he could not afford to buy agricultural machinery or call on the services of a farmers' co-operative or a land bank. In short, craftsmen, shopkeepers, and farmers were all incapable of coping with the new situation, for lack of capital, credit, machinery, and education. How then could they have failed to applaud the man who asserted in the year of Marx's death that the grave of the middle class was bound to become the grave of all personal freedom?[22] Their anxieties were reflected in the tragi-comedy of the forelock-touching village of Köpenick, where the hapless Wilhelm Voigt enjoyed a moment of glory in October 1906 when, disguised as an officer, he went there in search of the papers without which his very existence was threatened. In that world, you could no longer get on without donning one mask or another; you had ceased to be the master of your own fate and floundered in the moral shallows so sensitively described by the great Swiss writer Gottfried Keller.

The attitude of members of the new middle class was considerably tougher. Their economic and social dependence on finance capital had practical as well as intellectual consequences. They could not simply sit back like the old and wait for a measure of prosperity to fall into their laps; they had to fight for it remorselessly by grasping every chance

229

the new hierarchy offered them. And because they had to climb up on the backs of the workers, they could only afford to be humane once they had reached the top. Their world has been described realistically in Zola's *Au bonheur des dames* (1883), pitilessly in S. Siwertz's *Selambs*, sardonically in Arnold Bennett's Clayhanger Trilogy, scathingly in Karl Sternheim's plays, and oppressively in Heinrich Mann's *Der Untertan* — oppressively, because of the prophetic account of the rise of Diederich Hessling and, through him, of the new middle class in Wilhelminian Germany and its offshoots twenty years later. But all these writers blamed the alienation they decried on absolute human shortcomings, and ignored or failed to appreciate its true social causes.

The old middle class had evinced an aggressive conservative spirit, even in its decline. It was too deeply rooted in the past to do otherwise. The policies it advocated betrayed its desperation: opposition to the gold standard, to the banks, to the stock exchanges, to political coalitions, to universal suffrage, to social insurance, to the emancipation of women, and to advertising — in short, to capital and labor at once. The bitter draught of envy was reflected in its claim that department stores made spend-thrifts of their customers and that co-operatives were selfish institutions designed to rob decent people of their means of livelihood.[23] In its anti-capitalist movements, it would turn against the Jews, particularly in Austria and Germany but also in France, vilifying them as the pacemakers of capitalism. This attitude often went hand in hand with neo-romanticism, the Schopenhauer cult, and a host of other *fin de siècle* ideas, all signs of decay and collapse. For the old middle class was made up of men of the past, men who were forced to wear the tough mask of intemperate hatred the better to disguise their "natural" kindness.

The new middle class, on the other hand, was sped on its way by the wind of progress. Its members were determined to succeed in the world, come what may. They were men of action, who would rather do evil than nothing at all, champions of the neo-renaissance and of the Nietzsche cult. If the new men, too, wore a mask, it was the mask of imperturbable self-assurance, behind which they hid their unrelenting fear of failure.

The difference between the independent, but dying, old and the dependent, but rising, new middle class cannot be ignored by anyone concerned with the radical changes that took place at the time. The differences, however, were largely theoretical; in practice, the boundaries between the two groups were blurred. In any case, they were not based on birth, education, or wealth; so that there was no real obstacle to the merging of one group into the other or to social intercourse between them. Even the most important theoretical difference — dependence versus independence — did not weigh heavily in the balance, because the old middle class in its decline had felt dependent rather than independent, and the new in its rise was beginning to spread its wings. The differences became even more blurred as both groups began to share the same mixed feelings of contempt and envy toward the organized working class, feelings that were at first confined to the social sphere, but would eventually determine political attitudes as well. This development has been recorded in England[24] but was by no means confined to that country. *The upper middle class*

Much sharper than the difference between the old and the new middle class was the contrast between both and the modern patricians, the "haute bourgeoisie" as they were called in France or the "upper middle class" as they were known in Britain. The time when the bourgeoisie considered itself one, when it fought a united campaign against the nobility, was long past; the French Revolution, which had helped to elevate one section of the bourgeoisie into the ruling class, had merely underlined a process begun much earlier: the separation of a prosperous from a struggling branch of the bourgeoisie. The rise of modern industry and commerce had accentuated this separation, creating a class of industrial magnates and powerful merchants, a class open to all comers in principle but closed to most in practice. For though the new ruling class lacked the official privileges of the nobility, it was nevertheless highly privileged in all but name, the more so as wealth had begun to replace birth or education as the chief hallmark of social distinction. As a result, an ever deeper wedge was driven between the new haves and the new have-nots, the former, or rather their children, growing as proud of their names as any feudal lord of his. People were "distinguished," "*très correct,*"[25] or "respectable" because they came from "good homes."

Another new criterion of distinction was dress — clothes bought with money. Much as did its growing wealth, so also its sartorial elegance set this new class increasingly apart from the rest. For these men the battle had been won, the wealth was theirs, the seats of power had been conquered. Wealth, it appeared, would keep flowing into their pockets in an ever-swelling stream, now that industry, trade, and traffic were expanding so rapidly. The road back, even had it existed, had been cut off. For what was left to attract these men to the way of life of an ousted and impoverished feudal aristocracy, now that money had become the key to culture and to the elegant habits it had taken the nobility centuries to perfect? Moreover, increasing numbers of the new men were beginning to live on unearned income, and in this, too, they resembled the old

231

nobility, for it made little difference whether such income was derived from landed estates or from stocks and shares.

This is how it was in France under the Second Empire, and in Britain and Germany in the 1880s. And in whatever part of Europe capitalism had advanced far enough by the turn of the century, a bourgeois culture with aristocratic pretensions came to the fore. English "respectability" was merely a late-Victorian variant of "gentility." Just as the English bourgeoisie had no scruples about calling themselves "gentlemen," so their Continental cousins called themselves "aristocrats," conveniently forgetting that "real" aristocracy had been their most unyielding enemy. In addition, wherever they saw a chance to do so, they married their sons or daughters into titled families, however seedy or unattractive the holders of the noble name might be. The nobility, for its part, also missed no chance of escaping financial ruin by marrying into industry or banking, so much so that the ennobled upstarts resulting from such unions have been called the typical representatives of that period.

The partial fusion of these two classes, like most social processes, had wide repercussions.[25] Specifically, the upper middle class in general and the *rentiers* in particular became increasingly divorced from the rest of the bourgeoisie and were left in a social and political vacuum. They had deliberately cut their ties with the lower middle class in order to mark their superiority, so much so that "petit-bourgeois" became a term of abuse in their mouths, applied to people who were servile and over-ambitious and hence even more despicable than the working class. Paying lip service to the ideals of the nobility, they came to equate the "solidity," which was the unmistakable hallmark of the bourgeois life, with pusillanimity, insensitivity, and narrow-mindedness.

The distinction became so sharp that the French writer P. Coudert, who was not ashamed of his bourgeois origins, refused to apply the label "bourgeois" to this new class of "plutocrats" and "oligarchs."[27] The national wealth was shared by several hundred thousand property owners, about one half of it falling to a few hundred plutocrats, the "deux cents familles," the "upper ten," or "die oberen Zehntausend" as they were called. This class, he believed, grew alarmed at the slightest shift toward independence in the broad base of the social pyramid of which it itself formed the apex.[28] The threat this new class posed to the middle class at large had been noted by many writers[29] and — according to Coudert — might well lead to a fusion of the rest of the bourgeoisie with the lower classes.[30] As an antidote, he proposed to foster a new class-consciousness among the bourgeoisie, which, once alerted, would have to organize and thus avert the danger.[31] According to André Siegfried,[32] the main polit-

232

ical consequence of the abandonment by the "bien pensant" French
bourgeoisie of its original base was the rejection of progressive ideas
in favor of a narrow conservatism. This had happened in the wake of
three social upheavals, the last of which had occurred in 1899 and was
the emergence of a united Left following the Dreyfus Affair.

Wallraf has described the same process of alienation in Germany,[33]
where the upper middle class found it easiest to scramble to the top
by discarding the characteristic simplicity of its forebears and opting
for feudal pomp. As a result it lost a great deal of its former self-
confidence for, try as it might, the German bourgeoisie never lost its
hankering for the genial burghers' existence in the Biedermeier period.
Hence the genteel tone of so many German family periodicals, with
their nostalgia for "the good old days." Wallraf did not continue his
analytical study of the *Gartenlaube* and *Daheim* beyond the year 1890,[34]
but if we look at later issues we see that little was changed during the
next decade; the art supplements remained as blissfully rustic, the verses
as saccharine, and the stories as sentimental as ever. The only difference
was the glorification of everything nationalistic, imperialistic, and militaristic; the glowing description of the trooping of the colors in the Berlin
Arsenal on New Year's Day,[35] for instance, was a striking departure
from the usual enthusiasms of the bourgeoisie. Another sign of its growing
uncertainty was the belief, then very much in vogue, that a family is
used up in three generations: the simple grandfather who founds the
family business is followed by the well-to-do son who consolidates it,
and the luxury-loving grandson who abandons it all for a university,
a country estate, an artist's studio, or a life of idleness and profligacy.[36]
Uncertainty turned into insincerity just as soon as the turbulent times
called for greater exertions, and when *Kitsch* alone seemed able to paper
over the cracks in the crumbling walls of bourgeois self-confidence.

The political consequences in Germany resembled those in France,
except that in Germany industrialization was faster and hence more
traumatic. Moreover, the German, unlike the French bourgeoisie, could
not look back on a long tradition.[37] Otherwise, it, too, turned its back
on all the progressive ideals it had once held; such patrician burghers
as the Buddenbrooks were ousted by the upstart Hagenströms; and the
bourgeoisie was transformed into what Brinkmann has called a "secondary
or capitalist aristocracy"[38] — thanks largely to the fact that monopoly
capitalism was highly concentrated in Germany.

In Germany that transformation was all the smoother because the
German bourgeoisie, unable or unwilling to shake off the yoke of the
feudal caste, greatly preferred a marriage of convenience with it to an

alliance with the rising proletariat.[39] For this reason the Liberals under Bennigsen, including the left wing under Eugen Richter, sided with Bismarck against the Labor movement, if only to prove their fitness to rule.[40] For the rest, the German bourgeoisie grew ever more conservative, supplying the members or the funds for a host of nationalist, militarist, naval, and colonial leagues. Nor was it coincidence that the same small clique that held commanding posts in industry and banking should also have held the whip hand in these leagues, with the friendly encouragement of a number of time-serving academics.[41]

Britain, too, was experiencing similar changes; and in a speech he delivered in 1907 entitled "How the Middle Class Is Fleeced," Shaw said much the same thing as Coudert had said in France.[42] A class of "gentlemen of independent means" had emerged from the old middle classes in Britain also.[43] The process had, however, been more gradual because the English nobility had at no time cut itself off from the rest of society. The custom of knighting deserving commoners was a time-hallowed practice; and we have but to open our Thackeray to read about Lady Anne's and Lady Clare's marriages into bankers' and brewers' families. Within another generation or two this trend had become so common that it no longer excited the attention of novelists.[44] According to Beatrice Webb, the new capitalist aristocrat "tended to prefer the welfare of his family and personal friends to the interests of the companies over which he presided, the profits of these companies to the prosperity of his country, the dominance of his race to the peace of the world."[45] Yet in Britain as well, a new generation arose and felt revolted. For what Freud has said of individuals applies also to social classes: they are not as black as they have been painted, and pay with neuroses for their repressed instincts. One clear sign of British middle-class "neurosis" was the formation of the Fabian Society; another, the fact that so many middle-class intellectuals should have tried to join the trade unions, which at a conference held in 1900 agreed to support non-working-class parliamentary candidates provided they were nominated by affiliated bodies and "sympathetic with the needs and demands of the Labor movements."[46] Those who met these qualifications shared Ruskin's belief that "gentlemen have to learn that it is not part of their duty or privilege to live on others' toil."[47] It is no wonder that Lewis and Maude should have referred to this period, which followed the "Golden Age," as the "Age of Guilt."[48] And there is a great deal of truth in Schwarzschild's observation in his biography of Karl Marx that, in the final analysis, socialist and communist theories were not formulated by workers

234

but by members of the nobility and the middle classes, by manufacturers, businessmen, and intellectuals.

It would, however, be incorrect to imagine that the guilt feelings of the bourgeoisie, compounded as they were of alienation, uncertainty, and bad conscience, were deep or generally held. They existed, no doubt, but only as counterpoint to a familiar melody. They were responsible for the pessimistic undercurrent that had begun to blunt the edge of nineteenth-century optimism in part, but no more. Philanthropists and patrons of the arts may have tried to salve their guilty consciences, but they too, did nothing to stem the further accumulation of capital — nor were they particularly numerous. Brown has rightly deplored the fact that so few writers felt the need to look beneath the surface of a society that served their interests so well.[49] By the side of the few who suffered from a bad conscience there stood the many who lived too well to bother about the lot of those who did not.

As a class the British bourgeoisie did not act very differently from the French or the German, and this need not surprise us. As a class, it entertained no guilt feelings, unless the repeated denials of its true ambitions can be described as tacit admissions of guilt. Such denials go a long way toward explaining what Dangerfield has described as the "strange death of liberal England."[50] The liberal bourgeoisie had turned conservative and proved as hostile to reforms — Lloyd George came to feel it — as were its French and German counterparts. The middle class was the founder of, and provided the leaders for, the Primrose League; there were fewer than a thousand members in 1884, 900,000 in 1890, and more than 1.5 million in 1900, and each had to promise faithfully to ensure "the maintenance of religion, of the constitution of the realm and of the unity of the British Commonwealth and Empire" — none of which sounded particularly liberal. After 1909, the Conservative Party became less and less the party of landed privilege and more and more the bulwark of urban business, which purged it of most of its Tory philosophy and indoctrinated it with a "peculiar blend of Whiggery and laissez-faire Liberalism."[51]

This self-alienated middle class, which liked to describe itself as "society," "le monde," or "die Gesellschaft," set the tone in la belle époque. All those who differed were opinionated fools; the bourgeois view alone was true and hence not a matter of opinion. All those with different aims were merely playing at politics; bourgeois politics alone were fair to all and hence in the general interest. Theirs were the politics of the non-political, and the rest only counted so long as they toed the line

235

or pretended to do so. And because everyone who could tried to follow their lead, everyone had a drawing-room in which he never set foot unless there were visitors, a drawing-room darkened with heavy curtains and drapes, full of plush armchairs, tassels, and antimacassars. On the mantelpiece stood an ornate clock and other more pointless knick-knacks, and no home was complete without a grand piano, or at least an upright, with candles in crystal holders. The room was considered all the more elegant if the dark wallpaper was completely obscured by oil paintings in gilded frames, especially of the owner's parents and grandparents, provided these were in the least presentable. For the same reason, the pier-table invariably held a leather-bound album with a gilt lock and impressively thick cardboard pages, full of old family photographs: martial fathers, one foot on an imposing papier-mâché rock; elegant mothers complete with parasols standing behind imitation hedges with ivy tendrils fashioned of paper; lovable children in a great deal of lace or half-naked on all sorts of fur rugs with or without their favorite toys.[52] The nobility no longer had a style of its own but shared the love of superfluous embellishment and trinkets adopted by the middle class, as witness the furnishings of Tsarskoe Selo or the residence of Kaiser Wilhelm II in Doorn.

It was a world of appearances even when it was perfectly genuine. The "woman of the world" was not so much a creature of flesh and bone as a shape describing an S-line. Her natural contours were disfigured by corsets; she was swathed in yards of fine lace and boas, and wore bird-of-paradise or ostrich feathers on hats of an inordinate size on her head. In addition, she was expected to feign complete unworldliness and yet be an entertaining conversationalist and hostess. Just as the woman was hidden behind the mask of the lady, so her husband hid behind that of the gentleman, a type that, with moustache, top hat, quilted waistcoat, double gold watch chain, beige trouser straps and, last but not least, kid gloves, has lived on in the person of the ringmaster.[53] Children were taught to play the little aristocrat, and it was the boast of the most famous English public schools (Rugby, Eton, and Harrow) that they turned out perfect gentlemen, with all this equivocal word could be understood to mean. To foster their conversational skills, young ladies were encouraged to read Lamb's *Tales from Shakespeare;* the unexpurgated original was considered unsuited to their delicate sensibilities.

It goes without saying that these few general glimpses cannot completely recapture a world in which, more than in any other perhaps, nuances played so important a part. For though that world changed little from one Western country to the next, it nevertheless expressed itself

236

in various forms, each with historical and social roots of its own. We shall return to the subject in later chapters; here we are chiefly concerned to show that the new upper middle class, unaccustomed to luxury and power and lacking the time to develop a style of its own, simply took over the customs of its predecessors. Needless to say, few of these people were conscious of their lack of authenticity — quite the contrary. When they were driven in their carriages to the races or to other public or private amusements during the day, or to balls, concerts, or operas in the dim light of the gas lanterns at night, they never questioned their right to so much privilege and entertainment, and revelled in the "gay nineties" or "*la belle époque.*" This may explain why there are so few sociological studies of the lives they led, and why even those few deal largely with women: men, their authors, considered women, not themselves, to be the chief problem.

Yet we know their lives perhaps better than any others'. Seen in retrospect, the novelists to whom we owe this knowledge seem to have labored under a delusion as well, since, except for the few great masters who rejected the identification of "bourgeois" with "human" on psychological grounds, most of them took it for granted that their narrow bourgeois world was the only one that mattered. It was for that reason that they took such pains to describe trivial scenes of everyday life in much detail and at great length, and why they wrote of not just one generation but of two or even three; in a rapidly changing world, each generation developed interesting characteristics of its own. Often the setting was no longer a single country; their travels and connections had made these writers familiar with other lands. However, no matter what milieu or country they chose, the chief characters were invariably members of the one class that mattered — their own. Many writers tried to delve as deeply as they could into the souls of their characters, employing all the intuition, experience, and new psychological insights they commanded. Their range was very wide indeed, covering history, sociology, and psychology, and sometimes spilling over into the *roman fleuve* or continuous novel. In 1904, the *Cahiers de la Quinzaine*, founded by Charles Péguy on January 5, 1900,[54] published one of the first serial novels with a universal appeal: Romain Rolland's *Jean Christophe.* In the same year, Thomas Mann finished the manuscript of *Buddenbrooks.* In 1906, *The Man of Property*, the first volume of John Galsworthy's *Forsyte Saga*, came off the presses. *Du côté de chez Swann*, the first part of Marcel Proust's *A la recherche du temps perdu*, was published in 1913, the same year in which Robert Musil began his great but unfinished *Der Mann ohne Eigenschaften* ("The Man Without Qualities"), Part I of which was not

237

published until 1930. In the interval, Roger Martin du Gard had published the first part of his Thibault series (1922). Jules Romains's *Les Hommes de bonne volonté*, a monumental work running to twenty-seven volumes, was published in 1932.

Each of these writers, and of the hundreds of others who delved less deeply but were all the more typical for their lack of sophistication, provides us with a vast panorama in which we can savor almost at first-hand bourgeois thoughts, attitudes, viewpoints, and beliefs at the turn of the century. Whatever these writers may have lacked in sociological sophistication and conceptual clarity they more than made up with their experience, imagination, and artistic skill. Moreover, the best among them had begun to stand aloof from their class: alienation within alienation. Thus Rolland was forced to abandon the quiet life of the scholar when he was drawn into the Dreyfus affair, as was Martin du Gard. The first was thirty-two years old in 1900, the second just nineteen. Mann, who turned twenty-five that year, was both at one and at odds with his environment. His break with tradition may have been hastened by his descent from a Creole grandmother. Thomas Buddenbrook, the senator, was modelled on the author's own father, a good burgher with a bad conscience, as Mann has explained.[55] Mann abjured his patrician origins with a series of articles in the satirical *Simplicissimus;* in any case, he would not have gone in constant search of the good burgher had he remained true to his spirit.[56] Galsworthy, too, rebelled against his patrician background. We only need to look at his portrait — he was thirty-three in 1900 — to see that he himself was a born Forsyte. Yet when he had to choose, he preferred to side with the losers, and his sound instinct turned him into the good Samaritan — no Forsyte by any stretch of the imagination. He advocated reform both in his plays and in his novels, a belief he did not share with the Forsytes.[57] In particular, no Forsyte could ever have written *The Island Pharisees* (1904). Proust, who was twenty-nine at the start of the new century, gave alienation a more complex but also much clearer expression. His asthma and homosexuality presented this son of a Catholic professor of medicine and a Jewish mother with special problems, so much so that in 1909 he withdrew into a sick room, its walls lined with cork, to devote himself exclusively to his writing. He must have planned to do so as early as 1907, when he hinted at it in an article on the Eulenburg affair commissioned by *Le Figaro*.[58] His *Jean Sauteuil*, a novel first discovered in 1952, which was his pretext for withdrawing from society, was completed in 1911. As for Musil, like Rolland and Martin du Gard, he was not only a scientist by inclination but also by training. While Rolland was a musicologist and

Martin du Gard a physician, Musil trained as an engineer and then went on to study philosophy in Berlin. In his first book, published in 1906, *Die Verwirrungen des Zöglings Törless* ("Young Törless"), he described the sexual problems of adolescents with what was, at the time, quite unpardonable frankness, thus demonstrating that he knew his Freud more than superficially.[59] Rolland, for his part, may be said to have abandoned his love of literature in favor of social criticism; and we know that Martin du Gard did not write his three-part *L'Eté 1914*, the seventh group in his cycle, until he had done years of practical research.[60] Mann and Proust, too, were deeply inspired by scientific and philosophic ideas. It is impossible to read *Buddenbrooks* without sensing the influence of Schopenhauer and Nietzsche; and it was not verbosity that turned R. Green's *The Mind of Proust* into a work of close to 550 pages.[61] Jules Romains's *Manuel de déification*, published in 1910, was a theoretical justification of the views he had absorbed in Crétiel Abbey in 1907 or 1908, and his *unanimisme*, an attempt to surmount individual atomism by endowing social groups with a "soul" of their own. It was on this principle that he wrote *Les Hommes de bonne volonté*, with its ten thousand pages and more than a thousand characters. These very figures suggest that he was writing a cultural history of the year 1908 in novel form and not purely a work of art.

The philosophical aspects of the *roman fleuve* were as symptomatic as was its length. The world these authors set out to describe had grown too complex and problematic to be depicted in simple narrative style or in black and white. Romains's "unanimism," for instance, reflected his experience that the parts were interdependent and less important than the whole they constituted. Nor was he the only one to take this view. Similar ideas were also propounded by the sociologists Durkheim and Tarde and by such contemporary writers and poets as Zola, Verhaeren, and Paul Adams, and even earlier by Walt Whitman. Other literary-*cum*-philosophical credos, such as Barzun's "simultaneism" and Beauduin's "synoptism," had similar aims.[63] Later, the film was to prove a much more potent medium for conveying such messages.

By the side of this generalizing approach, literature at the time also began to use a relativizing attitude, the dialectical opposite of the former.[64] Thus Proust dissected the overall human nature of his characters to reveal a host of superposed layers, each the result of gradual process and experience. Proust's characters keep changing inwardly as well as outwardly.[65] Man wears not one but several masks, so that no one can hope to understand himself, let alone others.[66] Proust thus foreshadowed what was to become a favorite literary motif among later writers: man's total isolation. Again, he did not produce that motif out of a vacuum: Schopenhauer and Wagner influenced him as deeply as they had influenced Mann, and even a stranger in this Jerusalem will think of the names of Bergson, Paulhan, and Freud. In short, Proust was not alone in his receptiveness to what was later distinguished from the superficial psychology of earlier times and came to be known as "stereopsychology."

Yet the very factors that helped to make these writers famous in later days made them highly unpopular among their contemporaries. Rolland has told us that he originally saw no chance of publishing his *Jean Christophe* other than in Péguy's obscure little paper,[67] and Mann's *Buddenbrooks* was panned by all the critics, with the honorable exception of Lublinski, who praised it in the *Berliner Tageblatt.*[68] Although Galsworthy's *The Man of Property* was widely acclaimed, it was not nearly as successful as the sentimental novels of Marie Corelli — ten years earlier the whole of Windsor Castle had devoured her *Sorrows of Satan*, queens had asked for her signed portrait and Gladstone had complimented her for two long hours on the "magnetism of her pen."[69] Just as Galsworthy did not write for the Forsytes, so Proust did not write for the Guermantes, who, he pointed out, were much less liberal than trade unionists.[70] Musil, for his part, has remained a relatively unknown writer to this day.

The resistance was understandable. Those who wear masks do so for good reason, and do not like to have them stripped off by writers who were pessimists to a man, so that the best one can say of them is what was said of Duhamel on the publication of his *Chronique des Pasquiers;* namely, that though full of despair he had not given up all hope in mankind. At their worst, they evinced a kind of defeatism all the more devastating for its sweet reasonableness — the same reasonableness that had led the bourgeoisie from victory to victory in Descartes's day. Ultimately, these subdued discords had a much more paralyzing effect on high society than such more strident attacks as Paul Hervieu's romanticized *Peints par eux-mêmes;* Edmund Jaloux's *Une Âme d'automne* (1896), which likened the lives of the haute bourgeoisie to a macabre carnival of lunatics; or Arthur Schnitzler's *Der grüne Kakadu* (1899), which likened the upper middle class to the effete aristocrats of the *ancien régime.*

No one remains unchanged once he has gained knowledge, and this explains why not only individuals but classes, too, are less than grateful to anyone rash enough to hold up a mirror to them. The upper middle class wanted nothing less than change, and this precisely because it had become divorced from its bourgeois roots. It wanted to retain its certainty precisely because it had begun to be troubled by uncertainty. It wanted to have a clear conscience precisely because it was beginning to have a bad one. It preferred acting a part to living in the light of truth. It knew perfectly well that its world was riddled with hypocrisy, but felt vaguely that illusions were better than the bitter truths their prodigal sons were proclaiming. Did not the comfortable life of the present hold the promise of an even brighter future? Was not Marshall's suggestion, first made in 1890, that the hundred most important commodities be treated as a general yardstick of value[71] an idle intellectual game when the gold standard did its job so well?[72] Alas, all these treasures turned out to be so much fool's gold in the end, as transitory as a rainbow, a gilded mask at a fashionable fancy-dress ball. Yet so well did this mask fit the upper middle class that it mistook it for its own face. It was perhaps wise to do so, for when the storm of war tore the mask away, the face underneath appeared disfigured, and the taste on the solid burgher's lips was as bitter as ashes.

An unfair appraisal of the upper middle class: after all, there must always be an elite, even in a Communist state, and the elite must have its symbols, yes, its masks

CHAPTER XVI

THE ALMANACH DE GOTHA

October 29, 1900, was the day set for the wedding of the Archduchess
Maria Immaculata, daughter of Archduke Karl Salvator, to Prince
Ruprecht of Württemberg. In a sense, this occasion was of no great
importance: at the time there were at least thirty archdukes and fifty
archduchesses, all more or less in direct line of succession to the Hapsburg throne. People used to joke that half the Austrian army was
needed to guard the archducal palaces,[1] and all these exalted personages
married, sooner or later, happily or more often unhappily. However,
everything that happened in their circle, even of much less importance
than a wedding, was celebrated with great pomp and circumstance. Count
Paar was there to ensure that protocol was observed scrupulously and seen
to be so observed by the entire world. For though palaces and castles had
inordinately thick walls, these walls were as if made of glass.

On the eve of the festive event, a special concert was given in the
ceremonial hall of the Imperial Opera House, and the account of this
musical feast in the memoirs of the Princess Fugger may serve us as a
model of thousands of similar occasions, alike as drops of water. The
flower of the Austro-Hungarian nobility was there: dark uniforms set
off gold braid and glittering medals; elegant silk, satin, or velvet dresses
embellished with mother-of-pearl sequins or gold spangles, yards of
embroidery, lace, and ribbon. Perfumed fans and pink ostrich feathers
were *de rigueur*. The hair of the noble ladies was held in place with tiaras
and diadems reflecting the light of the ten thousand candles in their
crystal chandeliers. All of those present sat in places allocated by rank
according to the strictest rules of precedence, while they listened — en-
chanted, bored, or totally indifferent — to musicians who while never
below average in skill were very rarely above. On this occasion the star
was Madame Saville, whose performance caused more of a stir than did
any of the similar performances that took place almost every day; for just
as she was hitting a resonant high C, the attention of the audience was
distracted from her prodigious skill by the entrance of a mouse which

made straight for the Emperor and sat staring at him[2] as if determined to enjoy the majestic spectacle while it lasted.

The Viennese court was only one facet of the brilliant world celebrated in the Almanach de Gotha, a world that, like the Church, had remained a symbol of that universal Christianity which had held sway before the bourgeoisie divided the European community into different nations, each jealous of the loyalty of its citizens. In aristocratic society, the old tradition, which had largely disappeared from the political life of these nations and from industrial and cultural life in general, had found its last refuge. The 1900 French edition of the Almanach was also the 137th. At the time, visiting cards in three or even four languages were not unusual.[3] What was "chic" in the Viennese Prater was equally chic in the Nevski Prospekt, in Unter den Linden, in the Bois de Boulogne, and in Hyde Park; and everywhere you could watch the same padded carriages with liveried coachmen on the box and liveried grooms in the rumble. Nobility from all over Europe made for Biarritz in March, Paris in April, London in May and for the Derby and Ascot in June, Cowes in August, and Marienbad in September. In October, the Prince of Wales's "set" went to Balmoral for the annual shoot. Although there were a number of variations — the Russians preferred to visit their villas or hotels in Nice, the English theirs in Cannes; some chose Ems as their favorite watering place, while others chose Vichy or Spa — very few spent the entire year in one place. To mention an example, Prince Yussupov reported, as if nothing could be more natural, that his family used to while away most of the winter in St. Petersburg, Tsarskoe Selo, or Moscow; the summer in Archangel; and the autumn hunting in Rakitnoye; whence to another country estate in the Crimea at the end of October.[4] Similarly, the Sitwells would spend the winter on their Surrey estate, move to their Yorkshire estate in the summer, and spend the autumn in Londesborough Lodge, Scarborough.[5] House parties lasting for weeks and sometimes for months were the order of the day; as were visits, even over considerable distances. Visiting was a daily occupation in the season set aside for that purpose; the gentlemen in frock coats or uniform and the ladies in hats burgeoning with flowers or bird-of-paradise feathers were just as pleased when those they called on to exchange pleasantries, to condole with, or to congratulate were not at home and they could leave cards with turned-down corners. For what mattered most in this world was doing the right thing.

The evenings, too, were spent away from home more often than not. Those who could gave regular dinner parties, and this included most of society; for those who could not did not count in any case. Count Boni de Castellane gave a dinner almost every Sunday in Paris for two hundred and fifty guests, who were served on Sèvres or Dresden china. Other marquesses, dukes, and counts followed his example, though on a somewhat more modest scale; for even their great fortunes, amassed over decades, were in danger of being frittered away by too lavish a style of living, particularly now that the source — the exploitation of the peasants — had begun to dry up. De Castellane himself ended up across the "Big Pond" in search of a dollar princess, and the Americans marveled at his extravagance.[6]

One of these great dinners, given by Prince Braganza for five hundred guests, had been described in some detail by the Countess of Iowa — whose real name was Lilie Bouton and who came from Hamburg, Iowa. She was called "the Countess" because she had married Count Nostitz, Commander of the Russian Imperial Guard. The dinner was held in one of the palaces on the Avenue d'Iéna, and the guests included the easy-going Infanta Eulalia of Spain; her son Don Luis Fernandos, nephew of the king; the Marquise del Muni; Count René de Rougemont; Elsa de la Tour d'Auvergne; the Marquise du Bourg de Bozas; Mathilde de Rothschild; the Duke and Duchess of Gramont; the Princess Ruspoli; and many other exalted personages. The lady who has preserved the memory of this occasion finished her evening by dancing a cotillion with Baron Peter Wrangel — the very man who was to be routed in the Crimea by the Red Army in 1920. The most spectacular parties of all, although in this superlative world you could always find a higher superlative, were those given by Prince Alexei Orlov in his castle at Fontainebleau. There the revels were reminiscent of A Thousand and One Nights: golden bowls and plates, heavy crystal, delicacies from every corner of the world, an army of servants in blue velvet and silver braid. The illusion must have been complete when this fat sultan sat down among his favorites and hangers-on.[7] It was not, however, the honor of his house alone which ensured that no guest ever left sober.

Even much simpler dinners were inordinately expensive and extravagant. Lord Frederic Hamilton devoted more than half a page of his memoirs to a dinner he was given by a Moscow merchant, adding that, knowing what was in store for him, he had borrowed the suit of his fattest friend for the occasion.[8] Nor were the reserved English less lavish in their entertainments than the most impulsive of Russians. "If you have to give a dinner for a friend, a brother or a cousin returning from voluntary service in South Africa," so ran an advertisement in the *Daily Mail* in 1900, "and if you want to make it the best London has to offer, why not call on Escoffier? The price will be about three guineas per person." Indeed, the menu was something to satisfy the most discriminating palate: Caviar frais de sterlet, Sigui de Ladoga, Consommé aux nids d'hirondelles, Velouté d'oursins aux crevettes roses, Tonnelet de sole au Chambertin, Berquettes de laitances, Florentines, Filet mignon de poulet Alexandra, Crème de petits pois, Selle de chevreuil maréchal Roberts, Cèpes muscovites, Mousseline d'écrevisses, Neige au Cliquot, Cailles cocottes aux raisins, Brochette d'ortolants, Truffes sous la cendre, Asperges nouvelles, Suprême de foie gras, Mandarines soufflées, Pêches voilées orientales, Mignardises, Diablotins, Bénédictine, Fruits.[9] Yet all this was frugal compared with the dinner given in July 1900, by Prince Galitzin, president of the wine jury of the Paris Exposition. At this dinner the host served sixteen different wines and liqueurs, the vintages ranging from 1754 to 1891.[10]

If there was no dinner, there was always a ball where tiny feet — all ladies had tiny feet — skimmed the floor to the compelling tempo of a Viennese waltz, whose melancholy undertones they failed to hear. Best of all were the fancy-dress balls where pretence wore the guise of authenticity, the many *bals blancs* given for debutantes in search of husbands and dressed in white as a symbol of their purity and innocence, or the *bals roses* which included young married ladies and at which elation was often tempered by fears that you might turn into a wallflower, particularly when you were slightly less noble, rich, or beautiful than the rest. For name, money, and beauty were the only things that mattered in a world that asserted rather than lived its abhorrence of materialism. These select personages could sham indifference to wealth only because they still possessed it in such abundance.

During those evenings when there was no dinner or ball, there was always the opera, a concert, a charade, or a *tableau vivant*, generally inspired by the past. Wilhelm II once ordered his court to bring the Sans Souci flute concerto to "life" by enacting a scene painted by Adolf Menzel half a century earlier. Similarly, the Grand Duchess Catherine once staged a Venetian festival at the Russian court, based on Titian's famous painting and enlivened with historical dances.[11]

Indeed, where else could all these people, who despite their self-assurance must have sensed vaguely that they had no future, have taken refuge except in the past? Sir George Reresby Sitwell, the father of Osbert, Edith, and Sacheverell, was not the only one to be more at home in the Middle Ages than in his own day, living as he did behind the invisible barriers of pedigrees, coats-of-arms, shields, and banners, hearing in his mind the battle cries of armored men and the discordant sound of trumpets. As he walked about his great garden at Renishaw, he would sometimes plan a dragon in lead, or a colonnaded pavilion, or study decorative motifs, or note that the Byzantines used to gild the trunks of cypress trees up to the height of a man.[12] Without this nostalgia for the Gothic, neo-Gothic archi-

245

tecture would never have been able to set its stamp on the British landscape. Indeed, the leaden weight of the ancestors pressed so heavily upon the
descendants that their idea of culture became the very antithesis of
creativity.

For one thing, their lives were so filled with empty busyness that they
had little time for truly creative pursuits. In addition to the diversions we
have mentioned, racing and betting — at Auteuil and Longchamps, at Ep-
som and Ascot — took up much of their energy. A variant of this sport was
the new thrill of motoring, and though the everyday driving was usually
done by a chauffeur, quite a few aristocrats took the wheel themselves in
order to enjoy what was, for the time, sensational sport. We are speaking
of France in particular, for English lords, not to mention ladies, still considered the whole thing *infra dig*. The Duchess d'Uzès went to the other
extreme. She not only held an official driving license, but "without losing
her admiration for the noble horse" invariably drove to the hunt in her
automobile and did so with remarkable skill.[13] Another lady motorist was
the Viscountess Milhau, who employed Guillaume Apollinaire as a tutor —
to which fact we owe the knowledge that she drove her car from Paris to
Honnef in 1901.

Equally, but much more morbidly, active were those who played games
of chance in the casinos that could be found in most of the fashionable
watering places. Wherever the croupier's cry of "*faites vos jeux . . . rien ne
va plus*" could be heard, be it in Ostend, Monte Carlo, or elsewhere, fortunes were often won — and more often lost, a disaster described at length
in many of Edward Phillips Oppenheim's long-since forgotten novels.

More popular still was the autumn shoot, when wholesale slaughter
could be enjoyed. In his diary, Count von Waldersee tells us that he once
stayed with the Duke and Duchess von Donnersmarck in Neudeck, and that
the illustrious company bagged 4,200 pheasants in one day.[14] It was, no
doubt, good training for his "shoot" in China where his soldiers "bagged"
an even larger number of Boxers. Lord James of Hereford did nearly as
well: 4,000 carcasses including 1,324 pheasants.[15] No less bloodthirsty
were the French "meutes" of the Marquis de l'Aigle in Compiègne, of the
Duchesse d'Uzès in Bonnelles, or of the Duc d'Aumale. France still had 350
hunts in 1900.[16] Hunting, incidentally, was not only confined to the
thoughtless; Count Leo Tolstoy, too, felt its fascination before his conversion. One cannot help thinking that hunting was the only way left to
give free rein to violent instincts now that private wars had become things
of the past. It was also far less risky than war: pheasant, hare, rabbit, and
deer are the mildest of animals; and foxes and wild boar were, after all,

246

flushed by the beaters. But St. Hubert was a sadistic old saint and St. Catherine, another patron of the hunt, not much better.

More dangerous than motoring, hunting and shooting, and even roulette was the duel, which, though no longer the fight to the death it had been, was still considered an integral part of a code of honor to which all nobles and officers (often the same) were expected to subscribe. *Les Coulisses du boulangisme*, a book by Terrail published in 1890 under the nom de plume of Mermeix, led to no less than fifteen duels. As a rule, however, the cause was less intellectual: amorous escapades, gambling debts, insults or supposed insults were some of the most common motives.

However, as the nobility began to adopt bourgeois manners, the duel lost favor. In Britain, the Army Act of 1879 laid down that "any officer who fights or promotes a duel shall be cashiered or suffer such other penalty as a general court-martial may award." In France, where Floquet, the Prime Minister, fought a duel with Boulanger in 1888 and where the passions aroused by the Dreyfus affair still led to countless other duels, the fashion began to fade, possibly because the sensational press had begun to make too much of it. Thus at about the turn of the century, when convoys of carriages used to carry spectators to the duelling grounds, the scandal sheet *Le Gil Blas* printed accounts in full detail of every duel. Some achieved fame as duellists, chief among them Thomegueix, who at the age of fifty-seven probably held the record.[17] In Berlin, Baron Kotze, who was wrongly blamed for purveying obscene photographs to the court — the real culprit was much closer to the throne — was able to vindicate his name and achieve great notoriety by a series of duels during one of which he killed the man who had laid the false information against him.[18] Yet even in Germany, lawsuits and other less bloody forms of arbitration increasingly took the place of the "divine oracle." When a lieutenant in the Forty-Third Regiment was killed in a duel by a major, incensed public opinion forced the dismissal of the culprit.[19] The Eighth International Peace Congress, held in Hamburg in 1897, also expressed its opposition to duelling;[20] and when General Abdullah Pasha challenged the Young Turk exile, Ahmet Riza, to a duel at The Hague Peace Conference in 1899, Riza refused the challenge, saying that he would rather sacrifice his life for his fatherland and that duelling was, in any case, against Mohammedan law.[21] Again, when Putnam Weale challenged a brutal junior officer on von Waldersee's staff during the Boxer rebellion, a senior German officer intervened and made sure that the duel was called off.[22] Nevertheless, the mystical belief in the purifying powers of blood remained widespread in Germany. As late as April 1912, the otherwise mild Walter Rathenau challenged Maxi-

milian Harden to a duel; nothing came of it, simply because Harden refused on principle.[23]

Outwardly far less exciting but all the more satisfying were those other
two great sources of entertainment: the ladies' "at homes" and the gentlemen's clubs. For at both the latest scandal — and there was seldom a lack —
could be discussed at leisure, and the always fascinating game of making
and breaking reputations played with a smile over a glass. London was club-
land *par excellence*, with White's, Boodle's, Brooks's, the Turf Club, the
Bachelors', St. James's, the Reform, and some fifty others, with a thousand
times as many members. The twenty-five most expensive of these "High
Life" establishments — the phrase was coined during these years — charged
entrance fees of thirty guineas or more, and five of them were reserved
for senior officers.[24] Paris had the Jockey Club, the Agricole, and the
Union of Balkan Diplomats. Less exalted were the Volney for notaries
and the Épatant for modern painters.[25] Even foreigners had a special
club in the former town-house of Thérèse Lachmann, who was the Marquise of Pavia and the Countess of Henckel von Donnersmarck, at 25
Avenue d'Antin, the same premises in which Cubat, an enterprising
Russian, was to open an extremely expensive restaurant in 1900,[26] where
people would sit on the balconies surrounding the "court of honor" ignorant of the fact, or amused by the thought, that the intimate atmosphere of the place had been created by the Marquise's still more intimate
sins.

It goes without saying that the kind of life we have been describing
was based on unimaginable wealth. Admittedly, there have been massive
accumulations of capital since those days, but the part devoted to conspicuous consumption has dwindled dramatically and has, moreover,
been shared much more equitably. J. H. Huizinga, who studied this process in Britain, has called it the "bloodless revolution." In 1900, he
points out, the richest Englishmen had an average annual income of
£100,000, or 1,500 to 2,000 times that of the coal miner; fifty years
later the differential had shrunk to between 12 and 15. A similar fate
had befallen the lesser ranks of the traditional ruling class, i.e., the banker,
the industrialist, and the landed proprietor, the purchasing power of
whose income had shrunk from 340 times to a mere 9 times that of the
coal miner during the same period. Similarly, the top-ranking judges were
only five times better off in 1952 compared with a differential of approxi-
mately 70 in 1900.[27] What could be done with that sort of differential
may be gathered from the case of the Sitwells, who though well off were
by no means amongst the richest in the land. However, during the annual
summer exodus, part of the family would, by arrangement with the Great

Northern Railway Company, travel in a private car, while the three maids, the butler and his wife, the coachman, the footman, as well as the carriage, the horses, and the six Samoyed dogs were assigned to another.[28] The Sitwells were scarcely more modest when they travelled to London to have their portrait painted by the fashionable John Singer Sargent, a pupil of Carolus Duras and of Boldini, Duras's Italian rival in painting fashionable and beautiful women. The Sitwells set off on February 20, 1900, with a seventeenth-century panel of Brussels tapestry measuring thirty by twenty feet, a large commode designed by Robert Adam and made by Chippendale, and a silver racing cup won by an ancestor in 1747, for all these objects were to be immortalized on Sargent's vast canvas, for which he therefore charged £1,500.[29] Later Sargent doubled his prices, and his Marlborough family portrait executed in 1905 was even more ostentatious.[30] The Russian nobility, on the other side of Europe, was probably no richer than the English, but if anything even more open-handed. On the occasion of his marriage in 1907, Count Nostitz made over land worth more than $100,000 to a village in one of his seven domains, and gave his bride a pin-money allowance of 30,000 roubles.[31] Many Austrian, French, and German aristocrats also aspired to such largesse, though few of them were rich enough to follow Nostitz's example.

Nevertheless, even the poorest could still cash in on the magical prestige of their noble titles and contract desirable marriages with rich middle-class heiresses, preferably from America. This phenomenon attracted the attention of many contemporary writers, among them Gertrude Atherton, whose satirical *His Fortunate Grace*, published in 1897, was followed a year later by her even more caustic *American Wives and English Husbands*. Lady Sykes Algernon Castleton expressed the belief that English society was being corrupted by these women no less than by German financiers; and Frances Hodgson Burnett, the author of *Little Lord Fauntleroy*, said in a letter dated December 4, 1900, that she was not so much against foreigners as revolted by this kind of international market. That same year, Mrs. Humphry Ward portrayed the adaptable "New England girl" in her *Eleanor*.[32] One of these newly ennobled ladies was not above speaking of the great fight "our forebears" had put up at Agincourt, or deploring "our losses" in the wake of that "Stuart business."[33] Shaw, contrary as ever, called this custom a process of regeneration.[34] Consuela Vanderbilt, who married the ninth Duke of Marlborough in 1905 and who blamed the failure of that marriage on her inability to come to terms with her rigid new environment, was perhaps the most famous of those who tried to make the best of a difficult job. Another was Mrs. Hammerstay, a widow, who married the older Marlborough and whose ardent wish it was to learn by heart the names and titles of two hundred families and all their ramifications.[35] May Galet, who married the Duke of Roxburghe; Anne Meredith, the actress, who became Lady Sackville; Minnie Stevens, who became Lady Paget; and Jennie Jerome who became Lady Randolph Churchill and the mother of Winston — all were American girls, and were known as the Prince of Wales's set. Nor was this phenomenon confined to England. In France, Anna Gould became the Countess Boni de Castellane; Mrs. Blumenthal, the Duchess of Montmorency; and Sybil Durfort, the Marchioness of Bourg de Bozas — to mention just a few examples. The Germans were doing likewise: Miss Thayer from Boston became the Countess von Moltke; Kitty Spotswood, the Countess Schönborn; Clara Huntington, the Princess Hetzfeldt. Among the Russian nobles, Count Grisha Nostitz married Lilie Bouton from Iowa, whom we have had the pleasure of meeting; Prince Beloselski married Susie Whittier; and the Silesian Duchess of Hess, who has left us her vivid memoirs, used to be a simple Daisy before her marriage. An interesting and characteristic case was the marriage of Fräulein Bertha Krupp to Baron Gustav von Bohlen und Halbach in 1906. Here the money bags were so heavy that the union did not so much elevate the bourgeois partner to the ranks of the nobility as raise the nobility to the bourgeois estate. And much as nobles contracted marriages with middle-class daughters, so many industrial and commercial magnates tried to enhance their status by marrying noble ladies. The world of these people as immortalized in a host of diaries and memoirs seemed a mixture of eccentricity and inanity, possibly because centuries of inbreeding had led to far greater mental instability among the aristocracy than was common among the bourgeoisie, but more probably due to sociological reasons. In fact, the nobility as a class had ceased to play any role in society, though they themselves, of course, continued to believe that they were its undisputed masters. It was precisely this gap between fancy and reality that was, no doubt, the chief cause of their eccentricity. The scions of the great families had traditionally been diplomats and officers, yet even these professions had begun to lose much of their old glamor. Count von Waldersee, who was himself married to the American Miss Lee, realized it earlier than perhaps any of his peers, when he wrote that diplomatic work had lost much of its former importance and fascination; indeed, just like the soldier, the career diplomat was increasingly expected to satisfy technical and technological demands, and that was something a nobleman simply could not be expected to do. This may explain why so many of them, and their ladies in particular, took to writing novelettes and memoirs, from which it appears that though their supply of self-confidence was

250

still as great as their wealth, it, too, was fast ebbing away. Their whole world had begun to shrink, even in numerical terms. By 1895, no more than about seven hundred of the original 3,000 famous Swedish noble families were left.[36] Similarly, of the six hundred or so peers England could boast at the beginning of the century, only about sixty had at least ten ancestors with the same title and a mere seven had twenty such forebears. One of them, Lord Clifford, could extend the series to twenty-five.[37] The occasional sale of titles may have provided the peerage with fresh blood, but this practice did not assume important proportions until well after our period. Lloyd George, for instance, created 74 baronets and 294 knights during the last eighteen months of his term in office,[38] but by then even the English were beginning to question the right, not only of these upstarts, but also of the nobles from the past, to govern them, the more so as the merits of so many could be called into question. W. E. H. Lecky, the British historian, had said of the Anglo-Irish nobility that its historical past was more shameful than honorable, and he was an unbiased witness: not only was he a Conservative but through his marriage to Elizabeth, Baroness Dedem, he was allied to the nobility. The term "titled corruption" was widely bandied about in the struggle between the Commons and the still mighty House of Lords;[39] and, like so many similar indictments, it served to undermine the confidence of the nobility even further.

The first rule of the nobles' game had been to hold the peasantry down; the second not to waste their capital on agricultural machinery; the third to demand exemption from taxation and death duties; and the fourth to insist on privileges as a right. All these rules were increasingly challenged by the other players, and in Britain they were officially changed at the 1906 elections.[40] The program on which the Liberals were then elected with a large majority, and which they tried to implement with the help of the fifty Labour members, included land reform, licensing reform, workmen's compensation, insurance, old-age pensions, and the repeal of the Tory Education Act of 1902. When the House of Lords refused to pass this legislation, Campbell-Bannerman declared that a way must be found "by which the will of the people expressed through their elected representatives will be made to prevail." This threat did not go unheeded; but though the House of Lords made several attempts to reform its constitution in 1907 and 1908, a collision between the two Houses had become inevitable. When Lloyd George as Chancellor of the Exchequer produced his 1909 budget, Conservative papers and periodicals denounced the measures as confiscation and robbery. The Duke of Rutland, who owned large portions of London, declared that he would like to place a gag in the mouths of all the members of the Labour Party in the House of Commons;

the Duke of Beaufort stated publicly that he would dearly like to see Winston Churchill and Lloyd George "in the middle of twenty couple of dog hounds," and the Duke of Somerset threatened to discharge all his estate hands if the budget were passed.[41] In spite of such protests, it was passed by the House of Commons; and when the Lords threw it out, Parliament was dissolved. There followed new elections and new clashes, and it was only on August 10, 1911, after Asquith had threatened to create more tractable peers, that the Parliament Bill, which reduced the legal authority of the House of Lords was finally passed. The bitterness of the clash had helped to disguise the very moderate nature of the reforms — a fact that was recognized by many, even at the time.[42] The Parliament Act merely set the seal of statutory authority upon generally recognized custom, as the Lords had long ago ceased to throw out tax bills, and the fight the noble House had fought was thus lost even before it was begun.

In Russia, where the nobles still spent their roubles with unrestrained zest, things had not yet come to this pass, nor, for that matter, had they in Austria, where blue bloods still lorded it over the kind of world for which Johann Strauss the younger had composed his "Emperor" waltz, Opus 437. When Strauss died on June 3, 1899, Eduard Kremser was conducting a concert in the Volksgarten and, hearing of the sad loss, at once struck up "The Blue Danube," *pianissimo* and *con sordino*. A hundred thousand Viennese carried flowers to the freshly dug grave.[43] The German nobility, finally, though many of them were in economic difficulties, could console themselves with the fact that almost all court officials, diplomats, and officers, as well as the majority of state adminstrators, still belonged to their caste. As late as 1905, the Prussian Minister of the Interior, Count von Hammerstein, told an astonished Reichstag that in his view even junior government posts should be reserved for the lower nobility and former members of the student corps.[44] However, though some nobles in Germany and elsewhere still thought nothing of losing a thousand pounds at the gaming tables in the course of one night; though the young Marquess of Anglesey, who spent a thousand pounds on an overcoat, managed to squander a million pounds;[45] though Prince Friedrich Heinrich of Prussia lavished eighteen thousand marks a year on his wardrobe,[46] and more than one noble lady was quite happy to pay fifty guineas for the trimmings of her Ascot frock, worn once only, the great majority could no longer indulge such whims with an easy conscience. Those were the days in which Mrs. Alfred Lyttelton's play *Warp and Woof* showed forcefully the abuses in the clothing industry.[47] Moreover, if their consciences were not bruised by such plays, then their class-consciousness certainly suffered blow after blow from their ever-increasing dependence on the stock mar-

252

ket, which they were forced to play in a desperate attempt to stave off financial collapse. In this dance around the golden calf, at which the bourgeoisie were past masters, the nobility naturally came off second best. No wonder that their memoirs make such pitiable reading, however ludicrous their complaints may have been. When Count Vico Voss presented a vase embossed with life-size orchids, the only one of eighteen not to have cracked in the kiln, to Princess von Pless, she made the following philosophical observation: "Life is just like that. To produce one perfect man or woman, millions have to suffer and be broken."[48] Although these remarks may have been inspired by Nietzsche, they sound very much like a desperate, if laughable, attempt at self-justification. This was equally true of Consuela Marlborough's remark, on the occasion of a Christmas dinner she gave for two hundred children and five hundred old people, that she would gladly have done much more were it not that her gardens and stables swallowed up all her money.[49] "Laugh and the world laughs with you, cry and you cry alone," she wrote elsewhere,[50] and the very triteness of this remark made it sound like the honest *cri de coeur* of a desperately lonely woman. The rulers who no longer ruled had clearly lost the self-assurance of the Duchess Isabella, who died in 1799, and who, when suffering from a bad tooth, had a sound tooth pulled from the pretty mouth of a country girl to replace it.[51] The idea of the divine right to rule for one's own benefit was fast being eroded. There was, moreover, one noblewoman who refused to drown her awakened sensibilities in a vain hunt for pleasure: the Infanta Eulalia of Spain. She was a democrat; and when Filippo Ferrari, the son of the Duke of Galliera, renounced his noble title, she greeted the news with obvious satisfaction[52] — not because the title would now pass to her father-in-law, the Duke of Montpensier, but because someone had for once had the courage to refuse privileges that revolted him as much as they oppressed her. Needless to say, most of her kind thought otherwise; once someone has been placed on a pedestal he tends to take a superior view, no matter whether the pedestal is of marble or of papier mâché. The nobility as a whole remained as arrogant, and was as universally detested by the other classes, as ever it had been.[53] As a whole. But the exceptions became increasingly common, and the critics ever more vociferous. One of these, Elizabeth Mary Beauchamp, who was the daughter of an Englishman who had made his fortune in Australia, the niece of Katherine Mansfield, and the wife of the Count von Arnim and later of Lord Russell (older brother of Bertrand), gently but all the more effectively poured ridicule on the German nobility in *Elizabeth and Her German Garden* (1898) and in four subsequent novels. Nor did it need a whole novel to make the point: Oscar Wilde managed it in a few words, when he said

253

that the typical Tory squire was a red-cheeked, white-whiskered creature who, like so many of his class, was under the impression than an inordinate jocularity could atone for an entire lack of ideas.[54] Writers such as von Polenz with his *Der Grabenhäger* (1897), Wolzogen with his *Ecce Ego* (1895), and Fontane with his *Effi Briest* (1895), two of them noblemen, did not spare their own class.[55] The first was the only naturalist writer to give a valid account of the economic, political, and social life of the Prussian Junker with all his self-seeking, but also with all the self-discipline needed in order to survive in a rural world invaded by capitalism.[56]

When Osbert Sitwell, born in 1892, overheard his nurse telling his mother's maid how lucky he was to be the elder son of such parents and to be growing up in a world which had improved, owing to Queen Victoria and the benevolence of all members of the British race, he already felt "a very strong doubt arising from the wisdom of the blood, that fragile scarlet tree we carry within us."[57] He sensed the same doubt in others as well, particularly after 1900, the great turning point. Before 1900, he pointed out, "the esthetes alone had shown an interest in the rooms in which they so beautifully existed; ordinary people had been content to live in the houses in which they lived, with their possessions, ugly or beautiful, about them." They accepted what fate had decreed, as they accepted gas light; but with the turn of the century, they began to feel a "conscious need for self-dramatisation" because "their confidence had all of a sudden wilted." Sitwell concluded that the recent rage for interior decoration could be "related to the enormous social changes that were only hidden from them [the rich] by the still shadowy outline of the new century."[58] The new house into which the Sitwells moved at the time contained the first electrical fan young Osbert had seen. His family did not yet worship at the shrine of the new transatlantic goddess Comfortia, but, like Europe at large, it was already preparing to bend its knee to her.

Oddly enough, it was during these very years, when their tarnished image stared back at the nobility from every social mirror, that political and social conservatism made great headway. But while it was odd, this development was by no means incomprehensible; conservatism could only harden into a faith once it had ceased to be taken for granted. The same trend was inherent in Burke's *Reflections on the Revolution in France* — the names may have changed but the views were the same. Even Kirk, who wrote one of the few serious studies on the conservative mind, attributed the rejection of conservatism as a way of life in favor of conservatism as a conscious political and social faith to "the decay of Victorian confidence and the swelling influence of socialism."[59]

It was the threatened collapse of a world which, according to Kirk,[60] believed that "a divine intent rules society as well as conscience, forging an eternal chain of right and duty which links great and obscure, living and dead" — of a world in which political problems were, at bottom, religious and moral problems; of a world convinced that civilized society requires orders and classes; of a world longing for leadership and the preservation of natural distinctions; of a world persuaded that property and freedom are inseparably connected and that man is governed more by emotion than he is by reason and that tradition and sound prejudice provide checks upon his anarchistic impulses; of a world to which innovation is a devouring conflagration more often than it is a torch of progress; of a world that had faith in prescriptions and distrust of "sophisters and calculators" — that tried to perpetuate a set of values doomed to destruction.

Just as odd and yet comprehensible was the fact that the bourgeoisie, too, should have shared this longing for the past. In England, W. H. Mallock bewailed the fact that the days of the ancient manors and the peace of the untrodden road were numbered, and blamed it all on social changes and such "intellectual barbarians" as Huxley, Spencer, Jowett, Kidd, the Webbs, Shaw, and, above all, Ruskin. In his anger he claimed that the same calamity had fallen upon the British Empire as upon that of Rome — "real knowledge" had made way for "real ignorance." Mallock was, however, unable to discover a cure. Moreover, in his *Aristocracy and Revolution* (1898) he argued eloquently against social equality as the destroyer of progress, conveniently forgetting that, as an enemy of the latter, he ought to have welcomed the former with open arms.

Like Mallock, so Maurras and Barrès, too, tried vainly to place conservatism on a sound theoretical footing — a task clearly beyond anyone determined to reject the present for no better reason than his fear of the future. Walter Frank, their National-Socialist descendant, failed similarly to come up with a theory to support the "social kingship" and the "white Jacobinism" of the Action Française,[61] and Louis Dimier testified that Maurras, his former mentor, was a hollow man, who had tried vainly to fill his own emptiness with wild dreams of a "new state," in which he quite likely never believed. Barrès, also, was driven to conservatism by despair. All these men were convinced royalists, despite the fact that, in their hearts, they had to agree with Clemenceau's dictum that kings would soon be confined to packs of cards.[62] But people so often seek glory by fighting for lost causes.

Toward the end of our period, in 1912, Prince Yussupov paid a visit to Spasskoye Selo near Moscow, one of his family's oldest estates,

long since deserted. At the edge of a pine wood, he came upon a colonnaded ruin. The doors and windows had gone and the ceilings had
collapsed, but here and there were signs of a resplendent former existence:
pieces of finely chiseled stucco and the pastel remains of old wall paintings. Hall after hall was littered with broken marble pillars and with
fragments of ebony paneling inlaid with mosaic in soft pink or violet.
The wind whistled through the long corridors, owls had nested in the
cracks.[63]

Castles have been crumbling ever since they were first built. Ruins
are no tragedy. The real tragedy is the life of those who cannot imagine
a world without castles or castles without kings to rule the world and are
yet forced to make do without either. By 1914, it had come to that.

This chapter portrays vividly the decline of the aristocracy. But it was still powerful in England & Germany and even in the other European countries it enjoyed prestige of honour.

CHAPTER XVII

NEWS FOR EVERYONE

In his address to the Institute of Journalists, delivered in the Guildhall on September 10, 1900, the chairman, James Henderson, complained about the influence of American sensationalism on the British press.[1] He was not the only one to complain, nor was the American influence confined to journalism or even to England. One year later W. T. Stead wrote *The Americanization of the World* with the significant subtitle *The Trend of the Twentieth Century*;[2] and in 1902, F. A. MacKenzie published a series of articles he had originally written for the *Daily Mail*, under the title of *The American Invaders*, which, despite its title, was an attempt to examine the subject objectively. MacKenzie's conclusion was that so far as the printing presses, particularly those manufactured by Hoe & Co. of New York, the paper, and the ink were concerned America had taken the lead.[3] MacKenzie was also the author of *The Mystery of the Daily Mail*,[4] and one of the few to know that the man who had tried to buy *The Times* in 1893 and had recently acquired the *Pall Mall Gazette* was none other than the American multimillionaire William Waldorf Astor.[5] Astor's acquisitiveness was merely a sign of the times: Pierpont Morgan bought up all the ships of the Leyland Company a few years later, and the American Tobacco Trust took over most of the British tobacco companies at the beginning of the new century.[6] All this was only a symptom of a much wider trend: while two-thirds of all American exports before 1900 had been agricultural produce, the balance had shifted so rapidly since that date that before the outbreak of the First World War America as supplying Europe with industrial and agricultural goods in the same proportion.[7]

In these circumstances, it was not in the least surprising that America should have seized leadership of the modern press, and later of the film industry, both of which rest on the twin pillars of capital and technology. America's predominance in these two fields was based mainly on the development of labor-saving machinery so essential in a country short of cheap manpower, and on the combination, among the masses, of high literacy and a relative lack of taste.

However, the American influence on the press should not be exaggerated, for even without it Europe would have produced a popular press of her own at the time. Here, too, the accumulation of capital was great enough to permit the expensive installation of typesetting machines and rotary presses. Here, too, communications were rapidly improving and consequently the means of providing better and faster news services. In addition, European cities were growing in size, and the masses in them sought distraction in papers that did not make too great demands on their powers of thought or concentration.

In fact, the French boulevard press had existed long before 1883, the year in which Joseph Pulitzer bought Jay Gould's *World* as a potential mass medium. For example, the first issue of the *Petit Journal* had come out as early as February 2, 1863, and soon afterward it had enjoyed the then unprecedented circulation of 100,000. Its impressive growth was due to the same factors as were later to encourage so many similar papers: money (provided by the banker Moïse Billaud), technical expertise (provided by Hippolyte Marinoni, to whom Avenel has attributed the invention of the rotary press[8]), and journalistic flair (provided by Emile de Girardin of *La Presse*). The *Petit Journal* was a paper that, though conservative in essence, was not tied to any political party, and was in any case much more concerned with profits. To that end, it devised a host of advertising campaigns aimed at the "little man" and adopted the motto of Villesmessant, editor of *Figaro*: "Each morning, a new pebble into the pond."[9] The only specifically French thing about the *Petit Journal* was perhaps the fact that its most famous editor was the natural son of a count.[10]

The *Petit Journal* was so successful that it was quickly copied, in France and elsewhere. The Netherlands could boast a "small daily" in 1870, one year after the abolition of stamp duty on newspapers. It went by the name of *Het Nieuws van den Dag* ("Daily News") and was edited by Simon Gorter.[11] In Paris even the leading political papers were more or less forced to follow the lead of the popular press, both in content and in price. While Parisians could buy twenty-three politically committed papers in 1881 which cost five centimes, and twice as many more expensive ones, by 1889 they had a choice between sixty cheap papers and roughly the same number of expensive ones.[12] Oddly enough, even this development was dubbed "American." Thus Edouard Lockroy said as early as 1889, in his preface to the *Annuaire de la presse*, that French papers were daily becoming more "americanized."[13] However, all he meant was that these papers were run on efficient lines and that they lacked certain literary embellishments.

Germany followed the trend some ten years later; here the stamp duty on newspapers was not abolished until 1873.[14] The German pioneer in popular journalism was Rudolf Mosse, whose *Berliner Tageblatt* was edited by Arthur Levysohn. The first issue was published toward the end of 1872, and Mosse's reward for this "lapse from good taste" was a vast circulation. Within another ten years, August Scherl, too, had seized the new chance. He was one of those to whom the pursuit of personal advantage lends second sight. Thus, when he founded the *Berliner Lokal-Anzeiger* ("Berlin Local Advertiser") he hit upon an effective technique of jacking up the number of advertisements with the number of subscribers, and vice versa — a practice that every modern paper has had to adopt. The question remains, however, whether Scherl could have constructed the necessary financial machinery had he not possessed so pronounced and intuitive a grasp of mass psychology. The reason he did have that grasp was probably that he was a shy eccentric, a man with a private staircase to his own offices, who — so the story goes — would rent three boxes in the theater and sit in the central one, lest he be disturbed by inquisitive neighbors.[15] At any rate, he was one of the first to realize that the time for long and erudite leading articles, liberally sprinkled with classical quotations, was long over, and that the popular press, this new "elementary school," had to concentrate on the man in the street and to supply him with the latest news from Berlin, Paris, London, or New York — real news if necessary, fresh news if possible, and blood-curdling news in any event. Others may have had the same idea, but Scherl also handled the distribution of his paper: "his" women sold no other newspapers and were personally interested in boosting the sales of the *Lokal-Anzeiger*. Advertising was central to his whole enterprise. Later, his paper was to become the official mouthpiece of the military party, but that is another chapter, though not unconnected with the first.[16] Scherl was one of the first great modern organizers, a man who took care of the details while leaving the big editorial decisions to others; who got the best out of his staff by encouraging them to compete with one another; who could make decisions on the spot and see that they were implemented yet who could also, when necessary, adopt a wait-and-see policy and then strike at the right moment; who was always restless yet outwardly composed; and who, despite all his eccentricities, was certain of himself and his understanding of men.

Scherl's unique success was a thorn in the flesh of his chief competitor, Leopold Ullstein of the *Berliner Zeitung*, the *Berliner Abendpost*, and the weekly *Berliner Illustrierte Zeitung*. Toward the end of the century, when the circulation of mass dailies was still rising quickly and the *Lokal-Anzeiger* was obviously determined to have the lion's share, Ullstein, though past seventy, decided to stake his own claim: on September

259

20, 1898, after long and thorough preparations, he brought out the first issue of the *Berliner Morgenpost*. Its original editor-in-chief, Arthur Brehmer, was another eccentric. One day, the story goes, he decided to make a wedding trip to Paris, although he had already been married for ten years. He travelled in an open car that looked, with its tall, spoked wheels, more like a horse-drawn carriage than a modern automobile. It was wreathed in garlands for the occasion, and twenty similar vehicles gave Brehmer a royal send-off. Rumor had it that he got no further than Potsdam. He was helped to survive the rigors, not of this trip but of the early days of the *Morgenpost*, by the Viennese journalist Leopold Jacobson, a renowned Bohemian, whose fame rested largely on his libretto for *Walzertraum*.[17] The new paper sold for a mere ten pfennigs a week, and not surprisingly its circulation shot up by leaps and bounds: the 100,000 mark was passed on April 19, 1899, and advertising pillars throughout Berlin were plastered with graphs, large enough to catch the eye of even the most hurried passer-by, of the respective circulation figures of the *Morgenpost* and the *Lokal-Anzeiger* People began to make bets on the outcome until, precisely one year after the first appearance of Ullstein's paper, the issue was settled: the *Morgenpost* had 160,000 subscribers, the *Lokal-Anzeiger* but 120,000. Scherl continued the fight for another three months. Then, early in 1900, the "old king" sent an ambassador to Ullstein with an offer to buy shares in the *Morgenpost* to the amount of one million marks, on condition that Ullstein ceased broadcasting his circulation figures. It was probably Scherl's salvation, and certainly was Ullstein's; for the sale of both papers at give-away prices plus the cost of the special advertising campaigns had swallowed up vast sums of money. On May 11, 1900, the price of the *Morgenpost* was increased from ten to fifteen pfennigs a week.

This story has been related here, not because it was unique but because it was so typical, both of the growing competition between two groups of capitalists for the favor of the public and also of the growing tendency, not only among newspaper owners, to settle their disputes at the buyer's expense. Old Leopold Ullstein did not live to see the triumph of his enterprise; he died on December 3, 1899, just over a month before the contract was signed.[18] While less of an eccentric than Scherl or Brehmer, he was no less typical of the older press lords of his day. He was a baptized Jew, who felt that the difference between Judaism and Christianity could safely be ignored as Jesus, like the Jewish prophets before him, had preached neighborly love; and whether his appearance on earth as God's son had to be interpreted symbolically or literally was a matter each man had to decide for himself.[19]

In Britain, too, the rise of the popular press had to await the accumulation of enough capital to allow the installation of expensive machinery. Compulsory education, introduced in 1870, gradually accustomed the British masses to the art of reading; moreover the extension of the franchise, first in 1867 and again in the 1880s, caused the man in the street to take a genuine interest in certain aspects of national life. Yet it was true in Britain also that the best-known papers were written by gentlemen for gentlemen. The leading political articles — often running to one-and-a-half columns of small print, often devoted to remote countries with unpronounceable names and full of classical and literary allusions; the long reports of boring debates in the House of Commons or the House of Lords; the expert articles on the Stock Exchange or banking affairs were not able to capture the interest of those who dragged themselves to work half asleep in the morning and had great difficulty in keeping their eyes open in the evening. What they needed was a paper that did not demand an active response from them, one that made them feel that merely by reading about the men who made history they themselves were participating in the process.

W. T. Stead, of the *Pall Mall Gazette*, who had one foot in the past and another in the present (as witness the fact that while he still wore a beard, he already wrote with a fountain pen), had an inkling of this need. He not only appreciated the general value of stunts, but also performed a notorious one of his own: to substantiate the charges he had made in his "Maiden Tribute of Modern Babylon," a series of articles written in July 1885 purporting to show that there was a brisk trade in fourteen-year-old, and even younger, white slaves, he bought one such girl himself. A bill outlawing this vile practice, which the government had at first refused to consider, was quickly passed after the publication of these articles; and Stead went to prison with a good conscience.[20] T. P. O'Connor, of the *Star*, founded in January 1888, was another to try his hand at popular journalism.[21] In particular, he used simpler language and eschewed politics, though as a radical he constantly attacked privilege. Still, neither of these two men could be said to have revolutionized the British press, or even to have realized how drastic a change was just around the corner.[22]

Before it came, destiny made a strange detour, which led it past a vegetarian restaurant in Manchester. This was owned by George Newnes, a man who since 1881 had been publishing *Tit-Bits*, a weekly collection of anecdotes, incidents, jokes, verses, and other items of interest, under the heading of "Did you know that . . .?" Newnes simply followed his nose and printed what he and his wife thought interesting, only to discover that a host of others shared their tastes. That was not, however, the sole expla-

nation of his success. He also introduced two innovations: he insured his
readers against railway accidents, and he ran competitions in which the
prize was either a villa, provided it was named after the paper, or a job on
the paper itself. One man who won the second of these prizes was Arthur
Pearson, who founded the *Daily Express*[23] in 1900, as a rival to Harmsworth's *Daily Mail*.

There was another, tenuous, link between George Newnes and Alfred
Harmsworth, later Lord Northcliffe; for in 1885, Harmsworth, then twenty
years old and the Dublin-born son of an English lawyer and a beautiful
Irishwoman, called on Newnes and offered his services to *Tit-Bits*.[24] Three
years later, in 1888, Harmsworth brought out his own imitation of *Tit-Bits*
called *Answers to Correspondents*, which, though successful, was far from
a sensation. Harmsworth's real breakthrough came on May 4, 1896, when,
after eighteen months of careful preparation, he started his *Daily Mail* —
"the busy man's paper," "the penny paper for a halfpenny," the paper
that "beats every other paper every day."

Indeed, it did just that. The *Daily Mail* was everything a popular paper
could be: banner headlines every day across a never-ending procession of
new stories, news items both large and small but always red-hot and carefully edited to capture the reader's attention — not forgetting that of his
wife. There were interviews, scandals, and crimes. The *Daily Mail*, too, ran
insurance schemes and competitions. Instead of the usual one-and-a-half
column leaders, it published three leaders running to half a column each.
The very first issue contained one extolling the glorious future of the
motor car, at the time the butt of mocking tongues, its speed and mobility
severely curtailed by law. Ten years later, the paper was the first to hail
the new era of aviation; and flying would, in fact, have developed much
more slowly than it did without the constant encouragement of the *Daily
Mail*. In 1906 the paper offered a prize of £10,000 to the first person to
fly from London to Manchester in one day; in 1911 the same amount was
offered for a flight around Great Britain; and in 1913, for a transatlantic
flight. "Nothing can conceal the fact," the *Daily Mail* commented in 1911,
"that man has gained a new capacity, a new power." The paper was as
enthusiastic about sport as it was about attacking Germany. It stupefied
its readers even while rousing their passions by offering just a little bit
more for just a little bit less. It also paid its staff a little better; while
the chief editor of a quality paper was being paid six guineas a week, and
while Astor of the *Pall Mall Gazette* had been accused of wasting money
when he increased the pay to seven guineas, Harmsworth added another
few guineas. People have tried hard to discover the secret of his spectacular success, mentioning his early study tours in America; his intuitive

262

grasp of mass psychology; the fact that unlike other press lords he had no political axe to grind; his close co-operation with his brother Harold, later Lord Rothermere, a financial genius who converted 3,400,000 square miles of Newfoundland forest into paper; and the fact that his intellectual faculties were no greater than those of his readers. Although there was much to be said for every one of these explanations, it fell to H. G. Wells to point out the real reason for Alfred Harmsworth's meteoric rise: "He felt the looseness and insecurity of things about him and he tried in his impatient way to get something constructive and stabilizing." For his experience had been, Wells continued, that you only have to advertise a thing well or offer a prize to get all you want, whether it be world peace, or a cure for cancer or tuberculosis, or a machine to fly around the world.[25] Notwithstanding his success, Harmsworth failed to build anything lasting or stable, and his quest ended in 1922 with insanity. Though he had filled millions of his readers with a false sense of security, he had clearly been quite unable to conquer his own anxieties.

In any case, much of the "mysterious" success of the *Daily Mail* was due to Harmsworth's single-mindedness and to the great hold he exerted over his staff, from Kennedy Jones, the editor, down to the youngest reporter. The paper's motto was "first with the news"; and it was, in fact, the first paper to have a direct line to New York. To leave its competitors behind, it would think nothing of keeping the lines busy, if necessary by transmitting the Book of Genesis in full. For a time Manchester readers were supplied with the *Daily Mail* from London by train; but then the management discovered that telephoning the whole issue was cheaper, and the old practice was dropped. The main thing was to purvey the news, and "news" was everything that was in the least unusual. The story of the "Aden," which had been wrecked off Socotra, and of the forty survivors who were saved after seventeen days of misery on a sea-swept rock, was the paper's greatest scoop during the second year of its existence. The Boer War helped to boost circulation ever further — Harmsworth was an admirer not only of Rhodes and Kitchener but even of Jameson. The average daily sales which had been 610,323 in 1899 and had risen to 989,255 in 1900,[26] rose by a further 300,000 on March 2 of that year when the paper published the story of the first British successes. It was therefore not by chance that Pearson's *Daily Express* chose April 21, 1900, as the most propitious date to join in the dance round the golden calf.

Not that the *Daily Mail* invariably told its readers what they wanted to hear — far from it. During the Boer War, in particular, it felt in duty bound to point out the seriousness of the situation; from the outset it had argued that no fewer than a hundred thousand well-equipped men would be needed to subdue the Boers. The first to lead this campaign was W. G. Steevens, who had previously been with Kitchener in the Sudan and who died in besieged Ladysmith in January 1900. The *Mail's* attempt to tell the nation how precarious the situation in South Africa really was led to a head-on collision with the government, which decreed that the paper should be cut off from all War Office news. However, the other dailies, outraged by this interference with the freedom of the press, rallied to the support of the *Mail*, and handed news to its South African correspondents, Lady Sarah Wilson, who represented the *Daily Mail* in Mafeking and was the first woman war correspondent, among them. The success of his campaign gave Harmsworth a lasting taste for political battle. It stayed with him until his death, and was largely responsible for the exaggerated view he took of his own importance and his choice of the Northcliffe title. Like Napoleon, he could now sign himself with a capital N — a clear indication of his impending mental breakdown. In any case, his behavior gave the lie to the legend that his newspaper was apolitical; Northcliffe's political line may have been improvised, but it was there all the same.

However, as far as he was concerned, politics always took second place to scoops and stunts. The paper's greatest scoop during the first decade of its existence was its coverage of the Peace of Vereeniging in 1902. Military guards prevented any outsiders from approaching the camp in which the negotiators were isolated, nevertheless the *Daily Mail* and the *Daily Mail* alone was able to publish a progress report every day. Everyone was completely baffled until it came to light that the paper had a representative inside the camp, a man who would wave one of three handkerchiefs, red, blue, or white, as the train carrying a second representative passed by the camp. Red meant no progress; blue meant that things were beginning to move; white, that agreement was certain. The next problem was to get the reports past the censor; and to that end a secret code for cabling had been arranged well in advance. All the *Daily Mail* Special Correspondent had to do, in fact, was to cable from Johannesburg to a private address in London messages apparently dealing with gold mining and Stock Exchange transactions. Since large numbers of such messages were transmitted every day in the ordinary course of business, the censor had no cause to suspect them.[27]

At the beginning of 1905, the paper brought off a similar scoop, this time based on sound news-sense. Charles E. Hands, a *Daily Mail* correspondent, returning from the Russian front through St. Petersburg, was present during Bloody Sunday (January 22, 1905) and naturally sent a dispatch to his paper. The editorial office at once realized — and in these matters hours count and sometimes even minutes — that if there was fighting in St. Petersburg, there would almost certainly be an outbreak else-where, most probably in Warsaw. F. A. MacKenzie, who had just returned from Manchuria, was immediately sent to the Polish capital, and arrived there on a Saturday morning, just before the storm burst. The follow-ing Monday morning his dispatch, covering several columns, appeared in the *Daily Mail*, the only report to have slipped past the censor. The paper's circulation rose by 50,000 that day.[28]

All this expenditure of money and thought on getting the news in more quickly than anyone else would have been quite pointless in the ab-sence of machinery capable of printing it more quickly. The old hand-presses could not possibly cope — it would have taken some 5,000 of them and some 20,000 printers, not to mention an army of setters to produce a six-page newspaper with a circulation of 1.2 million in ten hours. Such a task was also quite beyond the nineteenth-century fly-press or even the prototype rotary press developed by the Times Printing Works about 1860. Mass circulation demanded not only the modern rotary press capable of printing 200,000 eight-page newspapers every hour, but also the development of modern typesetting techniques, a task to which some 200 inventors are known to have devoted their skill and energy before 1904. The one best suited to the new needs was the linotype machine of Ottmar Mergenthaler, a German-American who died in 1899. It came on the market in 1886, and was followed, one decade later, by the monotype machine invented by Tolbert Lanston, another American, who died in 1913.[29] If we ask who paid for all these costly news-services, the even more costly printing presses, and provided the enormous profits of the press lords, the answer is the reader, though not in his capacity as buyer or subscriber, for the papers put through his letter box or bought in the street cost more to produce than he paid for them. He made good the deficit, however, when he bought the goods advertised in "his" paper by manufacturers, who more than recouped the costs of their expensive advertising campaigns out of his pocket. Such profits to advertisers were not, of course, reflected in the account books of the newspaper industry; what they showed all the more clearly, however, was that without adver-tisements no modern newspaper could survive for long. The *Economist*[30] once calculated that the revenue of a great daily was in the region of £4.5 million per annum, of which £1.5 million came from sales and £3 million from advertisements. The fact that these figures bore on newspaper pub-lishing in the 1920s makes little difference in principle. The hunt for new readers was therefore not so much inspired by the wish to influence their opinions, let alone act as their spokesman, as by the compelling need to sell more advertising, which could only be done by increasing the circulation figures.[31] Newspapers had become big business, and what they printed was almost wholly determined by its effect on sales.

This mighty intellectual, technological, and commercial machine was, however, not large enough to collect and sift the avalanche of news that poured in from an ever-shrinking world. Moreover, while the cost of gathering news kept mounting, the press lords, for their part, were increasingly forced to economize. Hence the rise of the press agencies, the first of which, the Agence Havas, was founded as early as 1835. Wolffs Telegraphisches Correspondenz-Büro followed in 1849 and Reuters Telegram Company Ltd. in 1851. Although the *Times* still saw fit to turn down Reuters's offer in 1858 to supply it with news, and although the *Morning Advertiser* did likewise, the three agencies in 1859 signed a first agreement on the delimitation of sources and markets and on the mutual exchange of news.[32] The resulting network was predominantly Anglo-American: in 1913, 54% of the international cable system was in British, 20% in American, and 8% each in French and German hands. There is scarcely need to mention that this network has continued to expand in scope and intensity.

The big papers continued to employ correspondents and leader writers, but the news items themselves were increasingly provided by the news agencies. This source of news was anything but pure, for it was highly selective, the more so as Havas had covert links with the French government, Wolf with the German, and Reuters with the British. No wonder, then, that these agencies were called "semi-official," notwithstanding the fact that they were wholly or partly in private hands. The links were most obvious in Germany, where Otto Hammann ran the information division of von Bülow's Foreign Office, and to a lesser extent in France, where Robert de Billy pulled the strings of the *Bureau de la Presse et des Informations* in the Quai d'Orsay.[33] In Britain, the relationship between the government and the press, through Reuters or others, was far more obscure, but there is little doubt that it existed, if only because the British, like every other government, could ill afford to neglect public opinion. Thus we know from Northcliffe's brother Cecil, that in 1909 Lloyd George, that other human dynamo, gave Northcliffe an exclusive preview of the draft of his Highways Bill on the eve of its presentation to Parliament, in order to gain, in exchange, the full backing of the *Daily Mail* for this pet project.[34]

Governments also relied on news agencies and the press in general to whip up popular support for their foreign policies. In a special study devoted to this subject, Hale has shown how faithfully the British press reflected and supported what he calls the "diplomatic revolution,"[35] i.e., the shift in the British alliances in 1902–1907. Thus, in 1902, the British press grew perceptibly warmer toward Japan, and shortly before

266

1904 its attitude to France became as friendly as it had been hostile at the turn of the century. Again, much as the once decadent Marianne was restored to public favor in 1904, so the uncouth Russian bear was converted into a friendly pet in 1907. At almost the same time, benevolence toward Germany made way for sharp antagonism, not least due to Northcliffe, who was said to have sworn that none of the papers of his Associated Newspapers Limited — the *Daily Mail*, the *Evening News*, the *Weekly Despatch*, and the *Overseas Daily Mail* — would publish a single good word about that country. Similarly, Italy's withdrawal from the Triple Alliance was partly the work of the Italian press.[36] All in all, most governments would try to keep the press at bay while deciding on the next political step; but once they had made up their minds, they would bend over backward to gain favorable publicity. As for the attitude of the press toward the government, it cannot be described in so simple a way, if only because the press rarely spoke with one voice. In any case, it is hard to find a single example in which the press was able to force a determined government to change its foreign policy. If its influence was nevertheless great and sometimes decisive, it was because ministers paid heed to the papers while they were still of two minds.

As a result — a fact that was rarely remarked upon — official diplomacy became allied to an improvised and semi-official type of foreign policy that, precisely because it was improvised, hampered international understanding even more than did the traditional secret methods. Moreover, just as the press interfered in the diplomatic sphere, so it also meddled with Parliament, gaining in power while Parliament increasingly lost influence.[37]

The relations between the government and the press lead us quite naturally to the much wider problem of the general role of the press in modern society. This is a problem no historian of the period can ignore; for one of its main characteristics was the rise of the masses, who, except for being allowed to express their views periodically at the polls, would have remained as voiceless as ever they had been had the press not spoken up on their behalf.

This brings us to one of the most difficult questions raised by modern history: is the press, and particularly the popular press, correct in claiming that it speaks for the masses, or are its critics right in contending that it merely fills the masses with whatever ideas the press lords wish them to have? The answer is that there is a great deal of truth to both claims.[38] Kennedy Jones has shown that the press reflects public opinion honestly and completely in no more than 20% of its coverage; partly in 50% of its coverage; and not at all in the remaining 30%.[39] This discrepancy may even arise when the readers themselves think that their paper merely prints what they themselves have been thinking all along, for they far too often forget that the paper put these ideas into their heads in the first place. Nor was it the popular press alone that played such tricks upon them.[40] However, then as now, not even the most unscrupulous papers could ram anything they liked down their readers' throats — to succeed, their suggestions had to strike at least some chord in the majority. It is this very fact which validates our theory of the interaction between press and mass opinion, and which partly explains the growing influence of the masses at the turn of the last century. It is important to stress this development, because it, probably more than anything else, added greatly to the uncertainty of the bourgeoisie.

Was the unmistakable and growing influence of the press a blessing or a curse in the world of 1900? Nineteenth-century historians would have rejected this question as unscientific, unlike modern historiographers, who place man and his fate at the center of their investigations. Now, moral objections to the press are not a recent phenomenon. Apart from J. Lukas, who in 1867 called the press "a piece of modern simplification,"[41] the chief critic was Mehring, with his *Kapital und Presse*, published in 1891.[42] It was followed in 1892 by a pamphlet exposing the seamy side of the daily press, and claiming that newspapers were ousting literature and hence real thought.[42] In 1900, J. Henderson, like so many others, inveighed against the growing sensationalism of the press, which he called an American import, though it would surely have flourished had America never existed. In 1902, S. Munzinger produced his critical study of press advertising.[44] Peterson was even more outspoken in 1906. "The newspapers," he wrote, "represent in the domain of culture and enlightenment the mob spirit, a vast impersonal, delirious, anarchic, degenerating and disintegrating force."[45] In 1911, Frances Fenton wrote a thesis on the influence of newspaper presentation upon the growth of crime and other antisocial activity,[46] and showed in particular that the six newspapers of which she had made a special study devoted from 18.90% to 42.47% of their columns to antisocial material, and from 5.91% to 20.02% to suggestive material.[47] Though her study was confined to America, she would undoubtedly have found that things were not very different in Europe. In 1918, Bertrand Russell, then still in his radical phase, endorsed Mehring's opinion that the capitalist character of the press turned it into an agent of war.[48] Nor was this sort of criticism confined to the Left: Joseph Eberle's attack on the power of the press, one of the fiercest of all, came from the opposite camp.[49] His book was not published until 1920, but much of the material on which it was based was far older. This Austrian Catholic objected to the nefarious effects on the press of "Jewish" capitalism, and, like all anti-Semites he was not too particular about his evidence. Moreover, when he published a long attack on the advertising business in Richard Strauss's newspaper, he conveniently forgot that he had culled the revealing material for his article from that very paper.[50]

An objective attempt to evaluate the good of the press and the bad was made by Löbl in 1903.[51] He distinguished two functions of the press — leadership and information — and discussed the pros and cons of each. Thanks to press leadership, it was no longer possible to suppress ideas for good (Löbl was obviously not anticipating the advent of the Nazis with their state-controlled press). A second advantage was the faster dissemination of political and social truths and hence the acceleration of progress. One disadvantage was a levelling down of individual contributions and the growth of dependence on the opinion of others, a fault the press shared with the educational establishments. The advantages of the information service, now that messages poured in from all parts of the globe, included the broadening of the readers' mental horizons, as well as employment for writers. The disadvantages were that, as it was being assailed with a never-ending stream of news items, the readers' memory was being stretched too far, calm and reflection were undermined, and literary talent wasted.

While Löbl was undoubtedly right to argue that the modern press comprises a great deal of good and a great deal of bad, he failed to realize that the two cannot possibly be separated. Like every discovery and every advance, the modern press is no more than an extension of man's faculties and, as such, an expression of his dialectical potential for good and evil. Those who would eradicate the evil must also destroy the good, and those who would preserve but the good must find themselves saddled with the evil as well. This is particularly true of the press. Tavernier has shown that, in 1900 in Paris alone, there were 2,800 newspapers, large and small, giving employment to more than 125,000 people.[52] Even so, the supply of hands still exceeded the demand to such an extent that the wages of both journalists and administrative staff remained very low. In other words, while the rise of the popular press offered new opportunities to a host of gifted men and women, it also filled them with social dissatisfaction, and caused them to voice radical demands which society would not yet satisfy. What these people wrote was mostly trivial or worse, but the very machinery that enabled them to do so also offered them a chance to spread true knowledge to an extent that earlier generations could not have imagined. Sensationalism, too, has a positive as well as a negative function: it helps to rid man of a false sense of shame and hence to face some unwelcome truths. Thus, though Arthur Bernstein's courageous "Last Warning" in the *Berliner Morgenpost* of July 30, 1914, could not prevent the First World War, his concluding words did state bluntly that the only outcome of this "glorious" adventure would be a million corpses, two million maimed, and a vast national debt.[53]

Camille Desmoulins once said of the journalist that he has the love of truth of an historian addressing future generations, the fearlessness of an advocate attacking the mighty, and the wisdom of a legislator ruling over his contemporaries. The real journalist falls far short of this ideal, so much so, in fact, that we must ask ourselves whether the truth did not rather lie with another, who wrote at the beginning of our period that one of the chief effects of the modern press was the idealization of public life.[54] But then, did the historian, the advocate, and the legislator measure up to Desmoulin's ideal? Perhaps the fact that such an ideal was set up in the first place is more characteristic of this period than the fact that it was never attained.

If we bear in mind that the stormy development of the popular press took place against a background of extreme nationalism, rampant imperialism, and growing international tension, then we see why Desmoulin's ideal could not be implemented and also why the previous and the next five chapters of this book can be fully understood only in the light of what we have said in the present one. It was not by chance that we have placed it in the center, for in 1900 the press itself took the center of the public stage.

CHAPTER XVIII

THE STATE ENCROACHES UPON SOCIETY...

From July 25 to July 29, 1900, there took place one of the seemingly countless congresses that met in the French capital in connection with the impending universal exposition. This one was devoted to international labour legislation. Six countries were represented by government nominees; many others either by trade union delegates or by individuals with a social conscience. It was Luzzatti, the Italian spokesman, who laid the greatest stress on the need for *international* co-operation. His own campaign against night work, he explained, had foundered not so much on obstruction by Italian employers as on their inability to compete with foreign rivals who continued the practice.[1] And what applied to night work applied equally to a host of other social evils. The most important decision taken by the congress was the creation of an International Association for Labor Legislation. It was succeeded one year later by the International Labor Bureau with headquarters in Basel where similar congresses were now held every year, most of them attended by fourteen government delegations. The Bureau comprised fifteen sections and sub-committees which dealt with child labor, industrial poisons, maximum hours, sweated labor, transport and allied topics.[2]

These efforts could be dated from 1881, when the Swiss Federal Assembly first proposed a series of treaties governing international labor protection. This initiative was buried under a mountain of objections, the chief of which was that relations between employers and employees were not the business of the state.[3] In the years that followed, many individuals, including particularly Count de Mun in France and Count Hertling in Germany, tried to counter these objections,[4] but when Switzerland eventually had her way in 1889 it was not so much because of their intervention as because the proposals suited the political ambitions of the new Kaiser. A special conference was summoned in Berlin in March 1890, and though it produced no concrete results, the idea of international labor legislation had taken firm root, especially in the famous German *Verein für Sozialpolitik*, whose conference in Cologne in September 1897 is generally believed to have paved the way for the Paris

congress with which we began this chapter.[5] The main achievements
of the latter were a bilateral treaty between France and Italy, signed
on April 15, 1904, followed, before 1914, by thirteen further such treaties, and also by the Berne Conventions of 1905 and 1906.

Despite the widespread belief that social legislation must needs lead
to an increase in manufacturing costs, act as a brake on competition and
hence foster unemployment — a view also advanced by quite a few
"representatives of the people" in various parliaments — several countries
nevertheless introduced such legislation independently before 1900.
From E. Brooke's "Tabulation of the factory laws of European countries
in so far as they relate to the hours of labour and the special legislation
for women, young persons and children,"[6] we not only know that important labor legislation was passed before 1889 — she mentions twelve
initial measures in as many countries — but also that the process was
greatly speeded up in 1890–1910. When she wrote her account, labor
legislation in seven countries was based on laws passed before 1889 and
in nine countries on laws passed after that date, but in any case well
before international co-operation had become an established practice.

A full account of the laws passed would, even if it were confined
to the leading European countries, take up too much space, be misleading
and, in any case, be irrelevant to the purpose of this chapter, which is
to show how considerably state and society had begun to interpenetrate
each other during this period, and for what reasons.[7] We shall see that
labor legislation was only one of several factors responsible for this development, though one of the most important.

There was a clear ethical element in the increasing concern of the
state with social and socio-economic relations, even though, as we can
gather from Goodwin's account,[8] the chief motive was greater productivity. This is borne out by the order in which most labor legislation was
usually enacted: protection of children, followed by protection of ju-
veniles and women and finally of adult males, through accident prevention, industrial hygiene, the fight both against the truck system and for
fair, guaranteed wages, and the regulation of contracts, together with
insurance against sickness, unemployment and old age, and finally a
maximum hours act.[9] Some writers have subsumed all labor legislation
under three headings: indemnification, restoration, and prevention. The
first was said to be purely humanitarian and hence almost indistinguish-
able from poor relief, the second was said to be designed to restore full
productive capacity, and the third to prevent loss of productivity.[10]
This very classification underlines the fact that our period was one of

transition from the "charitable" concessions of yesterday to what has since come to be recognized as the worker's inalienable right.

The links between state intervention and the growth of social awareness were also reflected in the creation on September 15, 1899 — to mention just one example — of the Amsterdam Education Institute for Social Work, renamed the "School for Social Work" a few years later. Its curriculum comprised poor relief, home visiting, social assistance, child care and, if possible, social work in factories and workshops. It was the first institution of its kind in Europe and, to all intents and purposes, in the whole world, since the New York School of Social Work, founded in 1898, did no more at first than run summer courses. The leaders of the Dutch school included A. Kerdijk, Hélène Mercier, M. W. F. Treub, and Louise Went,[11] who had been trained in Octavia Hill's Charity Organization Society in London. While their work helped to spread their fame, poor relief generally was gradually passing from the church and private institutions into the hands of the state. In the Netherlands, for instance, the state contribution was increased from 35.7% in 1890 to 38.2% in 1900 and to 49.3% in 1910.[12] This was something the founders of the various charities had neither foreseen or intended — most of them had acted from purely sentimental motives. By saying this we in no way detract from their merit, for their sentiment helped to found a new science, based on a new ideal.

To say that increasing state intervention in social affairs was the direct result of the decline of economic liberalism and the consequent transformation of the state from a bad into a good fairy, and hence into the new mediator between man and his salvation, is telling no more than part of the story. We come much closer to the whole truth when we say that, in contrast to the untrammeled individualism of laissez-faire liberalism, the majority principle of political liberalism contained an inherent limitation of individual freedom that was bound to express itself as soon as circumstances allowed. Now, chief among these circumstances were, as we saw, the massive increase in the number of unskilled workers on the one hand, and the rise of trusts and cartels on the other. And we also saw that under the growing influence of socialism and anarchism, the "outcasts of the earth" were no longer prepared to submit.

When that happened, the state was forced to take social work out of the hands of childless women whose maternal instinct impelled them to help the needy, if only — and most social legislation at the time had no higher aim — to prevent the entire social system from breaking down. The old fable that the socially weak had to go to the wall as part of an

273

inevitable process of social regeneration had lost whatever shred of credibility it may have had in the past, and even those who still clung to it on purely economic grounds were prepared to make provisions against its worst consequences. One of their favorite arguments was that precisely because labor contracts, wages, and the right of association were free in principle, they had to be set certain legal bounds.[13] The only problem was where these bounds were to be drawn: minor state intervention left the capitalist system largely intact but could not eradicate the worst abuses; major intervention would convert the capitalist state into a socialist one.[14]

In the event, the bounds proved to be elastic in the extreme. State intervention, however mild, set off a chain reaction until, in the end, the state began to encroach upon what had previously been the church's exclusive province. It also began to concern itself, if not with social science as such, at least with its development and applications. In July 1901, the *Caisse des Recherches Scientifiques* was founded in France,[15] a modest beginning of what was to become a major trend fifty years later, and not in France alone. Hellpach argued in 1906 that this was a crucial development and called on the state to foster studies in mass-psychology which, he believed, were in more urgent need of government subsidies than the more platonic delights of polar expeditions.[16] He was also a typical product of his age when he asserted that the "great intellectual epidemics" had been eradicated once and for all. But though he thus failed to anticipate the rise of fascism, the greatest mass delusion the world has ever known, he, like so many of his contemporaries, realized full well that the alpha of state intervention would eventually be followed by the omega — even the idea of state medicine had been broached in his day.

In Britain, too, though Thomas Hill Green and his fellow neo-Hegelians in Oxford still considered property a necessary expression of the human personality, they nevertheless believed that the state represents a "general will" to foster the common good.[18] And the common good was to become the chief concern of Green's pupil David Ritchie (died 1903) and, of course, of the Fabians.[19] It was in their name that Sidney Webb wrote a masterly thirty-page account of state intervention in social life[20] and particularly in a number of industrial functions previously reserved for private enterprise. All the attempts by liberal industrialists to protect the underprivileged had proved so ineffective that the state had been forced to intervene in the end. As the liberty of the property owner to oppress the propertyless began to be circumscribed and pared away, and as slice after slice was cut off the incomes from rent and interest,

274

the political and industrial power of the state kept increasing to such an extent that eventually the Postmaster-General became the largest employer of labor. "Besides our international relations and the army, navy, police and the courts of justice, the community now carries on for itself, in some part or another of these islands, the post office, telegraphs, carriage of small commodities, coinage, surveys, the regulation of the currency and note issue, the provision of weights and measures, the making, sweeping, lighting and repairing of streets, roads and bridges, life insurance, the grant of annuities, shipbuilding, stockbroking, banking, farming and money-lending. It provides for many thousands of us from birth to burial — midwifery, nursery, education, board and lodging, vaccination, medical attendance, medicine, public worship, amusements and interment. It furnishes and maintains its own museums, parks, art galleries, libraries, concert-halls, roads, streets, bridges, markets, slaughter-houses, fire engines, lighthouses, pilots, ferries, surfboats, steamtugs, lifeboats, cemeteries, public baths, washhouses, pounds, harbours, piers, wharves, hospitals, dispensaries, gasworks, waterworks, tramways, telegraph cables, allotments, cow meadows, artisans' dwellings, schools, churches and reading rooms. It carries on and publishes its own researches in geology, meteorology, statistics, zoology, geography and even theology." Every one of these functions, Webb went on to explain, had at one time been left to private enterprise, and had been a source of legitimate individual investment of capital. Moreover, besides its direct supersession of private enterprise, the state also "registers, inspects and controls nearly all the industrial functions it has not yet absorbed."[21]

Webb went on to give a list of these supervisory functions, much too long to be repeated here; the reader need only look around to compile a much longer list for himself. All we need add is Webb's conclusion that there is no "apparent prospect of a slackening of the pace of this unconscious abandonment of individualism."

It may be true that Webb with his quite un-Fabian enthusiasm underestimated the strength of the opposing forces, but this fact merely increases our admiration for his astuteness — most of his thirty or so demands for further "socialist legislation" covering such wide-ranging topics as revision of taxation, extension of factory acts, educational reform, reorganization of poor law administration, extension of municipal activity and amendment of political machinery have become the law of most civilized countries — even without the advent of socialism in the strict sense.

Nor were Sidney Webb and his wife Beatrice Potter the only pioneers in this field. By their side stood the other leaders of the Fabian Society,

275

founded in 1883: George Bernard Shaw, H. G. Wells, Graham Wallas, Chiozza Money, Annie Besant, J. R. MacDonald, Philip Snowden, and three guild socialists: S. G. Hobson, G. R. S. Taylor and G. D. H. Cole, all of whom attained world renown in one way or another. In 1884, they may have declared that they preferred civil war to another century of suffering by the working class, but they are remembered for their profound social studies more than for their revolutionary stance.[22] Their renunciation of dreams of barricades in favor of the far more prosaic reality of the reading room was as typical of the period as were the great achievements that stand to the credit of this small band — for to the extent that the chances of armed uprising decreased in what was then called the "civilized world," so the chances of peaceful reform multiplied, and they were quick to seize them. The popularity of their own and similar ideas may perhaps be gathered from the sales of Robert Blatchford's *Merrie England* — a sequel to his *Dismal England* under capitalism. In 1894, when the new book in which he claimed that the era of socialism had already begun had sold twenty thousand copies, he reduced the price to one penny, whereupon an even larger number was immediately snatched up.[23] Just how far state intervention had progressed by the end of the period may also be gathered from a book by Davies, the first impression of which was published a few days before the fatal July 28, 1914.[24] His list was much more extensive than the Webbs', and he mentioned a number of reasons for the difference. To begin with, the public had become afraid of the growing power of private monopolies; secondly, the state needed more money to pay for the arms race and the new social benefits; thirdly, there was the general need for cheap power, a need, incidentally, that turned even industrialists into champions of nationalization. If we add to that an increased concern with public safety and health and with the fact that prices were increasing together with labor unrest, then we realize that state intervention was dictated more by political expediency than by the Webbs' idealistic wish to protect the socially underprivileged. History, it so happens, is not swayed by good intentions, neither in Britain, nor for that matter in Germany, where the *Verein für Sozialpolitik* argued that economic progress need not be built on the backs of innocent victims, and that capitalism need not destroy itself, as Marx had taught. Firmly convinced — so in brief ran their proclamation, which preceded the Fabian by ten years — that the future of the German Reich no less than of civilization as a whole depended on the shape of social conditions, certain that this shape, in turn, was profoundly affected by the attitude of the educated and possessing classes, of public opinion, of the press and the government toward

276

the social problem, the signatories called for a discussion with men from all political parties who had an intellectual and moral interest in the problem and did not believe in a policy of "laissez-faire, laissez-aller."[25] This proclamation did not commit anybody to anything very much, and, collectively, the signatories were quite prepared to leave it at that, both before and after 1890, the year in which Gustav Schmoller assumed the leadership. But individual members went much further, and they have entered history as "academic socialists" or "state socialists."[26] Schmoller himself belonged to the first group, and so did Schönberg and Brentano. None of them was a true socialist: they were sympathetic to the workers but not hostile to the employers. They believed that since society had grown rich enough to allow even the poor to share in its prosperity, the state must ensure that it do just that. Their approach may be called the historico-ethical.[27] The state socialists went one step further. They considered the accumulation of private capital a threat to economic, social, cultural and political life, and hence advocated the transfer of private property to the state whenever this was technically and economically justifiable. Apart from nationalization they also advocated progressive income and property taxes; high death duties amounting to total confiscation in the case of bequests by distant relatives; drastic levies on unearned increment of land and on speculative profits; and a ground rent. The flight of capital which was bound to ensue could easily be prevented if tackled with enough resolution. These temperate demands were considered extremely radical at the time.[28] Adolf Wagner, the leader of the state socialists, fought his whole life long — he died at the age of eighty-two in 1917 — for his ideals[29] in a society that, as he realized full well, felt anything but sympathy for them.[30]

In the long run, of course, his views came to be widely shared. Thus while Spencer still wrote his *Man versus the State* in 1884, Sidney Webb could declare a mere five years later that no Member of Parliament would have second thoughts about translating what used to be considered "anarchist principles" into law. And he added that not even the most determined attempts by the Liberty and Property Defence League could stop even the most conservative parliament from passing further socialist legislation.[31] In this phrase, only the second "even" seems misplaced for, in a sense, the conservatives who had always treated the state as an institution *sui generis* were not all that averse to state intervention in spheres that the old Liberals alone considered the special preserves of private enterprise. And since the democrats, too, to whom the state was but a manifestation of society, could raise no basic objections to government intervention in social affairs, most political parties, their

277

fundamental theoretical differences notwithstanding, were able to cooperate when it came to social legislation. The only exceptions were the "Conservative Liberals"[32] who, as a direct result, were forced off the political stage — perhaps the clearest proof that state intervention had become inevitable. In Britain, the Conservatives worked in close collaboration with the Progressive Liberals under the leadership of Salisbury and Balfour (1895-1905); in Germany the Catholics and Conservatives were supported by the left-wing of the National Liberals and the "Progressives", who thus continued the policies inaugurated by Bismarck: now that the stick had failed, they decided to try the carrot.

Child legislation and child care, in particular, became highly topical subjects — in the Netherlands alone some eight theses were devoted to them in 1890-1900. The result was a Bill — probably the most advanced of its kind — introduced in May 1900 and passed on February 12, 1901. Its importance is clear when we remember that, as late as 1894, 686 Dutch children below the age of sixteen and 1,213 Dutch children between the ages of sixteen and eighteen were still pining away in prison.[33] Other countries, too, were moving in the same direction. In Britain, the National Society for the Prevention of Cruelty to Children was founded in 1889 and the first preventive law was passed in the same year. That year, the Swiss Canton of Vaud also adopted a similar law, and France followed suit a year later.[34] Protective laws were also passed in Belgium and, in 1896, Norway made provision for the removal of neglected children from the care of their parents. Germany, Sweden, Denmark and the Netherlands followed soon afterwards.[35] Before 1914, the same countries also placed the protection of juvenile employees on the statute book.[36]

Even more typical of state intervention was the introduction of social insurance schemes. On January 1, 1900, Belgium passed an Old Age Pensions Bill, and though it cost no more than 300,000 francs it was a step in the right direction: in 1895 the state had contributed a mere 20,000 francs to the mutual insurance societies. Belgium, however, was not the leader in this field; she merely followed the example of France, where such legislation had become indispensable: small families were unable to practise the kind of self-help rendered by the larger families of the past. By contrast, France lagged behind in the field of industrial accident insurance. In 1901, Artibal wrote a special report on the subject to persuade French senators and deputies to bring France into line with Germany, Britain, Austria, Hungary, Russia, Italy, Norway, Sweden and Switzerland.[37] In Germany compulsory accident and sickness insurance together with an old age pension, had been introduced as early

278

as 1881. A disablement scheme was added soon afterwards, and thirty years later all these provisions were combined into a single law.[38] In 1898, 18,240,000 German workers with an annual income of less than $300 were insured against accident, the state paying out $10.5 million to 582,000 workers. Of the total contributions of $13.5 million — of which the employers provided close on $12 million — just under $2 million went on administrative costs. On the personal level, we know what happened to a bricklayer with an annual wage of $200 who injured his chest falling off a scaffold. For the first thirteen weeks after his fall he was paid sickness benefits and for the next ninety days he drew accident insurance. His wife and children were paid $25, and when he was still unable to work after twenty-six weeks' sick leave he was awarded an annual pension of $135. After his death, his wife and minor children were paid an annuity of $105.[39]

A brief glance at conditions in Britain may serve to round off our picture. It is important because it illustrates how the second phase of the industrial revolution, which attracted vast numbers of unskilled laborers into the towns, also forced the pace of social legislation.[40] In ideological respects, Britain was probably better prepared for this sort of legislation than any other country, for here the way had been cleared by a long series of illustrious pioneers, including particularly Shaftesbury, Owen, Carlyle, Maurice and Kingsley, Pusey, Newman and Manning, Ruskin, Toynbee, Chamberlain and the Fabians. The trade unions and the friendly and co-operative societies did the rest. But though the Workmen's Compensation Act of 1897 merely crowned their achievements, it was bitterly opposed not only in the House of Lords but also by many orthodox Liberals. According to them, accident insurance was bound to encourage carelessness at work.[41] In any case, the Act was confined to compensation for injuries sustained in notoriously dangerous occupations. In 1908, however, Asquith introduced a bill to extend it to other industries and to agriculture, and by then the idea of social responsibility had become so firmly entrenched that he carried the House with him.[42] Lloyd George wanted to go much further still; in 1914, he asserted that British social legislation was a palliative and that what was really needed was preventative legislation.[43] Hamon, for all his Latin rhetoric, did not exaggerate when he wrote that the spark of national assistance, lit by Napoleon III, had become a conflagration and was sweeping through great countries and small, all of which now worshipped at the shrine of insurance and social science.[44]

Closely linked with the establishment of insurance schemes — the cost of which was kept as low as possible by the introduction of appropriate safety measures — and also with the population increase, was the development of social medicine. In July, 1900, the *Tijdspiegel* published an article by Dr. P. Kopperburg on the running of municipal health services. Two years earlier, Professor Saltet told the Third Public Health Congress held in the Netherlands that in his view public health would make little progress if it were left in private hands and that, in this field, he fully agreed with the socialists. A public health bill was passed in 1900, and the Dutch example was soon followed elsewhere. That year a widely-read textbook on public health was published in Germany[45] and the death of von Pettenkofer attracted attention to his demand that public hygiene be treated as a special branch of medicine. Associations to further this objective were set up in most countries, and worked in close collaboration with central health councils, health inspectors and school doctors. There were many international congresses — the one held in Paris in 1900 was by no means the first, a congress devoted to hygiene on the railways and on ships having been held in Amsterdam in 1895, followed by congresses on tuberculosis and syphilis. Pestilence and cholera had largely disappeared from Europe, and people began to realize that money spent on the prevention of infectious diseases was so much money saved.[46] But though the "crusade against disease" was never to let up, we must not exaggerate its early achievements. In Norway, which had the lowest infant mortality rate of all European countries in 1901–1905, 81 infants in a thousand still died every year; in Austria, where the rate was highest of all except for Russia, the figure was 230.[47] The rate did not drop until 1904–1914, and then only in countries with special infant care legislation. In 1907, the first international congress devoted to infant care was held in Basel and an international bureau established. "Mental hygiene," a phrase coined by Clifford W. Beers, an inmate himself of several Connecticut institutions from 1900 to 1902, had also ceased to be a vague concept.

Better health provisions went hand in hand with better housing. In March 1910, a draft housing bill before the Dutch Parliament was examined at length by A. van Gijn in *De Economist*. Belgium passed its first housing act in 1889, authorizing the municipal authorities, though not yet the government, to inspect houses and if necessary order improvements and repairs. France had tackled the same problem as early as 1894 According to a report published in 1898, eighteen in every thousand industrial workers in Germany lived in homes built by their employers. The widespread hopes that this would encourage private builders to provide better workers' homes were, however, sadly disappointed. Luckily, the mutual insurance companies began investing some of their funds in more adequate housing projects. In 1900, they were able to rent out some twenty-four thousand homes to tenants who included people of small means, and even to paupers. British efforts went further still, but then the housing shortage was much more acute. By the Housing Act of 1890, local authorities were empowered to give financial support to registered building societies; a complete revision of the Public Health Act one year later rightly took into account the links between public health and housing.

The state intervened even more incisively in personal life when it introduced compulsory education and compulsory military service. Compulsory education was pioneered by Norway as early as 1860; Denmark followed suit in 1864, not without a great deal of resistance from those who called it a modern form of tyranny;[49] Italy followed in the late 1870s, France and Sweden in 1882, the Netherlands in 1900, and Russia in 1908.[50] This list, though correct, is also misleading, not only because of the absence of Germany, which made no special provisions for compulsory education but was, in fact, well ahead of most other countries, but also because elsewhere, too, law and reality rarely coincided. Belgium, for instance, drafted a compulsory education bill as early as 1883, but opposition to it proved so fierce that it did not become law until 1914, and Italy, though fairly high up in the list, nevertheless still had a 78% national illiteracy rate in 1900, and an even greater one in the south. The Netherlands came late, but then here no more than 9% of all children had to be compelled to go to school. It is even more difficult in this short space to give a complete chronological survey of the introduction of compulsory military service. Prussia led the way: having been forced by necessity to introduce universal conscription in 1813, she decided to make a virtue of necessity, and never abolished it again. Austria followed suit after her defeat, and France after hers. Russia and Italy also introduced conscription in the 1870s; Italy did it by stages during 1876–1892.[51] By 1914 all European countries had introduced compulsory military service, except for Britain.

At the same time, taxes began to bite deeper. While the opponents of social legislation eventually resigned themselves to the inevitable, they nevertheless continued to fight stubbornly against the financial consequences. They did so in their writings no less than in speeches at public meetings and in Parliament. Nor was their reaction surprising, for to the bourgeoisie all taxation was a compulsory form of charity, and a breach of the sacrosanct rights of private property. It hit them all the harder during the period of the "armed peace" when the various treasuries forced them to dip ever deeper into their pockets to pay for the arms race.

The reader would, however, be wrong to think that governments had really begun to soak the rich until it hurt. Even Adolf Wagner, for all his state socialism, never devised so drastic a tax policy. His long book on the history of taxation from antiquity to his day, apart from affording tangible proof of his diligence and exceptional learning, called for no more, in fact, than a modest and graduated tax on incomes and inherited wealth.[52] True, there was already a great deal of talk about taxing people according to their capacity to pay, but the reality was very different. Thus of the 500 million marks the German exchequer collected from taxes, excise, and import duties at the beginning of our period, a mere 130 million of 26% was contributed directly by the rich;[53] most of the rest came from indirect taxation. Nor was the state likely to change this situation at a time when greater prosperity ensured that indirect taxes filled its coffers more amply with every passing year. But the consequences of this policy were nevertheless disastrous. Thus Wagner calculated that a man with an annual income of 1,000 marks of which no more than 200 marks was "free" and 100 marks "relatively free" — because it took him from 700 to 800 marks to keep alive — had to hand over 30–40% of his "free" income and 60–80% of his "relatively free" income in taxes, whereas a man with an annual income of 200,000 marks paid taxes amounting to no more than 14.6% of his free income and 24.2% of his relatively free income.[54] Even if these blatant abuses had been corrected, it would still have been impossible to speak of a graduated, let alone a truly progressive, taxation policy. Wagner himself would have been the first to oppose it; indeed, he warned against the taxation policies of "communist levelers."

Other countries, except for Britain, the Netherlands and Scandinavia, were even further behind on the "leveling" road than Germany. In Britain,[55] a curious exception, income tax was introduced in 1799, during the Napoleonic wars. It was reintroduced in 1842, never to disappear again. In 1890–1893 the British income tax stood at 2.5%; it was increased to 2.91% in 1893–1894, to 3.33% in 1894–1900, to 5.0% at the beginning, and to 6.25% towards the end, of the Boer war.[56] In 1889 came a luxury tax, followed in 1894 by an increase in succession duty and a graduated estate duty. At the same time, the limit of exemption from income tax was fixed at £160. In his Budget of 1909, Lloyd George added a supertax in an attempt to bring tax more into conformity with the new ideas of equity. As a result, people with an income of £1 million

282

had to hand £150,000 over to the Exchequer. Taxes on unearned increments in land were raised to 20%, and a 5% tax on mining rights was also added. In 1913–1914, an attempt was made to increase the revenue from direct taxes to the level of indirect taxes.[57]

In the Netherlands, a tax on unearned incomes greater than 13,000 guilders was introduced in 1892. A year later followed a modest but graduated tax on all incomes above 650 guilders. Direct taxation accounted for 30% of the total tax bill and 30% of the direct taxation was obtained from estate duties.[58] In Denmark, it took another ten years and a great deal of parliamentary discussion, before direct taxation was raised to roughly 20% of the total tax bill.[59] Sweden, too, moved towards a progressive tax system: two out of every nine crowns came from direct taxation.[60] Norway introduced a modest property and income tax as early as 1880, but here direct taxation brought in no more than 12.5%.

France held out longest against this development,[61] for though the deputies first urged the government to tax incomes in 1887, it was not until twenty years later that a bill to that effect was drafted, and not until twenty-two years later that it was passed. Even then, the Senate held it up for another two years and when it finally became law on January 1, 1915, it appeared that quite a few important details had been neglected, so that it was not until 1917 that it could be put into effect.

The historian is able to take advantage of these delays, for they enable him to follow the arguments for and against state intervention step by step. During all these thirty years, French property owners produced an unending stream of objections, and did so with rare eloquence. In particular, they pleaded for a non-graduated tax on all incomes, large and small, from whatever source derived, on the grounds that a graduated tax, the exemption of incomes below a fixed minimum, and the distinction between earned and unearned income, encouraged the state to meddle in what were essentially private matters. Worse still, a graduated tax was bound to lead to a serious flight of capital and threaten to become a political weapon by which the untaxed majority could fleece the minority of tax payers at their will.[62] And in 1899, Leroy Beaulieu dismissed the case for direct taxation with the laconic remark that no merchant made his rich customers pay more and his poor customers less for the same goods. But others welcomed direct taxation, and Caillaux did so at length in 1903 and more formally in 1907. The turning point, however, did not come until 1909, when Edgar Allix declared that the state was not an artifical institution, but a natural organism to which individuals were bound by an iron law and not by personal choice.[63]

And indeed, as the state encroached more and more upon society, the view that it was an organic whole of which the individual was only a part began to take root in France, just as it had done elsewhere. To the modern historian, conscious of the functional connection between theory and practice, the question of which of the two came first is as irrelevant as the problem of the chicken and the egg is to the modern evolutionist. Wagner, in particular, realized that once the state had adopted his very modest proposals, it could never again go back, and would end by setting an upper limit to any one man's income and wealth. He saw it all so much earlier than most others because he was less afraid of it than they were. Things had not yet come to that pass in 1900, but the road was wide open now that the state itself had come to appreciate that, besides its old and generally accepted fiscal concerns, it also had a right to impose new taxes to pay for the many social tasks recent history had allotted to it.

. . . and SOCIETY ENCROACHES UPON THE STATE

On May 15, 1900, Sir H. H. Fowler delivered a lecture on municipal finance and municipal enterprise to the Royal Statistical Society in London.[1] In so doing, he helped to fulfill Laplace's prophecy in the *Essai philosophique sur la probabilité* (1814), that probability theory and statistics would one day be applied to the law, to economics, to politics and to management. That same year, Karl Pearson made final arrangements for the publication of *Biometrika*, a journal whose first appearance one year later gave a great boost to the application of mathematical statistics to problems of practical living.[2] Soon afterwards, a phalanx of scholars turned to the quantitative study of social phenomena, amongst them Levasseur, de Foville, Bloch, Juglar, Cheysson and Bertillon in France; Wappaeus, Engel, Mayr and Neumann in Germany; Inama-Sternegg and Ranchberg in Austria; Leone Levi, Craigie, Giffen and Ogle in Britain; Bodio in Italy, and N. G. Pierson in the Netherlands. It was thanks to the last-named that the *Centraal Bureau voor de Statistiek* was opened one year before the turn of the century.

The subject of Fowler's lecture was thus of great topical interest. Two months later, a joint committee of both Houses of Parliament published a report on municipal enterprise; two young Frenchmen, Montet and Stehelin, were writing a thesis on the same subject, while Karl Blücher, a well-known German authority, examined the economic tasks of urban society.

Questioned though it still was in 1900, state participation in social life was no longer "gray theory." In the 1880s, the German government had taken over the railways, and by 1909 the number of state railway officials, excluding workers, had risen to 150,000.[3] In fact, the German railways had become the largest industry in the world.

Nevertheless, state-run industries were still the exception and far less widespread than the municipal enterprises. Most of the latter were designed to protect the socially underprivileged against the worst excesses of monopoly capitalism — excesses they resented more fiercely than the state, if only because many urban communities had retained vestiges of the old social ties. But though some writers, for instance J. S. Mackenzie in his

Introduction to Social Philosophy (1890), considered the result a sign of a new spirit and even spoke of an advance from industrialism to humanitarianism, the reality was much more complex than that. Neither Joseph Chamberlain, one of the leaders of the movement in Birmingham, nor Lueger, its chief spokesman in Vienna, could be said to have acted from purely charitable motives; both were primarily interested in drumming up mass support for their anti-Liberal politics.

In any case, the idea of municipal enterprise was taking root almost everywhere. Manchester had made an early start: by 1824, Parliament had grudgingly endorsed the city's decision to buy the local gasworks.[4] Birmingham, Liverpool and Glasgow followed suit, and ninety years later, at the end of our period, 40% of all gasworks in the United Kingdom were municipally owned.[5] Much the same happened with city transport — towards the end of our period no fewer than sixty-eight of the seventy-four largest British cities ran their own tramway systems. By the end of the century, similarly, more than six hundred of the close on one thousand districts into which the United Kingdom had been divided for that purpose, drew their water from municipal water works, and by 1914 the ratio had been increased to 2:3.[6] In about the middle of the 1890s it also became generally accepted that the municipality should both plan and construct roads. And though in 1900 private enterprise still built 467 miles for every 520 miles of road built by the municipalities, the vast investment of capital needed for electric street lighting insured that, by 1914, three-quarters of all road-building was in municipal hands.[7]

Here we touch upon an objective cause of the rise of public industries: the intensive capitalization demanded by technological development. Thus while private enterprise could finance the generation and distribution of electricity when the demand was relatively small, municipal funds were increasingly needed as the system was extended. Britain, for instance, had 62 municipally-owned power stations in about 1900 but, by the end of our period, that number had risen to 323, only 230 stations remaining in private hands. In the twentieth century, municipal ownership and control also spread to the docks, markets, public baths, washhouses, cemeteries, savings banks, and a host of other economic spheres that had traditionally been the preserve of private enterprise.

This development was important for two main reasons. First, it demonstrated that the profit motive was not a *sine qua non* of efficient industrial organization, thus exploding yet another bourgeois myth. Second, it made clear that the provision of civilized standards had ceased to be a utopian ideal — and not in the United Kingdom alone. Thus Leyden, too, had a municipal gasworks as early as 1848, and of the 186 Dutch gasworks that existed in 1911 no less than 136 were municipally owned. Altogether these works supplied 53% of the gas piped to the 60% of the population who were served by gas mains. That same year, 45 of the 100 Dutch waterworks were in municipal hands, and so were 25 of the 37 telephone networks, and some 50% of the power stations. Germany had by then caught up with Britain, with Belguim and Italy following close on her heels, and though Austria-Hungary as a whole was rather backward, Vienna and Budapest were not. In 1890, Lueger, the Mayor of Vienna, took over the city's gas, water and public transport systems as part of a radical reorganization campaign,[8] and in 1900 he opened the first municipal bakery. Only the French washed their hands of what many of them called "municipal socialism" or more jocularly "gas and water socialism." They even proscribed it by law, except in Paris, and while this exception seemed to prove the inevitability of the rise of public utilities in large cities, so the general ban was a symptom that France was misreading the signs of the times and hence in danger of losing her dominant position.

In 1911, the Budapest municipality opened fourteen provision stores, but since only 60% of the capital was supplied by the municipality and the rest by private enterprise, these stores may be called early examples of "mixed enterprise." The term dates back to 1905,[9] but the process was begun in Prussia during the first quarter of the eighteenth century, though on a very small scale. It comprised all enterprises in which capital and management were provided by the authorities and private enterprise in varying proportions, and in fact, the concept of "mixed enterprise" was more indicative of the symbiosis of state and society than perhaps any other development at the time. We cannot tell whether the driving force was the attempt by the state to break the stranglehold of private monopoly or what threatened to degenerate into one, or whether it was rather the attempt by private enterprise to benefit from the growing industrial strength of the public sector, though the history of the Rheinisch-Westfälisches Elektrizitätswerk in 1898 suggests that it was the former rather than the latter: that year the mayor of Essen began to play an important official role in what was to all intents and purposes a private monopoly.[10] Another pointer in the same direction was the fact that mixed enterprises were particularly prevalent in Germany, where they provided an effective counterweight to the growth of trusts and cartels. Not that mixed enterprises were confined to that country. Switzerland, too, applied the idea, in 1898, and to an industry in which public interest was closely involved, namely the exploitation of hydro-electric power, or "white coal" as it was also called. In Britain mixed enterprise helped to rescue many a lame duck; an example is the Cunard Line, which in 1903 was in peril of suc-

cumbing to the pressure of an American trust. The Manchester Ship Canal
Company was another example of mixed enterprise. Austria passed a law
in favour of mixed enterprise in 1906, and France did likewise, although
she confined the new law to the building of cheap houses. In 1907 Belgium joined the rest by setting up a number of "mixed" waterworks.[11]

The problem of mixed enterprises has attracted the attention of many
scholars. According to Friedrich Engels (1891), no nationalized, let alone
mixed, enterprise can hope to put an end to man's exploitation by man so
long as the possessing classes remain in power — at best they can change
the method of exploitation.[12] In 1892 Julius Wolf, though agreeing that
mixed enterprise was a capitalist innovation, went on to extol the social
benefits of the capitalist system which, he claimed, the various schools of
socialism, however divided otherwise, were at one in misrepresenting.
Singer, in 1912, not only argued that nationalization, even in a capitalist
society, was greatly to the workers' benefit, but also that state control
of profits in industries where monopolistic practices had interfered with
natural competition would go a long way toward restoring social justice.
In other words, there was a clear correlation between the erosion of the
old capitalist order and the rise of reformist ideas in the trade union and
labor movements. And to that extent, we must agree with Wolf — without dismissing Engels. For, during the period under review, the rise of the
labor movement was as much the result of state penetration of society and
vice versa as these processes were the result of the growth of the labor
movement.

The consequences were momentous. In particular, the new process
was inseparably linked to three phenomena: the rise of a new scientific
ideal, the structural change of industry, and the rise of the modern bureaucracy. All three changed the prevailing political, economic, social and
cultural structure so incisively that they have been rightly called the shib-
boleths of the twentieth century.

The emergence of a new scientific ideal was the least noticeable of the
three, but probably the most far-reaching. Adolf Wagner put it very succinctly when he said that science, like the state, can be misused, but that
both have the power of self-regeneration. He believed that the regeneration of science, which had hitherto confined itself to the elucidation
and systematization of the past and the present, demanded a deep concern in the goal of future human development and the paths along which
that development must take place.[13] To that end, science must not only
mediate between the present and the future, but also between the state
and labor.

288

And this was indeed the path science took, though not at all in the way this learned dreamer had imagined. Moreover, it was not in the social sciences that the new light first dawned, as he had imagined it would, but in the technological sphere. It was technology which was chiefly responsible for the structural change to which we refer as "scientific management", and which is, in fact, the child of applied science and of time and motion studies. Its midwife was F. A. Taylor, an American engineer whose *Shop Management* and *Principle of Scientific Management* were both published in 1911. At that time productive capacity had begun to exceed the capacity of the market, and this situation demanded a more efficient use of the productive machine. While Taylor himself dwelt at some length on the treatment of materials, the selection of workers, and the most effective use of their time, his collaborators, Frank and Lillian Gilbreth, improved time and motion studies with the help of the newly-invented stop-watch and the equally new development of cinematography. More or less as a reaction — for the workers subjected to these studies looked upon them, with some justification, as a new type of slave-driving system — H. L. Gantt investigated the effect of workers' morale on productivity and based his target-and-bonus system on the findings. Thus when Ford introduced his first conveyor belt in 1913, he was persuaded to increase wages to roughly twice the customary level and moreover to reduce the working day to eight hours. Morris L. Cooke, finally, discovered that the principles and techniques of scientific management could also be applied to such non-industrial spheres as city management.[14] The movement soon spread to Europe, thanks largely to Fayol and Rathenau. Rathenau's name alone shows how integral a part scientific management had become of the general development described in this chapter. During the war, as comptroller of raw materials, Rathenau applied the new industrial method to Germany's needs most effectively. More generally, the chief consequence of his and other scientific management techniques was to render the relationship between employers and workers even more impersonal than before. An ever larger chain of command was interposed between them, consisting not only of managerial staff but also of various official agencies, and as industrial power became increasingly impersonal so also was the road opened for the even more impersonal intervention of the state. There were many who tried to resist this new trend but who were unable to locate the enemy. They shared the sad experience of the chief character in Kafka's *Trial.* In particular, it was the tragedy of the anarchists, the fiercest opponents of state power, that they should have attacked it in the person of princes, men who had long since ceased to wield it. They failed to realize that having become impersonal, the power of the state had also become irrepressible. It was like a hydra, growing a thousand new heads for each one that was cut off.

This increase in the power and facelessness of the state was called "bureaucratization." In 1888, Benjamin Tucker, the libertarian anarchist who as an American was even more violently opposed to it than his European comrades, gave so glaring an account of what he called state socialism as to make all subsequent attacks pale in comparison.[15] The new system, he claimed, held society responsible for the health, welfare and intellectual development of the individual, whose independence and sense of responsibility it was bound to destroy. It was all fated to end in a State religion at the altar of which all mankind would have to bow down; a State school of medicine by whose practitioners the sick must invariably be treated; a State system of hygiene, prescribing what all must and must not eat, drink, wear and do; a State code of morals which would not content itself with punishing crime, but would prohibit what the majority decided to be vice; a State system of instruction which would do away with all private schools, academies and colleges; a State nursery, in which all children would be brought up in common at the public expense; and, finally, a State family in which no man and woman would be allowed to have children if the State prohibited them, and no man and woman could refuse to have children if the State so ordered. "Thus will authority achieve its acme and monopoly be carried to its highest power." According to Tucker, the only alternative was the complete abolition of the State.

Tucker may have carried his argument to extremes, but he lived in an extreme age and his views were shared by quite a few people who were anything but radicals. Thus, some twenty years later, Eugène d'Eichthal threw all his eloquence into attacking a bill introduced in April 1906 by the socialist Vaillant and fifty-one of his comrades. That bill called for a four-hour day for sixteen-year olds, an eight-hour day for adult workers and a five-and-a-half day week for all, not only in industry but also in agriculture and in domestic service. At the same time another bill demanded a minimum daily wage of five francs and a minimum weekly wage of 35 francs for all state employees and for a paid annual holiday of fourteen days. Needless to say, the times were not ripe for such "radical" demands, and both bills were thrown out. Nevertheless, d'Eichthal was so incensed by the very introduction of these bills and by official trade union support for them, that he spoke of a new form of ancient slavery with the State lording it over all Frenchmen.[16] And he asked himself in dismay whether France was not inexorably moving to the point where the tyranny of the collective puts an end to individual choice and hence to all genuine social endeavor. When that happened, French industry and with it the welfare of the French nation was bound to collapse.[17]

Two years later, Ramsay Muir described the average Englishman's attitude to the new bureaucrats.[18] Although more moderate than Tucker and more objective than d'Eichthal, he, too, did not mince his words. The Englishman, he claimed, believes that bureaucracy is a logical development of the despotism that prevails in Russia, of the priggish official meddling in every detail of private life characteristic of the Germans; he finds it rampant in France, a country bristling with petty officials who behave as if they were the masters and not the servants of the public. But he believes it to be essentially hostile to the English idea of liberty and feels that bureaucracy is a more real antithesis to liberty than either monarchy or aristocracy. Even so, bureaucracy had crept into England, for the Englishman had also become scornful and distrustful of government by amateurs, and was every day learning to rely more and more upon the silent and unresting services of innumerable public servants, each expert in his own sphere. Both Houses of Parliament and the Cabinet might almost be described as a "complicated and decorated garment, clothing and concealing the real working body of bureaucracy." Bureaucrats directed, practically without control, nine-tenths of the work of the administration; in Britain they were mainly responsible for the character and increase in the amount of the national expenditure; they directly wielded immense legislative powers, and were indirectly responsible for a large proportion of the parliamentary legislative output. The only reason why the average Englishman was almost unconscious of this development was that no one had been bold enough to shatter the illusion that the Cabinet and Parliament, rather than the permanent officials, took all the important decisions. According to Muir, the change was best described as one from government by amateurs of a ruling caste to government by experts under the ultimate control of popular representatives. The change had been inevitable because the complex business of governing a modern state could only be conducted by skilled professional administrators.[19] For the same reasons bureaucracy was also beginning to encroach upon industry and the trade unions and, according to Sir H. H. Cozens-Hardy, even upon the judicial system. There had been a time, he said on May 3, 1911, when the great danger against which the judicature had to guard was the encroachments of the Crown. Happily there was no longer that danger, but there was another danger which was much more real than that, namely encroachment by the Executive. "For administrative action generally meant something done by a man whose name they [the Bench and the Bar] did not know, sitting at a desk in a government office, very apt to be a despot if free from the interference of the Courts of Justice."[20] Daniel Warnotte dealt with the rise of bureaucracy in France[21] and Cahen-Salvador, too, showed to what extent the State had encroached upon the economic sphere and was meddling in social problems.[22] Rabany, like Muir, made a study of bureaucracy, but used a different approach. People speak of democracy, he remarked in 1901, because the nobility has ostensibly disappeared. But though the real aristocrats may have gone, all the higher posts are still held by a caste best described as the "republican nobility."[23] Moreover all state officials had the unfortunate habit of looking upon their "officium" as a "beneficium,"[24] which was the more deplorable as most of them were incompetent. This situation would, however, change with the continued interpenetration of state and society though, as the officials became more efficient, the freedom of the individual was increasingly constricted. When applied to the political and social spheres, the medical tenet that prevention is better than cure meant that the maintenance of order was better than the eradication of abuses which, in turn, meant that the arrest of a potential criminal was better than allowing him to commit a crime. This attitude, too, was characteristic of a transitional age. For while people had begun to call for the isolation of potential criminals, far too few had turned their attention to the social causes of crime. Worse still, attempts to prevent dangerous acts far too often led to attempts to prevent the expression of dangerous thoughts.[25] As moral norms were increasingly replaced with legal rules, resentment and lawlessness increased, and with them the prevailing sense of uncertainty. It was in this climate that the practice of bertillonnage — a system of identifying criminals by measurements, developed by M. Bertillon, a Parisian police expert, and later extended to include fingerprinting — spread from France to Bengal and then to the United Kingdom, where it was first used in 1900. While it was originally designed for the identification of criminals, there is nevertheless no more telling symbol of the complete hold the modern state can exert over all its subjects.

Quantitively the rise of bureaucracy was reflected in a general increase in the number of officials. Alfred Weber, who made a sociological study of this phenomenon in Germany, put the number of officials at 700,000, 450,000 of them employed by the state. This was in 1900. In 1889, the second figure had been well below 100,000, but by 1927, the year in which Weber published his work, it had risen to 850,000, and the total number of officials to 2,000,000.[26] Other sources put the number of German officials at 39,000 in 1895, 51,000 in 1907, and 648,000 in 1925, in a working population of, respectively, 25,750,000, 26,850,000 and 32,000,000.

In 1908, Chardon put the number of French officials wholly or partly paid by the state at 608,510, and wholly or partly paid by local authorities at 262,078. Though other sources produced lower figures — 1866: 288,000; 1896: 501,000; 1906: 549,000; 1921: 734,000[27] — we can see that in France, too, the number of officials grew much more rapidly than the working population which was, respectively, 15,143,000, 18,970,000, 20,721,000 in the years we have just listed. The British figures, finally, cannot be compared with those of other countries because they include the army and the navy. For 1911, the total was put at 903,000 and for 1921 at 1,336,000, while the working population rose from 16,284,000 to a mere 17,187,000.

Unreliable and incomplete though these figures may be, taken all in all, they nevertheless express quantitatively what the authors we have mentioned in the last two chapters and a host of others, as well, tried to say qualitatively. The entire process of the interpenetration of state and society can, in fact, be subsumed under one heading: organization, considered as the deliberate creation of new structures in all spheres of life: in production, distribution and consumption; in industry, finance, trade and agriculture; in transport, education and art, but above all in the state which binds, co-ordinates, and controls; which imposes duties and draws up plans and leaves few if any human activities untouched. It was organization that replaced older methods of social cohesion, that arranged the parts so as to ensure the smoothest possible working of the whole, that tried to prevent friction within while trying to extend its influence without, and that, ultimately, called for ever more organization, on the grounds that the more organization there is the less chaos there will be.[28] That something unusual was happening did not, as we have seen, escape a number of contemporary writers. By way of a conclusion, we shall quote two who delved deeper into the process than most. As early as 1906, Alfred Weber complained that German art and science had become sterile, and blamed it all on the rise of the specialist, of the "placeman," a phenomenon that had caused even old Mommsen to speak of the "dehumanization" of man.[29] The irresistible magnet of rational organization had drawn man not only into industrialization but also into bureaucratization, the first involving the masses and the second the higher strata of society.[30] In protest against organization-man whose turpitude and dishonesty was sapping the roots of German civilization, there had appeared the equally unwholesome "cultural aesthete" with his cold contempt for politics and other social activities or concerns.[31]

More profound, because she was no subjective critic convinced of her own objectivity, Gertrude Bäumer[32] contended that her contemporaries were tackling the grave social problem facing them not with knowledge and resolution but with desperate vacillation, and this despite the fact that the rapid growth of social science had provided them with extremely effective new techniques. The trouble was that they could no longer distinguish social good from social evil. Neither politics, economics nor, for that matter, any special science could help them here: the individual's relationship to society could not be fitted into any special compartment. It was a highly practical problem based on his attitude to the community to which he belonged, on what he believed was its essence and importance and what privileges he was prepared to sacrifice for its sake. Gertrude Bäumer herself believed firmly that only by fusing their aims and work with society's could individuals live a meaningful life. This her fellow citizens had failed to do. Wavering as they did between individual and social motives, they lacked a sound system of ethics and a clear cultural policy. She drove this point home by underlining the contrasting nature of the attitudes so typical of her age: Nietzsche's superman morality, Tolstoy's Christian anarchism, Haeckel's theory of man's descent, and the ideas of Förster and Maeterlinck which we shall be discussing at greater length. Her conclusion, though expressed differently from Weber's, was essentially the same as his. Thus while Weber contended that the chief result of the interpenetration of state and society was the emergence of a group of men who had lost all interest in political or social ideals, Gertrude Bäumer, for her part, believed that the chief result was a return to conservative and orthodox attitudes. She herself realized only too well that these time-honored attitudes were unsuited to the needs of her day, let alone to producing order out of the prevailing intellectual chaos. But she nevertheless granted that they had the advantage of stability and of reflecting a respectable intellectual style and that they had stood the test of centuries. Gerald Heard, too, noted though much later, that the decline of intuitive and traditional attitudes and the rise of bureaucracy went hand in hand with a marked growth of scepticism among the educated classes. Conservative and pessimist that he was, he believed that he could demonstrate a decline in civilized standards, in law, education and national health.[33] Heard, too, was guilty of a flight from reality, simply because he, too, sought refuge in the old certainties for lack of anything better.

The love of certainty and of the peace it brings thus drowned the voices even of those who ought to have known better. "Progress," which at the beginning of our period was still an inviolable dogma, gradually lost its hold on the very class that had done so much to foster it and had derived the greatest benefit from it. The fact that they turned their backs on it the moment history decreed that those benefits should be shared out more equitably, is something that requires no special comment — all the historian need do is to point out that they were unable to halt further progress or, for that matter, the continued interpenetretation of state and society in which such progress was reflected.

CHAPTER XX

THE FESTIVAL OF HOPE AND FULFILMENT

On April 15, 1900, the long-awaited Universal Exposition, the eleventh in a series begun in London in 1851, was officially opened in Paris. President Loubet, and Millerand, the newly appointed socialist Minister of Trade, dressed in their Easter best, were driven in state through the *art nouveau* Monumental Gate to the Champs Elysées and on to the Grand Palais, specially built for the occasion between the Avenue d'Antin and the Avenue Nicholas II. Here, the Minister, using the grandiloquent style of Jules Roche, told an enthusiastic audience that the exhibition was intended to provide a synoptic view of all the achievements of the nineteenth century.[1]

The essential philosophy of that century was technological progress. Three weeks before the opening, this had become clearer than even the most eloquent words could have expressed. For on March 23, two 275-foot chimneys, adorned with pillars and wreathed in garlands as if they were the altars of a new religion, had puffed out their first thin columns of smoke into the bracing spring air. These chimneys flanked the cellars of the Palace of Electricity on the southern side of the Champ de Mars, and it was here that the first of the two brand new engines had been given a trial run.[2] With its companion, it would soon afterwards transform the heat generated in ninety-two boilers into motion and then, with the help of dynamos, into electric current. Not only would that current help to light up the 260 acres of open ground and buildings in the heart of Paris, but it would also drive all the machines and engines exhibited in the various halls, run the electric train, the moving staircase, the *trottoir roulant* (a double moving sidewalk circling the ground), and the great wheel with its eighty suspended cabins. Though the uses of electricity were not entirely unknown, the astonished world could only gape at this striking demonstration of its miraculous range and versatility. The flick of a finger was enough to release the power of 40,000 horses — 33,500 more than had graced the 1889 Exposition.[3] Man had demonstrated that he could produce tremendous effects at a great distance, and the immeasurable power released seemed as much a symbol of the age

296

as were its mysterious properties and apparent capriciousness. It was as if the times themselves had become charged with electricity.

Hence it was not in the least surprising that the old mythologizing love bestowed upon the new goddess should have been reflected in two impressive polychromes, one paying homage to her light and the other to her power. They loomed up where they could not be ignored: in the two niches of the gaudy building near the entrance of the Exposition, off the Place de la Concorde. It is also not surprising that the first floor of the Palace of Electricity, beneath which the engines were thudding and the dynamos purring, should have held the Hall of Honor, with a sweeping staircase to the largest of all the pavilions, stately and solemn like a cathedral, its curved walls covered with paintings and decorations. Here eighteen thousand visitors could sit down under a 230-foot stained glass dome.

It was in front of the Palace of Electricity, which was the real, if eccentric, center of the Exposition, that to the astonished delight of every visitor, the Water Palace stood: a glittering cascade some thirty feet across, falling from a height of 100 feet, its atomized mist of droplets sparkling like jewels with all the colours of the rainbow.

The Exposition of 1900 was, above all, a festival of light and movement. There was a profusion of light everywhere, and it almost seemed as if the exotic visitors from far-flung lands — from Central Asia, from the furthest North, from the tropical depths of Africa and South America — had been specially shipped to Paris to grace the festival with their wide-eyed admiration and to add more excitement to the bustling activity. And throughout the summer nights the whole Exposition was bathed in a lively, unprecedented profusion of light. Lights ran up the entire length of the newly bronzed Eiffel Tower, built in 1889 and towering 1,000 feet above the ground. There were lights in the Palaces of Education, Science, Letters and Industry, which were scattered along the Champ de Mars as if leading to a common source of all the light. There were lights in the colonial pavilions on the right bank of the Seine, lying between the Trocadéro and the river, the French to the east and those of the other European Powers to the west; in the Algerian, Tunisian, Sudanese and Senegalese pavilions; in the huts of the Ivory Coast and of Dahomey, in the pagodas of Cholom, Tonkin, Annam, and Cambodia; in the Byzantine pavilion of the Queen Mother and the Mosque of Samarkand; in the imitation Candi Sari; in the vestibule of Borobudur; in the two Sumatran houses and also over the two Buddhas at whose feet thirsty visitors could refresh themselves with Bols liqueurs or Blooker's cocoa.[4]

There were lights below the ground — in the imitation gold mine from

297

California — and above: in the hall of the South African Republics which had been relegated to the colonial section; in the Egyptian Temple of Daudurt and the ancient royal tombs beneath; in the graceful Japanese gardens and pagoda; in the semi-Moorish splendor of the British imperial pavilions; and in the models of every great lighthouse built since Fresnel's was opened in Cordouan in 1822.

Lights also shone over the Quai d'Orsay, on the left bank of the Seine, and from the twenty-two stucco buildings of the great foreign powers in the rue des Nations: the pseudo-Renaissance one of Italy; the imitation Moorish one of Turkey; the American one with its inevitable dome and eagle; the baroque one of Austria; the Tudor one of Great Britain; the imitation Gothic one of Belgium; the rustic wooden one of Norway; the baronial one of Germany with the highest tower of all; and the pseudo-Byzantine ones of the Balkan states.[5]

There was light also on the right bank, in the vast Congress Hall; in the Palais de Dance where every possible exotic dance, including the can-can, was performed by experts; in the Winter Garden surrounding the Palace of the Forestry Commission; and in the Palace put up by the City of Paris. There was light, lots of light, in the nearby amusement park, with its restaurants and cafés bearing such delightful names as Cadets de Gascoigne, Maison du Rire, and Jardin de la Chanson, with its theaters showing *tableaux vivants*, and with its host of reproduction taverns in the spirit of "Old Paris."

There was light both in the Grand Palais, where vast quantities of French nineteenth-century art had been crammed in together, with just enough room left over for both French and foreign examples from the last decade, and, across the road, in the Petit Palais designed by Girault, where there was a purely French retrospective exhibition. There was more light, too, in the Palaces along the Esplanade des Invalides on the left bank, with their exhibits of ornaments, furniture and crafts; and across the new bridge, specially built for the occasion, and named after France's latest ally, the Emperor Alexander III of Russia. There were five thousand light bulbs in the Palace of Electricity alone; eleven hundred of them along its coping; 4,500 more in the Festival Hall to the rear; over 3,000 in the Water Palace to the front; and 500 on the new bridge.

What the magic wand of the new fairy failed to brighten was lit up by the violet, silvery and carmine fairy lights and their reflection in the Seine.[6] It was as if no single source of light was brilliant enough to illumine the new path that mankind had entered.

And just as all the electric lights were symbolic of the new age, so also was the colossal scale of the exhibition, which was not only bigger than any that had gone before but also than any that followed. Forty nations were represented officially; there were more than 83,000 exhibitors including 38,000 from France; and there were more than 48,000,000 visitors.[7] It had all been designed for the masses. Binet's "modern" entrance gate, called hideous even in its day, had been so constructed as to allow a ring of thirty-six ticket offices to admit a thousand people a minute.[8] Though the monster banquet held in two gigantic tents on the terraces of the Tuileries towards the end of the Exhibition, and attended by 22,000 of the more than 36,000 French mayors and council chairmen who had been invited, had been arranged for the express purpose of cementing republican solidarity now that the Dreyfus affair was finally settled,[9] its very size made it an apt inauguration of the new century of the masses. In every way, the Paris Exposition of 1900 may be said to have excelled all the rest, for even though the 1893 Chicago Exhibition may have cost more, the differences in price levels were such as to make the Parisian the more expensive of the two.[10] Luckhurst, who made a comparative study in 1939 of world exhibitions from 1851 (London) to 1939 (New York), thought he could tell why the Parisian marked the climax of them all:[11] it celebrated the peak of nineteenth-century material progress at a time when faith in future prosperity and a peaceful world was still largely unshaken. However, the chief attraction of the Exposition, namely the chance it offered exhibitors to gather information and to do business with others, and the opportunity it gave to visitors to widen their horizons and to enjoy themselves, was about to be replaced with more effective techniques of mass communication. In particular, the growth of the advertising industry would soon afterwards enable businessmen to canvass customers at much lower costs and so would the international trade fairs; the thirst for knowledge could be quenched in a thousand different ways, by illustrated books and journals, by schools and special courses; the love of enjoyment could be satisfied in much greater comfort by visiting the cinema, by listening to the radio or by watching television. Once people had only to pick up a telephone to contact customers or suppliers in the most far-flung parts of the globe; had only to open the mail to be inundated with catalogues; had only to go to the nearest library to look up any information they needed; and, finally, had only to stare at a screen in order to amuse themselves every day of the year, they were quite content to forego the pleasure of world fairs. Moreover, private initiative waned as state concern in exhibitions increased. Julius Lessing, for instance, remarked that whereas it used to be taken for granted in 1850 that exhibitions were private affairs, this view no longer prevailed in 1900.[12]

The Paris Exposition, despite its great success, already bore witness to a decline. In particular, the entertainment industry was bitterly disappointed. Thus when Picard, the exhibitions's chief organizer, demanded the full rental, they protested so violently that Picard was forced to bring in the army. He took this step reluctantly, for he, too, realized that the standholders had had good reason to think that they would do much better than in fact they did, the more so as the pursuit of pleasure had recently spread to groups previously quite immune to it. Evgeny Markov, a Russian journalist, may have exaggerated when he wrote in 1900 that he took a dark view of the future, now that the cook, the flunkey, and the maid demanded such entertainment as had been traditionally reserved for the rich, a development which — and this was even worse — caused all of them to think that no normal life was possible without daily amusements and diversions,[13] but the facts on which he based his pessimistic forecast were real enough. Julius Lessing thought he could observe the same influence in the very character of recent exhibitions. The purity of the design of the 1851 Exposition, he claimed, had not been maintained by its successors, all of which had catered to the thirst for cheap pleasures.[14] In these circumstances, it seems quite incredible that Paris should have disappointed the entertainment industry as sorely as it did. Possibly, their high expectations had persuaded the organizers to set rentals at such high levels that visitors preferred to seek their pleasures elsewhere, and particularly in such "classical" places of entertainment as the café-concerts and café-chantants of Montmartre. For though the Chat Noir and the Quat'z Arts had passed their heyday, Aristide Bruant was still producing his popular ballads and Yvette Guilbert was still singing them despite the fact that in the summer of 1900 she had only just risen from her sick bed, and had to be taken to the Exposition in a wheelchair.[15] Loïe Fuller still performed her dance of the lilies and she, like Bruant and Guilbert, was only one of many. The public, and foreign visitors in particular, obviously failed to distinguish between genuine talents and cheap imitation.

Another possible cause of the stallholders' discomfiture was Picard's determination to make the Exposition as instructive and educational as he possibly could. It has been calculated that of the thirty-three attractions offered at the Exposition no fewer than twenty-one were devoted to knowledge of the world.[16]

All in all, the Paris Exposition fills us with a mixture of admiration for its unprecedented display of the marvels of the earth and contempt for its undeniable vulgarity. This may explain why de Vogüé said before the Exposition that it would treat visitors to a gigantic store of ideas;[17]

and why he complained after its closure that it had added nothing significant to the 1889 exhibition.[18] Isay, among many others, took a much
more somber view.[19] The Paris Exposition, he declared, had tried to
disparage the nineteenth century with its bourgeois materialism, but in
so doing it had fallen into the other extreme: it had ended up with the
baroque and with sheer affectation. And, indeed, there was hardly a
building without arcades, pilasters, domes and arabesques, without garlands and festoons; no line was left straight that could possibly be curved.
For the rest, however, the exhibition was a mixture of all styles, of which
the baroque was just one.

The visitors included many labor delegations, all of which had made
lengthy preparations for the great event. H. L. Boersma, representing
the former students at the Hague Technical School, later compiled a
comprehensive report on what the Exposition had to offer workers in
various trades.[20] Berlin sent some hundred municipal officials and teachers, and their findings ran to a thick volume.[21] This was the less surprising when we recall that the official catalogue covering the eighteen
groups and the 121 classes into which the exhibits were divided consisted
of thirty-six parts.

The division itself shows how much importance Picard attached to
education: he devoted all six classes of the first group to it. Education,
he claimed, was the gate through which man enters life, and, moreover,
the source of all progress. The second group, divided into four classes,
was dedicated to art which, Picard claimed, should be assigned its traditional place of honor. He was as good as his work: the ten galleries of
the Grand Palais were crowded with contemporary masters. Alas, most
of them are long since forgotten and we would have looked in vain for
names recorded in any history of modern art.[22] Near the bottom of
the list came two groups whose inclusion was of equal historical importance. The twelve classes of Group XVI, devoted to economics and to
the new science of social hygiene, had been assigned a place "worthy
of their actual importance." New also was Group XVII, devoted to the
work of colonization which, curiously enough, was not justified by the
benefits it ostensibly bestowed upon the colonial people but by Europe's
"need to expand."[23]

Much that was new and informative was also found in the other
groups. Sometimes information went hand in hand with diversion but
this did not make it the less instructive or detract from its ability to
depict scenes with which people were unfamiliar, not only because they
did not travel as far afield as we do today, but also because the world
was pictured far less. Highly entertaining and just as informative was

301

the exhibit of Old Paris, the city of dreams and folly. Robida had made a good job of it. On the 400 square meters put at his disposal he had constructed the most remarkable landmarks that had graced Paris from the Middle Ages, and had surrounded them with small houses, shops and taverns.

Also both instructive and enjoyable was the sea-water aquarium, containing a shipwreck and many kinds of exotic fish and maritime plants. It was honored with an entry printed in heavy type in the catalogue. There was also the cinerama and quite a few panoramas, among them the Trans-Siberian Railway exhibit, in which the visitor could sit and enjoy the passing scenery: a countryside studded with monasteries, onion domes and Russian crosses. To Morand, who saw it as a child, this exhibit was the star turn of the entire exhibition.[24] The cinerama, for its part, attempted to depict Europe as an air traveler might see it. There was also a mareorama with a rolling ship from which one could watch the Mediterranean coast slip by, and an excitingly novel phonocinema where one could not only watch but even listen to an actor, or observe the Rostand family take their box for the recent première of *L'Aiglon*. There was moreover a stereorama, an extended panorama depicting the Algerian coast from Bône to Oran.

But the most beautiful of all these exhibits was the world cruise, to which a special building had been assigned. The exterior was uglier than most: a chaotic mixture of Chinese, Japanese, Indian, Indonesian and old-European styles — enough to make most people avert their eyes. But once inside, it was well worth keeping one's eyes open. Standing on a central platform, one could "travel" for one or two francs across the Old World, beginning with a Japanese flower garden and ending up with a glimpse of the Spanish coast, just off Marseilles. And how much there was to see on the way! The recently discovered ruins of Angkor-Wat and — naturally — the Acropolis above Athens, were but two of the highlights. The painter, Dumoulin, had designed it all from memory and from more than four thousand photographs, and it had taken scores of other artists many months to put it all together.

Intended for purely instructive purposes but nevertheless enthralling was the celestial globe. Here the motion of the earth (the 27-foot hollow sphere in which the visitor sat) through the solar system was made perfectly clear, and so was everything that happened in the northern sky, from the origin of the nebulae to the course of the comets. The whole hemisphere had a diameter of 150 feet and was profusely decorated with mythological motifs.

Expert visitors flocked first to other exhibits. In the Civil Engineering

302

Palace, for instance, they could admire Ader's model aeroplane — a gigantic bat with a wingspan of 50 feet.[25] In the Optical Palace with its 140-foot dome, they could marvel at the greatest telescope ever exhibited or manufactured: it had a diameter of five feet and a length of 200 feet, and through it even laymen could watch the moon as if it were no more than one kilometer away.[26] Elsewhere, professionals could enthuse over new precision instruments capable, for instance, of measuring weights down to a tenth of a milligram, or over a host of self-registering thermometers and barometers, microscopes, typewriters, calculators and all sorts of technical and musical devices, including automatic concertinas, edeophones, auto-harps, bigophones and other long-forgotten objects.[27] The larger exhibits of the Palace included a crane capable of lifting weights of more than forty-five tons, and in the neighboring Palace of Navigation one could gaze at hundreds of models of the latest steamers, sloops, anchors, and wharves.[28] The Palace of Mining and Metallurgy supplied the latest proof of man's control over nature in the shape of gigantic steamhammers and rollers. All these were of German make, as was the most up-to-date pump. The German achievements in general left the French workers, who had had to erect them, with a bitter aftertaste, and so did the American exhibits, not least the fascinating *trottoir roulant*. But what probably worried the French most, and the other European exhibitors as well, was the evidence of Japan's growing industrial skills. For while European novelists and playwrights had continued to enthuse over cherry orchards and temples, geishas and daimyos, the Japanese themselves had, within just a few decades, and unbeknown to the rest of the world, succeeded in transforming their country into an industrial giant that could match up to the Ruhr.

It was national rivalry that, despite all the peace oratory poured forth during the Exposition, had created the most ingenious examples of modern technology. For though the army and the navy had been relegated to the bottom of the catalogue, they were housed in a conspicuously large Palace fronting the Seine. The Hachette Guide took eight columns to catalogue its contents.[29] There was, for instance, a new 32-cm monster cannon, fifteen and a half meters long, and complete with shells. Here the visitor could also admire the latest explosives, torpedoes, machine guns, armored trains, pontoon bridges, motor cars, airplanes and wireless equipment, and thus gather what future wars held in store for mankind. He could follow the competition between firepower and armor at close quarters, and though many of the latest inventions were on the secret list and hence not on display, those that were shown left no doubt but that a great deal of "progress" had been made since the 1889 Exposition.[30] The latest marine engine developed for the French navy astonished laymen and experts alike — it could develop twelve thousand horse power. Germany had understandably been somewhat reticent in displaying her most recent contributions to the art of war; one of her most striking exhibits was a large collection of the Kaiser's own uniforms. Schneider-Creusot, by contrast, had sent in so many exhibits that the Palace could not encompass them all; the overflow was housed in a model of the company's own 145-foot dome-shaped fort. It weighed 400 tons, was painted vermilion and held such peaceable objects as a steam locomotive capable of pulling a load of 200 tons at a speed of 120 kilometers per hour, and an electric train that could haul a load of 300 tons up a gradient of one in eleven at a speed of 50 kilometers per hour. But it also displayed a 24-cm gun with a revolving turret; a quick-firing gun of the same caliber; a grenade weighing 202 kilograms; and a host of other exhibits that were as ingenious as they were murderous. Those who could not have enough of war, could delight in a "naval battle" near the Porte des Ternes where two miniature fleets went through their paces in a "real" sea.[31] "It is in no way to be regretted that the Netherlands were not represented in this group," the Dutch guide ended its all too summary description of this exhibit.[32]

To gain an impression of the state of cultural life at the turn of the century, we need only look at the congresses held in association with the Exposition, for which purpose a special Palace had been set aside on the right bank of the Seine, near the Pont de l'Alma. From van Dongen's sketch of the building[33] we know that it was one of the most modern of all, despite the presence of the inevitable Louis XVI festoons beneath the cornices. According to Mèwes, the architect, these festoons were meant as homage to Turgot and Necker, the two great eighteenth-century economists. And the Palace was, in fact, devoted not only to congresses but also to the study of economics and of social problems, and had moreover been constructed by builders' co-operatives.

The Palace contained the richest collection of exhibits bearing directly or indirectly on the "social question" that had ever been assembled. It was described as a "social inventory of the century" with the kind of pride that far too often goes with a bad conscience.

Above this collection, which occupied the ground floor, lay the Congress Hall. Along the entire breadth of the building, facing the Seine, was an antechamber, its walls decorated with socio-economic motifs. The main hall, capable of seating 800, faced the street. Four smaller committee rooms occupied the space between the two, and none was empty throughout the six months that the Exposition was officially open. At least 130 congresses were held in the Palace and, with the exception of the one devoted to the care of the blind, none took less than two days. Several continued for a whole week and one, the geological, lasted for twelve days. If we could read the reports of their proceedings, we should undoubtedly obtain an unsurpassed picture of all the knowledge and ambition Europe shared in 1900. That picture would, however, fail to reflect the lowest depths or the greatest heights of the intellectual life of the time. This point was made more or less explicitly in the *Encyclopédie du siècle* which argued that though congresses do not solve a single problem or discover a single new fact, they nevertheless provide an excellent opportunity for making new contacts and for renewing old.[34] Israels has catalogued the congresses held during the Exposition in alphabetical as well as in chronological order. Alphabetically, they covered every letter from A to Z, beginning with *acetyleengas* (acetylene) and ending with *zondagsrust* (Sunday rest).[35] Chronologically they opened on May 24 with a congress on paleography that took a week — and which included discussions on graphology — and ended on October 13 with a congress on fruit pressing.[36]

From a cultural and historical point of view, however, a third list based on the importance attached to the various topics seems greatly preferable. Such a list would make it clear that problems connected with private property still weighed heavily on the delegates' minds. Special congresses were devoted to private houses, shares, limited companies, private land, industrial property, insurance, inventors' associations, and literary and artistic property, and it is possibly no accident that five of these eight congresses were held during the first two months of the Exposition, in May and in June. Next we are struck by the fact that social questions in the broadest sense attracted all the attention they deserved. There were more than twenty such congresses: on mutual aid, young workers' associations, cheap housing, women's institutions, women's rights, industrial accidents, labor and general insurance, savings banks, the after-care of prisoners, producers' and consumers' co-operatives and international co-operation between them, profit sharing, inspection of steam tools, legal protection of workers, care of the blind and the deaf, life-saving, slavery, the Red Cross, poor relief and private charities, and social education. There was also the famous Peace Congress.

That Picard was merely reflecting the spirit of the time when he gave education and learning pride of place is also proved by the number of congresses devoted to these two subjects: more than a dozen to education alone. There were congresses on the teaching of agriculture, of living languages, of social science, of commerce, of crafts and of drawing; on lower, middle and higher general, technical and commercial education; on the training of teachers, on physical education, on social education and even on elementary education by untrained staff. The sciences alone accounted for close on forty entries, including congresses on electricity, ornithology, chronology, chemistry, mathematics, physics, meteorology, botany, and psychology, not to mention numismatics. There was a congress on comparative history, one on comparative law, one on philosophy with special reference to the fate of the individual; one on the history of religion, one on geology, one on anthropology and prehistory, one on economic geography and one on "colonial economics," which dealt with the duties of the colonizing powers; even one on Basque studies. There were congresses on geography, librarianship, folklore, and maritime law. Special congresses were devoted to medicine, phototherapy, dermatology, hygiene, hypnotism, homeopathy, and the medical press. Pharmacists and dentists held their own congresses, including a special one on secret dental cures. The scientific congresses also included that of the Americanists, which was attended by delegates from all over the world.

A final series of congresses covered economic life in general: agriculture, horticulture, viniculture and forestry, with separate congresses on experimental agriculture, cattle feeding, dendrology, apiculture, the cultivation of the ramie plant, and fishing. Industry was less fully represented than one might have expected. There was a congress on mining and metallurgy, one on applied chemistry, and one on applied mechanics. There were congresses on shipbuilding, aviation, bakery, butchery, two on industrial gases, and one on the testing of materials. Commerce in the strict sense was only discussed at the congresses of grocers, commercial travellers and victuallers, unless we include the congress on customs regulations among this group. Trade and industry were covered by a single congress which, oddly enough, demanded free trade while calling for a measure of protection. This group also included several congresses devoted to railway and tramway affairs, and another three congresses remarkable for the fact that they anticipated the practice of standardization. They were devoted respectively to hallmarks, fabrics and musical notation.

The remaining congresses could perhaps be lumped together under the general heading of "odds and ends." There was a congress of vegetarians, a congress of alpinists and a congress of motorists. Less singular, but difficult to fit into any one group, were the congresses of photographers, journalists, architects, actuaries, stenographers and swordsmen. If, having reached the end of our survey, we add that a firemen's congress took five days to inveigh against the fire-risks caused by smokers, we may have exhausted the list of topics discussed and, no doubt, the reader's patience as well.

The reader would, however, be wrong to underestimate the historical importance of these international meetings, nearly 150 in all. Never before had Europe displayed its achievements and aspirations in so short a time and so convincingly, as she did during this intellectual review held in the summer of 1900. She was then at the peak of her power, and oblivious of the impending catastrophe that was soon afterwards to cast her from the greatest heights to the lowest depths. As we reflect upon this fact we cannot but be struck by the tragic element in all this spate of congresses, with their solemn delegates in frock coats and top hats, men who, soon afterwards, were to be crushed by the juggernaut of history. Their busy comings and goings were celebrated in two of Georges Récipon's statues, gracing the Grand Palace on either side of the Champs Elysées. Few visitors thought them particularly tasteful — Récipon was no Rodin and his name was quickly forgotten; even Springer omitted it from the 1912 edition of his *History of Art*. The ideas these statues symbolized — Immortality overcoming Time, and Unity toppling Discord — have lost their hold on mankind as well. And yet as the visitor saw the two teams of four heroic stallions rise from their plinths to a height of more than 70 feet, prancing impatiently as if eager to tear the terrestial sphere apart — eight solid giants in nervous motion whose romantic fieriness denied and yet recalled the classical spirit — he could not help being impressed by their sheer bulk and might. And the radiant, sweet-faced young women in their chariots — Immortality holding a history book in one hand and a garland intended for Genius in the other, and Harmony, her twin sister — though both were as conventional as could be, conveyed by their very conventionality something of the spirit of the age, which may have been bourgeois and inflexible but was forward-looking all the same. These figures were symbolic of the congresses no less than of the entire Exposition which, in turn, symbolized a world whose dreams had come true and which, for that very reason, looked forward to an even greater and safer future.

A safe world with Paris at its hub. In 1649, the Duc de Bouillon had called this city the capital not only of France but of the whole world; 250 years later Paris was still the world's capital and had probably never been as beautiful and vivacious as she was during that summer: with peace at home and abroad, there was nothing to threaten the idyll of undisturbed progress. Yet the end was, if not in sight, nevertheless close at hand. On November 11, 1900, when the Exposition began to be dismantled, it was just eighteen years before Europe herself was to suffer a similar fate. Then, too, the triumph turned out to be an illusion. But do we really detract from the essence of a triumph when we unmask it as an illusion? Or is illusion the unmistakable hallmark of every triumph, at least in historical retrospect?

On top of the flamboyant arch of the monstrous entrance gate rising to a height of well over 100 feet and flanked by two gigantic minarets, a plaster Parisienne in a floating evening gown of fake ermine stood on a sphere of gold. When she was hastily pulled down that wet day in November, her smiling head came away from the torso. Yet even this damaged idol was not without admirers — some say that an American shipped it home in 1920; others that it was acquired by a Hungarian tycoon. Of all the many gates and of all the palaces only the memory remained in November, 1900. Not even Paris is immune to the ravages of time.

CHAPTER XXI

THE PROMISED LAND

Time: 3 A.M., June 14, 1900. Place: Ville d'Avray, between Paris and Versailles. Scene: the start of the Paris–Lyon motor race. Dramatis personae: a group of motoring enthusiasts, drivers, or rather racing drivers, wearing their special peaked caps and cranking their engines at first light before leaping into automobiles that afforded them no protection from wind or rain — or indeed from the dust of roads that were still as poorly made as the tires. The number of competitors is hard to establish, but we do know that a far more modest race held on November 9, 1900, attracted 111 entries. In any case, at noon, Ferdinand Charron, driving a Panhard & Levassor — a car that came first in nearly every race held at the time — was the first to cross the finish line, having covered a distance said to be 355 miles at an unprecedented speed in nine hours and ten minutes. This record was broken a few months later on November 2, when two competitors in the Paris–Rouen race covered part of the route at a slightly higher speed. Charron's was nevertheless an incredible achievement; few of us can even imagine the noise, the jolting ride and the stench of the first automobiles, no more perhaps than we can the excited enthusiasm of the good Lyonnais who, braving the June heat wave, turned out almost to a man to welcome him.[1]

Barely three weeks later — at 7.30 P.M. on July 2 — the first "Zeppelin" was dragged out of its hangar near Manzell on the German side of Lake Constance. As soon as the wind had dropped, this colossal cigar-shaped monster — just under 380 feet long and about 33 feet in diameter — was released and rose solemnly into the air. On board were Count Zeppelin, Baron Bassus, Eugen Wolf, the explorer, Dürr, the engineer, and Grass, the mechanic. And though the airship proved difficult to steer, it kept to a height of more than 1,000 feet for some twenty minutes. On September 24 and October 17 there followed a further two flights, neither of which was completely satisfactory.[2] This may explain why the public, so enthralled by motor-racing, greeted the first ascent of a German airship with so little enthusiasm that the popular *Gartenlaube* felt the event merited no more than the briefest mention.[3]

Another event, at which few eyebrows would be raised today, was referred to in a report of the Boxer rebellion dated August 20, 1900: "We stepped in just as the Japanese photographers had started to 'cinemato-graph' the parade [of the victors]."[4] What was new here, however, was the object of their activities, not the method. Thus, as early as 1898, the Danish court photographer, P. Elfelt, had filmed the Danish royal family and their summer guests: Princess Alexandra of England, and the Czar with the Czarina holding the pale Czarevitch in her arms.[5] One year later, one of the first professional film directors, Georges Méliès, went much further than straight reportage when he reconstructed the Dreyfus drama on film, paying scrupulous attention to detail.[6]

On November 28 of that year, a New York newspaper published news of yet another milestone in scientific progress. "Thanks to recent advances," it declared, "England and the United States will be on 'speaking terms' well before Christmas."[7] The paper was referring to an invention of Guglielmo Marconi, the pioneer of what was then called wireless telegraphy. In the event, it was not before March 1901 that contact between the transmitter in Cornwall and St. John's in Newfoundland could be established.

We have picked out four highlights in a process which, more than any other, bears out Charles Péguy's dictum in 1913 that the world had changed more during the previous thirty years than it had in any other period since the birth of Christ. The motor car, aviation, the film and radio and all they implied — the internal combustion engine, oil, rubber, the film camera, celluloid and, last but not least, the technical exploitation of invisible waves — were the most important though by no means the only revolutionary discoveries made in the period under review.

The electric motor, though invented before the internal combustion engine — the first working model was built by Ferrari in 1885 — had turned out to be rather unreliable at first, but more recently it had been improved so considerably that it had found a permanent place in light, and to a lesser extent in heavy, industry. Together with the electric motor and the internal combustion engine, in which air is mixed with an easily inflammable substance and exploded with the help of a spark plug, there now also stood the diesel engine, in which a mixture of air and oil is so strongly compressed as to give rise to spontaneous combustion. Rudolf Diesel had described it as early as 1893,[8] but it was only in 1897–1903 that his engine was developed into a practical proposition.[9] Here and there, the reciprocating steam engine began to make way for the steam turbine, in which the steam moves the turbine blades by its impact. Though de Laval had built the first steam turbine in 1882, it took him more than eight years to perfect it. In 1897, Charles Parsons built his

Turbinia, the first ship to be powered by a steam turbine. It became the pride of the British merchant navy and its remarkable speed and capacity for maneuvering quickly attracted the attention of the Admiralty.[10] The same was true of the submarine, which had ceased to be a figment of Jules Verne's imagination by 1900. The American and French navies immediately set about building or buying this latest piece of equipment, as we know, for instance, from a newspaper report published on November 20, 1900, which mentioned the impending voyage from New York to Lisbon of a submarine recently built by John P. Holland and bought by Washington.[11] The British themselves were far less enthusiastic, a lapse for which the *Nineteenth Century* took them to task in May, 1900.

All these inventions may rightly be called the technical implementation of Marinetti's futurist manifesto of 1900, glorifying speed. But beside these inventions stood a whole series of others that were no lesser portents of the new century, chief amongst them man-made materials. Synthetic rubber was developed in 1901 – 1912; in 1913, Bergius discovered the first of the two common methods of synthesizing oil; in 1905 – 1907 Baekeland perfected the manufacture of bakelite, a substance that, together with celluloid and cellophane, helped to create the artificial resin industry, which in its turn opened the way for the "plastics age." The search for synthetic materials was crowned by the development of artificial fibers as useful substitutes for natural fibers on a large scale.[12]

Needless to say, the list of discoveries and inventions mentioned here and in subsequent chapters is far from complete. The lure of discovery is as great as man's curiosity, and it is not surprising that a German book on inventions should have sold 100,000 copies within a year of its publication.[13] If we mention several more contributions to the list, we do so only in order to stress how deeply the present is rooted in the recent past. In 1890, Dunlop produced the first bicycle tire, Fischer produced synthetic sugar, and Ulrich and Vogel invented three-colour printing. In 1891 came the invention of the rotary copperplate press,[14] and of the high-tension transformer. In 1895, Ramsey was able to isolate the "noble" gas helium, which had previously been observed in the solar spectrum and which Kamerlingh Onnes was to liquefy thirteen years later. In 1898, Waldemar Poulsen built the first wire-recorder; five years later he gave radio technology a fresh impetus with his invention of the arc converter which can oscillate up to a frequency of the order of 100 kHz. In 1902 came the first hot water heater; and solar energy was first used in Los Angeles to pump up water, an invention for which Wilhelm Ostwald foresaw a great future.[15] That same year, Orville Wright built a device for harnessing the energy of the tides.[16] In 1903 came the invention of glass capable of passing ultra-violet rays; in 1905, acetylene welding, bottle-making machinery and the tungsten filament lamp; in 1906, the artificial use of pneumo-thorax first described by Forlanini in 1882; in 1907, the widespread use of reinforced concrete, telephotography, the first serviceable caterpillar track; in 1909, the first slow-burning motion-picture film, safety glass, the 45-cm Krupp's gun, the 5-foot reflector in Mount Wilson Observatory; in 1910 the vacuum cleaner, the anti-rolling tank and the mine-thrower; in 1912, the discovery of cosmic rays, Krupp's stainless steel, and Siemens's high-speed telegraph capable of transmitting a thousand signals per minute; in 1913, the large-scale production of radio valves. The Deutsche Machi-nenfabrik built its first mobile crane in 1914, the year in which Britain produced the first armored car, and the brand new rotary press with its six rollers capable of printing 200,000 eight-page newspapers every hour,[17] but only just fast enough to keep up with the war news that had begun to stream steadily from almost every front.

Even with these additions to the list, however, we have only skimmed the surface, nor can we even claim that our list is reliable. For no inven-tion appears *ex nihilo*; each is a link in a long chain. Thus we can always date a discovery at will from the enunciation of the principle on which it is based, from the first successful experiment, from the first practical application, or from the beginning of large-scale-production. If we bear this in mind, then we are struck all the more forcibly by the feverish search that distinguished our period, that of emerging imperialism, from any that had gone before. Henceforth neither the tempo nor the volume of production could ever be great enough.

It has been claimed, and with some justification, that unlike the period of "pure" capitalism, that of "organized" capitalism and imperialism which began in about 1895 produced nothing but adaptations of older inventions and discoveries.[18] Thus the discovery of electricity as a source of light and power in transport and industry was made well before our period, which nevertheless fully deserves the name of "electric age" because it applied the new source of power on a vast scale: in tramway systems, home and street lighting, the telegraph and the telephone. The same is true of the in-ternal combustion engine. Its origins go back to Huygens's "gunpowder engine" of 1673 and it should in any case not be forgotten that in 1863 Lenoir covered the fifteen kilometres between Paris and Joinvoille-le-Pont in a vehicle powered by a gas engine, or that Daimler and Maybach built the first gasoline-driven engine in 1882. Petroleum, too, had been known for centuries, and as for rubber, the Mexicans had played with rubber balls long before the arrival of the Spaniards.[19] And, finally, the idea of underwater travel was as unoriginal as that of flying above the earth. After all, Cornelius Drebbel had demonstrated a submarine on the Thames in 1622. But what is not fundamentally new in science may very well prove to be of fundamental historical importance. This applies to all the discoveries and inventions we have listed and particularly to the first four: the car, the aircraft, the film and the radio. They have all caused space and time, and hence the intensity of social contacts, to change quantitatively to such an extent that life before 1900 came to differ qualitatively from life after 1900. A short survey of the development of these four new acquisitions is therefore indispensable to any chronicle of the quarter century to which this book is devoted.

First, however, we must mention another point, just as essential to any proper grasp of this period: the fact that every phase of a discovery or invention calls for a discoverer or inventor. And the transitional and revolutionary nature of our period which, as we saw and shall see further, was probably its deepest essence, found one of its most striking manifestations in the new type of discoverer it produced. Now, as Wilhelm Ostwald has said with full justification, the inventor is the most important human type to have sprung up because, in him, the characteristically human faculty of progress has been developed to its highest point.[20]

During our period, the inventor not only enjoyed an ever more intensive degree of scientific training and an ever larger pay packet, but was also expected to cope with a host of new technical or industrial processes and to do so increasingly by team work. At the same time the old type of inventor had not yet disappeared, and in fact will always be with us: the lone wolf obsessed with an idea in the pursuit of which he far too often crosses the borderline between reality and delusion, between brilliance and insanity and who, even when he is successful, usually dies poor and forgotten, not least because shrewder men know how to make money and earn renown from his discoveries.

One such inspired "dilettante," not to say fanatical dreamer, was John Worell Keely. He was a carpenter by trade and invented an engine of which Madame Blavatsky said in 1890 — eight years before he died — that "if Keely succeeds he will be able to smash the whole world into atoms within one second." Since the precise nature of his engine was never disclosed, we cannot tell whether it was perhaps a forerunner of the atomic pile.[21] No less remarkable a man was Hermann Ganswindt, the "Edison of Schöneberg" and a pioneer of space travel. For the spaceship he designed on paper was propelled by rockets, as indeed the modern spaceship was to be when it was eventually perfected. However, the power then available to him — a dynamite cartridge — was far too little to lift his machine from the ground, let alone carry it beyond the earth's gravitational field. And

313

when Professor Roman Gostowsky objected in 1900 that a rocket machine could not possibly work within and without the atmosphere, Ganswindt's most ingenious reply, which was also correct in principle, was: "In that case I shall take it to the limits of the atmosphere in a specially built flying machine and send it off from there." On May 27, 1891, Ganswindt, then thirty-four years old, tried with grim determination to defend his idea at a public meeting in the Berlin Philharmonic Hall, only to be greeted, then as later, with laughter and disbelief. The series of pamphlets he wrote and the many direct appeals he obstinately made to the Ministry of War had no effect at all, but Ganswindt's only reaction to such rebuffs was to produce new plans, each based on the same mixture of scientific understanding and the failure to grasp what was and was not feasible in his day. These plans included helicopters and heavier-than-air flying machines, and Ganswindt was not simply boasting when he headed his writing paper with "Hermann Ganswindt, inventor of the airship, the airplane, the automobile, the freewheel drive, etc." He died a lonely, embittered and poor old man in 1935, at the age of seventy eight — hero and victim of the technological age.[22]

More successful and hence less extreme but just as determined and unbending were such inventors and pioneers as Edison, Daimler, Diesel, Zeppelin, Farman — who progressed from cycle and motor racing to the design and construction of airplanes — and the brothers Wilbur and Orville Wright, two bicycle makers from Dayton, Ohio, who were obsessed with aviation. That all of them were of the modern breed of inventor may be gathered from the fact that they were either, like Diesel and Zeppelin, wealthy men to begin with, or else became so through their work. But they were all of them transitional figures as well, because the links between their inventions and capital were already unbreakable but still highly personal. It is to this type of man that mankind owes the four chief discoveries with which this chapter opened and which interest the historian, not only because they held the key to what looked very much like the Promised Land, but also and above all because they illustrate so well how one period grows out of another.[23] The concept of discontinuous continuity or continuous discontinuity which plays so important a part in the study of all transitional periods and which because of its dialectical nature is so hard to grasp *in abstracto*, can here be seen at work *in concreto*, in what, in retrospect, seems a gradual development toward ever more perfect solutions, but what, at close quarters, seems a series of sudden jumps. The study of the discontinuous aspect brings us into closer contact with the human agents, with their magnificent triumphs and quiet satisfactions and also with their blind spots and failures. The continuous aspect, by contrast, brings home to us how closely mankind as a whole is involved in scientific progress. Neither of these two aspects is of more or less historical importance than the other.

The chronological order in which our four discoveries have been introduced is rather misleading. For, at the time, aviation was still in its infancy; motoring was still no more than a sport; radio had already begun to benefit from the fusion of technology and science; and cinematography, though purely technical at its inception, had developed into a new art form even before the end of our period.

All four discoveries led to faster speeds, either as ends in themselves or else as means. All have become integral parts of human life, and no sphere of human activity lending itself to greater speed has escaped from this development. Early in 1900, the Paris–Calais express traveled at an average speed of 58 miles per hour; at the end of October this figure had increased to close on 60 mph.[24] Of all European trains the French were indeed the fastest, with an average speed of 59 mph; the British followed with 56.5, the Germans with 50, the United States topping them all in 1900 with 67.[25] That same year plans were drawn up to cross the Atlantic in four days;[26] they led to the competition for the Blue Ribbon and to an increase of the maximum speeds attained at sea from 20.75 knots in 1891, to 23.5 knots in 1900, and to 25.3 knots in 1907[27] — a race in which sport was not the only motive and to which the passengers of the *Titanic* fell victims on April 15, 1912.

Oddly enough, aviation, which would eventually produce speeds many times greater than that of sound, did not originally aim at swiftness, certainly not during the development of the lighter-than-air ships on which all hopes were first centered. The dirigible airship need not delay us long, for it was invented before our period: as early as 1884, the French Captains Krebs and Renard made a successful flight from Meudon to Petit-Bicêtre and back in the fish-shaped *La France* built and manned by them.[28] Ferdinand von Zeppelin, too, whose airship caused such a stir in 1900, began his attempts to conquer the air as early as 1887.[29]

The development of a heavier-than-air and mechanically propelled aircraft, by contrast, falls wholly into our period, at least if we ignore Henson's machine of 1843 which never actually took off.[30] On October 18, 1899, a contributor to *The Spectator* expressed his belief that the solution of the problem was in sight, because Percy Sinclair Pilcher, a British glider pilot, had constructed a 4.5 hp petrol engine so light that he could easily have powered his glider with it. Unfortunately, however, he had since had a fatal accident.[31] Whether this explanation was correct cannot, of course, be determined; what is certain, however, is that Pilcher had shown that heavier-than-air flight demanded the development of light engines. Thus while an internal combustion engine still weighed several hundred lbs. per horse power in 1880, by 1905 the weight had been reduced to under 10 lbs. per horse power.[32] The Wright brothers were quick to take advantage of this development and on December 17, 1903, Orville became the first man to make a sustained flight in a heavier-than-air machine. He kept his machine airborne for 59 seconds and covered a distance of 1,025 feet, while flying against a wind of just under 30 mph.

Before this flight, the Wright brothers had made the most careful preparations. Having decided to conquer the new dimension when they heard of the tragic death of Otto Lilienthal in 1896, they not only made a thorough study of his machine and gliders, but also of the designs of Chanute[33] and Langley. Moreover, for three long years, from 1900 to 1903, they familiarized themselves with the art of gliding, and it was only when they had mastered it that they added an engine.[34] At the time, however, their great feat did not attract the attention it deserved: Americans were not yet very keen on the new sport, and Europeans were still more or less skeptical about everything that came from America.

In 1908, Wilbur Wright went to France, where the biggest prizes could then be gained and, taking off from Le Mans airfield, he made the series of spectacular flights that earned him world-wide acclaim. On New Year's eve, for instance, he stayed in the air for two hours and twenty minutes and covered a distance of well over 70 miles.[35] By way of comparison we might mention that in 1914 the longest flight was over a distance of just under 1,200 miles and, with refueling stops, took 25 hours and 12 minutes.[36] Henry Farman's flight from Châlons to Reims on October 30 was another spectacular achievement. The same day, Louis Blériot nearly crashed, which did not, however, prevent him from taking off, one day later, in his Type VIII to cover the distance from Toury to Artenay and back, a total of 17 miles, at an average speed of 53 miles per hour, having stopped twice on the way and taken off again without assistance. In 1909 came two spectacular cross-Channel flights: that of Latham who crashed near his destination, and that of Blériot who completed the course on July 25 in 31 minutes and won the £1,000 prize offered by the *Daily Mail*. If we add that in August of that year the first international "air week" was held near Reims[37] and that all previous records were broken on that occasion, we see why the conquest of the air is generally dated 1909, despite the growing list of fatal accidents — according to Berget, aviation claimed the lives of sixteen balloonists and sixteen aviators before the nineteenth century was out,[38] and in 1912 alone there were 136 victims.[39] What was still wrong, however, was speedily put right by further experiments, by expert discussions in such journals as *L'Aérophile*, founded in 1893, and the *Zeitschrift für Luftschiffahrt und Physik der Atmosphäre*, founded as early as 1881, by the work of aeronautical associations and, not least, thanks to the big prizes offered by the press and industry, which at the end of 1908 stood in total at more than $300,000.[40]

The motor car, too, did not spring ready-made from the brain of a single inventor, but then no great discovery has ever been made except through the exertions of several generations. All great discoveries, in fact, reflect a change of quantity into quality.[41] The idea of a self-propelled vehicle was even older than Stevin's sailing car. Originally, the wind had been the only available motor force but, at the turn of the eighteenth century, the development of the steam engine allowed an alternative source of power. At this stage, Britain had the edge on the rest of the world, but as a result of what we have called the "law of the diminishing lead" and also of the speed limits imposed in the United Kingdom — 14 miles per hour until 1896 — the advantage passed to the Continent in about 1870: in 1875, Siegfried Samuel Marcus succeeded in driving a carriage with a gasoline engine through Vienna.[42] Better known and much less primitive were the gasoline driven cars built in 1885 and 1886 by the two German engineers Gottlieb Daimler and Carl Benz. At the Munich machinery exhibition of 1888 Benz's car was greatly admired and soon afterwards the Benz company began to advertise "horseless carriages from 1,200 marks" in the *Fliegende Blätter* and other papers.[43] Electrically propelled automobiles were also first mooted during the first half of the last century, and at the beginning of the 1890s it looked as if the electric car and the electric traction engine[44] would be the vehicles of the future. Jeantaud built the first electric car in 1881;[45] and the "tractor" idea was staunchly championed by the Comte de Dion and his engineer, E. Bouton.[46]

At about the turn of the century, however, the petrol engine carried the day, France taking the lead from Germany just as soon as Panhard and Levassor fitted the Daimler engine, and other engineers the Benz engine, into vehicles of their own make. Not that there were no French attempts to develop an internal combustion engine of their own — Pierre Ravel, for instance, took out a patent for a petrol engine as early as 1868[47] — but the 1870 war put a temporary stop to these indigenous efforts. Nevertheless France alone had a proper automobile industry before 1900, no doubt because of the traditional French predilection for small enterprise: the twelve hundred motor cars which made French roads so hazardous in 1898 were built in sixty factories, of which the largest produced no more than three cars per week. Another factor was the

317

equally traditional French love of luxury, for the first motor cars were still extremely expensive — despite the fact that the advertisements claimed they were cheaper to run than horses and carriages.[48] In any case motoring was, to start with, an exclusive affair. In the earliest records we meet many noble names, including that of the Duchess d'Uzès, of whom we mentioned before that she always drove to the hunt — for she was also a lover of noble animals — in an automobile that she handled with exceptional skill.[49] This lady and all the other motoring enthusiasts deserve our respect, if only because of the hazards they braved. The state of the roads, for instance, was such that during the 1903 Grand Prix from Paris to Madrid, so many drivers were blinded by the dust and crashed that the race had to be called off. A whole series of other races was organized by the motor industry in an effort to boost business. It all began with the Paris – Rouen race in 1894, and the Paris–Amsterdam race held on July 3–11, 1898, was the twentieth in the series. Of these twenty, listed by Carteret, one half was held in 1898, the same year in which motoring began to spread to every part of Western Europe.[50]

It was the thrill of the races more than the cars themselves which attracted the crowds, and it was not by chance that Jonkheer Jan Feith published his *Boek der Sporten*, a hymn of praise to sport, in the year 1900. The new cult of beauty and health which we shall be discussing in Chapters XXIV and XXXIII was the mother of the new enthusiasm for everything connected with sport. Whether or not that child eventually became estranged from its parent is a question the historian cannot but answer in the affirmative. Sport escaped the general search for ever greater speeds as little as did transport. And while better transport facilities enabled hundreds of thousands to participate actively in one sport or another, they also enabled millions more, to whom sport was, at best, nothing but a way of passing the time and, at worst, a sort of intoxication not so much with the sport itself as with gambling, to become involved as spectators. One of the leading champions of sport was Pierre, Baron de Coubertin, who considered physical training an instrument of peace and, in 1894, called on all sportsmen to help him revive the Olympic Games. His faith and his money enabled him to turn his dream into reality: in 1896 the first of the modern Olympic Games were held in Athens.[51] And while it was certainly not the intention of the President of the International Olympic Committee, it was as a direct result of his efforts that athletics degenerated into an extreme and unhealthy form of specialization. Thus when the first six-day bicycle race was run in 1900 in Madison Square Garden, New York City;[52] or when the first Tour de France dreamed up by the sensation-hungry brains of Desgrange and Goddet of *L'Auto* was launched in July 1903, it was difficult to ignore the mercenary motives — the second event boosted the circulation of *L'Auto* by one-and-a-half million copies. The cry of "assassin", flung by one of the cyclists at Desgrange during a later tour,[53] has resounded ever since: "the world's most hazardous race", run over a distance of 2,400 kilometers in six stages, each taking an average of fifteen hours, is nothing if not murderous; it was one of the first symptoms of the dehumanization and commercialization that were to become so characteristic of sport in the twentieth century.

Just as radio waves make less noise than a car, so also the development of wireless telegraphy proceeded more quietly than that of the internal combustion engine. It also provided the clearest possible demonstration of how closely science and technology began to be linked in this period. Maxwell's hypothesis, in about 1873, that electro-magnetic phenomena can be propagated in non-conducting media was still pure science, and so was Hertz's attempt in 1880 to put this hypothesis to the empirical test. However, as these experiments were continued in various laboratories — including Hertz's own in Germany, Lodge's in Britain and Righi's in Italy — the technological aspects became increasingly important, especially in 1892 when Sir William Preece discovered that signals could be transmitted between points not directly connected by an electrical conductor. That year, Sir William Crookes, who was not only a spiritualist (see Chapter XXXIII) but also a great physicist and chemist — he was awarded the Nobel Prize in 1907 — coined the term "wireless telegraphy"[54] and two years later, Sir Oliver Lodge succeeded in transmitting and receiving "wireless telegrams" over a distance of some fifty yards. By 1896, when Righi's pupil, Guglielmo Marconi, encouraged by his mother's English relations,[55] came to London and took out a patent on his system of wireless communication, so much progress had already been made that one of the objections to his patent was that it contained nothing new. On May 10, 1897, Marconi and Preece succeeded in sending wireless signals nearly nine miles across the Bristol Channel. As a result of a similar experiment in Germany later that year, the distance could be extended to just under 12 miles. In 1898 a wireless link was established between England and France, and Marconi planned to make wireless contact with the United States by Christmas, 1900. He did not, however, succeed until 1901, by which time Marconi's Wireless Telegraphy Company was busily negotiating for the construction of wireless stations on various capes and islands, with the intention of linking Britain and Australia.[56] Within a further ten years, wireless telegraphy had made so much progress that radio contact could be maintained with any ship at sea and with any airplane in the sky.

The modern cinema, too, had its precursors, so many in fact that there is probably no theatre large enough to hold everyone connected with its prehistory. It may all be said to have begun with Lucretius's description of drawings on very thin leather, which a revolving device caused to appear in such quick succession as to produce the illusion of motion.[57] Though the idea was developed over the centuries, for a long time it remained a mere toy for children or for childish adults. The various names of this toy mark a great future: the thaumatrope; the phaenakitoscope; the zootrope; the mutoscope; the stroboscope; the phantoscope; the kaleidorama; the kinetoscope; and the kinetograph. Then, in the middle of the nineteenth century, Baron Uchatius, an Austrian pioneer, transcended the most primitive stage by projecting "living pictures" on a rotating disc from a magic lantern. Twenty-five years later came the first "bioscope", in which a quick succession of drawings was projected onto a screen to suggest motion. The "real" cinema, however, had to wait for the development of the perforated film[58] and, above all, of the photographic gun with which Marey recorded the flight of birds in 1888. It is not clear who takes credit for the first public film show. Was it Emile Reynard who first used his praxinoscope to show *pantomimes lumineuses* in the Museum Grevin, Paris, in October, 1892;[59] was it Robert Paul[60] in London in 1896; or was it, as is so widely claimed, the brothers Auguste and Louis Lumière? All we do know for certain is that the latter showed ten 17-meter flicker films, including *La Sortie de lumière*, which may well be called the first film, on a radically improved projector to thirty-five interested spectators in the cellar of the Grand Café, Boulevard des Capucines, Paris, on December 28, 1895.

The complicated history of the cinema shows that it did not spring up overnight: illustrated books and journals had prepared the world for at least fifty years for the victory of the picture over the word. For that reason, the cinema would probably have superseded the fairground stage, the cafés chantants, and the vaudeville theaters even in the absence of brilliant business men with an intuitive grasp of the vast profits to be gained from this type of mass entertainment. As it was, these men did exist, particularly in America where, besides the Edison Trust, many Jewish immigrants from Eastern Europe realized which way the wind was blowing, amongst them Laemmle, Zukor, Fuchs (Fox), Goldfish (Goldwyn) and the Warner brothers. In France, there were the Pathé brothers and other film magnates who later became famous. The chances were there for the seizing: 75 dollars for a projector, a few dimes for renting a shed or a cellar, was all the "capital" needed to start the business; later something better could be acquired on cheap credit.[61] And, indeed, the industry swallowed up ever-increasing sums of money. In 1910, when the Gallic cock of Pathé Frères still crowed supreme over the European market, the firm could declare a dividend of 90% on what was still a paltry capital investment; one year later the capital had to be increased to fifteen, and two years later to thirty million francs.[62] The picture palaces, which had become permanent structures by then, multiplied like mushrooms: on January 1, 1900, only two of the 33 leading German cities had a cinema, and Berlin was not yet amongst them, but ten years later Berlin alone had 139 cinemas, and the 33 leading German cities shared no less than 480 between them, slightly more than New York. That same year, five million people a day went to the cinema in the United States.[63] The cinema had become a craze: the masses sought distraction and preferred to find it in melodramatic dreams of power and love, the more so as they sadly lacked either in real life. By then the cinema had gone a long way beyond the newsreel and the slapstick comedy. In particular, the influx of capital during the first decade of the twentieth century had not only produced the most splendid picture palaces but also far more professional films than had ever been made, two factors that persuaded the middle classes, not without a struggle, incidentally, to drop many of their original objections.[64] According to the film historians Bardèche and Brassillach, the first period in the history of the film ended in 1908,[65] to turn in 1909 into what Georges Sadoul, possibly the greatest of all the experts on the subject, has called a new art form.[66] The first "art film" ever to be made was probably *The Murder of the Duc de Guise*. The screenplay was by Henri de Lavedan, and it could be said to have ushered in the so-called *séries d'art* in 1907. But all these films were still cinematographic versions of well-known plays and novels — sometimes with such great actors as Sarah Bernhardt (in her only film, *Queen Elizabeth*) or Bassermann in Germany (where such productions were known as *Autorenfilme*) — and not yet original creations of the "tenth muse." Not even in 1909 did the ugly young duckling realize that it was destined to turn into a beautiful swan, and seen in retrospect, all the old plays and serialized novels on film made before 1914 did, indeed, bear out Jordaan's view that they were all a terrible mistake.[67] The first art film with an original script was probably Stellan Rye's *The Student of Prague* (1913) with Paul Wegener, from the Reinhardt Company, in the leading role and Hans Heinz Ewers, of *Golem* fame, as the co-author.[68]

The development of the cinema into the great institution it has since become was the work of a host of people and involved a host of preliminary stages. In France, Georges Méliès, the only pioneer to consider himself an artist and to write his own screen plays (in 1896 – 1914) also enriched the cinema with the fade-out and with slow and fast motion. In the United States, David W. Griffith was not only the first to introduce close-up techniques but also to use editing to artistic effect. Dupont, Lumière's representative in Vienna, was one of several film directors to use a mobile camera. Charlie Chaplin, the little man with the small moustache and the baggy trousers, who was to rise from the slapstick comedy to greater heights than even Buster Keaton or Harold Lloyd, and who, like tens of thousands of other talented slum children, forged his way to the top, has carved himself a permanent place in the history of the motion picture. Another famous figure of working class origins was to become the Eleanora Duse of the cinema and the first great film star: Asta Nielsen, to whom the Danish film owed so much of its great charm, but who had to learn to her cost how hard the life of a film actress was: all the nervous haste and tension, all the exploitation and dehumanization of talent for the sake of profit are immortalized in the few pages of her memoirs.[69] In 1912, as the final prelude to the modern cinema, came the first great outdoor film. It relied on crowd scenes rather than on elaborate sets, and its director was the Italian painter Enrico Guazzoni.[70] That film was *Quo Vadis*, based on Henryk Sienkiewicz's famous novel (1896), and the first "spectacular" in a long series of historical films, at which the Americans and the Russians were to excel not so long afterwards.

In 1912 there also appeared Walter Rathenau's *Zur Kritik der Zeit*. Technology and mechanization, its author claimed, were making their influence felt increasingly in production, administration, politics, science, and art; indeed in every sphere of daily life. A year later, he published its sequel, *Zur Mechanik des Geistes*, in which he assessed the repercussions of this trend on intellectual life, and expressed the view that faith in the infinite worth of the human spirit was the only way out of the impasse.

What happened at about the turn of the century to cause so astute an observer as Rathenau to write in this strain?[71] Had the intellect really succumbed to technology, as so many later commentators have claimed regretfully that it did? Alberès, for one, refused to accept this shallow interpretation. It was not because technology had gained a lead over the intellect but rather because vast new intellectual horizons were opened up at the time that the intellect had grown uncertain of itself to the point of paralysis. To a young structure such as technology, growth is normal and harmless; to an old one such as thought it may prove noxious.[72] The progress of technology was the gate to the Promised Land, to prosperity and fraternity, but whether or not man could enter through it depended on the spirit in which he approached. For, in the final analysis, it is not man's handiwork but man himself who writes history. Technology is indivisible: those who want one part of it must take the whole, and this at the risk of becoming enchained to its rich promises. For when it is presented with a plethora of choices, the intellect far too often wavers and grows unsure. In the second part of this book (beginning with Chapter XXII) which deals with science, art and interpersonal relationships, we shall encounter this profusion of choices and the intellectual uncertainty to which it gave rise, on almost every page.

THE TRIUMPH OF THE ATOM

"If one views this phase of development of theory critically, one is struck by the dualism which lies in the fact that the material point in Newton's sense and the field as continuum are used as elementary concepts side by side . . . H. A. Lorentz knew this very well . . . The revolution begun by the introduction of the field was by no means finished. Then it happened that, around the turn of the century, independently of what we have just been discussing, a second fundamental crisis set in, the seriousness of which was suddenly realized due to Max Planck's investigation into heat radiation (1900)."[1]

"The first phase, reaching from 1895 to 1916, might be called the heroic or, in a different aspect, the amateur stage of modern physics. In it new worlds were being explored, new ideas created, mainly with the technical and intellectual means of the old nineteenth-century science. It was still a period primarily of individual achievement: of the Curies and Rutherford, of Planck and Einstein, of the Braggs and Bohr. Physical science, particularly physics itself, still belonged to the university laboratory; it had few close links with industry, apparatus was cheap and simple, it was still in the 'sealing-wax-and-string' stage."[2]

In 1895, Wilhelm Röntgen, Professor of Physics at Würzburg, was examining electrical discharges in a glass tube when he made the unexpected discovery that, apart from the cathode rays that appeared inside the tube and that had been known since 1859, something was also taking place *outside* the tube: something that made fluorescent screens shine in the dark. Not knowing what this "something" was, he gave it the name of "X-rays." It quickly appeared that these new rays could also fog photographic plates through black paper to produce remarkable photographs, and even penetrate fairly thick metal plates.

Röntgen's discovery made headlines all over the world. Physicists performed X-ray experiments before admiring audiences, and much fun was had with the subject; "indeed no recent discovery — not even Hertz's experiments,[3] or the discovery of argon and helium[4] — was talked or written about so much," Lorentz explained to the readers of *De Gids* in 1896. In his specially commissioned article, he compared X-rays with cathode rays, showed that the two differed in many respects, and concluded with: "Perhaps much of the riddle will have been solved within a few months." When it was eventually solved, many even greater riddles arose. The discoveries that followed were so sensational that we have good reason to speak of a revolution in physics beginning with Röntgen's discovery. On January 20, 1896, Henri Poincaré exhibited X-ray plates, lent to him by Röntgen, at the Académie Française, of which he was a member. When another member, Henri Becquerel, asked for further particulars, he was told that the mysterious rays emerged from a spot in the tube that had been hit by the cathode rays. That spot itself appeared to be fluorescent. Becquerel decided to find out whether other fluorescent substances might not exhibit a similar luminosity. Thanks to his father, Alexandre Edmond Becquerel, Henri had gained familiarity with this type of material, and he decided to begin his investigations with certain uranium salts.

He quickly found that these salts did not require prior irradiation with light to produce pictures on photographic plates wrapped in dark paper. He had, in fact, discovered radioactivity, and his report of that discovery to the Académie on March 2, 1896 caused a sensation and has been commemorated on a stone in the laboratory wall in the Jardin des Plantes, Paris, which remains to this day.

Discovery now followed upon discovery. Becquerel established that radioactive energy was given off by the element uranium, regardless of its combination with other elements. This merely served to compound the mystery, for how could an element, immutable by definition, emit radiation and hence energy? To make things worse, other radioactive elements were discovered soon afterwards. In 1898, Marie and Pierre Curie isolated polonium and radium, both much more radioactive than uranium. They found that radium salts, in particular, could shine in the dark by themselves and that their radiation could cause serious tissue damage.

Between 1893 and 1903, E. Rutherford and F. Soddy came up with a new and most astonishing theory, namely that radioactivity occurs during the spontaneous disintegration of atoms: "Radioactivity may be considered a manifestation of subatomic chemical change." They produced a whole series of transformations, in all of which one radioactive element became changed into another, with lead as the end product. In the process three types of radiation were emitted which they called alpha, beta and gamma rays respectively. Alpha rays turned out to be fast-moving particles which were ultimately identified as helium nuclei. Beta rays, like cathode rays, appeared to be electrons, the negatively charged particles of earlier theories. Gamma rays, finally, were short-wave electromagnetic radiations, similar to X-rays. Man had at last succeeded in transforming the elements — the age of the alchemists seemed to have dawned all over again, albeit no gold was produced.

The discovery that cathode rays consist of negatively charged particles was made by Jean Perrin in 1895 and confirmed by J. J. Thomson in 1897. Thomson determined their velocity and also the ratio of their charge to their mass, which appeared to be 1/1840 that of a hydrogen atom. He then advanced the hypothesis that these particles were present in all atoms; in cathode rays, matter is found in a new state, one in which it is subdivided much further than in the normal gaseous state.[5] These discoveries bore out the views of those physicists who had come to believe that electricity had an atomic structure, H. A. Lorentz chief among them. In the 1880s he had started to revise Maxwell's theory on the assumption that electricity was conducted by small charged particles which, in about 1900, he began to call "electrons," a term suggested by G. J. Stoney (1891). "We imagine the presence in all ponderable bodies of countless extremely small, electrically charged particles, it being understood that every substance in its natural state contains equal positive and negative charges. These particles we call electrons," Lorentz wrote in 1901. Despite grave obstacles, he was able to use his theory to solve various apparently intractable problems. His explanation of the so-called Zeeman-effect (the splitting of spectral lines when the source of light is placed into a strong magnetic field, 1896) was greatly admired. "How easily the new Zeeman-effect has been accommodated, even helping to explain the Faraday-effect which has resisted all Maxwell's efforts," Henri Poincaré wrote appreciatively in 1900.[6] In Lorentz's electron theory, atomic particles were the only possible carriers of electric charges; between these particles lay empty space, the electromagnetic field set up by the charges. Here, too, the dualism introduced by the combination of Newton's material particles with Maxwell's continuous field continued to cause problems, but the experimental and theoretical successes of the corpuscular interpretation of matter and of electricity had proved so spectacular that by 1910 most physicists had joined the "atomist" camp, a camp that had seemed doomed to oblivion during the second half of the nineteenth century. At the same time, however, the relative certainty most physicists had felt in the nineteenth century made way for the uncertainty of new worlds. Indeed the discovery of X-rays, of radioactivity, of the atomic structure of matter and of alpha and beta rays, and the achievements of electron theory, all introduced fresh elements of uncertainty. What was one to make of an electron that was possessed of "ponderable" mass as well as of charge? Was its mass, too, a form of electricity, and should the generally accepted view that electricity was a form of matter perhaps be replaced with another, for instance that matter was a form of electricity? Moreover, what was one to make of the transmutation of elements? And whence came the energy that appeared during the emission of rays associated with radioactive decay — could this phenomenon be reconciled with the preservation of energy, one of the chief pillars of nineteenth-century science? What was the true explanation of "matter"? And now that the difficulties began to multiply, the thoughts of many physicists reverted to other unresolved problems of the past to which only a few had paid attention while confidence in classical physics had prevailed.

In the peaceful period Europe enjoyed during most of the second half of the nineteenth century, it had been widely believed that the foundations of physics were secure for all time. On these foundations a solid and impressive edifice had been built up: the mechanics established by Isaac Newton in 1687 and extended into a great mathematical system by Lagrange and Laplace in the eighteenth century. In the nineteenth century, electromagnetic theory based on Faraday's experiments had come to hold a special position, thanks largely to Maxwell's equations, whose precision equaled that of classical mechanics. Most physicists agreed with Maxwell that his electromagnetic theory could be verified with the help of mechanical models. As late as 1894, Heinrich Hertz, the discoverer of electromagnetic waves (whose existence had been foreshadowed by Maxwell's equations — Maxwell himself had already described light waves as electromagnetic waves) and one of the most critical physicists of his day, put forward the view that the problem of science was the reduction of natural phenomena to the simple laws of mechanics. All that mattered was the discovery of these laws.

And, indeed, it was astonishing how many varied spheres could be reduced to mechanics: heat, sound, light, hydrodynamics, aerodynamics, diffusion, osmosis, viscosity, and capillarity, together with a host of electric and magnetic phenomena. All were bound up with the great universal law of the conservation of energy, which also governed the conversion of heat into electrical energy, etc. Moreover, all energy was, at root, mechanical energy — potential or kinetic.

There were differences of opinion, of course. Was the corpuscular or atomic structure of matter the only possible explanation of natural phenomena? Belief in atoms had been handed down from the Greeks, and was happily embraced by many seventeenth-century philosophers. Boyle, the chemist, and Newton, the physicist, had been firm supporters of the corpuscular structure of matter. At the beginning of the nineteenth century, Dalton and others had presented the corpuscular structure of matter so convincingly that an entirely new science of chemistry was built up on the existence of atoms and molecules, or more precisely on the ratios of their weights. For many chemists, however, atoms and molecules were no more than symbolic entities, and most physicists had a horror of these, though quite a few could no longer imagine nature without them. The kinetic theory of gases, propounded by Daniel Bernoulli as early as 1738, continued to enjoy wide support because of the elegant way in which it provided mechanical explanations to many known properties of gases. In 1865, Loschmidt used the theory to determine the number of molecules in a cubic centimetre of gas — a number that, according to Avogadro's law (1811), was independent of the nature of the gas. Then, in 1873, Maxwell, himself a champion of the kinetic theory, having examined electrolysis with the help of a theory of molecular charges, went on to express the view that, once the nature of electrolysis was fully explained, the theory of molecular charges was likely to fall by the wayside.[7] The ablest defender of the kinetic theory of gases towards the end of the nineteenth century was Professor Ludwig Boltzmann, but he was considered to be something of an eccentric. The subsequent decline of support for the corpuscular structure of matter was partly due to the successes of Faraday's field theory. Faraday had tried to explain electromagnetic phenomena by postulating the existence, round electric currents and magnetic poles, of fields of force that, under certain conditions, could be derived from potential fields. These fields were said to exist in a rarefied substance, the ether, distributed evenly in space, and it now appeared that Newton's theory of gravitation, which involved the actions of particles through empty space, could also be treated as a field theory. Henceforth, science would have to consider gravitational, electric and magnetic fields, all of them continuous magnitudes involving electric charges and ponderable bodies.

One of the physicists who believed he had to reject the existence of atoms or molecules as so many metaphysical concepts, was Ernst Mach, who ended up in the neo-positivist camp which Lenin and Planck were to attack so fiercely. Another opponent of atomic theory was Wilhelm Ostwald who believed that all natural phenomena were the expressions of various forms of energy. Though his "energetics" did not prevail, it nevertheless reflected the fact that most nineteenth-century physicists

328

placed energy, and particularly the conservation of energy, at the center of their speculations. This was the nineteenth-century version of — or substitution for — the law of the conservation of mass, first formulated in the eighteenth century.

The new mechanistic approach went hand in hand with a specific philosophy. In theory, it was possible to take a causal view of all natural phenomena, and to express this causality in mathematical terms. In the simplest case — a system of material points acted upon by central forces — the future behavior of the system could be said to be fully determined once the position and velocity of every point at any one moment were known. All that had to be done was to define these magnitudes in terms of absolute time and space, as postulated by Newton.

Despite the grave problems this solution introduced, problems that Huygens and Leibniz had seized upon in their critique of Newton, the achievements of Newtonian mechanics were so great that most physicists and mathematicians were prepared to leave it at that. They took much the same view of Newton's gravitational force, which represented an action between two bodies at a distance from each other in absolute space, something to which Huygens and Leibniz had objected as well, eliciting Newton's now famous rejoinder: "Gravity exists and hypothesis non fingo". In this sphere, too, the theory of the continuous field helped to ease a great many troubled minds.

The upholders of the corpuscular theory, however, did not remain idle, and their activities were to bear rich fruit in Boltzmann's interpretation of the second law of thermodynamics, a branch of physics that had assumed increasing importance following the development of the steam engine about 1850. This law, a true Proteus which insinuated itself into all branches of physics, can be expressed as follows:[8] — If A and B are two states of a body in equilibrium and if a quantity of heat dQ must be added to transform A into B at a temperature T, its entropy is said to have increased by an amount dQ/T. Again, if no heat is added or removed from a system of bodies, there can be no reduction in its total entropy (the sum of all the entropies). In other words, entropy tends to increase, or, in special cases, to remain constant. To put it even more simply: changes in a system of bodies (isolated from the rest of the world) cannot result in mere heat exchanges.

The remarkable thing about the second law of thermodynamics is that it involves the *direction* of natural processes. In that way it differs strikingly from Newton's and Maxwell's laws. The new problem was to derive that direction from the classical laws. Ludwig Boltzmann succeeded in doing just that by combining kinetic with probability theory.

Now, the kineticists had arrived at the gas laws (e.g., Boyle's Law) by considering the motion of small particles colliding with one another and with the wall of the containing vessel. Boltzmann, for his part, considered the probability of a certain distribution of the gaseous particles, and based the second law of thermodynamics on their tendency to attain a more probable state. He defined entropy as a function of that probability ($k \log W$, where W is the statistical probability of the system). With great mathematical skill he was thus able to establish the second law of thermodynamics on corpuscular foundations. Unfortunately, many of his colleagues refused to take this theory — and even kinetic theory as a whole — seriously. This explains why he introduced his *Vorlesungen über Gastheorie* (1896) with the remark that he had written the book so that "when subsequent generations restore the kinetic theory to honor, they will not have to rediscover everything all over again."

We cannot leave the kinetic theory of matter without mentioning the contribution of the American physicist, Josiah Willard Gibbs, as set forth in his *Elementary Principles in Statistical Mechanics* (1902). It differed from Boltzmann's theory in various respects. Gibbs's starting point was Newtonian mechanics in its classical form: he considered individual systems, and tried to determine their evolution from given positions and velocities. This being an arduous task, Gibbs preferred to assume a probability distribution, and to investigate how that distribution changes with time. His new approach, which, like Boltzmann's, raised serious mathematical difficulties, nevertheless proved extremely valuable, not least because of its application to Brownian movement and in communication theory. As we shall see, the mathematical difficulties were partly resolved in the course of the twentieth century.

We must mention yet another difficulty that gave rise to keen discussion at the turn of the century. It sprang from attempts to probe more deeply into the links between the absolute space of classical mechanics and the ether of electrodynamics. To that end, Michelson and Morley (1887) performed their famous Cleveland experiment to measure the motion of the earth through the ether. Now it is obvious that the time a swimmer takes to cross a river differs from the time he takes to cover the same distance up or down stream. In the Cleveland experiment, the swimmer was a beam of light and the river was the ether which, if it coincided with absolute space, would have to stream past the earth as the latter moved through space. Two beams of light were accordingly made to shuttle between mirrors, one beam travelling in a direction vertical to the other. No difference could be detected between the time it took either beam to cover an equal distance, and the relationship between ether and absolute space looked more inexplicable than ever.

Of the various *ad hoc* explanations proffered at the time, the Fitzgerald-Lorentz contraction hypothesis (1892, 1897) achieved great renown thanks to Einstein's interpretation of it in 1905 and Minkowski's in 1908. It was based on the fact that all bodies moving through the ether must experience the same degree of compression. Lorentz, who assumed that the cohesion of bodies is due to the forces set up by the electric charges in the molecules, calculated that changes in the lengths of all bodies moving in the direction of the motion of the source of light could be expressed by $l = l_0 \sqrt{1 - v^2/c^2}$ (l_0 being the length at velocity $v = 0$ and c being the velocity of light). Clearly, such contractions can only be detected when v is very great, as in the case of the electrons in cathode rays. Lorentz also found that time must be transformed in a similar way. But how did all this fit in with the doctrine of absolute space and time on which classical dynamics was based? Did it affect only bodies with velocities much smaller than that of light? And how did the new approach affect the recurring problem of the relationship between ponderable matter and electric charge, between particles and fields?

In this period, when unexpected and sensational discoveries followed one another in quick succession, an astonishing application of corpuscular theory to a field that had previously been treated as a part of classical thermodynamics gave rise to a new theory so revolutionary, and at the same time so strange, that it took quite a few years before it could make its full impact felt. In Berlin, Max Planck had been working on the theory of thermal radiation (not to be confused with the radiation theory studied by Röntgen, Becquerel and the Curies). Now, as early as 1860 Kirchhoff had deduced from thermodynamic principles that in an evacuated space, surrounded by impenetrable walls and kept at (absolute) temperature T, the energy density and the frequency of the radiation are independent of the composition of the walls. Kirchhoff's law, like Avogadro's hypothesis governing the number of molecules in unit volume, was thus independent of the special nature of the material (the walls, or the gas). This peculiar feature of thermal radiation attracted the attention of many physicists, who studied it experimentally and tried to place it on sound theoretical foundations. One of them was Boltzmann who, also using a thermodynamic approach but coupling it to Maxwell's theory in 1884, was able to elucidate Stefan's law (1879), which states that the total energy emitted from unit area of a black body per second is proportional to the fourth

331

power of the absolute temperature (T). Later still, Wilhelm Wien, using much the same approach, discovered certain oddities about the connection between the function ρ (ν,T) and T. In 1900, having examined all the experimental values he could obtain for ρ (ν,T), Planck arrived at a precise formula, namely $\rho = A\nu^3 \, [\exp B\nu/T-1]^{-1}$ where A and B are constant. Planck, who, as he put it himself, "considered the quest of the absolute the most beautiful part of all scientific endeavor," did his utmost to adduce a theoretical justification of this formula.

It quickly appeared that it was impossible to base this justification on classical thermodynamics, and though Planck had carefully eschewed recourse to kinetic theory, he now decided to follow in Boltzmann's footsteps and to base the entropy of the radiation on probability theory. This conversion to the corpuscular theory led him to consider the radiation as being the product of a large number of oscillators, each emitting a "quantum" of energy $\epsilon = h\nu$, h being a constant. As a result he was able to determine the probability of the states, and to obtain an experimental formula for ρ (ν,T). The result: $\rho = \dfrac{8\pi h\nu^3}{c^3} \, [\exp h\nu/kT-1]^{-1}$ was published in December 1900 and marked the beginning of quantum theory. The odd thing was — and Planck drew particular attention to this fact — that the formula demanded the introduction of an energy quantum, that is, assumed the corpuscular structure of the emitted energy, when the laws of thermodynamics called for a continuous energy distribution. The quantity h (Planck's constant) appeared to be a new universal constant, and as such took its rightful place by the side of Avogadro's number and Boltzmann's constant (k). It proved to be extremely small: $h = 6.55 \times 10^{-27}$ erg sec., according to Planck's own calculations.

It was in this highly technical way that quantum theory saw the light of day, and although Planck's contribution was welcomed by a number of his colleagues, including Boltzmann, it was many years before it was generally accepted. At the time, most physicists still preferred Rayleigh's solution, which involved the principle of equipartion of energy, but in which the energy density tended to infinity as the frequency of the radiation increased. That solution, however, showed considerable discrepancy with the experimental finding that the energy tends to zero. It was this very discrepancy, which has been described as the ultra-violet catastrophe, which persuaded Planck to advance his revolutionery hypothesis; his own formula was in excellent accord with the experimental results, even at very high frequencies.

It was not until 1905-1906 that quantum theory gained its next success. For it was then that Einstein showed that not only the energy of the oscillators but also the radiation itself must be considered from the corpuscular point of view. In so doing, he brought out the sharp opposition between the new theory and classical dynamics and electrodynamics. For the rest, he was able to provide solutions to many previously intractable problems. In particular, he elucidated the so-called photo-electric effect by the introduction of photons or light quanta. In so doing, he apparently reopened the gulf between the two classical theories of light (based respectively on the Newtonian particle and the Huygens-Fresnel wave), though it gradually became clear that these were two complementary *viewpoints* rather than mutually exclusive descriptions of the *properties* of light. A few decades later, the fundamental character of the particle-wave dualism was recognised by de Broglie, and his hypothesis received a sensational confirmation when bundles of electrons (i.e., particles) were shown to exhibit undular behavior during refraction experiments.

The next important step in the revision of physics was Rutherford's description of the atom as a miniature solar system: a heavy, central, positive nucleus surrounded by a large enough number of (negative) electrons neutralizing its (positive) charge (1911). In 1913, when Niels Bohr produced his quantum-theoretical extension of this model, the anxiously awaited synthesis of atomic and quantum theory seemed to have been achieved, at least in principle. It was also in 1912 and 1913 that von Laue did his famous work on the structure of crystals, vindicating the corpuscular theory of matter; many other studies with which Einstein's name was associated had the same effect. Jean Perrin even succeeded in "measuring" the dimensions of atoms, summing up all the theoretical findings in such books as *Les atomes* (1913). In 1910 Planck was able to write that "in the theory of heat, in chemistry and in electron theory, the kinetic energy of atoms is no longer a mere working hypothesis but has become a solid fact." Further corroborations of atomic theory came in such quick succession that in 1909 even Ostwald gave up his opposition and joined the atomists' camp. Atomic theory had prevailed — in the form of quantum theory.

In 1905, Einstein published his first paper on relativity. In it he tried to come to grips with such difficult problems as absolute space and absolute time. He also pointed the way to a reconciliation between Newton's dynamics and Maxwell's theory, in which Lorentz's electron theory was not only retained but stripped of some of its *ad hoc* assumptions. This solution was inherent in Einstein's treatment of the Fitzgerald-

Lorentz contraction, which is a natural consequence of relativity theory. It led him to his famous formula connecting mass and energy, namely $E = mc^2$, which has become a symbol of the atomic age. The mathematical space and time of relativity theory were investigated by H. Minkowski in 1908.

As a result of all these studies, the new physics was able to weather the storms of 1895–1905. In 1925 it was refurbished with the quantum mechanics of Schrödinger and Heisenberg, thanks to which the concept of entropy became the very crux of theoretical physics. What energy had been in the nineteenth century, entropy became in the twentieth: fact and symbol in one.

In the period under discussion new ideas also entered mathematics. Though more of a piece with the older concepts and far less spectacular, these new ideas were nevertheless so incisive that within a few years people began to talk of a crisis. The nineteenth century not only widened the scope of mathematics with such innovations as group theory, but had also witnessed an upsurge of interest in the foundations of mathematics. The need to place differential and integral calculus on a sound footing, first felt in the eighteenth century, presided over the work of a whole series of mathematicians from Bolzano and Cauchy to Riemann and Weierstrass. Their work was based on what was called the arithmetization of mathematics, i.e., on the reduction of its foundations to those of arithmetic. There was also another current inspired by G. Boole, namely the mathematization of logic. The two currents became confluent in the work of Professor G. Frege of Jena, who in a number of writings published between 1879 and 1903 constructed an axiomatic arithmetic in which he defined rational numbers by means of logical concepts. Because he eschewed Boole's symbolic logic, his work was not fully appreciated until the publication of Bertrand Russell's *Principles of Mathematics* in 1903. During 1895–1905, the Italian mathematician G. Peano wrote the *Formulaire de mathématiques*, a series of studies in symbolic logic, in which he derived the theory of natural numbers from five axioms.

The reduction of mathematics to number theory, of numbers to natural numbers, and of natural numbers to logical concepts is known as symbolic logic and found its most perfect expression in a three-part standard work: the *Principia mathematica* by B. Russell and A. N. Whitehead, of which the first volume appeared in 1910. That work was written almost exclusively in logical symbols and formed an impressive and somewhat awe-inspiring whole, whose main purpose it was to demonstrate the identity of logic and mathematics.

After this logical extension of the axioms of mathematics, a second approach, based on the foundations of geometry, made itself felt as well. During the second half of the nineteenth century, the discovery of non-Euclidean geometries on the one hand and of projective geometry on the other, led to a re-examination of the foundation of Euclid's ancient science. While Frege was scrutinizing the axioms of arithmetic in Jena, his colleague Moritz Pasch of Giessen was examining the axioms of "elementary" geometry and discovered that this alleged paradigm of an axiomatic system no longer satisfied the demands of modern studies. His findings persuaded David Hilbert to construct an entirely new axiom system in his *Grundlagen der Geometrie*, the first impression of which appeared in 1899. The fact that this book was recently republished in amplified and revised form (the eighth edition) speaks eloquently for its continued importance.

To Hilbert, points, lines and surfaces were so many names for the elements a, A, a, defined purely by their internal relations: two elements a and b define element A, etc. Theorems are relations between elements derived from the axioms. A geometry, all of whose propositions can be proved, must have a set of consistent (non-contradictory) axioms and form a self-sufficient or closed system. Whether or not these demands were satisfied could be established by certain representations of one system in another. Thus analytical geometry can be used to translate Euclidean geometry into algebra, which, in turn, derives its consistency from arithmetic. In this way, Hilbert was ultimately led to investigate the axioms of arithmetic, a task he tackled in a way that differed strikingly from Frege's and Russell's.

One of the reasons for this difference was a third, more sensational development: Georg Cantor, a contemporary of Frege and Pasch, had meanwhile developed the theory of sets, and shown that it was possible to construct a mathematical system with closed sets. In so doing he had entered the almost undisputed preserve of theologians: the study of the relationship between potential and actual infinity. One remarkable result of set theory is the fact that the set 1, 2, 3, 4 . . . has the same number of elements as the set 2, 4, 6, 8 . . . , because the two sets can be put into one-to-one correspondence.[9] Thus 1 can be made to correspond with 2, 2 with 4, 3 with 6, etc. And yet the second set is part of the first! For infinite sets, therefore, the Euclidean postulate that the whole is greater than any of its parts no longer holds. Cantor assigned a transfinite number to such sets and then showed that the number of transfinite numbers is infinite. The transfinite number associated with continuum, e.g., the set of points of a linear segment, is greater than that of the set 1, 2, 3, 4 . . . , the so called denumerable set.

Once the study of transfinite numbers was begun, it quickly appeared that this branch of mathematics introduced, or rather seemed to introduce, a most disturbing effect. Thus between 1895 and 1905 all sorts of contradictions came to light, and contradictions in mathematics are, of course, intolerable. That ugly term was accordingly replaced with the more acceptable "paradox", in the hope that all would eventually turn out for the best. Several of these paradoxes were so technical that we cannot discuss them here; others can be stated in more popular form. Some were related to such famous classical paradoxes as that of the Cretan who claimed that all Cretans are liars (if all Cretans are liars, then the Cretan who made the claim was lying). Another paradox was J. Richard's, which went something like this: it is possible to define every natural number and count the number of letters in the definition. Consider the smallest number definable with "no fewer than a hundred letters." But then you have defined that number with fewer than a hundred letters! Similarly there were the paradoxes of G. Peano, C. Burali Forti and Bertrand Russell. We might also mention the paradox of the village barber who shaves all men M who do not shave themselves and no others. Does the barber himself belong to the set M? If he does, he cannot shave himself, when, according to the definition, he must do so!

In about 1900 it was realized that these paradoxes were no mere subtleties but that they were deeply embedded in the theory of infinity. Moreover, they suggested that there was a close link between mathematics and semantics. Logicians had always tried to construct their systems in such a way that no paradoxes could occur in them, and Hilbert and his formalist school now took the same path. They did so by consistent treatment of the concept of unnamed elements. More precisely, they tried to construct a formal mathematics with symbols that had no meaning in themselves but were joined together by such abstract relations as "and," "or," etc. The formalists refused to grant that mathematical concepts could be reduced to logical concepts with their logical paradoxes. Mathematics, to them, was a science that examined the structure of objects with the aid of systems of signs. In the construction of such systems, certain rules must be observed and all that was required of these rules was that they should be consistent. Though Hilbert and his pupils worked for many years on the construction of this type of mathematics, neither they nor Russell were able to bring the work to a really successful conclusion. More recently it has become clear that if this path is followed rigorously it is bound to lead to very great if not insurmountable difficulties.

There was yet another school of mathematics — the intuitionist — which treated the logical and the formalist alike with suspicion and took particular exception to Cantor's set theory. In the nineteenth century, the German mathematician Kronecker was the chief spokesman of this school, but in 1907 his mantle fell on the Dutch mathematician L. E. J. Brouwer, who contended that mathematics was an intellectual activity, and as such had to work with ideas rather than with symbols. Instead of continually defining new mathematical objects as Cantor had done, the mathematician must accompany every one of his definitions with a clear set of instructions about the construction of the objects of his definitions.

The name "intuitionist" was derived from Kant's doctrine that space and time as *a priori* concepts are based on pure intuition. True, after the discovery of non-Euclidean geometry (1820 to 1840), this doctrine could no longer be safely applied to space, but Brouwer continued to uphold the apriority of time. In particular, he insisted that moments of life can be split up into qualitatively different parts that can only be recombined while remaining separate in time, a fundamental feature of the human intellect. The mind is capable of abstracting its emotional contents and advance to the fundamental aspect of mathematical thought, which is the intuitive grasp of pure bi-unity. That intuitive grasp not only creates the numbers 1 and 2, but also all finite ordinal numbers: any one of the elements of this bi-unity can be considered a new bi-unity, a process that can be repeated *ad infinitum*.[10]

"Primitive intuition" was said to preside over the generation of the natural numbers with which all mathematical concepts must be constructed. This view recalled Kronecker's dictum of 1886: "The integral numbers were made by God; everything else is man's work." Hence the intuitionist insistence that none but intuitively understandable constructions may be used for mathematical existence proofs, and that only in this way can paradoxes be avoided. It also explains why Brouwer denied that the law of the excluded middle (a mathematical object is either A or non-A) exhausted all the possibilities of mathematics. "The law of the excluded middle does not apply to the case of infinite sets. Here it is no longer true that a proposition is either true or false — there is also a third possibility. As long as we have no means of establishing whether or not π contains 37 successive zeros we cannot say that the proposition 'the decimal expansion of π includes 37 successive zeros' is true or false."

The various mathematical schools were thus deeply immersed in two problems: the nature of mathematics, and the truth of mathematical propositions. At about the turn of the century these problems, together with the physical problem of the nature of matter, were responsible for throwing mathematics and physics into disarray. One result of the crisis in mathematics was the emergence of metamathematics, a new discipline concerned with the possible forms of mathematical thought; one of the results of the crisis in physics was the emergence of quantum theory (after 1925) and of general relativity theory (after 1915), two doctrines that have not become fully reconciled to this day. What mathematics, in particular, reaped from all these developments, apart from a number of general principles (for instance the demand that a definition of a mathematical object must as far as possible go hand in hand with a rule for its construction) was a set of special symbols to express its fundamental concepts. The incisive changes in mathematical language we are witnessing today are the direct result of the crisis that occurred in about 1900.[11] Most mathematicians, while paying their respects to intuitionism, now agree with Hilbert that "no one will expel us from the paradise into which Cantor has led us" (1925).

We end this chapter with yet another mathematical innovation to appear at the turn of the century. It, too, was a consequence of discussions of Cantor's set theory, this time among French mathematicians, who developed several ideas of their own.[12] Basing himself on the theories of denumerable sets and of the continuum, Henri Lebesgue, in his Paris thesis of 1902, advanced a revised theory of integration which was more comprehensive than Riemann's (1854). One of the theories that could be formulated more generally and also more simply with its help was that governing trigonometrical series. These series, also known as Fourier series, had been introduced in the eighteenth century to express the vibration of strings, and had raised the difficult question of the general nature of the state of motion of a system that can be constructed linearly from simple vibrations. The coefficients of these series represent certain mean values, and mean values are characteristic concepts of probability theory. It follows that Lebesgue's theory had a direct bearing on the development of mathematical statistics.

Probability theory, first propounded by Christiaan Huygens and others in the seventeenth century, still stood on shaky foundations. This seemed the more regrettable as its usefulness was increasingly being brought home to scientists at the turn of the century. Boltzmann's, Gibbs's and Planck's contributions had proved their worth in the theoretical sphere, and the use of statistical methods in everyday life (the census, traffic control, communications, etc.) had shown that its practical applications were no less far-reaching. Now Lebesgue's theory of integration went a long way toward eradicating many of the mathematical

338

difficulties of probability theory and of Boltzmann's and Gibbs's kinetic theories in particular. It also helped to improved the mathematical treatment of Brownian movement.[13]

All in all, therefore, many of the new ideas that had emerged independently in physics and mathematics at the turn of the century were increasingly being fitted into a coherent whole during the subsequent period. In what follows, we shall have many more occasions to draw attention to this process, so typical of the modern age.[14]

CHAPTER XXIII

MYSTERY REGAINED

On Monday, 17 September 1900 the Director of the Anatomical and Biological Institute of Berlin University, Professor Oscar Hertwig, addressed
a meeting of German naturalists in Aachen. It had been specially convened
to present members with a review of the latest achievements of natural
science.[1]

It was probably more than accident that, a physicist having delivered
the opening address, the chairman should have called on Professor Hertwig, whose subject — biology — had made such phenomenal progress
during the past century. A year later, Krogh estimated the number of
biological publications at some 3800 per annum — a modest enough figure
compared with the 18,000 that were to appear within a quarter of a century, but quite remarkable all the same.[2] Biology had come to hold a
special position among the sciences not only because it relied increasingly
on chemistry and physics, but also because of its close links with psychology and sociology and even with ethics and religion. The speaker was
therefore quite right to stress the central position of his science which, as
he pointed out, provided a bridge between the world of matter and the
world of the intellect, and to conclude his lecture by expressing the firm
belief that, if only it eschewed every kind of bias, biology was bound to
carry human civilization to unprecedented heights in the century to come.[3]

Nor could it have been an accident that it was as an embryologist
that Professor Hertwig had been chosen to present the case for biology.
For was not his discipline and its ally, genetics, the most auspicious branch
of biology and had not the discovery of chromosomes, just over a decade
ago, promised to unveil one of nature's most intriguing mysteries? And
was Hertwig not just the man to speak in the name of his colleagues? He
was about fifty and hence too old to be accused of hypermodernism, but
also young enough to feel in touch with current trends.

In one respect he was decidedly modern: he was no longer dazzled by
Darwin, whose ideas had dominated biology for forty long years and
whose views had been popularized just one year earlier in *Die Welträthsel*
(The Riddle of the Universe), a book by Ernst Haeckel, probably Darwin's

most capable, and in any case his most enthusiastic, disciple on the Continent. Hertwig, for his part, rejected Darwin's theory of natural selection, though not the theory of evolution as such, and he was to reiterate his views forcefully some sixteen years later in his *Das Werden der Organismen* (The Development of Organisms).

In his rejection of Darwin, he came close to Lamarck, whose name, after having been forgotten for fifty years, was coming back into prominence at the turn of the century: the term neo-Lamarckism was coined in 1901.[4] Darwin and Lamarck were indeed the two names, the two flags under which a fierce battle was being fought. In that battle few holds seem to have been barred. At the time it looked very much as if Darwin's inspired love of scientific truth coupled to his nineteenth-century experimental approach were bound to prevail over the genial but whimsical intellect of Lamarck, who seemed more a child of the eighteenth century. Moreover, Darwinism had absorbed the most brilliant of Lamarck's contributions: his idea of evolution. When all is said and done, Darwin had done no more — but no less — than to propound a theory on its precise mechanism.

Still, there were good reasons why the dispute should have been so bitter. Darwinism had developed into much more than a scientific explanation of the origin of species. In practice, Darwin's chief postulates — the struggle for existence, the survival of the fittest and natural selection, vaguely defined as they were — seemed to lend themselves to applications far outside the biological field for which they had originally been designed. They were increasingly being insinuated into broader scientific realms and even into sociology and politics, so much so that Rádl devoted a separate chapter of his book to the influence of Darwinism on chemistry, astronomy, linguistics, pedagogy, sociology, history, poetry and even on criminology.[5]

In the political field, oddly enough, that influence extended in two diametrically opposed directions. Inasmuch as Darwinism rejected all forms of supernatural control, it served to undermine the authority of the clergy and hence of the ruling class, and thus had a pronounced democratic effect, especially in absolutist and still semi-feudal Germany. In particular, Darwin's doctrine of the mutability of species seemed to suggest the mutability of social classes. In any case, there could be no doubt that most Darwinists, led by Haeckel, were to be found in the progressive camp. Darwin himself and Huxley and Spencer no less were known to have been democrats at heart. Small wonder then that social democrats as a whole should have been convinced Darwinists.

On the other hand, however, the Darwinist doctrine seemed to sanction the most aggressive aspects of capitalism no less than of nature herself. Did it really make sense to prop up the socially weak and impede the strong when nature herself proved that the progress of species was based on a struggle for existence and the consequent eradication of the unfit? These political inferences may have been impermissible; they were certainly less fundamental than the basic agreement between Darwin and Marx that evolutionary processes in nature and society take place regardless of man's will and consciousness. In any case, this controversy helps to explain why there should have been a crisis in Darwinism at the turn of the century, a crisis that had little bearing on its purely scientific validity. In particular, while the democrats and the socialists used Darwinism as a platform for their attacks on social privilege, the upper classes, aghast at the increasing power of the workers, inveighed bitterly against the deterministic and materialistic foundations on which both Darwinism and Marxism were built. And though no one could say how these developments affected individual men of science, it is obvious that, inasmuch as they were also citizens, they could not stay aloof from the struggle.

Sometimes they even lifted the tip of the veil that normally covers their non-scientific views. Two examples may serve to illustrate this point. There was first of all Oskar Schmidt, a Haeckelian, who to save Darwinism, stated as early as 1878 — the year of Bismarck's first socialist law — that though the egalitarian ideas of socialists and communists may have their natural parallel in primitive colony-forming animals, the emergence of the higher animals was the result of natural selection which is based on natural *inequality*.[6] On a higher level was the related but diametrically opposite argument advanced by the man with whom we introduced this chapter. Unlike Schmidt, Hertwig ended up as an anti-Darwinist, quite possibly because of antipathy to the prevailing anti-humanist adaptations of Darwinism. In the address we have mentioned he was still being temperate, perhaps because his rejection of Darwinism was not yet complete, or perhaps because he had decided to spare the many Darwinists in his audience. Darwin's and Haeckel's discoveries of the "true causes of evolution," he explained on that occasion,[7] had been greeted as grandiose solutions of the mystery of the origin of species. But he could not refrain from censuring the hyper-Darwinism of August Weismann, who had proclaimed the "omnipotence of natural selection"[8] by quoting Spencer's remark of 1893 that this hypothesis was wholly inadequate.[9] He went on to point out that Weismann had, that self-same year, been forced to admit that while there seemed little doubt that certain variations gained the upper hand in the struggle for existence it was impossible to pinpoint these variations in advance. Similarly Weismann had had

342

to concede that though there was no doubt that the fittest survive, no one could say in practice who the fittest were or how many of them must survive in any one generation.[10] Hertwig's comment on these heretical concessions sounded rather crushing: "This can only mean that we know nothing at all about the complex of causes responsible for a given trend."[11] Elsewhere Hertwig called it a weakness of natural selection that it was based on observations of human practices, not of natural processes. Thus the plant breeder does indeed select suitable variations, but in so doing creates nothing new but merely chooses what suits him best, something that does not happen in nature. It was in order to dispel such confusions that Hertwig published his *Zur Abwehr des ethischen, des sozialen, des politischen Darwinismus* (On the Rejection of Ethical, Social and Political Darwinism) in 1918. It was a belated response to a competition sponsored by Haeckel as early as 1900: "What bearing does the theory of evolution have on international political developments and legislation?" The jury was made up of the economist Conrad, the historian Schäfer and the zoologist Ziegler.[12] Besides the prize-winner, one Schallmayer, Hertwig also attacked a number of contributors who had misused Darwinist ideas to reject Christian charity and to glorify war, child mortality, social inequality and ruthless competition as so many means of eradicating the weak and fostering human progress. Thus one contributor, a certain Tille, had likened the East End of London, which others had called "darkest England," to a national sanatorium.[13] Others, like Ploetz, had carried this particular interpretation so far as to demand the destruction at birth of all weak or supposedly weak infants, and compulsory sterilization. The philosopher von Ehrenfels from Prague had even advocated polygamy as a mass aid to natural selection. This was also more or less the view of August Forel, the world-famous author of *Die sexuelle Frage* (The Sexual Question). Let it not be said that these sadistic designs by a host of armchair radicals remained without practical repercussions: sterilization was, in fact, adopted in some states in America, and it is a fact that the German general Bernhardi, in his notorious *Deutschland und der nächste Krieg* (Germany and the Next War, 1913), relied heavily on Darwin, on whom he thus placed the responsibility for many of his outrageous suggestions.

But natural phenomena, Hertwig asserted, cannot be elevated into norms of civilization; justice and morality are grounded exclusively in human life; nature knows no such principles. War and poverty are anything but elevating. And poor Hertwig lived long enough — he died in 1922 — to find his views confirmed by the tragedy of the First World War.[14]

From these two examples — Schmidt and Hertwig — however disparate

343

in importance, it will have become clear why the misuse of Darwinism should have led to its decline as a philosophy: a speculative scientific theory was fast degenerating into religious fanaticism with all the consequences that process entailed. In these circumstances it was perhaps understandable why Abraham Kuyper, speaking on the subject of evolution in 1899, should have begun his address with: "Our century is dying, hypnotized by the dogma of evolution."[15]

But while there was a tangible link between the crisis of Darwinism and the simultaneous transformation of social ideals that opened peoples' eyes to the plight of the underprivileged and the possible role of the state in alleviating their condition, the second development was by no means the full explanation, let alone the sole cause, of the first. Had that been the case, the more recent revival of Darwinism would have been completely inexplicable. For it is a fact that though capitalism is still the dominant system of the West, it is no longer the wild beast that Darwin's disciples, so to speak, took for the biological counterpart of social reality in their day.

Apart from the "exogenous" causes of the crisis of Darwinism, there was also a number of endogenous ones, rooted in the doctrine itself. The first of these was the same that had originally helped Darwinism to rise to such great heights: once ushered in, the theory of evolution was able to call on comparative anatomy, physiology and embryology for corroboration of its claims and for countless contributions to the construction of the "family tree of species" — an incomplete, indeed uncompletable, edifice to which even the most modest students could add their little building-stones with due pride. The resulting patchwork, of necessity, fell far short of their expectations, which may explain why the more talented became increasingly disillusioned and began to look for more rewarding solutions. Looking back at these developments, Nordenskiöld, one of the greatest historians of biology, has said that the mechanistic speculations of modern biologists make a rather monotonous impression.[16] Even at the time, Curt Grottewitz wrote a pamphlet on the history of nineteenth-century science as part of *Am Anfang des Jahrhunderts* (At the Beginning of the Century, 1902), a series of short books addressed to working-class readers, lamenting the fact that the mechanical handling of a single idea had led science to an impasse and that only "some new viewpoint, some new idea can help us out of the morass."[17]

However, the realization that no one had succeeded in correlating the main phyla, let alone in deriving them from one another — neither in botany where the algae, the mosses, the ferns, the angiosperms and the gymnosperms continued to lead their separate existences, nor in zoology where the same thing was happening with the protozoa, the coelenterata, the echinodermata, the nematoda, the athropoda, the mollusca and the vertebrata — was not enough to produce the new approach so many were demanding so passionately. When it did come it entered from without. One of its pioneers was Wilhelm Roux, who was not conscious of the least deviation from the orthodox Darwinism he had learned from Haeckel. On the contrary, when his first studies had shown him that apart from the struggle for existence that was waged by the species, a similar struggle took place between the various parts of the individual organism, "all" he wanted to do was to elucidate the mechanism of that process.[18] And his difference from Haeckel consisted only in the simple fact that he considered his teacher's vague phylogenetic approach less suited to that elucidation than a careful study of ontogenesis. He accordingly designed a series of special embryological experiments, a method to which he gave the name of "developmental mechanics" in the 1880s. Later, when the "mechanical" approach lost its appeal, he rechristened it "developmental physiology."

In his studies, Roux had encountered the phenomena of organic regulation, i.e., the fact that, after partial mutilation of the fertilized egg, the surrounding zones seem capable of making good the damage. And it was subsequent work in this field that suggested the existence of forces that could no longer be described as "mechanical" even in the broadest sense of that term. For though the effects Roux had obtained might still have been explained by mechanical theories — as indeed he tried to do — the processes themselves could not. Vitalism was about to be resurrected, albeit in the form of neo-vitalism — one more illustration that the history of science is like a wheel; whenever the old returns it does so at another point along the road.

For a time, however, orthodox Dawinists were not in the least disturbed by Roux's discoveries, the less so as the circle of his disciples in Germany — unlike in America — remained fairly small and silent.[19] "Normal" Darwinism was still too entrenched for anything else to happen. Nevertheless, the international congress of zoologists held in Berlin in 1901 set aside a special section for experimental biology, which according to one of its leading representatives was also the most popular branch of all.[20]

This man was Hans Driesch, and he was to go far along the path of Darwinist heresy; no one in fact could have gone further. At first, however, he, too, was a loyal disciple of Haeckel. In his memoirs he tells us that he met A. Pauly in Munich in 1888 when he was just twenty-one, but it is doubtful whether he would have remembered that meeting or thought it worth recording had he had not discovered much later that the older man was a kindred spirit. For Pauly eventually came to identify the driving force of evolution with a purposive striving by the organism as a whole and by all its parts.[21] In Munich, Driesch also made the acquaintance of Gustav Wolff, famed not only for his critique of natural selection,[22] begun early in his career,[23] but also for his now classical regeneration experiments, experiments that did not apparently allow of a mechanistic explanation: he showed that when the lens of an axolotl is extirpated, the iris is capable of producing a substitute. But once again it is questionable whether Driesch would have attributed so much importance to their meeting had he not engaged in similar work during a later phase of his career.

Driesch called 1890 his turning-point; it was then that he began to study the writings of Wigand, His and Goette, three vociferous opponents of Haeckel. Wigand, who had died in 1886, had been an evolutionist, but one who believed in evolution according to a plan involving neither accident nor finality. In the thirteen hundred pages of his *Beiträge zur Methodik der Naturforschung* (*Contributions to Scientific Methodology*) he had laid bare every possible flaw in the Darwinist doctrine, and it was perhaps because of this fact that he had fallen into oblivion by 1890, so much so that Reich twice misspelt his name.[24] Wilhelm His, a generation younger than Wigand but nevertheless fifty-nine in 1890, was one of those who opposed Haeckel's biogenetic law with the argument that the embryo of every species is as distinct as the species itself, and Alexander Wilhelm Goette, finally, slightly younger still, caused a great stir with his dogmatic, hypermechanistic ideas.

Thus equipped, and having also acquainted himself with the work of Roux, Driesch proceeded in 1891 to perform the first of his famous experiments on the eggs of sea urchins, creatures with which he had become familiar during a stay in Naples where his work in the Zoological Station had earned him the nickname of "dottore di pesci." Having vigorously shaken one such egg at the two-cell stage in a test tube until the two cells separated, he discovered that each half was capable of developing into a larva — a so-called pluteus — which was whole and normal though only half the "true" size. The same thing seemed to happen after violent shaking of the egg at the four-cell stage, and so on — in every case a complete larva was produced, be it a quarter or whatever fraction of the normal size. The fact that this result was in conflict with Roux's experimental findings — the emergence of half a tadpole of normal size — persuaded Driesch to repeat his own experiments over and over, until the least doubt had been removed.[25] Clearly such forcibly induced divisions

ushered in structural changes in both halves of the egg, enabling each
to take over the function of the whole, albeit on a reduced scale. He called
this process "prospective potential," by which he wanted to express the
fact that the germ has a greater developmental potential than it normally
deploys. In 1900, after a further series of experiments, he formulated
it all by saying that the four-cell stage of the sea urchin egg is "harmoni-
cally equipotential" inasmuch as any three cells *together* produce the
whole, and "complexly equipotential" inasmuch as every quarter cell produces the whole — if on a reduced scale.[26]

The fact that the contradiction between Roux's and Driesch's findings
was eventually resolved — it appeared that in the initial phase of its development the egg has the anisotropic properties discovered by Driesch, and
at a later stage the isotropic properties discovered by Roux, which meant
that the conflict between "preformation" (the egg is a mosaic of primor-
dia) and epigenesis (the egg possesses no more organization than is apparent) was resolved as well — did not prevent these two pioneers from
going their separate ways. For despite their public reconciliation, Roux
continued to uphold the mechanistic view, while Driesch developed into
a vitalist, though by stages. Thus in 1893, when he still demanded a
special place for biology among the sciences,[27] he was not yet calling
for a clear break with the mechanical approach. At the time, he still considered that all biological processes were physical or chemical and merely
believed that the organization of matter in the organic world was of a
purposive kind. The organism may have been a machine, but it was run
by an engineer.[28] He later described this phase in his intellectual development as "static teleology."

Only in 1899 did he take the step that was to divide him from most
of his colleagues and that, strictly speaking, carried him out of his own
discipline into philosophy: writing on the localization of morphogenetic
phenomena, he added the sub-title "a demonstration of vitalist processes."[29] So carried away was he by the vitalist idea that he immersed
himself in the writings of its precursors, beginning with Aristotle, from
whom he had previously borrowed the idea of entelechy, of an inbuilt
purpose, though in slightly changed form. Similar ideas were also advanced
by the American palaentologist E. D. Cope, who placed consciousness at
the beginning of all organic activity, arguing for instance that digestion
might well originate in the feeling that one's stomach was full. According
to Sorel, this theory was simply a reflection of American life.[30] In any
case, Dewey's stimulus-response theory, in which the "response" incites
the "stimulus,"[31] was closely related to Cope's idea, and both, in turn,
could easily be traced back to Bergson's *évolution créatrice*.

347

In 1905, Driesch devoted a whole book to all his predecessors,[32] but when he revised it in 1922 he elaborated the historical part and omitted the rest. The second edition ended with a most astonishing mental somersault. Much as he now placed his hopes in the future of psychology on parapsychology — in 1926 he was elected president of the Society for Psychical Research — so he now placed his hopes in the future of biology on "paraphysics."[33]

Driesch had, in fact, come to look upon a mysterious "vital force" as the ultimate guide of organic development. But which precise "vital force" of his own had persuaded him to abandon the safe plain of experimental biology for the giddy heights of parapsychology? This is not the place to probe deeply enough into his life and intellectual development to provide an answer to so personal a question. All we can hope to do is to give a brief indication of the spiritual attitude that Driesch eventually adopted. This attitude also serves to explain why he and so many others turned their back on Darwinism. Tell me who your friends are and I will tell you who you are. Bonds of friendship are indeed the cause and result of many of our intellectual habits. In 1891 Driesch had already met von Uexküll; by 1905 he had also met Count Hermann Keyserling and, in the order in which he mentions them in his memoirs, he also made the more than superficial acquaintance of Max Weber, who incidentally did not like him, of Boutroux and of Külpe, Bergson and Windelband, who did, of Jacques Maritain and his Jewish-Russian wife, Raïssa Umantsov, whom Bergson had sent to Germany in 1906 to study the vitalist movement, of the British biologist W. Bateson, one of the re-discoverers of Mendel,[34] of Husserl and Max Scheler, two kindred spirits who believed in the autonomy of the organic world and in the dualism of body and soul, and lastly — in 1913 — of Mrs. Sidgwick, the sister of Lord Balfour, who convinced him of the attractions of parapsychology, of which he himself confessed that it had made little impression on him beforehand.[35]

Driesch might well have remained a lone voice, in which case this "conversion" to vitalism would not have greatly mattered. But he did not, and was less and less one as the years went by. Although the number of his direct disciples may have been very small, there was a large number who, while they did not openly embrace his doctrine, nevertheless fell under its spell. Many of them now declared that the laws of life could not possibly be based on inanimate processes, and that the mechanistic approach was no more than a straitjacket imposed on science by the arrogant positivists.[36]

Their views did not, of course, go unchallenged. In 1901 the zoologist Otto Bütschli of Heidelberg declared that, while he was perfectly willing

348

to abandon the purely mechanistic interpretation of life, he had to insist that the organic world could only have been derived from the inorganic, for what other explanation could there possibly be?[37] And he warned biologists not to "revert to the romanticism of a hundred years ago." A closely related view was expressed one year later in the *Sozialistische Monatshefte*, the journal of the Marxist revisionists. Its author drew attention to the links between neo-romanticism and neo-vitalism.[38] In 1909 the Russian biologist Cholodenko examined the contributions of Driesch, J. Reinke and P. N. Cossmann, and criticized all three in his *Die teleologische Betrachtung in der modernen Biologie* (The Teleological Approach in Modern Biology).[39] Of these three, Cossmann was apparently the most extravagant. For while Reinke with his "dominants" and Driesch with his "entelechy" were still aiming at a causal explanation, Cossman had abandoned that approach altogether: though granting causality as such, he denied that it was the sole explanation of biological processes.[40] Cholodenko, for his part, concluded that the biological sciences did not stand or fall by the elucidation of the inbuilt purposes of organic beings but that these purposes stood in need of a more satisfactory explanation.[41]

Between the two extremes of Weismann and Haeckel on the one hand and Driesch and Pauly on the other, there was a whole host of intermediate viewpoints. This was only to be expected since biology stood at the crossroads: scientific solutions to new problems are rarely pat and straightforward, and less so as scientists, too, are men of flesh and blood. Two of these intermediate solutions may serve to illustrate this point.

One was advanced by G. Bunge, a physiologist who had opposed the mechanistic theory of life as early as 1899, but had retained enough of it to relegate the "vital force" to the work of the cells.[42] Another intermediate solution was proffered by the Viennese palaeontologist Neumayr. Following in the footsteps of his colleague and fellow citizen Waagen, who as early as 1867 had associated the variation of species with the idea of mutation, Neumayr, who was a staunch Darwinist, nevertheless argued that his view in no way undermined the orthodox Darwinist concept of species.[43] That was also, more or less, the opinion of W. Bateson, who abandoned the Darwinian postulate of gradual transitions amongst the species in 1894,[44] and also of S. Korzjinski, a botanist, who in 1899 and again in 1901 drew attention to the fact that many stable new forms appear quite suddenly.[45] Kölliker and Nägeli also took the view that species change discontinuously and even Huxley, Darwin's leading champion, agreed.

In short, by 1900 the theory of mutation was "in the air" and it was only a matter of time before it came down to earth. When it did, it was accompanied by the rediscovery of Mendel. It is difficult to find more telling proof of the fact that theories do not appear or re-appear by pure chance. Independently of one another — at least as far as we can tell — no fewer than three scientists rediscovered, within four months of the year 1900, the importance of Mendel's forgotten researches — the Dutchman Hugo de Vries on 14 March, the German Karl Correns on 24 April, and the Austrian E. von Tschermak on 2 June.[46] They laid the foundations on which the Dane W. L. Johannsen, the Englishman William Bateson and the American Thomas Hunt Morgan were to construct genetics during the first decade of the new century. Of the pioneers of the theory of mutation, de Vries has remained the best known, thanks to his famous experiments with the American evening primrose. In 1900 he published his *Hoe soorten ontstaan* (Origin of Species); one year later came his *Die Mutationstheorie* (The Theory of Mutation).[47] That he intended no break with Darwinism is proved, *inter alia*, by the fact that Max Verworn was able to accept his conclusions even while rejecting Mendelism and remaining a faithful disciple of his teacher Haeckel.[48] In any case, from then on it was generally accepted that nature could engage in sudden leaps, the more so as Planck's quantum theory of 1900 had drawn attention to the occurrence of just such leaps in the propagation of light.

By the side of the revival of Lamarckism, and particularly of the doctrine of the inheritance of acquired characteristics — which was not necessarily anti-Darwinist; by the side of the mutationists and the vitalists, there now also appeared a biological trend, repeated in psychology, which stressed the vital link between organisms and their environment, or their "Umwelt," as Jacob von Uexküll, its leading exponent, called it. In the wake of this new trend, orthodox Darwinism receded from sight, almost imperceptibly so. In his *Umwelt und Innenwelt der Tiere* (The Environment and Inner World of Animals; 1909)[49] von Uexküll gave clear expression to what, at the time, was a daringly sceptical view: that "scientific truth" was simply the embodiment of the misunderstandings of a particular age.[50] In 1913 L. J. Henderson went even further along the same road when he pointed out that the power of the environment to produce new organisms was at least as remarkable as the power of those organisms to adapt themselves to the environment.[51]

Just as in psychology, this emphasis of the interdependence of individual and environment was responsible for the claim that the study of vital processes must be based on the investigation no longer of the parts, but of the whole. This doctrine became known as "holism,"[52] a term coined by the South African J. C. Smuts, or as "emergent evolutionism"[53] a term preferred by the American C. Lloyd Morgan. Its disciples not only argued that any organic whole is greater than the sum of its parts, but also that biological effects are never adequately explained by their causes. Holists made the "principle of life" a cardinal principle and, moreover, one, as Gemelli put it in 1910, of which it was impossible to say whether it worked *in* matter, *on* matter, *through* matter or *with the help* of matter.[54] The British physiologist and philosopher John Scott Haldane was an early convert to this doctrine, and made it the basis of his outright rejection of the mechanistic theory of life and mind (1913).[55] In his opinion, any attempt to explain vital phenomena by chemical causes was comparable to the attempt to explain a painting by the chemical properties of its canvas or oils. As for the vitalist theory — in so far as it could be called a theory at all — he believed that it did no more than record this failure, i.e. man's ignorance of the precise way in which the parts of the living organism respond to physical and chemical changes.[56] Thus while such processes as secretion, absorption growth, nerve stimulation, and muscular contraction had hitherto been treated as independent physical or chemical processes, they were, in fact, so many interconnected aspects of a single if complex metabolic activity.[57] He also expressed the view that the world of consciousness and its elements — everything we perceive — constitute an indivisible whole.[58]

Haldane could no longer be called a Darwinist by the wildest stretch of the imagination. Nor was he the first to express such heterodox views, even in England where respect for Darwin was most deeply entrenched. Bateson had preceded him some of the way and so had Samuel Butler, that *enfant terrible*, whom we shall have occasion to discuss in a different context and who had tried — vainly — to prove as early as 1879 that the theory of evolution advanced by Erasmus Darwin, the grandfather, was sounder than that developed by Charles, the grandson.[59] Butler's views may not have mattered very greatly, for he was a jack-of-all trades — a mathematician, a classical scholar, a musician, a painter and a writer — and not a biologist, and also because his original mind made him reject authority wherever he encountered it. If I mention him here, it is only because as an historian I am not so much concerned with the rights and wrongs of Darwinism, a subject on which I am, in any case, poorly qualified to speak, as with the "variation" or "mutation" of the intellectual climate at the turn of the century and its untoward repercussions on Darwinism. For the rest, it is only fair to add that, far from causing an upheaval in the normal routine of biological laboratories or research, these repercussions merely led to a gradual re-examination of problems that had been swept under the carpet, a process that was so gradual that it was barely noticed at first.

Nevertheless a change had occurred, and it can even be dated fairly accurately. It took place between 1891 and 1909, the first year marking the start of Driesch's experiments and the second the emergence on the historical plane of a man who realized that, for all their differences and contradictions — which caused some to assume the existence of a functional plan and others to reject it — the new school was united in its refusal to advance mechanistic explanations of life.

That man was Emanuel Rádl, a Bohemian biologist. When the second part of his *Geschichte der biologischen Theorien* (History of Biological Theories) was published in 1909, it not only enriched the history of biology but also the history of science in general.[60] In the chapter devoted to Darwinism, Rádl showed clearly how that doctrine lost its hold in one sphere after another during the 1880s.[61] If we summarize his findings, even though most of them have already been described or will be discussed in subsequent chapters, it is because Rádl was one of the first to remark on the great changes that were taking place and to bring out their effects on so many different branches of human learning.

Rádl began with Paul Bourget, who in his preface to *Le Disciple* of 1899 rejected Zola's naturalism of instincts and at the same time opposed the exaggerated cult of science. He went on to discuss F. Brunetière, who also attacked Zola, rejected the scientific ideals advanced by Renan and Berthelot, and spoke of the "bankruptcy of science" in his *La Science et la réligion* (1895). This was also the period in which Max Nordau deplored the growing number of "decadents," of mystics and of Nietzscheans in his widely-read *Entartung* (Degeneration). In philosophy, Spencer and Haeckel were making way for a revival of Kant and for Schopenhauer; religion had found new champions in Harnack and Sabatier, the Protestant hagiographer of St. Francis of Assisi, and in Loisy and Schell. History, too, was taking the same path: Buckle and Taine were being ousted by Dilthey, Windelband, and Rickert. In 1899, examining the crisis of Marxism, Masaryk was able to show that it contained as many "variations" and "mutations" as also bedeviled psychology and biology.

In short: the fate which befalls all those theories that remain theories, namely that they degenerate into philosophical speculation, had visited Darwinism as well. Its younger disciples, unlike Huxley, Spencer, Weismann, and Haeckel, no longer felt at home in it and found its atmosphere stifling. However, a new lamp had begun to shine, and though — *de mortuis nil nisi bene* — it derived its radiance from the past, it seemed all the more glorious for being rekindled, rather than left to smolder. Darwinism as a doctrine that tried to impose itself by force was, as Rádl put it, a thing of the past. But, he was quick to add, it would continue to live on as a

Cyclopean creation in the minds of Darwin's descendants who would en-shrine it for all time by the side of mankind's greatest achievements.[62] Even had he added, as indeed he should have done, that Darwin's laws continued to apply to a host of phenomena, and that indeterminism never gained an unconditional victory, or that the new bounds set on adaptation did not invalidate the theory of cause and effect in biology (just as little as quantum and relativity theory invalidate classical mech-anics on the macrocosmic plane), he would still have been perfectly right to conclude that the days of Darwinism as a philosophy were numbered.

And so in biology, too, the moment of truth had arrived, the moment of which Max Weber said in 1904, when he was constructing his great methodological system, that "at some time or another the color changes: the importance of uncritically accepted viewpoints is put in doubt, the path is lost in the twilight, the light of the great cultural problems re-cedes."[63] A new light was shining on the mystery that is life. Far from dismantling science, it simply opened men's eyes to some of its short-comings. The myth that man was the center of the universe may have been buried for good, but man had not been relegated to the opposite pole: he was clearly much more than just a "successful amoeba." He had to be allocated a place between the two. The only problem was where.

CHAPTER XXIV

IN VITRO AND *IN VIVO*

On Friday August 24, 1900 at 5:00 P. M., Dr. Thomas Colvin was called
to a back street in Glasgow. Having stumbled in the dark up the ram-
shackle stairs, he entered a one-room tenement and discovered that he
had not one but three patients. And, indeed, it appeared that during
a meal four days earlier a fourth member of the family — a girl of ten —
had died. The symptoms of all four cases were identical, and he diagnosed
enteric fever. His mistake was discovered a day later in Belvedere Hospital,
where the three survivors were found to be suffering from bubonic
plague.[1]

It had been possible to diagnose that disease with certainty for six
years: in 1894 Yersin, a pupil of Pasteur, and Kitasato, a pupil of Koch,
working in Hong Kong where the plague was then raging, had, independently of one another, discovered the plague bacillus almost simultaneously. And it was also known, though not yet generally accepted, that
this bacillus had a predilection for rodents and that it was a flea that
carried it from the rat to humans, and then from one person to the next.
This had been suspected earlier but it was fully confirmed in Bombay by
Liston, a member of the Plague Research Commission appointed in 1905
by the British Secretary of State for India.[2] And now this new-found
knowledge was being applied. The Russian Chavkin, a pupil of Pasteur
who had also been involved in fighting the plague in India for many
years, had developed a method of preparing a vaccine from dead plague
bacilli. It may have been less potent than the vaccine that was later produced from live bacilli, but it nevertheless decreased the number of deaths
by from $33\frac{1}{3}\%$ to 50%.[3] Microscopic studies, the culture of bacteria,
serological investigations, inoculations and compulsory notification,
followed by isolation of the patient and his contacts, quickly became
common practice all over the so-called "civilized world." An international
health conference held in Venice in 1897, disturbed by the plague epidemic of 1895, had brought most of these measures to the attention of
the medical authorities.[4] And it is certain that, even if the outbreak
in Glasgow had been more virulent than in fact it turned out to be, these

measures would have brought it under control fairly quickly. In the event, the Glasgow outbreak was confined to twenty-seven cases, more than half of which were cured. Within three months the threat had been averted, and much the same happened following minor outbreaks of plague in other parts of Europe.

Simple though it has been to record these facts, it would take volumes to detail the vast amount of painstaking research that had led up to them. Bacteriology, serology, immunology and epidemiology are mere words, but behind them stand the names of hundreds of scientists with a thirst for knowledge, a will to succeed and a passion — be it only on Sundays — to alleviate the suffering of mankind. Behind them stand many great thinkers determined to dispel the time-hallowed misconception that disease is the direct result of sin and to rebuild their profession on the exact foundations of biology, chemistry and physics; behind them stand an endless series of experiments and an army of experimental animals whose corpses punctuated the search for the *therapia sterilisans magna* which even Paracelsus had sought in vain. Add the many gaps between thought and action, between speculation and discovery, between discovery and practical application, and the fight against prejudices that were often more resistant and virulent than the tiny organisms all these discoveries were meant to eradicate — as witness the writings of de Kruif[5] among many others — and the fact that as soon as one problem seemed to be solved a host of new ones arose, and we have the story of medical discovery in the period under review. Here, as in every other branch of human endeavor, the final answers proved much more elusive than anyone could at first have imagined. And even when it was thought that the answers had been found, research often had to start all over again, for instance when human patients failed to respond to a drug that had proved infallible with guinea-pigs.

Without the modern form of asceticism which is experimental science, the plague epidemic at the end of the nineteenth century might well have wrought the same havoc as did the "Black Death," estimated to have wiped out a quarter of the population in the middle of the fourteenth century. And not only the plague, but many other sorts of infectious diseases might also have done their dreadful work without let or hindrance. Thanks to laboratory studies, however, and the fundamental discoveries of Pasteur, Koch, Virchow, and Bernard in the 1860s up to the 1880s, one bacillus and carrier after the next had been isolated by the turn of the century and its effects rendered harmless.

In 1890 Emil Behring discovered the diphtheria antitoxin and thus became the founder of serotherapy. His discovery was the direct result of the recent isolation of the diphtheria bacillus. Behring was thirty-six at the time, and this and other discoveries were to earn him the first Nobel Prize for medicine and physiology eleven years later.

Even yellow fever, that frightful scourge which according to legend had turned the "Flying Dutchman" into a ghost ship that people beheld at their peril, and which in the seventies struck down twenty-two of the twenty-seven doctors and nurses working in Senegal, no longer posed an inescapable threat. It was the Americans Walter Reed, James Carroll, Jesse Lazear, and their fellow workers who, working in Havana in 1900, produced incontrovertible proof of something Carlos Juan Finlay had merely suspected twenty years earlier, namely that yellow fever was transmitted by the infected *Stegomyia fasciata* mosquito. The proof even claimed a victim: Lazear, accidentally infected, died of the disease. Carroll, by contrast, who had deliberately allowed himself to be infected, made a full recovery:[6] he exposed his arm to the mosquito on the same day that horrified Glaswegians learned that the Mallory family was stricken with the plague. Hemmeter, one of the most thorough medical historians, devoted a lengthy article to Carroll's self-sacrifice and vainly pleaded that his hero be awarded the Nobel Prize.[7] In 1902 that distinction was bestowed on Sir Ronald Ross for his discovery in 1897 that the anopheles mosquito was the carrier of the flagellating organism which causes malaria, a disease then still rife all over the world.[8] Ross's studies are a prime example of how much international co-operation underlay medical progress at the time. That co-operation, deliberate or otherwise, extended not only between research workers, but also between them and the authorities and industry. The malarial parasite itself had been discovered as early as 1880 by Alphonse Laveran in Constantine, Algeria, in the red blood corpuscles of malaria patients. The study of its habitat and life cycle — so many prerequisites for its eradication — was undertaken by the Italians E. Hore Marchiafava and Angello Celli in 1886. Ross's own work was confined to bird malaria, and it was the Italians Grassi, Bartinelli, and Bignami who, in 1898, showed that the same carrier infected birds and men, thus confirming a suspicion first expressed by Patrick Manson (1879) and A. King (1883). Although this story may seem highly involved, it is merely a brief summary of the true events.[9] The fight against malaria also provides an excellent illustration of the repercussions of medical discoveries on society, now as then: in the 1850s, malaria patients accounted for between twelve and sixty cases in a thousand treated in St. Thomas's Hospital, London; but soon after the turn of the century malaria had almost disappeared from most of Europe.[10]

A very similar story can be told about sleeping sickness. The causative organism was discovered by Aldo Castellani in 1902; in 1903 Bruce established that it is transmitted by the tsetse fly. We might also add the discovery in 1900 by Schott-Muller that paratyphus and typhus are caused by two distinct bacilli; and the discovery by Charles Nicolle in 1904 that body lice are the carriers of typhus fever.[11] Thanks to the unflagging efforts of these and other workers, by the end of the nineteenth century medicine had identified the causative agents of botulism, cholera, dysentery, gonorrhea, meningitis, pneumonia, malaria, Malta fever, leprosy, foot-and-mouth disease, bubonic plague, tetanus, and typhus.[12] The early twentieth century was to extend that list even further with the discovery of the causative agents of yaws (1905); of yellow fever and whooping cough (by Bordet and Gengou in 1906); of measles and smallpox (by Paschen in 1906); of scarlet fever and sleeping sickness; and finally of syphilis.

The last discovery, with its far-reaching diagnostic and therapeutic consequences, marked one of the most striking and widely-discussed episodes in the history of medicine, not only because of the exceptional perspicacity and persistence of the men responsible, and the mysterious and horrible nature of this disease, but also because, in the Wilhelmian period, the German press was quick to trumpet German successes throughout the world. During a series of tests performed in 1903 and 1904, Elie Metchnikoff and Emile Roux had succeeded in infecting apes with syphilis — which at the time was considered one further proof of the common descent of man and these animals. More important was the discovery in May 1905 by Fritz Schaudinn and his collaborator Erich Hoffmann,[13] with the help of the ultra-microscope invented in 1903, that spirochetes, tiny spiral and rod-shaped bacteria, were the causative agents of this disease, a scourge that more often than not led to general paralysis and a pitiful death. Protozoologists having thus taken the first steps towards the eradication of syphilis, the next and crucial step was taken by one who, though trained as a doctor, had, in fact, been devoting his energies to chemistry and pharmacology. His name was Paul Ehrlich,[14] and in 1900, when he was forty-seven, his fame had already spread so wide that the Royal Society of London invited him to deliver that year's Croonian Lecture. This he did, on 22 March of that year, and his lecture makes fascinating reading even today, not only because of the clear picture he drew of the state of immunology in 1900, but also and above all because of the modesty with which he veiled his own genius.[15]

His first step had been a purely theoretical one: on the basis of August Kekulé's model of the benzene molecule,[16] Ehrlich had postulated that the living protoplasm of cells consists of a fixed nucleus to which are attached certain atom complexes which he called "side chains" or "receptors". The latter combine chemically with food substances and also neutralized poisons by increasing their normal activity and sending antibodies into the blood stream. Though this theory was widely criticized, it nevertheless helped August Wassermann to develop his antibody-reaction test for the diagnosis of syphilis in 1906. That test, which has since been greatly improved, is still known by Wassermann's name.

Ehrlich's second step was the discovery, with the collaboration of Sahachiwo Hata, of a specific cure for syphilis: namely Salvarsan, or 606, an arsenic preparation so called because 606 tests were needed to produce it. The calendar had meanwhile moved on to 1909, and it was 31 August before the first rabbit was injected — and cured. Soon afterwards it was the turn of the first human patient, and during the next year no fewer than 65,000 shots of Salvarsan were administered.

The cry of "Paracelsus redivivus" now went up, for had Paracelsus's great dream of a *therapia sterilisans magna* not been fulfilled at last? Had not Ehrlich's "magic bullet" hit the parasite while sparing the host? In fact, the answer is yes and no. Yes, because the improved neo-Salvarsan of 1912 is being used to this day; no, because, even in improved form, it never fulfilled the original hope that a single injection would lead to a complete cure. That only happened with rabbits. No, too, because Salvarsan is not completely safe. Whether this justified the bitter recriminations that ensued is another question. There is no question, however, that it aroused high enough hopes for the Reichstag to discuss it at length on March 10, 1914. For the rest, its discoverer, who had the characteristic modesty of so many Jewish scholars, succumbed six years later to the onslaught of anti-Semitic attacks, the misery of the World War and the ravages of tobacco, for which even his own magic bullet provided no antidote. Two things are certain in any case. One is that the world owes him and Hata a great debt; the other is that though Ehrlich never sought glory or money, he earned world-wide acclaim when his discovery was published in 1900, and again in 1908 when he shared the Nobel Prize with Metschnikoff. And money? He bought books and cigars aplenty, but he had few other material needs. And yet money played a large part even in his discovery, and indeed a double role. Without the generosity of Frau Speyer, the widow of a Jewish banker from Frankfurt, he would not have been able to set up his institute, and without his institute he would certainly not have been able to produce his Salvarsan. Moreover, without the Hoechster Farbwerken, who acquired the first German patent on June 10, 1909, Salvarsan would never have gone into large-scale production. Medicine had not only allied itself to science, it had also become dependent on the chemical industry, that new herbalists' paradise.[17] Ehrlich himself joked that his discovery took four capital Gs: *"Geld, Geduld, Geschick und Glück"* (Money, Patience, Skill and Luck). True enough, but his success rested chiefly on the two middle Gs, on the fortunate combination of flashes of intuition with practical skill; the same combination that also informed the work of Marx, Freud, and Einstein.

Though immunology, serotherapy, and chemotherapy thus supplied convincing proof that medical science, like physics and chemistry, was growing more complex as human knowledge expanded, even more convincing proof of this trend was provided by endocrinology, vitaminology, chromosome research, blood grouping, and even by modern surgery — so many new branches grafted to the ancient stem of medicine in our period. Thus surgery was increasingly abandoning the sterilization of wounds, a field in which Semmelweis and Lister had made their names, in favour of aseptic methods aimed at preventing impurities from reaching the wound in the first place. The surgeon with his aseptic white coat, rubber gloves, sterile instruments and equally sterile assistants and nurses, was the symbol of the new age. Rubber gloves, for instance, used since 1890 in the U.S.A., became compulsory in Europe seven years later. In 1894 the electric filament lamp was first used for internal examinations and two years later the advent of inhalation anaesthetics further eased the surgeon's task and the patient's suffering. Morphine and scopolamine were first used as basic anaesthetics in 1900.

Modern brain surgery was born in 1905, although its basic principles are traced back to the Egyptians. Radiations too were increasingly employed both in diagnosis and in therapy. This had started when the Dane Niels Ryberg Finsen successfully treated *lupus vulgaris* with concentrated light radiation; the Finsen Institute, Copenhagen, whose methods were quickly copied elsewhere, was opened in 1895. That very year, however, it became clear that other radiations could prove of even greater therapeutic importance, following Roentgen's discovery of the remarkable fact that an electric discharge passing through a vacuum emits extraordinarily penetrating rays. The first attempts to cure cancer of the uterus with X-rays were made in 1902, and the first artifical sun lamp was brought into use in 1905. Soon after the Curies succeeded in separating radium from pitchblende in 1905, their discovery, too, was put to medical use. The jubilation with which all these new cures were greeted was, however, muted — just as happened with Salvarsan — by the realization that radiotherapy posed dangers for patient and doctor alike. And

359

by the side of these brand-new methods, many of the old — like medical gymnastics and massage, which had existed as long as human suffering — were being brought up to date, sometimes so fast as to become caricatures of their former selves. Practically no town of any significance was devoid of a Mensendieck, Müller, Sander or similar institute.[18]

Endocrinology and vitaminology really deserve chapters of their own. The honor of discovering that the endocrine glands preside over the functional balance of the human organism falls to Switzerland. And not by chance, for cretinism, which results from hypothyroidism due to iodine deficiency, was so prevalent in that country that Swiss doctors were the first to seize the chance of combating it with the latest medical weapons. The Bernese physician Professor Kocher, perhaps the most famous surgeon of his day, had previously tried to treat hypothyroidism by removing the malfunctioning thyroid gland of some of his goiter patients. These patients had not died, but contracted tetany, so-called because their condition resembled the muscular spasms associated with tetanus. What Kocher had already suspected, Moritz Schiff and von Eiselsberg now demonstrated by animal experiments:[19] the thyroid gland secretes a substance essential for normal life. If part of the patient's gland was left in place or if he was injected with a thyroid extract, no muscular spasms occurred. Addison's disease, first described in the middle of the nineteenth century, was now shown to have a comparable cause: the destruction of both adrenal glands.

Much more sensational but not necessarily less important was an experiment performed by Brown-Séquard, the son of an American and a Frenchwoman, and Claude Bernard's successor at the Sorbonne. In 1889, at the age of seventy-two, he concocted a brew of animal sex hormones, injected it into his skin, and appeared before a learned society with the news that he had been rejuvenated. Another Paracelsus! Though the poor man was ridiculed at the time, Garrison has coupled his name to that of Claude Bernard as the co-founder of endocrinology.[20] The path of science is clearly paved with strange ideas, though not many as striking as those of Brown-Séquard.[21] In any case, a new discipline was making fast progress, and it soon appeared that not only the thyroid gland, the gonads and the adrenals, but quite a few other endocrine glands, too, performed indispensable functions. In 1902, Bayliss and Starling complicated matters even further when they discovered a duodenal secretion capable of stimulating the pancreas via the bloodstream. And at the very end of our period, Kendall succeeded in isolating thyroxin. At about the same time, Starling was the first to use the term "hormones" for the secretions of the endocrine glands.

The word "vitamin" was coined by Casimir Funk in 1913.[22] The realization that certain vague substances are essential for health or even for survival, and that their deficiency causes such diseases as scurvy, rickets, beriberi and pellagra was of older, and often much older, provenance — Dutch East-Indiamen would never have been able to found the Cape Colony had they not carried fresh fruit and fresh green vegetables against scurvy. Nor did James Cook have his crew drink lemon juice for nothing. But acting and understanding are two different things. Some of the understanding came at the beginning of the 1880s when it was discovered that the main elements of man's diet — proteins, carbohydrates and fats — even when eaten in proper quantities and proportions, can cause deficiency diseases and death if they are too highly refined. Thus C. Eijkman showed in 1897 that white rice lacked a certain substance present in natural rice and that its absence was the cause of beriberi. Physicians now began to pay as much attention to vitamins as they did to hormones, and, incidentally, discovered a close connection between the two: the main effect of some vitamins — and their number kept growing apace — was to stimulate the hormone secretions of the endocrine glands.

A similar story can be told about the discovery of blood groups. In 1900 the Austrian Karl Landsteiner discovered that blood is much more than the "special juice" Goethe had called it. In particular, he found that if the red blood corpuscles of certain people were mixed with the blood serum of certain others, clotting occurred. This, he explained, was because different blood groups, as he called them, were incompatible. Landsteiner distinguished three such groups, two years later a fourth one was added, and in 1911 it appeared that the first (the A-group) could be further divided into two sub-groups. The identification of blood groups proved of great theoretical importance in genetics — membership of a certain blood group is transmitted in accordance with Mendel's laws — and of great practical importance as well, because it appeared that blood transfusions between different groups could prove fatal.[23]

Even more involved and astonishing, finally, was the complex of phenomena known as "allergies," hypersensitive reactions of the body to specific substances. This hypersensitivity was brought to light in the years 1903 to 1905, when Pirquet discovered serum allergies and serum diseases, and in 1914 when Richet began to draw attention to anaphylaxis, i.e., lessened resistance to a toxin resulting from previous inoculation with the same material. All this happened long before the first allergic infection was described in the literature.

The fact that medical science should have become so exceptionally complicated during this period may perhaps be explained by the vast number of detailed clinical studies on which its progress was based: hundreds and hundreds of students were systematically gathering thousands and thousands of disparate facts and it was left to a few exceptionally talented men to discover the hidden links between them and to fuse them into a coherent whole. For, appearances to the contrary, medical science, too, was built on a small number of central themes, or rather sets of observations that had hardened into conceptions.

One of the great conceptions of the last decade of the nineteenth century, as we have seen, was the belief that the exact sciences held the key to the causes and cures of illnesses, and the results of this conception were indeed such as to fill medical men with justified pride. That was, in any case, the gist of a lecture delivered by Hemmeter on April 24, 1900.[24] But the fact that the only prediction he made on that occasion — that the cancer problem would be solved in the first half of the twentieth century[25] — did not come true, makes one suspect that all this optimism was exaggerated. One reason was the impersonal bias of the new approach, essential perhaps to success, but one-sided none the less: after all, the patient is more than his illness and his body more than a complex of chemical reactions. Hemmeter also paid tribute to a great new — and at the same time, old — idea, when in the same lecture he advised government-sponsored laboratories to examine the possible nexus between psychological aberrations and the appearance of certain pathological conditions.[26] Such entities as constitution and disposition, which had been held in such contempt for so long, were thus restored to honor, albeit in a new setting. The holistic approach which had made itself felt in other sciences, had at last appeared in medicine: just one more symptom of the decline of nineteenth-century liberalism.

No doubt the many complaints voiced by contemporary medical writers about the spread of quackery were bound up with this change in medical thought, not as a direct consequence but rather as a reaction to the coldly scientific attitude of "official" medicine. Although many of these complaints merely reflected a "closed shop" attitude on the doctors' part and although quackery was not nearly as rampant as it was said to have been, it is nevertheless a fact that a spate of charlatans suddenly burst forth upon unhappy humanity, birds of different plumage, but all united in the belief that their particular nostrum was better than anyone else's. There were naturopaths, faith healers, masseurs, vegetarians, homeopaths, naturists, magnetizers, herbalists, Christian Scientists, occultists as well as common or garden quacks. Thus Pagel, the medical historian, cited some twenty books dealing with medical occultism, all published from 1893 to 1905, and his list covered German publications alone![27] Moreover, while no more than twenty-eight quacks had been registered with the Berlin police in 1879, that number had risen to 1,013 by 1903 and to 1,349 by 1909: more than half the number of registered doctors.[28] This is not at all surprising when one considers that quacks could now earn more money than ever before. There was a whole industry selling cheap "cures" in unlimited quantities and there was a press that was only too happy to advertise their magical properties to the masses — for a fee. The happy beneficiaries needed no Aladdin's lamp now that they could build palaces out of *pilules orientales* and pink tablets. One of their better-known victims was the English writer Harold Frederic, whose death in 1898, as Bernard Shaw put it, was "a sort of sealing with his blood of the contemptuous disbelief in and dislike of doctors he had bitterly expressed in his books."[29] Nor was Frederic alone, and many doctors, too, appreciated his dislike of their profession. Though they did not, of course, opt for quackery, they nevertheless realized that man can no more live by science than he can live by bread alone.[30] For the rest, however, medicine had become so dizzy with success that Wassermann felt free to declare that "we are now in a position to diagnose and prescribe cures by the mere examination of a patient's body fluids and secretions without having to see the patient himself."[31] Similarly, the Parisian neurologist Binet-Sanglé produced "incontrovertible evidence" that the prophet Samuel had suffered from cerebral degeneration.[32]

It was against this background that a new stage in the history of medical psychology was reached at the turn of the century, so new that Zilboorg, its historian, has called it a revolution.[33] The proceedings of the first world congress of psychiatrists held in 1900 give us no more than the vaguest account of this development. The change centered, in fact, around two men, Kraepelin and Freud, who though both born in 1856 nevertheless symbolized two worlds apart. In the sixth edition (1899) of his *Compendium der Psychiatrie*, first published in 1883 and later expanded into a textbook, Emil Kraepelin explained his system at length. It was still filled with the great nineteenth-century conception of mental diseases and its author was much more concerned with their classification into curable and incurable types than with the individual patient and his suffering. Not for him the personal, romantic or metaphysical approach to human madness; all mental "abnormality" was the direct result of brain disorders and, for the rest, he was certain of his distinction between what constitutes normal and abnormal behaviour. Every age has its own certainties which

363

it accepts without question, and its passing away in general, and in psychiatry in particular, can generally be traced back to the shaking of just these certainties. Kraepelin's certainty was that mental diseases could be clearly described and that they followed a set course. But the very clarity of his system contained the germs of its destruction; its benefits had been bought at too high a price: an oversimplification of human reality, by virtue of which the human personality was obscured by the very science whose aim it was to restore it to health. But to leave it at that would be another oversimplification. For the mere distinction of mental disease from sin led to a radical improvement in the treatment of people who had previously been likened to criminals or labeled as "lost souls." Even the most one-sided scientific approach was better than superstition, and sedatives a great advance over exorcisms and straitjackets.

But the times were changing. And however often Kraepelin's classical textbook may have had to be reprinted, new trends were busily undermining its central message. In the seventies, Heinrich Schüle's plea that the psychiatrist had far better consider sick individuals than sick brains or glands,[34] had still fallen on deaf ears, and so had Samuel Butler's profound remark that we cannot reason with our cells because they know so much more than we do.[35] But by 1894 Eduard Reich, the pioneer of social medicine, already felt free to speak of the immaterial causes of illness.[36] At about the same time Paul Möbius, who called himself a *dégénéré supérieur*, was causing something of a sensation with his *pathographies* of great men and his protests against the abuses of depersonalized psychology, while Gruhle described the doctrines of the leading school of psychiatry as "brain mythology." The anti-personal bias of that school was also adopted by numerous writers who were not afraid of looking squarely at the *bête humaine;* their exaggerated fears of romantic interpretations led to the emergence of neo-romanticism; and their revulsion from metaphysics produced a Nietzsche — three manifestations of a single determination to depict man as he was really thought to be.

All this must be borne in mind by anyone anxious to discover how Kraepelin's "clarities" turned into Freud's "obscurities" — all this, and also the fact that, oddly enough, the material conception of mental disease contained germs of the older view that man's immortal and God-given soul could not possibly be sick; if anything was amiss with it, the fault must necessarily lie with the body, that "foul sac" in which the soul was imprisoned.[37] Freud — and this was probably his greatest feat — was free of even *this* delusion. It was in any case Freud and Breuer who turned clinical psychopathology into a respectable branch of medicine by making the causes, symptoms, and treatment of mental diseases the subjects of thorough investigations — the fact that they used hypnosis and later analysis to achieve these ends need not concern us here. The word "psychotherapy", first used by P. Dubois in 1903, became common usage within a year. The great process of secularization, begun soon after the Middle Ages, was proceeding apace.

Of Freud it has also been said that his interest in the individual prevented him from dwelling on the environmental factors, with the result that he went astray whenever, in later years, he discussed the social implications of his psychological theories. Like so many such sayings, this is no more than a half-truth. For though Freud's doctrine did make the repression of individual human instincts the central cause of neuroses and psychoses, he was quick to point out that such repression was the direct result of social taboos. In other words, he was anything but blind to the nexus between mental disease and society.

The appreciation of this nexus was also responsible for the emergence, at the turn of the century, of a third great medical current, by the side of the purely somatic and the psychosomatic: that of social medicine, to which we shall be devoting the rest of this chapter. Much as society and the state had begun to penetrate each other, so had society and science. The primary cause was no doubt the fact that society badly needed the aid of science, which met that need willingly or otherwise, and having once met it began to influence society in turn, and most profoundly so. The repercussions were particularly marked in the field of public health — while the presence of sewers and piped water used to cause interested comment in the past, such comment was now reserved for their absence. Throughout western Europe housing and health were increasingly covered by stringent regulations; public wash-houses and baths became commonplace institutions, and so did municipal refuse-disposal services.

While doctors as a whole played a largely advisory part in these developments, they took the lead when it came to the prevention and control of epidemics through the compulsory notification and isolation of suspected cases, the closure and disinfection of public places, and the immunization of potential victims.

In addition, doctors were increasingly placed in charge of public health education: they did yeoman work in teaching the public to identify and guard against the most common infectious diseases, particularly tuberculosis, that great scourge of the period, and the venereal diseases. The first T. B. center, in which diagnosis went hand in hand with education, was established by Sir Robert Philip in Edinburgh in 1887. Another was opened independently by Ernest Malroz in Liége in 1900, and a third by Albert Calmette in Lille in 1901.[38]

Medical education was also the subject of a host of pamphlets and books. Those written by Krafft-Ebbing, Havelock Ellis, Forel and Magnus Hirschfeld, founders of modern sexology, a subject to which we shall be returning in another connection, lifted the veil under which the Victorians had hidden sexuality. They inveighed against the fiction of the "ignorant young girl" and the prevailing double standard of morality. Even had this type of education had no other result than to make people suffering from venereal diseases less reluctant to consult their doctors, it would still have been wonderfully beneficial. The dangers of alcoholism, too, were, if anything, brought home still more forcibly by what can only be called a literary crusade.

Yet another form of medical education came from the famous Russian physician, Pirogov. After the cholera epidemic of 1891 to 1892, he gathered together a host of illustrations, posters, photographs and lantern slides and made them the basis of a series of public lectures. In 1910 he ran mobile exhibitions and also set up a health museum. One year later a national health week was held in England,[39] and a national health exhibition in Dresden was attended by five million visitors who could study the structure and function of the human body on photographs, models, and ingenious machines. In 1912 this exhibition became a permanent institution,[40] and with it mass health education was given a solid platform. From the outset, it pointed to the ultimate goal of social medicine, namely to preventive medicine, as it began to be called. While social medicine as such is concerned with the social causes and effects of diseases, preventive medicine tries to keep them at bay. In 1900 George Meyer gave an impressive example of its achievements when he wrote in a pamphlet that due to its contributions the mortality figures for Prussia had decreased by 70,000 within a quarter of a century.[41] This pamphlet was a sign of the times in yet another respect. "Social achievement" was still being identified with "economic achievement." The cult of efficiency that had come to distinguish the modern capitalist system from all previous economic systems was understandably at pains to reduce the losses in production caused by the illness, invalidism, and premature old age of workers, and this the more so as social legislation placed increasingly onerous financial burdens on the employers in the form of insurances. It was no accident that people began to speak of industrial medicine, what with the growing army of factory doctors and of special government inspectors who ensured that the safety laws were being applied. The first chair of social medicine was established in Berlin in

1902.[42] Though the employers' self-interest was still its mainspring, a factor contributing to the rise of preventive medicine was the increasing cost of medical services, and another was the growing conviction that the blessings of scientific and technical progress ought to be brought within everyone's reach.[43] Thus Gaetano Pieraccini, writing just five years after Meyer, struck a new note: according to this Florentine professor, the benefits of modern medicine should be made widely available to the working masses and its aims should be prevention rather than cure; moreover its efforts should be directed at the social, not the individual, organism.[44] Much the same views were put forward by Alfred Grotjahn, a great physician who attended Schmoller's lectures and later became a socialist. He was the first to take his doctorate with a thesis on social medicine, and he was one of the founders of the Gesellschaft für Soziale Medizin, Hygiene und Medizinalstatistik (Society for Social Medicine, Hygiene and Medical Statistics). The first edition of his *Soziale Pathologie* was published in 1911.[45]

True preventive medicine must begin with the child and it was not merely because people began to realize that children's diseases were different or followed a different course from those of adults that pediatrics developed into an independent branch of medicine during our period. In 1894 Otto Heubner of Berlin became its first professor; in 1911 Berlin was also the venue of the first international pediatrics congress. Although we shall return to the subject in the chapter devoted to child care, no survey of preventive medicine would be complete without some mention of the growing practice to provide extra medical care for expectant mothers. Pinard's Maternité Baudelocque was founded for that purpose in 1890; similar institutes were opened by Spencer in London in 1891 and by Ballantyne in Edinburgh in 1901.[46] The first baby care centers, those run by Comby, Variat, and Dufour, were also set up in the 1890s, followed soon afterwards by centers for pre-school age children.[48] School medical services were of even earlier provenance; according to Sand the first of these was founded in Brussels in 1874. Though they were still few and far between before 1914, children's hospitals (the first of which was opened at the beginning of the nineteenth century)[49] and school medical services were becoming increasingly common.[50] The famous Waldschule in Charlottenburg in Berlin was set up in 1904, and the first open-air school in one of London's poorer districts was opened in 1914, thus giving concrete expression to one of Rousseau's greatest dreams. All these endeavors would, however, have come to nothing had they not gone hand in hand with noticeable improvements in the building and equipment of hospitals and in the selection and education of nurses.

These developments, incidentally, were far from smooth, as we may gather from a lecture delivered by Dr. Aletrino on 17 November 1900[51] or from some of the realistic novels and short stories by the same author. Dr. Aletrino gave his lecture to Nosokomos, the Dutch society of professional nurses, founded on 30 May. The society published a journal by the same name and the early issues make it clearer than perhaps anything else how hard nurses had to fight for their elementary rights, and for the transformation of what used to be an unpaid "vocation" into a (badly paid) "occupation" — and this in relatively progressive Holland![52] In Germany things were no better; here student nurses received a monthly pay of from 10 to 30 marks, qualified nurses a monthly pay of from 31 to 50 marks, and sisters a monthly pay of from 62.50 marks, mere pittances even though nursing staff received free board and lodging, free laundry services and free medical care. The pay was all the more deplorable as their working day stretched from 6.00 A.M. to 9.00 P.M., with meal breaks that amounted to a total of one-and-half hours a day. Worse still, they were given just one day and one evening off every three weeks.[53]

If, at the end of this chapter, we look back at the development of medical science during the quarter century with which this book is concerned, we gain the impression of a succession of great triumphs, so dazzling that no words can do them justice. In probably no other sphere of human endeavor did the spectacular achievements capture mankind's imagination so strongly, and this not only because medical skills affect man so intimately but also because the advances in this field were indeed extraordinary. In a secularized society the doctor had to replace the clergyman as man's father confessor and spiritual guide. "The capable doctor is the hero of modern literature," wrote Brandes, "no doubt because he may be considered the embodiment of modern ideas in all their rigor."[54]

If there was anything that could still underpin the security of the European bourgeoisie then it was surely the new horizons medical progress had just opened up: the prospect of a life without illness, perhaps even without old age, if not without death. But just as systematically as it underpinned bourgeois security, so medical progress also helped to undermine it.

By that we do not mean that every new certainty must sooner or later conjure up new uncertainties as it opens up ever-larger tracts of unexplored reality, for that feeling is confined to a small circle of initiates. Nor do we mean that greater familiarity with bacteria, microbes, and viruses caused the bourgeoisie to suffer from a kind of parasitophobia that turned every kiss into an act of daring and every sip from a cup of tea, let alone the communal cup at Holy Communion, into a perilous adventure. We are not even thinking of the impression spread by modern medicine that life is a simple chemical process, a view that gave rise to a secularized form of mysticism, with unfortunate repercussions not only in literature and art but also in medicine itself.[55]

No, we are thinking of the two uncertainties to which the European bourgeoisie had begun to succumb even before 1914, due on the one hand to the growing power of the working class which had taken the bourgeoisie completely by surprise, and on the other hand to the awakening of the people of Asia, exemplified by the rise of Japan. The balance of power had clearly been tilted and the achievements of medicine in general and social and preventive medicine in particular benefited its two opponents as much as they benefited the European bourgeoisie that had made them possible in the first place. Thus those who looked on every extension of the suffrage as just another inroad into sacred privileges must have been equally appalled by the decline in infant mortality, though few of them were bold enough to voice that opinion. Similarly, those who went in fear of the "yellow peril" because they considered European domination a guarantee of what to them was the only possible form of civilization, must have shuddered at the thought that the latest discoveries in bacteriology and the new health measures did anything but contain that peril. Moreover, the idea of the welfare state was already in the air and caused the bourgeoisie fresh shudders. What had looked so beautiful *in vitro* had turned into a monster when it was inspected *in vivo*.

CHAPTER XXV

WEAL AND WEALTH

It was on April 17, 1900 that Gustav Cohn finished a study that was soon afterwards to hold a conspicuous place in what was popularly called *Schmollers Jahrbuch* (Schmoller's Year Book). Thanks to the breadth of his philosophical outlook and his brilliant style, Cohn, who was sixty and had been professor of economics in Göttingen for sixteen years, had become the best economic essayist of his day.[1] The subject of his latest study was: "Ethics and Reaction in Economics."[2] He had clearly struck a new note, for at the time it was anything but fashionable to link the down-to-earth teachings of economics with the more ethereal speculations of ethics. Worse still he described the untrammeled expansion of German industry and commerce as an essentially reactionary phenomenon.

However Cohn was not entirely alone in his views. That same year Georg von Mayr, the statistician and systematist, published a book on moral obligation in economic life,[3] and the pugnacious Adolf Wagner was propounding similar ideas from the heights of his chair at Berlin University. At the time, Wagner was just finishing the last part of his monumental *Finanzwissenschaft* (Financial Science), a branch of economics that included Cohn among its founders. Part of that work was later translated by Veblen.[4] By far the greatest number of leading economists, however, took quite the opposite view, especially Werner Sombart, then thirty-seven years old, and the chief butt of the older Cohn's scorn. For three years earlier Sombart had warned against the dangers of ethical speculation in economics, which he called a reactionary phenomenon.[5] He had even repeated that view at a three-day meeting of the Society for Social Policy held in Breslau in September 1899.[6] "We must simply accept," he said on that occasion, "those organizational forms of economic life" — he was dealing with the burning question of the rise of department stores and the threat they posed to small shopkeepers — "that are the most efficient, and for the rest we can be as moral as we like. But to be moral at the expense of economic progress is the beginning of the end of civilization."[7]

The case was all the more complicated because the young and impetuous Sombart based his rejection of the ethical approach on no less an authority than Marx, and this with some justification for, at the time, Marx's early writings had not yet been rediscovered, and his doctrine of scientific socialism was generally identified with determinism. For all that, Sombart could easily have discovered strong ethical impulses in the work of one to whom the exploitation of man by man was the very linch-pin of all economic, social and political behavior in a capitalist society. Cohn, for his part argued that all sound social legislation must be based on an ethical ideal: the implementation of man's full humanity, if nec-essary at the expense of the maximization of productivity. And it was understandable that he should have confronted his adversary with the writings of F. A. Lange, whose history of materialism was still being widely read. For though Lange, too, was an admirer of Marx, sympa-thized with the aspirations of social democracy, and looked down on the academic socialists, he was not generally identified with the ethical cur-rent. It was equally understandable that Cohn should have asked Sombart why it was that, even while calling for protective labor legislation,[8] he should frown on the protection of underprivileged sections of the pop-ulation in general.

What made these discussions so important and at the same time so terribly complex was the difficult problem of assessing the scientific validity of the various premises on which they were based. For ultimately what was at stake was the crucial question of whether or not economics was a true science, i.e., whether or not its methods were objective. In the first article Max Weber published in 1904 in his and Sombart's *Archiv*, he examined the objectivity of socio-scientific and socio-political ideas,[9] and tried to save objectivity precisely by stressing their unavoidable subjective element. That article was largely inspired by the kind of arguments we have just been describing and at the same time provided a solution to them, albeit a temporary one.

From the stir this clash of opinions caused at the time, the reader may wrongly conclude that it played a paramount role in the development of economics at the turn of the century. In fact, another clash takes up very much more space in most textbooks devoted to the history of economics. This was the notorious methodological struggle which began in the 1880s and was still going on in 1900. If we nevertheless started this chapter with the moral question, we did so because, seen in socio-historical per-spective, the "methodological struggle" was essentially of a piece with the "ethical." Ritzel, one of its historians, gave his paper on that struggle the telling title of *Schmoller versus Menger*.[10]

By mentioning this controversy, we seem to have abandoned our principle of not referring back beyond 1889. This is not, in fact, the case, for Carl Menger, the founder of the Austrian school, may have opened the discussion in 1883 and 1884, but his arguments only became important when Wieser, his successor in Vienna, and Böhm-Bawerk entered the lists on Menger's behalf; in 1889, even so shrewd an observer as Sombart still failed to appreciate Wieser's importance.[11] Brinkmann, who has stressed this fact in his book on Schmoller, also examined the most significant contribution of the Austrian school — the subjective theory of value — and concluded that, at the time, Marxism held much greater sway in the economically sophisticated circles of Austria than it did in the national-liberal climate of Germany.[12] He based that view largely on an Austrian history of literature, and the sections devoted to Richard Kralik and Hermann Bahr in particular.[13]

That a rejection of Marxism was at the root of Menger's doctrine was also the opinion of Bukharin, the "veteran Bolshevik," who took part in the 1905 revolution while still a schoolboy, later studied under Böhm-Bawerk, became the leading Bolshevik economic theorist and was ultimately crushed under Stalin's steamroller. In 1919 he put forward a socio-historical interpretation of the subjective theory of values: he called it an intellectual product of the international rentier class.[14] When Stark rejected that interpretation on the grounds that the subjective theory had made its entry a quarter of a century before the emergence of the rentier class, he conveniently forgot that, on the socio-historical plane, what matters is not so much the date of the origin of a theory as its general adoption which, in the event, did not come until shortly before 1900,[15] even according to Spann, who referred his readers to Rudolf Stammler's *Wirtschaft und Recht* (Economics and Law) which appeared in 1896.[16] This was also the conclusion of a recent study by Braeuer, who observed that Menger considered Ricardo's — and Marx's — objective theory of value, when applied to profits, ground rent, and dividends, "an implicit and quite inadmissible attack on property and one that introduced insurmountable difficulties."[17] Hence the attention the Austrian school paid to individual psychological behaviour: that school was, in fact, much more concerned with consumption than with production.

The belief that Menger's pen was ultimately guided by his dislike of Marxism gains further credence when one asks oneself whether his adversary, Schmoller, was not motivated in the same way. If he was, as he seems to have been, then even Brinkmann's astonishing and indeed quite unacceptable distinction between the Austrian and German attitudes can be dropped: in the methodological struggle, it was their common fear of socialism which impelled both parties to deviate from classical economics, albeit in fundamentally different ways. For the rest, the ethical, academic socialists of the younger historical school were as anti-socialist as the marginalists and mathematicians Schnat and Wagner, and as anti-Marxist as Menger and Walras. Léon Walras of Lausanne, just like Menger of Vienna, adopted the subjective theory of value and, moreover, introduced the theory of equilibrium and the mathematical method into economics long before our period. Like Menger, he did not receive recognition until much later and even then it came from abroad. By that time he was seventy-five and it was 1909,[18] too late to wipe out the bitter ending of his autobiography.

The anti-Marxism of the academic socialists took quite a different form: they suited Bismarck's tactics to their own purpose. They, too, were trying to take the wind out of socialists' sails by meeting them halfway or even quarter-way. Thus Schmoller favored the idea of social justice, as Herkner, another academic socialist and Schmoller's successor to the presidency of the *Verein für Sozialpolitik* made clear in his memorial address.[19] According to Ritzel, moreover, Schmoller's whole work was based on the appreciation of social need. Even so, all these "ethicists" must be counted among the intellectual bodyguard of Kaiser Wilhelm, no matter how great the differences between them.

That the "ethical" current in economics was not the expression of a mere whim but an inevitable reaction to the social situation in Europe as a whole is proved by the fact that it also made itself felt outside Germany and Austria, and again took the form of a rejection of Marxism. There was the difference, however, that the atmosphere in the rest of Europe was slightly more liberal; while no academic economist in Germany or Austria could have professed socialism and retained his chair, other countries were more tolerant, though socialist professors were still exceptional. One such exception was Frank van der Goes, who was appointed a lecturer in economics at the University of Amsterdam in 1900, not without opposition, and had very little joy of his post.

In Belgium it was the venerable Laveleye, who, until his death in 1892 at the age of seventy, led the "ethical" school. He was certainly no socialist, for he believed in the value of private initiative, though he consistently upheld the right of the state to intervene where and whenever the private interest ran counter to that of the community. Moreover, he argued that political equality was quite meaningless without economic equality and accordingly considered the fair distribution of earthly goods a *sine qua non* of healthy democratic life. Such less well-known figures as Ansiaux, Mahaim, and Vaxweiler followed in his footsteps. In Italy Vito Cusumano, a professor at the Palermo Technical Institute (he died in

1908) disseminated the ideas of his teacher, Adolf Wagner, but laid greater stress than most academic socialists on the fact that the scope of social legislation was restricted by the employers' need to maximize the productivity of their industries. In his book on wage theory, published in 1900, Ricca Salerno, another Italian economist, gave a detailed historical analysis of the transition from strict state neutrality to increasing state intervention. Mention should also be made of Professor Cossa of Pavia, who was greatly influenced by the older historical school and particularly by Stein and Roscher, [21] and who brought economic history to Italy. He himself did not live to see the century out, but in 1900 the leading academic posts in economic history were held by his pupils Vivante, Ferraris, and Supino.

In Britain it was T. E. C. Leslie who, as early as 1876, published the school's manifesto. He was followed by Ashley, Rogers, and Ingram, and the school became so successful that according to Ingram, England was second only to Germany in the field of economic history. [21]

French economists did not develop a "historical school" of their own, and the only French book on the subject mentioned by Gonnard is that of the Frenchified Dutch anarchist, Christaan Cornellissen. However, economic individualism did not go unchallenged in France — far from it. Apart from the socialists, there were many other Frenchmen to question this facet of classical economics, though the French movement as a whole was inspired by philosophical rather than historical ideas. Gaëtan Pirou has described this development in his concise and instructive book on economic doctrines in France since 1870. [23] In it, he examined socialist as well as individualist doctrines, distinguishing an extreme and a temperate current in the second, and finally listing all doctrines based on an intermediate approach. And it was the latter and the temperate individualist current that concern us most for, at the end of the day, the historical school in the rest of Europe, too, took its stand somewhere between individualism and socialism. To accommodate ethics in this system was something French economists did not find difficult, the less so as the socialists among them had a long ethical tradition. Proudhon had even wanted to base all human certainty on man's inherent sense of justice. Malon, too, believed that socialism was as much a moral tenet as it was an economic conception, a view he expressed most forcefully in his *Le Socialisme intégral* of 1890. In his thesis on the origins of German state socialism (1897) Charles Andler, for his part, rejected the term "scientific socialism" out of hand: people become socialists for emotional reasons, and this was also the gist of a lecture he delivered in 1911. [24] To the young Edouard Berth things seemed different, although not essentially so. Thus he concluded his *Dialogues socialistes* of 1901 — probably his most re-

374

markable book[25] — with the observation that true Marxism, far from doing away with morality, helps to underpin it. And this was also the view of Jaurès, who had learned what he could from his three predecessors and who more than once (not least in his 1895 debate with Paul Lafargue, Marx's son-in-law)[26] went out of his way to stress the role of idealism in the historical conception. All four of these men, no matter how far they may have strayed from the Catholic Church, would presumably have acknowledged their debt to its moral doctrine. And what was true of them, was true *a fortiori* of the bourgeois economists. Even those whom Pirou ranged among the extreme individualists at no time dismissed the moral factor from their arguments. Thus when Molinari, who from 1881 to 1909 was editor-in-chief of the *Journal des Economistes*, searched for the causes of the modern social crisis, he found one of them in the general flagging of the moral impulse.[27] In 1896 his successor and pupil Yves Guyot wrote an article in *La Nouvelle Revue* and it was characteristic of him that he chose as his subject the "morality of competition."[28] And when Pirou placed Leroy Beaulieu, who had been writing the leading article in the weekly *Economiste Français* for close on half a century and had thus become an institution, among the temperate individualists, he did so because Beaulieu, almost despite himself, placed the national interest, or what he considered as such, above individual gain. While it is only be stretching the term to its limit that this kind of approach can be called "temperate individualism," there were others who went so far in their "temperance" as to render that term completely meaningless. One who did so was Charles Renouvier, not so much by virtue of his Kantian and Humean philosophy, as because of his social ideas, though the two were, of course, closely linked.[29] Renouvier was the founder of personalism, and his book on that subject, which was also his last, appeared in 1903, the year he died. In all his writings he was quick to proclaim his moral convictions. No wonder then that he called his *Science de la morale* his most important book, or that his wage theory was rooted much more strongly in ethics than in economics. To implement justice even while respecting the individual[30] was the guiding thread of all his thoughts. For his disciples Henri Michel and P. Archambault, too, "individualism" stood more for the protection of the economically underprivileged than for the endorsement of the economic self-seeking of powerful individuals. In his *Essai sur l'individualisme*, which appeared in 1913, Archambault even accepted the paradoxical conclusion that the individual has the right to forfeit all his rights when justice or supra-individual necessity is at stake.[31] And in his 1896 thesis, *L'Idée de l'état*, Michel declared that he had discovered to his astonishment — and to his delight — that in the view of

375

the eighteenth-century "individualist" Montesquieu it behooved the state to assure all its citizens of a dignified existence.[31] Whether or not Bouglé was right to claim that Michel did more than anyone else in his day to effect a fusion between the individualist and the socialist currents[33] is something we prefer to leave an open question, but no one can doubt that he aimed at achieving just that.

From Michel and Archambault it was but a small step to solidarism. Léon Bourgeois was the first to take it in his *Solidarité*, published one year after Michel's thesis, and in his *Essai d'une philosophie de solidarité* which appeared five years later.[34] He distinguished solidarity as a fact from solidarity as a norm and tried to apply the norm to his complex political and social work of statesman and legislator. He did not live long enough to see the gradual implementation of his solidarist thesis: that society gave as much to every one of its members as it receives in return.

As the last in our long series of intermediate figures we shall mention Maurice Bourguin. Of his writings, which have rightly been called the finest products of French economic thought in our period,[35] the most important was *Les Systèmes socialistes et l'évolution économique*, which was published in 1904. In a polemic of 1908[36] he himself summarized its main historical conclusion: social policies must aim at the free unfolding of the personality through economic democracy, free association and protective legislation. "To fall short of this aim is to ignore the rise of the popular masses in a civilized and democratic society; to go beyond it is to pursue a mirage." These were also the intermediate aims of "Social Democracy," a group founded in 1905, and which, as Pirou has pointed out,[37] was more directly inspired by Bergsonism and syndicalism than by the latest economic doctrines. This group conjures up the name of Georges Sorel, to whom violence was a creative force capable of establishing the new order of modern, productive, man. However, many other strands, too, ran between this type of "social radicalism" and what Charles Gide in 1890 called the "new school": new because it preferred the banner of solidarity to the liberal, Catholic, and socialist banners of freedom, authority, and equality.[38] Much as biology became increasingly interested in the "social" interdependence of lower animals, so sociology increasingly delved into the same phenomenon on the human plane: Emile Durkheim, the most famous sociologist of his day, also spoke of "organic solidarity" in his moral rather than economic studies of the ever-increasing division of labor. Philosophy, in the person of Alfred Fouillée, declared at about the same time that solidarity and individualism developed *pari passu*. Finally, there were even links between the solidarity movement and jurisprudence: no summary of the work of Léon Duguit, however short, can fail to mention that, for all his positivism, he considered the claims of social solidarity the source of all objective laws.

Just as in France, so elsewhere, too, the various disciplines overlapped to produce a kind of crystal structure in continuous motion. Thus the methodological conflict, and especially the German disputes about a value-free science of economics, cannot be grasped without the contributions of the Neo-Kantians or the idealist positivism of Vaihinger and his "as if" philosophy. Spencer, too, greatly influenced the economic thought, not only of Marshall and other economists in England, but also of Walras and Pareto, who, at least in the early stages of their work, were as indebted to him as they were to Comte and Cournot.[39] And there were many other examples as well; indeed, there was a spate of "reciprocal contacts" which can only be brought out in full by a detailed study of every one of the economists concerned.

Although the invasion of the house of classical economics by modern philosophical, sociological, and psychological currents, by ethicism and statism, by objectivism and mathematics did not affect the arrangement of the furniture, the simultaneous influence of such contemporary currents as dynamism and holism did just that. For while we can agree with Sombart[40] that the first four "heresies" did not yet run counter to classical economics inasmuch as they, too, made the discovery of laws their ultimate goal, the last two produced laws so "unorthodox" that their disciples could no longer be described as rebels within the "church" but only as complete outsiders.

One such disciple was Joseph Schumpeter, who made the dynamics of economic life the crux of his new theory of interest. According to him, it was the application of new discoveries that earned the creative entrepreneur a surplus over his costs from which he could repay the interest on the capital he had borrowed. In a static or semi-static society, there could be neither profit nor interest.[41] Schumpeter published this discovery in his *Theorie der wirtschaftlichen Entwicklung* (Theory of Economic Development), which did not appear until 1912 and which he defended a year later against Böhm-Bawerk's attacks.[42] He himself, however, dated his discovery back to 1905,[43] and it was with some justice that he said in the preface to the Japanese edition that his dynamic conception was likely to throw fresh light on the workings of capitalism. In particular it could explain a number of phenomena more satisfactorily than the theories of Walras or Marshall.[44]

The same blurring of the boundaries of classical economics that we find in Schumpeter (who made the extra-economic concept of "technology" his cornerstone and who was, not by chance, more renowned as a sociologist than as an economist) can also be found in the writings of many other contemporary economists. Thus few readers of Schmoller's *Grundriss der allgemeinen Volkswirtschaftslehre* (Outline of General Economic Theory), the first edition of which appeared in 1900, will be able to tell with certainty whether the author was an economist or a sociologist. Such men as Philippovich or Brentano were even more difficult to place. Both defended the Austrian theory of value — they lectured in Vienna for some time — but both nevertheless had close ties with the academic socialists and may be called "social reformers." The blurring of the boundaries was, of course, even more apparent with such holistic or "integral" economists as Pareto and Spann.

Vilfredo Pareto was forty-five in 1893 when he was called to Lausanne as Walras's successor, having devoted much of his earlier life to mathematics and physics, and having earned his living as a railway and mining engineer and as an entrepreneur. It is probably not too far-fetched to consider his early life as the key to his integralism. For although he started his economic career as a pupil of Walras, whose positivism he accepted and whose theory of equilibrium and mathematical method he extended, he soon realized that the science of economics cannot be self-sufficient: economic facts are inseparably bound up with social facts.[45] His first economic work of importance, the *Manuale di economia politica* (1906), with its sub-title "Introduction to Social Science", already pointed the way, and hence it is not surprising that his second great work should have been a general sociology, and that it should have been so crucial to the understanding of his *Manuale* that Suranyi-Unger discussed the second before the first.[46] And it was integralism, finally, that earned Pareto the honorary title of "father of modern economics", a title which, according to his compatriot Demaria, was bestowed on him almost unanimously.[47]

Othmar Spann was an integralist, or a universalist as he himself called it, from the very start; in his *Haupttheorien der Volkswirtschaftslehre* (Main Theories of Political Economy), he called the conflict between individualism and universalism the basic problem of sociology. That book was full of praise for the romantics, particularly Adam Müller, and full of scorn for the classics and anyone else who could be called an individualist; not even Marx escaped Spann's censure. The history of his book was highly instructive, too. Its author was twenty-five in 1903, when he produced the first draft, but it was not until 1910 that he was able to publish it. By 1919 the fifth edition had appeared, and since then reprints have followed one another in ever quicker succession: in 1931 the twenty-first edition came off the presses and the total sales had passed the 100,000 mark.[48] For all that, it is open to question whether Spann did much more than simplify the ideas of Gottl, his less well-known teacher at the Brno Technical High School.[49] Gottl was much more subtle, in any case, and anyone interested in the transformation of nineteenth-century economic theory can hardly do better than peruse his *Wirtschaft als Leben* (Economy as Life).[50] Despite his rugged independence, he had strong intellectual bonds with Rickert, Windelband, Dilthey, and above all with Max Weber. Thus Weber's attempts to come to grips with socio-scientific methodology in his *Roscher and Knies* followed Gottl's publication of two essays, subsequently re-issued under the title of *Herrschaft des Wortes* (The Reign of the Word). The first of these two essays, the *Ueber die Grundbegriffe der Nationalökonomie* (On the Basic Concepts of Political Economy), had originally been presented as a "Habilitationsschrift" — an essay written on the admission of an academic teacher into the faculty — and the second had been delivered as a lecture in Heidelberg that same month.[51] In these two essays Gottl dismissed — alas, rather verbosely — quite a few nineteenth century dogmas as so many ill-fitting children's shoes.[52]

But when all is said and done, science, however rigorous, and scholarship, however extensive, are but two mirrors of life. That is why we shall conclude our account of the decline of classical economics and the emergence on its ruins of new ideas not with the German Gottl, renowned for his theoretical approach, but with the Englishman J. A. Hobson, who was anything but remote from life and whose work clearly showed that modern economic ideas were reflections of changes in the economic process.

Hobson's name does not figure among those of the greatest. It appears neither among the twelve most important late nineteenth-century economists selected by Schumpeter[53] nor among the twenty chosen by Spiegel, though Spiegel does mention him as the author of a book on Henry George.[54] However, Hobson was more human than most of the rest and had the courage of his heterodox convictions: *Confessions of an Economic Heretic* was the title of his modest autobiography.[55] And we also choose him in preference to Gottl because he had a keen ethical sensibility, a holistic perception, and a dynamic approach. If there was one man who was the living embodiment of Sombart's "cognitive economics"[56] then it was surely Hobson, though, good Englishman that he was, he may not even have heard of Sombart's classification of economics.

Hobson became a rebel very early on in his career. He was not yet thirty when he wrote his *Physiology of Industry* (1889) in which he already propounded his highly unorthodox theory of savings. Five years

379

later he published his *Evolution of Modern Capitalism*, which would have made him famous had his critics but known what the history of economics held in store for them. In that book, he described monopolies, trusts, and crises not as oddities but as irreversible trends of a type of capitalism that was well on the way to imperialism. His own *Imperialism* (1902) examined that development in closer detail, and, characteristically, it, too, was not the result of mere theoretical speculation. He contributed an article by the same title to the *Contemporary Review* of March 1899, and it was thanks to this article that the *Manchester Guardian* sent him as war correspondent to South Africa, where he could study the phenomenon at close quarters. He concluded that imperialism was the result not of capitalism as such, but of some of its flaws.[57] We cannot tell whether Rosa Luxemburg[58] and Hilferding[59] were familiar with Hobson's work, though it would certainly have stood Luxemburg in good stead when she developed her theory of monopoly capitalism and its need for expansion, and Hilferding for his theory of the fusion of industrial with financial capital. Just as uncertain is his influence on two other socialist "classics", namely Parvus's *Die Kolonialpolitik und der Zusammenbruch* (Colonial Policy and the Collapse) and Kautsky's *Kolonialpolitik*, both of which appeared in 1907. Lenin, by contrast, confessed his indebtedness to Hobson in his own book on imperialism.[60] Hobson did, in any case, not exaggerate in his *Confessions* when he claimed that his early work contained all his later deviations from economic orthodoxy.[61] He himself described these deviations as "human" interpretations of the process of production and consumption and consequently as critiques of liberal laissez-faire policies. And he, indeed, gave a "human" twist to the theory of marginal utility: to him "final utility" was not at all the "final futility" it seemed to the Socialist Hyndman: he accepted it but stripped it of its scientific justification by arguing that marginal utility was based on irrational, not rational, choices, and hence an arbitrary and unpredictable factor. To him, the industrial wizard was a creative artist rather than someone good with figures.[63] Human, too, was his attribution of crises to underconsumption, not overproduction, and his heretical theory of supply and demand, propounded shortly before the turn of the century.[63] According to that theory, there is a gap between the lowest wage the worker is prepared to accept and the highest wage the employer is prepared to pay, and that gap is not determined by supply and demand but by the relative position of the two contenders on the labor market. Now, since the position of the employer is always the stronger, the wages he actually pays out leave him with an "extorted profit." Flux hastened to challenge this interpretation with views close to Marshall's.[64] Hobson, for his part, developed his own conception further, and in 1900 declared that it was the basis of all price-fixing.[65] Most profits were based on monopolistic advantages; the part that fell to the inventive or dynamic leader of industry was insignificant by comparison. Hence the lion's share ought to be taxed all the more heavily.[66]

Isolated though his many heresies rendered him, Hobson was by no means a voice crying in the wilderness, nor did he consider himself to be one. His tone was never bitter, even when the many other books he wrote before 1914 were left on the shelf, and he was typically English even in his lack of resentment. He did not have the ear of his contemporaries, nor did he have an academic position. And yet he was only speaking for a growing movement when he proposed subordinating economics to the common weal rather than to the accumulation of wealth, or when he concluded his book on modern capitalism with a calm but forceful plea for the collectivization of all those industries that provide for man's daily needs. Here the influence of socialism was unmistakable. And yet his tune did not harmonize with the Marxist chorus, for he sang it in quite a different key. To begin with, some of his teachers had been orthodox economists; Marshall, in particular, was not nearly as remote from him as may appear on superficial examination. For though Marshall was rightly famed for his rigorous mathematical approach, he was, in fact, drawn to economics in the 1860s, when he went visiting the slums and "looked into the face of the poorest." And even the mature Marshall was critical enough of the classics to assert that economic theory as such is not a set of concrete truths but merely one instrument for their discovery. Pigou was even closer to Hobson, as his *Wealth and Welfare* made abundantly clear.[67] In it, he quoted Hobson five times, and Hobson for his part quoted Pigou in his defense of state planning and state control which he published as an appendix to his autobiography.[68] He also learned from such men as Tarde, Henry George, Veblen, and especially from Ruskin who taught him to appreciate the importance of aesthetics in industrial production. In his autobiography he also mentions such men as J. M. Robertson and Bradlaugh, two republicans and free thinkers associated with the *National Reformer*; William Clarke, Herbert Samuel, Charles Trevelyan, and Ramsay MacDonald, with whom he edited *The Progressive Review* (from 1896 to 1898); and J. H. Muirhead and Bernard Bosanquet of the London Ethical Society. He was, moreover, a member of the Fabian Society until he turned his back on the Fabians for their failure to denounce the Boer War. In short, he lived in the small world — for that was what it was — of the English radicals who, in their turn, lived with the illusion that man was an honest and moral being at heart:

381

an illusion that seemed justified in their day more than perhaps in any other, but that remained an illusion for all that. This became clear in 1914, a year which for that reason alone constitutes a watershed.

All in all, the history of economics in our period forms a motley and confused picture reminiscent of some Impressionist paintings — and not of the best of them, either. But that is not the spectator's fault, for there was method in this chaos. No single old dogma had been left unchallenged, no old method unquestioned; there was a struggle on all fronts. Sartorius saw economics despised and respected all at once: despised because there were as many opinions as there were economists; respected because the demand for trained economists was becoming keen; and he called this one of the many contradictions with which the years 1890 to 1914 were beset. He concluded his summary of the intellectual movement in this period with the observation that though technology was riding high in all the arts and sciences, that lack of common conception and purpose robbed it of vital power.[69] And he was speaking about Germany alone. Sombart, too, writing in 1912, deplored the general uncertainty caused by the market economy,[70] as did a great many less encyclopedic minds in the economists' camp: the fact that periodic crises were undermining the very foundations of capitalism was increasingly being brought home at the turn of the century, and not by Marxists alone. Worse still, the intervals between successive crises seemed to decrease from ten or eleven years to seven or even less. Thus the crisis of 1890–1893 was followed by that of 1900–1902, which was followed by the crisis of 1907–1908 from which no country was spared.[71] True, the subject of economic crises had been attracting the attention of economists ever since the Napoleonic wars, so much so that in 1895 Bergmann was able to write a whole history of crisis-theories,[72] but the output of such theories was perceptibly stepped up under the pressure of the crises of 1900 and 1907.[73] Thus the first great work by the Russian economist Tugan-Baranovski (1894) was devoted to the British crisis, but by the time it became known in the West in Schapiro's French translation,[74] Aftalion, writing in 1911,[75] had already cast fresh light on the problem, taking much the same line as another Russian — Bunatyan. In Germany it was Spiethoff, in Sweden Cassel, and in Belgium Ansiaux who dealt with the crisis phenomenon, and that list could be greatly extended. Pohle, too, mentioned a crisis in 1911, but he was referring to the crisis within economics. This time he selected the academic socialists for special criticism, and called for the total expulsion of politics from economic science. But he made his own cause highly suspect when he based his plea for a value-free science of economics on Treitschke,[76]

382

a man who was much more of a political theorist than an economist. In any case Herkner was quick to retort that covert value judgments are much more dangerous than overt ones.[77] In short, a crisis was raging in economics, much as it raged without.

This was, indeed, understandable. Economics does not become a natural science merely by pressing its claims to that exalted position, the less so when most economists are at loggerheads with one another. In the preface to his *Finanzkapital* (Finance Capital), Hilferding declared that the mystical fog surrounding capital in general becomes totally impenetrable when it reaches finance capital and its vagaries.[78] Economics itself seemed to have grown no less impenetrable. It behaved as if it were an independent discipline, and that was how most economists saw it. Yet economics is of necessity a reflection of social life. If the latter becomes confused, for instance because one class no longer *wants* to put up with the prevailing state of affairs and the other *can* no longer maintain it, then even the science devoted to their interaction is bound to burst at the seams. For every society has the science it deserves — just one more case of supply and demand. What society demands, science supplies; and if society presses conflicting claims, science cannot but offer contradictory solutions. To the contemporary observer the result is utter confusion; to the historian it is this very confusion which illuminates the scene.

CHAPTER XXVI

WITH NEITHER BLINDFOLD NOR SWORD

On August 17, 1900 Maurice Hauriou celebrated his forty-fifth birthday.
This great jurist had reached the middle point of his career: for more
than twenty years he had been professor at Toulouse, and he was to
remain at that post for as many years more. It was at about this time
that he recorded his opinion of a decision the *Conseil d'Etat* had taken
on January 13, 1899. That decision concerned the Lepreux case,[1] and
it is thanks to Hauriou's more celebrated colleague, Duguit, that we
can recall it here.[2] In the Lepreux case the plaintiff, who had been hit
in both eyes and blinded while watching a shooting display at the fair
at Maison-Alfort in the Seine Department on August 8, 1886, was seeking
damages from the state. The *Conseil d'Etat* found against him and it
was to their decision that Hauriou had objected in his now famous opinion. True, not even he held the state responsible for all such accidents,
but he contended that it was responsible in this particular case because
the police had given permission for the shooting display and ought to have
ensured the spectators' safety. This was an entirely novel idea, and it
was not until ten years later that the state adopted it by awarding damages
to one Pluchard, whose leg was broken when he was accidentally knocked
down by a detective pursuing a suspect.[3]

Hauriou's opinion was all the more remarkable because, unlike Duguit,
he was not intent upon revolutionizing jurisprudence. As a staunch Catholic he was, in fact, a traditionalist and a disciple of Tarde, and as such
he advocated the curtailment of the powers of, and acceptance of greater
responsibility by, the state for the sake of the individual, not of society.
Tarde himself had declared as early as 1892 that he could not share the
growing enthusiasm for complete national independence, which merely
encouraged the various states to arm themselves to the teeth, a vicious
spiral that was bound to lead to ever higher taxes and to impose many
other burdens on the citizen, whose liberties would consequently be
whittled away. And he also pointed to the paradox that the very people
who welcomed the expropriation of private wealth for the general good

should frown upon the "expropriation" of the national state for the good of Europe at large.[4]

Much more original and radical than Hauriou was Léon Duguit, whom we have already mentioned. Though he spent most of his academic life as a professor of jurisprudence in Bordeaux, his influence could hardly have been greater had he held the chair in Paris. His theories in public and private law were so original, so consistent, so lucidly presented and so ably defended that, when they were eventually accepted, Duguit had changed the very foundations of jurisprudence. This does not mean that the philosophical cornerstone on which his entire edifice was constructed was also new, for at a time in which positivism had begun to waver, Duguit remained a positivist at heart, so that his legal innovations were, paradoxically, based on an antiquated approach. That paradox probably arose from the fact that it had taken positivism a very long time to gain a foothold in jurisprudence, one of the most conservative of all disciplines.

In the preface to his *Les Transformations du droit public*, the first edition of which appeared in 1913, Duguit summed up the prevailing legal approach clearly and succinctly: "Sovereign power, which is the subjective law of the nation organized as a state; limitation of that power by the natural rights of the individual; the obligation of the state to protect individual rights as best it can, not to limit these rights further than is necessary, to protect the rights of all, and to organize and run the defense, police, and judicial services, in short, the whole system of public law, the end result of a long historical process, as formulated with perfect concision in the laws of the Revolution."[5] The fact that a changing society was bound to turn all this into *vieux jeu* and that not even the law had been spared from the general crisis of confidence, had not escaped him either. "We find ourselves," he wrote just before setting down the above quotation, "in a critical period, a term borrowed from medicine, but which has no pejorative connotation for us whatsoever. Like it or not, everything seems to point to the fact that the fundamental ideas that, until recently, were the basis of our legal institutions are disintegrating; that the legal system by which our modern society has been living so far is out of joint and that a new system is being constructed on entirely different conceptions." Deliberately refraining from going beyond the facts, which his positivism would not allow him to do, he concluded with: "Is it progress or regress? We cannot say. In social science such questions make but little sense. All we do know is that things have changed, and fundamentally so."[6] Two years earlier, in a series of lectures delivered in Buenos Aires, he had argued that whereas the old legal system had been metaphysical and individualistic, the new one would be realistic and socialist.[7] What had been the subjective right of the individual — property for instance — was about to become "objective", a social function; what had been the subjective right of the state — the sovereign exercise of political and legal power — would also become "objective"; the state would turn into a public service. By "subjective" he was thus referring to the idea that the individual — be he a natural or a legal person — has the right to do as he wishes; by "objective" to the idea that justice is no more than the regulation of social relations. And he used "socialist" in the same sense as Charmont did in 1903, when he spoke of the "socialization of the law,"[8] and as Emmanuel Lévy did when he conjured up a *vision socialiste du droit.*

These new ideas did not remain confined to France, and how could they have been? They were the direct result of the interpenetration of state and society, a process that, as we saw earlier, was making itself felt throughout Europe at the turn of the century. Hence it is only fair to say that Duguit's great influence was ultimately based, not on any innovation, but on the impressive manner in which he formulated and systematized existing trends. The first real step along the new path had already been taken by Rudolf von Jhering,[9] first in a rather polemical lecture he delivered in Vienna as early as 1872 — "Der Kampf ums Recht" (The Struggle Around Law) — and then more systematically in his famous *Der Zweck im Recht* (Purpose in Law), the first part of which was published five years later. In it he maintained that purpose was just as important in human conduct and law as cause was in the exact sciences. Jurisprudence was based on value judgments, or more precisely on moral choices between conflicting interests, and legislation was an ethical rather than a legal process. Strangely enough Jhering had arrived at his particular "socialization" of the law by a deviation from positivism, while Duguit, as we have said, was led to similar ideas by his positivist approach — telling proof, incidentally, that it is not the philosophical basis but the social situation which constitutes the real breeding ground of new ideas. For ultimately all the developments we have been discussing can be considered so many adaptations of the law to changed social circumstances. Jhering, however, failed to appreciate the full consequences of his contribution. Being a German, he was chiefly concerned with upholding the rights of the free citizen vis-à-vis the authoritarian state: it was not by chance that he praised the English traveler who, insisting on his rights, refused to allow the railways to cheat him out of single shilling.[10] It was Georg Jellinek,[11] Jhering's compatriot, a man who had spent his early life in Vienna absorbing much of the liberal outlook of the

Austrian intelligentsia, who took the next step on the new road. To a man with Jellinek's philosophical and sociological training the central problem was to arrive at a more precise definition of the respective rights of the individual and society. Having accepted a chair in Heidelberg, he devoted his full energy to this problem, possibly with the help of Max Weber, who later became his colleague and friend.[12] Jellinek discovered the solution in his theory that the state must practice self-restraint in the interest of the individual citizen, an idea he developed further in three books: *System der subjectiven öffentlichen Rechte* (System of Subjective Public Rights; 1892); a famous historical treatise entitled *Die Erklärung der Menschen- und Bürgerrechte* (The Elucidation of Human and Civil Rights; 1894); and the more systematic *Allgemeine Staatslehre* (General Politics; 1900), a book that was to become a classic of political sociology within a decade, and that stood Duguit and many others in good stead.

Jellinek's benevolent state, which held itself in check for moral reasons, was a very long jump from Hobbes's Leviathan. In Jellinek's view, any failure by the state to practice such self-restraint was an abuse of justice that could only be repaired by "self-punishment." Even so Hugo Krabbe, the Dutch political theorist, contended that Jellinek had not gone nearly far enough. For what with the almost unlimited extension of its influence on social life, the "self-restraint" of the state was no guarantee of personal liberty, the less so as there was nothing to compel the state to observe tomorrow the self-restraining laws it had passed today. The Dutch professor accordingly proposed to replace the idea of the sovereignty of the state with that of the sovereignty of the law, whose binding force was not derived from political decisions but from man's innate sense of justice. In 1906 he presented that idea in his *Die Lehre der Rechtssouveränität* (The Doctrine of the Sovereignty of the Law) and he developed it further still in his *Die moderne Staatsidee* (The Modern Idea of the State) which, though written before the war, was not published until 1915. The whole problem could not have been more topical than it was at the time, for Krabbe had meanwhile extended his theory to international law. The influence on Krabbe of Heymans, another professor from Groningen, was unmistakeable — both were anxious to face the facts yet both could also see beyond them.

Krabbe's arguments had far-reaching repercussions. If the ultimate source of law was not the state — be it absolutist, constitutional, or even parliamentary — but man's sense of justice, then it behooved jurists to probe more deeply into that source. And was that work not a resurrection in modern form of the ancient idea of natural law, an idea that nineteenth-century man had rejected as unscientific? In a scholarly

387

study,[13] Haines has shown that this was precisely what was happening. He made special reference to Krabbe,[14] whose views were supported by a growing band of jurists, all opposed to the positivists, to the sociological school, and above all to the "classics" who in 1900 still shared Treitschke's belief that the state was the ultimate source of sovereign power. One of the first to challenge them had been Otto Gierke,[15] whose profound studies of German constitutional law and of natural law had prepared him for this task, as had his anti-positivist and anti-Marxist convictions. Another pioneer was Rudolf Stammler, who, though closer to Marxism, as witness his *Wirtschaft und Recht nach materialistischer Geschichtsauffassung* (Economics and Law in the Materialist Conception of History; 1896), was too much of a Neo-Kantian to embrace it unreservedly. Haines placed him among the founders of the modern school of natural law, because Stammler, unlike the old school, did not believe that the sense of natural justice has been implanted in man once and for all and immutably so, but rather that it changes with the times. The evolution of natural law was the basis of his *Lehre von dem richtigen Rechte* (The Doctrine of True Law; 1902). One may call his approach typical of the dynamic age in which he lived, notwithstanding the fact that similar ideas had been propounded two centuries earlier by Vico,[16] for Vico too, had lived at a time of rapid change.

In France it was Charmont who came closest to Stammler in his attempt to forge a link between natural law and social evolution.[17] Charmont's new, social interpretation of natural law became an inspiration to a growing movement, whose aims he himself summed up in 1910 in his *La Renaissance du droit naturel.* R. Saleilles had advanced similar ideas as early as 1902 in an article entitled "Some Recent Contributions to the Historical School of Natural Law."[18] According to him, it was only a matter of time before these ideas were generally accepted. "It is no accident," Roscoe Pound wrote in 1911, "that something like a revival of natural law should be sweeping the world."[19] He listed four main causes: the desire to introduce ethical conceptions into jurisprudence; the search for ideal or philosophical norms to underpin positive laws; the attempt to establish criteria that judges and administrators could apply in their legal and legislative functions; and finally the attempt to discover a justification for the limitation of the sovereign powers of the state.

It is easy to show that Pound's etiology was correct. All the four factors he listed had indeed become topics of keen discussion. The ethical current which, as we saw, was also making itself strongly felt in economics and sociology was, as we are about to see, particularly pronounced in the

388

domain of criminal law. Moreover, the growing conviction that it was essential to curb the power of the state gave rise to a call for a close scrutiny of all its administrative functions: an unavoidable development at a time when the state was increasingly encroaching on social and private life. All in all, people had ceased to look upon the state as the remote and exalted sovereign of former years, and this precisely because of its meddling with the problems of daily life. Few, however, would have gone as far as Franz Oppenheimer, the neo-liberal, who in 1912 called the modern state a "mechanism of oppression," adding that the sooner it disappeared in its present form the better. "Our age has lost the happy optimism of the classicists and humanists: sociological pessimism is our dominant theme," he added by way of an apology.[20]

"Sociological pessimism" also informed the search for new norms and criteria. Thus, in 1909, Martin Beradt voiced grave doubts about the present state of the law now that the old norms had fallen into disrepute.[21] The jurist and historian Hermann Kantorowicz, who wrote under the pen name of Gnaeus Flavius, had taken much the same view in 1906 when, as a young man, he wrote that only a more liberal approach based on social equity could create acceptable legal norms.[22] Ernst Fuchs's caustic attacks a few years later on "pandectology" and "cryptosociology" — by which he referred to the fact that judges base their decisions, willy-nilly, more on their own social attitudes than on the law book — helped to spread the influence of the school of Liberal Law even outside Germany.[23] Eugen Ehrlich used much the same approach with his call for "living justice." When his *Freie Rechtsfindung und freie Rechtswissenschaft* (Free Legal Decisions and Free Jurisprudence) was published in 1903, he became one of the founders of the German school of sociological law.[24] It was largely responsible for the fact that judges and advocates came increasingly to be seen in the sometimes less than flattering light of psychology. As a result the majesty of the law, just like the sovereignty of the state, began to look tarnished: we have only to read Anatole France's little masterpiece, *Crainquebille*, published in 1904, to realize just how badly. Others, afraid of total chaos, stuck desperately to the old norms or appealed to a "higher law" as the final arbiter.

This may explain the great attraction of the new doctrine of natural law, even to many traditionalists. Thus though both Hauriou and Duguit rejected the new doctrine on the grounds that it could not be reconciled with positivism, they, too, were not averse to placing the law above the state. The strongest support for the new idea came, understandably enough, from Catholic circles: Georgio del Vecchio of Rome, who enjoyed a great deal of active support,[25] carried the message to Italy in his

I presupposti filosofici della nozione del diritto (The Philosophical Presuppositions of the Idea of Law) published in 1905, and Cathrein, a German Jesuit, who before being expelled from Germany during the "Kulturkampf" was editor of the *Stimmen aus Maria-Laach* (Voices from
Maria-Laach) and later held the chair of moral philosophy at Ignatius
College in Valkenburg, brought the new idea to the Netherlands with his
Recht, Naturrecht und positives Recht (Law, Natural Law and Positive
Law) in 1901.[26] These Catholics not only welcomed the new movement,
but considered it a vindication of Thomistic views. Haines did not exaggerate when he claimed that at the turn of the century the repeated
attempts to re-classify the concept of natural law appealed to so many
European jurists that they gave rise to a great national and international
movement.[27] And so much headway did this movement make, in fact,
that the great Francois Gény of Nancy felt free in his *Méthode d'interprétation et sources en droit privé positif*, which appeared as early as
1899, to include among the sources of law not only social circumstances,
authority, logic and legal dialectics, but also natural law and intuition.[28]

If constitutional law was under attack from so many sides, what,
may we ask, was happening in the field of civil law, which is so much
less abstract but affects the citizen all the more intimately. "Socializing
the law," Charmont asserted, "means rendering it more comprehensive,
extending it from the rich to the poor, from the proprietors to the wage
earners, from man to woman, from father to child — in short, making
it an instrument from which all members of society can benefit."[29] He
followed this instructive introduction to a lecture on civil law delivered
in Montpellier with a set of examples, all showing how far short of these
objectives society still fell. Even so, he felt optimistic about the near
future: "It is difficult to imagine more exciting times . . . the whole world
is coming to realize that the great social transformation has already been
initiated."[30] According to him, the illusion that the *Code Civil* had ushered in equality had been shattered by the advent of scientific socialism
and by the growth of social concern in legal circles.[31] Had not Glasson
said as early as 1886 that the *Code Civil* had as good as forgotten the
worker?[32] And had not Rudolf Sohm told the International Congress for
Comparative Law, held in 1900, that both codes — the French framed
at the beginning, and the German framed at the end of the nineteenth
century — were bourgeois codes not only legally but socially as well?[33]

In corroboration, Sohm might well have mentioned Anton Menger's
Das bürgerliche Recht und die besitzlosen Klassen (Civil Law and the
Unpropertied Classes), published ten years earlier.[34] It was a critique
of the proposed new civil code presented in draft form in 1888 and

destined to be adopted, after modification, on the first day of the last year of the outgoing century. Menger held the chairs of constitutional and civil law in Vienna, a fact that, quite apart from the influence of both Marx and von Gierke, helps to explain his radicalism: at the turn of the century, it was no longer the capital on the Seine but that on the Danube in which the most original ideas were being put forward. Menger deliberately refrained from basing his critique on the socialist principles of jurisprudence that he had developed four years earlier,[35] choosing instead the more widely accepted principles of civil law.[36] Even on these principles, he argued, it was easy to show that the code adopted at the end of the last century protected the interest of the unpropertied classes no better than had the *Code Civil* adopted at the beginning of that century. This failing had become all the more obvious now that the proletariat had grown into a powerful political and economic force. But instead of meeting its demands, the new draft law passed the workers over in silence, as the remaining two hundred pages of Menger's book proved convincingly. In particular, Menger demonstrated that, because the income of the poor was not only absolutely but relatively smaller than that of the rich, the poor having to spend a much larger percentage on necessities, their claims on the law were absolutely and relatively smaller as well. The two fictions, that everyone is deemed to know the law and that the law is perfect, worked to the disadvantage of the poorer classes, and so did the judge's class prejudice. Things were no better with the legal profession at large, and Menger accordingly called for the replacement of the *pro deo* advocate by a state official.[37]

In fact the bourgeois nature of the doubly "bourgeois" civil code also made itself felt in other deplorable ways. Thus it largely glossed over the problem of illegitimate children, many of whom were conceived during a temporary liaison between a rich man and a poor woman, and it did so despite the fact that some 9% of all births fell into that category — in Germany, where the percentage was relatively small.[38] In particular, the code had little to say about compensation; indeed, if the girl was over the age of sixteen the man was perfectly free to seduce her, unless he happened to be her guardian or teacher.[39] And if she had accepted presents or money from him beforehand, he was absolved from all further responsibility. Canon Law and even Roman Law were less retrograde in this respect. And the new code was even less helpful when it came to the wage contract, on which the livelihood of most citizens depended.

To what large extent Menger had already adopted the sociological approach to the law appears from a passage he wrote about the monarchy. In it he claimed that while German jurisprudence considered that institution a social instrument for preserving the *status quo*,[40] the real importance of the monarchy resided in its power to narrow social contrasts, thus preparing the way for the transformation of the legal system to the benefit of the lowest strata of the population.[41] This was clear proof that his sociological insight was somewhat restricted, in practice at least, if not in theory, for in the rectoral address he delivered five years later he sang the praises of a sociology whose task it was "to discover the general doctrine which those engaged in the various branches of science have been missing so painfully for so long."[42]

Not everyone went as far as Menger, even though the sociological approach — whose beginnings have been wrongly traced back to Eugen Ehrlich, Schumpeter's colleague in Czernowitz[43] — was making undoubted headway. Thus Kantorowitz, who was afraid to abandon dogmatics in 1910, as witness his dictum that sociology without dogmatics is blind, nevertheless added that dogmatics without sociology was an empty vessel.[44]

Menger's ideas may have seemed extreme in his day, but he was anything but a lone wolf. We have already mentioned Sohm and Glasson. Raymond Saleilles, too, hit out at the *Code Civil* with the comment that there is no such thing as absolute right, not even the absolute right to property,[45] and Charmont was no less radical than Menger. Moreover, many legal historians have since come to appreciate the justice of Menger's critique. "The prevailing laws do but little to curtail privileges derived from laissez-faire economic practices," Eric Wolf remarked in 1933.[46]

It was Duguit, once again, who first grasped the full import of all the new currents and who tried to incorporate them into his attempt to transform the prevailing metaphysical and individualistic system of civil law into a realistic and "socialist" one. This he did in the six lectures he delivered in Buenos Aires in September 1911.[47] Duguit, like Durkheim, had discovered that looking at things in the round helped one to go beyond particular facts, and this realization may be said to have taken him beyond positivism: just as soon as he realized that the facts could not be isolated, a synthesis emerged almost by itself. In the event, that synthesis was the social approach to the law. "Purpose" and "social function" were its core and it helped to bring jurisprudence back to earth from the inaccessible heavens to which it had been banished for so long. And having become an earthly creation, it was also seen to be as mutable as the rest. In this connection, Duguit referred to the Waldeck-Rousseau union law of July 1, 1901. That law contained not a word about the "collective will" or "legal personality" of unions; it had been drafted exclusively to protect the rights of the members to pursue a common aim.[48] Property, too, had ceased to be inviolable. True, there was no law to safeguard the social function of property, for instance by ensuring the proper cultivation of landed estates, but few people would object to such legislation if this evil grew to even larger proportions.[49] In England and Germany, moreover, a beginning had already been made with the imposition of taxes on unearned increments in the value of land.[50] And Duguit was anything but an enemy of property; he believed that it could only benefit from such measures.[51] Furthering the class struggle — which, strangely enough, he refused to admit as a fact — was nothing short of a crime, for Duguit believed "that far from being on the road to the destruction of one class by another, we are moving towards the co-ordination and hierarchization of the different classes."[52] This was a prophetic message, even though the wish had clearly been father to the thought.

In any case Duguit had gone a very long way beyond the idea that the sole purpose of the law was to protect the individual from the state. This takes us back to the crisis of bourgeois liberalism.

As we read all these attacks on property and privilege we can only marvel that property and privilege have survived to this day. But the number of critics in the world of law was insignificant when compared with that of the champions of the established order, and even the critics, apart from a handful of socialists, were not so much concerned with the abolition of property and privilege as with ameliorating their effects. Nevertheless this legal revolution, however vaguely it filtered through to the public, served to make the bourgeoisie much more uncertain than it need have been. The middle classes could not help but notice that as jurists learned to face the social facts, Justice was gradually dropping the blindfold which, for centuries, had served to hide the bias of her pronouncements.

More obvious still than the revolution in constitutional and civil law was the revolution in criminal law. During the night of July 5, 1900, Marie-Julie V., unmarried, from V. in the parish of S., was delivered of a child. In hiding her "shame," this deserted and inexperienced woman omitted to tie off the infant's umbilical cord, with the result that the child bled to death. Marie-Julie was arrested and brought to trial under Article 319 of the *Code Pénal*. But her judge happened to be Magnaud, the *bon juge*, as Clemenceau called this president of the *tribunal correctionel* of Château-Thierry.[53] On 24 August he passed the minimum sentence on the "child murderess": he bound her over in the sum of sixteen francs. "Whereas . . . and whereas . . . but also bearing in mind that before

393

meting out punishment, the judge has the right and the duty to arrive with scrupulous care at the true causes of the crimes society has charged him to suppress," Magnaud came to the conclusion that most of the responsibility for such cases lay with a society that despises the unmarried mother while showing leniency towards the seducer.[54]

This was by no means the only sentence of the "good judge" to cause a sensation. Not surprisingly, therefore, he was as widely admired by some as he was execrated by all those opposed to reforms of the criminal law. Leyret discussed both camps, and especially mentioned Tolstoy, who had apparently heard of Magnaud, and Advocate-General Mazeau, who missed no chance to pillory the "good judge" as the leader of that "sentimentalist sect" which — as he claimed in a speech on 16 October 1900 — "is currently making so much of their pity for the poor criminal and claims that schools, charitable institutions and hospitals are all we need to protect the citizen or at least to produce a marked reduction in the number of those gentlemen whom the stringent laws we now enjoy help to bring to book."[55] The kind of "just" sentences that were more to Mazeau's taste, sentences that "dealt with each case in accordance with the precise letter of the law," were in any case in far greater abundance than Magnaud's more humane pronouncements.

Mazeau versus Magnaud — that formulation might easily sum up the spate of writings devoted to criminal law reform at the turn of the century. For the times were rapidly changing even in this field. The intransigence of the judiciary was crumbling along with its arrogance,[56] or rather with the self-assurance of which that arrogance was the social expression. Their self-assurance was being assailed from two quarters: by greater awareness of the social roots of criminal behavior, of which we have just read a striking example in the legal preamble to the sentence of Marie-Julie; and by the latest developments in criminology, to which we shall now turn our attention.

Modern criminology can be divided into two main schools: one that considers criminal behavior hereditary, and the other which blames it on the environment. There was also a third school that adopted an intermediate position between these two. But no matter which of the three he chose, the criminologist who wanted to keep abreast of his time had to use a sociological or determinist approach,[57] and on both these grounds to reject the old view that crime was a result of a deliberate choice, a conscious violation of God's commandments and hence a sin — a view that earlier generations had also applied to disease, and to mental diseases in particular. And there was another striking parallel with modern medicine. Much as, under the influence of the historical approach, the sick individual began to displace the illness from the center of medical attention, so legal discussions of crimes made way for discussions of the individuals who had committed them. Moreover, prevention had become a watchword in both disciplines.

But once the freedom of the will was put in doubt, so also were the responsibility and the accountability of the individual. The resulting uncertainty about the very basis of criminal law can only be described as a crisis. G. A. van Hamel, a Dutch professor in criminal law, summed it up lightheartedly when, at the tenth congress of the *Internationale Kriminalistische Verein* held in 1906, he remarked that three concepts were badly troubling criminologists: responsibility, crime, and punishment; only if all three were eliminated would clarity be restored.[58]

This sense of helpless uncertainty was understandable enough. David Simons, another Dutch professor of criminal law, was deeply worried by it throughout his career, and more specifically by the fact that, though on determinist grounds the delinquent was not to blame for his crime, the law was nevertheless forced to punish him.[59] But what was punishment if not a retribution for, or punishment of, a misdemeanor? Did it aim at deterrence or at rehabilitation? Was it meant to protect the criminal from himself, or society from the criminal? And if it was the second, must prevention not take precedence over repression and re-education over firmness? Many people at the time were in favor of granting judges greater latitude in interpreting the criminal code, with powers to pass indeterminate sentences, or to acquit and even to pardon the accused.

Eugen Ehrlich called for the "release of the judge from the law";[60] the famous Italian jurist Garofalo advocated indeterminate sentences as early as 1880;[61] and so did Kraepelin in Germany and Havelock Ellis, the famous sexologist, in England.[62] In his *The Criminal*, Ellis contended that modern science was at one with the Christian injunction not to judge others, and that the only effective reaction to crime was a social one.[63] There were many who shared his view. Thus Gauckler, one of the speakers at the International Congress of Criminal Anthropology held in Amsterdam in September 1901,[64] distinguished between punitive and corrective measures. Dorado, who also addressed the Congress, called for an end to the dualistic approach. "We must abolish punishments once and for all," he declared, "and have recourse, in no matter what case, to curative and protective measures only. Away, not only with revenge, but even with 'meet' punishment: the delinquent is an unfortunate who needs nothing so much as help and compassion."[65] Forel, if anything, went even further when he declared that the future of criminal law lay in its abolition.[66]

Parallel with the attempt to reform the criminal law went the effort to reform the prison system. Charles Cook, the Howard of his day, made a tour of prisons and found nothing good to say about any of them.[67] Kropotkin[68] and Gautier[69] wrote about their own prison experiences and all those prepared to open their eyes began to recognize that prisons were so many foci of moral infection, so many causes of recidivism — in short, nothing but schools for criminals. The American Griffith J. Griffith founded the Prison Reform League and dedicated a book to Leo Tolstoy which was widely read in Europe.[70]

But all that was so much theory; in practice, prison reform was an exceedingly slow process. Now, the practical difficulties arose precisely because the prison authorities were in a cleft stick as one new idea after the next found its way sporadically into the statute book, thanks not only to the agitation of the reformers, but also to the conciliatory spirit that was gaining ground even in the "classical" camp. For though there were striking differences between the two schools, both were suffused with liberal ideas and were therefore much less divided than they themselves would have acknowledged.[71]

Moreover, quite a few new questions began to be asked. What about the reliability of witnesses, and of children in particular? And what about the impartiality of lawyers[72] and judges? Were they not human, all too human? Many judges must have been put in mind of the colleague who, as Rabelais relates, made a point of examining every case with scrupulous attention before determining the sentence — with the help of dice.

The deepest source of uncertainty, however, was crime itself, which had ceased to be considered a misdemeanor to which Article so-and-so of the criminal code applied, but had become the action of an individual. Or not even that; for was not crime, first and foremost, a symptom of a sick society that deprived the criminal of legal means to satisfy his needs? And yet, to Manouvrier[73] and his disciples, the criminal remained an individual who differed sharply from the "ordinary" citizen. Different in essence? Caesare Lombroso answered this question with an emphatic yes. He claimed that he could recognize the *deliquento nato*, the born criminal, without fail from a set of physical characteristics. Many believed him, although not for long, and in any case not all without reservation. Detailed studies by Näcke and Hamel, and by Lacassagne and Manouvrier, did a great deal to dampen the enthusiasm of the rest. "Today,

Lombroso's ideas strike us as antiquated," wrote the medical criminologist Armand Ferester in 1897.[74] Lombroso's own daughter, Gina, watered down her father's doctrine when, at the congress in Amsterdam we mentioned earlier, she produced two case histories to demonstrate that it was possible to be led by sickness into crime even in later life.[75] Enrico Ferri, Lombroso's pupil, took a similar view when he admitted that, apart from born criminals, there were also habitual and occasional criminals, thus admitting the influence of social factors on criminal behavior.[76] Others, W. A. Bonger in the Netherlands amongst them, held these factors alone responsible for all crimes.[77] Bonger first expounded this doctrine in 1900, in response to a competition, and later elaborated it in a thesis entitled *Criminalité et conditions économiques.* But the problem of the criminal's responsibility remained as acute as ever it had been. In 1903, Tarde devoted a long chapter to the causes of crime in a comprehensive book that examined the whole problem from a philosophical point of view.[78] He devoted a further chapter to the problem of responsibility.[79] For the rest, most lawyers continued to be vexed by the problem of the diminished responsibility, not only of children and mental patients, but also of "normal" criminals.[80] This was not at all surprising when one considers that what was involved was not just a legal question, but one that was, at heart, a psychological and even a philosophical one: the problem of the freedom of the will, one that no one has managed to solve satisfactorily to this day.

It was a far distant land that Franz von Liszt must have envisaged when, following Jhering's footsteps, he sent the manuscript of his *Der Zweckgedanke im Strafrecht* (The Idea of Purpose in Criminal Law) to the printer in 1882. For, according to Tarde, the modern jurist was like the ancient geographer who gave names to semi-explored stretches of land.[81] And yet Jhering's belief that purpose was the mainspring of all jurisprudence seemed to express the nature of the land most precisely. Unintentionally, and indeed unwillingly, all social institutions and with them all branches of human learning including jurisprudence, had fallen under the spell of technology with its doctrine of maximum efficiency. This was the true historical import of Duguit's assertion that the law was destined to become realistic and socialist and cease to be metaphysical and individualistic. Could the purposive idea have been more clearly expressed than in the claim that the state was about to be transformed from a "sovereign power" into a "public service", and property into a "social function"? In criminal law, though no one could have given a precise theoretical definition of criminal responsibility, the new approach served its purpose well enough in practice. The absolute number of crimes did not decrease — every age has the criminals it deserves — but the number of total misfits did, at least relatively so.

This was the kind of partial success of which history abounds in examples. At a time when the most progressive section of the European intelligentsia was seriously entertaining the hope that in the foreseeable future all men would be able to do as they pleased, there were brief moments when it seemed that *Justitia* could not only dispense with her blindfold, but as a direct result, with her sword as well. Brief moments of hope, but more than man had enjoyed at any other period, or was to enjoy in the years to come.

CHAPTER XXVII

THE RIDDLE OF THE SPHINX

On January 6 and 13, 1900 the Viennese daily, *Die Zeit*, published a superficial but damning review of a book that had been published six weeks earlier, but bore the year 1900 on its title page. Although the critic had no qualifications other than that his name was Burckhardt and that he was the director of the Burgtheater, his name and position carried sufficient weight in Vienna to ensure that the modest sales of the book came to an almost complete halt. The book, of which the remaining 477 copies — out of a total edition of 600 — seemed doomed for repulping, was entitled *Traumdeutung* (The Interpretation of Dreams), and its author was a young and unknown psychiatrist, Sigmund Freud.[1]

Four months later Freud wrote a letter to his friend Wilhelm Fliess in which he said, with the typical mixture of pride and modesty of the misunderstood genius: "No critic . . . can see more keenly than I do the disproportion between the problems and the solutions, and I shall suffer the just punishment that none of the undiscovered provinces of mental life which I was the first mortal to enter will bear my name or follow the laws I have formulated."[2]

In the event, that punishment, just or otherwise, was not meted out, though for many years it looked very much as if it would be. At the Fourth International Congress of Psychology, opened by Ribot on August 20, 1900 — as one of the countless congresses held in Paris at the time — where no fewer than 185 papers were read and the proceedings covered some 800 big pages, Freud's name was mentioned just twice, both times by Dr. Hartenberg from Paris. The first time was in Hartenberg's address on "anxiety neuroses," and the second in his reply to Tokarski from Moscow, in which he granted that sexuality played an important role in the etiology of certain neuroses, though by no means of all, as Freud had claimed.[3]

If we look at the year 1900 through the eyes of the two leading psychological periodicals of the time, we arrive at an even more negative result. In the one, *L'Année Psychologique*, Freud's name does not appear at all; in the other, the *Zeitschrift für Psychologie und Physiologie*, it is mentioned twice, but disparagingly.

The first mention was in a review by R. Gaupp of Freud's article "On Repressed Memories", published during the previous year. Gaupp admittedly called its author a lively writer, but thought it all the more deplorable that with this quality he should have proffered "such subjective and far-fetched interpretations as 'psychological analyses' and, moreover, by arguments that have little claim to being called scientific."[4] The second mention of Freud, again by Gaupp, came at the end of a review of a book on castration by one Rieger, who had dismissed Freud's ideas as "old wives' tales,"[5] a view with which Gaupp was happy to concur.

That Freud's ideas should have aroused opposition is not surprising. for such is the fate of most fundamentally new insights. Writing on the subject many years later, Freud himself contended that this opposition was due to the psychic tension new concepts invariably set up because of the uncertainties and anxious expectations they arouse.[6] The nature of his own discovery — the fundamental role of sexuality in all psychological disturbances — did not improve matters at a time when nearly everyone was interested in the subject, but had to pretend that he was not. Worse still, Freud had spoken of the sexual feelings of children, something with which, as he himself put it, every nursemaid was familiar,[7] but which ran counter to the popular concept of the "innocent child." What was left of that concept when little children were shown not only to have sexual feelings, but also to be filled with "impermissible" longings for their parent of the opposite sex and with "impermissible" hostility towards the other parent? And was not the innocence of children one of the few survivals of the biblical claim that God had made man in his own image? Worse still, if children were "like that", was not the esteemed "ego" of the adult, too, shamefully transparent to anyone who cared to look? Few people at the time had the courage and resolution to engage in the kind of self-analysis that had led Freud, after an unimaginable psychological struggle, to the certainty of his own interpretation.

True, Krafft-Ebing, Havelock Ellis and Magnus Hirschfeld had already paved the "evil" way for what was later called "sexology"; Krafft-Ebing with his *Psychopathia sexualis*, the first edition of which had appeared as early as 1886; Havelock Ellis, with his *Studies in the Psychology of Sex*, the first of whose seven parts was published in 1897; and Hirschfeld with his committee for the social and legal equality of homosexuals founded in 1897, and more brazenly still with his *Jahrbuch für sexuelle Zwischenstufen* (Yearbook for Sexual Borderline Cases), first published in 1899. But, to begin with, this trio had at least spared the tender souls of children, and secondly, Professor Krafft-Ebing, when told of Freud's theory, had commented that it sounded like a "scientific fairytale." The fact that the self-same man soon afterwards proposed Freud for the position of associate professor is not usually mentioned in this connection.[8] No, Freud realized only too well that, more so even than Hebbel, he had "disturbed the sleep of the world."[9]

His colleagues — the neurologists, physiologists, psychopathologists, psychiatrists, and psychologists — were particularly disturbed by the fact (and this was no small matter to an age that had set science on a pedestal) that, although psychoanalysis in its initial phase claimed to be no more than a new method of treating mental illness, it nevertheless seemed to make short shift of everything science had taught them. Blinded by the new light, these men overlooked the fact that Freud had built his entire edifice on the very scientific premises his adversaries now accused him of having betrayed. And he not only started out from these premises but defended them throughout his life, so much so that Ortega y Gasset alleged that Freud had turned the intellectual process into a mechanical one, albeit one involving psychological as well as physical forces.[10]

To appreciate the historical significance of this apparent contradiction we must take a closer look at the well-trodden path of early twentieth-century psychology. For though there was good reason to start this chapter with Freud, one of the few pioneers in this field whose name carries authority to this day, indeed the only one of whom the "man in the street" is likely to have heard, it would be a complete misrepresentation to pretend that Freud belonged to the psychological mainstream in his day — the preceding remarks may have served to show that he was anything but that.

Had we wanted to start with one whom his own contemporaries considered the leading psychologist in their midst, then we should have had to choose, not a Viennese physician but a German professor, not Sigmund Freud but Wilhelm Wundt. For Wundt's psychological laboratory in Leipzig, founded in 1879 and the forerunner of many others to follow, was the clearest possible practical expression of psychological thinking at the turn of the century. In 1912, when the American psychologist G. S. Hall, another of the great of his day, published a selection of his lectures on the founders of modern psychology, five of the six men he discussed — Zeller, Lotze, Fechner, van Hartmann, and von Helmholtz — had died, and only the sixth, Wundt, was still alive and continued to live until 1920. Hall devoted 150 pages to him, more than to any of the others.[11] Moreover, in his *Historical Introduction to Modern Psychology*, published in 1929, Murphy included a long chapter entitled *"Psychology in the Age of Wundt.*"[12] If that were not praise enough, Brett, the great historian of psychology, tells us that, thanks to his longevity, his un-flagging application, and his great skill, Wundt held almost unchallenged pride of place among psychologists for close on half a century.[13]

Wundt's, like Freud's, most famous work was published in 1900. It was the first part of his *Völkerpsychologie* (Ethnopsychology). But the two authors belonged, and this was more crucial than the coincidence of their literary debut, to two different generations: Freud was forty-four in 1900; Wundt, sixty-eight. Brett was right to stress the latter's longevity and perserverance: during the sixty years that Wundt put pen to paper, he is said to have covered no fewer than 16,000 pages.

However, Brett had a few reservations about him, and indeed, Wundt lies buried today beneath the weight of the many heavy tomes he created in his lifetime. His chief importance, unlike Freud's, was that he did not so much break new ground as summarize the achievements of psychology and consolidate the results. The currents that joined together in the broad bed of Wundt's gigantic river of thought were Weber's and Fechner's experimental studies of vision and hearing; the quantitative determina-tion of sensations and reaction times; Darwin's genetic approach; and finally the evolutionist idea that had entered psychology via Galton, and thanks to which exclusive concern with those nuclear mental processes that could not be subsumed under the heading of "soul," made way for the study of emotion and volition so characteristic of modern psychology.[14]

Much as Freud's work throws light on the revolution in psychological thought at the turn of the century, so Wundt's work throws light on the even more complex process that went before: a subtle shift of empha-sis that, in retrospect, seems the direct if unintended result of his attempt to rebuild the entire corpus of physiological and psychological knowledge of his day on solid scientific foundations. But even while building on his predecessors he had started something entirely new. Thus he had be-gun the study of child and animal psychology in his laboratory, though not experimentally, because the sacrosanct method of introspection did not lend itself to that approach; moreover he had begun to look at the psychological interpretation of linguistic phenomena, and he had finally launched ethnopsychology. The fact that the thirteen volumes of his work have since been forgotten does not diminish his importance, which was so great in his day that E. W. Scripture, head of the Yale psychological laboratory, dedicated his *New Psychology* (1897) to Wundt, his teacher.[15] Those who want to know more about the subjects Wundt selected for study, the methods he applied, and finally about the extremely optimistic expectations people had of him, can do no better than page through Scripture's book, with its hundreds of illustrations of instruments and statistical tables, then deemed the last word in scientific sophistication.

The better to apply the scientific method consistently in psychology and the better to arrive at a causal and mechanistic theory of consciousness, Wundt freed psychology from its philosophical shackles, though, being a philosopher himself, he saw no reason for divorcing the two disciplines completely. As a result, he not only provided psychology with solid foundations but also helped to fit it into a wider context, and with such great success that pupils from far and wide poured into Leipzig. The first to arrive the very year Wundt opened his laboratory was the American Stanley Hall, who later became a professor of psychology and helped to train no less than eighty-one of Wundt's intellectual grandchildren. A second visitor, also from the United States, was James McKeen Cattell, who pioneered the idea of psychological tests and the utilization of psychological techniques in industry. A third caller, Titchener, was an Englishman who later became a professor in America. He was one of Wundt's most devoted disciples who turned a deaf ear to the growing clamor of Wundt's opponents. Together with their pupils, these men were the founders of American experimental psychology: by 1900, twenty-six psychological laboratories had been opened in the United States — more than in the whole of Europe. In all of them, great stress was laid on the genetic approach; there was a growing suspicion that introspection was an unreliable method, and a tendency to dwell on individual differences and no longer on the general properties of the human psyche, as Wundt had done. Emil Kraepelin, another of Wundt's well-known pupils, was responsible for a further shift in emphasis: he became more famous as a psychiatrist than as a psychologist, not least because he showed that a number of mental conditions that had previously been treated as distinct could all be combined under the heading of *dementia praecox*. Hugo Münsterberg abandoned the master's path even further, so much so that he even found favor in the eyes of William James, one of the first to look down on all that experimentation with ironic disdain. James brought Münsterberg to Harvard where the latter, a behaviorist *avant la lettre*, followed the call of applied psychology — he devoted the rest of his life to psychotherapy, criminology, and industrial psychology. Another of Wundt's pupils, Ernst Meumann, made a systematic study of the psychology of learning, while yet another, Alfred Lehmann, became the director of the psychological laboratory in Copenhagen, where he developed the psychology of expressive behaviour.[16]

Our list is by no means complete,[17] even if we add the name of Felix Krueger, Wundt's successor in Leipzig, whose "developmental" psychology made him one of the founders of cultural psychology and indirectly of Gestalt psychology;[18] or the name of Willy Hellpach, who extended ethnopsychology into geopsychotopy, a branch of social psychology concerned with the effects of the physical environment on the human psyche (his *Geopsychische Erscheinungen* [Geopsychological Phenomena] was first published in 1911); or even if we add the name of T. Zicken, who dared to contradict the master in the preface to his study of physiological psychology published as early as 1891, albeit he claimed that all he was trying to do was to extend Wundt's scientific psychology. He rejected Wundt's distinction between apperception and perception and called the former the "over-soul," something that science could discard as readily as it could dispense with the soul.[19]

And we have still not yet mentioned one man who must be included in even the briefest historical survey of psychology at the turn of the century, namely Oswald Külpe, Wundt's assistant until 1894, when he himself was given a chair in Würzburg and founded the Würzburg school. That school, too, introduced a shift in accent, of the kind we are beginning to recognize as typical of the gradual change in climate that was taking place all round. For though Külpe retained Wundt's general approach, he did so with a small difference: much as Wundt had freed psychology from its philosophical ties, he, in turn, now liberated it from its bonds with physiology and biology. To Külpe, who was thirty-eight in 1900, psychology was "the science of the facts of experience in their dependence on experiencing individuals" — no more and no less. Physiology, he believed, cannot explain purely psychic processes. The point had been reached within less than twenty intensive years when the labors of many men, but above all of Wundt and his school, had completed the process of turning psychology into an independent discipline. This process that may be said to have been begun by James Ward in 1886, when he wrote the first separate article on psychology for the ninth edition of the *Enclyopaedia Britannica* — in the footsteps of Wundt, perhaps, but in a manner that demolished rather than extended the impressive edifice Wundt had erected.

Other members of the Würzburg school completed this creative work of demolition. Thus Marbe showed that, no matter how many ideas or feelings were involved in the judgment that something is lighter or heavier, these ideas or feelings were not essential to the judgment itself. The latter was made of much flimsier stuff, was much more impulsive and intangible than the logical comparison of two objects, one found to be "light" and the other "heavy." Watt came to much the same conclusion when treating of the subordination or superordination of words.

Similarly K. Bühler's protracted studies of the cognitive process persuaded him that factual thought cannot be recovered by introspection: the same conclusion Binet had reached a few years earlier, in 1903.[20] N. Ach finally summed up all these findings by postulating that passive and associative tendencies played at least as decisive a part in guiding our actions as did active and purposive tendencies. In short, the subconscious will seemed to preside over consciousness. Ach called it the determining tendency. For our study of the mechanism of the "small revolutions" within the main revolution, it is not without significance that an extremely gradual shift should have occurred even in this field, so gradual, in fact, that it could not be detected with the naked eye, so to speak. Thus G. E. Müller originally looked on Ach's "determining tendency" not as something fundamentally different from the association principle but as its indirect result. We, who have become familiar with the idea of "wishful thinking," an idea of which Ach's "determining tendency" may be considered a forerunner, and who are no longer ensnared in the association dogma, have great difficulty in imagining how hard it was at the time to bid farewell to the second and to welcome the first.

That Ach's discovery was not the chance result of an arcane or isolated research project, but sprang from a shift in the general psychological approach and the increasing dynamism of the historical process as a whole is shown by the, apparently independent, discovery of similar psychic mechanisms by McDougall and Freud at about the same time.

At the turn of the century many others rushed forward as well to join in the demolition of the "old" school, a school that had been calling itself the "new psychology" since its recent inception. These men, too, were impelled from without rather than from within, just like those of Wundt's pupils who had decided to go their own way. For though Wundt had aimed at the consolidation of everything he deemed relevant to contemporary psychology, he had failed to attain anything like the encyclopedic unity to which he had devoted 16,000 pages. Beyond, animal and child psychology were pursuing their independent courses, and so was most of psychiatry, bound up as it still was with treatment of hysteria by hypnosis and suggestion. The idea that normal psychology had anything to learn from abnormal psychology was something that not only Wundt but all contemporary psychologists, with the exception of the egregious Freud, would have rejected with indignation, let alone the suggestion that, in the long run, it would prove impossible to separate the two groups unfailingly. Beyond, there also lay criminology, which was still considered a branch of psychopathology, and pedagogy, a subject that would vainly seek admittance to the sciences for many decades to come. Pedagogy was making increasing use of intelligence tests, which were being ignored by the most authoritative — and at the time that meant German — psychologists. This may explain why Binet and Simon presented the first of these tests in 1905 not as psychologists working in their own field, but on behalf of a French government commission charged with examining the problem of retarded children. And beyond Wundt's horizon — though not completely so, as witness his ethnopsychology — loomed social psychology and the psychology of religion, which, having apparently having had its day, had ceased to interest the professionals.

It was no accident that all these disciplines should have remained wholly or partially outside the frame of what one might call academic psychology. For none of them were suited to the introspective method. This was wholly true of animal psychology and to a slightly lesser extent of child psychology, abnormal psychology, and criminology. Nevertheless all these disciplines assumed fresh importance at the turn of the century when psychology increasingly turned its back on the abstract properties of the human psyche and looked afresh at concrete man in a concrete environment. It was as if psychology had recovered the subject of classical philosophy but, thanks to the interregnum of the exact sciences, on a higher plane. Even so, it now appeared that, for all their patient labors, the men who had presided over this interregnum had been too precipitate: they had tried to solve the problems with a set of improvised instruments unsuited to the purpose. As a result, they had caused a short-circuit, not unlike the one that paralysed Marxism at about the same time — Marxists, too, had been overhasty in deriving the ideological superstructure from the economic infrastructure without taking full account of the intermediate social and intellectual layers responsible for transforming economic into idealogical processes.

Better understanding of concrete man was, in any case, the direct upshot of this new interest. It was reflected in thousands of long-forgotten papers on sensation, perception, cognition, emotion, attention, memory, and thought. Other disciplines, too, produced an unprecedented spate of writings, but none more than modern psychology, whose very foundations were being laid during the period under review. Thus E. L. Thorndike, a student of William James, was one of the first to make a serious study of animal psychology, still following the path Wundt had opened in 1892 — he was mainly concerned with animal learning. Small and Yerkes joined him soon afterwards. Yerkes's book on the subject falls outside our frame of reference because it was not published until 1925, but nevertheless its very title — *Almost Human* — expressed the results of his protracted behavior studies of anthropoid apes so poignantly that we feel we must mention it here. Its comparative approach, which was to become the hallmark of so many scientific studies in the new century, is best brought out by the rejoinder that the new studies, especially by Freud and McDougall, demonstrating the importance of man's instinctive drives, might well have been published under the title of "Almost a Beast."[21] When Margaret Washburn published her *Animal Mind* in 1908, animal psychology, too, could be said to be growing up, the more so as the two great Russians, Bechterev and Pavlov, had already cast much fresh light on the subject with their work on association and conditioned reflexes in dogs.

From the study of animal behavior it was but a small step to behaviorism, i.e. to the objective study of human responses. John B. Watson was the first to take that step with a now famous article in the *Psychological Review* of March 1913 entitled "Psychology as the behaviorist views it."[22] The date of its publication and the fact that the influence of behaviorism remained chiefly confined to America, make it unnecessary to review that article at length in a book on European civilization at the turn of the last century. All we need add, therefore, is that behaviorists, much more than even Wundt or anyone else whom they accused of subjectivism, were chiefly concerned with turning psychology into an exact science. This meant discarding not only the "soul" which even Wundt had cast out, but also consciousness, the central element of Wundt's doctrine.[23]

Child psychology too was no longer virgin land, as witness the issue of December 1899 of the *Zeitschrift für pädagogische Psychologie*.[24] It listed no less than sixty child psychologists in Europe, and this at a time when, according to the author, the United States was the chief center of child psychology.[25] After two prior attempts, the first of which dated back to the end of the eighteenth century but had come to nothing for lack of general interest, child psychology had at long last found a hearing in Europe, thanks to Wilhelm Preyer's great classic, *Die Seele des Kindes* (The Soul of the Child, 1882). What Preyer was in the German-speaking world, Bernard Perez was in the French, and Paola Lambroso in the Italian. It was also in Italy that Marro published his *La puberta* in 1897, the forebear of the endless line of books on puberty that were to see the light of day in our century.[26]

Outside America, where Hall reigned supreme, although he himself rightly repudiated the title of "father of child psychology",[27] most of the work in this field was being done in England where the study of child psychology had its origins in Darwin's *Biographical Sketch of an Infant* (1877).

To rediscover that famous name in this context is not nearly as astonishing as it might seem. Darwin's evolutionary approach led almost automatically to "preliminary studies" of adult European psychology based on the psychology of animals, primitive races, and children. Thus, according to Stanley Hall's "recapitulation theory," every child must repeat the stages which have been passed through in the evolution of the race. This doctrine was not unlike the psychoanalytic theory that the original structure of human society was that of the primal horde, or unlike Haeckel's basic phylogenetic law, according to which the embryo repeats the evolutionary stages of the species.[28]

The best known English child psychologist, however, was not Darwin but James Sully, whose *Studies of Childhood* (1895) was a most valuable and readable contribution. The author's pragmatic approach was typically English, and this was reflected in the subtitle of the German edition which followed soon afterwards: "Psychological Essays for the Use of Teachers and Progressive Parents."[29]

For there was no lack of societies with the declared aim of applying the new discoveries to practical problems. Ever since 1894, one year after Hall had charted the new course, the United Kingdom could boast a British Child Study Association, which published its own journal, *The Paidologist*. Germany followed on November 18, 1899 with the Berlin Society of Child Psychology.[30] Paris did not lag behind either: the French Institute of Experimental Pedagogy and two similar bodies were founded that same year. Before 1914 Europe could count twenty-four such institutions and almost as many journals.[31]

The topics examined by their various members, be it in Europe or in America, may be gleaned from the bibliography published by the *Zeitschrift für pädogogische Psychologie* during the first year of its existence. It covered books and papers on the language, play, geographical interests, reasoning, sense of justice, social responsibility, punishment, and fears of normal as well as abnormal children. In 1896 Witmer opened the first "clinic" for problem children in Philadelphia, and his example was quickly copied in other parts of America and in Europe.[32]

It was also in the 1890s that social psychology began to forge ahead. W. H. Rivers, though better known for his anthropological studies of the Todas of South India and of the structure of Melanesian society, was a psychologist at heart; in 1897 he was appointed lecturer in physiological and experimental psychology at Cambridge, and at the end of his life — he died in 1922 — he turned his attention to the psychological aspects of politics. Most social psychologists at the time, however, were less interested than Rivers in primitive society; they preferred to examine their own.

This was particularly true of Tarde, Sighele, and le Bon, who tried to place social and mass psychology on scientific foundations. Their fundamental work, which will be discussed in another context, was done during the years 1890 to 1895. Cooley's *Human Nature and the Social Order* followed in 1902. It may be considered a direct precursor of the first book to carry the name of social psychology on its title page. Its author was Cooley's American compatriot, E. A. Ross, who argued that instinct was the mainspring of all social activity. Ross's book was published in 1908, a year that, as we shall see, proved of great importance in the history of social psychology.

In the psychology of religion, too, the turn of the century saw a shift towards a more empirical and systematic approach. Here, too, interest was originally focussed on primitive people, not surprisingly so since the evolutionist doctrine was being systematically applied to every conceivable sphere. It was E. B. Tylor, an anthropologist who had been associated with Oxford University since 1883, who took the first great step when he declared that animism was the most primitive form of religion. But already in the 1890s his views had to be "amplified" following Codrington's studies of the Melanesians — Marett was to go much further still in 1909 with his *Threshold of Religion*. These amplifications were, in fact, in conflict with what they set out to amplify; a characteristic of the age. Thus, whereas Tylor had based his animism on the attribution of a living soul to inanimate objects, Codrington found that the Melanesians endowed these objects with "mana," a spiritual *cum* material force, of which man could only gain mastery, for his own benefit or the destruction of his enemies, by magic.

However, in the psychology of religion as in social psychology, interest shifted quickly from primitive people to one's own. Thus Hall examined the religious experiences of American children, although his questionnaires — which had become a hobby with him — were far from suited to probing into the child's psyche. Just before the turn of the century, Starbuck, another American, tackled the subject in a different way: he assembled a famous collection of manuscripts in which various people had recorded their religious experiences. As was to be expected from Americans in his day, most of the contributors mentioned their guilt feelings and their longing for conversion and for the unification of the soul with God. Starbuck himself was chiefly interested in the phenomenon of conversion, which he attributed to the need for a safe anchorage from the storms and stresses of adolescence. He summed up his findings in his *Psychology of Religion*, published in 1899.

It was on this work that the more famous one of William James was

409

based. It appeared three years later under the title of *The Varieties of Religious Experience* and, like Starbuck's study, it approached religion with unprecedented detachment.

While the specific results of all these new studies, no more than hinted at in the last few pages, are examined in the relevant chapters: those of child psychology in the chapter on children; those of criminology in the chapter on law; those of social psychology in the chapter of sociology; those of the psychology of religion in the chapter on religion; those of modern psychology in the chapter on medical science; and those of animal psychology in the chapter on biology — three new methods that were cause and consequence alike of all the rest must be discussed in this chapter, devoted to the general state of psychology at the turn of the century.

The first of these new methods was Gestalt psychology. It was part and parcel of a much wider principle that was making itself felt not only in other branches of science but in social life as a whole: the principal of organization, which Roderick Seidenberg, among many others, has called a characteristic of the twentieth century.[33] In psychology, in particular, there was great dissatisfaction with the atomism and the associationism of the reigning school. Just as biologists had come to revive the old idea that the whole is more than the sum of its parts, so psychologists, too, had come increasingly to appreciate that the psyche is more than a bundle of disparate perceptions, ideas, and sensations and more even than Wundt's synthesis of them all. The psyche, they believed, is a structured whole of psychological elements, much as a melody is a structured whole of notes or as a painting is a structured whole of colors and shapes.

This approach was not, of course, brand new. As early as 1874 Franz Brentano — not to mention many earlier writers — had asserted that perceptions do not constitute mental activity as such.[34] Ernst Mach had argued in 1886 that three points make us think of more than just three points — they suggest the idea of a triangle.[35] Four years later C. Ehrenfels and his Prague school, studying responses to sound, discovered that the listeners constituted a "Gestalt" — an integrated whole — out of the tones they had heard.[36] Janet, the French psychiatrist, must also have been thinking of an integral whole when, in 1892, he published his *Etat mental des hystériques*. For how else could he have held the disassociation of certain parts of the mind responsible for psychasthenia or, when highly pronounced, for hysteria? And even the then famous Carl Stumpf realized that the mental "elements" he had so indefatigably pursued throughout his life constituted the "skin" not the "kernel", of psychic life. He simply believed that the skin must be fully explored before going on to the kernel — as he himself put it in 1907.[37] This was merely Stumpf's way of rationalizing his reluctance to abandon the old approach for the new, which he knew deep down was by far the better. No wonder that most of Stumpf's pupils turned to experimental phenomenology, one of the cornerstones of Gestalt psychology.[38] A revolution was clearly in the air, with the result that when Ehrenfels, who was anything but a revolutionary, and, who at the time attracted little attention, first introduced his new ideas, he threw the reigning psychology of consciousness into total confusion.

Here, too, there was a revolution within a revolution. For while Mach and Ehrenfels had merely stressed the relationship of the parts, K. Bühler went much further when he said in so many words what Brentano had merely alluded to, namely that psychology must introduce a new kind of structural element, a mental element that transcended the senses, and that, by and large, coincided with the mental process.[39] With this contribution — the calendar had meanwhile moved on to 1907 — Gestalt psychology began to stand on its own feet. The double revolution brought it inevitably into conflict with the official doctrine which, as we know, recognized but three elements of consciousness, namely perception, conception, and sensation. But the new heresy was there to stay,[40] and to live on long beyond our period. Max Wertheimer was still part of that period, for his attack on the doctrine of sensory atomism was launched in 1912.[41] He used a novel weapon, the film, to demonstrate the error of that doctrine: when we are shown distinct pictures, separated by short enough an interval, we do not gain isolated impressions but have the sensation of watching a moving scene. Wertheimer accordingly rejected psychology in the form it had existed ever since Hume's day. Our perceptions transcend the things we perceive. W. Köhler was to make the same point later. In particular, he argued that the objections to Wertheimer's interpretation — that the film nevertheless consisted of separate pictures — were quite irrelevant: what matters to psychology is precisely that we experience these pictures as a continuous whole. "Gestalten" — organized wholes — underlay all our experiences. Wertheimer worked in Frankfurt with Köhler and K. Koffka, who were to become the best-known Gestalt psychologists, and he also founded the Berlin school before emigrating to the United States.[42]

Quite clearly the new approach threw fresh light on the human personality. It ceased to be considered a bundle of discrete characteristics and came to be seen as, an integral whole determined by the specific organization of these characteristics. It was this organization which made

411

it possible to distinguish one individual from the next, not the characteristics themselves which all men shared with one another. This "total"
approach also became the basis of modern characterology. It marked the
great difference between Heymans and Spranger. Thus while Heymans,
though not entirely deaf to the new trend,[43] still based his eight types on
the dogma of characteristics,[44] Spranger's "living forms" were a first, if
awkward, attempt to classify men by their total personalities.[45]

While Gestalt psychology thus emphasized the "whole" man but, for
the rest, did little to change the old, more static, conception of psychic
processes, William McDougall's purposive or teleological psychology laid
particular emphasis on their dynamic aspect, even while retaining the
idea of separate characteristics, so dear to the old psychology.[46] Building
on Wundt's studies of volition, on Ach's "determining tendencies," on
animal psychology, on behaviorism, and on the older social psychology of
Tarde, Sighele, le Bon, and Ross, this British psychologist, who later
moved to America, arrived at a social psychology based on "purpose"
guided by "instinct." He distinguished seven main instincts man shared
with animals, namely: flight, repulsion, curiosity, aggression, submission,
dominance, and parental care — the sources of the primitive emotions
of fear, disgust, wonder, rage, humility, self-assertion, and tenderness.

The book in which he presented these ideas in 1908, his *Introduction
to Social Psychology*, was reprinted thirteen times within as many years,[47]
more than any other psychological textbook.[48] This may seem surprising
since Descartes, Hobbes, and Spinoza — to name only three — had already
expounded these basic features of man's nature, be it in a less precise
and elaborate way, so that McDougall was more a keeper of an ancient
heritage than an innovator. While this is undoubtedly true, when we
review his work against the backcloth of the centuries and the immediately preceding centuries in particular, its attraction becomes obvious.
Here there was — apparently for the first time — a psychology in which
concrete man with all his emotions, sentiments and ambitions could
recognize himself; a dynamic psychology, moreover, that suited the
accelerating tempo and drive of Western society to perfection.

Though later "purposive" psychologists such as Tolman and Hull and
even McDougall himself, scrapped most of his original system, they in
no way detracted from the historical importance of his *Introduction*. It
may be true that McDougall exaggerated the scope of his discovery and
that many of his arguments were vague and mystical,[49] but then all
science, and *a fortiori* the most complex of all sciences — the science of
man's mind — limps from hypothesis to hypothesis, its very progress
residing in the verification, and consequent amendment, of what, time

and again, turns out to have been biased, inadequate, or mistaken.

By the side of McDougall, William James, who was a far better thinker and writer, did a great deal to advance the new dynamic and concrete approach. He did this as a pragmatic philosopher, but here we are only concerned with his contribution to psychology, however closely bound up with his philosophy it may have been. James, like Freud, may be considered the very embodiment of the intellectual revolution that was then proceeding and, what is more, he was so from a fairly early age. Having studied medicine in his native America and in Germany, he became a materialist and a determinist, and remained one until a crisis occurred in his life; he was thirty at the time, having been born in 1842. He began to study the writings of the French philosopher Charles Renouvier on free will, and was led to what he thought was a more satisfactory approach. But he never became an idealist;[50] all he did was to discover his true self — even as a psychologist. Having concluded that physiology was busily trying to elucidate what, in fact, it obscured, he went on to postulate that mental activity was not built up of disparate elements but constituted a "stream of consciousness." Not only the physiologists had failed to grasp that fact, but the psychologists as well; their introspective method simply divorced mental representations from what they represented. James dismissed this approach as a tiresome abstraction; he himself "preferred to be systematically erratic rather than give up his opposition to systems."[51] When his *Principles of Psychology*, conceived as early as 1878, appeared in 1890, it caused if anything, an even greater stir than McDougall's *Intoduction* did in 1908. And that, too, was understandable. James was a brilliant writer and was admired as much for his prose as he was for his psychological insights. Thus even when he introduced difficult physiological concepts to elucidate the phenomena of consciousness, he was careful not to bore his readers. For the rest, he paid unprecedented attention to the role of the unconscious, the discovery of which he attributed to Janet.[52] According to James, some men at least have, not only consciousness, but also a series of unconscious memories, ideas and sensations that cannot be reached by the narrow beam of introspection, but are nevertheless part and parcel of mental life, inasmuch as they are capable of revealing their presence by unmistakable signs. He felt that this discovery was of the utmost importance because it revealed an unexpected peculiarity of human nature.[53] The fact that he attributed these processes to "some men at least" shows that James's unconscious was not so much Freud's as a paranormal phenomenon. Now James was taking an increasing interest in just such phenomena, as witness his founding of the American Society for Psy-

413

chical Research in 1884, two years after the establishment of a similar society in England. For all that, he remained close enough to Janet not to relegate the unconscious to physiology; instead he described it as "a secondary self" which though distinct from the "primary self," was nevertheless part of the human personality.

The names of James and McDougall may suggest that dynamic psychology was an exclusively American affair, but the contributions of Alfred Fouillée and Emile Boutroux, although they may have been less famous men, and of Léon Brunschvicg, show that this was not at all the case. Fouillée, who, like Wundt, had also dabbled in ethnopsychology, as witness his *Psychologie du peuple français* (1898) and his *Esquisse psychologique des peuples européens* (1903), was no less dynamic in his approach than McDougall. He, too, believed that the fundamental fact of psychic life was not a mechanical reflex, but intent, and he distinguished intellectual consciousness from an intentional consciousness which he described as the urge or will to live. According to him, every idea is guided by the intention of the thinking subject. It turns his every thought into an *idée force*, whose evolution he discussed in 1890 and whose psychology he described in 1893. Fouillée also worked with such immeasurables as psychological intensity, but unlike Bergson, who owed him a great debt, he did not treat that intensity as a quality. Though Fouillée's doctrine was suffused with the ideas of the romantic philosophers — after all, he was born in 1838 — it nevertheless suited the climate of 1900, in which a host of romantic buds came into late blossom.[54] It was no accident that the last of Fouillée's books to be published during his life should have examined the most recent anti-intellectual trends (1911). Brunschvicg, for his part, never became an anti-intellectual. But his *Introduction à la vie de l'esprit* of 1900 nevertheless makes it clear that he could not dispense with a "spirit." Man's choice of ideas could not possibly be mechanical or random, but reflected his overall conception; every act of consciousness sent out waves in all directions. Each individual was an original, unique and indivisible whole.[55]

Much as McDougall's dynamic psychology had its European counterparts, so James's and his compatriot Leuba's psychology of religion found its European equivalent in the ideas of Janet and Boutroux. Like the Americans, these Frenchmen were convinced of the importance of religious experiences, in normal no less than abnormal mental life. For Janet, however, this branch of psychology was at most a subsidiary one. Boutroux, who, like Brunschvicg, was a philosopher, published just one purely psychological study — *La Psychologie du mysticisme*, which appeared in the same year as James's book.[56]

414

The third new intellectual current bore Freud's name. It was so revolutionary that its full effects did not make themselves felt until much later. Light can illuminate but it can also blind. The almost unanimous rejection of Freud's doctrine was not due primarily to genuine or alleged resentment of the emphasis he placed on the sexual etiology of mental illness, or even on the sexual stirrings in children. On the contrary, what aroused the greatest opposition was the fact that Freud did not confine his "libido," the central element of his doctrine, to the purely sexual sphere, as Marx did not confine his economic ideas to the economy. In other words, what the anti-Freudians resented most bitterly was Freud's attempt to synthesize all the latest psychological currents: the organizational idea, the indivisibility of the psyche, the dynamic approach, the idea of purpose, and the stress of the concrete elements of psychological life.

Tracking down predecessors can just as easily bring out the greatness of an innovator as it can reduce him to human dimensions. In the history of nineteenth-century psychology and psychiatry it is possible to point to a number of discoveries — we have mentioned some already — that might have served Freud as a starting point, and quite often did just that. His links with such admired colleagues as Breuer, Charcot and Fliess proved a help and a hindrance all at once. He must have gleaned a great deal from literature as well, not only from Sophocles and Shakespeare but even from nineteenth-century writers. For Freud was a great reader, absorbing fresh insights from books much as he absorbed them from his medical practice, his self-analysis and from everything else that his unquenchable thirst for knowledge settled upon. Of Nietzsche who, with some clairvoyance, had arrived at many of Freud's later ideas (for instance sublimation) in purely intuitive ways, Freud said with great honesty: "Nietzsche . . . whose pronouncements and insights are so often in astonishing agreement with the difficult findings of psychoanalysis, is someone I avoided for a long time for that very reason. For, ultimately, I was not so much concerned with my own priority, as with keeping an open mind."[57] Beerling summed up Nietzsche's role as a precursor of Freud when he said: "Nietzsche destroyed the rational nucleus of human subjectivity, and made the complex of drives the true organ of the interpretation of reality."[58] Even so, Freud himself needed a great deal of creative power, not to mention tenacious work, to develop a theory that went so much against the grain, albeit, as Freud himself put it, it was no more than discovering "what was right under my nose." By that he meant that he had done no more than complete a revolution, no more than fit all the previous discoveries into a sweeping panorama of the human intellect.

415

But he was being far too humble, for it took a great deal of courage to proceed from the nineteenth-century mechanistic approach, via physiology and neurology, without slighting scientific precepts, to a new science concerned with something as tangible as the psyche, to a science that his colleagues dismissed as nothing short of fantasy and divination; it took much courage, through long years of financial difficulties, while working in a precarious practice and while being thwarted by professional hostility, to keep putting forward such apparently far-fetched ideas as displacement, Oedipus complex, infantile sexuality, dream analysis, flight into illness, the psychology of error, and self-punishment, most of which have since become household words in intellectual and even in semi-intellectual circles. These ideas could only have been gained after a deep inner struggle, for Freud was anything but a revolutionary. Worse still, he was proposing to apply to "normal" people what insights he had gained from his dealings with mental patients. Montessori, too had been reproached for propounding ideas she had acquired from her work with "idiots."

Karl Bühler, no less, has denied that Freud should be numbered among the "holistic" thinkers. Bühler condemned him as thinking in terms of substance rather than form ("structure"), and went so far as to say that the modern Gestalt idea is at the opposite pole to Freud's thinking.[59] But this charge was unjust, if only because every school of psychology that adopts a central principle must needs apply that principle to the whole personality. What possible justification was there for accusing a man who held that all man's actions were guided by the unconscious, indeed who denied that the least lapse of the tongue or of the pen was due to chance, of ignoring the "whole"? It is even more difficult to deny that Freud's doctrine must be included among the "purposive psychologies," what with its explanations of human behavior in terms of pleasure, pain, desire, needs, drives, and impulses. McDougall, for one, considered Freud an ally, albeit one who was obsessed with sex.[60] Freud's psychology must also be called dynamic. It did away with the idea that human consciousness is no more than a passive mirror of the external world and with the dissection of the human personality into abstract properties or separate instincts, and this despite the fact that he called his method psychoanalysis.

We cannot enter into the fascinating history of psychoanalysis in greater detail, not merely because space prevents us from doing so but also because what concerns us here above all is the wider effect of Freud's great discovery. Hence the briefest mention of his school must suffice, the more so as, though Rank, Reik and Ferenzi, Adler and Jung in Vienna or nearby, Abraham in Berlin, Brill in New York and Jones in Toronto and London, all began their careers before the First World War, though they participated in the many psychoanalytical congresses held since 1908, and though most of them helped to found the International Psychoanalytical Association in 1910, they did not achieve world fame until well after our period.

All in all, it is clear that the fundamental changes that overtook psychology at the turn of the century in the form of the three new methods of thought we have examined, could not have been smooth, if only because all three were introduced in the relatively short space of less than twenty years. Thus when Wundt's experimental psychology called itself the "new psychology" at the turn of the century, it was new in name only. Anyone looking for the contributions of Ehrenfels, Janet, McDougall, or Freud in Scripture's *New Psychology*, published in 1897, will be disappointed. True, the last chapter, devoted to the current state of psychology, does mention James's name and even his *Principles*, but only to add the derogatory remark that the book attracted some public attention.[61] Psychology was undoubtedly in the public eye. Ribot, the chairman of the fourth international congress, held in Paris in 1900, estimated the number of books, reports and articles on psychology published since the last congress (held in Munich in 1896) at between nine and ten thousand, and he added that the process was accelerating.[62]

We know of the many shock waves caused by this surprising development not only from the countless polemics that were raging at the time, but more particularly from two books. Karl Willy's *Krisis in der Psychologie*[63] ("Crisis in Psychology") appeared in 1899. He did not, it is true, perceive the crisis with which we are concerned, yet it is revealing that Willy leaned toward a psychology that would take serious account of both Nietsche and Bergson. He himself thought that his results harmonized with those of Bergon's *Essai sur les données immédiates de la conscience*, which had appeared in a second printing the year before.

The other book was published thirty years later: it was Karl Bühler's *Die Krise der Psychologie*.[64] It deserves special mention here not only because Bühler traced the crisis in psychology back to 1890, but also because he showed that its repercussions still made themselves felt twenty-five years after the turn of the century. Bühler himself considered that crisis not a sign of decay, but as one of great constructional activity reminiscent of the erection of the Tower of Babel.

So the optimistic days of 1890, the days of Wundt, when leading

417

psychologists had a common program and a shared hope, and when the first edition of the *Zeitschrift für Psychologie* saw the light of day, had ended in a grave crisis. All the countless studies and experiments, all the research and speculation, had been unable to solve the riddle of the Sphinx, the riddle of man's essence. That riddle remains unsolved to this day, and perhaps it is as well that it does.

CHAPTER XXVIII

INSIGHT THROUGH IMPOTENCE

On January 9, 1900 André Antoine, leader of the avant-garde theater movement in Paris, produced, directed and played the lead in *En Paix*, a new play by L. Bruyère, in his own theater. Here we are not so much concerned with the play, the author or even with the actor, as with a much more remarkable fact. In its January issue that year — the eighth of its existence — the *Revue Internationale de Sociologie* devoted one-and-a-half pages to a review of Bruyère's play by Oscar d'Araujo.[1] One reason for the review may have been that the play dealt with the fate of a normal person who had been sent to a lunatic asylum by a family anxious to get rid of him, but this does not explain why the same issue also carried reviews of other plays, or why the column was con-tinued in the February issue. The answer is that everything under the sun had become grist to the sociologist's mill. Thus the same journal also published an article that year on the seventh-century Chinese Queen, Ou-ch'eh.[2] It came from the versatile pen of C. Letourneau, one of the great sociologists of his day, albeit his name is missing from Barnes's exhaustive history of sociology,[3] which runs to close on a thousand pages.[4] The *Revue* also held an enquiry into its readers' views of Tolstoy's philosophy — something no modern sociological journal would consider worthy of inclusion in its pages,[5] and a *projet de tableau du progrès des sciences morales et politiques* drawn up by the Parisian Academy of Moral and Political Science and based on an idea of the French Revolu-tion: the compilation of periodic reports to the nation on the progress of the sciences.[6] The journal, moreover, kept its readers informed of Novikow's plan to set up a European federation, printing long selections from his forthcoming *La Féderation de l'Europe*.[7]

While these are but random examples, the systematic efforts of Emile Durkheim, generally considered the leading sociologist of his day, leave us in no doubt whatsoever that in the proliferating phase it had entered at the turn of the century, sociology was usurping the functions of ethics, cultural history, economics, religious studies, aesthetics, demography, politics, and anthropology. For in *L'Année Sociologique*, a journal of which Durkheim was the editor and which first appeared in 1896–1897, we can follow this proliferating process from year to year simply by consulting the systematic bibliography. In 1900 it already ran to seven sections: general sociology, the sociology of religion, of law, of morals, of crime and of economics, and social morphology, in addition to a "miscellaneous" section, inevitable in all classifications, and in this case comprising aesthetics and technology. It need not be stressed that, in view of the omnivorous appetite sociologists evinced at the time, the table of contents devoted to each of the sections should have been divided and subdivided, each entry being provided with Roman and/or Arabic numerals, and that the subdivisions should have been studded with capital letters.[8] All these "analyses," as the brief descriptions (and often even the mere mention of books were called somewhat extravagantly in the bibliography, covered nearly five hundred pages in 1899–1900, providing a nearly complete survey of contemporary sociological literature in the widest sense of the term: close on six hundred authors were mentioned. The first item listed was, ironically enough, de Martini's book on the impossibility of constructing a general sociology; the last was Girod and Massénat's text on human settlements during the reindeer period in the Vézère and Corrèze valleys,[9] something we should now consider a contribution to archaeology or prehistory, not to sociology.

The lectures delivered by the Italian sociologist Achille Loria in January to May 1900 at the University of Padua also make it clear how prolix sociology had become in his day. "Sociology," he had an imaginary opponent declare, "has not arrived at a single truth on which the various authors can agree." But Loria consoled himself with the fact that the older disciplines were no better off, not even mathematics, where certain century-old geometric ideas were being challenged with growing success. "Allez en avant," he exhorted his colleagues, "la foi vous viendra."[10]

S. R. Steinmetz, who delivered his inaugural address before Leyden University in 1900 — a clear sign that the Dutch academic world, too, had at long last opened its doors to the youngest and most curious of the sciences — called for some restriction when he proposed that sociologists should grant economics the status of an independent discipline, but that was his only concession. "I consider that, for the time being, the entire sphere of non-economic phenomena constitutes a single whole, and that all studies devoted to them can be subsumed under the heading of sociology. Sociology is the hitherto undifferentiated part of social science." Nevertheless, he considered that some of its subdivisions — for instance, religious science and ethnology — had grown mature enough to be hived off from the mother science in the near future.[11]

But if this dogmatic declaration were to suggest some measure of unanimity among sociologists, that impression would be totally misleading. Thus one contributor to *L'Année Sociologique,* dealing with the place of morals, or "elementary sociology" as he called it, in the hierarchy of the abstract sciences — Comte's ideas were still rife at the time — summed up the situation correctly when he wrote that, in sociology, system follows upon system, with every sociologist feeling obliged to correct the views of his colleagues on one point or another. This explained why there were at least thirty theories on what sociology really was or had to be. And he concluded sadly with the classical *tot capita tot sensus.* As during the blessed reign of the scholastics, there were again as many heads as there were ideas, the only apparent solace being that now, at least, the sociological textbooks which were becoming as numerous as pebbles on the beach could fill their emptiness with lists of conflicting ideas.[12]

There were others, too, who noticed this proliferation and deplored it. Charles Bouglé, the reviewer of the above-named book by de Martini, who also achieved renown as an independent collaborator of Durkheim, freely admitted that general sociology was still nothing more than a tower of Babel.[13] He did so in the same annual in which he also tried to suggest the correct approach, as exemplified in his own study of the caste system, the results of which were by no means confined to India or even to Aryan civilizations.[14] For his readings of de Martini had persuaded him that sociologists were agreed neither on the subject nor on the method nor even on the classification of their discipline, let alone on the characteristics of social phenomena, and he believed that this very failure was the best possible argument in favor of more methodical studies.

Had Bouglé also been able to show why this confused situation had to be as confused as it was, he could have taken an even more decisive step. Seeing through confusion, after all, means discovering a regulating principle. Here the historian has the advantage of hindsight. Comte and Spencer, who laid the foundations of sociology, still believed that they could survey the entire social process with the help of a few more or less arbitrary concepts, an approach that however brilliant, was bound to render sociology sterile in the long run. The parallel development of economics, psychology, religious studies, cultural history, and above all of anthropology (Tylor's *Anthropology* was published in 1881) made it clear to anyone who cared to look — and sociologists wanted nothing more — that their great predecessors had not derived their general concepts from real processes but, anxious to improve upon the prevailing ideas, had ended up with so many abstractions.

421

The "social" tendency was still rife in the social sciences at the turn of the century. But something had nevertheless changed. Thus while Bouglé still tried to lay down guidelines for society, he had begun to realize that to do so effectively sociology must first become a completely disinterested discipline.

Like late nineteenth-century philosophical sociology, the analytical sociology that emerged at the beginning of the twentieth century tried to throw light on the changing social scene. However, being suffused with the relativizing tendency so characteristic of our period, it gradually abandoned the search for an unequivocal explanation, and contented itself instead with the isolation of the "genuine scientific" elements needed for that explanation.

The main source of confusion in sociology was the fact that social developments were increasingly undermining the existing social relationships. How could sociology which — no matter how we describe its methods, aims, or classifications — was primarily concerned with these relationships in one way or another, possibly have escaped this fate? It had to be confused, and the confusion became all the greater because, at the time, sociologists fell into two camps: those who still looked for a general theory and those who were convinced that no such theory could be found.

So, at the turn of the century, sociology was a no-man's-land, unexplored territory, an eldorado without visible or defensible borders, where every comer could stake his claim. This may explain why some considered "social Darwinism" a purely academic approach, while others mistook it for a call to political action, and used this shaky platform to launch their campaign of intolerance.[15] Unfortunately, their views did not fall on deaf ears, particularly during the last quarter of the nineteenth century and the first decade of the twentieth, when racial, national and social conflicts abounded. This faction included Bagehot, who died in 1877, and Benjamin Kidd, who was as outspoken a hyper-Darwinist in sociology as Weismann was in biology. Despite, or rather thanks to, the light weight of his scientific luggage, his *Social Evolution* of 1894 and his *Control of the Tropics*, which appeared four years later[16], became the guidebooks of the "young lions" in the Radical Party, led by Chamberlain. The second book argued that imperialism reflected the will of the age, and the first attracted attention with its virulent attacks on rationalism. According to Kidd, all progress was the result of national struggle — the fiercer the struggle the faster the progress. Reason, by contrast served only to impede the struggle, fostering nothing so much as narrow self-interest. Reason, to Kidd, was like fire: useful if under control but all-consuming if left to itself. It was the very anti-thesis of religion, that irrational but powerful source of order.[17]

Of greater scientific standing were such men as Gumplowicz and Ratzenhofer, to mention only two who made the headlines. It was not without significance that both should have been born in Austria-Hungary, the breeding ground of racial conflict. In his youth Gumplowicz, who came from Cracow, was a member of the "Young Poles," and although in 1893 he became a professor in Graz, he never recanted his rebellious ideas.[18] The result was an uncompromising approach, one that even Barnes dismissed as being purely subjective.[19] Ratzenhofer, too, knew what social strife meant from personal experience. The son of a Viennese watchmaker, he managed to rise to the rank of Lieutenant-General and President of the War Council, not without being hurt in the process in more than one sense: after a series of duels over politics and women, still *de rigueur* throughout continental Europe, he received a wound from which he died years later, on his return from the United States in 1904.[20] It is not surprising, therefore, that, according to him, every living creature was born with a tendency to live out its instincts; after all, Ratzenhofer's home was in Freud's Vienna and though eventually forced to bridle his passions, he continued to be guided throughout life by "bread envy," as he called the instinct of self-preservation, and "blood love." Nor was that all. The rest was said in a long-forgotten brochure by a long-forgotten author: C. von Kelles-Krauz, professor at the Collège des Sciences Sociales in Paris, and also at the University of Brussels. According to Krauz, Gum-plowicz (and we might add Ratzenhofer as well) was anything but a social Darwinist. For though the social Darwinists were "hard" they were nevertheless socially progressive in their own way, while Gumplowicz was a "sceptical counter-revolutionary."[21] In his cynical mouth, bour-geois society was denying the very possibility of reform, and continued to chew the bitter fruit of a pessimism born of loss of faith in its mission.

However, the bitterest fruit of this tree, which spread more knowledge of evil than it did of good, was something our pamphleteer could not have foreseen in 1902: from Gumplowicz a series of twisting paths led on to Hitler's intellectual mentors. One of these paths was geopolitics. Its first exponent was F. Ratzel, whose *Das Meer als Quelle der Völker-grösse* (The Sea as Source of National Greatness) was published in 1900.[22] Durkheim, who reviewed it for *L'Année Sociologique*, and objected to the German author's rapacity, found that it had far more sinister political overtones than even the same author's *Politische Geographie* (Political Geography) which had appeared three years earlier. At the time similar ideas were being propounded outside Germany as well; Sir Halford Mackinder, for instance, applied the terms "heartland" and "world island" to the Sino-Russian land mass and Eurasia respectively, adding that whoever controlled the heartland also controlled the world island, and whoever controlled the world island controlled the world. America, too, added its voice: Admiral Mahan's famous *The Influence of Sea Power Upon History* was published in 1890.[23] In Sweden R. Kjellén, professor in Göteborg since 1901, discussed geopolitics in his *Stormakterna* (The Great Powers) of 1905; he called it one of the five great divisions of politics, the other four being demopolitcs, sociopolitics, eratopolitics, and ecopolitics. With Karl Haushofer, this approach became frankly poisonous, but only after the First World War. Before that, he was a staff officer and a leading expert on modern Japan, where he was stationed from 1908 to 1910.[24]

However great the influence of these "social Darwinists" may have been, there were many to challenge their views. One of them was Franz Oppenheimer. In his *Soziologische Streifzüge* (Sociological Excursions),[25] which, incidentally, he did not commit to paper until long after the war because his medical practice left him little time for other pursuits, he argued that all monopolies were based on power. According to this liberal socialist, they used their power for evil, not for good, a view he shared with the neo-liberal Alexander Rüstow, with his "superimposition" theory.[26] But the true challenger of the militant and explosive sociologies of Gumplowicz and Ratzenhofer was that most peaceful of peaceful men, the Russian Jacques Novikow, whom we mentioned earlier. Not that he denied the importance of the "struggle for existence"; he simply believed that it, too, was subject to evolutionary change. His four stages of human development were physical, economic, political, and intellectual struggle, and although all four still existed in his day, he considered it a sign of progress that the last was becoming increasingly important. Comte and Spencer left their traces on his work as well, not surprisingly since Novikow was just fifty in 1900. His main work, *Les Luttes entre sociétés humaines et leur phases successives*, published in 1893 and reprinted three years later, stands as a lasting monument to him and to his ideas. From it strands ran directly to Kropotkin and to Norman Angell and the peace movement in general. In short, sociology was the servant of good or evil, depending on one's point of view.

Novikow was no more a champion of value-free science than were his social Darwinist opponents. His Russian youth had filled him with hatred of despotism in every form; his experiences in Western Europe (he arrived there during the Bismarck period) with a horror of militarism. The case of Novikow and his opponents corroborated the main law of the sociology of knowledge: that every scientific idea reflects the general social situation of its propounder.

We can go further, and say that this realization had entered the consciousness of the age, and it was not by chance that it should have done so from Russia, where the intelligentsia was locked in mortal battle with Czarism and the orthodox church. For it was in Russia that P. L. Lavrov (died 1900) and N. K. Mikhailovsky (died 1904) founded the so-called subjective school of sociology. They anticipated the future when they wrote that there are certain truths that cannot be grasped when they are first presented because of the subjective unpreparedness of society to see things as they actually are.[27] That was a tremendous step forward, and, moreover, a striking example of the "spur of backwardness," for Czarist society seemed the worst possible environment for the growth of academic sociology. Indeed, the first sociological textbook published in Russia had done little more than review the leading sociological theories of the day. It was published in 1894, and its author, N. I. Kareyev, was also the only member of the "subjective" school to hold a chair — not in sociology but in the philosophy of history — at the University of St. Petersburg.[28] M. M. Kovalevski, too, was a professor, and in Moscow, but of jurisprudence and not for long. Being a liberal, although anything but revolutionary, he was dismissed in 1887 for teaching that political developments were essentially the same all over the world and that Russia was accordingly due for a constitution.[29]

The dependence of sociological insights on socio-political developments was also appreciated by many not directly involved in the development of the sociology of knowledge. Thus Kovalevski became one of the most influential sociologists of his day in and outside Russia thanks precisely to his attempt to abolish this oppressive dependence. Being a man of independent means and unmarried, he settled in France, and in his Mediterranean villa built up a library of 50,000 volumes. For the rest, he wrote articles for the *Revue Internationale de Sociologie*, or went on lecture tours that took him from Stockholm to California. With his own money he founded a Russian school of social science in Paris (1900), before being elected chariman of the renowned International Sociological Institute. During the 1905 revolution he returned to Russia, where he held the first chair of sociology from 1908 until his death during the First World War — in Bechterov's Psycho-Neurological Institute.[30] To the historian of sociology, Kovalevski's fame, which during his lifetime was based on his wealth and "interesting" life abroad as much as it was based on his contributions to economic history, lies rather in his vacillation between the old and the new conceptions. This also explains why we have drawn his intellectual portrait at some length: Kovalevski was the embodiment of the confusion in the sociological camp to which this chapter has been devoted. A pupil of Maine, the great legal historian, of Tylor, the anthropologist, and personally acquainted with Spencer and Marx, he started his career as a staunch evolutionist and a firm believer in progress. And though he modified his original ideas over the years, he never abandoned them altogether: he always believed that mankind evolved in a positive direction. But he was no longer as certain as he had been, and this uncertainty caused him to abandon the attempt to demonstrate that population growth was the central factor of evolution. "I believe that modern sociology attaches such importance to this problem because it is looking for a way out of the maze of unpredictable actions and reactions that constitute the social process," he wrote in 1905.[31] Though life in Czarist Russia had taught him that evolution was not the nostrum for social ills he had thought it to be, his opposition to monistic theories also embraced the Marxists. For like the rest of his colleagues, he, too, was a politician at heart: he became leader of the democratic reform movement, a member of the first Duma and later of the Council of State. The only school he founded had been built on money, not on new insights. For all that, Kovalevski exerted a great deal of influence on his younger compatriots Kondratiev and, in particular, Sorokin, who escaped the terror of the Civil War, on the two Webers in Germany, on L. T. Hobhouse in England and on American sociology in general.[32]

Sorel and Pareto, probably the two most original sociologists of their day, did not help to reduce the confusion either. Rather did they add to it by turning what had been a mere reorientation and shift in emphasis into a complete transformation. But though their work struck a dissonant note, it remained part of a symphony played to an audience that was no longer afraid of discords. Pareto himself was a paradox, and as such typical of the impending cultural crisis. For while there was no stauncher champion of the scientific method in social science, he just as resolutely made short shrift of the idea that truth was a useful guide to social organization. At the same time as Freud discovered that man can easily come to terms with lies about himself, indeed that such lies are an indispensable aid to social adaptation, Pareto concluded that society thrived on untruths, that the scientific verities by which men swore could lead them to hell just as well as to heaven. Such current ideas as faith in progress, in democracy, or the benefits of general suffrage, struck him as being no more logical than the old belief that dreams can help men to pick winners, or that 3 or 7 are sacred numbers. Equally

426

modern was his relativistic theory of knowledge. The mainsprings of our actions are not logical decisions but "residues," indirect expressions of our sentiments, mere "derivates," whose very nature prevents us from identifying them as such. Modern, too, was his rejection of human solidarity and of sentimental ethics. Force is more important than reason; all governments are oligarchies. Hence his élitist approach which, as we saw earlier, was another sign of "modernism." Pareto's celebrated compatriot and contemporary, Gaetano Mosca, used much the same approach and also shared Pareto's disdain of monistic theories.[33] To him, history was a cemetery of aristocracies that appear and vanish in an apparently pointless series of cycles. That these, the most "modern" ideas in sociology, should have come from Italy was partly due to the fact that the old had maintained its hold on that country longer than on most others. Here, the old philosopher and sociologist Roberto Ardingò, who was seventy-two in 1900 and who was to live for another twenty years, reigned supreme as a Comte redivivus. The only "old-fashioned" thing about Pareto, who was fifty in 1898, was probably the fact that he, too, tried to construct a system — in the *Trattato di sociologia generale*, his main work, which ran to more than two thousand paragraphs, and the first volume of which was published in 1915. It was the last, mistaken attempt at general system-building — no sociologist ever tried it again.[34]

Sorel, too, was a highly controversial figure. He was a friend of Pareto, and like him he started out as an engineer. His intellectual pedigree was more twisted than even the most gnarled of oaks: Proudhon, Bakunin, Marx, but also Vico and Bergson. No wonder that the resulting cocktail with its almost indescribable taste could only be sipped, and that the intellectuals were almost unanimous in rejecting it, as witness their reaction both to his first important book, *Le Procès de Socrate*, which appeared at the very beginning of our period, and also to his second *Les Illusions du progrès*, published in 1908. In this last book Sorel challenged the idea of automatic progress more incisively than even Pareto had done. Matters did not improve with his publication, also in 1908, of the *Réflexions sur la violence*, a book that became the gospel of the militant syndicalists, and in which he upheld violence as a creative force needed to usher in the age of modern, productive man. Moreover, Sorel stressed the importance of "myths" as mainstays of the militancy and morale of the workers.[35] Not that he was particularly interested in furthering the interests of the working class as such; he turned to them simply because he had ceased to believe in the future of the bourgeoisie.

Distrust of the bourgeoisie, of the intelligentsia, of the idea of prog-

427

ress of democracy, of parliament, and of humanitarianism; glorification
of violence, of myths and the élite, together with unreserved approval of the
untrammeled expression of man's deepest instincts — it was hard to
find a doctrine more opposed to the apparent spirit of the age. So contrary was it, in fact, that one might easily gain the impression that all
Sorel did was to stand the prevailing ideas on their head. On closer inspection, however, it appears that the spirit of the age had itself begun to change. The First World War and its aftermath had, so to speak,
cast their ominous shadow before them on Sorel, who, shortly be-
before his death in 1922, was able to see his teachings bear fruit in Lenin
and Mussolini, with, incidentally, grim satisfaction rather than great hope.

Every age is, however, more than what it bequeaths to future generations; its products crumble into dust and can only be resurrected by
careful excavation and reconstruction. Thus while the ideas of Sorel
and Pareto now look antiquated and confused, they seemed most original
to many of their contemporaries. Tired of seeking for the one great
explanation, the one great abstract system, sociology had begun to look
more closely at concrete reality and was bravely assisted in this task
by anthropology, which, more generously endowed with funds than ever
before, had begun to open up vast new territories and to explore them
in depth. As a result, the whole world had become Europe's workshop,
from the Shamans in the extreme north of Siberia to the Fuegians in the
extreme south of America, and from the Eskimos of Greenland to the
aborigines of Tasmania, the last of whom died in London in 1877. What
all this meant to sociology we may gather from Tylor's *Primitive Culture*,
first published in 1871 but regularly reprinted; from Frazer's famous
Golden Bough, the second edition of which was published in 1900; from
Lucien Lévy-Bruhl's *Les Fonctions mentales dans les sociétés inférieures*
(1910) or finally from Franz Boas's *The Mind of Primitive Man* (1911).[36]
These books were crammed with new data and hypotheses.[37]

Just at the turn of the century, moreover, anthropology entered
a new phase which helped to turn it into an even closer ally of sociology,
but for the rest did little to diminish its own problems. That phase was
bound up with the names of W. Foy, F. Graebner, Father Wilhelm Schmidt, and Leo Frobenius. Under the influence of Ratzel, who believed
that man's inventiveness was not nearly as great as man thought, these
scholars turned their backs on evolutionism which, in anthropology,
meant explaining the similarities between various cultures in terms of
parallel development. The new school, by contrast, propounded the
idea of cultural diffusion, i.e., that all cultures of significance originated
in a single center. This interpretation faced sociologists with grave dif-

ficulties. To take but one example, when Frobenius "showed" that the cultures of West Africa and Oceania could be traced back to a common source,[38] Ratzel, his teacher, who concurred with him, nevertheless realized that the new approach raised grave new problems.[39] The "diffusionist" school made its greatest impact in Germany and Austria, and left two great monuments to its ebbing fortunes, namely the international journal *Anthropos*, edited by Wilhelm Schmidt, which was to stand missionaries in such good stead from 1906 onwards, and the *Kulturgeschichtliche Bibliothek* (Library of Cultural History) founded by Foy. Its first volume, edited by Graebner, was published in 1911 under the title of *Methode der Ethnologie* (The Method of Ethnology).[40] The term "cultural history" had been chosen very deliberately, for the problem of dating, which had been of no more than passing interest to the evolutionists, was of paramount importance to the diffusionists. We shall be returning to the subject in the appropriate chapter.

So sociologists were presented with a mass of new and indigestible data. Their impotence to survey a field that looked so much greater than it had ever been, almost persuaded them to doubt its existence, but these very doubts eventually brought them fresh insight into tens of thousands of details, the existence of which the great system builders had not even suspected. Everything appeared to be similar but everything also appeared to be different. There was nothing novel under the sun and yet everything seemed new. Everything had been thought of before and nothing had been thought out properly.

The almost interminable series of sociological studies assembled in thousands of books and articles, of which only the titles survive in bibliographies and on card indexes, would merely have served to add to the confusion had sociology been no more than a mirror of the society in which it was practised and not an autonomous discipline, thus resembling the individual who is both the product of his environment and at the same time an independent being. From the confusion sprang the call for order. Because this quest for order and organization in science, a symptom of our age, made itself felt with such great force at the turn of the century, the rest of this chapter will be devoted to its effects in sociology. When Durkheim first tried to set its house in order, he was no doubt guided by Descartes's "I know very little or nothing at all." The upshot was *Les Règles de la méthode sociologique* of 1895, revised and extended in 1901. In it Durkheim set out his refusal to start with any presuppositions, be they positivist, evolutionist, or spiritualist. And he would be a naturalist only in the sense that he considered the phenomena under review as open to a natural explanation on principle. The worldly

successes sociology had scored with Comte and Spencer meant nothing
to him. Durkheim was almost ascetic in his quest for esoteric knowledge.
He refused to be a pure sociologist, one who produced nothing but pure
sociology. The passion with which he defended the scientific approach
makes one suspect that he was at pains to repress the opposite tendency
in himself, and a recent study has, in fact, shown that the links between
philosophy and sociology, so sacred to Comte, were present in Durkheim's
work as well, albeit implicitly.[44] This great innovator, too, was thus
tied to the past. In particular, he never denied his own beginnings: he
was originally intended to become a rabbi, and his early training stood
him in good stead. For despite everything he never became the dupe
of his claim that sociology is an autonomous science; he knew much
too much about the close relationship between society and the knowledge it produces. This awareness made him, like the Russians we mentioned earlier, a pioneer of the sociology of knowledge. Meillet, the
famous linguist, was deeply impressed by him. Just as oddly, Durkheim,
his quest for a value-free science notwithstanding, was not blind to the
importance of values in social behavior. Thus he argued that the individual
adheres to the norms of his group, not through fear of punishment but
because he accepts its system of values. The sociology of knowledge
and the theory of values were the main achievements of Durkheim's attempt to bring order into sociology, much more so than the doctrine of
solidarity which he advanced in his book on education and sociology
(published after his death) or his earlier study of suicide. It was thanks to
these two achievements that his name was spared the oblivion that has
overtaken his school.[42]

Compared with Durkheim, Bouglé, Mauss, Parodi, and Simiand —
the group round *L'Année Sociologique* — the Germans were latecomers.
Bouglé, who recorded the state of German sociology in the mid-1890s,
found that Germany still lacked a "true" sociology. This was not surprising since illiberal regimes are invariably hostile to a discipline that
lays bare what most autocrats prefer to sweep under the carpet. But
when Aron reviewed the position forty years later, German backwardness
had been transformed into a lead.[44] Long before that date Ferdinand
Tönnies had tried to put the sociological house in order with his *Gemeinschaft und Gessellschaft* (Community and Society), a book that was
published in 1887 but did not attract the attention it deserved until
much later. Although his distinction between the organic and mechanical
conceptions of social groups was far from exhaustive, it gave German
sociology an excellent starting point, one that Max Weber would perpetuate in his "ideal types." And though Georg Simmel's early writings

430

on moral and social differentiation, which appeared at the beginning of the 1890s, may still have been Spencerian, though he may have called his *magnum opus* of 1900 the *Philosophy* (rather than the Sociology) *of Money*, and though besides being an expert on finance he was also a cultural and literary historian, he was nevertheless the first German to make a serious attempt at putting some order into the masses of data that constituted sociology in his day. To that end, he deliberately limited its scope, arguing that sociology was exclusively concerned with the *forms* of social interactions. Aron has emphasized that this abandonment of the two old pillars of sociology — the individual and society — was the sign of an age in which the hostile classes were agreed on one thing only, namely the fiction of a single society.[45] This was true, but only if we add that the impotence to which the situation condemned even so great a thinker as Simmel also provided him with fresh insights. For the theoretical gain of Simmel's attempt was great indeed. Not only did it help to bridge the gap between the individual and society, but it also demonstrated that social behavior remains largely unchanged even in the face of dramatic social changes. In particular, he showed that such attitudes as dominance and subjection, loyalty and competition, social agreement and discord, class distinction and class collaboration, are lasting expressions of the behavior of individuals in organized groups.[46]

This explains why Simmel is often called the founder of the "formal" school of sociology, though his right to that title has been challenged.[47] What is certain is that all his books and articles published before and after 1908, the year in which he presented his ideas systematically in his *Soziologie*,[48] no matter whether they dealt with super- or subordination, with intellectual life in the great cities, with general sociology or with the sociologies of human conflict, religion, fashion, or sociability, were based on a formal approach. It was his brilliant powers of presentation rather than his "formalism" which earned him, in contrast to Tönnies, an international renown which his works extended over the entire Western world before his death in 1918. This was all the more remarkable because it was not until 1914 that he was offered a Chair (in Strasbourg). At the time anti-Semites were already muttering about the "Judaization" of German intellectual life, but their views were not yet taken into account by those making academic appointments.

His realization that social attitudes were not necessarily dependent on time and space also helped Simmel to explain why so many "great men" lived isolated lives. He did this convincingly in his *Kant* (1904), *Schopenhauer und Nietzsche* (1907), *Goethe* (1913), *Rembrandt* (1916) and finally in his own reflections which he published in 1918 under the title of *Lebensanschauung* (View of Life). Von Wiese and Vierkandt were to continue the work he had so ably begun.

But not these two alone: all German sociology in the decade before the First World War is inseparably bound up with Simmel's name. We do not wish to detract from the renown of other contemporary German sociologists — Werner Sombart, Ernst Troeltsch, Max Scheler, Othmar Spann, Hans Freyer, Ludwig Stein, or Alfred Weber, some of whom we shall meet again in other sections of this book — when we pass straight on from Simmel to Max Weber. For only someone with Weber's gigantic intellect could have tried to encompass all the problems besetting sociology in his day. We say "could have tried" for, as so often happens with the very greatest, Weber, too, had not completed his life's work when he died in 1920 at the age of fifty-six. It was Weber whom Rilke had in mind when he spoke of the man who invariably returns when a dying age re-examines its values.[49] Indeed, Weber was full of the tensions of his age. He was torn by the tension between science and politics, which he had distinguished so clearly, precisely because he tried to bring them closer together[50] with the help of a value-free science that alone could serve as a guide to the good life. He also bore the tension between knowledge and the will and between objectivity and subjectivity, attempting to preserve the first by admitting the claims of the second. He bore the tension between science and his own ambition, for he felt that he was cut out, not to be a great scholar,[51] but a statesman, a role that was never assigned to him. He bore a further tension because he felt impelled to agree with Rickert that the social sciences were not governed by strict laws, only to resurrect these laws with his postulate that causal relations could not be demonstrated except by explicit or implicit reference to generalizing theoretical categories[52] — his famous "ideal types."

He also bore the tension between rationality and irrationality, not in the sense that he ever wavered between them, but inasmuch as, unlike Marx with whose shadow he seemed to struggle without respite, he recognized that the irrational influences the course of history during critical periods (*cf.* his concept of "charisma"). He did so at about the same time that Freud detected the same influence in the life of the individual. Strangely enough, Weber, whom Salomon called a "bourgeois Marx"[53] for that very reason, had no illusions about the future, although his "charisma" might easily have persuaded him that a highly gifted personality could break the fatal chain of history. At heart he was a defeatist, in science no less than in politics. He no longer believed that knowledge could advance to the "true essence" of things or even to "laws." He

432

was afraid that the individual was doomed to be swallowed up by the bureaucratic apparatus and by the masses, and that freedom would vanish in a rationalized economy. He was without illusions about the future, and yet prepared to fight for it to the bitter end, as witness the deep furrows on his forehead, his rather laborious style, and perhaps also the final tension of this tortured man: his attempt to reconcile the two scientific currents of his age — integration and specialization. If anyone could have reconciled these two it was assuredly Weber with his encyclopedic mind; after all he had only become a sociologist because he was a jurist, an economist, and a historian. It was this very combination that made his work, abstract though it was, so extraordinarily true to life.

Max Weber, in the short span allotted to him, did more than anyone else to bring order into three distinct spheres: the definition of sociological concepts and methods which he treated in his *Gesammelte Aufsätze zur Wissenschaftslehre* (Collected Essays on the Theory of Science);[54] the sociology of religion as treated in his *Gesammelte Aufsätze zur Religionssozioligie* (Collected Essays on the Sociology of Religion)[55], of which he can be considered the founder; and finally the analysis of current social trends as presented in his *Wirtschaft und Gesellschaft* (Economy and Society).[56] With these books and all the many others space prevents us from listing here, Weber had met Abel's four conditions for turning sociology into an autonomous discipline: he had provided a sharply defined territory, a sharply defined set of objectives, a sound basis for systematizing the data, and, finally, adequate methods of investigation.[57] If Weber's influence has not yet been fully assessed to this day, it is only because it had such wide repercussions. His brother Alfred, no less than Troeltsch and Sombart still felt that influence through personal contact with the master; many, many others felt it more indirectly, Karl Mannheim chief among them. Not only bourgeois sociologists but even such social democrats as Emil Lederer or such communists as Georg Lukács can be understood as little without Marx as they can without Weber, as we may gather from Lukács's *Zur Soziologie des modernen Dramas* (On the Sociology of the Modern Drama).[58]

Weber produced order where confusion had reigned. It was as if he anticipated his early death, and so hastened to complete his life's work in the short span of fifteen years. His haste was symptomatic not only of the man but also of the age in which he lived. Another symptom of that age was the fact that science had begun to demand personal sacrifices that only religion could have expected in earlier times. "No one but God prevails above man's will, and so he hates Him with a distant love," to quote Rilke once again. Finally Weber symbolized his age in his own nervous breakdown. His breaking point came at the turn of the century.[59] For all these reasons neither the nineteenth nor the twentieth century, and hence the transition between the two, can be fully grasped without Weber. Conversely Weber's sociology cannot be grasped without some knowledge of the two centuries and of their meeting point.

[CHAPTER XXIX]

LANGUAGE AS SYMBOL

On December 3, 1900 Michel Bréal (a pupil and the translator of the great German pioneer, Franz Bopp, and himself the father of comparative philology in France) celebrated the silver jubilee of his election to the Institut Français, that greatest of all learned societies in France. Antoine Meillet, his own pupil, who was substituting for him at the Collège de France,[1] marked the great occasion by presenting a beautifully bound encomium to the hero of the day.[2]

That encomium interests us less than the address with which Meillet, now Bréal's successor, opened his lectures on comparative grammar in 1906. Having once again paid tribute to his teacher, he went on to explain with unusual candor how he had come to concern himself with the social causes of linguistic processes. Linguistic regularities, he believed, were not governed by the autonomous laws in which the "neogrammarians" or "Junggrammatiker" took such great pride; these regularities were mere potentialities and it was social influences alone that had turned them into actualities. Bréal had anticipated part of this conclusion in his *Essai de sémantique* of 1897, in which he had argued that the individual's freedom of expression was restricted by his need to grasp the meaning of words and that this restriction was a social phenomenon. He now added that the nineteenth century had been the century of history, and that linguistics, too, had adopted the historical point of view, to its own great benefit. But now that the social sciences were making such great strides, linguistics itself was due for renovation.[3]

For all that, Meillet did not usher in a revolution in linguistics, either with this program or with its implementation during a long and fruitful academic life. Nor was he the man to do so. What he did, and did remarkably well, is what he himself had called for during his inaugural lecture: to introduce just one more degree of precision into a number of problems. The result was a shift in emphasis which became a veritable revolution in the hands of his great contemporary, Ferdinand de Saussure, on whose death in 1913 Meillet wrote an appreciative obituary.

To explain the full import of that revolution, we must first take stock of the state of linguistics at the turn of the century. If we do that, we find that Meillet was by no means the only one or even the first to introduce "one more degree of precision." In Germany, which, at the end of the century no less than at the beginning, held the lead in linguistics, Herman Hirt explained in the preface to his *Der indogermanische Ablaut* (Indo-Germanic Vowel Gradation), which was published in 1900, that dissension in linguistics had assumed such ominous proportions that many scholars had begun to despair of its future.[4] The reason why he laid so much emphasis on vowel gradation becomes clear from the subtitle of the book: "with particular reference to its relationship with stress," for the novel idea that the key to phonetic changes lay in stress struck him as offering a way out of the impasse. That idea was gratefully taken up by his colleague Berthold Delbrück, who dug right down to the foundations in his *Grundfragen der Sprachforschung* (Basic Questions of Philology) of 1901. In particular he examined Wundt's linguistic psychology (the reader may remember that the first two parts of Wundt's *Völkerpsychologie*, which dealt with language, had appeared one year earlier) and remarked that the grand old man had stressed the need for extending the research from the Indo-European languages to primitive languages, something that could easily be done with the help of Friedrich Müller's *Grundriss der Sprachwissenschaft* (Outline of Linguistics), the last part of which had been published in the 1880s. "And who would cavil at that?" Delbrück exclaimed. Anyone writing about language ought really to be acquainted with all languages, but this was an impossible task. Nor would it remove all the difficulties, since even the classification of languages was beset with pitfalls. Unlike Schmidt,[5] who had died in 1901, Delbrück did not think it was possible to reconstruct the reciprocal relations of the Proto-Indo and Indo-European languages. Still, he went on to concede that his sceptical attitude may not have been fully justified; it merely reflected his own ignorance of primitive languages.[6]

These were so many voices expressing the prevailing uncertainty in no uncertain terms. No less eloquent, however, were those who called for a completely new start. Before we discuss their work in greater detail, we must first explain what particular certainty was beginning to crumble under the impact of "one more degree of precision."

This certainty was a bequest of late nineteenth-century historical linguistics as developed in Germany, a bequest that, as we saw, Meillet had begun to question implicitly when he argued that language was a social phenomenon. However, in his encomium to Bréal he had still been careful to hint at, rather than spell out, his objections. For the "difficulty" to which he had referred in that address was the problem of deciding whether or not the similarities between the various Indo-European languages stemmed from their common descent, as was still widely believed, or from their parallel but independent development. It was not until twenty years later that he openly declared for the second solution.[7]

The certainty Meillet and others challenged had existed ever since 1875, when Karl Verner had shown in a famous article that an apparently irregular phonetic change could be accounted for by the law now bearing his name. He had previously written in a letter that the old adage "no rule without an exception" must be replaced with "no exception without a rule". The certainty had begun to look even more certain in 1878, when Karl Brugmann and Hermann Osthoff, prior to publishing the first issue of their *Morphologische Untersuchungen* (Morphological Studies), had issued an exuberant manifesto in which they used the authority of Wilhelm Scherer to attack the older school of Georg Curtius, boldly asserting that they intended to abandon the "fog" of academic presuppositions for the brighter light of tangible reality.[8] They were happy to accept the sneering epithet of "Junggrammatiker" (neogrammarians), a name under which they became the leading school of linguistics during the two last decades of the nineteenth century. Brugmann's *Grundriss der vergleichenden Grammatik der indogermanischen Sprachen* (Outline of Comparative Grammar of the Indo-Germanic Languages), which ran to close on 4000 pages and was completed in 1893 except for the sections on syntax which Delbrück, not yet a sceptic, was to add in 1900, was perhaps the greatest achievement of the school, though pride of place might equally well be given to Hermann Paul's repeatedly reprinted classic *Principien der Sprachgeschichte* (Historical Principles of Linguistics), first published in 1880.

In any case, it was from 1880 to 1900 that the fruits of this tree, which can be briefly characterized as "positivist," were harvested. To savor them without delving into the 4000 pages of Brugmann's work, we need merely to look at such contemporary journals as Brugmann and Streitberg's *Indogermanische Forschungen* (Indo-Germanic Studies), Bezzenberger and Prellwitz's *Beiträge zur Kunde der indogermanischen Sprachen* (Contributions to Indo-Germanic Linguistics), E. Kuhn and J. Schmidt's *Zeitschrift für vergleichende Sprachforschung auf dem Gebiete der indogermanischen Sprachen* (Journal of Comparative Linguistics in the Field of the Indo-Germanic Languages), and the previously mentioned *Bulletin de la Société de Linguistique de Paris*. All contained detailed studies of a remarkable standard, a Sisyphean labor conducted with unflagging enthusiasm.

Is intellectual fare like normal food? Does the intellect suffer from too monotonous a diet? Does science, too, need vitamins? While it is extremely difficult to answer these questions in general, it seems certain that the crisis of linguistics at the turn of the century was partly the result of the dull fare it had been served by the triumphant neogrammarians. The very rigor that was celebrated as their greatest achievement now helped to usher in a more relaxed approach. Meillet put it all very well when he acknowledged the debt linguistics owed to the Germans. An overworked and tired machine, he said, was grinding to a halt, and as it did the young began to turn away from what, in the mistaken belief that it had solved all the crucial problems, had incapsulated itself in a shell of intolerable self-satisfaction.[9] Indeed, the process of transformation was perhaps more obvious in linguistics than in any other sphere of learning with the possible exception of biology, where Haeckel's alleged solution of the "riddle of the universe" had produced the same sort of soporific effects as those with which Paul's *Principien* had lulled linguistics. It now appeared that, much as uncertainty can lead to a search for new assurance, so certainty can begin to pall and make way — temporarily — for the more exciting attractions of uncertainty.

A sign of fatigue, if you like, but one that also gave rise to bursts of creativity, of the kind familiar to anyone whom overtiredness keeps wide awake. That one additional degree of precision led linguists to question many things they had previously taken for granted, for instance the functions of certain suffixes, and the links between grammatical and biological gender or between grammatical tenses and historical time. It was discovered that linguistic phenomena, be they ever so physiological, are nevertheless anthropomorphic. The fact that the "sun" was masculine to the Romans and feminine to the Germans no doubt had good reasons but these did not lie in the sun. Indeed the dogma of evolution had suffered such severe setbacks that many linguists began to wonder whether the existence of primitive and non-primitive languages was more than a figment of the imagination.

Speaking in Heidelberg on November 22, 1899, Osthoff even applied the term "poetic play of the imagination" to the fact that, in certain adjectives, the positive, comparative, and superlative degrees are derived from the distinct stems, as in *bonus, melior, optimus*, or that the same happens with the present, the perfect and the participle of certain verbs, e.g. *fero, tuli, latum*.[10] His Heidelberg address was topical in yet another respect: in it he drew attention to a host of cracks in the smooth linguistic façade. He did so by reference to the past for, like so many academic addresses at the time, his, too, was delivered to mark the birthday of the reigning prince, the "most blessed" Grand Duke Karl Friedrich of Baden. For the title page, the setter had pulled out every

438

type he could lay his hands on: large and small, long and short, thick and thin, carefully ensuring that the name of the speaker was a respectful size or two smaller than that of the celebrant. This utterly dull and apparently interminable address, which was carefully shorn of much of its philolological ballast when it was actually delivered, conjures up the image of the Great Hall of this famous University, crowded with learned professors, all with flowing beards and gold-rimmed spectacles, as we know them from the *Festschrift*, published in 1903,[11] the whole atmosphere redolent of the lavender scent of grandmother's linen chest. To complete the picture, we must also imagine the hammer blows in the distant Friedrichsbau of the Castle, which was then being restored like every other famous building in Wilhelm's prosperous Germany.

The learned men assembled in the Hall wanted nothing so much as to continue basking in their old certainties. Yet the worm of uncertainty had begun to gnaw even at them. Some of the august assembly no doubt recalled that, as long ago as 1885, Hugo Schuchardt had argued that if one was forced, as he firmly believed one was, to treat the phonetic law as products of space and time and hence as individual manifestations, one as good as abolished them, since, as Ludwig Tobler had remarked in 1879, "individual phenomena can never be subsumed under laws." In the same article Schuchardt also claimed that the universal and lasting validity of the linguistic laws could not be proved deductively or inductively and that anyone who denied this was a pure dogmatist.[12] Those present may also have remembered the aged Graziadio Isaia Ascoli, the leading Italian linguist who, like Schuchardt, was still alive in 1900. He, too, had rejected the claims of the neogrammarians, possibly due, at least in part, to his resentment of German leadership. This famous Romanist had explained that what mattered was not so much the diffusion of linguistic changes as the emergence of so many different languages on the cultural soil of the Roman Empire.[13] It would not be long before even earlier scholars were restored to honor, a return to the penultimate phase so characteristic of scientific progress. In this particular case, one of the beneficiaries was Heymann Steinthal, that lonely mid-nineteenth-century genius who had been the first to speak of "interior linguistic form" (the overlapping of mental form and linguistic structure), an idea that was not fully appreciated until much later. Indeed, even the shadow of Wilhelm von Humboldt was given fresh substance: Arens mentioned him twelve times in his review of our period, although in 1900 sixty-five years had passed since von Humboldt's death. People had begun to look at his teachings with fresh eyes: that language was the creation of individuals and of races, that linguistics affords man a glimpse into the essence of

439

the latter and hence was an integral part of human civilization.[14] By 1902 it was already being said that, at the turn of the century, linguistics, though it still applied the known laws in practice, had ceased to formulate general principles.[15]

We might also say that the attention of linguists had shifted from enquiry into the "what" and "how" of linguistic change to asking "why." But this does not explain why the shift should have taken the particular direction it did. That failure need not surprise us. The rejection of old certainties can do no more than create uncertainties and hence lead to a search for fresh certainties, and that search is fostered not by negative but by positive impulses. As Meillet put it so well, linguistic laws are mere potentialities, not necessities, and it is society which determines which of the many possibilities are actualized. And though the results of this search differed markedly — this too was socially determined — all those involved in it aimed at a single effect: the elucidation of the essence of language. Arens agrees that this re-appraisal came at the end of the century.[16] To him it even seemed like a bolt from the blue, and he noted that, as in so many fundamental crises, the chief impetus did not come solely or even primarily from those working in the field.[17]

In 1899 the linguist Franz Nikolaus Finck, then twenty-two years old (and the generation gap was as important in the linguistic revolution as it was in all others), published his eight lectures in which he asserted that the structure of the German language was an expression of the German "Weltanschauung," in the literal sense of "world view." This was a novel approach, though it, too, was based on the teachings of von Humboldt. It was novel inasmuch as the dominant positivist school had never deigned to examine the subject. According to Finck, it was possible to deduce from a language what view its speakers took of the surrounding world and what emotions it aroused in them, and hence to proceed to a classification of languages based on the respective predominance of conceptual or emotional expressions.[18] The fact that his ideas fell on deaf ears does not detract from the fact that, by treating language as the expression of responses to the environment, Finck prepared the way for many others, including Karl Vossler, who in 1913 published a book on French culture as mirrored in the development of the French language.

Like Finck, but even more directly so, Wilhelm Wundt, the oldest among the innovators, celebrating his sixty-eighth birthday in 1900, also looked for the essence of language in psychology. Conversely he looked to language for the key to the secrets of psychology, so much so that he devoted to it Part I of his great *Völkerpsychologie*.[19] Perhaps "key" is the wrong word, for he said in 1300 pages what he could easily have

440

compressed into 300. But when, having hacked one's way through it, one can make out the wood for the trees once again, the vista is clear enough. It is easy to see that, in Wundt's voluntary psychology, language was bound to be treated as the expression of ideas, emotions, and the will and that, just as in Finck's closely related approach, this meant introducing new linguistic forms. Günther Ipsen, to whom we owe a very brief but penetrating analysis of Wundt's successes and failures in this field, drew a favorable balance sheet. For though Wundt had but one direct successor in linguistic psychology (Ottmar Dittrich, whose rather indigestible book on the outlines of linguistic psychology ran to 2200 paragraphs and proved nothing so much as that linguistics was bogged down in physical psychology[20]), Wundt's indirect influence on linguistics was beyond doubt. In particular the discussions he initiated cast fresh light on a host of fundamental problems and threw up many new ideas.[21]

We said earlier that Berthold Delbrück returned to the fundamental problems of linguistics, largely inspired by Wundt. The same inspiration also made itself felt in the work of Anton Marty, like Husserl a pupil of the philosopher and psychologist Franz Brentano. With Meinong and von Ehrenfels, he was a member of the "Prague school." During a lecture on the central problems of linguistic philosophy, delivered in 1903, Marty first propounded his own ideas, which, though prompted by Wundt's, ran counter to the latter's axiom of the parallel development of thought and speech, and hence went largely unheard. Much the same fate befell his attempt to construct an abstract "general grammar," a subject he discussed at greater length four years later. Less specifically, the rejection of his ideas was also due, at least in part, to the fact that Marty was no less a positivist than Brentano and Wundt, at a time when positivism had begun to lose its hold. Hence it was not until much later that linguistics began to appreciate the full importance of Marty's theory of meaning. In any case, Marty was quite right to argue that, with Wundt, "language" as such had ceased to be the central issue. So was Ipsen when he claimed that Wundt was not so much concerned with language or even with psychology as with the renewal of social philosophy. He might equally well have pointed a finger at Konrad Burdach, a Germanist and cultural historian to whom the history of language was social history, molded by the "suggestive force of social intercourse," a force that was intellectual rather than physical.[22] In any case this particular interpretation of language proved a most fruitful attempt to grasp language as a meaningful whole.[23]

Much more radical than the approach of Wundt and his disciples or critics was the contribution of those who rejected positivism on principle.

They, too, made their voices heard at about the turn of the century, under the leadership of Benedetto Croce in Italy and of his prophet Karl Vossler in Germany. Croce was not so much interested in language, of which he knew little, as in the place of aesthetics in philosophy. In 1900 he delivered a lecture to the Neopolitan Accademia Pontaniana on aesthetics as the theory of expression and language. That lecture was published in 1902 as Part I of his *Filosofia come scienza dello spirito* (Philosophy as the Science of the Spirit), in which he declared boldly that whosoever deals with linguistics is in fact dealing with aesthetic problems. Linguistics and the philosophy of art were one and the same thing.[24] As with Finck, this approach marked a return to the pre-positivist stage, or more precisely to von Humboldt, for though Croce did not mention him by name, von Humboldt, too, had described language not as "ergon," physical work, but as "energeia," the creative activity of the mind.

That is precisely what it was for Vossler, whose *Positivismus und Idealismus in der Sprachwissenschaft* (Positivism and Idealism in Linguistics; 1904) was dedicated to Croce. His anti-positivism was most clearly reflected in the chapter on phonetics, since the positivist method had done best in that sphere, though, according to Vossler, it had also committed the cardinal error of postulating the existence of phonetic laws.[25] If one rejects these laws, as Vossler himself suggested one should, then linguistics became a branch of aesthetics, and the task of linguists, like that of aestheticists, became the demonstration that the mind is the only effective source of linguistic forms.[26]

Indeed, the development of phonetics enables us to follow the general transition from positivism to anti-positivism step by step. In 1900 Eduard Wechssler, in a very thoughtful article 180 pages long,[27] opposed the prevailing practice of replacing the term "phonetic law" with the term "phonetic change."[28] Moreover, he refused to use "phonetic law" in its "classical" sense. In particular, he contended that the term must be stripped of its animistic overtones: like Rudolf Eucken some twenty years earlier, Vossler, too, insisted that a "law" was not something imposed from the outside.[29] He also invoked the authority of Wundt, who had said that "phonetic laws" apply not to particular, but to general, phenomena; that they are based on causal relationships and prove their heuristic value in the face of new experiences.[30] A different, intermediate, position was adopted by Delbrück one year later. In his review of the current discussions, though he granted the existence of certain phonetic laws that admitted of no exceptions, he added that these laws proved of very little practical help because the material was so diffuse and awkward and also because far too little work had been done on living languages.[31]

Finck and Wundt, who tried to rob linguistics of its autonomy by incorporating it into psychology, or Croce and Vossler, who tried to incorporate it in aesthetics, were not the only ones to proclaim their views at the turn of the century. There was also Fritz Mauthner, whose three-part *Beiträge zu einer Kritik der Sprache* (Contributions to a Critique of Language; 1901–1902) pointed linguistics towards sociology. In 1907 he published a more popular account of his views in Martin Buber's series, *Die Gesellschaft* (Society), a reliable mirror of intellectual life at the time.[32] Mauthner was opposed not only to neogrammarians — the common descent of the so-called Aryan languages struck him as being no more than a fable — but also to Wundt and Vossler. To him, as to Steinthal and Lazarus in the 1860s and 1870s, language was a social phenomenon, for even if it were an individual creation it would be nothing if there was no one else to understand what the individual was trying to convey with it. Language was the *sensorium commune*, mankind's "common center of feeling," much as the brain was the "common center of feeling" of individuals.

At the same time, he had a deeply rooted suspicion of words and concepts. Language was tyrannical, a means by which the majority oppressed the minority. It served as a powerful social bond, the richest of all men's social possessions, but it was also the chief culprit in perpetuating man's social misery. His tone clearly reflected the anguish of his age: Mauthner viewed language as an anarcho-communist disciple of Gustav Landauer, much as Vossler viewed it though the eyes of the hyperindividualist threatened by the rise of mass culture. Mauthner was a mirror of his age in his versatility (he was journalist, novelist, parodist, agnostic, atheist, mystic and philosopher all rolled into one) no less than in his confusion. For in the end, far from mastering the countless problems he set out to solve, he became their slave.

As if the situation were not confused enough, there was also the phenomenologist Edmund Husserl who, though not primarily interested in language as such, nevertheless felt obliged to establish the "precise" meaning of words in his *Logische Untersuchungen* (Logical Investigations; 1901–1902). Then there was Jacobus van Ginneken, who tried vainly to lessen the confusion with the help of a new synthesis expounded in the conclusion to his *Principes de linguistique psychologique* of 1907: the fusion of the solid methods of the positivists with the vision of the idealists, the analytical approach to linguistic change of the historians, and the study of language formation of the phoneticists and dialectologists.[33] Marty, whom we have met before, made a much more radical effort to master the prevailing confusion and, indeed, pointed the way to the most fruitful solution of all. For if the publisher of his literary bequest was right to claim that Marty was the first to take a clear stand against Paul's purely historical standpoint by substituting the synchronic for the diachronic approach,[34] and if it is also true that his undated contributions to the theory of meaning were written between 1900 and 1907,[35] then Marty may be said to have charted the course of twentieth-century linguistics.

The main innovator, in his own day, however, was another Swiss linguist, Ferdinand Saussure, who was not only much more lucid than Marty and went much further in the attempt to systematize linguistics, but was not even familiar with Marty's work, which was published in 1926 when Saussure had been dead for thirteen years. Like Marty, Saussure was not fully appreciated by his contemporaries. Thus when Meillet, though he greatly admired the famous *Mémoire sur le système primitif des voyelles dans les langues indo-européennes*, published in 1879 when Saussure was twenty-one, wrote Saussure's obituary, he felt impelled to confess: "Saussure has not fulfilled his promise."[36] This was an understandable mistake, for Saussure had published very little after his first essay, something Meillet in particular must have found exceedingly strange. For the obituary was his own 171st article in a series that had grown to just under 550 by the time he himself died in 1937, not to mention the twenty-four books he also published.[37] Saussure, by contrast, was the kind of scholar who, possessed by an essential idea, has neither the wish nor the energy to write academic dissertations, let alone popular articles or lectures. Meillet's "error" was thus a classical example of how even his best-informed peers can misjudge the true importance of a man's work. Still, we must not exaggerate Saussure's obscurity or Meillet's mistake: on his fiftieth birthday, Saussure was presented with a collection of tributes by fifteen of his colleagues, including Meillet.[38] True, his star did not rise until after his death, but when it did it waxed much more quickly and brightly than Marty's. Within three years, C. Bally and A. Sèchehaye, two of his leading pupils in Geneva, where he had been teaching since 1891, had published his lectures, and his name became a household word in all interested circles.

His use of the word "system" held the essential key to his entire approach. To Saussure, language was a system, whose interdependent parts determine one another and combine to delimit the whole. It was a system of signs, as it had also been for Pott in the 1830s and 1840s, of signs that give voice to an idea and define it by their sound; linguistics was nothing but the study of conventional systems for the production of meanings. Saussure arrived at this revolutionary conception with the help of three distinctions. The first of these was the distinction between "language," i.e., language as a system, and the actual manifestations of language in speech or writing, the first being a suprapersonal, social phenomenon and the second a personal one. This distinction was not unlike von Humboldt's distinction between "ergon" and "energeia." The second of Saussure's distinctions was that between the diachronic and synchronic studies of language, the first being an attempt to trace the historical development of language through various stages, and the second being an attempt to reconstruct a given language system as a functional whole. The first approach was dynamic, the second static. Marty introduced a similar distinction at about the same time. Saussure's third and most difficult distinction was probably the most fruitful of all: it was the distinction between the value and the signification of a word, the value being that part of the signification on which the latter is dependent in a given context. Value cannot be read off from the signification as such but can only be determined by comparisons with related values. It must therefore be considered a part not only of the signification of every word, but also of the system of a whole. Meaning, thinking, and believing each have significations of their own, but every member of that trio derives its value from the "field" in which it appears with the remaining two.

Highly illuminating though Saussure's view of language undoubtedly was, for he was not only a brilliant innovator but also a great systematist, he was unable to put an end to the crisis in linguistics for the simple reason that only his immediate pupils were familiar with his ideas — at the time. So linguistics remained an extremely many-sided and vague discipline, the more so as it proliferated in all sorts of directions, embracing the philosophy of language, the psychology of language, the sociology of language and the biology of language. Thus at the third international congress of psychology, held in 1897, one of the speakers dealt with the language of children and primitive people, and in 1900 another speaker dilated on language and ethics, a third on speech defects while a fourth — Trombetti — still dwelt on the unity and origins of language, and Freud threw fresh light on slips of the tongue. Then there were semantics and stylistics, two old acquaintances, but now infused with fresh life by the "one additional degree of precision." In the case of semantics or semasiology, the study of the meaning of words, this renewal led to the introduction of the idea of the "conceptual field"; stylistics owed much of its modernization to Albert Sèchehaye, one of

445

Saussure's pupils, who, in the jubilee presentation of tributes we mentioned earlier, claimed that its chosen field lay between grammatical rigor and belles-lettres or rhetoric.[39] These are only a few random pickings from a garden full of exotic and more humble blooms, the second (the countless etymologies) outnumbering the first by far. But then there was also a proliferation of new hybrids, for instance the new semasiology, which clearly betrayed its descent from the recent marriage of cultural history to cultural morphology. The garden itself was being extended as well, not least by Hendrik Kern, a famous sanskritist and an even more famous expert on the Indonesian and Polynesian languages,[40] and by C. C. Uhlendeck, a student of the Basque, Eskimo, and American Indian languages.[41] The fresh light thrown on the Tocharian language by the Prussian expedition to Turkestan in 1905, or on the Hittite language by H. Winckler and O. Puchstein's discovery of the Royal Archives at Boghazköy in Asia Minor, deciphered by Bedrich Hrozný, that modern Champollion, shortly after our period, faced even students of the Indo-European languages with fresh problems,[42] just when they were feeling so inordinately sure of themselves. Finally, in the same period an entirely new field was opened up by Hermann Hirt's theory (1894) of "linguistic substrata," according to which irregularities and change in the Indo-European languages were due to the absorption of indigenous populations by the "Aryan" conquerors.[43] Previously, in 1884 and again in 1891, the Orientalist, Hommel, had already mentioned the influence of old Armenian on Greek. Kretschmer applied the new approach carefully, but all the more successfully, in 1896 when he wrote his introduction to the history of the Greek language. At about the same time, Pauli threw himself into the study of the Pelasgian, Etruscan, Basque, Ligurian, and other more or less extinct languages.

So, at the turn of the century, the proud edifice of linguistics seemed to be on the point of collapse, just when its foundation had apparently been shored up so securely. As it turned out, however, the main structure was far from uninhabitable, and its well-timbered wings — the study of the Germanic, Romance, and Slavonic languages — had remained more or less intact. For all that, the transience of human achievement finds no better illustration than it does in linguistics, that great monument to man's creative power. For the crisis in linguistics, of which this chapter tried to catch a brief glimpse, was indeed a crisis, but one of growing pains. The course of history happens to be a succession of broken equilibria. Thus the turmoil in linguistics was but a symbol of the critical years in which it occurred. Hence the title of this chapter: language as symbol.

CHAPTER XXX

THE EXCITABLE AGE

On the morning of Tuesday, July 24, 1900, Henri Houssaye opened the first session of Section One — General and Diplomatic History — of the first International Congress of Historians held in the frame of the Paris World Exposition. He did so with the kind of eulogy that was expected of an "academician": the historical method, he proudly declared, had been thoroughly overhauled during the past century; it was no longer a set of vague hypotheses, trivial compilation, idle systems, brilliant but misleading theories, empty moralizations, but had become a solid body of facts and more facts, revealing the truth, the whole truth and nothing but the truth. Interest in history was indeed growing apace: no fewer than three hundred people had registered for this Section. Was this due to the charms of Clio? Only in part, for patriotism was involved as well: the more you learned about your country, the more you learned to love it, and the more you loved it, the more you wanted to learn about it. That patriotism might one day clash with the search for truth was something the speaker preferred to gloss over; instead he added that even great novelists — Zola was a case in point — were increasingly helping to spread the new gospel. He ended with the obligatory quotation, this time from Victor Hugo, who had compared literature to a magnificent edifice built up of documents, charters, letters, minutes, treaties, military reports, confidential notes, marriage contracts, and death certificates. "And our congress will bear witness to the fact that you have not wasted your time and energies."[1]

Be that as it may. What the congress certainly did reflect was the rise of national fervor, if not the love of truth and nothing but the truth. An exception, perhaps, was a lecture delivered that very morning on "hypotheses in history." It had been written in May in distant Jassy and was given by A. D. Xénopol, a fifty-three year old Roumanian historian.

History, he argued, was concerned with facts unique not only in time but also in space, and hence stood in urgent need of a special hypothesis, one that could be confirmed by direct reference to the sources. When no such sources could be found, as in the case of Roumanian history

447

from ca. 400 to ca. 1300, then logical argument must take over. He tried to illustrate this point by weighing up two arguments, namely that the Roumanians had left Dacia after the Slavonic invasion only to return in their own good time, or that they had never left in the first place. The speaker himself favored the second alternative. It was an attempt, once the "facts and more facts, the truth, the whole truth and nothing but the truth" had led to a blind alley, to reach a solution along a different route. He concluded his address with an appeal: the theory of history must become a special part of every university syllabus.[2]

Though Xénopol failed to make a direct impact there and then, the theoretical approach he advocated gradually gained ground. Thus, at the beginning of August 1900 subscribers received the first issue, 120 pages long, of the bimonthly *Revue de Synthèse Historique*.[3] Its editor was the thirty-seven year old Henri Berr, who, having graduated the year before with his thesis "Outline of a Synthesis of the Sciences Based on History," had just taken the first steps along a road he was to follow all his life. Fifty years later he was still editing "his" journal,[4] and still voicing his basic opposition to historical specialization. Not that he advocated a return to speculative philosophy; what he proposed was a synthesis based on more direct contacts between history and Durkheim's young sociology.

The July–August issue also carried an article on historical developments in Germany. It was written by the famous Professor Karl Lamprecht of Leipzig, and summarized his own arguments in favor of the socio-historical approach he had developed at greater length in a special paper published earlier that year.[5]

The same issue also mentioned the recent foundation of the Kulturwissenschaftliche Gesellschaft (Society of Cultural Science) in Freiburg, which Heinrich Rickert had set up for the express purpose of offsetting the influence of the local Verein der Naturforscher (Natural Science Society). According to Berr, Rickert's Kulturwissenschaft was simply the German equivalent of his own "synthèse historique."[6] If we go on to read the October issue, we shall find an article by Xénopol entitled "The Repetition or Succession of Historical Events" and written in reply to Paul Lacombe's lengthy critique of Xénopol's recent *Principes fondamentaux de l'histoire*,[7] and if, finally, we also read Paul Mantoux's report in the same issue of an interview on the present state and immediate future of historical research granted to the editor of *Le Temps* by Gabriel Monod,[8] we gain a far better idea of the state of historical research than we could glean from the lengthy reports of the International Congress.[9]

All these writers bore witness to the growing crisis of confidence among historians, to a loss of faith in those nineteenth-century certainties Houssaye had propounded with so much rhetoric just a short while before. In referring to this crisis it seems only right to stress the crucial contribution of Lamprecht, whose controversial work was probably more symptomatic of it than that of any other contemporary historian.

During the first forty years of Lamprecht's life there was nothing to suggest that he would one day attempt to strip Clio of her last secrets. The son of a parson, like so many other nineteenth-century intellectuals from Protestant countries, Lamprecht at first followed the straight and narrow academic path — neither his ineradicable optimism, his unquenchable thirst for knowledge, nor even his studiousness made him in any way exceptional. The only unusual thing about him even then was the breadth of his interests, and an intellectual agitation shared by few of his colleagues. In the 1870s and 1880s he devoted himself not only to economic history but also to the history of art: excellent preparation for the integralist approach he was to apply later.

It was not until 1891, by which time he was forty-five and held a Chair in Leipzig, that he published the first part of his *Deutsche Geschichte* (German History) and first attracted the attention he was still enjoying in 1913, when the twenty-fourth and last part of his *magnum opus* came out at long last. It was his life's work, even in the sense that one can say without fear of contradiction that he made the book just as much as the book made him. At the end of his labors he had come a very long way indeed, changing his mind not only about the aims but also about the method of history. It had all started with his rejection of what he called the "individualist" current, and its replacement with his own "collectivist" ideal. But this was not his only about-turn. Having started out as a positivist he ended up as a psychologist. This was his most profound change: his broadest was the abandonment of specialism in favor of universalism.

It was these three innovations that made Lamprecht a symbol of the crisis in history he witnessed all around him. For in the struggle he had to wage he was both isolated and also ably supported, often by those who attacked him most fiercely.

The Lamprecht controversy raged from 1896 until the end of the century, and was the subject of more than a hundred publications.[10] Despite the length of the struggle and the number of papers and books devoted to it, the issue was never settled; neither Lamprecht's collectivist school nor the old individualist doctrine of his opponents scored a decisive victory. At best we can say that the new idea was able to hold its own by the side of the old.

449

This achievement was certainly due, at least in part, to the man who was both the subject and the object of the protracted struggle. From his *Alte und neue Richtungen in der Geschichtswissenschaft* (Old and New Directions in History) of 1896 to his *Die kulturhistorische Methode* (The Cultural Historical Method) of 1900, Lamprecht defended his cause consistently and with growing conviction. The five lectures he delivered in 1904 in America, to which his fame had spread, and which were published a year later under the title of *Moderne Geschichtswissenschaft* (Modern Historical Science), were perhaps the best summary of his general approach.

Nevertheless, Lamprecht's partial victory was not entirely due to his own zeal and self-confidence. There were two reasons for this. In the first place, the cause was much better than its defense. So good a cause really deserved a much better champion, for though the twenty-four parts of his main work often reflected an astonishing breadth of knowledge, the reader's astonishment rarely makes way for enthusiasm. Moreover, his polemical writings were extremely vague. Lamprecht may have chosen this presentation deliberately so as to outwit his critics, but the gap between his vague assertions and the self-assured tone in which they were expressed was nevertheless glaring. He may have escaped criticism from such non-theoretical specialists as F. Rachfahl, H. Oncken, Max Lenz, and H. Finke but not from such thoughtful historians as Georg von Below, Hans Delbrück, Otto Hintze, and Friedrich Meinecke. The condescending tone in which Meinecke dismissed him may seem rather misplaced in the light of subsequent developments, but it was certainly not an expression of narrow professional pride.

More than to Lamprecht himself, the revolution in historical thought was due to the times, in which mass movements and impersonal powers had begun to play so important a role that the study of "conditions" came to take precedence over the study of "events." It was perhaps Lamprecht's greatest achievement that, aware of the influence of his period on his own intellect, he not only introduced the concept "temporal subjectivism," but even made it the cornerstone of social history. One can agree or disagree with his division of history into six periods: the animistic; the symbolic, which prevailed until ca. 900 A.D.; the typical, which prevailed until ca. 1200 A.D.; the conventional, which prevailed until ca. 1400 A.D.; the individualistic, which prevailed until ca. 1750 A.D., and the subjectivist, which lasted until 1900, and partly coincided with the current "age of excitability" — but one cannot dispute that it reflected Lamprecht's growing conviction that historical truths change with the times, and that every period must rewrite history.

450

One of Lamprecht's opponents dismissed his love of innovation as a mere whim. Seeing that the entire guild of historians was then ranged against him, this view was understandable enough. In retrospect, however, Lamprecht appears as the leader of a broad current that could not be stemmed for long, as witness the enthusiastic reception accorded to his *Deutsche Geschichte*, several parts of which had to be reprinted time and again. Lamprecht's fate was thus not so very different from that of Spengler twenty years later, or that of Toynbee fifty years on. Moreover his importance is also vouchsafed by the controversy he started: people do not react so violently and for so long if they do not feel that they are meeting a real challenge. Finally, his idea that the combined effect of collective factors was the mainspring of history was infecting even literary historians, as witness Taine's *Histoire de la littérature anglaise*, Brandes's *Hovedströmninger i det nittende aarhundredes litteratur* (Main Currents in Nineteenth-Century Literature), the work of Scherer and his school,[11] or A. Brückner's *Geschichte der russischen Literatur* (History of Russian Literature), first published in 1905. There were many others too, who tried to fit literature into history, or who divided it up by style and genre rather than by individual writers.

Lamprecht may even be said to have gone further in depersonalizing historical developments than such socialist historians as Plekhanov, Kautsky, Mehring, Labriola, or Jaurès. For had Jaurès not acknowledged the threefold inspiration of Marx, Michelet, and Plutarch? And had Mehring not acknowledged the role of individuals, albeit implicitly, in all his works and especially in his biography of Marx? Others had done so quite explicitly, Labriola in his *Del materialismo storico* (On Historical Materialism; 1896), in which he referred to the attempt to gloss over the contributions of eminent personalities as "pure perverseness"; Kautsky a year later in an essay on the aims and scope of the materialist conception of history ("Was kann und will die materialistische Geschichtsauffassung leisten");[12] and Plekhanov another year later in a special treatise on "The Role of the Individual in History."[13] At the same time, the extreme views of Carlyle and Nietzsche, the two hero-worshipers, also made a reappearance, particularly with such writers as George Bernard Shaw and Stefan George, and not even Spengler was entirely immune to them. Bentley made a special study of their superman cult because, with the evidence of Mussolini and Hitler before him, he realized that "heroic vitalism" was part and parcel of the pre-history of fascism. He attributed this kind of hero worship to lack of self-assurance (the intellectual's reaction to increasing mechanization) and to the quest for excellence in an age of mediocrity, for individuality in the age of the

451

masses, for organic in an age of mechanism, in short, for quality in an age of quantity.[14]

To what great extent the struggle round Lamprecht was a sign of the times is, however, proved by nothing so much as by the fact that a similar struggle had taken place shortly before. In the event the chief antagonists had been Eberhard Gothein and Dietrich Schäfer. At the beginning of our period, in 1889, Gothein had published his *Aufgaben der Kulturgeschichte* (Tasks of Cultural History)[15] in reply to Schäfer's inaugural address delivered a year earlier and entitled *Das eigentliche Arbeitsgebiet der Geschichte* (The True Field of History).[16] To Schafer that field was and remained political history; to Gothein it was social history, as based on Dilthey's interpretation of the study of society and culture. Cultural history was the study of the human intellect: philosophical if one paid attention to its permanent foundations, cultural if one paid attention to intellectual changes and developments in time. The struggle ended with Schäfer's reply of 1891,[17] only, as we know, to be revived soon afterwards in the new round of polemics initiated by Lamprecht.[18]

The final and most conclusive proof that Lamprecht's progress from political to cultural history (or in his own terminology, from an individualist to a collectivist view) was indeed a sign of the times, was the simultaneous emergence of sociological tendencies in many other disciplines. Nor was it at all surprising that historical research should have fared no differently from economics, jurisprudence, medicine, biology, psychology and linguistics, or that, beside drawing closer to sociology, the study of history should have been about to draw closer to economics as well. John Clapham, for one, was aware of this, for in 1897 Marshall had asked Lord Acton to help him convert Clapham from a political into an economic historian.[19] The story of modern economic history has still to be written, but its beginnings were clear enough: they lie with Bücher, Schmoller, and Sombart in Germany; Inama-Sternegg in Austria; Ashley, Cunningham, and Unwin in Britain; Des Marez, van Houtte, and Pirenne in Belgium; and Posthumus and van Ravesteyn in the Netherlands, all of whom produced their best work in the two decades around the year 1900.

The new trend was exemplified in the very title of a book by Paul Barth published in 1897: *Die Philosophie der Geschichte als Soziologie* (The Philosophy of History as Sociology). It was an attempt to construct a bridge between the "official" German historical school — Lamprecht's opponents — and the most unofficial school of historical materialism. Both these schools were, in fact, the offshoots of Hegelianism, the first

452

through Ranke and the other through Marx. In their reunion, Barth, a former student of philosophy under Avenarius and Wundt and now a lecturer by Lamprecht's side, saw the true task of history. By basing itself on sociology, history must become more than the mere digging up of facts, and also more than the presentation of these facts in elegant writings. Barth's was thus another synthetic attempt, different from Lamprecht's or Berr's, but no less a symptom of the times.[20]

Barth was even less of a Marxist than Lamprecht, who was wrongly accused of being one in the heat of the struggle, not only by Rachfahl but also by one of the *dii minors*, a certain Friedrich Aly.[21] In fact, Barth and Lamprecht merely nibbled at the fruit of the Marxist tree of knowledge, but that was enough to earn them the enmity of loyal German historians. Luckily, Lamprecht did not have to face them unaided. Quite apart from the far from negligible group round Maximilian Harden's *Die Zukunft* (The Future), his supporters also included quite a few of the older and many more of the younger historians. In his famous textbook,[22] a faithful mirror of the theoretical debates at the turn of the century, Bernheim mentions Lamprecht in no less than thirty places — clear proof that he took him seriously enough despite all the criticisms he voiced. One of these, incidentally, was that Lamprecht was exaggerating his own contribution to the new outlook. For the rest, Ludo Moritz Hartmann, G. Winter, E. Rothacker, and even Hintze had quite a few kind words to say either about Lamprecht himself or else about his views. His fame had even spread beyond the borders of Germany, Monod and Pirenne[23] more or less favoring him, and Henri Berr, as we saw, even offering him space in the first issue of his new journal.

Even Lamprecht's drift into psychologism was not unique. This tendency was carried to extremes by S. N. Patten, an American of Scots-Irish descent who had studied in Germany. In 1896, by which time he was a professor of economics at the University of Pennsylvania, he published his *Theory of Social Forces*, an early attempt to replace the old scarcity economics with the new economics of plenty. But he carried his psychologism so far that he attributed the difference between these two to the difference between man's sensory and motor nerves.[24] In his other works, too, he used so unconventional an approach that most of his colleagues found him a scandal. The central problem, he argued, was no longer production but consumption; life was dynamic, and economic truths, like all others, were relative.[25] Another great "psychologizer," or even "biologizer" was Ottokar Lorenz whose *Lehrbuch der gesamten wissenschaftlichen Genealogie* (Textbook of Comprehensive Scientific Genealogy; 1898) was an attempt to corroborate the findings

453

of genetics by establishing clear breaks in the succession of the generations. For Croce and Dilthey, too, the structure of the human intellect was a fundamental aspect of historical understanding; for Dilthey because that "understanding" was an act of the intellect, and for Croce because he identified intellectual intuition with historical "understanding," arguing that the historian "creates" the past in his mind. It would also seem that the scientific treatment of biographical problems, so popular at the end of the last century, was not unconnected with the "psychologistic" approach.[26]

Lamprecht's universalist tendency was another manifestation of the same trend. It must have been forced upon him almost against his better judgment. For while he had discovered psychological "dominants" and named his cultural periods accordingly, he had also argued in his fifth and last American lecture that every deeper (read cultural-historical) approach must be universalistic, so that the historical development of other nations — be it with many variations — ought to fit readily into the "German" scheme. Consistent man that he was, he called the organizational center he founded in Leipzig in 1909 the Institut für Kultur- und Universalgeschichte (Institute of Cultural and Universal History). And though it became quite famous in its day, one is entitled to wonder whether this institutionalization of his problems was not, in fact, an escape from them. Lamprecht had caught a glimpse of the Promised Land, but lacking the courage to enter it he contented himself with planting its flag on the map.

However, Lamprecht's conversion to universalism was not purely the result of his theoretical reflections. His affiliations with the German Near East Commission, where he rubbed shoulders with Albert Ballin (a friend of the Kaiser and the world's largest shipowner), Goltz-Pasha of Volk in Waffen fame, and a host of other imperialists,[27] was no accident, nor was his presence in the Verband für internationale Verständigung (League for International Understanding) founded in 1910. Hallgarten called this equivocal attitude a typical expression of Lamprecht's antinomic universalism.[28] In any case Lamprecht followed the path from specialism to universalism with great determination. He shifted his interest not only to non-European civilizations but also pleaded for a restoration of Herder's broad historical vision, though he was prevented by the burden of his positivist past from adopting it himself. He was not the only one to hark back to the inspiration of the eighteenth century. Dilthey, too, succumbed to its attractions both in his account of Hegel's youth (1905), and also in his Aufbau der geschichtlichen Welt (Structure of the Historical World, 1910). But a hundred years had passed since

454

the eighteenth century had made way for the nineteenth, and by 1900
the Enlightenment and the Romantic Age lay far enough away for a
more objective appreciation. At the same time, historians had begun
to take a more critical look at the nineteenth century. Croce, in particular,
voiced his criticisms and it was no accident that he, like Bolland in the
Netherlands, should have returned to Hegel — to take what he needed,
but no more. As the star of neo-Hegelianism began to wax, so did that
of neo-Kantianism, which was destined to become one of the most important philosophical currents in our period.

In any case, universalism had come back into vogue, and Breysig,
among others, welcomed it. His *Geschichte der Menschheit* (History of
Mankind), begun in 1905 when he was forty, was meant to cover the
political and social history of all known civilizations.[29] No one could
be more universalistic than that and it is not surprising that, when he
died in 1940, Breysig's work was left to be completed by his widow.
Others also paid tribute to the new approach, but with much greater
reluctance. Thus Troeltsch, while granting that "universal history" was
a valuable attempt to come to grips with the past, added that what really
mattered "to us" was European civilization, on which universal history
might at best throw fresh light. In any case, it was only the European,
with his cultural versatility, his blazing intellect, and his ceaseless quest
for self-discovery, who could attain to a "universal historical consciousness."[30] This was merely one way of lending intellectual respectability
to the aspirations of the imperialists.

Yet others made more modest contributions by editing or writing
"world histories," thus following in the footsteps of Voltaire, who —
once again in the eighteenth century — had written his world-historical
Essai in answer to Bossuet's narrowly European *Discours.* This time
the Germans were the pacemakers. After all, the Kaiser's country had
to be the first in every field, and knowledge of foreigners and of their
history was bound to cement economic relations. They discovered the
word "Weltgeschichte" long before the French and English produced
their own equivalents. Helmolt, a pupil of Ratzel, divided his "world
history" of which the first part appeared in 1899, into geographical
sections, thus skating over the difficult problem of the reciprocal influence of the various civilizations. Baldamus, when revising Weber three
years later, went a step further by including what elements of non-
European history he considered relevant to "world civilization," with
ancient China and India taking precedence over Babylonia, Syria and
Egypt.[31] Pflugk-Harttung's *Weltgeschichte* of 1907 also falls into our
period. But even earlier, in 1902, the *Cambridge Modern History*, con-

ceived by Acton, had begun to pay homage to the new current. In France the indefatigable Berr followed suit not long afterwards, for though the first volume of his *Evolution de l'humanité*, intended to run to a hundred volumes, did not appear until 1921, the introduction was written as early as 1913 and would have come off the presses in October 1914 had the war not intervened.[32]

No matter what the particular objectives of any of these historians, the result of their combined efforts was to expand their discipline in all directions. Not only was something new added every day, but the past, too, was further and further revealed, as archaeologists delved deeper and deeper. According to Daux, the first forty years of the new century witnessed a marked diversification and extension of archaeological research,[33] and we have only to read the textbooks of Déchelette or Michaelis[34] to see how right he was. Daniel, for his part, called the year 1900 a turning point in archaeology, and took more than a hundred lines to list the most important archaeological and prehistorical contributions made over the twenty-five years of our period, by Abercromby, d'Arbois de Jubainville, Breuil, Cartailhac, Dörpfeld, Evans, Meyer, Montelius, de Morgan, Myres, Petrie and Reinach[35] — and then he omitted Maspero. More impressive by far than even these famous names, of which there was, after all, a surfeit even before and after our period, were the results of their excavations. From Crete in the west, where Evans began his work in Knossos in 1900, to Persia in the east where de Morgan discovered Hammurabi's Code of Laws near Susa in 1901, unsuspected worlds rose up from the ashes of the past. These achievements were partly due to the institutionalization of archaeology: the Deutsche Orient Gesellschaft was founded in 1899, the Ecole Francaise d'Extrème Orient in 1900. So much progress had archaeology made by the end of the century that Maspero's famous book on the subject, written in 1875, had to be expanded into a three-part work within twenty-five years.[36] And what had been happening since then was brought home to the world at large when Bruce Ingram, at the age of twenty-two, took over the editorship of the *Illustrated London News* from his father and grandfather, and was quick to benefit from a series of recent technical advances. In 1906 the first aerial photograph of Stonehenge revealed what had remained hidden to the investigators on the ground; in 1910 the Easter issue of the *Freiburger Zeitung* published a number of illustrations produced by the new screen printing technique, and when Ingram adopted the same method in his paper two years later,[37] he helped to make archaeology more popular than it had ever been before. Indeed, archaeology had begun to play an important cultural-historical role, not least because the latest discoveries cast doubt on the idea of continuous historical progress by showing that Greco-Roman civilization had by no means been the only civilization to rise to great heights only to decline again.

Together with this horizontal extension went a vertical extension, due primarily to the unprecedented accumulation of fresh material by increasingly more extensive and intensive studies of the archives. As a result, historians, for all their universalist and synthetic inclinations, were forced increasingly into specialization and analysis. So strong was this force even before our period that Baumgarten, the biographer of Charles V, succumbed to it as early as 1885.[38] The vertical extension also took the form of a more profound attack on historical problems, as witness particularly the contributions of Dilthey and Croce, whose refined theories may have influenced historical research less immediately than Lamprecht's, but who left a much more lasting impression on it in the long run.

We have to be brief about these two men because their chief contribution was to philosophy rather than to history. In 1900, when Wilhelm Dilthey was sixty-seven, his work was only just beginning to come into prominence, and it was not until after 1918, seven years after his death, that its full importance began to be appreciated. Benedetto Croce, by contrast, made a strong impact even in our period, at least in his native Italy, although in 1900 he was only half Dilthey's age.

Though they were philosophers first and foremost, it is impossible to ignore the part these two men played in revolutionizing historical thought in our period. In Dilthey's case the repercussions made themselves felt in no less than four facets of that revolution. In the first place, he "legitimized" the universalist approach, so to speak, by rediscovering it in eighteenth-century historical thought — his article on the eighteenth century and the historical world was published in the *Deutsche Rundschau* in August–September 1901. In the second place, he drew attention to the unbridgeable gulf between the natural and human sciences (or between the nomothetic and idiographic sciences, as Windelband called them). According to Rickert, that gulf reflected the distinction between the study of repetitive and of "unique" events — a distinction he examined at length in his *Die Grenzen der naturwissenschaftlichen Begriffsbildung* (The Limits of Scientific Conceptualization; 1896), a book repeatedly reprinted and revised, and still a classic. Dilthey, however, went much further than Rickert, if we are to believe Ortega y Gasset, his Spanish translator, who maintained that whereas Rickert, though distinguishing mind from nature, put both on a par as static concepts, Dilthey held that the "mind" *qua* "historical reason" represented an entirely different type of dynamic reality. In other words, Ortega y Gasset considered Dilthey a precursor of existentialism.[39] Thirdly, and closely following the last point, Dilthey introduced a clear distinction between "explanation" and "understanding" in his two types of science. "Understanding" was re-experiencing by analogy even what one had never experienced oneself (e.g., historical facts). This was because of the existence of an objective mind to which all experiences are not only personal but also communal. It was doubtless in this way that Huizinga, who ever since 1905 had ensured that the historical revolution in the Netherlands followed an anti-positivist course, "understood" history. Fourthly, and finally, there was Dilthey's theory of value. Being a relativist, Dilthey believed in the possibility of a relative degree of historical objectivity, "relative" in the sense that history cannot be a true "copy" of reality, but must "evaluate" the material it examines, its evaluations changing with time. Historians ever since have been unable to shake off this universalist, or even vitalist (inasmuch as "understanding" is ultimately based on a subjective feeling), approach, or the holistic tendency it reflected, dispite the fact that Mandelbaum has shown conclusively that Dilthey became trapped in his own relativism.[40]

Croce was much more conscious of his break with the century into which he was born than were Lamprecht or Dilthey. He was one of the first to strike up a tune since repeated in every possible key: that his age was one of cultural, religious, and moral decay, and that its downfall had begun with the decline of romantic philosophy at the beginning of the nineteenth century. The age was confused, superficial, lacking in synthetic force, and incapable of providing liberalism (which was Croce's gospel) with the theoretical structure it so urgently needed. For although the four decades that had passed since 1870 had witnessed the triumph of liberty, its fruits had turned rotten the moment they were harvested.[41] Oddly enough, Croce's philosophical and historical views were much more deeply rooted in the nineteenth century than those of either Lamprecht or Dilthey. His conclusions, however, were much more revolutionary than theirs, though he introduced no new elements. He abominated Bergson's intuitionism, James's pragmatism, and vitalism, and preferred to return to the past, sometimes distorted by a mind that lacked the clarity of the nineteenth century but was filled with the dynamics of the twentieth, as witness the importance he attached to dialectics. Croce like Dilthey, distinguished between two types of knowledge: the intuitive, which he called the aesthetic and which bore on particulars, and the conceptual, which he called the logical,

458

and which bore on universals. He, too, considered history as falling into the first group. But, in addition, he also introduced the distinction — and this was characteristic of him — between the work of the "chronicler" and that of the true historian. The first dealt with dead history, with past actions; the second, by contrast, was the historiographer of the present, and as such reflected its intellectual structure through a creative thrust of the intellect. Because the intellect never stands still, it creates its own past even while creating itself. Hence Croce's identification of philosophy with history.

It is not difficult to see that the draught prepared in Croce's dispensary served many as an anodyne, particularly in his native Italy, which was hard put to it to present itself as a great power, and all the prouder once again to boast "a great man" admired by the world at large. That man, moreover, was reminiscent of Spaventa, and through him of the imperishable tradition of the Renaissance, the more so as he helped Italy to shake off the baneful influence of the positivist, Andigó.

The world outside, by contrast, was more attracted by Croce's synthetic approach and by his highminded but dynamic sentiments, for highmindedness always helps to soothe frayed nerves, and dynamism was felt to be consolingly modern. In particular, Croce's idealism seemed to offer an escape from a world full of strife, from an atomosphere heavy with the smoke of revolution and war.

This may explain why the Viennese art historian Julian Schlosser not only translated Croce's self-analysis of 1915[42] but also confessed in his own commentary on that book that Croce had helped him to a better understanding of his discipline and hence to the introduction of some order where chaos had previously reigned supreme.[43] The serious art historian at the time was in much the same quandary as the criminologist, psychologist, or physician. For just as criminology failed to see the criminal behind the crime, psychology the psyche behind the associations, and the doctor the patient behind the disease, so the history of art had lost sight of the artist behind the styles, schools, and the forms that were taking up so much of the attention of a Wölfflin, an Alois Riegl and a Worringer. Not surprisingly so, for now that the classical ideal had become so tarnished, this approach afforded them the only chance of being open to all new trends, and hence of keeping abreast of the uncertain times.

Schlosser was not the only one to raise the alarm. His colleague, Hans Tietze, also said that whoever had witnessed scientific or artisitc developments during the first few years of the second decade of the twentieth century knew or suspected that an intellectual crisis was im-

459

minent, that revolution was in the air.[44] In his *Methode der Kunstgeschichte* (Method of Art History; 1913) he tried to divert this revolution into safe channels. All in all, Lamprecht had thus been right to call his period the "excitable age." To him, excitability was a symptom of all major historical transformations, and he agreed with Croce that this symptom was unusually clear in his own day. This was understandable. For he himself had defined "excitability" in 1903 as the creative response to new and previously unexpressed inner stimuli caused by a series of successive and unresolved tensions.[45] These tensions, he believed — for despite his psychologism he had remained enough of a realist to appreciate this fact — were set up in talented individuals by the social and economic changes of the age in which they lived.[46]

Indeed they were. Social and economic changes and all the tensions and uncertainties they produce, together with the quest for new certainties, order and synthesis — all these were reflected in the frantic activity of historians. Small wonder, for history is never completed and must always seem to be emulating Münchhausen's attempt to pull himself out of the swamp by his own hair.

CHAPTER XXXI

THE CRISIS OF VALUES

On Saturday, August 25, 1900, at his home in Weimar, Friedrich Nietzsche closed his eyes for the last time — those shrewd eyes with their jutting brows that had looked, perhaps too clearly, into the depths of the world around him.

For the last eleven or twelve years of his life he had plummeted ever deeper into the dark abysses of madness. But during the twice twelve years that he had been at the height of his powers, he had toppled many idols with grim bitterness and had upset the values in which European culture had trusted for twice twelve centuries — a demolition of ideals and values that culminated in the notorious assertion: God is dead.

Indeed, the nineteenth century had known no cultural crisis as radical as the one he had ushered in, nor any man so convinced of his own mission. We live in an age whose culture is threatened by its own cultural products — that is how he himself characterized his age. He realized that "in him, time was being rent in two, and history cleft for the parting of the ways; that he was an explosive charge on the dividing line of two centuries." Beerling was perfectly right to add that Nietzsche's self-assurance cannot be dismissed as a sympton of his incipient insanity.[1] The prophet's calling does not happen to be a healthy one, and if we were to eliminate all human creations that had a touch of madness about them, we should be left with very few great achievements.

One cannot dismiss Nietzsche's contribution as an individual aberration for the further reason that it would leave us with two completely inexplicable phenomena: the intriguing parallelism between Nietzsche's ideal man and the capitalist *condottiere*, and the great impact Nietzsche himself made on some of his contemporaries and on so many among the next two generations. A whole library could be filled with books proving this point; moreover, people had begun to speak of a Nietzsche cult even before the end of the last century. In 1933 Gisela Deesz wrote at length on the "development of the Nietzsche image in Germany," and in 1956 Kaufmann made it his business to purge that image of the many myths surrounding it.

For it is a fact that the Nietzsche image has been badly distorted by a host of myths, and especially by the deliberate mythologizations of his sister and intellectual testatrix, who was quick to pick from his works whatever seemed to serve her own racist and pre-Fascist ideas. As a result it has become almost impossible to separate Nietzsche fact from Nietzsche fiction. In any case, the capitalist *condottiere* could not really have modeled himself on the Nietzschean ideal if only because no one becomes a superman by reading about it. Nevertheless, it remains a fact that at the turn of the century, "empire builders" and industrial magnates, no matter what their nationality, could not have been less "compassionate" and "masterful" in their attitude to their slaves, or more convinced that they were "beyond good and evil," ideas they had taken straight from Nietzsche. He could serve as the great glorifier of the deed precisely because he saw himself as a powerless thinker, while the "masterful" men who looked to him for justification could permit themselves the luxury of glorifying the intellect even while behaving like savages. To some extent, at least, the relationship can be reversed without doing violence to the facts. Thus, as we said earlier, no one contributed more than Nietzsche to what Lütgert has called "the decline of idealism." In so doing he cut off the branch bearing the authority of the "poets, philosophers, and prophets," and hence his own. Seen in this light, his superman was no more than a super-ego born of a philosopher's disgust with an Establishment that despised him as a mere intellectual. Did this man of pure thought not draw close to the men of pure action when he avowed that great deeds can only be performed by those who have the strength and determination to injure others?[2] Or when with the characteristic pathos he proclaimed that life must be glorified above everything else and that the basis of life was the will to power?

This explains why Franz Mehring entitled his essay on Nietzsche (1891) "On the Philosophy and Poetry of Capitalism,"[3] and why he later described Nietzsche's philosophy as "subjectively, a desperate delirium of the intellect; and objectively, a glorification of big capital."[4] Hence, Mehring felt, the appeal of Nietzsche's philosophy, which was given a powerful new impetus in 1888 when Georg Brandes, that great talent scout, delivered a series of lectures on Nietzsche in Copenhagen, and which had grown so fast by 1897 that Ferdinand Tönnies, a former disciple, could write a critical essay on the "Nietzsche cult."[5] That same year, Alios Riehl published his *Friedrich Nietzsche, der Künstler und der Denker* (Friedrich Nietzsche, the Artist and Philosopher), and in 1903, he again discussed Nietzsche's contribution in his *Zur Einführung in die Philosophie der Gegenwart* (Introduction to Contemporary Philosophy).[6] If Mehring referred by "objectively" to the fact that, regardless of Nietzsche's real intentions, there was a striking agreement between his ideas on morality and the "moral" activities of the modern *condottieri*, between what he despised and they violated, then it is impossible to deny the justice of Mehring's critique. But this does not yet establish a structural connection.

That connection did, however, exist, albeit below the surface. A catalogue of Nietzsche's objections to the spirit of the age is quickly written. In essence, these were identical with the objections voiced by all conservative thinkers since the French Revolution. Nietzsche was opposed to everything that was or seemed to be democratic: universal suffrage, woman's rights, tolerance, and even the reading of newspapers. Most particularly he disliked the idea of human equality and its logical consequence:socialism. Even the "causes" of the "decline" he had diagnosed were far from new: a lack of moral discipline, of authority, of temperance, of a hierarchy of values. The effects he listed were not surprising either: the rise of the stupid and commonplace; the substitution of feelings for principles; the uprising of slaves ("petty minds" who no longer believe in saints); citizens who reject the ideal of a ruling caste; scientific drudges who despise the philosophers — in short, a "domesticated type of barbarism." His critique of contemporary culture would have been little more than run-of-the-mill antidemocratic claptrap, had his intellect not elevated him far above that of the ordinary reactionary. In fact, his critique did not spare the ruling classes either — he had nothing but scorn for the Bismarcks, the Hohenzollerns, and the Wagners, and "Deutschland, Deutschland über alles" spelled to him the end of German culture. Indeed, he went further still when he spoke of "factualism" — the slavish respect for "facts" evinced by "objective" science no less than by the naturalistic art of his day — and of inner emptiness, reflected in a frantic search for consolation in alcohol, music, and hedonism.[7]

Among all these objections there was one that, so to speak, summed up his entire outlook. The twentieth century, he claimed, had two faces: one of decay and one of rebirth. And the two were inseparable. For the same causes "that now make it possible for mightier spirits to emerge than have ever appeared before, spirits far less beset with prejudices and antiquated moral ideas, also foster decay in weaker characters."[8] What else could these "causes" be but the unprecedented economic expansion of the new German Reich and the new chances it held out to every "powerful nature" that wished to seize them?

Seen in this light, his alleged revulsion from this type of man looks more like mistaken love, in which case Nietzsche, like so many other intellectuals, while despising the celebrated successes of the vulgar place-seekers so common in Wilhelminian Germany, nevertheless, and as it were despite himself, must have looked up to these "gentlemen" as examples whose flawed greatness he tried to remodel in the marble of his prose. Here we have what it perhaps the greatest difference between Nietzsche and Burckhardt. Burckhardt was not German but Swiss, not the son of a village parson but a patrician, one who could brave his own age and the future, albeit he too was a pessimist. Moreover, he succeeded in fusing his scientific to his artistic interests, and, all in all, had no cause for resentment, while Nietzsche had a long list of grievances from his interrupted academic career to his syphilis.

One can adopt this view and yet maintain that Mehring was as wrong with the first part of his characterization (" . . . subjectively, a desperate delirium of the intellect") as he was right with the second (" . . . objec-tively, a glorification of big capital"). Nietzsche's philosophy was no "delirium of the intellect" either objectively or subjectively, if only because it was not nearly as incomprehensible as many of his superficial critics have made it out to be.[9] True, Nietzsche's thought was difficult to follow and lent itself to a host of divergent interpretations, but this was something he shared with the greatest philosophers. His belief that man is capable of developing into a higher type was in keeping with the evolutionary outlook of his age, and was as little a sign of delirium as were his attempts to topple the existing values, which were, in any case, overthrowing themselves. Nor was he alone in rejecting the atomistic approach of the positivists. His glorification of life, which might very well have been a compensation for his illness, was nevertheless "objective" enough to give rise to an entirely new current in philosophy at the turn of the century. Even his strange doctrine of "eternal recurrence" cannot be called a delirium. Nietzsche may have exaggerated its importance, but if we consider it a revival of the cyclical ideas of the Greeks, then it simply made him a conservative, one who wanted no changes because he was afraid of change, but nevertheless had to allow for change in his philosophy. For the cyclical idea acknowledges change, but tempers its effects, by holding that change merely helps to restore the old.[10]

Two weeks before Nietzsche's death, Vladimir Soloviev, the great Russian philosopher, died in a village near Moscow. The two deaths were coincidental, but it was no coincidence that two philosophers who started from entirely different premises and arrived at diametrically opposite conclusions should have had so much in common. Both were hypersensitive to the signs of the times, and both voiced their objections to the present in such a way as to make them appear heralds of the future. Both alike rejected positivism (on the shortcomings of which Soloviev had dilated in his 1874 thesis), rationalism and materialism, and both advanced a philosophy that was more than an academic specialty; both inveighed against socialism, or rather against the process of levelling downwards. And both were voicing the views of much broader circles, so much so that they may be said to have initiated a general search for new values and new truths. They themselves failed in the attempt. For though Soloviev set out to revitalize Christianity by the resurrection of mystical and gnostic elements, he found no lasting satisfaction; indeed, towards the end of his life he was as pessimistic as he had previously been optimistic, and spoke of the imminent arrival of the Antichrist.[11] Nietzsche's nihilism was no less symptomatic of the crisis he had helped to usher in than was his convulsive attempt to surmount it with the help of a superman, of whom one could say that he, too, was the Antichrist, albeit a welcome one.[12]

Nor was it astonishing that philosophy should have suffered a crisis in the last decades of the nineteenth century. Positivism had become totally discredited, and Nietzsche and Soloviev were not the only ones to argue that it had strayed far from the "love of wisdom." Thus Burckhardt and Dilthey were opposing positivism in the historical sphere, Driesch in biology, Gierke in jurisprudence,[13] and Paul de Lagarde in theology. Lagarde had been one of the first to voice his objections (he died in 1891) and he, incidentally, revealed the reactionary character of the anti-positivist current: he was one of the fathers of both modern anti-Semitism and also of "German Christianity," and even went so far as to describe St. Paul as "nothing better than a Pharisee." Somewhat later, in 1907, Josef Kohler, another lawyer, likened the positivist to the man who hears nothing but isolated sound waves in a piece of music, and who, though he may analyse these waves down to the finest detail, utterly fails to grasp the meaning of the composition.[14] Moreover, though most practical scientists remained positivists, even they would have found it difficult to explain why as a philosophy, positivism was fast losing its hold even on them. For positivism was no longer modest enough to claim that its sole objective was to ensure that science did not stray beyond the visible and measurable, and had also abandoned the great dream that the thousands of modest scientific contributions would one day provide the answer to all the world mysteries. For the rest, the growth of industry and technology had ensured that what to Hegel was still the mother of science was cut off from most of her daughters: first of all from physics, but also

465

from psychology, pedagogy, sociology, cultural history, anthropology, and finally even from the theoretical discussion of the proper role of these various disciplines.

It is understandable why these developments should have become the source of new philosophic life; why they should have persuaded those attracted to the subject either to "elevate" philosophy into the scientific study of epistemological or ethical problems or else to rise "above" all the sciences and seek new answers to the riddle of "being."

The first solution was adopted by almost the whole of academic philosophy, or at least by those among the philosophers who glossed over the difficulties by adopting a purely historical approach. Thus Gerard Heymans, in his inaugural professorial address of 1890, described philosophy as "the study of problems posed by the realization that all human knowledge is relative"; philosophy, according to him, was a discipline whose problems, methods, and theories differed in no way from those of the sciences.[15] Though his view was shared by quite a few leading philosophers, it did not have a great future. The rising trend of specialization helped to split epistemological studies into as many special branches as there were sciences, so much so that only the expert could have said what his particular discipline knew or set out to discover.

However the very specialization that fragmented philosophy into as many philosophies as there were sciences also stressed the need for a new approach, one that might help one to see the wood for the trees once again. This holistic approach, which we have mentioned on more than one occasion, became known as "life philosophy." Of the two prevailing currents, it was the one that made a much more radical break with the rationalist tradition of Descartes and the idealistic tradition of Kant and Hegel. It was also a clearer mirror of society, and this in two respects. In the first place, all its disciples were entranced by movement, words, and life, sometimes to the point of exultation. They were actualists. It was no accident that, like Dilthey, they should have based themselves on historical studies, or, like Bergson, on biology. "Life philosophy" could only have flourished in a society shaken to its foundations by the dynamics of industrial and technological expansion. In the second place, it was nothing if not a reaction against the progressive rationalization, organization, and bureaucratization of human relationships. It opposed reason with intuition, theory with practice, the abstract with the concrete, quantity with quality, analysis with synthesis, the part with the whole. As against monism, be it of materialist or of idealist origins, it adopted a pluralist or personalist approach, dismissing determinism as an attack on human freedom and responsibility.[16]

That this was no *post hoc* construction is shown by a collection of forty-eight philosophical autobiographies published in Germany in the 1920s[17] but confined to men who were already at work in 1900. We shall look at the philosophical development of Karl Joël — one of these forty-eight — to see how the conversion of anti-positivism was effected in one concrete case.[18] Joël's starting point was neo-Kantianism which he considered a serviceable weapon against naturalism. He confessed that he, like so many of his contemporaries, had discovered to his dismay that the historical, objectivist specialism inherited from the nineteenth century was in conflict with the speculative spirit of the new age; that too much attention to detail stood in the way of the growing urge to embrace the whole. In a public lecture on the future of philosophy he delivered in Basel, where he became a lecturer in 1893, he described contemporary culture as "monumental barbarism." In Berlin, where he vacationed from 1894 onwards, he came into contact with people of like mind: with Zeller, Paulsen, Lazarus, Steinthal, and above all with Dilthey and Simmel.[19] He came to look upon the ethical reformers as his closest allies in the fight against naturalism, and tried to effect a synthesis between power and love as respectively exemplified by Nietzsche and Tolstoy; between philosophy and fantasy, a marriage of which it was said that it could produce nothing but loathsome abortions; between monism and dualism, and more generally between explorer and writer, historian and observer, specialist and humanist. This made him a romantic almost despite himself. Philosophizing meant liberating oneself by drawing on the "spirit of the times" with all one's strength the better to surmount it. To him, philosophy was a living activity, not the mechanical passivity of his predecessors: the past century had been static but the new one would be dynamic. This was in accord with his later theory that all the odd centuries that had elapsed since the heyday of Ancient Greece had been static, while all the even centuries had been dynamic.[20]

In the writings he published during the first decades of the new century, his change of attitude was reflected even more clearly than in his autobiographical summary. They included a collection entitled *Philosophenwege* (Philosophers' Paths; 1901); a series of essays on Schopenhauer, Nietzsche and romanticism (1905), on free will (1908), on the soul and the world (1912), and finally his *Weltanschauung* (World View, 1928), and a collection called *Antibarbarus* (1928) which included his design of a "culture for a hundred years."

Joël was not one of the very great, but it was just this fact that enabled him to record the philosophical life of his period with great detachment, thus making him a most trustworthy guide. This is particularly true of the rectoral address he delivered in Basel in November 1913 on "the philosophical crisis of today,"[21] in which he dealt with the two main currents we have just distinguished and pointed to their dangers: the splitting up of philosphy into epistemology, logic, psychology, or history at the expense of an overall, synthetic approach; and the surrender to the call of power and the intoxication of life — an irrational, emotional, and pragmatic response in which the objective "experience" of the positivists had yielded to the subjective lure of mysticism. And he added that Rudolf Eucken was the only one to share his view of the situation.

Enlightening though Joël's analysis of the state of philosophy in 1913 may have been, he was nevertheless quite wrong to think that specialization and mystical vitalism had become the only philosophical alternatives. Once the old values had been thrown into disarray by rapid social changes, the choice became much wider than it had been before, the more so as the new society differed from the old by its even greater complexities and more rapid strides. Thus while Nietzsche, Bergson, Husserl, Croce, and Russell, the great masters of philosophy at the turn of the century, may have retained various ingredients of the two major trends, they nevertheless opened four new windows: Bergson as the spokesman of the philosophy of life, Husserl as the spokesman of the philosophy of being, Croce as the spokesman of the philosophy of the spirit, and Russell as the spokesman of the philosophy of matter. If, in addition, we recall the two no less influential currents which Delfgaauw distinguished as "traditional solutions" from what he called the "transformational solutions"[22] — namely dialectical materialism and neo-Thomism — then we have drawn a still incomplete but broadly correct picture of philosophy in the certain and yet uncertain, apparently peaceful but in fact highly agitated, period with which we are concerned. For all that, this picture was not the one students of philosophy at the turn of the century would have drawn themselves. Of the six normative figures we have mentioned, only one — Croce — is found among the forty-eight autobiographical sketches published in the 1920s (see p. 467). And in Ludwig Stein's discussion of the main philosophical currents of his day,[23] which was published in 1908 and ran to 450 pages, only the name of Husserl was mentioned, but not discussed. Frischeisen,[24] who wrote in 1907, did exactly the same, while Schjelderup[25] only mentioned Bergson, although his book was published in the 1920s. Wright[26] listed them all except for Lenin, an omission made good by Bochénski.

Bergson was probably the clearest mirror of the problems that beset philosophy at the turn of the century. The year 1900 was a watershed

468

in his own life as well; he was then forty-one years old and was to live on for another forty-one. He owed his special place not to that accident but to the brilliance of his philosophical style, rivalled only by Plato, or perhaps by Nietzsche. He first displayed it in 1899, in a thesis entitled *Essai sur les données immédiates de la conscience* and next in his *Matière et mémoire* of 1896 and above all in his *L'Évolution créatrice* of 1907, the work that brought him fame, and incidentally, detracted from his professional standing. For had he written less brilliantly he might not have been lumped together with the irrationalists, nor would so many lesser lights have invoked his name in support of critiques of reason that, in their case, were so many signs of their own lack of rationality. Bergson himself, who came to philosophy from biology, carried the ideas of positive science and evolution in his intellectual luggage, but rejected the deterministic and mechanistic approach and substituted human freedom of choice, or more precisely the unpredictable effects of *élan vital*. He at no time questioned the value of rationality; he merely contended that the "duration" of vital phenomena was inaccessible to reason and could only be grasped by intuition. This was merely a reformulation of the old Heraclitean doctrine that all things in the universe are in ceaseless flux and that "becoming" prevails over "being."

Bergson had a sharp eye, and first of all for the dangers of specialization from which his contemporaries expected nothing short of miracles. As early as 1882, when he was only twenty-three years old, he wrote in *La Spécialité*[27] that we can only perfect any of our qualities if we develop all the rest, and that this was precisely what distinguished human intelligence from the instincts of animals, each animal being a kind of specialist. He also had an eye for the irreducible uniqueness and hence the inexhaustible potential of the individual, though he did not overlook man's social attachments or the rational roots of his actions and ideas. Ultimately, he did no more than introduce Meillet's extra degree of precision,[28] no more than call for closer understanding of the tools needed to grasp complex reality. In this respect Bergson may rightly be compared with Freud, who also used reason to advance a sphere of reality beyond reason.[29]

To pragmatism, too, life was the central problem, not as an object as it was for Bergson, but as a starting point: William James, the founder of this school, also referred to it as "radical empiricism." Pragmatism (the term was coined by Peirce, James's predecessor) was of Anglo-Saxon origin, but about 1900 it also exerted a more than superficial influence on the continent of Europe — on Bergson and Sorel in France, and on Simmel and Vaihinger in Germany. Moreover, the appeal of James's

Varieties of Religious Experience (1901–1902) extended far beyond this small circle of professional philosophers; it was one of the few contemporary books mentioned in Huizinga's *Herfsttij*. James's influence was largely spread by John Dewey, who, being an educational reformer, moved in much wider circles. James himself, who was fifty-eight in 1900, had come to reject idealism and monism in favour of a realistic, dynamic, and pluralistic approach, largely under the influence of European critics of the philosophy of science. Partly under their influence, he was carried so far from determinism that he came to speak of himself as a proponent of tychism — the rule of chance.

However, he is much better known for his pragmatism, which, as its names suggests, assigns a central role to action, something Blondel had earlier done in his thesis, *L'Action*, of 1893. How unusual this approach was considered to be at the time may be gathered from the stiff resistance Blondel met at the Sorbonne: action was the last thing a true philosopher thought about.[30] James mentions Blondel as an ally in the preface to his *Pragmatism* (1907). To the pragmatists, action was central, inasmuch as they held that ideas are only correct if they lead to new observations and experiences, and attitudes only right if they prove to be of practical worth. Usefulness thus determines not only value but also truth. Though James, with characteristic American forthrightness, even spoke of the "cash value" of ideas, he did not confine himself to the narrow sphere of material needs; religion was of practical value as well since men could not do without it.[31] James, too, was a mixture of the old and the new; "old" in respect of his empiricism and belief in progress, but "new" because his empiricism was not fragmented but structured, and also because his belief in progress was not deterministic but voluntaristic.

In England pragmatism made its appearance with *Personal Idealism*, a collective work published in 1902 by eight young philosophers, of whom the thirty-eight year old F. C. S. Schiller was probably the best known. To him, unlike to Pythagoras, man was not only the measure but also the creator of all things: a fact only becomes a fact through the intervention (the action) of man. He took much the same view of truth: there is not only no absolute truth, but no truth at all, for truth being human, never *is* but always *becomes*. This explains why Schiller liked to refer to his particular brand of pragmatism as "humanism."[32]

The typically German form of life philosophy bore the name of historicism. Its founder was Wilhelm Dilthey, who, chronologically speaking, must be considered a nineteenth-century philosopher — he was born in 1833 and died in 1911 — but whose influence only made itself felt during the first decade of the twentieth century to become very great indeed during the next fifteen years. Like James, he too was a mixture of the old and the new, but in quite a different manner. His historicism, an attendant phenomenon of the spectacular development of historical research in the nineteenth-century, was "old"; what was "new" in his vision was that he no longer dwelt on historical *phenomena* but on historical *structures* and their origins; "new" also was his recognition that these structures, though necessary, were quite "fortuitous," and his conclusion that it was its values that determined the historical picture of a particular age; and "new" finally was his intuitive method of coming to grips with history. Historical "understanding", he believed, differed in principle from the rational "explanations" of natural science. In this respect Dilthey did what Rickert, Simmel, and Windelband had done as well: he stressed the fundamental difference between the human and natural sciences, the better to free the first from the shackles of the second. For "understanding" was only possible through "empathy." "Old" again was the fact that Dilthey, despite the relativizing subjectivism which was the unavoidable consequence of this method, held fast to the objectivism on which contemporary historians so prided themselves. This indigestible positive remnant set up an intellectual tension in him, which he was unable to resolve.[33] What was most in keeping with the mood of the times and at the same time Dilthey's most lasting contribution, was probably his structual conception. At the end of his life, it led him to consider successive philosophies as so many temporary systems in the eternal current of history. Thus history became the history of the human spirit, of man's ever-changing "attitudes" and life situations. Though he did not say it in so many words, Dilthey was in fact pleading for an integral construction of history, in which the various sectors are of equal importance.[34]

Neither Bergson, James nor Dilthey were irrationalists unless we apply that label to anyone who holds that certain spheres of reality cannot be plumbed by reason alone. However, at the turn of the century the general crisis of confidence had grown so acute that it also gave rise to irrationalism in the true sense of the word, namely to the belief that reason itself is unreliable and that it can only reflect reality in distorted form, if at all. This was the view, above all, of the Russian "intuitivists" led by N. O. Losski, who launched the movement in 1906, and of S. L. Frank, who became its best-known spokesman in western Europe.[35] Even before the revolution of 1905, Losski, with the help of Berdyaev and Bulgakov, founded the journal *Problems of Life*, which preached a related philosophy. But more important by far was the contribution of Lev Shestov, who like Berdyaev, Bulgakov, and Frank, started off as a Marxist only to end up as an extreme anti-Marxist. He not only described reason as an unsound guide but considered reality contradictory and absurd, thus becoming a precursor of existentialism. "Protest against reason" is what Suys has called this philosophy,[36] and Shestov himself referred to it in 1905 as the apotheosis of the unfathomable. Few others made a more radical *volte-face* than he did, partly, no doubt, under the influence of the political and social revolution in his country of origin. However this could not have been the full explanation, for the Spaniard Miguel de Unamuno (who was thirty-four in 1898, the year of the Spanish cultural revival) must also be counted among the precursors of modern existentialism, not least thanks to his *Del sentimiento trágico de la vida* (*The Tragic Sense of Life*), published in 1913.

To understand how it came about that the German Edmund Husserl, a number of Russians, and a Spaniard should have come to feel, albeit on different grounds, that the crisis in philosophy had grown so severe that it could only be remedied by a radical new start, we must look briefly at the state of science at the time. Here not only the old values but also the entire methodology were under increasing attack as it became clear that the foundations of positivism were not nearly as "objective" as they had previously seemed to be. Even the strictest scientific theories appeared to be no more than useful instruments, and hence "neither true nor false," as the great French mathematician, Henri Poincaré, put it quite bluntly. According to other critics, the infallibility of science was no more than a nineteenth-century fable. That was, in any case, the express opinion of Emile Boutroux, who had spoken of the "fortuitous character" of natural laws as early as 1874, and that was also the view of Pierre Duhem, and of perhaps the most important of all these critics, the Pole Emile Meyerson, born like Bergson and Husserl in 1859, that memorable year in which both Darwin's *On the Origin of Species* and Marx's *Zur Kritik der politischen Ökonomie* (Critique of Political Economy) saw the light of day.

Related to the critique of science, to pragmatism and finally to fictionalism as expressed in Vaihinger's "as if" philosophy, was the empirio-criticism of the Austrian Ernst Mach and the Swiss Richard Avenarius. It was probably no accident that the climate should not have been right for Mach's ideas until he was no longer a young man: although he was not unknown as a physicist, his philosophy did not make an impact until 1895, when he was offered the Chair of Philosophy in Vienna. By then he was fifty-seven and had acquired an influence that went far beyond philosophy, no doubt because his doctrine of the "economy of thought" (according to which concepts were abbreviated, and hence inadequate,

472

but nevertheless convenient reflections of reality) seemed to provide a bridge between idealism and materialism.

Be that as it may, Mach's influence on his contemporaries was in any case undeniable. To mention only two striking examples: Einstein fell under his spell and Lenin did his utmost to fault him in his *Materialism and Empirio-Criticism* of 1908.

To bridge the gulf between idealism and materialism was also Husserl's objective.[37] To that end, he decided to start right from the beginning, to go back to the objects themselves and to describe them with an open mind. This attempt was not unlike Dilthey's in psychology. According to Husserl, the fact that phenomena cannot be described, except as they manifest themselves to consciousness, did not mean that phenomena (be they ideal or real) were mere manifestations of consciousness, as the idealists contended. Nor was consciousness simply a reflection of matter, as the materialists taught, if only because consciousness is always intentional, i.e., directed at something, no matter whether its content is a perception, a conception, an image, an idea, or a desire. However, an exhaustive description of phenomena is impossible, and in any case pointless; what matters is to grasp their essence and this we can do only by intuition. Husserl presented these phenomenological ideas in a work with the modest title of *Logische Untersuchungen* (Logical Investigations), and when it was published in 1900 to 1901, it, too, made its impact felt far beyond the circle of academic philosophers.

Mach's and Husserl's attempts to take a position between idealism and materialism may well have reflected their national origins: both were born in Moravia, had their heads crammed full of the battle of Sadowa and were naturally opposed to the dominant German philosophy whose anti-materialism reflected a desperate anxiety to throw up a dam against Marxian socialism. These German "philosophers of the spirit," no matter whether they were neo-Kantians or neo-Hegelians, had returned to idealism with a vengeance as soon as they realized that the social consequences of materialism and positivism posed a serious threat to all they stood for. This was particularly obvious with F. A. Lange, who took a keen interest in the "social problem" and who devoted two thick tomes to a classical history of materialism — only to reject it.[38] Although he died in 1875, before our period, we mention him here because he is generally considered the father of the "back to Kant" movement, which promised salvation from materialism. Hermann Cohen, the leader of the Marburg neo-Kantians, thus knew what he was doing when he saw to the fourth reprinting of Lange's book. Not that Social Democrats were not affected by the Kant revival: Eduard Bernstein, Karl Vörlander, and

Max Adler are the best known but by no means the only example of this swing. Whether or not it made them anti-Marxists may be irrelevant here, but that their views were incompatible with Marx's is in any case beyond question. The Marburg neo-Kantian school of Cohen and Natorp differed in many respects from the Baden school of Windelband and Rickert, and this despite their common positivist starting point. From about 1890 to 1910 the Baden school was by far the more influential of the two, probably because it attached great importance to values, whereas the Marburg school adopted a purely epistemological approach. For the rest, the Marburg school, too, was suffused with other philosophic currents; towards the end of his life — he died in 1924 at the age of seventy — Natorp came out in support of both life philosophy and phenomenology, while conversely Husserl's overtures to idealism in 1913 were due, at least in part, to Natorp's influence. Moreover, the Marburg school had a fairly close affinity with Hegel, with whom it shared the quest for logical unity.

In fact, at the turn of the century, Hegelianism experienced a revival side by side with Kantianism, particularly in Italy and Holland. Here, too, the chief attraction was the idealist message, the primacy of the spirit over matter. That revulsion from Marxism played an important part in all this is shown by the fact that the new doctrine did not take root in England where Marxism had made a very small impact. In Germany and France, too, neo-Hegelianism found few adherents of any importance, in the former because neo-Kantianism already played a satisfactory anti-materialist role; in the second because it had idealist traditions of its own. In Italy and the Netherlands, though neo-Kantianism had made great strides, Marxism gained an increasing hold on the young intellectuals. Bolland wanted no truck with socialism or even with the sovereignty of the people, that "topsyturvy society in which the lowest rises to the top." Croce's conversion from Marxism to idealism was a step along the same road, and took him five years. In a series of articles written in 1900 and collected in his *Historical Materialism and Economics of Karl Marx*, he abandoned once and for all what he had embraced so ardently five years earlier under the influence of Antonio Labriola.[39]

The fact that Croce adopted neo-Hegelianism rather than neo-Kantianism as a substitute for historical materialism was due on the one hand to the Italian philosophical tradition which had had its neo-Hegelian precursors in Vera and Spaventa, and on the other hand to Croce's historical training; after all Hegel had called history the workshop of the universal spirit. However important his aesthetics and ethics may have been (no less than the other purely philosophic ideas he expounded in

474

his four-part work on the philosophy of the spirit, published between 1902 and 1917) it was probably his historical relativism that earned him lasting influence beyond his country and period. Croce was a historical relativist in the sense that he welcomed the idea of the "plasticity" of the past. History was the reflection of the dynamics of human thought, so that all historical knowledge was time-bound, an idea he himself expressed most poignantly when he said that any history that is more than a chronicle is the history of one's own time.[40] This view, which was strongly reinforced by his study of historiography, was not necessarily based on Hegelian conceptions; in any case it shows that the period under review, with its growing uncertainties, sharpened perceptions, and increasing knowledge, was bound to lead to relativism, to throw up identical problems in most branches of learning, and hence to encourage a search for unity amid all this disparate and desperate diversity. Nietzsche had foreshadowed this development when he spoke of historical perspectivism, a term Scheler was to borrow; we also meet it (and at about the same time as with Croce) in Bergson and M. Stern, who coined the term "the plastic past."[41]

Neo-idealism in various forms had become the predominant trend in philosophy not only in Germany and Italy but also in England and France. In England, as in Italy, it took the form of neo-Hegelianism under F. H. Bradley, B. Bosanquet, J. Royce, a Californian, and J. E. McTaggart (the youngest of the four, born like Croce in 1866). In Germany it took the form of neo-Kantianism which had its precursor in Lange, while French idealism found its precursor in Charles Renouvier, who was eighty-five in 1900. The leading French idealist in the 1920s was Léon Brunschvicg who, though he was just thirty in 1900, did not make his full impact felt until well after the First World War, possibly because the philosophy of this "spiritualist without God" bore clear traces of Bergsonism. His *Introduction à la vie de l'esprit* of 1900 was perhaps one of the most important intellectual contributions made during a year of exceptionally prolific intellectual activity.[42]

It was no accident that an island should have withstood the force of the anti-materialistic tide that washed an entire continent during this period of revolutionary changes. That island was Britain with its unshakable empiricist tradition. What came to be known as the neo-realistic movement was inaugurated with a famous article by G. E. Moore in 1903, written when he was thirty years old. It was published in *Mind* under the title of "Refutation of Idealism". Moore may have been less-known than James or Bergson but his influence was hardly less than theirs, thanks chiefly to Bertrand Russell, who throughout his long life remained more faithful to Moore's doctrine than any of Moore's many other pupils.[43] What Russell expected from philosophy was the kind of certainty others sought in religion.[44] In particular, he was anxious to discover a truth that was independent of human experience. He thought he had found it in mathematics, which was both true and elegant at the same time. In the *Principia Mathematica*, which he published in 1910 to 1913 in collaboration with Whitehead, his elder by eleven years, he opposed Hilbert's formalism no less than Brouwer's intuitionism, both of which had cast doubt on the "superhuman" certainty of mathematics. However, his own honesty forced him to admit soon afterwards that man's need for certainty was an intellectual sin, the greatest obstacle to unprejudiced thought, and that his own certainty was in the long run just another illusion. Space, time, matter, and force, those pillars of Newton's natural philosophy, had been swept away by modern science, which no longer considered space and time as absolutes, but as systems of relations, matter as a series of events, force as energy, no longer made a sharp distinction between matter and energy, and placed less emphasis on causality. Russell was, moreover, exceptionally receptive to modern sociological ideas, but since this particular facet of his work did not come to the fore until after the First World War it falls outside our survey.

Of the many materialist currents there was only one that stuck unreservedly to its nineteenth-century foundations: dialectical materialism, the doctrine of Marx and Engels. This was thanks not so much to Social Democrats in western Europe as to two Russian Marxists: Plekhanov and Lenin. Like the founders, they were emphatic in their rejection of both mechanical materialism and idealism, and in upholding the dialectical character of reality. Plekhanov's chief objective was to preserve Marxist theories intact; Lenin's to preserve the unity of theory and practice which he considered the most fundamental contribution of Marxist philosophy. In particular, he stressed that every philosophy has a class bias. In the event, dialectical materialism remained a philosophical undercurrent until the October Revolution when it proved to be the most influential philosophy of all, bearing out the truth of Marx's dictum that the true philosopher not only interprets the world but also changes it.[45] Another undercurrent, and one that would long remain a bulwark against dialectical materialism, was neo-Thomism. It, too, had its precursors — in early nineteenth-century Italy — but it did not make its full impact felt until 1897, when Pope Leo XIII published his encyclical *Aeterni Patris* on the initiative of the Jesuit Liberatore,[46] and declared it to be the "official" church response to the growing materialism of science. Marxism, which was a product of nineteenth-century thought, found it much easier to adapt itself to the new age than did Thomism, which dated from six centuries before. The leading light among the priests anxious to infuse Thomism with fresh life at the turn of the century was Desiré Mercier, later Cardinal-Archbishop of Malines. In 1893 he founded the Institut Supérieur de Philosophie at Louvain University, which has been one of the most important neo-Thomist centers ever since. At the turn of the century, the new doctrine began to attract the general attention of intellectuals, and particularly of Eucken, who developed it further in his *Thomas von Aquino und Kant* (Thomas Aquinas and Kant).[47] This sudden swing to conservatism underlined rather than refuted the idea that change had become inevitable in 1900.

Philosophy in our period was thus characterized by a great diversification. Positivism had been the last unified philosophic style of the western bourgeoisie, whose apparently unassailable Cartesian *cum* Newtonian edifice, piled up brick by brick through three centuries, had begun to show irreparable cracks in the wake of socio-political developments that had undermined bourgeois self-confidence. Nietzsche had been the petrel heralding the impending storm. A tide of anti-intellectualism that spilled over into irrationalism and mysticism threatened to erode all the foundations of intellectual life. Neo-idealism and neo-realism were but temporary defences. Only two small islands withstood the force of the raging waters: neo-Thomism and dialectical materialism, the first because it rested on the solid foundations of a tradition that went back to Descartes and Newton, the second because it represented the aspirations of a new class, heir to the bourgeoisie and as confident in the future as its predecessors had been in theirs.

CHAPTER XXXII

BABEL AND BIBLE

"A word in haste . . . The Archbishop of Paris has *publicly* banned the publication of further articles by Firmin on the history of Israel, on the grounds that his first article ran counter to the Constitution *Dei Filius* and to the encyclical *Providentissimus Deus.* I was not given the slightest warning. The Cardinal was simply shown the first two pages, and the good man was so horrified to learn that the world was not created in 4004 B.C. . . . that he banned . . . the publication there and then." These remarks were contained in a letter written on October 29, 1900 by the Abbé Alfred Loisy,[1] the leading French Catholic modernist, to Baron Friedrich von Hügel, the international spokesman of progressive Catholicism.[2] The quotation has been chosen at random from a vast number, all illustrating the quandary of traditional Christianity, both in the Catholic and the Protestant camp, at the turn of the century.

The crux of the matter was the massive defection from the churches in an industrial society that increasingly questioned their dogmas. The defectors came from both classes. The liberal bourgeoisie was so satisfied with its own progress that it felt free to dispense with the benefits of religious solace if not altogether then at least in its old form, and the working class, touched by the spirit of revolt, could not but despise a faith that had always preached acquiescence to earthly misery against the promise of heavenly salvation.

The "bankruptcy of Christianity" was greeted with satisfaction by some and with horror by others, but denied by few. Nietzsche had already prophesied "the death of God"; like him, Vacher de Lapouge now declared that Christianity was an unnatural religion and an unnatural morality with disastrous consequences for the future of mankind. He blamed it not only for the current crisis of confidence but also for the "sickness of the age": the "inability to believe coupled to charitable impulses."[3] Since Vacher de Lapouge was one of the creators of the Aryan myth, anti-Semitism was certainly part and parcel of his rejection of Christianity. But so temperate a man as Stanley Leathes, who succeeded Lord Acton as editor of the *Cambridge Modern History*, must have had quite different motives when, shortly after the turn of the century, he stated soberly that religion had lost its hold over the European mind, and that the young would replace it with practical efforts to usher in social reforms.[24] Small wonder that this period was the heyday of "free thought," that freethinkers should have banded together — the International Free-thinkers' League was founded in Brussels in 1880 — or that so many freethinkers should have been workers and artisans and with socialist leanings at that. Feuerbach, Darwin and Huxley, Büchner, Vogt and Moleschott, Multatuli, Gerrit Jan Mulder and Haeckel were their great prophets. It was Haeckel himself who convened an International Free-thinkers' Congress in Rome in 1904, partly in response to the vicious attacks on his *Welträthsel* (The Riddle of the Universe) of 1899. His name was something to be conjured with in those years, not only thanks to the remarkable success of that book — it sold some three million copies in more than twenty languages[5] — but even more so because certain clerics had been forced to retract their libelous allegations that he had falsified illustrations of embryos in several of his books. Libel is always a two-edged sword. Another leading light in the movement was John MacKinnon Robertson, who wrote a *Short History of Free Thought* in 1899.[6]

A much more comprehensive picture of the "spirit of the age" emerges from an inquiry into the crisis of religion launched by the *Mercure de France* in 1907. In explaining its purpose, Frédéric Charpin argued that the problem of religion had become the topic of keen scientific, political, and sociological discussions; and that new schools and ideas bore witness to the fact that every religious denomination was in ferment. Everywhere voices were being raised for or against religion. In France there was the hotly contested separation of Church and State; in England, the schools controversy; in Germany, the fight between the government and the Center Party; in Russia, the struggle between autocratic orthodoxy and liberalism. In Italy and Spain anticlericalism was on the increase; through-out the Orient there was a clash of races divided on religious lines, and Charpin concluded the list by reminding his readers of the recent Japanese victory over a Christian nation. He might well have added that interest in religious problems was also reflected in a number of new journals and reference works: the *Revue de l'Histoire des Religions* founded in 1818; the *Archiv für Religionsgeschichte* founded in 1898; the *Catholic Encyclopedia* of 1907–1912 and the *Realenzyklopädie für protestantische Theologie und Kirche* of 1908–1913.

The replies to the inquiry by some 150 leading personalities showed that, in their view, religion was on the decline, but by no means in complete disarray, and that religious sentiments were innate in man. Religion, they felt, must be completely reformed, though they differed sharply about the means. Paul Sabatier, known as a catholicizing Protestant by virtue of his book on St. Francis (1892), thought he could detect signs of the emergence of a Universal Church — an ideal that had been kept alive ever since the Reformation. Nicolai Berdyaev, for his part, looked forward to the creation of a Church that would embrace not only the various denominations but also the idea of salvation on earth — that much at least he had still retained from his Marxist past. Scipio Sighele, the Italian sociologist, also anticipated the emergence of a single religion and a single morality which he, however, identified with a rational philosophy that would prove its scientific validity by accepting the fact that it could never hope to discover the ultimate causes of the universe. Michel Revon, professor of the history of far eastern civilization, made no private confessions; instead he pointed out that a Japanese journal had recently held an investigation into the thoughts of its readers on religious developments in Japan during the next hundred years. The replies had shown that most readers believed that the various religions would become fused into a single ethical code.

In Europe, too, the idea of a syncretic religion was taking root, even among some of the clergy. In his memoirs, Loisy mentions a letter he received in 1908 (by which time he himself had been excommunicated) from a young parson. "I do not know whether I am reading the signs of the times correctly," the young man had written, "but I believe that it would be a good thing for Protestantism no less than for Catholicism if they made way for something better than either." Loisy did not add any comments of his own, but the fact that he concluded Part II of his memoirs with this letter shows how important he felt it to be.[7]

In some, this quest assumed very peculiar forms, as we shall show at greater length in the next chapter. Here we shall confine ourselves to two further replies to the French inquiry. The first was by Merezh-kovsky whose trilogy, *Christ and Antichrist*, was completed in 1905. His new religion was that of a "Third Testament," the Testament of the Spirit: the old idea of Joachim of Fiore in barely new guise. The second was by Minsky, whose ideal was rather more difficult to present. But this much is certainly clear from his comprehensive reply to the inquiry: that he was no more original than his compatriot. For while Merezh-kovsky had turned back to medieval Christianity, Minsky found his mystical inspiration indirectly in Buddhism and directly in the work of Philipp Mainländer, whose *Philosophie der Erlösung* (Philosophy of

Redemption; 1876) was based on the belief that the aim of becoming was non-being.

That the old was finished and something new had to take its place was also the view of more worldly spirits, among them Gabriel Monod and Baldassare Labanca, a Roumanian professor of religious history: both felt that religion must evolve into moral and social idealism. The reply of Ellen Key, famed for her *Century of the Child* (1900) clearly reflected her own romanticism: the collapse of dogmatic religion would lead to irreligion which, in turn, would give rise to a true religion based on genuine religious sentiment. Her authorities were the moral philosopher Jean Marie Guyau, whose *L'Irreligion de l'avenir* (1886) was still widely read, Marcel Hébert, the author of *Le Divin*, Maeterlinck and the poet Verhaeren. George Brandes took a much more sober view: if orthodox Christianity was declining, it was doing so very slowly, for had the process not started three hundred years ago? Indeed had it not perhaps been reversed? For while Frederick II and the leading politicians of his day had openly called themselves freethinkers, during the nineteenth century no prince had dared to copy their example, not even Napoleon, nor any important statesman, not even Bismarck. On the contrary, Bismarck was proud to call himself "God's soldier" in which capacity he had succeeded in combining his *Realpolitik*, his "natural egoism of the state" with Lutheran pietism, so much in vogue with the German landed nobility as we know from Bismarck's own letters, particularly those addressed to his fiancée. Brandes's acuity turned him into a pessimist: the old *odium theologicum* might be on the wane, but what was about to take its place — race, class and national hatred — was no better and at bottom religious as well.

Though quite a few respondents to the inquiry declared themselves atheists, they were vastly outnumbered by the rest, which suggests that the inquiry was not as representative as it might have been. In any case, all those who rejected religion in every shape or form, amongst them Plekhanov, Domela Nieuwenhuis, and the Parisian professor of medicine, P. Naquet, looked forward to a better society in which people no longer had any need for opiates. One of them, Yves Guyot, the author of the *Étude sur les doctrines sociales du Christianisme*, first published in 1873, having discussed the status of religious dogma, worship, and preaching in contemporary France, concluded that dogma was continuously losing ground to science; worship had fallen victim to the doctrine of formalism — "Who of us still believes in the power of the sign of the Cross?" — and as for preaching: "Is there a young man left who shivers at the portrayal

481

of hell or swoons with happiness at the mere mention of heaven?" And
he added that Joseph de Maistre had known what he was doing when
he had opposed Bacon so fiercely. For there was no doubt that one of
the causes of the religious crisis was the widening gulf between traditional
Church dogma and the insights of modern science, which continued to
shore up its truths with more truths while religion clung to the skirts of
past authorities. As Troeltsch had put it: people no longer wanted to
wear the "yellow hat" of any ecclesiastical epistemology.[8] The American
Andrew Dickson White also devoted his well-known *History of the War-*
fare of Science with Theology (1896) to this widening gulf. This former
President and professor of history at Cornell, a university he had helped
to found, and former United States ambassador to Petersburg and Berlin,
was a freethinker, but not in the negative sense that people so often
attached to that label. To him, true Christianity lay not in the miraculous
legends of the Bible, not in falsely or deceitfully interpolated texts, not
in dogmas and rites, let alone in the horrible and barbarous threats attributed to a bloodthirsty and vengeful divinity, but in the simple message
that all men are the children of one father, creatures destined to turn their
backs on lies and deception, wickedness and injustice, and to look squarely
at the truth, the better to help man love others as he loves himself.[9]

White's bible of modernism devoted every one of its twenty chapters
to comparisons of the positive achievements of modern science with
the specious relics of antiquated doctrine. Thus he contrasted evolution
with creation, universal laws with signs and miracles, the latest geological
and astronomical findings with the ideas presented in Genesis. He also
reviewed human prehistory in the light of recent discoveries by Egyp-
tologists, Assyriologists and archaeologists, and showed that the "Fall"
was incompatible with anthropology and history; he contrasted the
magical conception of thunder and lightning with the findings of modern
meteorology, magic with chemistry and physics, miracles with medicine,
fetishism with hygiene, "possession" with mental illness, and Leviticus
with modern economics — all without parading his scholarship or making
use of cheap effects. His book is as instructive and pleasant to read today
as it was when it was first published, if only because it reveals what
prejudices were still rife amongst his contemporaries, great scholars
included. Chapter XVII deserves special mention for it dealt with man's
progress from Babel to comparative linguistics, and "Babel and Bible"
is an excellent summary of the crisis discussed in this chapter, a crisis
that involved almost every other branch of human learning.

First there was biology, which, basing itself increasingly on geology,
paleontology and comparative anatomy during the nineteenth century,

482

had built up an impregnable wall round the theory of evolution; archaeology and prehistory had brought to light civilizations that were both older and more highly developed than those of which the Bible constitutes the literary deposit; history, more broadly based than ever before and now no less evolutionist than biology itself, had shown that intellectual and moral norms and general behavior patterns were so many temporary phases of human development; anthropology under Tylor, Frazer, and Lang had produced new ideas on the origins and development of religion, much as philology had done under Friedrich Max-Müller; sociology under Spencer, Durkheim and Weber had shown that religious attitudes, like all others, were specific behavior patterns of groups in search of values they could live by; finally psychology, and what went under the name of "ethnopsychology" in particular, had contributed more than any other discipline to the relativization of religion by treating it as one of many means for satisfying personal and social needs (Lazarus, Steinthal, Wundt, *et al.*).

The more these new disciplines enriched human knowledge, the more difficult it became to uphold the old dogmas. A case in point was the psychological explanation of the religious phenomenon. Originally, psychologists had held that religion was nothing but an "exaggeration" of empirical psychological facts,[10] an argument theologians could readily counter with one of their own, namely that this very "exaggeration" reflected the existence of a metaphysical reality behind the facts. However, Simmel had robbed them of even that consolation: he had simply replaced the simplistic "exaggeration" with another, more profound but no less relativizing psychological explanation which proved much more difficult to brush aside.[11] In short, the vast masses of material assembled by the various sciences at the end of the last and the beginning of this century had shaken theology to the core, so much so that the resulting crisis could only be resolved by the emergence of a radically new approach, one more in keeping with the holistic tendency of the age. It has been said that religious sociology was not born until the turn of the century,[12] because not until then were conditions ripe for its emergence.[13] But when it was eventually inaugurated by Professor Tiele of Leyden,[14] far from ending the crisis it merely aggravated tensions by adding inside to outside pressures that built up to an explosion. First of all, modern biblical criticism had made it increasingly plain that Christianity was not the unique religion it had always been thought to be. Biblical criticism as such was nothing new and may even be said to have found a fitting conclusion before our period in the work of Professor Abraham Kuenen of Leiden. It now received an ever increasing store of extra-biblical ammunition. In particular, it became obvious that there were close parallels between the Old Testament and Babylonian and Egyptian traditions — for instance in the stories of the Creation, of Paradise and of the Flood — and that the Jewish version was not only a derivation of, but according to some, even inferior to the others.

The New Testament, too, was shown to be an unreliable historical document. Here, too, more and more parallels were discovered, between the dead and resurrected God and the Sacraments on the one hand, and certain elements of contemporary Hellenistic mystery religions on the other; and as far as the Apocalypse was concerned it bore a strong resemblance to certain features of contemporary Judaism. Or, as one of these modern theologians put it resignedly: "Let us not forget that our dear Lord has taught us absolutely nothing new."[15]

During our period the findings of "higher criticism" were accepted by most Protestant thinkers without demur. The difficulties that Strauss, F. C. Baur, and Renan had still encountered no longer dogged the steps of Chantepie de la Saussaye, Bacon, Cumont, Cheyne, Drews, Holtzmann, Jastrow, Kuenen, Nash, Schweitzer, Troeltsch and Weiss or any other leading biblical critics or religious historians at the turn of the century. True, W. Robertson Smith lost his Chair in Aberdeen because of the articles on biblical subjects he had contributed to the *Encyclopaedia Britannica*. But that had happened in 1881, and soon afterwards he was appointed Lord Almoner's Professor of Arabic in Cambridge. Adolf von Harnack, who traced the rise of dogma back to the Reformation, and Friedrich Delitzsch were held in high regard by their Kaiser. Julius Wellhausen, theologian and orientalist at various German universities, continued Professor Kuenen's biblical criticism and was given a free hand in turning scores of German theologians into "Wellhausians."

Cheyne[16] and Nash[17] became the leading historians of the new movement. Even the layman can gain an impression of the peaceful and sedate approach and tone of these modernists by reading Hinneberg's *Geschichte der christlichen Religion* (History of the Christian Religion), which was part of an excellent series, *Die Kultur der Gegenwart*, (Contemporary Culture),[18] or the encyclopedic *Die Religion in Geschichte und Gegenwart* (Religion in History and the Present), published in the years of 1909 to 1913, with Hermann Gunkel as its first editor.

Not that these writings failed to cause a commotion. In particular, the last of a series of three lectures delivered by Delitzsch to the Deutsche Orient Gesellschaft in the Berlin Singakademie from 1902 to 1904, raised a storm of protest. In a later book, which like the *Babel and Bible* series printed and sold many thousands of copies, he tells us how he came to adopt a radical position very early on in his career. He was born in 1850, and as a student he heard one of his professors declare in a lecture that the Fifth Book of the Bible must have been written seven centuries after Moses, its alleged author. When he later asked the professor in private whether the book must therefore be considered a fabrication, he was told that it was indeed just that, but that he had best keep the knowledge to himself.[19] This persuaded Delitzsch to reject as rank prejudice a host of biblical ideas.[20] Needless to say a flood of repudiations greeted his revelations: Delitsch himself mentioned fifteen large piles of newspaper articles and pamphlets.[21] However, the new truths continued to stand out like Mount Ararat above the Flood, and one would have nothing but praise for Delitzsch if he had acted out of pure love of truth, and not from darker motives. In fact it became clear during and after the First World War that Delitzsch was riddled with anti-Semitic prejudice and that his earlier ideas must have been infected with the same virus, his own denials notwithstanding.[22] That other non-scientific currents, too, affected the results of biblical criticism is particularly clear from successive interpretations of the character of Jesus Christ. Renan's "liberal" Jesus image had evaporated, though it made a brief reappearance in Gustav Frenssen's widely read novel *Hilligenlei* of 1906. Many modern critics, for instance Robertson,[23] Drews[24] or G. A. van den Bergh van Eysinga, denied his historicity; others "updated" him to accord with modern ideals: thus while certain freethinking clergymen described him as a "socialist," less enlightened spirits tried to "aryanize" him into a germanic God. This was, for instance, the approach of the influential theologian and orientalist Paul de Lagarde, whose "harmonization of Christianity with the German spirit" meant "purging it of Jewish elements," and also of Houston Stewart Chamberlain, who became a naturalized German and followed in the racialist footsteps of Richard Wagner, his father-in-law. At about the same time, Johann Weiss[25] and Albert Schweitzer[26] drew a picture of Jesus that was as far removed from that of the gentle harbinger of salvation as it was from the *bondieuserie* of the *bienpensants* whom Léon Bloy so heartily despised.[27] Their Jesus was full of heroic passion and Dostoevskian despair and hence far more "real" than the Savior of the milk and water pietists. In fact he looked much more a superman than an incarnate God. In short, even the central figure of Christianity had been "relativized." Moreover, so had his deeds: studies of the almost unknown Mythra mysteries[28] and of the influence of eastern myths on Roman paganism[29] by Cumont, the Belgian historian of religion, had made it increasingly hard to credit Christianity with essentially new contributions. It also became clear

485

that Christianity had continued to borrow from alien religions; Harnack's studies of Christian dogmas showed that many of them were Hellenic derivates.[30] The impact of this message was not limited to narrow academic circles: his *Wesen des Christentums* (Essence of Christianity; 1900) sold over 72,000 copies within thirty years.

It goes without saying that the Protestant, the Anglican, and the Roman Catholic establishments did not sit by with folded arms while these "besmirchers" of the faith were doing their sordid work of demolition. In the struggle between Bible and Babel, they tried to buttress their own position with a dike of anti-criticism. But the old has never been able to maintain itself by the mere rejection of the new. It needs more positive defenses, and the best of these is always the partial absorption of the new. Thus Protestant modernism may be described as the attempt to make certain concessions to science, the better to save the faith, and the Catholic variant was, if anything, even more blatant. Many Catholics realized only too clearly that the age of the *ecclesia triumphans* had gone for ever and that it was high time to replace it with the age of the *ecclesia defendens.* To that end, Monsignor le Camus, Bishop of La Rochelle, prepared a new syllabus for his seminary, of which Bible and dogma formed the core. The prescribed reading list, remarkably enough, included works by German and English Protestants for, as the bishop explained, "God's blessing is precisely that He imparts to us what is good in the works of our opponents, the better to rebut them."[31] Modernist Catholic philosophers (Laberthonnière, Blondel, and le Roy chief amongst them) had similar objectives: to lead an irreligious world back to the one true religion.[32] This was the chief purpose of le Roy's *Dogme et critique*, a book that, despite its 400 pages, was widely read at the time.[33] Houtin, one of the historians of this movement, followed George Tyrell, one of its chief leaders, in describing the modernist as "a religious man of whatever Church, who believes in the possibility of synthesizing the essential truth of his own religion with the essential truth of the modern age," namely science and the scientific approach.[34]

At first, these men seemed to have the ear of Rome. At the end of 1902 Pope Leo XIII appointed an International Bible Commission which included many of the modernists. But all too soon it turned out that the chief concern of the commission was to define the limits Catholic scholars must not overstep in their biblical criticism. This is not in the least surprising when we reflect that in 1899 Leo XIII already described the tactics of accepting the results of science in order to save the faith as "a dubious and dangerous weapon," recalling his own encyclical, *Providentissimus Deus* of 1893.[35]

486

The antimodernists, or integralists as they preferred to call themselves, rejoiced too early. It was precisely during the twenty years around
the turn of the century that international modernism had become a
burning issue with Rome, whose influence was then at its nadir following
not only the secularization of France but also mass defections in other
countries. Most of the defectors had left the church very quietly; others
had done so with a great deal of noise, among them the leaders of the
Bohemian "Away from Rome" movement, who accused the Vatican
of favoring the Slavs in the Danube monarchy. The number of defectors
in Bohemia, from 1898 when the movement began to 1908 when it began
to subside, was estimated at some 50,000.[36] Although this mass conversion to Protestantism had nothing to do with modernism, it nevertheless encouraged the integralists to press Rome for further sanctions
against the innovators on the grounds that, in essence, modernism was
nothing other than a Protestant infiltration of the Roman Catholic
Church.

Like all such arguments, this one, too, had a semblance of truth.
It could, in any case, be turned against an even greater danger, one that
the integralists honored with the name of "Americanism." The Catholic
minority in the United States had, in fact, been highly exposed to the
influence of the many Protestant sects that flourished in that country,
and had fully accepted the prevailing ideology of individual freedom.
Moreover, the Roman shepherds were exceptionally democratic in America because their flock consisted almost entirely of working-class immigrants of Irish, Polish or Italian descent. Both influences converged
in the ideas of Father Isaac Thomas Hecker, a convert who set out to
win the United States for the Mother Church. His efforts, too, were
originally approved by the Vatican, until it became clear that the Paulist
Fathers, a missionary organization founded by Hecker, were nothing
like traditional monks: they had no wish to be martyrs, hermits, or
ascetics but preferred to go out to meet ordinary Americans in market
places, offices, and factories. Monsignor Ireland, Archbishop of St. Paul
in Minnesota, lent them his support both by a preface he wrote in 1891
to the *Life of Father Hecker* by the Paulist, Father W. Elliot,[37] and also
by a series of lectures he delivered a year later in Paris on "the church
and the century." In these lectures he voiced the prevailing feeling that
a radical change was needed, and his remarks were received with approbation, as was the French translation of his book in 1897.[38] Even Cardinal
Gibbons, Archbishop of Baltimore, the first Chancellor of the Catholic
University of Washington and adviser to successive Presidents of the
United States on Catholic affairs, and Monsignor O'Connell, Rector of

the American College in Rome, spoke up for the movement. But in vain. In a letter he addressed to American priests in 1899 (*Testem benevolentiae*), Leo XIII set forth his own views. The letter was as temperate as ever, but quite final: the Pope was opposed to the new movement.[39]

Even closer to modernism in the strict sense of the word were the views of Hermann Schell, a Catholic professor of theology in Würzburg. For though Schell harked back to Aristotle and the Schoolmen, he did so the better to assure the Church a place in the modern world. The title of his most controversial pamphlet, which appeared in 1897, speaks for itself and for his times: *Der Katholizismus als Prinzip des Fortschritts* (Catholicism as the Principle of Progress). Many Catholic intellectuals realised that Schell was merely putting into words here — and even more so a year later in his *Die neue Zeit und der alte Glaube* (The New Age and the Old Faith) — what they had been thinking all along. Schell's triumph, too, was great but short-lived: by the end of 1898 all his writings had been placed on the Index. As a faithful son of the Church he submitted, and kept his silence until his early death in 1906. Then slanderous rumors began; by slighting his memory, the integralists were, in fact hitting out at the German *Reformkatholiken* who, they believed, were continuing his work in *Die Renaissance*, a journal founded in 1900, and also at the fifth congress of Catholic scholars in Munich. The integralists need not have worried: Schell's fate had proved so great a deterrent that German modernism never dared to march openly into battle against Rome.

Things were quite different in Italy, England, and France.[40] Ernesto Buonaiuto, George Tyrrell, and Alfred Firmin-Loisy were made of stronger stuff than Schell, Joseph Müller, and Franz Xaver Strauss. Buonaiuto, who was just nineteen years old in 1900, was appointed Professor of Church History in the Seminario Romano a mere three years later, only to be dismissed in 1908 for his liberal views. He, for one, was not cowed by the Pope's condemnation of modernism as set forth in the encyclical *Pascendi dominici* of 8 September 1907,[41] and countered with his own *Il programma dei modernisti* (The Programme of the Modernists). Although both this book and also his *Lettere di un prete modernista* (Letters of a Modernist Priest; 1908) were published anonymously, their militant author did not escape excommunication for long. Later still, he was to prove as great a thorn in the flesh of the Fascist system as he had earlier been in that of the Church.[42]

Tyrrell, too, was a born fighter, despite his unselfish nature, lack of self-assurance, and mystical inclinations.[43] Like Manning and Newman he was a convert and retained elements of his Anglican past, not only as a priest but even as a Jesuit. The last book published in his lifetime, *Through Scylla and Charybdis, or the Old Theology and the New*, was sent on its way with a motto by Milton. In 1904, when he was forty-three, he showed the first signs of dissatisfaction with the traditional approach of the Church. Two years later this dissatisfaction culminated in a break following his *Much Abused Letter*, addressed to a fellow scholar who was having religious doubts, and which made a number of concessions to modern science. Tyrrell was denied the sacraments. He submitted, but with reservations — he had not been a Jesuit for nothing. A year later, when the *encyclica ferox* was issued, he broke his vow of silence and published a fierce attack on the Pope, both in the *Giornale d'Italia* of 30 September and also in *The Times* of 1 October. In a letter he revealed his motives: "I did not want people to say that this encyclical was received without protest, and that the modernists were as cowardly as the minority in the Vatican Council."[44] Tyrrell persisted in his attempts to keep the faith free of the shackles of theology until death put an early end to his life in 1909. Short though it was, that life had been exceedingly rich — and tragic, too — for Tyrrell could never bring himself to disown the mother who had rejected him. On his deathbed, he asked for Brémond, his brother-Jesuit to help him in his difficult hour. Brémond, who prized humanity above all injunctions, came over from France — but this was the last deed he performed as a Jesuit.

The most important modernist of all was Loisy, not because his great scholarship and passion for truth[45] made him the most intransigent of all, nor even because he was the very embodiment of Catholic modernism (radical, but faithful to the Church), one who had been called the "father" of the movement,[46] but rather because Rome had so much more at stake in France than anywhere else. Loisy was forty-three when the conflict with his Church which we mentioned at the beginning of this chapter took place. Nor had that been his first skirmish. It all began with his thesis of 1890 — the Roman Church had no wish for a Wellhausen of its own, least of all in France — and there were almost continuous clashes in the decades that followed. Loisy's keen interest in New Testament studies following the publication of Harnack's *Wesen des Christentums* (Essence of Christianity) to which Loisy himself had replied in 1902 with his *L'Évangile et l'église*, did not improve matters either. True, he tried to counter Harnack's argument that Catholicism had increasingly departed from original Christianity with the claim that this development had been both justified and inevitable, but he drove out one devil with another: unlike Harnack, Loisy described the historical Jesus, not as the savior, but as a Jewish Messiah, and one who had never

489

wanted to be anything else. Moreover, Loisy abandoned the traditional ideas of the origin of the Bible, of Christianity, of the Catholic Church and of its dogma, which he considered so many stumbling blocks in the path of his beloved Church. Despite all the other concessions he made, it was obvious that his excommunication was only a matter of time. On July 3, 1907, the Holy Office published the decree *Lamentabili* and condemned sixty-five theses[47] of which thirty could be traced back to Alfred Loisy. Rome waited six months for his contrite submission, but when it was not forthcoming the Holy Office pronounced the major excommunication on him on March 7, 1908.[48] Loisy devoted the more than thirty years that remained to him to church history and to writing his memoirs, which are as readable today as they were when they first appeared.

So by the end of our period the power apparatus of the Church had succeeded in killing Catholic modernism. Its Protestant counterpart succumbed by itself, at least in its old rationalist form, for the so-called "malcontents" had become increasingly disillusioned with the optimistic and progressive ideas that had so inspired them at first.[49] Jesus once again became the Christ, the good once again became God and the restoration of orthodoxy in both the Roman and the Protestant camps seemed imminent. But as Niebuhr has pointed out, by emphasizing the historical relativity of religious ideas previously taken for absolute truths, modernism has rid religion of the dead weight of traditional authority, and hence remains a lasting historical truth.[50]

This explains why the crisis in Christianity was not resolved with the decline of modernism. For when it became clear that this remedy could not cure the calcification of the Church, a more effective nostrum appeared on the market, namely active social commitment. Church charities had had their day, for the State had increasingly taken over their role, and those who wanted to infuse new breath into the fossilized life of the Church were forced to set their sights much higher: they tried to stand the old idea that men must live for the sake of the Church on its head.[51] This, they claimed, could only be done by casting out the spirit of unctuous self-satisfaction that had taken possession of the Church. The leading spokesmen of this new current were Bloy, Péguy, Claudel, and Bernanos, those revered "neo-evangelists,"[52] and many other members of the French "neo-Christian" movement founded in the 1890s.[53] A considerable proportion of the profuse religious and ethical writings produced during these years was devoted to the social problem, that is to the needs of the working class,[54] the authors ranging from socialist preachers to fervent anti-socialists.

After a long period of preparation, which began in November 1848 with Monsignor von Ketteler's six famous sermons in the Cathedral of Mainz on "the great social problem of the age," and was continued by le Play, the Comte de Mun, and René de la Tour du Pin in France, Freiherr Karl von Vogelsang in Austria, Don Bosco in Italy, A. Ariëns in the Netherlands, Cardinal Manning in Britain, Cardinal Gibbons in America and, Professor Décurtins (who called for international labor legislation) in Switzerland, and again by the social congresses of 1886, 1887 and 1890 in which the majority came down in favor of state intervention in social problems, and by the special study circles set up in Rome with the encouragement of Pope Leo XIII, the work of the movement culminated in the publication of the encyclical *Rerum novarum* on May 15, 1891. The social policies of the Roman Church laid down in that document and also in its amplification, the *Graves de communi rei* of January 18, 1900, were thus anything but improvised, even if their publication was hastened by the notorious anarchist riots in Chicago (1886), the great dock strike in London which involved a quarter of a million workers (1889), the spread of organized Marxism, and the massive defection of the French proletariat. Though both documents were aimed at communism rather than at laissez-faire capitalism, they were thought to be so "radical" that quite a few Catholic employers tried to persuade their priests not to read the encyclical from the pulpit, lest it gave their workers revolutionary ideas.[55]

With social policies imposed from above by such powerful political machines as the Catholic Church or the German Empire, it is, of course, impossible to say just where social compassion ended and fear of socialism or of other "subversive" currents began. Bismarck bestowed the name of "Christian socialism" on a movement that conformed with his anti-socialist laws, and was, in effect, little more than a charitable effort, with no interest in limiting Sunday work or in the protection of working women and children. Treitschke wrote: "Only through the Christian faith can the lowest strata of the population be prepared for the frugality that the indispensable aristocratic and idealistic order of society imposes upon them."[56] And Schmoller, the academic socialist, added: "If any nation on earth is destined to reach its objectives by inner change and peaceful reform rather than by bitter social conflict and violent revolution, it is ours, and this because we are a nation devoted to righteous thinking and filled with strong religious sentiments."[57] It would not be difficult to assemble a large collection of similar pronouncements from all over the world, without detracting from the merit and honesty of the many more who actually put their shoulders to the wheel.

In Protestant countries, which were also the most highly industrialized, the social reform movement within the Church was much more incisive than in the Catholic world, but also much more varied and uncoordinated because here the initiative did not usually come from the hierarchy. Even a brief history of this movement would fill a volume.

In Germany, there was the Evangelical Social Congress, of which Harnack was both a founder and President from 1903 to 1905; in the Netherlands there was the Social Congress organized by Abraham Kuyper and the Blijde Wereld (Happy World) movement;[58] in France there were the Cercle Socialiste de la Libre Pensée Chrétienne and the Union des Libres Croyants pour la Culture Morale, whose 1907 program stated that social progress was dependent on moral regeneration, and which had its German counterpart in the Gesellschaft für Ethische Kultur founded in about 1890 by Förster and Gizycki;[59] in Britain, finally, there was the Labor Church Movement. None of these organizations, not even the last, achieved anything like lasting success.

More influential were the countless weekly and monthly papers, many of which disappeared without a trace after a fleeting existence, and the many books which examined the relationship between social and religious attitudes from an historical angle, amongst them Yves Guyot's *Étude sur les doctrines sociales du christianisme* (1873) and Nash's *Genesis of the Social Conscience*, both of which emphasized that to the founders of Christianity the fatherhood of God had implied the brotherhood of man, and above all Troeltsch's *Die Soziallehren der christlichen Kirchen und Gruppen* (The Social Teachings of Christian Churches and Groups), first published in 1912.

Ultimately, however, it was left to a handful of compassionate Christians, agitated by the miserable lot of urchins and appalled by the airless slums of the overcrowded cities, to declare that the fight for social justice must take precedence over all other religious activities. The world of these part-socialist, part-humanitarian and pacifist churchmen was exemplified by Albert Kalthoff, a parson from Bremen, whose sermons of 1898 placed the kingdom of God squarely on earth,[60] and by Friedrich Naumann (an opponent of the anti-Semite, H. Stöcker), editor of the *Die Hilfe* since 1895, albeit his *Jesus als Volksmann* (Jesus as a Man of the People), *Arbeiterkatechismus* (Workers' Cathechism) and somewhat harebrained scheme of a democratic Reich under the Kaiser,[61] caused some to consider him a forerunner of the Nazis.[62] Then there was the Swiss, Hermann Kutter, whose *Sie müssen* (They Must) of 1903 put fresh wind into the socialist sails, and his compatriot, Leonhard Ragaz, then still professor of theology, and much more radical than Kutter in that he actually joined the Social Democratic Party. His journal

Neue Wege (New Paths) first appeared in 1906. The influence of these two men on Karl Barth and his many disciples is quite unmistakable.

For many other Protestants, social action became a substitute for the religious certainties they had lost, an escape from doubt and spiritual discontent.[63] A famous example was the departure in 1913 of Albert Schweitzer for Lambarene in the French Congo. Even earlier, in 1888, Mary Humphry Ward, niece of Matthew Arnold, had published her famous *Robert Elsmere*, a novel whose hero was said to have been modeled on a real clergyman who abandoned theology, left the church and devoted all his energies to founding a "church without creed" for the workers. Strangely enough, just such a church was established three years after the publication of the book, first in Manchester and later in various other British cities; in London it even called itself the "Socialist Church." The founder of this movement was John Trevor, to whom the workers' movement was a religious crusade. However, despite active support from Keir Hardie, Tom Mann, Ben Tillett, and Stanton Coit,[64] the workers' church was stifled almost at birth.

History is impenetrable while it is still the present. But once it has become the past, it often reveals itself as the future. The religious crisis at the turn of the century produced two failures. The first, the failure of modernism, led to a permanent decline of faith in the absolute authority of the churches; the second, the failure of the churches to identify itself with the social reform movement, has, on the contrary, helped it to remain an important social factor to this day.

CHAPTER XXXIII

A HUNDRED AND ONE PROPHETS

Reporting on the Third International Congress of Spiritualists held in Paris on September 29, 1900, the Dutch daily newspaper *De Telegraaf* also disclosed that the poet Willem Kloos, having discussed the hereafter with the dying Jacques Perk, and having asked him for some sign from the beyond, had an extraordinary experience: on the night after the discussion, at about half-past two, Kloos was awakened by knocking at his bedroom door, yet when he inquired next morning, it was clear that no one staying in the house had been anywhere near his room. Soon afterwards, on passing Perk's house and seeing the curtains drawn, he learned that his friend had passed away during the night, at about half-past two.[1]

Max Dessoir, the historian of the occult sciences, recorded, with a great many details that were meant to guarantee the authenticity of the story but need not delay us here, that on August 29, 1900 a thirteen-year old boy was bitten by a horse on a wharf; the strange part of the story was that the boy dreamt some two months earlier that he was being chased along a wharf by a savage gray. He had obviously had a "proscopic" dream. A great deal was written about the case and a thorough investigation made.[2]

On August 25, 1900 a lady from Brussels, who signed herself v. K. and was a co-editor of *Het Toekomstig Leven* (Future Life), a "fortnightly journal for the study of experimental psychology and supernatural phenomena," wrote a letter reporting that Sadi Carnot, the later President of France but at the time a minister, had been presented with a Hindu idol by Gustav le Bon, who had himself received it from the Rajah of Khajraho. Honest man that he was, le Bon had explained that, according to local legend, the idol would bring its owner not only power and esteem but violent death as well. Carnot, who was no more superstitious than le Bon, was delighted to accept the gift. Soon afterwards he was elected President, and seven years later, as the reader will recall, he was stabbed to death by the anarchist Cesario during a visit to an industrial exhibition in Lyons.[3]

We need not dwell on the veracity of these three anecdotes, for even if they were pure fiction they were tokens of a widespread resurgence of interest in occultism. That resurgence is amply documented. We have already mentioned the International Congress of Spiritualists held in Paris in 1900. Earlier that year, on June 22, various spiritualist associations had given a public demonstration of their skills in the Tonhalle, Berlin, in response to a challenge issued by the arch-conservative Adolf Stöcker at a meeting of clergymen in the same hall. Stöcker, not content with being an anti-Semite and an antisocialist, had no love for spiritualism either; indeed, he had called for a crusade against "these satanic doctrines from the fourth dimension."[4] The spiritualists' June meeting was followed by two antispiritualist lectures delivered in Berlin on 24 October and 6 November, and subsequently issued in print. The spiritualists hit back with at least four further public meetings, all of them announced in the November issue of the *Spiritistische Rundschau*. *Het Toekomstig Leven* published a full report of Stöcker's challenge and the various responses, including the two antispiritualist lectures we have mentioned. Both had been delivered by Pastor Otto Riemann of St. Nicolas Church, Berlin, a rational opponent. He was perhaps the first to formulate the paradox of spiritualism, or for that matter of theosophy, when he described it as "an attempt to replace faith with what went for deeper knowledge but far too often proved a witches' sabbath of credulity and self-deception."[5] We shall see time and again that what at first sight appears to be protest against the prevailing rationalism, turns out on closer examination to be an attempt, with the help of reason, to open up territories that by their very nature are inaccessible to reason. Hence all these attempts were nothing if not irrational. Here we have one of the most obvious manifestations of the "changeable" character of our period. That it should have produced Riemann's paradox not only among the disciples of the hundred and one prophets of the day, but, as we saw, in philosophy and the sciences as well, is therefore not in the least surprising.

A better token of the revival of interest in the occult than any number of anecdotes or "demonstrations" on the part of its devotees, is the fact that even "official science" felt compelled, during the summer of 1900, to examine the claims of the various occult schools. When the Institut Psychique International was founded on 30 June, it adopted a program presented by Pierre Janet, the most famous French psychiatrist of the day. It called for the study of hypnotism, telepathy, telekinesis, lucidity, mediumicity and what other paranormal phenomena may have occurred or were likely to occur. The British Society for Psychical Research, which had been founded in 1882 for the express purpose of making a methodical and systematic study of all these topics, was another beehive of activity, graced with such renowned scholars as William Crookes, Oliver Lodge, Frederick W. H. Myers, and Alfred Russell Wallace. Crookes had been brought into the occultist camp by his realization that all human knowledge is relative: had men only been capable of making small enough measurements, they would never have concluded that water tends to produce a perfectly horizontal surface; under the microscope every dewdrop appears as a flattened sphere. Myers wrote his *Human Personality and its Survival of Bodily Death* before 1903; the impact it made when it was published was so great that Gerald Heard, whose knowledge of this period was almost unsurpassed, said that its author had contributed more to the discovery of the extra-individual, supra-personal consciousness and of its sway over human behavior than Freud, who had laid bare no more than a part of it, and the lowest part at that.[5] How Wallace, who discovered the central idea of Darwinism, came to embrace occultism so warmly that he was elected chairman of the International Congress of Spiritualists in 1898, is explained in Chapter XXI of his autobiography,[7] a book which is also the best by far to illustrate the close links between occultism and radicalism in our period. Wallace had been interested in Owenism from early youth; he later advocated the nationalization of land, and in 1889, having read Bellamy's *Looking Backward*,[8] became a declared socialist. Annie Besant followed a similar path. For many years she had been a collaborator of Charles Bradlaugh, the freethinker, and a friend of George Bernard Shaw; in 1884 she joined the Fabians, and began to speak and write in support of neo-Malthusianism, advocated the eight-hour day, helped to organize strikes and, while in India, identified herself so closely with the Freedom Movement that the Indian National Congress chose her as its president in 1907, and the British later interned her. She, too, has described her parallel interest in occultism and socialism in her autobiography.[9] In this connection we might also mention the Dutch theosophist, A. J. Resink, who published a brochure on the links between theosophy and the class struggle in 1908,[10] in which he identified the occult laws of motion with the impersonal forces that governed society according to Karl Marx.[11] "Occult" in this sense, one could argue, simply meant "not yet discovered," or only just discovered as by Marx. Driesch was to go further still when he spoke approvingly of parapsychology and "paraphysics" and claimed that they were wrongly called "occult"; their subject matter had long since ceased to be "hidden."[12]

To some extent these people were atypical, because only a minority among the occultists was attracted to socialism. But it was a vociferous minority, as we may also gather from a collection of seven articles published in the same year as Resink's brochure.[13] In fact, since both occultism and socialism were descendants of the Enlightenment, they were bound to have much in common. Theosophy, in particular, was not a rejection of science, but rather a precipitate hankering after it, as witness the last two of the three main objects of the Theosophical Society, first formulated in 1875. The first object was "to establish a nucleus of the universal brotherhood of humanity regardless of race, sex, caste, or color"; the second "to promote the study of comparative religion and philosophy"; the third "to make a systematic investigation into the unexplained laws of nature and into man's unrevealed powers." According to Annie Besant, who later led the movement, theosophy was philosophy and science rather than religion in the ordinary sense of the word, because its doctrines were open to verification[14] — Riemann's paradox once again.

France, too, took a keen interest in the occult. Thus Fréderic Paulhan was widely applauded when he wrote in his *Nouveau mysticisme* of 1892 that to extract the miraculous from nature was both a token of man's irrepressible thirst for knowledge, and also of his ever-growing respect for science.[15] Apart from Janet and Paulhan, Paris, still in the forefront even in this field, could also boast Gibier, later director of the Pasteur Institute in New York; de Rochas; and Charles Richet, who, in 1891, became the editor of the first learned French publication devoted to occult studies.[16] Germany did not lag far behind. Here the pioneers were Karl du Prel,[17] Zöllner, Braune, Weber, Scheibner, and Thiersch, all professors except for the first two, who, incidentally, became the best known.

Coste, who has listed all their names, added that, had he presented his thesis (which, as he himself puts it, aimed at gaining "official admittance for the miraculous," i.e., for "all the facts that are in apparent conflict with the known natural laws and hence closed to science") but ten years earlier, it would have been thrown out by every medical faculty.[18] Dankmar, the author of a book on the cultural situation in Europe during the revival of occultism, tried to explain why what was happening at the time was altogether new, though the subject itself was quite old. He was no blind adherent of the movement, albeit he mentioned Swedenborg's name with approval. He shared Paulhan's view that the study of hidden truths does not violate the demands of science. "Occultism," he claimed, "must be transformed into the science of those borderline concepts whose content is truth and whose form is logic. Thanks to this purified form of occultism, even the miraculous will one day be converted into the natural."[19] He attributed the revival of interest in the occult to man's "thirst for inwardness in the desert of our present cultural comedy." Richard Humphrey was to delve more deeply into the matter, for though he was more concerned with the revival of anti-intellectualism, especially by Sorel,[20] than with the revival of occultism, what he discovered was applicable to the latter as well. Living as he did in an age of unprecedented mechanization, Humphrey contended that, though machines supplied pragmatic corroboration of the mechanistic, i.e., the deterministic, world view, they also showed that man can intervene in the natural process at will, and hence feel free to take a voluntarist view of their actions.

To all these occultists, the universe was an indivisible whole and had to be treated as such. Was this simply a reaction against positivism? Or must we rather take the holistic view ourselves and conclude that this sudden hankering after the "whole" was, at least partly, a reflection of the unique situation of western civilization at the turn of the century, when its superiority still seemed so obvious, and its horizons so vast that everything appeared within its grasp? Writing about the "unknown" guest," that is about the unconscious or the occult, Maeterlinck had this to say: "As soon as one comes to think about it, one realizes how horrible and absurd it would be if we were no more than what we seem; if we were nothing but ourselves, self-sufficient, separated, divided, and bounded by our bodies, by our spirit, by our consciousness, by our birth, and by our death. We are only possible and probable provided we transcend ourselves and project ourselves into space and time."[21]

Then there was the unique idealism of our period, ranging from saccharine love for all that exists to a sense of bitter frustration at the failure of immensely high-pitched expectations to materialize. The literature of the period, inasmuch as it is not purely scientific or factual, teems with such words as "light," "quest," "joy," "betterment," "ennoblement," "ulterior," "communal spirit," and "divine consciousness." More even than by disclosing the existence of a paranormal reality behind the normal, spiritualism tried to bring solace with the "irrefutable" proof that one's "dear departed" not only continued to exist after their "passing over," but that, under certain circumstances, one could maintain regular contacts with them. Such famous mediums as Home, Henry Slade, Mrs. Marshall and her daughter-in-law, Kate and Florence Cook, Eusapia Palladino, Anna Rothe (the flower medium), Mesdames Piper and Thompson, the prophetess of Geneva, and whatever other titles or names they may have borne, were all revered as benefactors of mankind. Then there were the hundreds of somnambulists, the many "materializations," and the countless predictions of men and women who were themselves much more sensational than any of their works. Finally there were such humbugs as Zanzig, Hicks, and Svengali,[22] who all had one thing in common:

though they may not have been believers themselves, they helped to keep the spiritualist banner aloft.

If the spiritualists flew high, the theosophists and adherents of the many other "petites religions" flew even higher. The "ennoblement of mankind" and universal brotherhood were, so to speak, their minimal aims, to be implemented if not tomorrow then certainly the day after that. Thus Annie Besant argued that man's fate was not the result of a divine whim but, thanks to karma, the immutable law of cause and effect, shaped by man himself. Karma also presided over reincarnation "until the effects of every error are expunged, every fault repaired, until perfect compassion, perfect resolution and perfect tenderness reign on earth, until self-denial has become a law of life, and self-sacrifice the joyful driving force of all nature."[23] Better still, the doctrine of reincarnation "removes the unbearable feeling of oppression that besets all those to whom the cosmos has become nothing but the embodiment of injustice." In short, theosophy provided balm to a world that was licking its wounds.

Idealism, and indeed holism, were typical reflections of the age in which they flourished. The first fourteen years of the twentieth century were years of peace, if we ignore the Sino-Japanese war of 1894 and the series of modern imperialist ventures that followed and that only too few saw in the lugubrious light more recent historians have cast upon it. There was great prosperity, albeit confined to an upper crust in a relatively small part of the world. Even so there was peace and prosperity enough at the turn of the century for people to indulge in the luxury of dreaming the great dream of world improvement without being immediately disillusioned by the stark facts.

This explains why the new anti-materialism (though some materialism entered into the "materializations" of the spiritualists),[24] the new anti-positivism and the new anti-intellectualism, the new holism and idealism, spread far beyond the small band of vociferous occultists, so far in fact, that even a brief summary of the most important writings they inspired would turn into a thick catalogue. Countless authors were visited by Maeterlinck's "unknown guest"; innumerable people experienced the effects of the "silent power" mentioned by Couperus in a book by that title.

Countless, in any case, was the number of treatises on what was later called parapsychology; countless, too, the number of oracles, prophecies, omens, magical formulae, revivals of the dead, manifestations, ghosts, miraculous cures, levitations, thought transferences over long or short distances, palmists' feats, meddlings with magical names or numbers, efforts to "decipher" the language of birds, and all sorts of similar efforts that often bordered on insanity. Though not quite so numerous, there were also quite a few who felt tempted to attend the black masses of the satanists, luciferists, palladists or similar strange sects, but who, unlike J. K. Huysmans, must have held back at the last moment. Huysmans himself tells us in *Là-bas*: "Lucifer, a young man with open wings, seemed to descend on the altar out of a burning sky. His right hand bore a torch, his left a horn of plenty. His foot rested on a crocodile bearing a tiara and crown, symbols of Satan's dominion over the lords spiritual and temporal."[25] We have said that many were tempted. There must have been very many, indeed. For why else should *La Semaine religieuse de Paris*, an official publication of the church, have taken notice of their activities, why else would it have identified Lemmi, the leader of the palladists, with the antipope and Antichrist, whose reign, according to some prophecies, was due to begin in the twentieth century?[26] At the safe distance of more than half a century, it all seems childish rather than blood-curdling. At the time, however, it looked very much as if the eighteenth and nineteenth centuries had been completely forgotten and all the lamps of the Enlightenment suddenly dimmed.

Occultism, however widespread, was only one province of the empire of the spirit to reflect the mood of the age. We could describe the rest as petty or semi-official religions, though they had a greater hold on "questing souls" than the official ones at a time that anarchist currents ran much deeper than the actual size of the anarchist movement suggested. Anarchism in this very broad sense was, just like idealism, an approach to life that "society" could still shrug off with a smile. For fiercely though the members of the bourgeoisie reacted to the political manifestations of anarchism, they proved extremely tolerant of its ideological constructions — perhaps because they felt highly tempted by both. For ultimately anarchism, in both forms, was the ideal of freedom and tolerance, in extreme form, and it was to that ideal that the bourgeoisie itself had rallied a century earlier in its fight against the absolutism of kings and princes.

Jules Bois has described a number of the new sects in his *Petites Religions de Paris*. There were, first of all, the worshippers of Zeus Olympios, and one wonders whether the gigantic *Jupiter and Semele*, a composition in deep crimson, blue and gold-leaf, with the mighty god enthroned in a fantastic architectural setting,[27] was not a tribute to that sect. If it was, then Gustave Moreau, who painted it in 1898, must have been a spiritual kinsman of Joris Karl Huysmans. Then there were the servants of Isis, who looked upon themselves as priests of beauty and

500

goodness and the sincerity of whose prayer: "Blessed art Thou, Oh Isis . . . who hast suffered so much that Thou alone hast the right to forgive," . . . "Oh, Creator of immutable certainties, Thou whose heart is above the pitfalls of reason,"[28] sounds strangely misplaced to the modern ear. Thirdly, there were the essenianists, members of a sect resurrected in Paris by Marie Gérard, and to which E. Schuré, the best-known authority on the new mysticism, must have belonged. Theirs was a form of feminist religion and as such it rejected the Pauline doctrine. The disciples worshipped the divine principle as the father and mother of mankind, and its two Messiahs were Jesus and Joan of Arc. The sect was particularly opposed to cruelty to animals, on the grounds that animals were "incipient human beings." Marie Gérard and her disciples were firm believers in reincarnation and, moreover, in the extreme form that recognizes but one distinction: "higher" and "lower." Next, there were the gnostics, who also found their mystical inspiration in the distant past, the Swedenborgians, the light worshippers, the worshippers of humanity, and finally the Buddhists.

European Buddhism was by far the most important of the currents we have mentioned, particularly if one takes into account how much theosophy owed to the Buddha. Ever since 1903, it has been possible to speak of an organized Buddhist mission to Europe, but the names of Schopenhauer, Wagner, Eduard von Hartmann, and S. van Houten suffice to show that the influence of Buddhism, in the broader sense, made itself felt much earlier. However, that influence increased markedly as the nineteenth century drew to its close,[29] not least thanks to Friedrich Max-Müller, who began to publish the first of the *Sacred Books of the East* series in 1879.[30] H. Kern, one of the leading Dutch Orientalists, wrote his *Geschiedenis van het buddhisme in Indie* (History of Indian Buddhism) in 1882–1884, while Karl Eugen Neumann, the Viennese Pali expert, published the three long volumes of his *Die Reden des Gotamo Buddho's* (The Sayings of Gautama Buddha) during the years 1896 to 1902, at about the same time that the German historian of philosophy, Paul Deussen, a disciple of Schopenhauer and a friend of Nietzsche, immersed himself more deeply in ancient Indian philosophy than any European had done before.[31] Finally, there was Theodor Schultze (who died in 1898), a German jurist whose study of Buddhism was reprinted in 1901 under the telling title of *Die Religion der Zukunft* (The Religion of the Future). That year also saw the publication of the second edition of A. Pfungst's life of Schultze, *Ein deutscher Buddhist* (A German Buddhist). Schultze, we are told in the biography, had studied the philosophy and religion of ancient India, not, like so many others, "to provide the

501

militant servants of Jahve with fresh weapons in their fight against 'blind heathendom,' but in order to learn more about the meditative practices of a nation that had produced the most fruitful religious ideas of all." This period of positive but passive interest was followed, in 1903, by a phase of active Buddhist propaganda. On August 13 of that year, the Buddhistischer Missionsverein (Buddhist Missionary Union) was founded in Leipzig, later to be renamed the Buddhistische Gesellschaft (Buddhist Society) to avoid what had by then become a term of opprobrium. *Der Buddhist*, the first Buddhist journal to appear in Europe, was published by the Society. It was also in 1903 that the International Buddhist Society in Rangoon conceived the idea of training Europeans as *bhikshus*, and that Huizinga delivered his public lecture, "On the Study and Evaluation of Buddhism," at Amsterdam University. The Buddhist Society of England, later "of Great Britain and Ireland," was chaired by Thomas William Rhys Davids, who, with his wife, made an immense contribution to European Buddhism. This group, too, began to publish a journal — the first issue of the *Buddhist Review* appeared in 1909.

All these bodies, of which the Young Men's Buddhist Association was by no means the least, helped to produce a temporary endosmosis[32] between Buddhism and Christianity, a hybrid religion that, in 1900, according to the *Journal des Débats*, numbered as many as 30,000 disciples in Paris alone;[33] Boas had previously mentioned more than 100,000 "friends" and at least 10,000 adherents.[34] At least a page could be filled with the titles of the novels and plays that made up Europe's original Buddhist literature, and Bähler did just that, his list even including an opera: M. Vogrich's *Der Buddha* of 1901.

This unusual success story must obviously have had unusual causes. Chief amongst them was the revival of Buddhism in the east and defections from orthodox Christianity in the west. The need for an integral vision, which we have encountered so often in these pages, also played its part and racism no doubt added further fuel to the flames. We are no Jews, these racists must have told themselves; our racial roots go back to India rather than to the Middle East. Thus L. Ménard, the "Jupiterist," argued that a healthy return to heathenism called for the destruction of the *Jewish* idea of monotheism.[35] Above all, this endosmosis offered critical Christians an opportunity to remain believers while yet dispensing with the untenable idea of a personal god. This was certainly what Deussen did. Lastly Buddhism provided a welcome combination of mysticism[36] and scholarship, something that was both "exalted" and yet down to earth. Had not the Buddha's message to his first disciples been both beautifully vague and also reassuringly precise: to avoid the two extremes

502

of worldly pleasure and abstinence; to walk the noble, eight-fold path of right belief, right aspirations, right speech, right action, right living, right effort, right meditation, and right concentration?

Moreover, the exotic had a strange appeal to the jaded palate of Europeans. On November 13, 1893 a number of Parisians at least were able to savor it to the full. On that day, the Buddhist High Priest, Horion-Toki, stopping in Paris on his return from the Parliament of Religions,[37] presided over a special ceremony in the Museum Guimet. His small pagoda, the Buddha image, the white chrysanthemums, the holy water, the incense, the tinkling bell and resonant gong, his priestly gestures and sacral murmurings, must have made a deep impression on those present.

So the world at the turn of the century had its hundred and one prophets, great or small, holy or profane, gifted or grasping. There were one-eyed kings in the land of the blind, and quacks in the Land of Cockaigne. There were some with tarnished reputations, amongst them the American seer Bart Reese, originally from Pobiedziska in Poland, who haunted Berlin in 1907 and claimed that he knew everything, absolutely everything, thanks to his highly developed sixth sense.[38] There were some with other talents, for instance Joséphin Péladan, nicknamed le Sar, whose series of novels on Latin decadence have rightly been forgotten, but whose open-air plays, performed in Orange in 1903 and 1904, are still remembered by some with pleasure; he was also the first to join the Cabbalistic Order of Rosicrucians and, in 1891, became the founder of the Salon de la Rose-Croix, only to end up in the neo-Catholic camp like so many of his contemporaries.[39] There were also such well-intentioned men as Emile Coué, a pharmacist from Nancy, who took up where Mesmer had left off a hundred years earlier, and whose magical formula, based on auto-suggestion and faith in the subconscious: "Every day, in every way, I am getting better and better," led to many cures where other methods had failed.[40] His religious counterparts were the American Christian Scientists with the "scientific system of divine healing." Their leader, Mary Baker Eddy, died in 1910 at the age of eighty-nine, but only ten years before her death this indefatigable woman, who was perhaps even more energetic than Annie Besant, had founded a daily newspaper, *The Christian Science Monitor*, which quickly earned itself a permanent place in the front rank of the world press.[41] Her central idea was extremely simple. The gulf between God on the one hand, and matter, suffering, sin, illness, and death on the other, can be bridged by denying the reality of the last five elements, thus freeing man from his bondage to them. This was yet another example of religion trying to step into the shoes of science,[42] but oddly enough it proved more successful than most, not least because it took into account psychosomatic factors that nineteenth-century medicine preferred to ignore.

Health, which was a matter of increasing general concern during our period, was also part of the program of many other prophets, who, though they sought salvation in physical well-being, nevertheless did so on ethical grounds. This was in any case the inspiration of those who called for a return to nature, among them the nudist disciples of the notorious German clergyman, Pastor Kneipp, who, incidentally, still had enough Victorian inhibitions not to appear naked during mixed nature cures. Others who spring to mind were Gustav Nagel, Richard Jannasch, who was to die tragically in Brazil, Karl Kurzrock, Gustav Gräser and his Lake Como colonists, C. W. Diefenbach, R. Duncan (the brother of Isadora), Professor G. Herman, who in 1907 launched an international appeal for the funds he needed to establish a "nudonatio," and finally Johannes Guttzeit, who has immortalized all their deeds in numerous books and pamphlets on nudism.[43] In Germany the nudist movement produced several journals of its own: *Die Schönheit* (Beauty), *Kraft und Schönheit* (Strength and Beauty), *Geschlecht und Gesellschaft* (Sex and Society), and published a spate of brochures that sang the praises of the new trinity — nudity, beauty, and morality — in every possible register, down to near-naked pornography in the lowest. The tag *naturalia non sunt turpia* obviously lent itself to a variety of interpretations.

Germany may have been the leader in this field, but she was by no means alone. "Back to nature" was also the battle-cry of the French anarcho-individualist "naturiens,"[44] who sought escape from the strains and stresses of industrial life by returning to nature and rejecting everything that went by the name of culture. Science to them was nothing but a delusion, progress the fruit of slavery, and all man's sufferings the result of civilization. The best-known prophet of this movement was the illustrator Emile Gravelle, whose paper, *L'Etat Naturel*, was founded in 1894. His converts included Louis Martin (who built himself a hut of his own at 96, rue Lepic, Paris, to the dismay of his more discriminating neighbors), Henri Zisly and the popular poet, Paul Paillette, to whom we owe the following lines: *"Public, on te dit fatigué? Ton ennui seul en est la cause . . . Pour la chasser, o créature . . . écoute la mère nature. Ce monde menteur ne vaut rien. Couvert de crime il expire. Dans la nature tout est bien. C'est son livre qu'il faut lire."* Rejection of the modern world in favor of the "book of nature" was also reflected in Gauguin's escape from civilization in 1891, in Elie Reclus's glorification of "primitive" life, and in the growing interest of Europeans in Negro sculpture and music. Another broad, ethical, world-reforming, though at first

rather one-sided, movement — incidentally linked to the "secret" aspects
of freemasonry — embraced the Order of Good Templars and other
teetotallers, who had their work cut out for them in a society that drove
its wage slaves to drink by their thousands. Then there were the homeopaths, vegetarians, non-smokers, bare-footers, natural composters, earth-
rayers and simple-lifers, most of whom were also pacifists, anti-vivisec-
tionists and disciples of Tolstoy, the great prophet from Yasnaya Polyana.
Their concern with health and purity had something almost sickly about it;
their pursuit of higher goals was so single-minded and humorless as to
make them appear quite inhuman.

Some of them were blatantly so, for instance Lanz von Liebensfels,
founder of the "Order des Neuen Tempels," who died in 1954 at the age
of eighty. His doctrine, which was a strange mixture of occultism and
race delusion, was adopted by a sect that began to publish its own journal,
Ostara, in 1905, and it must have been in 1907 that their leader hoisted a
swastika over the ancient castle of Werfenstein on the Danube, near St.
Nikola. In 1909, he received one Adolf Hitler, who was greatly attracted
by the "secret ariosophic doctrine" or the "race-phrenology" of the
pseudo-intellectual lord of the manor.[45]

Sometimes, however, it was all innocent and healthy enough and only
seems peculiar because it was couched in such strange language. A case
in point was the protest against extreme individualism by the "mystic"
Jean Paul Mazoroz, a Parisian furniture-manufacturer, whose ideas were
so many pleas for economic and political corporatism, but who was also
antimasonic and fiercely anticlerical, and who presented his doctrine in a
mixture of Christian and Hindu terms. The greatest enemy and evil,
according to him, was individualism, the cause of a host of fraudulent
bankruptcies, of speculation, of litigation, of the class struggle, of the
disintegration of the family, of poverty, of juvenile delinquency, of
suicide, and, at its best, of poor health.[46]

Sometimes, again, it proved very frail, and all too human in its frailty.
This was especially true of the many sects that drew their inspiration from
the east, but unlike the theosophists, lacked an Annie Besant to lead
them. One such sect was the modern Sufi movement of Inayat Khan
(who died in 1927). It, too, laid stress on the unity of all religions, which
satisfied the holistic aspirations of many of its disciples no less than their
hankering after the occult, the mystical, the symbolic, the aesthetic, and
the aristocratic — the last above all. Another was the Baha'i faith, founded
during the second half of the ninteenth century by the Persian Baha'u'llah,
the successor of Bab and Babiism. It, too, prided itself on being a universalist religion. August Forel, famed since 1905 for his *Die sexuelle Frage*

505

(The Sexual Question), joined the Baha'i after the First World War, and said that his greatest wish was the the new religion should survive.[47]

In this welter of doctrines and emotions, Rudolf Steiner's "anthroposophy" was perhaps the most characteristic reflection of the general change in the intellectual climate of Europeans at the turn of the century. Steiner was thirty-five in 1896, when his mission first became clear to him. He, too, rejected the positivist and materialist approach, and he did so in a unique way. He rejected positivism for its narrow belief that only the visible world could be known, and dismissed materialism, not because it focussed attention on material phenomena, but because it failed to realize that all matter was "spiritual" in essence.[48] He accordingly proposed to abandon the prevailing scientific approach, but only in order to develop it further with the help of imagination, inspiration and intuition. Even his most unrelenting critics must admit that he was unusually astute when he wrote that man's thought and will had never before been so completely cut off from the spirit as they were in his day.[49] Anthroposophy, according to him, was not the subjective complement of science but its objective extension. In other words, in Steiner, the western influence outweighed the eastern. It was no accident that it was geometry which first suggested to him that side by side with the visible world there existed another, hidden from the senses but nevertheless accessible to man. Nor was it by chance that he was an ardent admirer, not only of Goethe, but also of Kepler and Darwin, that he should have held Haeckel in high regard, or that he should have had second thoughts about theosophy just as soon as Annie Besant declared that Krishnamurti was destined to become the world's great spiritual leader. In 1913 he was expelled from the Theosophische Gesellschaft, which he had led for more than ten years, and anthroposophy was born. With his exceptional synthetic gifts, but also with the characteristic self-conceit of all founders of esoteric doctrines, he brought to it a unique approach to man, the world, the universe, and not least to history.

It was also in 1913 that a thesis was written in Germany on the Salvation Army. It was published under the title of *Der Salutismus*,[50] and the term "salutism" could equally well have been applied to all the other ideas, emotions, currents and movements we have described in this chapter. There was probably no more conclusive proof of the fundamental uncertainty and dissatisfaction of the age than all this thirsting after salvation and sanctity. If, here and there, voices within the ranks of these idealists were raised in protest against the concomitant "impoverishment of ideals, and exaggerated enthusiasm,"[57] these voices generally belonged to those few who had remained sober enough to realize that many of the new prophets exploited rather than lived according to their ideals. The exploitation of idealism and of salutism was not confined to the petty herbalist or miracle-worker, the classic quack, the layer-on-of-hands, the magnetizer, the astrologist, or the chiromancer; it also infected many an authentic prophet, though in less obvious ways. Even the anarcho-communist colonies that sprang up during this period — for instance F. van Eeden's "Walden" or C. S. Kylstra's commune, both in Holland — were not above reproach. Their decline may ultimately have been due to the impossibility of setting up communal islands in a society based on private property, but the more immediate cause was the human, all too human urge of many of the colonists to turn their backs on all responsibilities and sponge on the labor of their fellow colonists — a privilege strictly reserved for capitalists. Clerical objections and the ingrained prejudice of the good Dutch burgher against "spinach-eaters" did the rest. When all is said and done, however, the exploiters no less than the vilifiers of salvationism were paying implicit tribute to its powerful appeal.

Riemann, who as we saw launched an attack on spiritualism in 1901, also admitted that its sudden growth was a sign that it "satisfies the spiritual needs of the present."[52] What these needs were, we have tried to set out as best we could in the preceding pages. Europe was passing through a phase that was even then described as "emotional anarchy,"[53] as "weariness with, rather than delight in, man's latest achievements."[54] That weariness was reflected, if not in an actual increase in mental illness, suicide and degeneracy, certainly in the belief that such an increase was taking place, and that belief was enough to inspire terrible fears, especially among the upper strata of society. These fears, with salutism and idealism as their antidotes, were so many manifestations of the bad conscience of a ruling class that was no longer convinced of its divine right to rule but not yet under sufficient threat to take full stock of its shortcomings. It recognized the flaws in the educational, welfare, and penal systems, in government, organized religion, in the modern way of running life and work, but did little about them. Some observers have argued that even the working class had become strangely susceptible to the same psychopathological virus. "We know to what alarming extent present-day social conditions are helping to increase the incidence of mental illness," was the view of a doctor whose job it was to cope with the misery of the fourth estate.[55] Otto Rühle, who took a critical look at the whole subject, discovered a direct connection between social conditions and salutism: chronic starvation and child labor were "creating a sickly generation, in which religious and sectarian fanaticism, spiritualism and similar foolishness easily take root."[56] That the lower classes were suffering from the spirit of the age must also have been the view of William Booth, who, for that very reason, must be bracketed together with such "salutists" as Tolstoy, Ghandi, Annie Besant and Rudolf Steiner, albeit he intended no more with his Salvation Army than to implement the social message of the Gospels. For did not all of them want to live "in tune with the infinite," as Ralph Waldo Trine put it?[57]

However, all these exalted aspirations, even, or precisely when they were genuine, foundered on the rocks of human frailty. Nothing like it had happened before, and nothing like it was ever to happen again. Most of these prophets threw either themselves, or else their ideals, under the juggernaut of the First World War. The fire blazed once again during the October Revolution, but briefly and only to be blown out, in its turn, by the harsh wind of reality.

CHAPTER XXXIV

BEFORE THE FOOTLIGHTS

January 15, 1900 was the date on which Emil Reich signed the preface
to the third edition of his *Ibsens Dramen* (Ibsen's Plays).[1] Two months
later, on March 15, Ibsen, the greatest playwright of his day, suffered
a stroke that left him with little more than his life. *Naar vi dode vaagner,*
which he himself called an "epilogue" and in which he honestly recorded
the failure of his life, had been finished just in time.[2] It had come
in the wake of years of vilification and a decade of profuse admiration
when hardly a week and certainly not a month went by without one
of his plays being staged in some theater somewhere in what was known
as the civilized world. Ever since the 1890s, critical essays and critical
books on his work had appeared, year in, year out — more than five
hundred all told in the two decades round 1900[3] — and most of them
widely read, even though some — for instance Reich's and Ehrhard's[4] —
ran to more than 400 pages each. Of the German books on Ibsen, which
are the most numerous, we shall only mention Eugen Heinrich Schmitt's,[5]
not because of its size — it, too, ran to 400 pages — but because one of
its chapters was devoted to the "demonic character of our age," a favorite
subject, and because of its title, *Ibsen als Prophet* (Ibsen as Prophet),
for that was how most of his contemporaries saw the man. This may
explain why his translators included such famous men as Prozor in France,
William Archer in England, and Christian Morgenstern, of *Galgenlieder*
fame, in Germany. Ibsen was not just a prophet, but so wonderfully
modern that when Mendes da Costa, one of the old school, wrote his
theatrical reminiscences in 1900, he lumped Ibsen together with Strindberg and Maeterlinck and relegated them all to the miscellaneous section,
thus demonstrating that he thought them unworthy of serious attention.[6]
It was because Ibsen lent himself to so many different interpretations —
a characteristic of all prophets — that every kind of heretic took him
for a spokesman of his own individualistic or socialistic, pessimistic or
optimistic, naturalistic or idealistic, romantic or symbolist, views. Some
declared him to be a mystic, others acclaimed him as a "successor" of
Kierkegaard, who had just been rediscovered. What was Ibsen's attitude

509

to women, what his attitude to men, and what precisely was the secret of his dramatic power? What was his social philosophy? Was he a purely intellectual rebel, or was he also an active enemy of the capitalist state? Even the Marxists joined in the fray, with Plekhanov at the helm.[7] It was probably Henri Lichtenberger, then a professor at the Sorbonne, who came closest to the truth when he claimed in 1909 that the real basis of Ibsen's fame was his "uncertain groping for truth and sincerity . . . one of the mightiest impulses of our age."[8] Thomas Mann traced Ibsen's love of truth back to Schopenhauer, who had challenged the faith of millennia by insisting that instinct took precedence over reason, that weak emanation of the will. "So truthful was the nineteenth century that, through Ibsen, it tried to show that even the 'lies of life' were indispensable."[9]

With Ibsen gone, a whole world came to an end and another took its place. On the same night that Ibsen had a stroke, Edmond Rostand's *L'aiglon* had its première in the Théatre Sarah Bernhardt, with "la divine Sarah" herself in the title role: a woman on the wrong side of fifty playing the young "eaglet" — a feat within a feat. Morand has given us a fictional account of the talk in the corridors during the interval: "If Rostand had only wanted to, he could have marched on the Elysée," and "Remember the date, my child: March 15, 1900."[10] Rostand's world seemed more worldly than that of the old Norwegian, but the appearances, as ever, were deceptive and Rostand's glory was, in any case, very brief. Unlike the great Ibsen, whose talents had ensured that the innermost secrets of the bourgeoisie were given a public airing, Rostand's only theatrical resources were the threadbare devices of rhetoric and chauvinism; the ranting verses of this "last romantic melodrama" were simply a glorification of Napoleon[11] and as such — this must be admitted — not without bearing on the coming century with its "popular" dictators.

So profuse was theatrical life in 1900 that it is easy to find two other premières that year which were to be long remembered by those fortunate enough to have attended them. On November 7 the Lessingtheater in Berlin staged the first performance of Gerhart Hauptmann's *Michael Kramer*.[12] This, too, was an "event," and another that has not stood the test of time. It was a tragic portrayal of the life of a brilliant but degenerate artist, and contained so many elements of the author's earlier plays that there was good reason to fear that his rather slight talents had been exhausted by his *Vor Sonnenaufgang* (1889), *Die Weber* (1892) and *Hannele's Himmelfahrt* (1893), three rightly famed naturalistic plays. Then, on Christmas Eve, the Hollandse Schouwburg in Amsterdam opened with *Op hoop van zegen* (The Good Hope), a play by Herman

510

Heijermans, who served his art without betraying his socialism, and his socialism without betraying his art. This was yet another "event," not least because Esther de Boer-van Rijk played the part of Kniertje, and also because it marked the only period in which the Dutch theater could stand on its own feet. Within less than half a year, the play had its hundredth performance in the Netherlands, and there was hardly a city of any importance in Europe or America, from Moscow to Los Angeles, in which the play was not staged. In Moscow, it was produced by the great Stanislavsky himself. To the tens of thousands who identified themselves with Kniertje in scores of theatres, were added the hundred of thousands more who, after the war, flocked to see *The Good Hope* and the social abuses it pilloried on the screen.[13]

Finally, anyone interested in the theater of this period will remember another date, November 30, 1900, the day of Oscar Wilde's lonely death following a series of triumphs as brilliant as the pit that opened up before him during the last five years of his life was somber. He will remember that date because Wilde — with Shaw — was the first to bring the British theater, after a long period of hibernation, back to life again, at about the same time that Morris revived British typography, Mackintosh reanimated British design and architecture, and Whistler and Beardsley revitalized British art. It was a marvelous year for the stage, for it was also in 1900 that Chekhov's *The Three Sisters*, and Gorky's *Lower Depths* made their debut, that Strindberg wrote his *Dödsdansen* (Dance of Death), that Sarah Bernhardt gave some of her finest performances, and that Eleonora Duse scored unforgettable successes in the very forgettable plays of Gabriele d'Annunzio.

The chronicler has no difficulty in showing how important a part the theater played in the period under review. He cannot mention a dramatist from any other period to whom, like Ibsen, a monument was set up in his own lifetime, or who, like Hauptmann,[14] had his sixtieth birthday marked by two thousand articles in the press; no other period in which a playwright, by virtue of his craft, was deemed capable of holding the highest office in the land, or was so widely celebrated. Nor will he be able to name any other period in which at least a dozen great or ostensibly great playwrights were at work in Europe, all of them venerated by a large public. Indeed, one might claim that the greater the gulf between their actual merits and the homage paid to them, the clearer it becomes how important a social need the stage was filling. But the historian, for one, cannot leave it at that: he wants to know why the theater should have soared to such great heights in just this period, and why it should have passed through three phases: first, the naturalist;

511

secondly, as a reaction to the first, the symbolist, neo-romantic, and expressionist; and thirdly, a strange marriage of naturalism with one of its antitheses.

Artificial though these terms are, they cannot be avoided by anyone concerned with the changes that took place in the theater during our period of general cultural transformation. The historian knows that every experiential datum hides an infinity of details and that he must delve deep beneath the surface if he is to discover what specific processes are at work and how they affect the wider problems.[15] It would be a grave mistake to conclude that general processes are of no more than subsidiary importance to the historian — quite the contrary. Those who claim that the macrocosm and microcosm of the past constitute one dialectical whole which provides the truest possible picture of historical reality, are stating no more than the truth.[16] Thus a closer study of everything that, historically, has been labeled "naturalism," shows that it embraced a wide spectrum of protest against traditions and conventions. "Naturalism" may be said to have been ushered in with the Goncourts' *Germinie Lacerteux* (1864), which argued that "the novel has assumed the work and the duties of science" and to have begun to wane as the dominant trend in 1891, when Deyssel published his notorious "The Death of Naturalism."

The primary aim of the movement was to be true to nature and in this it succeeded so well that we cannot but agree with Fechter, who, discussing Hauptmann's *Fuhrmann Henschel*, *Michael Kramer*, and *Die Ratten*, observed that whoever wants to write the history of the years 1880 to 1910 can do no better than use these three plays as his sources.[17] Wanting to be true to nature, however, is not the same as being true to it. No long arguments are needed to show that the writer, however honest he tries to be, is caught in the meshes of his own age. In our particular case these meshes were the belief that man is fully determined by his race, environment, and period, and is driven by irresistible instincts that render him a plaything of fate, turning his life into torture until he finds final release through mental and — especially on the stage — physical disintegration.

It would, however, be quite wrong to conclude that this form of "objective" art left no room for subjective differences among the artists or their creations. For what they saw and depicted were not so much the realities themselves — albeit many deluded themselves that they did — as their ever-changing interactions; indeed one can posit the paradox that the more accurately they tried to reflect the light and shadow of real life, the more they drew on their personal experience — in other

512

words, the more subjective they became. Hence it needed no more than the slightest change in course to land, as Kleinberg put it, on "quite different shores."[18] Was not that what Zola, too, had meant when he spoke of "nature perceived by temperament"? We shall see below how their "temperaments" led a number of playwrights from naturalism to one of its antitheses, in much the same way that quite a few poets and writers turned into symbolists and neo-romantics, or that so many painters veered from impressionism to symbolism or expressionism.

However, "temperament" does not operate in a vacuum. There was a close link between the shift from naturalism to some form of anti-naturalism and social conditions. Franz Mehring has examined this link in its particular effects on the theater, and has done so in depth. This was not by chance, for during the period under review he was a respected drama critic.[19] Between 1892 and 1912 he repeatedly returned to the problem of naturalism,[20] and his general conclusion was that naturalism must be considered a protest against withered traditions. This was particularly true in Germany, and we can gather how much the younger generation there despised the literature produced before 1880 from a brochure by Carl Bleibtreu in which he referred to the renewal of 1880 as nothing short of a revolution.[21] The marked anti-traditionalism of progressive German youth is also brought home in Albert Soergel's *Dichtung und Dichter der Zeit* (Poetry and Poets of the Age): "A generation of very young people, born between 1860 and 1870, supplies the enthusiasts who write program after program in noisy superlatives, found one society after another, and who, despite all their differences, are filled with one overriding urge: to break with traditions in life no less than in art. Even the best no longer satisfies us, we need a new technique, a different style, a different subject matter, a different relationship between the artist and the world he tries to portray. We need a new world view in keeping with the spirit of the times, a new type of writer, one who acts as a public force."[22] Mehring, too, took a positive view of the protest movement, which, he asserted, was directed against modern capitalism and all the misery it caused. One may agree with him and yet add that it took a particularly sensitive age to record all that misery, and that this hypersensitivity, in its turn, was the direct result of the fact that capitalism itself had created the material means of eradicating the worst of these abuses. However, Mehring blamed the naturalists for not going far enough. For though they had broken with a bad tradition, they had failed to create a new one; they pilloried social abuses on the stage but produced no cures; in short they were negative because they had no links with the modern labor movement and hence with the future.

513

This lack of political acumen caused them to tire of portraying social misery — of which the public, too, had had more than enough — and to seek solace in new, or, more correctly in old, forms of neo-romanticism, symbolism and mysticism. As a result, they were drawn increasingly into the paths of bourgeois decline.

In our examination of the problem of naturalism and its transformation we have come face to face with a much more general phenomenon. There is no better way of illustrating it than by examining a concrete case: that of Arno Holz, a man whose personality and work might have been designed for this very purpose.[23] This "hero" of the artistic revolution stepped into the limelight during the very year — he was twenty-two at the time — that Bleibtreu heralded the new age. He did so with a collection of poems that bore the proud title of *Buch der Zeit. Lieder eines Modernen* (Book of the Times. Poems of a Modernist). His verses were, however, modern only inasmuch as they made city life and work the proper objects of poetry, and also in their compassion for the poor, of whom the poet himself was one. Urged on by his own radicalism and prophetic aspirations, this self-styled "Baptist of the coming century" perfected a naturalist credo of his own, which he presented to the world in 1887 by way of three short stories written in collaboration with Johannes Schlaf and published under a Scandinavian pseudonym:[24] clear proof by the way, that Germany had already entered the age of Ibsen. But Holz was not yet satisfied. Three years later, in a short book entitled *Die Kunst. Ihr Wesen und ihre Gesetze* (Art: Its Essence and Laws)[25] he proclaimed himself a "consistent naturalist," one who went further even than Zola in that he had no need of "temperament." The true naturalist writer must be as unprejudiced about his subject matter as the scientist is about his.

So far so good. However, a closer look at Holz's work brings to light certain elements that not only give the lie to his theory but transform it into its very opposite.

Though a declared naturalist, Holz was, in fact, an effeminate aesthete, reminiscent of Huysmans after his "conversion" to anti-naturalism: he wrote in Indian ink because it was "so beautifully dark black" and, strange outcome of his "scientific approach," carefully counted all the dashes and colons that studded his writings. More characteristically still, the second of the three short stories we have just mentioned contained what can only be described as a surrealist scene: the child who has run away from school finds his grandfather dead in a chair, a tame raven perched on his bald head.

514

In 1898 Holz published a new collection of poems, entitled *Phantasus*, dedicated to the rediscovery of "the great path of nature," a path, he argued, that art had abandoned since the Renaissance (see Chapter XXXVI). What Holz now produced under Rousseau's motto was as far removed from nineteenth-century naturalism as it is possible to imagine: *"Ich liege noch im Bett und habe eben Kaffee getrunken"* (I am still in bed, and have just drunk coffee), or *"Im Tiergarten, auf einer Bank, sitz ich und rauche"* (In the Zoo, I sit on a bench and smoke).[26] A year later — still before the turn of the century — he published another collection with the same title, and one has only to dispense with some of the capital letters to be left with expressionist poetry: *Sieben Billionen Jahre vor meiner Geburt / war ich / eine Schwertlilie / Meine suchenden Wurzeln / saugten / sich / um einen Stern / Aus seinen wölbenden Wassern / traumblau / in / neue / kreisende Weltenringel / wuchs / stieg, stiess / zertströmte, versprühte sich / meine dunkle Riesenblüte* (Seven billion years before my birth / I was / a fleur-de-lis / my searching roots / sucked / themselves / to a star / from its vaulted waters / dreamblue / into / new / circling world whorls / grew / rose, thrusted / dissolved into spray / my dark giant blossom).[27] It was surely impossible to move further away from naturalism in so short a time[28] and without any avowed "conversion."[29] The reason we have included Arno Holz in this chapter is not so much because of his own play, *Berlin. Die Wende einer Zeit in Dramen* (Berlin. The Turning Point of an Epoch in the Theater),[30] as because, when "consistent naturalism" began its German stage career in 1889, it did so with a play by a young writer who dedicated it to Holz as a mark of respect. The name of the play was *Vor Sonnenaufgang* (Before the Dawn), its author was Gerhart Hauptmann, and the main subjects of this social drama, as it was expressly called, were capitalism, alcoholism, and hereditary weakness. It was written with the apparent detachment so characteristic of the new school. In fact it was anything but detached: the discerning spectator could easily discover something — and not the best — of Hauptmann's own character in Loth, the "hero." The play made a great impression, not only on the young, who, according to Heinrich Hart, one of their leaders, were beginning to withhold their applause from anything normal,[31] but also on their "normal" elders: Theodor Fontane considered *Vor Sonnenaufgang* the "consummation of Ibsen."[32] With *Die Weber* (The Weavers), which came three years later, Hauptmann's fame spread even further, not only because public performances of the play were banned at first, or because rightists considered its author the very imbodiment of evil and ugliness, but because

515

it was undoubtedly Hauptmann's best work, and one that, incidentally, inspired some fine drawings by Käthe Kollwitz. Samuel Lublinski extolled its "near-Shakespearean power."[33]

Both plays were first put on in the Kleines Lessingtheater before members of Die Freie Bühne (The Free Stage), founded in 1889, as we know from a pamphlet by Paul Schlenther.[34] Here the chronicler once again discovers some of the threads that, just as with Hauptmann's dedication of his first play to Holz, tie together the thousands of *dramatis personae* of our period, loosely but not at all arbitrarily: threads so strangely interwoven that they hide the secret motive force of that period but nevertheless reveal an overall pattern. In our particular case, that pattern throws some light on the objections to Hauptmann's work and to naturalism in general. After the performance of his third play in 1893, Chancellor Hohenlohe made the following entry in his diary: "A dreadful pot-boiler, social-democratic, realistic, suffused with a sickly and sentimental mystique, and horribly enervating, in a word, gruesome. When it was all over, we went to Borchardt's to restore our spirits with caviar and champagne."[35]

Another spectator was André Antoine, the producer, who had come all the way from Paris. In 1887 he had founded the Théâtre Libre, from which the Freie Bühne had borrowed more than its name. Hermann Bahr, the well-known author, took the occasion to write a vivid account of the rise to fame of this former Parisian gas works official with a salary of 150 francs a month.[36] Antoine's little theater in the Rue Blanche, with its fewer than 150 seats, was the very hub of the naturalist stage during its five or six palmy years. With Tolstoy's *Power of Darkness*, Ibsen's work in 1890, and Hauptmann's *The Weavers* in 1893, it broke the unchallenged reign of Dumas fils, Pailleron, and Sardou and, especially during the first decade of its existence, opened its doors to many new talents. One of these was François de Curel, author of such *drames d'idée* as *La Nouvell idole* (1895) in which he broached a highly topical subject: the authority of science, and *La Fille sauvage* (1902) in which, *à la* Rousseau, he questioned the value of civilization. The group also included Porto-Riche, whose *Amoureuse* (1891) and *théâtre d'amour* kept harping on the inevitable misunderstanding between men and women.[37] Then there were the anarchist Paul Hervieu, who showed that the law was responsible for most evils, and Eugène Brieux, another naturalist, whose social protests in the *théâtre à thèse*[38] marked the liberation of the stage from one of the most oppressive dogmas of naturalism: his comedy, *L'Évasion*, poked fun at the sacred theory of heredity.

The Théâtre Libre had several offshoots apart from the Berlin Freie

Bühne. J. T. Grein, a Dutch journalist and businessman, was so inspired by Antoine that he founded the Independent Theatre in London. It opened in February 1891 with Ibsen's *Ghosts* and it was here that Shaw made his debut on December 9, 1892 with *Widowers' Houses*, another social indictment, this time of slum landlordism. Much as the Freie Bühne gave rise to the Volksbühne, so the Théâtre Libre inspired the, incidentally abortive, attempt by Rolland and others to create a popular stage dedicated to the ideas of the French Revolution.[39] Antoine's influence was also noticeable in the renaissance of the Dutch stage during the 1890s: Jan C. de Vos has rightly been called the Antoine of Holland.[40]

Antoine's example was copied not only by those in sympathy with his views, but also by many who were not. The second group included the poet Paul Fort who opened his Théâtre de l'Art in 1890, and the actor and director Lugné-Poë who opened his Theatre de l'Oeuvre in 1893. Lugné-Poë produced Ibsen's later plays, Wilde, Verhaeren, Gorky, but above all Maeterlinck and other symbolists, as we know from his autobiographical *Parade*.

Let us return to Germany for a moment, where the theater was well ahead of the age. In 1908, Heijermans left Holland for Berlin in the hope of finding a more appreciative audience, and that year the British theatrical designer and actor Edward Gordon Craig declared that the German theater was impelling and methodical and that its example would sooner or later be copied in Britain.[41] Max Reinhardt helped to ensure that it was, at least to some extent; he himself was inspired by Craig and his journal, *Mask*. It was thanks chiefly to the German stage that the great Russians, Tolstoy, Chekhov, and Gorky, the great Scandinavians, Ibsen, Björnson, and Strindberg, and the Austrian, Schnitzler, achieved international renown, as did Frank Wedekind, without whom the theater would not have been what it was, though his talent was not immediately appreciated. Thus Richard Meyer failed to mention him in the comprehensive history of German literature he published in 1900. Yet *Frühlings Erwachen* (Spring's Awakening), Wedekind's first and probably most famous play, had been written in the winter of 1890. The reason for this neglect is not hard to find: Wedekind's honest treatment of the problems of puberty, far from clearing the broody *fin de siècle* atmosphere of erotic intoxication, struck most of his contemporaries as a perverse and sadistic ploy,[42] and this despite favorable reviews by Georg Brandes, Knut Hamsum, Max Nordau, Otto Julius Bierbaum, Arthur Moeller von den Bruck, and many other critics.[43] Heinrich Mann explained later that the age was not ripe for Wedekind's plays.[44] In the genteel atmosphere of the 1890s, when people still believed in goodness and in the imminent solution of all social problems, there was no place for one who placed truth before benevolence, and the promptings of the inner voice before naturalistic dogma, and who was something of what would later be called an expressionist, and later still, an existentialist. It was only in 1905, under Reinhardt's inspired direction and with Alexander Moissi as Melchior Gabor, that *Spring's Awakening* finally received the acclaim it so richly deserved: it was staged two hundred times within a few years. Since then, so many playwrights have followed the path paved by Wedekind that his truth — the sexual needs of adolescents — has become a commonplace, which does not make it any less of a truth, and, moreover, one that had to be discovered if the evil it pilloried was to be eradicated, just as *spirochaeta pallida* had to be discovered before syphilis could be cured. That the second discovery, too, was made in 1905 is a coincidence, but not the fact that it was only during this period that people found what courage it took to make either.

Those who know nothing more about Wedekind or his *Spring's Awakening* might think that the play was typical "slice of life" and its author a typical naturalist. Nothing could be further from the truth: Wedekind was never anything but an anti-naturalist. He used the subtle technique of leaving the appearances unchanged even while transforming the essence, a technique that had just been discovered by Bahr, who was exceptionally sensitive to the undercurrents of his age. In two articles, one dealing with the crisis of, and the other with the decline of, naturalism,[45] he not only described but helped to complete the shift from "without" to "within," from "environment" to "inner light" — a shift that went hand in hand with a new psychological approach. Though that new approach led the searching mind into unexplored territory, it spelled the end of naturalism: it drove art back from the "market-place of reality" into the "temple of dreams," and turned the artist from a tool of reality into an interpreter of his own nature. Maurice Maeterlinck was the most perfect embodiment of this transformation, which may explain why he was one of the first to be declared a genius overnight, a type that has since become so common. There was a great demand for neo-romanticism, for symbolism and mysticism, and Maeterlinck satisfied it as early as 1889 with his *Princesse maleine*. The play was "discovered" by Octave Mirbeau, who sang its praises to the world at large in *Le Figaro* during the summer of 1890.[46] He did it with characteristic eloquence: the Belgian, he declared, had produced "by far the most brilliant, by far the most singular, and by far the most ingenuous masterpiece of the age"; in short, a new Shakespeare had appeared on the horizon.

Exaggerated though this view may have been, Maeterlinck's effect on his contemporaries is hard to exaggerate, as witness the more than two thousand entries in an incomplete bibliography. Moreover, he had a profound influence on the work of Paul Claudel and of John Millington Synge, to mention just two famous literary figures, on a number of philosophers, and also on Debussy and Fauré; conversely the fame of Maeterlinck's *Pelléas and Mélisande* (1892) owed much to Debussy's opera by that name, to which it formed the libretto.

A special role in the renewal of the stage was played by the "Irish Theatre" founded in 1899 by W. B. Yeats and Lady Isabella Augusta Gregory, and eventually housed in the Abbey Theatre, Dublin. While Maeterlinck and others, who felt alienated from bourgeois civilization, turned to a world of fantasy built up from elements of a pre-bourgeois civilization, seen through rose-colored spectacles, Yeats and his friends found their idyll in the "backward" Irish countryside, and looked upon its preservation as an effective weapon against England, the oppressor and prototype of urban degeneration. Indeed, the "dramatic lyrics" staged in the Abbey Theatre, a struggling playhouse run by amateurs, stood the Irish Freedom Movement in good stead, not least by fostering living ties between the spectators and the actors. Its rendering of John Synge's *Playboy of the Western World*, for instance, made the dramatic effects of the neo-romantic school pale into insignificance.[47]

Maeterlinck, we have said, achieved great fame in his lifetime, but he influenced his period far less than did the great Swede, August Strindberg: the first was like moonlight, the second like a flash of lightning. Strindberg was, in any case, the more compelling of the two, historically as well as psychologically. In his desperate hankering after versatility, indeed after universality — he was also a painter and a very modern one at that[48] — Strindberg was symbolic of his age, which like him tried to throw all restraints to the winds in a frantic attempt to shake off its doubts, regardless of the consequences. Strindberg's bitterness may well have been the result of his schizophrenia; Jaspers, for one, thought that it was to some extent, though not as obviously as with Hölderlin and van Gogh.[49] For all that, Esswein may have exaggerated, but was nevertheless not far from the truth, when he said that since the prophets of Israel and the Church Fathers, no one had equaled Strindberg's portrayal of a world collapsing about his ears.[50] Strindberg himself was an embodiment of that fickle world, because he kept demolishing the very altars he himself had erected. Thus, no sooner had the socialists begun to quote him, than he was once again the remote aristocrat; no sooner had the church clasped him to her bosom than he became an outspoken atheist; and no sooner had the materialists applauded him than he turned mystical, abandoning naturalism for neo-romanticism.[51] What impressed his contemporaries most were not these sudden changes but his ability to portray his own, almost superhuman suffering: the hell of marriage in the *Dance of Death* of 1900, and the macabre and pathological aspects of family life in *The Father* of 1887, a play that seemed horribly true to life, if only because its characters were so "ordinary" and their hatreds so inevitable. Naturalist? Symbolist? The answer to both questions is Yes.

In the "marginal areas" of European culture — Russia, Austria, and Britain — naturalism and the reaction to it were not nearly as marked as they were in the "heartlands." The Russian bourgeoisie, in its numerical weakness and desperate struggle against Czarism, could not afford the luxury of indulging in purely literary differences of opinion, and with few exceptions, refrained from doing so. Indeed, what more could it have asked than the subdued voice of a Chekhov which, though open to any number of interpretations, was so manifestly humane that it offered solace for the loss of traditional certitudes and, almost imperceptibly, an intimation of better things to come? So they cheered the four great plays he wrote between 1897 and 1904: *Uncle Vanya, The Seagull, The Three Sisters,* and *The Cherry Orchard,* finished shortly before he succumbed to tuberculosis. Its sympathetic rendering by Stanislavsky in the Hermitage on October 14, 1898, faithfully recorded by Julius Bab,[52] did much to spread the fame of this almost silent masterpiece (in which moods are more telling than words, and the atmosphere more important than human actions — or rather inactions). Apart from the prophetic work of Tolstoy, and the revolutionary dramas of Maxim Gorky, Chekhov's plays were the only "messages" the Russian stage may be said to have emitted, but only inasmuch as they heralded a new age by ringing out the old. By their side, the plays of the Austrian masters — Hugo von Hofmansthal, Stefan Zweig, and Arthur Schnitzler — appeared like so many mirrors, and sometimes distorting mirrors, of their age, and so did the farces of Bahr. All of old Vienna, the city that was to fade away in 1914 to 1918, is reflected in Schnitzler's early work: its Slavonic baroque, its belated rococo, its elegant morbidity, and its melodious air of depravity. In his *Liebelei* 1895 (Playing with Love), and his *Reigen* (English translation: *The Reckoning,* later the film *La Ronde*), Schnitzler, with the deep humanity of the east European Jew and the sceptical melancholy of the worldly Viennese, brought to the stage, more grippingly and also more charmingly than anyone else, not only the loneliness and bitter aftertaste of the erotic, but also its omnipotent hold over the spoilt darlings of pre-war Europe. He did so reluctantly, for he refused to have his *Reigen* performed for a long time, and only changed his mind when inflation drove him to it after the war.[53] There is perhaps nothing that illustrates the decline of sexual taboos more convincingly than the fact that, when *Reigen* appeared on the screen after the Second World War no one seemed to object.

Message and mirror in one — England could still afford this form of self-criticism — was what George Bernard Shaw (forty-four in 1900) held out to his contemporaries, once William Archer had "discovered" him in 1889. Shaw owed a great deal to Ibsen — his *Quintessence of Ibsenism* was published in 1891 — and his strength, too, lay in his contrariety, and in his open mind, which even prevented him from falling prey to his own scepticism. He relied largely on "shock" and "show," two effects no one could handle better than he. Just as frankly as he exposed *Mrs. Warren's Profession* in 1894 — first staged in 1902 — so he deflated jingoism in his *Arms and the Man*. His *Caesar and Cleopatra* (1901) stripped the mask from yet another delusion, and foreshadowed a trend that would make itself felt insistently in a host of biographies, autobiographies and historical writings after the debacle of the First World War. *Candida*, of the same vintage as *Arms and the Man*, was perhaps pre-war Shaw at its very best: it, too, was message and mirror in one, for it showed that it needed no more than a sober look at conventional manners to shake the pre-war world of sham certainties to its foundations.

With the change of social conditions, the artist acquired a new status at the turn of the century. This was particularly true of actors, who were suddenly promoted from second-class citizens and comedians buried alongside prostitutes and suicides, to popular idols. Actresses ceased to be the prey of prosperous dressing-room prowlers, and the erotic antics of a Sarah Bernhardt raised no more eyebrows than did the virtuous family life of an Alida Tartaud-Klein.

The spectators, too, had been transformed. The élite, stepping in and out of their boxes, and the candy-sucking, beer-swilling "pit," became fused into a single great theater-loving audience. Those who insisted on more direct contact with the players, on joining in the choruses, on spontaneous outbursts of hilarity and catcalls, could always turn to the music halls and variety shows, whose latest products could be whistled and sung at home, at work and in the street.

The five Barrison sisters from the United States owed their triumphant reception in Europe during the 1890s to the incongruous nature of their act. These dear little girls with their rustling silk frocks, tantalizingly innocent lingerie, and loose blond curls, bounced about the stage singing naughty songs in their clear little voices, and appeared so spontaneous and natural compared with the chanteuses of the *cafés dansant* with their plush roses, dyed hair, obscene corsets, and lewd paradings of well supported bosoms and flashing thighs.[54] In the music halls, too, the lusty admirers of feminine beauty could enjoy a judicious mixture of spontaneous fun and erotic titillation.

It was in the variety theater and the café dansant that the can-can found its home, "that boisterous, scandalous and fashionable dance of the Second Empire popularized in Offenbach's operettas."[55] It had emerged as a country dance during the French Revolution, a massive display of joie de vivre and human solidarity, but once put on the stage it became just another facet of the Dionysian pursuit of ecstatic pleasure that was also erupting in the other arts. Such talented dancers as Saharet and Loïe Fuller created a can-can style of their own.[56]

It seems most unlikely that Isadora Duncan should have even heard of these two dancers in 1900 when, at the age of twenty, she appeared in Europe, filled with the mission that had brought her from the New World to the Old. Still, the atmosphere they had created must have rendered Europe receptive to the shock of her temperamental attack on the ossified classical ballet. Indeed it is unthinkable that dancing, of all arts, should have been left untouched by the spirit of the age, marked by a spontaneous breakthrough to the unconscious, free movement and hatred of prudishness and the hypocritical camouflage of the human body. There was a clear affinity between the billowing lines of Loïe Fuller's skirt dances, the undulating "natural" movements of Isadora Duncan and "Jugendstil." The desire to reveal the body as an instrument of the dance, to use it as a means of total expression and no longer as a display of feminine grace, was something many had felt even before the bare feet of Isadora became its sensational symbol. But her object was much wider than that; she was preaching a new philosophy and did so with typical American thoroughness: by public demonstrations, lectures and press conferences, which aroused a wave of enthusiasm but also a storm of derision. Although the dancing academies she founded all over the world were fairly short-lived, her appearances helped Fokine and Diaghilev to free the ballet from its straitjacket. Rudolf von Laban was of the same school, but his attempt to give direct expression to the unconscious was too philosophical and much too symbolic to make much headway.[57] It was left to his pupils, Mary Wigman chief among them, to give his ideas a more spontaneous and poignant airing. The expressionist ballet, like the expressionist stage, liked to dispense with elaborate decor: Isadora Duncan contented herself with a plain curtain. At about the same time, the Swiss composer Emile Jaques-Dalcroze extended the idea of the rhythmical expression from the ballet to eurhythmics, a system of musical education based on the rhythmical discipline of bodily movements.

A whole complex of nationalist, educational and anti-intellectual impulses also led, again in about 1900, to a revival of the folkdance. Cecil Sharp's collections and arrangements of folk songs and country dances were snatched up by a host of youth organizations, ranging from the blood and soil variety to the socialist. Simultaneously, the attractions of the exotic made themselves felt on the dance floor, where the cakewalk and the tango took their place by the side of the waltz which had so long enjoyed a near monopoly.

The appearance of Isadora Duncan in the Netherlands in 1908 has been recorded not only in the press but also in the songs of Koos Speenhoff,[58] the first Dutch cabaret artist. The cabaret was a Parisian creation of the 1880s (*Chat Noir, Mirliton, et al.*), later copied in many other great cities, not least in Berlin where Ernst von Wolzogen's *Überbrettl* attracted large crowds. Speenhoff, too, enjoyed great popularity for many years, though there were quite a few negative reactions as well. Thus the Dutch Young Catholic Men's Association, "Voor Eer en Deugd" (For Honour and Virtue), interrupted his "filthy" recitals with showers of pamphlets, and the *Maasbode* called upon its readers to "pay tribute to those brave young knights of Holy Chastity who fight so valiantly under the lily-white banner of the Immaculate Conception."[59]

The cabaret artist was the street-singer of former years, a modern troubadour, who serenaded his fellow citizens, not the lady of his choice, in the backrooms of obscure little cafés. He was also the heir of those daring non-conformists who suddenly popped up on a market square, sang their rebellious songs, sold the text on tattered pieces of paper, only to vanish again as quickly as they had appeared. Aristide Bruant, probably the most talented of their modern descendants, would pillory society while dressed in flowing robes and a slouch hat. At first, he addressed himself exclusively to "les gars et les filles du quartier", but then all Paris seemed to crown into his *Mirliton*, delighted to hear their own way of life abused in Bruant's juicy argot, to the wild applause of his regular clients. Bruant was modern, too, in that he exploited his talents to full economic advantage: in later life he retired to a country house where he spent his time hunting and writing a dictionary of French slang. Much more versatile than Bruant was Yvette Guilbert, who deliberately paraded her lack of feminine beauty to emphasize that personality mattered more than the perfect vital statistics every teenage girl was enjoined to develop. She has been immortalized on Toulouse-Lautrec's posters: dressed in shapeless white or sea-green gowns, gangly arms in black gloves, turned-up nose, tight lips and flaming red hair. Audiences from all over the world came to marvel at her artistic temperament, her extremely subtle powers of expression, and her liberating eroticism.

We can now attempt to answer the question we raised at the beginning of this chapter: why it was that the stage held such a special position in our period. The stage showed people what they wanted to see or what they abhorred, and the "people" were no longer the select few theatergoers of former years, but the much wider public that was beginning to read the popular dailies and to make its voice heard. The stage was the only place in which it could live out its dreams, its fears, and illusions in almost tangible form. The film, the radio, and the highly capitalized amusement industry which were to take the place of the theater after the First World War, had not yet risen to prominence. When they did, the cinema in particular proved to be a more democratic form of art and entertainment than the stage had ever been, for the stage had never shed its class prejudice[60] and the psychological subtleties of its set drawing-room pieces had been largely lost on the masses. But the isolated spectator sitting in a dark cinema, unable to express his feelings and even denied the satisfaction of applauding his favorite stars, has lost something in the process.

He no longer has the old stalls with their red plush and gilt, the fairy lights lit by candles, oil, gas, or electricity, or even the indirect stage lighting invented by the Spanish painter, Fortuny.[61] He no longer leaves the theater, gallery or stalls, crushed in a single throng that has shared the same emotions up to the final, all-too-regretted, curtain, no matter whether he went on to a restaurant, or back home, in his own carriage (by then equipped with rubber tires), or in a rattling hansom cab, or even on foot.

CHAPTER XXXV

EVERY MAN A PHOENIX

A neglected shop in a sad little back street; that is what the bookstore and
publishing firm from which Charles Péguy launched his *Cahiers de la
Quinzaine* looks like on a contemporary photograph. Péguy's passionate
love of truth and justice had turned him into a socialist at an early age,
and later into an enthusiastic Dreyfusard and supporter of Jaurès, whom
he worshipped as a standardbearer of honesty and humanity. In one
of the first *Cahiers*, he congratulated Jaurès on his defense of reason and
science against Brunetière, a convert to Catholicism and one who, in his
notorious "Après une visite au Vatican",[1] had spoken of the "bankruptcy
of science." (Later Péguy himself was to repent and return to Brunetière's
fold.)[2] Once Dreyfus had been vindicated and the victors were preparing
to reap the political fruits of their triumph, Péguy was suddenly struck
by "the conflict between the mystical and political elements of Drey-
fusism."[3] Supported by a group of young, but by no means kindred
seekers after the truth, including Rolland, Daniel Halévy, the brothers
Tharaud, and Julien Benda, he devoted his *Cahiers* to defence of a "mystique" that, at first, he identified with "disinterested and whole-hearted
devotion to a cause, unto death." For fifteen years he and his paper
lived in blessed poverty, years in which his "mystique" was transformed
from what he himself later called "the notorious metaphysics of progress" into Catholicism outside the church and a fervent type of nationalism that, in fact, he had never completely forsworn.

Péguy's work did not have any formative or revolutionary influence
on the literature of this century. His main aim was to hammer home his
own ideas, and the only original thing about him was that occasionally,
and especially in his *Mystères*, he broke through the dam of traditional
verse to let his ideas pour forth as free verse or rhythmic prose. But
then, so did Claudel, Suarès, Yeats, and Arno Holz. Holz, though he
liked to think of himself as an entirely independent innovator,[4] had an
obvious precursor in Walt Whitman, whose *Leaves of Grass* had appeared
in 1855. "Verse is wherever rhythm is found," wrote Mallarmé, "except
in advertisements and on the last page of the newspaper."[5] The true

renewal of form had to come from men who wrestled with their alienated emotions and perceptions, not from a Péguy who, if he is read at all today, is read exclusively for his defence of a church he himself had rejected for its opportunism and total lack of *caritas*. Yet he deserves to stand at the head of this chapter if only because his obstinate attachment to purity was so typical a reflection of the spirit of the age: the rebellion against the rule of reason. When we call Péguy a *pure* representative of that rebellion, we do so because his conversion from socialism to religion and nationalism was based on conscientious scruple, not on opportunism and, in fact, gained him no personal advantage. Nor was it a mere attempt to shift personal responsibility on to impenetrable metaphysical forces; like all the greatest symbolists, he tried to go beyond rationalism in order to reach a rational understanding of the irrational. This is precisely what Bergson and Freud, too, tried to do in their particular spheres. Small wonder that Péguy's last essay in the *Cahiers* was a passionate defense of his teacher, Bergson, whose work had just been placed on the Index, and he had far more right to call himself Bergson's pupil than the large numbers who flocked to the master's fashionable lectures and believed that they were participating in an "attack on the monster of Intellectualism."[6] "Bergsonism has been telling modern society precisely what it wants to hear," wrote Benda;[7] what he should have said was that modern society heard in Bergson what it wanted to hear. Like Bergson, Péguy veered from rationalism to "Intuitionism," to recapture the mystical tendencies of his youth. Like Bergson, who, in his *Évolution créatrice*, acknowledged that the industrial revolution had given rise to valuable new ideas and new human relationships, Péguy at no time rejected reason as a tool of knowledge. In this respect, at least, he enjoyed the support of Leo XIII (one of the pioneers of neo-Thomism), who, afraid that the baby might be thrown out with the bathwater, defended "natural reason" against "subjective thought" in one of his encyclicals.[8]

Words like "rebellion" and "revolution" are not too strong to describe the changes in literature that occurred at the turn of the century, and were, in fact, frequently used, especially in Germany, where new ideas mushroomed as nowhere else and were all the vaguer for it, as we may gather from Carl Bleibtreu's *Revolution der Literatur* (1886) and Arno Holz's *Revolution der Lyrik* (1899).[9] Outside Russia, this "revolution" rarely had socio-political implications, and, if it did, often no more than incidentally and, so to speak, symbolically as with Rimbaud. The movement included widely divergent trends, reflecting a broad spectrum of opinion and national backgrounds. But all who belonged to it were agreed on one thing: that there must be absolute freedom to express every possible truth in every possible form.

526

Among young intellectuals, respect for the bourgeois founders of the French Revolution had been swept away by contempt for their time-saving heirs who profited from the enormous technical and economic developments for which their elders had paved the way, but ignored their humanitarian ideals. This explains why so many of the young rebels ended up in or near the socialist camp. Not for them the lures of purely literary innovations; they preferred to follow in the footsteps of the great nineteenth-century masters, though at a different tempo. Anatole France, Thomas Hardy, George Bernard Shaw, H. G. Wells, Heinrich Mann, and also such poets as Richard Dehmel and Herman Gorter, must be placed in this group.

The great dramatic tensions (even of some socialist writers) remained so many bourgeois tensions, with two unfortunate but inevitable consequences. The first was a hankering after social distinction: many adopted more or less fictitious noble pedigrees and identified themselves and their work with the scions of an ancient race or with figures from the romanticized Middle Ages. Their ranks included Rilke, George, Proust, Huysmans, Villiers de l'Isle Adam, Maeterlinck, Wilde, and Nietzsche. Erich Heller has rightly said of Rilke and Nietzsche that both were uprooted and homeless.[10] The first wrote: "He who is homeless now, no longer builds a home," and the second: "Woe to him who lacks a home." In their detestation of the democratic vulgarity of their age, both harped on their own nobility. They looked to the past for the answers to their own artistic problems: "I believe in all that was left unspoken / . . . / What no one dared to say, / will one day be instinct."[11]

All these hankerers after an aristocratic past thought of themselves as "disinherited souls," unhappy in the bourgeois world because "the whole man moves at once."[12] Even D. H. Lawrence, one of the few great writers with working-class origins — his *The White Peacock* of 1911 was the first of a long series of books challenging the mores of the bourgeoisie — was not free of the bourgeois yearning for distinction, while Gide, with his sermons on morals without morality (begun with his *Nourritures terrestres* of 1897) and his postulate of absolute honesty, was irresistibly thrown back upon the hypocrisy of his bourgeois ancestors. The same is true of Thomas Mann, whose *Buddenbrooks* (1901) was a melancholy but unsentimental analysis of the decline of a patrician family, but whose *Tod in Venedig* (Death in Venice), 1913, produced a super-bourgeois, semi-autobiographical hero with an unmistakable touch of snobbery.

The second consequence of the literary rebellion we are examining here was the espousal of Evil, the deliberate attempt to stand bourgeois ethics on its head by what were often grotesque glorifications of satanic

527

forces. It had all begun as far back as 1857 with Beaudelaire's *Fleurs du mal*[13] — it was not by chance that his work was not generally appreciated until shortly after 1880. Its true high priest was J. K. Huysmans, who completed the transition from naturalistic to diabolic prose within a few years, and whose novel, *Là-bas*, reads almost like a reference work on demonolatry.[14] Oscar Wilde used similar ideas in his *The Picture of Dorian Gray*, which appeared that same year, to be greeted as the quintessence of *fin de siècle* decadence. Originally — and especially in the poetry produced during the last decades of the century — these shifts in attitude went hand in hand with almost frenzied attempts to discover new forms of expression for inexpressible experiences. Much as nineteenth-century science owed its most striking advances to the adoption of an evolutionary approach, so the ideas of continuous change, this entirely novel interpretation of the *panta rei*, together with the urge to delve ever more deeply into every possible phenomenon, led to a tremendous broadening of literary horizons. Yet as literature probed more deeply, it found life itself increasingly impenetrable, its meaning increasingly obscure, and personal responsibility ever more onerous to bear. This explains why so many writers at the turn of the century preferred to drift along on a wave of emotional and mystical impulses. "Nowadays, two things seem to be modern: the analysis of life and the escape from life . . . Many are deeply immersed in anatomical studies of their own psyche or their dreams . . . Modern, too, are old furnishings and youthful irritation . . . Modern is . . . the splitting of atoms and the playing of ball-games with the universe; modern the dissection of moods, passions, and doubts; and modern, finally, the instinctive, almost somnambulistic surrender to Beauty in all its manifestations," wrote Hugo von Hofmannsthal in an article on Gabriele d'Annunzio.[15] Modern was every form of rejection of anything that had gone before, and the word "modern" replaced "old" and "antique" as a token of excellence. The uncertainty that weighed on European life during this period had a stimulating as well as a paralysing effect: it stimulated such disciplines as economics, sociology, and psychology but it also suggested the "bankruptcy of reason"; it encouraged poets and novelists to fathom the unfathomable and the magical power of the word, but it also encouraged them to put their faith in all sorts of false gods and supernatural forces. Thus the French poet, Paul Adam, saw fit to abandon materialism for "the reality of the supernatural world, the influence of the planets, the Chaldean tradition, the Cabbala, chiromancy and graphology."[16] This type of conversion was entirely to the taste of a large section of the reading public, who sought spiritual salvation in a "thousand and one prophets," and literary solace in the romances of a Marie Corelli.

528

Another characteristic of the times was the isolation of the poet. Resistance, unless it is practiced under the banner of a unifying cause, always spells isolation. Those who failed to find the cause in a new religious, nationalist or socialist ideal, felt like fledglings thrown out of their nests. The gulf between citizen and poet was, however, nothing new. Yeats, who was exceptionally sensitive to it, uttered the following plaint: "Had not Europe shared one mind and heart, until both mind and heart began to break into fragments a little before Shakespeare's birth?"[17] This sense of isolation had already been marked in the romantic school, a group of anti-bourgeois outsiders buffeted by the cold winds of Bohemia. At the end of the century, isolation began to look like total excommunication: utter loneliness in the midst of a crowd. No wonder that it was the central theme of the work of Thomas Mann, whose chief concern, according to Josef Kunz, was "to rediscover, at the highest level of consciousness, the human bonds that used to be taken for granted in the pre-bourgeois period."[18] The gradual process of alienation had reached crisis point: all European poets of note turned their backs on their own cultural background and either dreamed of a golden future of human solidarity based on the pre-bourgeois, general human pattern[19] of medieval or primitive man, or rather on what they mistook for it, or else withdrew completely into themselves.

Now, this was not the first time that a cultural crisis should have encouraged a return to the past: the Renaissance had done just that, but far from denying reality it had tried to refurbish old norms. Nietzsche's Superman may have been an idealized self-portrait, but it was also a desperate appeal for recognition, for the resurrection of Renaissance man, one who did not have to share the fate of a Rimbaud — whose *Bateau ivre* Clouard called a "song of extreme loneliness"[20] — or of a Mallarmé, whose mystical writings were a response to his isolation: "At this moment," he had declared, "we are witnessing a truly exceptional spectacle: every poet is playing what music he likes best on his own flute and in his own little corner; for the first time poets have ceased to sing in chorus."[21] He added a strange explanation of what he meant by "exceptional spectacle": "Balanced or positive art cannot flourish in a society devoid of balance or cohesion. Our imperfect social organization, which also explains our intellectual unrest produces that mysterious need for individuality of which present-day literature is the direct reflection." Valéry, for his part, withdrew for twenty years to perfect his own imagination before returning to poetry. The deliberate isolation of Stefan George assumed a more aristocratic form; and so did that of Huysmans, with his medieval reminiscences, or of Villiers de l'Isle Adam, with his Wagnerian *Axel*. In general, too, it was becoming increasingly obvious that the poet had abandoned lyricism, with one clear exception: Yeats, who never laid down his Irish harp. Rilke, harking back to the enchantment of Love and Death, rationalized his fear of life with the sacrifice of the poet who renounces his fate: "Perhaps the poet has been placed above fate and becomes ambiguous, imprecise and implausible whenever he heeds its call. The hero was brought to truth by fate: the poet is rendered mendacious by it."

All of them were haughty individuals, shut in on themselves, and cut off from their environment: "Every man alone . . . a phoenix."[22]

Unique was the response of W. B. Yeats and his younger compatriot, John Synge. For Yeats, the pre-bourgeois world was not a dream beckoning from the past, but a tangible reality surviving in "backward" Ireland, the paradise of his youth, where people still lived in mystical union with nature, treasuring time and refusing to barter it away. To him, the struggle against England was one of natural human decency against the vulgarity and materialism of the modern, bourgeois world. To him, as to Gorter, for whom the Promised Land lay in a socialist future, life and poetry were fused into an indivisible whole, and like Gorter, he traveled the length and breadth of his country to proclaim his message. As against Rilke's rejection of fate, and as against Villiers de l'Isle Adam's dictum, "Living is something we leave to our servants," he declared roundly: "I shall, if good luck or bad luck make my life interesting, be a great poet."[23] He stood out like Gorter, a vital figure in the midst of a generation of listless poets (many of whom died young) who had turned their listlessness into a virtue. Nor was he the only vitalist on whom fascism would later cast its spell.

The ambivalent desire to make one's every nuance felt even while shutting oneself away either with a chosen élite or in a closed dream world of one's own, sometimes led to obscurity and mysticism or, as with George and several later poets, to the creation of a special language that, being the true vehicle of primitive emotions, was alleged to be universally understandable. In general, poetic language gained tremendously in tension, meaning, and expressive force from the obsessive wish to give new depths to all, even the most ordinary words. Rilke asserted that the poet would infuse fresh color into even such humble, everyday words as "und," "der," "die" and "das": "Die armen Worte, die im Alltag darben, / die zagen, blassen Worte lieb ich so. / Aus meinen Festen schenk ich ihnen Farben, / da lächeln sie und werden langsam froh."[24] It was in France that poets first embraced symbolism, and traced its roots back to Baudelaire and Lautréamont and, through them, to Poe, in whom Baudelaire claimed he could recognize himself. Baudelaire also discovered many of the concepts that were later called "symbolistic" in the works of Swedenborg and E. T. A. Hoffman. Mallarmé, the leading French symbolist, found his earliest inspiration in Keats and the Pre-Raphaelites. "Naming an object," he asserted, "means forfeiting three quarters of the pleasures of a poem, for that pleasure springs from the satisfaction of guessing by stages: to suggest, to evoke — that is the true delight of the imagination."[25]

With symbolism we have barely touched on the essence of the renewal of poetry. For our common speech, too, teems with symbols, and poets had always used symbols to evoke emotions. The symbols of Dante, for example, were traditional and hence generally accessible, logical and clear. The new symbolists, by contrast, tried to develop a "primitive symbolism": one so basic that it would strike a chord in every man's heart. But as Proust, who considered himself a defender of traditional French clarity against the "obscurity" of symbolism, put it: "By pretending to ignore the 'accident of time and place' and to present us with eternal truths, symbolism ignores another law of life, the command to realize the general and eternal, but only in the individual. In literature, no less than in life, those men are most individualistic who have most to give to others (*cf. War and Peace* and *The Mill on the Floss*), and we can say of them that they represent the universal spirit in the widest sense when they are most themselves."[26] Proust refused to see that this was precisely what the symbolists were trying to do, and that, as a result, the greatest poems of Rimbaud, Mallarmé, Appolinaire, Yeats, Rilke, and Gorter were able to convey flashes of illumination in a few, bare words. Gorter has been called "a blaze, / a wave, a flame, / an eruption of nature,"[27] and Rimbaud said that the true poet was a prophet, indeed had to turn himself into one, for "the poet truly steals fire."[28]

It is fascinating to follow the parallel but often widely separated paths of the various "symbolists": what Rimbaud discovered in an outburst of visionary fire, Yeats found in the primitive symbols of Celtic mythology, Rilke in a highly personal form of Christian mysticism, and Gorter in what might be called a pantheistic mystique, based on Man and Reason. All of them expressed what has been called rather superficially a reaction to naturalism and rationalism, but what in the most important of them was, rather, a way of carrying these doctrines to their ultimate conclusions, and in the greatest of them never a denial of reason. Even Maeterlinck, whom Yeats, his great admirer, censured for being one of a group that had perfected the art of "picking stories and symbols where it pleased,"[29] believed firmly that he was doing no more than plumbing the mysteries of life and death. He owed his tremen-

531

dous but short-lived fame not only to the part he played in the development of the modern theater, but also to his unusually profound view of life, which offered the questing soul liberation through the fusion of modern science with modern mysticism.[30]

The greatest of these poets were appalled at the decay they observed all around them, at the total divorce of emotion from reason. The creative explosion of a Rimbaud may be considered a deliberate *dérèglement de tous les sens*, which, he believed, was a prerequisite of the full unfolding of his creative powers. Valéry, no less haunted, but more controlled — one might almost say, more careful — placed the creative process above what it created, and devoted twenty years of his life to its study and to the discovery of the link between poetic emotion, intellectual reflection, and even mathematics. To him, poetry became an intellectual game, a methodical distillation of essences and a total renunciation of such arbitrary devices beloved of epic poets as "La marquise sortit à cinq heures."[31]

He must have been deeply angered by Anatole France, whose satirical novel *Histoire contemporaine* had recently been published, and who had written to a friend: "Least of all can I forgive the symbolists their deep obscurity; I cannot believe in a literary school that expresses difficult thoughts in obscure language."[32]

France's own Latin *clarté* was derided by Valéry rather ungenerously in 1927, when he took his place in the Académie with the customary *éloge* to France, his predecessor,[33] and suggested that the latter's *clarté* was synonymous with superficiality. The generation gap this remark revealed was wide indeed. France, the great sceptic and naturalist, could not conceive of *clarté* without the certainties of nineteenth-century science, and, like so many of his contemporaries, refused to look into the abyss of the irrational that the symbolists were busily exploring, not for the purpose of becoming lost in its dark caverns but to map it more carefully. Valéry, obsessed with his introspective quest, failed to realize that the intellect knows no upper or lower limits and that it can scan the heights of human destiny no less searchingly than it can probe into the darkest recesses of man's soul. "The greatest objection that can be leveled against the symbolist school," wrote Gide, who had gone back on his own symbolist work, *Les Cahiers d'André Walter*, in his *Les Nourritures terrestres*, "is that it lacks curiosity about life" — a remark that could equally well have been made by the symbolist Yeats. In this remark, incidentally, he was being unjust to those symbolists — in the broad sense — who had gone far beyond individualism to tackle existential problems of life that had previously been the preserve of philosophers. Much more radical even than the symbolists, whom he rejected as "com-

532

promisers," was René Ghil, the "founder" of the *école instrumentiste*. Basing himself on Helmholtz's theory of resonance, he tried to develop a "purely scientific form of poetry" through "analysis followed by synthesis" — an attempt that was bound to lead to the most esoteric form of subjectivism.

The slumbering rational element in symbolism surfaced most clearly in its affinity with music, that combination of indefinable sensations and strict constructions. Whereas poets of the preceding generation had had a particularly intimate bond with painting, Valéry wrote in 1920: "What is called symbolism can be summarized as the common inclination of various groups of poets . . . to seek salvation in music."[34]

"Comme de longs échos, qui de loin se confondent . . ./ Les parfums, les couleurs et les sons se répondent,"[35] Baudelaire had written earlier, thus anticipating later speculations on *audition colorée*. In his *Art poétique*, Verlaine looked to poetry for *"de la musique avant toute chose,"*[36] and he entitled one of his collections of poems *Romances sans paroles*. And Mallarmé said: "The young [i.e., the symbolists] have turned directly to music, as if nothing had gone before."[37] Yeats explained that the symbolist movement had found perfection in Germany with Wagner, in England with the Pre-Raphaelites, and in France with Villiers de l'Isle Adam (whose dramatic prose poem *Axel* had a marked Wagnerian touch), Mallarmé and Maeterlinck. The titles of some of his own poems — *The Wind Among the Reeds* and *The Shadowy Waters* — are reminiscent of Debussy. That the symbolists should have been drawn to Wagner is as inexplicable today as is their attraction to Nietzsche.[38]

By contrast, Tolstoy inveighed bitterly against the erotic fascination of music in his *Kreutzer Sonata* (1889), a book that was considered too "revealing" and had to be sold under the counter in Germany — and, no doubt, elsewhere as well.[39]

It is hard to prove that a number of young intellectuals at the turn of the century committed suicide because they could not bear their isolation, thus acting like so many fictional heroes — seven of Fontana's short stories end in suicide. What is quite certain is that the sense of isolation, the longing for greater fellowship, the nostalgic hankering after the irrational, and the exaltation of traditional solutions were responsible for the large number of religious conversions among poets and writers, especially in France[40] (Bourget, Coppée, Brunetière, Jammes, and Claudel) but also in England (Oscar Wilde, Aubrey Beardsley, Lionel Johnson, and Ernest Dowson). A related but even more absolute *Credo quia absurdum* — the title of a novel by Nico van Suchtelen — was the adoption of faith for faith's sake. A highly talented Dutch spokesman of that creed was

Frederik van Eeden, who in the course of his life espoused a variety of contemporary intellectual causes: irrationalism, or rather anti-rationalism, in his novel *De kleine Johannes* (1885), social humanitarianism in his colony, Walden, and a saccharine form of theosophy, only to end up in the safe bosom of Mother Church. But midway in his career he wrote what, in retrospect, appears to be his most important work: at the exact turn of the century, the then forty-year old van Eeden produced *Van de koele meren des doods*, a shrewd literary and psychological, indeed psychiatric analysis of the emotional life of a woman, at odds with the times.[41]

Paul Bourget, the fervent anti-Dreyfusard, might be called a political convert to Catholicism, for his *Le Disciple* of 1889 and *L'Étape* of 1902, far from advocating a return to a mystical faith, called for the restoration of order through the rejection of the Revolution, of the general franchise, and of "nihilism." Catholicism and science must oppose democracy. His individualism expressed itself in his traditionalism; much the same was true of Maurice Barrès, whose trilogy *Le Culte du moi* (1888-1891) was an attempt to probe the "ego" to its fullest depths. Barrès's Nietzschean rejection of "mass man" led him into the shifting sands of corporatism: the body of the Church, according to him, was the ground of man's individuality. He, too, fell under the spell of Wagner's dreams, but, unlike Yeats and Villiers de l'Isle Adam, he was more attracted to the nationalist and racist doctrines of the magician of Bayreuth. Thus, in his second cycle, the *Roman de l' énergie nationale* (1897-1902), Barrès propounded a purely French version of racism and of blood-and-soil ideology, and became one of the fiercest of French revanchists.

The search for certainty and the hypertrophied individualism that went with it also marked the long series of novels written by J. K. Huysmans, whose hesitant conversion occurred midway in his literary career. Huysmans tried to recover certainty, especially in *À Rebours* (1885) which made a great impression on his contemporaries, by declaring personality the sovereign and central force of man's existence, and by advocating a return to a collective life that, in his case, too, was based on a pre-bourgeois and pre-capitalist pattern.

Such attempts to find release from the vulgar masses by more or less mystical union with a new collective, and detachment from the lures of society, often went hand-in-hand with the adoption of vague ideals or of words as magical incantations, an art in which Mallarmé excelled. It all went with respect for the closed cultural pattern of the Golden Age (Proust, Brunetière, Faguet), the Gothic cathedral (Ruskin, Proust, Huysmans), a hankering after the monastic life (Huysmans, Rilke), and a withdrawal from, indeed a challenge to, the utilitarian and hypocritical bourgeois ethos and the fatalism of psychological determinism — "escape from the deadly slavery of materialism and threadbare conventions into a meaningful, intense, beautiful, personal and if necessary daring, life, which alone vouchsafes deep satisfaction and the most exciting experiences";[42] not only to be a poet but also to live as one, to bridge the gulf between the poet's dream and existence through true communion. " . . . That name is royal. / And to wear it like a queen I dare not,"[43] Elizabeth Barrett Browning wrote of the poet's title. Now that the name had lost so much of its royal luster, it was being flaunted as a princely title, one that placed its owner above the law and above society. It transformed his isolation magically into a deliberate escape from the "profane masses," a dedicated acceptance of the "rule of life" (George) or, as with Rilke before his "conversion" in about 1914, changed his fear of life into a conscious renunciation of Fate: "Denn irgendwo ist eine alte Feindschaft / zwischen dem Leben und der grossen Arbeit."[44] This aristocratic approach persuaded Rilke to describe himself as a "pure poet"; in Wilde, it was tempered with irony and an irrespressible urge to deflate pomposity. George, for his part, appointed himself "priest-king" and d'Annunzio went to bed in his buskins, a demigod in his own day.

Nietzsche believed that the poet's role in and against society must become the central theme of poetry, essay-writing and poetic conversation .[45] To Yeats, who appears to have been familiar with Nietzsche, poetry was a spiritual vocation; he spoke of the "infallible church of the poetic tradition" made up of artists, philosophers and theologians — a parallel to Nietzsche's "poets, philosophers and prophets." Donne's "Everyman . . . a phoenix" had become "Every poet a superman." Treitschke spoke of the poets' "impotent delusion of grandeur, the sickness of our century."[46]

The poet's aloofness needed to be given outward expression by such trappings as slouch hats, velvet jackets and billowing cloaks, not to mention a host of more personal idiosyncrasies. Oscar Wilde set all London talking with his clothes no less than with his epigrams.

His surroundings, too, had to accentuate the poet's personality and set him off from the vulgar horde outside. It was the age of fanciful and exotic studios and attics, with draperies on all the walls. In Berlin, George read his poetry to select circles in Rembrandtesque candlelight from elegant *Jugendstil* volumes set in type styled on his own handwriting, dressed all the while in the most outlandish clothes.

The inconstant hero of Huysmans's *À Rebours*, a decadent scion of a noble race, had his sitting-room so divided and furnished that he could recapture the emotional atmosphere of each of his favorite books at will. The valet wore Flemish dress that reminded his master of his ties with the Middle Ages. We also find accounts of such bizarre quarters in Henry James,[47] in Yeats's *Temple of the Alchemical Rose*, and in George Moore's *Confessions of a Young Man*, which contains a detailed description of the author's bizarre apartment in one of the old houses in Rue de la Tour des Dames, Paris. Its windows "overlooked a bit of tangled garden with a dilapidated statue." The drawing room was "in cardinal red, hung from the middle of the ceiling and looped up to give the appearance of a tent; a faun, in terra cotta, laughed in the red gloom, and there were Turkish couches and lamps. In another room you faced an altar, a Buddhist temple, a statue of Apollo and a bust of Shelley. The bedrooms were made unconventional with cushioned seats and rich canopies; and in picturesque corners there were censers, great church candlesticks and palms . . . I bought a Persian cat and a python that made a monthly meal of guinea pigs; Marshall, who did not care for pets . . . used to sleep beneath a tree of gardenias in full bloom."[48] Could anything be more redolent of decadence than this description?

Moore was not a great writer, but a hyper-individualist and an extremely sensitive seismographer, and hence more typical of his age than many a great author. He savored the poetry of Baudelaire, Verlaine, Mallarme, and Rimbaud and was highly susceptible to the magic of words and symbols. Verlaine, in particular, appealed to him for his withdrawal from "all commerce with virtue and vice . . . a licentiousness more curiously subtle and penetrating than any other; and the licentiousness of the verse is equal to that of the emotion; every natural instinct of the language is violated and the simple music native in French metre is replaced by falsetto notes sharp and intense."[49]

He jotted down ideas of the kind Proust would later elaborate into a carefully devised system (which was the more remarkable in that Proust was probably unfamiliar with Moore's writings and, moreover, had a pronounced dislike of all the symbolists Moore so greatly admired). One of these ideas was what Moore called "echo-augury," "words heard in an an unexpected quarter, but applying marvellously well to the besetting difficulty of the moment."[50] Like so many of his contemporaries, Moore abandoned Zola's sober art of "scientific" observation, for the more highly metaphysical and somewhat irrational art of "heightened perception." He drew on the same sources to which Proust was to turn to a few decades later: listening to conversations with the "patience of a cat before a mousehole," the better to develop his "instinct for a rapid

536

notation of gestures and words,"[51] and to recapture the "magnetic, intense and vivid" memories of youth they evoke.[52]

When Moore returned to London in the 1880s as an artist manque with an empty purse, and tried, in the spirit of the sport of kings on which he had been nurtured, to make his way in literature, his Parisian past gained him entrance to the *fin de siècle* "decadents" — the symbolists who in the 1890s gathered round the *Yellow Book* of which Aubrey Beardsley was the art editor for a time. "Moore hated his own past in Zola," wrote Yeats,[53] and he went on to quote Moore's remark on the death of his former idol: "Anyone can get himself asphyxiated."

The whole tone of young England in the nineties was one of provocation and playful naughtiness. Oscar Wilde's circle, copying the example of Verlaine, drank nothing but absinthe, and liked to boast about their real or imaginary "purple sins." When Wilde went to hear sentence pronounced upon him for immoral conduct, he drove to court in an elegant carriage drawn by two horses, and carried a book under his arm. The daily press headlined the news that it had been *The Yellow Book*, to which, in fact, Wilde had never contributed a single word, and the lovers of decency smashed the publisher's windows.[54] "Young England," for its part, was determined to smash the Victorian Age with its moral and religious hypocrisy and insular self-satisfaction. This "self-criticism" may explain why British writers looked up much more to France than they were historically justified in doing. French romanticists, naturalists and symbolists had always followed a clearly defined theoretical program and hence seemed of purer metal than their English counterparts, though, in fact, what was now being welcomed so enthusiastically as a French innovation had been flowing for centuries in the undercurrents of English literature. Verse had been freed from its traditional shackles by that "great Barbarian" William Shakespeare — and the symbolists could have discovered many other familiar bonds with him as well. The courageous publisher, Vizetelly, had to pay for his translations of Zola's naturalist novels with fines, a spell in prison and, ultimately, because of his weak constitution, with his life, but Hardy's *Tess of the D'Urbervilles* (1891) and *Jude the Obscure* (1896) were no less naturalistic, except perhaps in declared intent, and produced a similar shock to Victorian sensibilities and especially to the owners of the great lending libraries who greatly preferred "decent" novels in three parts and the extra custom they brought. Moore, too, offended them with his *Esther Waters* (1894), a highly moral work in the best nineteenth-century English tradition, but one whose heroine was an unmarried mother, and which included a scene in a maternity ward. Some of Moore's neighbors pushed a torn copy of the book through his letter box in an envelope on which they had written: "Too foul to keep in a decent home."

Vizetelly's Zola was not the only attempt to put an end to the insular character of English literary life: translations poured from British presses, in particular of Ibsen,[55] the destroyer not of shrines but of whole temples, and of the other great Scandinavians and Russians. The Russians were also snatched up in France and Germany; in fact, the whole of western Europe seemed anxious to rejuvenate itself with the help of these "barbarians," much as the Roman Empire had done with its own. Here, too, it was a long time before it became clear that Kierkegaard, J. P. Jacobsen, Tolstoy, Turgenev, Dostoyevsky, and Chekhov were not so much innovators as interpreters of existing ideas and attitudes. Nietzsche, too, made his influence felt in England, if gradually. He was first mentioned in George Egerton's *Keynotes*, of 1893, and one of the first reviews of his work was published in *The Savoy* (successor to *The Yellow Book*) in 1896. (By the end of the century the attempt at a complete English edition of his work had to be abandoned for lack of interest.)[56]

Because of the lack of a formal program and of proper "schools," the children of the new spirit were more heterogeneous in Britain than they were on the Continent. In France, the symbolists in the widest sense were, by and large, uncommitted, meaning that they recognized no tradition and generally preferred the seventeenth or sixteenth century or even the Middle Ages to the rationalist eighteenth century they despised.

In England, by contrast, even the most divergent currents became fused in a common insistence on freedom: "If the one demanded freedom for an individual expression tending towards degeneration and perversion, the other demanded a freedom which should give the common man opportunities for the redemption of himself and his kind. Side by side with the *poseur* worked the reformer, urged on by the revolutionist."[57] All of them collaborated in a journal that declared proudly: "We are not Realists, or Romanticists or Decadents. For us all art is good which is good art."[58] The same atmosphere also lent itself to mockery and self-derision: "Though the Philistines may jostle, / you will rank as an apostle / in the high aesthetic band, / if you walk down Piccadilly / with a poppy or a lily / in your medieval hand."[59] No one could call Wilde, for all his worship of beauty, a completely uncommited writer, let alone such rationalists as Shaw, who in his *Quintessence of Ibsenism* praised Ibsen's naturalistic and didactic plays above his more poetic and symbolic products, or H. G. Wells. Such words as "new" and "renewal" were the order of the day in England (and elsewhere), and Walter Pater ushered in a new period with his: "Not the fruit of experience, but experience itself, is the end."[60] By experience he was not referring to the "experiments" of a later period, but to experience in the widest sense, which comprised the symbolists' probing of the unconscious no less than the conscious evaluation of one's relationship with one's fellow men and society. The thirst for experience extended even to the music hall and the variety theater and, as it were, culminated in a passion for the nonsensical: the nonsense refrain of "tarara-boom-de-ay" remained a hit for many years. The famous Parisian cabaret showed a similar predilection for puns, for bluntness (both in the risqué *chansons* of Yvette Guilbert and also in the social satires of Aristide Bruant) and for derision, something that was greatly appreciated even by bourgeois spectators who, as we saw, could not applaud these attacks on their own foibles loudly enough. Jean-Claude Carrière devoted a special chapter of his book on the humor of *la belle époque* to the *goût de l'absurde*, and another, incidentally, to *l'humour noir*.[61]

In Germany the division between socially committed writers and those exclusively concerned with the salvation of their own souls was much sharper. It was no accident that the central figures in both currents should have played the roles of Olympian and Priest-king so perfectly: Gerhard Hauptmann, who gave the German conscience such a sharp jolt with his *The Weavers* — but then, it was a historical drama, or was it? — and who, for many years, could remain the leading German writer because he absorbed later currents so impartially; and Stefan George, the narcissistic, purposeful, and revered leader of an élite made up of politically immature, and chiefly academic, intellectuals. After the First World War not a few of them, intoxicated with George's "New Reich" and by such verbiage as "The solution . . . will never [dawn upon] the many and least of all through words,"[62] marched blithely into the Third Reich, and though they were not propelled there by their prophet they were certainly not discouraged by him either.

On the sidelines stood Rilke, his face averted, for he believed that the poet had to withdraw from life "as far as possible," and also the many social critics who mocked at the Establishment in such papers as *Simplicissimus*. And then there were those two Austrian "outsiders," Hugo von Hofmannsthal and Schnitzler. Von Hofmannsthal had started as a "decadent," but, put on his guard by the enthusiasm with which George had tried to enlist him as a junior member of his "Circle," he became conscious of his duty "to open his soul to everything that sought admission," and went on to cast off the "burden of life" in a metaphysical

539

solution that found its climax in *Jedermann*. Schnitzler, for his part, took the detached view of the physician and arrived at the melancholy conclusion that all things were transitory and vain, and as fleeting as the Viennese waltz.

The rebellion against paternal authority, which in other countries went back to the 1880s, only touched Germany in the shadow of the First World War, and hence became all the fiercer: it could no longer be contained in the well-trodden paths of the singing Wandervogel youth movement, but exploded in the very names of such ephemeral expressionist journals as *Aktion*, *Sturm* (Storm), *Revolution*, *Neues Pathos* (New Pathos), *Der Brenner* (The Burner), *Der Ruf* (The Call),[63] all of which made their debut in about 1910, and loudly proclaimed their rejection of coercion in every form. Hauptmann, whose importance and glory, as we saw, stemmed from his spontaneous absorption of all the currents of his age, wrote: "Worte sind verwirrte Sprache. Schrei ist Klarheit, Schrei ist Wahrheit" (Words are confused speech. The scream is clarity, the scream is truth).[64] The only thing this "scream" made "clear" in the event, however, was that freedom had once again become an end in itself, regardless of the consequences. Those who went to war in 1914 were a generation without idealism and without heroes, and they would have to pay dearly for it.

It was an age without heroes or hero-worship, but not without a hidden longing for both. Kipling owed his renown to his ability to glorify the British Empire, and to do so sincerely. In France such disparate figures as Georges Sorel, Maeterlinck, and Rolland were all appalled by the spiritual vacuity of the age in which they lived. "Materialism without greatness . . . is asphyxiating the world. Let us throw open the windows and admit the fresh air. Let us breathe the breath of heroes,"[65] wrote Rolland at the beginning of his *Vie des hommes illustres*. All of them may have been chasing after shadows, but the need for devotion was nevertheless an essential antidote to the dissecting spirit of the age — how else explain the enthusiasm for the Boers even in such exclusive clubs as George's Circle? Rarely has the longing for the hero been depicted as poignantly as it was in Alain Fournier's *Le Grand Meaulnes* (1914).

At the turn of the century there occurred another shift in European literature, so marked, in fact, that many writers who were admired for their innovations by their contemporaries, for instance Maeterlinck, Huysmans, George, Wilde, d'Annunzio, Wells, Kipling, Hauptmann, and Rolland, came to be looked upon as second or even third-rate writers, men too involved in their age to stand the test of time. Thus the fame of Maeterlinck and George in their day rested on their "victory over rationalism", but that triumph was something that only a great poet and visionary of Rilke's stature could celebrate without losing his soul, and not even he without sometimes impairing the lucidity and living warmth of his work; or a Yeats, who was rooted in a pre-rationalist world and urged on by the spur of Irish nationalism. All great poets, like all great philosophers, are a mixture of rational and irrational motives.

Incomprehensibility was another facet of our period; it reflected the split between writers who addressed a literary élite and those who wrote for the masses. That split was quite different from the old distinction between great literature and the penny novelette. Such great writers as Dickens and Hugo had been read by all classes, but now a fresh boundary was drawn: on the one side Flaubert and the Pre-Raphaelites, together with Huysmans and Swinburne, Wilde and Mallarmé, George and Rilke, Proust and Gide, authors and poets who focussed attention on the artist in his relationship with, and isolation from, the bourgeoisie; and on the other hand writers and poets of varied renown who were chiefly concerned with the world around them, a group in which we must include all the great nineteenth-century Russians. They fell into that category either because they were not yet ready to deal with purely intra-bourgeois conflicts, or else because they refused to chase after individual fame, to be lured by the call of "Every man a phoenix." But the true miracle of the Russians was that, despite the social backwardness of their country, they did not produce naive peasant tales, but that, beginning with Pushkin and continuing with Gogol, Turgenev, Tolstoy, Dostoyevsky, and Chekhov, they continued to supply Western writers and the Western stage with new impulses, with new literary forms and fresh psychological insights.

Thomas Mann made the following entry in his diary, after having read the reminiscences of a Bavarian art critic: "Nothing but personalities! I do not think *I* am one. I shall be no more remembered than, say a Proust." This may seem a strange view of two authors whose work was so highly personal, and of whom one was, in later years, to personify the "good Germany," while the personality of the other has been the subject of hundreds of special studies. Yet it is true that these two recorders of the life of the French and German bourgeoisie, no less than their English counterpart, Galsworthy, remained hidden behind their work and did not become "personalities" in the sense that Wilde, Anatole France, Ibsen and Hauptmann did. There was an even more essential similarity between the two: both — and Proust much more than Mann — had a rejuvenating effect of the literature of their respective countries and the outside world, and this *without turning their backs on tradition*.

541

Both were essentially conservative. In politics, Mann was a *German* liberal, in contrast to his brother Heinrich, who was attracted to French influences, eventually embraced communism and abhorred the German spirit (*Der Untertan*). It was certainly not from democratic, let alone revolutionary, motives that Proust came to side with the Dreyfusards. Like Mann, he was a bourgeois writer who tried in vain to escape from his isolation in a bourgeois environment, not by rebellious attacks on society, by expressionist "screams" or a total rejection of the past, but by adopting an aristocratic stance and by returning to the pre-bourgeois period. He expressly rejected the symbolists' "lack of clarity."[66] Being much too original to be called anyone's successor, Proust nevertheless studied his beloved French classics, and the great seventeenth-century writers in particular, and in a lyrical paean to his mother tongue extolled the "antiquated" Anatole France as "one of the few who are still capable of using it."[67] He also admired George Eliot, whom most of his contemporaries scorned but in whom he discovered something of his *seconde mémoire*, and spoke highly of Ruskin, another innovator with an eye for the past.

Neither Mann nor Proust were directly responsible for the transformation of literature in their day, and their influence made itself felt much later: Proust's great work did not appear until 1913. Of the two new ideas and the associated literary techniques Proust applied with near-maniacal determination, that of the *seconde mémoire* or *mémoire involontaire* was anything but "original"; like all great ideas that are more than sleight-of-hand, it was rooted in its age. All Proust did was to systematize what had been foreshadowed not only by George Eliot, whom he mentioned by name, but also by Tolstoy, and what Moore had tried to formulate many years before.

No less incisive was Proust's second great idea, immortalized in the title of his *magnum opus*. Here, too, he was neither the first nor the only one to advance it: Couperus's *Van oude menschen, die dingen die vorbijgaan* (Old People and the Things that Pass) was published in 1906; Jens Peter Jacobsen's *Fru Marie Grubbe* had appeared as early as 1876, and though his work was not nearly as well-known in France as it was in Germany, Proust may well have come across it, and if he did he would certainly have recognized his own approach in it. Proust tried for more than twenty years to plumb the bottomless depths of his age; he had ceased to create characters, and instead paraded an endless series of tiny snapshots revealing the relativity of perceptions, attitudes and character. "And so it was she," he said of an old servant "who first suggested to me that a person does not, as I had believed, stand before one clearly and

542

motionless with all his virtues and failings . . . . but that he is a shadow, as likely to cover hatred as it is to cover love."[68] Proust, like no one else, reflected the two great motifs of his period: that of the *mémoire involontaire* and that of *temps perdu*; and no one has recorded the itinerary of his *recherche* as conscientiously as he did — at the cost of readability. It was the great tragedy of this lover of seventeenth-century clarity that he should have been one of the great unreadables, that though we tend to dip into Proust, we do not read him with the breathless fascination we bring to, say, a Dickens or a Tolstoy. He has not become dated like some of his contemporaries (Maeterlinck or d'Annunzio for example, men whose fame was much greater in their day) but of the many copies of his work in public libraries, only the first volume is usually well-thumbed. One of the most fascinating representatives of an age that rejected classicism has thus taken his place amongst the classics he so greatly admired, even in this respect.

CHAPTER XXXVI

NOA-NOA

One of the many letters the French painter Camille Pissarro, the oldest of the Impressionists — he was due to celebrate his seventieth birthday in July 1901 — wrote to his son Lucien, bore the date April 21, 1900. In it he spoke of a special Impressionist hall at the World Exposition. It would be set up in the Grand Palais, reserved for "modern" art, and would follow upon the work of the 1830 school. The art dealer Durand-Ruel had promised to see to everything. Durand's business associates, the Bernheims, father and son, had told him only yesterday that the idea was excellent and that it would cause a sensation. Even Cézanne would be hung. He was becoming highly popular, just imagine! His canvasses were fetching from 5000 to 6000 francs, but it was true that Sisleys and Monets were fast changing hands at 6000 to 10,000.[1]

This letter tells us a great deal about official recognition of modern art — modern in the sense of unfamiliar — to which people were taking the more readily as they had come to realize that Art Nouveau had been greatly overrated.

Yet it is open to doubt whether Pissarro's confidence in the victory of the art of light-and-color he had considered the only true form of art to have emerged during the past thirty years, was not somewhat premature. Paul Morand, the chronicler of the Exposition, took quite a different view. He mentioned a dozen or so names of now forgotten masters, but as for the Impressionists, Neo-Impressionists, and Nabis, he merely reported that none of them had been invited to exhibit their work, or else it had been tucked away under the stairs. He, too, mentioned a few prices, as if in response to Pissarro's letter: Monets had fetched 310 francs and Cézannes 150 francs at an auction.[2] The last price is more in keeping with the somewhat condescending protection Zola used to extend to Cézanne, the friend of his youth. In 1900 those who are now considered the great leaders of the last revolution in art still worked behind a wall of silence.[3]

Thus Pissarro himself wrote in a letter of slightly later date — 17 June — that he had visited the Exposition two days before and that he

had seen no more than two decent paintings: a Watts and a Chassériau —
the first an English painter of grandiose allegorical schemes; the other
a French Creole who tried to combine the classicism of Ingres with the
romanticism of Delacroix, and who had died as far back as 1856.[4]

We should not be dwelling at such length on art appreciation at the
turn of the century if it did not afford us an unexpected opportunity
to broach a subject that crops up in every chapter of this book: the two
distinct faces of a period that produced a Boldini and a Sargent as well
as a Cézanne and a van Gogh. It was not because of the generation gap
between them that the public prized the first two — both of them fashionable painters — above the two modernists, for van Gogh was three years
older than Sargent. Much the same was also happening to sculpture.
Thus while the art of the anecdotal, of optical illusions, sham decorations,
allegory, history, in short the whole waxwork display of a Dubois, a
Mercié, a Marqueste or even a Falguière, could be admired at the Exposition itself, Rodin was relegated to the corner of the Avenue de
l'Alma.[5]

Remarkable in this connection are the comments on art old and new
by the German art historian, Karl Woermann, in a book that appeared in
three impressions in as many months in 1894.[6] Woermann distinguished
the two faces of his age with the aid of the somewhat simplisitc device
of tracing all mid-ninteenth-century German painting back to Menzel
or Böcklin respectively (both advanced in years but still alive in 1900).
The first was said to represent "nature," the second "imagination" in
art. The "natural" group included Max Liebermann; the "imaginative"
group Max Klinger and the generation of Franz von Stuck and Ludwig
von Hofmann, who in 1900 were approaching their forties. In this way
the difference between the two "faces" was transformed from a historical into a philosophical or even a psychological distinction. However,
the young painters also had something else that set them off from the
older ones, something Woermann considered a justified reaction to the
antiquated academicism of the latter, although he regretted their lack
of inner balance and — naturally — of "contact with the German soul
without which no German art can achieve a lasting effect." His first
objection was not altogether invalid, at least if we bear in mind that
Georg Kolbe, for instance, had written, well before he became Germany's
most popular sculptor, that he "did not offer his work as a finished
product, but as something in the process of becoming, something kinetic
and dynamic."[7]

The two faces appeared most clearly of all in the polemics of the
period, and quite especially in the extreme views adopted by Erich Wich-

mann and Professor C. L. Dake respectively.[8] Their exemplary value is, however, greatly diminished by the fact that the modernist, Wichmann, produced considerably better arguments than the traditionalist, Dake, unless that very difference is considered symptomatic of the death rattle of the old spirit. For the good professor took the view that modern art was a clear manifestation of madness or of rank dishonesty, so that, sad though its products indubitably were, ordinary people did well to laugh them off. The more serious, however, of whom the professor was, of course, one, "saw an ogre of destruction the likes of which history had not produced for centuries." Curiously enough, he too blamed materialism, that scapegoat for all the evils of the day.[9]

The chronicler may leave it there, but the historian must go on to determine the precise moment, or rather the series of moments, in which the "center of gravity" of the age began to shift. This was the approach Pierre Francastel used in his profound study of the evolution of the spatial idea during the Renaissance, and its destruction, in our period. Finding it impossible to attach this transformation to a given person or place, he concluded that the real problem was to discover which works were true milestones in the history of art, lasting expressions of a given society.[10]

But Francastel said nothing at all about the social forces responsible for the transformation which, in our particular case, led to the emergence of modern art. On closer examination, we find that these forces were produced by the collapse of values accepted by the West for the past five hundred years, that is, since about the time of the Renaissance. The idealized view of the true, the good, and the beautiful from which the Greeks had derived the meaning of life and the form of their art, proved untenable during the last decade of the nineteenth century and hence lost its universal appeal.

In Burckhardt, that ideal was still unimpaired, as witness his unshakable faith in Raphael. Nietzsche's first-born, his *Geburt der Tragödie*, (Birth of Tragedy) took a different line: it shifted the stress from Apollo to Dionysus. Still, Nietzsche, too, remained a Greek, though not a classical one, and in this he was like Maillol and Braque, two modern champions of "order," so much so that Guillaume Apollinaire, "that impresario of the avant-garde," said of the second that his renewal of art had restored the social element to the society in which it had originated.[11] The first to forswear the Greek ideal explicitly was Gauguin, who wrote in October 1897 that "*the* great error was the Greek approach, however beautiful it may be."[12] Indeed the Greek influence oppressed him, perhaps more than anyone else, precisely because he was not blind to its quality and

546

realized how revoltingly spurious were its contemporary French imitators. It was from their lack of authenticity that he tried to escape by running off to Tahiti in 1891.

His flight was the unconscious and symbolic expression of two tendencies that presided over the birth of modern art: the search for the genuine, the original, and the true, and the quest for primitive values. Gauguin himself said just that, and as early as 1890. Having inveighed against the "abominable error of naturalism" which "started with the Greeks from Pericles onwards," he went on to argue that truth resides in the purely cerebral art of the Egyptians, which was primitive and yet the most erudite of all.[13]

As if to bear him out, our period witnessed an almost general growth of appreciation of primitive "originality," reflected both in a revulsion from the "poison" of the prevailing attitude and also in a return to the unpoisoned sources of the past. Much as Gauguin looked to the Egyptians, so others began to look to the medieval Flemish artists for "primitive" qualities. "Primitive" had suddenly become a fashionable term, even in England, where it was first applied to art in 1892.[14] The appreciation of Japanese art, and of colored woodcuts in particular, was of somewhat earlier provenance. Van Gogh had been deeply impressed by it all, and admiration for Hokusai grew apace at the turn of the century.[15] Bonnard, one of the five painters of the Nabis, a group in Paris which Félix Vallotton immortalized on canvas in 1902, even earned himself the nickname of *Nabi très japonard*.[16] This trend was encouraged further by the expansion of the historical horizons with which we have dealt in Chapter XXX. Museums became crowded with objects from distant times and lands, collected as curios but suddenly elevated into great works of art. It was thus that Ernst Ludwig Kirchner, later renowned as an abstract painter, "discovered" while still an architectural student at the Technical High School in Dresden that the Negro sculptures he came across in the local museum in 1904 were parallels of his own work.[17] Toulouse-Lautrec, Degas, Picasso, and Matisse made similar discoveries when they unearthed various prehistoric and primitive treasures in Parisian antique shops. Modigliani, in particular, found inspiration in "Negro art," and especially in the demonic, dramatic, or tranquil ancestral masks that kept pouring into Europe in the wake of imperialist advances in Africa and the Pacific islands. An exhibition of Oriental art held in 1903 made a deep impression on Matisse and on many other artists.[18] The link between primitivism and modernism was brought to unique perfection in the work of Henri Rousseau, nicknamed "le douanier".[19] Growing interest in folk art, children's paintings, and the work of mental patients

547

had the same source: the appreciation of primitive ideas. The influence of folk art was particularly pronounced in those marginal areas of Europe where the "universal human pattern" had not disappeared entirely: in Norway, Russia, and Spain. It was most noticeable in the work of Jawlensky, Kandinsky, and Chagall. A similar trend also appeared in music, in the works of the Spanish composer Pedrell, who began to apply it consistently in 1890, of de Falla,[20] Stravinsky, but also of Ravel, to mention only a few, and in literature with the poetry of Yeats. This whole revival, based on a return to a primitive past, would have been impossible without a renunciation of the ideals of the Renaissance and the rejection of historicism. Gauguin, who at times when his spirit gained the better of his poverty, sickness, and neglect, showed the qualities of a great writer, once expressed this radical transformation with inimitable brevity and precision: "Back to the horses of the Parthenon, indeed right back, back to my rocking horse." Apollinaire put it more learnedly but no less incisively when he wrote that traditional was to modern painting as literature was to music — an allusion to the abstract qualities of modern art. Another characteristic of the latter was its extreme subjectivity. The change from objectivity to subjectivity has been examined at length by Max Raphael, whose *Von Monet zu Picasso* was published in 1913. Of the Impressionists he said that, even while adhering to realism, they allowed their own vision of color and form to prevail above the "natural"; theirs was a preparation for modern art — not yet modern art itself.[21] A further step towards more extreme subjectivism was taken with Neo-Impressionism, or Pointillism and Divisionism, as the Italians liked to call it. It was ushered in when Seurat exhibited his *Baignade à Asnières* in the "Salon des Indépendants" in 1884. In this group of painters, the mixture of two conflicting currents — subjectivism and scientism — was so strange that one suspects it may have crept in as an uninvited guest. For all that, the Neo-Impressionists could have justified themselves by referring to a scientific theory advanced by Fénéon and Sutter, based on the optical studies of Chevreul and Helmholtz, Maxwell's experiments and N. O. Rood's measurements.[22] But Max Raphael was right to assert in 1913 that a scientific theory could not bridge the gulf between the rational determination to create order and the surrender to momentary and individual sensations. Neo-Impressionism, he added, was a first and, according to him, mistaken, step away from naturalism; Seurat and Signac paid much more attention to the subject than the Impressionists had done, even though they still prized rational detachment.[23] All that would change, not so much with Cubism as with Futurism, two movements built on the foundations of Neo-Impressionism.

Other characteristic features of the two decades round the turn
of the century were also reflected in modern art, and plainly so. They
cannot easily be reduced to a common denominator, for they were often
in conflict, and their common factor can only be inferred from their
dialectical interactions. Thus there was, on the one hand, the aestheticism
of the art for art's sake school: "Art never expresses anything but itself,"
Oscar Wilde proclaimed. On the other hand, there was the socially committed school to whom art was a means of expressing something greater
than itself.

The first school betrayed its social attitudes not despite but because
of its aloofness from society. In fact, it was not so much that the artist
had deliberately withdrawn from society as that society had stripped
him of his social role. Art no longer had eternal values to bestow upon
society, and, thrown back upon itself, it became a personal philosophy,
indeed a way of life.[24] True, isolated individuals such as the young Baudelaire had already played the refined dandy, whose highest law was
Beauty, but now this attitude was adopted on a much broader scale.
It was no accident that Baudelaire only attained fame in the 1880s —
twenty years after his death. The dandies at the turn of the century,
by contrast, acquired fame in their own lifetime, albeit they were hated
by "decent" society. Baudelaire found a worthy successor in Mallarmé,
whose "hermetic" poetry was widely acclaimed soon after Huysmans
had sung his praises in A Rebours (1885). Oscar Wilde, in his fame no
less than in his notoriety, was perhaps the most striking figure of this
strange world, unless he had to cede pride of place to Stefan George with
his esoteric circle of disciples. The Netherlands, anything but fertile soil
for this exotic lifestyle, nevertheless boasted a Couperus: a declared
aesthete, but like Wilde too much the artist not to be more than that,
and a van Deyssel, too much the pure aesthete to make a lasting impression. The ideal of a sacrosanct cenacle was warmly embraced by
many, even though in the cold light of lack of talent and money it often
looked rather threadbare. Young men like Arnold Zweig's fictional student, Karl Steinitz, could be found in every European city by the score,
if not by the hundreds. Most of them provided modern psychiatry with
a welcome series of experimental subjects, until the storm of 1914 cured
them of their aesthetic intoxication or cut short their young lives.[25]

Their detestation of existing society drove a number of artists —
and not the least among them — to join a protest movement that had
arisen not out of pity or even compassion for, but simply out of feelings
of solidarity with, the working class — feelings, as we saw, that were
not confined to artistic circles alone. Gauguin gave voice to this protest

549

in his own way: by his escape in 1891 from the "refined civilization" he abhorred, first to Tahiti and a primitive "barbarism" in which the essential values had been preserved, and when it appeared that western influences had crept in even there, on to the Marshall Islands in 1900. Van Gogh's protest was more direct, as witness his *Sorrow*, a melancholy drawing of a "pale, slender woman's figure" produced during his Dutch period, and the unsentimental drawings of seamy neighborhoods he produced at about the same time. Even when he painted a bare bed in a cheap hotel, or a pair of old shoes, he was obviously moved by the same spirit. This sense of bearing the burden of the world on one's own shoulders had become quite general, and was something different from fascination with somber themes, as we know them from Israels's canvasses. It was direct participation in the misery the artist saw all round him; expressionism within impressionism. Edvard Munch, the Norwegian, knew it as well (*The Scream*, 1893; *The Dead Mother*, 1900), and so, each in his own way, did the Belgians Eugène Laermans and James Ensor, who after 1885 hid his sense of outrage behind savage masks, skeletons, death and demons. In France there was Théophile Steinlen. His name conjures up a world of illustrations that would have been impossible before the 1880s and would not be resurrected again: the world of the satirical cabaret (Steinlen obviously identified himself with Aristide Bruant), of daring posters, but above all of caricatures in a host of such papers as *Gil Blas*, the *Assiette au Beurre*, and probably the most famous of all, *Simplicissimus*, which had been published in Munich since 1896 with drawings by T. T. Heine and the Gulbranssons, to mention only the best-known. (Heinrich Zille did similar work in Berlin.) The socio-political satires published in these papers, available weekly at a very small cost, were so caustic and often so crude that a conformist age like ours can barely imagine what they were like.

In Germany, Fritz von Uhde, a disciple of modern Protestantism, endeavored to alleviate human misery by bringing the figure of Christ down to earth; Ernst Barlach was another great painter filled with social unrest. However, the greatest heights of all were reached by Käthe Kollwitz, who began her work in 1894 with the incomparable series *The Weavers*, inspired by Hauptmann's play.[26]

The same current also ran through literature — as, incidentally, did its opposite: aestheticism. Gorky has often been called the father of social and proletarian literature, but there were many others like him: Charles Louis Philippe in France, the young Gerhart Hauptmann in Germany, Herman Heijermans in Holland and, to some extent, Thomas Hardy in England and Jack London in America.[27]

550

A synthesis between the barren muse of art for art's sake and the fruitful muse of social responsibility[28] was attempted by a third group, which at the time attracted as much attention as the other two. It embraced artists such as Ruskin and Morris, who devoted themselves to applied art and tried to improve society through beauty. Their ideal has been called "noa-noa", fragrance, for unlike Gauguin they did not fly from the hideousness of reality but attempted to reform it. There were many other antithetical currents, too, and we mention their existence to emphasize the extreme breadth of modern art, a quality by which it was set off from the art of all earlier periods. The nodal points on which, perspectively speaking, all its lines seemed to converge, were no longer rest and eternity, but the fleeting moment and motion. This aspect of modern art does not belie that other truth, namely that in motion the moment is abolished, so that motion is experienced as an eternal principle: a belief Marinetti's Futurism did not derive from historicism but shared with it.

As a reaction to its alienation from society there was also the deification of art, but the revered divinity was rarely the radiant Balder of Gorter's poem *Mei*, and far more frequently a dark and unpredictable demon, even in many artists who stopped far short of J. K. Huysmans's satanism.[29]

The attitude of modern art to science and technology was equally uneven. Thus while some artists rejected science out of hand, and looked to dreams for the ultimate revelation of artistic truths, others were fervent admirers of the latest scientific achievements. I am not thinking so much of the fact that Pierre Bonnard, for instance, long before Braque or Léger, saw and depicted the beauty of a radiator — for that might simply have been an individual quirk. Nor am I thinking of the creation in 1907, a most fruitful year in the history of modern art,[30] of the *Werkbund*, a working alliance inspired by Art Nouveau and hence by the interpenetration of art and technology.[31] I am thinking of a broader current that at times washed over the entire field of the fine arts. For next to Neo-Impressionism, of which we have already said that it was an "amalgam" of subjectivism and scientism, and which Seurat wanted to call "chromo-luminarism" — what could have been more scientific? — there was Cubism. Though its effect was less direct, it was nevertheless the more decisive and consistent current of the two. For the first time the spirit of mathematics had come to replace literary and philosophic conceptions in aesthetics. Cézanne must have had some inkling of this fact when he argued that all natural forms are built up from basic geometric shapes. In 1908 this new insight gained ground so suddenly, and became so widespread, that we can safely say that no other trend delivered a more serious blow to the tradition of the Renaissance than did Cubism.[32]

Deeper than all the contrasts we have mentioned, however, was the gulf between the modern artist and the world in which he lived. Even this thesis and antithesis was, however, synthesized into a whole that, as we have tried to show in previous chapters, also manifested itself in a great many other spheres of intellectual endeavor during our period. In art, that whole was juxtaposition and simultaneity. Artists discovered the simultaneity of non-concurrent processes each in his own way: they saw it and painted it (a head that faced two ways at once; a young girl and the woman she had become) at about the same time that Breysig, Spengler, and the young Toynbee began to speak of the recurrent phases of civilizations (turning Homer into a "contemporary" of Dante) and that Jung introduced the concept of synchronism.[33] Paul Valéry (stimulated by Wells's *Time Machine* and by Alfred Jarry) wrote a long theoretical article on this subject in 1899.[34] Equally deep and dialectically inter-linked was the antithesis between the artist's conscious and unconscious efforts. If we ignore the "scientistic" current, all these artists shared the view that consciousness was something that had to be surmounted, and that this process called for keener consciousness. The result was a host of hybrid ideas whose existence is difficult to demonstrate in art but easily shown in the poetry of Rimbaud and Gérard de Nerval. Having examined the case of Jarry, Robert Shattuck went on to explain that, in the modern writer, the conscious and the unconscious constitute a single dialectical continuum, similar to the continuum formed by thought and deed, art and life, childhood and maturity.[35]

So broad was the spectrum of modern art that it is impossible to speak of a modern style, however loosely defined. All we can do is to consider this breadth in the light of what we have been saying about the inherent contradictions of modern art. Werner Haftmann did just that in his *Malerei im 20. Jahrhundert* (Painting in the Twentieth Century).[36] His "retrospective review," which appeared at the end of the fourth and last volume, is hard to better in insight or penetration.

In the second of his "retrospections,"[37] he explains what to him are the two extremes of object-experience and intellectual conception between which modern painting had begun to oscillate before the out-break of the First World War. At one pole he placed Marcel Duchamp, the first French Dadaist, who, being no more than thirteen in 1900, only just fits into our scheme. The work Duchamp produced before his departure for the United States in 1915 already shows what to Haftmann made him so typical a representative of his age: the isolation of objects by their translation to the wrong environment so that they assume the strange and magical aspects of fetishes. Haftmann no doubt had in mind a painting first exhibited in 1912: *The King and Queen Traversed by Quick Nudes.*[38]

The opposite pole, which might be described as psychic primitivism (inasmuch as it is closely related to the primitive "participation" discovered by Lévy-Bruhl), was extreme rationalism, which, according to Haftmann, was exemplified during the pre-war period in the work of Kazimir Malevich from Kiev, who was some nine years older than Duchamp. What was so peculiar about him was not so much that in 1908, when he still lived in Russia, he should have painted in the manner of the Fauves, or that after a visit to Paris in 1911 he should have adopted the style of Léger — which, incidentally, was also reflected in Duchamp's canvas we have just mentioned — but the fact that, as early as 1913, he should have exhibited a painting in Moscow of a black square on a white background. Malevich did not yet refer to this painting as "abstract" but spoke of suprematism, by which he referred to the supremacy of the inner experience. We may take it that Kandinsky, too, was not a stranger to this current, although he remained much too much the expressionist to convey his own "inner experiences" by means of geometrical forms.[39] Malevich explained his approach in his *The Non-Objective World*, first published in Russian in 1915, and in German translation in 1926, by which time the Soviet government had severed all links with modern art.[40]

Hans Sedlmayr agreed by and large with Haftmann's interpretation, but went a step further.[41] For while Haftmann had argued that the starting points of both Duchamp (the worship of the absolute object) and of Malevich (the worship of absolute form) had little to do with art, albeit both men had paved the way for a new aesthetics, Sedlmayr claimed that aesthetics cannot be founded on extra-artistic principles, and concluded that the closer art approaches the two extremes we have mentioned, the more it ceases to be art. According to him, the emergence of "modern" art not only marked a break with the history of European art, but with art in general.[42] The historian can leave this an open question, though not without remarking that this blurring of the boundary between art and non-art was one of the great uncertainties with which the turn of the century was so clearly beset. What he must, however, record is that in its development modern art did indeed converge on Haftmann's two extremes, and increasingly so — witness the emergence of the surrealist and abstract schools. At the same time he must also note that the seeds of this development germinated in our period, which is thus once again, and irrefutably, shown to have been one of incisive change.

The change, in this particular case, was that art, abandoning its traditional role of consoler and sanctifier of the existing order, drew so far apart from society that the artist and the world could no longer meet. To bring them together again was a social challenge, and modern art was a direct response to it. Seen in that light, even the ultimate contrast — that between surrender to the absolute object (or the absolute dream) and surrender to absolute form (or absolute color) — became fused into a single desire to come to terms with the world, or at least with its loss of peace. If this is true, then it is not surprising that currents, groups, circles, coteries, and lone wolves should have succeeded one another in ever quicker succession during a period when the tempo of social change was so greatly accelerated. Indeed, the pulse of modern art beat even faster than that of society at large, so fast, in fact, that we can discover a continuous succession of contemporary art critics and art historians who described every year, from 1899 to 1914, as "crucial." Here we can do no more than mention the most important turning points.

The new sense of vitality reflected by the Impressionists ("Impressionism is not a school but a world view," said Max Liebermann, the German Impressionist who in 1899 became chairman of the "Berlin Secession")[43] was followed in the middle of the 1880s by the Neo-Impressionism of Seurat and Signac. This was the beginning of the first revolutionary phase of modern art, and so it was still being described twenty years later. In 1908 an exhibition entitled "From Cézanne to Picasso" caused a sensation in Munich, once an outpost of modern art.[44] Paris was by then once again in the van, even though the giants of the early phase, whose greatness appeared to grow as time went by, had gone — Van Gogh had died in 1890, Seurat in 1891, Gauguin in 1903, and Cézanne in 1906 — and the early, symbolist form of Expressionism, influenced by Gauguin and Maurice Denis, had become *vieux jeu* by the turn of the century.[45] Though symbolism was by no means confined to France — in Holland, for instance, its leading lights were Toorop, Prikker, der Kinderen and Roland Holst[46] — and Art Nouveau at about the turn of the century had a European rather than a specifically French character, Paris nevertheless remained the center of the art revolution to the very end of our period and, like a flame bewitching a moth, held almost all artists of later fame under her spell for at least a time, and sometimes throughout their lives. We may mention but a few examples: Breitner arrived in 1884; Van Gogh lived there from 1886 to 1888; Francois

Kupka and Ernst Barlach came in 1895; Kees van Dongen in 1897; Braque, Dufy, and Chagall in 1900; the Polish painter, Marcoussis, and Picasso in 1903; Brancusi, the Roumanian painter, and Arp in 1904; Gris, Modigliani, and Severini in 1906; Archipenko in 1908; Lipchitz in 1909 and the sculptor Zadkine in 1911. In short, at the turn of the century, Paris was to modern artists from all over the world what Italy had been four hundred years earlier — and this comparison may be more profound than it at first appears.

The Nabis, or "prophets," who also appeared shortly after 1900 with Denis, but above all with Bonnard and Vuillard, were typically Parisian, even though the Swiss painter Félix Vallatton also belonged to the group. In 1904 they were temporarily overshadowed by the "Fauves" round Matisse, de Vlaminck, André Dérain, and Kees van Dongen. Although "Die Brücke" (The Bridge) of Dresden, the first German group of Expressionists (led first by Ernst Ludwig Kirchner and later by Pechstein and Emil Nolde) was much talked about that same year, Paris was and remained the true home of the avant-garde.

The year 1907 was what we might call a "vintage" year:[47] it saw the birth of Cubism, not unrelated to the retrospective Cézanne exhibition in the autumn, and the opening of Kahrweiler's gallery. That year the world first heard of Picasso, with his *Demoiselles d'Avignon*, and of Braque. It was also the year of the first biography of Van Gogh, written by Meier-Graefe who still bracketed Van Gogh with Manet, Pissarro, Cézanne, and others.[48] Three years later the chapter devoted to Van Gogh was published separately and with profuse illustrations.[49] Rewald's selected Van Gogh bibliography published half a century later included over 260 items[50] — more than five publications a year devoted to "pauvre Vincent."[51] It was also in 1907 that the German painter, Lovis Corinth, began to move towards Expressionism, that Munch painted his famous portrait of Walter Rathenau — more revealing of the man than his own writings — and that Maillol sculpted Renoir's head. It was also the year in which Bergson's *L'Évolution créatrice* was published. The modern artist too, more perhaps than anyone else, saw himself as a creative evolutionist capable of shaping the future. This made him the extreme representative of a feeling widespread among the European bourgeoisie of his day. For Europe was suffused with a pioneering *élan;* it seemed briefly as if the *fin de siècle* spirit, tired of itself, had changed, all unawares, into the spirit of the Renaissance. The omens may have been most unpropitious, but had they been all that different in the quattrocento and cinquecento? Cubism did not remain static for long; soon afterwards it was possible to distinguish an analytic and a synthetic phase, and as for Robert Delaunay and Fernand Léger, they were Cubists in little more than name.

However influential, Cubism never held absolute sway. From February 20, 1909, when Marinetti published the first Futurist manifesto in *Le Figaro*, Futurism began to take pride of place in the art columns — its founder causing sufficient noise to ensure that it did — at least for a time. Though a clear sign of the times, Futurism as a philosophy is difficult to define. One does not have to dwell too deeply on the antecedents of its poet-founder, who was thirty-three in the year his manifesto appeared, to appreciate that his anarchistic — and chaotic — outbursts were but the obverse of his decadent past. That does not dispose of Futurism — quite the contrary: by sweeping the detested tradition away as brutally as it did, it paved the way for the glorification of violence and war and the fanfares of a Fascist future could be heard in the distance. Nor did this movement affect painting alone. Boccioni wrote a manifesto — for such was their style — on sculpture, Severini on dynamism in the fine arts, and Carrà resurrected Baudelaire's idea of the intimate relationship between sound and color. Sant'Elia pleaded for a new architecture, and Prampolini for a new theatre.[52] Yet one of the most important hallmarks of the whole school was a love of noisy publicity, reflecting the penetration of art by capitalism. It was to culminate in the investment, for speculative or other reasons, of fixed sums in the work of certain painters or authors, with an eye to the maximization of profits. Futurism unwittingly or otherwise contributed to this process.

Another current worthy of attention was "Der Blaue Reiter" (Blue Rider) movement, founded in December 1911 in Munich as a breakaway group from the Neue Künstlervereinigung (New Artists' Society). Kandinsky, its leader, with Marc, Macke, Klee, Jawlensky, and Kubin as his leading — if independent — disciples, recorded his views of art in *Über das Geistige in der Kunst* (Concerning the Spiritual in Art), written in 1910 and published in 1912. Here, too, much more was involved than art alone: Kandinsky was determined to ring in a new cultural era. His book was, above all, anti-materialist and anti-subjectivist, and reflected an undogmatic religiosity, influenced not only by Madame Blavatsky and Rudolf Steiner, but also by eastern pantheism. It enjoyed an enormous success: three editions of the German edition within one year and a host of translations, even into Japanese,[53] so much so that the author might have merited a place in Chapter XXXIII. In his book we can catch glimpses of the moonscape of "magical realism" at which we have hinted in our comments on the Duchamp-Malevich clash.

Sculptors, who depend more on commissions than painters, were, by that very fact, impeded from casting off the shackles of tradition quite as quickly as the painters. Much as Dostoyevsky once said that every nineteenth-century Russian writer was descended from Gogol, so the modern sculptor might have claimed that he and his fellows had all been cradled by Rodin. Auguste Rodin, the Impressionist among contemporary sculptors, was alone great enough to rebuff the snub of the organizers of the World Exposition by holding an exhibition of his own at the corner of the Avenue de l'Alma. Both Bourdelle, whom Anatole France considered his most famous French contemporary, and also the Belgian sculptor, Minne, were strongly influenced by Rodin, albeit the first gave his work an archaic, and the second a Gothic, twist.[54] Aristide Maillol, by contrast, was a true innovator, and we may rightly call him the first modern sculptor, not least by virtue of his *Méditerranée* (1902), produced at the age of forty, though there were many other sculptors at the time — Mendes da Costa and Zijl in Holland, for instance — who also rejected both Academicism and Impressionism in favor of new, monumental forms. The joint influence of Rodin and Maillol informed the work of another great French sculptor, Charles Despiau, who was twenty-seven in 1900.

The "vintage" year of 1907 also witnessed the rise of Expressionism in German sculpture: Ernst Barlach and Wilhelm Lehmbruck, both opposed to Maillol, the second because of his emphatic rejection of Maillol's tranquil and tranquillizing, spiritualized and elongated, forms: a late manifestation of the painters' "distortions." German Expressionism, in painting no less than in sculpture and literature, was the tacit or "screaming" witness of the rebellion of an entire generation.

At the end of our period a number of east Europeans appeared abruptly on the scene to lend modern sculpture a whole series of new impulses. They were the Russians Alexander Archipenko, Nahum Gabo and Antoine Pevsner, the Pole Jacques Lipchitz, and the Roumanian Constantin Brancusi. The oldest of them, Brancusi, was twenty-four in 1900; the youngest, Lipchitz, just nine. If we mention them here it is because their work, even before 1914, showed that sculpture would stray even further from the inspiration of the Renaissance than it had strayed with Rodin. The importance of the young Archipenko was, first of all, that his machine-like constructions made him a precursor of the constructivism of Pevsner and Gabo. With Brancusi, who, like Hans Arp, never lost sight of the primitive natural forms, for all his modernity, it is impossible to say whether his work was a reaction to what had gone before or an individual effort to reach the goal of all modern artists along an original path.

All art strives towards a goal. It is perhaps the greatest achievement of the art historian Alois Riegl, professor at the University of Vienna from 1897 to 1905, to have expressed this idea in his theory of "Kunstwollen" (the autonomous will to art), albeit in somewhat obscure language. His theory can be briefly stated as follows: the dependent variable — style — is an expression of the independent variable — the will to art derived by the artist, consciously or unconsciously, from a philosophy determined by his personality, group, place and time.[55] Riegl thus expressed, without saying so explicitly, indeed perhaps without even knowing it, the contemporary idea of voluntarism, i.e. the rejection of mechanical determinism.[56]

"Kunstwollen" was the re-integration of the artist's "ego" into the world, by the restoration of lost contact, if possible with *the* whole, and if not, with *some* whole. The artist can never renounce his goal, not even for the sake of personal success, a goal that is both the source of his uncertainty and the meaning of his quest.

CHAPTER XXXVII

ART NOUVEAU

On January 20, 1900 John Ruskin died at the age of eighty. A fervent
admirer of Carlyle, he, too, had swum against the tide, but unlike Carlyle
he had received recognition in his lifetime, and, on his death, was honored
as a prophet in both the New World and the Old. "A very great man,"
was what that other prophet, the sage from Yasnaya Polyana, called him,
"one who resembled a Russian peasant" — high praise indeed from those
lips.[1] Gandhi confessed that his life had been changed by Ruskin's *Unto
This Last*, and Berdyaev learnt English, chiefly to read Ruskin in the
original.[2] In the obituary he wrote for the *Mercure de France*, Marcel
Proust compared Ruskin to the biblical prophets, and he even "translated" him, although, not having any English himself, he used a draft
prepared by his mother. Bernard Shaw had pointed out somewhat earlier
that the secret of such writers as Ruskin, Morris, and Kropotkin was that
they saw through the lies of society with its façade of wealth, splendor,
nepotism, conformity, piety, and high moral pretensions.[3] Soon afterwards Ouida, herself a celebrity by then, claimed that Ruskin's death
had also spelled the death of gentleness, and the birth of a new cruelty.[4]
Heinrich Herkner, a professor from Zurich who spent his 1900 summer
vacation in Arosa, confessed in his autobiography that Ruskin's books
had been his faithful companions on his lonely walks through the very
mountains where many of them had, in fact, been conceived, and that
he shared their author's eye for landscape, art and social injustice.[5]
Even Henry van de Velde, who so prided himself on his independent
spirit, conceded that Ruskin and Morris had had a decisive influence on
his intellectual development.[6]

Ruskin aimed his shafts at industrialism, which in his day was making
ever deeper inroads into the life of society, divorcing art from the needs
of the people. His reaction was artistic and social at once. Half a century
before his death he had argued that the noblest buildings are generally
those which reveal the secret of their structure to the intelligent eye,[7]
an idea also expressed in the title of one of the many books devoted

to early twentieth-century art: Bøe's *From Gothic Revival to Functional Form*.[8]

But before architecture in particular and art in general could appeal to more than a small circle of prosperous art-lovers, a further step had to be taken, and it was taken not by Ruskin or his disciples but by others who made a detour, as short and as twisting as the new style they created. It lead them to "new art," known at different times and in different places under different names, including whiplash style, vermicelli style, *style nouille* and *Schnörkel-Stil*. However, it was more generally referred to as "Art Nouveau," a term coined in 1896, except in Germany where they stuck to *Jugendstil*, so called after *Jugend*, a journal that began publication in Munich that same year.[9]

When Ruskin died, Art Nouveau, which had come into bud in the 1890s, was still in full bloom. Yet less than ten years later, it suddenly faded away. The fact that it remained confined in the main to decoration, that it did not spread beyond western and central Europe, and above all that it was a protest movement, all doomed Art Nouveau to a transitory existence. Its protest was directed first and foremost against the historicism that had lain upon the nineteenth century like a lead weight. But it was also the protest of youth against old age, of light against darkness, of simplicity against ostentation, of nature against the academic establishment and the museum. It *was* a new style: a specific expression of the time, as witness the inscription above the portals of the Vienna Sezession: *Der Zeit ihre Kunst, der Kunst ihre Freiheit* (To time its art and to art its freedom). As such, it is hard to exaggerate the importance of Art Nouveau: it was a "transformation *in actu*," with all the ambiguity and fickleness this entailed. For its attitude to technology still wavered between the total rejection of Morris and Ruskin and the total acceptance of the futurists: van de Velde fully appreciated the danger though he no longer blamed it on the machine, but on the self-seeking of its owners whose only aim was profit. He lived in high hopes that machines would one day make up for all the misery they had caused: the smoke of the furnaces would, in due course, spread like angels' wings over society.[10] This remark reflected the socio-political radicalism of many of these innovators, most of whom were socialists in their youth, but fickle in that they embraced socialism for purely individualistic reasons.[11] Moreover, their anti-historicism had a touch of the baroque or rococo — a fact that was recognized even at the time;[12] their determination to stay young was often reminiscent of the aspirations of a tired old age; their simplicity often degenerated into artificiality, so much so that many Art Nouveau products seem highly contrived, the more so as the conscious quest for originality imposed by an unprecedented need to compete and to advertise, encouraged cheap imitation. The best were fully aware of the pitfalls, and later even described them as "tragic,"[13] and Herbert Croly referred to all their restless pursuit of the unusual as rank escapism.[14]

However many national nuances the new style may have had, it was truly international in essence. It began everywhere as decoration, and decoration it remained: decoration of bookbindings and title pages, of headings and margins, of initials and letters, and, proliferating from these, of posters, furniture, carpets, and walls. Diversity in unity seemed to be its first command: the product was always asymmetrical and the leading motifs rarely repeated. The motifs themselves were strictly limited in number: plant stalks and twisting flowers, sinuous reflections, slim feminine outlines imprisoned in the serpentine coils of their own hair, or else draped in veils, trails of mist or clouds of incense. The picture was usually fused with the frame. The new element was not the natural form, stylized or otherwise; branches, leaves, flowers and female shapes had been used in much earlier illustrations. What was decidedly new was the immuring tendency achieved with the aid of hair, waves, flames or lianas, and so marked was it that it seemed a desperate effort to shut off the realm of beauty, the soul's own sphere, from the noisy world outside. New also was the fluidity and softness: water merging into lilies, lilies merging into swans, snakes into flames or plumes of smoke. These devices were intended to suggest motion but generally failed to do so — only Cassandre was able to lend his posters true mobility. The rest had a somewhat gelatinized aspect, reminiscent of the tentacles of polyps, radiolaria and other primitive organisms. It was probably not by chance that in 1899, the year of his *Welträthsel*, Ernst Haeckel should also have published his *Kunstformen der Natur* (Art Forms of Nature). At the same time, this style seemed a materialization — in its own way, for there was not a great deal of material — of Maeterlinck's "soul vapor" or of the liquid element in the work of Debussy.

Whatever else it may have tried to express, Art Nouveau aimed chiefly at delicacy and sensitivity,[15] as we know them from *fin de siècle* literature, from Maeterlinck and Huysmans, from Wilde, from Rimbaud and Mallarmé, and from the music of Debussy and Delius. That aim was exotic, even when it was not directly reminiscent of Japanese, Egyptian, Celtic, or Javanese art, and erotic even when — as with Beardsley — it did not set out deliberately to be so. Sternberger, who claimed the new century had revealed new erotic values, *inter alia* in Puccini's *Bohème*, Wedekind's *Lulu* and *Erdgeist*, and in the work of Félicien Rops and Toulouse-Lautrec — he might well have added Oscar Wilde — discovered the same element in the languid convolutions of Art Nouveau.[16] This was the eroticism of the "primitive feminine form," something that tried to be exalted and profound at once in the twilight atmosphere of the beauty it worshiped, laying bare sin in innocence and innocence in sin, as if it took Freud's discovery of the unconscious stirrings of the infantile psyche for granted. It was an escape from normality, but lacked the strength to proceed to an open attack on conventional morality.

From the exalted to the ridiculous it is but a short step, as it is also from the profound to the meaningless, and the exponents of Art Nouveau did not always avoid taking it since, if anything, they were exceedingly serious. Thus Jan Veth, the artist and poet, wrote the following exalted passage in super-eighties style about Toorop's drawing, *The Three Brides*, which had been exhibited that year: " . . . swaying undulations . . . which soar, swell, inter-mingle and sing, like gushing springs, seeking a bed from which they may arise in harmony — lines that twist and turn, grapple and wrestle, burst asunder, join in kneeling worship, fleetingly touching the earth . . . vibrant lines of deep resonance, piercing lines of sonorous flight . . . " No one could say that this verbiage was not a fitting description of Toorop's creations, for instance of his poster for "Calvé's Delft Salad Oil."[17] One does not have to rummage among the writings of the opponents of this type of exaltation, one of whom said of a typographical exhibition that the "solution will no doubt be provided next time," and another who, on seeing an Art Nouveau interior, sighed that he would rather have bare cell walls than this "imperative mood," to discover its ridiculous aspects. Friedrich Ahlers, who quoted the last opinion, began his book on the subject by claiming that the vision the word *Jugendstil* conjured up was both ridiculous and grisly, and he went on to speak of "improbable masses of hair on concavely twisted heads of women representing ashtrays"; of "lilies that have succeeded in taking root on stoves"; and he added that when modern youngsters see such objects in their parents' homes they can only shake their heads at an age that produced such monstrosities, the parents joining in the laughter with some embarrassment.[18]

Jugendstil was given a great boost by the Paris Exposition of 1900. Both the entrance gate and the leading restaurant, the Pavillon Bleu, were overpowering specimens of Art Nouveau. However, the exhibition also gave a boost to industrial vulgarization and hence accelerated the decline of the new style. Despite its excesses, its short-lived fame and its transitional character, its radicalism and idealism earned Art Nouveau a lasting place in the history of art. One only has to imagine the kind of interior the well-to-do still relished in 1900 to grasp its liberating influence. Then: a room stuffed with over-ornate furniture, with gloomy paintings in weighty gold frames against a somber wall paper; real or imitation Oriental carpets on the floor, and every window and doorway hung with dark curtains and heavy drapes; countless knick-knacks in copper, ivory, or china on a host of pier-tables, whatnots, and chests — in short a chaotic confusion of shades and shapes that was rendered only slightly less unpleasing by the half-light in which all of it was bathed. Now: a room that, however cold and uncomfortable it might seem to the modern eye, nevertheless attempted to recapture nature in its floral aspect, in which all the planes were true planes, in which the colors, however gaudy, were nevertheless colors, and in which wall, floor and furniture knew the stillness that springs from unity and simplicity.[19]

However original that style may have been, it too was not created *ex nihilo*. It was not by chance that we opened this chapter with Ruskin, or that we mentioned the revival of interest in Japanese prints. We might safely have added the renewal of interest in folk art with all its naive directness, or the work of such contemporary painters as van Gogh, Gauguin, Seurat, Toorop, Hodler, and Edvard Munch, and such modern engineering feats as the Eiffel Tower of 1889, to arrive at the intellectual sources from which the new stream sprang up in five places, almost at the same time and yet independently: England, Scotland, Belgium, France, and the United States, which last thus made its first independent contribution to international art[20] at about the same time that Walt Whitman's *Leaves of Grass* did so in literature.

It was no accident that England should have taken the lead. Here industrialization had come first, and here the loss of artistic values it brought in its wake was felt most strongly. Here Arthur H. Mackmurdo and C. R. Ashbee established craftsmen's guilds in the eighties; here C. F. A. Voysey pioneered the cottage style in architecture and designed his greatly admired wallpapers and fabrics, and here Aubrey Beardsley, during the eight years of feverish activity that were granted to him, helped to lay the foundations of Art Nouveau with his famous illustrations. Ever since 1893 their endeavors had enjoyed the full support of Gleeson White's *The Studio*. The versatility of the new trend was further exemplified by the stained-glass windows of Ford Madox Brown, the fabrics of Walter Crane, the book-bindings of Cobden-Sanderson, and last but not least the products of the Kelmscott Press, founded in 1891 by Morris.[21] In neighboring Scotland, the movement was led, quite independently, by the brilliant architect and furniture designer Charles Rennie Mackintosh, ably assisted by his wife, Margaret Macdonald.

In America there were Louis C. Tiffany, whose glassware with its un-

563

dulating lines resembled long-stemmed flowers, and two architects who were greater perhaps than any other in their day and age: Louis H. Sullivan and Frank Lloyd Wright. They all spoke the new language of forms, the first with a peculiar accent: a burgeoning ornamentation and tautness of design that, even in the nineties foreshadowed the next phase. The American school developed on independent lines, although what Ruskin had said and Morris had done did not remain entirely unknown across the Atlantic. Curjel has tried to explain the near-simultaneous and ubiquitous emergence of Art Nouveau by a biological change in man,[22] much as Dagobert Frey tried to do when he spoke of the "changed imagination" of Renaissance man. Both hypotheses are highly improbable.[23]

Unlike America, Belgium found the ground for Art Nouveau well prepared, for here two well-to-do lawyers, Octave Maus and Edmond Picard, had been publishing the weekly *L'Art Moderne* since 1891, and had founded the circle of *Les XX*, in 1880, thus turning Brussels into a leading center of contemporary art. *Les XX* provided a forum and a gallery for many talented men who had not yet made their mark, including Cézanne, Debussy, Gauguin, van Gogh, Meunier, Rops, Renoir, Rodin, Seurat, Toulouse-Lautrec, but also Verhaeren, Vincent d'Indy, and Whistler. However much they differed from one another, all of them endorsed the declaration of war on academicism and classicism which an anonymous member of their group had issued in the first volume of *L'Art Moderne*: "Art is the antithesis of rote and formulas; it is the eternal, spontaneous and free reaction of man to his environment and to new ideas."[24] No wonder that the house and famous vestibule, full of "blossoming" wrought-iron tendrils, which Victor Horta built in Brussels, proved to be as great a wonder as Sullivan's first skyscraper. It was ready in 1893, before any trace of modern architecture could be detected elsewhere in Europe. "Not a single detail has been borrowed from anything that went before," a Hungarian critic on the *Wiener Tageblatt* wrote five years later.[25] Horta was just thirty when he designed the house; his spiritual kinsman, Henry van de Velde, was two years younger. Although perhaps less talented, the latter was to become more famous because he coupled his many other gifts with that of great oratory,[26] found a more fruitful field of activity in fast-expanding Germany, and above all because, to the end of his life — he died in 1957 — he remained true to his ideals and did not become an upstart baron like Horta. Van de Velde was perhaps the most striking exemplification of the all-round versatility that was so characteristic of the whole movement and so reminiscent of Renaissance man. He was a painter, a keen student of Ruskin and Morris, an illustrator and an architect — he built his own house in Uccle (completed in 1896) and made everything in it, including the wallpaper, the curtains, the furniture, and the glass, "the better to banish ugliness from his surroundings."[27] We might add that he also designed the clothes for the woman who was to be the center of the house.

In the Netherlands, Art Nouveau had a face of its own. The most probable explanation of the emergence of this particular variant is, on the one hand, the absence of a baroque or rococo tradition, and, on the other, the presence of Javanese influences: Wayang puppets, Japara woodcuts, and Jogja silverwork with their floral motifs and, of course, the intricately patterned batik-work. It is remarkable that every Chinese furniture maker in Indonesia at the beginning of the new century should have fashioned furniture with floral decorations that used to be known locally as the "Toorop style." Jan Veth gave the Dutch Art Nouveau movement a great impetus in the early 1890s with his magnificently bound translation of Crane's *Claims of Decorative Art*.[28] In the first half of the 1890s, Dijsselhof, Lion Cachet, and T. Nieuwenhuis broke with the traditional system of decoration by cutting elaborate motifs in wood, scorning illusionist depth effects. New potteries produced ceramics in the style pioneered by T. Colenbrander. Toorop, Thorn Prikker, and der Kinderen were working as early as 1893 on the decorations of the van Gogh issue of the Belgian journal *Van Nu en Straks*, and R. N. Roland Holst made a worthy addition to that trio. De Bazel and Lauweriks set up a "Studio for Architecture, Crafts and Decorative Art" in 1895, which was copied by many others. During the first year of its publication, Tak's *Kroniek* devoted a special column to "decorative art"; one year later there appeared a short-lived monthly wholly devoted to the applied arts.[29] The end of Dutch Art Nouveau can be put at 11 September 1898, when Berlage wrote an article for the *Kroniek*, in which he warned against van de Velde's influence, and forswore the entire Art Nouveau movement.[30] What the Dutch exhibited at the Turin exhibition of 1902 was no longer Art Nouveau.

This early demise was not the result of lack of talent, but reflected the very nature of the movement. The Dutch artist, as a rule, stands firmly on his low ground. When he declares his sincerity he cannot also put on airs and graces, and when der Kinderen, Roland Holst, and Berlage claimed that they wanted to create a monumental form of social art, they could not at the same time offer sacrifices on the altar of hyper-individualism. The ambiguity of Art Nouveau was resolved in the Netherlands by the rejection of that style. But not of ambiguity as such — it proved impossible to be unambiguous in an ambiguous age. Dream and deed are two hostile twins. Dutch Art Nouveau found its fiercest critic in one of its own descendants, one who turned on his own past and who by sacrificing his own life in the Dutch Resistance proved that the deed mattered more to him than the dream — in Arondéus.[31]

In France the movement started with Emile Gallé from Nancy and his pupils, of whom the furniture designer Louis Majorelle and the architect Emile André were probably the most famous. In this school, the Japanese influence was more obvious than in the others: the floral decorations follow the grain of the wood and even mother-of-pearl inlays are quite common. More important still, was the exceptionally close relationship between French Art Nouveau and contemporary French literature. Gallé's glasswork was occasionally etched with aphorisms by Baudelaire, Verlaine and Maeterlinck, and the work bench he submitted to the World Exposition of 1900 bore the marquetry description *Travail est joie* — a brief summary of the unclouded delight in craftsmanship that was so typical of the whole movement. But there was much more to these "literary" craft products than that: the belief in the fundamental unity of the arts that had persuaded Wagner to fuse them into an indigestible hotchpotch, had clearly not yet lost its hold. In modern architecture it would soon afterwards — albeit in more controlled and sober form — preside over the unity of exterior and interior, of form and function, of structure and decoration.

In Paris, Art Nouveau had an active leader in Samuel Bing, an art dealer from Hamburg, who dealt chiefly in Japanese prints. He was also a cabinet maker and had his workshop built in modern style by Bonnier and van de Velde, with Julius Meier-Graefe as adviser, and had a stand of his own at the World Exposition, designed and decorated by G. de Teure amongst others.[32] Hector Guimard made a more lasting impression, thanks chiefly to the Art Nouveau motifs for the Paris Metro stations he presented in 1898 and 1901, some of which exist to this day. But the greatest of French Art Nouveau architects was undoubtedly Auguste Perret. French Art Nouveau poster design, for its part, found a leading representative in Eugène Grasset from Switzerland. He was one of the many artists who had been contributing to *Jugend* since 1896; other leading contributors were the famous Théophile Steinlen, the Czech-Parisian Mucha, the Swiss-Parisian Vallotton, renowned for his woodcuts in continuous white and black planes, and Henri Jossot, whose caricatures bordered on the grotesque.

When we look at the German *Jugendstil* movement, we find that it was strongly influenced not only by the French artists we have just mentioned but even more so by Belgians, Austrians, Dutchmen, and Scandinavians, not to mention the English, whose influence extended to the whole of Europe. Van de Velde, in particular, was a leading light in Germany. Encouraged by Bing, he exhibited his hotel room at the Dresden exhibition of 1897, and once he had been called to Berlin in 1899, he continued to spend most of his time in Germany — until 1914, when he opted for his invaded fatherland and returned to Belgium.

This prolonged stay was no accident. Germany, which, as we saw in an earlier chapter, inaugurated the monopolistic phase of capitalism at the turn of the century, boasted a class of extremely wealthy nouveaux riches, who, not hampered by any tradition, were only too ready to parade their generosity and love of progress by employing modern artists. As in France, Art Nouveau held sway in two main centers: Munich and Darmstadt. It was through the second center that the Viennese school entered Germany.

That school, too, was older than the German. The Viennese influence was the more important in that it reflected two currents which, however contradictory, combined into one: the sinuous and decorative current with which the name "Art Nouveau" is so intimately linked, and a strictly functional current, which, as we shall see below, gave rise to modern architecture. The first current had been associated with the name of Koloman Moser since 1893; the second was represented from 1895 onwards by the architects Otto Wagner and Adolf Loos. Those artists who, in the highly traditional Hapsburg Empire, hankered after the new, split off from their conservative fellows in 1897 to form the so-called Vienna Sezession, under the chairmanship of Gustav Klimt. Their visible symbol was their meeting place with its telling inscription: *Der Zeit ihre Kunst, der Kunst ihre Freiheit* (To time its art, to art its freedom). No less expressive of their high ambition was the name of their journal: *Ver Sacrum* (Sacred Spring).

When the Vienna Sezession first emerged, the new fire was already burning in the Bavarian capital, the artistic Paris of the rising Wilhelminian Germany. The flaming fabrics the Swiss artist Hermann Obrist submitted for the Munich exhibition of 1894 may be considered so many sparks in this powder barrel. As soon as he had seen these designs, Otto Eckmann threw away his brush, burnt all his pictures and began his series of decorative drawings: flat patterns with licking flames forming long curves gracefully intertwined. Richard Riemerschmid, too, abandoned his palette for the designer's drawing board, and August Endell became the third of this pioneering trio. Bernhard Pankok and Bruno Paul, Patriz Huber and Hans

567

Christiansen, were to follow soon afterwards. The journals *Jugend* and, to a lesser extent, *Simplicissimus* (with T. T. Heine) quickly popularized the new art form.

One result of all this popularity was the fact that the last Grand Duke of Hesse, in the manner of an enlightened despot, engaged seven modern artists to work at his Darmstadt court in 1899. Chief among them were Joseph Olbrich from Vienna, who had been involved in the Sezession-House, and Peter Behrens from Munich. Behrens brought the new art with him, but was careful to leave his social criticism at home. The group held its first exhibition in 1901, and that exhibition deserves special notice because it was the first sign of opposition to the flourishes of the *Jugendstil*, whose sinuous lines the Darmstadt school replaced with the formal language of taut, geometrical patterns.

The end of Art Nouveau was drawing near. We saw that in 1898 Berlage proclaimed his opposition to van de Velde, who in his turn, was to reject Eckmann's purely emotional lines upon the latter's death in 1902. The heyday was over, but the original impulse which had welled up from a deep social need lived on. The road back to historical styles had been closed for good. *Art Nouveau* and *Jugendstil*, the appeal of the new and the youthful, had made a lasting impression on a society changing too rapidly and too incisively to retain the old respect for tradition and antiquity.

The new approach was based on the conviction that art was not an "embellishment" of life, but must satisfy one of man's most elementary needs, and that the sincerity of art presupposes an honest craftsmanlike and functional approach to the material. Form follows function, Sullivan had taught. Obviously, the machine was ultimately invincible. Now, that idea was essentially an engineering precept translated into artistic language. Even C. R. Ashbee, a direct disciple of Ruskin and Morris, ended up by declaring that "modern civilization rests on machinery and that no system for the encouragement or the endowment of the teaching of the arts can be sound that does not recognize this fact."[33]

The greatest advantage of this realization was reaped by architecture. Here, a new tradition had grown up from the beginning of the "machine age," largely ignored by "official" art. As early as 1796, Ditherington, near Shrewsbury in England, could pride itself on a flax mill with iron beams and props, probably built by Charles Bage. Abraham Darby constructed the first cast-iron bridge, across the Severn at Ironbridge, as early as 1779. The Machine Hall built by Contamin and Dutert at the Paris World Exposition of 1889 and the Crystal Palace of Sir Joseph Paxton and Fox & Henderson at the London World Exposition of 1851, were probably the best-known examples of the new trend in industrial architecture.[34]

Architecture in the narrower sense was still concerned simply to build with modern materials, examples of which were plentiful and ready to be applied. If we classify architects by decades, we shall need four subdivisions to cover their gradual meeting with the engineers. For it was during our period that functional architecture first emerged, small though its share in the general building activity may still have been. The first group, born between 1840 and 1850, the decade which also saw the birth of Cézanne, Redon, Rousseau, Gauguin, Contamin and Dutert, was dominated by Otto Wagner from Vienna. Wagner who designed, among many other buildings, the "Majolika House" towards the end of the century[35] and the Post Office Savings Bank in 1906,[36] both in his native Vienna, was also the author of *Moderne Architektur*.[37] His basic premise was the belief that artistic creativity must be the expression of everyday life; he fully agreed with Goethe that the artist must not create what the public esteems, but what it ought to esteem. Yet Wagner had many more opponents than disciples, and one of his critics called him a "pall-bearer of fashion," a "sensation hunter" and "a follower of the hideous materialism of Gallic architecture."

The second group, born between 1850 and 1860, was bigger. It included, in order of birth, four of the greatest architects of the period: the American Louis Sullivan, the Spaniard Antoni Gaudí i Cornet, the Dutchman Berlage, and the Englishman Voysey. Sullivan designed the earliest (and perhaps the best) skyscrapers in Chicago, the first of which went up in 1890 and still had a decorative roof line, however sober; the last, built in 1904, was practically devoid of ornamentation.[38] The work of Gaudí, the only Art Nouveau architect to emerge south of the Pyrenees, was so original that even people without a visual memory would always remember his petrified waves. As early as 1880, when he was twenty-eight, Gaudí constructed the first house based on his own design — the home of Don Manuel Vicens. But though its flamboyance was reminiscent of medieval Spain, Gaudí struck a most personal note with his iron work, which is best described as proto-Art Nouveau. The same effect was repeated in Palau Güell, a house he built for a wealthy merchant in 1889.[39] No one familiar with Spain's isolation would be surprised to learn that Gaudí retained his unique Art Nouveau style even in his twentieth-century work.[40] There was, however, this difference, that the Casa Milá, an apartment house he built in 1907 — and all his other buildings in Barcelona — looked exceedingly modern when compared with his earlier contributions. Strangely enough, they bore a certain resemblance to the fantastic productions of the later work of the Amsterdam School, work that could not have been more unlike Berlage's. For like Adolf Loos, fourteen years his junior, Berlage, despite the unmistakable influence of Art Nouveau on his early designs, ended up as one of its staunchest opponents. The Calvinism that runs so deep in every Hollander's blood caused him to make short shrift of all decorations, except for those sober enough to fit the rigid structure of his buildings. He also refused to camouflage the building material he used, be it brick, iron, concrete or glass. His most individual creation was the Produce Exchange in Damrak, Amsterdam, which was completed in 1903. In those years, his name was something to conjure with far beyond the borders of his native Holland. His belief in the superiority of the strictest and purest functionalism did not drop into his lap: we can follow his inner struggle in the four preliminary drafts for the Exchange, the first submitted in 1885, still wholly in romantic and Renaissance style, the subsequent ones increasingly pared down toward the economy of the last.[41] Was the final product a true reflection of his ideal? This will be doubted by anyone who compares the finished work with his dream. His greatest ambition — building for the community — was something neither his period nor his patrons were willing to grant him. He probably came closest to it in his plans for the expansion of Amsterdam. They show that he had moved a very long way from Sitte, who had sought salvation from the misery of nineteenth-century life in a return to the Middle Ages. The entire transformation of ideas on urban reconstruction in our period is comprised between Sitte's book of 1889 and Berlage's of 1913.[42] The British architect, Voysey, finally, though a lesser figure than Wright, was more important to the evolution of modern architecture because, being twelve years older, he enjoyed an international reputation as early as 1900, when his American colleague was not yet well known. His most progressive project, Ward House, dates back to 1890, the year in which the French architect Paul Sédille drew the attention of all Europe to modern English architecture.[43] The plans for one of Voysey's many cottages, on Lake Windermere, were published in 1904 by the German architect Muthesius in his book on the English house[44] and Hitchcock thought it quite possible that these plans may have inspired Adolf Loos and other continental architects.[45]

Even larger was the phalanx of avant-garde architects born between 1860 and 1870, the contemporaries of Ensor, Klimt, Munch, Vallotton, and Kandinsky, and of Croce and Romain Rolland. In 1900, when the oldest among them were just forty, most were, if not more radical, certainly more impetuous than the earlier two groups. This is also one of the reasons why van de Velde is usually considered the leading member

570

of this group, even though Horta and Mackintosh, Behrens and Bazel and, of course, Wright, were greater architects, and even though Hermann Muthesius, the oldest of the group, was a far better theorist.[46] Van de Velde was, in any case, a typical expression of the sudden change in attitude that occurred in his day and age. As a high-school boy he was enraptured by the symbolic poet, Ekskamp, whose work he later illustrated; he became a keen member of *Les XX* even while he admired Tolstoy and Nietzsche, but throughout his career he remained a staunch rationalist. The dividing line he himself drew between modern and pre-modern man was close to that drawn by Muthesius. He identified "pre-modern" with sentimental, lyrical and romantic behavior, which was in sharp contrast with that of modern man, a product of the machine age, who eats, sleeps, works and plays realistically, ignoring irrelevant diversions, however fascinating.[47]

And it was to sober reality, later known as functionalism, that most architects of this group turned sooner or later, each contributing part of his personal and national past. Victor Horta may have done so less than the others, but he neverthless made that contribution with his *Maison du Peuple* (People's House) in Brussels, completed in 1896, and quite particularly with its large hall, which was no less daring than Berlage's Exchange.[48] Charles Rennie Mackintosh did so more unreservedly, though he was the last person of whom one might have expected it. The room he was invited to exhibit at the Vienna Sezession in 1900 must have persuaded many architects, already suspicious of Art Nouveau, to turn their backs on it much more resolutely than they might otherwise have done.[49] Even earlier, Mackintosh had been chosen to design the Glasgow School of Art. It was no less puritanical than Berlage's Exchange, and only the strange metal stalks at the base of the upper floor windows were reminiscent of the old Mackintosh and his Cranston Tearoom in Buchanan Street. Of the German architects who broke with the past, Peter Behrens was probably the most important. He was a painter turned craftsman, which, in his day, meant a Jugendstilist. But he could not bear that sultry atmosphere for long, and found his true vocation in architecture. His first house, which he built for his own occupation in Darmstadt in 1901, already showed a hardening of the tender curves of Art Nouveau, and was thus reminiscent of the work Mackintosh and Berlage produced during the same period. From 1904 onwards, all his industrial buildings — the most prominent were the turbine factory and the factory for the production of small motors he built for AEG, one of the big German electrical combines — had an elegant compactness and an unmistakable classical touch. Pevsner called the turbine factory "perhaps the most beautiful

571

industrial building ever erected up to that time."[50] It was certainly no accident that Walter Gropius, the greatest architect (apart from Corbusier) to emerge in the twentieth century, should have been trained in Behrens's office. The American architect Frank Lloyd Wright can only be mentioned in passing here — his work before 1914 was practically unknown in Europe. When Berlage spoke about him in Zurich, after his return from America in 1911, it was a revelation to the audience.

The fourth and last group, born between 1870 and 1880, was, by and large, still too young in 1900 to have played an important role in our period. Two exceptions, however, confirm the rule that no one younger than thirty can make truly fundamental contributions to art or the humanities: Adolf Loos and Auguste Perret. Perret was of Burgundian descent, but was born in Brussels where his father, a Communard, had sought refuge. Most of his work was done in Paris, and although his artistic renown was not very great, he deserves special mention for having been the first architect to use reinforced concrete consistently — not surprisingly, for the family firm dealt in it. Concrete had been known since the middle of the nineteenth century, but it had rarely been used in large buildings and never in undisguised form. In the apartment houses he built at the beginning of the twentieth century, Perret left concrete as concrete, although he did not yet dare to dispense with all forms of decoration. Adolf Loos from Vienna was, with Otto Wagner and Wagner's pupil Joseph Hoffmann, the most outspoken opponent of Art Nouveau. As early as 1898, two years before the exhibition of Mackintosh's interior in Vienna, he designed a completely plain and rectangular shop interior. More important, though not unconnected with his rectilinear approach, was the fact that his work was the first to make it clear that the new architecture built from the inside out, so to speak, and no longer attached central importance to the external appearance. Loos's façades — *inter alia* that of the Gustav Scheu Haus of 1912 — had the "cubist" form which was to become an integral part of twentieth-century architecture. Loos disliked the ornate in any shape or form; no more radical departure from Art Nouveau was possible, nor could that dislike have been expressed more forcefully than it was in Loos's "Ornament is crime."[51] He was not, however, alone in his thinking. "The result of the machine," Muthesius wrote as early as 1902, "can only be the unadorned, factual form."[52] Still, Loos's pronouncement must be considered a most fitting epitaph of the nineteenth century, and a motto for the twentieth — more down to earth than any that had gone before.

CHAPTER XXXVIII

DAYBREAK AFTER *GÖTTERDÄMMERUNG*

Musical life in Europe at the turn of the century was still cast in the
shadow of Richard Wagner, the great prodigy who had died in 1883.
Perhaps we should rather say that the light of Bayreuth, his creation,
had been irradiating musical life ever since 1875: thousands of west
Europeans were enraptured not only by the music of Wagner's operas
but also by their emotional and intellectual appeal, many despite themselves. In an age when royal patronage had begun to wane, Ludwig of
Bavaria nevertheless risked a government crisis rather than cut his generous subsidies to the capricious master, and when the overstretched prince
was forced to back down, a form of limited company (subscriptions
with exclusive rights of admission to the *Festspiele*) was launched to
finance the great Bayreuth project. In various German cities Wagner
societies sprang up for the express purpose of organizing local Wagner
concerts, not entirely to the liking of the master, who felt anything but
attracted to the life of a traveling conductor.[1] The first Bayreuth *Fest-
spiel*, at which Hans Richter conducted the *Ring der Nibelungen*, was
much more than an important musical event: it ushered in a cult the
like of which the world had never seen, and one that — it is only fair
to say — was largely inspired by the great magician's delusions of grandeur. The German deification of Wagner is readily explained by the
nationalist soil in which it was rooted. However, if that nationalism
had been a purely German phenomenon, enthusiasm and snobbery alone
would not have carried the Wagner cult so far beyond Germany's borders.
The Dutch variety arose in 1884; Paris had its own Wagner circle, the
Petit Bayreuth,[2] whence Wagner extended his influence over French
nationalists and symbolists, who admired his "sultry suggestiveness."[3]
Chicago invited the master to build a *Festspielhaus* within its precincts,
and even the Sultan of Turkey and the Viceroy of Egypt purchased
"certificates of patronage."[4]

So much for Wagner's appeal to concertgoers. If we now look at
the creative aspects of his music, then the dark side of his character
begins to loom large, for Wagner's musical importance cannot be isolated

from his pan-Germanic ideas, cloaked in veiled mysticism and undisguised eroticism. For the rest, he tried to escape from the oppressive pettiness of life by substituting high-flown images for the threadbare norms which Nietzsche, too, considered it his duty to overthrow in his "transvaluation of all values." But though Nietzsche discerned the *fin de siècle* character of the Wagner phenomenon,[5] and, moreover, pointed out with frightening clarity of what process this phenomenon was the beginning and the end, practically all of Wagner's younger contemporaries and direct successors fell under the master's spell and then developed their own character in trying to shake it off. Thus Debussy, in his later years, spoke of the time when he was still so much the Wagnerian that he "forgot the most basic principles of civility";[6] Mahler earned his spurs as a conductor of Wagner's works, and Diepenbrock was an enthusiastic Wagnerian, at least until 1914 when, somewhat over-emotionally, he threw out the musician with the nationalist.

There are many other elements of late nineteenth-century music that can be attributed to Wagner's influence. One of these was the tremendous growth of the orchestra, connected with both the gradual disappearance of court musicians and private concerts and with the construction of large concert halls. Another was the rise of nationalism in music, and the rivalry it gave rise to. In an article in the *Revue des Deux Mondes* on the relative backwardness of British industry, we can read: "Even the opera to which you listen is an opera made in Germany, performed by musicians trained in Germany, with instruments and scores imported from Germany."[7] National sentiments manifested themselves particularly in compositions based on traditional folk themes: we have only to think of the Czech composer Smetana, with his *Má vlast*, (My Country) a cycle of symphonic poems about his fatherland with such subtitles as "Vltava" and "From the Bohemian Woods"; his compatriot Dvořák; the Finn Sibelius; the Norwegian Grieg; or the "mighty little band" of Russians, of whom the bearded Mussorgsky was the most prominent. In Spain, folk music was the inspiration of Felipe Pedrell and Manuel de Falla, and in the Netherlands of Zweers, with his symphony *Aan mijn vaderland* (To My Fatherland, 1890). The latter, though anything but a call to arms, nevertheless spoke in the national voice; it had all the musical characteristics of the Dutch people: part folk song and part solemn diatonic melody, firmly anchored in a compact, homophonous score with broad cadences, in which austere dissonances were often added to functional harmonies.[8] Even in the Netherlands, where, under the Republic, musical life had retired indoors and where no composer of any importance can be mentioned beside Sweelinck, there was a national revival, however slow.

Meanwhile German music continued to reign supreme: such composers as Mendelssohn and Schumann were copied everywhere zealously but without marked success. Preoccupation with the local product led to a ridiculous sense of self-importance, to a lyrical passion for compositions that were faded and antiquated even while they were still being written.

Even in the nineteenth century, the Netherlands could boast a great many amateurs who played to select audiences. In every Dutch city of any size, people could listen to the performances of at least one, and sometimes of several orchestral societies, as well as a host of ad hoc ensembles. The underrated position of the conductor — he was often referred to as the "bandmaster" — and the non-professional status of many of the musicians were two of the chief causes of the low standard of public performances. Adorno has drawn attention to the lowly social status of both the musician and the actor: "Until far into the century, with capitalism in full sway, composers were anachronistically kept in a servile state because their work, though long since marketable, failed, due to retrograde legislation, to gain them an adequate living, even while the impresarios waxed fat on them." He cited the case of Wagner, from whose *Tannhäuser*, *Lohengrin* and *Der fliegende Holländer*, opera houses earned fortunes, and claimed that Puccini and Strauss were the first composers to exploit their work like good capitalists.[9] At the same time, oddly enough, touring virtuosos were greatly admired: Liszt and Paganini were acclaimed throughout Europe for their solo performances. We do not know what these celebrities thought of the orchestras accompanying them, particularly in the Netherlands; only Brahms has been recorded as saying that the Dutch were better at serving up good food than good music.[10]

It was thus something of a shock for Dutch music lovers when the Meininger Hofkapelle made its first appearance under the baton of the great Hans von Bülow in 1885. At last they had come face to face with a famous orchestra, conducted by a truly great artist. At last they could hear what a disciplined and well-trained ensemble could achieve when it was led by a great personality, one who could and did make demands on the players.

Von Bülow's appearance strengthened the hands of those who insisted that Amsterdam, too, must have a symphony orchestra and a concert hall of which it could be proud; their efforts bore fruit in 1888 when the *Concertgebouw* was opened to the public. On that occasion, the newly formed orchestra was conducted by Henri Viotta, founder of the Dutch Wagner Society. Under the able leadership of the youthful

575

Willem Kes, the orchestra went from strength to strength, and the standard of performance and repertoire improved dramatically. Kes also made a number of drastic changes in an effort to retain a public that had become used to savoring its musical fare in the affable atmosphere of a society gathering: he banned the sale of refreshments in the body of the hall, ordered the removal of the little tables from the floor, and stopped people from talking or taking their seats while the performance was in progress — two ingrained habits.[11] Apart from introducing a host of foreign soloists and compositions not previously heard in the Netherlands, Kes also helped the national musical cause by performing a work that stood out far above its immediate predecessors: Bernard Zweers's *Mijn vaderland.* In 1895 Kes was succeeded by Willem Mengelberg, who in a long and glorious career — alas, cut short by his behavior during the Second World War — earned the Amsterdam orchestra lasting renown. His Mahler festivals, in particular, and his systematic performances of Richard Strauss, helped to turn Amsterdam into a leading music center during the 1920s.

Dutch creative music was initially no more than a pale shadow of that produced in Germany, Austria, France and Russia. In the last, Glinka and Dargomizhsky were able to draw freely on the inexhaustible treasure of folk tunes. The spell of Italian music, which had turned musical life in the great Russian cities into an elegant, but anything but "popular" affair, was finally broken when a small group of composers under the leadership of Balakirev threw up a dam against the Italian current. A prominent member of this group was Modest Mussorgsky, unquestionably the most brilliant and original of them all. However unusual his musical education may have been — he remained a dilettante throughout his tragic life, plagued by drink, mental decline and poverty — his works were, and still are, strangely compelling. The national flavor of his compositions did not so much reside in his choice of subjects — such operas as *Boris Godunov* and *Sorochintsy Fair* (after Gogol) — as in his exuberant strength and unpolished roughness. Even the adaptations of his work, which were no improvements, by his friend Rimsky-Korsakov, were unable to detract from the strong appeal of this type of popular music. It was through Rimsky-Korsakov that the Russian line was continued by Igor Stravinsky in Paris. The Russians, and all the other composers who relied on national themes, provided new melodic, and above all rhythmical, impulses. This was particularly true of Sibelius who endowed his music with a highly original sonority — with impressionist overtones one might say — and who, despite his close relationship with the Romantic, Bruckner, reflected the culture and atmosphere of his native Finland in all his music. There was only one other country in which the same clear national strains could be heard, namely England. Here Parry's *Prometheus Unbound* (1880) was a first step towards the birth of a truly native school of music. Next came the impressionist work of Delius and above all of Vaughan Williams, followed by a composer of international renown: Elgar, whose *Dream of Gerontius* (1899) and later symphonic works reserved for English music, with its very particular charm, a prominent place in the European "concert of nations."

However, the real revolution in music was wrought in the German-speaking world and in France. In 1882 Wagner produced his swan song with *Parsifal*, which to his many admirers was his highest and most spiritual achievement, and to Nietzsche the *Götterdämmerung* of his decadence. It was a work charged with mystical power, but lacked the strength of his *Ring der Nibelungen.* In 1885, Brahms completed his fourth and last symphony and in 1886 the greatest pianist of his day, Franz Liszt, died. Much more than in his symphonies, his importance to subsequent generations of musicians lay in the piano compositions he bequeathed to them. He and Chopin are the twin pillars of the art of modern piano playing.

As an unexpected challenge to the oppressive sway of Wagner's "total art," Bizet's *Carmen* blossomed into full flower in France as early as 1875, revealing the opposition between the Latin and German spirits in the clearest possible way. Besides Bizet, Verdi, who put the final touches to his *Otello* in 1887, was the only composer to steer a steady course through the musical eddies churned up by Wagner's tidal wave. Verdi's unshakable faith in grand opera and, above all, his unflinching determination to create a more incisive musical language, helped to stamp a unique imprint on each of his works — his operas have stood the test of time far better than those of his great opponent. Bizet's Carmen, for all that, had a host of admirers in Italy; Mascagni with his *Cavalleria rusticana* (1890), Leoncavallo with *Pagliacci* and, above all, Puccini with *La Bohème* (1896), *Madame Butterfly* (1904), and *Manon Lascaut* (1893), all wrote deliberately popular and tuneful works that linked the old to the new, as exemplified in the short operas of Menotti, who works in America.

Richard Strauss, who began writing operas as a disciple of Wagner, later found his way back to the more Italianate, conventional opera, *inter alia* in the *Rosenkavalier* (1911), having first displayed an extreme form of musical imagination in his *Salome* and *Elektra*, two works with a pronounced atonal approach. This expressionist genre was concluded, via several of Schönberg's operas, with Alban Berg's *Wozzeck* (1924), a moving, somber and highly personal work.

The spread and democratization of musical life in the nineteenth century was particularly marked in northern Europe where, so to speak, it revolved round the piano: "It is not by chance", wrote Max Weber, "that the pianist's art is so highly developed among northern nations, tied to their homes, as they are, by the weather . . . "[12] Democratization proceeded by stages: from the small concert hall to the larger, a process that culminated in London with the famous "Proms," which began in 1895.

Another gain was the revival of interest in musicology, one of the seven "liberal arts" of the medieval academic syllabus. The Société Internationale de Musicologie was founded in 1899;[13] a musicological congress was held in the Netherlands in 1912; and before the nineteenth century was out musicology had recaptured its place in the universities. Thus Hugo Riemann, who is considered the father of modern musicology, began to lecture in Leipzig in 1895; even earlier, Sir George Grove had made his influence felt in England, not least with his classic *Dictionary of Music and Musicians* (1879–1889). Expert knowledge was now expected of even the music critic on the daily press; it was no longer done to employ any supernumerary member of the staff who happened to be available. Unfortunately, his very expertise often misled the critic into paying more attention to the performance than to the work, with the result that his public pronouncements could make or break careers and thus became an element in the commercialization of music.[14] Light music in particular degenerated into the writing of "hits," which for the sake of profit were aimed at the broadest, and hence the lowest, taste.[15] Still, the worst excesses did not appear until well after the First World War.

Possibly because music is so strongly dependent on execution, the composer who believes that he can make an entirely new start is a very rare exception. Nevertheless, music, too, experienced sudden changes, many of which appear in retrospect as the convergence of a series of interconnected developments. At the close of the nineteenth century these were, first of all, the expansion of the orchestra, sometimes to colossal proportions, and the associated increase in instrumental inventions and in what may be called the sense of musical color. In the second place, there was a return to folk music as a source of inspiration and of melodic and rhythmical motifs, to which the work of nearly every composer of the period bears witness. Hand in hand with all this went a keen interest in exotic music. In western Europe this inspiration came chiefly from Russia and from Spain, with its Moorish themes — as witness, quite particularly, the work of Ravel. Then there was the even more remote African music, that reached Europe *via* the detour of jazz, and Asian music, as reflected in Debussy's *Pagodes*, or his dictum that, compared with Javenese counterpoint, Palestrina's was mere child's play. "And if you listen to their percussion without European prejudice, you will have to admit that our own is no more than the barbaric noise of a fairground merry-go-round."[16] The same exoticism, as we saw, also invaded the other arts at the time.

Closely connected and related to this development was the growing sense of "discontent with civilization," a kind of longing for the general human pattern, for nature, and for escape from city life with its confusing contradictions. This was clearly reflected in Mahler's annual flight from Vienna to his lonely forest refuge as soon as the season was over, and in many of Debussy's letters, in Ravel's withdrawn rural existence, and also in the closer association of musicians with other artists. Much as the painter deployed "tonal elements," so the musician became filled with the "color" of his sounds and the poet demanded *de la musique avant toute chose*. Writers, musicians and painters joined together, for instance, round Mallarmé in Paris, in the old artists' quarter in Vienna, or round such papers as *The Yellow Book* in London or *De Nieuwe Gids* in Amsterdam. Wagner's "total art" had, as it were, helped to fuse the various arts, though the Pre-Raphaelites might well have denied his priority in that field. In any case, the work of poets and musicians now appeared in editions set and illustrated by friends; Maeterlinck collaborated with Debussy, for instance, in *Pelléas et Mélisande*, and their partnership was quite different from the relationship between the old opera composer and his librettist. Moreover, Ronner's set and costume designs for Mahler at the Vienna Opera were a refreshing change from the fixed sets and the few baskets of costumes of the past. Berlage involved the artists Toorop, Roland Holst, Zijl, and der Kinderen, and the poet Verwey, in the design of his Exchange, and Cuypers called in Diepenbrock for the dedication of his Rijksmuseum. A much closer collaboration between poets and composers also took place in song-writing, as witness the appealing Mörike and Goethe songs of Hugo Wolf, who almost turned singing into intoned speech, thus becoming a precursor of Schönberg with his *Sprechgesang*, and laying particular emphasis on the independent poetry of the piano score. Debussy, for his part, opened up new and totally unexpected musical horizons in 1892 with his *Prélude à l'après-midi d'un faune*, based on a poem by Mallarmé. For although it took

579

up the old idea of the symphonic poem, its musical language was
so highly original that it may be called one of the great moments of
musical history. His *Trois nocturnes* (1898) and *La Mer* (1905) also
contained all the elements of a new musical style: impressionism. In
Debussy's work the symphonic idea had made way for an extremely
subtle form of tonal painting or musical poetry, reflecting his mastery
of orchestration, largely under the influence of Berlioz. Debussy's music
was, however, so Latin in orientation and so opposed to the prevailing
German spirit — despite his confession that he had started out as a Wagnerian — that his influence remained largely confined to his native France,
where his musical expressionism was adopted by Dukas and Ravel. Thus
Ravel's enchanting *Mother Goose* (1908) is hardly conceivable without
Debussy. But then Ravel was original enough to advise men of talent
to copy a worthy example.[17] Still, he was so basically different from
Debussy that one is bound to conclude that their common traits — for
instance the organic association of music and words — must have been
one of the characteristics of the age. One of the few lines running from
Debussy beyond the borders of France ended in Italy with Respighi,
whose *Pini di Roma* and *Fontane di Roma* are a curious mixture of
impressionism with elements from the music of Liszt and Strauss. Oddly
enough, in England, too, traces of musical impressionism could be found
in the work of Cyril Scott and above all in the somewhat ethereal compositions of Delius. The English love of eclecticism — reflected even
nowadays in the work of Benjamin Britten — was clearly not averse to
this influence.

Impressionism had its last and very interesting offshoot in Skriabin
(died 1915), who tried to weld impressionism to mysticism in his tone-
poem *L'Extase*.

Like each of his symphonic works, Debussy's lone operatic composition
Pelléas et Mélisande, based on a text by Maeterlinck, was a unique creation. It had its first performance in 1902, but it was as early as 1892
that he had chanced upon a copy of the book, just published, in a bookstore, and even earlier that he had taken the first step away from Wagner —
"after several years of passionate pilgrimages to Bayreuth."[18] In 1889
his former teacher, Ernest Guiraud, invited Debussy and another ex-
pupil, Maurice Emmanuel, to luncheon in a bistro, and Emmanuel realized
that the occasion was important enough and the conversation exciting
enough to be recorded in his pocket-diary.[19] "I have not given way to
the temptation of imitating what I admire in Wagner," Debussy declared.
"I am aiming at a different dramatic form: a form in which music begins
where the word has become impotent. Music is there to express the

unspeakable." He was looking for a poet who "by leaving things half unsaid allows me to graft my own dream to his."[20] He wished to write music "après Wagner and yet not après Wagner,"[21] and when he objected that, with Wagner, "every person, so to speak, had his own leitmotiv,"[22] it was not because he disliked leitmotivs on principle, but only the over-emphatic, German manner in which Wagner presented all his discoveries. This explains why Debussy signed his scores *"Musicien français."*

In the new century, Paris and Vienna remained the chief centers of European musical life. Igor Stravinsky, the leading composer in the first half of that century, made his home in Paris. He was a highly original pupil of Rimsky-Korsakov and his ballet music attracted attention from the very outset. His work, too, reflected the drawing together of the arts which, as we saw, was a typical, innovating feature of our period. For Stravinsky enlisted the support and collaboration of Diaghilev, the great choreographer also resident in Paris, whose work was then in great vogue. Together they put on the first performances of the *Firebird* (1910), *Petrushka*, and *Rite of Spring* (1913). In all these ballets, Stravinsky expressed an idiom of his own, rooted in the oriental splendor of the instrumental art of Rimsky-Korsakov. In the *Rite of Spring*, which caused a furor in Paris, he deployed an incredible wealth of rhythmic patterns, a minimum of thematic development and an extraordinary sensitivity to orchestral sonorities the better to achieve a shocking impact on the ear. His *Soldier's Tale* (1916–1917), a short work combining opera with declamation, and *Oedipus Rex* were important postwar additions that continued to intrigue by their constant change of intent and the complete unpredictability of their musical language.

Musical life in Vienna revolved round Gustav Mahler, who was ap-pointed director of the Court Opera at the age of thirty-seven. Guido Adler, speaking of the constant bickerings that eventually drove Mahler to America in the wake of sore disappointments, has blamed the "ir-ritability of the age," which in the musical world found a "sickly ex-pression" in the "lower instincts and hatred of his opponents" — no doubt an allusion to their anti-Semitism — but also in the "remorseless will of Mahler, who spared neither himself nor others when it came to imple-menting what his deepest and highest artistic convictions demanded."[23] Mahler had already made his mark when he accepted his post in Vienna and this may well have contributed to his exacting demands on the orchestra. He had started out as a genuine nineteenth-century band-master at the age of eighteen in an open-air theatre in Bad Hall, where his duties included placing the music on the stands, clearing it away again, dusting the piano, and taking the director's baby out for walks in its pram.[24] Not surprisingly, he reacted by taking a somewhat exalted view of the conductor's social and artistic position, which explains why he abolished the claque as an unworthy institution.[25] In his Viennese years, he wrote his *Lieder eines fahrenden Gesellen* (1883) and his symphonies, including the colossal Eighth, in which he carried the choir, the soloists, and the orchestra to unprecedented heights, thus following a line begun by Wagner, although he, too, strove to write music "après and not après Wagner," but without ever denying his debt to the master of Bayreuth. Thus he told a colleague who refused to hear a Wagnerian opera "lest I become too much like him," that he was being unnecessarily cautious: "After all, you go on eating beef without turning into an ox."[26]

Mahler and Debussy had certain common traits characteristic of the age they lived in: a longing for nature and a search for new sonorities. Both owed a great debt to national music, though Debussy, the declared *musicien français*, was also influenced by east European music, having spent some time in Russia, by jazz and by the Indonesian gamelon, which, to him, was the great surprise of the World Exposition of 1889. Compared with Debussy, the Austrian Mahler was a typical German composer who for all his Viennese jollity and love of life found it hard to rid himself of his German Weltschmerz and who at the same time — another typical German trait — "tried in his compositions to plumb the depths of existence, to fulfill his highest ends and, following the titanic example of Beethoven, to express the quintessence of primitive wisdom in a few lines of music."[27] While Debussy and Ravel were impressionists, who *heard* music in everything, Mahler was an expressionist who wanted to *say* everything through music. He was a split personality and the most glittering jewels of his art were wrought out of passionate despair, as in the *Kindertotenlieder* (1902) or out of the reconciliation of his inner conflicts, as in *Das Lied von der Erde*, the musical credo, partly based on Chinese texts, he wrote during the last year of his life. With it, Mahler took his leave from a world that had made life so hard for one who had done his utmost to be true to the composers he interpreted, and to infuse both orchestra and audience with his own enthusiasm.

It was also under the spell of Wagner, indeed as a fiery Wagnerian, that Arnold Schönberg, born in 1874, began his musical career — as witness such early works as *Verklärte Nacht* (1899) and *Gurrelieder* (1911). Instead of adopting the growing practice of using monstrously large choirs and orchestras (Mahler's *Symfonie der Tausend*), Schönberg preferred to express his unique personality in a logical extension of the chromatic ideas that had dominated everything else before his time. Tonality disintegrated in his hands — we noticed a similar development in Debussy — so much so that his *Drei Klavierstücke* (1908), the *Fünf Orcheststücke* (1909) and *Pierrot Lunaire* (1912) have been described as masterpieces of "atonal music" — a rather equivocal term.

His *Pierrot Lunaire*, based on Hartleben's translations of Giraud's poems, was a particularly striking example of this new approach which eventually led Schönberg, after four years of silence during the war, to his twelve-note music, in which each element of the chromatic scale has exactly the same weight as any other. No doubt the importance of this "system" has been exaggerated; for all that, it inspired a number of master works written by two of Schönberg's pupils, who, with him, set the tone in Vienna, and moreover posed a great challenge to Paris and its influence. Alban Berg (1885–1935) and Anton von Webern (1883–1945) both broke away from their master's somewhat rigid system to infuse it with a brilliant spirit of their own. The first, apart from producing a number of minor compositions during the years preceding the First World War, composed the most tragic, nostalgic opera written in the twentieth century, *Wozzeck*, in which romantic passion tempers the sober structure of the twelve-note scale and lends it content.

Anton von Webern reacted against the unbridled expansion of the post-romantic orchestra in his *Sechs Orcheststücke* (1909) and *Fünf Orcheststücke* — straightforward titles characteristic of the man. His piano and orchestral works were marvels of expression, whose terseness was not only highly effective but also reminiscent of the pre-classical composers.

Of Béla Bartók (1881–1945) we can say with little exaggeration that he was reared on folk music — not at all surprisingly for a Hungarian. With his friend and compatriot, Kodály, he has preserved a veritable treasure trove of traditional Hungarian and Roumanian airs. In addition he was a great pianist and a composer whose work at no time denied his debt to his source of inspiration in either melody or rhythm. A first period, during which his work was still strongly influenced by Liszt, quickly made way for a second, highlighted by such striking compositions as *Allegro barbaro* (1911) and the sublime one-act opera *Bluebeard's Castle* (1911), in which the orchestral section produces the characteristic sonorities so intimately associated with Bartók's later work.

In the Netherlands, the "après Wagner" did not begin until after our period, with Willem Pijper. This may explain the "passionate discussions about Wagner that took place whenever Verwey, Diepenbrock and der Kinderen got together in Den Bosch."[28] Diepenbrock (1862–1921), holds a very special place in the history of the Dutch musical revival. Educated as a classicist, and a musical autodidact who had to contend his whole life long with the label of "dilettante," he developed, not entirely without Wagner's influence, into an over-refined composer with a mystic touch, one who wrote all his work with the utmost attention to detail. His *Missa* (1891), and above all his songs, bear witness to an intellectual independence, and his sudden and total rejection of Wagner on the outbreak of the First World War to a certain naiveté.

In the Netherlands, as elsewhere, Wagner's "total art" started the conscious quest for artistic unity (as an antidote to social disintegration?) that was so characteristic of the turn of our period and that, by way of an additional complication, drove many artists to reject the idea of social commitment and to embrace the idea of art for art's sake instead. It took Marx's sharp insight to grasp the nexus between art and society. And it took all the acumen — the razor-sharp intellect, the psychological insight, and the hypersensitivity — of a Nietzsche to demonstrate the nexus between the most sensual and the most spiritual of the arts on the one hand and pan-Germanic delusions on the other.

Debussy was right to call himself a *musicien français*, for the brighter sources of the new music could only well up beyond the frontiers of Germany.

CHAPTER XXXIX

THE WAY OF ALL FLESH

On November 20, 1900 Oscar Wilde, the former lion of English society, died a repentant Catholic in the Hôtel d'Alsace, Rue des Beaux-Arts, Paris. A tragic shadow of the "irresistible, insufferable" aesthete he had been, he nevertheless protested with his last strength against the hideous furnishings of his dingy hotel room. Though the ultimate cause of his death was alcohol, his real downfall was not absinthe but his trial, three years earlier, for immoral conduct, at which he had been sentenced to two years' hard labor. The furor the trial had caused in England and beyond was only stifled by the Boer War. Before Wilde, thousands of unfortunates had been sentenced with far less noise but all the more savagely for the same "lapse" — in England, the death penalty for homosexual offenses was not abolished until 1861. What earned Wilde's case its notoriety, however, apart from his prominence in literary and society circles, was the fact that he himself was responsible for the whole affair by deliberately pressing a libel action, thus entering an arena in which Christian morality was locked in deadly battle with a code that placed responsibility to one's fellow men above the idea of sin. This clash was made unusually complicated because the old morality had never been applied and the new was not truly new. For the temptation to break the seventh and tenth commandments had always been stronger and more widespread than transgressions against, say, the sixth. The result was a double moral standard designed to paper over the cracks. Thus men were, in practice, granted far greater sexual license than women, and prostitution was looked upon as an unavoidable evil, a quagmire of sin, and yet a source of undeniable pleasure. In the nineteenth century it may no longer have been true that many lords spiritual derived part of their private income from the profits of the licensed town brothel, but prostitution was nevertheless recognized by the Code Napoléon — and by many other legal codes based upon it — which confined it to regular *maisons de tolérance* under medical and police supervision, with all the chicanery that entailed. Concubinage, too, unless in the very highest circles, redounded to the discredit of the female, not generally of the male, partner. Another facet of the prevailing double standard was that society tolerated marriages for money, but frowned upon free love and divorce. Many a promising career was broken as a result, for instance that of the Irish nationalist Charles Stewart Parnell (1890), and as late as 1906 two doctors were sentenced by a Berlin medical court for the crime of adultery.[1] At about the same time, two great scholars, Lombroso and Ferrero, defended the prevailing standard by adducing "incontrovertible" scientific evidence that prostitutes represented a "typically feminine form of criminality," adding the classical nineteenth-century rider that their function met a certain social need, inasmuch as it deflected male sensuality outside decent society and hence prevented crime.[2]

The late nineteenth-century revolt against this attitude was rooted in eighteenth-century ideas of human dignity, as reflected in Voltaire's angry protest when the clergy refused to bury Adrienne Lecouvreur, an actress and hence apparently no better than a prostitute, in sacred ground. Christian social workers trying to save the souls of such "depraved" women became gradually filled with the compassion and sense of human kinship we see expressed in the work of Dostoevsky, de Maupassant and Shaw, and also in Margarethe Böhme's tremendously successful *Tagebuch einer Verlorenen* (Diary of a Lost Soul). That book, edited by a physician, first appeared in 1905 and its idea was quickly "elaborated" by a host of lesser writers, some of them preferring to present it in pornographic guise.

For the rest, the new morality fitted well into what Holbrook Jackson[3] has called the age of experiment and curiosity about life, an age dominated by Ibsen, who had once written to Brandes: "The great thing is not to allow oneself to be frightened by the venerability of an institution."[4] It was an age in which no words had higher intellectual standing than "new" or "modern," both of which were used with great frequency in the titles of journals, books, and organizations.

Three currents in particular stimulated the change in sexual attitudes: naturalistic pessimism, which painted the existing conditions in black on gray and dispensed with all sentimental or idealistic circumlocutions; socialism, with its insistence that society must bear full responsibility for the misdeeds of the underprivileged and which took particular issue with the Christian idea of indissoluble marriage vows; and finally Darwinism, which for the first time treated man as part of nature at large.

One of the earliest literary onslaughts on the old morality in general, and on Victorian hypocrisy in particular was Samuel Butler's *The Way of All Flesh*. It was written in the 1870s but — and this was characteristic of the spirit of the age no less than of the author's pessimism — not

586

published until 1903, one year after his death. V. S. Pritchett called it a literary time-bomb, one that had lain in Butler's desk in Clifford's Inn for thirty years, ready to blow up the Victorian family.[5] Butler was anything but a revolutionary; his book was a plea for honesty, not for social reform. His pessimism, no less than that of his compatriot Thomas Hardy, was irrational, and it was not by chance that at the end of the book he had his hero, "a sadder and a wiser man," write an essay on "irrational rationalism."

Hundreds of contemporary writers shared his pessimistic view of contemporary society: Ibsen in *A Doll's House* and *Ghosts*; Zola and Shaw in all their work; Wedekind in *Frühlings Erwachen*, Brieux in *Les Avariés*, A. Forel in *Die sexualle Frage*,[6] Havelock Ellis in *Sex and Society*[7] and I. Bloch in *Das Sexualleben unserer Zeit*.[8] However, all these works, unlike Butler's, were suffused with faith in the perfectibility of man, so much so, in fact, that many seemed to contemplate the future through rose-colored spectacles. Thus I. Bloch, otherwise so objective in his approach, claimed that "all the currents of the age are moving towards a more radical perfection of love, to its free and individual expression." And elsewhere: "Place the free woman by the side of the free man, fill both with a deep sense of responsibility . . . ", only to end his book, a veritable compendium of the sexual frustrations suffered by his contemporaries with: *Und Liebe blüht nur in dem Doppel-Leben/Verwandter Seelen die nach oben streben* (Love only flourishes in the double life of upward-striving, kindred souls).

This quotation, which could only have been found in a German book, brings us to the typically national aspects of the sex reform movement. Its English champions had little of the rigidity one might have expected from a country in which prudishness had become a hallmark of the age. The tone of such men as Havelock Ellis, G. B. Shaw and H. G. Wells was realistic, forward-looking and candid (*Candida* was not by chance the name Shaw gave to one of his most unforgettable characters). Candid, too, was the tone of George Egerton (Chevalita Dunne), a now forgotten writer who introduced her countrymen to Nietzsche and Knut Hamsun and who was the first writer to allow an Englishwoman to express her own sexual feelings.[9] Scandinavia produced true "problem" literature, with Ibsen, Björnson, Strindberg, Ellen Key, Amalie Skram, as did Germany, where the tendency to combine thoroughness and profundity with passion and fervor sometimes led to the most exaggerated products, including the writings of Lou Andreas Salomé, Laura Marholm, Gabriele Reuter, Rosa Mayreder, and the German-Swiss A. Forel. Things were quite different in France, a "Catholic" country that traditionally took a much more candid view of sexual love than did "Protestant" countries, where love was rarely allowed to step out of married quarters. Nowhere else did the bourgeoisie keep more consistently to the double standard or discard it with such cynical abandon than they did in France. Nevertheless, George Sand, following in the footsteps of the Saint-Simonists, defended free marriage in her novels *Lélia* and *Jacques*, and could get away with it because she was both a *grande dame* and a *bohémienne*. After her, Théophile Gautier and Guy de Maupassant, among many others, wrote equally courageous books on sexuality. In about 1900 French women still had very little to say for themselves and those who had, did so in an extremely serious, if not bitter, vein.[10] By contrast, one of the leading male sex reformers, Léon Blum,[11] interspersed his serious reflections with the same lighthearted and cynical comments as can be found in Marcel Prévost's novels about contemporary society,[12] or in Paul Bourget's traditional "analyses" of love, which, lightly scented as they were with *fin de siècle* perfume, his contemporaries considered extremely astute.[13]

For the rest, it cannot be said with too much emphasis that, with few exceptions, all these writers dealt with, or at least reflected, the attitudes of the bourgeoisie, adding at most a paragraph or two on the deviant behavior of workers and peasants, and that the emancipated man of whose advent all of them dreamed was the cultured intellectual or artist who lived with his wife, a woman dressed in a charming "reform" dress with art nouveau motifs, in a suburban villa with the most fashionable interior. The socialist Blum defended this preoccupation with a very small élite on the grounds that the bourgeoisie determined the character of the nation, and that peasants and workers were, if anything, less inhibited in their sexual lives.[14] This was also the view of Adrienne Thomas, who showed how their sexuality was held against the *pétroleuses* in the monster trial of the Communards.[15] Moreover, though the tragic results of the clash between the old and the new morality had been the subject of keen debate for half a century, it was not until our period that the sexual problem was first treated as a complex of interconnected tensions by Mantegazza, Forel, Havelock Ellis, and Bloch. The reception of their books was no less sensational than the contents. On the one hand they were snatched up as soon as they appeared — Bloch's book, for instance, sold 60,000 copies within three years, and Forel was translated into sixteen languages. On the other hand they were fiercely attacked by obscurantists from every quarter. Part I of Ellis's *Sex and Society* was confiscated on publication in England, and the subsequent parts had to be published in America. And while Shaw and many others rallied to Ellis's defence, Sir Theodore Martin, author of the official *Life of the*

Prince Consort, sent a letter to the press in which he urged the suppression of a doctrine that was likely to change society into "a band of whores."[16] Forel, for his part, when attacking the practice of questioning confessants about their sexual behavior, thought it prudent to quote the actual questions in the original Latin[17] and, in the French edition, replaced the dedication to his wife with *exposée aux adultes cultivés*. Though Bloch wrote defiantly that a natural conception of nudity was certain to take root in the future,[18] in the naughty — and hypocritical — nineties, nudity served to titillate and was anything but a natural form of behavior. It was the age of the can-can, the precursor of the strip-tease, and of "art photography" which relied on a great deal of bare flesh and on even more suggestive garments placed against a backcloth of Art Nouveau velvet drapes. It was also the dawn of "mixed bathing," with very little nudity and that little under strict police supervision — for instance in the Wansee, Berlin, and on the Baltic beaches; the age in which Isadora Duncan caused a furor by dancing in bare feet, in which no "decent" woman took pleasure in sex, and in which no bad woman took her pleasure in anything else.[19] It was the age in which no respectable French girl ventured onto the streets unaccompanied,[20] and in which the organizers of the exhibition "Woman — 1813–1913", where all the work was done by their own sex in accordance with feminist principles, nevertheless felt they would damage their good name by employing female staff in the exhibition restaurant, for waitresses were considered little better than harlots, and their recruitment an integral part of the white slave traffic.[21] It was the age when engaged young people of good family were kept on the paths of virtue by the presence of an innocent younger sister, albeit some of the novels they read made a mockery of that very virtue. It was the age in which *De Groene Amsterdammer* announced a book on sexual hygiene in the following words: "Much recent literature has been censured for not turning a blind eye to the more intimate aspects of human behavior, treating them as blandly as the far more familiar. Now, however, a well-known physician, Dr. J. Rutgers, has given young men and women an acceptable account of everything concerning sexuality."[22] It was also the age in which the *Fliegende Blätter* could publish a cartoon showing young Karl staring at a lady on a bicycle and exclaiming: "Aber Mutter, die Tante had ja Beine!" (But Mother, auntie has legs!)

Central to the clash between the old and the new morality was the erosion of the concept of sin through the growing realization that human behavior is socially determined (Zola: *Les Rougon-Macquart*; Thomas Hardy: *Tess of the D'Urbervilles*) or doubts about the validity of the old moral norms (the "good murderer" in Galsworthy's *The First and the Last* or the saintly prostitute in Dostoyevsky's *Crime and Punishment*, a book which, like Tolstoy's *Anna Karenina* took so profound a look at the whole problem of the "fallen woman" that neither of the contending parties could cite it in support of their case). In great novels doubt was increasingly ousting the certainty of sin, and not only in novels: the diaries of Grillparzer and Kierkegaard reflected the same trend, and so did the diaries of Maria Bashkirtseff and Sonya Kovalevsky. An ironic and fatalistic attitude to eroticism was reflected in the work of the Viennese physician Dr. Arthur Schnitzler, whose *Liebelei* and *Reigen* looked at the intensity and evanescence of love with melancholic humor. The sex reform movement in general took issue with the Christian view that all sexuality was sinful, and tolerable only in the context of a Christian marriage. So strong was their revulsion that most of them came to reject Christianity as a whole, with the result that the fight for a purer sexual morality was fought entirely outside the church. Its champions were determined to replace the double standard with the absolute norm of the individual's conscience and the absolute demands of honesty, so absolute as to be totally impracticable and to usher in a new type of "as if" behavior: men and women who had not been brought up on the new morality made it a point to parade their "free attitudes," yet parents who had rejected the old morality were deeply grieved when their children put the new ideas into practice.

In about 1900 the number of divorces in Western Europe showed a gradual increase and this despite the fact that legislators still held the view that a relaxation of the divorce laws was tantamount to state recognition of free love. In 1906 a marriage reform committee was set up in Paris and Vienna followed suit that same year. The twin problem of marriage and free love was now on everyone's lips. "Free marriage," as an alternative to the "immoral" and unbreakable fetters that the combined forces of state and church tried to impose upon love was courageously embraced by the so-called "marriage-protestants" who proudly proclaimed themselves as "freely-weds" in marriage announcements. These champions of a less oppressive union made it a point to cite the authority of such precursors as William Godwin[23] and Ruskin, both of whom had pointed out that it was not marriage that justified love but quite the opposite. Bloch, who favored a form of trial marriage (for a term of five years, renewable by mutual consent) observed that the Japanese had been using a similar arrangement since time immemorial, and also pointed to Goethe's *Wahlverwandtschaften* (Elective Affinities) and his free union with Christiane. This search for historical support was only too under-

590

standable: marriage reform needed the support of every possible authority it could dig up, if it was to topple the false morality and hypocrisy that held sway. Like all just causes it, too, produced a hypocrisy of its own: infidelity was no longer justified by an appeal to a double standard, but by the alleged benefits of a second or third alliance with a woman who at last understood her partner.

Arranged marriages, designed to join money to money or youth to money, were still common in well-to-do bourgeois circles. Léon Blum[24] has described a typical French marriage of an older man to a girl just out of boarding-school who after her marriage flits from one man to the next until she is mature enough to enter into a permanent alliance with a lover of her own choice. He proposed a simple solution to this problem: shift the period of searching to before the marriage, allow the woman, like the man, to satisfy her natural non-monogamous instincts, which are a source of delight and yet *un vice, une tare originelle*, and both parties will eventually be ready for a harmonic marriage. The rejoinder, "But what about the children?" was blithely brushed aside with: "Children? There won't be any."[25]

Forel attacked yet another current practice: young officers were not given leave to marry any but girls from a "suitable" family, rich enough to allow their future husbands to live according to their station.[26] He also objected to the fact that students, who were permitted to share their rooms with a girl friend, had to postpone marriage until they, too, could afford "decent" married quarters.

The new attitude to the relationship between the sexes was reflected in a host of lengthy dissertations on women and often by women, for Simone de Beauvoir's dictum that man is the Absolute and woman the Other, applied then even more than it does today.[27] Thus it was argued that "the combination of erotic and economic factors in the course of cultural development has greatly increased the teleological differentiation of the sexes,"[28] so much so, in fact, that all human actions and institutions could be said to be subject to specifically male or female influences. This may explain why Bismarck distinguished male (dominant, German) from female (submissive, Slav) people in 1895. Moreover, our period was "sex-determined" in yet another way. No longer shackled by the old morality but not yet truly candid about sexual matters, people at the turn of the century lived in a strange atmosphere of smutty allusions, sniggers and giggles, of peeping behind bedroom curtains, under skirts and into the open bodices of vaudeville charmers, of suggestive drawings, toilet jokes, can-can dances, and "funny" postcards.[29]

Many writers attributed the sexual behavior of men and women to the

591

behavior of the sperm and the ovum and the position adopted during copulation. Rosa Mayreder was quick to put her finger on the "philistine narrow-mindedness" of this kind of would-be scientific approach.[30] Forel, too, was guilty of this sin, with his "scientific" contrast between active and passive sexual characters.

How divided opinions were is shown by a series of fierce attacks by women on man as he was and by men on woman as she was, but even more so as each threatened to become. For the rest, most writings by women were devoted to women rather than to attacks on men. One of the most famous was Laura Marholm's often reprinted and widely translated *Buch der Frauen*, in which she described the lives of six women, including the child prodigy Maria Bashkirtseff and the mathematician and writer Sonya Kovalevsky.[31] All their lives were said to be tragic because woman was essentially "a void with man as the content," and because the talented, thoughtful, and high-minded woman allows her emotional life to run to seed in a materialistic age that encourages her to develop her intellectual faculties to the full and to gamble away her chances of finding happiness in love. This book and many similar writings were warmly welcomed by oversexed contemporaries because, however progressive they may otherwise have been, they considered intellectual achievement a prerogative of the active male and hence something modern women had best eschew. In the Netherlands the same spirit informed the writings of Anna de Savornin Lohman,[32] Ina Boudier-Bakker,[33] and Annie Salomons, but with this essential difference that, unlike Laura Marholm, they failed to see that modern woman was a divided being, one who had been forced by society to adapt herself to male intellectual norms. No less representative of the period than Laura Marholm's oppressed woman was Lou Salomé's self-confident woman, who openly challenged the age and the world she lived in. What was new about this writer was that she tried to analyze the emotions of man *and* woman and that she explicitly rejected the traditional active-passive antithesis. Woman "still participated in the universal life that spoke within her," enjoying permanently what the restless male had lost in his quest for the absolute or could only achieve in his highest moments. Despite all her intellectual ambitions, woman, basically, wants nothing more than a broadening and enrichment of her own personality. She has a much deeper disdain for tradition than man. Man, not woman, has the greater need for a home, morality, and a closed family circle, for such is the creative power of woman that she can build all these out of her inner resources. In this she resembles the ovum, which "maintains a closed circle around itself . . . For that very reason, the feminine principle contains . . . pure harmony, is more rounded and has a self-assured perfection and wholeness."[34]

The attacks on (modern) woman by such psychologists as P. J. Möbius and Otto Weininger, by such philosophers as Nietzsche, or by such writers as Strindberg, strike us as so many "oversexed" reactions by oversensitive men to such "emancipated women" and Lou Salomé, who, it so happened, had been friendly with Nietzsche for many years. These men refused to see that the emancipation of women was simply the granting of basic human rights to one half of humanity; they considered it a total rejection of the female essence, the "resting pole in the flux of phenomena." This was a cry from the agitated hearts of many men: Nietzsche's rather unphilosophical pronouncements on "woman" were perhaps the most frequently quoted of his sayings, and Weininger's *Geschlecht und Charakter* (Sex and Character),[35] written in similar vein, the work of a talented but rather unbalanced young man who gave up the struggle at the age of twenty-three, came out in its twenty-sixth "popular" edition in 1925. It was a typical youthful effusion, a desperate effort to demonstrate that all woman's intelligent, active, talented — in short, human — qualities were so many individual "masculinizations."[36] Strindberg's misogynism, too, was the result of vague fears of female ascendancy.

Rosa Mayreder, who analyzed contemporary views on the male-female relationship in the most original way, received all the scholarly acclaim she deserved. But the fasionable public preferred to read some of the books we have just mentioned, and especially Ellen Key's *Ethics of Love and Marriage*, a "declaration of human rights in the field of love and a gospel for all those who are determined to harmonize love with the latest cultural changes and advances."[37] Bloch took more than fifteen pages of his textbook to sing the praises of this Swedish writer, whom he singled out above all for her realism and strict evolutionary approach,[35] and Forel, too, gave a detailed account of her ideas. After more than half a century, her book strikes us as a typical example of Butler's "irrational rationalism." In particular, her "erotic monism" took the form of a purely monogamous, free marriage as "practised by the most developed, high-minded and spiritual individuals." "The development of erotic life cannot be based on this or that divine commandment or transcendental concept. Its norm can only be found in man's mysterious longing for perfection that, in the course of evolution, has raised instinct into passion, and passion into love, and that is now striving toward ever greater love."[39]

Two elements in Ellen Key's gospel touched a deep chord in her readers' hearts. The first was her declared opposition to coercion, hypocrisy, and imitation in love, that is to unbreakable marriages, the double standard of morality, and prostitution. The second was her assertion that silence on the subject of sexuality was just another form of hypocrisy, particularly at a time when many great minds were still arguing that sex was sinful and impure. Thus Tolstoy, after a stormy youth and a fruitful and tempestuous marriage, concluded that the only answer to the temptations of the flesh was its subjugation — as witness his *Kreutzer Sonata*. Against him and others, Ellen Key upheld the unity of natural instinct and a spiritualized, "higher" love, a "spiritual sensuality" by which, according to George Sand, the soul did not deceive the senses nor the senses the soul. In the place of procreation as a duty and expiation, Ellen Key set the idea of the spiritual force of love, and man's obligation to his "species" which renders deliberately childless marriages immoral. Those who refuse to marry because of disappointed love, or to have children, "follow their subjective feelings at the expense of the future generation and allow their love to serve their self-interest."[40]

This evolutionist approach also explains the demand that the "new" man and woman should "refrain voluntarily or compulsorily from producing life in circumstances that would render it inferior," with the optimistic addendum that these circumstances might well be eradicated in the foreseeable future. Needless to say, Ellen Key's program comprised such items as medical checks before marriage with possible sanctions against, or official encouragement of motherhood even for unmarried women — a burning issue in emancipationist circles at the time. However, her sense of responsibility was such that she confined that encouragement to "high-minded" women. There was a general tendency to exaggerate the significance of motherhood and to underplay the role of the father. Thus Forel called the father "at best, his children's best friend,"[41] and considered it only right and proper that children should bear their mother's family name.[42] Rosa Mayreder, for her part, drew a glaring picture of the "motherly" but egoistic and frigid woman, which clearly foreshadowed the dominant American "mom" of the future,[43] and Ellen Key, finally, drafted a highly idealistic new marriage law, many of whose more reasonable proposals have since been adopted in most western and many other countries.

Forel, too, called for a new morality and for many of the other reforms demanded by his fellow writers. But while his was the most widely read book of all, it strikes the modern reader as the most outdated. Its fame rested on its appeal to the "educated layman" — a fastgrowing section of the adult population — and to its "scientific" approach.

594

Forel was a trained psychiatrist, for many years the highly progressive director of what was still called a lunatic asylum, a man who liked to present even his most doubtful assertions as so many established statistical facts, for instance the claim that most mental defectives born in Switzerland were conceived during the carnival and grape harvest.[44] For the rest, his book was so widely read because of its comforting conservative pronouncements: the male was the active, the female the passive partner, a large number of women were frigid by nature and, normally, sexual sensations in women were solely aroused during intercourse.[45] The "normal" woman adapts herself to her partner and the spinster, who finds no substitute for this sacrifice, becomes an intolerable creature.

Forel was a typical all-round reformer of the type we have met before in Chapter XXXIII, and his stable was full of a number of hobby-horses, of which the favorite was the fight against alcoholism, and another, and much more dangerous, was genetics.

At the turn of the century the discoveries of Charles Darwin and Hugo de Vries and the rediscovery of Mendel's experiments awakened great public interest in genetics and the wildest speculations about that subject. If it was possible to improve seeds and flowers beyond all expectations, then surely eugenic engineering opened up a radiant future for mankind. The ideas of the biologists A. Weismann, A. R. Wallace and F. Galton were taken up and spread with great enthusiasm. Wallace had arrived at the survival of the fittest independently of, and at the same time as, Darwin. In his plea for selective breeding, he argued that personal erotic feelings were an essential element in the improvement of the race. Galton, whose writings included *Eugenics: Its Definition, Scope and Aims"* (1905), was the founder of the biological discipline named in that title.[46]

Forel not only rejected the "immoral constraint" of the Christian marriage vows and advocated civil marriage based on equality of men and women, equal property rights, and so on,[47] but also called for legal sanctions to protect future generations by the preservation of the germ plasm so valuable to the "race." A detailed examination of the general admissibility of polygamy and the exceptional admissibility of polyandry led him to the conclusion that, in barren marriages, which were still almost exclusively blamed on women, polygamy was admissible for race-hygienic reasons; on the same grounds, the "social Darwinist" C. von Ehrenfels, Professor of Philosophy in Prague, claimed that polygamy was the only admissible form of marriage.[48]

The admirer who showered Forel with letters of gratitude for the "salvation and cure" his book had brought him[49] was obviously not bothered by his hero's paradoxical combination of respect for individual freedom in sexual matters and coercive methods of safeguarding the future of mankind. In particular, Forel insisted on the medical and genetic investigation of all marriage candidates, so that the doctor could compute the "mean quality" of the descendants and then advise how many, if any, children the couple should have.[50] Rational selection, he contended, must preserve mankind from the procreation of mentally and physically handicapped children, and the grave economic problems they posed. Moreover there must be close collaboration between specially trained lawyers and psychiatrists to determine which criminals should be castrated. "Our hypersensitive civilization may not like this idea, but the Turks have few qualms about their eunuchs, and the Papal Court is only just reconsidering the castration of choirboys."[51]

This kind of humanitarian "concern" became highly dangerous — and we have since learned to what extent — when it was coupled with racism. Thus Forel was bitter in his reproaches of American women, who preferred a life of idle luxury to looking after their homes and families, thus helping the intellectually inferior Chinese or Negro races to gain the upper hand in America.[52] Like so many sociologists of his day, he kept returning to the "race problem" with pronouncements that were said to be based on scientific studies, or, even more "scientifically," were being offered as provisional hypotheses. He wondered "to what extent the Mongolian and possibly the Jewish race could mix with the Indo-Germanic cultures without . . . displacing or even destroying them,"[53] and wrote a note in his memoirs: "Which races can be considered for the further development of mankind, and which cannot? And if the lower races are unsuitable, how can they be gradually eradicated?"[54]

Closely associated with the campaign for sex reform were the movement for the protection of unmarried mothers and their children, the fight against venereal disease, and the demand for birth control, sex education, and the more humane treatment of homosexuals.

The protection of unmarried mothers and their children had become a concern of Christian philanthropic associations as early as the 1850s, though their principles unhappily caused them to lump this category of "unfortunates" together with discharged criminals and prostitutes, and hence to treat them with exemplary strictness. In the Netherlands, the Vrouwenbond tot Verhooging van het Zedelijk Bewustzijn (Woman's League for the Improvement of the Moral Consciousness), founded in 1884 after a visit by Josephine Butler, the English campaigner against state-controlled prostitution, was affiliated to an international federation with the same objectives. The Union Internationale des Amis de la Jeune Fille, founded in 1887, was more specifically concerned with combating

the white slave traffic. The Mutterschutz (Mother-Care League), founded
in Berlin in 1905 with the support of such leading public figures as Lily
Braun, Werner Sombart, A. Forel, R. von Liszt, Franz Oppenheimer, and
Max Weber, was built on quite different foundations.[55] It held its first
public meeting that same year, under the chairmanship of Helene Stöcker,
who also edited the League's official journal: *Mutterschutz*, Journal for
the Reform of Sexual Ethics. It published articles on every aspect of
sex reform and in particular on its socio-economic implications. Helene
Stöcker was an enthusiastic follower of Nietzsche and liked to quote his
"Nicht fort sollt Ihr Euch pflanzen sondern hinauf!" (Let regeneration,
not reproduction be your aim!). In 1907 a similar league was founded
in Vienna with the support of Freud and Rosa Mayreder.[56]

No point in the program of the sex reformers proved more contentious than birth control, partly, no doubt, because the subject aroused
such strong atavistic emotions. Moreover, while the fight against prostitution could be waged safely on paper, birth control called for the most
intimate and personal involvement. Nevertheless, the first to interest
themselves in the subject, the neo-Malthusians, followed a purely social
objective: the abolition of poverty through family planning. This was
also the aim of Aletta Jacobs, who became the first doctor to hold special
family planning sessions (in the Jordaan district, Amsterdam). In England,
the trial in 1877 of Annie Besant and Charles Bradlaugh, which had
ended in a formal acquittal, had earlier opened the door to a constructive
propaganda campaign in which Marie Stopes was quickly to play a leading
role.

It is a striking fact that women, whose reputation was particularly
susceptible to attack, should have borne the brunt of a struggle that
earned them little but slander, derision, and persecution. In America,
where the notorious Comstock laws of 1873 stood in the way of all
birth-control propaganda and practical help even on medical grounds, the
neo-Malthusian idea had to be spread illegally, until Margaret Sanger
threw herself openly into the struggle in 1912. In various European
countries, by contrast, birth-control propaganda was tolerated until
after the First World War, when various governments grew anxious about
the problem of population decline.

In about 1900 the chief contenders in the birth-control struggle were
still the old rationalist and social reformers on the one hand, and the
Christian champions of the biblical "Be fruitful and multiply" on the
other. But there was one innovation: such race-improvers as Forel wished
to leave nothing to chance and demanded "a rational and well-considered
selective choice." "The sick, the incompetent, the dumb, the criminal

597

and inferior races will have to be taught neo-Malthusianism consistently. The strong, the good, the healthy and intellectually superior races must be enjoined to multiply energetically."[57]

One of the worst consequences of nineteenth-century prudery and double morality was the refusal to deal squarely with the problem of venereal disease, or the prescription of a cure that was worse than the malady: state-controlled prostitution. It was not until September 1899 that the first international congress for the prevention of venereal diseases was held in Brussels, attracting a wide audience of doctors, lawyers, clergymen, authors and philanthropists, many women among them. No satisfactory cure was discovered until 1907, when Ehrlich produced his "magic bullet," but the public airing of the subject was almost as revolutionary, and rarely was faith in future progress more justified than it was in this field. (In her memoirs, Aletta Jacobs tells us how, while working in Groningen Hospital, she became filled with pity for a lonely tabes dorsalis patient, doomed to death, and registered in the hospital files as a "meretrix." The Latin dictionary told her that this meant "public woman," and since she had no idea what that might be, she consulted an older colleague, only to find great difficulty in eliciting a more satisfactory explanation.[58]) A second congress followed in 1903, once again in Brussels. One of the resolutions it adopted was that "chastity and abstinence are not only harmless to health, but virtues that should be recommended on medical grounds." These and similar injunctions were aimed on the one hand against the usual quasi-medical justifications for state brothels, and on the other hand served as concessions to religious pressure groups, who considered the medical eradication of venereal disease an unwarranted attempt to meddle with what God had intended as a fitting scourge. In a widely read handbook of "practical psychology,"[59] chastity was exalted as the greatest safeguard against venereal disease and contrasted with the great evil of fornication. The book considered venereal diseases together with alcoholism and tuberculosis (!) under the heading of "diseases caused by the passions," and not even in the 1921 edition was there any mention of the existence of a *bona fide* cure, but only of quacks who cash in on the credulity of the public. So "science," too, helped to keep a veil of silence and ignorance over sexual life, exacting a heavy toll in human misery. Well-brought-up young girls were supposed to enter marriage "undefiled"; young men were supposed not to have any sexual feelings before their initiation — and often sexual education — by dirty jokes and brothels. In 1892 Frank Wedekind shocked the more thoughtful section of the reading public with his *Frühlings Erwachen* (Spring's Awakening), in which he discussed the sex life of adolescents and its consequences. But it was not until the dawn of the new century that people began to take a more honest look at this problem, one that had been deliberately brushed under the carpet throughout "nineteen centuries of Christian morality." I. Bloch devoted an entire chapter of his book to sex education, and the 1909 edition refers to more than twenty other German books on the subject written between 1904 and 1907.[60] Bloch pointed to Freud, who had argued that the mixture of smuttiness and prudery with which mankind habitually deals with sexual problems was one of the gravest threats to the minds of the young.[61] Like all branches of education, sex education, too, spawned a number of systems, many based on natural history. F. W. Förster voiced his strong objections to this approach on the grounds that it tended to bracket man with animals and plants and hence did violence to the "sacred idea" of human superiority.[62] While Förster and others felt that sex education should be the task of parents or primary school teachers, there were many who insisted that the subject must not be broached before adolescence. In short, most sexual reformers at the turn of the century had an attitude to youth that can only be called vague and hesitant. Bloch, like many of the pedagogues he quoted, praised the beneficial effects of co-education, and made the "avoidance of the first opportunity and of the first contact, and the guarding of children and young people from adult diversions and pleasures" the first rule of sex education — nothing but negative advice.

Those who were concerned about the victims of the antiquated moral code — about prostitutes, illegitimate children, and those tied down in unhappy marriages — may have been denounced as airy idealists, but their personal reputations were rarely under attack. Things were quite different with those who, towards the end of the century, questioned the common belief that homosexuals must be hounded out of society — they ran the very real danger of being mistaken for "one of them" and of being ostracized as defenders of the most perverse form of immorality, of something unmentionable outside police dossiers and court records. Hence it took a great deal of courage for Magnus Hirschfeld to found a "scientific and humanitarian committee" in 1897 and to try, with the help of his *Yearbook for Sexual Borderline Cases* and more popular writings, to gain wider public sympathy for the homosexual. Guy de Maupassant, who examined every aspect of sexual life with great objectivity and acuity, dealt with lesbian love in his *La Femme de Paul*, and Marcel Proust rid the novel of one of its last fig leaves with his *À la recherche du temps perdu*, the first part of which appeared in 1913.[63] The Wilde and Krupp scandals aroused fresh interest in homosexuality, but also a host of sensational rumors and sanctimonious condemnations from the pens of "normal sinners." "He will never lift his head again," said the London art critic Gleeson White of Oscar Wilde, "for he has against him all men of infamous life," and Yeats tells us in his autobiography that when the court had passed sentence on Wilde, the "harlots in the street outside danced upon the pavement."[64] The belief that the homosexual was a depraved libertine, a man who, tired of his excesses with the opposite sex, sought new sensations with his own, gradually made way for the belief — not least among the medical profession — that he was a disastrously unbalanced mental case. It took Krafft-Ebing and Bloch a great deal of time and thought before they came to share Hirschfeld's view that homosexuality was a natural deviation.

Forel, for his part, refused to the end to "treat as normal a completely purposeless sexual drive."[65] All the achievements and failures of the sex reform movement at the turn of the century were embodied in this exceptional man, whose favorite subject was entomology, who reorganized a mental home in accordance with the best model available in his day, played a most beneficial role in the temperance movement, and brought solace to millions of people shackled by sexual taboos, but whose own irrational rationalism provided the ammunition with which callous obscurantists assailed anyone with progressive views on homosexuality or on the race question.

CHAPTER XL

THE IDOL BEHIND GLASS

The Congrès des Oeuvres et Institutions Féminines, held in Paris on
June 18, 1900, one of many congresses with a more or less international
flavor associated with the World Exposition, was not the first of its kind.
It had been preceded by a feminist congress in Washington, and a host
of minor congresses in other parts of the United States, where the War
of Independence and frontier life had greatly stimulated the emancipation movement.

What strikes the modern observer most as he pages through the reports
of all these gatherings, ostensibly attended by viragos and militant suffragettes, is the decorum and restraint of all the participants. Moreover,
press reports suggest that some of the most progressive women still considered the National Exhibition of Women's Work held in The Hague
in 1898 an extremely daring venture. Even the organizers were astonished
at its success and at the profit: 20,000 guilders could be set aside for a
permanent National Bureau.

There was a marked contrast between the organizers' diffidence
and the worship women had enjoyed in the previous century, when they
were fêted as in the days of the troubadours. But while the troubadours
had revered women as objects of love, nineteenth-century veneration
had been chiefly focussed on the innocent maiden and the wife and
mother. A whole thesis could be written on the treatment of ladies'
feet by just one poet (Pushkin), and quite a few others on the recurrence
of high-minded women in nineteenth-century novels and poems, whose
perfection was constantly contrasted with the misdeeds of the *femme
fatale*, Eve the temptress. The whole approach can be summed up in
one sentence: nothing was more shameful than to defame or to take
advantage of woman's innocence, nothing worse than to fail one's mother.

It was this veneration that most impeded the social emancipation of
women, an urgent problem in the nineteenth century. Such women as
George Sand, who, having grown up in aristocratic homes, dared to assume
the rights to which she felt entitled, or as Elise van Calcar, who had
the audacity to address public meetings (even on so innocent a subject

601

as nursery school education), were looked down upon as sinners and contrasted with the idol man had made of woman: an idol under glass. The women's emancipation movement was ultimately directed against this type of idolatry, for it felt that even the strictest moral code was less oppressive than something that forced talented and adventurous women to live lives of dull domesticity in arranged marriages or, if fate and the lack of a dowry so decreed it, to serve as unpaid maids-of-all-work. How many brothers did not sigh as they paid the insurance premiums for their unmarried sisters against the day when they could no longer share mama's frugal widow's table, and how many of these sisters did not accept this sacrifice with a sigh? Deification forced even the most original and independent wives to heed every least demand of their righteous husbands, or else to employ petty ruses that often robbed them of their dignity.

The greatest gain of these women's congresses, in which, as in most congresses, there was more talk than action, was therefore the fact that they granted women a measure of self-respect.

In 1900, two other feminist congresses were also being held in Paris, and this trinity tells us a great deal about the feminist movement. In May, the Congrès Catholique des Oeuvres de Femmes had met under the patronage of the Archbishop of Paris; in September it was the turn of "leftists" to attend the Congrès de la Condition et des Droits de Femmes. Charles Turgeon, a contemporary author of an unnecessarily voluminous book on French feminism,[1] considered this division clear proof of the weakness of the feminist camp. In fact, however, the Catholic congress was a watershed in the feminist movement and a victory as incisive as that achieved by the labor movement when it induced Leo XIII to issue the encyclical *Rerum novarum* in 1891.

"Inasmuch as the parties do honor to themselves by honoring their opponents," one of the participants had said at the opening of the May Congress, "I, whom it has pleased God to make a firm believer, should like to pay tribute to those women who, expecting nothing from God's righteousness and His leadership of this world, nevertheless have faith in human righteousness and have devoted their lives to its furtherance."[2] These words reflected a complete change of front by the Catholic church, which had come to accept the inevitable: increasing entry of (unmarried) women into the world of trade, industry and education.[3] In the circumstances the best thing to do was to give them the vote, the more so as women, to a greater extent than men, were inclined to follow the directives of the church and were thus likely to strengthen the conservative side. Moreover, a moderate defense of women's rights, surprisingly enough, seemed to have as many good biblical arguments in its favor as did the domination of women by men. But this was only a minor point pressed at the Catholic congresses. For the rest, it was almost exclusively devoted to what until recently had been the only public works permitted to women: charity and the best means of preserving such "feminine" qualities as self-sacrifice, loving service, and similar superhuman attributes. At the June congress, too, two of the five days were devoted to charitable works, and no resolution on universal suffrage was submitted. A Dutch delegate was warned in the corridor about the "inflammatory language" she was likely to hear in September at the third congress devoted to the conditions and rights of women (also held in conjunction with the Exposition) where "suffrage would be pressed as a demand and the sanctity of marriage totally ignored."[4]

The third congress, also held in the Congress Hall of the Exposition, was much more modern and down to earth. It had been organized by the small but very active circle of middle-class women associated with *La Fronde*, a daily paper produced entirely by women. It called openly for what the June congress had merely hinted at, and most gingerly at that: civil equality, co-education, preparation of girls for the university, and so on. Foreign delegates noted the "backwardness" of France and the sharp contrast between the aristocratic delegates at the Catholic congress, and the predominantly working-class and bourgeois delegates at the two others, whereas in England aristocratic women could always be found to lend their authority and money to feminist congresses of every description.

There was yet another sign that women were determined to smash the glass case in which they were kept and to turn from idols into creatures of flesh and blood: a rising flood of protests that ranged from cartoons to "purely scientific demonstrations" of women's equality. Opposition to the feminist movement fell into two groups: those who pointed to the erotic confusion that was bound to follow the entry of women into assembly and university halls, and those who looked upon all feminists as dragons. The otherwise pleasant tone of Speenhoff's poetry was only too apt to degenerate into strident abuse when he turned to the "new woman." "The feminist wears short-cut dresses, / And lets you glimpse her knobbly knee / As through the busy streets she presses, / Shapeless, charmless but so free! / Not a curve and nothing tender, / Skin and bones is this poor hag, / Men would just as soon surrender / To a walking piece of scrag." This specter of a woman was indeed a specter, a pure delusion or at best an exception that proved the rule, but one that far too often obscured the true picture of the feminist.[5] For no women were more concerned about their outward appearance than those who had stepped into the spotlight of the emancipationist movement. They were most insistent that the congress reports mention the evening gowns they wore at late functions, and they made it a point of honor to attend all sessions in distinguished "petites robes noirs," or tailor-made suits, with feather boas or boaters, or — in the more artistic and modern circles — in hyperfeminine gowns incorporating the latest art nouveau motifs: "Remember, ladies, everything must be slender, delicate, soft, glowing, misty and light."[6]

The journalist Jeanne Rival issued the following exhortation: "In all your demands and in stepping into what used to be male preserves, always remain perfectly feminine in character, in behavior, and not least in appearance — here lies the secret of our success. Why, in a struggle in which it behoves us to use all our powers, should we reject our most powerful aid: our charm?"[7] Needless to say even this attitude was turned into a reproach by the enemy, and the clamorous references to "Eve's bag of tricks" were, in their turn, responsible for the somewhat nun-like reserve of the first women students and for the decorum the pioneers of the movement observed even in their own circles. This may explain why a Dutch feminist allowed herself to be talked into having an abortion "for the good name of the Movement."

More "scientific" opponents of the feminist movement may have used different terms, but they did not differ in outlook. S. R. Steinmetz[8] began his attack with what was meant to be an objective, but was in fact a sadly distorted, summary of the "feminist program," ending with such cantankerous remarks as "Point 11 - complete misrepresentation of the facts," and "quick and thorough decline of the nation through the childlessness or family planning of talented women." Otto Weininger took a similar line in his *Geschlecht und Charakter* (1903), mentioned earlier, and so, to a slightly more judicious extent, did Lombroso and Ferrero.[9] A typical product of rational-irrational German science was a book published as part of a series of treatises by famous professors and medical consultants. It was entitled *Sammlung zwangloser Abhandlungen aus dem Gebiete der Nerven- und Geisteskrankheiten* (Selection of Informal Papers on Nervous and Mental Diseases),[10] and Möbius, its author, proved "conclusively" that the female was a simpleton, and intended to be so by Providence, particularly in advanced cultures, because "cultural man alienated from nature" needs "natural" woman as his counterpart, not least for the sake of future generations. The author accordingly advised that all higher educational establishments for women be razed to the ground,[11] and he went on to inveigh against women who neglect their "natural" duties: "These modern fools are bad child-bearers and bad mothers . . . The children of brainy women are weak and deficient in mother's milk".[12] This crude kind of polemic, of a piece with the arguments later advanced by racist "scholars," was characteristic of the attitude of a host of German intellectuals. To them feminism was a sign of decadence, and one that infected both men and women: "The feminist movement is less influenced by the activities of women than by the effeminacy of men. Here lies the greatest danger, and one whose spread can only be halted by war, epidemics or other natural phenomena."[13]

Yet their fear was anything but justified by the actual position of German women. In a comparative survey of the development of girls' education in the nineteenth century, Lily Braun referred to the shameful backwardness of Germany, pointing out, *inter alia*, that in 1898 an attempt to open a municipal girls' high school in Breslau — at the time girls still used to attend private classes — was thwarted by the Prussian Minister of Culture who considered it his duty to "douse this little flame before it turns into a raging conflagration." Similarly, in 1849 one of his predecessors had closed a girls' high school in Hamburg, an action he followed in 1851 by closing a kindergarten, in which quite a few young women were earning a fair living, on the grounds that it was a "hotbed of pernicious ideas."[14] "And this," wrote Lily Braun, referring to the Breslau incident, "was happening at a time when Russia had had a state high school for girls for a good thirty years and when China was about to copy the Russian example."[15]

In France, too, there were quite a few misogynists, T. Joran amongst them. He liked to quote Möbius, set down his pique in a whole series of books[16] and claimed that "feminism spells the bankruptcy of French chivalry."[17] This was also the basic theme of a great many other books and pamphlets, and of a host of novels that Frenchmen (including Victor Hugo and Alexandre Dumas) contributed to the emancipation of women. All of them were afraid that feminism might undermine woman's time-hallowed role as mother, and that as a result she might lose some of her attractions for man. Faguet's attitude was typical of all those of his compatriots who were prepared to make a few concessions, but for the rest expected women to play the game — the game in which they remained the dear little creatures who, using "feminine" wiles, are able to benefit from male benevolence without ever taking advantage of it: "I am in favor of every woman being allowed to have a vocation, but not engaging in it."[18] The same spirit of benevolent conservatism also informed the answers to a questionnaire on the dangers of feminism, issued by the literary monthly, *Revue Naturiste*.[19]

National character, tradition, history, and the socio-political circumstances impressed a special stamp on the feminist movement in each particular European country. In America, feminism had a much smoother passage: here liberal professions had been opened to women before the end of the nineteenth century — the legal profession in 1869 — and so had education, though not yet in the greatest of American universities. In 1898 the United States could boast 250 women lawyers as against a mere two in France, and these two, moreover, had to brave a solid wall of hostility. American women were also the first to be organized in a national body that eventually founded the International Woman's Council.[20]

In France, what few feminist "explosions" there were during the Great Revolution and that of 1848 (and also during the Commune)[21] yielded few long-term results. In business, and particularly in the family business and the control of the family fortune, French women had always played an important role as of right, and this fact was accepted all the more readily because it was so exceptional. Similarly, a George Sand, who would have been quite inconceivable in Victorian England, let alone in Küchen-Kinder-Kirchen (kitchen-children-church) Germany, was tolerated in France because she was quite unparalleled.

Apart from the rapid increase in the number of women in the lowlier occupations, which was economically inevitable even in France, organized French feminism remained confined to a small group in Paris with barely 3,500 members, and even then fragmented into several splinter groups.[22] As for education, those well-to-do parents who did not prefer to send their daughters to the traditional convent schools, could, from 1880 onwards, send them to state lyceums where they were taught exclusively by women trained in special *écoles normales.*[23] Worse still, these lyceums did not prepare their pupils for the universities, thus forcing them to complete their education with private lessons. The result was that when the doors of the universities were thrown open to girls in 1868, more Russian and Polish women than French entered through them, so that quite a few of the twenty women doctors practising in Paris at the turn of the century were foreigners. Much more than by laws and official prohibitions, however, the life of the great majority of French women was governed by fears of engaging in unladylike behavior. Thus at the June Congress a somewhat rhetorical Italian delegate exclaimed: "Women ought sooner to die than grant favors to men, who repay them with slavery or dishonor." Turgeon added his voice with: "If a woman reaches this degree of depravity, there is every chance that she will go on to demand the abolition of marriage and the introduction of free love."

606

Still, because French women had traditionally been admitted to business life, they were able to publish *La Fronde.* For the rest, Simone de Beauvoir, born in 1908,[24] tells us in her memoirs that she had to fight hard for the privilege of going out on her own. The Scandinavian countries and the Netherlands had never known the chaperon's profession, and the Scandinavian countries were also the first to grant women the franchise: Finland in 1907, Norway in 1913. The Netherlands for their part led in the educational field — in 1900 Scandinavia still had no state schools in which women were prepared for the universities,[25] while some sixty Dutch headmasters and rectors gave a favorable reply to a questionnaire on co-education sent out one year earlier,[26] though Hertogenbosch Municipal Council voted that same year against the admission of girls to secondary schools.[27]

England struck a remarkable balance between the Victorian spirit, liberalism and necessity, thanks to which the transformation of the over-protected young girl of good family into the young woman about town, and perhaps into the militant sufragette, could be completed within the two decades round the turn of the century.[28] The liberal outlook was reflected in repeated attempts ever since 1867 to obtain a parliamentary majority for woman's suffrage. This struggle was led by John Stuart Mill, who wrote *The Subjection of Women* in 1869. At first the franchise was demanded exclusively for tax-paying women in accordance with the old English maxim of no taxation without representation, but later this restriction was dropped. An important factor in this development was the Boer War and the sudden shortage of manpower it brought in its wake. Another was the Corrupt Practices Act (1883), which not only put a stop to the bribing of voters, but also granted educated women an active part, and valuable political training, in electioneering campaigns. One of the leading opponents of women's suffrage, the writer Mrs. Humphry Ward, explained her absence from an anti-suffragette meeting by the fact that she had to campaign for her son who was a candidate in another division.

Secondary and higher education for girls had always been in private hands in England. In 1869 a highly unfavorable report by a Royal Commission on the Education of Girls set off a determined campaign to remedy this evil, and that same year, and again in 1871, the first two women's university colleges were opened: Girton and Newnham, whence small groups of students supervised by "chaperons" were allowed to proceed to lectures in various Cambridge and Oxford colleges, though only in certain faculties. The strangely closed English university system made sure that these rights were not "abused." Thus until 1920 and

1948 respectively, though the names of women appeared in the honors lists published by these two universities, they were not allowed to hold degrees — on the tenuous grounds that graduates had the right to parliamentary representation so that degrees would have granted women an illicit say in the affairs of state. Moreover as "Fellows" of the universities they would have had an automatic right to college rooms and free access to the private lawns of these venerable institutions. As late as 1929, Virginia Woolf[29] still characterized the inferior position of women in the English universities with her priceless description of two meals she was offered in "Oxbridge": the first, a luncheon party in an atmosphere of feudal splendor given by a men's college and including sole "over which the cook had spread a splendid counterpane of the whitest cream," followed by partridges "many and various," and a "confection which rose all sugar from the waves"; the second a dinner in the drab hall of a women's college and consisting of the "homely trinity" of beef, greens, and potatoes, followed by prunes and custard.

The feminist movement assumed a unique form in Russia, where the emancipation of women was proceeding faster, at least in certain respects, than in the highly advanced west. In certain respects — for nowhere else was the emancipation of women so clearly confined to a small circle of intellectuals. After Peter the Great had smashed the "twenty-six bolts"[30] of the closed women's quarters, and the Empress Catherine had founded the famous Smolny, the first "institute for young ladies," the way was opened for the kind of life led by the gay young Russian things we know from nineteenth century novels: a life filled with balls and operas during the winter season in Moscow and Petersburg, al fresco parties in the summer, and French novels and dreams of romance and the noble life all the year round. Through little more than a whim on the part of the Empress Maria Alexandrovna, the first proper lyceum for girls was opened in Petersburg in 1857 (by 1900 there were 300 such schools in Russia),[31] and a few years later the first ex-pupils were knocking at the gates of the universities, which, despite government opposition, were happy to run lecture courses for them, especially in medicine. The great shortage of doctors in the countryside, but also the radical attitude of a large section of the intelligentsia, ensured that these women did not encounter the kind of tough opposition from male academics for which their western counterparts had become notorious. Nor did these women have to contend with the anti-feminist traditions of an established bourgeoisie. In Russia women were accepted by their male colleagues as welcome fellow-fighters in the common cause, and many of them were, in fact, expelled by the authorities during the recurring crises. Then they would cross the border to share the austere life of their fellow emigrés in Swiss and Parisian universities. Of the thousand or so women students who attended Swiss universities at the turn of the century, fewer than a hundred were Swiss, the rest being predominantly Russian and Polish, and of these, two-thirds were studying medicine.[32] Back at home these girls had less difficulty in finding work than their west European colleagues: fifteen of the thirty-six district physicians working in Saint Petersburg in 1900 were women and most had a larger number of patients than the men. Nor were they afraid of rural seclusion, the less so as in the countryside they could enjoy the company of pioneer women agronomists.[33]

The progressive Russian woman at the turn of the century was a phenomenon that greatly intrigued western Europeans. Some spoke of her as a self-sacrificing angel; others saw her as a smoking and drinking virago in trousers, amongst them Nicolaas Beets who told the Utrecht Provincial Association with great trepidation that if this process spread to Holland it would not be long before he would have to stop addressing even this august assembly as "Gentlemen." In fact, the Russian woman was neither an angel nor a shrew, but someone who had one advantage over her western sisters: the weakness of the Russian bourgeoisie spared her the heavy burden of a tradition that would have every woman behave as a lady. The Russian woman felt free to draw water from the river in men's boots and this at a time when the "liberated" woman in the west still anxiously wondered whether she could permit herself the liberty of crossing the street with a shopping basket.

However great the differences between the ideal and the reality of womanhood may have been at the turn of the century in the west, the differences between women in the various social classes were greater still. The women's movement everywhere pretended (and often sincerely intended) to speak for all women. That ideal was voiced passionately in a large number of emancipationist novels, of which the notorious *Hilda van Suylenburg*[34] was a paradigm in Holland. Exploited women workers and defenseless, unmarried mothers were supposedly championed with the same zeal as girls from middle-class homes who wanted to study or earn an honest living instead of sponging on their families or marrying for status or money. But it was no accident that the middle class should have constituted the core of the feminist movement and that the typical "emancipated" woman was a lady, albeit one whom many considered degenerate. For the basic aims of the movement — full civic rights and the right to work — were of direct concern to these women alone, or to a select group among them.

609

The working man had long since come to look upon cheap women's labor as a dangerous means of depressing his wages, while the working woman forced by harsh necessity to do menial factory chores had little interest in fighting for something that struck her as little short of forced labor. This explains why the socialist movement continued to waver and to be divided in its attitude to feminism: in public it demanded protective legislation for women but in secret it nurtured the — justified — fear that women's suffrage, at least in the beginning, would serve the cause of reaction. Only a few of the more far-sighted socialist leaders, for instance Léon Blum,[35] August Bebel,[36] and Keir Hardie, who ranged himself unreservedly behind the suffragette movement,[37] spoke up for the civil equality of the sexes, and this at a time when the British Liberal Party and even the Conservatives, if chiefly for tactical reasons, had already gone a long way toward meeting some of the most pressing feminist claims.

The women's movement for its part was too bourgeois to take up the cudgels for the working-class woman and — particularly in Germany — too afraid of becoming infected with socialist ideas. Not that it opposed the struggle — we have only to think of Aletta Jacobs's fight to provide seats for Dutch sales clerks — but it took a rather patronizing attitude to the lower classes. Thus when the handful of delegates from the still very small women's trade union movement submitted reports to the "labor" section of the 1900 Paris Congress and several resolutions on factory conditions and night shifts, part of the assembly protested that these proposals were incompatible with the general resolution in support of free employment. In 1895, when a new labor law was being considered by the British Parliament, the Women's Liberal Federation waged a fierce compaign — in the name of freedom — against all forms of labor protection and even against the extension of paid leave for pregnant women or women in childbed.[38] At the International Women's Congress in Berlin in 1896, an address on the servant problem was cut short in mid flow; outside, the League of Berlin Housewives was waging a campaign for police supervision of the obligatory "service books" carried by domestic servants, in which the characters issued by previous employers — favorable or otherwise — were recorded for their successors.[39] Even in the radical *Groene Amsterdammer*, the Dutch paper that repeatedly spoke out against the low wages of women, the woman editor of the "ladies' column" protested against the "sickly wails about the alleged injustices suffered by our servants."[40]

As a consequence, the "servant question" became the Achilles' heel of the feminist cause: after all, the freedom of movement of the lady of the house was in direct proportion to the enslavement of her servants, no matter whether Madam used her freedom to follow a vocation, to work for the great cause or to fulfill an unbroken round of social engagements. Throughout our period — right up to the First World War, which had a revolutionary effect — the British aristocracy with their estates and houses in which a few dozen open fires had to be tended constantly would have been horrified at the suggestion that an annual day off might bring some relief in the almost endless round of duties of the male servants tending the fires and lamps, of the maids who had to fill bathtubs twice daily and carry hot water to all the bedrooms, and of the cooks who had to prepare enormous quantities of lamb, venison, and puddings. Worse still was the fate of urban maids-of-all-work, many of them country girls washed up in the city. Lily Braun has painted a horrifying picture of the total defenselessness, the deplorable housing conditions — often no more than a board fixed to the wall of a stairwell — and the frequent recourse to prostitution of these slaves of "good housewives."[41] Even in the idealized atmosphere of feminine solidarity that prevailed at the Paris Congress of 1900 there was a marked drop in temperature during the discussion of a motion calling for fixed hours, rest periods, and free days for domestic servants, and a special inspectorate. Amidst "numerous demonstrations of agreement," one of the delegates remarked that it was "totally unnecessary to demand legal protection for women working in our homes, where no stranger has the least right of entry." The resolution was an "affront to individual liberty."

While most working-class women were indifferent to the movement because it ignored their most pressing needs, aristocratic ladies kept aloof because, for the time being at least, they had no need for civil rights. The right to work, so fundamental for bourgeois women without property, was something that left their noble sisters quite cold. Proust's countesses and duchesses and all their living prototypes[42] felt completely free in a world in which the fashionable *mariage de raison* went hand in hand with a total disregard of marital fidelity. As long as they did not violate their code in public, these women had little need to curb their passions, the less so as marriages into *haute finance* provided them with luxurious settings for their purple sins. Anna de Noailles, the daughter of the Princess de Brancovan, would receive the friends who came to listen to her youthful poems while reclining in bed. "I have never seen a girl leap about so much on a bed," wrote one of the visitors.[43] The women's movement was much less interesting to these women than the Dreyfus affair, on which they could take sides with much more abandon.

In England, too, the Victorian spirit was much more firmly entrenched

611

in the middle classes than in the "honorable" members of society. True, that select group included quite a few who played a leading role in the women's movement and with English thoroughness, even among the radical suffragettes, but for the great majority of them the emancipation of women was already a *fait accompli* — they had seized what liberty they needed one generation earlier. In the memoirs of Lady Diana Manners, the famous society beauty who was born in 1893 and later married the diplomat and statesman Duff Cooper,[44] we are told that her mother, the artistic wife of the eighth Duke of Rutland (remarkable, in the House of Lords, only for his insignificance) was a member of a circle which was known as the "Souls," not simply because of the ethereal nature of its members but because they were exceptionally intelligent, cultured men and women "who knew how to live and love and serve and savour the best." When the beautiful Diana "came out" she was described, not without malice, as "the Soulful daughter of a Soulful mother" by a "cheap paper,"[45] soon afterwards to earn herself the reputation of scalp-collector in a circle that was bluntly called the "corrupt coterie" and that caused tongues to wag not only in London but as far away as Venice. Her mother tried vainly to keep her in line with lengthy remonstrations on the need for chaperons, on the indiscriminate consumption of cock-tails and cigarettes, and on "eligible" and "non-eligible" young men.[46] It all seemed an endless midsummer night's round of luxury and pleasure with the added and heady pungent flavor of rebellion and emancipation. The declaration of war in 1914 threatened to put a sudden end to it all, though not for long: by 1915, the "coterie" could make a come-back, despite the taste of death and ashes on the distant horizon of the blazing front. After a vain attempt to persuade some of her friends to stop the war by initiating peace talks (!), and after she, together with a great many other "honourables," had gone to the front as a nurse, Diana volunteered for service in a London hospital, feeling most independent and self-confident while her protesting mother wept bitter tears, not least about her "hideous" clothes.[47] Within a year, she allowed her mother to entice her away with a plan to open a hospital for officers in a French chateau, but this plan was thwarted by the Red Cross — after the names of the unqualified departmental heads had already been painted on the oak doors![48]

In retrospect, it is an open — and ironically enough a somewhat embarrassing — question whether the doings of the Comtesse De Noailles of Diana's "coterie" did not contribute as much to the emancipation of women as even the most stout-hearted and persistent activity of the feminist pioneers. Similarly we are entitled to wonder whether the in-

clination to dress in loose liberty gowns designed by artist acquaintances
was not more directly responsible for the disappearance of whalebone
stays than all the propaganda of the reform movement: "There was a
general new look in everything in those last years before the first war —
a Poiret Bakst blazon and a budding freedom of behaviour that was
breaking out at the long last end of Victorianism. We felt it and revelled
in it."[49] This effect was due not least to the fact that the doings of the
"honourables" were discussed at great length in the society columns of
the daily press and in such illustrated papers as *The Sketch*, whose en-
ticing stories and portraits, churned out with the latest reproduction
techniques, were devoured by upper and middle-class readers alike, while
the women's movement received but scanty and rarely favorable mention.
The publicity given to the English suffragettes was in any case paid for
much more dearly than that of the "honourables." In general it was also
much more negative. A virago, a *pétroleuse*, a hysteric, who at mass
meetings and demonstrations, hidden in the House of Commons or
chained to the railings of Buckingham Palace, emitted her shrill cries
of "Votes for women," who practised stone-throwing on Brighton beach
the better to fling bricks at the windows of public buildings and shops
in London, who started fires, threw petitions into the King's carriage,
placed bombs on railway tracks, destroyed paintings in galleries and
fought like an alley cat with the policemen who tried to apprehend
her — that was the common view the press took of these women. But
there was another picture as well: that of the fragile Mrs. Emmeline
Pankhurst, always dressed in loose gowns, gauze veils and voile and
crowned with spring-fresh flower hats, who, with her two no less stalwart,
intelligent, and artistic daughters, waged a campaign, bolstered by iron
discipline and devotion, that sent shivers through the British Establishment. Members of the aristocracy and the City helped to boost the
movement's income to close on £37,000 in 1913, the most successful
year. In 1912 a meeting in the Albert Hall brought in £3,600.[50] Hundreds of women worked in a fever of enthusiasm preparing posters, flags,
and special costumes for a host of processions and demonstrations.
Dozens of young girls, and older women too, courted arrest and prison
sentences with acts of public defiance, braving the horrors of forced
feeding, administered by callous prison doctors accustomed to dealing
with jail birds. The delicate Lady Constance Lytton, whose ambitions
to become a useful and educated woman had been thwarted, and who
ended up as a "useless old maid," joined the suffragettes when she was
forty, and had herself arrested disguised as a seamstress, in order to
gain her cause the full publicity due to one of her name and position.

She was carried half-dead to a hospital after several forced feedings.[51]
In June 1913 Emily Davison wrapped herself in the flag of the movement, threw herself in front of the King's horse at the Derby and was
trampled to death. Her funeral turned into an impressive demonstration.[51]
The government kept vacillating between severity and indulgence and
for the rest was practically powerless. The "cat-and-mouse" law made
it possible to suspend sentences until the victims of forced feeding had
recovered, whereupon the suffragettes set up medical services of their
own and organized escape lines.[53] England would not have been England
if the courage of the suffragettes had not earned them, apart from resentment, a great deal of public sympathy and admiration. Thus when
Sylvia Pankhurst suddenly materialized at a meeting surrounded by
policemen and began to speak, scores of sturdy East End workers rushed
up on the stage, formed a cordon and carried her outside as soon as the
police stormed into the hall.[54]

Besides the militant group, England also had a larger union of suffrage associations which, in 1912, ranged itself behind the Labour Party.
In the wave of patriotic enthusiasm that washed over England in 1914,
both groups suspended all their activities and the suffragettes, in particular, brought all their organizational experience to the Women's Emer-
gency Corps.[55]

Did they perhaps abondon the struggle with a sigh of relief? It would
have been more human to do so than to prolong the outburst of energy,
or if you like, of hysterical enthusiasm and sacrifice that had preceded it
all. How had they kept it up with no other objective than a ballot? The
indomitable will of the slight Emmeline Pankhurst and her outstanding
leadership were certainly part of the explanation. "I have tried to destroy
the portrait of the most beautiful woman in mythology, because the
government is destroying Mrs. Pankhurst, the most beautiful character
in modern history," declared Mary Richardson, after having attacked
Velasquez's *Venus* with an axe in 1914.[56]

But then, "the vote" as a symbol meant infinitely more than the
ballot-paper. A pamphlet written by an Austrian delegate to the International Women's Congress held in London in 1898,[57] was published
under the slogan "Woman is a symbol of higher things" (Carlyle). It
would not be difficult to produce a collection of similar dicta from
nineteenth-century writers, for never had woman been more admired
for her virtues and supernatural qualities than she was in the Victorian
era. She was an idol under glass, and man was only too happy to get
down on his knees to worship her, provided only she remained in her
show case. It was with good reason that van Gogh wrote Michelet's

rhetorical question under a study of an aging nude: "Comment est-il possible qu'il y ait sur la terre une femme seule, délaissée?" The misogynist strain that made itself heard in the literature of the end of the century, especially in the writings of such naturalists as Nietzsche and Strindberg, was chiefly directed at women who broke out of their glass cases, at the "modern" educated woman and her alleged claims to a common humanity. If woman discarded her divinity, all that would be left was a carnal creature. But the woman of 1900 who had discarded the paralyzing constraints of family supervision and nineteenth-century clothing and who reached for her bicycle[58] and short skirts the better to move about in a society in which she was determined to choose her own tasks, opposed the idea of the carnal creature with an ideal of her own. That ideal was more abstract than the old; women now expected less of the "courtesy man owes to them," were prepared to forgo concessions to their frailty, and instead demanded a say in the shaping of the world, and that meant the ballot paper. We find them depicted on posters advertising handicrafts, feminist and socialist demonstrations and on murals by Roland Holst of der Kinderen: slender but healthy, in loose dresses and footwear, charming but with a wilful line around the mouth and often holding a couple of strapping children by the hand. Though as feminine as the old, the new woman, liberated by modern education from the short-sighted and egoistic preoccupation with her own family, could at long last pour out her maternal love over all mankind. With American "momism," this new form of woman and mother worship turned into a caricature of itself, but even the less exalted forms brought smiles to the lips of the sober generation that followed.[59] The new woman, her elders had explained, would use her vote to make war impossible, for no mother would allow her sons to kill the sons of other mothers. The woman who had felt the scourges of poverty, hunger, prostitution, and discriminatory marriage laws in her own life or that of her children would use her new powers to change society from top to bottom. In literature the new woman had first appeared in the work of such rationalists as Shaw (Candida) and Wells (Ann Veronica, The New Machiavelli) and in the poems of Henriette Roland Holst. Women's congresses had been customarily opened by ladies from the highest circles, distinguished by their noble "feminine" qualities. Thus the London Congress of 1900 (where "many thousands of women . . . treated one another as sisters") was opened by Lady Aberdeen, "a woman wreathed in sweetness and charm" and an "example of true femininity," who laid great emphasis on the fact that the last thing the movement wanted women to do was to neglect their role of wife and caring mother;[60]

615

and the Berlin Congress of 1904 was opened by the wife of Chancellor von Bülow, who expressed her heartfelt delight that "women were once again determined to be women."[61]

However, during the first decade of the new century there was a marked change — people spoke of a reaction — in the women's movement, and especially in educated circles, which, on closer examination, turns out to have been a sign of growing confidence. The number of women in public office, in schools and universities continued to increase steadily, while one social barrier after the next went down. The woman of 1905 could move freely in society; no one looked askance when she asked to be heard; no one was astonished at the contents of her handbag: front-door keys, traveling season tickets and checkbook, as well as a variety of cosmetics. If anyone took offense at her daring language and behavior, it was probably her grandmother, an ex-official of the suffragette movement. Work outside the confines of the home and study had become so common that they had ceased to be privileges; they were now looked upon as duties, or a way of filling one's time before marriage, which was still widely considered the most rewarding task of womankind. In short, the movement had lost its vital spark even before it had reached its goal: the franchise would come by itself wherever it had not yet come as a result of horse trading by the political parties.

Emancipationist movements usually have two platforms: equality and respect for one's own uniqueness. In the women's movement, the second took the form of an appeal for greater appreciation of the feminine essence and the transformation of women from sexual objects into subjects with a place in society that was in keeping with what was considered woman's immutable and primordial nature. Even in the nineteenth century, there had been quite a few who, apparently flying in the face of reason, had frankly declared that woman could only have a full share of life if she were free to express her loving instincts.[62] Presented in the somewhat lugubrious tones of the novels of Anna de Savornin Lohman, that message had been greeted with derision by the reading public, to whom a woman who openly confessed her quest for love was little better than one who undressed in the marketplace. The same reactions had been evoked even earlier by such courageous women writers as Elizabeth Browning and Hélène Swarth.

Their successors took a more "scientific" line. Thus Ellen Key accused the women's movement in 1904 of concentrating on civil rights at the expense of erotic, religious and social emancipation.[63] Her irrational worship of the theory of evolution had convinced her that the improvement of the human race would cause eroticism to lose its irrational nature, for was the irrational anything other than what had not yet been grasped by science?

Laura Marholm caused a sensation with her *Buch der Frauen* (The Book of Women; 1894) and *Zur Psychologie der Frau* (The Psychology of Woman; 1897), which were translated into most European languages. Thousands of women who had only the slightest inkling of the new intellectual horizons the emancipation had opened up for them, were only too happy to agree with her that the greatest evil of the age was the "declining inwardness of women's emotional life"[64] — a direct consequence of the ascendancy of reason. These women dreamed of a responsible life in the shadow of the male, where their intuitive sagacity would earn them what real power some were about to barter away for that mess of pottage which was women's rights. Laura Marholm's ideal came straight out of the Middle Ages, and readers of her books would not have been surprised to learn that she ended up in the arms of Mother Church.

To many women of 1905, who also liked to bask in Annie Salomons's romances and who believed that they had outgrown the emancipation, all these books, which caricatured the life of the women pioneers, were so many cries from their own hearts. Not that they hankered after the old-fashioned ideal; they accepted all the freedoms the emancipation had brought them, but they projected a new feminine image which, though it no longer stood under glass, nevertheless had something of the loftiness of the impenetrable feminine spirit. They had made too few personal sacrifices to appreciate the battles fought on their behalf, and they idealized the past too much to grasp that the status of woman (like that of man) changes with the times and the environment, but that changes in the essence of humanity are as slow as the growth of stones. The naive political program of the pioneers had made way for an equally naive chase after happiness by their disillusioned daughters.

CHAPTER XLI

THE CENTURY OF THE CHILD

Kaiser Wilhelm II was clearly predestined to play the part of *deus ex machina* when, with his imperial decree of November 26, 1900, he put an end to the dominance of the classical gymnasium, and thus opened the doors of the universities to pupils from all secondary schools. For Wilhelm this was first and foremost a nationalist decision: in an address, he enjoined German teachers to educate their pupils not as ancient Greeks or Romans but as good Germans, and one of his closest advisers put it even more bluntly: "Germany's world position assures her a steadily increasing share in the world market . . . In this struggle, that nation has the greatest chance of success which has the widest knowledge of foreign countries."[1] Two years later, an Educational Reform Act was passed in France to established a new *baccalauréat* without Greek and even, for certain faculties, without Latin, and with more science and modern languages.[2]

The French Reform Act and the Kaiser's decree were two milestones on a road that ran far back into the nineteenth century: the attempt by all western governments to mold the education of children, from the primary school to the university, to the demands of a quickly developing society. Hand in hand with the broadening of education went a host of pedagogical studies and experiments that, at the beginning at least, were mainly aimed at discovering the best method of imparting to a hundred children, crammed into a single classroom in which you could hear a pin drop, the rudiments of reading, writing, arithmetic, and the history of their country.

Much more far-reaching than the partial replacement of the gymnasium by schools of a more "practical" nature, was the gradual takeover by the German state of elementary schools previously run by municipal or other charitable institutions. Another practical need — the demand for crèches and nursery schools for working mothers — was ignored by that state and left to the churches, anxiously fishing for souls.

It was also practical considerations that presided over the introduction of compulsory education in most other European countries at the end of the century, though here, too, educationalists were divided as to "whether tradition or economic need ought to preside over education."[3] That the gymnasium should have been hotly defended even by many who were not particularly interested in a classical education, was entirely in keeping with the élitist aspirations of the bourgeoisie, which, after all, treated even the nobility as a bourgeois institution. The philosopher and educationalist F. Paulsen drew attention to the growing class structure of nineteenth-century German high-school and university education. Originally the educational establishment had been largely staffed with the sons of the clergy and promising country stock (Paulsen himself was a farmer's son) who, having enjoyed a rather informal education at the local vicarage, followed by one or two years at a provincial gymnasium, usually went on to a university, not infrequently as "mendicant students" (Luther) or on a scholarship (Erasmus).[4] In countries with an older bourgeoisie — France, England and the Netherlands — the training of an élitist educational corps was inaugurated even earlier, especially in the exclusive Jesuit colleges, "public" schools, and universities.

The back door to higher education, through which country boys had slipped into the universities formerly, was systematically closed as the state gradually took charge of examinations, the training of teachers, and of all other facets of public education. Hand in hand with this process went the decline of monastery schools in Catholic countries and of clerical supervision in the Protestant world. In France there was growing opposition to the Falloux Law of 1850, which entitled members of monastic orders without a teacher's diploma to engage in lower education, and members of the clergy to teach in secondary schools. In 1871 England abolished religious tests for admission to the universities,[5] tests that had hampered Shelley's academic career.

This change was accompanied by a bitter struggle between those determined to maintain the sacred traditions and those determined to see modernism win. Germany had been the pioneer in the extension of higher education and the transformation of the classical university into an institute of scientific research. France and England followed suit with the establishment of provincial universities and high schools, which prepared students for the universities and thus provided an alternative to costly "public" schools like Eton and Harrow. This did not, of course, alter the fact that Eton boys and Oxford and Cambridge men have retained a socially privileged position to this day. What was at heart a social conflict was rationalized into a dispute about the "subject matter of education" between the champions of the old system, who were firmly convinced that Plutarch's *Lives* in the original offered the best possible education even for colonial adminstrators, and the reformers, who fought

619

under the blessed banner of "general evolution." To show how deep-rooted was the faith of the former in the moral influence of the classics we need merely mention that, in British Borstal detention centers, where young delinquents have been kept in segregation from hardened criminals ever since 1902 and where the emphasis is placed on training rather than on punishment, the teaching of Roman history was declared an integral part of the moral rehabilitation program.[6]

The attempts to adapt the "classical gymnasium," that double crown of the pedagogue, to the demand of a basically altered society, led, particularly in Germany, to an overloaded curriculum and to the petrification and dehuminization of all the subjects taught, and this produced the most divergent reactions. Treitschke declared that without classical education, youth would lose touch with the moral forces of human existence, [7] while more religiously minded conservatives argued that, though the classical authors had grown in pagan soil, they had nevertheless anticipated Christianity in their unconscious thoughts and desires.[8] Paulsen called upon the state to stamp out the current anti-classicist trend in education,[9] while the "radical conservative" Paul de Lagarde claimed that "we no longer gain ideas despite all our education,"[10] and endorsed Nietzsche's view that the new education was breeding journalists, not scholars. Nietzsche, however, was no less fiercely opposed to the "christianization" of antiquity: "The humanist conception of the world of antiquity is an 'enlightened' adulteration by Christianity . . . True Hellenism was not humane, but natural, human, and naive."[11]

Only a few weeks after Kaiser Wilhelm's edict, the Swedish teacher Ellen Key published her *Barnets aarhundrede*[12] (The Century of the Child), which her contemporaries considered another milestone in the history of education (translations and reprints followed one another in quick succession) and which was based on quite different assumptions. These assumptions, incidentally, were far less new than one might have gathered from the sensation her book caused, for they could be traced back directly to Rousseau. The opinion of the latter of a benevolent critic could equally well have been applied to her: "Theory run mad."[13] But for all that it was a theory based on the realization that all those educators anxious to turn the child into a "useful member of society" were oblivious of the fact that society was totally alienated from the child, who comes into the world as a *bon sauvage* and, just like the primitive placed into modern society, runs all the moral and psychological risks that threaten the "marginal man." These risks were much greater in Ellen Key's day than they had been in Rousseau's — society had grown so fluid and so contradictory that it could no longer provide the child with fixed norms. Travelers in "primitive" lands kept bringing back reports that children there were spoiled beyond anything known in Europe and yet grew into adroit adults. G. Heard reported that the Eskimos allow their children to pick the best morsels from the bowl because "they will learn soon enough to do as we do."[14] In 1900 Ellen Key voiced the same longing for a return to the pre-bourgeois pattern of civilization that we have met in so many literary and other reactions to the mechanization, over-organization and denigration of life in modern society. She was an enthusiastic believer in progress — with a retrospective ideal. That is why she was so widely read, praised, and quoted, and also attacked by frightened conservatives. She was largely responsible for the reduction of drilling, coercion, and corporal punishment of children, which, together with insistent appeals to ambition and competition, too often led to the sad spectacle of juvenile suicide,[15] particularly in schools were children learned to "behave like cattle, an attitude that is the hallmark of the mob."[16] In short she helped to abolish a system of education in which, despite all the good intentions of the theorists, the harshness of the Puritans was allied to the cruel demands of mass efficiency. For the rest, many of her ideas could be found not only in Rousseau but also in her immediate predecessors, Pestalozzi and Fröbel, and in many of her contemporaries. She "enthused" about the renewal of religion, love, art, social harmony, marriage, and family life in the near future, when the child's initial education would be handed back to its mother — which explains why she considered the emancipation of women, which would draw them out of the home, "the most egoistic movement of our time."[17] She at no time appealed directly to the authority of her predecessors, let alone of her contemporaries, although she did mention the growing interest in child psychology as a positive sign; instead she repeated vague rumors about the permissive educational practices of "our Norse ancestors" — and the Japanese.

The most important of her ideas were developed by others more soberly, systematically and subtly. Herbart, who died in 1841, had still made the teacher the pivot of education, but in the wake of the many educational child-psychological studies that poured over Europe and North America from the 1850s onwards, the emphasis shifted gradually to the child itself and the scientific study of its behavior.[18]

At the end of the century, the United States began to play a special part in this development. Before then, the fame of the German universities had attracted a large number of Americans, and German methods quickly took root in America. The founder of American psychology, G. Stanley Hall, taught originally at Johns Hopkins University, which was founded on the German model,[19] and in his autobiography[20] he devoted a special chapter to his student years in Bonn and Berlin. Others, who had sat at Herbart's feet, brought back his ideas to the United States. But the next generation was much more alive to the cultural and pedagogic needs of a new country with a large frontier. The old humanities had lost their traditional authority in a land of pioneers whose children grew up in an unintellectual atmosphere, with little or no formal education, but with all the healthy and practical training the pioneer's life has to offer, and which appeals so strongly to the child. If we add that American educators were forced to deal with the entirely new problem of transforming the children of the growing stream of immigrants from all over the world and with widely differing cultural backgrounds, into loyal American citizens, then the reader will appreciate that this challenge produced a number of original teachers and psychologists whose influence made itself felt even in Europe. Stanley Hall, who founded the first laboratory for experimental psychology in America at Johns Hopkins in 1888, stressed the fact that the child's character was much "older" than the adult's,[21] and that the "mass and class system" of contemporary education stood in need of a Copernican revolution. In an article on his youth in the Massachusetts countryside during the 1850s, he stressed all the educational benefits and happiness such a life produces and compared it with the sterile existence of the urban child.[22] John Dewey, who as Professor of Philosophy and Pedagogy at the University of Chicago founded his famous and widely copied Laboratory School in 1894, also extolled the benefits of child upbringing in a natural environment.[23]

Dewey, as a convinced democrat, wanted his Laboratory School to become the prototype of a public school system in which these benefits could be reclaimed. The tasks of cleaning and cooking, of tending the garden, feeding the animals, and running the several workshops, including a weaving mill, were distributed by the children among themselves, and the curriculum linked as far as possible to the solution of practical problems. This system, based on learning by doing, on mutual aid, on teachers who acted as comrades, on contacts with nature and on individual development, in the place of mass education imparted to a passive group of children in the typical "idler's attitude" of crossed arms, was also welcomed and, to some extent, developed independently in Europe. Here, educationalists remembered that Pestalozzi, too, had been taught by poverty the advantages of mutual aid, something that "normal" schools punished as a form of cheating. They also recalled that Itard and Séguin had taught retarded children by individual methods. The natural unfolding of the powers of the individual child and the method of learning, not through listening but through individual activity, were the leading principles of three great European pioneers: O. Decroly,[24] with his theory of globalization, "learning from the fullness of life" and *centres d'intérêt*; Maria Montessori,[25] with her concept of "free discipline" and the use of special educational material; and Georg Kerschensteiner, with his "Arbeitsschule" (work school).[26]

The philosophy underlying or apparently justifying the "new education" was the vitalism of Simmel and Bergson, who had taught that "there are no finished things but only things in the process of becoming, no permanent states but only changing conditions".[27] The child was no longer treated as a ragbag of positive and negative qualities that had to be fostered or suppressed, not as a mere intellect that had to be "formed," but as a unity of sensations, instincts, ambitions, and talents, that must be allowed to develop through activity if greater awareness, independence, and social involvement were to be fostered.

Once it was accepted that education was concerned with the child and its individual potentialities, psychology, and particularly psychological tests, became of central importance in education. The great pioneers in this field were K. Rieger of Würzburg, J. McKeen Cattell, who introduced the idea of "mental tests" to the United States, and A. Binet, on whose "intelligence scale" the growth of child intelligence could be read off month by month.

European education at the turn of the century presented an extremely complicated picture, thanks partly to differences in national and religious traditions, but above all to the intereffects of two opposed currents: mass education based on practical needs on the one hand, and, on the other, Rousseau's romantic approach, which, though overwhelmed by the successes of mass education, nevertheless kept surfacing from time to time in the work of such "eccentrics" as Pestalozzi and Fröbel. The picture was further confused, firstly by the conflict between the champions of state education and the advocates of church or private schools for the privileged classes, and secondly by the fact that teachers, despite their Platonic love for the "new education," felt in duty bound to satisfy the "demands of society" (by which they referred to the demands of big business), which needed an army of docile and well-trained workers.

The height of confusion was reached whenever traditional methods of education, or what were taken for such, were adapted to the child's "natural" needs. Thus model schools were set up to provide their urban pupils with a "natural" environment in the countryside, while others crammed the study of natural science into an already overcrowded and antiquated syllabus. As for the gymnasium, it was often impossible to

tell to what extent its antiquated approach went back to monastic asceticism or to nineteenth-century rational drilling methods. Gurlitt[28] has
shown that the barrack system of the Wilhelminian gymnasium had been
preceded by an older, less martial tradition with a curriculum that, though
confined to the classics, nevertheless had a more humane approach and
a staff that dispensed with such orders as "Open books! — Read! — Look
up! — Repeat!", etc. The atmosphere of the barrack school has been
brilliantly recaptured in Thomas Mann's *Buddenbrooks*.

Another "natural" ideal, prescribed by Ellen Key, Gurlitt, and many
others, was education in the bosom of the family, first by the mother,
then by the versatile and leisured father. This sort of education may
have suited the intellectual élite of previous centuries (Hugo Grotius,
Constantijn Huygens and his family, Goethe, and, of course, the families
of rustic clergymen), but was anything but "natural" under the new
conditions.

The growth of state intervention in education, which was particularly
marked in Prussia but also spread to Scandinavia and the Netherlands,
was a gradual process that stretched over several centuries. England,
traditional even in this field, clung as long as was humanly possible to
private and church education. In France the process was much more
sudden. Here the thirst for revenge after the defeat of 1870 presided
over the determination to overtake the better-schooled Germans. To
that end, the syllabus and the examination were standardized and the
status of teaching staff greatly improved: the highly trained product of
a recognized normal school increasingly ousted the unqualified monk or
nun, or the traditional shoemaker and carpenter who combined his
teaching job with that of bellringer or gravedigger and whose authority
was based on the stick, the dunce's cap, and the special awards he issued
once a year. This meant that in France — as elsewhere — proper schools
came to replace superannuated storerooms, old monasteries, and the like.
In secondary education, the monopoly of the Jesuit colleges with their
antiquated classical program was broken; their solemn displays of ostentatious gowns and Ciceronian eloquence during the prizegivings, their
"recreation," which took the form of supervised paradings through the
streets, their unhygienic and gloomy housing conditions — one bath a
term[29] — no longer suited the times, though, having adapted themselves
reluctantly even to the demands of physical education, they survived
(just as did the traditional public schools in England) as *the* educational
establishments of the élite. For a long time to come, however, the pupils
of the colleges and lyceums which, in 1902, adopted a form of grammar
school program in the hope of "turning out triumphant generations of

businessmen," were despised as "grocers" and treated as poor relations.[30]

French state control of secondary education for girls — the first law was passed in 1880 — was sabotaged by the bourgeoisie even more than the state education of boys. They considered it an extremely dangerous step, despite the fact that it did not even lead to a *baccalauréat* (university matriculation). In other countries, too, girls continued to be debarred from the universities. In Germany it took a protracted tug of war before a law governing the preparation of girls for university was finally passed in 1908. For years, girls' education outside the expensive boarding schools was confined to the daughters of petty officials who — dreadful thought — might one day have to earn their own living.

British "public" schools were — and despite everything remain — inviolable pillars of the Establishment. Though attempts to reform them were begun with some success early in the nineteenth century, they continue to be a law unto themselves. The appointment of Dr. Thomas Arnold as headmaster of Rugby in 1828 was intended to usher in a thorough, two-pronged reform program: the introduction of a more modern curriculum adapted to the needs of the century — the very program Kaiser Wilhelm was to implement in Germany seventy years later — and the raising of the moral tone of a system that has been described as "anarchy tempered by despotism":[31] the undermanned teaching staff presided passively over a lion's den in which a few hundred boys from twelve to eighteen engaged in vicious fights, bullying, and coarse practical jokes, and compensated for their meager social status by chastising the young gentlemen with the cane. Improvements of the system would, however, be suggested long after Dr. Arnold has gone, and despite his reputation as a reformer and teacher of "gentlemen and Christians" — built largely on his appointment of the senior pupils as "praeposters" over the younger ones — memoirs and novels based on experiences in these schools, written in about 1900, suggest that they remained dens of iniquity (vicious corporal punishment, wholesale bullying of the weak and noncomformist, and homosexual entanglements) and that there had been no basic changes.[32] At the end of the century Rugby was much more renowned for its athleticism than for its educational reforms in the modern sense — neither of which, incidentally, was among Arnold's ideals.

Criticism of secondary education, as it was voiced everywhere at the end of the century, can be divided into the possibilist and the impossibilist, both camps appealing to nature and reason. The possibilist school, especially in Germany, turned against the sacrosanct traditional syllabus and the way in which morale was maintained by distinctions and punish-

625

ments. Gurlitt reports how he plowed through the classics at his gymnasium totally ignorant of their contents and treating them as a jumble of grammatical tricks "spiced with slaps, detentions, and lines,"[33] and he quotes the archaeologist Ernst Curtius as saying: "In my youth, transgressions against the Latin rules of gender were punished as if they were incest."[34]

Systematic castigations at school and at home were regular and highly-prized instruments of German and English education, though in the Netherlands they were not applied by rote. How reluctant people were to renounce them may be gathered from the attitude of the Swiss educationalist, F. W. Förster, who attacked Rousseau's "superstitious belief in human nature" and considered Gurlitt a wild individualist, but who nevertheless admitted that many teachers had discovered that "the old school discipline is inadequate, because most pupils have an entirely different psychological disposition." What with youth's quest for independence and its touchy sense of honor, he continued, repressive discipline could only lead to indiscipline.[35] But he had strong reservations about the more liberal British, and in particular, American experimental schools, and about the democratic "school city system," because they wasted too much time on trying to foster "character training" and "discipline" without corporal punishment. It was not by chance that he dwelled at such lengths on the educational advantages of military discipline: "The great traditions must not be forgotten,"[36] he warned, adding that much greater strictness and army discipline was needed in all spheres of life if society was to become truly productive.[37] As late as 1919, a little booklet by the socialist teacher Julian Borchard on the education of children without the use of corporal punishment still filled a very real need. Oddly enough, this degrading form of "correction" usually went hand in hand with a systematic appeal to the child's sense of honor: position in class, prizes, competition in games, etc.

In 1912 A. Graf published a collection of school reminiscences by more than 125 prominent Germans.[38] It does not take a long search to cull a somber selection from it: "Drill sergeant spirit . . . deadly, formal education . . . spankings that we in Prussia receive in droves . . . the most horrible time of my life . . . torture . . . nightmares, which I remember with shivers . . . penitentiaries," the general deception of teachers considered as "natural enemies." The teachers were "petty, vicious, envious, false and embittered men with bad manners, unkempt and shabby in appearance . . . plebeians," men who, being socially inferior, took delight in denigrating their socially superior charges. Hermann Hesse, too, said of his teachers that they were "hated and feared, mocked and despised,"[39] and he went on to say: "School was considered an enemy in the fight against whom every means was acceptable and justified." German children were particularly incensed at the formal confirmation classes, which lent German education its national stamp, and of which Max Weber wrote that they were "conventional and dogmatic and did nothing to quench the thirst for knowledge." We might add that they left the emotions even more unsatisfied.

Not without bitter humor is the fact that what few favorable opinions are found in Graf's selection came from the pens of theologians and classicists, and that one of the most positive appreciations should have taken the guise of a reactionary rejection of contemporary life: "The century of the child has blown up self-consciousness to grotesque pro- portions, and where a good spanking used to help in the past, our humane age is wont to assert that the strictures of the conscientious teacher drive his pupils to suicide."[40] The problem of juvenile suicide was mentioned elsewhere too, but more often than not in less cynical tones. Gurlitt, in one of his bitter philippics, called it a side effect of the treatment of "final examinations as regimental exercises" and he quoted a report in the *Dresdner Nachrichten* of July 7, 1905 about a fourteen-year-old boy who had drowned himself while holding a hymnal, whose contents he had been unable to memorize.[41] "Teachers take a different view of dead pupils than they do of living ones," Herman Hesse wrote in *Unterm Rad* (Under the Wheel),[42] a sober account of a scholastic tragedy ending in suicide.

The incidence of juvenile suicide, a rare event before the nineteenth century, increased in all west European countries towards the end of that century: between 1869 and 1873 one in 666,028, and between 1894 and 1898 one in 497,815, schoolchildren took their lives. The reasons were almost invariably fear of chastisement and of poor school reports.[43] Nowhere was dismay at this phenomenon more marked than in Germany. This does not mean that Germany punished or humiliated pupils more abjectly than other countries; rather does it suggest that there were growing doubts — naturally confined to a progressive group — about the rightness of a system that the young no less than these dis- turbed educationalists were increasingly rejecting as a personal injustice and humiliation. Moreover, in the "reformed" Wilhelminian school system, punishment and competition lacked the support of a tradition rooted in the medieval practices of the monastic orders. Gurlitt, who knew how to combine Prussian patriotism with a spirited attack on all forms of coercion and "unnatural" methods, implicitly betrayed his regret in Germany's lack of a sound educational tradition when he at-

627

tributed "the hard educational methods" of the preceding period to the political and material needs of Prussia during her period of consolidation, which "found its clearest and strongest expression in Kant's catergorical imperative,"[44] but — a strange parallel with Ellen Key! — went on to say: "Now we clamor for the old freedom, the old sense of responsibility, the old voluntary obedience . . . We demand our ancient Germanic right, a right that has never died in England and North America."[45] Gurlitt himself had grown up in a pre-capitalist environment: in a castle with all its appurtenances, assigned by a ducal patron to his father, who was a painter with an independent outlook, and Gurlitt's past informed all his educational ideas. However, his attempts to implement at least some of them in the Berlin-Steglitz gymnasium were deeply resented by his superiors and, like a second Socrates, he was dismissed as a despoiler of youth.

The first school born out of the protest against the bourgeois-rationalist spirit was the one Leo Tolstoy set up for peasant children in Yasnaya Polyana shortly after the Crimean War. It was a winter school — during the summer these children were still thought to acquire all the learning they needed while working the land. Without demonstrable contacts with Tolstoy's system, England, France, and Germany also gave concrete expression to the idea of the "free school" at the end of the century. Though they may have differed in approach, all these schools had a number of common traits: they were anti-intellectual, laid great stress on contact with nature and the cultivation of the emotional life, emphasized the value of physical exercise, favored self-government and self-sufficiency, and did their best to nourish artistic gifts. England led with Abbotsholme, founded in 1899, and Bedales, founded as early as 1892, the latter even pioneering co-education. Both schools had a host of successors and imitators on the Continent. In France, Ferrière founded the Bureau Internationale des Écoles Modernes in 1899, and the École des Roches was opened in the same year. In Germany G. Wyneken, a great idealist, championed the Freie Schulgemeinde, a Germany copy of the American community school, which he eventually set up in Wickersdorf in 1906 but from which he was expelled in 1910 after representations from Saxe-Meiningen's reactionary government. A few years later a press and parliamentary campaign against him was unleashed by the Bavarian clergy, who were particularly incensed at the alleged anarchism and immorality of *Der Anfang*, a paper for young people influenced by him and which, to the dismay of the Bavarian Landtag, was written and edited by schoolboys.[46] In 1899 Dr. Lietz founded Landerziehungsheim in Ilsenburg, and in 1910 Paul Geheeb opened his Odenwaldschule. Before the First World War there were at least twenty such "reform schools" in Germany and some eighty in western Europe, including Decroly's *École pour la vie et par la vie* in Brussels, and Montessori's Casa dei Bambini in Rome, both founded in 1907.[47] (Rudolf Steiner's Freie Waldorf Schule was not opened until 1919, and Kees Boeke's Werkplaats not until 1926.)

All in all, however, few of these model or laboratory schools had a marked influence on mass education at the time, if only because of the high fees they charged. Moreover, all of them mistook the "natural" for the rational. Those reformers who made the greatest practical impact all worked in the cities and adapted themselves to the demands of urban schools: Decroly in Brussels, Kerschensteiner in Munich, Jan Ligthart in the Netherlands, and Montessori in Rome. It is difficult to gauge what influence these educators had on schools that were not directly associated with them. Decroly's open system possibly had a wider effect than Montessori's with its dogmatic approach, but even his *École pour la vie et par la vie* did not suit the needs of an industrialized society. Thus the socialist educationalist, Otto Rühle, rightly argued that the trade schools taught their pupils to prize antiquated forms of labor, because the "natural" form of work in a capitalist society, i.e., wage labor, is "totally devoid of ethical and pedagogic values, of any qualities that have an elevating or liberating effect."[48] Kerschensteiner, in a preface to the 1925 edition of his book, which had meanwhile been translated into eleven European and three Asian languages, complained that when foreign visitors asked him in which state schools they could see his system work, he had to confess: not a single one.[49] Even in these educationalists, the fundamental conflict of modern man was rarely resolved: Maria Montessori, who aimed at the natural development of the child's intellect, nevertheless advocated a Catholic education; she banished fairy tales from her school, and with rationalist consistency replaced free drawing with the copying out of figures, designed to improve the child's handwriting. Moreover, she trained the senses, not with the help of natural sounds and colors but with special "educational apparatus" of her own invention.

The new attitude was clearly reflected in the development of children's books. Before the eighteenth century, children would advance from the spelling primer straight to books written for adults, which at best were occasionally set aside *ad usum delphini*. In the Netherlands, van Alphen was the first to write a book of poems for children that did not include the usual nursery rhymes. Children continued, of course, to be told all sorts of fairy stories, not thought worthy of setting down on

paper until the advent of the Grimm brothers. As late as 1900, a rationalist critic still objected to the nonsense children were being offered in
Nelly Bodenheim's *Handje-plak*.[50] At the time there also poured forth
a stream of edifying and patriotic poems for children, including *Struwwel-
peter* and the rhymes of J. P. Heije, and, in the nineteenth century, the
romantic novels of Walter Scott, Victor Hugo, Felix Dahn, J. van Lennep,
and others like them were increasingly held up as choice reading for the
young. There were also many abridged editions of such classics as *Don
Quixote*, *Gulliver's Travels*, *Robinson Crusoe* and *Monsieur Cryptogame*.

   Children's newspapers, which began to appear in the second half of
the century, were uplifting and romantic in tone and reflected the attitude
of the affluent bourgeoisie, with a strong emphasis on virtue and charity.
However, the *Magasin de l'Education et de Récréation* broke new ground
when it began to publish the travelogues of Jules Verne in 1863. In 1867
another pioneer, Louisa M. Alcott, published her *Little Women*, which
despite its educational overtones was nevertheless written from the child's
point of view. Similarly Mark Twain's *The Adventures of Tom Sawyer*
(1870) and *Huckleberry Finn* (1885) were free of adult condescension,
as was Hector Malot's *Sans famille* (1878). The best children's books to
appear at the time were, in fact, good enough to be classed as great
literature. Soon after the turn of the century Jan Ligthart published his
widely acclaimed *Ot en Sien* reading books, and there also appeared
another classic of Dutch children's literature, Nienke van Hichtum's
Afke's tiental (Afke's Ten). At about the same time, other publications
in which the child's world was evidently prized above the adult's, first
appeared, the most famous of all being J. M. Barrie's *Peter Pan*, which
bore the challenging subtitle "The Boy Who Wouldn't Grow Up." Peter
Pan's statue graces Kensington Gardens to this day. In his stage directions
Barrie enjoined all players, adults no less than children, to express the
child's outlook on life.[51] The growing autonomy of children's literature
was also reflected in the work of Lewis Carroll, Beatrix Potter, Alain
Fournier, Frederick van Eeden, Top Naeff and a host of others, and
invited imitation on the part of lesser lights who had their eye on the
market. For in the capitalist system, youth had become a purchasing
force with whose tastes the writer had to reckon. Side by side with books
written expressly to satisfy the wishes and dreams of the child, there also
appeared new children's clothes: simple, washable and tough, so that
children no longer had to feel guilty about "messing" their pretty suits
or dresses. The same was true of toys; not only were they specifically
designed to meet the child's needs, but they also appealed to status-

seekers among the parents, and were, moreover, the first example of built-in obsolescence: no sooner had they been bought than they were out of fashion again. Hand-me-down toys became as rare as hand-me-down clothes. German industry became the great toy supplier; for the rest, Germany contributed little to youth beyond a series of hypocritical young ladies' novels and the hollow romances of Karl May with their ugly racial delusions.

The emancipated child appeared in yet another literary genre: biography and autobiography. This was due not only to the growing impact of psychology but also to the fact that writers no longer felt that life begins at maturity. Autobiographers before Butler's *The Way Of All Flesh*, and often much later as well, generally kept silent about their youth, or else resorted to such clichés as "the happy years of childhood," "my beloved father," or "my loving and self-sacrificing mother." In a series of autobiographies written in Germany during the twenties, mostly by elderly philosophers,[52] such clichés and lists of presentable ancestors still took pride of place over the sketchiest accounts of the authors' childhood or youth. The sole exception was Leopold Ziegler, who claimed that the only good memory he had of his school years was a teacher who "took our youth seriously."[53] In another series of reminiscences, however, a number of teachers did dwell at some length on their youthful experiences.[54] But it was novelists in particular that now poured forth their childhood memories. Quite apart from Tolstoy, who was a pioneer in so many fields, and whose *Childhood* and *Boyhood* date back to the 1850s, the work of Marcel Proust, André Gide, D. H. Lawrence, Katherine Mansfield, W. B. Yeats and Thomas Mann bore out Freud's view that youthful impressions had a crucial effect of man's later life. Julien Green exclaimed that "Everything I write springs straight from my youth"; Jean Cocteau declared that "Poetry is the elaboration of youthful memories," and Péguy wrote: "All the essential elements of life have been assembled before the age of eleven."[55]

Their drab life at school and the urgent need for reforms persuaded many German secondary-school pupils to take "evasive action" during the nineties: the boys of the Berlin-Steglitz Gymnasium, in which Gurlitt had waged his vain campaign, followed the lead of an ex-pupil, the "dashing Karl Fischer" and started to make regular Sunday and holiday excursions into the countryside, carrying rucksacks, stout sticks, and guitars, and wearing hobnailed boots and loose clothing — the hallmarks of the *Wandervogel*. The movement spread across Germany like a flame through dry grass. The first Germany youth hostel was founded in 1909. Because an independent youth organization was bound to be prohibited by the authorities, the members worked under the protective screen of an innocuous council of respectable but sympathetic adults.

It is almost inconceivable today how much exhilaration this escape into nature, this return to a more or less artificial form of primitive life — roaming about, sleeping under the open sky, and the romance of campfires — brought to young people longing for release from the constraints they were made to suffer at school and at home. Those who expected a democratic or perhaps even an anarchist reaction were greatly mistaken. A new type of conformism, albeit self-imposed, replaced the old, and the new principles were amply reflected in such terms as "royalist leadership," "Führer principle," "loyal comradeship" and so on. Homosexuality and accusations of sexual misdemeanor played an important part in the endless fight between the various factions, and when Karl Fischer, originally revered as a god, saw his following decline he reported for naval service in Kiaochow, to stem the yellow peril in the Kaiser's name. Needless to say, there also emerged a host of pseudo-*Wandervogel* organizations under denominational control, and few people nowadays would be surprised to learn that the historian of the *Wandervogel* Movement should have concluded his extremely affecting and widely-read account with the observation that "the *Wandervogel* was always of good Germanic race, often with a Slavic touch which, as is well known, produces a new and outstanding type," and that he should have gone on to dish up the well-worn obligatory anti-Semitic arguments.[56]

In France, nineteenth-century youth, students no less than young workers, were strongly under the spell of rationalism and its offshoots: socialism, anticlericalism, and agnosticism, tempered by *fin de siécle* pessimism. The École Normale was "the citadel of agnosticism," and so were many teachers' training colleges in neighboring countries, not least in the Netherlands. However, soon after the turn of the century, a counter-current, set off by the Dreyfus affair, washed over French youth partly in the form of the "rational irrationalism" exemplified by Péguy's *mystique républicaine*, and more generally in the form of the antirationalist nationalism of Barrès's *Appel au soldat* (1900) and of Maurras's *Action Française*. In 1905 some three or four boarders of the École Normale used to attend Mass; by 1912 that number had increased to forty, a third of the total body of students. This trend reflected the growing influence of the Association Catholique de la Jeunesse Française, which had 30,000 members in 1900 and which extended its hold on French youth with the help of circulating libraries, lectures, and sports clubs.[57] The results are recorded in three books: Etienne Rey's *Renais-*

sance de l'orgueil français (1912), Gaston Riou's *Aux écoutes de la France qui vient* (1913) and Amélie Gayraud's *Les Jeunes filles d'aujourd'hui.* From the answers to a questionnaire — not always the most reliable source — it appeared that French youth was "spoiling for action" and subscribed to a form of nationalist pragmatism that was perfectly compatible with a religious revival. In short, it was filled with the spirit of the volunteers who sold the *Action Française* in the streets, called themselves *camelots du roi* and looked forward to evening the score with Germany, a chance they were offered in 1914.

Related to the German *Wandervogel*, but even more closely with the patriotic and denominational organizations that emerged in competition with it, was the Boy Scout Movement, founded in 1908 by Lord Baden-Powell, a British general who, during the Boer war, came to appreciate the military value of Christiaan de Wet's scouts, those strapping Boer lads, familiar with horses since early childhood, who had played so important a part in the field. It was on them that he modeled his movement which, just like the *Wandervogel*, satisfied youth's romantic hankering after the primitive life, and was intended to educate youngsters in such bourgeois and paramilitary virtues as a sense of honor, patriotism, service, and obedience.

The free youth movement, by contrast, was the overt expression of a growing distrust of authority, a process that affected all personal relationships, especially those between parents and children. In the Netherlands, where authority was less of a problem than in Germany, the Young Abstainers' League became the forerunner of various "red" youth organizations associated with the radical political parties,[58] which, here as elsewhere, had grasped the importance of influencing and organizing an increasingly vociferous sector of the population. To that end, they copied the example of such clerical organizations as the YMCA, the YWCA, and other Christian youth associations. In Britain the political youth movement (Red Dawn) was of small importance, quite possibly because British youth was more interested in sport than in politics, and in Catholic countries it was conspicuous by its absence. Things were quite different in Russia, where the generation conflict had found its classical expression as early as 1861 in Turgenev's *Fathers and Sons*; by the 1880s and 1890s western Europe had come to look upon every Russian student as a dangerous nihilist.

The transformation of the relationship between the young and the old reflected a radical shift in value judgments, due in turn to rapid socioeconomic developments. Youth, which accepts and welcomes change much more readily than its "elders and betters", suddenly felt superior.

insisted on its rights, and turned with great and sometimes exaggerated idealism towards the future. "Old" was no longer synonymous with "wise" and "experienced" but became equated with "stale." Long trousers, long skirts, elaborate hairstyles, the status symbols of adulthood, lost their appeal not least because these "elders" themselves now dressed and behaved as youthfully as they could.

Despite the impact of social legislation, the turn of the century still saw a sharp distinction between workers (the "poor" objects of charitable endeavor) and gentlemen (the prosperous classes). The rich lived in the best districts and did not have to share their front door with others; they dressed differently — not for them the illustrated mail order catalogues of various Parisian stores with special sections devoted to *articles de bienfaisance* (serviceable but unfashionable and cheap clothing); they were addressed not by their first names, but as "sir," and their children could look forward to an infinitely brighter and longer future. It was extremely rare for even the most talented working-class child to rise above his circumstances. The new science of statistics, first applied to anthropometry by Quetelet in Brussels in 1870 and soon afterwards extended to schoolchildren in Belgium and elsewhere, made it clear that working-class children were shorter and thinner than the children of well-to-do parents and more likely to succumb to such typical diseases of the poor as tuberculosis and scrofula. Infantile mortality, predominantly due to intestinal disorders, was particularly rife among children of working mothers.

The children of the poor went to Poor Board or Charity schools (in Germany, for instance, these took care of the education of 95% of all children). When modern educators (Dewey, Natorp, Kerschensteiner, Ziegler, Gurlitt, *et al*) advocated comprehensive schools,[59] they did so for national no less than for humanitarian reasons. This explains why the idea was first mooted in the USA and in Germany, where national unity had still to be cemented. A meeting of teachers held in Kiel in 1914, having heard an address by Kerschensteiner, called for an "organically constituted comprehensive school, with equal opportunities for all children, with a highly trained and preferably academic staff in all branches of education and without social or denominational distincitions."[60] In the United States these demands had already been met to a large extent — although southern and black children still lagged far behind the rest. In Germany they were satisfied only inasmuch as all schools were equal in evincing patriotic sentiments. In Scandinavia the low population density favored democratic reforms, but elsewhere the champions of privileged

634

or church education still held the upper hand and were not unduly worried by the "impossible" demands of their opponents.

The idea of the comprehensive state school was closely connected with that of compulsory education. In Britain the Elementary Education Act was passed as early as 1870; France adopted compulsory education in 1882; the Netherlands in 1900, Belgium in 1914, and Germany in 1920. But at first there were a great many loopholes and the strict enforcement of the new laws depended on whether or not they were mere *post facto* endorsements of what had long since been the general practice, as in the Netherlands and Scandinavia. The education of physically and mentally handicapped children was still widely neglected, though a first attempt to cope with their special problems had been made in the eighteenth century. It was no accident that such educators as Montessori and Decroly should have started their work with abnormal children. Most absenteeism from school was still caused by economic factors: harvest and potato holidays were common practices and, on Prussian estates for instance, they lasted throughout the summer: "Child labor in agriculture is not only admissible, but useful and even commendable," said Count Bülow, and the Prussian Junker Parliament was asked to decree that rural children should have their schooling between the hours of 6:30 A.M. and 9.00 A.M., so that they could be "usefully employed" during the rest of the day.[61] Nor were things much better in the German industrial centers; the captains of industry were as deaf to the needs of the lower classes as the Junkers on their estates, and far too often ignored the child labor laws of 1839, 1903, and 1908, taking advantage of a host of escape clauses. An inquiry by a teachers' congress in 1898 showed that school absenteeism in industrial centers ran at from 10% to 80% — a government commission had arrived at 6.53%! — and that children earned from 2 to 2½ pfennigs per hour. In Friedrichshafen the clergy ran an annual "child-market," where little cowherds, some under the age of ten, could be hired for summer work and conveyed in cattle trucks to the Tyrolean meadows.

What was new was not the phenomenon itself — centuries earlier little slaves had been regularly conveyed from southern Belgium to the textile centres of Holland — but the many public protests against what was now considered a certain method of stifling the great potential inherent in every child.

Interest in child welfare manifested itself in many other ways as well: school medical services, school meals, crèches, preparatory schools and day nurseries sprang up everywhere. However, state penny-pinching and perverse ideas of charity ensured that the actual achievements fell far short of the objectives of the enthusiastic sponsors. This was particularly true in Germany: in 1908, that country spent 585,000 marks on school meals, while London alone spent 1,240,000 and Paris had spent more than 1,460,000 in 1904.[62] There were repeated and bitter confrontations. A society that was shifting its attention from the crime to the criminal[63] realized increasingly that the children it ostracized were the potential criminals of the future.

Until the end of the nineteenth century however, the only remedies for the antisocial behavior of youth were the practically unrestricted right of parents to punish and chastise their children (in France, parents were even entitled to send recalcitrant children to prison for a few days),[64] and trial by judges who went strictly by the book and, at best, considered the age of very young offenders a mitigating circumstance. Worse still, the neglected or abandoned child was placed under the same "care" and subjected to the same regimen as the one sentenced by the courts. Children between the ages of ten and sixteen who were caught roaming the streets of France or begging disappeared, until their twenty-first birthday, into a *maison de correction* or a "reformatory" run by some brutal ex-sergeant,[65] to be unleashed on society as unhealthy and badly trained misfits. An international congress for the protection of children held in Antwerp in 1890 was responsible for a number of improvements in various countries. One year earlier, the Loi Roussel had been passed in France. It curtailed the unlimited power granted to French fathers by the Code Napoléon, but it was only in 1900 that the worst abuses were tempered, not least by taking the *maisons de correction* out of private hands. In the Netherlands (and in Germany) the first child protection acts were passed in 1900,[66] a preparatory commission having had its recommendations rejected in 1886; Belgium followed in 1912. The first Dutch children's court was set up as late as 1921, while Chicago had one as early as 1889.[67] The schooling and training of antisocial children was greatly impeded by the fact that urban society cannot provide youngsters with a natural environment. It used to be customary to send "good-for-nothing" boys to sea or to the colonies, not only to avoid scandal, but also as a positive outlet for their misdirected energies, but this was no longer a solution: the modern transatlantic liner or even the navy offers few romantic outlets. Or else these boys used to be sent to some farmer to find moral regeneration on the land, an idea on which van den Bosch had based his agricultural colonies. This, too, was no longer an acceptable practice. Britain was trying out the Borstal system — a modified form of prison treatment with schools, provision for technical training, and a

636

fixed scale of rewards and promotions. However, Russell and Rigby, who have described it,[68] showed that Borstals were not the answer: the same urge that sends more prosperous youngsters into the hikers' or the scout movements, drives the neglected urban child into criminal adventures. Their book had nothing of the sanctimonious tone with which nineteenth-century writers used to dilate on the subject of young sinners. Moreover, their plea for the rehabilitation of young offenders was not based on abstract ethics, but on sympathy with young men and women who, after having been educated in an "institution," however innocuously named, have to step into a world that offers them unaccustomed outlets for their repressed energies and thus tends to upset their already tenuous equilibrium. The general desire to do something for the neglected and criminal youngster, and the meager results that all these well-intentioned attempts have so far yielded, show that the break which occurred at the turn of the century was nowhere else as abrupt or as blatant. For this volatile group, whose spontaneous reactions were so often even more repressed than those of other children, was, so to speak, an enlarged projection of the gaping chasm between the noble — or, if you like, amoral — savage who enters this world at birth, and the acceptable member of modern society he is expected to become in due course and at any cost.

[CHAPTER XLII]

THE DARK GATE

On November 16, 1900 the *New York Herald* quoted the claim by Professor Goldwin Smith from Toronto, an Englishman by descent, that sea-sickness was a great blessing for America. Without that affliction, he said, all rich Americans would surely be living in their castles in Europe, thus reducing America to an ant heap of workers, busily maintaining a plutocracy ensconced across the Atlantic. Professor Smith had no doubt meant it as something of a joke, but not entirely. Ever since 1861 he had been afraid of the threat the mighty United States posed to Canada, alerting his friend, Lord Rosebery, in England, and America at large in his *Commonwealth of Empire* (1902).[1] Most other observers had barely noticed the transformation of a poor colony into a land of a thousand wonders. As late as 1856 D. C. Gilman, later President of Johns Hopkins University, complained that the United States lagged far behind Europe in agricultural and industrial productivity and in the exploitation of her natural wealth.[2] Fourteen years earlier Charles Dickens in his *American Notes*, and shortly afterwards in *Martin Chuzzlewit*, incensed Americans with his jibes and boasts about the superiority of old England. In 1868, however, after a second American tour, during which he was widely fêted, he felt obliged to acknowledge, at a public dinner in his honor given by the American press, "the amazing changes I have seen around me on every side," and to declare that as long as he and his descendants had any legal rights in his works he would cause this statement to be included in future editions of both his American books.[3]

By the end of the century it had become clear that the "amazing changes" were, in fact, a complete reversal of the relationship between the (former) mother country and her colony. As early as 1894 Conan Doyle, writing from America, had argued that the center of gravity of the Anglo-Saxon race had shifted to that side of the Atlantic Ocean and that England would have to sit up and take notice,[4] and on June 16, 1900 the *Westminster Gazette* explained that British and American imperialism were not the same thing, and that even those who defended imperialism at home had good reason to protest against the imperialism of a country as large as the United States.[5]

Of somewhat later date — March 1905 — was the publication of two articles in two German journals about the American peril, both from the pen of one L. M. Goldberger. It was not too late, he believed, to stem American trade supremacy by intelligent counter-measures.[6] He must have been thinking of the fact that, while two thirds of all U. S. exports before 1900 had been agricultural produce, that trend was being rapidly changed, so much so that by 1914 America would be exporting agricultural and industrial products in roughly the same proportions.[7] We cannot be sure, but it is quite possible that Goldberger's articles were inspired by the Kaiser himself, who, as we know, was greatly concerned about the American "problem." In 1901 Albert Ballin turned, not by chance and not in vain, to his imperial friend for help in averting the threat posed by the Morgan Trust to German shipping in general and to the Hamburg America Line in particular.

That threat was real enough. For the rest, however, Professor Smith was right: in the "crude land of pioneers" there were still many Americans who hankered after Europe to the point of nostalgia: we have only to think of Henry James, who adopted British nationality and enthused about European civilization in *The Sense of the Past*. After the First World War he was to find quite a few successors, T. S. Eliot among them, and inevitably, there were enough snobs among the American upper-middle classes to ape their attitude. Many more, however, prided themselves on their pioneering stock, and their pride was given solid foundations in the increasing wealth of their country.

Let us take the case of John Pierpont Morgan, the banker and founder of the American equivalent of the House of Rothschild. Morgan gained control of the American railways at the end of the century, thus foreshadowing a new trend that was to make itself felt in Europe as well, and particularly in Germany: the fusion of industrial and finance capital and the concomitant sacrifice of the principle of competition. In short, Morgan was the classical representative of the transformation of laissez-faire into monopoly capitalism, and he made no secret of it either, as witness his declaration of 1899.[8]

Once he had the railroads under his thumb, he went on to gain control of ocean transportation companies which had fallen on bad days after losing the handsome subsidies certain railroad companies had been paying them for special harbor rights. Morgan acquired two American shipping lines to Europe, reduced freight charges and brought the English Leyland

Line to its knees. He then bought up their shares and though he paid more than the market value, he was able to sell the company at a large profit to the International Mercantile Marine Company — his own creation.[9] He did much the same with the White Star Line, which he took over in 1902 from the Ismay family, who had previously declared that they would never sell "Britannia's pride." It was only because the German government threw its full weight behind the Hamburg-America Line and the North German Lloyd that he failed to gain control of these companies as well.

The lesson was nevertheless clear, and it was by no means the only one. In a speech at the Guildhall on December 5, 1901, the Prince of Wales stated quite bluntly that unless the old country woke up, foreign competitors would undermine her preferential position in colonial trade.[10] Though he may have included the Germans among the "foreign competitors," it was the Americans he had in mind first and foremost. British blood and British money had planted the British flag from Tanganyika to Cape Town, but now it looked very much as if the Americans would reap the financial benefits. Stead declared that he had heard Cecil Rhodes say more than once that when he had organized the Jameson Raid he was less worried about Paul Krüger than about the Uitlanders who were trying to set up an "American republic" in the Transvaal.[11] This may have been an exaggerated fear, and yet when Rhodes expressed it he caused few eyebrows to be raised, and it is a fact that, during the Boer War, American money and American technicians poured into the mining districts of South Africa, while American bankers and manufacturers were falling over themselves to meet South Africa's post-war needs. Within five or six years of the peace they had, in fact, invested £30,000,000 in South African gold and diamond mines. Moreover, the *British and S.A. Export Gazette* reported of a Cape Town brewery that everything in it had come from the USA, except for the bricks and mortar.[12] The new Cape government set another "bad" example: if British tenders for railway lines were 10% higher than American tenders, then the orders went to the United States.[13]

If that sort of thing could happen in dependent South Africa, no one should have been surprised that the Dominion of Canada, let alone independent states on the American Continent should have acted in similar ways. In 1875 Canada still bought 50% of her imports from Great Britain. But this percentage had begun to decline and no amount of imperial preference was able to halt the process: by 1900, more than 60% of the Canadian imports came from her mighty neighbor in the south.[14]

Much the same happened in Central and South America. How much was at stake for Great Britain here may be gathered from the fact that she had invested £500,000,000 in these regions — very little when one considers their enormous size, but a vast amount for a relatively small island to spend, the more so as American investment, most of which was placed in South America, did not exceed $500,000,000.[15] For the rest, the Americans were not the only ones to compete with the British — the French, too, had gained a foothold in Columbia and Mexico, and the Germans were not far behind. But political events illustrate the situation better than any figures can hope to do. Most readers will have some knowledge of the story of the Panama Canal, and it needs no great historical perspicacity to deduce that these happenings marked a decisive change. In 1891 the de Lesseps had gone bankrupt — a company that had allowed its workmen to die of yellow fever for an entire decade but had achieved little else. Its successors had fared no better, and in 1902 they tried to sell all their shares. In 1901 the United States, no longer bound by the pro-British Clayton-Bulwer treaty of 1850, forced Great Britain to sign the second Hay-Pauncefote treaty, by which Great Britain renounced all her rights in the canal zone — the Monroe doctrine was easily interpreted in that way. Next, the United States obtained permanent control of the canal zone by a treaty with Colombia signed in 1903. When Colombia hesitated to ratify it, a revolution was staged in Panama. The new Panamanian leaders were quick to reach an understanding with Washington: the United States was granted jurisdiction over a zone five miles wide on each side of the canal, while Panama was to receive $10,000,000 in cash and a $250,000 annuity to begin nine years after ratification. The canal could now be built, and it was finally opened to traffic on August 15, 1914, as the roar of guns started to resound over Europe.

The second event was less spectacular, but because it was repeated time and again it was, if anything, more characteristic of the way in which North America was gaining a dominant hold over the center and the south of the continent. In 1899 Morgan, who had done so well out of rails and ships, concluded negotiations for the first loan of its kind with the Mexican government, a loan that proved highly beneficial to the financiers and extremely costly to the Mexican peons. At the time the United States had not yet changed from debtor into creditor nation; this would not take place until the end of the First World War. In 1913, no more than four American banks were engaged in foreign dealings (that number had increased to eighty-one by 1920[16]) but anyone with the least imagination could already see which way the wind was blowing, and Stead was both correct and prophetic when he spoke of the "Americanization of the world."

The fact that Cuba and the Philippines had been conquered from Spain in 1898 is generally known; what is perhaps less well known is that American influence was even then extending to Asia and Australia.

All this affected none but those directly involved. However, the American factories that Europeans saw rising in their own countries were quite a different matter. The British, who had for so long been exploiting gas and tramway concessions on the Continent, and the other Europeans, who had set up factories in colonies and semi-colonies where cheap raw materials and cheap labor abounded, saw the tables being turned on them when the Americans began to do the same thing in the Old World. The American encroachments were all the more glaring because they came so suddenly and involved revolutionary techniques that left stolid Europeans quite speechless. We need only look at the proud report of D. N. Dunlop of the Westinghouse Company,[17] which was commissioned to build a factory for electrical equipment near Manchester in 1900. The British workman traditionally laid 450 bricks during his nine-hour working day, a rate that was stepped up under the supervision of American foremen to between 1800 and 2500 bricks, so that the factory complex, which needed ten million bricks to build, was finished in record time. That American businesses should have opened branches in Europe was not a new phenomenon — Tiffany, Pullman, and Singer had started as early as the 1850s — but their number kept increasing rather alarmingly: between 1880 and 1900 twenty-eight American factories sprang up in Europe, and almost double that number between 1900 and 1910.[18] This did not include the big American tobacco combine in Dresden, on which the *Sozialistische Monatshefte* published a lengthy report in 1902.[19]

Much more incisive still was the effect of a series of American inventions made during the 1870s and 1880s, most of which were adopted by Europe within the space of twenty years. This process had started long before our period with the sewing machine (1846). But now electric light, the telephone, the typewriter, and the composing-machine lengthened the day of Europeans and lent it fresh excitement, while the phonograph helped to make it noisier. Gone was the soft glow of candles and oil-lamps, the quiet of pen and copybook, the domestic bliss of the harmonium, the tinkling sounds of the music box. What was to prove the most far-reaching American innovation was the least noticeable when it first appeared in Europe: the conveyor belt, introduced here in 1914 by Ford, in celebration, one might say, of the tenth anniversary of its invention.[20]

Most incisive of all, perhaps, was the strange American idealism, which contrasted so wonderfully with, and yet fitted so well into, the prevailing European mood. Was it not characteristic that one of the many contingents of young Englishmen the Westinghouse Corporation sent for management training in Pittsburgh, became known as the "Holy Forty"?[21] And was not Henry George, the champion of land nationalization, that "wild man from California," an idealist par excellence?

It was the idealism of a young nation, in a new world bursting with new possibilities, unhampered by traditional inhibitions but thrown back on its own resources and hence clinging all the more stubbornly to the oldest tradition of all, namely religion. It was a country in which everything (space, distances, dangers, and chances) was larger than life and hence encouraged bustle, inventiveness, passion, independence, ambition, and a gigantic thirst for adventure. Here we have the secret of American literature, the cultural expression of an uncultured country that continued to look up to the more civilized mother continent and yet produced such men as Cooper, Emerson, Hawthorne, Poe, Thoreau, and, in our period Whitman and Henry James. America even became a maker and breaker of playwrights: Shaw did not capture the British stage before his *Man and Superman* had received an enthusiastic reception in America. Conversely, William James, Henry's brother, and the founder of pragmatism with its typically American overtones, was celebrated in Europe as a great philosopher and psychologist.

America also made her influence felt on the woman's rights movement, which was a relatively recent development in Europe; across the Atlantic it had a long history in contrast to the country's relative youth. As early as 1787 the wives of the colonists, less burdened with historical scruples than their European sisters and fully conscious of the part they had played in the struggle for independence, petitioned Congress in Philadelphia for full suffrage — in vain on that occasion. But when the first women's rights congress met in Seneca Falls in July 1848 it received wide and sympathetic publicity; the Civil War later liberated white women no less than it did the Negro, and the women's fight was no longer an uphill struggle. By 1913 fourteen states (almost all of them in the west) had granted women full voting rights, Wyoming leading the way in 1869. Outside America, full women's suffrage had been adopted by only four countries (Australia, New Zealand, Norway, and Sweden).

And was not the celebration of the first of May as Labor Day as much an American institution as Sunday school? Were not European pacifists given as much encouragement from their American comrades[22] as those who devoted their lives to prison reform?[23] The current of educational innovations that had originally flowed from Europe to America, was reversed toward the end of the century, and the same process made itself felt in psychology and, in the long run, in all the sciences. From America came the impulse for more effective hygienic measures; the American Sanitary Bureau was founded in 1902, the European Office Internationale d'Hygiène Publique in 1906.

Even the Vatican, which in practice though not in theory was an exclusively European and even a purely Italian institution, could not stand up to Catholic pressure from the United States, however weak it still was. According to Huret of the *Figaro*, Leo XIII not only approved the policies of Monsignor Ireland, but even held them up as an example to Europe.[24] (Which, incidentally, did not prevent His Holiness from condemning even the slightest attempt to suit the hierarchical structure of the Church to the more democratic needs of American Catholics, with his *Testem Benevolentiae* of January 1899, an apostolic letter to Archbishop Gibbons.)[25] In this connection it should be noted that it was in America that the Knights of Columbus sprang up as the first Catholic laymen's organization anywhere in the world.[26]

The American success struck the fascinated European observer as something that was as obvious as it was easily explicable. Everyone knew the "causes": the varied climate, the natural wealth, the relatively sparse population and consequent shortage of manpower that made it essential to invent and employ all sorts of labor-saving machinery. In addition there were the long working hours and the high tariff walls that protected American industry against foreign competitors. Finally there was a psychological factor: the success that success invariably brings in its wake. That success was, as it were, symbolized in the coronets that an ever-increasing number of "dollar princesses" was entitled to don as a reward for the restoration of shaky family fortunes. The Duchess of Marlborough and Lady Curzon may have been among the best known of these benefactresses, but a list published in 1906 mentioned some five hundred others who had married into the European aristocracy since 1870, bringing with them some $208,000,000. American success was also reflected in a whole series of books, including Frances Hodgson Burnett's *Little Lord Fauntleroy* and the novels of Gertrude Atherton, or in the family portraits of English high society by John Singer Sargent, an American by descent and as such obviously best qualified to array all the trappings of feudal life that exerted so powerful an attraction on the nouveaux nobles, to present an imposing whole.

To these "known" causes of success we must add another three, each one of which was probably more important than any we have mentioned. The first was that America did not waste her substance on an expensive defense establishment. If Britain was afraid of naval competition, she must have cast anxious glances at France, Russia, or Germany, but not at the United States. America left her immensely long frontier with Canada undefended from the very outset. As late as 1899 the army protecting her 75 million inhabitants numbered a mere 25,000 men.

The second cause of America's success was her educational system.[27] Much as Americans came to fear Russian education and the thorough training of Russian technicians fifty years later, so the British were envious of American educational progress at the turn of the century. This was true even of classical studies, which Americans were still treating with due seriousness, chiefly out of respect for the Old World. The differences were particularly marked in the education of girls – English society ladies found the American girl a marvel of ignorance when it came to manners, but were staggered to discover that Lucy "could read Horace and Virgil and all the rest."[28]

This was not the real explanation of the "secret" of the United States. That secret was revealed by a leading article in the New York *Evening Journal.* It suggested that an Englishman who wished to understand what America was all about could do no better than stand in Delaware-Lackawanna Station in Hoboken during the morning rush hour, when the commuter trains poured in from the suburbs. For even while the trains were still moving at a dangerous speed, the passengers had already jumped off onto the platform where they jostled one another in their eagerness to be first on the ferry. No one walked slowly or sedately: everyone joined in the tumultuous chase after business; it was one long rush throughout the day, and another at night on the way back home. Stead, who quoted this article at the end of his *The Americanization of the World*, went on to show that the American businessman is a machine that must needs wear out before its time: he is bald and gray even in youth, a victim of poor digestion, of his nerves, and of drugs. The American mother, Stead added, kept supplying the demand for fresh machines that run at dangerous speed. "The American succeeds because he is constantly under high pressure." It is a mere detail, but a telling one for all that, that the English vocabulary was enriched with the word "doping" shortly after 1899, when the American jockey Tod Sloane celebrated his triumphs in Britain.[29] Here we have the ultimate psychological deviation from the "general human pattern" on which European civilization is based. Looking at America, Europe could catch a glimpse, as if in a distorting mirror, of the end of the road that, held back by cultural inhibitions, it had never been able to reach.[30]

Oddly enough, no one except Stead realized, as far as we can tell, that the real difference between Americans and Europeans was one of tempo. McKenzie failed to notice it, and so did Furness,[31] Sorel,[32] and Plenge.[33] But then all of them focussed their attention on the "backward" elements of American capitalism. Even Péguy, the ex-socialist and nascent mystic, preferred to dwell on other matters in his *Cahiers*, and especially on the rationalist views of M. Mangasarian from Chicago.[34] The novelist, Gertrude Atherton, who was so keen to contrast American with English personalities, was as unaffected by the difference in tempo[35] as the historian Lamprecht, one who had said in a different context that man's attitude to time was characteristic of the age he lived in, and had made a wide study of the subject. He did, however, allude to the matter indirectly when he mentioned the role of the typical German in American comedy: the man who always turns up late.[36] The aim of Hugo Münsterberg, author of *Die Amerikaner*[37] — friendship between the Germany of the Hohenzollern and the America of Theodore Roosevelt — was probably too official to allow him such critical remarks, though as one who became a professor at Harvard and settled in the United States (and moreover collaborated with Taylor) he ought to have known the conveyor-belt system better than anyone else. But, as happens to so many over-enthusiastic physicians, he found the American "potion" too beneficial for Europe to bother about its less salubrious side effects.

Though America had become a competitor and sometimes even an opponent, she was nevertheless the child of Europe, part of one's own familiar flesh and blood. The powers which challenged European domination in Asia, by contrast, had nothing of America's ambivalent attitude to the "mother continent." For centuries they had been subjugated, exploited, repressed, and treated with boundless arrogance. Their slumbering resistance was given a powerful shot in the arm when Japan scored a decisive victory in the relentless struggle she had waged ever since 1868: in 1902 Britain was forced to accept her as an ally and to recognize her as one of the great powers. Previously, all that had mattered was how the white world reacted to colonial repression, either by voicing moral objections (Douwes Dekker) or by political opposition, or by a combination of both, as for instance during Leopold II's all too blatant behavior in the Congo. But now the attitude of the "colonies" had to be taken into account as well, however semi-officially. Asia was turning restive, in apparently small things at first: in 1905 the Japanese baseball team was beaten in the United States, and from that moment on sport became a subject of great national importance to the Japanese. But Asia showed restiveness in great matters also: that same year Japan beat Russia soundly on land and at sea. It is said that the report of the first great victory of a colored race over a white spread like wildfire and penetrated even to deepest Africa via the jungle drum. The year 1905 also saw the first great uprising in India in protest against Lord Curzon's division of Bengal, and it became clear that the Indian nationalists were determined not only to gain political independence but also to benefit from modern technology and social reform. The founding of the Jadavpur College of Engineering in Bengal was just a straw in the wind.[38]

In 1908, after the Turks had been made to feel the superiority of the West in all possible ways, *inter alia* by an American ultimatum following the abduction of Miss Stone, a missionary, in 1901,[39] a young officers' rebellion broke out in Macedonia. Whatever else became of the Young Turks, it is certain that this rebellion was as much directed against the plan of the western powers to wrest Macedonia from the Turkish Empire as it was intended to force Sultan Abdul Hamid to implement the constitution he had proclaimed as long ago as 1876. At about the same time, the modernization of Indonesia and Burma was begun. In Indonesia the Budi Utomo educational organization was set up, followed four years later by the more aggressive and influential Sarekat Islam; in Burma, where American missionaries enjoyed great influence, a Medical Institute was founded in 1907, and the Young Men's Buddhist Association, modeled on the YMCA, in 1908.

In Persia there had been unrest ever since 1905 when the young nationalists drawn to the Russian revolutionaries had ceased to be frightened of the Cossack threat. A year later the corrupt Ayn-al-Dawal had to be dismissed and the Shah was forced to recognize the authority of parliament — the Majlis. True, once the support of the Russian revolutionaries could be increasingly discounted, the Shah felt confident enough to reverse the tide, aided by the Czar, in accordance with the time-honored principle of all princes and great men in semi-colonial territories: to exploit the national movement when foreign rulers had to be kept in check, but more often than not to plot with the foreign rulers against the popular movement. An American citizen, Morgan Shuster, was charged with the modernization of the treasury during one of the liberal waves, but two Russian ultimata called for his dismissal in 1911, and the invading Cossacks underwrote these demands with the kind of strength Persia could not yet resist. But despite the division of Persia into a northern, Russian, and a southern, British sphere of influence, the perceptive observer could see clearly enough that while western domination would continue for some time it would not prevail forever.

In China, which joined the liberation movement late in the day, the year 1911 proved a watershed. The suppression of the Boxer Rebellion was the last chance the European powers had of imposing their will, though even then they had to put a good face on Hay's open-door policy, which stood the Chinese in good stead: America greatly preferred to sell her lamps and her oil on China's near-inexhaustible market to joining in the unpromising division of that country. After a series of vain attempts, Sun Yat-sen succeeded on October 9, 1911 in starting a mutiny in Hankow that soon afterwards put an end to the rule of the Manchus. He could not have known that his Japanese-trained Kuomintang, with their call for "nationalism, democracy, and socialism," had begun a revolution that was to last for more than half a century and was to reform China beyond recognition. Nor did the ambassadors of the Great Powers realize what was happening; they did not even grasp the fact that their merchants would soon lose their last chance of making "celestial" profits in a country about to relieve them of the "white man's burden."

But the most remarkable event from the European point of view, at least in retrospect, probably occurred in hitherto "quiet" Arabia. Here, at the end of our period, Abd al-Aziz ibn al-Saud, who was later to unite the peninsula under his scepter, wrested the maritime province of al-Hasa (south of Kuwait) from Turkish overlordship. It seemed to be nothing more than a struggle between the Rashid dynasty and the Turks, as indeed it was, but it had greater significance. Nascent Arab nationalism had triumphed with the help of the Great Powers, and while the latter were attempting to use this triumph in order to weaken the Turkish empire and, *en passant*, to lay their hands on vast oil resources, London, Paris and Saint Petersburg failed to appreciate that they had helped an enemy into the saddle, a saddle that, good desert horseman that he was, he would never again abandon.

Though events in darkest Asia during the first decade of the twentieth century may have escaped the attention of the European public, the more perspicacious were beginning to feel increasingly uneasy. Still, very few would have gone as far as the French deputy, Jules Delafosse, who, protesting in December 1885 against the conduct of his government in Indochina, declared that he was convinced that no European colony would survive on the coast of Asia for more than half a century.[40]

Many more were afraid of the American challenge to European supremacy. Thus the "idealist," Jean de Bloch, had predicted as early as 1898 that the United States and Russia were bound, sooner or later, to outstrip all the other powers, because they alone had enough space to absorb their excess population.[41] What he could not have foreseen in 1900, nor anyone else for that matter, was that the New World was later to be confronted with an even newer world in ancient and backward Russia. All the European of 1900 was anxious to do was by putting up a united front to stem the "peaceful" tide of American domination.

But Europe was far from united. The gentlemen who played first fiddle in London, Paris, Berlin, Saint Petersburg and Vienna were about to change the famous "European Concert of Nations" into a cacophony. Few could read the storm signals, and those who could were promptly denounced as Cassandras. There was Tangier in 1905; Bosnia and Herzegovina in 1908; Agadir in 1910 and again in 1911, immediately followed by the war between Italy and Turkey over Tripoli and then by the Balkan wars. How united the world has become since then, albeit in a more sinister way than anyone expected, may be grasped by anyone disturbed by recent events in Korea, Cuba, or Vietnam, and who happens to read how little concern most Europeans felt about "some powder barrel in the far-away Balkans." Even the shot fired in Sarajevo, the little pebble that set off a huge avalanche, did not cause nearly as great a stir as has so often been suggested. Otherwise so many Europeans would not have blithely chosen that diplomatically tense month of July to holiday abroad. In Austria-Hungary both the government, after some vacillation, and the press hinted increasingly at Serbian complicity, although all that seemed certain was that the secret society "Union or Death," which aimed at the unification of all southern Slavs, had had a "black hand" in the affair. Von Wiesner, incidentally, was sent out as late as July 13 to declare that this was not the case. A day later the opposition of Count Stephen Tisza, the Hungarian premier, was overruled in the Austrian Crown Council, which now demanded the exemplary punishment of Serbia. The upshot was a 48-hour ultimatum, still couched in fairly temperate language. Within a day, Russia let it be known that she would not countenance an Austrian attack on Serbia. Though the Austrians immediately declared that they had no intention of annexing Serbian territory, the Russian Crown Council ordered precautionary measures against Austria. The French, for their part, promised the Russians support, while the Germans ranged themselves behind the Austrians. Belated

649

attempts at mediation on the part of Britain could no longer stem the tide: on August 1 Germany declared war on Russia and on August 3 on France. German troops invaded Belgium, and one day later Britain had joined the war. While the guns blazed away between the trenches, a clash of ideologies, inflamed by the press, was unleashed behind the lines. The war was declared to be a struggle between two irreconcilable cultures: the "democratic" one of the Entente and the "authoritarian" one of the Central Powers. Russia was conveniently forgotten, but then an ideology is an ideology, and facts may be easily glossed over. Within the great clash of ideologies, which remained rather vague and meant little to the man in the street — the less so as democracy could also be described as lawlessness, and autocracy as national discipline — the smaller hatreds loomed up all the more fiercely: the loathing the Austrians felt for the Balkan barbarians, and the Serbians for the Austrians and above all for the Hungarian oppressors of their race and nationality. Then there was French resentment about the defeat of 1870, German envy of British world supremacy and British doggedness in the face of a crisis coupled to righteous indignation at the rape of neutral Belgium, and equally righteous German indignation at Britain's failure to appreciate that the invasion of that country had been an unavoidable stratagem. So everyone waved flags, and carried flowers on their rifles, while roaring the *Marseillaise, Deutschland über alles, God Save the King* or *Tipperary* at one another. The churches blessed all guns indiscriminately, and pastors prayed for the triumph of their particular sheep, while the Second International fell apart into national sections, whose respective leaders — Kautsky, Vaillant, and Henderson — supported the war and joined the various war cabinets.[42] The odd protesting voice — for instance, that of Liebknecht in the Reichstag — was quickly silenced. Bernstein, the "father of revisionism," was to follow him into the wilderness soon afterwards. Those who felt horrified by their leaders' "betrayal of socialism" — and not they alone — had been walking about with closed eyes for decades, else they would surely have realized that an International which had demanded compulsory arbitration and disarmament during so many pre-war congresses (Stuttgart in 1907, Copenhagen in 1910 and Basel in 1912) but had done little else to fulfil its intention to "fight the war with all the means the parties (!) may deem fit," would do nothing when the time came. In an article in the *Bremer Bürger Zeitung* of November 1914 the Russian socialist Axelrod had this to say: "The war has destroyed an *illusion* rife among social democrats. All of us had been under the misapprehension that at least the *socialist* workers in the various countries were filled with the spirit of international sol-

650

idarity."[43] This may have been true of the oldest pioneers of socialism who had indeed been "unpatriotic scum" and of their first disciples. But, as Axelrod went on to explain, the very means socialists had used to oppose the state had made them its ally. Thus one of the most important platforms in the workers' struggle had been the demand for a full share in the cultural achievements of the nation at large. This was not just because of the suffrage and parliamentarianism. One of the most important weapons of the workers in emancipating themselves had become their participation in the culture (through school and press, above all), and this was achieved precisely in the period when the culture became thoroughly nationalistic.

The social democrat's betrayal of their ideals was, however, only one facet of the general decline of idealism in the late nineteenth century, an idealism the vestiges of which, together with the balloon sleeves, the pigtails, and the *Jugendstil*, struck subsequent generations as the clearest possible signs that our period was antiquated even while it was still in full sway.

In his *Civilization and its Discontents*[44] Freud has traced the historical and psychological roots of man's cultural malaise back to prehistory. It was no accident that he should have examined this phenomenon — by the turn of the century Western man had succumbed to a paralyzing crisis of confidence. At the root of this crisis was the disintegration — a word that was to come into increasing use — of the bonds between emotion and reason, to the detriment of the former. Ever since the industrial revolution and the consequent rationalization of industrial life, Europeans had been greeting the accumulation of human knowledge and skills and the control of natural and social forces it brought them, with as much astonishment as pride. Rationalization and industrialization were the two sources of what nineteenth-century man so confidently described as Progress. The human intellect was plumbing the mysteries of nature more thoroughly than ever before, while technical advances were bringing Western man unprecedented prosperity. The new dream of a golden future had displaced the old dream of the Golden Age; "new" and "modern" became terms of approbation and "seasoned" a recommendation for nothing but cheese and wine.

The European felt acutely that he was participating personally in the very process of historical growth. Here we have another source of disintegration, for while the idea that historical developments can be influenced by man persuaded some to cling all the more firmly to their historical roots, to historicism in the narrower sense, which mythologized the past in an irrational, conservative, and nationalist way, it drove others into the arms of what is best described as "historical meteorology," the prediction and planning of the future by an analysis of the present and the past, a methodology of which Marxists became the leading exponents.

It has been said — and with some justification — that Marxism became a new religion, one that offered a fresh panacea for all man's ills, though no one can say to what extent history was actually influenced by the nineteenth-century conviction, not only among Marxists but also, though to a lesser extent, among other economists, that the future can be planned and controlled. All that is clear is that this belief (coupled with the growing confidence of the advancing working class) produced uncertainty and fear. There was first of all the fear of "the specter of communism" which was not confined to the propertied classes but was also shared by intellectuals, who saw culture threatened both by mechanization and also by the growing class consciousness of the masses. Secondly there was the fear of responsibility, an essentially different and graver responsibility than any leading group had ever known. Men could no longer allow God's rain to fall on God's acre. They were now not only responsible for building dikes against floods but also against economic crises and unemployment — until recently treated as just punishment for indolence — against epidemics, housing shortages, crime, and so on; and it was once again the intelligentsia that felt the brunt. Some simply closed their eyes, among them such bourgeois aesthetes as Marius Bauer and Lodewijk van Deyssel who, with almost deliberate dishonesty, defended the prodigality and the cruelty of the Czarist regime against the attacks of a number of socially committed writers.[45] Similarly, Huizinga complained as late as 1940 that "the total usurpation of our intellectual heritage by political and economic forces, causes one to have serious fears about the health of our civilization".[46]

We have repeatedly referred to the transformation of Western culture at the turn of the century, a transformation that was so sudden and so rare in history that we are entitled to call it a dialectical change of quantity into quality. There had always been a contrapuntal line in the triumphant score of reason: Romanticism, religious revival movements such as the *Réveil*, such figures as Kierkegaard and Bilderdijk, but not until the end of the century did the counterpoint assume the nature of an overriding theme, a sign of growing discontent with the tempo of modern life. Man may have acquired such powers over matter that he could look down condescendingly on Prometheus and Icarus as mere tyros, but in the process he had become "a god by means of artificial limbs, so to speak, quite magnificent when equipped with all his accessory

652

organs; but they do not grow on him and they still give him trouble from time to time."[47] The liberal belief that "progress" was necessarily for the best was unmasked as an illusion, for the power progress bestows on man can serve evil just as devotedly as it can serve good, if not more so. Discontent with a civilization that had become infatuated with its own skills caused many to cast off the oppressive burden of responsibility and reason in favor of "spontaneity" and what has been called "the germinal power of the irrational enshrined in the human spirit."

"Her mother," Albérès said of the twentieth century, "died in labor — by 1900, universal reason, which had protected previous generations, had ceased to be the womb of art and philosophy."[48] But was the real cause of the crisis not rather the fact that the nineteenth century had stayed alive, even while it was being disowned by some of its children? There was no question of a break in the normal development of industrial life, in human communication, or in science, albeit, as ever, that development went hand in hand with the rejection of old certainties and, in our period, even with doubts about the absolute validity of natural laws. But the new physics, which destroyed so many previously unquestioned axioms, left it to the layman to seek metaphysical solace for this disappointment and, for its own part, continued to work on rational lines. For the rest, mankind at large, too, clung firmly to its rationality, at least in public, though man had come to appreciate how little sway the rational ego held over the irrational id in his private thoughts. The ego, Thomas Mann declared, was a tiny, precocious and vigilant part of the id — much as Europe was a small, enlightened province in the vast continent of Asia.[49] While so many still clamored for social progress, the irrational countercurrent in philosophy, art and education could not make the triumphant breakthrough so many had counted on, and was confined to personal attempts at liberation and at best to a tragic penetration of the deeper layers of the psyche. It would, however, erupt with a vengeance in politics, in the abominations of jingoism and anti-Semitism. True, these impulses were not new, but they had previously either been kept in check by idealism or else swept under the carpet. In that sense, they could be called a form of liberation from old constraints and particularly from the repression of the emotions by the intellect. To the enemies of nineteenth-century rationalism, of "dry reason," the "arid, dehumanized science," the supremacy of the mind was a myth, a hypocritical attempt to denigrate human spontaneity, so as to make man a slave to the so-called higher needs of the captains of industry, the builders of empires, or the anonymous leaders of big business. It is difficult to deny that Nietzsche's superman was a projection, born out of the burning

653

self-consciousness of a shy, sickly professor, a mighty super-ego with which to confront the arrogant new masters of society. It is just as understandable that lesser figures than Nietzsche, ready to worship anyone with power, should have identified these unscrupulous empire builders and similar embodiments of primitive strength and irrational violence with his superman. For heroes were undoubtedly needed by an intellectual bourgeoisie which could no longer, as it had been accustomed to do for centuries, live on the élitist concepts of classical antiquity and the Middle Ages, and which, as we have said, was bound, at a time in which democracy held the winning hand, to be filled with apprehensions about the stultifying results of what they liked to describe as materialism — something that appealed to none but the "gray masses" with their vulgar and egalitarian ambitions.

The confused and blurred character of our period is also reflected in the way in which it attacked or annexed the ideas of the great nineteenth-century rationalists. Thus Freud was decried as a crude materialist and an exorcist, but also worshiped as the great diviner of dreams by the droves who plagiarized his ideas and his terminology. Similarly, William James was variously attacked and praised for his conversion from objectivism to subjectivism, or from determinism to voluntarism, as was Bergson for his intuitionism and *élan vital.*

The same process that undermined the authority of reason, also brought liberation from the hollow authority of the older generation, which was now blamed for everything. This may have been no more than the normal generation gap, and the rebels of 1900 would be blamed just as vigorously by the post-war generation as they had blamed their own fathers. But youth was increasingly gaining the upper hand and with every new generation it felt more and more that it alone had right on its side.[50]

There was a sense of personal liberation and of self-discovery as only the Renaissance had experienced it: "What distinguished me from the rest, was what mattered; what no one but myself said or could say, was what I had to say," Gide explained.[51] "The uppermost fact, the most seminal and liberating fact was that everyone could speak his own truth," wrote Unamuno.[52]

The fact that the precious jewel of freedom was bought at the cost of disintegration could not have been formulated more clearly than in this exultant cry of Unamuno. It was a tragic triumph because only the rarest of men can live without idealism, and without faith in the harmony of emotion and reason. Much as the high demands of idealism had bred nineteenth-century hypocrisy, so twentieth-century love of

654

truth turned into mere lip service. Those who were not part of the intellectual élite and yet could not live by bread and circuses alone, constituted a new phenomenon in human civilization: the culturally homeless in search of a life philosophy in which they could take shelter like a naked hermit crab in a mollusc shell.

After discussing bourgeois loss of faith in reason, Albérès went on to say: "Rationalism has never been able to recover the public esteem it lost: *twentieth-century man lives with fear and a guilty conscience because he has killed his faith in the intellect.* Still, the battlefield has not remained empty for the Marxist idea has stepped into the breach ... "[53] But in so doing, had not the Marxists themselves been forced to embrace irrationalism? Can anyone say that theirs is purely rational doctrine? At most, it can be claimed that the Marxists were the first to provide a rational theory of social transformation. Even if that should make all the communist pioneers from Babeuf to Marx and Engels men of pure reason, it is nevertheless a fact that communism met all the irrational longings of the outcasts of this earth, and that, as a result, it was changed from a theory into an ideology, into what Heine was the first to describe as a secular religion. For the homeless on the threshold of the twentieth century, and long afterwards as well, had two dwellings prepared for them, two great ideologies, both promising to restore the sorely missed harmony of reason and emotion: Mother Church and communism. The church, her faith rooted in the irrational, had realized ever since St. Thomas that she could not survive without stone walls built of reason. This explains why she was not entirely happy with those new converts who sought her out solely to regain peace of mind by suppressing their own doubts, and why she expressly declared herself against all attacks on reason.[54] It also explains why the "conservative" church no less than the "revolutionary" communists both rejected everything they felt as a threat to human dignity: the ideas of Nietzsche and Freud, who had stripped off so many veils, and the exponents of abstract art. It is also the reason why both refused to carry self-criticism beyond the slenderest limits. Personal inclination and experience, and age too, determined which of the two "dwellings" the homeless of 1900 chose as their own, but there were also quite a few smaller and less solid refuges. Many escaped all forms of tradition and the threat of becoming lost in the gray mass by adopting what was often a singularly bloodless form of aestheticism and individualism; others tried to transform their petty convictions into ideologies, amongst them the vegetarians, the feminists, and the spiritualists.

There were those, finally, who in their isolation were no longer able

to embrace any ideology or pseudo-ideology, and who in their hunger
for safety and their passion for unity, embraced hero worship and self-
sacrifice for their own sakes:

"The times are black. / We were born out of season, too late. / Wrapped
in a coat / by an angel lost in a storm / filled with bitter longing / for
the King whose champion I aspired to be / I walk to my Death . . ."[55]

The collapse of the old norms in the wake of material progress at an
unprecedented rate, the loss of faith in the unity of emotion and reason,
its replacement by two great ideologies and a host of pseudo-ideologies,
were the most characteristic features of European intellectual life on
the threshold of the new century. It is impossible to gauge to what
strata of the population the ultimate ramifications of that dissolution
had percolated. What is certain is that the general disintegration of the
norms by which European man had been living until then was not confined to those who felt a shock of recognition on reading Gide's: "Nothing
is good for all, but only for certain persons; nothing is true for all but
only to those who believe in it." How many people, and intellectuals
in particular, had not taken him for a prophet and an apostle of the
truth during the first half of our century!

The anxiety felt by a Kafka was not shared exclusively by just the
handful of those who read his work. For Kafka not merely reflected
all the fears of the oppressed East European Jew threatened by new
waves of anti-Semitism, and the anguish of all intellectuals who realize
that their world is built on shifting sands, but also the intangible terror
of all those ordinary men and women who felt that every scientific
advance posed a threat to their existence: the farmer who had to re-
organize his whole way of life with the advent of artificial fertilizers
and the introduction of farm machinery on a massive scale; the worker
who was suddenly faced with conveyor-belts and time-and-motion studies
in his factory; the shopkeeper who was being bankrupted by the department store; the slum-dweller who lived in the shadow of rehousing
schemes; the old generation, which was threatened by the rebelliousness
and lack of understanding of the next, and the young generation which
was sickened by the delusions and hypocrisy of the old. All this went
hand in hand with vague fears of the "specter of communism," of the
"yellow peril," the "black peril", and the decline of European hegemony.
"From the very outset, the century was existentialist," Albérès explained.

Not only the intellectual — who still had some self-assurance because
he believed he knew what it was all about — felt betrayed by the kind
of science that turned everything upside-down, while looking ironically
over its shoulder at the "absolute" platinum meter in the Bureau Inter-

national des Poids et Mesures in Sèvres, but also the man in the street had lost his trust in science as the fountain of wisdom and the great exorcist of ghosts. All he could do was lament with Albert Einstein that everything is relative, although it remained a relative question how much this type of relativity was within his intellectual grasp. Even the dream had been stripped of its poetic appeal to become an irrational cover of quasi-rational forces — it was no longer a sweet escape into the Land of Cockaigne of the imagination, but a thorny path to the innermost recesses of man's repressed fears.

Finally, on the threshold of the new century, there appeared a number of further phenomena, all of them related to man's conception of time. It was as if man, as he approached the twentieth century, just when medical science could guarantee him a much longer life, first became conscious of the murmurings of Chronos. Man's concept of time in 1900 was quite different from that of previous centuries, with their promise of life eternal. Time on earth had ceased to be an uneconomic entity: whosoever disposed of time — his own or that of others — was the master; whosoever did not was the slave. No longer was time treated in a cavalier manner, as if it were inexhaustible. True, the work ethos was nothing new, as witness the many proverbs and the countless victims of forced labor in one form or another, but the tempo of work in the past had been slow, the performance lackadaisical, and technical progress too gradual to make itself felt. The twelve-hour day had not been labor-intensive, Monday absenteeism was a recognized institution, and the Suez and North Sea canals had still been dug with spade and wheelbarrow. The increase in productivity together with the eight-hour day changed man's attitude to time incisively, facing him with the paradox that the more intensely he worked the less satisfaction he obtained: mechanized labor became more monotonous, traveling on railroads that spanned the whole continent became a tedious wait for the end of a journey fixed to within minutes and no longer a means of meeting people, seeing cities, admiring villages and landscapes. How quickly this transformation was effected becomes clear when we recall that Napoleon still moved his *Grand Armée* in the same way that Julius Caesar had moved his legions. The watch, still a status symbol in the nineteenth century and an ornament proudly displayed by ladies and gentlemen, produced with due ceremony at the end of a long gold chain from the waistcoat pocket or pinned to the bosom in jeweled splendor, became an article of daily use for all but eccentrics and poets.

Twentieth-century man hears the sound of passing time wherever he goes. The chronometer tells the seconds of his work and his play. His is no longer the time of the hourglass, the time between transient life and eternity, but the time of Christian Morgenstern's *Zeitgedichte*; it dogs his steps with remorseless capriciousness. It is no longer time, but my time, your time, his time. "Bide your time" and "Fill your hour" were two injunctions by Verwey affixed to Berlage's Exchange in the same year that Einstein revealed the relativity of even this dimension, in the year that Proust wrestled to capture "lost time" in the meshes of his elaborate sentences and Joyce tested the possibility of spanning the infinite vastnesses of a single day, while art, abandoning the stillness of perspective, tried to capture motion and simultaneity. On the threshold of the twentieth century, European man, who only half a century earlier had believed he was about to embrace an almost totally safe existence, and paradoxically enough did so in many ways, found himself before the dark gate of utter uncertainty.

NOTES

Works indicated by shortened references are cited in full in the Bibliography.

1. 1900: A SYNOPTIC VIEW

1. England and Wales: 32.5 millions; Scotland and Wales *ca.* 4.5 millions each. *The Statesman's Yearbook*, 39 (1902), p. 14.
2. *Ibid.*, p. 901.
3. *Diaries* quoted in *Howe*, pp. 91-93. For a critical analysis of Blunt's poetry, see *Sampson*, p. 739.
4. *Cf. Romein* VI, pp. 117-152.
5. *Sykes, Baker,* and *Petermanns geographische Mitteilungen* 46 (1900).
6. *De Hollandsche revue*, 5 (1900), p. 642.
7. *Petermanns geographische Mitteilungen* 46 (1900), p. 173.
8. *Ibid.*, p. 146.

II. FIN DE SIÈCLE

1. *Jackson H.*, pp. 19-20.
2. *Howe*, p. 48.
3. *The Statesman's Yearbook*, 39 (1902), pp. 572 and 648.
4. *Ibid.*, p. 574.
5. *Ibid.*, pp. 566-567.
6. *Howe*, p. 253.
7. *Howe*, p. 33.
8. *Grousset*, p. 261.
9. *Romein* VI, pp. 12-40 and especially pp. 23-26.

III. THE DRAGON AWAKES

1. *De Hollandsche revue*, 5 (1900), pp. 436-437.
2. *Cordier*, Part III, 2, pp. 458-459. *Steiger*, pp. 162-163.
3. *Morse*, Part III, p. 186.
4. *Clyde*, pp. 257-273.
5. *Morse*, Part III, pp. 169-170.
6. *Chirol* II, pp. 199-200.
7. *Morse*, Part III, p. 326.
8. *Johnson*, p. 44.
9. *Clyde*, p. 300.
10. *Borel*.
11. *Clyde*, p. 298. *Cf. Krausse*, pp. 258-378 and especially p. 362.
12. *Waldersee*, Part III, p. 2.
13. *Steiger*, p. 182.
14. *Allen*, pp. 78, 80, 83. *Cf. Steiger*, p. 221.
15. *North China Herald*, June 20, 1900.

16. *Weale.*
17. *Cordier*, Part III, 2, pp. 520–522.
18. *Weale*, p. 302.
19. *Chirol* II, p. 206.
20. *Bland*, p. 144 (note).
21. *Anthouard*, p. 291.
22. *Zabel*, p. 288.
23. *Mohs*, p. 417. Meisner (see *Waldersee*) has omitted this passage.
24. *Mohs*, p. ix.
25. *Steiger*, Appendix I, p. 316.
26. *Journal des Economistes* (September, 1900), pp. 507–508.
27. *Steiger*, p. 260.
28. *Zabel*, pp. 412–431.
29. *De Hollandsche revue*, 5 (1900), pp. 436–437.
30. *Borel*, p. 36.
31. Quoted in *Cordier*, Part III, 2, pp. 553–554.

IV. CAPE TO CAIRO

1. Postgate, R. in *Picture Post*, January 7, 1950, p. 20.
2. *Annual Register 1900–1901:* "The War in South Africa," pp. 392–410.
3. *Visscher*, p. 63.
4. *Grosclaude*, p. 54f.
5. *Darcy*, p. 349.
6. *Hilsenbeck.*
7. *Batts*, p. 177.
8. *Batts*, p. 184.
9. Spender, H. quoted in *Bouman P. J.* II, pp. 30 and 443 (note).
10. *Rompel*, p. vii.
11. *Adams*, p. 98.
12. *Williams*, p. 51.
13. *Leyds*, Part II, p. 191.
14. *Hole*, pp. 299–329.
15. *Sayers*, p. 43.
16. *Mustafa*, pp. 63–123.
17. *Williams*, p. 236f.
18. *Huxley*, Part I, p. 11.
19. *Thomas, H. B.*, p. 1f.
20. *Hennig*, p. 172. All the other data concerning the Cape to Cairo railway line are taken from this book.
21. *Grosclaude*, p. 86; *Poel*, p. 201.
22. *Adams*, p. 15.
23. *Darcy*, pp v–vi.
24. *Grosclaude*, p. 84.
25. *Depelley.*
26. *Grosclaude*, p. 84 (note).
27. *Adams*, p. 49f.
28. *Daily Mail*, November 25, 1899, quoted in *Picture Post*, January 7, 1952, p. 9.
29. *Seeley*, p. 350.
30. *Schuiling.*
31. *Adams*, p. 50.
32. *De Hollandsche revue*, 5 (1900), p. 218.
33. *Friedjung*, Part I, p. 16.

1. *Schulthess' Eur. Gesch. Kalender*, N. F. 16 (1900), Munich, 1901, p. 26.
2. The first set of figures is taken from *Schulthess' Eur. Gesch. Kalender*, N. F. 16 (1900), Munich, 1901; the second set from *New York Herald Tribune*, Eur. ed., January, 22-23, 1950.
3. *Sartorius*, pp 378-632.
4. *Sombart* III, p. 530.
5. *Ancel*, p. 228f.
6. *Keynes*, p. 15.
7. *Gagliardi*, Part II, p. 195.
8. *Gagliardi*, Part II, p. 496.
9. *Gagliardi*, Part II, p. 213.
10. *Gagliardi*, Part II, p. 205.
11. *Gagliardi*, Part II, p. 238.
12. *Schaefer*, p. 52; *Earle* I, p. 34.
13. *Schulthess' Eur. Gesch. Kalender*, N. F. 16 (1900), Munich 1901, p. 278.
14. Summary of report in *Diplomatic and Consular Reports*, 3140, London, 1903, p. 26ff. See also *Report of the Anatolian Railway*, 1899, p. 9, and *Hennig*, p. 140.
15. *Netscher*, pp. 724-725.
16. *De Hollandsche revue*, 5 (1900), p. 807.
17. *Heyd*.
18. *Buxton*, p. 118.
19. *De Hollandsche revue*, 5 (1900), pp. 8-11.
20. *Buxton*, p. 23 ff.
21. *Buxton*, pp. 24 and 25.
22. *Pears*.
23. *De Hollandsche revue*, 5 (1900), pp. 8-11.
24. *De Hollandsche revue*, 5 (1900), p. 508ff.
25. *Gaulis*.
26. *Helfferich* II, Part III, p. 29.
27. *Helfferich* II, Part III, p. 32.
28. *Helfferich* II, Part III, p. 33.
29. *Hoskins*, p. 451.
30. *Helfferich* II, Part III, p. 35.
31. *Gaulis*, p. 130.
32. *Schaefer*, p. 16ff.
33. *Grothe*, p. 251.
34. *Helfferich* II, Part III, p. 76.
35. *Sax*, p. 526.
36. *Hallgarten*, Part I, p. 406, quoting *Verwey*, p. 224.
37. *Helfferich* II, Part III, p. 85. *Cf. Lindow*.
38. *Helfferich* II, Part III, p. 86.
39. *Helfferich* II, Part III, p. 88.
40. *Schulthess' Eur. Gesch. Kalender*, N. F. 16 (1900), Munich 1901, pp. 29-30.
41. For the text of the contract and the appended "Cahiers des charges" and statutes, see *Fraser* I, pp. 375-379 and *Ragey*, pp. 127-203; for the financial and technical details, see *Schmidt H*.
42. *Schaefer*, p. 21.
43. *Lewin*, p. 66 and note.
44. *Hennig*, p. 147 and map on p. 137.
45. *Hennig*, p. 136 (figures for 1909).
46. *Seton, R. W.*, pp. 385 ff. *Cf. Sprenger*.

47. *Wiedemann,* p. 10.
48. *Wiedemann,* pp. 15-20.
49. *Hallgarten,* Part I, p. 500 (note 4).
50. *Hennig,* p. 141.
51. *Helfferich* II, Part III, p. 111.
52. *Helfferich* II, Part III, pp. 119-125.
53. *Ragey,* p. 43 f.
54. *Helfferich* II, Part III, pp. 125-130.
55. *Schaefer,* p. 47.
56. *Chirol* I, p. 215.
57. *Wolf, J. B.*
58. *Schaefer,* p. 23.
59. *Wolf, J. B.,* p. 55.
60. *Schaefer,* p. 25.
61. *Wichmann, H.,* p. 113f.
62. *Wiedemann,* pp. 37-39.
63. *Hakki,* pp. 251, 266, 270, 284.
64. *Bülow,* Part I, p. 253.
65. *Wolf, J. B.,* p. 95f.

VI. ORIFLAMME AND TRICOLORE

1. *Reinach,* Part IV, p. 592ff.
2. *Herzog,* p. 833.
3. *Reinach,* Part V, p. 260 (note 2).
4. *Morand,* pp. 16, 17, 350; *Reinach,* Part V, p. 308ff.
5. *Morand,* pp. 149-157.
6. *Herzog,* p. 357.
7. *Herzog,* p. 362f.
8. *Herzog,* p. 353f.
9. *Herzog,* p. 354.
10. *Charensol,* p. 11.
11. John 11: 49-50.
12. *Clemenceau,* p. 553.
13. *Romein* I, p. 211.
14. *Axa,* p. 272.
15. *Axa,* p. 271.
16. *Axa,* p. 50.
17. *Gobier,* p. vi.
18. *Herzog,* pp. 351-968.
19. *Kayser,* pp. 411-421.
20. *Desachy.*
21. *Charpentier* II.
22. *Charpentier* II, pp. 171-205.
23. *Fréville,* p. 126.
24. *Herzog,* p. 132.
25. *Fréville,* p. 127.
26. *Baschwitz* I.
27. *Leyret* I, p. 9f.
28. *Leyret* I, p. 153.
29. *Schwartzkoppen,* p. 3ff.
30. *Hamilton,* p. 275.
31. *Avenel* I, p. 801.

32. *Lazare* II.
33. *Lazare* I.
34. *Clemenceau.* (Article published on January 10, 1898.)
35. *Zola* IV, Part I, pp. 57-69.
36. *Bracq*, p. 259.
37. *Herzog*, p. 331f.
38. *Ajalbert*, p. 26f.
39. *Ajalbert*, p. 28.
40. *Delhorbe.*
41. *Morand*, p. 158.
42. *Charpentier* II, pp. 246-277.
43. *Leyret* I, p. 153.
44. *Herzog*, p. 53.
45. *Guyot* II, p. 165, quoted in *Bracq*, p. 259.
46. *Cornilleau*, p. 63ff.
47. *Zévaès*, p. 212; *Delhorbe*, p. 270; *Rolland* IV, Part I, p. 46.
48. *Hedenström*, p. 66.
49. *Die grosse Politik*, 5890, quoted in *Hallgarten*, Part I, p. 455.
50. *Michon*, p. 35 quoted by E. W. Fox in *Earle* II, p. 132.
51. *Byrnes*, pp. v–vi.
52. *Dutrait.*

VII. CHAUVIN'S LEGACY

1. *Almanach Hachette*, Appendix p. lvi.
2. *Viau*, p. 270.
3. *Viau*, pp. 271-274.
4. *Stenographisches Protokoll der Verhandlungen des IV. Zionisten Congresses in London*, Vienna 1900, p. 3.
5. *Bein*, p. 574.
6. *Bloch, J. S.*, Part III, pp. 1ff, 15.
7. *Baron*, Part II, p. 291.
8. *Baron*, Part II, p. 291.
9. *Bloch*, Part III, p. 15.
10. *Tager.*
11. *Byrnes*, pp. 118-121.
12. *Baron*, Part I, p. 285.
13. *Valentin*, pp. 7, 211.
14. *Valentin*, p. 211.
15. *Lütgert*, p. 373.
16. *Oertzen.*
17. *Hayes* I, p. 262.
18. *Parkes*, pp. 200-202.
19. *Byrnes*, pp. 157-158.
20. *Brynes*, p. 164; *cf.* p. 156.
21. *Byrnes*, p. 227; *cf. Donos.*
22. *Byrnes*, p. 249.
23. *Byrnes*, p. 176.
24. *Byrnes*, pp. 205-212.
25. *Gayraud*, p. 191, quoted in *Gurian.*
26. *Finkelstein*, Part I, pp. 287, 409.
27. *Wischnitzer*, p. 98.
28. *Bein*, p. 619.

29. *Parkes,* p. 195; *Zweig A.* I, p. 30.
30. *Simmel, E.* and *Ackerman.*
31. *Novicow* I.
32. *Lazare* I.
33. *Lombroso* II.
34. *Bloch, J. S.,* Part I.
35. *Bloch, J. S.,* Part II, p. 123.
36. *Bloch, J. S.,* Part I, p. 246.
37. *Bloch, J. S.,* Part III, p. 73.
38. *Bloch, J. S.,* Part III, pp. 71-119.
39. *Scholz.*
40. *Cf. Baron,* Part II, p. 311.
41. *Dubnow* II, p. 124. (The German translation has been greatly condensed.)
42. *Pinsker.*
43. *Dubnow* II, p. 139.
44. *Kaplan,* Table III, p. 19.
45. German translation, Berlin 1925-1929.
46. *Nordau* III, p. 325.
47. *Bein,* p. 283.
48. *Herzl* II, Part I, pp. 19-105.
49. *Gelber; Sokolow.*
50. *Cohen,* p. 69.
51. *Herzl* II, Parts II-IV *(Tagebücher).*
52. *Cohen,* p. 80; *Nordau* III, p. 230f; *Nordau* II, pp. 140-153.
53. *Theodor Herzl Jahrbuch,* Vienna 1937, p. 284.
54. *Wischnitzer,* p. 98.
55. *Stenographisches Protokoll der Verhandlungen des IV. Zionisten Congresses,* Vienna, 1900, p. 5.
56. *Cohen,* p. 89ff.
57. *Hayes,* II, p. 165.
58. *Hayes* I, Chapter 7.
59. *Schulthess' Eur. Gesch. Kalender,* N. F. 16 (1900), Munich, 1901, p. 61.
60. *Schamelhout,* Part III, pp. 241-243.
61. *Chastenet,* p. 51.
62. *Vermeil,* p. 19.
63. *Hayes* I, p. 253.
64. *Hayes* I, p. 259.
65. *Nordau* I, Part II, p. 402.
66. *Hayes* I, p. 257 (note 14).
67. *Curtis,* p. 403.
68. *Hayes* I, p. 279.
69. *Vermeylen.*
70. *Schamelhout,* Part II, p. 298ff.
71. *Schamelhout,* Part II, p. 156.
72. *Schamelhout,* Part II, p. 62ff.
73. *Hayes* I, p. 284.
74. *Schamelhout,* Parts I and III.
75. *Hayes* I, p. 272ff.
76. *Bloch, J. S.,* Part III, p. 14.

VIII. THE GREAT ILLUSION

1. *Passy.*
2. *Fried,* Part II, p. 178.

3. *Fried*, Part II, p. 177.
4. *Bloch, J. von*, Part VI, p. 200.
5. *Suttner* II, p. 586.
6. *Suttner* I.
7. *Suttner* II.
8. *Suttner* II, p. 608.
9. *Ligt*, Part II, p. 309.
10. *Suttner* II, pp. 606-614.
11. *Fried*, Part II, pp. 310-422.
12. *Fried*, Part II, pp. 426-462.
13. *Beales*, pp. 238-242.
14. *Joyce*, p. 92. *Lange, C. L.*, p. 409, gives 645 and 790 respectively.
15. *Derry*, pp. 169-185.
16. *Nippold* and *Ralston*.
17. *Nippold*, p. 94ff; *Schücking*, p. 21.
18. *Langer* II, pp. 581-592.
19. First published in 1909 as *Europe's Optical Illusion*.
20. *Schück*.
21. *Lysen*.
22. *Mandere*, pp. 95-128.
23. Until 1889.
24. *Ligt*, Part II, pp. 44-46.
25. *Ligt*, Part II, pp. 147-155.
26. *Ligt*, Part II, p. 309.
27. Proceedings of the Stuttgart Congress, pp. 421-424.
28. *Ravesteyn*, Part II, pp. 231-264, and especially p. 263.
29. *Andler* III, p. 204.
30. *Drachkovitsch*, pp. 323-330.
31. *Liebknecht*, p. 43.
32. *Langer* I, p. 481.
33. *Seligmann*, under "armaments."
34. *Himer*, Part II, p. 81.
35. *Wehberg*, p. 351ff. Text of letter in *Lehmann*, p. 19.
36. *Lewinsohn* II, p. 185.
37. *Brailsford*, p. 90.
38. *Lewinsohn* I.
39. *Menne*, p. 187.
40. *Wehberg*, pp. 341-360.
41. *Wehberg*, pp. 348-349.
42. *Wehberg*, p. 347.
43. *Nordau* III, p. 256.

IX. LET CANDLES BE BROUGHT IN

1. *Cauchy*.
2. *Benoist* III, p. 5.
3. *Benoist* I, p. viii.
4. *Benoist* IV.
5. *Thuillier*.
6. *Morer*, pp. 85-103.
7. *Micelli*, pp. 441-462.
8. *Seligman*, under "Sighele."
9. *Maitron*, p. 184.
10. *Destrée*, p. 24.

11. *Destrée*, p. 12.
12. *Zenker* I.
13. *Zenker* II, p. 189.
14. *Norikus*, pp. 3, 8.
15. *Godkin*, p. 117.
16. *Laveleye*, p. 824ff. and Preface; *cf. Destrée*, pp. 11-12.
17. *Destrée*, pp. 13-14.
18. *Weber, Marianne*.
19. *Kropotkin* I, pp. 197-200.
20. *Domela* I.
21. *Ofner*.
22. *Domela* I, p. 14.
23. *De Hollandsche revue*, 5 (1900), p. 678.
24. *Ritchie* II, p. 255.
25. Sorel, G. in Preface to *Merlino* II.
26. *Elbow*, pp. 81-121.
27. *Schäffle*, p. 120ff; *Herrfahrdt*, p. 86 (note 2), p. 87 (note 1).
28. *Kautsky* II.
29. *Destrée*, p. 37. *Cf. Herrfahrdt*.
30. *Rittinghausen*.
31. *Kautsky* II, p. 139.
32. *Esmein*, p. 227ff.
33. *Domela* I, pp. 73-80.
34. *Lafitte*.
35. *Laski* II, p. 79; *cf. Romein* VI, pp. 309-310.
36. *Ferri* III, October 29, 1901. *Cf. Destrée*, p. 40 (note).
37. *Schmitt, C.*, p. 7.
38. *Domela* I, p. 85.
39. *Brandenburg; cf. Gerlach*, pp. 53-61.
40. *Faguet* II.
41. *Arendt*, p. 133.
42. *Milner*, Part II, p. 291. Letter of January 4, 1902 to E. B. I. Müller, author of
    Lord Milner in South Africa.
43. *Nietzsche* II.
44. *Delafosse*.
45. *Michels*.
46. *Spitz*, p. 19.
47. *Hayes* I, p. 249ff.
48. *Seligman*, under "Machayski."
49. *Shaw* VIII. See *Lippincott*, p. 207.
50. *Lippincott*, pp. 207-243.
51. *Spitz*, p. 287 (note 19).
52. *Spitz*, p. 165.
53. *Spitz*, pp. 197-201.
54. *Spitz*, p. 106.
55. *Norman*, p. 189.
56. *Cameron*, p. 25.
57. *Ursyn*.
58. *Cameron*, p. 100.
59. *Trotsky*, pp. iv, 32.
60. *Dolléans*, Part II, p. 62.
61. *Howe*, p. 236.
62. *Dolléans*, Part II, p. 72.

63. *Trotsky*, p. 59.
64. *Seton, H.*, p. 222.
65. *Seton, H.*, pp. 245–247, 251.
66. *Kropotkin* I, pp. 259–260.
67. *Fraser* II, p. 18.
68. *Bérard* II, p. 6.
69. *Bérard* II, p. 7.
70. *Sarrou*, p. 12; *Bérard* I, p. 350.
71. *Sarrou*, p. 19. For the program of the Committee, see especially pp. 40–43.
72. *Buxton*, pp. 75–84.
73. *Azoury*, p. 227.
74. *Buxton*, p. 68.
75. *Chirol* II, p. 138.
76. *Sarrou*, p. 21.
77. *Emin*, p. 87.
78. *Fehmi*, pp. 237–271.
79. *Chirol* II, p. 139.
80. *Mackenzie, K. R.*, p. 135.

X. UNDER THE BLACK FLAG

1. *Maitron*, p. 393.
2. *Huret* I, p. 246f.
3. *Maitron*, pp. 195–209; *Enthoven*, pp. 156–166.
4. *Enthoven*, p. 100.
5. *Maitron*, p. 196.
6. *Maitron*, p. 216, and index under "Vaillant"; *Enthoven*, p. 166.
7. *Maitron*, p. 226, and index under "Henry"; *Enthoven*, p. 178.
8. *Maitron*, p. 229, and index under "Caserio"; *Enthoven*, p. 190.
9. *Enthoven*, pp. 216–217.
10. *Maitron*, p. 196.
11. *Maitron*, index under "Vaillant"; *Enthoven*, pp. 172–178.
12. *Enthoven*, pp. 169–172.
13. *Maitron*, p. 534 (note 1).
14. *Fénéon*.
15. *Varennes*, p. 235ff.; *Maitron*, Annexe III, pp. 528–534.
16. *Vizetelly*, p. 138 (note).
17. *Nettlau* II, pp. 50–56.
18. *Nettlau* II, pp. 70–75.
19. *Vizetelly*, pp. 240–250.
20. *Hoek*, p. 32.
21. *Raymond*, p. 22ff.
22. *Vizetelly*, p. 252–253.
23. *Roller*.
24. *Archer* II.
25. *Romein* VII, p. 31ff.
26. Romein, J.: "Syndicalisme" in *Winkler Prins Encyclopaedie*, sixth impression, and bibliography therein. See also J. Maitron: *Le Syndicalisme révolutionnaire et Paul Delesalle*, Paris, 1952.
27. *Schellwien*.
28. *Zoccoli*, p. 18; *Seligmann* under "Stirner."
29. *Eltzbacher* I, pp. 82–124.
30. *Basch*.

31. *Sergent*, pp. 149–160.
32. *Woodcock*, pp. 49–91.
33. *Hamon, A. F. A.*
34. *Oppenheimer* III, Part II, p. 143.
35. *Kropotkin* IX.
36. *Kropotkin* IX, p. 46.
37. *Kropotkin* IX, p. ix.
38. *Kropotkin* IX, p. 304ff.
39. *Howard.*
40. *Kropotkin* VII, pp. 6–8.
41. *Laurentius.*
42. *Laurentius*, pp. 12, 75.
43. *Laurentius*, p. 98 (note).
44. *Laurentius*, pp. 35–36.
45. *Laurentius*, p. 80.
46. Published in 1912 but set in about 1907.
47. *Nettlau* III.
48. *Mackay*. Preface dated Rome, 1891.
49. *Rocker.*
50. *Mackay*, p. 59. *Flexner* I, p. 26 calls this figure a clear exaggeration.
51. *Mackay*, Condensed from Chapter III.
52. *Plekhanov* I, p. 87.
53. *Shaw* III, p. 32.
54. Romein, J. & A: *Erflaters van onze beschaving*, Amsterdam, 1959, p. 795ff.
55. Facsimile in catalogue of the Domela Nieuwenhuis exhibition, December 1959 - January 1960.
56. *Nettlau* I.
57. *Nettlau* I, p. vi.
58. *Stammhammer.*

XI. THE RED TIDE ADVANCES

1. *Vandervelde* II, p. 388.
2. *Spiekman.*
3. See *De Hollandsche revue*, 5 (1900), p. 838.
4. *Goes* I.
5. *Genet*, p. 9.
6. *Morand*, p. 65.
7. *Compte-rendu* I and *Compte-rendu* II
8. *Lenz*, pp. 39–51.
9. *Ravesteyn*, Part II, pp. 191–208.
10. *Michels.*
11. *Luxemberg* II.
12. *Ravesteyn*, Part II, p. 195; *Compte-rendu* I, p. 118.
13. *Compte-rendu* II, p. 201.
14. *Ravesteyn*, Part II, p. 203.
15. *Ravesteyn*, Part II, pp. 205–206; *Compte-rendu* I, p. 105.
16. *Compte-rendu* II, p. 207.
17. Published jointly with *Kautsky* IV. *Cf. Bernstein* III. For Bernstein, see *Bernstein* I and *Meiner*, who also mentions Kautsky.
18. *Valarché.*
19. *Sorel* II, p. 368.
20. *Ravesteyn*, Part I, pp. 99–159.

21. *Diehl*, p. 314.
22. *Weisengrün* I.
23. *Weisengrün* I, p. 73.
24. *Weisengrün* I, p. 78.
25. *Weisengrün* II.
26. *Masaryk* III, p. 303.
27. *Masaryk* III, pp. 303–308.
28. *Sorel* III.
29. *Kadt.*
30. *Treub* II.
31. *Bülow*, Part I, p. 600.
32. *Deville*, p. 239 quoted in *Ravesteyn*, Part II, p. 367.
33. *Merlino* I. French translation (*Merlino* II) with Preface by Sorel.
34. German translation: *Tugan* I.
35. Revised French edition (*Tugan* IV).
36. *Vorländer* I.
37. *Mehring* II, p. 33. Reprinted in *Mehring* IV, Part VI, p. 215.
38. *Vorländer* II.
39. *Adler, M.* III and *Adler, M.* I.
40. *Woltmann*, pp. 396, 398.
41. *Untermann.*
42. *Roland* II.
43. *Croce* III. French edition: *Matérialisme historique et économie marxiste*, Paris, 1901.
44. *Croce* III, p. 266.
45. *Ferri* I.
46. *Njewski*, p. 384. The book contains a summary of Bogdanov's writings.
47. *Simkhovitch.*
48. *Nomad*, Chapter V.
49. *Lozinsky*, p. 127.
50. *Lozinsky*, p. 127.
51. *Clayton.*
52. *Hintze*, p. 194; *cf. Jaurès* I.
53. *Jaurès* II; *cf. Posse.*
54. *Millerand*, quoted in *Louis*, p. 273.
55. *Hilton.*
56. A. Labriola in *Giornale d'Italia*, July 16, 1917, quoted in *Bezemer*, pp. 67–68.
57. *Masaryk* III, pp. 401, 402.
58. *Vandervelde* I.
59. *Kampffmeyer, P.* II, p. 104.
60. *Kampffmeyer, P.* I, p. 354.
61. Romein, J. in *Winkler Prins Encyclopaedie*, sixth impression, under "Bolsjewisme." For the London Congress, see *Jarowslawski*, pp. 90–112.
62. *Andler* III, p. 172.
63. *Mehring* III, Part IV, p. 355.
64. *Ravesteyn*, Part II, pp. 208–231.
65. *Sombart* II, p. vi; *Beckerath* under "Sombart."

XII. MODERN MAGNATES

1. *Laur.*
2. *Laur*, Part I, p. vii.
3. For the causes, see *Dillen*, p. 850.

4. *Kuczynski, J.* IV, pp. 86, 90.
5. *Rousiers.*
6. *Wibaut,* p. 14.
7. *Singer, I.,* p. 294.
8. *Rousiers,* p. 9.
9. *Rousiers,* p. 15.
10. *Colliez,* p. 3, motto.
11. See last note.
12. *Colliez,* p. 609.
13. *Colliez,* pp. 611, 620.
14. *Kleinwächter.*
15. In 1879: 14; in 1884: 54. See *Kuczynski, J.* IV, p. 86.
16. *Kleinwächter,* p. 111.
17. *Braun, A.*
18. *Braun, A.,* pp. 43-45.
19. *Braun, A.,* p. 46.
20. *Braun, A.,* p. 48.
21. *Wibaut.*
22. *Meyer, R.*
23. *Meyer, R.,* p. 303 (note).
24. *Meyer, R.,* p. 188.
25. *Schmoller* I.
26. *Meiner,* pp. 3, 4.
27. *Liefmann* I.
28. *Liefmann* II.
29. *Liefmann* III.
30. *Jeans.*
31. *Jeans,* p. 26.
32. *Laur,* Part I, p. 63.
33. *Singer, I.,* p. 113.
34. *Ufermann,* quoted in *Kuczynski, J.* IV, p. 126
35. *Laur,* Part II, p. 3.
36. *Huber,* p. 13.
37. *Ely.*
38. *Jenks.*
39. *Colliez.*
40. *Sombart* IV, p. 520.
41. *Riesser.*
42. *Riesser,* pp. 184, 203.
43. *Riesser,* pp. 244-278.
44. *Riesser,* pp. 204-226.
45. *Riesser,* p. 231; *cf.* p. 317.
46. *Riesser,* p. 170, and Appendix II, pp. 310-316.
47. *Lysis.*
48. *Westermann.*
49. *Sombart* IV, pp. 872-883.
50. *Hilferding,* p. ix.
51. *Hilferding,* p. 510.
52. *Lenin* II.
53. *Singer, I.,* p. 261.
54. *Huber,* pp. 98-99.
55. *Eggmann.*

56. *Drucker*, quoted in *Seidenberg*, p. 3.
57. *Eggmann*, pp. 1-53.
58. *Kuczynski, J.* IV, pp. 74-79.
59. *Sombart* IV, p. 941.
60. *Lexis*, p. 332ff.; *Böhm*.
61. *Sombart* IV, pp. 941-948.
62. *Huber*, pp. 7, 8.
63. *Zitzmann*, pp. 35-36.
64. *Sombart* IV and *Sombart* VI.
65. *Polak, F. L.*, pp. 245-258.

XIII. URBI ET ORBI

1. *Meuriot*, p. 30ff.
2. *Legoyt*.
3. *Meuriot*, p. 30ff.
4. *Fircks*.
5. *Sombart* IV, p. 390.
6. *Sombart* IV, p. 359.
7. *Clough*, p. 671.
8. Hollander, A. N. J. den, in *Winkler Prins Encyclopaedie*, sixth impression, under "Amerika."
9. *Gonnard* I, p. 290.
10. *Graham*, p. 3; *cf. Clough*.
11. *Sombart* IV, p. 417.
12. *Wirminghaus*, p. 11.
13. *Seligman* under: "Agriculture, International Institute of" and "Lubin."
14. *Hellpach* IV, p. 1.
15. *Daniels*, quoted in *Clough*, pp. 671, 672.
16. *Weber, A. F.*, p. 368.
17. *Longstaff*, p. 416.
18. *Hansen*.
19. Quoted in *Clough*, p. 693.
20. *Wirminghaus*, p. 175.
21. *Ammon* I, p. 183ff; *cf. Ammon* II.
22. *Bauer, L.*, p. 61.
23. *Bertillon* I.
24. *Rühle* III, p. 384.
25. *Rühle* III, p. 496.
26. *Rühle* II, p. 182.
27. *Bouman, P. J.* I, p. 59.
28. *Hermans*, p. 49.
29. *Bauer, L.*, p. 61.
30. Report on the state of large towns and populous districts (1845), quoted in *Mumford*, p. 165.
31. *Hermans*, p. 71.
32. *Rühle* III, p. 386.
33. *Weber, A. F.*, p. 410.
34. *Hermans*, p. 43.
35. *Rühle* III, p. 385.
36. *Rénon*, Part III, pp. ix, x.
37. *Rühle* III, p. 496.

38. *Braun, L.*
39. *Rühle* III, p. 504.
40. *Rénon*, Part III, p. 105.
41. "Résultat du referendum" in *Revue moderne de médecine et de chirurgie* (April 1904), p. 576.
42. *Rénon*, pp. 128-129.
43. *Simon*, p. 73.
44. *De Wegwijzer*, 3 (1900), pp. 189-191.
45. *Gruber, G. B.*, p. 14.
46. *Gruber, M.*, p. 306.
47. *Kautsky* I, p. 107.
48. *Weber, M.* I, p. 777.
49. *Grotjahn* I, p. 282.
50. *Bertillon* II, p. 76.
51. In *The Times*, July 3, 1895, quoted in *Rénon*, p. 80.
52. *Rénon*, Part II, p. 83.
53. *Rowntree, J.*, p. 7f.
54. *Gruber, G. B.*, p. 12.
55. *Gruber, G. B.*, Table facing p. 108.
56. *Grotjahn* I, p. 292.
57. *Pieper*, p. 17. *Cf.* Blocher.
58. *Pfeiderer.*
59. *Proost* III.
60. *De Volksbond* (Journal of the Dutch Association against Drink Abuse), Jubilee issue, 1875-1900; *Proost* III; *Brom*.
61. *Johnson.*
62. *Rénon*, Part I, pp. 161-166.
63. *Flexner* I, p. 26.
64. *Schneider, C. K.*, p. 41, gives an estimate of 16,500 unofficial prostitutes in Berlin.
65. *Flexner* I, p. 27.
66. *Ellis* II, p. 302.
67. Bordewijk's term.
68. *Blaschko* I, pp. 430-435; *Blaschko* II.
69. *Fiaux.*
70. *Lombroso* I; *Tarnowsky*.
71. *Hellpach* I, p. 169.
72. *Bloch, I.*, pp. 339-391.
73. *Fuchs* II, pp. 386-424.
74. *Durkheim* II.
75. *Wijnaendts.*
76. *Masaryk* I.
77. *Krose* I.
78. *Krose* I, pp. 55-56.
79. *Krose* II, pp. 88-89.
80. *Ungern.*
81. *Forbes* I, p. 644.
82. *Fritsch.*
83. *Kampffmeyer, H.*, p. 259.
84. *Howard.*
85. *Weber, A. F.*, p. 58.
86. *Vandervelde* III, pp. 288-298.
87. *Bauer, L.*, p. 164ff.

1. *Seilhac*, pp. 171–172.
2. *Bazin.*
3. *Seilhac*, p. 174.
4. *Seilhac*, pp. 152–170.
5. *Huret* I, pp. 16, 42.
6. *Bauman, P. J.* I, p. 82.
7. *Hours; Meyer, M.; Bernstein* IV.
8. *Lavollée*, Part II, p. 188.
9. *Nostitz.*
10. *Pelloutier.*
11. *Wurm; Rühle* III.
12. *Roland* I.
13. *Lavollée.*
14. *Booth.*
15. *Rowntree, E. S.*
16. *Money.*
17. Davis, W. J.: Presidential Address to the Labour Representation Committee Conference, February 1902.
18. *Adams*, p. 27.
19. *Nostitz*, p. 732.
20. *Money*, p. 272ff.
21. *Adams*, p. 34.
22. *Blatchford* II, p. 135.
23. *Nostitz*, pp. 522–525.
24. *Jacobs*, p. 119ff.
25. *Nieuwe Rotterdamse Courant*, October 16, 1954.
26. *Kuczynski, R., passim.; Kuczynski, J.* I, p. 133.
27. *Kuczynski, J.* II, p. 201; *cf. Kuczynski, R.*
28. *Hobson* III, pp. 64, 76, 89ff.
29. *Hobson* III, p. 149.
30. *Report of the Select Committee of the House of Lords on the Sweating System*, 1890. *Cf. Nostitz*, pp. 583ff.
31. Collet, C.: *Report on the Money-wages of Indoor Domestic Servants*, London, 1899.
32. Quoted in *Adams*, p. 32.
33. *Stillich.* A review of the subject can be found in *Sozialistische Monatshefte*, 6 (1902), p. 238.
34. *Braun, L.*, Chapter VIII, *passim.*
35. *Rühle* III.
36. *Tyszka*, p. 66.
37. *Rowntree, E. S.*, p. 298.
38. *Rowntree, E. S.*, p. 304.
39. *Kuczynski, J.* II, p. 210ff.
40. *Clarke, A.*, pp. 69, 70.
41. *Money*, p. 138.
42. *Bauman, P. J.* I, p. 75.
43. *Beveridge.*
44. *Money*, pp. 116–117.
45. *Reports from the Select Committee on Distress from Want of Employment*, London 1895–1896.

46. Quoted in *Nostitz*, p. 686.
47. *Die Not*, p. 11.
48. *Die Not*, pp. 96–115.
49. *Die Not*, p. 96.
50. Quoted in *Rühle* II, p. 55.
51. *May* I and *May* II.
52. *Michel, E.*, p. 146.
53. *Nostitz*, p. 449.
54. *Halma*, p. 671.
55. *Money:* Conclusion.
56. *Die Not*, p. 92ff.
57. *Michel, E.*, p. 133.
58. *Nostitz*, p. 453ff.
59. *Düwell*, p. 45.
60. *Rühle* II, p. 120.
61. *Money*, p. 283.
62. *Düwell*.
63. *Diesel, E.* II, p. 240.
64. *Money:* Conclusion.
65. *Nostitz*, pp. 762–763.
66. Chapter XI: The Red Tide Advances.
67. *Dolléans*, Part II, pp. 30–31.
68. *Sombart* IV, p. 691.
69. *Helfferich* I, p. 17; *Sombart* III, p. 530; *Clapham*, p. 329.
70. *Sombart* IV, pp. 609–691.

XV. THE SLIPPING MASK

1. *Wernicke* I, p. 648; *Wernicke* II, p. 36.
2. For a fuller account , see *Goes* II, pp. 126–127.
3. *Cohn, H.*, p. 532.
4. *Goes* II, p. 129.
5. Biermer in *Beckerath*, Part VII, p. 658.
6. *Grävéll*, p. 82.
7. Quoted in *Goes* II, p. 105.
8. *Waentig*, p. 480, quoted in *Prager*, p. 38.
9. *Reichsbote*, September 22, 1905, quoted in *Wernicke* I, p. 328 (note 1).
10. Aristotle's *Politica*, Book IV, quoted as motto in Jowett's translation for *Lewis*, Chapter XI.
11. *Pyfferoen*.
12. *Dungen*, p. 17.
13. *Schmoller* II.
14. *Schmoller* II, p. 32.
15. *Vorster*.
16. *Masaryk* II.
17. *Treub* I.
18. *Böttger*.
19. *Böttger*, p. 9ff.
20. *Sombart* III. pp. 534, 531.
21. *Pohle* I. p. 37, quoted in Prager, p. 18.
22. *Hitze*, p. 33, quoted in *Brants*, p. 11.

23. *Prager*, p. 48.
24. *Masterman*, pp. 70-73.
25. *Goblot*, p. 78.
26. *Wallraf*, p. 33.
27. *Coudert.*
28. *Coudert*, p. 230.
29. *Coudert*, p. 108.
30. *Coudert*, p. 195.
31. *Coudert*, p. 184.
32. *Siegfried*, p. 426.
33. *Wallraf*, pp. 31-66.
34. *Wallraf*, p. 5.
35. *Die Gartenlaube*, 1900, pp. 45, 51.
36. *Wallraf*, pp. 46-48.
37. *Plessner* I, pp. 66-78.
38. *Brinkmann* I, pp. 30-34.
39. *Gitermann*, p. 273.
40. *Mehring* IV, Part V, p. 227.
41. *Kuczynski, J.* III, p. 311.
42. Shaw, G. B.: *How the Middle Class is Fleeced*, quoted in *Lewis*, p. 75.
43. *Ensor*, p. 114.
44. *Seligman*, under "Aristocracy," contributed by L. T. Hobhouse.
45. Webb, B.: *My Apprenticeship*, quoted in *Lewis*, p. 67.
46. *Lewis*, pp. 68-69.
47. *Lewis*, p. 108.
48. *Lewis*, pp. 65-85.
49. *Brown*, p. 72.
50. *Dangerfield.*
51. *Lewis*, p. 74.
52. *Musil* II, Part I, p. 730.
53. *cf. Burnand* I.
54. Facsimile in *Rolland* IV, Part I, facing p. 80.
55. *Bauer, A.*, p. 19.
56. *Lukács* II.
57. *Ould*, p. 121ff.
58. *Hindus*, p. 235.
59. *Lejeune.*
60. *Rice.*
61. *Green, F. C.*
62. *Clouard*, Part I, p. 594.
63. *Clouard*, Part I, pp. 556-557.
64. *Romein* IV, pp. 205-206.
65. *Green, F. C.*, p. 15.
66. *Hindus*, p. 164.
67. *Rolland* IV, Part I, p. 303 (note 2).
68. *Bauer, A.*, p. 27.
69. Hilborne, R.: "Amazing Marie Corelli" in *Everybody's Weekly*, 32, December 1944.
70. *Hindus*, p. 193.
71. *Marshall.*
72. *Clouard*, Part II, p. 405.

1. *Radziwill*, p. 48.
2. *Fugger*, pp. 139–140.
3. *Daisy*, p. 30.
4. *Youssoupoff*, p. 59.
5. *Sitwell*, pp. 114, 148.
6. *Morand*, chapter entitled "High Life."
7. *Fernandez*, pp. 104, 120.
8. *Hamilton*, p. 164.
9. *Horeca*, 15, November 10, 1950.
10. *Burnand* II, pp. 116, 117.
11. *Narischkin*.
12. *Sitwell*, pp. 3, 100.
13. Hepp, A., quoted in *Grand*, p. 384.
14. *Waldersee*, Part III.
15. *Cudlipp*, p. 16.
16. *Morand*, p. 219.
17. *Morand*, p. 146.
18. *Chirol* II, p. 273ff.
19. *Waldersee*, Part III, p. 175.
20. *Mandere*, p. 29.
21. *Netscher*.
22. *Weale*, pp. 307, 308.
23. *Kessler*, p. 158.
24. *Ponsonby*, p. 77.
25. *Morand*.
26. *Burnand* II, p. 95.
27. *Huizinga, J. H.*, p. 255ff.
28. *Sitwell*, p. 148.
29. *Sitwell*, pp. 206–244.
30. *Vanderbilt*, p. 145.
31. *Fernandez*, p. 67.
32. *Heindel*, p. 349.
33. *Fernandez*, p. 112.
34. Shaw, G. B.: *Prefaces*, London 1934, p. 654.
35. *Vanderbilt*, p. 45.
36. *Fahlbeck*.
37. *Stead* III, p. 35.
38. *MacMillan*.
39. *Stead* III, p. 39.
40. *Muir*, p. 112.
41. *Allyn*, p. 180.
42. *Baumann*, p. 597.
43. *Kuringer*, p. 212.
44. *Lotz*, p. 621, first column.
45. *Cudlipp*, pp. 15-16.
46. *Zedlitz*, p. 25.
47. *Money*, p. 151.
48. *Daisy*, p. 66.
49. *Vanderbilt*, p. 71.
50. *Vanderbilt*, p. 70..
51. *Sitwell*, p. 70.

52. *Eulalia*, p. 217.
53. *Ponsonby*, p. 27.
54. *Huizinga, J. H.*, p. 337.
55. *Kohn*, p. 232ff.
56. *Niemann*, p. 28.
57. *Sitwell*, p. vi.
58. *Sitwell*, pp. 218, 219.
59. *Kirk*, p. 330.
60. *Kirk*, pp. 7, 8.
61. *Frank, W.*
62. *Benjamin.*
63. *Youssoupoff*, pp. 80–81.

XVII. NEWS FOR EVERYONE

1. *Heindel*, p. 12.
2. *Fischer*, p. 32. See particularly Chapter III: "The Americanization of the World," pp. 78–97.
3. *MacKenzie, F. A.* I, pp. 178–189.
4. *MacKenzie, F. A.* II.
5. *Robertson Scott*, pp. 271–272.
6. *Stead* II, pp. 144–146.
7. *Fischer*, p. 81.
8. *Avenel* I, pp. 491, 854–859.
9. *Fyfe* I, p. 43.
10. *Winkler Prins Encyclopaedie*, sixth impression, under "Girardin."
11. *Schneider, M.*, p. 163.
12. *Avenel* I, p. 859.
13. *Boivin*, pp. 81–82.
14. *Sury*, p. 111.
15. *Ullstein* II, pp. 63–64.
16. *Chambure*, p. 188.
17. *Ullstein* II, p. 68 and *Ullstein* I, pp. 159–160.
18. *Ullstein* II, p. 70 and *Ullstein* I, pp. 42, 45, 147ff.
19. *Ullstein* II, p. 71.
20. *Robertson Scott*, pp. 124–145.
21. *Stutterheim*, p. 47.
22. *Fyfe* II, pp. 68–71.
23. *Stutterheim*, pp. 47, 48.
24. *Fyfe* I, p. 9.
25. *Wells* IV, p. 272ff.
26. *Fyfe* I, p. 113.
27. *MacKenzie, F. A.* II, p. 31ff.
28. *MacKenzie, F. A.* II, p. 33ff.
29. *Ensie*, Part IX, pp. 256–258.
30. "The Contemporary British Press" in *The Economist*, November-December 1928, quoted in *Stutterheim*, p. 122.
31. *Stutterheim*, pp. 122–124.
32. *Baschwitz* II, pp. 156–162; *Storey;* and *Jones, R.*
33. *Eltzbacher* II; *Hale*, pp. 6, 11.
34. *Clarke*, T., pp. 87, 88.
35. *Hale, passim.*
36. *Eltzbacher* II, p. 21.

37. Frederick Greenwood to Goldwin Smith in 1905, in *Correspondence of Goldwin-Smith.* pp. 439, 440, quoted in *Salmon,* pp. 447, 448.
38. *Bücher,* pp. 52-64.
39. *Jones, K.,* p. 307.
40. *Eltzbacher* II, p. 128.
41. *Lukas* II.
42. *Mehring* I.
43. *Koch,* pp. 5, 6.
44. *Munzinger.*
45. Peterson, F.: "The Newspaper Peril," in *Colliers Weekly,* September 1, 1906, No. 37, pp. 12-13, quoted in *Salmon,* p. 427.
46. *Fenton.*
47. *Fenton,* p. 91.
48. *Russell, B.* III, pp. 143-144, quoted in *Salmon,* p. 438.
49. *Eberle.*
50. *Eberle,* pp. 122-124.
51. *Löbl.*
52. *Tavernier,* p. 270ff.
53. *Ullstein* I, p. 175.
54. Lilly, W. S.: "The Ethics of Journalism" in *Forum,* July 1889, pp. 503-512, quoted in *Salmon,* p. 466.

XVIII. THE STATE ENCROACHES UPON SOCIETY...

1. *Lowe,* p. 38.
2. *Ritzmann,* p. 26.
3. *Ritzmann,* p. 24.
4. *Ritzmann,* p. 24.
5. *Brentano,* pp. 202-203.
6. *Brooke.*
7. *Poelje.*
8. *Goodwin.*
9. *Ritzmann.*
10. *White, R. C.,* p. 8ff.
11. *Problemen,* pp. 395-400.
12. Figures for 1910-1940, as published by the Netherlands Central Bureau for Statistics.
13. *Borght,* p. 42.
14. *Saitzew,* pp. 331-332.
15. Bret, P. L.: "La recherche scientifique en France" in *Rapports France-Etats Unis,* No. 74, May 1953, pp. 19-20.
16. *Hellpach* II, p. 97.
17. *Vogel,* p. 364.
18. *Green, T. H.*
19. *Ritchie* I and *Ritchie* II; *cf. Schlatter,* p. 259.
20. *Webb* II.
21. *Webb* II, pp. 47, 48.
22. *Montgomery,* pp. 179-185.
23. *Wingfield,* p. 1226.
24. *Davies.*
25. *Bäumer,* p. 342.
26. *Wagner, A.* II.
27. *Wagner, A.* II, p. 16.

28. *Wagner, A.* II, pp. 18–23.
29. *Thier.*
30. *Webb* II, p. 53.
31. *Wagner, A.* II, *passim.*
32. *Vries, C. W.*, p. 398.
33. *Toorenburg.*
34. *Coenen.*
35. *Toorenburg*, p. 134.
36. "Der Jugendschutz der Welt. Übersicht über den Stand der Jugendschutzgesetz-
    gebung in den verschiedenen Ländern"; Vol. 3 of a series published by the
    Verlag des internationalen Gewerkschaftsbundes, Amsterdam, 1922.
37. *Artibal.*
38. *Dawson.*
39. *Artibal*, p. 23.
40. *Walter.*
41. *Bielefeld*, p. 18ff. The text of the Compensation Act is given on pp. 91–107.
42. *Bielefeld*, p. 47.
43. *Walter*, p. vi.
44. *Hamon, G.*, p. 3.
45. *Rapmund.*
46. *Rapmund*, Part I, pp. 33–34.
47. *Rapmund*, Part II, p. 524.
48. *Vries, C. W.*, p. 347ff.
49. *Lukas* I.
50. *Heller, T.* and *Petersilie*, Part II, pp. 157–188.
51. *Herre*, p. 561.
52. *Wagner, A.* I.
53. *Wagner, A.* I, pp. 316–317.
54. *Wagner, A.* I, pp. 345–347.
55. *Wagner, A.* I, pp. 415–424.
56. *Vragen van den dag.* 17 (1902), pp. 127ff.
57. *Grossmann*, p. 311.
58. *Boissevain; cf. Wagner, A.* I, pp. 446–448.
59. *Wagner, A.* I, pp. 448–449.
60. *Wagner, A.* I, pp. 450–451.
61. *Lemcke.*
62. *Bocquet*, pp. 29, 30.
63. *Lemcke*, pp, 2–5.

XIX. ...and SOCIETY ENCROACHES UPON THE STATE

1. *Fowler.*
2. Gaudswaard, G., *Winkler Prins Encyclopaedie*, sixth impression, under "Statistiek."
3. *Lotz*, pp. 573, 574.
4. Robson, W. A.: "The Public Utility Services" in *Laski* I, pp. 299–331.
5. *Laski* I, p. 308ff.
6. *Laski* I, p. 317ff.
7. *Laski* I, p. 320ff.
8. *Hayes* I, p. 212.
9. *Moor.*
10. *Moor*, p. 23.
11. *Moor*, p. 57; *Poelje*, p. 73ff.
12. *Mayer*, Part II, p. 492.

13. *Thier*, p. 111.
14. *Filipetti*, p. 5.
15. Tucker, B. R., in *Liberty*, March 1888.
16. *Eichthal*, p. 201.
17. *Eichthal*, p. 202.
18. *Muir*.
19. *Muir*, p. 27.
20. *Hewart*, pp. 150-151.
21. *Warnotte*, pp. 219-260.
22. *Cahen-Salvador*, p. 319.
23. *Rabany*.
24. *Worms* I, p. 56, quoted in *Warnotte*, p. 250.
25. *Heard*, pp. 187-223.
26. *Weber, A.*, pp. 81-101.
27. *Chardon*, p. 136.
28. *Seidenberg*, pp. 1-31.
29. *Weber, A.*, p. 72.
30. *Weber, A.*, p. 84.
31. *Weber, A.*, p. 77.
32. *Bäumer*, pp. 6-8.
33. *Heard*, pp. 187-223.

XX. THE FESTIVAL OF HOPE AND FULFILMENT

1. *Tamir*, p. 134, wrongly attributes the words to Millerand himself. See *Encyclopédie du siècle: L'exposition de Paris de 1900*, introductory article by A. Picard.
2. *Encyclopédie du siècle: L'exposition de Paris de 1900*, Part III, p. 60.
3. *Lapauze*. This guide differs from the many others because it makes constant comparisons with the Paris Exposition of 1889.
4. *Israëls*, p. 125.
5. Illustrations in *Paris*, pp. 226-230.
6. *Morand*, p. 77.
7. *Luckhurst*, pp. 220, 221.
8. *Israëls*, p. 58.
9. *Burnand* II, p. 248ff.
10. *Luckhurst*, pp. 220-221, gives £5,222,000 for Chicago and £4,650,000 for Paris, and receipts of £6,029,000 and £4,600,000 respectively.
11. *Luckhurst*, p. 213.
12. *Lessing*, p. 30.
13. Quoted in *Howe*, p. 97.
14. *Lessing*, p. 4.
15. *Guilbert*, p. 134.
16. *Burnand* II, p. 237.
17. *Paris*, p. 171.
18. *Vogüé*, II, p. 396.
19. *Isay*, p. 212.
20. *Verslag*.
21. *Berichte*.
22. *Morand*, pp. 97, 98.
23. *Encyclopédie du siècle*, Part I, p. 1.
24. *Morand*, p. 122.
25. *Paris*, p. 312.
26. *Paris*, pp. 271-272.

27. *Encyclopédie du siècle*, Part III, p. 254.
28. *Israëls*, p. 141.
29. *Paris*, pp. 251-255.
30. *Lapauze*, pp. 279-284.
31. *Lapauze*, pp. 374-376.
32. *Israëls*, p. 181.
33. *Israëls*, p. 88. But *cf.* the illustration on p. 96. Van Dongen shows a wing.
34. *Encyclopédie du siècle*, Part III, p. 230.
35. *Israëls*, pp. 96-100.
36. *Israëls*, pp. 92-95.

XXI. THE PROMISED LAND

1. *New York Herald Tribune*, European edition, June 14 and 15, 1950: "Fifty Years Ago." The distance between Paris and Lyon is less than is given here, but there may have been detours. For the reception after the race from Paris to Marseille in October, 1896. see *Grand*, pp. 328-337. For the race of November 9, see the "Fifty Years Ago" column in the *New York Herald Tribune* of that date. For the heat-wave, see the same source, June 13, 1950.
2. *Nimführ*, pp. 85-88. *Die Gartenlaube*, 1900, pp. 517-519 is the source of our figures.
3. *Die Gartenlaube*, 1900, pp. 517-519.
4. *Anthouard*, p. 289.
5. *Bardèche* II, p. 8.
6. *Chattuck*, p. 13 and Plate 2.
7. *New York Herald Tribune*, European edition, November 28, 1950. Marconi apparently shared the common misconception that the twentieth century began on January 1, 1900, when in fact it started one year later. Much ink and paper was expended on this question at the time.
8. *Diesel, R.*
9. *Diesel, E. I.*
10. *Forbes* I, pp. 644-645.
11. *New York Herald Tribune*, European edition, 1950, on the date mentioned.
12. *Forbes* II.
13. *Samter.*
14. *Ovink*, p. 25.
15. *Ostwald* II, p. 47, quoted in *Sombart* IV, pp. 1011, 1012.
16. *Coppersmith*, pp. 123-124.
17. All these data are taken from *Stein, W.*
18. *Kleinberg*, p. 182.
19. *Romein* II.
20. *Ostwald* I, p. 18.
21. *Coppersmith*, pp. 124-126.
22. *Gartmann.*
23. *Usher*, Chapter IV, p. 56ff.
24. *New York Herald Tribune*, European edition, January 18 and October 30, 1950. "Fifty Years Ago".
25. *Guth*, p. 23.
26. *New York Herald Tribune*, European edition, November 22, 1950, "Fifty Years Ago".
27. *Blum, O.*, pp. 120-121.
28. *Fries*, pp. 548-566.
29. *Bogeng*, Part II, p. 766.

30. *Sazerac*, p. 10, with illustration.
31. Quoted in *Picture Post*, January 1, 1950, p. 49. *Cf. Nimführ*, p. 113.
32. *Kress*, p. 48.
33. *Chanute.*
34. *Wright, W.*
35. *Tilgenkamp*, p. 13.
36. *Tilgenkamp*, p. 16.
37. *Feith* II gives a vivid description of the second international "air week" held in Reims in 1910.
38. *Berget*, pp. 208–212. The list is incomplete.
39. *Tilgenkamp*, p. 14.
40. *Sazerac*, pp. 88–90.
41. *Usher*, p. 83.
42. See *Bogeng*, Part II, p. 739, illustration 754 on p. 735.
43. Aertnijs, M. W.: "Automobielsport" in *Feith* II, p. 183.
44. *Grand*, p. 182.
45. *Grand*, p. 211.
46. *Grand*, p. 182.
47. *Grand*, p. 191.
48. *Grand*, p. 390.
49. Hepp, A., in his column "Quotidiennes" in *Le Journal*, quoted in *Grand*, p. 384. For illustration see p. 383.
50. *Grand.*
51. *Coubertin.*
52. *Morand*, p. 142.
53. *Het Vrije Volk*, July 27, 1953, p. 2.
54. *Crookes.* See also *De Hollandsche revue* 6 (1901), pp. 778–783: "Telegrafeeren zonder draad" ("Wireless Telegraphy"), from which the information has been taken.
55. *Samter*, p. 256.
56. *Bräuer*, p. 228.
57. *Fawcett*, p. 11.
58. *Schmitt, W.*, pp. 11–16; Wolf-Czapek, pp. 33–34; Panofsky, pp. 40–80.
59. *Panofsky*, p. 47ff.
60. Gath, P. G., *Ensie*, Part IX, p. 606, no sources given.
61. *Fülöp-Miller*, pp. 11–23.
62. *Sadoul* II, p. 95ff; *Moreck*, p. 30. For the capital of other film companies, see *Altenloh.*
63. *Moreck*, pp. 21–23.
64. *Panofsky*, pp. 50–66.
65. *Bardèche* I.
66. *Sadoul* I.
67. *Jordaan*, pp. 9–18.
68. *Kracauer*, pp. 20–21.
69. *Moreck*, pp. 218–223.
70. *Sadoul* I, Part III, pp. 158–160.
71. *Rathenau* III, p. 12.
72. *Alberès.*

XXII. THE TRIUMPH OF THE ATOM

1. A. Einstein: "Autobiografisches" in Schilpp, P. A. (ed.): *Albert Einstein, Philosopher-Scientist*, Evanston (Illinois), 1949, p. 36.

2. *Bernal*, Chapter 10, Introduction, p. 518.
3. These were the experiments performed by Heinrich Hertz from 1887 to 1888, in which electromagnetic waves differing from light were produced for the first time. The possibility of producing such waves had been suggested by Maxwell's equations. These waves became a subject of popular and even of government concern once Marconi began to experiment with wireless telegraphy in 1896.
4. By W. Ramsay and Lord Raleigh, 1889-1895. *Cf. Lorentz* I, p. 510.
5. *Thomson.*
6. *Poincaré*, p. 25.
7. *Maxwell*, p. 351.
8. *Lorentz* II.
9. This remark can also be found in Galileo.
10. *Cf. Brouwer* II, pp. 11-12.
11. *Freudenthal.*
12. *Baire.*
13. *Cf. Wiener.*
14. *E. g.* tensor composition, operator theory and quantum mechanics.

XXIII. MYSTERY REGAINED

1. *Hertwig* I, p. 1.
2. F. le Lionnais: "Sciences in *Béguin*, p. 175.
3. *Hertwig* I, pp. 30-31.
4. *Packard*, p. 396 (footnote).
5. *Rádl*, Part 2, pp. 212-230.
6. *Schmidt, O.*
7. *Hertwig* I, p. 13.
8. *Locy.*
9. *Spencer* II. *Cf. Hertwig* I, p. 14.
10. *Weismann*, p. 60; *Hertwig* I, p. 15, footnote 1.
11. *Hertwig* I, p. 15.
12. *Hertwig* III, p. 49.
13. M. Harden, in *Zukunft*, Vol. 5 (1893), p. 268.
14. *Nordenskiöld*, p. 569.
15. *Kuyper.*
16. *Nordenskiöld*, p. 606.
17. *Grottewitz*, p. 37.
18. *Roux* I, p. 5. *Cf. Roux II.*
19. *Rádl*, Part 2, p. 521.
20. *Driesch* VII, p. 120.
21. *Nordenskiöld*, p. 571; *Pauly.*
22. *Wolff.*
23. *Driesch* VII, p. 44.
24. *Driesch* VII, p. 67.
25. *Driesch* VII, p. 74.
26. *Driesch* II.
27. *Driesch* V.
28. H. Driesch: *Die Maschinentheorie des Lebens*, Leipzig, 1898.
29. *Driesch* Ia and Ib.
30. *Sorel* VI, p. 370.
31. *Mead, G. H.*, p. 389.
32. *Driesch* III.
33. *Driesch* VI, p. 209.

34. *Bateson* II.
35. *Driesch* VII.
36. *Heymans,* p. 414, quoted in *Buytendijk,* p. 14.
37. *Bütschli; cf. Rádl,* Part 2, p. 560.
38. *Sozialistische Monatshefte,* 6 (1902), p. 235.
39. *Cholodenko.*
40. *Cholodenko,* p. 46.
41. *Cholodenko,* p. 59.
42. *Bunge; cf. Meyer, A.,* p. 35.
43. *Rádl,* Part 2, p. 368.
44. *Bateson* I.
45. *Rádl,* Part 2, p. 484.
46. M. J. Sirks: "Erflijkheidsleer bij planten en dieren" in *Ensie,* Part 6, p. 116.
47. *Vries, H.* II and *Vries, H.* III; *cf. Stomps* and *Went,* p. 263ff.
48. *Nordenskiöld,* p. 603.
49. *Nordenskiöld,* p. 612ff.
50. *Uexküll,* p. 1.
51. *Henderson: cf. Umbgrove,* p. 110.
52. *Smuts.*
53. *Morgan.*
54. *Umbgrove,* p. 72.
55. *Haldane.*
56. *Haldane,* pp. 64ff and p. 26.
57. *Haldane,* p. 70.
58. *Haldane,* p. 108.
59. *Butler.*
60. *Rádl,* Part 2.
61. *Rádl,* Part 2, pp. 40–43.
62. *Rádl,* Part 2, p. 565.
63. *Weber, M.* III, p. 214.

XXIV. *IN VITRO* AND *IN VIVO*

1. *Colvin.*
2. *Sand,* p. 181; *Sticker,* p. vi.
3. W. Kouwenaar in *Winkler Prins Encyclopaedie,* sixth edition, under "Pest."
4. *Procès verbaux de la conférence sanitaire internationale de Venise contre l'invasion de la peste.* Rome, 1897.
5. *Kruif* I and *Kruif* II.
6. *Singer, C.,* p. 280ff and *Lloyd,* p. 136ff.
7. *Hemmeter* I.
8. *Stevenson.*
9. *Garrison,* p. 617.
10. *Singer, C.,* p. 276.
11. *Aschoff; Sand,* p. 181.
12. *Lloyd,* pp. 116–117.
13. *Hoffmann,* pp. 174–199.
14. *Loewe.*
15. *Ehrlich, P.*
16. *Deventer.*
17. *Shryock.*
18. For all these data see *Aschoff* and the chronological survey in *Garrison,* p. 793ff.
19. *Eiselsberg,* pp. 483–494.

20. *Garrison,* p. 587.
21. *Kruif* II, pp. 35–58.
22. *Funk.*
23. *Spek.*
24. *Hemmeter* II, p. 160–169.
25. *Hemmeter* II, p. 169.
26. *Hemmeter* II, p. 168.
27. *Pagel.*
28. *Garrison,* p. 779.
29. *Garrison,* p. 779, footnote 2.
30. *Honigmann,* pp. 64–69.
31. *Honigmann,* p. 29 and pp. 80–81, footnote 27. Quotation from *Die Woche,*
   No. 2, 1912.
32. *Pagel,* p. 47.
33. *Zilboorg,* pp. 479–510.
34. *Schüle.*
35. Quoted in *Zilboorg,* p. 454.
36. E. Reich: *Immaterielle Ursachen der Krankheiten,* quoted in *Sand,* p. 139, footnote 5.
37. *Zilboorg,* pp. 466–467.
38. *Sand,* p. 231.
39. *Sand,* p. 133.
40. *Sand,* p. 132.
41. *Meyer, G.,* p. 30.
42. *Sand,* p. 511.
43. *Sand,* p. 510.
44. *Pieraccini,* quoted in *Sand,* p. 509.
45. *Grotjahn* III.
46. *Sand,* p. 219.
47. *Sand,* p. 221.
48. *Sand,* p. 224.
49. *Sand,* p. 84.
50. *Herderschee.*
51. *Aletrino.*
52. *Wortman.*
53. *Stoffers; Vernède,* p. 362ff.
54. *Brandes* II, p. 515.
55. *Müller, F. von,* pp. 35–36.

XXV. WEAL AND WEALTH

1. *Seligman,* under "Cohn."
2. *Cohn, G.*
3. *Mayer.*
4. Under the title of *The Science of Finance,* Chicago, 1895 (from the 1889 edition).
5. W. Sombart: "Ideale der Socialpolitik" in *Archiv für Sociale Gesetzgebung und
   Statistik,* Vol. 10 (1897), pp. 1–48.
6. *Sombart* I.
7. *Sombart* I, p. 253.
8. *Sombart* I, p. 157.
9. Cf. *Weber, M.* III.
10. *Ritzel.*
11. Cf. *Brinkmann* II, pp. 131–132.

12. *Brinkmann* II, p. 133.
13. *Cf. Brinkmann* II, p. 133.
14. *Bukharin*, p. 31.
15. *Stark*, p. 55, footnote 2.
16. *Spann*, p. 178.
17. *Braeuer*, pp. 188–189.
18. *Schumpeter, J. A.*, p. 76. For the Walras *cf. Boson.*
19. *Herkner* III, p. 12.
20. *Ritzel*, p. 133.
21. For the two German schools of history, *cf. Lifschitz.*
22. See *Gonnard* II. *Cf.* index, pp. 687ff.
23. *Pirou.*
24. *Andler* II.
25. *Pirou*, p. 17.
26. *Jaurès* I.
27. *Pirou*, pp. 116–117.
28. Published as a pamphlet, Paris, 1896.
29. *Picard.*
30. *Pirou*, pp. 129–130.
31. *Pirou*, pp. 133–135.
32. *Pirou*, pp. 131–133.
33. *Bouglé* III.
34. *Pirou*, pp. 158–165.
35. *Seligman*, under "Bourguin"; *Pirou*, pp. 166–167.
36. *Bourguin* II.
37. *Pirou*, p. 167, footnote 2.
38. *Gide, C.* I; *cf.Gide, C.* II.
39. *Suranyi*, pp. 16–34.
40. *Sombart* V, pp. 151–152.
41. *Whittaker*, p. 560.
42. *Cf. Zeitschrift für Volkswirtschaft, Sozialpolitik und Verwaltung* 23 (1913); *cf. Spiegel*, pp. 568 and 734.
43. *Haberler* on Schumpeter in *Spiegel*, p. 740.
44. *Haberler* in *Spiegel*, p. 752.
45. *Bousquet*, p. 88.
46. *Suranyi*, p. 141.
47. *Demaria* on Pareto in *Spiegel*, p. 629.
48. *Cf. Gossel*, pp. 33–49.
49. *Gossel*, p. 7.
50. See *Gottl-Ottlilienfeld.*
51. See *Gottl-Ottlilienfeld*, pp. 18–148 and 151–241.
52. *Gottl-Ottlilienfeld*, p. 238, footnote.
53. *Schumpeter, J. A.*
54. *Spiegel*, pp. 329ff. The article was originally published in *The Fortnightly Review* of December 1897.
55. *Hobson* VI.
56. *Sombart* V, pp. 140ff.
57. *Winslow*, pp. 92ff.
58. *Luxemburg* III.
59. *Hilferding.*
60. *Lenin* II.
61. *Hobson* VI, p. 37.

62. *Peck,* pp. 217ff.
63. *Suranyi,* p. 269.
64. *Flux,* p. 380.
65. *Hobson* IV.
66. *Suranyi,* p. 309.
67. *Pigou; cf.* C. Clark on Pigou in *Spiegel,* pp. 779ff.
68. *Hobson* VI, p. 213.
69. *Sartorius,* pp. 338 and 390.
70. *Sombart* III, pp. 398–399.
71. *Hinte,* pp. 60–63.
72. *Bergmann.*
73. *Gide, C.* II, p. 806; *cf.* "Bibliographie der Konjunktur- und Krisenforschung" in *Archiv der Fortschritte betriebswirtschaftlicher Forschung und Lehre* 4 (1927), pp. 183–199.
74. *Tugan* IV.
75. *Aftalion.*
76. *Pohle* II, p. 188, footnote 2.
77. *Herkner* II.
78. *Hilferding,* p. v.

XXVI. WITH NEITHER BLINDFOLD NOR SWORD

1. *Hauriou,* p. 54ff.
2. *Duguit* II, pp. 258ff.
3. *Duguit* II, p. 261.
4. *Tarde I,* pp. 159–161; *cf.* H. E. Barnes: "The Philosophy of the State in the Writings of Gabriel Tarde" in *Philosophical Review,* 28 (1919), pp. 248–279.
5. *Duguit* II, pp. xiv–xv.
6. *Duguit* II, p. x.
7. *Duguit* I, pp. 1–22.
8. *Charmont* I, p. 403, reprinted in *Charmont* II, pp. 38–80.
9. *Seagle,* pp. 306ff.
10. *Seagle,* p. 323.
11. *Sinzheimer,* pp. 201ff.
12. *Weber, Marianne,* pp. 481ff.
13. *Haines.*
14. *Haines,* pp. 274–277.
15. *Wolf, E.* II.
16. *Croce* II.
17. *Haines,* p. 258.
18. *Saleilles.*
19. *Pound,* p. 162, quoted in *Haines,* p. 309, footnote.
20. *Oppenheimer* II, p. 160.
21. *Beradt.*
22. *Flavius.*
23. *Seligman,* under "Fuchs."
24. *Sinzheimer,* pp. 231ff.
25. *Haines,* pp. 279ff.
26. *Haines,* pp. 286ff.
27. *Haines,* p. 244.
28. I. Kisch, in *Winkler Prins Encyclopaedie,* sixth edition, under "Gény."
29. *Charmont* II, p. 39.

30. *Charmont* II, p. 48.
31. *Charmont* II, p. 50.
32. *Charmont* II, p. 59.
33. *Charmont* II, p. 60.
34. *Menger* II.
35. *Menger* I.
36. *Menger* II.
37. *Menger* II, p. 35.
38. *Menger* II, pp. 57–58.
39. *Menger* II, p. 64.
40. *Menger* II, p. 212.
41. *Menger* II, p. 214.
42. *Menger* III, p. 24.
43. *Seligman*, under "Eugen Ehrlich."
44. *Kantorowicz.*
45. *Charmont* II, p. 96.
46. *Wolf, E.* I, p. 19.
47. *Duguit* I.
48. *Duguit* I, p. 77.
49. *Duguit* I, p. 162; *cf.* Appendix IV, pp. 198ff.
50. *Duguit* I, Appendix III, p. 192ff.
51. *Duguit* I, p. 160.
52. *Duguit* I, p. 161.
53. G. Clemenceau in *L'Aurore*, March 1898.
54. *Leyret* II, pp. 77–80. The first part appeared in 1900.
55. *Leyret* II, p. 4.
56. *Leyret* II, p. 8.
57. *Hymans*, p. 182.
58. *Pompe*, p. 374.
59. *Pompe*, p. 388.
60. *Ehrlich, E.*
61. *Garofalo.*
62. *Ellis* I.
63. *Ellis* I.
64. *Congrès*, p. 39.
65. *Congrès*, p. 89.
66. *Pompe*, p. 403.
67. *Ellis* I, pp. 240ff.
68. *Kropotkin* II.
69. *Gautier.*
70. *Griffith.*
71. *Wolf, E.* I, p. 23.
72. *Fuchs* I.
73. *Ferester.*
74. *Ferester.*
75. *Congrès*, p. 3.
76. *Ferri* II.
77. *Bonger.*
78. *Tarde* II, pp. 85–149.
79. *Tarde* II, pp. 151–215.
80. *Schaffstein.*
81. *Tarde* I, p. 3, in the 1894 edition.

1. *Jones, E.*, Part 1, p. 395. *Cf.* Freud's letter to Fliess of January 8, 1900 in *Bonaparte*, p. 328.
2. *Jones, E.*, Part 1, p. 383. The letter of May 7, 1900, is reprinted in *Bonaparte*, p. 341.
3. *Janet* II, pp. 518–521.
4. *Gaupp* I, p. 234.
5. *Gaupp* II, p. 400.
6. *Freud* IV, p. 99.
7. *Jones, E.*, Part 1, p. 384.
8. *Jones, E.*, Part 1, p. 289.
9. *Jones, E.*, Part 1, pp. 298–299.
10. *Ortega* I.
11. *Hall* I, pp. 311–458.
12. *Murphy*, pp. 160–187.
13. *Peters*, p. 487.
14. *Murphy*, p. 160.
15. *Scripture.*
16. *Flügel*, pp. 206–214.
17. For an almost complete list, see *Boring.*
18. *Flügel*, p. 245.
19. *Peters*, p. 623.
20. *Flügel*, pp. 233–240.
21. *Peters*, p. 661.
22. *Watson.* The word first occurs on p. 166.
23. *Cf. Tilquin.*
24. *Stimpfl*, pp. 344–361.
25. *Stimpfl*, p. 354.
26. *Murphy*, p. 281, footnote 2.
27. *Hall* III, p. 378.
28. *Murphy*, p. 282.
29. *Stimpfl*, p. 352, footnote 2
30. *Zeitschrift für pädagogische Psychologie*, I (1899), p. 362.
31. *Bühler, C.*, pp. 219–220.
32. *Murphy*, p. 284.
33. *Seidenberg*, Chapter I.
34. *Brentano, F.*, as mentioned by *Flügel*, pp. 144ff.
35. *Mach.*
36. *Ehrenfels* I, pp. 249ff; *cf. Peters*, p. 678.
37. *Bühler, K.*, p. 4.
38. *Boring*, p. 359.
39. *Murphy*, p. 241.
40. For a survey of Gestalt psychology, see *Köhler, W.*
41. *Wertheimer.*
42. *Peters*, p. 677.
43. G. Heymans, in *Schmidt, R.*, Part 3.
44. *Schmidt, R.*, Part 3, special pages 1–13.
45. *Spranger.*
46. *Murchison*, pp. 191ff.
47. *Murphy*, p. 295, footnote 2.
48. *Flügel*, p. 271.
49. *Peters*, p. 673.

50. *Murphy,* pp. 208-209.
51. *Peters,* p. 653.
52. *Murphy,* p. 209.
53. *James,* W. II, p. 233.
54. *Dwelshauvers,* pp. 156-166.
55. *Dwelshauvers,* pp. 191-194.
56. *Boutroux; cf. Dwelshauvers,* p. 176.
57. *Freud* V, p. 86.
58. *Beerling* I, p. 62.
59. *Bühler,* K., p. 178.
60. *McDougall* II, pp. 19-20.
61. *Scripture,* p. 471.
62. *Congrès,* pp. 41 and 46.
63. *Willy.*
64. *Bühler, K.*

XXVIII. INSIGHT THROUGH IMPOTENCE

1. *Araujo,* pp. 65-66. For Antoine, see *Kalff.*
2. *Letourneau,* pp. 481-487.
3. *Barnes.*
4. *Achelis,* p. 27, however, numbers Letourneau among his most important colleagues.
5. *Revue internationale de sociologie,* 8 (1900), pp. 181-195.
6. *Revue internationale de sociologie,* 8 (1900), pp. 241-255.
7. *Revue internationale de sociologie,* 8 (1900), pp. 561-577.
8. *L'année sociologique,* 4 (1899-1900), pp. 601-610.
9. *L'année sociologique,* 4 (1899-1900), pp. 106 and 596.
10. *Loria,* pp. 11-13.
11. *Steinmetz* II, pp. 21-22. Steinmetz's italics.
12. *Roberty,* p. 402.
13. *Bouglé* II, p. 106.
14. *L'Année sociologique,* 4 (1899-1900), p. 63.
15. *House,* pp. 158-178.
16. *Kidd* I; *Kidd* II.
17. *Mackintosh.*
18. *House,* p. 163.
19. *Barnes,* p. 191.
20. See biography in *Gumplowicz. Cf. Barnes,* Chapter 19, pp. 374ff; *House,* Chapter 14, pp. 174ff.
21. *Kelles,* p. 42. The work is part of the series *Am Anfang des Jahrhunderts,* especially written for workers, in which various nineteenth-century phenomena are reviewed from a progressive standpoint.
22. *L'Année sociologique,* 4 (1899-1900), p. 565.
23. *Livezey; Walsh.*
24. *Walsh.*
25. *Oppenheimer* I.
26. *Rüstow.*
27. N. S. Timasheff, in *Barnes,* Chapter 23, p. 442; *cf. Hecker,* pp. 75-174.
28. *Hecker,* p. 149.
29. N. S. Timasheff, in *Barnes,* p. 443.
30. N. S. Timasheff, in *Barnes,* p. 444.
31. *Kowalewski,* Chapter 8.
32. *Worms* II; *Sorokin,* Chapter 7.

33. *Burnham.*
34. *Schoeck,* pp. 229-243. For a review *see Barnes,* pp. 555-568.
35. *Freund.* His bibliography, by P. Delesalle, in *International Review for Social History,* 4 (1939), pp. 463-487.
36. *Lowie,* pp. 128-155.
37. *Davie.*
38. *Frobenius* I; *cf. Frobenius* II.
39. *Frobenius* II, p. 153.
40. *Graebner.*
41. *Cuvillier.*
42. *Cf.* E. Benoit-Smullyan, in *Barnes,* p. 499; *Alpert:* fragments in *Schoeck,* pp. 195-199.
43. *Bouglé* I.
44. *Aron.*
45. *Aron,* p. 10.
46. A. Salomon, in *Gurvitch,* Part 2, Chapter XX, p. 614. *Cf. Spykman.*
47. R. Heberle, in *Barnes,* p. 250, quoting *Sorokin,* pp. 497-498.
48. *Simmel G.* III.
49. *Weber, Marianne.*
50. *Aron,* pp. 97-98.
51. *Weber, Marianne,* p. 175.
52. Talcott Parsons, in *Barnes,* Chapter XIII, pp. 287-308.
53. A. Salomon, in *Gurvitch,* Part 2, Chapter XX, p. 605.
54. *Weber, M.* III.
55. *Weber, M.* II.
56. *Weber, M.* V.
57. *Abel,* pp. 156-159.
58. A. Salomon, in *Gurvitch,* Part 2, Chapter XX, pp. 608-616.
59. *Weber, Marianne,* pp. 239-277.

XXIX. LANGUAGE AS SYMBOL

1. *Vendryes,* p. 6.
2. *Meillet* II, Part 1, pp. 36-43.
3. *Meillet* II, Part 1, pp. 2-3, 15, 17-18.
4. *Hirt,* p. iii.
5. *Arens,* p. 279.
6. *Delbrück,* pp. 44-48.
7. *Meillet* II, Part 1, p. 103; *cf. Arens,* pp. 455-458.
8. *Pedersen,* pp. 282-293.
9. *Meillet* II, Part 2, p. 157.
10. *Osthoff,* p. 52.
11. *Heidelberger.*
12. *Schuchardt,* quoted in *Arens,* pp. 325-332.
13. *Cf. Arens,* pp. 332-335.
14. *Arens,* pp. 324-325.
15. *Thompsen,* p. 98. *Cf.* translator's preface.
16. *Arens,* p. 352.
17. *Arens,* p. 353.
18. *Finck.*
19. *Wundt,* Part 1.
20. *Dittrich.*
21. *Ipsen,* p. 8.

22. *Burdach,* pp. 52–53.
23. *Ipsen,* p. 9.
24. *Arens,* p. 372.
25. *Vossler,* p. 47.
26. *Vossler,* p. 63.
27. *Wechssler.*
28. *Wechssler,* p. 349.
29. *Eucken* I.
30. *Wundt,* Part 2, 2, p. 138.
31. *Delbrück,* pp. 93–102; *cf.* Hermann, pp. 104–105.
32. *Mauthner* II.
33. *Ginneken,* p. 532; *cf. Weynen.*
34. "Ueber Wert und Methode einer allgemeinen beschreibenden Bedeutungslehre," in *Marty.*
35. *Marty,* p. 11.
36. *Meillet* I, p. 123.
37. *Beneviste,* pp. 43–68.
38. *Mélanges.*
39. *Mélanges,* p. 153.
40. *Caland.*
41. *Josselin.*
42. *Arens,* p. 403.
43. *Wheeler,* p. 105.

XXX. THE EXCITABLE AGE

1. *Annales,* pp. 5–8.
2. *Annales,* pp. 39–49.
3. *Cf. Revue de synthèse historique,* 1 (1900), p. 23 and *Revue de synthèse* 67 (1950), p. 5.
4. *Revue de synthèse,* Part 67 of the entire series, and Part 16 of the new series (January-June 1950). with H. Berr's "Le cinquantenaire de la Revue," p. 5.
5. *Lamprecht* III.
6. *Revue de synthèse historique,* 1 (1900), p. 112.
7. *Revue de synthèse historique,* 1 (1900), pp. 28ff.
8. *Revue de synthèse historique,* 1 (1900), pp. 230ff.
9. *Lamprecht* VII.
10. *Lamprecht* I. See Part 1, second impression, 1901.
11. *Kleinberg,* p. 173.
12. *Kautsky* III, pp. 230ff.
13. *Plekhanov* II.
14. *Bentley,* p. 261, p. 262.
15. *Gothein.*
16. *Schäfer* I.
17. *Schäfer* II.
18. *Seifert; cf. Barth,* pp. 262–267.
19. *Powicke.*
20. *Schmidt, R.,* Part 1, pp. 1–20.
21. *Aly,* pp. 199ff.
22. *Bernheim.*
23. *Pirenne,* pp. 50ff.
24. *Patten; cf. Barth,* 1915 edition, pp. 613–627.
25. *Seligman,* under "Patten"; *cf. Tugwell.*

26. M. Schütt: "Zur Theorie der Biographie" (typescript), Hamburg, p. 1.
27. *Winterstetten.*
28. *Hallgarten,* Part 2, p. 314; *cf.* footnote 1.
29. *Breysig* II. Completely revised in 1955 from his notes.
30. *Troeltsch* III, p. 710.
31. *Weber, G.*
32. *Perrier,* p. xxv.
33. *Daux.*
34. *Déchelette; Michaelis.*
35. *Daniel.*
36. *Maspero* I; *Maspero* II.
37. *Ovink,* p. 19, column 2. For B. Ingram see M. Harris: "Doyen of British Editors" in *Printing News,* July 11, 1957.
38. *Baumgarten,* Part 1, p. iv.
39. *Ortega* II and *Ortega* III.
40. *Mandelbaum,* pp. 58-67. *Cf. Hodges* for Dilthey. For Rickert, see *Mandelbaum,* pp. 119-147.
41. *Burks,* pp. 89ff.
42. *Schmidt, R.,* Part 4, pp. 1-44.
43. *Jahn,* pp. 1-40 (95-134); for Croce, see p. 12.
44. *Jahn,* pp. 1-16 (183-198). The passage quoted is found on p. 1 (183).
45. *Lamprecht* IV, Part 2, p. 386.
46. *Lamprecht* IV, Part 2, p. 461.

XXXI. THE CRISIS OF VALUES

1. *Beerling* I, p. 8.
2. *Salin,* p. 114.
3. *Mehring* I, Chapter 9, reprinted in *Mehring* IV, Part 6, pp. 170-177.
4. *Mehring* IV, Part 6, p. 187. The idea is elaborated in *Lukács* III, pp. 244-317.
5. *Tönnies* II. *Cf. Mehring* IV, Part 6, pp. 178-188.
6. *Deesz.*
7. *Nietzsche* III, pp. 71-99.
8. *Nietzsche* III.
9. Of the vast number of works devoted to Nietzsche, special mention should be made of *Jaspers* I, with bibliography, and of the more recent *Kaufmann.*
10. *Romein* IX, pp. 99-124.
11. *Frank, S.; Gelder; Graaf; Lossky.*
12. *Bentley.*
13. *Wolf, E.* II, p. 669.
14. *Kohler, J.,* p. 10.
15. *Plessner* II, pp. 105-106.
16. *Cf. Bochenski* and *Delfgaauw.*
17. *Schmidt, R.*
18. *Schmidt, R.,* Part 1, pp. 71-90.
19. *Schmidt, R.,* Part 1, p. 80.
20. *Joël* IV.
21. *Joël* III.
22. *Delfgaauw.*
23. *Stein, L.* II.
24. *Frischeisen.*
25. *Schjelderup.*
26. *Wright, W. K.*

27. Speech published in Angers in 1882.
28. See Chapter XXIX.
29. For books on Bergson published in our period, see particularly *Drisch* IV, *Roy* II and *Maritain*.
30. *Delfgaauw*, p. 119.
31. *Bochenski*, p. 122.
32. *Bochenski*, p. 123; *cf. Leroux*.
33. *Mandelbaum*, pp. 58-67.
34. *Romein* IX, pp. 25-42.
35. *Lossky*, pp. 251-292.
36. *Suys; Beerling* II.
37. *Plessner* III, p. 23.
38. *Lange, F. A.*, preface to the third edition (1873).
39. *Schmidt, R.*, Part 4, pp. 17-19.
40. *Mandelbaum*, pp. 39-57.
41. *Kuypers*, p. 154, but neither Croce nor Bergson are mentioned.
42. *Etcheverry*.
43. *Wahl*, pp. 214-234.
44. *Russell, B.* IV.
45. See *Jackson, T. A.*, p. 631.
46. *Schmidt, R.*, Part 4, p. 6 (52).
47. *Eucken* II.

XXXII. BABEL AND BIBLE

1. *Loisy* III, Part 1, p. 573. Firmin was one of Loisy's pseudonyms; for the article in question, see *Firmin*. For the prohibition of further publications, see the November 1 issue of the same journal. *Cf. Loisy* III, Part 1, pp. 563ff. Despite this prohibition, the entire series was published under Loisy's own name (see *Loisy* I; *cf. Rivière*, p. 155).
2. *Kübel*, p. 144; *cf. Holland*.
3. *Colombat*, Chapter 3, p. 95.
4. *Howe*, p. 97.
5. *McCabe*, p. 275.
6. *Robertson* II and *Robertson* III.
7. *Loisy* III, Part 2, p. 651.
8. *Troeltsch* II, pp. 56-57.
9. *White, A. D.*
10. *Simmel, G.* IV, p. 17.
11. *Simmel, G.* IV, pp. 20-21, 100.
12. *Schoeck*, pp. 255-256.
13. *Seligman*, under "Comparative Religion."
14. *Tiele* I and *Tiele* II.
15. *Du Bose*, p. 115, quoted in *McCabe*, p. 335.
16. *Cheyne*.
17. *Nash* II.
18. *Hinneberg*.
19. *Delitzsch*, Part 1, preface, p. 5.
20. *Delitzsch*, Part 1, pp. 6-7.
21. *Delitzsch*, Part 1, p. 5.
22. *Delitzsch*, Part 1, p. 126, and preface to Part 2. *Cf. Baron*, Part 2, pp. 303-304.
23. *Robertson* I.
24. *Drews*.

25. *Weiss* I and *Weiss* II.
26. *Schweitzer.*
27. *Heppenstall,* p. 9.
28. *Cumont* I and *Cumont* II.
29. *Cumont* III.
30. *Harnack* II.
31. *Kübel,* p. 87.
32. *Kübel,* p. 103.
33. *Roy* I.
34. *Houtin,* p. vi.
35. The encyclical *Depuis le jour* of September 8, 1899, on the training of the clergy in France.
36. *Schrieke.*
37. *Elliott.*
38. *Kübel,* pp. 6-15.
39. *Cf. Huret* I, pp. 315-326.
40. For modernism in these countries see *Kübel, Houtin* and *Rivière* (bibliography); for more recent publications see *Aubert.*
41. *Condamnation du modernisme. Document.* Latin and French text of *Pascendi dominici gregis.* Tournai, 1907.
42. Buonaiuti was the probable author of this letter, although his authorship is not authenticated. See *Houtin,* p. 381, footnote 3, and *Poulat,* pp. 668-669 and 674-675.
43. *Stam,* p. 8; *cf. Petre.*
44. See *Revue moderniste internationale,* 1 (1900), p. 23, in which this letter was published.
45. *Loisy* III, Part 3, p. 550; *cf. Rivière,* p. 389.
46. *Heiler.*
47. *Condamnation du modernisme,* Tournai, 1907, pp. 102-112.
48. *Loisy* III, Part 2, pp. 642-643. *Cf. Lagrange.*
49. *Lindeboom,* pp. 59-72.
50. H. R. Niebuhr, in *Seligman* under "Higher Criticism."
51. *Atkins,* p. 297.
52. *Béguin,* p. 26.
53. *Klein,* quoted in *Gurian.*
54. *The history,* p. 743.
55. *Oirschot; Schilling.*
56. *Treitschke* II, Part 3, p. 490.
57. *Schmoller* IV, p. 31.
58. *Lindeboom,* pp. 86ff.
59. *Kleinberg,* p. 171.
60. *Kalthoff.*
61. *Naumann* I and *Naumann* II.
62. *Voet.*
63. *Atkins,* p. 313.
64. *Lindeboom,* pp. 167-170.

XXXIII. A HUNDRED AND ONE PROPHETS

1. See *Het toekomstig leven,* 4 (1900), p. 324. *Cf.* p. 374, where Kloos tries unconvincingly to retract the published report.
2. *Dessoir,* p. 59. From p. 132 it appears that part of the book was written before 1914.

3. *Het toekomstig leven,* 4 (1900), pp. 315–316.
4. *Het toekomstig leven,* 4 (1900), p. 260.
5. *Riemann,* p. xxvi.
6. *Heard,* p. 146.
7. *Wallace.*
8. *Wallace,* pp. 326–327.
9. *Besant* I; *cf. Nethercot.*
10. *Resink.*
11. *Resink,* p. 13.
12. *Driesch* VI, pp. 208–209.
13. *Theosofie.*
14. *Besant* II, pp. 1–2.
15. *Coste,* p. ix.
16. *Coste,* p. 39.
17. *Prel.*
18. *Coste,* p. vii.
19. *Dankmar,* p. xxxiii.
20. *Humphrey.*
21. See *Tielrooy,* pp. 176–177.
22. *Dessoir,* p. 117.
23. *Besant* II, pp. 23–25.
24. *Schultze,* F.
25. *Bois* II, p. 162; *cf. Bois* III
26. *Bois* II, p. 155.
27. Gustave Moreau Museum, Paris. In the summer of 1961 an exhibition of the work of this symbolist and surrealist *avant la lettre* was held in the Louvre.
28. *Bois* I, quoted in *Bois* II, pp. 214–215.
29. *Cf. Bibliographie, March* and *Heldt.*
30. *Müller, F. M.*
31. *Deussen.*
32. *Bähler.*
33. *Bähler,* p. 35.
34. *Bois* II, p. 41.
35. *Bois* II, p. 8.
36. *Nes.* This author examined the mystical element in theosophy, literature and art at the turn of the century.
37. *Hugenholtz.*
38. *Dessoir,* p. 128.
39. *Dantinne.*
40. *Mourik,* pp. 189ff.
41. *Zweig, S.* I; *cf. Mourik,* pp. 126ff.
42. *Slotemaker,* p. 24.
43. *Guttzeit,* pp. 130–136.
44. *Voo.*
45. *Daim.*
46. *Elbow,* pp. 97ff.
47. *Forel* II, p. 293.
48. *Steiner,* pp. 34–35.
49. *Steiner,* p. 258.
50. *Clasen.*
51. *Mayreder,* p. 1.
52. *Riemann,* p. 1.
53. *Stein, L.,* pp. 300ff.

54. *Steiner*, p. 282.
55. *Die Not*, p. 39.
56. *Rühle* II, p. 255.
57. *Trine*.

XXXIV. BEFORE THE FOOTLIGHTS

1. *Reich.*
2. *Lavrin*, p. 134.
3. *Ten Eyck*. For later bibliographies see *Meyer, F.; Petterson*.
4. *Ehrhard.*
5. *Schmitt, E. H.* II, pp. 118-143.
6. *Mendes*, p. 15.
7. *Flores*. Plekhanov's article (pp. 35-92 in this edition) was first published as a Russian book in 1908. An expanded German form was published a year later.
8. *Einiges*, p. 48.
9. *Mann, T.* III, p. 16.
10. *Morand*, p. 157.
11. *Presser*, p. 545.
12. *Proost I*, p. 134.
13. *Hunningher*, pp. 133, 169-172.
14. *Proost* I, p. 2.
15. *Teggart*, pp. 60, 132.
16. *Romein* IX, pp. 63-83.
17. P. Fechter in *Berliner Lokal-Anzeiger*, September 15, 1910.
18. *Kleinberg*, p. 176.
19. *Mehring* IV, Part 2. For Mehring the social democrat see *Höhle*.
20. *Mehring* IV, Part 2, pp. 103-111, 247-268, 294-300. *Cf.* p. 396 in which a number of articles related to the subject and not reprinted in the *Gesammelte Schriften* appear.
21. *Bleibtreu.*
22. *Soergel*, p. 3. Quoted in *Proost I*, p. 24.
23. *Mehring* IV, Part 2, pp. 131-143, 285-294.
24. *Hanstein*, pp. 146-159.
25. *Holz* II, *cf. Hanstein*, pp. 146-159, 229.
26. *Mehring* IV, Part 2, p. 293.
27. *Holz* VI, Part 1, p. 7; *Döblin*, p. 87 (later expanded in *Rappl*, p. 84).
28. *Turley*, pp. 14-17.
29. Letter to K. H. Strobl of June 25, 1900, in *Holz* V, p. 127.
30. *Schär*, p. 80.
31. Quoted in *Proost* I, p. 28.
32. *Tank*, p. 166.
33. *Lublinski;* see *Tank*, p. 166.
34. *Schlenther.*
35. *Hohenlohe*, Part 2, p. 507.
36. *Bahr*, pp. 199-211.
37. *Brugmans.*
38. *Rossum*, pp. 30-33.
39. *Rolland* I.
40. *Prince*, title of Chapter 5, p. 69.
41. *Craig, E. G.*, pp. 125, 127; reprinted in 1957.
42. *Goldmann*, pp. iii ff, quoted in *Proost* II, p. 37, footnote.
43. *Proost* II, pp. 37-38; *Moeller* I.

44. *Mann, H.* II, pp. 75-95.
45. *Bahr*, pp. 65-72 and 152-158.
46. *Bahr*, pp. 189-198; *cf.* Lecat II and Lecat I.
47. *Yeats*, pp. 559ff.
48. *Les Sources du XXe siècle.* Catalogue of the exhibition *Les Arts en Europe de 1884 à 1914,* Paris 1960-1961, p. 231.
49. *Jaspers* II.
50. *Esswein.*
51. *Poritzky.*
52. *Bab.*
53. *Specht*, p. 140.
54. *Moeller* II, p. 167.
55. *Höweler.*
56. *Moeller* II, pp. 183, 192.
57. *Schultink*, pp. 220ff.
58. *Speenhoff*, pp. 30-35.
59. *De Maasbode*, February 9, 1907.
60. *Panofsky*, p. 10.
61. *Michael*, p. 78. *Cf.* p. 94.

XXXV. EVERY MAN A PHOENIX

1. *Brunetière* II.
2. *Roland* IV, Part 1, p. 21.
3. *Roland* IV, Part 1, p. 77.
4. *Holz IV; cf. Döblin.*
5. *Huret* III, p. 57.
6. William James, after reading *L'Évolution créatrice.*
7. *Cahiers de la quinzaine*, November 23, 1913.
8. *Depuis le jour.*
9. *Cf.* Chapter XXXIV.
10. *Heller, E.*, p. 128.
11. *Rilke* I, p. 12 (from the 1922 edition).
12. *Hofmannsthal* II, Part 2, p. 329.
13. *Cf. Ruff*, who traces this trend back to 1750.
14. J. W. Oerlemans: "Het kwaad als bondgenoot" in Weekly Supplement to the *Nieuwe Rotterdamse Courant*, May 25, 1963.
15. *Hofmannsthal* II, Part 1, p. 149.
16. *Huret* III, p. 42.
17. *Yeats*, p. 191.
18. *Friedmann*, p. 210.
19. *Romein* IX, pp. 63-83.
20. *Clouard*, Part 1, p. 63.
21. *Huret* III, p. 56.
22. *Donne*, p. 238: " 'T is all in pieces, all cohaerence gone; /All just supply, and all Relation: /Prince, Subject, Father, Sonne, are things forgot, /For every man alone thinkes he hath got /To be a Phoenix, and that than can bee /None of that kinde, of which he is, but hee."
23. *Yeats*, p. 103.
24. *Rilke* III, p. 207.
25. *Huret* III, p. 60.
26. M. Proust: "Contre L'obscurité" in *Proust* III, p. 143.
27. Marsman on Gorter in *Verzamelde gedichten*, Amsterdam 1946, p. 127.

28. In a letter to Paul Demeny of May 15, 1871.
29. *Yeats*, p. 193.
30. *Tielrooy*.
31. See André Breton: "Premier manifeste du surréalisme" in *Le Sagittaire*, 1955, p. 10.
32. From a letter to Charles Morice, included in *Morice* I.
33. *Valéry*, Part 4, pp. 9–48.
34. In the preface by Fabre included in *Valéry*, Part 1.
35. In the sonnet "Correspondances" in *Les Fleurs du mal*, Paris, 1857.
36. In the collection *Jadis et naguère*, Paris, 1884.
37. *Huret* III, p. 59.
38. See *Fabre*.
39. *Lütgert*, p. 359.
40. *Sageret*.
41. *Eeden* II; *Rümke*.
42. *Gallienne*, p. xv.
43. *Gallienne*, p. 4.
44. *Rilke* II, Part 2, p. 333.
45. *Lange* V.
46. Quoted in *Lütgert*, p. 353.
47. *James, H.*, p. 147.
48. *Moore, G.* II, p. 61.
49. *Moore, G.* II, p. 83.
50. *Moore, G.* II, pp. 2, 97.
51. *Moore, G.* II, p. 30.
52. *Moore, G.* II, p. 113.
53. *Yeats*, p. 452.
54. *Gallienne*, p. xviii.
55. For other playwrights see Chapter XXXIV.
56. *Jackson, H.*, p. 128.
57. *Jackson, H.*, p. 22.
58. Introduction to *The Savoy*, 1896.
59. Quoted in *Daiches*, Part 2, p. 1103.
60. *Pater*.
61. *Carrière*.
62. *George*, p. 40.
63. *Friedmann*, p. 118.
64. Quoted in *Friedmann*, p. 110.
65. *Rolland* II, introduction.
66. M. Proust: "Contre l'obscurité" in *Revue blanche*, 1896, reprinted in *Proust* III, p. 137.
67. *Proust* III, p. 141.
68. *Proust* I, Part 2, pp. 66ff.

XXXVI. NOA - NOA

1. *Rewald* I, pp. 474–475.
2. *Morand*, pp. 98–99.
3. *Mellquist*.
4. *Rewald* I, p. 477.
5. *Morand*, p. 99.
6. *Woermann*.
7. *Trier*, p. 26.

8. *Wichman,* E.
9. *Wichman,* E., p. 31.
10. *Francastel,* p. 151.
11. *Apollinaire,* pp. 41, 43. For Apollinaire, see *Shattuck,* pp. 195–248.
12. *Monfreid,* p. 190. A better edition (Paris, 1950) is mentioned in *Rewald* II, p. 565 (No. 45).
13. *Morice* II, pp. 25–29. *Rewald* II (p. 489) gives 1890 as the year of this celebration, not 1899, the date given by Morice.
14. *Seligman,* under "Primitivism."
15. Catalogue of the Hokusai Exhibition, 1949, Stedelijk Museum, Amsterdam, p. 13.
16. *Hahnloser,* p. 135.
17. *Trier,* pp. 36, 37.
18. F. Elgar' "Arts et cinéma" in *Béguin,* p. 145.
19. *Shattuck,* pp. 37–87.
20. *Höweler,* p. 293.
21. *Raphael,* p. 57.
22. G. C. Argan: "Les Arts plastiques" in *Les Sources du XXe siècle,* Introduction, p. xxx.
23. *Raphael,* p. 81.
24. See footnote 22.
25. *Zweig, A.* II.
26. These figures are given particular weight in *Myers, B. S.,* whose book is subtitled "A Generation in Revolt." Reproductions of Käthe Kollwitz's work in *Het werk van Käthe Kollwitz,* introduction by W. J. de Gruwter, The Hague, 1932.
27. *Romein* IX, pp. 125–155; cf. *Poulaille* and *Ragon.*
28. *Romein-Verschoor* I.
29. *Bricaud.*
30. See catalogue No. 176, "Europe 1907," held in the Stedelijk Museum, Amsterdam, in the summer of 1957.
31. J. Cassou, in *Les Sources du XXe siècle,* Introduction, p. xix.
32. *Vermij,* pp. 149–156.
33. *Breysig* III.
34. P. Valéry: "Méthodes" in *Mercure de France,* May, 1899, quoted in *Shattuck,* p. 267, footnote. Cf. *Shattuck,* pp. 157, 161, 269–270.
35. *Shattuck,* p. 157.
36. *Haftmann.*
37. *Haftmann: Textband,* pp. 281–282.
38. *Haftmann: Tafelband,* p. 145. For M. Duchamp see also the catalogue mentioned in footnote 31.
39. *Malewitsch.*
40. *Myers, B. S.,* p. 216.
41. *Sedlmayr* I, pp. 110–115.
42. *Sedlmayr* I, p. 110.
43. *Raphael,* p. 55.
44. *Zweig, A.* II, p. 206.
45. *Rookmaker,* pp. 160–164.
46. *Polak, B. H.*
47. "1907" was also the title of a commemorative exhibition in the Stedelijk Museum, Amsterdam, held in 1957. See the introduction to the catalogue.
48. *Meier* I.
49. *Meier* II.
50. *Rewald* II, pp. 570–579.
51. *Stéphane.*

700

52. G. C. Argan: "Le futurisme" in *Les Sources du XXe siècle*, Introduction, pp. 5-7.
53. *Myers, B. S.*, p. 208, quoting *Zehder*.
54. *Trier*, pp. 20, 36, 38.
55. *Riegl. Cf. Sedlmayr* II, pp. 14-34.
56. *Riehl, H.*

XXXVII. ART NOUVEAU

1. Letter by Tolstoy in *Daily Chronicle*, August 4, 1903. Quoted in *Leon*, p. 578.
2. *Leon*, p. 578.
3. *Shaw* III.
4. *Horrix*, pp. 351ff.
5. *Herkner* I. *Cf.* his autobiography in *Meiner*.
6. *Velde* II, p. 23.
7. *Ruskin*, Chapter 2, paragraph 7, quoted in *Madsen*, p. 89.
8. *Bøe*.
9. *Madsen*, pp. 75-83; *Schmalenbach*, pp. 12-22.
10. *Velde* I, chapter entitled: "Wie ich mir freie Bahn schuf," written in 1890.
11. *Scheffler*, pp. 65-67. *Cf. Hobson* II, Chapter 14, pp. 368-372.
12. *Madsen*, p. 110, footnote 17.
13. *Knuttel. Cf. Engelman*, pp. 17-18.
14. See *Lenning*, pp. 118, 128.
15. *Pevsner* I, p. 100.
16. *Sternberger*, pp. 114ff.
17. *Dooijes*, p. 326. For Veth, see *Huizinga* III.
18. *Ahlers*, p. 5.
19. For the first interior, see *Ahlers*, p. 13; for the second interior, see *Ahlers passim*.
20. See H. Curjel: "Vom neunzehnten zum zwanzigsten Jahrhundert" in the catalogue *Um 1900* of the exhibition held in the Kunstgewerbe Museum, Zurich, in 1952, pp. 7-20. The best bibliography covering Art Nouveau is found in *Madsen*, pp. 451-470.
21. *Schmalenbach*, pp. 52-54.
22. See footnote 20 (Curjel, p. 12).
23. *Frey*, p. 292. *Cf. Romein* III, p. 200.
24. *Giedion*, p. 200.
25. *Giedion*, pp. 202ff.
26. *Velde* III.
27. See footnote 20 (Curjel, p. 12).
28. *Radermacker*, pp. 4-5.
29. *Gans*.
30. *Spaanstra*, p. 357.
31. *Arondéus. Cf. Engelman*.
32. Illustration in *Lenning*, p. 58.
33. *Pevsner* I, p. 28.
34. *Hitchcock*, pp. 116, 117, 118, 124-126, 283. *Cf. Giedion* and *Pevsner* II, Chapter 5.
35. Illustration in *Hitchcock*, p. 183 of the plates.
36. *Hitchcock*, p. 154.
37. *Wagner, O.*
38. *Hitchcock*, Plates 118-121.
39. *Hitchcock*, Plate 96.
40. *Hitchcock*, Plates 135-137.
41. *Gratema*.

42. *Sitte; Berlage. Cf. Giedion,* pp. 445ff.
43. *Sédille,* quoted in *Hitchcock,* p. 281.
44. *Muthesius* II, quoted in *Hitchcock,* p. 281.
45. *Hitchcock,* p. 277 and Plate 129.
46. *Muthesius I,* quoted in *Schmalenbach,* p. 19.
47. *Lenning,* p. 24.
48. *Hitchcock,* Plate 132.
49. *Hitchcock,* p. 297.
50. *Pevsner* II, p. 114. *Hitchcock,* Plates 148–149.
51. A. Loos: Ornament und verbrechen" in *Loos. Cf. Hitchcock,* p. 453, footnote 2.
52. *Ahlers,* p. 115.

XXXVIII. DAYBREAK AFTER *GÖTTERDÄMMERUNG*

1. *Loeser,* p. 279.
2. *Onnen,* p. 9.
3. *Shattuck.*
4. *Loeser,* p. 282.
5. *Nietzsche* IV and *Nietzsche* V.
6. Quoted in *Onnen,* p. 22.
7. Quoted in *Grosclaude.*
8. *Reeser,* p. 212.
9. *Adorno,* p. 68.
10. *Reeser,* p. 151.
11. *Mengelberg,* p. 10.
12. *Weber* V, p. 928, quoted from the 1956 edition.
13. *Lang,* p. 989.
14. *Lang,* p. 985.
15. *Adorno,* pp. 33ff.
16. Quoted in *Ketting,* p. 41.
17. *Onnen,* p. 14.
18. From a letter sent to the General Secretary of the Opéra Comique.
19. *Vallas,* p. 43.
20. *Emmanuel,* pp. 35–36.
21. See footnote 18.
22. *Emmanuel,* p. 133.
23. *Adler, G.,* p. 7.
24. *Mahler,* p. 135.
25. *Adler, G.,* p. 29.
26. *Mahler,* p. 68.
27. *Adler, G.,* p. 44.
28. *Cronheim,* p. 7.

XXXIX. THE WAY OF ALL FLESH

1. *Bloch,* I, p. 259.
2. *Ellis* II, p. 267.
3. *Jackson, H.*
4. *Jackson, H,* p. 132.
5. Quoted on the jacket on the Dolphin Books edition of *The Way of All Flesh.*
6. *Forel* I.
7. *Ellis* II.
8. *Bloch* I.

9. *Egerton.*
10. *Deflou.*
11. *Blum, L.*
12. *Prévost* I and *Prévost* II.
13. *Bourget, P.* II.
14. *Blum, L.*, p. 338.
15. *Thomas, A.*
16. *Craig, A.*, p. 128.
17. *Forel* I, p. 369.
18. *Bloch, I.*, p. 176.
19. *Mead, M.*, p. 293.
20. *Beauvoir* II.
21. *Forel* I, p. 358.
22. *De Groene Amsterdammer*, 1900, p. 1214.
23. Quoted in *Ellis* II, p. 483.
24. *Blum, L.*
25. *Blum, L.*, p. 312.
26. *Forel I*, p. 314.
27. *Beauvoir* I, Part 1, p. 15.
28. Quoted in *Mayreder*, p. 53.
29. *Mayreder*, p. 123.
30. *Mayreder*, p. 42.
31. *Marholm* II.
32. *Savornin: Salomons.*
33. *Boudier.*
34. Summary after *Mayreder.*
35. *Weininger.*
36. Summary after *Mayreder.*
37. *Key* III.
38. *Bloch, I.*, p. 297.
39. *Key* III, p. 40.
40. *Key* III, p. 17.
41. *Forel* I, p. 61.
42. *Forel* I, p. 410.
43. *Mayreder*, p. 176.
44. *Forel* I, p. 285.
45. *Forel* I, p. 91.
46. *Galton.*
47. *Forel* I, p. 416.
48. *Ehrenfels* II.
49. *Forel* I, preface.
50. *Forel* I, pp. 469 and 505.
51. *Forel* I, p. 421.
52. *Forel* I, p. 354.
53. *Forel* I, p. 554.
54. *Forel* II, p. 158.
55. *Bloch, I.*, p. 297.
56. *Bloch, I.*, p. 302.
57. *Forel* I, p. 504.
58. *Jacobs.*
59. *Eymieu*, Part 3, p. 44.
60. *Bloch, I.*, p. 747.
61. *Freud* II, p. 216.

703

62. *Förster* I.
63. *Clouard*, Part 2, p. 123.
64. *Yeats*, p. 291.
65. *Forel* I, p. 258.

XL. THE IDOL BEHIND GLASS

1. *Turgeon.*
2. Quoted in *Turgeon*, Part 1, p. 101.
3. *Turgeon*, Part 1, p. 101.
4. *Zuylen*, p. 164.
5. *De Groene Amsterdammer*, 1900, p. 1183.
6. *Rival.*
7. *Couvee.*
8. *Steinmetz* I.
9. For both, see Chapter XXXIX.
10. *Möbius.*
11. *Möbius*, p. 41.
12. *Möbius*, p. 40.
13. *Möbius*, p. 145.
14. *Braun, L.*, p. 117.
15. *Braun, L.*, p. 146.
16. *Joran* I and *Joran* II.
17. Quoted in *Faguet* I, p. 364.
18. *Faguet* I, p. 358.
19. *La revue naturiste*, July, 1897.
20. *Schirmacher*, p. 24.
21. *Thomas, A.*
22. *Schirmacher*, p. 35.
23. *Schirmacher*, p. 37.
24. *Beauvoir* II.
25. *Belang en recht*, 4 (1900), p. 105.
26. *Belang en recht*, 3 (1899), p. 14.
27. *Belang en recht*, 4 (1900), p. 142.
28. *Goodwin*, pp. 83ff.
29. *Woolf.*
30. From a Russian folksong.
31. *Schirmacher*, p. 63.
32. *Belang en recht*, 4 (1900), p. 198; *Belang en recht*, 5 (1901), p. 195.
33. *Braun, L.*, p. 137.
34. *Goekoop.*
35. *Blum, L.*
36. *Bebel.*
37. See *Pankhurst.*
38. *Webb* I, p. 83.
39. *Braun, L.*, p. 475.
40. *De Groene Amsterdammer*, 1900, p. 1204.
41. *Braun, L.*, Chapter 8, *passim.*
42. Fully catalogued by *Painter.*
43. *Painter*, p. 240.
44. *Cooper.*
45. *Cooper*, p. 72.
46. *Cooper*, pp. 72, 84.

47. *Cooper*, p. 101.
48. *Cooper*, p. 119.
49. *Cooper*, p. 94.
50. *Pankhurst*.
51. *Pankhurst*, p. 330.
52. *Pankhurst*, p. 467.
53. *Pankhurst*, p. 477.
54. *Pankhurst*, p. 472.
55. *Anthony*, Part 6, p. 738.
56. *New York Herald Tribune*, November 8, 1961.
57. *Suess*.
58. In the *Revue des revues*, Paris, July 1900, Zola defended women's bicycling dress as follows: "Without relinquishing any of the courtesy they owe her, men should not, in my view, treat woman as an idol whom they can only approach with diffidence and reverence."
59. See *Key* V, *passim* and Marholm II.
60. *Suess*, pp. 6, 8, 9.
61. Quoted in *Soesman*.
62. *Savornin*.
63. *Key* III, p. 63.
64. *Marholm* II.

XLI. THE CENTURY OF THE CHILD

1. *Gurlitt*, p. 94.
2. *Chastenet*, p. 148.
3. *Kleinberg*, p. 168.
4. *Paulsen*, Part 2, p. 687.
5. *Cumberley*, p. 635.
6. *Russell, C. E. B.*, p. 123.
7. *Treitschke* I, p. 256.
8. This and similar views quoted in *Lütgert*, pp. 147ff.
9. *Paulsen*, Part 2, p. 689.
10. *Lagarde*, p. 239.
11. See *Lütgert*, p. 159.
12. *Key* I.
13. *Cumberley*, p. 509.
14. *Heard*, p. 153.
15. *Key* IV, p. 113; *cf. Rühle* II, p. 256.
16. *Key* IV, p. 158.
17. *Key* IV, p. 58.
18. *Prins*, p. 9.
19. *Cumberley*, p. 577.
20. *Hall* III, p. 186.
21. *Hall* II, p. v.
22. *Hall* II, p. 300.
23. *Dewey*, p. 22.
24. *Philippi* contains a bibliography of his work.
25. *Montessori* and many other writings.
26. *Kerschensteiner* gives a summary of his ideas.
27. *Bergson* III, p. 25.
28. *Gurlitt*, p. 76; *cf.* a quotation in *Rühle* II in which Brautigam, professor of pedagogy in Bremen, calls the modern school "a penitentiary."

29. *Burnand* I, p. 61.
30. *Chastenet*, p. 148.
31. *Strachey*, pp. 180, 181.
32. See *Graves* and *Walpole* among others.
33. *Gurlitt*, p. 7.
34. *Gurlitt*, p. 5.
35. *Förster* II, p. 69.
36. *Förster* II, p. 74.
37. *Förster* II, p. 77.
38. *Graf.*
39. Quoted in *Zeller*, p. 18.
40. *Graf*, p. 215.
41. *Gurnitt*, pp. 146–200.
42. *Hesse*, pp. 152–156, quoted from the 1951 edition.
43. *Rühle* II.
44. *Gurlitt*, p. 154.
45. *Gurlitt*, p. 158.
46. See *Wyneken* I and *Wyneken* II.
47. See *Ehm*, p. 128ff.
48. *Rühle* I, p. 25.
49. *Kerschensteiner*, p. 6.
50. *Bodenheim.*
51. *Barrie* I, *cf. Barrie* II, p. 505.
52. *Schmidt, R.*
53. *Schmidt, R.*, Part 4, p. 166.
54. *Hahn.*
55. These quotations are taken from *Gusdorf*, p. 411.
56. *Blücher*, p. 164.
57. In 1906 as many as 60,000; *Chastenet*, pp. 218, 220.
58. See *Harmsen.*
59. *Kühnhagen*, p. 10.
60. *Kühnhagen*, p. 16.
61. This figure and those following from *Rühle* II.
62. *Rühle* II, p. 124.
63. See Chapter XXXIX.
64. *Russell, C. E. B.*, p. 179.
65. See *Coppée*, who describes the vicious regime at La Petite Roquette.
66. *Toorenburg*, p. 72.
67. *Russell, C. E. B.*, p. 165.
68. *Russell, C. E. B.*, p. 118.

XLII. THE DARK GATE

1. *Heindel*, p. 87.
2. *Flexner* II, p. 9.
3. *Dickens* I and *Dickens* II.
4. *Fischer*, p. 32.
5. *Heindel*, p. 87.
6. *New York Herald Tribune*, March 29, 1955, in its reprint of a report first published fifty years before.
7. *Fischer*, p. 81.
8. F. L. Allen: *The Great Morgan*, p. 47, quoted in *Mandel*, Part 2, p. 25.
9. *MacKenzie, F. A.* II, Chapter 3, pp. 25–32.

10. *MacKenzie, F. A.* II, p. 202.
11. *Stead* II, p. 28.
12. *MacKenzie, F. A.* II, p. 204.
13. *MacKenzie, F. A.* II, p. 206.
14. *Stead* II, p. 44.
15. *Stead* II, p. 87; *Fischer*, p. 86.
16. *Fischer*, p. 87.
17. *MacKenzie, F. A.* II, pp. 157–164.
18. *Southard*, p. xiii.
19. *Lebius*, p. 131.
20. "Vijftig jaar Ford auto's" in *Nieuwe Rotterdamse Courant,* June 13, 1953.
21. *Heindel*, p. 281.
22. *Fried*, Part 3, p. 133.
23. *Lekkerkerker.*
24. *Huret* I, p. 315.
25. *Fischer*, p. 153.
26. *Beard*, p. 153.
27. *Snethlage.*
28. *Ward* II, p. 6.
29. *Heindel*, pp. 397–398.
30. *Romein* IX, p. 63.
31. *Furness.*
32. *Cadt*, p. 81; *cf.* G. Sorel in *Sozialistische Monatshefte,* 2 (1898), pp. 537–543.
33. *Plenge.*
34. C. Péguy in IIe Cahier (Series 5), March, 1904; *cf. Rolland* IV, Part 1, p. 69.
35. *Atherton* II.
36. *Lamprecht* VI, p. 25.
37. *Münsterberg.*
38. Preface by K. M. Panikkar, in *Romein* XI.
39. *Stead* II, p. 73.
40. See footnote 38.
41. *Bloch, J. von.* The original Russian edition appeared in 1898.
42. W. van Ravesteyn: *De oorlog en de internationale,* Baarn, 1915, p. 29.
43. W. van Ravesteyn: *De oorlog en de internationale,* Baarn, 1915, p. 30.
44. *Freud* III.
45. Part of this polemic can be found in *Bauer, M.*
46. *Huizinga* IV, p. 37.
47. *Freud* III, p. 53.
48. *Alberès*, p. 13.
49. *Mann, T.* III, p. 19.
50. *Romein-Verschoor* II, p. 51.
51. *Gide, A.* II, p. 145.
52. Quoted in *Alberès*, p. 15.
53. *Alberès*, p. 44.
54. *Depuis le jour.*
55. "Heimwee" in H. Marsman: *Verzamelde gedichten,* Amsterdam, 1946, p. 54.
56. *Alberès*, p. 224.

BIBLIOGRAPHY

References given are not necessarily to first editions.

Abel, Th.: *Systematic sociology in Germany.* New York, 1929. *Abel*

Achelis, Th.: *Sociologie.* Leipzig, 1899. *Achelis*

Ackerman, N. W. & M. Jahoda: *Anti-Semitism and emotional disorder. A psycho-analytic interpretation.* New York, 1950. *Ackerman*

Adams, W. S.: *Edwardian heritage. A study in British history, 1901-'06.* London, 1949. *Adams*

Adler, G.: *Gustav Mahler.* Vienna, 1916. *Adler G.*

Adler, M.: *Marx als Denker.* Berlin, 1908. *Adler M.* I

Adler, M.: *Kausalität und Teleologie im Streite um die Wissenschaft.* Vienna, 1904. *Adler M.* II

Adler, M.: *Kant und der Marxismus.* Berlin, 1925. *Adler M.* III

Adorno, Th. W.: *Einleitung in die Musiksoziologie.* Frankfurt a.Main, 1962. *Adorno*

Aftalion, A.: *Les crises périodiques de surproduction.* 2 parts. Paris, 1913. *Aftalion*

Ahlers-Hestermann, F.: *Stilwende. Aufbruch der Jugend um 1900.* Berlin, 1941. *Ahlers*

Ajalbert, J.: *Sous le sabre.* Paris, 1898. *Ajalbert*

Alberès, R. M.: *L'aventure intellectuelle du XXe siècle, 1900-'50.* Paris, 1950. *Alberès*

Alcott, L.: *Little Women.* London, 1869. *Alcott*

Aletrino, A.: *Het leven der verpleegster.* Amsterdam, 1900. *Aletrino*

Allen, R.: *Siege of the Peking legations. A diary.* London, 1901. *Allen*

Allyn, E.: *Lords versus commons. A century of conflict and compromise 1830-1930.* Philadelphia, 1931. *Allyn*

Alpert, H.: *Emile Durkheim and his sociology.* New York, 1939. *Alpert*

Altenloh, E.: *Zur Soziologie des Kinos.* Jena, 1914. *Altenloh*

Aly, F.: 'Der Einbruch des Materialismus in die historischen Wissenschaften' in *Preussische Jahrbücher,* Vol. 81 (1895), pp. 199-214. *Aly*

Ammon, O.: *Die natürliche Auslese beim Menschen.* Jena, 1893. *Ammon* I

Ammon, O.: *Die Gesellschaftordnung und ihre natürlichen Grundlagen,* Jena, 1895. *Ammon* II

Ancel, J.: *Manuel historique de la question d'Orient, 1792-1923.* Paris, 1923. *Ancel*

Andler, Ch.: *Les origines du socialisme d'état en Allemagne.* Paris, 1897. *Andler* I

Andler, Ch.: *La civilisation socialiste.* Paris, 1912. *Andler* II

Andler, Ch.: *Vie de Lucien Herr (1864-1926).* Paris, 1932. *Andler* III

Angell, N.: *The great illusion. A study of the relation of military power in nations to their economic and social advantage.* London, 1910. *Angell*

Annales internationales d'histoire. Congrès de Paris 1900. Première section: Histoire générale et diplomatique. Paris, 1901. *Annales*

Anthony, S. B. & I. H. Harper (ed): *The history of woman suffrage.* 6 vols. Rochester (N. Y.), 1886-1922. *Anthony*

Anthouard, A. F. I. d': *La Chine contre l'étranger. Les Boxeurs.* Paris, 1902. *Anthouard*

Apollinaire, G.: *Les peintres cubistes. Méditations esthétiques.* Geneva, 1949-'50. *Apollinaire*

Araujo, O. d': 'La vie sociale contemporaine: Théâtre' in *Revue internationale de sociologie*, 8 (1900), pp. 60-67. *Araujo*

Archambault, P.: *Essai sur l'individualisme.* Paris, 1913. *Archambault*

Archer, W. (ed.): *Henrik Ibsen, Prose dramas.* 5 vols. London, 1890-'91. *Archer* I

Archer, W.: *The life, trial and death of Francisco Ferrer,* London, 1911. *Archer* II

Arendt, H.: *The burden of our time.* London, 1951. *Arendt*

Arens, H.: *Sprachwissenschaft. Der Gang ihrer Entwicklung von der Antike bis zur Gegenwart.* Munich, 1955. *Arens*

Aron, R.: *La sociologie allemande contemporaine.* Paris, 1949-50. *Aron*

Arondéus, W.: *Figuren en problemen der monumentale schilderkunst in Nederland.* Amsterdam, 1941. *Arondéus*

Artibal, J.: *L'assurance ouvrière à l'étranger.* Paris, 1901. *Artibal*

Aschoff, L. & P. Diepgen: *Kurze Übersichtstabelle zur Geschichte der Medizin.* Munich, 1940. *Aschoff*

Atherton, G.: *His fortunate Grace.* London, 1897. *Atherton* I

Atherton, G.: *American wives and English husbands.* Leipzig, 1899. *Atherton* II

Atkins, G. G.: *The making of the Christian mind.* London, 1929. *Atkins*

Aubert, R.: 'Recente publikaties rond het modernisme' in *Concilium. Internationaal tijdschrift voor theologie*, 2 (1966), no. 7, pp. 87-104. *Aubert*

Avenel, H.: *Histoire de la presse française depuis 1789 jusqu'à nos jours.* Paris, 1900. *Avenel* I

Avenel, H.: *La presse française au XXe siècle.* Paris, 1901. *Avenel* II

Axa, Z. d': *Les feuilles.* Paris, 1900. *Axa*

Azoury, N.: *Le réveil de la nation arabe dans l'Asie turque.* Paris, 1905. *Azoury*

Bab, J.: *Das Theater der Gegenwart. Geschichte der dramatischen Bühne seit 1870.* Leipzig, 1928. *Bab*

Bähler, L. A.: Het boeddhisme in Europa. Baarn, 1911. *Bähler*

Bahr, H.: *Die Überwindung des Naturalismus, als zweite Reihe von 'Zur Kritik der Moderne'.* Dresden, 1891. *Bahr*

Baire, R., E. Borel, J. Hadamard, H. Lebesgue: 'Cinq lettres sur la théorie des ensembles' in *Bulletin de la Société Mathématique de France*, 33 (1905), 261-273. *Baire*

Baker, J. N. L.: *A history of geographical discovery and exploration.* London, 1931. *Baker*

Bardèche, M. & R. Brasillach: *Histoire du cinéma.* Paris, 1935. *Bardèche* I

Bardèche, M. & R. Brasillach: *History of the film,* London, 1938. *Bardèche* II

Barnes (ed), H. E.: *An introduction to the history of sociology.* Chicago, 1948. *Barnes*

Baroja, P.: *¡El mundo es ansi!* Madrid, 1912. *Baroja*

Baron, S. W.: *A social and religious history of the Jews.* 3 vols. New York, 1937. *Baron*

Barrès, M.: *Le culte du moi. Examen de trois idéologies.* Paris, 1888-'91. *Barrès* I

Barrès, M.: *Le roman de l'énergie nationale.* Paris, 1897-1902. *Barrès* II

Barrès, M.: *L'appel au soldat.* Paris, 1900. *Barrès* III

Barrie, J. M.: *Peter Pan in Kensington Gardens.* London, 1906. *Barrie* I

Barrie, J. M.: *The plays of J. M. B. in one volume.* London, 1945. *Barrie* II

Barth, P.: *Die Philosophie der Geschichte als Soziologie.* Leipzig, 1922. *Barth*

Basch, V.: *L'individualisme anarchiste. Max Stirner.* Paris, 1904. *Basch*

Baschwitz, K.: *Du und die Masse. Studien zu einer exakten Massenpsychologie.* Amsterdam, 1938. *Baschwitz* I

Baschwitz, K.: *De krant door alle tijden.* Amsterdam, 1949. *Baschwitz* II

Bateson, W.: *Materials for study of variations and discontinuity.* London, 1894. *Bateson* I

Bateson, W.: *Mendel's principles of heredity. A defence.* London, 1902. *Bateson* II

Batts, H. J.: *Pretoria from within during the war, 1899-1900.* London, 1901. *Batts*

Baudelaire, C.: *Les fleurs du mal.* Paris, 1857. *Baudelaire*

Bauer, A.: *Thomas Mann und die Krise der bürgerlichen Kultur.* Berlin, 1946. *Bauer A.*

Bauer, L.: *Der Zug nach der Stadt und die Stadterweiterung.* Stuttgart, 1904. *Bauer L.*

Bauer, M.: *Brieven en schetsen van zijn reizen naar Moskou en Constantinopel, gevolgd door enige polemieken tussen socialisten en estheten.* Amsterdam, 1964. *Bauer M.*

Baumann, A. A.: 'A Tory plea for the Parliament Bill' in *The fortnightly review,* 89 (1911), new series, pp. 597-607. *Baumann*

Bäumer, G.: *Die soziale Idee in den Weltanschauungen des 19. Jahrhunderts. Die Grundzüge der modernen Sozialphilosophie.* Heilbronn, 1910. *Bäumer*

Baumgarten, H.: *Geschichte Karls V.* 3 delen. Stuttgart, 1885-'92. *Baumgarten*

Bazin, R.: *De toute son ame.* Paris, 1897. *Bazin*

Beales, A. C. F.: *The history of peace: the organised movements for international peace.* London, 1931. *Beales*

Beard, C. A. & M. R.: *The rise of American civilization.* Cambridge (Mass.), 1948. *Beard*

Beauchamp. E. M.: *Elizabeth and her German garden.* London, 1898. *Beauchamp*

Beauvoir, S. de: *Le deuxième sexe.* 2 vols. Paris, 1949. *Beauvoir* I

Beauvoir, S. de: *Mémoires d'une jeune fille rangée.* Paris, 1958. *Beauvoir* II

Bebel, A.: *Die Frau und der Sozialismus.* Stuttgart, 1912. *Bebel*

Beckerath, E. von, C. Brinkmann e. a. (ed.): *Handwörterbuch der Sozialwissenschaften.* Stuttgart, 1952. *Beckerath*

Beerling, R. F.: *Het wankele Westen. Nietzsche en de critiek op de Europese cultuur.* Arnhem, 1950. *Beerling* I

Beerling, R. F.: *Uren met Sjestow.* Baarn, 1950. *Beerling* II

Béguin, A. e.a.: *Cinquante années de découverte. Bilan 1900-1950.* Paris, 1950. *Béguin*

Bein, A.: *Theodor Herzl.* Vienna, 1934. *Bein*

Bellamy, E.: *Looking backward, 2000-1887.* London, n.d. *Bellamy*

Benjamin, R.: *Clemenceau dans la retraite.* Paris, 1929. *Benjamin*

Benoist, C.: *Sophismes politiques de ce temps. Etude critique sur les formes, les principes et les procédés de gouvernement.* Paris, 1893. *Benoist* I

Benoist, C.: *L'organisation du suffrage universel. La crise de l'état moderne.* Paris, 1897. *Benoist* II

Benoist, C.: *L'organisation de la démocratie.* Paris, 1900. *Benoist* III

Benoist, C.: *La crise de l'état moderne.* Paris, 1936. *Benoist* IV

Bentley, E.: *The cult of the superman. A study of the idea of heroism in Carlyle and Nietzsche.* London, 1947. *Bentley*

Benveniste, E.: 'Bibliographie des travaux d'Antoine Meillet' in *Bulletin de la Société de linguistique de Paris,* 38 (1937), pp. 43-68. *Benveniste*

Beradt, M.: *Der Richter.* Frankfurt a.Main, 1909. *Beradt*

Bérard, V.: *La révolution turque.* Paris, 1909. *Bérard* I

Bérard, V.: *Révolutions de la Perse.* Paris, 1910. *Bérard* II

Berget, A.: *La route de l'air. Aéronautique. Aviation. Histoire. Théorie. Pratique.* Paris, 1909. *Berget*

Bergmann, E. von: *Die Wirtschaftskrisen. Geschichte der nationalökonomischen Krisentheorien.* Stuttgart, 1895. *Bergmann*

Bergson, H.: *Essai sur les données immédiates de la conscience.* Paris, 1889. *Bergson* I

710

Bergson, H.: *Matière et mémoire. Essai sur la relation du corps à l'esprit.* Paris, 1896. *Bergson* II

Bergson, H.: 'Introduction à la métaphysique' in *Revue de métaphysique et de morale,* 11 (1903), pp. 1–36. *Bergson* III

Bergson, H.: *L'évolution créatrice.* Paris, 1907. *Bergson* IV

Berichte über die Welt-Ausstellung in Paris im Jahre 1900. Berlin, 1902. *Berichte*

Berlage, H. P.: *Amerikaansche reisherinneringen.* Rotterdam, 1913. *Berlage*

Bernal, J. D.: *Science in history.* London, 1954. *Bernal*

Bernhardi, F. von: *Deutschland und der nächste Krieg.* Stuttgart, 1913. *Bernhardi*

Bernheim, E.: *Lehrbuch der historischen Methode und der Geschichtsphilosophie.* Leipzig, 1914. *Bernheim*

Bernstein, E.: *Die Voraussetzungen des Sozialismus und die Aufgaben der Sozial-demokratie.* Stuttgart, 1899. *Bernstein* I

Bernstein, E.: *Wie ist wissenschaftlicher Socialismus möglich?* Berlin, 1901. *Bernstein* II

Bernstein, E.: *Zur Theorie und Geschichte des Socialismus. Gesammelte Abhand-lungen.* 3 vols. Berlin, 1904. *Bernstein* III

Bernstein, E.: *Der Streik. Sein Wesen und sein Wirken.* Frankfurt a.M., 1906. *Bernstein* IV

Bernstein, E.: *Aus den Jahren meines Exils. Erinnerungen eines Sozialisten.* Berlin, 1918. *Bernstein* V

Berth, E.: *Dialogues socialistes.* Paris, 1901. *Berth*

Bertillon, J.: *Essai de statistique comparée du surpeuplement des habitations à Paris et dans les grandes villes européennes.* Paris, 1895. *Bertillon* I

Bertillon, J.: *L'alcoolisme et les moyens de le combattre jugés par l'expérience.* Paris, 1904. *Bertillon* II

Besant, A.: *An autobiography.* London, 1893. *Besant* I

Besant, A.: *Kort begrip der theosofie.* Amsterdam, 1903. *Besant* II

Beveridge, W. H.: *Unemployment. A problem of industry.* London, 1909. *Beveridge*

Bezemer, J. W.: *De Russische revolutie in westerse ogen.* Amsterdam, 1956. *Bezemer*

Bibliographie bouddhique. 31 vols. Paris, 1930–'61. *Bibliographie*

Bielefeld, O.: *Eine neue Ära englischer Sozialgesetzgebung.* Leipzig, 1898. *Bielefeld*

Bier, A.: *Über die Berechtigung des teleologischen Denkens in der praktischen Medizin.* Berlin, 1910. *Bier*

Bland, J. O. P. & E. T. Backhouse: *China under the Empress Dowager.* London, 1914. *Bland*

Blaschko, A.: 'Zur Prostitutionsfrage' in *Berliner klinische Wochenschrift,* 29 (1892), pp. 430–435. *Blaschko* I

Blaschko, A.: *Hygiene der Prostitution und der venerischen Krankheiten.* Jena, 1900. *Blaschko* II

Blatchford, R.: *Merrie England.* London, 1894. *Blatchford* I

Blatchford, R.: *Dismal England.* London, 1899. *Blatchford* II

Bleibtreu, C.: *Revolution der Literatur.* Leipzig, 1886. *Bleibtreu*

Bloch, I.: *Das Sexualleben unserer Zeit in seinen Beziehungen zur modernen Kultur.* Berlin, 1909. *Bloch* I.

Bloch, I. von: *De oorlog en de toekomst.* Haarlem, 1899. *Bloch I. von.*

Bloch, J. von: *Der Krieg.* 6 vols. Berlijn, 1899. *Bloch J. von*

Bloch, J. S.: *Erinnerungen aus meinem Leben.* Vienna, 1922. *Bloch J. S.*

Blocher, H. & J. Landmann: *Die Belastung des Arbeiterbudgets durch den Alkohol-genuss.* Basle, 1903. *Blocher*

Blondel, M.: *L'action. Essai d'une critique de la vie et d'une science de la pratique.* Paris, 1893. *Blondel*

711

Blücher, H.: *Wandervogel. Geschichte einer Jugendbewegung.* 2 vols. Charlottenburg, 1919. *Blücher*

Blum, L.: *Du mariage.* Paris, 1937. *Blum L.*

Blum, O.: *Die Entwicklung des Verkehrs.* Berlin, 1941. *Blum O.*

Boas, F.: *The mind of primitive man.* New York, 1911. *Boas*

Bocheński, I. M.: *Europäische Philosophie der Gegenwart.* Berne, 1947. *Bocheński*

Bocquet, L.: *L'impôt sur le revenu cédulaire et général.* Paris, 1921. *Bocquet*

Bodenheim, N. (thesis): *Handje-plak* in *De Hollandsche revue*, 5 (1900), p. 869. *Bodenheim*

Bøe, A.: *From gothic revival to functional form. A study in Victorian theories of design.* Oslo, 1957. *Bøe*

Bogeng, G. A. E. (Hrsg.): *Geschichte des Sports aller Völker und Zeiten*, 2 vols. Leipzig, 1926-'27. *Bogeng*

Böhm-Bawerk, E. von: *Einige strittige Fragen der Capitalstheorie.* Vienna, 1900. *Böhm*

Böhme, M.: *Tagebuch einer Verlorene. Von einer Toten.* Berlin, 1905. *Böhme*

Bois, J.: *Cours d'occultisme.* Paris, 1893. *Bois I*

Bois, J.: *Les petites religions de Paris.* Paris, 1894. *Bois II*

Bois, J.: *Le satanisme et la magie.* Paris, 1895. *Bois III*

Boissevain, G. M.: 'Die neueste Steuerreform in den Niederlanden im Anschluss an die Finanzgeschichte des Landes seit der Verfassungsrevision im Jahre 1848' in *Finanzarchiv*, II, 2 (1894), pp. 1-328 and 419-704. *Boissevain*

Boivin, E.: *Histoire du journalisme.* Paris, 1949. *Boivin*

Boltzmann, L.: *Vorlesungen über Gastheorie.* 2 vols. Leipzig, 1896-'98. *Boltzmann*

Bon, G. le: *Psychologie des foules.* Paris, 1895. *Bon*

Bonaparte, M., A. Freud, E. Kris (ed.): *Aus den Anfängen der Psychoanalyse.* London, 1950. *Bonaparte*

Bonger, W. A.: *Criminalité et conditions économiques.* Amsterdam, 1905. *Bonger*

Booth, Ch.: *Life and labour.* 2 vols. London, 1889-'91. *Booth*

Borchhardt, J.: *Wie sollen wir unsere Kinder ohne Prügel erziehen?* Berlin, 1919. *Borchhardt*

Bordewijk, F.: *Rood paleis. Ondergang van een eeuw.* Rotterdam, 1936. *Bordewijk*

Borel, H.: *De Chineesche kwestie.* Amsterdam, 1900. *Borel*

Borght, R. van der: *Grundzüge der Sozialpolitik.* Leipzig, 1904. *Borght*

Boring, E. G.: *A history of experimental psychology.* New York, 1929. *Boring*

Bos, G. M.: *Mr. S. van Houten, Analyse van zijn denkbeelden voorafgegaan door een schets van zijn leven.* Purmerend, 1952. *Bos*

Boson, M.: *Léon Walras. Fondateur de la politique économique scientifique.* Lausanne, 1951. *Boson*

Böttger, H.: *Vom alten und neuen Mittelstand.* Berlin, 1901. *Böttger*

Boudier-Bakker, I.: *De moderne vrouw en haar tekort.* Amsterdam, 1922. *Boudier*

Bouglé, C.: *Les sciences sociales en Allemagne. Les méthodes actuelles.* Paris, 1895. *Bouglé I*

Bouglé, C.: 'Méthodologie. Conceptions générales de la science'. Book review of van G. de Martini: 'Delli impossibilità di esistere di una scienza sociologica generale' in *L'année sociologique*, 4 (1899-1900), p. 106. *Bouglé II*

Bouglé, C.: 'Une doctrine idéaliste de la democratie. L'oeuvre d'Henry Michel' in *Revue politique et parlementaire*, 12 (1905), tome 43, p. 562-576. *Bouglé III*

Bouman, L.: *De wetenschappelijke beoefening der psychiatrie.* Kampen, 1907. *Bouman L.*

Bouman, P. J. & W. H.: *De groei van de grote werkstad. Een studie over de bevolking van Rotterdam.* Assen, 1952. *Bouman P. J. I*

Bouman, P. J.: *Revolutie der eenzamen. Spiegel van een tijdperk.* Assen, 1953. *Bouman P. J.* II

Bourgeois, L.: *Solidarité.* Paris, 1896. *Bourgeois* I

Bourgeois, L.: *Essai d'une philosophie de solidarité.* Paris, 1902. *Bourgeois* II

Bourget, L.: *Quelques erreurs et tromperies de la science médicale moderne.* Paris, 1907. *Bourget L.*

Bourget, P.: *Le disciple.* Paris, 1889. *Bourget P.* I

Bourget, P.: *L'amour moderne.* Paris, 1891. *Bourget P.* II

Bourget, P.: *L'étappe.* Paris, 1902. *Bourget P.* III

Bourguin, M.: *Les systèmes socialistes et l'évolution économique.* Paris, 1904. *Bourguin* I

Bourguin, M.: 'Un nouvel essai sur le régime socialiste' in *Revue politique et parlementaire,* 15 (1908), tome 55, pp. 365–391. *Bourguin* II

Bousquet, G. H.: *Essai sur l'évolution de la pensée économique.* Paris, 1927. *Bousquet*

Boutroux, E.: 'La psychologie du mysticisme' in *Revue bleue,* tome XVII (March 1902), pp. 321–327. *Boutroux*

Bracq, J. C.: *France under the republic.* London, 1911. *Bracq*

Braeuer, W.: *Handbuch zur Geschichte der Volkswirtschaftslehre. Ein bibliographisches Nachschlagewerk.* Frankfurt a.Main, 1952. *Braeuer*

Brailsford, H. N.: *The war of steel and gold. A study of the armed peace.* London, 1917. *Brailsford*

Brandenburg, E.: *Die parlementarische Obstruktion.* Dresden, 1904. *Brandenburg*

Brandes, G.: *Hovedströmninger i det 19de aarhundredes litteratur.* 2 vols. Copenhagen, 1872-'73. *Brandes* I

Brandes, G.: *Moderne Geister.* Frankfurt a.Main, 1901. *Brandes* II

Brants, V.: *La petite industrie contemporaine.* Paris, 1902. *Brants*

Bräuer, H. J.: *Die Entwicklung des Nachrichtenverkehrs. Eigenarten, Mittel und Organisation der Nachichtenbeförderung.* Nuremberg, 1957. Bräuer

Braun, A.: *Die Kartelle.* Berlin, 1892. *Braun A.*

Braun, L.: *Die Frauenfrage. Ihre geschichtliche Entwicklung und wirtschaftliche Seite.* Leipzig, 1901. *Braun L.*

Bréal, M.: *Essai de sémantique.* Paris, 1897. *Bréal*

Brentano F.: *Psychologie vom empirischen Standpunkte.* Part 1. Leipzig, 1874. *Brentano F.*

Brentano, L.: *Mein Leben im Kampf um die soziale Entwicklung Deutschlands.*Jena, 1931. *Brentano, L.*

Breysig, K.: *Kulturgeschichte der Neuzeit.* 2 vols. Berlin, 1901. *Breysig* I

Breysig, K.: *Die Geschichte der Menschheit.* Berlin, 1907. *Breysig* II

Breysig, K.: *Der Stufenbau der Weltgeschichte.* Berlin, 1950. *Breysig* III

Bricaud, J.: *J. K. Huysmans et le satanisme, d'après des documents inédits.* Paris, 1913. *Bricaud*

Brieux, E.: *L'évasion. Comédie en trois actes.* Paris, 1897. *Brieux* I

Brieux, E.: *Les avariés.* Paris, 1901. *Brieux* II

Brinkmann, C.: 'Die Aristokratie im kapitalistischen Zeitalter' in *Grundriss der Sozialökonomie,* IX, vol. 1, pp. 22–34. Tübingen, 1926. *Brinkmann* I

Brinkmann, C.: *Gustav Schmoller und die Volkswirtschaftslehre.* Stuttgart, 1937. *Brinkmann* II

Brom, G.: *De nieuwe kruistocht. Drankweergeschiedenis van Rooms Nederland, 1895-1907.* Helmond, 1909. *Brom*

Brooke, E.: *A tabulation of the factory laws of European countries in so far as they relate to the hours of labour and the special legislation for women, young persons and children.* London, 1898. *Brooke*

Brouwer, L. E. J.: *Over de grondslagen der wiskunde.* Amsterdam, 1907. *Brouwer* I
Brouwer, L. E. J.: *Intuïtionisme en formalisme.* Amsterdam, 1912. *Brouwer* II
Brown, A.: *The fate of the middle classes.* London, 1936. *Brown*
Brückner, A.: *Geschichte der russischen Litteratur.* Leipzig, 1905. *Brückner*
Brugmann, K. & B. Delbrück: *Grundriss der vergleichenden Grammatik der indogermanischen Sprachen.* 3 vols. Straatsburg, 1886-1900. *Brugmann*
Brugmans, H.: *Georges de Porto-Riche. Sa vie, son oeuvre.* Amsterdam, 1934. *Brugmans*
Brunetière, F.: *La science et la religion. Réponse à quelques objections.* Paris, 1895. *Brunetière* I
Brunetière, F.: 'Après une visite au Vatican' in *Revue des deux mondes,* 127 (1895), pp. 97-118. *Brunetière* II
Brunschvicg, L.: *Introduction à la vie de l'esprit.* Paris, 1900. *Brunschvicg*
Brusse, M. J.: *Boefje.* Rotterdam, 1903. *Brusse*
Bücher, K.: *Gesammelte Aufsätze zur Zeitungskunde.* Tübingen, 1926. *Bücher*
Bühler, Ch. & H. Hetzer: 'Zur Geschichte der Kinderpsychologie' in *Beiträge zur Problemgeschichte der Psychologie. Festschrift zu K. Bühler's 50. Geburtstag,* pp. 204-224. Jena, 1929. *Bühler Ch.*
Bühler, K.: *Die Krise der Psychologie.* Jena, 1927. *Bühler K.*
Bukharin, N. J.: *Economic theory of the leisure class.* New York, 1927. *Bukharin*
Bülow, B. von: *Denkwürdigkeiten.* 4 vols. Berlin, 1903-'31. *Bülow*
Bunge, G.: *Lehrbuch der physiologischen und pathologischen Chemie.* Leipzig, 1889. *Bunge*
Burdach, K.: *Wissenschaftsgeschichtliche Eindrücke eines alten Germanisten. Festgabe zum 250 jähr. Jubiläum der Weidmannschen Buchhandlung.* Berlin, 1930. *Burdach*
Burks, R. V.: 'Benedetto Croce' in B. E. Schmitt (ed.): *Some historians of modern Europe.* Chicago, 1942, pp. 66-99. *Burks*
Burnand, R.: *La vie quotidienne en France de 1870 à 1900.* Paris, 1947. *Burnand* I
Burnand, R.: *Paris 1900.* Paris, 1951. *Burnand* II
Burnett, F. H.: *Little Lord Fauntleroy.* Leipzig, 1887. *Burnett*
Burnham J.: *The Machiavellians, defenders of freedom.* New York, 1943. *Burnham*
Burns, J.: *The nineteenth century.* London, 1892. *Burns*
Butler, S.: *Evolution old and new.* London, 1879. *Butler*
Butler, S.: *The way of all flesh.* London, 1903. *Butler S.*
Bütschli, O.: *Mechanismus und Vitalismus.* Leipzig, 1901. *Bütschli*
Buxton, C. R.: *Turkey in revolution.* London, 1909. *Buxton*
Buytendijk, F. J. J.: *Oude problemen in de moderne biologie.* Haarlem, 1919. *Buytendijk*
Byrnes, R. F.: *Antisemitism in modern France.* Vol. 1. New Brunswick, 1952. *Byrnes*

Cahen-Salvador, G.: 'La situation matérielle et morale des fonctionnaires' in *Revue politique et parlementaire,* 33 (1926), tome 129, pp. 315-338. *Cahen-Salvador*
Caland, W.: 'Levensberichten van H. Kern' in *Handelingen en levensberichten van de Mij. der Ned. Letterkunde te Leiden (1917-'18),* 11 Levensberichten, pp. 1-30. *Caland*
Cameron, M. E.: *The reform movement in China (1898-1912).* Stanford, 1931. *Cameron*
Carrière, J. C.: *Humour 1900.* Paris, 1963. *Carrière*
Cathrein, V.: *Recht, Naturrecht und positives Recht.* Freiburg, 1901. *Cathrein*
Cauchy, G.: *L'organisation du suffrage politique.* Paris, 1900. *Cauchy*
Cervantes Saavedra, M. de.: *Don Quichote.* Madrid, 1605. *Cervantes*

714

Chamberlain, H. S.: *Die Grundlagen des neunzehnten Jahrhunderts.* 2 vols. Munich, 1899. *Chamberlain*

Chambure, A. de: *A travers la presse.* Paris, 1914. *Chambure*

Chanute, O.: *Progress in flying-machines.* London, 1894. *Chanute*

Chardon, H.: *L'administration de la France.* Paris, 1908. *Chardon*

Charensol, G.: *L'affaire Dreyfus et la troisième république.* Paris, 1930. *Charensol*

Charmont, J.: *'La socialisation du droit'* in *Revue de métaphysique et de morale,* 11 (1903) pp. 380-405. *Charmont* I

Charmont, J.: *Le droit et l'esprit démocratique.* Paris, 1908. *Charmont* II

Charmont, J.: *La renaissance du droit naturel.* Montpellier, 1910. *Charmont* III

Charpentier, A.: *Historique de l'affaire Dreyfus.* Paris, 1933. *Charpentier* I

Charpentier, A.: *Les côtés mystérieux de l'affaire Dreyfus.* Paris, 1937. *Charpentier* II

Chastenet, J.: *Une époque pathétique. La France de M. Fallières.* Paris, 1949. *Chastenet*

Cheyne, T. K.: *Founders of Old Testament criticism.* London, 1893. *Cheyne*

Chirol, V.: *The Middle Eastern question or some political problems of Indian defence.* London, 1903. *Chirol* I

Chirol, V.: *Fifty years in a changing world.* London, 1927. *Chirol* II ✓

Cholodenko, D.: *Die teleologische Betrachtung in der modernen Biologie.* Berne, 1909. *Cholodenko*

Clapham, J. H.: *Economic development of France and Germany (1815-1914).* Cambridge, 1921. *Clapham*

Clarke, A.: *The effects of the factory system.* London, 1899. *Clarke A.*

Clarke, T.: *Northcliffe in history. An intimate study of press power.* London, 1950. *Clarke T.*

Clasen, P. A.: *Der Salutismus. Eine sozialwissenschaftliche Monographie über General Booth und seine Heilsarmee.* Jena, 1913. *Clasen*

Clayton, J.: *The rise and decline of socialism in Great Britain, 1884-1924.* London, 1926. *Clayton*

Clemenceau, G.: *Vers la réparation.* Paris, 1898. *Clemenceau*

Clouard, H.: *Histoire de la littérature française du symbolisme à nos jours.* 2 vols. Paris, 1947-'49. *Clouard*

Clough, S. B. & Ch. W. Cole: *Economic history of Europe.* Boston, 1947. *Clough*

Clyde, P. H.: *The Far East. A history of the impact of the West on Eastern Asia.* New York, 1952. *Clyde*

Coenen, F.: *De Fransche wet ter bescherming van verwaarloosde en mishandelde kinderen.* Amsterdam, 1892. *Coenen*

Cohen, I.: *The Zionist Movement.* London, 1945. *Cohen*

Cohen-Portheim, P.: *Die Entdeckung Europas.* Berlin, 1933. *Cohen-Portheim*

Cohn, G.: 'Ethik und Reaktion in der Volkswirtschaft' in *Jahrbuch für Gesetzgebung, Verwaltung und Volkswirtschaft im Deutschen Reich,* 24 (1900), pp. 839-886. *Cohn G.*

Cohn, H.: 'Das preussische Gesetz betreffend die Warenhaussteuer' in *Archiv für soziale Gesetzgebung und Statistik,* 15 (1900), pp. 529-553. *Cohn H.*

Collier, W. M.: *The trusts.* New York, 1900. *Collier*

Colliez, A.: *Les coalitions industrielles et commerciales d'aujourd'hui. Trusts, cartels, corners.* Paris, 1904. *Colliez*

Colombat, J.: *La fin du monde civilisé. Les prophéties de Vacher de Lapouge.* Paris, 1946. *Colombat*

Colvin, Th.: 'A preliminary note on the outbreak of bubonic plague in Glasgow' in *The lancet,* 87 (1900), II, pp. 762-764. *Colvin*

Compte-rendu analytique, officiel, (du) cinquième congrès socialiste international, tenu à Paris du 23 au 27 septembre 1900. Paris, 1901. *Compte-rendu* I

Compte-rendu sténographique, non officiel, de la version française du cinquième congrès socialiste international, tenu à Paris du 23 au 27 septembre 1900. Cahiers de la quinzaine IV, 2e série. Paris, 1901. Compte-rendu II

Congrès int. d'anthropologie criminelle. Compte rendu des travaux de la 5me session tenue à Amsterdam. Amsterdam, 1901. Congrès.

Conrad, M. G.: Von E. Zola bis G. Hauptmann. Erinnerungen zur Geschichte der Moderne. Leipzig, 1902. Conrad

Cooley, C. H.: Human nature and the social order. New York, 1902. Cooley

Cooper, D.: The rainbow comes and goes. London, 1958. Cooper

Coppée, F.: Le coupable. Paris, 1896. Coppée

Coppersmith, F.: Luchtkastelen der techniek. Avontuur en romantiek in het rijk der techniek. Amsterdam, 1948. Coppersmith

Cordier, H.: Histoire générale de la Chine et de ses relations avec les pays étrangers depuis les temps les plus anciens jusqu'à la chute de la dynastie Mandchoue. 4 vols. Paris, 1920. Cordier

Corelli, M.: The sorrows of Satan or the strange experience of one Geoffry Tempest millionaire. 2 vols. Leipzig, 1896. Corelli

Cornilleau, R.: De Waldeck-Rousseau à Poincaré. Chronique d'une génération (1898-1924). Paris, 1926. Cornilleau

Coste, A.: Les phénomènes psychiques occultes. Etat actuel de la question. Paris, 1895. Coste

Coubertin, P. de: Les batailles de 'l'éducation physique'. Une campagne de 21 ans (1887-1908). Paris, 1909. Coubertin

Coudert, P.: La bourgeoisie et la question sociale. Essai pour la formation d'une 'conscience de classe'. Paris, 1914. Coudert

Couperus, L.: Van oude menschen, de dingen die voorbijgaan. 2 vols. Amsterdam, 1906. Couperus

Couvee, D. H. & A. H. Boswijk: Vrouwen vooruit! The Hague, 1962. Couvee

Craig, A.: The banned books of England. London, 1937. Craig A.

Craig, E. G.: On the art of the theatre. London, 1914. Craig E. G.

Crane, W.: Claims of decorative art. London, 1892. Crane

Croce, B.: Filosofia come scienza dello spirito. 4 vols. Bari, 1902-'17. Croce I

Croce, B.: The philosophy of Giambattista Vico. London, 1913. Croce II

Croce, B.: Materialismo storico ed economia marxistica. Bari, 1941. Croce III

Cronheim, P.: Gedenkboek van de Wagner-vereeniging. Amsterdam, 1934. Cronheim

Crookes, W.: 'Some possibilities of electricity' in The fortnightly review, 51 (1892), pp. 173-181. Crookes

Cudlipp, H.: Publish and be damned. The astonishing story of The Daily Mirror. London, 1953. Cudlipp

Cumberley, E. P.: The history of education. London, 1920. Cumberley

Cumont, F.: Textes et monuments figurés relatifs aux mystères de Mithra, avec une introduction critique par F. Cumont. 2 vols., Brussels, 1895-'99. Cumont I

Cumont, F.: Les mystères de Mithra. Brussels, 1913. Cumont II

Cumont, F.: Les religions orientales dans le paganisme romain. Brussels, 1929. Cumont III

Curel, F. de: La nouvelle idole. Paris, 1895. Curel I

Curel, F. de: La fille sauvage. Paris, 1902. Curel II

Curtis, E.: A history of Ireland. London, 1952. Curtis

Cuvillier, A.: Où va la sociologie française? Avec une étude d'Emile Durkheim sur la sociologie formaliste. Paris, 1953. Cuvillier

Daiches, D.: A critical history of English literature. 2 parts. London, 1960. Daiches

Daim, W.: *Der Mann, der Hitler die Ideen gab. Von den religiösen Verirrungen eines Sektierers zum Rassenwahn des Diktators.* Munich, 1958. *Daim*

Daisy, Princess of Pless: *From my private diary.* Ed. D. Chapman-Huston. London, 1931. *Daisy*

Dangerfield, G.: *The strange death of liberal England (1910–1914).* London, 1936. *Dangerfield*

Daniel, G. E.: *A hundred years of archaeology (1840–1940).* London, 1950. *Daniel*

Daniels, G. W. & H. Campion: *The distribution of national capital.* Manchester, 1936. *Daniels*

Dankmar, G. L.: *Die kulturelle Lage Europas beim Wiedererwachen des modernen Okkultismus.* Leipzig, 1905. *Dankmar*

Dantinne, E.: *L'oeuvre et la pensée de Péladan. La philosophie rosicrucienne.* Brussels, 1948. *Dantinne*

Darcy, Jean: *L'équilibre africain au XXe siècle. La conquête de l'Afrique.* Paris, 1900. *Darcy*

Darwin, C.: *On the origin of species.* London, 1859. *Darwin* I

Darwin, C.: *Biographical sketch of an infant.* London, 1877. *Darwin* II

Daux, G.: *Les étapes de l'archéologie.* Paris, 1942. *Daux*

David-Sauvageot, A.: *Le réalisme et le naturalisme dans la littérature et dans l'art.* Paris, 1899. *David*

Davies, A. E.: *The State in business. The collectivist State in the making.* London, 1920. *Davies*

Davy, G.: *Sociologues d'hier et d'aujourd'hui.* Paris, 1949–'50. *Davy*

Dawson, W. H.: *Social insurance in Germany 1883–1911. Its history, operation, results and a comparison with the National Insurance Act, 1911.* London, 1912. *Dawson*

Déchelette, J.: *Manuel d'archéologie.* 2 vols. Paris, 1908–'15. *Déchelette*

Deesz, G.: *Die Entwicklung des Nietzsche-Bildes in Deutschland.* Würzburg, 1933. *Deesz*

Deflou, J.: *Le sexualisme.* Paris, 1900. *Deflou*

Defoe, D.: *Robinson Crusoe.* London, 1719. *Defoe*

Delafosse, J.: *Psychologie du député.* Paris, 1904. *Delafosse*

Delbrück, B.: *Grundfragen der Sprachforschung. Mit Rücksicht auf W. Wundts Sprachpsychologie erörtert.* Strassbourg, 1901. *Delbrück*

Delfgaauw, B.: *De wijsbegeerte van de 20e eeuw.* Baarn, 1957. *Delfgaauw*

Delhorbe, C.: *L'affaire Dreyfus et les écrivains français.* Paris, 1932. *Delhorbe*

Delitzsch, F.: *Die grosse Täuschung.* 2 vols. Stuttgart, 1921. *Delitzsch*

Del Vecchio, G.: *I presupposti filosofici della nozione del diritto.* Bologna, 1905. *Del Vecchio*

Depelley, J. M.: 'Les cables télégraphiques en temps de guerre' in *Revue des deux mondes,* 157 (1900), pp. 181–201. *Depelley*

Depuis le jour. Encycliek van paus Leo XIII van 8 september 1899 over de vorming der geestelijkheid in Frankrijk. Ecclesia docens serie. Hilversum, 1953. *Depuis le jour.*

Derry T. K. & T. L. Jarrman: *The European world. 1870–1945.* London, 1950. *Derry*

Desachy, P.: *Bibliographie de l'affaire Dreyfus.* Paris, 1905. *Desachy*

Dessoir, M.: *Vom Jenseits der Seele. Die Geheimwissenschaften in kritischer Betrachtung.* Stuttgart, 1918. *Dessoir*

Destrée, J.: *La fin du parlementarisme. Discours.* Brussels, 1901. *Destrée*

Deussen, P.: *Mein Leben.* E. Rosenthal-Deussen (ed.). Leipzig, 1922. *Deussen*

Deventer, C. M. van: *August Kekulé.* Haarlem, 1897. *Deventer*

Deville, G.: *Principes socialistes.* Paris, 1896. *Deville*

717

Dewey, J.: *The school and society*. Chicago, 1900. *Dewey*

Deyssel, L. van: 'De dood van het naturalisme' in *De nieuwe gids*, 6 (1890–'91), vol. 2, pp. 114–122. *Deyssel*

Dickens, Ch.: *American notes*. 2 vols. London, 1842. *Dickens* I

Dickens, Ch.: *Martin Chuzzlewit*. London, 1849. *Dickens* II

Die Not des vierten Standes, von einem Arzte. Leipzig, 1894. *Die Not*

Diehl, K.: *Über Sozialismus, Kommunismus und Anarchismus*. Jena, 1922. *Diehl*

Diesel, E.: *Diesel. Der Mensch, das Werk, das Schicksal*. Hamburg, 1937. *Diesel E.* I

Diesel, E.: *Jahrhundertwende. Gesehen im Schicksal meines Vaters*. Stuttgart, 1949. *Diesel E.* II

Diesel, R.: *Theorie und Konstruktion eines rationellen Wärmemotors*. Berlin, 1893. *Diesel R.*

Dietzgen, J.: *Das Wesen der menschlichen Kopfarbeit*. Berlin, 1869. *Dietzgen*

Dilke, Ch.: *Greater Britain*. London, 1868. *Dilke* I

Dilke, Ch.: *Problems of Greater Britain*. London, 1890. *Dilke* II

Dillen, J. G. van: 'Rivalités économiques. Expansion économique et financière, in *L'Europe du XIXe et du XXe siècle (1870–1914). Problèmes et interprétations historiques*. Vol. II. Milan, 1962. *Dillen*

Dilthey, W.: *Die Jugendgeschichte Hegels*. Berlin, 1905. *Dilthey* I

Dilthey, W.: *Der Aufbau der geschichtlichen Welt*. Berlin, 1910. *Dilthey* II

Dilthey, W.: 'Das achtzehnte Jahrhundert und die geschichtliche Welt' in *Wilhelm Dilthey Gesammelte Schriften*. Vol. 3. Stuttgart, 1962, pp. 209–268. *Dilthey* III

Dimier, L.: *Vingt ans d'Action Française*. Paris, 1926. *Dimier*

Dittrich, O.: *Grundzüge der Sprachpsychologie*. Vol. I. Halle, 1903. *Dittrich*

Döblin, A.: *Arno Holz. Die Revolution der Lyrik. Eine Einführung in sein Werk und eine Auswahl*. Wiesbaden, 1951. *Döblin*

Dolléans, E.: *Histoire du mouvement ouvrier*. 2 vols. Paris, 1946. *Dolléans*

Domela Nieuwenhuis, F.: *Het parlementarisme in zijn wezen en toepassing*. Amsterdam, 1906. *Domela* I

Domela Nieuwenhuis, F.: *Van christen tot anarchist*. 2 vols. Amsterdam, 1910. *Domela* II

Donne, J.: *Poems*. Ed. H. J. C. Grierson. Oxford, 1912. *Donne*

Donos, Ch. de: *Morès, sa vie, sa mort*. Paris, 1899. *Donos*

Dooijes, D.: 'De Nederlandse typografie en de ⟨Jugendstil⟩' in *Forum. Maandblad voor architectuur en gebonden kunst*, 10 (1958), pp. 324–329. *Dooijes*

Dostoyevski, F.: *The brothers Karamazov*, London, 1922. *Dostoyevski*

Doughty, C. M.: *Travels in Arabia deserta*. 2 vols. Cambridge, 1888. *Doughty*

Drachkovitch, M.: *Les socialismes français et allemand et le problème de la guerre (1870–1914)*. Geneva, 1953. *Drachkovitch*

Drews, A.: *Die Christus-Mythe*. Jena, 1909. *Drews*

Driesch, H.: 'Die Lokalisation morphogenetischer Vorgänge. Ein Beweis vitalistisches Geschehens' in *Archiv für Entwicklungsmechanik*, 8 (1899), pp. 35–112. *Driesch* Ia

Driesch, H.: *Die Lokalisation morphogenetischer Vorgänge. Ein Beweis vitalistisches Geschehens*. Leipzig, 1899. *Driesch* Ib

Driesch, H.: *Die organischen Regulationen*. Leipzig, 1901. *Driesch* II

Driesch, H.: *Der Vitalismus als Geschichte und als Lehre*. Leipzig, 1905. *Driesch* III

Driesch, H.: 'Henri Bergson, der biologische Philosoph' in *Zeitschrift für den Ausbau der Entwicklungslehre*, 2 (1908), pp. 48–55. *Driesch* IV

Driesch, H.: *Die Biologie als selbständige Grundwissenschaft*. Leipzig, 1911. *Driesch* V

Driesch, H.: *Geschichte des Vitalismus*. Leipzig, 1922. *Driesch* VI

Driesch, H.: *Lebenserinnerungen. Aufzeichnungen eines Forschers und Denkers in entscheidender Zeit*. (ed.) J. Tétaz-Driesch. Basle, 1951. *Driesch* VII

718

Drucker, P. F.: *Future of industrial man. A conservative approach.* New York, 1942. *Drucker*

Drumont, E.: *La France juive.* 2 vols. Paris, 1886. *Drumont*

Du Bose, W. P.: *Turning points in my life.* London, 1912. *Du Bose*

Dubnow, S.: *Weltgeschichte des jüdischen Volkes von seinen Uranfängen bis zur Gegenwart.* Berlin, 1925. *Dubnow* I

Dubnow, S.: *Mein Leben.* (ed.) E. Hurwicz. Berlin, 1937. *Dubnow* II

Dückershoff, E.: *Wie der englische Arbeiter lebt?* Dresden, 1898. *Dückershoff*

Duguit, L.: *Les transformations du droit public.* Paris, 1921. *Duguit* II

Duguit, L.: *Les transformations générales du droit privé depuis le Code Napoléon.* Paris, 1912. *Duguit* I

Duhamel, G.: *Chronique des Pasquiers.* Paris, 1945. *Duhamel*

Dungen, P. A. van den: *De middenstandsbeweging in Nederland.* Tilburg, 1938. *Dungen*

Durkheim, E.: *Les règles de la méthode sociologique.* Paris, 1895. *Durkheim I*

Durkheim, E.: *Le suicide.* Paris, 1897. *Durkheim* II

Dutrait-Crozon, H.: *Précis de l'affaire Dreyfus.* Paris, 1924. *Dutrait*

Düwell, W.: *Wohlfahrtsplage. Eine eingehende Studie über die sogen. Wohlfahrtsein-richtungen in den verschiedenen Grossbetrieben.* Dortmund, 1903. *Düwell*

Dwelshauvers, G.: *La psychologie française contemporaine.* Paris, 1920. *Dwelshauvers*

Earle, E. M.: *Turkey, the Great Powers and the Bagdad railway. A study in imperialism.* New York, 1923. *Earle* I

Earle (ed.), E. M.: *Modern France. Problems of the Third and Fourth Republics.* Princeton, 1951. *Earle* II

Eberle, J.: *Grossmacht Presse. Enthüllugen für Zeitungsgläubige. Forderungen für Männer.* Vienna, 1920. *Eberle*

Eeden, F. van: *De kleine Johannes.* The Hague, 1887. *Eeden* I

Eeden, F. van: *Van de koele meren des doods. Een verhaal.* Amsterdam, 1900. *Eeden* II

Egerton, G.: *Key-Notes.* London, 1893. *Egerton*

Eggmann, E.: *Der Staat und die Kartelle. Eine international vergleichende Untersuchung.* Zürich, 1945. *Eggmann*

Ehm, A.: *L'éducation nouvelle.* Sélestat, 1937. *Ehm*

Ehrenfels, C. von: 'Ueber ⟨Gestaltqualitäten⟩' in *Vierteljarhrsschift für wissenschaftliche Philosophie,* 14 (1890), pp. 249-292. *Ehrenfels* I

Ehrenfels, C. von: 'Die konstitutive Verderblichkeit der Monogamie und die Unentbehrlichkeit einer Sexualreform' in *Archiv für Rassen-und Gesellschaftsbiologie,* 4 (1907), pp. 803-830. *Ehrenfels* II

Ehrhard, A.: *Henrik Ibsen et le théâtre contemporain.* Paris, 1892. *Ehrhard*

Ehrlich, E.: *Freie Rechtsfindung und freie Rechtswissenschaft.* Leipzig, 1903. *Ehrlich E.*

Ehrlich, P.: 'On immunity with special reference to cell life' in *Proceedings of the royal society of London,* 66 (1900), pp. 424-448. *Ehrlich P.*

Eichthal, E. d': *La liberté individuelle du travail et les menaces du législateur.* Paris, 1908. *Eichthal*

Einiges über Ibsen. Ibsenvereinigung zu Düsseldorf. Berlin, 1909. *Einiges*

Eiselsberg, A. von: *Lebensweg eines Chirurgen.* Innsbruck, 1940. *Eiselsberg*

Elbow, M. H.: *French corporative theory 1789-1948. A chapter in the history of ideas.* New York, 1953. *Elbow*

Elliott, W.: *The life of Father Hecker.* New York, 1891. *Elliott*

Ellis, H. H.: *The criminal.* London, 1890. *Ellis* I

719

Ellis, H. H.: *Studies in the psychology of sex*. Vol. 6. *Sex in relation to society*. Philadelphia, 1919. *Ellis* II

Eltzbacher, P.: *Der Anarchismus*. Berlin, 1900. *Eltzbacher* I

Eltzbacher, P.: *Die Presse als Werkzeug der auswärtigen Politik*. Jena, 1918. *Eltzbacher* II

Ely, R. T.: *Monopolies and trusts*. New York, 1900. *Ely*

Emin, A.: *The development of modern Turkey as measured by its press*. New York, 1914. *Emin*

Emmanuel, M.: *Pelléas et Mélisande*. Paris, 1926. *Emmanuel*

Encyclopaedisch handboek van het moderne denken. Edited by W. Banning *et al*. Arnhem, 1950. *Encyclopaedisch*

Engelman, J.: 'Een monumentale kunst' in *Provinciaal Utrechts Genootschap van Kunsten en Wetenschappen. Verslag van de algemene vergardering gehouden de 25ste mei 1950*, pp. 9-26. Utrecht, 1950. *Engelman*

Ensor, R. C. K.: *The Oxford history of England, 1870-1914*. London, 1936. *Ensor*

Enthoven, F. B.: *Studie over het anarchisme van de daad*. Amsterdam, 1901. *Enthoven*

Esmein, A.: *Eléments de droit constitutionnel francais et comparé*. Paris, 1896. *Esmein*

Esswein, H.: *August Strindberg im Lichte seines Lebens und seiner Werke*. Munich, 1909. *Esswein*

Etcheverry, A.: *L'idéalisme français contemporain*. Paris, 1934. *Etcheverry*

Eucken, R.: *Geschichte und Kritik der Grundbegriffe der Gegenwart*. Leipzig, 1878. *Eucken* I

Eucken, R.: *Thomas von Aquino und Kant. Ein Kampf zweier Welten*. Berlin, 1901. *Eucken* II

Eulalia, H. R. H. the Infanta: *Court life from within*. London, 1915. *Eulalia*

Eymieu, L.: *Le gouvernement de soi-même. Essay de psychologie pratique*. 3 vols. Paris, 1921. *Erymieu*

Fabre, L.: *Connaissaince de la déesse*. Paris, 1920. *Fabre*

Faguet, E.: *Le féminisme*. Paris, 1910. *Faguet* I

Faguet, E.: *Le culte de l'incompétence*. Paris, 1914. *Faguet* II

Fahlbeck, P. E.: *Der Adel Schwedens (und Finlands). Demographische Studie*. Jena, 1903. *Fahlbeck*

Fawcett, E.: *Die Welt des Films*. Zürich, 1930. *Fawcett*

Fehmi, Y.: *La revolution ottomane (1908-'10)*. Paris, 1911. *Fehmi*

Fehr, A. J. A.: *De Franse symbolisten en de muziek*. Groningen, 1960. *Fehr*

Feith, J.: *Een week als vliegmensch*. Amsterdam, 1910. *Feith* I

Feith, J.: *Het boek der sporten*. Amsterdam, 1900. *Feith* II

Fénéon, F.: *Oeuvres*. Paris, 1948. *Fénéon*

Fenton, F.: *The influence of newspaper presentations upon the growth of crime and other anti-social activity*. Chicago, 1911. *Fenton*

Ferester, A.: *Sur la responsabilité dans les crimes*. Paris, 1897. *Ferester*

Fernandez-Azabal, Señora Lilie (Bouton) de: *The countess of Iowa*. New York, 1936. *Fernandez*

Ferri, E.: *Socialismo e scienza positiva. Darwin, Spencer, Marx*, Rome, 1894. *Ferri* I

Ferri, E.: *La justice pénale. Son évolution, ses défauts, son avenir*. Brussels, 1898. *Ferri* II

Ferri, E.: *La force du parlementarisme*. Paris, 1901. *Ferri* III

Fiaux, L.: *La prostitution 'cloitrée'. Les maisons de femmes autorisées par la police, devant la médecine publique. Etude de biologie sociale*. Brussels, 1902. *Fiaux*

Filipetti, G.: *Industrial management in transition*. Chicago, 1947. *Filipetti*

Finck, F. N.: *Der deutsche Sprachbau als Ausdruck deutscher Weltanschauung.* Eight lectures. Marburg, 1899. *Finck*

Finkelstein, L.: *The Jews. Their history, culture and religion.* 2 vols. New York, 1949. *Finkelstein*

Fircks, A. von: *Bevölkerungslehre und Bevölkerungspolitik.* Leipzig, 1898. *Fircks*

Firmin (ps. van A. Loisy): 'La religion d'Israël' in *Revue du clergé français,* 7 (15 October 1900), pp. 337-363. *Firmin*

Fischer, E.: *The passing of the European age. A study of the transfer of Western Civilization and its renewal in other continents.* Cambridge (Mass.), 1948. *Fischer*

Flavius, G.: *Der Kampf um die Rechtswissenschaft.* Heidelberg, 1906. *Flavius*

Flexner, A.: *Prostitution in Europe.* New York, 1919. *Flexner* I

Flexner, A.: *Daniel Coit Gilman, creator of the American type of university.* New York, 1946. *Flexner* II

Flores, A. (ed.): *Henrik Ibsen. A marxist analysis by Engels, Mehring, Plekhanov, Lunacharsky.* New York, 1937. *Flores*

Flügel, J. C.: *A hundred years of psychology (1833-1933).* London, 1933. *Flügel*

Flux, A. W.: Bespreking van J. A. Hobson 'The economics of distribution' in *The economic journal,* 10 (1900), pp. 380-385. *Flux*

Fontaine, Th.: *Effi Briest.* Berlin, 1896. *Fontaine*

Forbes, R. J.: 'Uitvindingen en ontdekkingen' in *Ensie.* Vol. 9. Amsterdam, 1950. *Forbes* I

Forbes, R. J.: *Man the maker. A history of technology and engineering.* New York, 1950. *Forbes* II

Forel, A.: *Die sexuelle Frage.* Munich, 1907. *Forel* I

Forel, A.: *Rückblick auf mein Leben.* Zürich, 1935. *Forel* II

Förster, F. W.: *Jugendlehre.* Berlin, 1906. *Förster* I

Förster, F. W.: *Schule und Charakter.* Zürich, 1908. *Förster* II

Fouillée, A.: *Psychologie du peuple français.* Paris, 1898. *Fouillée* I

Fouillée, A.: *Esquisse psychologique des peuples européens.* Paris, 1902. *Fouillée* II

Fournier, A.: *Le Grand Meaulnes.* Paris, 1914. *Fournier*

Fowler, H. H.: *Municipal finance and municipal enterprise.* London, 1900. *Fowler*

Francastel, P.: *Peinture et société. Naissance et destruction d'un espace plastique. De la Renaissance au cubisme.* Lyon, 1952. *Francastel*

France, A.: *Crainquebille.* Paris, 1904. *France*

Frank, S.: *De Russische wereldbeschouwing.* Amsterdam, 1932. *Frank S.*

Frank, W.: *Nationalismus und Demokratie im Frankreich der dritten Republik (1871-1918).* Hamburg, 1933. *Frank W.*

Fraser, D.: *The short cut to India. The record of a journey along the route of the Baghdad railway.* Edinburgh, 1909. *Fraser* I

Fraser, D.: *Persia and Turkey in revolt.* Edinburgh, 1910. *Fraser* II

Frazer, J. G.: *The golden bough. A study in comparative religion.* 2 vols. *London, 1890.* Frazer

Frenssen, G.: *Hilligenlei.* Berlin, 1908. *Frenssen*

Freund, M.: *Georges Sorel. Der revolutionäre Konservatismus.* Frankfurt a.Main, 1932. *Freund*

Freud, S.: *Die Traumdeutung.* Vienna, 1900. *Freud* I

Freud, S.: *Sammlung kleiner Schriften zur Neurosenlehre; 1893-1906.* Vienna, 1906, *Freud* II

Freud, S.: *Das Unbehagen in der Kultur.* Vienna, 1930. *Freud* III

Freud, S.: 'Die Wilderstände gegen die Psychoanalyse' in *Gesammelte Werke.* Vol. 14, pp. 99-110. London, 1948. *Freud* IV

Freud, S.: 'Selbstdarstellung' in *Gesammelte Werke.* Vol. 14, pp. 31-96. London, 1948. *Freud* V

Freudenthal, H.: 'Trends in modern mathematics' in *I.C.S.U. Review of world sciences*, 4 (1962), pp. 54-61. *Freudenthal*

Fréville, J.: *Zola, semeur d'orages*. Paris, 1952. *Fréville*

Frey, D.: *Gotik und Renaissance als Grundlagen der modernen Weltanschauung*. Augsburg, 1929. *Frey*

Fried, A. H.: *Handbuch der Friedensbewegung*. 2 vols. Berlin, 1913. *Fried*

Friedjung, H.: *Das Zeitalter des Imperialismus, 1884-1914*. 3 vols. Berlin, 1919-'22. *Friedjung*

Friedmann, H. & O. Mann: *Deutsche Literatur im zwanzigsten Jahrhundert*. Heidelberg, 1954. *Friedmann*

Fries, G.: 'De geschiedenis en het tegenwoordig standpunt der luchtscheepvaart en haar gebruik in oorlogstijd' in *Vragen van den dag*, 11 (1896), pp. 548-566. *Fries*

Frischeisen-Köhler, M.: *Moderne Philosophie. Lesebuch zur Einführung in ihre Standpunkte und Probleme*. Stuttgart, 1907. *Frischeisen*

Fritsch, Th.: *Die Stadt der Zukunft*. Leipzig, 1897. *Fritsch*

Frobenius, L.: *Der Ursprung der afrikanischen Kulturen*. Berlin, 1898. *Frobenius I*

Frobenius, L.: *Ein Lebenswerk aus der Zeit der Kulturwende. Dargestellt von seinen Freunden und Schülern*. Leipzig, 1933. *Frobenius II*

Fuchs, E.: *Recht und Wahrheit in unserer beutigen Justiz*. Berlin, 1908. *Fuchs I*

Fuchs, E.: *Illustrierte Sittengeschichte*. Vol. 3. *Das bürgerliche Zeitalter*. Munich, 1912. *Fuchs II*

Fugger: *The glory of the Habsburgs. The memoirs of Princess Fugger*, translated by J. A. Galston. London, 1932. *Fugger*

Fülöp-Miller, R.: *Die Phantasiemaschine. Eine Saga der Gewinnsucht*. Berlin, 1931. *Fülöp*

Funk, C.: *Die Vitamine*. Wiesbaden, 1914. *Funk*

Furness, C.: *The American invasion*. London, 1902. *Furness*

Fyfe, H.: *Northcliffe. An intimate biography*. London, 1930. *Fyfe I*

Fyfe, H.: *Press parade*. London, 1936. *Fyfe II*

Gagliardi, E.: *Bismarck's Entlassung*. 2 vols. Tübingen, 1927-'41. *Gagliardi*

Gallienne, R. de: *The romantic '90s*. London, 1951. *Gallienne*

Galsworthy, J.: *The island pharisees*. London, 1904. *Galsworthy I*

Galsworthy, J.: *The man of property*. London, 1906. *Galsworthy II*

Galton, F.: 'Eugenics: its definition, scope and aims' in *Sociological papers*, 1904, pp. 45-99. London, 1905. *Galton*

Gans, L.: 'Nieuwe kunst. De herleving van de Nederlandse kunstnijverheid' in *Forum. Maandblad voor architectuur en gebonden kunst*, 10 (1958), pp. 314-323. *Gans*

Garofalo, R.: *Di un criterio positivo della penalità*. Naples, 1882. *Garofalo*

Garrison, F. H.: *An introduction to the history of medicine*. Philadelphia, 1917. *Garrison*

Gartmann, H.: *Vlucht in de ruimte*. Amsterdam, 1956. *Gartmann*

Gaulis, G.: *La ruine d'un empire. Abd-ul-Hamid, ses amis et ses peuples*. Paris, 1913. *Gaulis*

Gaupp, R.: Bespreking van S. Freud's 'Ueber Deckerinnerungen' in *Zeitschrift für Psychologie und Physiologie der Sinnesorgane*, 1900, Vol. 23, pp. 233-234. *Gaupp I*

Gaupp, R.: Bespreking van C. Rieger's 'Die Castration in rechtlicher, socialer und vitaler Hinsicht' in *Zeitschrift für Psychologie und Physiologie der Sinnesorgane*, 1900, Vol. 24, pp. 398-400. *Gaupp II*

Gautier, E.: 'Le monde des prisons' in *Archives de l'anthropologie criminelle et des sciences pénales*, 3 (1888), pp. 417-436 en 541-563. *Gautier*

Gayraud, A.: *Les jeunes filles d'aujourd'hui*. Paris, 1914. *Gayraud, A.*

722

Gayraud, H.: *Les démocrates chrétiens*. Paris, 1889. *Gayraud, H.*

Gedenkboek van 'Toonkunst'. Amsterdam, 1929. *Gedenkboek*

Gelber, N. M,: *Zur Vorgeschichte des Zionismus. Judenstaatsprojekte in den Jahren 1695-1845*. London, 1927. *Gelber*

Gelder, G. M. de: *Russische denkers*. Haarlem, 1934. *Gelder*

Genet, L.: *Cinquante ans d'histoire (1900-'50)*. Paris, 1950. *Genet*

Gény, F.: *Méthode d'interprétation et sources en droit privé positif*. Paris, 1899. *Gény*

George, S.: *Der Teppich des Lebens und die Lieder von Traum und Tod mit einem Vorspiel*. Godesberg, 1949. *George*

Gerlach, H. von: *Das Parlament*. Frankfurt a.Main, 1907. *Gerlach*

Gibbs, J. W.: *Elementary principles in statistical mechanics*. New York, 1902. *Gibbs*

Gide, A.: *Les nourritures terrestres*. Paris, 1897. *Gide A.* I

Gide, A.: *L'immoraliste*. Paris, 1902. *Gide A.* II

Gide, A.: *Les cahiers et les poésies d'André Walter*. Paris, 1952. *Gide A.* III

Gide, C.: 'L'école nouvelle' in *Quatre écoles d'économie sociale*. Geneva, 1890. *Gide C.* I

Gide, C. & C. Rist: *Histoire des doctrines économiques depuis les physiocrates jusqu'à nos jours*. Paris, 1909. *Gide C.* II

Giedion, S.: *Ruimte, tijd en bouwkunst*. Amsterdam, 1954. *Giedion*

Ginneken, J. van: *Principes de linguistique psychologique. Essai de synthèse*. Amsterdam, 1907. *Ginneken*

Gitermann, V.: *Die historische Tragik der sozialistischen Idee*. Zürich, 1938. *Giterman*

Gobineau, J. A. de: *Essay sur l'inégalité des races humaines*. 4 vols. Paris, 1853-'55. *Gobineau*

Goblot, E.: *La barrière et le niveau. Etude sociologique sur la bourgeoisie française moderne*. Paris, 1925. *Goblot*

Godkin, E. L.: *Unforeseen tendencies of democracy*. London, 1898. *Godkin*

Goekoop-de Jong van Beek en Donk, C.: *Hilda van Suylenburg*. 2 vols. Amsterdam, 1897. *Goekoop*

Goes, F. van der: *De arbeidskracht*. Amsterdam, 1900. *Goes* I

Goes, F. van der: *Grootkapitaal en kleinhandel. Bijdrage tot de kennis der middenstandspolitiek*. Amsterdam, 1902. *Goes* II

Goeverneur, J. J. A.: *Reizen en avonturen van mijnheer Prikkebeen*. Amsterdam, 1858. *Goeverneur*

Gohier, U.: *L'armée contre la nation*. Paris, 1899. *Gohier*

Goldmann, P.: *Vom Rückgang der deutschen Bühne*. Frankfurt a.Main, 1908. *Goldman*

Goltz, C. von der: *Das Volk in Waffen*. Berlin, 1884. *Goltz*

Goncourt, E. & J. de: *Germinie Lacerteux*. Paris, 1864. *Goncourt*

Gonnard, R.: *L'émigration européenne au XIXe siècle*. Paris, 1906. *Gonnard* I

Gonnard, R.: *Histoire des doctrines économiques*. Paris, 1930. *Gonnard* II

Goodwin, M.: *Nineteenth century opinion*. London, 1952. *Goodwin*

Gorter, H.: *Mei. Een gedicht*. Amsterdam, 1889. *Gorter*

Gossel, F.: *Gebildetheorie und Universalismus in der theoretischen Nationalökonomie. Eine methodologisch vergleichende Untersuchung der Theorien von Fr. von Gottl-Ottlilienfeld und O. Spann*. Hamburg, 1933. *Gossel*

Gothein, E.: *Die Aufgaben der Kulturgeschichte*. Leipzig, 1889. *Gothein*

Gottl, F.: *Die Herrschaft des Wortes. Einleitende Aufsätze*. Jena, 1901. *Gottl*

Gottl-Ottlilienfeld, F. von: *Wirtschaft als Leben*. Jena, 1925. *Gottl-Ottlilienfeld*

Gougenot des Mousseaux, H. R.: *Le juif, le judaïsme et la judaïsation des peuples chrétiens*. Paris, 1869. *Gougenot*

Graaf, J. de: *De anthropologie in de moderne Russische wijsgerige theologie*. Assen, 1949. *Graaf*

723

Graebner, F.: *Methode der Ethnologie*. Heidelberg, 1911. *Graebner*

Graf, A.: *Schülerjahre*. Berlin, 1912. *Graf*

Graham, P. A.: *Rural exodus. The village and the town*. London, 1892. *Graham*

Grand-Carteret, J.: *La voiture de demain. Histoire de l'automobilisme. (Passé, présent, techniques, caricatures.)* Paris, 1898. *Grand*

Gratama, J.: *Dr. H. P. Berlage, bouwmeester*. Rotterdam, 1925. *Gratama*

Grave, J.: *La société mourante et l'anarchie*. Paris, 1893. *Grave*

Grävéll, A.: *Zum Kampfe gegen die Waarenhäuser!* Dresden, 1899. *Grävéll*

Graves, R.: *Goodbye to all that*. London, 1929. *Graves*

Green, F. C.: *The mind of Proust*. Cambridge, 1949. *Green F. C.*

Green, T. H.: *The works of T. H. Green*, ed. R. L. Nettleship. 3 vols. Vol 2, pp. 335–553: 'Lectures on the principles of political obligation'. London, 1885–'88. *Green T. H.*

Griffith, C. J.: *Crime and criminals*. Los Angeles, 1910. *Griffith*

Grosclaude, E.: *Une politique européenne. La France, la Russie, l'Allemagne et la guerre au Transvaal*. Paris, 1899. *Grosclaude*

Grossmann, E.: 'Die Kunst der Besteuerung' in *Festgabe Fritz Fleiner*, pp. 299–320. Zürich, 1937. *Grossmann*

Grothe, L. H.: *Auf türkischer Erde. Reisebilder und Studien*. Berlin, 1903. *Grothe*

Grotjahn, A.: *Der Alkoholismus nach Wesen, Wirkung und Verbreitung*. Leipzig, 1898. *Grotjahn* I

Grotjahn, A.: *Soziale Pathologie*. Berlin, 1912. *Grotjahn* II

Grotjahn, A.: *Erlebtes und Erstrebtes. Erinnerungen eines sozialistischen Arztes*. Berlin, 1922. *Grotjahn,* III

Grottewitz, C.: *Die Naturgeschichte im 19. Jahrhundert*. Berlin, 1902. *Grottewitz*

Grousset, R.: *Bilan de l'histoire*. Paris, 1946. *Grousset*

Grove, G.: *A dictionary of music and musicians (1450-1880), by eminent writers*. 4 vols. London, 1879–'89. *Grove*

Gruber, G. B.: *Der Alkoholismus. Ein Grundriss*. Leipzig, 1911. *Gruber G. B.*

Gruber, M.: 'Der oesterreich. Gesetzentwurf zur Bekämpfung der Trunkenheit' in *Archiv für soziale Gesetzgebung und Statistik*, 1 (1888), pp. 293–319. *Gruber M.*

Gruyter, W. J. de: *Het werk van Käthe Kollwitz*. The Hague, 1931. *Gruyter*

Guilbert, Y.: *La chanson de ma vie. Mémoires*. Paris, 1927. *Guilbert*

Gumplowicz, L.: *Grundriss der Soziologie*. Vienna, 1905. *Gumplowicz*

Gurian, W.: *Die politischen und sozialen Ideen des französischen Katholizismus 1789-1914*. Mönchengladbach, 1929. *Gurian*

Gurlitt, L.: *Der Deutsche und seine Schule*. Berlin, 1906. *Gurlitt*

Gurvitch, G.: *La sociologie au XXe siècle*. 2 vols. Paris, 1947. *Gurvitch*

Gusdorf, G.: *Mémoire et personne*. 2 vols. Paris, 1951. *Gusdorf*

Guth, H.: *Die Schnelligkeit im Eisenbahnpersonenverkehr*. Zürich, 1948. *Guth*

Guttzeit, J.: *Schamgefühl, Sittlichkeit und Anstand, besonders in geschlechtlicher Hinsicht*. Dresden, 1909. *Guttzeit*

Guyau, J. M.: *Esquisse d'une morale sans obligation ni sanction*. Paris, 1885. *Guyau* I

Guyau, J. M.: *L'irreligion de l'avenir. Etude de sociologie*. Paris, 1886. *Guyau* II

Guyot, Y. & S. Lacroix: *Etude sur les doctrines sociales du christianisme*. Paris, 1873. *Guyot* I

Guyot, Y.: *Le bilan social et politique de l'église*. Paris, 1901. *Guyot* II

Haeckel, E.: *Die Welträthsel. Gemeinverständliche Studien über monistische Philosophie*. Bonn, 1899. *Haeckel* I

Haeckel, E.: *Kunstformen der Natur*. 2 vols. Leipzig, 1899-1904. *Haeckel* II

Haftmann, W.: *Malerei im 20. Jahrhundert*. 2 vols. Munich, 1954–'55. *Haftmann*

Hahn, E. (Hrsg.): *Die Pädagogik der Gegenwart in Selbstdarstellungen.* 2 vols. Leipzig, 1926-'27. *Hahn*

Hahnloser, H. R.: 'Félix Vallotton' in *Hauptwerke des Kunstmuseums Winterhur,* pp. 121-137. Winterthur, 1949. *Hahnloser*

Haines, C. G.: *The revival of natural law concepts. A study of the establishment and of the interpretation of limits on legislatures with special reference to the development of certain phases of American constitutional law.* Cambridge (Mass.), 1930. *Haines*

Hakkî bey Bâbân Zâdé, I.: 'De Stamboul à Bagdad. Notes d'un homme d'état turc' in *Revue du monde musulman,* 14 (1911), pp. 185-296. *Hakkî*

Haldane, J. S.: *Mechanism, life and personality. An examination of the mechanistic theory of life and mind.* London, 1913. *Haldane*

Hale, O. J.: *Germany and the diplomatic revolution. A study in diplomacy and the press (1904-'06).* Philadelphia, 1931. *Hale*

Halévy, D.: *La république des ducs.* Abbeville, 1937. *Halévy*

Hall, G. S.: *Founders of modern psychology.* New York, 1912. *Hall* I

Hall, G. S.: *Aspects of child life and education.* New York, 1921. *Hall* II

Hall, G. S.: *Life and confessions of a psychologist.* New York, 1923. *Hall* III

Hallgarten, G. W. F.: *Imperialismus vor 1914.* 2 vols. Munich, 1951. *Hallgarten*

Halma, F.: 'De natuurlijke historie der misdadigers en het stelsel van Lombroso' in *Vragen van den dag,* 8 (1893), pp. 668-677. *Halma*

Hamilton, F.: *The vanished pomps of yesterday.* London, 1937. *Hamilton*

Hamon, A. F. A.: *Psychologie de l'anarchiste-socialiste.* Paris, 1895. *Hamon A. F. A.*

Hamon, G.: *Les assurances sociales en Europe.* Paris, 1900. *Hamon G.*

Hansen, G.: *Die drei Bevölkerungsstufen. Ein Versuch, die Ursachen für das Blühen und Altern der Völker nachzuweisen.* Munich, 1899. *Hansen*

Hanstein, A. von: *Das jüngste Deutschland.* Leipzig, 1901. *Hanstein*

Hardy, T.: *Tess of the D'Urbervilles.* 3 vols. London, 1891-'92. *Hardy* I

Hardy, T.: *Jude the obscure.* London, 1896. *Hardy* II

Harmsen, G. J.: *Blauwe en rode jeugd.* Assen, 1961. *Harmsen*

Harnack, A. von: *Das Wesen des Christentums.* Leipzig, 1900. *Harnack* I

Harnack, A. von: *Lehrbuch der Dogmengeschichte.* 3 vols. Tübingen, 1931. *Harnack* II

Haspels, G. F.: *De weerloosheid. Een hoofdstuk van levensleer.* Amsterdam, 1901. *Haspels*

Hauptmann, G.: *Vor Sonnenaufgang. Soziales Drama.* Berlin, 1889. *Hauptmann* I

Hauptmann, G.: *Die Weber.* Berlin, 1892. *Hauptmann* II

Hauptmann, G.: *Hannele's Himmelfahrt.* III

Hauriou, M.: 'Notes sur ⟨le cons.⟩ d'état, 13 janvier 1899' in *Recueil Sirey,* 20 (1898-1900), vol. 3, pp. 54-58. Paris, 1906. *Hauriou*

Hayes, C. J. H.: *A generation of materialism. 1871-1900.* New York, 1941. *Hayes* I

Hayes, C. J. H.: *The historical evolution of modern nationalism.* New York, 1949. *Hayes* II

Heard, G.: *Morals since 1900. Twentieth century histories.* London, 1950. *Heard*

Hébert, M.: *Le divin. Expériences et hypothèses. Etudes psychologiques.* Paris, 1907. *Hébert*

Hecker, J. F.: *Russian sociology.* London, 1934. *Hecker*

Hedenström, A. von: *Geschichte Russlands von 1878 bis 1918.* Stuttgart, 1922. *Hedenström*

Heidelberger Professoren aus dem 19. Jahrhundert. Festschrift der Universität. 2 vols. Heidelberg, 1903. *Heidelberger*

Heiler, F.: *Der Vater des katholischen Modernismus, Alfred Loisy (1857-1940).* Munich, 1947. *Heiler*

725

Heindel, R. H.: *The American impact on Great Britain, 1898-1914. A study of the United States in world history.* Philadelphia, 1940. *Heindel*
Heldt, H. L.: *Deutsche Bibliographie des Buddhismus.* Munich, 1916. *Heldt*
Helfferich, K.: *Deutschlands Volkswohlstand, 1888-1913.* Berlin, 1915. *Helfferich* I
Helfferich, K.: *Georg von Siemens. Ein Lebensbild aus Deutschlands grosser Zeit.* 3 vols. Berlin, 1923. *Helfferich* II
Heller, E.: *The disinherited mind.* New York, 1959. *Heller E.*
Heller, Th. (Hrsg.): *Enzyklopädisches Handbuch des Kinderschutzes und der Jugendfürsorge.* 2 vols. Leipzig, 1911. *Heller Th.*
Hellpach, W.: *Nervosität und Kultur.* Berlin, 1902. *Hellpach* I
Hellpach, W.: *Die geistigen Epidemien.* Frankfurt a.Main, 1906. *Hellpach* II
Hellpach, W.: *Die geopsychischen Erscheinungen.* Leipzig, 1911. *Hellpach* III
Hellpach, W.: *Mensch und Volk der Groszstadt.* Stuttgart, 1939. *Hellpach* IV
Helmolt, H. F. (ed.): *Weltgeschichte.* Leipzig, 1899-1907. *Helmolt*
Hemmeter, J. C.: 'The U.S. Army Yellow Fever commission of 1900 and the discovery of the transmission of yellow fever' in *Master minds in medicine.* New York, 1927, pp. 297-336. *Hemmeter* I
Hemmeter, J. C.: *Master minds in medicine.* New York, 1927. *Hemmeter* II
Henderson, L. J.: *The fitness of the environment.* London, 1913. *Henderson*
Hennig, R.: *Bahnen des Weltverkehrs.* Leipzig, 1909. *Hennig*
Heppenstall, R.: *Léon Bloy.* Cambridge, 1954. *Heppenstall*
Herderschee, D.: 'Schoolverpleging' in *Vooruitgang op medisch en verplegingsgebied in de laatste 25 jaar. Herdenkingsbundel bij 25 jaar Tijdschrift voor ziekenverpleging.* Amsterdam, 1916, pp. 158-163. *Herderschee*
Herkner, H.: 'John Ruskin als Sozialreformer' in *Neue deutsche Rundschau,* 12 (1901), 225-237. *Herkner* I
Herkner, H.: 'Der Kampf um das sittliche Werturteil in der Nationalökonomie' in *Jahrbuch für Gesetzgebung, Verwaltung und Volkswirtschaft im Deutschen Reich,* 36 (1912), pp. 515-555. *Herkner* II
Herkner, H.: 'Gedächtnisrede auf Gustav von Schmoller' in *Verhandlungen des Vereins für Sozialpolitik in Regensburg,* 1919, 159 (1920), pp. 11-22. Munich, 1920, *Herkner* III
Hermann, E.: *Berthold Delbrück. Ein Gelehrtenleben aus Deutschlands grosser Zeit.* Jena, 1923. *Hermann*
Hermans, L. M.: *Krotten en sloppen. Een onderzoek naar de woningtoestand te Amsterdam.* Amsterdam, 1901. *Hermans*
Herre, P.: *Kulturgeschichte des Krieges.* Leipzig, 1916. *Herre*
Herrfahrdt, H.: *Das Problem der berufsständischen Vertretung von der französischen Revolution bis zur Gegenwart.* Stuttgart, 1921. *Herrfahrdt*
Hertwig, O.: *Die Entwicklung der Biologie im 19. Jahrhundert.* Jena, 1900. *Hertwig* I
Hertwig, O.: *Das Werden der Organismen.* Jena, 1916. *Hertwig* II
Hertwig, O.: *Zur Abwehr des ethischen, des sozialen, des politischen Darwinismus.* Jena, 1918. *Hertwig* III
Hervieu, P.: *Peints par eux-memes.* Paris, n.d. *Hervieu*
Herzl, Th.: *Der Judenstaat.* Vienna, 1896. *Herzl* I
Herzl, Th.: *Gesammelte zionistische Werke.* 5 vols. Tel Aviv, 1934-'35. *Herzl* II
Herzog, W.: *Der Kampf einer Republik. Die Affäre Dreyfus. Dokumente und Tatsachen.* Zürich, 1934. *Herzog*
Hess, M.: *Rom und Jerusalem. Die letzte Nationalitätsfrage.* Leipzig, 1862. *Hess*
Hesse, H.: *Unterm Rad.* Berlin, 1905. *Hesse*
Het vraagstuk van den godsdienst. Ontbinding of evolutie. Beantwoord door de grootste denkers ter wereld. Met een inleiding van F. Charpin. Amsterdam, 1908. *Het vraagstuk*

Hewart, G. (Lord Bury): *The new despotism.* New York, 1929. *Hewart*

Heyd, U.: *Foundations of Turkish nationalism. The life and teachings of Ziya Gökalp.* London, 1950. *Heyd*

Heijermans, H.: *Op hoop van zegen.* Amsterdam, 1901. *Heijermans*

Heymans, G.: *Die Gesetze und Elemente des wissenschaftlichen Denkens.* Leipzig, 1905. *Heymans*

Hichtum, N. van (S. M. D. Troelstra-Bokma de Boer): *Afke's tiental. Een schets uit het Friesche arbeidersleven.* Groningen, 1903. *Hichtum*

Hilbert, D.: *Grundlagen der Geometrie.* Göttingen, 1899. *Hilbert*

Hilferding, R.: *Das Finanzkapital. Eine Studie über die jüngste Entwicklung des Kapitalismus.* Vienna, 1920. *Hilferding*

Hilsenbeck, W.: *Die Deckung der Kosten des Krieges in Südafrika von 1899–1902 auf Seite Englands.* Thesis, Munich, 1904. *Hilsenbeck*

Hilton-Young, W.: *Italian left. A short history of political socialism in Italy.* London, 1949. *Hilton*

Himer, K.: *Geschichte der Hamburg-Amerika Linie im 6. Jahrzehnt ihrer Entwicklung, 1897–1907.* Hamburg, 1907. *Himer*

Hindus, M.: *The Proustian vision.* New York, 1954. *Hindus*

Hinneberg, P. (Hrsg.): *Geschichte der christlichen Religion mit Einleitung: die israelitisch-jüdische Religion.* Berlin, 1909. *Hinneberg*

Hinte, E. van: *Kapitalistische crises. Een beschouwing over het karakter der groote economische storingen van de laatste eeuw.* Amsterdam, 1924. *Hinte*

Hintze, H.: 'Jean Jaurès und die materialistische Geschichtstheorie' in *Archiv für Sozialwissenschaft und Sozialpolitik,* vol. 68, Tübingen 1933, pp. 194–218. *Hintze*

Hirt, H.: *Der indogermanische Ablaut, vornehmlich in seinem Verhältnis zur Betonung.* Strassbourg, 1900. *Hirt*

Hitchcock, H. R.: *Architecture. Nineteenth and twentieth centuries.* London, 1958. *Hitchcock*

Hitze, F.: *Schutz dem Handwerk!* Paderborn, 1883. *Hitze*

Hobson, J. A. & A. F. Mummery: *The physiology of industry.* London, 1889. *Hobson* I

Hobson, J. A.: *The evolution of modern capitalism. A study of machine production.* London, 1894. *Hobson* II

Hobson, J. A.: *Problems of poverty. An inquiry into the industrial condition of the poor.* London, 1896. *Hobson* III

Hobson, J. A.: *Economics of distribution.* New York, 1900. *Hobson* IV

Hobson, J. A.: *Imperialism. A study.* London, 1904. *Hobson* V

Hobson, J. A.: *Confessions of an economic heretic.* London, 1938. *Hobson* VI

Hodges, H. A.: *Wilhelm Dilthey. An introduction.* London, 1944. *Hodges*

Hoek, K. van: *Kruger days. Reminiscences of W. J. Leyds.* London, 1939. *Hoek*

Hoffmann, E.: *Lebenserinnerungen aus einer Wendezeit der Heilkunde. I. Wollen und Schaffen 1868–1932.* Hanover, 1948. *Hoffmann*

Hofmannsthal, H. von: *Jedermann.* Berlin, 1911. *Hofmannsthal* I

Hofmannsthal, H. von: *Prosa.* H. Steiner (ed.). 4 vols. Frankfurt a.Main, 1951–'56. *Hofmannsthal* II

Hohenlohe-Schillingsfuerst, C. zu: *Denkwürdigkeiten.* F. Curtius (ed.). 2 vols. Stuttgart, 1906. *Hohenlohe*

Höhle, T.: *Franz Mehring. Sein Weg zum Marxismus, 1869–1891.* Leipzig, 1956. *Höhle*

Hole, H. M.: *The making of Rhodesia.* London, 1926. *Hole*

Holland, B.: *Baron F. von Hügel. Selected letters, 1896–1924.* London, 1924. *Holland*

Holz, A.: *Das Buch der Zeit. Lieder eines Modernen.* Zürich, 1886. *Holz* I

Holz, A.: *Die Kunst. Ihr Wesen und ihre Gesetze.* Berlin, 1891. *Holz* II

727

Holz, A.: *Phantasus.* 2 vols. Berlin, 1898-'99. *Holz* III
Holz, A.: *Revolution der Lyrik.* Berlin, 1899. *Holz* IV
Holz, A.: *Briefe. Eine Auswahl.* A. Holz en M. Wagner (ed.). Munich, 1949. *Holz* V
Holz, A.: *Werke.* (ed.) Wilhelm Emrich & Anita Holz. 6 vols. Neuwied, 1961. *Holz* VI
Honigmann, G.: *Ärztliche Lebensfragen und ihre moderne Lösung. Für Ärzte und Laien.* Wiesbaden, 1913. *Honigmann*
Hoppe, H.: *Die Thatsachen über den Alkohol.* Berlin, 1904. *Hoppe*
Horrix, P.: 'De eigenschap van medegevoel' in *Vragen van den dag,* 17 (1902), pp. 351-363. *Horrix*
Hoskins, H. L.: *British routes to India.* New York, 1928. *Hoskins*
Hours, A.: *Essai sur la légitimité du droit de coalition. Les grèves en 1900 en France et à l'étranger.* Paris, 1903. *Hours*
House, F. N.: *The development of sociology.* New York, 1936. *House*
Houtin, A.: *Histoire du modernisme catholique.* Paris, 1913. *Houtin*
Howard, E.: *Tomorrow: a peaceful path to real reform.* London, 1898. *Howard*
Howe, Q.: *World history of our own times. I. From the turn of the century to the 1918 armistice.* New York, 1949. *Howe*
Höweler, C.: *Inleiding tot de muziekgeschiedenis.* Amsterdam, 1947. *Höweler*
Huber, F. C.: *Die Kartelle. Ihre Bedeutung für die Sozial-, Zoll- und Wirtschaftspolitik.* Stuttgart, 1903. *Huber*
Hugenholtz, F. W. N.: *Het parlement der godsdiensten.* Rotterdam, 1893. *Hugenholtz*
Huizinga, J.: *Over studie en waardering van het boeddhisme.* Haarlem, 1903. *Huizinga* I
Huizinga, J.: *Herfsttij der middeleeuwen. Studie over levens- en gedachtenvormen der 14e en 15e eeuw in Frankrijk en de Nederlanden.* Haarlem, 1919. *Huizinga* II
Huizinga, J.: *Leven en werk van Jan Veth.* Haarlem, 1927. *Huizinga* III
Huizinga, J.: *De mensch en de beschaving.* Amsterdam, 1946. *Huizinga* IV
Huizinga, J. H.: 'The bloodless revolution' in *The Fortnightly,* 171 (1952), new series, pp. 255-261 and pp. 335-341. *Huizinga J. H.*
Humphrey, R.: *Georges Sorel. Prophet without honor. A study in anti-intellectualism.* Cambridge (Mass.), 1951. *Humphrey*
Hunningher, B.: *Toneel en werkelijkheid.* Rotterdam, 1947. *Hunningher*
Huret, J.: *Enquête sur la question sociale en Europe.* Paris, 1896. *Huret* I
Huret, J.: *Enquête sur la grève et l'arbitrage obligatoire.* Paris, 1901. *Huret* II
Huret, J.: *Enquête sur l'évolution littéraire.* Paris, 1901. *Huret* III
Husserl, E.: *Logische Untersuchungen.* 2 vols. Halle, 1901-'02. *Husserl*
Huston (D. Chapman): *The private diaries of Daisy Princess of Pless, 1873-1914.* London, 1950. *Huston*
Huxley, E.: *White man's country. Lord Delamere and the making of Kenya.* London, 1935. *Huxley*
Huysmans, J. K.: *A rebours.* Paris, 1885. *Huysmans* I
Huysmans, J. D.: *Là-bas.* Paris, 1891. *Huysmans* II
Hymans, I. H.: 'Geschiedenis der rechtswetenschap' in *Geschiedenis der wetenschappen.* Vol. 2, pp. 150-187. Baarn, 1917. *Hymans*

Il programma dei Modernisti. Risposta all' enciclica di Pio X. Rome, 1907. *Il programma*
Ipsen, G.: *Sprachphilosophie der Gegenwart.* Berlin, 1930. *Ipsen*
Isay, R.: *Panorama des expositions universelles.* Paris, 1937. *Isay*
Israëls, H. L.: *Nederlandsche gids op de Parijsche tentoonstelling in 1900.* Amsterdam, 1900. *Israëls*

Jackson, H.: *The eighteen nineties. A review of art and ideas at the close of the century.* London, 1950. *Jackson H.*

Jackson, T. A.: *Dialectics. The logic of marxism and its critics. An essay in exploration.* London, 1936. *Jackson T. A.*

Jacobs, A. H.: *Herinneringen.* Amsterdam, 1924. *Jacobs*

Jacobsen, J. P.: *Fru Marie Grubbe. Interieurer fra det syttende aarhundrede.* Copenhagen, 1876. *Jacobsen*

Jahn, J. (ed.) *Die Kunstwissenschaft der Gegenwart in Selbstdarstellungen.* Leipzig, 1924. *Jahn*

James, H.: *What Maisie knew.* London, 1898. *James H.*

James, W.: *Principles of psychology.* 2 vols. London, 1890. *James W.* I

James, W.: *Varieties of religious experience.* London, 1902. *James W.* II

James, W.: *Pragmatism. A new name for some old ways of thinking.* London, 1907. *James W.* III

Janet, P.: *État mental des hystériques: les stigmates mentaux.* Paris, 1893. *Janet* I

Janet, P. (red.): *Quatrième congrès international de psychologie. Compte rendu des séances et textes des mémoires.* Paris, 1901. *Janet* II

Jarowslawski, E.: *Aus der Geschichte der Kommunistischen Partei der Sowjetunion.* Vol. 1. Berlin, 1930. *Jarowslawski*

Jaspers, K.: *Nietzche. Einführung in das Verständnis seines Philosophierens.* Berlin, 1950. *Jaspers* I

Jaspers, K.: *Strindberg und van Gogh. Versuch einer pathographischen Analyse unter vergleichender Heranziehung von Swedenborg und Hölderlin.* Munich, 1950. *Jaspers* II

Jaurès, J.: *Idéalisme et matérialisme dans la conception de l'histoire. Conférence de Jean Jaurès et réponse de Paul Lafargue.* Lille, 1895. *Jaurès* I

Jaurès, J.: *Les deux méthodes. Conférence par Jean Jaurès et Jules Guesde.* Lille, 1900. *Jaurès* II

Jaurès, J.: *L'organisation socialiste de la France. L'armée nouvelle.* Paris, 1911. *Jaurès* III

Jeans, J. S.: *Trusts, pools and corners as affecting commerce and industry.* London, 1894. *Jeans*

Jellinek, G.: *System der subjektiven öffentlichen Rechte.* Freiburg, 1892. *Jellinek* I

Jellinek, G.: *Die Erklärung der Menschen- und Bürgerrechte.* Leipzig, 1896. *Jellinek* II

Jellinek, G.: *Allgemeine Staatslehre.* Berlin, 1900. *Jellinek* III

Jenks, J. W.: *The trust problem. Facts regarding large private corporations and the conditions affecting them.* New York, 1900. *Jenks*

Jevons, W. S.: *The coal question.* London, 1865. *Jevons*

Jhering, R. von: *Der Zweck im Recht.* 2 vols. Leipzig, 1877-'83. *Jhering*

Joël, K.: *Philosophenwege. Ausblicke und Rückblicke.* Berlin, 1901. *Joël* I

Joël, K.: *Antibarbarus.* Jena, 1914. *Joël* II

Joël, K.: *Die philosophische Krisis der Gegenwart.* Leipzig, 1922. *Joël* III

Joël, K.: *Wandlungen der Weltanschauung.* 2 vols. Tübingen, 1928-'34. *Joël* IV

Johnson, J.: *The Gothenburg system of public-house licensing. What it is and how it works.* London, 1893. *Johnson*

Johnston, R. F.: *Twilight in the forbidden city.* London, 1934. *Johnston*

Jones, E.: *Sigmund Freud. Life and work.* 3 vols. London, 1953-'57. *Jones E.*

Jones, K.: *Fleet Street and Downing Street.* London, 1920. *Jones K.*

Jones, R.: *A life in Reuters.* London, 1951. *Jones R.*

Joran, Th.: *Le mensonge du féminisme.* Paris, 1905. *Joran* I

Joran, Th.: *Autour du féminisme.* Paris, 1908. *Joran* II

Jordaan, L. J.: *Dertig jaar film.* Rotterdam, 1932. *Jordaan*

Josselin de Jong, J. P. B.: 'In memoriam C. C. Uhlenbeck' in *Lingua,* 3 (1952), pp. 243-269. *Josselin*

Joyce, J. A.: *World in the making. The story of international cooperation.* New York, 1953. *Joyce*

Kadt, J. de: *Georges Sorel. Het einde van een mythe.* Amsterdam, 1938. *Kadt*

Kafka, F.: *Der Prozess. (The Trial)* Berlin, 1935. *Kafka*

Kalff, J.: *André Antoine.* Haarlem, 1901. *Kalff*

Kalthoff, A.: *An der Wende des Jahrhunderts.* Berlin, 1898. *Kalthoff*

Kampffmeyer, H.: *Die Gartenstadtbewegung.* Leipzig, 1913. *Kampffmeyer H.*

Kampffmeyer, P.: 'Historisches und Theoretisches zur social-demokratischen Revisions-bewegung' in *Sozialistische Monatshefte*, 6 (1902), pp. 345–354. *Kampffmeyer P. I*

Kampffmeyer, P.: *Wandlungen in der Theorie und Taktik der Sozialdemokratie.* Munich, 1904. *Kampffmeyer P. II*

Kandinsky, W.: *Über das Geistige in der Kunst, insbesondere in der Malerei.* Munich, 1912. *Kandinsky*

Kantorowicz, H. U.: *Rechtwissenschaft und Soziologie.* Tübingen, 1911. *Kantorowicz*

Kaplun-Kogan, W. W.: *Die jüdischen Wanderbewegungen in der neuesten Zeit (1880–1914).* Bonn, 1919. *Kaplun*

Kaufmann, W.: *Nietzsche: philosopher, psychologist, antichrist.* New York, 1959. *Kaufmann*

Kautsky, K.: 'Der Alkoholismus und seine Bekämpfung' in *Die neue Zeit*, 9 (1891), pp. 1–8, 46–55, 77–89 and 105–116. *Kautsky I*

Kautsky, K.: *Der Parlamentarismus, die Volksgesetzgebung und die Sozialdemokratie.* Stuttgart, 1893. *Kautsky II*

Kautsky, K.: 'Was will und kann die materialistische Geschichtsauffassung leisten?' in *Die neue Zeit*, 15 (1896–'97), pp. 228–238. *Kautsky III*

Kautsky, K.: *Bernstein und das sozialdemokratische Programm.* Stuttgart, 1899. *Kautsky IV*

Kautsky, K.: *Sozialismus und Kolonialpolitik.* Berlin, 1907. *Kautsky V*

Kayser, J.: *The Dreyfus affair.* London, 1931. *Kayser*

Kelles-Krauz, C. von: *Die Sociologie im 19. Jahrhundert.* Berlin, 1902. *Kelles*

Kern, H.: *Geschiedenis van het Buddisme in Indië.* Haarlem, 1882–'84. *Kern*

Kerschensteiner, G.: *Begriff der Arbeitsschule.* Leipzig, 1928. *Kerschensteiner*

Kessler, H.: *Walther Rathenau. Sein Leben und sein Werk.* Berlin, 1928. *Kessler*

Ketting, P.: *Claude-Achille Debussy.* Amsterdam, 1941. *Ketting*

Key, E.: *Barnets aarhundrede.* 2 vols. Stockholm, 1900. *Key I*

Key, E.: *De ethiek van liefde en huwelijk.* Leiden, 1904. *Key II*

Key, E.: *De vrouwenbeweging.* Leiden, 1909. *Key III*

Keynes, J. M.: *The economic consequences of the peace.* London, 1920. *Keynes*

Kidd, B.: *Social evolution.* London, 1894. *Kidd I*

Kidd, B.: *Control of the tropics.* New York, 1898. *Kidd II*

Kingsley, C.: *Alton Locke, tailor and poet.* Leipzig, 1857. *Kingsley*

Kirk, R. A.: *The conservative mind. From Burke to Santayana.* Chicago, 1953. *Kirk*

Kjellén, R.: *Stormakterna.* Stockholm, 1905. *Kjellén*

Klein, A.: *Le mouvement néochrétien dans la littérature contemporaine.* Paris, 1892. *Klein*

Kleinberg, A.: *Die europäische Kultur der Neuzeit. Umrisslinien einer Sozial- und Geistesgeschichte.* Leipzig, 1931. *Kleinberg*

Kleinwächter, F.: *Die Kartelle. Ein Beitrag zur Frage der Organisation der Volks-wirtschaft.* Innsbruck, 1883. *Kleinwächter*

Knuttel, G.: *De Nederlandse schilderkunst van Van Eyck tot Van Gogh.* Amsterdam, 1938. *Knuttel*

Koch, L.: *Die Schattenseiten unserer Tagespresse.* Bremerhaven, 1892. *Koch*

Kohler, J.: *Moderne Rechtsprobleme.* Leipzig, 1907. *Kohler J.*

Köhler, W.: *Gestalt psychology. An introduction to new concepts in modern psy-chology.* New York, 1947. *Köhler W.*

Kohn-Bramstedt, E.: *Aristocracy and the middle classes in Germany. Social types in German literature, 1830–1900.* London, 1937. *Kohn*

Kovvalewski, M. M.: *Sowremennye sotsiologi.* St. Petersburg, 1905. *Kovvelewski*

Krabbe, H.: *Die Lehre der Rechtssouveränität. Beitrag zur Staatslehre.* Groningen, 1906. *Krabbe* I

Krabbe, H.: *De moderne staatsidee.* The Hague, 1915. *Krabbe* II

Kracauer, S.: *Von Caligari bis Hitler. Ein Beitrag zur Geschichte des deutschen Films.* Hamburg, 1958. *Kracauer*

Kraepelin, E.: *Compendium der Psychiatrie.* Leipzig, 1883. *Kraepelin*

Krafft-Ebing, R. von: *Psychopathia sexualis.* Stuttgart, 1886. *Krafft*

Krausse, A.: *China in decay. The story of a disappearing Empire.* London, 1900. *Krausse*

Kress, W.: *Aviatik. Wie der Vogel fliegt und wie der Mensch fliegen wird.* Vienna, 1905. *Kress*

Kropotkin, P.: *Paroles d'un révolté.* Paris, 1885. *Kropotkin* I

Kropotkin, P.: *In Russian and French prisons.* London, 1887. *Kropotkin* II

Kropotkin, P.: *La morale anarchiste.* Paris, 1889. *Kropotkin* III

Kropotkin, P.: *La grande révolution.* Paris, 1893. *Kropotkin* IV

Kropotkin, P.: *Fields, factories and workshops or industry combined with agriculture and brainwork with manual work.* London, 1898. *Kropotkin* V

Kropotkin, P.: *Memoirs of a Revolutionist,* London, 1906. *Kropotkin* VI

Kropotkin, P.: *Mutual Aid. A Factor of Evolution.* London, 1902. *Kropotkin* VII

Kropotkin, P.: *La grande révolution, 1789–1793.* Paris, 1909. *Kropotkin* VIII

Kropotkin, P.: *La science moderne et l'anarchie.* Paris, 1913. *Kropotkin* IX

Krose, H. A.: 'Der Selbstmord im 19. Jahrhundert, nach seiner Verteilung auf Staaten und Verwaltungsbezirke' in *Ergänzungshefte zu den Stimmen aus Maria Laach,* 90. Freiburg i.Br., 1906. *Krose* I

Krose, H. A.: 'Die Ursachen der Selbstmordhäufigkeit' in *Ergänzungshefte zu den Stimmen aus Maria Laach,* 91. Freiburg i.Br., 1906. *Krose* II

Kruif, P. de: *Microbe hunters.* London, 1927. *Kruif* I

Kruif, P. de: *The male hormone.* New York, 1945. *Kruif* II

Kübel, J.: *Geschichte des katholischen Modernismus.* Tübingen, 1909. *Kübel*

Kuczynski, J.: *Short history of labour conditions under industrial capitalism.* IV. *France 1700 to the present day.* London, 1946. *Kuczynski J.* I

Kuczynski, J.: *Die Geschichte der Lage der Arbeiter unter dem Industrie-Kapitalismus.* Vol. 1. Berlin, 1947. *Kuczynski J.* II

Kuczynski, J.: *Studien zur Geschichte des deutschen Imperialismus.* II *Propaganda-organisationen des Monopolkapitals.* Berlin, 1950. *Kuczynski J.* III

Kuczynski, J.: *Studien zur Geschichte des deutschen Imperialismus.* I *Monopole und Unternehmerverbände.* Berlin, 1952. *Kuczynski J.* IV

Kuczynski, R.: *Arbeitslohn und Arbeitszeit in Europa und Amerika 1870–1909.* Berlin, 1913. *Kuczynski R.*

Kühnhagen, O.: *Die Einheitsschule im In- und Auslande.* Gotha, 1919. *Kühnhagen*

Kuringer, P.: *Johann Strauss.* Haarlem, 1952. *Kuringer*

Kutter, H.: *Sie müssen.* Zürich, 1904. *Kutter*

Kuyper, A.: *Evolutie* (address). Amsterdam, 1899. *Kuyper*

Kuypers, K.: 'Cultuur- en geschiedenisfilosofie' in *Ensie.* Vol. 1, pp. 145–165. Amsterdam, 1946. *Kuypers*

Labriola, A.: *Del materialismo storico: delucidazione preliminare.* Rome, 1896. *Labriola*

Lafitte, P.: *Lettres d'un parlementaire.* Paris, 1894. *Lafitte*

Lagarde, P. de: *Deutsche Schriften.* Göttingen, 1903. *Lagarde*

Lagrange, M. J.: *M. Loisy et le modernisme. A propos des 'Mémoires'.* Juvisy, 1932.
   Lagrange
Lamb, Ch. & M.: *Tales from Shakespeare.* Leipzig, 1863. *Lamb*
Lamprecht, K.: *Deutsche Geschichte.* 24 vols. Berlin, 1891–1913. *Lamprecht* I
Lamprecht, K.: *Alte und neue Richtungen in der Geschichtswissenschaft.* 2 vols.
   Berlin, 1896. *Lamprecht* II
Lamprecht, K.: *Die kulturhistorische Methode.* Berlin, 1900. *Lamprecht* III
Lamprecht, K.: *Zur jüngsten deutschen Vergangenheit.* 2 vols. Berlin, 1902–'04.
   Lamprecht IV
Lamprecht, K.: *Moderne Geschichtswissenschaft.* Freiburg, 1905. *Lamprecht* V
Lamprecht, K.: *Americana. Reiseeindrücke, Betrachtungen, geschichtliche Gesamtan-
   sichten.* Freiburg, 1906. *Lamprecht* VI
Lamprecht, K.: *Kindheitserinnerungen.* Gotha, 1918. *Lamprecht* VII
Lang, P. H.: *Music in Western Civilization.* London, 1940. *Lang*
Lange, Chr. L.: 'Histoire de la doctrine pacifique et de son influence sur le développe-
   ment du droit international' in *Recueil des cours de l'Académie de Droit Inter-
   national,* 1926, vol. 3, pp. 171–426. *Lange Chr. L.*
Lange, F. A.: *Geschichte des Materialismus und Kritik seiner Bedeutung in der
   Gegenwart.* Leipzig, 1896. *Lange, F. A.*
Lange, V.: *Modern German literature: 1870–1940.* London, 1945. *Lange V.*
Langer, W. L. (ed.): *Encyclopedia of world history.* New York, 1947. *Langer* I
Langer, W. L.: *The diplomacy of imperialism (1890–1902).* Cambridge, 1951. *Langer* II
Lapauze, H. e.a.: *Le guide de l'exposition de 1900.* Paris, 1900. *Lapauze*
Laski, H. (ed.): *A century of municipal progress.* London, 1935. *Laski* I
Laski, H. J.: *Parliamentary government in England. A commentary.* London, 1938.
   Laski II
Laur, F.: *De l'accaparement. Essai doctrinal.* 3 vols. Paris, 1900–'05. *Laur*
Laurentius, Dr.: *Kropotkins Morallehre und deren Beziehungen zu Nietzsche.* Dresden,
   1896. *Laurentius*
Laveleye, E. de: 'Le régime parlementaire et la démocratie' in *Revue des deux mondes,*
   54 (1882), pp. 824–850. *Laveleye*
Lavollée, R.: *Les classes ouvrières en Europe. Etudes sur leur situation matérielle et
   morale.* 3 vols. Paris, 1884–'96. *Lavollée*
Lavrin, J.: *Ibsen. An approach.* London, 1950. *Lavrin*
Lawrence, D. H.: *The white peacock.* London, 1911. *Lawrence*
Lazare, B.: *L'antisémitisme. Son histoire et ses causes.* Paris, 1894. *Lazare* I
Lazare, B.: *Une erreur judiciaire.* Brussels, 1897. *Lazare* II
Lebius, R.: 'Der americanische Cigarettentrust in Dresden' in *Sozialistische Monat-
   shefte,* 6 (1902), pp. 131–138. *Lebius*
Lecat, M.: *Bibliographie de M. Maeterlinck.* Brussels, 1939. *Lecat* I
Lecat, M.: *Le Maeterlinckisme.* Brussels, 1941. *Lecat* II
Lecky, W. E.: *Democracy and liberty.* 2 vols. London, 1896. *Lecky*
Legoyt, A.: *Du progrès des agglomérations urbaines et de l'émigration rurale en
   Europe et particulièrement en France.* Paris, 1870. *Legoyt*
Lehmann-Russbüldt, O.: *Die blutige Internationale der Rüstungsindustrie.* Hamburg,
   1930. *Lehmann*
Lejeune, R.: *Robert Musil. Eine Würdigung.* Zürich, 1942. *Lejeune*
Lekkerkerker, E. C.: *Reformatories for women in the U.S.A.* Groningen, 1931.
   Lekkerkerker
Lemcke, J.: 'Die Vorgeschichte und gegenwärtige Gestaltung des französischen
   Steuersystems' in *Finanzwissenschaftliche und volkswirtschaftliche Studien,*
   ed. K. Bräuer. Heft 8. Jena, 1927. *Lemcke*
Lenin V. I.: *Materialism and empirio-criticism,* London, 1928. *Lenin I*

732

Lenin V. I.: *Imperialism: the highest stage of capitalism*, London, 1933. *Lenin II*

Lenning, H. F.: *The Art Nouveau*. The Hague, 1951. *Lenning*

Lenz, J.: *Die Zweite Internationale und ihr Erbe (1889-1929). Beiträge zur Geschichte der Arbeiterbewegung*. Vol. 2. Hamburg, 1930. *Lenz*

Leon, D.: *Ruskin, the great Victorian*. London, 1949. *Leon*

Leroux, E.: *Bibliographie méthodique du pragmatisme américain, anglais et italien*. Paris, 1922. *Leroux*

Lessing, J.: *Das halbe Jahrhundert der Weltausstellungen*. Berlin, 1900. *Lessing*

Letourneau, Ch.: 'Une impératrice chinoise' in *Revue internationale de sociologie*, 8 (1900), pp. 481-487. *Letourneau*

Lettere di un prete modernista. Rome, 1908. *Lettere*

Levasseur, E.: *Questions ouvrières et industrielles en France sous la Troisième République*. Paris, 1907. *Levasseur*

Levy, H.: *Monopole, Kartelle und Trusts in ihren Beziehungen zur Organisation der kapitalistischen Industrie*. Jena, 1909. *Levy*

Lévy-Bruhl, L.: *Les fonctions mentales dans les sociétés inférieures*. Paris, 1910. *Lévy-Bruhl*

Lewin, E.: *The German road to the east. An account of the 'Drang nach Osten' and the Teutonic aims in the Near and Middle East*. London, 1916. *Lewin*

Lewinsohn, R. (Morus): *Der Mann im Dunkel. Die Lebensgeschichte Sir Basil Zaharoffs, des mysteriösen Europäers*. Berlin, 1929. *Lewinsohn I*

Lewinsohn, R.: *Les profiteurs de guerre à travers les siècles*. Paris, 1935. *Lewinsohn II*

Lewis, R. & A. Maude: *The English middle classes*. London, 1950. *Lewis*

Lexis, W.: Review of K. Wicksell: 'Über Wert, Kapital und Rente nach den neueren nationalökonomischen Theorien' (Jena 1893) in *Jahrbuch für Gesetzgebung, Verwaltung und Volkswirtschaft im Deutschen Reich*, 19 (1895), pp. 332-337. *Lexis*

Leyds, W. J.: *Het insluiten van de Boerenrepublieken*. 2 vols. Amsterdam, 1914. *Leyds*

Leyret, H.: *Lettres d'un coupable. Précédées d'un portrait du commandant Walsin-Esterhazy*. Paris, 1898. *Leyret I*

Leyret, H.: *Les nouveaux jugements du président Magnaud*. Paris, 1903. *Leyret II*

Liebknecht, K.: *Militarismus und Antimilitarismus unter besonderer Berücksichtigung der internationalen Jugendbewegung*. Leipzig, 1907. *Liebknecht*

Liefmann, R.: *Die Unternehmerverbände (Konventionen, Kartelle). Ihr Wesen und ihre Bedeutung*. Freiburg i.Br., 1897. *Liefmann I*

Liefmann, R.: *Die Allianzen, gemeinsame monopolistischen Vereinigungen der Unternehmer und Arbeiter in England*. Jena, 1900. *Liefmann II*

Liefmann, R.: *Kartelle und Trusts*. Stuttgart, 1905. *Liefmann III*

Lifschitz, F.: *Die historische Schule der Wirtschaftswissenschaft*. Berne, 1914. *Lifschitz*

Ligt, B. de: *Vrede als daad*. 2 vols. Arnhem, 1931-'33. *Ligt*

Ligthart, J. & H. Scheepstra: *Nog bij moeder*. Groningen, 1904-'05. *Ligthart*

Lindeboom, J.: *Geschiedenis van het vrijzinnig protestantisme*. Vol. 3. Assen, 1935. *Lindeboom*

Lindow, E.: *Freiherr Marschall von Bieberstein als Botschafter in Konstantinopel 1897-1912*. Danzig, 1934. *Lindow*

Lippincott, B. E.: *Victorian critics of democracy*. Minneapolis, 1938. *Lippincott*

Liszt, F. von: *Der Zweckgedanke im Strafrecht*. Marburg, 1883. *Liszt*

Livezey, W. E.: *Mahan on seapower*. Norman (Oklahoma), 1947. *Livezey*

Lloyd, W. E. B.: *A hundred years of medicine*. London, 1936. *Lloyd*

Löbl, E.: *Kultur und Presse*. Leipzig, 1903. *Löbl*

Locy, W. A.: *Biology and its makers*. New York, 1908. *Locy*

Loewe, H.: *Paul Ehrlich, Schöpfer der Chemotherapie*. Stuttgart, 1950. *Loewe*

733

Loeser, N.: *Richard Wagner.* Haarlem, 1948. *Loeser*

Loisy, A.: *La religion d'Israël.* Lyon, 1901. *Loisy* I

Loisy, A.: *L'évangile et l'église.* Paris, 1902. *Loisy* II

Loisy, A.: *Mémoires pour servir à l'histoire religieuse de notre temps.* 3 vols. Paris, 1930-'31. *Loisy* III

Lombroso, C. & E. Ferrero: *La donna delinquenta, la prostituta e la donna normale.* Turin, 1893. *Lombroso* I

Lombroso, C.: *L'antisémitisme.* Paris, 1899. *Lombroso* II

Longstaff, G. B.: 'Rural depopulation' in *Journal of the Royal Statistical Society*, 56 (1893), pp. 380-433. *Longstaff*

Loos, A.: *Trotzdem. Gesammelte Aufsätze, 1900-1930.* Innsbruck, 1931. *Loos*

Lorentz, H. A.: 'De door prof. Röntgen ontdekte stralen' in *De gids*, 60 (1896), Vol. 14., pp. 510-528. *Lorentz* I

Lorentz, H. A.: 'Thermodynamica' in *Lessen over theoretische natuurkunde*. Vol. 4. Leiden, 1921. *Lorentz* II

Lorenz, O.: *Lehrbuch der gesamten wissenschaftlichen Genealogie.* Berlin, 1898. *Lorenz*

Loria, A.: *Die Soziologie. Ihre Aufgabe, ihre Schulen und ihre neuesten Fortschitte.* Jena, 1901. *Loria*

Lossky, N. O.: *History of Russian philosophy.* New York, 1951. *Lossky*

Lotz, A.: *Geschichte des deutschen Beamtentums.* Berlin, 1906-'09. *Lotz*

Louis, P.: *Histoire du socialisme en France, 1789-1945.* Paris, 1950. *Louis*

Lowe, B. E.: *International protection of labor.* New York, 1921. *Lowe*

Lowie, R. H.: *The history of ethnological theory.* New York, 1937. *Lowie*

Lozinsky, E.: 'Das religiöse Problem in Socialismus' in *Sozialistische Monatshefte*, 6 (1902), pp. 123-131. *Lozinsky*

Lublinski, S.: *Die Bilanz der Moderne.* Berlin, 1904. *Lublinski*

Luckhurst, K. W.: *The story of exhibitions.* London, 1951. *Luckhurst*

Lukács, G.: 'Zur Soziologie des modernen Dramas' in *Archiv für Sozialwissenschaft und Sozialpolitik*, 38 (1914), pp. 303-345 and pp. 662-706. *Lukács* I

Lukács, G.: *Thomas Mann, Auf der Suche nach dem Bürger.* Berlin, 1953. *Lukács* II

Lukács, G.: *Die Zerstörung der Vernunft.* Berlin, 1954. *Lukács* III

Lukas, J.: *Der Schulzwang. Ein Stück moderner Tyrannei.* Munich, 1866. *Lukas* I

Lukas, J.: *Die Presse. Ein Stück moderner Versimpelung.* Regensburg, 1867. *Lukas* II

Lütgert, W.: *Das Ende des Idealismus im Zeitalter Bismarcks.* Gütersloh, 1930. *Lütgert*

Luxemburg, R.: *Miliz und Militarismus.* Leipzig, 1899. *Luxemburg* I

Luxemburg, R.: 'Die sozialistische Krise in Frankreich' in *Die neue Zeit*, 19 (1900-'01), 1, pp. 494-499, 516-525, 548-558, 619-631 and 676-688. *Luxemberg* II

Luxemburg, R.: *Die Akkumulation des Kapitals. Ein Beitrag zur ökonomischen Erklärung des Imperialismus.* Berlin, 1913. *Luxemburg* III

Lysen, A.: *History of the Carnegie foundation and of the Peace Palace at the Hague.* Leiden, 1934. *Lysen*

Lysis, (E. Letailleur): *Contre l'oligarchie financière en France.* Paris, 1908. *Lysis*

McCabe, J.: *A rationalist encyclopedia. A book of reference on religion, philosophy, ethics and science.* London, 1950. *McCabe*

MacDonald, J. R.: *Socialism and society.* London, 1906. *MacDonald*

McDougall, W.: *An introduction to social psychology.* London, 1908. *McDougall* I

McDougall, W.: *An outline of abnormal psychology.* London, 1926. *McDougall* II

Mach, E.: *Beiträge zur Analyse der Empfindungen.* Jena, 1886. *Mach*

Mackay, J. H.: *The anarchists. A picture of civilization at the close of the nineteenth century.* N. Y. 1891. *Mackay*

734

MacKenzie, F. A.: *The American invaders*. London, 1902. *MacKenzie F. A.* I
MacKenzie, F. A.: *The mystery of the Daily Mail, 1896-1921*. London, 1921. *MacKenzie F. A.* II
Mackenzie, J. S.: *An introduction to social philosophy. Lectures 1889*. London, 1890. *Mackenzie J. S.*
Mackenzie, K. R.: *The English Parliament*. London, 1950. *Mackenzie, K. R.*
Mackintosh, R.: *From Comte to Benjamin Kidd. The appeal to biology or evolution for human guidance*. London, 1899. *Mackintosh*
MacMillan, G.: *Honours for sale. The strange story of Maundy Gregory*. London, 1955. *MacMillan*
Madsen, S. T.: Sources of Art Nouveau. Oslo, 1956. *Madsen*
Maeterlinck, M.: La princesse maleine. Brussels, 1890. *Maeterlinck*
Mahan, A. T.: *The influence of sea power upon history, 1660-1783*. London, 1890. *Mahan*
Mahler, A.: *Gustav Mahler. Erinnerungen und Briefe*. Amsterdam, 1940. *Mahler*
Mainländer, Ph. (Ph. Batz): *Die Philosophie der Erlösung*. Berlin, 1876. *Mainländer*
Maitron, J.: *Histoire du mouvement anarchiste en France (1880-1914)*. Paris, 1952. *Maitron*
Malewitch, K.: *Die gegenstandslose Welt*. Munich, 1928. *Malewitch*
Mallock, W. H. : *Aristocracy and evolution*. London, 1898. *Mallock*
Malon, B.: *Le socialisme intégral*. 2 vols. Paris, 1890-'91. *Malon*
Malot, H.: Sans famille. 2 vols. Paris, 1878. *Malot*
Mandel, E.: *Traité d'économie marxiste*. 2 vols. Paris, 1962. *Mandel*
Mandelbaum, M.: *The problem of historical knowledge. An answer to relativism*. New York, 1938. *Mandelbaum*
Mandere, H. Ch. G. J. van der: *De vredesbeweging en hare geschiedenis*. Leiden, 1928. *Mandere*
Mann, H.: *Der Untertan*. Leipzig, 1918. *Mann H.* I
Mann, H.: *Sieben Jahre (1921-1928). Chronik der Gedanken und Vorgänge*. Berlin, 1929. *Mann H.* II
Mann, Th.: *Buddenbrooks. Verfall einer Familie*. Berlin, 1901. *Mann Th.* I
Mann, Th.: *Tod in Venedig*. Berlin, 1913. *Mann Th.* II
Mann, Th.: *Freud und die Zukunft*. Vienna, 1936. *Mann Th.* III
March, A. C.: *A Buddhist bibliography*. London, 1935. *March*
Marett, R. R.: *Threshold of religion*. London, 1909. *Marett*
Marholm, L.: *Zur Psychologie der Frau*. Berlin, 1897. *Marholm* I
Marholm, L.: *Das Buch der Frauen*. Berlin, 1899. *Marholm* II
Maritain, J.: *La philosophie Bergsonienne*. Paris, 1913. *Maritain*
Marr, W.: *Der Sieg des Judenthums über das Germanenthum*. Berne, 1873. *Marr*
Marro, A.: *La pubertà studiata nell' uomo e nella donna*. Turin, 1897. *Marro*
Marshall, A.: *Principles of economics*. London, 1890. *Marshall*
Martin du Gard, R.: *L'été 1914*. Paris, 1922-'28. *Martin*
Marty, A.: *Nachgelassene Schiften*. O. Funke (ed.). Berne, 1950. *Marty*
Marx, K.: *Zur Kritik der politischen Ökonomie*. Berlin, 1859. *Marx*
Masaryk, Th. G.: *Der Selbstmord als sociale Massenerscheinung der modernen Civilisation*. Vienna, 1881. *Masaryk* I
Masaryk, Th, G.: *Die philosophischen und sociologischen Grundlagen des Marxismus*. Vienna, 1899. *Masaryk* II
Masaryk, Th, G.: *Zur russischen Geschichts- und Religionsphilosophie. Soziologische Skizzen*. Jena, 1913. *Masaryk* III
Maspero, G.: *Histoire ancienne des peuples de l'Orient*. Paris, 1875. *Maspero* I
Maspero, G.: *Histoire ancienne des peuples d'Orient classique*. 3 vols. Paris, 1894-'99. *Maspero* II

735

Masterman, C. F. G.: *The condition of England.* London, 1909. *Masterman*

Mauthner, F.: *Beiträge zu einer Kritik der Sprache.* 2 vols. Stuttgart, 1901-'02. *Mauthner* I

Mauthner, F.: *Die sprache.* Frankfurt a.Main, 1907. *Mauthner* II

Maxwell, J. C.: *A treatise on electricity and magnetism.* Vol. I. Oxford, 1873. *Maxwell*

May, M.: *Zehn Arbeiter-Budgets. Ein Beitrag zur Frage der Arbeiterwohlfahrts-Einrichtungen.* Berlin, 1891. *May* I

May, M.: *Wie der Arbeiter lebt.* Berlin, 1897. *May* II

Mayer, G.: *Friedrich Engels. Eine Biographie.* 2 vols. The Hague, 1934. *Mayer*

Mayr, G. von: *Die Pflicht im Wirtschaftsleben.* Tübingen, 1900. *Mayr*

Mayreder, R.: *Zur Kritik der Weiblichkeit. Essays.* Jena, 1905. *Mayreder*

Mead, G. H.: *Movements of thought in the nineteenth century.* Chicago, 1936. *Mead G. H.*

Mead, M.: *Male and female.* London, 1950. *Mead M.*

Mehring, F.: *Kapital und Presse. Ein Nachspiel zum Falle Lindau.* Berlin, 1891. *Mehring* I

Mehring, F.: 'Die Neukantianer' in *Die neue Zeit,* 18 (1899-1900) 11, pp. 33-37. *Mehring* II

Mehring, F.: *Geschichte der deutschen Sozialdemokratie.* 4 vols. Stuttgart, 1919. *Mehring* III

Mehring, F.: *Gesammelte Schriften und Aufsätze.* 10 vols. Berlin, 1929-1933. *Mehring* IV

Meier-Graefe, J.: *Impressionisten.* Munich, 1907. *Meier* I

Meier-Graefe, J.: *Vincent van Gogh.* Munich, 1922. *Meier* II

Meillet, A.: 'Nécrologie. Ferdinand de Saussure' in *Annuaire de l'Ecole Pratique des Hautes Etudes (1913-1914).* pp. 115-123. *Meillet* I

Meillet, A.: *Linguistique historique et linguistique générale.* 2 vols. Paris, 1921-'36. *Meillet* II

Meiner, F. (ed.): *Die Volkswirtschaftslehre der Gegenwart in Selbstdarstellungen.* Leipzig, 1924. *Meiner*

Mélanges de linguistique offerts à Ferdinand de Saussure. Paris, 1908. *Mélanges*

Mellquist, J.: 'François Kupka: Om de absoluutheid in de schilderkunst' in *Elseviers Weekblad,* 27 September 1952, p. 25. *Mellquist*

Mendes da Costa, M. B.: *Toneelherinneringen.* Leiden, 1900. *Mendes*

Mengelberg, R.: *50 jaar Concertgebouw, 1888-1938.* Amsterdam, 1938. *Mengelberg*

Menger, A.: *Das Recht auf den vollen Arbeitsertrag in geschichtlicher Darstellung.* Stuttgart, 1886. *Menger* I

Menger, A.: *Das bürgerliche Recht und die besitzlosen Volksklassen. Eine Kritik des Entwurfs eines bürgerlichen Gesetzbuches für das Deutsche Reich.* Tübingen, 1890. *Menger* II

Menger, A.: *Über die socialen Aufgaben der Rechtswissenschaft.* Vienna, 1895. *Menger* III

Menne, B.: *Krupp, Deutschlands Kanonenkönig.* Zürich, 1937. *Menne*

Merezjkowski: *Christos i Antichrist.* 3 vols. Berlin, 1922. *Merezjkowski*

Merlino, S.: *Pro e contro il socialismo.* Milan, 1897. *Merlino* I

Merlino, S.: *Formes et essence du socialisme.* Paris, 1898. *Merlino* II

Meulen, J. ter: *Der Gedanke der internationalen Organisation in seiner Entwicklung.* The Hague, 1917-'40. *Meulen*

Meuriot, P.: *Les agglomérations urbaines dans l'Europe contemporaine.* Paris, 1898. *Meuriot*

Meyer, A.: *Krisenepochen und Wendepunkte des biologischen Denkens.* Jena, 1935. *Meyer A.*

Meyer, F.: *Ibsen-Bibliographie* in *Nordische Bibliographie.* Reihe I, Heft I, pp. 1-37 Brunswick, 1928. *Meyer F.*

736

Meyer, G.: *Die sociale Bedeutung der Medicin.* Berlin, 1900. *Meyer G.*

Meyer, M.: *Statistik der Streiks und Aussperrungen im In- und Auslande.* Leipzig, 1907. *Meyer M.*

Meyer, R.: *Der Capitalismus fin de siècle.* Vienna, 1894. *Meyer R.*

Micelli, V.: 'La tyrannie des chambres' in *Revue politique et parlementaire,* 3 (1896), vol. 7, pp. 441–462. *Micelli*

Michael, F.: *Deutsches Theater.* Breslau, 1923. *Michael*

Michaelis, A.: *A century of archeological discoveries.* London, 1908. *Michaelis*

Michel, E.: *Sozialgeschichte der industriellen Arbeitswelt, ihrer Krisenformen und Gestaltungsversuche.* Frankfurt a.Main, 1948. *Michel E.*

Michel, H.: *L'idée de l'état.* Paris, 1896. *Michel H.*

Michels, R.: *Zur Soziologie des Parteiwesens in der modernen Demokratie. Untersuchungen über den oligarchischen Tendenzen des Gruppenlebens.* Leipzig, 1911. *Michels*

Michon, G.: *La préparation à la guerre. La loi de trois ans. (1910–1914).* Paris, 1935. *Michon*

Mill, J. S.: *Subjection of women.* London, 1869. *Mill*

Millerand, A.: *Le socialisme réformiste français.* Paris, 1903. *Millerand*

The Milner papers. South Africa, 1897–1899. Ed. C. Headlam. 2 vols. London 1931– 1933. *Milner*

Möbius, P. J.: *Über den physiologischen Schwachsinn des Weibes.* Halle, 1907. *Möbius*

Moeller von den Bruck, A.: *Die moderne Literatur in Gruppen- und Einzeldarstellungen.* Berlin, 1902. *Moeller* I

Moeller von den Bruck, A.: *Das Variété.* Berlin, 1902. *Moeller* II

Mohs, H. (ed.): *General-Feldmarschall von Waldersee in seinem militärischen Wirken.* Berlin, 1929. *Mohs*

Money, L. G. C.: *Riches and poverty.* London, 1905. *Money*

Monfreid, G. D. de: *Lettres de Paul Gauguin, précédées d'un hommage par Victor Segalen.* Paris, 1920. *Monfreid*

Montessori, M.: *Il metodo della pedagogia scientifica.* Rome, 1909. *Montessori*

Montgomery, B. G. de: *British and continental labour policy. The political labour movement and labour legislation in Great Britain, France and the three Scandinavian countries, 1900–'22.* London, 1922. *Montgomery*

Moor, J. M. de: *De gemengde onderneming in hare economische beteekenis.* Amsterdam, 1923. *Moor*

Moore, G.: *Esther Waters.* London, 1894. *Moore G.* I

Moore, G.: *Confessions of a young man.* London, 1904. *Moore G.* II

Moore, G. E.: 'The refutation of idealism' in *Mind. A quarterly review of psychology and philosophy,* 12 (1903), pp. 433–453. *Moore G. E.*

Morand, P.: *1900.* Paris, 1931. *Morand*

Moreck, K.: *Sittengeschichte des Kinos.* Dresden, 1926. *Moreck*

Morer, P.: *La crise morale du parlementarisme. Un remède: la non-rééligibilité temporaire des députés.* Montpellier, 1930. *Morer*

Morgan, C. L.: *Life, mind and spirit.* London, 1929. *Morgan*

Morgenstern, C.: *Alle Galgenlieder.* Wiesbaden, 1950. *Morgenstern*

Morice, C.: *La littérature de toute à l'heure.* Paris, 1889. *Morice* I

Morice, C.: *Paul Gauguin.* Paris, 1920. *Morice* II

Morse, H. B.: *The international relations of the Chinese Empire.* London, 1910–'18. *Morse*

Mourik Broekman, M. C. van: *Geestelijke stromingen in het christelijk cultuurbeeld.* Amsterdam, 1949. *Mourik*

Muir, R.: *Peers and bureaucrats. Two problems of English government.* London, 1910. *Muir*

Müller, E. B. I.: *Lord Milner and South Africa.* London, 1902. *Müller E. B. I.*

737

Müller, F.: *Grundriss der Sprachwissenschaft.* 4 vols., Vienna, 1877-'88. *Müller F.*
Müller, F. von: *Spekulation und Mystik in der Heilkunde.* Munich, 1914. *Müller F. von*
Müller, F. M.: *My autobiography. A fragment.* London, 1901. *Müller F. M.*
Mumford, L.: *The culture of cities.* London, 1945. *Mumford*
Münsterberg, H.: *Die Amerikaner.* 2 vols. Berlin, 1904. *Münsterberg*
Munzinger, S.: *Die Entwicklung des Inseratenwesens in den deutschen Zeitungen.* Heidelberg, 1902. *Munzinger*
Murchison, C. (ed.): *A history of psychology in autobiography.* Vol. 1. London, 1930. *Murchison*
Murphy, G.: *An historical introduction to modern psychology.* London, 1928. *Murphy.*
Musil, R.: *Die Verwirrungen des Zöglings Törlesz.* Vienna, 1906. *Musil* I
Musil, R.: *Der Mann ohne Eigenschaften.* 2 vols. Berlin, 1930-'33. *Musil* II
Mustafa, O. M.: *Le Soudan Egyptien.* Thesis. Neuville-sur-Saône, 1931. *Mustafa*
Muthesius, H.: *Stilarchitectur und Baukunst.* Mühlheim, 1902. *Muthesius* I
Muthesius, H.: *Das englische Haus.* 3 vols. Berlin, 1904-'05. *Muthesius* II
Myers, B. S.: *Expressionism. A generation in revolt.* London, 1956. *Myers B. S.*
Myers, F. W.: *Human personality and its survival of bodily death.* 2 vols. London, 1903. *Myers F. W.*

Nagl, J. W., J. Zeidler, E. Castle: *Deutsch-Österreichische Literaturgeschichte.* 4 vols. Vienna, 1899-1935. *Nagl*
Narischkin-Kurakin, E.: *Unter drei Zaren. Die Memoiren der Hofmarschallin Elisabeth Narischkin-Kurakin.* R. Fülöp-Miller (ed.). Vienna, 1930. *Narischkin*
Nash, H. S.: *Genesis of the social conscience.* New York, 1897. *Nash* I
Nash, H. S.: *The history of the higher criticism of the New Testament. Process whereby the word of God has won the right to be understood.* New York, 1900. *Nash* II
Natorp, P.: *Sozialpädagogik.* Stuttgart, 1899. *Natorp*
Naudh, D. H.: *Die Juden und der deutsche Staat.* n.p., 1861. *Naudh*
Naumann, F.: *Jesus als Volksmann.* Göttingen, 1894. *Naumann* I
Naumann, F.: *Demokratie und Kaisertum.* Berlin, 1900. *Naumann* II
Nes, H. M. van: *De nieuwe mystiek.* Rotterdam, 1900. *Nes*
Nethercot, A. H.: *The first five lives of Annie Besant.* London, 1961. *Nethercot*
Netscher, F.: 'Karakterschets. Ahmed Riza. Leider der Jong-Turken' in *De Hollandsche revue,* 4 (1899), pp. 724-745. *Netscher*
Nettlau, M.: 'Bibliographie de l'anarchie. Préface de E. Reclus' in *Bibliothèque des 'Temps Nouveaux',* 8. Brussels, 1897. *Nettlau* I
Nettlau, M.: *Errico Malatesta. Das Leben eines Anarchisten.* Berlin, 1922. *Nettlau* II
Nettlau, M.: *Elisée Reclus. Anarchist und Gelehrter (1830-1905).* Berlin, 1928. *Nettlau* III
Neumann, K. E.: *Die Reden des Gotamo Buddho's.* 3 vols. Berlin, 1896-1902. *Neumann*
Niemann, L.: *Soziologie des naturalistischen Romans.* Berlin, 1934. *Niemann*
Nietzsche, F.: 'Die Geburt der Tragödie' in *Nietzsche's Werke.* Vol. I, pp. 33-204. Leipzig, 1906. *Nietzsche* I
Nietzsche, F.: 'Modernität' in *Nietzsche's Werke.* Taschen-Ausgabe. vol. II, pp. 71-99. Leipzig, 1906. *Nietzsche* III
Nietzsche, F.: 'Der Fall Wagner' in *Nietzsche's Werke.* Vol. II, pp. 175-225. Leipzig, 1906. *Nietzsche* IV
Nietzsche, F.: 'Nietzsche contra Wagner' in *Nietzsche's Werke.* Vol. II, pp. 227-255. Leipzig, 1906. *Nietzsche* V

738

Nimführ, R.: *Die Luftschiffahrt. Ihre wissenschaftlichen Grundlagen und technische Entwicklung.* Leipzig, 1909. *Nimführ*

Nippold, O.: *Die Fortbildung des Verfahrens in völkerrechtlichen Streitigkeiten.* Leipzig, 1907. *Nippold*

Njewski, W.: 'Der dialektische Materialismus und die Philosophie der toten Reaktion' in *W. I. Lenins Sämtliche Werke.* Vol. 13, pp. 383-393. Vienna, 1927-'35. *Njewski*

Nomad, M.: *Rebels and renegades.* New York, 1932. *Nomad*

Nordau, M.: *Entartung.* 2 vols. Berlin, 1893. *Nordau* I

Nordau, M.: *Zionistische Schriften.* Cologne, 1909. *Nordau* II

Nordau, M.: *Erinnerungen.* Leipzig, 1928. *Nordau* III

Nordenskiöld, E.: *The history of biology. A survey.* London, 1928. *Nordenskiöld*

Norikus, F.: *Gegen den Strom! Moderner Parlamentarismus oder berufsständische Vertretung? Ein Wort zur politischen und sozialen Misère.* Hamm i.W., 1904. *Norikus*

Norman, E. H.: *Japan's emergence as a modern State. Political and economic problems of the Meiji period.* New York, 1948. *Norman*

Nossig, A.: *Die Revision des Sozialismus.* 2 vols. Berlin, 1901-'02. *Nossig*

Nostitz, H. von: *Das Aufsteigen des Arbeiterstandes in England. Ein Beitrag zur socialen Geschichte der Gegenwart.* Jena, 1900. *Nostitz*

Novicow, J.: *Les luttes entre sociétés humaines et leurs phases successives.* Paris, 1893. *Novicow* I

Novicow, J.: *La guerre et ses prétendus bienfaits.* Paris, 1894. *Novicow* II

Novicow, J.: *Der ewige Krieg.* Berlin, 1899. *Novicow* III

Novicow, J.: *La fédération de l'Europe.* Paris, 1901. *Novicow* IV

Oertzen, D. von: *Adolf Stoecker. Lebensbild und Zeitgeschichte.* Schwerin, 1912. *Oertzen*

Ofner, J.: 'Die Gefahr des Parlementarismus für das Recht' in *Archiv für öffentliches Recht,* 18 (1903), pp. 219-246. *Ofner*

Oirschot, F. van: *Beknopte geschiedenis der sociale kwestie. Onstaan en oplossingen.* Roermond, 1950. *Oirschot*

Onnen, F.: *Maurice Ravel.* Amsterdam, 1948. *Onnen*

Oppenheimer, F.: *David Ricardos Grundrententheorie.* Berlin, 1909. *Oppenheimer* I

Oppenheimer, F.: *Der Staat.* Frankfurt a.Main, 1912. *Oppenheimer* II

Oppenheimer, F.: *Soziologische Streifzüge.* Munich, 1927. *Oppenheimer* III

Ortega y Gasset, J.: *Bespiegelingen over leven en liefde.* The Hague, 1935. *Ortega* I

Ortega y Gasset, J.: *Ideas y creencias.* Madrid, 1940. *Ortega* II

Ortega y Gasset, J.: *Historia como sistema.* Madrid, 1941. *Ortega* III

Osthoff, H.: *Vom Suppletivwesen der indogermanischen Sprachen.* Heidelberg, 1899. *Osthoff*

Ostwald, W.: *Erfinder und Entdecker.* Frankfurt a.Main, 1908. *Ostwald* I

Ostwald, W.: *Energetische Grundlagen der Kulturwissenschaft.* Leipzig, 1909. *Ostwald* II

Ould, H.: *John Galsworthy.* London, 1934. *Ould*

Ovink, G. W.: *Het aanzien van een eeuw.* Haarlem, 1959. *Ovink*

Packard, A. S.: *Lamarck, the founder of evolution. His life and work.* London, 1902. *Packard*

Pagel, J.: *Grundriss eines Systems der medizinischen Kulturgeschichte.* Berlin, 1905. *Pagel*

Painter, G. D.: *Marcel Proust.* London, 1959. *Painter*

Pankhurst, E. S.: *The suffragette movement.* New York, 1931. *Pankhurst*

Panofsky, W.: *Die Geburt des Films, ein Stück Kulturgeschichte. Versuch einer zeitgeschichtlichen Darstellung des Lichtspiels in seinen Anfangsjahren.* Würzburg, 1940. *Panofsky*

Pareto, V.: *Manuale di economia politica, con una introduzione alla scienza sociale.* Milan, 1906. *Pareto I*

Pareto, V.: *Trattato di sociologia generale.* 2 vols. Florence, 1916. *Pareto II*

Paris-Exposition, 1900. Paris, 1900. *Paris*

Parkes, J.: *The emergence of the Jewish problem, 1878-1939.* London, 1946. *Parkes*

Parvus: *Die Kolonialpolitik und der Zusammenbruch.* Leipzig, 1907. *Parvus*

Pascendi dominici gregis. (Papal encyclical on modernism of 8 September, 1907). Hilversum, 1948. *Pascendi*

Passy, F.: 'L'héritage du dix-neuvième siècle' in *Journal des économistes,* July 1900, 5e série, tome XLIII, pp. 3-12. *Passy*

Pater, W. H.: *Studies in the history of the Renaissance.* London, 1873. *Pater*

Patten, S. N.: *Theory of social forces.* Philadelphia, 1896. *Patten*

Paul, H.: *Principien der Sprachgeschichte.* Halle, 1880. *Paul*

Paulhan, F.: *Le nouveau mysticisme.* Paris, 1892. *Paulhan*

Paulsen, F.: *Geschichte des gelehrten Unterrichts.* 2 vols. Berlin, 1921. *Paulsen*

Pauly, A.: *Darwinismus und Lamarckismus.* Munich, 1905. *Pauly*

Peano, G.: *Formulaire de mathématiques.* 4 vols. Turin, 1894-1906. *Peano*

Pears, E.: *Life of Abdul Hamid.* London, 1917. *Pears*

Pearson, K.: *National life from the standpoint of science.* London, 1901. *Pearson I*

Pearson, K.: *Nature and nurture: the problem of the future.* London, 1910. *Pearson II*

Peck, H. W.: *Economic thought and its institutional background.* London, 1935. *Peck*

Pedersen, H.: *Linguistic science in the 19th century. Methods and results.* Cambridge (Mass.), 1931. *Pedersen*

Péguy, Ch.: *Le mystère de la charité de Jeanne d'Arc.* Paris, 1910. *Péguy I*

Péguy, Ch.: *Le mystère des saints innocents.* Paris, 1912. *Péguy II*

Pelloutier, F. & M.: *La vie ouvrière en France.* Paris, 1900. *Pelloutier*

Perrier, E.: *La terre avant l'histoire.* Paris, 1921. *Perrier*

Perrin, J.: *Les atomes.* Paris, 1913. *Perrin*

Peters, R. S. (ed.): *Brett's history of psychology.* London, 1953. *Peters*

Petersilie, A.: *Das öffentliche Unterrichtswesen im Deutschen Reiche und in den übrigen europäischen Kulturländern.* 2 vols. Leipzig, 1897. *Petersilie*

Petre (ed.), M. D.: *Autobiography and life of George Tyrrel.* 2 vols. London, 1912. *Petre*

Petterson, H. M.: *Henrik Ibsen.* Oslo, 1928. *Petterson*

Pevsner, N.: *Pioneers of the modern movement. From William Morris to Walter Gropius.* London, 1936. *Pevsner I*

Pevsner, N.: *Wegbereiter moderner Formgebung. Von Morris bis Gropius.* Hamburg, 1957. *Pevsner II*

Pfeiderer, A.: *Bilderatlas zur Alkoholfrage.* Reutlingen, 1910. *Pfeiderer*

Pflugk-Harttung, J. von (ed.): *Weltgeschichte.* 7 vols. Berlin, 1907-'25. *Pflugk*

Pfungst, A.: *Ein deutscher Buddhist (Oberpräsidialrat Theodor Schultze).* Stuttgart, 1901. *Pfungst*

Philippi-Siewertz van Reesema, C.: *Uit en over de werken van prof. dr. Ovide Decroly.* Groningen, 1931. *Philippi*

Picard, R.: *Les idées sociales de Renouvier.* Paris, 1910. *Picard*

Pieper, A.: *Mässigkeitsbestrebungen. Ihre Bedeutung, Aufgabe und Mittel.* Mönchengladbach, 1900. *Pieper*

Pieraccini, G.: *Patologia del lavoro.* Milan, 1905. *Pieraccini*

Pigou, A. C.: *Wealth and welfare.* London, 1912. *Pigou*

Pinsker, L. S.: *Autoemanzipation. Mahnruf an seine Stammesgenossen von einem russischen Juden*. Brno, 1913. *Pinsker*

Pirenne, H.: 'Une polémique historique en Allemagne' in *Revue historique*, 64 (1897), pp. 50-57. *Pirenne*

Pirou, G.: *Les doctrines économiques en France depuis 1870*. Paris, 1935. *Pirou*

Plechanow, G.: *Anarchismus und Sozialismus*. Berlin, 1894. *Plechanow* I

Plechanow, G.: *Über die Rolle der Persönlichkeit in der Geschichte*. Moscow, 1940. *Plechanow* II

Plenge, J.: *Die Zukunft in Amerika* in: *Plengiana* from the library of Max Adler; pp. 431-500. *Plenge*

Plessner, H.: *Das Schicksal deutschen Geistes im Ausgang seiner bürgerlichen Epoche*. Zürich, 1935. *Plessner* I

Plessner, H.: *Zwischen Philosophie und Gesellschaft*. Berne, 1953. *Plessner* II

Plessner, H.: *Husserl in Göttingen*. Göttingen, 1959. *Plessner* III

Poel, J. van der: *The Jameson raid*. Oxford, 1951. *Poel*

Poelje, G. A. van: *Osmose. Een aanteekening over het elkander doordringen van de beginselen van openbaar bestuur en particulier beheer*. Alphen aan den Rijn, 1931. *Poelje*

Pohle, L.: *Die neuere Entwicklung des Kleinhandels*. Dresden, 1900. *Pohle* I

Pohle, L.: *Die gegenwärtige Krisis in der deutschen Volkswirtschaftslehre. Betrachtungen über das Verhältnis zwischen Politik und nationalökonomischer Wissenschaft*. Leipzig, 1911. *Pohle* II

Poincaré, H.: 'Relations entre la physique expérimentale et la physique mathématique' in *Rapports présentés au congrès international de physique de 1900*. Tome I, pp. 1-29. Paris, 1900. *Poincaré*

Polak, B. H.: *Het fin-de-siècle in de Nederlandse schilderkunst. De symbolische beweging 1890-1900*. The Hague, 1955. *Polak B. H.*

Polak, F. L.: *Kennen en keuren in de sociale wetenschappen*. Leiden, 1948. *Polak F. L.*

Polenz, W. von: *Der Grabenhäger*. 2 vols. Berlin, 1899. *Polenz*

Pompe, W. P. J.: 'Geschiedenis der Nederlandse strafrechtswetenschap sinds de codificatiebeweging' in *Geschiedenis der Nederlandsche rechtswetenschap*. Vol. 2, pp. 219-478. Amsterdam, 1956. *Pompe*

Ponsonby, A. W. H.: *The decline of aristocracy*. London, 1912. *Ponsonby*

Poritzky, J. E.: *Dämonische Dichter*. Munich, 1921. *Poritzky*

Porto-Riche, G. de: *Amoureuse. Comédie en 3 actes*. Paris, 1891. *Porto*

Posse, E. H.: *Der Marxismus in Frankreich, 1871-1905. Klassenkampflehre des Marxismus und der parteipolitischen Arbeiterbewegung bis zur Gründung der Parti Socialiste*. Berlin, 1930. *Posse*

Poulaille, H.: *Nouvelle littérature prolétarienne*. Paris, 1931. *Poulaille*

Poulat, E.: *Histoire, dogme et critique dans la crise moderniste*. Tournai, 1962. *Poulat*

Pound, R.: 'The scope and purpose of sociological jurisprudence' in *Harvard law review*, 25 (1911-'12), pp. 140-168 and pp. 489-516. *Pound*

Powicke, F. M.: *Modern historians and the study of history*. London, 1955. *Powicke*

Prager, M.: 'Die Mittelstandsfrage' in *Volkswirtschaftliche Zeitfragen*. Vol. 201-202. Berlin, 1904. *Prager*

Prel, C. du: *Studien auf dem Gebiet der Geheimwissenschaften*. 2 vols. Leipzig, 1890-'91. *Prel*

Presser, J.: *Napoleon. Historie en legende*. Amsterdam, 1946. *Presser*

Prévost, M.: *Les demi-vierges*. Paris, 1894. *Prévost* I

Prévost, M.: *Les vierges fortes: Lea*. Paris, 1900. *Prévost* II

Preyer, W.: *Die Seele des Kindes*. Leipzig, 1882. *Preyer*

Prince, F.: *André Antoine et le renouveau du théâtre hollandais (1880-1900)*. Amsterdam, 1941. *Prince*

Prins, A.: *La démocratie et le régime parlementaire.* Brussels, 1886. *Prins A.*

Prins, F. W.: *Wisselende aspecten in de didactiek.* Amsterdam, 1957. *Prins F. W.*

Problemen van maatschappelijk werk. Gedenkboek ter gelegenheid van het vijftigjarig bestaan (1899-1949) van de School voor Maatschappelijk Werk. Purmerend, 1949. *Problemen*

Proost, K. F.: *Gerhart Hauptmann, zijn leven en werken. Een inleiding.* Zeist, 1924. *Proost I*

Proost, K. F.: *Frank Wedekind. Zijn leven en werken. Een inleiding.* Zeist, 1928. *Proost II*

Proost, K. F.: *Weg en werk. Een eeuw drankbestrijding.* Utrecht, 1941. *Proost III*

Proust, M.: *A la recherche du temps perdu.* 8 vols. Paris, 1913-'28. *Proust I*

Proust, M.: *Du côté de chez Swann.* Paris, 1913. *Proust II*

Proust, M.: *Chroniques.* Paris, 1927. *Proust III*

Proust, M.: *Jean Santeuil.* Paris, 1952. *Proust IV*

Pyfferoen, O.: *La petite bourgeoisie aux Pays-Bas.* Brussels, 1902. *Pyfferoen*

Rabany, C.: 'Les types sociaux - le fonctionnaire' in *Revue générale d'administration* (1907), pp. 5-28. *Rabany*

Radermacher Schorer, M. R.: *Bijdrage tot de geschiedenis van de renaissance der Nederlandse boekdrukkunst.* Utrecht, 1951. *Radermacher*

Rádl, E.: *Geschichte der biologischen Theorien.* 2 vols. Leipzig, 1909. *Rádl*

Radziwill, C. (Kolb-Danvin): *The Austrian court from within.* London, 1916. *Radziwill*

Ragey, L.: *La question du chemin de fer de Bagdad, 1893-1914.* Paris, 1935. *Ragey*

Ragon, M.: *Histoire de la littérature ouvrière du Moyen Age à nos jours.* Paris, 1953. *Ragon*

Ralston, J. H.: *International arbitration from Athens to Locarno.* Stanford, 1929. *Ralston*

Raphael, M.: *Von Monet zu Picasso. Grundzüge einer Ästhetik und Entwicklung der modernen Malerei.* Munich, 1913. *Raphael*

Rapmund, O.: *Das öffentliche Gesundheitswesen.* 2 vols. Leipzig, 1901-'14. *Rapmund*

Rappl, H. G.: *Die Wortkunsttheorie von Arno Holz.* Cologne, 1957. *Rappl*

Rathenau, W.: *Zur Kritik der Zeit.* Berlin, 1912. *Rathenau I*

Rathenau, W.: *Zur Mechanik des Geistes.* Berlin, 1913. *Rathenau II*

Rathenau, W.: *Von kommenden Dingen.* Berlin, 1917. *Rathenau III*

Ratzel, F.: *Politische Geographie.* Munich, 1897. *Ratzel I*

Ratzel, F.: *Das Meer als Quelle der Völkergrösse.* Munich, 1900. *Ratzel II*

Ratzenhofer, G.: *Soziologie.* Leipzig, 1907. *Ratzenhofer*

Ravesteyn, W. van: *Het socialisme aan den vooravond van den wereldoorlog.* 3 vols. Amsterdam, 1933-'60. *Ravesteyn*

Raymond, G. de: *Léopold II à Paris. Souvenirs.* Bruges, 1949-'50. *Raymond*

Reade, W.: *Martyrdom of man.* London, 1872. *Reade*

Reeser, E.: *Een eeuw Nederlandse muziek.* Amsterdam, 1950. *Reeser*

Reich, E.: *Henrik Ibsens Dramen.* Dresden, 1900. *Reich*

Reinach, J.: *Histoire de l'affaire Dreyfus.* 6 vols. Paris, 1901-'04. *Reinach*

Rénon, L.: *De drie volksziekten. Lessen gegeven aan de medische faculteit te Parijs,* vertaald door M. Kamerling. 3 vols. Amsterdam, 1906. *Rénon*

Renouvier, C.: *Science de la morale.* 2 vols. Paris, 1908. *Renouvier*

Resink, A. J.: *De Theosofische Vereeniging en de klassenstrijd.* Amsterdam, 1908. *Resink*

Rewald, J.: *C. Pissarro, lettres à son fils Lucien. Présentées avec l'assistance de L. Pissarro.* Paris, 1950. *Rewald I*

Rewald, J.: *Post-impressionism. From Van Gogh to Gauguin.* New York, 1956. *Rewald II*

742

Rey, E.: *La renaissance de l'orgueil français.* Paris, 1912. *Rey*

Rice, H. C.: *Martin du Gard and the world of the Thibaults.* New York, 1941. *Rice*

Rickert, H.: *Die Grenzen der naturwissenschaftlichen Begriffsbildung.* Freiburg, 1896. *Rickert*

Riegl, A.: *Stilfragen. Grundlegungen zu einer Geschichte der Ornamentik.* Berlin, 1923. *Riegl*

Riehl, A.: *Friedrich Nietzsche, der Künstler und der Denker.* Stuttgart, 1897. *Riehl A. I*

Riehl, A.: *Zur Einführung in die Philosophie der Gegenwart.* Leipzig, 1903. *Riehl A. II*

Riehl, H.: 'Die Bedeutung des ganzheitlichen Denkens für die Kunstgeschichte' in *Die Ganzheit in Philosophie und Wissenschaft. Othmar Spann zum 70. Geburtstag.* Edited by Dr. Walter Heinrich, pp. 270–278. Vienna, 1950. *Riehl H.*

Riemann, O.: *Ein aufklärendes Wort über den Spiritismus auf Grund praktischer Erfahrungen und wissenschaftlicher Studien.* Berlin, 1901. *Riemann*

Riesser, J.: *Zur Entwicklungsgeschichte der deutschen Grossbanken mit besonderer Rücksicht auf die Konzentrationsbestrebungen.* Jena, 1906. *Riesser*

Rilke, R. M.: *Das Studen-Buch.* Leipzig, 1905. *Rilke I*

Rilke, R. M.: *Gesammelte Werke.* Leipzig, 1927. *Rilke II*

Rilke, R. M.: *Sämtliche Werke.* Vol. 3. Frankfurt a.Main, 1963. *Rilke III*

Riou, G.: *Aux écoutes de la France qui vient.* Paris, 1913. *Riou*

Ritchie, D. G.: *Principles of State interference.* London, 1891. *Ritchie I*

Ritchie, D. G.: *Natural rights. A criticism of some political and ethical conceptions.* London, 1916. *Ritchie II*

Rittinghausen, M.: *La législation directe par le peuple et ses adversaires.* Paris, 1851. *Rittinghausen*

Ritzel, G.: *Schmoller versus Menger. Eine Analyse de Methodenstreits im Hinblick auf den Historismus in der Nationalökonomie.* Frankfurt a.Main, 1950. *Ritzel*

Ritzmann, F.: *Internationale Sozialpolitik. Ihre geschichtliche Entwicklung und ihr gegenwärtiger Stand.* Mannheim, 1925. *Ritzmann*

Rival, J.: 'La femme moderne par elle même' in *Revue encyclopédique*, 6 (1896), p. 883. *Rival*

Rivière, J.: *Le modernisme dans l'église. Etude d'histoire religieuse contemporaine.* Paris, 1929. *Rivière*

Robertson, J. M.: *Christianity and mythology.* London, 1900. *Robertson I*

Robertson, J. M.: *A short history of freethought, ancient and modern.* 2 vols. London, 1915. *Robertson II*

Robertson, J. M.: *History of freethought in the 19th century.* 2 vols. London, 1929. *Robertson III*

Robertson Scott, J. W.: *The life and death of a newspaper.* London, 1952. *Robertson Scott*

Roberty, E. de: 'Rapports de la morale (ou sociologie élémentaire) avec les autres sciences formant l'échelle du savoir abstrait' in *Revue internationale de sociologie*, 8 (1900), pp. 401–423. *Roberty*

Rocker, R.: *Johann Most. Das Leben eines Rebellen.* Berlin, 1924–'25. *Rocker*

Roelse, E.: 'Der Alkoholkonsum der Kulturvölker' in *Die Alkoholfrage*, 4 (1907), pp. 113–135. *Roelse*

Rohling, A.: *Der Talmud-Jude.* Münster, 1871. *Rohling*

Roland Holst, H.: *Kapitaal en arbeid in Nederland.* Amsterdam, 1902. *Roland I*

Roland Holst, H.: *Josef Dietzgens Philosophie gemeinverständlich erläutert in ihrer Bedeutung für das Proletariat.* Munich, 1910. *Roland II*

Rolland, R.: *Le théâtre du peuple.* Paris, 1903. *Rolland I*

Rolland, R.: *Vie de Beethoven.* Paris, 1903. *Rolland II*

743

Rolland, R.: *Jean Christophe*. Paris, 1904-'12. *Rolland* III
Rolland, R.: *Péguy*. 2 vols. Paris, 1944. *Rolland* IV
Roller, A. (S. Nacht): *Blätter aus der Geschichte des spanischen Proletariats zum zehnten Jahrestag der Hinrichtung Michel Angiolillos*. Berlin, 1907. *Roller*
Romains, J.: *Manuel de déification*. Paris, 1910. *Romains* I
Romains, J.: *Les hommes de bonne volonté*. 27 vols. Paris, 1932 e.v. *Romains* II
Romein, J.: *Dostojewsky in de westersche kritiek. Een hoofdstuk uit de geschiedenis van den literairen roem*. Haarlem, 1924. *Romein* I
Romein, J.: *Grondstoffen en politiek. Katoen, petroleum, rubber, staal.* Amsterdam, 1935. *Romein* II
Romein, J.: *Het ouvoltooid verleden. Cultuurhistorische studies.* Amsterdam, 1937. *Romein* III
Romein, J.: *In opdracht van de tijd. Tien voordrachten over historische thema's.* Amsterdam, 1946. *Romein* IV
Romein, J.: *Machten van deze tijd*. Introduced and revised by J. Presser. Amsterdam, 1950. *Romein* V
Romein, J.: *Tussen vrees en vrijheid. Vijftien historische verhandelingen.* Amsterdam, 1950. *Romein* VI
Romein, J.: *Carillon der tijden. Studies en toespraken op cultuurhistorisch terrein.* Amsterdam, 1953. *Romein* VII
Romein, J.: *In de ban van Prambanan. Indonesische voordrachten en indrukken.* Amsterdam, 1954. *Romein* VIII
Romein, J.: *Eender en anders. Twaalf nagelaten essays.* Amsterdam, 1964. *Romein* IX
Romein, J. & J. E.: *De eeuw van Azië. Opkomst, ontwikkeling en overwinning van het modern-Aziatisch nationalisme.* Leiden, 1956. *Romein* X
Romein, J. & J. E.: *The Asian century*. Berkeley, 1962. *Romein* XI
Romein, J. & A. Romein-Verschoor: *Aera van Europa. De Europese geschiedenis als afwijking van het algemeen menselijk patroon.* Leiden, 1954. *Romein* XII
Romein-Verschoor, A.: *De vruchtbare muze*. Amsterdam, 1949. *Romein-Verschoor* I
Romein-Verschoor, A.: *Spelen met de tijd*. Amsterdam, 1957. *Romein-Verschoor* II
Rompel, F.: *Heroes of the Boer War*. London, 1903. *Rompel*
Rookmaker, H. R.: *Synthetist art theories. Genesis and nature of the ideas on art of Gauguin and his circle.* Amsterdam, 1959. *Rookmaker*
Ross, E. A.: *Social psychology*. London, 1908. *Ross*
Rossum, C. P. van: *Het moderne Fransche toneel*. Leiden, 1918. *Rossum*
Rostand, E.: *Cyrano de Bergerac*. Paris, 1898. *Rostand*
Roth, J.: *Radetzkymarsch*. Berlin, 1932. *Roth*
Rousiers, P. de: *Les syndicats industriels de producteurs en France et à l'étranger. Trust, cartells, comptoirs.* Paris, 1901. *Rousiers*
Roux, W.: *Programm und Forschungsmethoden der Entwicklungsmechanik der Organismen*. Leipzig, 1897. *Roux* I
Roux, W.: 'Autoergographie' in *Medizin der Gegenwart in Selbstdarstellungen*. Leipzig, 1923. *Roux* II
Rowntree, E. S.: *Poverty. A study of town life*. London, 1901. *Rowntree E. S.*
Rowntree, J. & A. Sherwell: *The temperance problem and social reform*. London, 1899. *Rowntree J.* I
Rowntree, J. & A. Sherwell: *State prohibition and local option*. London, 1900. *Rowntree J.* II
Roy, E. le: *Dogme et critique*. Paris, 1907. *Roy* I
Roy, E. le: *Une philosophie nouvelle. H. Bergson*. Paris, 1912. *Roy* II
Ruff, M. A.: *L'esprit du mal et l'esthétique Baudelairienne*. Paris, 1955. *Ruff*
Rühle, O.: *Arbeit und Erziehung*. Munich, 1904. *Rühle* I
Rühle, O.: *Das proletarische Kind*. Munich, 1911. *Rühle* II

744

Rühle, O.: *Illustrierte Kultur- und Sittengeschichte des Proletariats.* Berlin, 1930.
    Rühle III
Rümke, H. C.: *Over Frederik van Eeden's 'Van de koele meren des doods'.* Amster-
    dam, 1964. *Rümke*
Ruskin, J.: *The seven lamps of architecture.* London, 1849. *Ruskin*
Russell, B.: *The principles of mathematics.* Cambridge, 1903. *Russell B.* I
Russell, B., & A. N. Whitehead: *Principia mathematica.* 3 vols. Cambridge, 1910-'13.
    Russell B. II
Russell, B.: *Roads to freedom, Socialism, anarchism and syndicalism.* London, 1918.
    Russell B. III
Russell, B.: *My philosophical development.* London, 1959. *Russell B.* IV
Russell, C. E. B. & L. M. Rigby: *The making of the criminal.* London, 1906. *Russell
    C. E. B.*
Rüstow, A.: *Ortsbestimmung der Gegenwart. Eine universalgeschichtliche Kultur-
    kritik.* 3 vols. Erlenbach, 1950-'57. *Rüstow*

Sabatier, P.: *Vie de S. François d'Assise.* Paris, 1893. *Sabatier*
Sadoul, G.: *Histoire générale du cinéma.* 3 vols. Paris, 1945-'51. *Sadoul* I
Sadoul, G.: *Histoire de l'art du cinéma des origines à nos jours.* Paris, 1953. *Sadoul* II
Sageret, J.: *Les grands convertis.* Paris, 1906. *Sageret*
Saitzew, M.: 'Der Interventionismus' in *Festgabe Fritz Fleiner.* Zürich, 1937. pp.
    321-346. *Saitzew*
Saleilles, R.: 'L'école historique et le droit naturel d'après quelques ouvrages récents'
    in *Revue trimestrielle de droit civil,* I (1902), pp. 80-122. *Saleilles*
Salin, E.: *Vom deutschen Verhängnis. Gespräch an der Zeitenwende: Burckhardt-
    Nietzsche.* Hamburg, 1959. *Salin*
Salmon, L. M.: *The newspaper and authority. With biographical notes.* New York,
    1923. *Salmon*
Salomons, A.: *Een meisjes-studentje.* Bussum, 1907. *Salomons*
Saltykow, M.: *Golowljows.* Amsterdam, 1927. *Saltykow*
Sampson, G.: *The concise Cambridge history of English literature.* Cambridge, 1945.
    Sampson
Samter, H.: *Das Reich der Erfindungen.* Berlin, 1905. *Samter*
Sand, R.: *The advance to social medicine.* London, 1952. *Sand*
Sarrou, A.: *La jeune-Turquie et la révolution.* Paris, 1912. *Sarrou*
Sartorius von Waltershausen, A.: *Deutsche Wirtschaftgeschichte, 1815-1914.* Jena,
    1923. *Sartorius*
Saussure, F. de: *Mémoire sur le système primitif des voyelles dans les langues indo-
    européennes.* Leipzig, 1879. *Saussure*
Savornin Lohman, A. de: *Het ééne noodige.* Amsterdam, 1897. *Savornin*
Sax, C. von: *Geschichte des Machtverfalls der Türkei bis Ende des 19. Jahrhunderts
    und die Phasen der 'orientalischen Frage' bis auf die Gegenwart.* Vienna, 1913.
    Sax
Sayers, G. F.: *The handbook of Tanganyika.* London, 1930. *Sayers*
Sazerac de Forge, L.: *L'homme s'envole. Le passé, le présent et l'avenir de l'aviation.*
    Paris, 1909. *Sazerac*
Schaefer, C. A.: *Die Entwicklung der Bagdadbahnpolitik.* Potsdam, 1916. *Schaefer*
Schäfer, D.: *Das eigentliche Arbeitsgebiet der Geschichte.* Jena, 1888. *Schäfer* I
Schäfer, D.: *Geschichte und Kulturgeschichte.* Jena, 1891. *Schäfer* II
Schäffle, A. E. F.: *Deutsche Kern- und Zeitfragen.* Berlin, 1894. *Schäffle*
Schaffstein, F.: *Die Nichtzumutbarkeit als allgemeiner übergesetzlicher Schuldaussch-
    liessungsgrund.* Leipzig, 1933. *Schaffstein*

Schamelhout, G.: *De volkeren van Europa en de strijd der nationaliteiten.* 3 vols. Amsterdam, 1929–'32. *Schamelhout*

Schär, O.: *Arno Holz. Seine dramatische Technik.* Berne, 1926. *Schär*

Scheffler, K.: *Der Architekt.* Frankfurt a.Main, 1907. *Scheffler*

Schell, H.: *Der Katholizismus als Prinzip des Fortschritts.* Würzburg, 1897. *Schell* I

Schell, H.: *Die neue Zeit und der alte Glaube.* Würzburg, 1898. *Schell* II

Schellwien, R.: *Max Stirner und Friedrich Nietzsche. Erscheinungen des modernen Geistes und das Wesen des Menschen.* Leipzig, 1892. *Schwellwien*

Schiller, F. C. S. (e.a.): *Personal idealism.* London, 1903. *Schiller*

Schilling, O.: *Die Gesellschaftslehre Leos XIII. und seiner Nachfolger.* Munich, 1951. *Schilling*

Schirmacher, K.: *Le féminisme aux Etats-Unis, en France, dans la Grande-Bretagne, en Suède et en Russie.* Paris, 1898. *Schirmacher*

Schjelderup, H. K.: *Hauptlinien der Entwicklung der Philosophie von der Mitte des 19. Jahrhunderts bis zur Gegenwart.* Kristiania, 1920. *Schjelderup*

Schlatter, R.: *Private property.* London, 1951. *Schlatter*

Schlenther, P.: *Wozu der Lärm? Genesis der freien Bühne.* Berlin, 1889. *Schlenther*

Schmalenbach, F.: *Jugendstil. Ein Beitrag zur Theorie und Geschichte der Flächenkunst.* Würzburg, 1935. *Schmalenbach*

Schmidt, H.: *Das Eisenbahnwesen in der asiatischen Türkei.* Berlin, 1914. *Schmidt H.*

Schmidt, O.: *Darwinismus und Sozialdemokratie.* Bonn, 1878. *Schmidt O.*

Schmidt, R.: (ed.): *Die Philosophie der Gegenwart in Selbstdarstellungen.* 7 vols. Leipzig, 1921–'29. *Schmidt R.*

Schmitt (ed.), B. E.: *Some historians of modern Europe. Essays in historiography by former students of the Department of History of the University of Chicago.* Chicago, 1942. *Schmitt B. E.*

Schmitt, C.: *Die geistesgeschichtliche Lage des heutigen Parlamentarismus.* Munich, 1926. *Schmitt C.*

Schmitt, E. H.: *Die Kulturbedingungen der christlichen Dogmen und unsere Zeit.* Leipzig, 1901. *Schmitt E. H.* I

Schmitt, E. H.: *Ibsen als Prophet. Grundgedanken zu einer neuen Ästhetik.* Leipzig, 1908. *Schmitt E. H.* II

Schmitt, W.: *Das Filmwesen und seine Wechselbeziehungen zur Gesellschaft. Versuch einer Soziologie des Filmwesens.* Freudenstadt, 1932. *Schmitt W.*

Schmoller, G.: *Über wirtschaftliche Kartelle in Deutschland und im Ausland. Fünfzehn Schilderungen nebst Anzahl, Statuten und Beilagen.* Leipzig, 1894. *Schmoller* I

Schmoller, G.: *Was verstehen wir unter dem Mittelstande? Hat er im 19. Jahrhundert zu- oder abgenommen?* Göttingen, 1897. *Schmoller* II

Schmoller, G.: *Grundriss der allgemeinen Volkswirtschaftslehre.* Leipzig, 1900. *Schmoller* III

Schmoller, G.: *Zwanzig Jahre deutscher Politik (1897–1917).* Munich, 1920. *Schmoller* IV

Schneider, C. K.: *Die Prostituierte und die Gesellschaft. Eine soziologisch-ethische Studie.* Leipzig, 1908. *Schneider C. K.*

Schneider, M.: *De Nederlandse krant. Van 'Nieuwstijdinghe' tot dagblad.* Amsterdam, 1944. *Schneider M.*

Schnitzler, A.: *Liebelei.* Berlin, 1895. *Schnitzler* I

Schnitzler, A.: *Der grüne Kakadu.* Berlin, 1900. *Schnitzler* II

Schnitzler, A., *Reigen.* 10 Dialoge. Vienna, 1903. *Schnitzler* III

Schoeck, H.: *Soziologie. Geschichte ihrer Probleme.* Munich, 1952. *Schoeck*

Scholz, A.: *Die Juden in Russland. Urkunden und Zeugnisse russischer Behörden und Autoritäten.* Translated from the Russian by A. Scholz. Berlin, 1900. *Scholz*

Schrieke, O.: *De los-van-Rome-beweging.* Baarn, 1910. *Schrieke*

Schuchardt, H.: *Über die Lautgesetze. Gegen die Junggrammatiker.* Berlin, 1885. *Schuchardt*

Schück, H. & R. Sohlman: *Nobel. Dynamit, Petroleum, Pazifismus.* Leipzig, 1928. *Schück*

Schücking, W.: *Der Staatenverband der Haager Konferenzen.* Munich, 1912. *Schücking*

Schuiling, R.: 'Zuid-Afrika' in *Tijdschift voor geschiedenis, land- en volkenkunde,* 15 (1900), pp. 41–55 and pp. 87–119. *Schuiling*

Schüle, H.: *Handbuch der Geisteskrankheiten.* Leipzig, 1878. *Schüle*

Schultink, J. W.: *Op de pointes. De Westeuropese dans als cultuurspiegel.* Amsterdam, 1948. *Schultink*

Schultze, F.: *Die Grundgedanken des Spiritismus und die Kritik derselben.* Leipzig, 1883. *Schultze F.*

Schultze, Th.: *Die Religion der Zukunft.* 2 delen. Frankfurt a.Main, 1901. *Schultze Th.*

Schumpeter, J.: *Theorie der wirtschaftlichen Entwicklung.* Leipzig, 1912. *Schumpeter J.*

Schumpeter, J. A.: *Ten great economists.* London, 1952. *Schumpeter J. A.*

Schwarzkoppen, M. von: *Die Wahrheit über Dreyfus.* B. Schwertfegen (ed.). Berlin, 1930. *Schwarzkoppen*

Schweitzer, A.: *Von Reimarus zu Wrede. Eine Geschichte der Leben-Jesu-Forschung.* Tübingen, 1906. *Schweitzer*

Scripture, E. W.: *The new psychology.* London, 1897. *Scripture*

Seagle, W.: *Men of law.* New York, 1947. *Seagle*

Sédille, P.: *L'architecture moderne en Angleterre.* Paris, 1890. *Sédille*

Sedlmayr, H.: *Die Revolution der modernen Kunst.* Hamburg, 1955. *Sedlmayr I*

Sedlmayr, H.: *Kunst und Wahrheit. Zur Theorie und Methode der Kunstgeschichte.* Hamburg, 1958. *Sedlmayr II*

Seeley, J. R.: *The expansion of England.* London, 1919. *Seeley*

Seidenberg, R.: *Posthistoric man. An inquiry.* Chapel Hill, 1950. *Seidenberg*

Seifert, F.: *Der Streit um Karl Lamprechts Geschichtsphilosophie. Eine historisch-kritische Studie.* Augsburg, 1925. *Seifert*

Seilhac, L. de: *Les grèves.* Paris, 1903. *Seilhac*

Seligman, E. R. A. & A. Johnson (ed.): *Encyclopedia of the social sciences.* 15 vols. New York, 1930–'35. *Seligman*

Sergent, A. & Cl. Hamel: *Histoire de l'anarchie.* I *De la Révolution Française à la Commune.* Paris, 1949–'50. *Sergent*

Seton-Watson, H.: *The decline of Imperial Russia.* London, 1952. *Seton H.*

Seton-Watson, R. W.: 'Pan-German aspirations in the Near East' in *Journal of the Royal Society of Arts,* 64 (1916), pp. 385–397. *Seton R. W.*

Shattuck, R.: *The banquet years. The arts in France (1885–1918).* London, 1959. *Shattuck*

Shaw, G. B.: *Quintessence of Ibsenism.* London, 1891. *Shaw I*

Shaw, G. B.: *Widowers' houses.* London, 1893. *Shaw II*

Shaw, G. B.: *Het onmogelijke van het anarchisme. (The impossibility of anarchism).* Amsterdam, 1894. *Shaw III*

Shaw, G. B.: *Candida.* London, 1894. *Shaw IV*

Shaw, G. B.: *Arms and the man: an anti-romantic comedy in 3 acts.* London, 1894. *Shaw V*

Shaw, G. B.: *Caesar and Cleopatra.* London, 1901. *Shaw VI*

Shaw, G. B.: *Man and superman.* London, 1903. *Shaw VII*

Shaw, G. B.: *Socialism and superior brains: a reply to Mr. Mallock. Fabian Tract 146.* London, 1909. *Shaw VIII*

747

Shryock, R. H.: *The development of modern medicine. An interpretation of the social and scientific factors involved.* Philadelphia, 1936. *Shryock*

Siegfried, A.: *Tableau politique de la France de l'ouest sous la Troisième République.* Paris, 1914. *Siegfried*

Sighele, S.: *La folla delinquente: studio di psicologia collettiva.* Turin, 1892. *Sighele*

Simkhovitch, V. G.: *Marxism versus socialism.* London, 1914. *Simkhovitch*

Simmel E. (ed.): *Anti-Semitism. A social disease.* New York, 1946. *Simmel E.*

Simmel, G.: *Philosophie des Geldes.* Leipzig, 1900. *Simmel G.* I

Simmel, G.: *Schopenhauer und Nietzsche.* Leipzig, 1907. *Simmel G.* II

Simmel, G.: *Soziologie. Untersuchungen über die Formen der Vergesellschaftung.* Leipzig, 1908. *Simmel G.* III

Simmel, G.: *Die Religion.* Frankfurt a.Main, 1912. *Simmel G.* IV

Simmel, G.: *Goethe.* Leipzig, 1913. *Simmel G.* V

Simmel, G.: *Lebensanschauung.* Munich, 1918. *Simmel G.* VI

Simmel, G.: *Rembrandt. Ein kunstphilosophischer Versuch.* Leipzig, 1919. *Simmel G.* VII

Simon, Dr.: 'Bladvulling' in *De wegwijzer. Maandschrift voor geheelonthouding,* 3 (1900), p. 73. *Simon*

Sinclair, U.: *The jungle.* London, 1907. *Sinclair*

Singer, Ch.: *A short history of medicine.* Oxford, 1928. *Singer Ch.*

Singer, I.: *Das Land der Monopole: Amerika oder Deutschland?* Berlin, 1913. *Singer* I

Sinzheimer, H.: *Jüdische Klassiker der deutschen Rechtswissenschaft.* Amsterdam, 1938. *Sinzheimer*

Sitte, C.: *Der Städte-Bau nach seinen künstlerischen Grundsätzen.* Vienna, 1889. *Sitte*

√ Sitwell, O.: *Left hand, right hand. An autobiography.* 5 vols. London, 1945-'50. *Sitwell*

Slotemaker de Bruïne, J. R.: *Buitenkerkelijke religie.* Groningen, 1919. *Slotemaker*

Smith, Goldwin: *Commonwealth or empire: a bystander's view of the question.* London, 1902. *Smith*

Smuts, J. C.: *Holism and evolution.* London, 1926. *Smuts*

Snethlage, J. L.: *De schoolopvoeding in Amerika en het vraagstuk der kennis.* Amsterdam, 1923. *Snethlage*

Snowden, P.: *The socialist's budget.* London, 1907. *Snowden*

Soergel, A.: *Dichtung und Dichter der Zeit.* Leipzig, 1922. *Soergel*

Soesman, F. J.: *De moderne vrouwenbeweging van psychologisch-philosophisch standpunt bezien.* The Hague, 1905. *Soesman*

Sokolow, N.: *History of Zionism, 1600-1918.* 2 vols. London, 1919. *Sokolow*

Sombart, W.: 'Die Entwicklungstendenzen im modernen Kleinhandel' in *Verhandlungen der am 25., 26 und 27. September 1899 in Breslau abgehaltenen Generalversammlung des Vereins für Socialpolitik,* 88 (1900), pp. 137-157. Leipzig, 1900. *Sombart* I

Sombart, W.: *Sozialismus und soziale Bewegung.* Jena, 1920. *Sombart* II

Sombart, W.: *Die deutsche Volkswirtschaft im neunzehnten Jahrhundert und im Anfang des 20, Jahrhunderts.* Berlin, 1921. *Sombart* III

Sombart, W.: *Der moderne Kapitalismus.* Vol. 3. *Das Wirtschaftsleben im Zeitalter des Hochkapitalismus.* Munich, 1927. *Sombart* IV

Sombart, W.: *Die drei Nationalökonomien. Geschichte und System der Lehre von der Wirtschaft.* Munich, 1930. *Sombart* V

Sombart, W.: Review by E. Schams 'Die ⟨zweite⟩ Nationalökonomie' in *Archiv für Sozialwissenschaft und Sozialpolitik,* 64 (1930), pp. 453-491. *Sombart* VI

Sorel, G.: *Le procès de Socrate.* Paris, 1889. *Sorel* I

Sorel, G.: 'Les polémiques pour l'interprétation du marxisme' in *Revue international de sociologie*, 8 (1900), pp. 262-284, 348-369. *Sorel* II

Sorel, G.: *La décomposition du marxisme*. Paris, 1908. *Sorel* III

Sorel, G.: *Les illusions du progrès*. Paris, 1908. *Sorel* IV

Sorel, G.: *Réflexions sur la violence*. Paris, 1908. *Sorel* V

Sorel, G.: *De l'utilité du pragmatisme*. Paris, 1921. *Sorel* VI

Sorel, G.: *Die Auflösung des Marxismus*. E. H. Posse (ed.). Jena, 1930. *Sorel* VII

Sorokin, P.: *Contemporary sociological theories*. New York, 1928. *Sorokin*

Southard, F. A.: *American industry in Europe*. Boston, 1931. *Southard*

Spaanstra-Polak, B. H.: 'Jugendstil in de Nederlandse schilderkunst en grafiek' in *Forum. Maandblad voor architectuur en gebonden kunst*, II (1958-'59), pp. 345-357. *Spaanstra*

Spann, O.: *Die Haupttheorien der Volkswirtschaftslehre*. Leipzig, 1931. *Spann*

Specht, R.: *Arthur Schnitzler*. Berlin, 1922. *Specht*

Speenhoff, J. H.: *Liedjes, wijzen en prentjes*. 4th set. Rotterdam, 1907. *Speenhoff*

Spek, L. A. M. van der: *Bloedgroepen en hare beteekenis voor de praktijk*. Amsterdam, 1941. *Spek*

Spencer, H.: *Man versus the state*. London, 1884. *Spencer* I

Spencer, H.: 'The inadequacy of natural selection' in *The contemporary review*, 63 (1893), pp. 153-166 and pp. 439-456. *Spencer* II

Spiegel, H. W. (ed.): *Development of economic thought. Great economists in perspective*. New York, 1952. *Spiegel*

Spiekman, H.: 'Arbeids-secretariaten' in *De nieuwe tijd*, 5 (1900), pp. 1-9 and 375-381. *Spiekman*

Spitz, D.: *Patterns of anti-democratic thought. An analysis and a criticism, with a special reference to the American political mind in recent times*. New York, 1949. *Spitz*

Spranger, E.: *Lebensformen*. Halle, 1914. *Spranger*

Sprenger, A.: *Babylonien, das reichtste Land in der Vorzeit und das lohnendste Kolonisationsfeld für die Gegenwart. Ein Vorschlag zur Kolonisation des Orients. Mit einem Anhang: Metrologie der Araber*. Heidelberg, 1886. *Sprenger*

Springer, A.: *Handbuch der Kunstgeschichte*. Vol. 5. Leipzig, 1912. *Springer*

Spykman, N. J.: *The social theory of Georg Simmel*. Chicago, 1925. *Spykman*

Stam, J. J.: *George Tyrrell (1861-1909)*. Utrecht, 1938. *Stam*

Stammhammer, J.: *Bibliographie des Socialismus und Kommunismus. Nachträge und Ergänzungen bis Ende 1898*. 2 vols. Jena, 1900. *Stammhammer*

Stammler, R.: *Wirtschaft und Recht nach der materialistischen Geschichtsauffassung*. 3 vols. Leipzig, 1893-1909. *Stammler* I

Stammler, R.: *Die Lehre vom dem richtigen Rechte*. Berlin, 1902. *Stammler* II

Starbuck, E. D.: *The psychology of religion*. London, 1899. *Starbuck*

Stark, W.: *The history of economics in its relation to social development*. London, 1945. *Stark*

Staudinger, F.: *Ethik und Politik*. Berlin, 1899. *Staudinger*

Stead, W. T.: *Mr. Carnegie's conundrum, £ 40.000.000*. London, 1899. *Stead* I

Stead, W. T.: *The Americanization of the world*. London, 1902. *Stead* II

Stead, W. T.: *Peers or people? The House of Lords weighed in the balance and found wanting. An appeal to history*. London, 1907. *Stead* III

Steiger, G. N.: *China and the Occident. The origin and the development of the Boxer movement*. New Haven, 1927. *Steiger*

Stein, L.: *An der Wende des Jahrhunderts. Versuch einer Kulturphilosophie*. Freiburg i.Br., 1899. *Stein L.* I

Stein, L.: *Philosophische Strömungen der Gegenwart*. Stuttgart, 1908. *Stein L.* II

Stein, W.: *Kulturfahrplan. Die wichtigsten Daten der Kulturgeschichte von Anbeginn bis heute.* Berlin, 1954. *Stein W.*

Steiner, R.: *Mein Lebensgang.* Dornach, 1925. *Steiner*

Steinmetz, S. R.: *Het feminisme,* Leiden, 1899. *Steinmetz I*

Steinmetz, S. R.: *Wat is sociologie?* Leiden, 1900. *Steinmetz II*

Stengel, K. von: *Der ewige Friede.* Munich, 1899. *Stengel*

Stéphane, N.: *Le pauvre Vincent.* Paris, 1954. *Stéphane*

Sternberger, D.: *Über den Jugendstil und andere Essays.* Hamburg, 1956. *Sternberger*

Stevenson, L. G.: *Nobel prize winners in medicine and physiology, 1901-'50.* New York, 1954. *Stevenson*

Sticker, G.: *Abhandlungen aus der Seuchengeschichte und Seuchenlehre.* I *Die Pest.* Giessen, 1907. *Sticker*

Stillich, O.: *Die Lage der weiblichen Dienstboten in Berlin.* Berlin, 1902. *Stillich*

Stimpfl, J.: 'Stand der Kinderpsychologie in Europa und Amerika' in *Zeitschrift für pädagogische Psychologie,* I (1899), pp. 344-361. *Stimpfl*

Stirner, M.: *Der Einzige und sein Eigentum.* Leipzig, 1845. *Stirner*

Stoffers, H. E.: 'Een terugblik' in *Vooruitgang op medisch en verplegingsgebied in de laatste 25 jaar. Herdenkingsbundel bij 25 jaar Tijdschrift voor ziekenverpleging.* Amsterdam, 1916, pp. 118-120. *Stoffers*

Stomps, T.: *Aus dem Leben und Wirken von Hugo de Vries.* Tübingen, 1928. *Stomps*

Storey, G.: *Reuters' century (1851-1951).* London, 1951. *Storey*

Strachey, L.: *Eminent Victorians.* London, 1918. *Strachey*

Stutterheim, K. von: *Die englische Presse von ihren Anfängen bis zur Gegenwart.* Berlin, 1933. *Stutterheim*

Südfeld, Max (Max Nordau): *Die Krankheit des Jahrhunderts.* 2 vols. Leipzig, 1889. *Südfeld*

Suess-Rath, H.: *Der Londoner Frauen-Congress.* Vienna, 1900. *Suess*

Sully, J.: *Studies of childhood.* London, 1895. *Sully*

Suranyi-Unger, Th.: *Economics in the 20th century. The history of its international development.* London, 1932. *Suranyi*

Sury d'Apremont, P. de: *La presse à travers les âges. Les origines et le développement de la presse en France, en Angleterre, en Allemagne et aux Etats-Unis.* Paris, 1929. *Sury*

Suttner, B. von: *Krieg und Frieden.* Munich, 1900. *Suttner I*

Suttner, B. von: *Der Kampf um die Vermeidung des Weltkriegs. Randglossen aus zwei Jahrzehnten zu den Zeitereignissen vor der Katastrophe (1892-1900 und 1907-1914).* A. H. Fried (ed.). Zürich, 1917. *Suttner II*

Suys, J.: *Leo Sjestow's protest tegen de rede. De intellectueele biografie van een Russisch denker.* Amsterdam, 1931. *Suys*

Swift, J.: *Gulliver's travels.* London, 1726. *Swift*

Sybil (Ch. Benoist): *Croquis parlementaires.* Paris, 1891. *Sybil*

Sykes, P.: *A history of exploration from the earliest times to the present day.* London, 1950. *Sykes*

Synge, J. M.: *The playboy of the western world.* London, 1907. *Synge*

Tager, A. S.: *Decay of Czarism: the Beiliss trial. A contribution to the history of the political reaction during the last years of Russian Czarism, based on unpublished materials in the Russian archives.* Philadelphia, 1935. *Tager*

Taine, H.: *Histoirie de la littérature anglaise.* 4 vols. Paris, 1863-'64. *Taine*

Tamir, M.: *Les expositions internationales à travers les âges.* Paris, 1939. *Tamir*

Tank, K. L.: *Gerhart Hauptmann in Selbstzeugnissen und Bilddokumenten.* Hamburg, 1959. *Tank*

Tarde, G.: *Les transformations du droit. Etude sociologique.* Paris, 1893. *Tarde* I

Tarde, G.: *La philosophie pénale.* Paris, 1903. *Tarde* II

Tarnowsky, B.: *Prostitution und abolitionismus.* Hamburg, 1890. *Tarnowsky*

Tavernier, E.: *Du journalisme. Son histoire, son rôle politique et religieuse.* Paris, 1902. *Tavernier*

Taylor, F. W.: *Principles of scientific management.* London, 1911. *Taylor* I

Taylor, F. W.: *Shop management.* London, 1911. *Taylor* II

Teggart, F. J.: *Theory and processes of history.* Berkeley, 1941. *Teggart*

Ten Eyck Firkins, I.: *Henrik Ibsen.* New York, 1921. *Ten Eyck*

Terrail, G. (Mermeix): *Les coulisses du Boulangisme.* Paris, 1890. *Terrail*

The history of christianity in the light of modern knowledge. A collective work. London, 1929. *The history*

Theosofie en het maatschappelijke vraagstuk door verschillende schrijvers. Amsterdam, 1908. *Theosofie*

Thier, E.: *Rodbertus, Lassalle, Adolph Wagner. Ein Beitrag zur Theorie und Geschichte des deutschen Staatssozialismus.* Leipzig, 1930. *Thier*

Thomas, A.: *Les pétroleuses.* Paris, 1964. *Thomas A.*

Thomas, H. B. & R. Scott: *Uganda.* London, 1935. *Thomas H. B.*

Thompsen, V.: *Geschichte der Sprachwissenschaft bis zum Ausgang des 19. Jahrhunderts.* Halle, 1927. *Thompsen*

Thomson, J. J.: *Conduction of electricity through gases.* Cambridge, 1903. *Thomson*

Thuillier, P.: *Le fonctionnement du régime parlementaire en France et en Angleterre.* Lyon, 1899. *Thuillier*

Tiele, C. P.: *Elements of the science of religion.* 2 vols. Edinburgh, 1897-'99. *Tiele* I

Tiele, C. P.: *Inleiding tot de godsdienstwetenschap.* Amsterdam, 1897-'99. *Tiele* II

Tielrooy, J.: *De levende gedachten van Maeterlinck.* The Hague, 1941. *Tielrooy*

Tietze, H.: *Die Methode der Kunstgeschichte.* Leipzig, 1913. *Tietze*

Tilgenkamp, E.: *Der Luftverkehr. Seine Entstehung und Entwicklung. Seine ökonomischen Grundlagen.* Usten, 1924. *Tilgenkamp*

Tilquin, A.: *Le behaviorisme. Origine et développement de la psychologie de réaction en Amérique.* Paris, 1942. *Tilquin*

Tönnies, F.: *Gemeinschaft und Gesellschaft.* Leipzig, 1887. *Tönnies* I

Tönnies, F.: *Der Nietzsche-Kultus. Eine Kritik.* Leipzig, 1897. *Tönnies* II

Toorenburg, P. A. van: *Kinderrecht en kinderzorg in de laatste honderd jaren.* Leiden, 1918. *Toorenburg*

Töpffer, R.: *Histoire de monsieur Cryptogame.* Paris, 1845. *Töpffer*

Toussenel, A.: *Les juifs, rois de l'époque.* 2 vols. Paris, 1847. *Toussenel*

Treitschke, H. von: *Zehn Jahre deutsche Kämpfe.* Berlin, 1879. *Treitschke* I

Treitschke, H. von: *Briefe.* 3 vols. Leipzig, 1912-'20. *Treitschke* II

Treub, M. W. F.: *Het economisch standpunt der vrijzinnig-democraten.* Amsterdam, 1901. *Treub* I

Treub, M. W. F.: *Het wijsgerig-economisch stelsel van Karl Marx.* 2 vols. Amsterdam, 1902-'03. *Treub* II

Tridon, G.: *Du molochisme juif.* Brussels, 1884. *Tridon*

Trier, E.: *Moderne Plastik. Von Auguste Rodin bis Marino Marini.* Berlin, 1954. *Trier*

Trine, R. W.: *In tune with the infinite; or, fulness of peace, power, and plenty.* London, 1899. *Trine*

Troeltsch, E.: *Die Soziallehren der christlichen Kirchen und Gruppen.* Tübingen, 1912. *Troeltsch* I

Troeltsch, E.: 'Der Modernismus' in *Gesammelte Schriften*, II, pp. 45-67. Tübingen, 1913. *Troeltsch* II

Troeltsch, E.: *Der Historismus und seine Probleme.* Tübingen, 1922. *Troeltsch* III

Trotsky, N.: *Russland in der Revolution.* Dresden, 1909. *Trotsky*

Tugan-Baranowsky, M.: *Geschichte der russischen Fabrik.* Berlin, 1900. *Tugan* I

Tugan-Baranowsky, M.: *Studien zur Theorie und Geschichte der Handelskrisen in England.* Jena, 1901. *Tugan* II

Tugan-Baranowsky, M: *Theoretische Grundlagen des Marxismus.* Leipzig, 1905. *Tugan* III

Tugan-Baranowsky, M.: *Les crises industrielles en Angleterre.* Paris, 1913. *Tugan* IV

Tugwell, R. G.: 'Notes on the life and work of S. N. Patten' in *The journal of political economy,* 31 (1923), pp. 153–208. *Tugwell*

Turgeon, C.: *Le féminisme français.* 2 vols. Paris, 1902. *Turgeon*

Turley, K.: *Arno Holz. Der Weg eines Künstlers.* Leipzig, 1935. *Turley*

Twain, M.: *The adventures of Tom Sawyer.* 1876. *Twain* I

Twain, M.: *The adventures of Huckleberry Finn.* 1885. *Twain* II

Tylor, E. B.: *Primitive culture.* 2 vols. London, 1871. *Tylor* I

Tylor, E. B.: *Anthropology. Introduction to the study of man and civilisation.* London, 1881. *Tylor* II

Tyrrel, G.: *Through Scylla and Charybdis, or the old theology and the new.* London, 1907. *Tyrrel*

Tyszka, C. von: *Die Lebenshaltung der arbeitenden Klassen in den bedeutenderen Industriestaaten: England, Deutschland, Frankreich, Belgien und Vereinigte Staaten von Amerika.* Jena, 1912. *Tyszka*

Uexküll, J. von: *Umwelt und Innenwelt der Tierre.* Berlin, 1909. *Uexküll*

Ufermann, P.: *Der deutsche Stahltrust.* Berlin, 1927. *Ufermann*

50 Jahre Ullstein, 1877–1927. Berlin, 1927. *Ullstein* I

Ullstein, H.: *The rise and fall of the house of Ullstein.* London, ca. 1944. *Ullstein* II

Umbgrove, J. H. F.: *Leven en materie.* The Hague, 1943. *Umbgrove*

Unamuno, M.: *Del sentimiento trágico de la vida.* Madrid, 1913. *Unamuno*

Ungern-Sternberg, R. von: 'Die Ursachen der Steigerung der Selbstmordhäufigkeit in West-Europa während der letzten hundert Jahre' in *Veröffentlichungen auf dem Gebiete der Medizinalverwaltung,* 44. Berlin, 1935. *Ungern*

Untermann, E.: *Die logischen Mängel des engeren Marxismus. Georg Plechanow et alii gegen Josef Dietzgen. Auch ein Beitrag zur Geschichte des Materialismus.* Munich, 1910. *Untermann*

Ursyn-Pruszynski, R. von: *Grundelemente der neuen chinesischen Staatsform.* Vienna, 1911. *Ursyn*

Usher, A. P.: *History of mechanical inventions.* Cambridge (Mass.), 1955. *Usher*

Vaihinger, H.: *Die Philosophie des Als ob.* Berlin, 1911. *Vaihinger*

Valarché, J.: 'E. Bernstein, marxiste national' in *Revue d'histoire économique et sociale,* volume 27 (1948), pp. 298–322. *Valarché*

Valentin, H.: *Antisemitenspiegel. Der Antisemitismus. Geschichte, Kritik, Soziologie.* Vienna, 1937. *Valentin*

Valéry, P.: *Variété.* 5 vols. Paris, 1930. *Valéry*

Vallas, L.: *Achille-Claude Debussy.* Paris, 1944. *Vallas*

Vanderbilt-Balsan, C.: *The glitter and the gold. Autobiography.* London, 1953. *Vanderbilt*

Vandervelde, E.: 'De groeikoorts van het socialisme.' Report of a lecture delivered on 22 Oct. 1900, in *Propria Cures,* 12 (1900–'01). pp. 65–66. *Vandervelde* I

Vandervelde, E.: 'Das Wachsthum des internationalen Sozialismus' in *Die neue Zeit,* 19 (1900–'01), pp. 388–395. *Vandervelde* II

Vandervelde, E.: *L'exode rural et le retour aux champs.* Paris, 1903. *Vandervelde* III

Varennes, H.: *De Ravachol à Caserio.* Paris, 1895. *Varennes*

Velde, H. van de: *Kunstgewerbliche Laienpredigten.* Leipzig, 1902. *Velde* I

Velde, H. van de: *Die Renaissance im modernen Kunstgewerbe.* Berlin, 1903. *Velde* II

Velde, H. van de: *Zum neuen Stil. Aus seinen Schriften ausgewählt und eingeleitet von Hans Curjel.* Munich, 1955. *Velde* III

Vendryes, J.: 'Antoine Meillet' in *Bulletin de la Société Linguistique de Paris,* 38 (1937), pp. 1–42. *Vendryes*

Verlaine, P.: *Jadis et naguère.* Paris, 1885. *Verlaine*

Vermeil, E.: *L'Allemagne.* Paris, 1940. *Vermeil*

Vermeylen, A.: *Kritiek der Vlaamsche beweging.* Bussum, 1905. *Vermeylen*

Vermij, M. O.: 'Het cubisme als geestesverschijnsel der twintigste eeuw' in *Centaur* (1947–'48), pp. 149–156. *Vermij*

Vernède, C. H.: *Geschiedenis der ziekenverpleging.* Haarlem, 1927. *Vernède*

Verney, N., & G. Dambmann: *Les puissances étrangères dans le Levant, en Syrie et en Palestine.* Lyon, 1900. *Verney*

Verslag der commissie tot uitzending van werklieden naar de wereldtentoonstelling te Parijs in 1900. (Report by H. L. Boersma.) N.p., 1901. *Verslag*

Viau, R.: *Vingt ans d'antisémitisme (1889–1909).* Paris, 1910. *Viau*

Visscher, J.: *De onder gang van een wereld. Historisch-economische studie over de oorzaken van den Anglo-Boer Oorlog (1899–1902).* Rotterdam, 1903. *Visscher*

Vizetelly, E. A.: *The anarchists. Their faith and their record.* London, 1912. *Vizetelly*

Voet, M. van der: *Friedrich Naumann. Een hoofdstuk uit de sociale ethiek.* Leiden, 1934. *Voet*

Vogel, H.: 'Zur Verstaatlichung des Medizinalwesens' in *Die neue Zeit,* 15 (1897), pp. 364–368. *Vogel*

Vogüé E. de: *Les Morts qui parlent.* Paris, 1899. *Vogüé* I

Vogüé E. M. de: 'La défunte exposition' in *Revue des deux mondes,* 142 (Nov.-Dec. 1900), pp. 380–399. *Vogüé* II

Vollmar, G. von: *Über Staatssocialismus.* Nuremburg, 1892. *Vollmar* I

Vollmar, G. von: *Über die nächsten Aufgaben der deutschen Sozialdemokratie.* (Rede in der Parteiversammlung, I.6.1891, im Eldorado zu München.) Munich, 1899. *Vollmar* II

Voo, B. P. van der: '⟨De Naturiens⟩, de bestrijders der beschaving' in *Vragen van den dag,* 13 (1898), pp. 662–681. *Voo*

Vorländer, K.: *Kant und der Sozialismus, unter besonderer Berücksichtigung der neuesten theoretischen Bewegung innerhalb des Marxismus.* Berlin, 1900. *Vorländer* I

Vorländer, K.: *Marx und Kant.* Vienna, 1904. *Vorländer* II

Vorländer, K.: *Kant und Marx. Ein Beitrag zur Philosophie des Sozialismus.* Tübingen, 1911. *Vorländer* III

Vorster, J.: *Die Grossindustrie. Eine der Grundlagen nationaler Sozialpolitik.* Jena, 1896. *Vorster*

Vossler, K.: *Positivismus und Idealismus in der Sprachwissenschaft.* Berlin, 1904. *Vossler*

Vries, C. W. de: 'Bijdrage tot de staatkundige geschiedenis der arbeidswetgeving in Nederland. Tien jaar sociale hervormingsarbeid onder leiding van een liberale regerring, 1891–1901' in *Themis,* 85 (1924), pp. 209–235, 273–318, 385–429. *Vries C. W.*

Vries, H. de: *Hoe soorten ontstaan.* Haarlem, 1900. *Vries H.* I

Vries, H. de: *Die Mutationstheorie.* 2 vols. Leipzig, 1901–'03. *Vries H.* II

Vries, H. de: 'The origin of the mutation theory' in *The monist,* 27 (1917), pp. 403–410. *Vries H.* III

Vijgh, S. E. van der: *Werkers.* Haarlem, 1900. *Vijgh*

Waentig, H.: *Gewerbliche Mittelstandspolitik. Rechtshistorisch-wirtschaftspolitische Studie auf Grund österreichischer Quellen.* Leipzig, 1898. *Waentig*

Wagner, A.: *Finanzwissenschaft.* 3 vols. Leipzig, 1910. *Wagner A.* I

Wagner, A.: *Die Strömungen in der Sozialpolitik und der Katheder- und Staatssozialismus.* Berlin, 1912. *Wagner A.* II

Wagner, O.: *Moderne Architektur. Seinen Schülern ein Führer auf diesem Kunstgebiete.* Vienna, 1914. *Wagner O.*

Wahl, J.: *Les philosophies pluralistes d'Angleterre et d'Amérique.* Paris, 1920. *Wahl*

Waldersee, A. von: *Denkwürdigkeiten.* (ed.) H. O. Meisner. 3 vols. Stuttgart, 1922-'23. *Waldersee*

Wallace, A. R.: *My life. A record of events and opinions.* London, 1908. *Wallace*

Wallraf, K.: *Die 'bürgerliche Gesellschaft' im Spiegel deutscher Familienzeitschriften.* Keulen, 1939. *Wallraf*

Walpole, H.: *Fortitude.* London, 1913. *Walpole*

Walsh, E. A.: *Total power. A footnote to history.* New York, 1948. *Walsh*

Walter-London, H. A.: *Die neuere englische Sozialpolitik.* Munich, 1914. *Walter*

Ward, M. H.: *Robert Elsmere.* 3 vols. London, 1888. *Ward* I

Ward, M. H.: *Eleanor.* London, 1900. *Ward* II

Warnotte, D.: 'Bureaucratie et fonctionnarisme' in *Revue de l'Institut de Sociologie,* 17 (1937), pp. 219–260. *Warnotte*

Washburn, M. F.: *The animal mind. A text-book of comparative psychology.* London, 1908. *Washburn*

Watson, J. B.: 'Psychology as the behaviorist views it' in *Psychological review,* 20 (1913), pp. 158–177. *Watson*

Weale, B. L. (Putnam): *Indiscreet letters from Peking.* London, 1900. *Weale*

Webb, S. & B.: *Problems of modern industry.* London, 1898. *Webb* I

Webb, S.: 'The basis of socialism: historic' in *Fabian essays in socialism* (G. B. Shaw et al.), pp. 30–61. London, 1911. *Webb* II

Weber, A.: *Ideen zur Staats- und Kultursoziologie.* Karlsruhe, 1927. *Weber A.*

Weber, A. F.: *Growth of cities in the 19th. century. A study in statistics.* New York, 1899. *Weber A. F.*

Weber, G. & A. Baldamus: *Lehr- und Handbuch der Weltgeschichte.* 4 vols. Leipzig, 1912-'14. *Weber G.*

Weber, M.: *Die Verhältnisse der Landarbeiter im ostelbischen Deutschland, dargestellt auf Grund der vom Verein für Socialpolitik veranstalteten Erhebungen.* Leipzig, 1892. *Weber M.* I

Weber, M.: *Gesammelte Aufsätze zur Religionssoziologie.* 3 vols. Tübingen, 1921-'23. *Weber M.* II

Weber, M.: *Gesammelte Aufsätze zur Wissenschaftslehre.* Tübingen, 1922. *Weber M.* III

Weber, M.: 'Roscher und Knies und die logischen Probleme der historischen Nationalökonomie' in *Gesammelte Aufsätze zur Wissenschaftslehre,* pp. 1–145. Tübingen, 1922. *Weber M.* IV

Weber, M.: *Wirtschaft und Gesellschaft.* Tübingen, 1925. *Weber M.* V

Weber, Marianne: *Max Weber. Ein Lebensbild.* Tübingen, 1926. *Weber Marianne*

Wechssler, E.: 'Giebt es Lautgesetze?' in *Forschungen zur romanischen Philologie. Festgabe für Hermann Suchier zum. 15. März 1900,* pp. 349–538. *Wechssler*

Wedekind, F.: *Frühlings Erwachen. Eine Kindertragödie.* Zürich, 1892. *Wedekind* I

Wedekind, F.: *Frühlings Erwachen.* Munich, 1892. *Wedekind* II

Wedekind, F.: *Erdgeist.* Munich, 1895. *Wedekind* III

Wehberg, H.: *Die internationale Beschränkung der Rüstungen.* Stuttgart, 1919. *Wehberg*

Weininger, O.: *Geschlecht und Charakter.* Vienna, 1903. *Weininger*

Weisengrün, P.: *Das Ende des Marxismus.* Leipzig, 1899. *Weisengrün* I

Weisengrün, P.: *Der Marxismus und das Wesen der sozialen Frage.* Leipzig, 1900. *Weisengrün* II

Weismann, A.: *Die Allmacht der Naturzüchtung.* Jena, 1893. *Weismann*

Weiss, J.: *Die Predigt Jesu vom Reiche Gottes.* Göttingen, 1892. *Weiss* I

Weiss, J.: *Die Idee des Reiches Gottes in der Theologie.* Giessen, 1901. *Weiss* II

Wells, H. G.: *The time machine.* London, 1895. *Wells* I

Wells, H. G.: *Ann Veronica.* London, 1911. *Wells* II

Wells, H. G.: *The new Machiavelli.* London, 1911. *Wells* III

Wells, H. G.: *Experiment in autobiography. Discoveries and conclusions of a very ordinary brain (since 1866).* New York, 1934. *Wells* IV

Went, F. A. F. C.: *Hugo de Vries.* Haarlem, 1900. *Went*

Wernicke, J.: *Kapitalismus und Mittelstandspolitik.* Jena, 1907. *Wernicke* I

Wernicke, J.: *Der Mittelstand und seine wirtschaftliche Lage.* Leipzig, 1909. *Wernicke* II

Wertheimer, M.: 'Experimentelle Studien über das Sehen von Bewegungen' in *Zeitschrift für Psychologie,* 61 (1912), pp. 161–265. *Wertheimer*

Westerman, W. M.: *De concentratie in het bankwezen. Een bijdrage tot de kennis der economische ontwikkeling van onzen tijd.* The Hague, 1919. *Westerman*

Weynen, A.: 'Jac. van Ginneken' in *Jaarboek van de Mij. der Ned. Letterkunde te Leiden,* 1946–'47, pp. 50–59. *Weynen*

Wheeler, B. I.: *The whence and whither of the modern science of language.* Berkeley, 1905. *Wheeler*

White, A. D.: *A history of the warfare of science with theology in Christendom.* 2 vols. London, 1896. *White A. D.*

White, R. C.: *The growth of German social insurance.* Bloomington, 1933. *White R. C.*

Whitman, W.: *Leaves of Grass.* 1855. *Whitman*

Whittaker, E.: *A history of economic ideas.* New York, 1940. *Whittaker*

Wibaut, F. M.: *Trusts en kartellen.* Amsterdam, 1903. *Wibaut*

Wichman, E. & C. L. Dake: *Nieuwe richtingen in de schilderkunst. (Cubisme, expressionisme, futurisme, etc.)* Baarn, 1914. *Wichman E.*

Wichmann, H.: 'Die englischen Bemühungen um Arabien und die Bagdadbahn' in *Petermanns Mitteilungen,* 1913, II, pp. 113–114. *Wichmann H.*

Wiedemann, M.: *Deutsche Orient Korrespondenz.* Berlin, 1911. *Wiedemann*

Wiener, N.: *Cybernetics.* Paris, 1948. *Wiener*

Wigand, A.: *Der Darwinismus und die Naturforschung Newtons und Cuviers. Beiträge zur Methodik der Naturforschung und zur Speciesfrage.* 3 vols. Brunswick, 1874–'77. *Wigand*

Wilde, O.: *The picture of Dorian Gray.* London, 1891. *Wilde*

Williams, B.: *Cecil Rhodes.* London, 1921. *Williams*

Willy, R.: *Die Krisis in der Psychologie.* Leipzig, 1899. *Willy*

Wingfield-Stratfield, E.: *History of British Civilization.* London, 1928. *Wingfield*

Winslow, E. M.: *Pattern of imperialism. A study in the theories of power.* Oxford, 1948. *Winslow*

Winterstetten, K. von: *Berlin-Bagdad. Neue Ziele mitteleuropäischer Politik.* Munich, 1915. *Winterstetten*

Wirminghaus, A.: 'Stadt und Land unter dem Einfluss der Binnenwanderungen. Ein Überblick über den gegenwärtigen Stand der Forschung' in *Jahrbücher für Nationalökonomie und Statistik,* III, 9 (1895), pp. 1–34, 161–182. *Wirminghaus*

Wischnitzer, M.: *To dwell in safety. The story of Jewish migration since 1800.* Philadelphia, 1948. *Wischnitzer*

Woermann, K.: *Was uns die Kunstgeschichte lehrt. Einige Bemerkungen über alte, neue und neueste Malerei.* Dresden, 1894. *Woermann*

Wolf, E.: *Krisis und Neubau der Strafrechtsreform.* Tübingen, 1933. *Wolf E.* I

Wolf, E.: *Grosse Rechtsdenker der deutschen Geistesgeschichte.* Tübingen, 1951. *Wolf E.* II

Wolf, J.: *System der Sozialpolitik.* Vol. I. *Sozialismus und kapitalistische Gesellschaftsordnung.* Stuttgart, 1892. *Wolf J.*

Wolf, J. B.: *Diplomatic history of the Bagdad railroad.* Missouri, 1936. *Wolf J. B.*

Wolf-Czapek, K. W.: *Die Kinematographie. Wesen, Entstehung und Ziele des lebendigen Bildes.* Dresden, 1908. *Wolf-Czapek*

Wolff, G.: *Beiträge zur Kritik der Darwin'schen Lehre.* Leipzig, 1898. *Wolff*

Woltmann, L.: *Der historische Materialismus. Darstellung und Kritik der marxistischen Weltanschauung.* Düsseldorf, 1900. *Woltmann*

Wolzogen, E. von: *Ecce Ego. Erst komme ich!* 2 vols. Berlin, 1896. *Wolzogen*

Woodcock, G. & I. Avakumović: *Anarchist prince. A biographical study of Peter Kropotkin.* New York, 1950. *Woodcock*

Woolf, V.: *A room of one's own.* London, 1945. *Woolf*

Worms, R.: 'Séance du Société de Sociologie de Paris, 12 décembre 1906' in *Revue internationale de sociologie,* 15 (1907), pp. 56–57. *Worms* I

Worms, R.: 'Maxime Kovalewsky' in *Revue internationale de sociologie,* 24 (1916), pp. 257–263. *Worms* II

Wortman, J. L. C.: 'De sociale positie der verplegenden' in *Vooruitgang op medisch en verplegingsgebied in de laatste 25 jaar. Herdenkingsbundel bij 25 jaar Tijdschrift voor ziekenverpleging,* pp. 111–117. Amsterdam, 1916. *Wortman*

Wright, W.: *Experiments and observations in soaring flight.* Chicago, 1903. *Wright W.*

Wright, W. K.: *A history of modern philosophy.* New York, 1941. *Wright W. K.*

Wundt, W.: *Völkerpsychologie.* 13 vols. Leipzig, 1900–'20. *Wundt*

Wurm, E.: *Die Lebenshaltung der deutschen Arbeiter. Ihre Ernährung und Wohnung. Nebst einem Anhang: Die Zusammensetzung der Nahrungsmittel.* Dresden, 1892. *Wurm*

Wijnaendts Francken, C. J.: *De zelfmoord. Een sociologische studie.* The Hague, 1899. *Wijnaendts*

Wyneken, G.: *Schule und Jugendkultur.* Jena, 1919. *Wyneken* I

Wyneken, G.: *Die neue Jugend. Ihr Kampf um Freiheit und Wahrheit in Schule und Elternhaus, in Religion und Erotik.* Munich, 1919. *Wyneken* II

Xénopol, A. D.: *Les principes fondamentaux de l'histoire.* Paris, 1899. *Xénopol*

Yeats, W. B.: *Autobiographies.* London, 1955. *Yeats*

Yerkes, R. M.: *Almost human.* New York, 1925. *Yerkes*

Youssoupoff, F.: *Avant l'exil, 1887–1919.* Paris, 1952. *Youssoupoff*

Zabel, R.: *Deutschland in China.* Leipzig, 1902. *Zabel*

Zedlitz-Trützschler, R.: *Zwölf Jahre am deutschen Kaiserhof. Aufzeichnungen.* Stuttgart, 1924. *Zedlitz*

Zehder, H.: *Wassily Kandinsky. Unter Benutzung der russischen Selbstbiographie.* Dresden, 1920. *Zehder*

Zeller B.: *Hermann Hesse.* Hamburg, 1963. *Zeller*

Zenker, E. V.: *Reform des Parlamentarismus.* Vienna, 1902. *Zenker* I

Zenker, E. V.: *Der Parlamentarismus. Sein Wesen und seine Entwicklung.* Vienna, 1914. *Zenker* II

Zenner, R.: *Die Not des vierten Standes. Von einem Arzte.* Leipzig, 1894. *Zenner*

Zévaès, A.: *L'affaire Dreyfus.* Paris, 1931. *Zévaès*

Zilboorg, G.: *History of medical psychology*. New York, 1941. *Zilboorg*

Zitzmann, G.: *Trusts und Antitrustbewegung*. Munich, 1928. *Zitzmann*

Zoccoli, H.: *Die Anarchie. Ihre Verkünder, ihre Ideen, ihre Taten*. Leipzig, 1909. *Zoccoli*

Zola, E.: *Au bonheur des dames*. Paris, 1883. *Zola* I

Zola, E.: *Germinal*. Paris, 1885. *Zola* II

Zola, E.: *Travail*. Paris, 1901. *Zola* III

Zola, E.: *Les oeuvres complètes. Oeuvres critiques: La vérité en marche*. Notes et commentaires de Maurice le Blond, texte l'édition E. Fasquelle. 3 vols. Paris, 1901. *Zola* IV

Zuylen-Tromp, N. van: 'Congresindrukken' in *Belang en recht*, 4 (1900), no. 92, pp. 164–165. *Zuylen*

Zweig, A.: *Caliban oder Politik und Leidenschaft. Versuch über die menschlichen Gruppenleidenschaften dargetan am Antisemitismus*. Potsdam, 1927. *Zweig A.* I

Zweig, A.: *Versunkene Tage. Ein Roman aus dem Jahre 1908*. Amsterdam, 1938. *Zweig A.* II

Zweig, S.: *Die Heilung durch den Geist*. Leipzig, 1932. *Zweig S.* I

Zweig, S.: *Die Welt von Gestern. Erinnerungen eines Europäers*. Stockholm, 1946. *Zweig S.* II

INDEX OF NAMES

Avenel, H.: 258
Avogadro, A.: 328, 331, 332
Axa, Z. d': 84

Bab, J.: 505, 520
Babbitt, I.: 135
Baboeuf, G.: 655
Bacon, F.: 22, 482, 484
Baden Powell, R. S.: 633
Badeni, K. F.: 133
Baekeland, L. H. A.: 311
Baer, K. M.: 201
Bage, C.: 568
Bagehot, W.: 422
Baha' u 'llah: 505
Bähler, L. A.: 121, 502
Bahr, H.: 372, 516, 518, 520
Bailly, Vincent de Paul: 92
Baker, S. W.: 17
Bakker, Reverend: 173
Bakunin, M. A.: 30, 151, 154, 158,
    159, 427
Balakirew, M. A.: 576
Baldamus, A.: 455
Baldwin: 21
Balfour, A. J.: 5, 75, 248, 348
Ballantyne, J. W.: 367
Ballin, A.: 73, 124, 454, 639
Ballou, A.: 121
Bally, C.: 444
Balzac, H. de: 85
Bardèche, M.: 321
Barin, A.: 61
Barlach, E.: 550, 555, 557
Barnes, H. E.: 419, 423
Baroja, P.: 158
Barrès, M.: 78, 90, 128, 255, 534, 632
Barrie, J. M.: 630
Barth, K.: 493
Barth, P.: 452
Bartinelli: 356
Bartlett, R. A.: 21
Bartók, B.: 583, 584
Barzun, 239
Basch, V.: 154
Basjkirtsewa, M.: 590, 592
Bassermann, A.: 321
Bassus, K. M. F.: 309
Bateson, W.: 348, 349, 350
Battenberg, E. von: 152
Batts, H. J.: 54
Baudelaire, C.: 528, 530, 533, 536, 549,
    556, 566
Bauer, M.: 652
Bauer, O.: 172, 207
Bäumer, G.: 293, 294
Baumont, M.: 168
Baur, F. C.: 484
Bax, B.: 176

Bayliss, W. M.: 360
Bazel, K. P. C. de: 565, 571
Bazin, R.: 209
Beales, A. C. F.: 118, 119
Beardsley, A.: 511, 533, 537, 561, 563
Beauchamp, E. M.: 253
Beauduin, N.: 239
Beaufort, Duke of: 252
Beaulieu, L.: 375
Beaunier, A.: 90
Beausoleil: 167
Beauvoir, S. de: 591, 607
Bebel, A.: 33, 73, 122, 176, 177, 178, 610
Bechterew, W.: 407, 425
Becquerel, A. E.: 325
Becquerel, H.: 325, 331
Beerling, R. F.: 415, 461
Beers, C. W.: 280
Beethoven, L. von: 582
Beets, N.: 609
Behrens, P.: 568, 571, 572
Behring, E.: 355
Beilis, M.: 96
Beleredi, Count: 99
Bellamy, E.: 496
Beloselski, Prince: 250
Below, G. von: 450
Benda, J.: 525, 526
Bennett, A.: 230
Bennigsen, R. von: 234
Benoist, C.: 167
Benson, A. C.: 62
Bentham, J.: 158
Bentley, E.: 451
Benz, C.: 317
Beradt, M.: 389
Berdyaev, N.: 174, 471, 480, 559
Berg, A.: 578, 583
Berget, A.: 316
Bergius, F. C. R.: 311
Bergson, H.: 36, 155, 240, 347, 414,
    417, 427, 458, 466, 468, 469, 471,
    472, 473, 475, 526, 527, 555, 623,
    654
Berlage, H. P.: 565, 568, 569, 570, 571,
    572, 579
Berlioz, H.: 573, 580
Bernanos, G.: 490
Bernard, C.: 355, 360
Bernard, T.: 161
Bernhardi, F. von: 343
Bernhardt, S.: 79, 321, 510, 511, 521
Bernheim: 544
Bernheim, E.: 453
Bernoulli, D.: 328
Bernstein, A.: 269
Bernstein, E.: 37, 168, 170, 171, 173,
    175, 176, 177, 473, 650
Berr, H.: 36, 448, 449, 453, 456

760

Berth, E.: 153, 374
Berthelot, M. P.: 352
Bertillon, A.: 198, 285, 292
Bertrand, Procurator-General: 148
Besant, A.: 276, 496, 497, 499, 503,
    505, 506, 508, 597
Beveridge, W. H.: 219
Bezzenberger, A.: 437
Bieberstein, Marshal von: 72, 77
Bierbaum, O. J.: 517
Biez, J. de: 97
Bignami, G.: 356
Bilderdijk, W.: 652
Billaud, M.: 258
Billot, General: 87, 89
Billy, R. de: 266
Binet, A.: 299, 405, 406, 623
Binet-Sanglé, C.: 363
Bing, S.: 566, 567
Biryukov, P.: 121
Birnbaum, N.: 103
Bismarck, H. von: 64
Bismarck, O. von: 8, 10, 52, 64, 65,
    66, 69, 70, 96, 159, 168, 234, 278,
    323, 342, 424, 463, 481, 491, 591
Bizet, G.: 577
Bialik, Ch. N.: 103
Björnson, B.: 517, 587
Blanqui, A.: 168
Blaschko, A.: 205
Blatchford, R.: 211, 276
Blavatsky, H. P.: 135, 313, 556
Bleibtreu, C.: 513, 514, 526
Bleichröder, G.: 163
Blériot, L.: 316
Bloch, I. or J. von, or J. de: 113, 117,
    119, 122, 205, 285, 587, 588, 590,
    593, 599, 600, 649
Bloch, J. R.: 90
Bloch, J. S.: 101, 102, 103, 104, 169
Blondel, M.: 470, 486
Blooker: 297
Bloy, L.: 485, 490
Blum, L.: 90, 161, 588, 591, 610
Blumenthal, Mrs., Duchess of Mont-
    morency: 250
Blunt, W. S.: 16
Boas, F.: 428
Bobrikow, N. I.: 138
Bobrinski, Count: 140
Boccioni, U.: 556
Bocheński, I. M.: 468
Böcklin, A.: 545
Boddaert, E. C.: 223
Bodenheim, N.: 630
Bodenheimer: 103
Bodio, L.: 285
Boeke, K.: 629
Boer-van Rijk, E. de: 511

Boersma, H. L.: 301
Boëx, J. H.: 109
Boëx, S. J. F.: 109
Bogdano: 173
Bohlen und Halbach, G. von: 250
Böhm-Bawerk, E. von: 171
Böhme, M.: 586
Bohr, N.: 324, 333
Bois, J.: 500, 502
Boldini: 249, 545
Bolland, G. J.: 135, 455, 474
Boltzmann, L.: 328, 329, 330, 331,
    332, 338, 339
Bolzano, B.: 334
Bon, G. le: 67, 86, 134, 409, 412, 494
Bonger, W. A.: 397
Bonghi, R.: 127
Boni de Castellane: 26, 244, 250
Bonnard, P.: 547, 551, 555
Bonnemain, Mme de: 80
Bonnier, L. B.: 566
Bontoux, E.: 98
Bonvalot, P. G.: 19
Boole, G.: 334
Booth, C.: 211, 213, 220
Booth, W.: 508
Bopp, F.: 435
Borchgrevink, C. E.: 22
Borchhardt, J.: 626
Bordet, J.: 357
Borel, H.: 43, 50
Bosanquet, B.: 381, 475
Bosch, J. van den: 636
Bosco, don G.: 491
Bossuet, J. B.: 455
Botha, L.: 51, 55
Böttger: 228
Boudier-Bakker, I.: 592
Bouglé, C.: 376, 421, 422, 430
Bouillon, Duke of: 307
Boulanger, G. E.: 6, 7, 8, 80, 81
Bourdeau, J.: 148
Bourdelle, A.: 557
Bourg de Bozas, Marchioness of: 244
Bourgeois, L.: 376
Bourget, P.: 163, 352, 523, 588
Bourguin, M.: 376
Bouton, E.: 317
Bouton, L.: 244
Boutonné: 82
Boutroux, E.: 348, 414, 472
Bower, H.: 19
Boyle, R.: 328, 330
Bradlaugh, C.: 381, 496, 597
Bradley, F. H.: 475
Braeuer, W.: 372
Braganza, Prince of: 244
Bragg, W. H.: 324
Bragg, W. L.: 324

764

765

Geheeb, P.: 628
Gelle: 127
Gemelli, A.: 351
Gengou: 357
Gentil, L.: 19
Gentile, G.: 174
Gény, F.: 390
George, H.: 381, 643
George, S.: 451, 527, 530, 535, 539, 540, 541, 549
Gérard, M.: 501
Gerber, S.: 101
Gerlache de Gomerie, A. de: 22
Gervex, H.: 205
Ghil, R.: 533
Gibb, D.: 338, 339
Gibbons, J.: 487, 491
Gibbs, J. W.: 330
Gibier, P.: 497
Gide, A.: 527, 532, 541, 654, 656
Gide, C.: 127, 376
Gierke, O. von: 388, 391, 465
Giffen, R.: 285
Gijn, A. van: 280
Gilbreth, F. B.: 289
Gilman, D. C.: 638
Ginneken, J. van: 443
Girardin E. de: 130, 258
Giraud, G.: 583
Girault, C.: 298
Girod, P.: 420
Gitermann, V.: 179
Gizycki, G. von: 492
Gladstone, W. E.: 59, 240
Glasier, J. B.: 110
Glasson, D. E.: 390, 392
Glinka, M. I.: 576
Gobineau, J. A. de: 96, 108
Goddet, J.: 318
Godwin, W.: 155, 158, 590
Goes, F. van der: 163, 373
Goethe, J. W.: 361, 431, 506, 569, 579, 590, 624
Goette, A. W.: 346
Gogh, V. van: 211, 519, 545, 550, 554, 555, 563
Gogol, N.: 541, 557, 576
Göhre, P.: 173
Gökalp, Z.: 67
Goldberger, L. M.: 639
Goldfish, S.: 320
Goldwyn, S.: 320
Goltz, C. von der: 69, 454
Goncourts, brothers and E. J. de: 512
Gonnard, R.: 374
Gonse, C. A.: 83, 87, 89
Goodwin, M.: 272
Gordon, C. G.: 58
Gorky, M.: 211, 511, 517, 520, 550

Gorter, H.: 258, 527, 530, 531, 551
Gorter, S.: 258
Gostowsky, R.: 314
Gothein, E.: 190, 452
Gottl-Ottlilienfeld, F. von: 379
Gould, A.: 250
Gould, J.: 250, 258
Gourmont, R. de: 161
Gouzer: 148
Graebner, F.: 428
Gramont, Duke of: 244
Grand-Carteret, J.: 318
Gräser, G.: 504
Grass: 309
Grasset, E.: 566
Graux, L.: 127
Grave, J.: 128, 132, 154, 158
Gravelle, E.: 504
Greef, G. de: 131
Green, F. C.: 239
Green, J.: 631
Green, T. H.: 274
Gregory, Lady: 519
Grein, J. T.: 517
Grevy, J.: 80
Grieg, E.: 574
Griffith, A.: 109
Griffith, D. W.: 322
Griffith, J.: 396
Griffuelhes, V.: 153
Grillparzer, F.: 590
Grimm, (brothers): 630
Gris, J., or J. Gonzáles: 555
Gropius, W.: 572
Grotius, H.: 624
Grotjahn, A.: 201, 202, 367
Grottewitz, C.: 344
Grove, H.: 578
Gruber, J. G.: 201, 202
Gruhle, H.: 364
Gruizel: 190
Guazzoni, E.: 322
Guérard. E.: 153
Guérin, J.: 78
Guesde, J.: 83, 97, 122, 165, 166, 174, 176
Guilbert, Y.: 523, 539
Guillaume, A.: 205
Guillaume, J.: 158
Guimard, H.: 566
Guiraud, E.: 580
Guitry, L.: 79
Gulbransson, G.: 550
Gulbransson, O.: 550
Gumplowicz, L.: 423
Gunkel, H.: 484
Gurlitt, L.: 624, 626, 627, 628, 631, 634
Guttzeit, J.: 504

767

768

771

772

774

Proust, M.: 237, 238, 239, 240, 527, 531, 534, 536, 541, 542, 599, 631, 658
Prozor, Count: 509
Puccini, G.: 561, 575, 577
Puchstein, O.: 446
Pulitzer, J.: 258
Pullmann, G. M.: 642
Pusey, E. B.: 279
Pushkin, A.: 541, 601
Putilov, K.: 125, 139

Quack, H. P. G.: 211
Quetelet, A.: 634
Quidde, L.: 120

Rabah, Sultan: 9
Rabany, C.: 292
Rabelais, F.: 396
Rachfahl, F.: 450, 453
Rádl, E.: 341, 352
Ragaz, L.: 492
Ramsay, W. M.: 311
Ranchberg: 285
Rank, O.: 417
Ranke, L. von: 453
Raphael, M.: 548
Rasmussen, K.: 21
Rathenau, E.: 73, 191
Rathenau, W.: 191, 247, 289, 322, 555
Ratzel, F.: 423, 428, 429, 455
Ratzenhofer, G.: 423, 424
Ravachol: 83, 145, 146, 147, 148, 150
Ravary, Commandant: 89
Ravel, M.: 548, 579, 580, 582
Ravel, P.: 317
Ravesteyn, W. van: 122, 164, 452
Reade, C.: 56
Récipon, G.: 307
Reclus, Elie: 90, 504
Reclus, Elisée: 129, 158, 161
Redfern: 163
Redon, O.: 569
Reed, W.: 356
Rees, J. van: 121
Reese, B.: 503
Régnier, H. de: 161
Reich, Eduard: 364
Reich, Emil: 509
Reik, T.: 417
Reinach, J.: 90
Reinach, J. de: 7, 81
Reinach, S.: 456
Reinhardt, M.: 517, 518
Reinke, J.: 349
Rekowski: 176
Rembrandt: 431
Renan, E.: 352, 484, 485

Renaudel, P.: 176
Renoir, A.: 555, 564
Rénon, L.: 199, 200
Renouvier, C.: 375, 413, 475
Resink, A. J.: 496
Respighi, O.: 580
Reuter, G.: 587
Reuter, J. de: 71, 266
Revon, M.: 480
Rewald, J.: 555
Rey, E.: 632
Reynaud, E.: 320
Rhins, de: 19
Rhodes, C.: 52, 56, 57, 58, 59, 60, 61, 62, 135, 263
Rhodes, F.: 60
Rhys Davids, C. A. F.: 502
Ribot, T. A.: 399, 417
Ricardo, D.: 372
Ricca Salerno, G.: 374
Richard, J.: 336
Richardson, M.: 614
Richet, C.: 113, 361, 497
Richter, E.: 234
Richter, H.: 573
Rickert, H.: 352, 379, 432, 457, 471, 474
Rieger, C.: 400
Rieger, K.: 623
Riegl, A.: 459, 558
Riehl, A.: 462
Riemann, G. T. B.: 334, 338
Riemann, H.: 578
Riemann, O.: 495, 497, 507
Riemerschmid, R.: 567
Rienzi: see Kol, H. H. van
Riesser, J.: 186, 187
Rigby, L. M.: 637
Righi, A.: 319
Rilke, R. M.: 195, 432, 434, 527, 530, 531, 534, 535, 539, 541
Rimbaud, A.: 526, 529, 531, 532, 536, 561
Rimski-Korsakov, N. A.: 576, 581
Riou, G.: 633
Ritchie, D.: 131, 274
Rittinghausen, M.: 130, 132
Ritzel, G.: 371, 373
Rival, J.: 604
Rivers, W. H.: 408
Riza bey, A.: 66, 67, 247
Roberts, F. S.: 51, 53, 54, 55
Roberts of Kandahar and Waterford, Lord: 51
Robertson, J. M.: 381, 479, 485
Robida, A.: 302
Rochas, A. de: 497
Roche, J.: 296

Rochefort, H.: 107, 128, 145
Rockefeller, J. D.: 181
Rockhill, W. W.: 19
Rodin, A.: 90, 545, 557, 564
Rogers, T.: 374
Roget, General: 7, 78
Rohling, A.: 96, 98, 100
Roland Holst, R. N.: 554, 565, 579, 615
Roland Holst-van der Schalk: 172, 177, 213, 615
Rolland, R.: 89, 163, 238, 239, 240, 517, 525, 540, 570
Romains, J.: 238, 239
Rompel, F.: 56
Ronner: 579
Röntgen, W. C.: 324, 325, 331, 359
Rood, N. O.: 548
Roosevelt, T.: 646
Rops, F.: 205, 561, 564
Roscher, W.: 374
Rosebery, A. P. F.: 60, 61, 202, 221, 638
Rosny, J. H.: 109
Ross, E. A.: 409, 412
Ross, J. C.: 23
Ross, R.: 356
Rossini G.: 150
Rostand, E.: 79, 510
Roth, J.: 27, 116
Rothacker, E.: 453
Rothe, A.: 498
Rothermore, H. S. H.: 269
Rothschild: 137
Rothschild family: 96
Rothschild, E. de: 105
Rothschild, H. de: 95
Rothschild, M. de: 244
Rougemont, R. de: 244
Rousiers, P. de: 181
Rousseau, H.: 547, 569
Rousseau, J. J.: 128, 367, 515, 516, 620, 626
Rouvier, M.: 73, 81
Roux, P. P. E.: 357
Roux, W.: 345, 346, 347
Rowntree, B. S.: 211, 213, 218
Roxburghe, Duke of: 250
Roy, E. le: 486
Royce, J.: 475
Ruel, D.: 544
Rühle, O.: 199, 213, 507, 629
Ruskin, J.: 145, 213, 234, 255, 279, 381, 534, 542, 551, 559, 560, 563, 564, 568
Ruspoli, Princess: 244
Russell, B.: 253, 268, 334, 335, 336, 468, 475, 476

Russell, C. E. B.: 637
Rüstow, A.: 424
Rutgers, J.: 589
Rutherford, E.: 324, 325, 333
Rutland, Duke of: 251, 612
Rye, S.: 321

Sabatier, C.: 127
Sabatier, J.: 127
Sabatier, P.: 352, 480
Sackville, Lady: 250
Sadoul, G.: 321
Saharet: 522
Saint-Simon, C. H. de: 96
Saleilles, R.: 388, 392
Salisbury, R. A. T. G. markies van, eig. R. A. T. G. Cecil: 39, 117, 278
Salome: 577
Salomé, L.: *see Andreas-Salomé, L.*
Salomon, B.: 432
Salomons, A.: 592, 617
Saltet, R. H.: 280
Saltykov, M.: 27
Samuel: 363
Samuel, H.: 381
Sand, G.: 588, 594, 601, 606
Sanderson, T. H.: 75
Sandherr, Lieutenant-Colonel: 81, 87, 91
Sanger, M.: 597
Santayana, G.: 135
Sant'Elia, A.: 556
Santos Dumont, A.: 131
Sardou, V.: 516
Sargent, J. S.: 249, 545, 644
Sartorius von Waltershausen, A.: 382
Saud, Abd al-Aziz ibn al-: 648
Saussure, F. de: 435, 444, 445, 446
Saville: 242
Savornin Lohmann, A. de: 592, 616
Sazonov, S. D.: 138
Schaaffhausen, A.: 187
Schäfer, D.: 343, 452
Schäffle, A. E. F.: 132
Schallmayer, W.: 343
Schapiro, J.: 382
Schaudinn, F.: 205, 357
Scheibner, K.: 497
Scheler, M.: 348, 432, 475
Schell, H.: 352, 488
Scherer, W.: 437, 451
Scherl, A.: 259, 260
Scheu, G.: 572
Scheurer-Kestner, A.: 88
Schiff, M.: 360
Schiff, W.: 198
Schiller, F. C. S.: 470
Schjelderup, H. K.: 468

778

779

Somerset, Duke of: 252
Sophocles: 415
Sorel, G.: 132, 135, 153, 169, 170,
  376, 426, 427, 428, 469, 498, 540,
  646
Sorokin, P. A.: 426
Spann, O.: 372, 378, 379, 432
Spaventa, B.: 459, 474
Speenhoff, J. H.: 523, 603
Speke, J. H.: 17, 19
Spence, T.: 207
Spencer, H.: 67, 116, 130, 158, 173,
  255, 277, 341, 342, 352, 367, 377,
  421, 424, 426, 430, 483
Spender, S.: 174
Spengler, O.: 451, 552
Speyer, Frau: 358
Spiegel, H. W.: 379
Spiethoff, F.: 382
Spinoza, B. de: 173, 412
Spitz, D.: 134
Spotswood, K.: 250
Spranger, E.: 412
Sprenger, A.: 74
Sprigg, G.: 52
Springer, A. H.: 307
Stalin, J. W.: 30, 372
Stammhammer, J.: 161
Stammler, R.: 171, 172, 372, 388
Stanislavski, K.: 511
Stanley, H. M.: 17
Starbuck, E. D.: 409, 410
Stark, W.: 372
Starling, E. H.: 360
Staudinger, F.: 172
Stead, W. T.: 56, 114, 120, 257, 261,
  642, 645, 646
Steevens, W. G.: 264
Stefan, J.: 331
Stefansson, V.: 21
Steffen, G. F.: 213
Stehelin: 285
Stein, A.: 18, 19
Stein, L.: 432, 468
Stein, L. von: 374
Steiner, R.: 506, 508, 556, 629
Steinlen, T. A.: 84, 205, 212, 566
Steinmetz, S. R.: 420, 604
Steinthal, H.: 439, 443, 467, 483
Stemrich: 66
Stengel, E.: 119
Stephen, J.: 135
Stern, M.: 475
Sternberger, D.: 561
Sternheim, C.: 230
Steur, J. A. van der: 120
Stevens, M.: 250
Stevin, S.: 317
Stirner, M.: 153, 154, 158

Stöcker, A.: 97, 98, 107, 492, 495
Stöcker, H.: 597
Stolypin, P. A.: 30
Stone, Miss: 647
Stoney, G. J.: 326
Stopes, M.: 597
Stössel, A. M.: 139
Strauss, D. F.: 484
Strauss, J.: 34, 252
Strauss, R.: 269, 575, 576, 577, 580
Stravinsky, I.: 548, 576, 581
Streitberg, W.: 437
Strindberg, A.: 509, 511, 517, 519,
  587, 593, 615, 634
Struve, P.: 139, 174
Stuck, F. von: 545
Stumpf, C.: 410, 411
Suarès, A.: 525
Suchtelen, N. van: 533
Südfeld, M.: 25
Sugiyama: 45, 49
Su I: 49
Sullivan, L. H.: 564, 568, 569
Sully, J.: 408
Sun Yat-sen: 41, 45, 50, 648
Supino, C.: 374
Suranyi-Unger, T.: 378
Sutter, J. de: 418
Suttner, B. von: 115, 116, 117, 120
Suys, J.: 472
Svengali: 498
Sverdrup, O.: 18, 20
Swarth, H.: 616
Swedenborg, E.: 497, 531
Sweelinck, J. P.: 574
Swinburne, A. C.: 541
Svjatopolk-Mirski, Prince: 138
Sybil: 127
Synge, J. M.: 519, 530

Taine, H.: 352, 451
Tak, P. L.: 162, 565
Tao: 121
Tarde, G.: 148, 237, 381, 384, 397,
  409, 412
Tarnowsky, B.: 205
Tartaud-Klein, A.: 521
Tattenbach, Count Von: 33
Taylor, F. W.: 646
Taylor, G. R. S.: 276, 289
Tchaikovski, P. I.: 158
Terrail, G.: 247
Tertullianus: 162
Teure, G. de: 566
Thackeray, W. M.: 234
Tharaud, Brothers: 525
Thayer, Miss: 250
Théry, E.: 180
Thiers, L. A.: 80

Wolf, Eugen: 309
Wolf, H.: 579
Wolf, J.: 288
Wolff, B.: 266
Wolff, G.: 346
Wolff, T.: 92
Wölfflin, H.: 459
Wolmarans, A. D. W.: 55
Wolseley, G. J.: 59
Woltmann, L.: 171
Wolzogen, E. von: 254, 523
Woolf, V.: 608
Worringer, W.: 459
Wrangel, P.: 244
Wright, F. L.: 564, 570, 571, 572
Wright, O.: 23, 311, 316
Wright, W.: 316
Wright, W. K.: 468
Wundt, W.: 401, 402, 403, 404, 405,
    406, 407, 410, 412, 414, 417, 436,
    440, 441, 442, 443, 483
Wurm, E.: 213
Württemberg, Prince R. of: 242
Wyneken, G.: 628

Xénopol, A. D.: 447, 448

Yeats, W. B.: 519, 525, 529, 530, 531,
    532, 533, 534, 535, 536, 537, 541, 548
Yerkes, R. M.: 406
Yersin, A.: 354
Yorck, Count: 64

Younghusband, F.: 19
Yü-hsien, Prince: 40, 44
Yü-lu:44
Yussopov (Prince): 243, 255
Yusuf Fehmi: 143
Yvetot, G.: 153

Zabel, R.: 50
Zadkine, O.: 555
Zaharoff, B.: 124
Zangwill, I.: 105
Zanzig, E.: 498
Zeller, E.: 401, 467
Zenker, E. V.: 128
Zeppelin, F. von: 21, 23, 31, 315
Zhitlovsky, C.: 102
Zicken, T.: 404
Ziegler: 21
Ziegler, H. E.: 343
Ziegler, L.: 631, 634
Zikni, Pasha: 73
Zilboorg, G.: 363
Zille, H.: 212, 550
Zisly, H.: 504
Zola, E.: 86, 88, 89, 90, 92, 109, 128,
    163, 211, 230, 239, 352, 447, 536,
    537, 538, 587, 589
Zöllner, J. K. F.: 497
Zukor, 320
Zweers, B.: 576
Zweig, A.: 549
Zweig, S.: 33
Zijl, L.: 557, 579